LET'S GO

PAGES PACKED WITH ESSENTIAL INFORMATION

"Value-packed, unbeatable, accurate, and comprehensive."

—The Los Angeles Times

"The guides are aimed not only at young budget travelers but at the independent traveler; a sort of streetwise cookbook for traveling alone."

—The New York Times

"Unbeatable; good sight-seeing advice; up-to-date info on restaurants, hotels, and inns; a commitment to money-saving travel; and a wry style that brightens nearly every page."

—The Washington Post

THE BEST TRAVEL BARGAINS IN YOUR BUDGET

"All the dirt, dirt cheap."

—People

"Let's Go follows the creed that you don't have to toss your life's savings to the wind to travel—unless you want to."

—The Salt Lake Tribune

REAL ADVICE FOR REAL EXPERIENCES

"The writers seem to have experienced every rooster-packed bus and lunar-surfaced mattress about which they write."

—The New York Times

"[Let's Go's] devoted updaters really walk the walk (and thumb the ride, and trek the trail). Learn how to fish, haggle, find work—anywhere."

—Food & Wine

"A world-wise traveling companion—always ready with friendly advice and helpful hints, all sprinkled with a bit of wit."

—The Philadelphia Inquirer

A GUIDE WITH A SPIRIT AND A SOCIAL CONSCIENCE

"Lighthearted and sophisticated, informative and fun to read. [Let's Go] helps the novice traveler navigate like a knowledgeable old hand."

—Atlanta Journal-Constitution

"The serious mission at the book's core reveals itself in exhortations to respect the culture and the environment—and, if possible, to visit as a volunteer, a student, or a teacher rather than a tourist."

—San Francisco Chronicle

LET'S GO PUBLICATIONS

TRAVEL GUIDES

Australia
Austria & Switzerland
Brazil
Britain
California
Central America
Chile
China
Costa Rica
Costa Rica, Nicaragua & Panama
Eastern Europe
Ecuador
Egypt
Europe
France
Germany
Greece
Guatemala & Belize
Hawaii
India & Nepal
Ireland
Israel
Italy
Japan
Mexico
New Zealand
Peru
Puerto Rico
Southeast Asia
Spain & Portugal with Morocco
Thailand
USA
Vietnam
Western Europe
Yucatan Peninsula

ROADTRIP GUIDE

Roadtripping USA

ADVENTURE GUIDES

Alaska
Pacific Northwest
Southwest USA

CITY GUIDES

Amsterdam
Barcelona
Berlin, Prague & Budapest
Boston
Buenos Aires
Florence
London
London, Oxford, Cambridge & Edinburgh
New York City
Paris
Rome
San Francisco
Washington, DC

POCKET CITY GUIDES

Amsterdam
Berlin
Boston
Chicago
London
New York City
Paris
San Francisco
Venice
Washington, DC

LET'S GO

GERMANY

RESEARCHERS

DANIEL K. BILOTTI JUSTIN KENNAN
AYLIN ERMAN ALEX MCADAMS
KAYALA M. HAMMOND SCOTT MCKINNEY
DANA KASE RACHEL NOLAN
LEAH SCHWARTZ

DWIGHT LIVINGSTONE CURTIS MANAGING EDITOR
ADAM CLARK EDITOR
ARIELLE FRIDSON ASSOCIATE EDITOR
DAVID ANDERSSON RESEARCH MANAGER
SARA S. O'ROURKE RESEARCH MANAGER
CLAIRE SHEPRO RESEARCH MANAGER

EDITORS

COURTNEY A. FISKE RUSSELL FORD RENNIE
SARA PLANA CHARLIE E. RIGGS
OLGA I. ZHULINA

HOW TO USE THIS BOOK

COVERAGE. In *Let's Go Germany,* each *Land* (province) is presented in its own chapter, starting with Berlin and moving clockwise around the map. The major city or transportation hub within each *Land* introduces its chapter, followed by other significant **cities, towns,** and **villages.** Because not every one of Germany's ancient castles or quirky museums is the sort of place you'd want to spend the night, we've also included tons of **daytrips,** single-day excursions from nearby towns. The book also features extensive coverage of **outdoor areas,** including national parks and adventure sites. For each area, we recommend gateway towns—nearby villages that offer easy access to the parks, lakes, and mountains where you'll really want to spend your time.

WHY PRAGUE? At the end of the book, we list everything you'll need to know to visit the mother of all gateway cities, **Prague.** We've included this essential coverage to enable you to sample one of Europe's sweetest destinations, readily accessible from Dresden, Munich, Berlin—or wherever, really.

PLANNING YOUR TRIP. Our **Discover** section is the best place to begin your trip preparations. Brimming with advice on when to go, where to go, and what to do, the chapter's tools include suggested itineraries—themed routes across the country—and **Let's Go Thumbpicks**—zany highlights carefully selected from an entire country's worth of castles, beaches, hostels, and clubs—to bring you to Germany's must-see destinations on and off the beaten path. The **Life and Times** chapter is a primer in German history and culture. Read that section of this book and you'll be able to order a Märzen from Rilke's favorite *Jugendstil* beer hall on Allerheiligen—and know what all of it means! To help you actually get yourself to Germany, the **Essentials** section will tell you more than you've ever wanted to know about passports, customs, airline tickets, railpasses, health, and safety.

LISTINGS. We list establishments in order from best to worst value, and assign food and accommodations a price diversity ranking from ❶ (cheapest) to ❺ (most extravagant). We've detailed the prices for each rank and the corresponding services you can expect, on our **price diversity** page (p. IX).

ABBREVIATIONS. In order to pack the book with as much information as possible, we have used a few **standard abbreviations.** Please note that "Pl." is short for "Platz," "Str." for "Straße," and "G." for "Gasse."

LANGUAGE. Because wildly gesticulating doesn't always cut it, we've included **essential phrases** on the inside back cover and a **glossary** in the Appendix. Whenever relevant, we translate phrases as such: *German* (English).

PHONE CODES AND TELEPHONE NUMBERS. Area codes for each region appear opposite the name of the region and are denoted by the ☎ icon. Phone numbers in text are also preceded by the ☎ icon.

A NOTE TO OUR READERS. The information for this book was gathered by Let's Go researchers from May 2008 through August 2009. Each listing is based on one researcher's opinion, formed during his or her visit at a particular time. Those traveling at other times may have different experiences since prices, dates, hours, and conditions are always subject to change. You are urged to check the facts presented in this book beforehand to avoid inconvenience and surprises.

CONTENTS

RESEARCHERS

Daniel K. Bilotti *Munich*

Fame seemed to follow this California-born Economics major wherever he went, bumping into both John Malkovich and Furious Pete (a record-holding competitive eater). We were a little concerned about sending him off to represent Let's Go, given that he said he was most looking forward to embarrassing America abroad—but we're pretty sure he failed in that regard, and succeeded in most others, including charming us with great coverage of Munich.

Aylin Erman *Nordrhein-Westfallen, Rheinland-Pfalz*

Taking on a challenging route, Aylin made her way from Trier to the quicksands of the Wattenmeer with grace. Finding time for morning jogs through palace gardens, she took her route in stride, impressing even the most seasoned *Let's Go* vets. Though she was easily seduced by free Wi-Fi, her critical eye ensured a unique candor in every word.

Kayla Hammond *Berlin and Brandenburg*

Passionately dedicated to her research, Kayla braved dark, techno-booming warehouses and remote, pickle-crazy towns alike. With a knack for fashion, she made it her mission to find the best boutiques so readers could hit the Berlin nightlife looking their best, while her Brandenburg research left no Stein unturned.

Dana Kase *Hamburg, Mecklenburg, Schleswig-Holstein*

A painter, sculptor, DJ, graphic designer, and traveler, Dana turned her attention to Germany's northernmost points and befriended locals at every stop—especially babies, as language wasn't an issue. Through technicolored glasses, she credits her success as an RW to an uncanny ability to recognize people who look like sea creatures.

Justin Keenan *Prague*

Justin coolly and confidently attacked Prague with all of his might and humor. A Let's Go veteran, he knew exactly how to find the hidden secrets about an establishment after only having set foot in it for a few moments. And he was never afraid to share his on-the-mark opinions---his snarky commentary had the office laughing for days. This English major only has one year left at Harvard, but he will grace it his newfound appreciation for subtle regional variations of goulash.

RESEARCHERS

Alex McAdams *Bayern*

Crew star and snowboarder-extraordinaire, Alew grew up in cities around the world, including two years in Bonn. He used his impressive German and adorable grin to woo the hearts of cute tour guides across Bavaria, charming the inside scoop out of every last one of them.

Scott McKinney *Niedersachsen, Sachsen, S.-Anhalt, Thüringen*

With wry wit and Watson-caliber investigative skill, Scott (the Leipzig lady-killer) ferreted out the real deal in every corner of the east. An accomplished musician, his unparalleled writing talent infuses listings with enough humor and charm to kill a small goat.

Rachel Nolan *Berlin*

There is perhaps no one more qualified than RaNo to write about Germany's capital city. An LG legend, '07 grad and freelance journalist by trade, Rachel has lived within the city's pulse for months—keeping company with both hipsters and students, professionals and the perpetually-wandering. For LG, she took on the city by storm—and bike—getting lost in (and rediscovering) its quirks, and blazing a trail of impeccable prose planted with quirks of her own.

Leah Schwartz *Baden-Württemberg, Rheinland-Pfalz, Hessen*

Vivacious, trilingual, and a world-class athlete, Leah conquered Germany's storied southern landscape and fairytale towns, from Bacharach to the Black Forest. Going the distance for original and honest coverage, she sought out the inside scoop with alarming efficiency and a mind like a trap. Just try asking her about cuckoo clocks.

STAFF WRITERS

Sanders Isaac Bernstein   Julia Cain   Megan Popkin   Madeleine M. Schwartz

CONTRIBUTING WRITERS

Dr. Angelika Lampert is a German neuroscientist studying the role of sodium channels in pain. She spent three years of postdoctoral training at Yale University, and now works at the University of Erlangen-Nuremberg, Germany.

Valerie Hartung is a freelancer in online marketing. She has lived and traveled all over the world, but home is where the heart is—Munich.

Dr. Richard Carr works at Ludwig-Maximilians University, where he specializes in Neurophysiology. He was born in Melbourne, Australia and has bween brewing and drinking beer in and around Bavaria for the past seven years.

ACKNOWLEDGMENTS

TEAM GERMANY THANKS: Our RWs for being the most attractive team of reseachers this company has ever seen. Dwight for his effortless leadership. Sammy for always knowing the answer. The Office for snacks and shenanigans. Jesse, for every -asse and -atz. And, Jonathan for the extra effort and dedication.

ADAM THANKS: Mom and Dad for bequeathing some good old Wanderlust. Brittany for putting up with it. Jonathan for his (endless) patience. That goes ditto for Elissa. Dwight for being an all-around gentleman. Samuel for making me jealous of Berlin life. The miles of copy that kept me entertained all summer long and the all-star RWs who wrote them. And the United States Congress for fronting the money for my first trip to Germany.

ARIELLE THANKS: Vanessa, Dwight, Nicklette, Elissa, and Sam for their enthusiasm and support. Shemesh et Sheleg pour leurs conseils avisés, leur perspicacité, et leur voix mélodieuse. Mom, Dad, Guy, Großmutti, and Bijou for their love, challah, and never-ending brunches. Mon chapin bien-aimé, whose dashing good looks and inexhaustible charm make me happy every single day. My grandfather, whom I miss, for his humor and wisdom.

Managing Editor
Dwight Livingstone Curtis
Editor
Adam Clark
Associate Editor
Arielle Fridson
Research Managers
David Andersson, Sara O'Rourke, Claire Shepro
Editors
Courtney A. Fiske, Sara Plana, Russell Ford Rennie, Charlie E. Riggs, Olga I. Zhulina
Typesetter
C. Alexander Tremblay

1 2 PRICE RANGES 3 4 GERMANY 5

Our Researchers list establishments in order of value from best to worst, honoring our favorites with the Let's Go thumbs-up (☒). Because the best *value* is not always the cheapest *price*, we have incorporated a system of price ranges based on a rough expectation of what you will spend. For **accommodations**, we base our range on the cheapest price for which a single traveler can stay for one night. For **restaurants** and other dining destinations, we estimate the average amount one traveler will spend in one sitting. The table below details what you'll *typically* find in Germany at the corresponding price range, but keep in mind that no system can allow for the quirks of individual establishments.

ACCOMMODATIONS	RANGE	WHAT YOU'RE *LIKELY* TO FIND
❶	under €15	Campgrounds and dorm rooms, both in hostels and actual universities. Expect bunk beds and a communal bath. You may have to provide or rent towels and sheets.
❷	€15-25	Upper-end hostels or lower-end hotels. You may have a private bathroom, or there may be a sink in your room and a communal shower in the hall.
❸	€26-35	A small room with a private bath. Should have decent amenities, such as phone and TV. Breakfast may be included in the price.
❹	€36-50	Should have bigger rooms than a ❸, with more amenities or in a more convenient location. Breakfast probably included.
❺	over €50	Large or upscale hotels. Rooms should elicit an involuntary "wow." If it's a ❺ and it doesn't have all the perks, you've paid too much.

FOOD	RANGE	WHAT YOU'RE *LIKELY* TO FIND
❶	under €5	Probably street or Imbiß food, but also university cafeterias and bakeries (yum). Simple dishes in minimalist surroundings. Usually takeout, but you may have the option of sitting down.
❷	€5-9	Sandwiches, pizza, appetizers at a bar, or low-priced entrees. Most ethnic eateries are a ❷. Either takeout or a sit-down meal (sometimes with servers!), but only slightly more fashionable decor.
❸	€10-14	Mid-priced entrees, seafood, and most traditional German fare. More unique and upscale ethnic eateries. Since you'll have a waiter, tip will set you back a little extra.
❹	€15-22	A somewhat fancy restaurant; you'll probably have a special knife. Entrees tend to be heartier or more elaborate, but you're really paying for decor and ambience. Few restaurants in this range have a dress code, but some may look down on T-shirts and sandals.
❺	over €22	Your meal might cost more than your room, but there's a reason—it's something fabulous, famous, or both. Slacks and dress shirts may be expected. Offers luxurious food and a decent wine list. Your experience should be memorable.

ABOUT LET'S GO

THE STUDENT TRAVEL GUIDE

Let's Go publishes the world's favorite student travel guides, written entirely by Harvard students. Armed with pens, notebooks, and a few changes of clothes stuffed into their backpacks, our student researchers go across continents, through time zones, and above expectations to seek out invaluable travel experiences for our readers. Because we are a completely student-run company, we have a unique perspective on how students travel, where they want to go, and what they're looking to do when they get there. If your dream is to grab a machete and forge through the jungles of Costa Rica, we can take you there. If you'd rather bask in the Riviera sun at a beachside cafe, we'll set you a table. In short, we write for readers who know that there's more to travel than tour buses. To keep up, visit our website, www.letsgo.com, where you can sign up to blog, post photos from your trips, and connect with the Let's Go community.

TRAVELING BEYOND TOURISM

We're on a mission to provide our readers with sharp, fresh coverage packed with socially responsible opportunities to go beyond tourism. Each guide's Beyond Tourism chapter shares ideas about responsible travel, study abroad, and how to give back to the places you visit while on the road. To help you gain a deeper connection with the places you travel, our fearless researchers scour the globe to give you the heads-up on both world-renowned and off-the-beaten-track opportunities. We've also opened our pages to respected writers and scholars to hear their takes on the countries and regions we cover, and asked travelers who have worked, studied, or volunteered abroad to contribute first-person accounts of their experiences.

FIFTY YEARS OF WISDOM

Let's Go has been on the road for 50 years and counting. We've grown a lot since publishing our first 20-page pamphlet to Europe in 1960, but five decades and 54 titles later our witty, candid guides are still researched and written entirely by students on shoestring budgets who know that train strikes, stolen luggage, food poisoning, and marriage proposals are all part of a day's work. This year, for our 50th anniversary, we're publishing 26 titles—including 6 brand new guides—brimming with editorial honesty, a commitment to students, and our irreverent style. Here's to the next 50!

THE LET'S GO COMMUNITY

More than just a travel guide company, Let's Go is a community that reaches from our headquarters in Cambridge, MA all across the globe. Our small staff of dedicated student editors, writers, and tech nerds comes together because of our shared passion for travel and our desire to help other travelers get the most out of their experience. We love it when our readers become part of the Let's Go community as well—when you travel, drop us a postcard (67 Mt. Auburn St., Cambridge, MA 02138, USA), send us an e-mail (feedback@letsgo.com), or sign up on our website (www.letsgo.com) to tell us about your adventures and discoveries.

For more information, updated travel coverage, and news from our researcher team, visit us online at www.letsgo.com.

DISCOVER GERMANY

While there is no shortage of images that characterize Germany—Lederhosen and busty barmaids, ultra-modern skyscrapers, unconscionable heaps of meat and potatoes—perhaps the most accurate explanation of this compelling country lies not in a preconception but in a word: *Gestalt*. This German term, literally meaning "shape," characterizes something that is distinctly more than the sum of its parts. *Gestalt*'s evocative brand of holism speaks both to Germany's geographical diversity, sweeping from the jagged snowy peaks of the Bavarian Alps to the sprawling sandy beaches of the north, and to its historical legacy and ever-evolving sense of national identity. A country split between Protestantism and Catholicism and forged from dozens of squabbling principalities, Germany has never been homogeneous. Yet a new influx of non-German immigrants and the challenge of collective guilt has forced an entire nation—once confident in its own ethnic heritage, if nothing else—to question what it means to be German in an ever-shrinking world and a rapidly diversifying *Land*. Poised at the juncture of common tradition and forward-looking cosmopolitanism, and facing tremendous uncertainty coupled with the uplifting potential of change, Germany is uniquely positioned to offer travelers culture, adventure, and the opportunity to discover the phantasmic *Gestalt* of contemporary Germany.

FACTS AND FIGURES

JAN. 18, 1871: The date of German unification, 95 years after the birth of the US.

27: The number of times Germany could fit inside the borders of the US.

82.5 MILLION: Germany's population.

107,000: The size of Germany's current Jewish community, the third largest in Western Europe.

80: The number of mosques in Berlin.

2.7 MILLION: The number of Turks living in Germany, of whom approximately one third have citizenship.

500,000: The estimated number of Berlin residents of Turkish descent, making it the third-largest Turkish city in the world.

120: The number of liters of beer consumed per German per year.

66: The percentage of German men who are overweight, making Germany the heaviest country in the EU.

INFINITY: The speed limit on the Autobahn. (130km/hr. is recommended).

4.3 MILLION: The number of passenger vehicles Germany exports in a year.

3: Germany's rank on a list of the world's largest economies, after the US and Japan.

1: Germany's rank as the world's largest exporter, ahead of the US and China.

14.2: Percentage of Germany's electricity made from renewable energy sources.

WHEN TO GO

Airfares and tourism increase with the temperature in July and August. May, June, and September have fewer vacationers and cooler, rainier days. Cold and wet weather is never a surprise in Germany: between one-third and one-half of the days each year bring some precipitation, and even in summertime hailstorms can blow across blue skies with no warning. In June and July, school groups overrun state-run HI hostels, bringing noise, confusion, and hallway soccer in their wake—don't say we didn't warn you. Larger cities typically sport better non-HI offerings. In the winter, some German hostels close and museum hours may be shortened. Winter sports gear up in November and continue through April; peak season for skiing is mid-December to March. For charts listing average temperatures and national holidays, see **Appendix,** p. 492.

WHAT TO DO

Germany's alpine wonderlands, seaside resorts, medieval relics, and cosmopolitan cities cohere to form one of Europe's most diverse destinations. The trademark of any German effort is its intensity: lively modern cities are hyperactive, droll storybook villages are fiercely provincial, and scenic wilderness preserves are thoroughly natural. Within each of the country's historically distinct cities and regions, travelers will find outdoor activities, intellectual wonders, aesthetic thrills, and drunken adventures. For regional attractions, see the **Highlights** section at the beginning of each chapter.

NAVES AND KNAVES

Early examples of fine German engineering can be seen in the resplendent castles and cathedrals scattered across the country. Two hundred years after rural fortresses went out of style, Mad King Ludwig II commissioned **Neuschwanstein,** the unfinished gem of the **Bavarian Royal Castles** (p. 360) and one of Germany's most recognizable landmarks. Set in a meticulously contrived (but still stunning) park in Potsdam, **Schloß Sanssouci** (p. 134) sports a frilly French Rococo style. In the cliffs over the Rhein River, the romantic half-ruins of **Burg Rheinfels** (p. 279) have underground passages that you can tour by candlelight. Check out our **Sloshed and Schloß-ed itinerary** (p. 5) for a tour of Germany's grandest residences (and a few beers along the way).

The epitome of Catholic extravagance, Cologne's unforgettable **Dom** (p. 231), is the largest High Gothic cathedral in the world, built between 1288 and 1880. Other important cathedrals include the imposing **Münster** (p. 316) in Freiburg, which rings the oldest bells in Germany; the **Frauenkirche** (p. 345) in Munich, whose two distinctive towers dominate the city skyline; and the **Münster** (p. 231) in Ulm, where the largest spire in the world rises 161m into the sky. Protestant houses of worship stake a claim to German skylines as well. Wittenberg is home to the **Schloßkirche** (p. 435), upon which Martin Luther nailed his *95 Theses* in 1517, sparking the Protestant Revolution. Hamburg's Große **Michaeliskirche** (p. 189) has a famous copper tower which is the city's symbol. The **Nikolaikirche** in Leipzig is doubly famous as the church in which Bach composed his *St. John's Passion* and as the rallying point for the demonstrations in early October 1989 that hastened the fall of communist East Germany.

FESTIVALS AND HOLIDAYS

Germany works hard but plays even harder—time your trip right, and you can hit a festival in every town you visit. Themes range from the humble (local produce) to the lofty (high culture) to the downright gratuitous (sex, drugs, techno, and pancakes). A few even claim international renown: Munich's

Oktoberfest (Sept. 18-Oct. 3, 2010) began as a wedding celebration centuries ago and continues to fill the city with reveling beer drinkers every year. Catch the infamous techno-wild **Love Parade** as it makes a 5-year tour around the Ruhr Region (Next stop: Bochum). In the early spring, Cologne hosts the yearly **Karneval** celebration (Feb. 11-17, 2010), where extravagantly costumed fools traipse in parades and generate revelry for the final week before Lent. During Advent, traditional **Christmas Markets** spring up all over Germany, serving *Glühwein* and other holiday spirits. Nuremberg's *Christkindlmarkt* with its glorious *Lebkuchen* (gingerbread) is the most famous. Finally, for film fanatics, Berlin hosts the young but prestigious **Berlinale Film Festival** (Feb. 11-21, 2010) every year.

LET'S GO PICKS

BEST ART-IS-LIFE EXPERIENCE: Subordinate form and function to a full night's sleep in Dessau's famous **Bauhaus** architectural school (p. 437).

BEST PLACE TO SLEEP IN YOUR CAR: Go nowhere fast in a VW Beetle-turned-bed in Berlin's **Bax Pax hostel** (p. 94).

BEST BATHROOM: Check out the bathroom "art" at the **Schwarzes Cafe** (p. 98) in Berlin's Charlottenburg—it's like peeing in a Prince video.

BEST TAKE ON WORSHIP: The monks at the **Andechs monastery** (p. 355) serve the holiest—and at 12%, the most potent—brew in Bavaria.

BEST PLACE TO MINE: Go deep in Rammelberg's thousand-year-old mine near the medieval town of **Goslar** (p. 208).

BEST PLACE TO WEIN: Nothing to complain about in **Neustadt** (p. 453), where a 2hr. sampling of Reisinger runs €6.

BEST PLACE TO FEEL LIKE A PRINCE(SS): Mad King Ludwig's magical **Neuschwanstein Castle** (p. 360), which inspired Disney's Cinderella Castle.

BEST AUTHENTIC CULTURAL EXPERIENCE: Book ahead for tickets to an opera in Wagner's **Festspielhaus** in Bayreuth (p. 410). Opened in 1876 with the Ring cycle premiere, this has been the site for the cult Bayreuth Festival ever since.

BEST GERMAN UNIVERSITY PARTIES: Every year, Munich's prestigious **LMU** opens its doors to host an enormous indoor/outdoor extravaganza for students and those who just want to party like them (p. 330).

BEST BEACHES: Sunbathe with the stars on **Sylt** (p. 173), avoid the crowds on nearby **Amrum** (p. 175), or dip into the Baltic Sea along **Rügen Island** (p. 155). The **Bodensee** (p. 322) is a favorite sun-filled destination on the Swiss border.

BEST DIRTY FUN (DAYTIME): Run across quicksand-dotted **Wattenmeer mudflats** (p. 170) between the islands of Sylt and Amrum at low tide.

BEST DIRTY FUN (NIGHTTIME): Try Berlin's techno-epic **Berghain** (p. 127), Hamburg's industrial **Fabrik** (p. 196), or Leipzig's subterranean **Moritzbastei** (p. 476).

GERMANY'S GREATEST (1 MONTH)

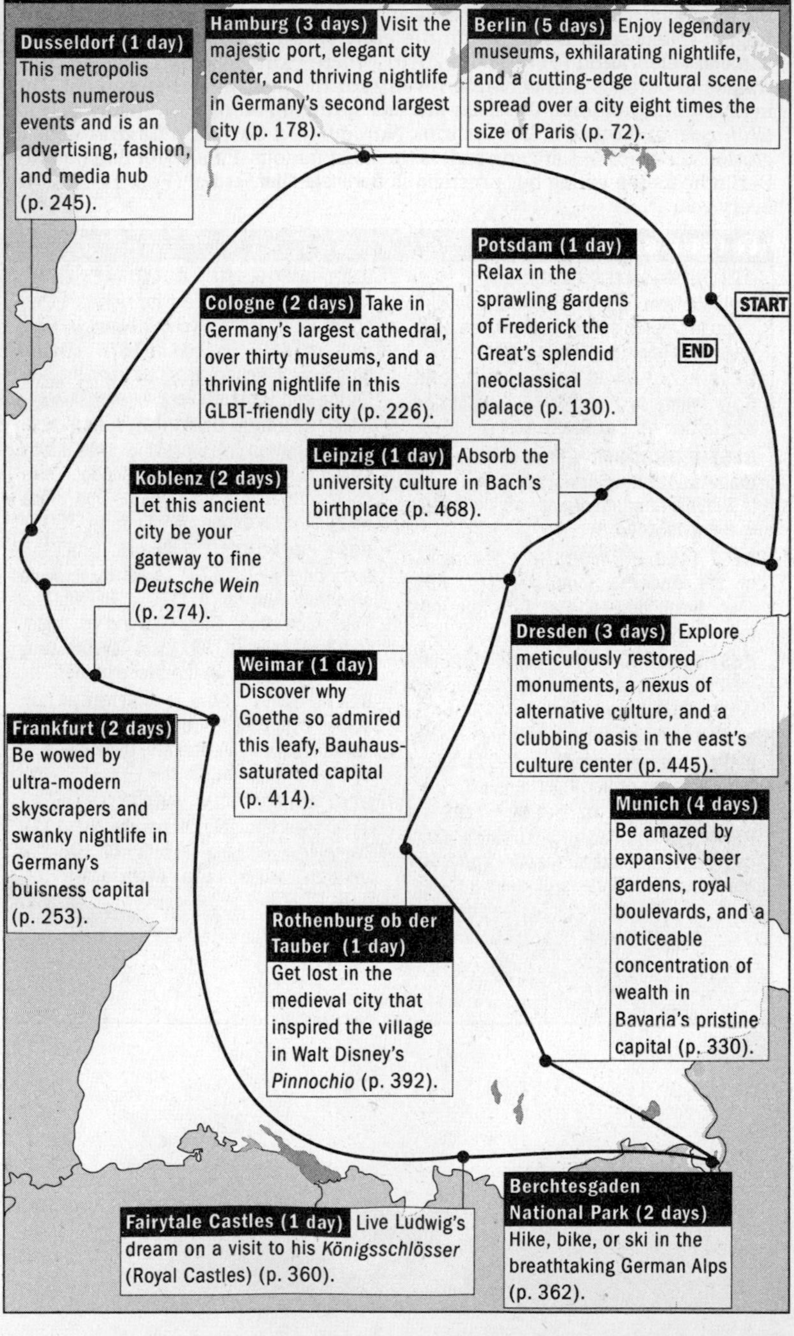
Dusseldorf (1 day) This metropolis hosts numerous events and is an advertising, fashion, and media hub (p. 245).
Hamburg (3 days) Visit the majestic port, elegant city center, and thriving nightlife in Germany's second largest city (p. 178).
Berlin (5 days) Enjoy legendary museums, exhilarating nightlife, and a cutting-edge cultural scene spread over a city eight times the size of Paris (p. 72).
Potsdam (1 day) Relax in the sprawling gardens of Frederick the Great's splendid neoclassical palace (p. 130).
START
END
Cologne (2 days) Take in Germany's largest cathedral, over thirty museums, and a thriving nightlife in this GLBT-friendly city (p. 226).
Leipzig (1 day) Absorb the university culture in Bach's birthplace (p. 468).
Koblenz (2 days) Let this ancient city be your gateway to fine *Deutsche Wein* (p. 274).
Dresden (3 days) Explore meticulously restored monuments, a nexus of alternative culture, and a clubbing oasis in the east's culture center (p. 445).
Weimar (1 day) Discover why Goethe so admired this leafy, Bauhaus-saturated capital (p. 414).
Frankfurt (2 days) Be wowed by ultra-modern skyscrapers and swanky nightlife in Germany's buisness capital (p. 253).
Munich (4 days) Be amazed by expansive beer gardens, royal boulevards, and a noticeable concentration of wealth in Bavaria's pristine capital (p. 330).
Rothenburg ob der Tauber (1 day) Get lost in the medieval city that inspired the village in Walt Disney's *Pinnochio* (p. 392).
Fairytale Castles (1 day) Live Ludwig's dream on a visit to his *Königsschlösser* (Royal Castles) (p. 360).
Berchtesgaden National Park (2 days) Hike, bike, or ski in the breathtaking German Alps (p. 362).

SLOSHED AND SCHLOß-ED (3 WEEKS)

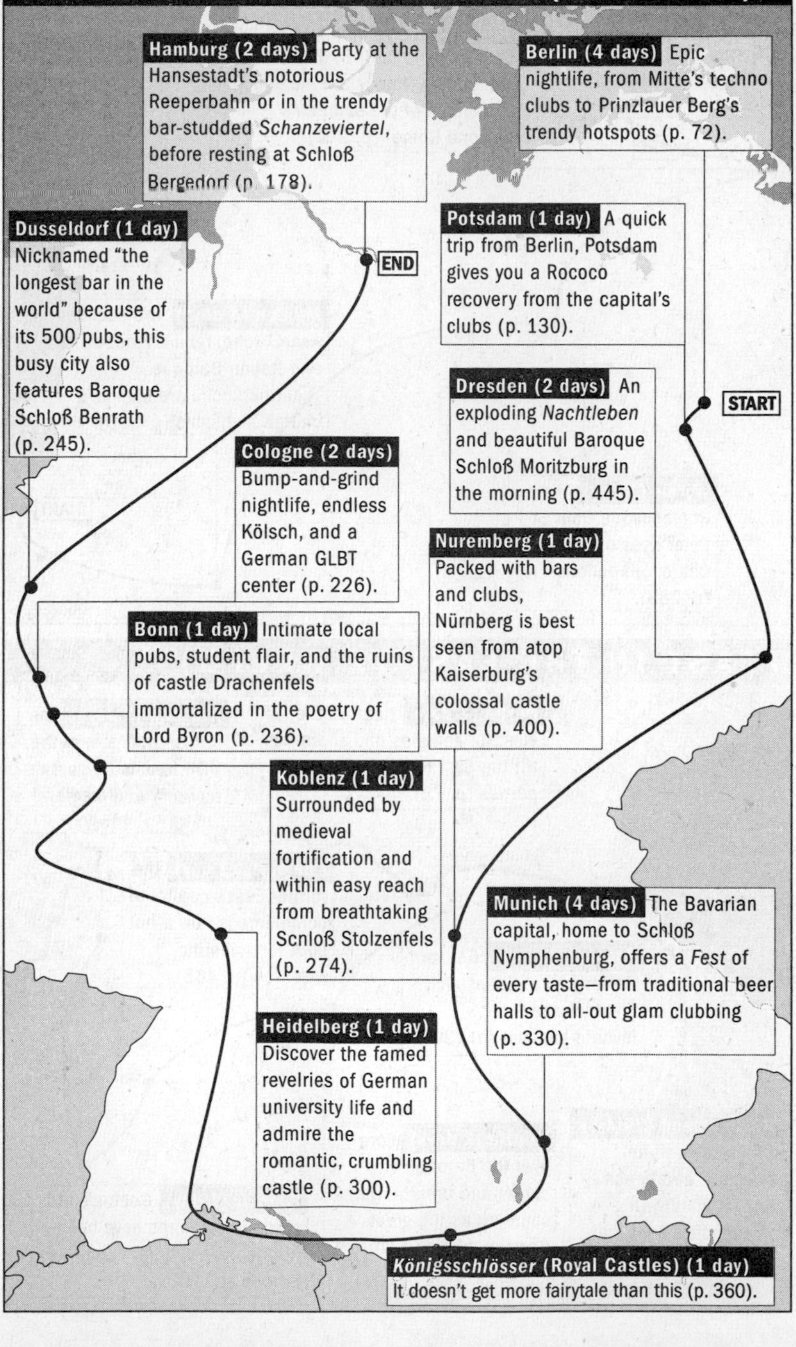

Berlin (4 days) Epic nightlife, from Mitte's techno clubs to Prinzlauer Berg's trendy hotspots (p. 72).

Potsdam (1 day) A quick trip from Berlin, Potsdam gives you a Rococo recovery from the capital's clubs (p. 130).

Dresden (2 days) An exploding *Nachtleben* and beautiful Baroque Schloß Moritzburg in the morning (p. 445).

Nuremberg (1 day) Packed with bars and clubs, Nürnberg is best seen from atop Kaiserburg's colossal castle walls (p. 400).

Munich (4 days) The Bavarian capital, home to Schloß Nymphenburg, offers a *Fest* of every taste—from traditional beer halls to all-out glam clubbing (p. 330).

***Königsschlösser* (Royal Castles) (1 day)** It doesn't get more fairytale than this (p. 360).

Heidelberg (1 day) Discover the famed revelries of German university life and admire the romantic, crumbling castle (p. 300).

Koblenz (1 day) Surrounded by medieval fortification and within easy reach from breathtaking Scnloß Stolzenfels (p. 274).

Bonn (1 day) Intimate local pubs, student flair, and the ruins of castle Drachenfels immortalized in the poetry of Lord Byron (p. 236).

Cologne (2 days) Bump-and-grind nightlife, endless Kölsch, and a German GLBT center (p. 226).

Dusseldorf (1 day) Nicknamed "the longest bar in the world" because of its 500 pubs, this busy city also features Baroque Schloß Benrath (p. 245).

Hamburg (2 days) Party at the Hansestadt's notorious Reeperbahn or in the trendy bar-studded *Schanzeviertel*, before resting at Schloß Bergedorf (p. 178).

CHOICEST CHURCHES (2 WEEKS)

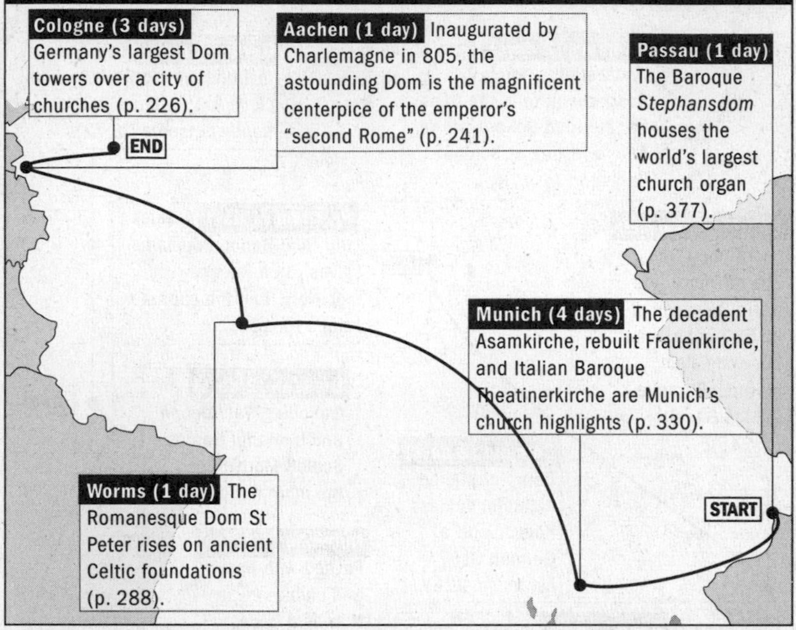
Cologne (3 days) Germany's largest Dom towers over a city of churches (p. 226).
Aachen (1 day) Inaugurated by Charlemagne in 805, the astounding Dom is the magnificent centerpice of the emperor's "second Rome" (p. 241).
Passau (1 day) The Baroque *Stephansdom* houses the world's largest church organ (p. 377).
END
Munich (4 days) The decadent Asamkirche, rebuilt Frauenkirche, and Italian Baroque Theatinerkirche are Munich's church highlights (p. 330).
Worms (1 day) The Romanesque Dom St Peter rises on ancient Celtic foundations (p. 288).
START

FEAST IN THE EAST (2 WEEKS)

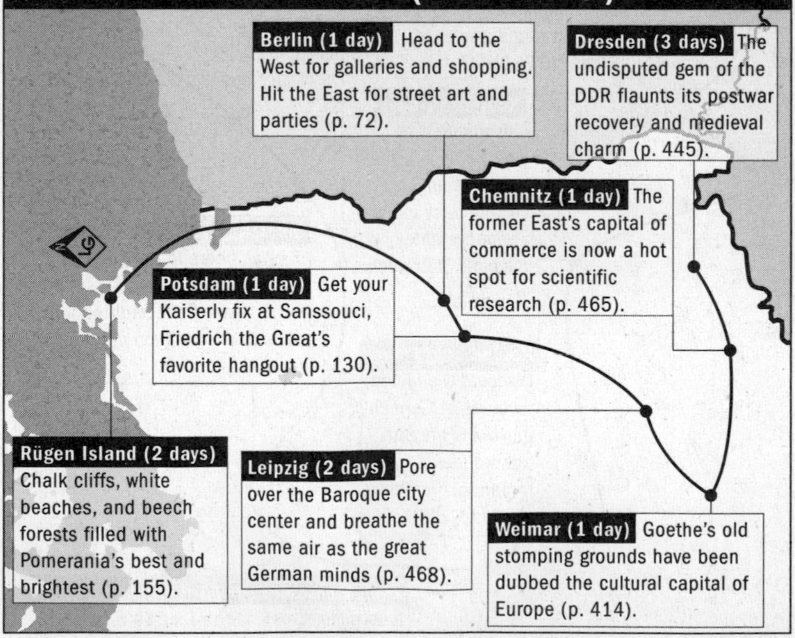
Berlin (1 day) Head to the West for galleries and shopping. Hit the East for street art and parties (p. 72).
Dresden (3 days) The undisputed gem of the DDR flaunts its postwar recovery and medieval charm (p. 445).
Chemnitz (1 day) The former East's capital of commerce is now a hot spot for scientific research (p. 465).
LG
Potsdam (1 day) Get your Kaiserly fix at Sanssouci, Friedrich the Great's favorite hangout (p. 130).
Rügen Island (2 days) Chalk cliffs, white beaches, and beech forests filled with Pomerania's best and brightest (p. 155).
Leipzig (2 days) Pore over the Baroque city center and breathe the same air as the great German minds (p. 468).
Weimar (1 day) Goethe's old stomping grounds have been dubbed the cultural capital of Europe (p. 414).

UNIVERSITY CROWNS (3 WEEKS)

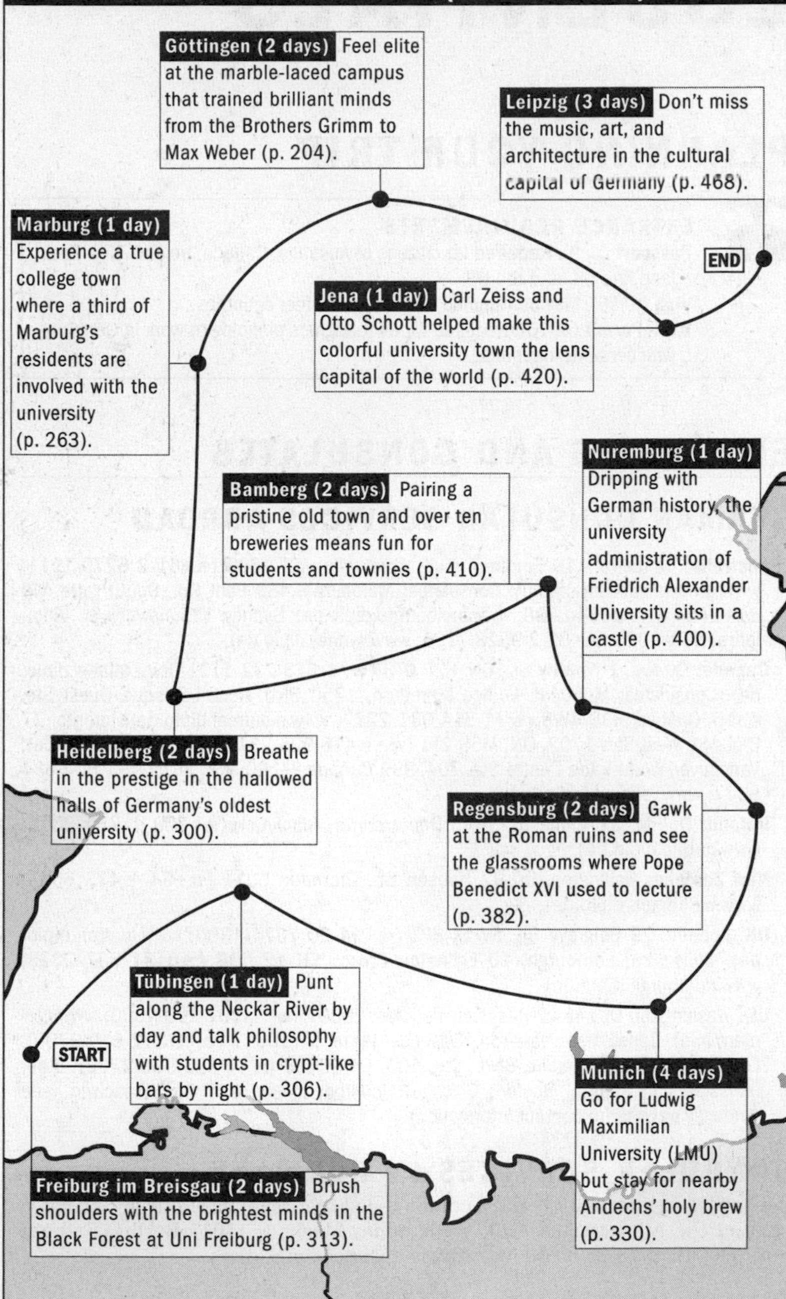

Freiburg im Breisgau (2 days) Brush shoulders with the brightest minds in the Black Forest at Uni Freiburg (p. 313).

Tübingen (1 day) Punt along the Neckar River by day and talk philosophy with students in crypt-like bars by night (p. 306).

Munich (4 days) Go for Ludwig Maximilian University (LMU) but stay for nearby Andechs' holy brew (p. 330).

Regensburg (2 days) Gawk at the Roman ruins and see the glassrooms where Pope Benedict XVI used to lecture (p. 382).

Nuremburg (1 day) Dripping with German history, the university administration of Friedrich Alexander University sits in a castle (p. 400).

Bamberg (2 days) Pairing a pristine old town and over ten breweries means fun for students and townies (p. 410).

Heidelberg (2 days) Breathe in the prestige in the hallowed halls of Germany's oldest university (p. 300).

Marburg (1 day) Experience a true college town where a third of Marburg's residents are involved with the university (p. 263).

Göttingen (2 days) Feel elite at the marble-laced campus that trained brilliant minds from the Brothers Grimm to Max Weber (p. 204).

Jena (1 day) Carl Zeiss and Otto Schott helped make this colorful university town the lens capital of the world (p. 420).

Leipzig (3 days) Don't miss the music, art, and architecture in the cultural capital of Germany (p. 468).

ESSENTIALS

PLANNING YOUR TRIP

ENTRANCE REQUIREMENTS

Passport (p. 9). Required for citizens of Australia, Canada, Ireland, New Zealand, the UK, and the US.

Visa (p. 10). May be required of citizens of other countries.

Work Permit (p. 10). Required for all foreigners planning to work in Germany with certain exceptions.

EMBASSIES AND CONSULATES

GERMAN CONSULAR SERVICES ABROAD

Australia: Canberra, 119 Empire Circuit, Yarralumla, ACT 2600 (☎+61 2 6270 1911; www.germanembassy.org.au). Consulates: Melbourne, 480 Punt Rd., South Yarra, VIC 3141 (☎+61 3 9864 6888; www.melbourne.diplo.de); Sydney, 13 Trelawney St., Woollahra, NSW 2025 (☎+61 2 9328 7733; www.sydney.diplo.de).

Canada: Ottawa, 1 Waverly St., ON, K2P OT8 (☎+1 613 232 1101; www.ottawa.diplo.de). Consulates: Montréal, Edifice Marathon, 1250 Blvd. René-Lévesque Ouest Ste. 4315, Québec, H3B 4W8 (☎+1 514 931 2277; www.montreal.diplo.de); Toronto, 77 Bloor St. West Ste. 1702, ON, M5S 2T1 (☎+1 416 925 2813; www.toronto.diplo.de); Vancouver, World Trade Centre Ste. 704, 999 Canada Pl., BC, V6C 3E1 (☎+1 604 684 8377; www.vancouver.diplo.de).

Ireland: Dublin, 31 Trimleston Ave., Booterstown, Blackrock (☎+353 1 269 3011; www.dublin.diplo.de).

New Zealand: Wellington, 90-92 Hobson St., Thorndon 6011 (☎+64 4 473 6063; www.wellington.diplo.de).

UK: London, 23 Belgrave Sq. SW1X 8PZ (☎+44 20 7824 1300; www.london.diplo.de). Consulate: Edinburgh, 16 Eglington Cresc., EH 12 5DG (☎0131 337 2323; www.edinburgh.diplo.de).

US: Washington, DC, 4645 Reservoir Rd., NW 20007 (☎+1 202-298-4000; www.germany.info). Consulates: New York, 871 U.N. Plaza, NY 10017 (☎+1 212-610-9700); Los Angeles, 6222 Wilshire Blvd., Ste. 500, CA 90048 (☎+1 323-930-2703); other consulates in Atlanta, Boston, Chicago, Houston, Miami, and San Francisco (see embassy website for contact information).

CONSULAR SERVICES IN GERMANY

For the latest information and a complete list of foreign missions in Germany, contact the Auswärtiges Amt, Wederscher Markt 1, 11017 Berlin (Federal Foreign Office ☎030 50 00; www.auswaertiges-amt.de).

Australia: Frankfurt, Neue Mainzer Str. 52-58, 60311 (☎069 90 50 80; www.germany.embassy.gov.au).

Canada: Düsseldorf, Bernratherstr. 8, 40213 (☎0211 17 21 70). Hamburg, Ballindamm 35, 20095 (☎040 460 0270). Munich, Tal 29, 80331 (☎089 219 9570). Stuttgart, Lange Str. 51, 70174 (☎0711 223 9678). All are listed at www.canada.de.

Ireland: Cologne, Frankenforsterstr. 77, 51427 (☎022 04 60 98 60). Frankfurt, Graefstr. 99, 60487 (☎069 977 883 883). Hamburg, Feldbrunnenstr. 43, 20148 (☎040 44 18 61 13). Munich, Denninger Str. 15, 81679 (☎089 20 80 59 90). More information at www.embassyofireland.de.

New Zealand: Hamburg, Domstr. 19, 20095 (☎040 442 5550; www.nzembassy.com).

UK: Düsseldorf, Yorckstr. 19, 40476 (☎0211 944 80). Munich, Bürkleinstr. 10, 80538 (☎089 21 10 90). All listed at www.britischebotschaft.de.

US: Düsseldorf, Willi-Becker-Allee 10, 40227 (☎0211 788 8927; http://dusseldorf.consulate.gov). Frankfurt, Gießener Str. 30, 60435 (☎069 753 50; http://frankfurt.usconsulate.gov). Hamburg, Alsterufer 27/28, 20354 (☎040 411 71 10; http://hamburg.usconsulate.gov). Leipzig, Wilhelm-Seyfferth-Str. 4, 04107 (☎0341 213 840. http://leipzig.usconsulate.gov). Munich, Königinstr. 5, 80539 (☎089 288 80; http://munich.usconsulate.gov).

TOURIST OFFICES

The German National Tourist Office (GNTO) is based at Beethovenstr. 69, 60325 Frankfurt (www.germany-tourism.de). This umbrella organization supervises Germany's international tourist infrastructure and provides trip-planning information. The website is a veritable goldmine for quick reference.

DOCUMENTS AND FORMALITIES

PASSPORTS

REQUIREMENTS

Citizens of Australia, Canada, Ireland, New Zealand, the UK, and the US need valid passports to enter Germany and to return home. Germany does not allow entrance if the holder's passport expires in under six months, and attempting to return home with an expired passport is illegal and may result in a fine.

NEW PASSPORTS

Citizens of Australia, Canada, Ireland, New Zealand, the UK, and the US can apply for a passport at any passport office or at selected post offices and courts of law. Citizens of these countries may also download passport applications from the official website of their country's government or passport office. Any new passport or renewal applications must be filed well in advance of the departure date, though most passport offices offer rush services for a very steep fee. "Rushed" passports still take up to two weeks to arrive.

PASSPORT MAINTENANCE

Photocopy the page of your passport with your photo as well as your visas, traveler's check serial numbers, and any other important documents. Carry one set of copies in a safe place, apart from the originals, and leave another set at home. Consulates also recommend that you carry an expired passport or an official copy of your birth certificate separate from other documents.

If you lose your passport, immediately notify the local police and your home country's nearest embassy or consulate. To expedite its replacement, you must show ID and proof of citizenship; it also helps to know all information previously recorded in the passport. In some cases, a replacement may take weeks to process, and it may be valid only for a limited time. Any visas stamped in your old passport will be lost forever. In an emergency, ask for immediate temporary traveling papers that will permit you to re-enter your home country.

VISAS, INVITATIONS, AND WORK PERMITS

VISAS

Citizens of Australia, Canada, Ireland, New Zealand, the UK, the US need a valid passport for entrance into Germany. The passport cannot expire any less than four months after your arrival in Germany. EU citizens, including individuals from Ireland and the UK do not need a visa and may stay indefinitely. Citizens of Australia, Canada, New Zealand, and the US do not need a visa for stays of up to 90 days, but this three-month period begins upon entry into any of the countries that belong to the EU's freedom of movement zone. Those staying longer than 90 days may purchase a visa at their local mission. A national visa costs €60 and allows the holder to live or study in Germany for a set period of time. A hybrid visa can also be obtained for €60, and it offers the benefits of a national visa with the freedom to stay in other countries in the EU. Double-check entrance requirements at the nearest embassy or consulate of Germany (see **German Consular Services Abroad,** on p. 8) for up-to-date information before departure. US citizens can also consult http://travel.state.gov.

WORK PERMITS

A traveler's admittance into a certain country does not grant the right to work, which is authorized only by a work permit. For more information on this, refer to the **Beyond Tourism** chapter (p. 61).

IDENTIFICATION

When you travel, always carry at least two forms of identification on your person, including a photo ID. A passport and a driver's license. Never carry all of your IDs together. Instead, split them up to protect against theft or loss and keep photocopies of all of them in your luggage and at home.

STUDENT, TEACHER, AND YOUTH IDENTIFICATION

The **International Student Identity Card** (ISIC), the most widely accepted form of student ID, provides discounts on some sights, accommodations, food, and transportation, access to a 24hr. emergency help line, and insurance benefits for US cardholders (see **Insurance,** p. 18). ISIC discounts on museums abound in Germany. Applicants must be full-time secondary or post-secondary school students at least 12 years old. Because of the proliferation of fake ISICs, some services (particularly airlines) require additional proof of student identity.

The **International Teacher Identity Card (ITIC)** offers teachers the same insurance coverage as the ISIC and similar but limited discounts. To qualify for the card, teachers must be currently employed and have worked a minimum of 18hr. per week for at least one full school year. For travelers who are under 26 years old but are not currently students, the **International Youth Travel Card (IYTC)** offers many of the same benefits as the ISIC.

Each of these identity cards costs US$22. ISICs, ITICs, and IYTCs are valid for one year from the date of issue. To learn more about ISICs, ITICs, and IYTCs, visit www.myisic.com. Many student travel agencies issue the cards; for a list of issuing agencies or more information, see the **International Student Travel Confederation (ISTC)** website (www.istc.org).

The **International Student Exchange Card (ISE Card)** is a similar identification card available to students, faculty, and children aged 12 to 26. The card provides discounts, medical benefits, access to a 24hr. emergency help line, and the opportunity to purchase student airfares. An ISE Card costs US$25; call ☎+1 800-255-8000 (in North America) or ☎+1 480-951-1177 (from all other continents) for more info or visit www.isecard.com.

CUSTOMS

Upon entering Germany, you must declare certain items from abroad and pay a duty on the value of those articles if they exceed the allowance established by Germany's customs service. Goods and gifts purchased at duty-free shops abroad are not exempt from duty or sales tax—"duty-free" just means that you won't pay tax in the country of purchase. Duty-free allowances were abolished for travel between EU member states on June 30, 1999, but still exist for those arriving from outside the EU. Upon returning home, you must likewise declare all articles acquired abroad and pay a duty on the value of articles in excess of your home country's allowance. In order to expedite your return, make a list of any valuables brought from home and register them with customs before traveling abroad. It's a good idea to keep receipts for all goods acquired abroad.

MONEY

CURRENCY AND EXCHANGE

The currency chart below is based on August 2008 exchange rates between local currency and Australian dollars (AUS$), Canadian dollars (CDN$), European Union euro (EUR€), New Zealand dollars (NZ$), British pounds (UK£), and US dollars (US$). Check the currency converter on websites like www.xe.com or www.bloomberg.com for the latest exchange rates.

EURO(€)		
	AUS$ = €0.59	€1 = AUS$1.70
	CDN$ = €0.62	€1 = CDN$1.62
	NZ$ = €0.47	€1 = NZ$2.15
	UK£ = €1.26	€1 = UK£0.79
	US$ = €0.65	€1 = US$1.54

As a general rule, it's cheaper to convert money in Germany than at home. While currency exchange will probably be available in your arrival airport, it's wise to bring enough foreign currency to last for at least a few days.

When changing money abroad, try to go only to banks or *Geldwechsel* (money exchange) locations that have at most a 5% margin between their buy and sell prices. Since you lose money with every transaction, it makes sense to convert large sums at one time (unless the currency is depreciating rapidly).

If you use traveler's checks or bills, carry some in small denominations (the equivalent of US$50 or less) for times when you are forced to exchange money at poor rates, but bring a range of denominations since charges may be applied per check cashed. Store your money in a variety of forms: ideally, some cash, some traveler's checks, and an ATM and/or credit card.

CREDIT, DEBIT, AND ATM CARDS

Where they are accepted, credit cards often offer superior exchange rates, up to 5% better than the retail rate used by banks and other currency exchange establishments. Credit card companies may also offer services like insurance or emergency help and are sometimes required to reserve hotel rooms or rental cars. **MasterCard** (a.k.a. EuroCard in Europe) and **Visa** are the most frequently accepted, and **American Express** cards work at some ATMs and at AmEx offices and major airports.

The use of ATM cards is widespread in Germany. Depending on the system that your home bank uses, you can likely access your personal bank account from abroad. ATMs get the same wholesale exchange rate as credit cards, but there is often a limit on the amount of money you can withdraw per day (usually around US$500). There is also typically a surcharge of US$1-5 per withdrawal. These fees vary and escalate as you move away from urban centers. In smaller villages, you will have limited options for withdrawls.

Debit cards are as convenient as credit cards but withdraw money directly from the holder's checking account. A debit card can be used wherever its associated credit card company (usually MasterCard or Visa) is accepted. Debit cards often also function as ATM cards and can be used to withdraw cash from associated banks and ATMs throughout Germany.

The two major international money networks are **MasterCard/Maestro/Cirrus** (for ATM locations ☎+1-800-424-7787 or www.mastercard.com) and **Visa/PLUS** (for ATM locations ☎+1-800-847-2911 or www.visa.com). American Express and Diners Club cards are not as prevalent in Germany as elsewhere, but may be accepted in upscale restaurants and hotels, or in heavily touristed areas. Most ATMs charge a transaction fee paid to the bank that owns the ATM.

GETTING MONEY FROM HOME

If you run out of money while traveling, the easiest and cheapest solution is to have someone back home make a deposit to your bank account. Otherwise, consider one of the following options.

PINS AND ATMS. To use a debit or credit card to withdraw money from a cash machine (ATM) in Europe, you must have a four-digit Personal Identification Number (PIN). If your current PIN is longer than four digits, ask your bank whether you can just use the first four or whether you'll need a new number. Credit cards don't usually come with PINs, so if you intend to hit up ATMs in Europe with a credit card to get cash advances, call your credit card company before leaving to request one.

Travelers with alphabetic rather than numerical PINs may also be thrown off by the absence of letters on European cash machines. Here are the corresponding numbers: 1 = QZ; 2 = ABC; 3 = DEF; 4 = GHI; 5 = JKL; 6 = MNO; 7 = PRS; 8 = TUV; and 9 = WXY. If you mistakenly punch the wrong code into the machine three times, it will swallow your card for good.

WIRING MONEY

It is possible to arrange a bank money transfer, which means asking a bank back home to wire money to a bank in Germany. This is the cheapest way to transfer cash, but it's also the slowest, usually taking several days or more. Note that some banks may only release your funds in local currency, potentially sticking you with a poor exchange rate; inquire about this in advance. German banks do not issue personal checks to their customers, and therefore won't cash a traveler's personal check unless that individual has an account with the bank. Other options include online banking and PayPal. Money transfer services like **Western Union** are faster and more convenient than bank transfers—but also much pricier. Western Union has many locations worldwide. To find one, visit www.westernunion.com, or call: in Australia ☎1800 173 833, in Canada and the US 800-325-6000, in the UK 0800 833 833, or in Germany +49 180 18 18 123. To wire money using a credit card (Discover, MasterCard, Visa), call in Canada and the US ☎800-CALL-CASH/225-5227, in the UK +44 0800 833 833. Money transfer services are also available to **American Express** cardholders and at selected **Thomas Cook** offices.

US STATE DEPARTMENT (US CITIZENS ONLY)

In emergencies only, the US State Department will forward money within hours to the nearest consular office, which will then disburse it according to instructions for a fee of US$30. If you wish to use this service, you must contact the Overseas Citizens Services division of the US State Department (☎+1-202-501-4444, from US ☎888-407-4747).

COSTS

STAYING ON A BUDGET

To give you a general idea, a bare-bones day in Germany (camping or sleeping in hostels/guesthouses, buying food at supermarkets) would cost about US$42 (€27); a slightly more comfortable day (sleeping in hostels/guesthouses and the occasional budget hotel, eating one meal per day at a restaurant, going out at night) would cost US$71 (€46); and, for a luxurious day, the sky's the limit. Don't forget to factor in emergency reserve funds (at least US$200) when planning your budget.

TIPS FOR SAVING MONEY

Some simpler ways include searching out opportunities for free entertainment, splitting accommodation and food costs with trustworthy fellow travelers, and buying food in supermarkets rather than eating out. Bring a **sleepsack** (p. 14) to save on sheet charges in hostels and do your **laundry** in the sink when possible. Museums often have certain days once a month or once a week when admission is free, so plan accordingly. If you are eligible, consider getting an ISIC or an IYTC (p. 10) to take advantage of reduced admission at museums and sights. For getting around quickly, bikes are the most economical option. Renting a bike is cheaper than renting a moped or scooter. Don't forget about walking: you can learn a lot about a city by seeing it on foot. Drinking at bars and clubs quickly becomes expensive. It's cheaper to buy alcohol at a supermarket and imbibe before going out. That said, don't go overboard. Though staying within your budget is important, don't do so at the expense of your health or a great travel experience.

TIPPING AND BARGAINING

Tipping is practiced less liberally in Germany than it is elsewhere. Most Germans only round up a euro or two in restaurants and bars as tip, no matter the bill, and may give a small tip when getting a service, like a taxi ride. Tips in Germany are not left on the table, but handed directly to the server. If you don't want any change, say *"Das steht so"* (dahs SHTAYT zo) or *"Das stimmt so"* (dahs SHTIMT zo). Germans rarely bargain except at flea markets.

TAXES

Most goods and services bought in Germany include a Value-Added Tax of 16% (7% for books, food, and agricultural products) called the *Mehrwertsteuer* (MwSt). Non-EU citizens can usually get MwSt refunded for large purchases (not services). Ask for a Tax-Free Shopping Form at points of purchase, and present it at customs upon leaving the country, along with your receipts and the goods (which must remain unused until you leave the country). Refunds can be claimed at Tax Free Shopping Offices, found at most airports, road borders, and ferry stations, or by mail (Tax-Free Shopping Processing Center, Trubelg. 19, 1030 Vienna, Austria). For more information, contact the German VAT refund hotline (in English, ☎0228 406 2880; vwww.bzst.de).

PACKING

Pack lightly: lay out only what you absolutely need, then take half the clothes and twice the money. The Travelite FAQ (www.travelite.org) is a good resource for tips on traveling light. The online **Universal Packing List** (http://upl.codeq.info) will generate a customized list of suggested items based on your trip length, the expected climate, your planned activities, and other factors. If you plan to do a lot of hiking, see **The Great Outdoors,** p. 34.

Luggage: If you plan to cover most of your trip on foot, a sturdy **internal-frame backpack** is unbeatable. (For the basics on buying a pack, see p. 35.) Unless you are staying in 1 place for a large chunk of time, a suitcase or trunk will be unwieldy. In addition to your main piece of luggage, a **daypack** (a small backpack or courier bag) is useful.

Clothing: No matter when you're traveling, it's a good idea to bring a warm jacket or wool sweater, a rain jacket (Gore-Tex® is both waterproof and breathable), sturdy shoes or hiking boots, and thick socks. Flip-flops or waterproof sandals are must-haves for grubby hostel showers, and extra socks are always a good idea. You may also want 1 outfit for going out and a nicer pair of shoes. If you plan on visiting religious or cultural sites, you will need modest and respectful dress.

Sleepsack: Some hostels require that you either provide your own linen or rent sheets from them. Save cash by making your own sleepsack: fold a full-size sheet in half the long way, then sew it closed along the long side and one of the short sides.

Converters and Adapters: In Germany, electricity is 230 volts AC, enough to fry any 120V North American appliance. 220/240V electrical appliances won't work with a 120V current, either. Americans and Canadians should buy an adapter (which changes the shape of the plug; US$5) and a converter (which changes the voltage; US$10-30). Don't make the mistake of using only an adapter (unless appliance instructions explicitly state otherwise). Australians and New Zealanders (who use 230V at home) won't need a converter, but will need a set of adapters to use anything electrical.

Toiletries: Condoms, deodorant, razors, tampons, and toothbrushes are often available, but it may be difficult to find your preferred brand, so bring extras if you're picky. Contact lenses are likely to be expensive and difficult to find in Germany, so bring enough extra pairs and solution for your entire trip. Also bring your glasses and a copy of your prescription in case you need emergency replacements.

First-Aid Kit: For a basic first-aid kit, pack bandages, a pain reliever, antibiotic cream, a thermometer, a multi-function pocketknife, tweezers, moleskin, decongestant, motion-sickness remedy, diarrhea or upset-stomach medication (Pepto Bismol® or Imodium®), an antihistamine, sunscreen, insect repellent, and burn ointment.

Other Useful Items: For safety purposes, you should bring a **money belt** and a small **padlock.** Basic **outdoors equipment** (plastic water bottle, compass, waterproof matches, pocketknife, sunglasses, sunscreen, hat) may also be handy. Quick repairs of torn garments can be done with a needle and thread and small tears in other materials can be patched with electrical tape. Other useful items include: an umbrella, sealable **plastic bags**, an **alarm clock,** safety pins, rubber bands, a flashlight, earplugs, garbage bags, and a small calculator. A **cell phone** can be a lifesaver on the road; see p. 29.

Important Documents: Don't forget your passport, traveler's checks, ATM or credit cards, adequate ID, and photocopies of all of the aforementioned in case these documents are lost or stolen (p. 8). Also check that you have any of the following that might apply to you: a hosteling membership card (p. 32), driver's license (p. 26), travel insurance forms (p. 18), ISIC (p. 10), and railpass or bus pass (p. 25).

SAFETY AND HEALTH

GENERAL ADVICE

In any type of crisis, the most important thing to do is **stay calm.** Your country's embassy abroad (p. 8) is usually your best resource in an emergency, and it is a good idea to registering with that embassy upon arrival in the country. The government offices listed in the **Travel Advisories** box (p. 17) can provide information on the services they offer citizens in case of emergencies abroad.

LOCAL LAWS AND POLICE

Abide by all locals laws while in Germany. Certain regulations might seem harsh and unusual—the police's keeness for ticketing jay-walkers, for instance. Many offenses will result in fines, and some will land you in jail. Most English-speaking countries will not be able to bypass the

TOP 10 WAYS TO SAVE IN GERMANY

10. Love Parade. Dance like it's the end of the world as Westphalian towns resurrect Berlin's epic street party.

9. Sacred Churches. Rid yourself of guilt but not *Gelt*, at some of Germany's greatest cultural landmarks, including Ulm's Minster, the world's tallest church.

8. National Parks. Hike the holy Alps, bike the beautiful Rhine, or swim the glacial lakes throughout the country (p. 34).

7. Händel's Organ, Halle. Enjoy free concerts where Händel honed his harmonies.

6. Spa Towns. Take a dip in the Roman baths at Baden-Baden, or breathe some soothing brine in Ramsau (p. 362).

5. Outdoor Concerts, Munich. Join the crowds in Olympiapark to see famous and home-grown bands (p. 346). Don't miss the Tollwood Festival in July p. 349).

4. Der BahnCard. This network discount card will save you loads of cash in Germany and in other European countries.

3. Museums. Skip admission prices at Berlin's East Side Gallery (p. 111) or most museums during their last hour of opening.

2. Döner Kebap. This delicious Turkish treat is an unbeatable and ubiquitous value.

1. Reichstag, Berlin. Climb to the glass dome at the top of Germany's historic house of parliament for a city panorama (p. 108).

local judicial system and get you off the hook. That said, the *Polizei* can be extremely helpful. Be sure to carry a valid passport, as police have the right to ask for identification.

DRUGS AND ALCOHOL

A meek "I didn't know it was illegal" will not fly in Germany. It is your responsibility to familiarize yourself with local laws. If you carry insulin, syringes, or any prescription drugs, you must have a copy of the prescriptions and a doctor's note. Avoid public drunkenness: it can jeopardize your safety and earn the disdain of locals. The drinking age in Germany is 16 for beer and wine and 18 for spirits. The maximum blood alcohol level for drivers is 0.08%.

Needless to say, illegal drugs are best avoided. The average sentence for possession in Germany is seven years. In 1994, the German High Court ruled that while possession of marijuana or hashish is still illegal, possession of "small quantities for personal consumption" is not prosecutable. Each Land has interpreted "small quantities" differently (anywhere from 6 to 30 grams). More liberal areas like Berlin and Hamburg tend toward the higher end of this range, while East Germany and more conservative provinces like Bavaria are less lenient. The worst offense is carrying drugs across an international border; not only could you end up in prison, but you could be marked with a "Drug Trafficker" stamp on your passport, which lasts for life. Embassies may be unwilling to help those arrested on drug charges.

PERSONAL SAFETY

EXPLORING AND TRAVELING

To avoid unwanted attention, try to blend in as much as possible. Respecting local customs (in many cases, dressing more conservatively than you would at home) can help ward off would-be hecklers. Familiarize yourself with your surroundings before setting out and carry yourself with confidence. Check maps in shops and restaurants rather than on the street. If you are traveling alone, be sure that someone at home knows your itinerary and never tell anyone you meet that you're by yourself. When walking at night, stick to busy, well-lit streets and avoid dark alleyways. If you ever feel uncomfortable, leave the area as quickly and directly as you can.

There is no surefire way to avoid all the threatening situations that you might encounter while traveling, but a good **self-defense course** will give you concrete ways to react to unwanted advances. **Impact, Prepare,** and **Model Mugging** can refer you to local self-defense courses in Australia, Canada, Switzerland, and the US. Visit www.modelmugging.org for a list of nearby chapters.

If you are using a **car,** learn local driving signals and wear a seatbelt. Children under 40 lb. should ride only in specially designed car seats, available for a small fee from most car-rental agencies. Study route maps before you hit the road and, if you plan on spending a lot of time driving, consider bringing spare parts. For long drives in desolate areas, invest in a cellular phone and a roadside assistance program (p. 26). Park your vehicle in a garage or well-traveled area and use a steering-wheel locking device in larger cities. Sleeping in your car is the most dangerous way to get your rest, and it's also illegal in many countries. For info on the perils of **hitchhiking,** see p. 29.

ESSENTIALS

POSSESSIONS AND VALUABLES

Never leave your belongings unattended. Bring your own padlock for hostel lockers and never store valuables in a locker. Be particularly careful on **buses** and **trains:** horror stories abound about determined thieves who wait for travelers to fall asleep. Carry your bag or purse in front of you where you can see it. When traveling with others, sleep in alternate shifts. When alone, use good judgment in selecting a train compartment: never stay in an empty one and use a lock to secure your pack to the luggage rack. Use extra caution if traveling at night or on overnight trains. Try to sleep on top bunks with your luggage stored above you (if not in bed with you), and keep important documents and other valuables on you at all times.

A few steps can take to minimize the financial risk associated with traveling. First, **bring as few belongings as possible.** Second, buy a few combination **padlocks** to secure your belongings either in your pack or in a hostel or train-station locker. Third, **carry as little cash as possible.** Keep your traveler's checks and ATM/credit cards in a **money belt**—not a "fanny pack"—along with passport and ID cards. Fourth, **keep a small cash reserve separate from your primary stash.** This should be about US$50 (US dollars or euros are best) sewn into or stored in the depths of your pack, along with your traveler's check numbers, photocopies of your passport, your birth certificate, and other important documents.

In large cities, **con artists** often work in groups and may incoprorate children. Beware of certain classic scenarios: sob stories that require money, rolls of bills "found" on the street, mustard spilled (or saliva spit) onto your shoulder to distract you while they snatch your bag. **Never let your passport and your bags out of your sight.** Hostel workers will sometimes stand at bus and train-station arrival points to recruit tired and disoriented travelers to their hostel. Be wary of strangers who tell you that theirs is the only hostel open. Beware of **pickpockets** in city crowds, especially on public transportation. Also, be alert in public telephone booths: if you must say your calling card number, do so very quietly; if you punch it in, make sure no one is looking over your shoulder.

If you will be traveling with electronic devices, such as a laptop computer or a PDA, check whether your homeowner's insurance covers loss, theft, or damage when you travel. If not, you might consider purchasing a low-cost separate insurance policy. **Safeware** (☎+1-800-800-1492; www.safeware.com) specializes in covering computers and charges $90 for 90-day comprehensive international travel coverage up to $4000.

TRAVEL ADVISORIES. The following government offices provide travel information and advisories by telephone, by fax, or via the web:

Australian Department of Foreign Affairs and Trade: ☎+61 2 6261 1111; www.dfat.gov.au.

Canadian Department of Foreign Affairs and International Trade (DFAIT): ☎+1-800-267-8376; www.dfait-maeci.gc.ca. Call for their free booklet, *Bon Voyage...But.*

New Zealand Ministry of Foreign Affairs: ☎+64 4 439 8000; www.mfat.govt.nz.

United Kingdom Foreign and Commonwealth Office: ☎+44 20 7008 1500; www.fco.gov.uk.

US Department of State: ☎+1-888-407-4747; http://travel.state.gov. Visit the website for a booklet, *A Safe Trip Abroad.*

PRE-DEPARTURE HEALTH

In your passport, write the names of any people you wish to be contacted in case of a **medical emergency** and list any allergies or medical conditions. Matching a prescription to a foreign equivalent is not always easy, safe, or possible, so, if you take **prescription drugs,** carry up-to-date prescriptions or a statement from your doctor stating the medication's trade name, manufacturer, chemical name, and dosage. While traveling, be sure to keep all medication with you in your carry-on luggage. For tips on packing a **first-aid kit** and other health essentials, see p. 15.

Common drugs such as aspirin, acetaminophen, and antihistamines (allergy medicines) are readily available in Germany. Many items will be much more expensive at a German pharmacies (*Apotheke*), however. Certain drugs like pseudoephedrine (Sudafed), some cough syrups, and diphenhydramine (Benadryl) are not available at all, so you should plan accordingly.

IMMUNIZATIONS AND PRECAUTIONS

Travelers over two years old should confirm that the following vaccines are up to date: MMR (for measles, mumps, and rubella); DTaP or Td (for diphtheria, tetanus, and pertussis); IPV (for polio); Hib (for *haemophilus influenzae* B); and HepB (for Hepatitis B). For recommendations on immunizations and prophylaxis, consult the Centers for Disease Control and Prevention (CDC; see below) in the US or the equivalent in your home country and ask a doctor.

INSURANCE

Travel insurance covers four basic areas: medical problems, property loss, trip cancellation and interruption, and emergency evacuation. Though regular insurance policies may well extend to travel-related accidents, you should consider purchasing separate travel insurance if the cost of potential trip cancellation, interruption, or emergency medical evacuation is greater than you can absorb. Prices for travel insurance purchased separately generally run about US$50 per week for full coverage, while trip cancellation/interruption may be purchased separately at a rate of US$3-5 per day, depending on length of stay.

Medical insurance (especially university policies) often covers costs incurred abroad. Check with your provider. **Homeowners' insurance** (or your family's coverage) often covers theft during travel and loss of travel documents (passport, plane ticket, railpass, etc.) up to US$500.

ISIC and **ITIC** (p. 10) provide basic insurance benefits to US cardholders, including US$100 per day of in-hospital sickness for up to 100 days and US$10,000 of accident-related medical reimbursement (see www.isicus.com for details). Cardholders also have access to a toll-free 24hr. helpline for medical, legal, and financial emergencies while overseas. **American Express** (☎+1-800-338-1670) grants most cardholders automatic collision and theft insurance on car rentals made with the card.

USEFUL ORGANIZATIONS AND PUBLICATIONS

The American **Centers for Disease Control and Prevention** (**CDC;** ☎+1-877-FYI-TRIP/394-8747; www.cdc.gov/travel) maintains an international travelers' hotline and an informative website. Consult the appropriate government agency from your home country for consular information sheets on health, entry requirements, and other issues for various countries. For contact information, see the listings in the box on **Travel Advisories,** p. 17). For quick access to information on health and other travel warnings, call the **Overseas Citizens Services** (from overseas +1-202-501-4444, from US ☎+1-888-407-4747;

line open M-F 8am-8pm EST) or contact a passport agency, embassy, or consulate abroad. For information on medical evacuation services and travel insurance firms, see the US government's website at http://travel.state.gov/travel/abroad_health.html or the **British Foreign and Commonwealth Office** (www.fco.gov.uk). For general health information, contact the **American Red Cross** (☎+1-202-303-4498; www.redcross.org).

ESSENTIALS

STAYING HEALTHY

Common sense is the simplest prescription for good health while you travel. Drink lots of fluids to prevent dehydration and constipation and wear sturdy, broken-in shoes and clean socks. Germany enjoys a fairly temperate climate and relatively safe landscape, so day-to-day activities might not seem taxing. The stress of traveling can take its toll, however, and you should always be mindful of your mental and physical wellness.

MEDICAL CARE ON THE ROAD

Germany has quality medical care readily accessible to travelers. EU citizens in possession of an E11 form can get free first aid and emergency services. Travelers from outside the EU may visit private practitioners and pay on a per-visit basis for non-emergency situations.

If you are concerned about obtaining medical assistance while traveling, you may wish to employ special support services. The **MedPass** from **Global-Care, Inc.,** 6875 Shiloh Rd. East, Alpharetta, GA 30005, USA (☎+1-800-860-1111; www.globalcare.net) provides 24hr. international medical assistance, support, and medical evacuation resources. The **International Association for Medical Assistance to Travelers** (**IAMAT;** US ☎716-754-4883, Canada 519-836-0102; www.iamat.org) has free membership, lists English-speaking doctors worldwide, and offers detailed information on immunization requirements and sanitation. If your regular insurance policy does not cover travel abroad, you may wish to purchase additional coverage (p. 18).

Travelers with medical conditions (such as diabetes, allergies to antibiotics, epilepsy, or heart conditions) may want to obtain a **MedicAlert** membership (US$40 per year), which includes among other things a stainless-steel ID tag and a 24hr. collect-call number. Contact the MedicAlert Foundation International, 2323 Colorado Ave., Turlock, CA 95382, USA (from US ☎888-633-4298, outside US +1 209-668-3333; www.medicalert.org).

WOMEN'S HEALTH

Women traveling in unsanitary conditions are vulnerable to urinary tract infections, including bladder and kidney infections. Bring supplies from home if you are prone to infection, as they may be difficult to find on the road. Tampons, pads, and contraceptive devices are widely available, though your favorite brand may not be stocked so bring extras of anything you can't live without. First-trimester abortion is legal in Germany, but in order to get one, a woman must undergo counseling and a three-day wait. Contact PRO FAMILIA Bundesverband (a family parenthood group; www.profamilia.de) or the state-supported BZgA (www.familienplanung.de).

GETTING TO GERMANY

BY PLANE

When it comes to airfare, a little effort can save you a bundle. Courier fares are the cheapest for those whose plans are flexible enough to deal with the restrictions. Tickets sold by consolidators and standby seating are also good deals, but last-minute specials, airfare wars, and charter flights often beat these fares. The key is to hunt around, be flexible, and ask about discounts. Students, seniors, and those under 26 should never have to pay full price for a ticket.

BUDGET AND STUDENT TRAVEL AGENCIES

While knowledgeable agents specializing in flights to Germany can make your life easy, they may not spend the time to find you the lowest possible fare—they get paid on commission. Travelers holding ISICs and IYTCs (p. 10) qualify for big discounts from student travel agencies. Most flights from budget agencies are on major airlines, but in peak season some may sell seats on less reliable chartered aircraft.

STA Travel, 5900 Wilshire Blvd., Ste. 900, Los Angeles, CA 90036, USA (24hr. reservations and info ☎+1-800-781-4040; www.statravel.com). A student and youth travel organization with over 150 offices worldwide (check their website for a listing of all their offices), including US offices in Boston, Chicago, Los Angeles, New York, Seattle, San Francisco, and Washington, DC. Ticket booking, travel insurance, railpasses, and more. Walk-in offices are located throughout Australia (☎+61 3 9207 5900), New Zealand (☎+64 9 309 9723), and the UK (☎+44 8701 630 026).

The Adventure Travel Company, 24 MacDougal St., New York, NY 10021, USA (☎+1-800-467-4595; www.theadventuretravelcompany.com). Offices across Canada and the US, including Champaign, New York, San Diego, Seattle, and San Francisco.

USIT, 19-21 Aston Quay, Dublin 2, Ireland (☎+353 1 602 1904; www.usit.ie). Ireland's leading student/budget travel agency has 20 offices throughout Northern Ireland and the Republic of Ireland. Offers programs to work, study, and volunteer worldwide.

COMMERCIAL AIRLINES

TRAVELING FROM NORTH AMERICA

The most common ways to cross the pond are those you've probably heard of. Standard commercial carriers like **American** (☎+1-800-433-7300; www.aa.com), **United** (☎+1-800-538-2929; www.ual.com), and **Northwest** (☎+1-800-447-4747; www.nwa.com) will probably offer the most convenient flights, but they may not be the cheapest. Check **Lufthansa** (☎+1-800-399-5838; www.lufthansa.com), **British Airways** (☎+1-800-247-9297; www.britishairways.com), **Air France** (☎+1-800-237-2747; www.airfrance.us), and **Alitalia** (☎+1-800-223-5730; www.alitaliausa.com) for cheap tickets from destinations throughout the US to all over Europe. You might find an even better deal on one of the following airlines, if any of their limited departure points is convenient for you.

Icelandair: ☎+1-800-223-5500; www.icelandair.com. Stopovers in Iceland for no extra cost on most transatlantic flights. New York to Frankfurt May-Sept. US$500-730; Oct.-May US$390-450. For last-minute offers, subscribe to Lucky Fares.

Finnair: ☎+1-800-950-5000; www.finnair.com. Cheap round-trip flights from San Francisco, New York, and Toronto to Helsinki. Connections throughout Europe.

Martinair: ☎+1-800-627-8462; www.martinair.com. Fly from Miami to Berlin, Düsseldorf, Frankfurt, Munich, and elsewhere mid-June to mid-Aug. US$1000.

TRAVELING FROM THE UK AND IRELAND

Cheapflights (www.cheapflights.co.uk) publishes bargains on airfare from the British Isles. Below is a short list of commercial carriers with special deals, but there is really no reason for British and Irish globetrotters not to fly on budget airlines (p. 21).

Aer Lingus: Ireland ☎+353 818 365 000; www.aerlingus.ie. Return tickets from Dublin, Cork, Galway, Kerry, and Shannon to Düsseldorf, Frankfurt, Munich (EUR€102-244).

KLM: UK ☎+44 8705 074 074; www.klmuk.com. Cheap return tickets from London and elsewhere to Frankfurt, Düsseldorf (UK£219). Traveling from Australia and New Zealand

Air New Zealand: New Zealand ☎+64 800 737 000; www.airnz.co.nz. Auckland to Frankfurt and Munich (NZ$2350-3150).

Qantas Air: Australia ☎+61 13 13 13, New Zealand ☎+64 800 808 767; www.qantas.com.au. Flights from Australia and New Zealand to Frankfurt for around AUS$2200.

Singapore Air: Australia ☎+61 13 10 11, New Zealand ☎+64 800 808 909; www.singaporeair.com. Flies from Auckland, Christchurch, Melbourne, Perth, and Sydney to Frankfurt (AUS$2600-2800).

Thai Airways: Australia ☎+61 1300 65 19 60, New Zealand ☎+64 9 377 3886; www.thaiair.com. Auckland, Melbourne, Perth, and Sydney to Berlin, Bremen, Cologne, Frankfurt, Munich, and others (AUS$1700-2300).

BUDGET AIRLINES

airberlin, (Germany ☎01805 737 800; www.airberlin.com). Germany's second largest airline boasts an extensive network of destinations from San Francisco to Russia, Cape Town to Reykjavik. One-way flights within Europe start at €29.

easyJet, (UK ☎0871 244 2366, 10p per min.; www.easyjet.com). London to Athens, Barcelona, Madrid, Nice, Palma, and Zurich (UK£72-141).

Ryanair, (Ireland ☎0818 30 30 30, UK 0871 246 0000; www.ryanair.com). Serves 72 locations across Europe including Berlin, Düsseldorf, Frankfurt and several more in Germany. Extraordinary fares regularly available (€0.01-100).

Sterling, (Denmark ☎70 10 84 84, UK ☎0870 787 8038; www.sterling.dk). The 1st Scandinavian-based budget airline. Connects Denmark, Norway, and Sweden to 47 European destinations. Copenhagen to Berlin (€40).

Germanwings, (Germany ☎020 7365 4997; www.germanwings.com). German subsidiary of Eurowings with flights across Europe. London to Berlin, Cologne, Dresden, Düsseldorf, Hamburg, Munich, and Stuttgart from €40 one-way.

TUIfly, (Germany ☎01805 757510; www.tuifly.com). Hanover-based travel agency with affiliates throughout Europe and the Mediterranean. Flights from the UK starting at €15. Endless menu of travel services available for budget prices. Check website.

FLIGHT PLANNING ON THE INTERNET. The Internet may be the budget traveler's dream when it comes to finding and booking bargain fares, but the array of options can be overwhelming. Many airline sites offer special last-minute deals on the web. Air Berlin (www.airberlin.com), Condor (www.condor.de), and Lufthansa (www.lufthansa.com) are the major German carriers and frequently offer fares not available on English flight search engines.

STA (www.statravel.com) and **StudentUniverse** (www.studentuniverse.com) provide quotes on student tickets, while **Orbitz** (www.orbitz.com), **Expedia** (www.expedia.com), and **Travelocity** (www.travelocity.com) offer full travel services. **Priceline** (www.priceline.com) lets you specify a price and obligates you to buy any ticket that meets or beats it, and **Hotwire** (www.hotwire.com) offers bargain fares but won't reveal the airline or flight times until you buy. Other sites that compile deals include www.bestfares.com, www.flights.com, www.lowestfare.com, www.onetravel.com, and www.travelzoo.com.

SideStep (www.sidestep.com) and **Booking Buddy** (www.bookingbuddy.com) are online tools that can help sift through multiple offers; these two let you enter your trip information once and search multiple sites.

Air Traveler's Handbook (www.faqs.org/faqs/travel/air/handbook) is an indispensable resource on the internet. It has a comprehensive listing of links to everything you need to know before you board a plane.

BY TRAIN

German trains are generally comfortable, convenient, and reasonably swift. Second-class compartments, which seat anywhere from two to six passengers, are great places to meet fellow travelers. Trains, however, are not always safe; for safety tips, see p. 16. For long trips, make sure you are on the correct car, as trains sometimes split at crossroads. Towns listed in parentheses on European train schedules require a train switch at the town listed immediately before the parenthesis.

You can either buy a **railpass,** which allows you unlimited travel within a region for a given period of time, or rely on buying individual **point-to-point** tickets. Almost all countries give students or youths (usually defined as anyone under 26) discounts on domestic rail tickets, and many also sell a student or youth card that provides 20-50% off all fares for up to a year.

RESERVATIONS. While seat reservations are required only for selected trains (usually on major lines), you are not guaranteed a seat without one (usually US$5-30). You should strongly consider reserving in advance during peak holiday and tourist seasons (a few hours ahead at the very latest). You will also have to purchase a **supplement** (US$10-50) or special fare for high-speed or nicer trains like Germany's ICE. InterRail holders must also purchase supplements (US$3-20) for trains like EuroCity and InterCity. Supplements are often unnecessary for Eurailpass and Europass holders.

OVERNIGHT TRAINS. On night trains, you won't waste valuable daylight hours traveling and you can avoid the expense of staying at a hotel. However, the main drawbacks include discomfort, sleepless nights, and the lack of scenery. Passengers on overnight trains also face a greater vulnerability to theft and assault. **Sleeping accommodations** on trains differ from country to country, but typically you can either sleep upright in your seat for a supplement of about $2-10, or pay for a separate space. **Couchettes** (berths) typically have four to six seats per compartment (supplement about US$10-50 per person); **sleepers** (beds) in private sleeping cars offer more privacy and comfort, but are considerably more expensive (supplement US$40-150). If you are using a railpass that is valid only for a restricted number of days, inspect train schedules to maximize the use of your pass: an overnight train or boat journey often uses up only one of your travel days if it departs after 7pm.

SHOULD YOU BUY A RAILPASS? Railpasses were conceived to allow you to jump on any train in Europe, go wherever you want whenever you want, and change your plans at will. In practice, it's not so simple. You still must stand in line to validate your pass, pay for supplements, and fork over cash for seat and couchette reservations. More importantly, railpasses don't always pay off. If you are planning to spend extensive time on trains, hopping between big cities, a railpass will probably be worth it. But in many cases, especially if you are under 26, point-to-point tickets may prove to be a cheaper option.

MULTINATIONAL RAILPASSES

EURAIL PASSES. Eurail is **valid** in most of Western Europe: Austria, Belgium, Denmark, Finland, France, Germany, Greece, Hungary, Italy, Liechtenstein, Luxembourg, the Netherlands, Norway, Portugal, the Republic of Ireland, Spain, Sweden, and Switzerland. It is **not valid** in the UK. Standard **Eurailpasses,** valid for a given consecutive number of days, are best for those planning on spending extensive time on trains every few days. **Eurailpass Flexi,** valid for any 10 or 15 (not necessarily consecutive) days within a two-month period, is more cost-effective for those traveling longer distances less frequently. **Eurailpass Saver** provides travel for travelers in groups (prices are per person). **Eurailpass Youth** and **Eurailpass Youth Flexi** provide second-class perks for those under 26.

EURAILPASSES	15 DAYS	21 DAYS	1 MONTH	2 MONTHS	3 MONTHS
1st class Eurailpass	US$796	US$1032	US$1281	US$1808	US$2232
Eurailpass Saver	US$673	US$876	US$1088	US$1537	US$1903
Eurailpass Youth	US$517	US$669	US$833	US$1177	US$1457

EURAILPASS FLEXI	10 DAYS IN 2 MONTHS	15 DAYS IN 2 MONTHS
1st class Eurailpass Flexi	US$939	US$1234
Eurailpass Saver Flexi	US$798	US$1050
Eurailpass Youth Flexi	US$612	US$803

Passholders receive a timetable for major routes and map with details on possible bike rental, hotel, and museum discounts. Passholders often also receive reduced fares or free passage on many boat, bus, and private rail lines.

The **Eurail Selectpass** is a slimmed-down version of the Eurailpass: it allows five to 15 days of unlimited travel in any two-month period within three, four, or five bordering countries. Eurail Selectpasses (for individuals) and **Eurail Selectpass Savers** (for people traveling in groups of 2 or more) range from US$383/325 per person (5 days) to US$850/723 (15 days). The **Eurail Selectpass Youth,** for those aged 12-25, costs US$249-553. Holders are entitled to the same freebies and discounts afforded by the Eurailpass, but only when the attractions are within or between countries valid on the railpass purchased.

SHOPPING AROUND FOR A EURAIL. Eurailpasses are designed by the EU itself, and can be bought only by non-Europeans almost exclusively from non-European distributors. These passes must be sold at uniform prices determined by the EU. However, some travel agents tack on a US$10 handling fee, and others offer certain bonuses with purchase, so shop around. Also, keep in mind that pass prices usually go up each year, so if you're planning to travel early in the year, you can save cash by purchasing before January 1 (you have three months from the purchase date to validate your pass in Europe).

It is best to buy your Eurail before leaving as only a few places in major European cities sell them, and do so at a marked-up price. You can get lost passes replaced only if you have purchased insurance under the Pass Security Plan (US$12). Eurailpasses are available through travel agents, **Rail Europe** (Canada ☎800-361-7245, US 888-382-7245; www.raileurope.com), **Flight Centre** (+1-866-967-5351; www.flightcentre.com), and student travel agencies like STA. You can also buy direct from Eurail's website, www.eurail.com.

INTER RAIL PASSES. If you have lived for at least six months in one of the European countries where Inter Rail Passes are valid, they prove an economical option. The Inter Rail pass allows travel within 30 European countries (excluding the passholder's home country), which are divided into eight zones. Passes may be purchased for one, two, or all eight zones. The one-zone pass (€286, under 26 €195) is good for 16 days of travel, the two-zone pass (€396, under 26 €275) is good for 22 days of travel, and the global pass (8 zones; €546, under 26 €385) is valid for a full month. Passholders receive free admission to many museums, as well as discounts on accommodations, food, and many ferries to Ireland, Scandinavia, and the rest of Europe. Passes are available at www.interrailnet.com, as well as from travel agents, at major train stations throughout Europe, and through online vendors (www.railpassdirect.co.uk).

FURTHER READING & RESOURCES ON TRAIN TRAVEL

Info on rail travel and railpasses: www.raileurope.com.

Point-to-point fares and schedules: www.raileurope.com/us/rail/fares_schedules/index.htm. Allows you to calculate whether buying a railpass would save you money.

Railsaver: www.railpass.com/new. Uses your itinerary to determine the best railpass for your trip.

European Railway Server: www.railfaneurope.net. Links to rail servers throughout Europe.

Thomas Cook European Timetable, updated monthly, covers major and minor train routes in Europe. Buy online. (www.thomascooktimetables.com).

Europe by Rail. by Tim Locke. Tenth Edition. Thomas Cook Publishing, 2008 (US$19.95)

BY BUS

Though European trains and railpasses are extremely popular, buses are sometimes a better—and cheaper—option. Amsterdam, Athens, Istanbul, London, Munich, and Olso are centers for private bus lines that offer long-distance rides accross Europe. **International bus passes** provide an affordable way to access unlimited travel between 40 European cities. The web resource **www.reisebus24.de** (in German) compares prices of different German bus lines. The prices below are based on travel during high-season.

Eurolines 4 Vicarage Rd., Edgbaston, Birmingham B15 3ES, UK (☎+44 8705 143 219 www.eurolines.com). The largest operator of Europe-wide coach services. Unlimited pass for 15 days under 26 €279, adult €329; for 30 days €359/439.

Busabout, 258 Vauxhall Brigde Rod., London SW1V 1BS, UK (☎+44 207 950 1661; www.busabout.com). Busabout is a hop-on hop-off travel network with 30 destinations in Europe in 10 countries. A Busabout Flexitrip Pass (6 or more flexistops) ($549, Flexi Days $59) will give you access to the entire Busabout coach network.

GETTING AROUND GERMANY

BY PLANE

With jet fuel prices on the rise, savvy travelers have to be clever when searching for the best deal on airfare. In addition to budget European companies like **RyanAir** and **easyJet**, here are some Germany-specific places to start looking:

Air Berlin, (UK ☎08070 738 88 80; www.airberlin.com). The second largest airline in Germany flies to over 140 destinations in Germany, Europe, and throughout the world. Took over Düsseldorf-based airline LTU in August 2007.

germanwings, (Germany ☎01805 73 71 00; www.germanwings.com). With 68 destinations in Germany and abroad, German Wings offers many special deals and reduced fares, especially for children.

TUI Fly, (Germany ☎0180 509 35 09; www.hlx.com). Formerly Hapag-Lloyd Express. Services Stuttgart, Cologne/Bonn, Hanover, Hamburg and Berlin, with routes extending to Greece and Israel.

Condor, (USA & Canada ☎+1-800-364-1667, Germany ☎+49 180 570 7202; www.condor.com). Operates out of major German airports in Germany. Condor City Flights start at €29 one-way, including all surcharges.

BY TRAIN OR BUS

RAILPASSES AND DISCOUNTED FARES

BASIC DISCOUNTS. Deutsche Bahn, the national German rail company, offers some terrific discounts to travelers. **Groups of at least six** can save up to 70% by reserving in advance, and **children** under 14 ride free with a guardian. Buyers who purchase tickets at least three days in advance are eligible for the **Sparpreis25** or **Sparpreis50** discounts: Sparpreis25 offers a 25% discount, while Sparpreis50 affords a 50% discount on trips that leave and return on a weekend.

DEUTSCHE BAHN PASS. Designed for tourists, this pass allows unlimited travel for four to 10 days within one month. Non-Europeans can purchase Deutsche Bahn passes in their home countries and—with a passport—in major German train stations. A second-class railpass costs €160 for four days of unlimited travel and €20 per extra day. The **German Rail Youth Pass,** for tourists under 26, costs €130 for four days and €10 per extra day. The second-class **Twin Pass,** for two adults traveling together, is €240 for four days and €30 per extra day.

BAHNCARD. A great option for those making frequent and extensive use of German trains for more than one month, the **Bahncard25** is valid for one year and entitles you to a 25% discount on all trains (even on already-discounted tickets). Passes are available at major train stations and require a passport-sized photo and mailing address in Germany. A second-class card costs €55. A newer **Bahncard50,** offering 50% discounts on tickets, now costs €220 (€110 for students up to 26 years old and seniors over 60). Bahncard holders can upgrade to **Railplus** and earn 25% rail discounts across Europe for an additional €15.

REGIONAL TICKETS. Deutsche Bahn offers two regional tickets: **Happy Weekend Tickets** enable up to five adults to travel together on local trains on any single Saturday or Sunday for €30, and **Länder-Tickets** grant up to five adults unlimited travel on a single day within any one of Germany's provinces (€22-29).

PRAGUE EXCURSION PASS. A useful purchase for holders of Eurail and German Rail passes—neither of which are valid in the Czech Republic—the **Prague Excursion Pass** covers round-trip travel from any Czech border to Prague and back out of the country within a period of seven days (2nd-class US$75, under 26 US$60). Available from **RailEurope** (p. 22) and from travel agencies.

RAIL-AND-DRIVE PASSES. RailEurope offers rail-and-drive passes, which combine two days of car rental with two days of rail travel. Prices range from US$155-320 per person, depending on the type of pass, type of car, number of people traveling, and ticket vendor, so shop around. Additional second-class rail days cost US$51, while extra car rental days run US$49-95.

BUS TRAVEL

The few parts of Germany that are inaccessible by train can often be reached by bus, which can be slightly more expensive than trains for comparable distances. Service between cities and outlying areas runs from the local main bus station, the **Zentralomnibusbahnhof (ZOB),** usually near the main train station. Although **Eurolines** (see **Getting to Germany: By Bus,** p. 24) mostly offers travel between countries, its German routes include Berlin-Hanover and Frankfurt-Munich, as well as routes covering the Romantic Road, Castle Road, and the Black Forest, all through **Deutsche Touring GmbH** (www.deutsche-touring.de).

BY CAR

Drivers in Germany benefit from supreme mobility—not to mention terrific, terrifying speed. Although a single traveler won't save by renting a car, four probably will. If you can't decide between train and car travel, try a combination railpass (see **Rail-and-Drive Passes** above). Fly-and-drive packages are also available from travel agents, airlines, and rental companies.

Before you take the wheel, make sure you read up on Germany's strictly-enforced driving laws (http://germany.usembassy.gov has good overview). It is true that there is no speed limit on the famed **Autobahn** and that cars in the left lane are expected to change lanes to let faster cars pass. For an informal primer on European Road signs and conventions, check out www.travlang.com/signs. **The Association for Safe International Road Travel (ASIRT),** 11769 Gainsborough Rd., Potomac, MD 20854, USA (☎301-983-5252; www.asirt.org) can provide specific information about road conditions.

DRIVING PERMITS AND CAR INSURANCE

INTERNATIONAL DRIVING PERMIT (IDP)

If you plan to drive, you must be 18 and have a valid driver's license accompanied by an International Driving Permit (IDP), an official 10-language translation of your license recognized across the world. Foreign licenses are valid for six months after entering Germany, after which a German license is required. Your IDP, valid for one year, must be issued in your own country, before you depart. An IDP application usually requires one or two passport-size photos, a current license, an additional form of identification, and a fee. To apply, contact your home country's automobile association. Be careful when purchasing an IDP online or anywhere other than your home automobile association. Some vendors sell permits of questionable legitimacy for higher prices.

RENTING

In comparison to other European countries, auto-obsessed Germany offers relatively affordable car rental. Still, when you factor in insurance costs and automatic transmission fees, you'll still be paying at least US$45 a day.

RENTAL AGENCIES

You can generally make reservations before you leave by calling major international offices in your home country. It's a good idea to cross-check this information with local agencies as well. The local desk numbers are included in town listings; for home-country numbers, call your toll-free directory.

To rent a car from most establishments in Germany, you need to be at least 21 years old. Some agencies require renters to be 25, and most charge those 21-24 an additional insurance fee. Small local operations occasionally rent to people under 21, but be sure to ask about the insurance coverage and deductible, and always check the fine print. Rental agencies in Germany include:

Auto Europe, US and Canada ☎888-223-5555; Germany 0800 22 35 55 55; www.autoeurope.com.

Avis, Australia ☎136 333; New Zealand 0800 65 51 11; UK 0870 606 0100; US and Canada 800-311-1212; Germany 01805 21 77 02; www.avis.com.

Budget, Australia ☎1300 36 28 48; Canada 800-268-8900; New Zealand 0800 283 438; UK 08701 56 56 56; US 800-527-0700; in Germany 01805 24 43 88, €0.14 cents per min.; www.budgetrentacar.com.

Hertz, US ☎800-654-3131; Germany 01805 93 88 14; www.hertz.com.

COSTS AND INSURANCE

Rental car prices start at around US$45 a day from national companies. Cars with **automatic transmission** generally cost more than cars with manual transmission (stick shift). In some places, **automatic transmission** is hard to find in the first place, and it is especially difficult to find four-wheel-drive vehicles.

If you are driving a conventional rental vehicle on an unpaved road in a rental car, you are almost never covered by **insurance;** ask about this before leaving the rental agency. Cars rented on an **American Express** or **Visa/MasterCard Gold** or **Platinum** credit card in Germany might not carry the automatic insurance that they would in some other countries; check with your credit-card company. Insurance plans from rental companies almost always come with an **excess** for conventional vehicles which can increase for younger drivers and for four-wheel-drive. This means that the insurance bought from the rental company only applies to damages over the excess while damages up to that amount must be covered by your existing insurance plan. Many German rental companies in Germany require you to buy a **Collision Damage Waiver (CDW),** which will waive the excess in the case of a collision. **Loss Damage Waivers (LDWs)** do the same in the case of theft or vandalism.

ON THE ROAD

There is no set speed limit on the **Autobahn,** only a recommendation of 130km per hour (81mph). For Germans, *schnell* (fast) is the name of the game. Watch for signs indicating right-of-way (usually designated by a yellow triangle). The Autobahn is indicated by "A" on signs; secondary highways, where the speed limit is usually 100km per hour (60mph), are noted as "B" on signs. Germans drive on the right side of the road and it is always illegal to pass on the right. If you are in the left lane and a car is trying to pass you, it is expected that you will change lanes. In cities and towns, speeds hover around 30-60kph (18-36mph). Wearing a **seatbelt** is the law in Germany, and children should sit in the rear seat. Children under 40 lb. (17 kg) should ride only in a specially-designed carseat, available from most car rental agencies. **The legal maximum for blood-alcohol level is 0.08%.** German police strictly enforce driving laws, and German motorists observe them almost religiously. Gasoline (petrol) prices vary, but average about US$5.57 per gallon.

CAR ASSISTANCE

The **Allgemeiner Deutscher Automobil Club (ADAC;** www.adac.de) is Europe's largest automobile association, offering support to motorists all over Germany. Members of worldwide partner organizations (including the American automobile associations) can contact the ADAC for assistance (☎0180 222 2222).

BY BICYCLE

Hop on a mountainbike and you're set to explore Germany's wondrous natural landscape. Many airlines will count your bike as your second free piece of luggage although a few charge extra (around US$80 one-way). Bikes must be packed in a cardboard box with pedals and front wheels detached. Many airlines sell bike boxes at the airport (US$15-25). Most ferries let you take your bike for free or for a nominal price, and you can always bring your bike on trains. Some youth hostels rent bicycles at good rates and Deutsche Bahn often rents them at train stations. In addition to **panniers** (US$10-40) to hold your luggage, you'll need a **helmet** (US$15-50) and a **sturdy lock** (from US$25). For country-specific books on biking through France, Germany, Ireland, and the UK try **Mountaineers Books,** 1001 S.W. Klickitat Way, Ste. 201, Seattle, WA 98134, USA (☎206-223-6303; www.mountaineersbooks.org).

Blue Marble Travel (Canada ☎519-624-2494; US 215-923-3788; www.bluemarble.org) offers small-group bike tours for ages 20 to 49 in Europe, including one that works its way through northwestern Germany. **CBT Tours,** 2506 N. Clark St. #150, Chicago IL 60614, USA (☎800-736-2453; www.cbttours.com), offers full-package culinary, biking, hiking, and sightseeing tours (around US$3000 for seven days, $250 deposit) to Germany.

BY MOPED AND MOTORCYCLE

Motorized bikes and **mopeds** don't use much gas, can be put on trains and ferries, and are a good compromise between costly car travel and the practical limits of bicycles. However, they're uncomfortable for long distances, dangerous in the rain, and unpredictable on rough roads. Always wear a helmet and never ride with a backpack. Expect to pay about $50 per day, $75 on the weekend. Try auto repair shops, and remember to bargain. Opt for a Vespa to fully realize your European-cool. Motorcycles are more expensive and normally require a license, but are better for long distances. Before renting, ask if the price includes tax and insurance, or you may be hit with an unexpected fee.

BY THUMB

LET'S NOT GO. Let's Go never recommends hitchhiking as a safe means of transportation, and none of the information presented here is intended to do so.

Let's Go strongly urges you to consider the risks of hitchhiking before you choose to stick out your thumb. Hitching means entrusting your life to a stranger and risking assault, sexual harassment, theft, and unsafe driving. For women traveling alone (or even in pairs), hitching is just too dangerous. A man and a woman are a less dangerous combination, two men will have a harder time getting a lift, while three men will go nowhere.

Germany does have a very popular rideshare service known as the **Verband der Deutschen Mitfahrzentralen** (www.mitfahrzentrale.de) which pairs drivers with riders. The fee varies according to the destination. Not all organizations screen drivers and riders so ask in advance. Offices are listed under the **Transportation** header of most large cities.

KEEPING IN TOUCH

BY TELEPHONE

CALLING HOME FROM GERMANY

Prepaid phone cards are a common and relatively inexpensive means of calling abroad. Each one comes with a Personal Identification Number (PIN) and a toll-free access number. You call the access number and then follow the directions for dialing your PIN. To purchase prepaid phone cards, check online for the best rates; www.callingcards.com is a good place to start. Online providers generally send your access number and PIN via email, with no actual "card" involved. You can also call home with prepaid phone cards.

CELLULAR PHONES

The international standard for cell phones is **Global System for Mobile Communication** (GSM). To make and receive calls in Germany you will need a GSM-compatible phone and a **SIM (Subscriber Identity Module) card,** a country-specific, thumbnail-sized chip that gives you a local phone number and plugs you into the local network. Many SIM cards are prepaid, and incoming calls are frequently free. You can buy additional cards or vouchers (usually available at convenience stores) to "top up" your phone. For more information on GSM phones, check out www.telestial.com, www.orange.co.uk, www.roadpost.com, or www.planetomni.com. Companies like **Cellular Abroad** (www.cellularabroad.com) rent cell phones that work in a variety of destinations around the world.

PLACING INTERNATIONAL CALLS. To call Germany from home or to call home from Germany, dial:

1. The **international dialing prefix.** To call from Australia, dial 0011; Canada or the US, 011; Ireland, New Zealand, or the UK, 00; Germany, 00
2. The **country code** of the country you want to call. To dial Australia, dial 61; Canada or US, 1; Ireland, 353; New Zealand, 64; the UK, 44; Germany, 49
3. The **city/area code.** *Let's Go* lists the city/area codes for cities and towns in Germany opposite the city or town name, next to a ☎, and in every phone number. If the first digit is a zero (e.g., 020 for London), omit the zero when calling from abroad (e.g., dial 20 from Canada to reach London).
4. The **local number.**

TIME DIFFERENCES

Germany is 1hr. ahead of Greenwich Mean Time (GMT), and observes Daylight Saving Time from late March through late October—the reverse is true for Australia. The following table relates Germany and other localities at noon GMT.

4AM	5AM	6AM	7AM	NOON	1PM	10PM
Vancouver Seattle San Francisco Los Angeles	Denver	Chicago	New York Boston Toronto	London	**BERLIN** Paris Rome Prague	Sydney Canberra Melbourne

BY MAIL

SENDING MAIL HOME FROM GERMANY

Airmail is the most efficient way to send mail home from Germany. **Aerogrammes,** printed sheets that fold into envelopes and travel via airmail, are available at post offices. Write "airmail," "par avion," or "luftpost" on the front. Most post offices will charge exorbitant fees or simply refuse to send aerogrammes with enclosures. Surface mail is by far the cheapest and slowest way to send mail. It takes one to two months to cross the Atlantic and one to three to cross the Pacific—good for heavy items you won't need for a while, such as souvenirs that you've acquired along the way. These are standard rates for mail in and from Germany.

The standard time for mail to be delivered from Germany to:

Australia: Allow 4-7 days for regular airmail home.

Canada and US: Allow 3-7 days.

UK: Allow 2-4 days.

SENDING MAIL TO GERMANY

To ensure timely delivery, mark envelopes "airmail" or "par avion." In addition to the standard postage system, whose rates are listed below, **Federal Express** (Australia ☎+61 13 26 10, Canada and the US +1-800-463-3339, Ireland +353 800 535 800, New Zealand +64 800 733 339, the UK +44 8456 070 809; www.fedex.com) handles express mail services between most countries and Germany.

There are several ways to arrange pick up of letters sent to you while you are abroad. Mail can be sent via **Poste Restante** (General Delivery; Postlagernde Briefe) to almost any city or town in Germany with a post office, and it is very reliable. Address Poste Restante letters like so:

Johann Schmidt
Postlagernde Briefe
City, Germany

The mail will go to a special desk in the central post office, unless you specify a post office by street address or postal code. Use the largest post office, since mail may be sent there regardless. It is usually safer and quicker, though more expensive, to send mail express or registered. Bring your passport (or other photo ID) for pickup. There may be a small fee. If the clerks say there is nothing for you, ask them to check under your first name as well. *Let's Go* lists post offices in the **Practical Information** section for each city and most towns.

American Express's travel offices throughout the world offer a free **Client Letter Service** (mail held up to 30 days and forwarded upon request) for cardholders who contact them in advance. *Let's Go* lists AmEx locations for most large cities in **Practical Information** sections; for a complete list, call ☎+1-800-528-4800 or visit www.americanexpress.com/travel.

ACCOMMODATIONS

HOSTELS

In 1908, German Richard Schirman, believing that life in industrial cities was harmful to the physical and moral development of Germany's young people, built the **world's first youth hostel** in Altena—a budget dormitory that would make travel possible for urban youth. Many hostels are laid out dorm-style, often with large single-sex rooms and bunk beds, although private rooms that sleep two to four are becoming more common. Hostels often have kitchens and utensils for your use, bike or moped rentals, storage areas, transportation to airports, breakfast and other meals, laundry facilities, and Internet. However, there can be drawbacks: some hostels close during certain daytime "lockout" hours, have a curfew, don't accept reservations, impose a maximum stay, or, less frequently, require that you do chores.

Hostelling in Germany is overseen by **Deutsches Jugendherbergswerk (DJH),** Bismarckstr. 8, 32756 Detmold, Germany (☎05231 740 10; www.jugendherberge.de). Its hostels are open to members of DJH or Hostelling International (see below), but travelers can join or buy guest passes at the hostels. DJH has initiated a growing number of **Jugendgästhäuser,** youth guest-houses that are generally more expensive, have more facilities, and attract slightly older guests. DJH has absorbed hundreds of hostels in eastern Germany, though some still lack the sparkling facilities of their western counterparts. DJH's German-language *Jugendherbergen in Deutschland*, a guide to all federal German hostels, can be purchased at German bookstores and major newsstands by writing to DJH, or from the **DJH webpage,** which also has pictures, prices, addresses, and phone numbers for almost every hostel in Germany. Contact information can also be found on most on most German cities' official websites, listed under the tourist office in the **Practical Information** section of cities

ESSENTIALS

in this guide. **Eurotrip** (www.eurotrip.com) has information on and reviews of budget hostels and international hostel associations.

HOSTELLING INTERNATIONAL

Joining the youth hostel association in your own country (listed below) automatically grants you membership privileges in **Hostelling International (HI),** a federation of national hosteling associations. Non-HI members may be allowed to stay in some hostels, but will have to pay extra to do so. HI hostels are scattered throughout Germany, and are typically less expensive than private hostels. HI's umbrella website (www.hihostels.com), which lists the web addresses and phone numbers of all national associations, can be a great place to begin researching hosteling in a specific region. Other comprehensive hosteling websites include www.hostels.com and www.hostelplanet.com.

Most HI hostels also honor **guest memberships**—you'll get a blank card with space for six validation stamps. Each night you'll pay a nonmember supplement (one-sixth the membership fee), and earn one guest stamp. Six stamps make you a member. A new membership benefit is the FreeNites program, which allows hostelers to gain points toward free rooms. Most student travel agencies sell HI cards, as do all of the national hosteling organizations listed below. All prices listed below are for one-year memberships.

Australian Youth Hostels Association (AYHA), 422 Kent St., Sydney, NSW 200 (☎+61 2 9261 1111; www.yha.com.au). AUS$52, under 18 AUS$19.

Hostelling International-Canada (HI-C), 205 Catherine St., Ste. 400, Ottawa, ON K2P 1C3 (☎+1 613 237 7884; www.hihostels.ca). CDN$35, under 18 free.

Hostelling International Northern Ireland (HINI), 22-32 Donegall Rd., Belfast BT12 5JN (☎+44 28 9032 4733; www.hini.org.uk). UK£15, under 25 UK£10.

Youth Hostels Association of New Zealand Inc. (YHANZ), Level 1, 166 Moorhouse Ave., P.O. Box 436, Christchurch (☎+64 3 379 9970, in NZ 0800 278 299; www.yha.org.nz). NZ$40, under 18 free.

Youth Hostels Association (England and Wales), Trevelyan House, Dimple Rd., Matlock, Derbyshire DE4 3YH (☎+44 8707 708 868; www.yha.org.uk). UK£16, under 26 UK£10.

Hostelling International-USA, 8401 Colesville Rd., Ste. 600, Silver Spring, MD 20910 (☎+1-301-495-1240; www.hiayh.org). US$28, under 18 free.

> **A HOSTELER'S BILL OF RIGHTS.** There are certain standard features that we do not include in our hostel listings. Unless we state otherwise, you can expect that every hostel has no lockout, no curfew, free hot showers, some system of secure luggage storage, and no key deposit.

OTHER TYPES OF ACCOMMODATIONS

YMCAS AND YWCAS

Young Men's Christian Association (YMCA) and **Young Women's Christian Association (YWCA)** lodgings are usually cheaper than a hotel but more expensive than a hostel. Not all locations offer lodging. Those that do are often located in urban areas. Many YMCAs accept women and families. Some will not lodge those under 18 without parental permission.

YMCA of the USA, 101 N. Wacker Dr., Chicago, IL 60606 (☎+1-800-872-9622; www.ymca.net). Provides a listing of the nearly 1000 Ys across the US and Canada, as well as info on prices and services.

YWCA of the USA, 1015 18th St. NW, Ste. 1100, Washington, DC 20036 (☎+1-202-467-0801; www.ywca.org). Provides a directory of YWCAs across the US.

YMCA Canada, 42 Charles St. E, 6th fl., Toronto, ON M4Y 1T4 (☎+1-416-967-9622; www.ymca.ca). Offers info on Ys in Canada.

European Alliance of YMCAs, Na Porici 12, CZ-115 30 Prague, Czech Republic. (☎+420 22 487 20 20; www.internationalymca.org). Maintains listings of Ys in Europe.

HOTELS, GUESTHOUSES, AND PENSIONS

Hotel singles in Germany cost about €25-40 per night, doubles €35-50. You'll typically share a hall bathroom, while a private bathroom will cost extra, as may hot showers. Some hotels offer "full pension" (all meals) and "half pension" (no lunch). Smaller guesthouses and pensions are often cheaper than hotels. If you make reservations in writing, indicate your night of arrival and the number of nights you plan to stay. The hotel will send you a confirmation and may request payment for the first night.

BED AND BREAKFASTS (B&BS)

For a cozy alternative to impersonal hotel rooms, B&Bs (private homes with rooms available to travelers) range from acceptable to sublime. Rooms in B&Bs generally cost €40-70 for a single and €70-100 for a double in Germany. Any number of websites provide listings for B&Bs in Germany: www.bandb-ring.de and www.bedandbreakfastgermany.com are good starting points. For more general listings, check out **Bed & Breakfast Inns Online** (www.bbonline.com), **InnFinder** (www.inncrawler.com), **InnSite** (www.innsite.com), **BedandBreakfast.com** (www.bedandbreakfast.com), or **BNBFinder.com** (www.bnbfinder.com).

LONG-TERM ACCOMMODATIONS

Travelers planning to stay in Germany for extended periods of time may find it most cost-effective to rent an apartment. A basic one-bedroom (or studio) apartment in Berlin will range €250-350 per month. Besides the rent itself, prospective tenants are also often required to front a security deposit (usually one month's rent) and the last month's rent. Shared houses in Germany, called **Wohngemeinschaften (WGs),** are a popular option for students and young professionals. German-language listings can be found online at a few sites including www.studenten-wg.de, www.wg-gesucht.de, and www.kijiji.de. Foreign visitors often find it easier to rent through **Mitwohnzentralen** (homeshare companies), which find rooms for individuals in shared appartments. These companies charge a percentage of each month's rent as commission. Shop around to find the best rates. Check the Practical Information sections of cities listed in this guide for information about specific *Mitwohnzentralen*.

CAMPING

The 26,000 campsites dotting the Alps, forests, beaches, and suburbs of major cities are testament to Germany's enthusiasm for the outdoors. Hiking trails wind through the outskirts of every German city, and a national network of long-distance trails weaves the country together. The Black Forest, Saxon, Switzerland, Harz Mountains and Bavarian Alps are especially well-traversed. The outdoor facilities in Germany are among the best-maintained in the world, usually accessible by public transportation and providing showers, bathrooms, and a restaurant or store. Camping typically costs €3-6 per person with a surcharge for tents and vehicles. Blue signs with a black tent on a white background indicate official sites. For information on campsites accross the country, check out the **accommodations** sections of the towns and outdoor areas listed in this guide. For more information on outdoor activities in Germany, see **The Great Outdoors,** below.

THE GREAT OUTDOORS

The **Great Outdoor Recreation Page** (www.gorp.com) provides excellent general information for travelers planning on camping or enjoying the outdoors.

USEFUL RESOURCES

A variety of publishing companies offer guidebooks to meet the educational needs of novice or expert hikers. For information about camping, hiking, and biking, write or call the publishers listed below to receive a free catalog. Campers heading to Europe should consider buying an **International Camping Carnet.** Similar to a hostel membership card, it is required at a few campgrounds and sometimes provides discounts. It is available in North America from the **Family Campers** and **RVers Association** and in the UK from **The Caravan Club** (below).

Camping Germany, (www.camping-germany.de). Offers information and pictures for campgrounds access the country. Contains charming English grammatical errors.

Sierra Club Books, 85 2nd St., 2nd fl., San Francisco, CA 94105, USA (☎+1-415-977-5500; www.sierraclub.org). Publishes general resource books on hiking and camping, as well as specific guides on Germany.

Woodall Publications Corporation, 2575 Vista Del Mar Dr., Ventura, CA 93001, USA (☎+1-877-680-6155; www.woodalls.com). Annually updates campground directories.

NATIONAL PARKS

The heaviest concentration of parks is in Bavaria and the former East Germany. Winter sports, especially skiing and tobogganing, are popular in Berchtesgaden and Bayerischer Wald (Bavarian Forest) parks; the Saxon Switzerland and Harz parks in the east are popular for their glorious hiking opportunities among chalk cliffs and forested peaks. Germans place strict limits on camping, firebuilding, and other activities that could potentionally harm the environment.

There are no entrance fees for German parks, although parking can be costly and camping is nearly always restricted to designated campgrounds, which charge around €5-10 per camper per night. Travelers can also stay at huts in some parks, which rarely require reservations and typically cost €10-20. For general information, contact **Nationalpark-Service**, Informationshaus, 17192 Federow, Germany (☎039 91 66 88 49; www.nationalpark-service.de). Listings of ranger offices can be found in specific national park's listings in this book.

WILDLIFE

Germany is home to a diverse array of wildlife. While beautiful birds, alpine butterflies, and oodles of fuzzy creatures are sure to delight the wilderness explorer, a few other animals—notably bears—are less than cuddly. (Except for baby **Knut,** of course; see p. 102). Always pack trash in a plastic bag and carry it with you until you reach the next trash receptical. **If you do encounter a bear, do not approach it.** Back away slowly while keeping your eye on the bear; bears are shy of humans and are likely not to attack if they do not feel threatened. For more information, consult *How to Stay Alive in the Woods*, by Bradford Angier (Black Dog & Leventhal Books; US $11).

CAMPING AND HIKING EQUIPMENT

WHAT TO BUY

Good camping equipment is both sturdy and light. North American suppliers tend to offer the most competitive prices.

Sleeping Bags: Most sleeping bags are rated by season: "summer" is designed for nighttime temperatures of 30-40°F (around 0°C); "4-season" or "winter" often means below 0°F (-17°C). Bags are made of **down** (warm and light, but expensive, and miserable when wet) or of **synthetic** material (heavy, durable, and warm when wet). Prices range US$50-250 for a summer synthetic to US$200-300 for a good down winter bag. **Sleeping bag pads** include foam pads (US$10-30), air mattresses (US$15-50), and self-inflating mats (US$30-120). Bring a **stuff sack** to store your bag and keep it dry.

Tents: The best tents are freestanding with their own frames and suspension systems, set up quickly, and only require staking in high winds. Low-profile dome tents are the best all around. Worthy 2-person tents start at US$100, 4-person tents at US$160. Make sure your tent has a rain fly and seal its seams with waterproofer. Other useful accessories include a **battery-operated lantern,** a plastic **ground cloth,** and a nylon **tarp.**

Backpacks: Internal-frame packs mold well to your back, keep a lower center of gravity, and flex adequately to allow you to hike difficult trails, while **external-frame** packs are more comfortable for long hikes over even terrain, as they carry weight higher and distribute it more evenly. Make sure your pack has a strong, padded hip belt to transfer weight to your legs. There are models designed specifically for women. Any serious backpacking merits a pack of at least 4000 cu. in. (16,000cc), plus 500 cu. in. for sleeping bags in internal-frame packs. Sturdy backpacks cost anywhere from US$125 to US$420. Either buy a rain cover (US$10-20), bring a heavy duty trash bag, or store all of your belongings in plastic bags inside your pack.

Boots: Be sure to wear hiking boots with good **ankle support.** They should fit snugly and comfortably over 1-2 pairs of **wool socks** and a pair of thin **liner socks.** Break in boots over several weeks before you go to spare yourself blisters.

Other Necessities: Synthetic layers, like those made of polypropylene or polyester, and a pile jacket will keep you warm even when wet. A **space blanket** (US$5-15) will help you to retain body heat and doubles as a **ground cloth.** Plastic **water bottles** are vital; look for shatter- and leak-resistant models. Carry **water-purification tablets** for when you can't boil water. Although most campgrounds provide campfire sites, you may want to bring a small **metal grate** or **grill.** For those places (including virtually every organized campground in Europe) that forbid fires or the gathering of firewood, you'll need a **camp stove** (starts at US$50) and a propane fuel bottle to operate it. Also bring a **first-aid kit, pocketknife, insect repellent,** and **waterproof matches** or a **lighter.**

SPECIFIC CONCERNS

TRAVELING ALONE

Traveling alone can be extremely beneficial, providing a sense of independence and a greater opportunity to connect with locals. On the other hand, solo travelers are more vulnerable to harassment and street theft. If you are traveling alone, look confident, try not to stand out as a tourist, and be especially careful in deserted or very crowded areas. Stay away from poorly-lit areas. If questioned, never admit that you are traveling alone. Maintain regular contact with someone at home who knows your itinerary, and always research your destination before traveling. For more tips, pick up *Traveling Solo* by Eleanor Berman (Globe Pequot Press; US$18), visit www.travelaloneandloveit.com, or subscribe to **Connecting: Solo Travel Network,** 689 Park Rd., Unit 6, Gibsons, BC V0N 1V7, Canada (☎+1 604 886 9099; www.cstn.org; membership US$30-48).

WOMEN TRAVELERS

Women exploring on their own inevitably face some additional safety concerns. Single women can often stay in hostels which offer single rooms that lock from the inside or in religious organizations with single-sex rooms. It is a good idea to stick to centrally located accommodations and to avoid solitary late-night treks or metro rides.

Always carry extra cash for a phone call, bus, or taxi. **Hitchhiking** is never safe for lone women, or even for two women traveling together. Look as if you know where you're going and approach older women or couples for directions if you're lost or feeling uncomfortable. Generally, the less you look like a tourist, the better off you'll be. Dress conservatively, especially in rural areas. Wearing a conspicuous **wedding band** can help to prevent unwanted advances.

Your best answer to verbal harassment is no answer at all: feigning deafness, sitting motionless, and staring straight ahead at nothing in particular will usually do the trick. Persistent aggressors can often be dissuaded by a firm, loud, and very public "Go away!" in the appropriate language. Don't hesitate to seek out a police officer or a passerby if you are being harassed. Memorize the emergency numbers in places you visit, and consider carrying a whistle on your keychain. A self-defense course will both prepare you for a potential attack and raise your level of awareness of your surroundings (see **Personal Safety,** p. 16). Also, it might be a good idea to talk with your doctor about the health concerns that women face when traveling (p. 19).

GLBT TRAVELERS

Attitudes toward gay, lesbian, bisexual, and trasgendered (GLBT) travelers are progressive and accepting in Germany. Listed below are contact organizations, mail-order catalogs, and publishers that offer materials addressing specific concerns. **Out and About** (www.planetout.com) offers a weekly newsletter addressing travel concerns and a comprehensive site addressing gay travel concerns. The online newspaper **365gay.com** also has a travel section.

Gay's the Word, 66 Marchmont St., London WC1N 1AB, UK (☎+44 20 7278 7654; http://freespace.virgin.net/gays.theword). The largest gay and lesbian bookshop in the UK, with both fiction and non-fiction titles. Mail-order service available.

Giovanni's Room, 345 S. 12th St., Philadelphia, PA 19107, USA (☎+1-215-923-2960; www.queerbooks.com). An international lesbian and gay bookstore.

International Lesbian and Gay Association (ILGA), Avenue des Villas 34, 1060 Brussels, Belgium (☎+32 2 502 2471; www.ilga.org). Provides political information, such as homosexuality laws of individual countries.

TRAVELERS WITH DISABILITIES

Those with disabilities should inform airlines and hotels of their disabilities when making reservations; some time may be needed to prepare special accommodations. Call ahead to restaurants, museums, and other facilities to find out if they are wheelchair-accessible. Guide-dog owners should inquire as to the quarantine policies of each destination country.

USEFUL ORGANIZATIONS

Accessible Journeys, 35 W. Sellers Ave., Ridley Park, PA 19078, USA (☎+1-800-846-4537; www.disabilitytravel.com). Designs tours for wheelchair users and slow walkers. Site has tips and forums for all travelers.

Flying Wheels Travel, 143 W. Bridge St., Owatonna, MN 55060, USA (☎+1-507-451-5005; www.flyingwheelstravel.com). Specializes in escorted trips to Europe for people with physical disabilities; also plans custom trips worldwide.

Mobility International USA (MIUSA), P.O. Box 10767, Eugene, OR 97440, USA (☎+1-541-343-1284; www.miusa.org). Provides a variety of books and other publications containing information for travelers with disabilities.

Society for Accessible Travel and Hospitality (SATH), 347 5th Ave., Ste. 610, New York, NY 10016, USA (☎+1-212-447-7284; www.sath.org). An advocacy group with free online travel information. Annual membership US$49, students and seniors US$29.

MINORITY TRAVELERS

Germany has a significant minority population composed mainly of about two million Turks. Travelers may notice that some Germans harbor resentment towards this burgeoning population, which first arrived in Germany during post-WWII years as *Gastarbeiter* (guest workers). Since then, many Turks have settled and prospered in Germany. Still, there have been significant cultural and religious clashes. Tensions between Turks and ethnic Germans are palpable in parts of major cities. In particularly tense neighborhoods, dark-skinned travelers and those of Middle-Eastern descent should be especially cautious.

In certain regions, especially in large cities in former East Germany, minority tourists may feel threatened by small but vocal neo-Nazi groups. While they represent only a small fraction of the population, neo-Nazi skinheads have been known to attack foreigners, especially non-whites. In these areas, common sense and caution will serve you best.

DIETARY CONCERNS

The travel section of the **The Vegetarian Resource Group's** website, at www.vrg.org/travel, has a comprehensive list of organizations and websites that are geared toward helping vegetarians and vegans traveling abroad. They also provide an online restaurant guide. For more information, visit your local bookstore or health food store and consult *The Vegetarian Traveler: Where to Stay if You're Vegetarian, Vegan, Environmentally Sensitive*, by Jed and Susan Civic (Larson Publications; US$16). Vegetarians will also find numerous resources on the web; try www.vegdining.com, www.happycow.net, and www.vegetariansabroad.com, for starters.

Travelers who keep kosher should contact synagogues in larger cities for information on kosher restaurants. Your own synagogue or college Hillel should have access to lists of Jewish institutions across the nation. If you are strict in your observance, you may have to prepare your own food on the road. A good resource is the *Jewish Travel Guide*, edited by Michael Zaidner (Vallentine Mitchell; US$18). For halal restaurants, check out www.zabihah.com.

LIFE AND TIMES

Located in the heart of Europe, Germany has played a central role in countless political, social, and cultural developments in the region and in the world. It is still Europe's most industrialized and populous country. Largely responsible for the outbreak of WWI and guilty of provoking WWII, Germany has successfully overcome its legacy of National Socialism and maintains a stable democracy. Today, Germany strives to secure its position as a leader in artistic and scientific advancement.

LAND

Germany's diverse landscapes offer travelers a wide range of vistas, from long beaches by the sea to vast lowland plains to Alpine peaks. Denmark lies to the north of Germany, The Netherlands, Belgium, Luxemburg, and France to the west, Switzerland and Austria to the South, and Czech Republic and Poland to the east. Germany's two coasts, on the Baltic Sea (Ostsee) and North Sea, are in the north, east, and west of the Jutland peninsula that joins Denmark.

Germany is about the size of Montana at 357,027 sq. km (137,849 sq. mi.). The country borders the outermost ranges of the Alps in the south, reaching an altitude of 9718ft. (2962m.) in the Zugspitze, and reaches across the plain on their northern edge, the *Alpenvorland* (Alpine Foreland). In the center of the country, the Central German Uplands, part of a European stretch of territory from France's Massif Central to the east, exhibits forested mountains, steep plateaus, and lowland basins. In the north, the North German Plain, or Lowland, part of the North European Plain, is bordered by jagged coastlines, sandy beaches, and the gorgeous island chains of the North and Baltic seas.

High population density and extensive agricultural use make nature conservation an important issue. Germany has 15 national parks, of which the oldest are in Bavaria: Nationalpark Bayerischer Wald (p. 371) and Nationalpark Berchtesgaden (p. 362). There are also 14 Biosphere reservations from the UNESCO program, which together cover 4.3% of the country's surface.

DEMOGRAPHICS

POPULATION

With over 82.5 million inhabitants, Germany is the most densely populated state in the European union. Apart from the city-states Berlin, Bremen, and Hamburg, the most populous states are North Rhine-Westphalia (capital: Duesseldorf) in the west, with 18.03 million, and Bavaria (capital: Munich) in the south with 12.49 million. The population of the former East Germany remains below the national average, with the exception of Saxony. Berlin, the capital, is the most densely populated city with 3.4 million inhabitants, followed by Hamburg and then Munich. Overall, there are 84 large cities with a population over 100,000. These were developed either in Roman times (Cologne, Bonn, Trier, Augsburg), according to bishop seats in the Middle Ages (Wuerzburg,

Hildesheim, Magdeburg and others), as imperial palaces (Aachen, Goslar, Quedlinburg), or as carefully planned Residenzstädte during the baroque period (Dresden, Karlsruhe, Mannheim). War destruction and reconstruction has dramatically changed the relative strengths of Germany's urban centers.

Germany's birth rate of 1.3 children per family is one of the lowest in the world. The negative population growth first registered in 1972. The population increase from 60.7 to 62.1 million between 1970 and 1989 was primarily due to immigration. However, with immigration decreasing, 2004 saw the first decrease in the German population by about 30,000 people.

ETHNIC MINORITIES

Germany has had a difficult history with ethnic minorities. The Nazi regime's persecution of six million Jews and a quarter of a million Gypsies during the Holocaust has left the country with a problematic legacy. In the 1950s, the first immigrant workers came from Italy, followed by Spaniards, Greeks, Turks and Yugoslavs. In the GDR, contract workers from other so-called socialist countries like Mozambique and Vietnam began coming in the 1960s, but most did not stay. In 2000, a new law facilitated naturalization for foreigners in Germany. Today, Turks represent the largest ethnic minority in Germany. In addition, there are 60,000 Sorbs, Slavic people who first settled in the abandoned region east of the Elbe and Saale Rivers in AD 600, about 50,000 Sinti and Roma people who live in small towns nationwide, 50,000 Danes in the Schleswig region of Schleswig-Holstein, as well as the 12,000 German Friesians, a North Sea coastal people who settled in North Friesia in the AD 7th century, and in the Saterland region between 1100 and 1400.

HISTORY

SIPPING CHARLEMAGNE

58 BC Roman Empire conquers Germanic tribes.

476 AD Roman Empire collapses.

800 Charlemagne is crowned Emperor by the Pope.

By 58 BC, the Roman Republic had expanded its borders to the Rhein, forcing pagan clans of the Germanic peoples in Central Europe (including the Saxons, Franks, Frisians, and Thuringians) to join forces for defense. In AD 9, when battles erupted in the Teutoburg Forest (near present-day Osnabrück), the allied Germans' resounding homecourt victory against the Romans earned them the nickname "Teutons" and marked the first assertion of a truly Germanic culture. After five centuries of mutual antagonism and several barbarian attacks on Rome, the weakened Roman Empire fell in 476. Without a common enemy to unify them, the clans dispersed. In 800, the Holy Roman Empire, founded by Charlemagne (known in Germany as Karl der Große) in France and western Germany, became the first major German state. Charlemagne initiated administrative reforms and cultural advancements in his kingdom (Reich), reviving European commerce along the way. He built his permanent residence in Aachen because of its soothing hot springs (p. 241). After Charlemagne's death in 814, the Franconian realm divided along the language separation between early Medieval French in the west and Old High German in the east (called "deutsch," meaning "as the people speak"—as opposed to Latin, the language of scholars). Charlemagne's son Louis I gained control of the empire, but after his death, his misfit sons spent three years tearing their grandfather's kingdom apart with civil war. The Treaty of Verdun in 843 finally brought peace by dividing the realm into three parts.

Otto I initiated a close relationship between the church and monarchy, but in the Investiture Crisis of 1075, the Pope demanded autonomy, specifically in appointing church officials, which sparked conflict that ravaged Germany for nearly 50 years. The Concordat of Worms (1122) restored peace, setting up checks and balances between pope and king.

War broke out time and again between the dozens of minor dukes and princes vying for power, while the bubonic plague of the 14th century killed roughly a third of Europe's population. The Golden Bull of 1356 declared that seven electors—three archbishops and four secular leaders—should approve the selection of the Holy Roman Emperor. Under the leadership of the House of Hapsburg which occupied the throne for five centuries, the empire began to define itself clearly. Manufacturing and sea trade transformed small North Sea towns into wealthy merchant oligarchies, which banded together in 1358 to form the Hanseatic League. This trade federation had outposts as far away as England, Norway, and Russia, and grew powerful enough to successfully defeat Denmark in war. Yet while German interests focused on wealthy towns, discontent roiled in rural regions, and outlying areas of the empire slipped out of the Hapsburgs' control entirely.

962
Otto the Great unifies Germanic Franks; proclaims himself Holy Roman Emperor.

1122
Concordat of Worms resolves Investiture Crisis, balancing power between the Pope and the King.
14th Century Bubonic Plague kills a third of German population.

LIFE AND TIMES

MARTIN'S MANY THESES

The Reformation (1517-1700), initiated by Martin Luther, a monk and Biblical studies professor at the University of Wittenberg (p. 434), split Germans according to religious beliefs. When German electoral princes adopted Lutheranism as a way to restrict the flow of money to the Vatican, things got messy. Hapsburg Emperor Charles V (Karl V), the most powerful leader since Charlemagne, resolved to destroy the subversive Lutheran doctrine, but he signed the 1555 Peace of Augsburg instead. Charles' successors were not happy about this, and when the Archduke Ferdinand of Austria imposed Catholicism on Bohemia, his Protestant subjects rebelled by throwing a papal representative out a window in the 1618 Defenestration of Prague. Violence between the German Catholics and Protestants reached its breaking point when Catholic France sided with German Protestants to oppose the Habsburgs, leading to the Thirty Years' War (1618-1648), which devastated the population. The Peace of Westphalia at the end of the war made each prince sovereign in his own territory. The treaty also served as the de facto constitution of the empire until its abolition by Napoleon in 1806.

1517
Martin Luther nails his 95 Theses to the door of Wittenberg's church.

1555
Karl V signs the Peace of Augsburg, allowing princes to determine the official religion of their own domains.

1618-48
The Thirty Years' War, fought primarily within Germany, involves most of continental Europe in a religious and political struggle.

OTTO WINS THE LOTTO

1756-63
Fredrick the Great expands his kingdom in the Seven Years' War.

1806
Napoleon conquers the remains of the Holy Roman Empire.

During the 18th century, flute-playing King Friedrich II (known as Frederick the Great) lead Brandenburg-Prussia to become the ascendant state in Germany. In 1806, Napoleon conquered the remains of the Holy Roman Empire, creating a subservient Confederation of the Rhein until the Wars of Liberation ousted Napoleon from Germany. The 1815 Congress of Vienna partially restored the pre-war German state system by establishing the Austrian-led German Confederation, which set up the Frankfurt National Assembly in 1848. Internal conflicts weakened this movement and the old order was restored when Prussian chancellor Otto von Bismarck lead three successful wars, the final one against France, between 1864 and 1871. Wilhelm Kaiser of the German Reich was crowned at Versailles, commencing the second reich.

STRIKE IT REICH

1815
The Congress of Vienna, convened in the wake of Napoleon's defeat, establishes the German Confederation to govern central Europe.

1848
The failed Revolution of 1848 results in the emigration of hundreds of thousands of German liberals as well as profound political instability.

In 1871, Bismarck founded the German Empire on his own terms: unification under an authoritarian monarchy. At the same time, Germany was industrializing at breakneck speed, but the aristocratic political system could not keep up. To consolidate power, Bismarck began a series of social initiatives known as the Kulturkampf, which included unemployment insurance for the working class, but repressed trade unions and imposed sanctions against Catholicism. This tactic allowed Bismarck to quell revolts, but he was forced to resign in 1890 over disputes with the new Kaiser Wilhelm II. Germany also accelerated its foreign adventurism with a policy derisively known as *Flucht nach vorn* (Forward escape). Disputes over colonial issues left Germany diplomatically isolated in Europe. Germany kept the most powerful army in the world at the turn of the century, prompting Britain, France, and Russia to unite and form the Triple Entente.

GERMANY WAR HERE

1862
Bismarck is named prime minister of Prussia, and in 1867, chancellor of Germany.

1871
Through careful political maneuvering by Bismarck, Germany founds the unified German Empire.

On the eve of WWI, Europe was balanced in a web of alliances so complex that minor disputes threatened to ignite continental war. The first domino fell in 1914, when a Serbian nationalist assassinated Archduke Franz-Ferdinand, Hapsburg heir to the Austrian throne. Austria marched on Serbia in immediate retaliation, and Russia ran to the aid of its Slavic ally. After Russia ignored Germany's ultimatum to retreat, Germany united with Austria to form the Central Powers, prompting France to mobilize. Germany declared war on France and demanded that the German army be allowed to march through Belgian territory. When Belgium refused, Britain (treaty-bound to defend Belgian neutrality) declared war on Germany. Despite this opposition, Germany advanced through Belgium and northern France, sweeping all of Europe into war.

The German offensive stalled at the Battle of the Marne. Four years of agonizing trench warfare ensued 50km outside of Paris. The rivals' technologically advanced weaponry—tanks, planes, flame-throwers, and poison gas—led to unprecedented slaughter. In 1917, Germany's policy of unrestricted submarine warfare provoked the US to entevr the war on the side of the Allies. A British naval blockade, coupled with US manpower, finally enabled Ally victory.

1914
The great powers of Western Europe plunge into WWII.

IF I HAVE TO SAY IT WEIMAR TIME

In late 1918, with the German army on the brink of collapse, workers and Socialists spearheaded revolt on the homefront in the November Revolution. On November 9, 1918, Social Democratic leader Philipp Scheidemann declared a republic in Berlin, with Friedrich Ebert as its first president. The young republic, named after the National Assembly in Weimar that drafted its constitution, was guided by its Social Democrat, German Democratic Party, and Catholic Center parliamentary majority. Marshal Ferdinand Foch, the Allied Commander-in-chief, and Matthias Erzberger, Germany's representative, signed an armistice in a railroad car outside of Compiègne, France, on November 11. Following this, the Treaty of Versailles called for staggering reparation payments, reduced the German army to 100,000 men, and ascribed full blame for the war to Germany. An Allied blockade literally starved the newborn republic into accepting the treaty.

1918
The Treaty of Versailles exact harsh reparation payments from Germany, leaving it demoralized and economically vulnerable. The Weimar Republic is declared.

By 1922-23, hyperinflation from war debts was so severe that the American Dawes Plan reduced the demand for war reparations in order to prevent total economic collapse in Germany. A period of remarkable cultural and scientific artistic flourishing ensued. It was during the abortive 1923 Beer Hall Putsch uprising in Munich that Adolf Hitler, then a frustrated artist and decorated Austrian corporal, was arrested. He received the minimum sentence of five years, but served only 10 months. During his imprisonment Hitler wrote *Mein Kampf* (My Struggle), attacking Communists and Jews and stressing the importance of *Lebensraum* ("living space"). Hilter believed that his party, the National Socialist German Workers Party (Nationalsozialistische deutsche Arbeiterspartei; NSDAP, also known as the Nazis), should seize power by constitutional means. Though the Nazis had nearly quadrupled its membership to 108,000 by 1929, it was still a fringe party, receiving only 2.6% of the vote. The same year, the Great Depression struck, leaving 25% of the population unemployed; membership in the party exploded to over a million. The SA (Sturmabteilung), its paramilitary arm, grew to match the German army by 1930. Hitler failed in a 1932 presidential bid against the aging Franco-Prussian war hero Paul von Hindenburg, but parliamentary elections made the Nazis the largest party in the Reichstag. After intense political maneuvering, Hindenburg reluctantly appointed Hitler chancellor of a coalition government on January 30, 1933.

1923
Inflation soars in the wake of WWI–US$1 is equal to 4.2 trillion marks. Citizens of Germany burn cash instead of firewood.

1932
Following the stock market crash on Wall Street, over 5 million Germans are unemployed.

NATIONAL SOCIALISM

1933
President Hindenburg appoints Hitler chancellor of Germany.

Although Hitler now held the most powerful government post, the Nazi party still had difficulty obtaining a majority in the Reichstag. Politically astute, Hitler used the mysterious Reichstag fire one week prior to the elections of 1933—then attributed to Communists—to declare a state of emergency and round up his opponents, many of whom were relocated to newly-built concentration camps. Within two months of taking control, Hitler convinced the ailing Hindenburg to dissolve the Reichstag and hold new elections, allowing him to invoke Article 48, a provision drafted by sociologist Max Weber that granted Hitler the power to rule by decree for seven weeks. During this reign of terror, he curtailed freedom of the press, authorized special security arms (the Special State Police or Gestapo, the SA Storm Troopers, and the SS Security Police), and brutalized opponents. In the ensuing election on March 5, 1933, the Nazis only got 44% of the vote. However, they arrested and browbeat enough opposing legislators to secure passage of an Enabling Act in 1933, making Hitler the legal dictator of Germany. Hitler proclaimed his rule the Third Reich, successor to the Holy Roman Empire (800-1806) and the German Empire (1871-1918).

Vilifying the Weimar government as soft and ineffectual, Hitler's platform played on post-war anxieties. Germany's failing economy forced greater uncertainty upon a country that was largely receptive to ideas of anti-Semitism and German racial superiority, gleaned from centuries of struggle for a national identity in an atmosphere of continental anti-Semitism. Nazi rallies were masterpieces of political demagoguery, and the Nazi emblem, the swastika (co-opted from Hindu tradition), appeared everywhere from propaganda films to the fingernails of loyal teenagers. "Heil Hitler" and the right arm salute became a legally required greeting.

1938
Kristallnacht, an early and brutal display of anti-Semitism, foreshadows the atrocities of the Holocaust, in which 6 million Jews and 5 million homosexuals, Gypsies, Slavs, Soviets, mentally disabled, and political dissenters were killed.

To restore the floundering economy, Hitler pushed for massive industrialization, creating jobs in munitions factories. He defied the Versailles Treaty, refusing to pay reparations and beginning rearmament. Next, he annexed Austria—staring down the Western Allies with the infamous "Anschluß Österreichs"—in 1938. He demanded territorial concessions from Czechoslovakia, claiming that ethnic Germans comprised the majority of the population in the Sudetenland. British Prime Minister Neville Chamberlain assured Hitler in the 1938 Munich Agreement that Britain would not interfere with this hostile takeover in exchange for future peace. The Allies continued to tolerate Germany's aggressive expansionism until war was inevitable. Not everyone kept silent, though: there were a few resistance movements, like the Weiße Rose (White Rose) student group.

1939
After steadily annexing territory, Germany invades Poland and initiates WWII.

On September 1, 1939, German tanks rolled across the eastern border into Poland. Britain and France, bound by treaty to defend Poland, declared war on Germany but did not attack. The Soviet Union likewise ignored the German invasion, having secretly divided up Eastern Europe with

Germany under the Molotov-Ribbentrop Pact. Within a month, Poland had been crushed by Germany's new tactic of *Blitzkrieg* (literally, "lightning war"), and Hitler and Stalin carved the country up between themselves. By April 9, 1940, Hitler had overrun Denmark and Norway. A month later, *Blitzkrieg* roared through Luxembourg and overwhelmed Belgium, the Netherlands, and France. Despite leveling most of the city, the Nazis failed to bomb London into submission in the aerial Battle of Britain. Hitler shelved preparations for a cross-channel invasion, turning his attention to the Soviet Union. The German invasion of the USSR in June 1941 ended the Hitler-Stalin pact, aligning the Soviets with France and Britain. Despite the Red Army's overwhelming manpower, the German invasion nearly succeeded. At his apex of power in late 1941, Hitler held an empire from the Arctic Circle to the Sahara Desert and from the Pyrenees to the Urals.

1940
British forces retreat from the continent at Dunkirk just before the Fall of Paris and the French surrender. Hitler believes the war will soon be over.

The Soviets suffered crippling casualties, but Blitzkrieg faltered in the Russian winter. Hitler's stubborn refusal to allow a retreat at the bloody battle of Stalingrad resulted in the death or capture of over 200,000 troops and represented a crucial turning point on the Eastern Front. Following the bombing of Pearl Harbor, Hitler declared war on the US. The Allies began their counterattack in North Africa, and soon Germany was retreating on all fronts. The Allied landings in Normandy on D-Day (June 6, 1944) preceded an arduous, bloody advance across Western Europe. The Third Reich's final offensive, the Battle of the Bulge, failed in December 1944. As part of the Allies' advance the following February, the firebombing of Dresden killed at least 35,000 Germans, mostly civilians and refugees. This was one of many assaults on civilian populations worldwide that exemplified 20th-century warfare and the concept of Total War. In March 1945, the Allies crossed the Rhein; in April, the Red Army took Berlin. With Soviet troops closing in, Hilter, along with Eva Braun, committed suicide. The Third Reich, which Hitler had boasted would endure for 1000 years, had lasted only 12.

1945
The Allies defeat Germany and divide the country and its capital into four distinct zones.

THE HOLOCAUST

The persecution of the Jews began years before WWII. The racial ideology that fueled Hitler's rise to power framed history in terms of racial confrontations with absolute winners and losers. Hitler believed the German *Volk* ("people") would either triumph universally or perish, and in his mind, Jews threatened his program of fanatic nationalism, militarism, and belief in the infallibility of the Führer. In 1935 the first anti-Semitic Racial Purity Laws deprived Jews of German citizenship. On November 9, 1938, known as Kristallnacht (Night of Broken Glass), Nazis across Germany destroyed Jewish businesses, burned synagogues, killed nearly 100 Jews, and sent 20,000 more to concentration camps.

Early on, German SS troops massacred entire Jewish towns as they rolled eastward, but as the war progressed, institutions of mass execution were developed as Nazis further expanded the persecution and deportation of minorities under their control. Seven extermination camps—Auschwitz, Buchenwald (p. 419), Chelmno, Treblinka, Mąjdanek, Sobibor, and Belzec—and dozens of "labor" camps such as Bergen-Belsen, Dachau (p. 355), and Sachsenhausen were operating before war's end. Nearly six million Jews (two-thirds of Europe's Jewish population), mostly from Poland and the Soviet Union, were gassed, shot, starved, worked to death, or killed by exposure, along with five million other Soviets, Slavs, Gypsies, homosexuals, the mentally disabled, and political dissenters as part of Hitler's atrocious and systematic "final solution."

HALT'S MAUER

1949 French, American, and British holdings in Germany are consolidated into the autonomous Federal Republic of Germany; East Germany becomes the socialist German Democratic Republic (DDR).

In 1949, conflict between the Allies and the Soviets lead to the division of Germany into a capitalist and democratic state in the west and a communist Soviet state in the east. This separation was most symbolically marked by the Berlin Wall, which stood until the Soviet Union fell in 1989. One year later, Reunification began and the two territories adopted the West German constitution. Thus was born the Federal Republic of Germany.

TODAY

ECONOMY

1992 The European Union is established.

2008 Unemployment falls below 8% for the first time in over 16 years.

Germany has the third largest economy in the world that is particularly influential on the overall EU economy and on central and eastern Europe. It also remains the biggest exporter in the world, with exports accounting for 40% of German GDP. Though economic performance has been slow in recent years, especially in the east, where it is aggravated by a complicated tax system, Germany's economy seems to be on the rebound. Inflation also remains a concern. However, unemployment continues to fall and overall trends in the economic and labor market are positive.

POLITICS

Though the Social Democrats (SPD) and the center-right Christian Democratic Union (CDU) have traditionally dominated the political arena, the framework for coalitions is changing dramatically in Germany. Though the SPD government, lead by Gerhard Schröder, tried to implement reforms between 1998 and 2005, a sluggish economy prompted early elections in October 2005. These elections resulted in a stalemate, which brought about a "grand coalition" of the SPD and CDU under the leadership of CDU's Angela Merkel. The new government engaged in ambitious foreign policy initiatives, but its domestic efforts were compromised by Germany's unstable internal structure and disagreements within the coalition. Merkel's popularity has declined as the SPD and the Left Party gain support..

RELIGION

After the Reformation divided Germans between Roman Catholics and Protestants in 1517, the Peace of Augsburg in 1555 decided that the ruler would determine regional religious affiliation, resulting in a mostly Roman Catholic South and a Protestant South and East. After WWII, however, population redistributions lessened this distinction. While citizens in the former West Germany paid an obligatory church tax levied with their income tax, church membership in the GDR was actually a barrier to career advancement. Today, there are approximately equal numbers of Lutherans and Roman Catholics in Germany. Five percent of the population is Muslim, mainly due to Turkish immigration, and though only a few thousand German Jews survived the Holocaust, about 100,000 Jews now reside in Germany.

CULTURE

FOOD AND DRINK

German food gets bad press. Maybe it isn't as "gourmet" as French cuisine or "delicato" as Italian fare, but deutsche Küche has a robust charm that meat-and-potato lovers find especially satisfying. And if the local food is not to your taste, Germany's cities offer a wide variety of quality ethnic restaurants.

Since the 1970s, vegetarianism has steadily gained popularity in Germany. Approximately one fifth of Germany's population now eats little or no meat, and in most cities vegetarian and Biokost (health food) restaurants and supermarkets are common. Be sure to mention *ich bin Vegetarier(en)* ("I am a vegetarian") when dining, or simply say *kein Fleisch* ("no meat"). As most vegetarian fare relies heavily on cheese, vegans may have a more difficult time. For more information, see **Dietary Concerns** (p. 37).

The typical German *Frühstück* (breakfast) consists of coffee or tea with a selection of *Brötchen* (rolls), butter, marmalade, wurst (cold sausage of myriad varieties), *Schinken* (ham), *Eier* (eggs, usually soft- or hard-boiled), *Käse* (cheese), and *Müsli* (granola). *Mittagessen* (lunch) is traditionally the main meal of the day, consisting of soup, sausage or roasted meat, potatoes or dumplings, and a salad or *Gemüsebeilage* (vegetable side dish). *Abendessen* or *Abendbrot* (supper) is a re-enactment of breakfast, with less Müsli and coffee, and more wine or beer. Dessert after meals is rare, but many older Germans indulge in a daily ritual of *Kaffee* und *Kuchen* (coffee and cakes), analogous to English "tea-time," at 3 or 4pm.

Germany's bakeries produce a delicious range of *Brot* (bread). *Vollkornbrot* is a heavy whole-wheat, *Roggenbrot* is rye, *Schwarzbrot* (black bread) is a dense, dark loaf, and *Bauernbrot* (farmers' bread) a lighter, slightly sour country recipe. Go to a *Bäckerei* (bakery) and point to whatever looks good. Bread is usually sold as a whole loaf; for half, ask for *ein Halbes*. German bread does not contain preservatives and will go stale the day after its purchase, so Germans typically make the *Bäckerei* a daily stop. *Brötchen* (rolls) come in a staggering number, starting with the simple, white *Wasserbrötchen* and extending to the hearty *Kürbiskernbrötchen* (pumpkin seed rolls). No visit to Germany would be complete without a taste of a *Bretzel*, the south German soft pretzel that puts ballpark vendors to shame, and that in larger bakeries also comes in roll and even baguette shapes.

Aside from breads, the staples of the German diet are wurst (sausage, in dozens of varieties; see **The Best Wurst,** p. 259), *Schweinefleisch* (pork), *Rindfleisch* (beef), *Kalbfleisch* (veal), *Lammfleisch* (lamb), *Huhn* (chicken), and *Kartoffeln* (potatoes). Sampling the various local specialties around Germany gives a taste of diverse culinary traditions. In Bavaria, *Knödel* (potato and flour dumplings, sometimes filled with meat or jam) are popular, as is *Weißwurst*, a sausage made with milk. Thuringia and northern Bavaria are famed for their succulent grilled *Bratwurst*, a roasted sausage eaten with potatoes or bought from a street vendor clasped in a roll and bathed in mustard and sauerkraut. Southwestern Germany is known for its *Spätzle* (rough, twisty egg noodles), and *Maultaschen* (pasta pockets) are popular in Swabia. Hessians do amazing things with potatoes; be sure to sample the *grüne Soße* (green sauce). The North and Baltic seacoasts harvest *Krabben* (shrimp) and *Matjes* (herring), as well as other fresh forms of seafood.

When Turks began immigrating to West Germany in the early 1960s, the German palate was first treated to such now-ubiquitous delights as *Döner Kebap*; thin slices of lamb mixed with cucumbers, onions, and red cabbage in a wedge of *Fladenbrot*, a round, flat, sesame-covered bread. Other well-known Turkish dishes include *Börek*, a flaky pastry filled with spinach, cheese, or meat; and *Lahmacun* (also called türkische Pizza), a smaller, zestier version of Italy's staple fast food. Turkish restaurants and *Imbiße*, popular and cheap fast-food stands, also offer *Kefir* (flavored yogurt drinks) and *Baklava* for dessert.

Beer and wine (p. 49) are the popular meal-time beverages. *Saft* (juice), plain or mixed with mineral water, is an alternative. Germans do not guzzle glasses of water by the dozen; instead, they will sip a (small) glass of carbonated mineral water—ask for *Wasser ohne Gas* to get the non-bubbly kind. If you ask for water in a restaurant, you'll get the expensive bottled type, so be sure to ask for *Leitungswasser* (tap water) if that's what you want.

With few exceptions, restaurants expect you to seat yourself. If there are no free tables, ask someone for permission to take a free seat by saying *Darf ich Platz nehmen?* (DAHRF eesh PLAHTS nay-men; "may I sit here?"). In a less formal setting, just say *Hallo.* It's standard for perfect strangers to sit next to you—they may or may not be interested in conversation. At the table, Germans eat with the fork in the left hand and the knife in the right and keep their hands above or resting on the table. While eating, it is polite to keep the tines of your fork pointing down at all times. When you're finished, ask the server *Zahlen, bitte* (TSAH-len, BIT-tuh; "check, please"); it's considered rude to bring customers the bill before they have asked for it. Taxes (*Mehrwertsteuer*) and service (*Bedienung*) are always included in the price, but it is customary to leave a small tip, usually by rounding up the bill to the nearest euro.

Eating in restaurants at every meal will quickly drain your budget. One strategy to save money at restaurants is to stick to the daily fixed-price option, called the *Tagesmenü*. A cheaper option is to buy food in grocery stores. University students eat in cafeterias called *Mensen*. Some Mensen (singular *Mensa*) require a student ID or charge higher prices for non-students. In smaller towns, the best budget option is to stop by a bakery (*Bäckerei*) for bread and garnish it with sausage and cheese from a butcher (*Fleischerei* or *Metzgerei*).

BEER

Beer brewers shall sell no beer to the citizens, unless it be three weeks old; to the foreigner, they may knowingly sell younger beer.
—German Beer Law, 1466

Germans have brewed frothy, alcoholic malt beverages since the 8th century BC, and they've been consuming and exporting them in prodigious quantities ever since. The state of Bavaria alone contains about one-fifth of all the breweries in the world. Germans drink more than 120L of beer per person every year. According to legend, the German king Gambrinus invented the modern beer recipe when he threw some hops into fermenting malt. During the Middle Ages, monastic orders refined the art of brewing, imbibing to stave off starvation during long fasts. It wasn't long before the monks' lucrative trade caught the eye of secular lords, who established the first *Hofbrauereien* (court breweries).

BEER	REGION	DESCRIPTION
Altbier	Düsseldorf	dark, top-fermented beer
Berliner Weiße	Berlin	light beer, often served with Schuß (raspberry syrup)
Bockbier & Doppelbock	Einbeck (near Hannover)	strong, bottom-fermented; many seasonal versions
Dampfbier	Bayreuth	fruity, top-fermented
Dortmunder Export	Dortmund	mild, bottom-fermented lager
Dunkles Lagerbier	Bavaria	dark lager, strong malt, bottom-fermented
Gose	Leipzig	top-fermented wheat beer with oats
Hefeweizen	Bavaria	wheat beer, more hops than Weißbier
Kölsch	Cologne (Köln)	pale, top-fermented beer (by law, served only in Köln)
Märzen	Bavaria	amber colored lager
Pils (Pilsner)	North Germany	clear, bitter taste (extra hops)
Radler (Alster)	Hamburg	mix of half beer, half lemon-lime soda
Rauchbier	Bamberg	dark and smoky
Weißbier (Weizenbier)	Bavaria/south	wheat beer, smooth and refreshing, rich brown color

To ensure the quality of this new phenomenon, Duke Wilhelm IV of Bavaria decreed in 1516 that beer could contain only pure water, barley, and hops. Wilhelm's Purity Law *(Reinheitsgebot)* has endured to this day, with minor alterations to permit the cultivation of Bavaria's trademark wheat-based beers. As a result, German beer contains no preservatives and will spoil relatively quickly. Most German beer is *Vollbier*, containing about 4% alcohol. Export (5%) is also popular, and stout, tasty *Bockbier* (6.25%) is brewed in the spring. *Doppelbock* is an strong malt reserved for special occasions. *Ein Helles* gets you a light-colored beer, while *ein Dunkles* can look like anything from Coca-Cola to molasses. The average German beer is maltier and thicker than Czech, Dutch, or American beers, hence the term "*flußiges Brot*": liquid bread. Generalizations are difficult, however, as each region boasts its own special brew.

The variety of places to drink beer is almost as staggering as the variety of brews. A traditional *Biergarten* consists of outdoor tables under chestnut trees; often, simple food is served as well. In the days before refrigeration, the broad leaves of the trees kept beer barrels cool—now they just shade the beer drinkers. A *Bierkeller* is a subterranean version of the *Biergarten*. To order *ein Bier*, hold up your thumb, not your index finger. Raise your glass to

A CLOSER LOOK

Beer Today, Beer Tomorrow

The beer-swilling stereotype can probably be attributed to the Romans, who made pretentious claims about the nobility of wine and depravity of beer. Fortunately, the Germans, in the tradition of Luther, have steadily dismantled this image. In fact, Germans have gone so far as to enshrine beer in innumerable gemütliche beer gardens. Germany lays claim to over 1200, collectively producing upwards of 5000 individual beers. As a lone consumer, holding this variety in check requires some familiarity with the beer-brewing essentials.

"Since 1516, Germany has limited the ingredients for brewing to water, malt, and hops."

Since 1516, Germany has limited the ingredients for brewing to water, malt, and hops. Water quality was pivotal in former times, its source determining both brewery location and taste. Although low-calcium, alkaline water is still favored for brewing with lighter malts (like that for Pils), most commercial breweries modify their brew water to maintain a uniform taste. The soul of the beer is the malt, a word that may derive from the indo-germanic mldu, meaning soft or tender, or from the initial "green-malt," resulting from the controlled budding of water-soaked barley. Kiln-drying the green yields numerous malt varieties from light Pils malt (at ca. 176°F) through to dark Munich malt (ca. 212°C). The malt mixture determines the beer both by influencing flavor and by setting the strength of the beer—malt is the sole source of Stammwürze (precious maltose sugars.) Hops, botanical relatives of cannabis, can be either aromatic or bitter. They give beer its distinctive bitter flavor and help the beer remain bacteriostatic during fermentation.

The original Reinheitsgebot (German beer purity law), adopted in 1516, made no provision for fermentation—a haphazard affair until 1866, when the hirsute Frenchman Louis Pasteur, working under Napoleon's decree to determine the cause of fouled wine, grounded the field of zymology (the study of fermentation), by demonstrating that single-celled fungi were responsible for the process. Yeast convert sugars to ethanol and those operating optimally around 15-20°C at the water's surface produce obergäriges (top-brewed) beer varieties, such as Weizen (originally and still known in Munich as Weißbier), Kölsch and Alt. The beer vandals in the north also serve a form of obergäriges beer to which they add a dollop of either raspberry, lemon, or woodruff syrup and call it a Berliner Weiße. Yeast strains that clump together and ferment at cooler (43-48°C) temperatures on the vats' floor, produce untergäriges (bottom-brewed) beer. The fastidious selection and maintenance of untergärige strains—initiated in the 1840's by Anton Dreher—is now the most guarded trade secret of many large breweries.

In the land of the Dichter und Denker (Poets and thinkers), the beer drinker is well provided for, and you can expect to chose from three basic sorts of beer: Schankbiere (<4.5%), Vollbiere, and Starkbiere (>6%). Amongst the vollbiere is the bitter Pils from Pilzen (Czech), helles (light colored), dunkles (dark), and the obergärige beers. Starkbier, often called Bock, has a strong clod of Stammwürze—and therefore alcohol—and is often strengthened in the form of Maibock or Eisbock. Still, these are not as strong as Doppelbock beer, which is identifiable by the suffix "–ator," and can be found en masse at Munich's 17-day-long Starkbierfest, beginning in late February. An ungespundetes beer is not carbonated and a Zwickel is not filtered. As for quantity, the Germans have got you covered: the standard quantity of beer is half a liter, a Mass is double, and if you are already filling up, Pils is titrated to 400ml and Kölsch to 200ml. But never fear, this Kölsch, Cologne's specialty, can also be ordered by the metre, offered in long wooden servers.

Dr. Richard Carr *works at Ludwig-Maximilians University, where he specializes in Neurophysiology. He was born in Melbourne, Australia and has been brewing and drinking beer in and around Bavaria for the past seven years.*

a *Prost* (cheers), make eye contact with your companions, and drink. Another option for drinking is the *Gaststätte*, a simple, local restaurant. It's considered bad form to order only drinks at a Gaststätte during mealtimes, but at other times friends linger for hours over beers. Many *Gaststätten* have a *Stammtisch* (regulars' table) marked by a flag where interlopers should not sit. The same group of friends may meet at the *Stammtisch* every week for decades to drink and play cards. *Kneipen* are bars where hard liquor is also served.

TIP **LIVING UNDER GLASS.** Most of Germany's beverage bottles—containing everything from cola to beer—are made of glass, and bars will often add a €1-2 Pfand (deposit) to the advertised price. Return the bottle, and you'll get your Pfand back. Grocery stores have collection bins for the absent-minded, but retail reimbursements are much lower.

CUSTOMS AND ETIQUETTE

Although Germans may seem reserved or even unfriendly, they are not as standoffish as they may first appear. Germans are very frank and will not hesitate to show disapproval. To the uninitiated this may come across as confrontational, but it stems mostly from honesty. Many Germans consider effusive chumminess insincere, and Americans are often perceived as disingenuous for being overly friendly.

The complex rules of German etiquette may seem excessive; however, most apply only with older Germans and in rural areas. In general, Germans are more formal than Americans, and punctuality is a huge deal. An invitation to a German home is a major courtesy—bring a gift for the host. Among the older generations, be careful not to use the informal *du* (you) or a first name without being invited to do so. *Du* is appropriate when addressing fellow students and friends, or with children. In all other circumstances, use the formal Sie for "you," as in the question *Sprechen Sie Englisch?* (Do you speak English)?

Addressing a woman as *Fräulein* is inappropriate in most instances; address all women as *Frau* (followed by a surname). While the average German will generally speak English, Germans will be more receptive to a traveler who knows at least a little German; learn some before you go (see the **Appendix**, p. 492, for help). In any case, remember at least two phrases: *bitte* (both please and you're welcome; BIT-tuh) and *danke* (thank you; DAHNK-uh).

The first time you see a German standing at an intersection in the rain, no cars in sight, waiting for the "walk" signal, you'll see what a law-abiding nation Germany is. Jaywalking is only one of several petty offenses that will mark you as a foreigner (and subject you to fines); littering is another. Drug use has yet to become publicly acceptable, even where penalties are more relaxed (see **Essentials, p. 8**).

ARTS

Germany is the land of *Dichter und Denker*—poets and philosophers. German humanities have had an enormous influence on the world and German research has produced innumerable advances in the natural sciences.

ARCHITECTURE

IT'S YOUR SCHLOSS. Churches and castles around Germany manifest stunning Romanesque, Gothic, and Baroque styles. The **Romanesque period,** spanning the years 800 to 1300, arose from direct imitation of Roman ruins. Outstanding Romanesque cathedrals can be found along the **Rhein** at **Speyer, Trier, Mainz,** and **Worms.**

MEDIEVAL CATHEDRALS. Gothic style, characterized by pointed rib vaulting, gradually replaced the Romanesque from between 1300 and 1500. The **Gothic cathedral at Cologne** (p. 231) is one of the most famous structures in Germany. Secular architecture at the end of the Middle Ages is best remembered through the *fachwerk* (half-timbered) houses that still dominate the Altstädte of many German cities. In the South, the Renaissance influence can be seen in the **Augsburg Rathaus** (p. 392) and the **Heidelberg Schloß** (p. 303).

I'M BAROQUE. By 1550, Lutheran reforms put a damper on the unrestrained extravagance of cathedrals in the north, while the **Counter-Reformation** in the Catholic south spurred the new Baroque style. The **Zwinger** in Dresden (p. 452) exemplifies Baroque fluidity, contrast, and exaggerated motion. This style eventually reached an opulent extreme with **Rococo,** as exemplified by **Schloß Sanssouci** in Potsdam (p. 134). Versailles' decadent precedent influenced Bavarian castles, notably the **Herrenchiemsee** (p. 371) and the **Königsschlößer** (p. 360).

NEOCLASSICAL CLASSICS. The late 18th century saw an attempt to bring Greco-Roman prestige to Germany in the form of Neoclassical architecture. This style was spurred on by the pomp of **Karl Friedrich Schinkel,** state architect of Prussia. The **Brandenburg Gate** and the buildings along **Unter den Linden** in Berlin (p. 104) all hailed from this period.

JUGENDSTIL. The **Mathildenhöhe buildings** in Darmstadt are products of a much more modern movement, **Jugendstil,** which took its name from *Die Jugend* magazine. In the 1920s and early 30s, **Walter Gropius** and the **Bauhaus school** of Weimar (p. 418) and Dessau (p. 435) came to the fore, seeking to unite the principles of form and function in sleek glass and concrete buildings.

NATIONAL SOCIALIST AND SOVIET STRUCTURES. Hitler disapproved of these new building styles. He named a design school reject, **Albert Speer,** as his minister of architecture, and commissioned large neoclassical buildings appropriate to the "thousand-year Reich." Many were intended for public rallies, such as the **congress hall** and **stadium** in Nürnberg (p. 405) and the **Olympic Stadium** in Berlin (p. 103). After the war, **Soviet architecture** began to clutter East Germany, reaching its pinnacle with the 368m **Fernsehturm** (TV tower) in Berlin (p. 107). Berlin's **Karl-Marx-Allee** (p. 111) is rich in **Plattenbauen,** the dispassionate pre-fab apartment buildings that can be found throughout eastern Germany.

POST-WALL AND THE SCENE TODAY. New construction has once again put Germany on the architectural map, although many buildings were designed by non-German architects. Berlin is home to many high-profile projects, such as **Sir Norman Foster's** glass dome on the **Reichstag** (p. 108) and the reconstruction of **Potsdamer Platz** (p. 105), anchored by the steel and glass **Sony Center. Daniel Libeskind's Jewish Museum** (p. 118) opened in 2002, and American architect **Peter Eisenman's** jarring **Holocaust memorial** (p. 108) was unveiled in 2005.

KUNST YOU HANDLE IT?

THE RENAISSANCE. German art first broke its Gothic fetters with Renaissance painters like **Matthias Grünewald** and **Hans Holbein the Younger,** who gave depth and realism to secular subjects. Their prolific colleague **Lucas Cranach** churned out pieces with historical and mythological themes. **Albrecht Dürer's** series of self portraits were among the first, and most influential, in Western art and his engravings and detailed work **A Young Hare** are highly recognizable.

GERMAN ROMANTICISM. During the **Protestant Reformation** and the Thirty Years' War, the visual arts suffered from lack of financial encouragement, but by the 19th century German critics were advocating Romantic painters' return to traditional, spiritual German masterworks. This idea was easily incorporated into the melancholy landscapes of **Philipp Otto Runge** and **Caspar David Friedrich,** who painted Rügen's chalk cliffs (p. 153) and Eldena's ancient ruins.

EXPRESSIONISM. In the 20th century, German art boomed. German Expressionism recalled the symbolist tendencies of **Viennese Jugendstil** and **French Fauvism.** Founded in Dresden in 1905, **Die Brücke** (The Bridge) was the earliest Expressionist group. Its artists, such as **Ernst Ludwig Kirchner,** used jarring outlines and deep color to make artwork loud and aggressively expressive. A 1911 exhibition in Munich entitled **Der Blaue Reiter** (The Blue Rider), led by Russian emigré **Wassily Kandinsky,** marked the rise of a second Expressionist school.

NEUE SACHLICHKEIT. WWI and its aftermath forced politics onto German art. **Max Ernst** started a **Dadaist** group in Cologne expressing artistic nihilism with collage and composition. The grotesque, satirical works of **Otto Dix** juggled Expressionism and Dadaism; ultimately, the artist embraced **Neue Sachlichkeit** (New Objectivity), an anti-fascist movement that sought to understand the rapid modernization of life through matter-of-fact representation. Perhaps its best-known proponent, **Max Beckmann,** expressed a tortured view of man's condition. The smaller **German Realist movement** devoted itself to bleak, critical works such as the social reform posters of **Käthe Kollwitz.** Sculptor **Ernst Barlach** infused realism with religious themes, inflaming Nazi censors.

NATIONAL SOCIALISM. Nazism drove most artists into exile. Themes of **Blut und Boden** (Blood and Soil) dominated Nazi visual arts, depicting mythical union of folkish blood and German soil through idealized images of workers, farmers, and soldiers. In 1937, the Nazis' infamous **Entartete Kunst** (degenerate art) exhibit ridiculed pieces by Kandinsky, Kirchner, and other masters by displaying them with paintings by psychotics and mental patients.

EAST OR WEST, WHO PAINTS THE BEST? After the war, German art made a quick recovery. In East Germany, state-supported **Socialist Realism** dominated, while West German art was characterized by **abstraction.** As time went on, installations, "happenings," and other new media art pieces, especially video, edged out painting, although **Sigmar Polke, Gerhard Richter,** and a few other masters kept the medium alive. Richter gained renown for his paintings of photos of the criminal **Baader-Meinhof group,** entitled "October 15, 1977." Polke also studied with **Josef Beuys,** known for his performance art happenings, at his **Constructivist sculpture school** at Düsseldorf.

A MODERN ART CAPITAL. Today, Germany produces and exhibits a huge range of modern art, from video and multimedia installations to avant-garde painting and sculpture. *Kunstfonds* (art funds) have supported artists since 1980, and the modern art school in Leipzig enjoys international renown. Kassel hosts the acclaimed **"Documenta"** exhibit every five years, showcasing contemporary art in installations throughout the town. Other museums to see are Berlin's **Hamburger Bahnhof** (p. 117), Cologne's **Museum Ludwig** (p. 233), and Düsseldorf's **Kunstsammlung im Ständehaus** (p. 250). Wolfgang Laib, a minimalist artist who uses materials from nature, and the unconventional painter **Günter Förg,** are among Germany's dynamic and prolific contemporary artists.

LITERATURE

MEDIEVAL AND RENAISSANCE WRITING. German literary history begins around 800 AD with **Das Hildebrandslied** (The Lay of Hildebrand), an epic poem describing the fatal struggle between the heroic **Hildebrand** and his son **Hadubrand.** The next several centuries showed an intriguing mix of Christianity and Germanic myth. As chivalry took hold in Germany, lyric poetry focused on unrequited love emerged, best represented by the work of **Walther von der Vogelweide.** In the 16th century, **Martin Opitz** and **Andreas Gryphius** insisted on strict rules for meter and stresses in poetry. The first significant German novel, **Hans J. C. von Grimmelshausen's** roguish epic *Simplicissimus*, was written during the **Thirty Years' War.** The long war hampered German literary efforts, which would slowly revive in the 18th century.

ROMANTICISM: LOST AND FAUST. Sentimental, unusually personalized verse arose in the mid-18th century, about the time **Johann Wolfgang von Goethe** was writing his early poetry (p. 417). Goethe later turned to the **Bildungsroman** (coming-of-age tale) and to classicism and orientalism. His masterpieces include a retelling of the **Faust** legend, considered the pinnacle of German literature.

In the early 19th century, Romanticism gained momentum, with the poetry of **Novalis** and **J. C. Friedrich Hölderlin,** who wrote mythical poetry until he succumbed to insanity. The Brothers Grimm documented fairy tales for the first time. **E.T.A. Hoffmann** wrote ghost stories (Bamberg, p. 410). Romanticism gave way to realistic political literature around the time of the revolutions of 1848. **Heinrich Heine** was the finest of the **Junges Deutschland** (Young Germany) movement and also one of the first German Jews to achieve literary prominence (Düsseldorf, p. 245). Dramatists **Georg Büchner** and **Gerhart Hauptmann** had an influence at the turn of the century with characteristic *fin-de-siècle* realism.

MODERNISM IN GERMANY. Hermann Hesse incorporated Eastern spirituality into his writings (his 1922 novel *Siddhartha* became a paperback sensation in the 1960s), while **Thomas Mann** carried the Modernist novel to a high point with *Der Zauberberg (The Magic Mountain)*, using the traditional **Bildungsroman** to criticize German culture (Lübeck, p. 162). Also vital to the period were German-language writers living in Austria-Hungary, among them Rainer Maria Rilke, Robert Musil, and Franz Kafka.

EXPRESSIONISM AND DESTRUCTION. In the years before WWI, Germany produced a violent strain of Expressionist poetry that mirrored developments in painting. The style was suited to depict the horrors of war, and several of its masters were killed in battle. The Weimar Era was filled with artistic production. Its most famous novel was **Erich Maria Remarque's** bleak portrayal of the Great War, *Im Westen nichts Neues (All Quiet on the Western Front)*. **Bertolt Brecht** presented mankind in its grotesque absurdity through literature (see Berlin, p. 109). The Third Reich burned more books than it published and the Nazi attitude toward literature was summed up by Nazi propaganda chief Joseph Goebbels: "Whenever I hear the word 'culture,' I reach for my gun."

HOLOCAUST LITERATURE. Famous authors who are themselves victims or survivors include Elie Wiesel, Jean Améry, Edgar Hilsenrath, and Anne Frank. Though philosopher Theodor Adorno pronounced that "writing poetry after Auschwitz is barbaric," poets such as **Paul Celan** have proven this statement false. Celan's famed *Todesfuge (Death Fuge)* exemplifies a powerful attempt to express that which is beyond expression.

GRUPPE 47. While the literature of the Weimar period seemed to succeed WWI almost effortlessly, WWII left Germany's artistic consciousness in shambles. To nurse German literature back to health, several writers joined to form Gruppe 47, named after the year of its founding. The group included such renowned authors as **Günter Grass** and Celan. Much of the ensuing literature dealt with the problem of Germany's Nazi past, while the poetry of **Hans Magnus Enzensberger** and the novels of Grass and **Heinrich Böll** turned a critical eye towards post-war West Germany's overly-bureaucratic tendencies.

LITERATURE OF THE DDR. Many expatriates, particularly those with Marxist leanings from before the war (such as Brecht), returned to the East with great hopes. But the communist leadership was not interested in eliciting free artistic expression, causing many talented writers to emigrate. Nevertheless, the literature produced during Soviet occupation from 1945 until 1989 has become a field of interest for scholars.

CONTEMPORARY LITERATURE. Günther Grass's receipt of the Nobel Prize for Literature in 1999 provided the newly reunited Germany with its first literary icon and propelled German literati back into an international spotlight. **W.G. Sebald's** novels pushed the boundaries of fiction and nonfiction in their focus on German history. For further happening German literature, look for **Monika Maron, Peter Schneider,** and **Bernhard Schlink.**

PHILOSOPHY

A GERMAN DELICACY. German philosophy is like wurst: thick and difficult to digest. **Immanuel Kant,** the foremost thinker of the German Enlightenment, argued for autonomous rational calculation, positing reason as our highest moral safeguard, and insisting that we ask if our motivating principles can at any time be made into a universal law. Meanwhile **Johann Gottlieb Fichte** spearheaded the new **German Idealist movement,** which stressed the importance of a spirit or Geist in interpreting experience (p. 423). **G. W. F. Hegel** proposed that history as well as the development of the individual consciousness could be understood as conflicts between thesis and antithesis, which produced synthesis—essentially the idea that from struggle comes growth. Hegel's view of world history would, after some distortion, eventually provide a theoretical backing for **German nationalism.** Meanwhile, **Johann Gottfried Herder** pushed for romantic nationalism, asserting that the spirit of a nation could be found in its folklore and peasant traditions. **Karl Marx** turned Hegel around, asserting that class conflict was the stage on which the world was made, profoundly altering the course of 20th-century history.

Similarly controversial, **Friedrich Nietzsche,** influenced by pessimist par excellence. **Arthur Schopenhauer,** scorned the mediocrity of "resentful" Judeo-Christian masses and advanced the idea of the **Übermensch** (superman), a man who creates a moral code without reference to the standards of others.

Around the turn of the century, Max Weber wrote that the world was trapped in a bureaucratic iron cage. Nazi sympathizer **Martin Heidegger** made his name with *Sein und Zeit* (Being and Time). This notoriously cumbersome book insists that man understand the significance of questioning the meaning of life in a world where one-sided technology development has led to a crisis of existential alienation. The most celebrated post-war exponent of this school, **Jürgen Habermas,** has criticized German reunification, citing the danger of joining two nations that had adopted two very different cultures.

MUSIC

German contributions to music have always been marked by three characteristic tendencies: striking creativity, thorough exploration, and a penchant for theory and explanation.

FIRST NOTES. Charlemagne introduced the Roman liturgy and its chant to German parts of his empire. German theorists aided in the development of **Western musical notation** and **polyphony,** which started as the addition of new musical lines to the original chant. **Hildegard of Bingen,** a 12th-century mystic, writer, composer, scientist, and correspondent with popes and kings, composed elaborate chants and liturgical dramas. The love poetry of the **Minnesänger** was written around the same time as the narrative epics *Tristan*, *Parzival*, and the *Nibelungenlied.* Together with the northern French trouvère songs and Provençal troubadour songs, they expressed chivalry and other medieval ideals of love.

BURROWING FROM THE ITALIANS. In the 17th century, German composers were impressed by the elaborate forms developed in Italy that involved choruses, soloists, and large groups of instruments: **cantatas, oratorios,** and **passions.** Composers like **Heinrich Schütz** produced glorious works, sometimes called sacred symphonies. Oratorios were sacred dramas not meant for church performance. The situation in Germany was made more complicated by the different observances of Catholics and Protestants, both of whom wrote passions, narratives of the suffering and death of Jesus Christ. Famous Passions include **J.S. Bach's** *St. Matthew Passion* and the *St. John Passion.* A cantata could be either sacred or secular. German writers around 1600 developed an elaborate correspondence between music and the classical rhetoric of ancient Greece and Rome. They thought every musical setting of a text was designed to make a particular impression and elicit an emotional response from the listener.

ENLIGHTEN ME. In the 18th century, Germany imported a great deal of Italian opera, and one of the greatest German composers, **George Frideric Handel,** lived in London and wrote operas in Italian and oratorios, such as *Messiah,* in English. **Frederick the Great** liked the French style in instrumental music, though he had his German composer **Johann Joachim Quantz** write it. He also employed Bach's son **Carl Philipp Emanuel.** When J.S. Bach visited Frederick the Great, the King gave him a theme to improvise on that couldn't be manipulated in the way Bach was famous for doing. Driven crazy by this, Bach wrote a collection of pieces based on the theme and sent it back to the King, calling it the *Musical Offering*, part of which was a trio sonata in the French style.

IN THEORY. Theory returned with a vengeance in the 18th century, when German philosopher **Alexander Gottlieb Baumgarten** invented aesthetics (coining the term *aesthetica.*) German composers wrote treatises on how to play instruments, compose music, and develop musical taste. **Bonn** became a hotbed of enlightenment thought. **Joseph Haydn** and **Wolfgang Amadeus Mozart,** although Austrian, were a crucial part of the Austro-German tradition of Classical and Romantic music. They developed and championed instrumental genres like the **symphony** and **string quartet. Ludwig van Beethoven** first made his name first as a brilliant improviser and pianist. When he was almost thirty years old, he wrote the long and difficult *Eroica symphony*, originally intending to dedicate it to Napoleon; however, with the latter's declaration of imperial ambition, he turned the second movement into a funeral march and changed the title.

ROMANTICISM AND ITS AFTERMATH. The ambition of German writers of the 1790s and early 1800s to create the "poetry of longing" (Schlegel) can be correlated with early 19th-century Romantic composers like **Franz Schubert** and **Robert Schumann,** who distilled something ineffable in their *Lieder* (songs) and piano pieces. The era of the generalist composer was ending and the specialist composer was a new feature of the 19th century. The **New German School** loved music with a story or "program." **Richard Wagner** wrote massive operas that reached back to the medieval German epics of *Tristan*, *Parsifal*, and the *Ring of the Nibelung*, as well as the stories of *Tannhäuser* and the *Meistersingers;* like Goethe in Faust, he wanted to create a uniquely national epic.

20TH CENTURY. The modern era saw a fragmentation of the grand dreams of the Romantics, and strong reactions to WWI. The Austrian **Arnold Schoenberg** took Wagner's chromaticism and turned it into more controlled forms of "composing with twelve tones" that he said would "insure the supremacy of German music for a hundred years." **Paul Hindemith,** on the other hand, headed a group of **German Neoclassicists** (a school of composing inspired by Russian **Igor Stravinsky**) that embraced the older instrumental forms like the sonata and the variation. At the same time, the unstable Weimar economy encouraged smaller, cheaper musical forms like **jazz.** Music hall works bred the **Singspiel,** satiric operettas. **Kurt Weill's** partnership with **Bertolt Brecht** mastered the genre with *Die Dreigroschenoper* (Three-Penny Opera) and the well-known song *Mackie Messer (Mack the Knife)*. A new movement of **Gebrauchsmusik** (utilitarian music) engendered music for amateur players and film scores. **Carl Orff,** Hitler's favorite living composer, is known for his *Carmina Burana*, a resurrection of bawdy 13th-century lyrics with a bombastic score. The immediate post-war period was dominated by schmaltzy **Schlagermusik** (pop music) on the popular side, and esoteric avant-garde "art" music of the **Darmstadt school.**

CURRENT TRENDS. Today, Germany is known for its influential **Krautrock** of the 60s and 70s, a blend of rock instrumentation and electronic textures, featuring artists **Can, Faust, Kraftwerk,** and **Neu!.** Germany also pioneered **techno,** an umbrella term for electronic music. Now there is a vital rock scene, with such notable acts as **Die Ärtzte, Wir Sind Helden, Einstürzende Neubauten** (Collapsing New Buildings), and **The Notwist.** After becoming a rock sensation in the 60s, **Herbert Grönemeyer** has enjoyed a comeback among younger generations. German **hip-hop** groups include **Die fantastischen Vier, Fünf Sterne Deluxe,** and **Fettes Brot.** Some popular Popular rappers include **Sabrina Setlur, Xavier Naidoo,** and **Illmatic.**

FILM

NEW ART. The newborn medium of film exploded onto the German art scene in the Weimar era thanks to a number of brilliant directors. **Das Cabinet des Dr. Caligari** (The Cabinet of Dr. Caligari) is an early horror film directed by **Robert Wiene. Fritz Lang's** remarkable films include **M., Dr. Mabuse der Spieler,** and **Metropolis,** a dark portrayal of the techno-fascist city of the future. Meanwhile, **Josef von Sternberg** extended the tradition into sound with his satiric **Der blaue Engel** (The Blue Angel), starring Berlin bombshell **Marlene Dietrich.**

PROPOGANDA FILM. Heeding Hitler's prediction that "without motor-cars, sound films, and wireless, (there can be) no victory for National Socialism," propaganda minister **Joseph Goebbels** became a masterful manipulator. Filmmaker **Leni Riefenstahl's** *Triumph des Willens (Triumph of the Will)* documented a Nürnberg Party Rally (p. 401), and her *Olympia* recorded **1936 Olympic Games** in Berlin (p. 103).

POST-WAR PROWESS. Germany's film renaissance began in 1962 with the **Oberhausen Manifesto,** a declaration by independent filmmakers demanding artistic freedom and the right to create new feature films. **Rainer Werner Fassbinder** told fatalistic stories of people corrupted or defeated by society, including an epic television production of **Alfred Döblin's** mammoth novel Berlin Alexanderplatz. Fassbinder's film *Die Ehe der Maria Braun (The Marriage of Maria Braun)* and **Volker Schlöndorff's** *Die Blechtrommel (The Tin Drum),* based on Günther Grass's novel of the same title, brought the new German wave to a wider, international audience. **Wolfgang Petersen** directed *Das Boot (The Boat),* one of the most famous submarine films ever made.

FILM IN THE DDR. East German film had to be produced under the supervision of the state-run German Film Corporation (DEFA). Slatan Dudow produced the first of the DEFA's films, *Unser täglich Brot (Our Daily Bread),* a paean to the nationalization of industry. After a brief post-Stalinist thaw, few East German films departed from the standard format of socialist heroism or love stories, with the exception of **Egon Günther's** feminist 1965 film *Lots Weib (Lot's Wife).* **Frank Beyer's** politically daring *Spur der Steine (Trace of Stones)* was a reflection on corruption and intrigue in a communal construction project. **Winfried Junge, Volker Koepp,** and **Jürgen Böttcher** made prominent documentaries which primarily glorified the East and vilified the West.

RECENT PRODUCTION. **Tom Tykwer** wowed international audiences in 1998 with stylish, high-energy *Lola Rennt (Run Lola Run);* a film that is, to many, iconic of a reunified and postmodernist Germany, apace with throbbing techno and bodies relentlessly in motion. **Wim Wenders's** hit documentary *Buena Vista Social Club* celebrates Cuban music. **Caroline Link's** dramatic *Nirgendwo in Afrika (Nowhere in Africa)* follows a Jewish family fleeing to Kenya in 1938, and won the 2002 Academy Award for Best Foreign Film. **Wolfgang Becker's** hit *Goodbye, Lenin!* is an affecting and hilarious portrait of life in the DDR after reunification. In 2007, **Florian Henckel von Donnersmarck's** *Das Leben der Anderen (The Lives of Others),* a gripping tale of Stasi surveillance in Berlin, also won the Academy Award for Best Foreign Film.

SCIENCE AND TECHNOLOGY

Imagining technology without the Germans is like making cake without the flour. Foundational discoveries by inventors, physicists, chemists, and biologists have profoundly altered world history in unimaginable ways. Around 1455, a humble, if mischievous, goldsmith named **Johannes Gutenberg** printed 180 copies of the Bible and launched a new epoch of human intellectual development. The movable type printing press that Gutenberg developed over 15 years facilitated the flow of information that gave rise to ideological revolutions from Martin Luther's *95 Theses* to the Mercedes-Benz Maybach 62.

The major contributions of German scientists after Gutenberg, produced a legacy of energy research that continues to influence technology. In 1650, **Otto von Güricke's** vacuum pump invention laid the groundwork formodern thermodynamics. A few decades later, **Gabriel Daniel Fahrenheit** created one of the first systems for measuring temperature, a system still in place in the Unites States. With the Age of Enlightenment, **Alexander von Humboldt** won international acclaim for laying the groundwork for the fields of physical geography and meteorology as well as producing one of earliest scientific accounts of the New World. Physics took center stage during the late 19th and early 20th centuries in the German academy. Drawing from Humboldt's geophysical work, **Hermann von Helmholtz** worked in chemical thermodynamics and eventually pioneered the modern field of electrodynamics. Helmholtz's star student, **Heinrich Rudolf Hertz** discovered the existence of electromagnetic waves, paving the way for the development of modern telecommunications technology. The international unit for measuring frequency was later named after him. In the related field of electromagnetic radiation, the discovery of X-rays earned **Wilhelm Conrad Röntgen** the first Nobel Prize in Physics in 1901.

Two decades later, another Nobel Prize in Physics was awarded to **Albert Einstein** for his Special Theory of Relativity. Einstein's research reacted to and drew from legendary Germany physicist, **Max Planck,** the founder of quantum theory and winner of the 1918 Nobel Prize in Physics. In fact, it was Planck who recognized the significance of the then-unknown Einstein's early work on relativity around the turn of the century. **Otto Hahn,** a member of the Max Planck Society, is credited as the founder of the atomic age, conducting the first successful nuclear fission experiments in 1938. By the 1960s, nuclear energy was in regular use throughout the country.

Today, a strong emphasis on renewable energy dominates the scientific dialogue in Germany. Along with the other countries of the European Union, Germany set a goal in 1997 that 12% of its energy would be renewable by 2010. The plan depended on an increasing use of **hydroelectric, solar, and wind power.** Germany surpassed the target in 2007 with 14% renewable resources and set out to reach 27% by 2020. Currently, Germany ranks first in the use of wind power and is nearly tied with Japan for the use of solar energy. Recycling has also become a chief priority, and practically everything can be recycled since the inauguration the nationally sanctioned **Grüne Punkt system.**

HOLIDAYS AND FESTIVALS

Stores, museums, and most tourist offices will be closed on the days listed.

2010	HOLIDAY	ENGLISH
Jan. 1	Neujahrstag	New Year's Day
Jan. 6	Heilige Drei Könige	Epiphany
Mar. 21	Karfreitag	Good Friday
Apr. 2	Ostersonntag	Easter Sunday
Apr. 3	Ostermontag	Easter Monday
May 1	Tag der Arbeit	Labor Day
May 13	Christi Himmelfahrt	Ascension Day
May 23	Pfingstsonntag	Whitsunday (Pentecost)
May 24	Pfingstmontag	Whit Monday
June 3	Fronleichnam	Corpus Christi
Aug. 15	Maria Himmelfahrt	Assumption Day
Oct. 3	Tag der deutschen Einheit	Day of German Unity
Nov. 1	Allerheiligen	All Saints' Day
Dec. 24	Heiligabend	Christmas Eve
Dec. 25-26	1. und 2. Weihnachtstage	Christmas Day and Boxing Day
Dec. 31	Silvester	New Year's Eve

A CLOSER LOOK

More Than Lederhosen

Growing up in a traditional Munich family, I was always aware that my Bavarian identity came first and foremost. Most Bavarians will say, "I am from Bavaria," before "I am from Germany." Kids in elementary school even learn to sing the Bavarian anthem before the German one. Extreme as it sounds, quite a few Bavarians would prefer restoring the Bavarian monarchy rather than remaining subjects of the Federal Republic. The head of the royal Bavarian dynasty, Prinz Franz von Bayern, still lives in Munich's Nymphenburger Schloß. The Bavarian dialect ("*Boarisch*") remains ubiquitous here. We greet people with *Grüß Gott* or *Servus* and say goodbye with *Pfiadi Gott* or *Servus.*

"Two brothers... bet Munich's mayor that they could steal the city's Maibaum."

My family was first mentioned in the city archives in 1304. They were "free farmers," meaning they did not have to pay landlords. Much later, they founded a company that manufactured wooden beer kegs, which became the "Royal Bavarian purveyor to the court." I proudly wear the ring with my family crest, displaying a knight's helmet, an eagle, and a heart. Like in the majority of Bavarian homes, a portrait of beloved King Ludwig II hangs over the dining room table at my mother's house. I spent a large part of my childhood in Garmisch-Partkirchen, a picturesque Bavarian hamlet nestled in the white-tufted Alps. Growing up in this oasis of splendor instilled in me a deep sense of attachment to the land and to its traditions. Looking back at my long familial tradition, I know this cultural inheritance is more than just wearing Dirndls drinking beer.

Our tradition is closely related to Roman Catholic beliefs—the pope himself is Bavarian, after all. On June 23rd, we build bonfires in the mountains for *Johanni-Feuer*, the holiday marking Jesus' arrival. Every other year, we set up the *Maibaum* (Maypole), a tradition dating back to at least the 16th century in Bavaria. In the late 60s, two brothers, Georg "Schorsch" and Valentin "Timo," bet Munich's mayor that they could steal the city's Maibaum. They went into the building yard, where the Maibaum was being finished, and told the workers they were needed to paint and decorate it. Their success made them local heroes: the Augustiner Bräu renamed a reserved area at Oktoberfest the Maibaumräuberbox (Maibaum-hijacker-box) and the brothers party there every year. Classic names, usually with religious and regional significance, are still commonly given to children in Bavaria. In my family, for example, many generations have the family names "Ludwig," "Franz-Xaver," and "Kaspar." The men have the middle name "Maria," in honor of mother Mary, the patron saint of Bavaria.

Oktoberfest, Munich's fifth season, was first held in 1810 at the Theresienwiese—which is why we call it *die Wiesn.* As early as July, Bavarians count the days to the festival. Women begin the "before-Oktoberfest diet," while men look amazing in *Lederhosen*, even if they have a *Bierbauch* (beer belly). Bavarians often say, "*A Mo ohne Wampn is koa gscheiter Mo*" ("A man without a belly is not a man at all.") Oktoberfest is the time when my family and friends gather to honor our heritage. On opening day, the public concert at the Bavaria statue ends in our anthem: "*Gott mit Dir, Du Land der Bayern!*" (God save you, country of the Bavarians.) Today, the slogan "Laptop and *Lederhosen*" describes Munich's unique blend of cutting-edge and traditional charm. Companies like Microsoft and BMW (Bavarian Motor Works) make their home in here. Audi, Puma, and Adidas are also home-grown Bavarian businesses. In fact, Puma and Adidas were launched by the rival Dassler brothers from the small town of Herzogenaurach.

Whether we're enjoying modern Munich or wearing heirloom *Trachten*, the bottom line is this: We are very proud of being Bavarian and we show it. A place where rich tradition, natural beauty, and technology combine, Bavaria is clearly more than *Lederhosen* and the world's best beer—but these are also some of the reasons that we love it so much.

Valerie Hartung *is a freelancer in online marketing. She has lived and traveled all over the world, but home is where the heart is—Munich.*

BEYOND TOURISM

So you've fallen for Germany. Whether it's the pervasive sense of history, the flowing founts of beer, the riverside grilling, or the culture of cutting-edge technological and scientific advancement, the point remains: Germany is the place for you. You want to stay. Lucky for you, we've done all the legwork to present you with a wide range of possibilities to allow you to transform a short-term gig a long-term stay. As a volunteer, worker, teacher, au pair, adventurer, or student, Germany has a wealth of longer-term opportunities to offer the savvy foreigner looking to go native.

A PHILOSOPHY FOR TRAVELERS

HIGHLIGHTS OF BEYOND TOURISM IN GERMANY

WORK ON AN ORGANIC FARM in the bucolic hills of Bavaria (p. 63).

PUT THE PEDAL TO THE METAL (literally) as you assemble German cars and perfect your mechanical engineering skills with International Cooperative Education (p. 69)

RECAPTURE THE SPLENDOR of a crumbling chapel as you help to rebuild it (p. 63).

As a tourist, you are always a foreigner. Sure, hostel-hopping and sightseeing can be great fun, but connecting with a foreign country through studying, volunteering, or working can extend your travels beyond tourist traps. We don't like to brag, but this is what's different about a *Let's Go* traveler. Instead of feeling like a stranger in a strange land, you can understand Germany like a local. Instead of being that tourist asking for directions, you can be the one who gives them (and correctly!). All the while, you get the satisfaction of leaving Germany in better shape than you found it (after all, it's being nice enough to let you stay over). It's not wishful thinking—it's Beyond Tourism.

As a **volunteer** in Germany, you can unleash your inner superhero with projects from saving Bavarian forests to championing disability rights. Work for peace side by side with like-minded German idealists! Fight for social justice! Empower the elderly! This chapter is chock-full of ideas to get involved, whether you're looking to pitch in for a day or run away from home for a whole new life in German activism.

The powers of **studying abroad** are beyond comprehension: it actually makes you feel sorry for those poor tourists who don't get to do any homework while they're here. German students famously live the good life. In fact, they enjoy the student community, university activities, communal living, and healthy student party scene so much that many stay students as long as they can. It is not uncommon to find happy, successful Germans who purposefully remained undergrads well into their late twenties. Now you too can find out what all the *Student Leben* hype is about by studying abroad in Germany.

Working abroad immerses you in a new culture and can bring some of the most meaningful relationships and experiences of your life. Yes, we know you're on vacation, but these aren't your normal desk jobs. (Plus, it doesn't hurt that it helps pay for more globetrotting.) Unemployment is an ongoing problem in Germany, so expect to encounter some difficulties when looking for work. Large cities like Berlin, Hamburg, and Munich might be more fruitful for those pursuing career-related experience or those with special skill sets. Travelers looking for short-term opportunities should have luck in seasonal tourist destinations, especially ski towns in the South and beach towns in the North. Always be mindful of your impact on the local culture and be sensitive to the sometimes volatile sentiment towards working foreigners.

SHARE YOUR EXPERIENCE. Have you had a particularly enjoyable volunteer, study, or work experience that you'd like to share with other travelers? Post it to our website, www.letsgo.com!

VOLUNTEERING

Feel like saving the world this week? Volunteering can be a powerful and fulfilling experience, especially when combined with the thrill of traveling in a new place. Many of Germany's volunteering opportunities involve environmental conservation—working on farms or in forests and educating people on protecting the environment. Other volunteers participate in community service camps that bring together Germans and foreigners to promote cultural exchange and tolerance. There are also placements available in social activist and community building organizations, particulary in Berlin.

Most people who volunteer in Germany do so on a short-term basis at organizations that make use of drop-in or once-a-week volunteers. The best way to find opportunities that match your interests and schedule may be to check with local or national volunteer centers. As always, read up before heading out. Those looking for longer, more intensive volunteer opportunities usually choose to go through a parent organization that takes care of logistical details and often provides a group environment and support system for a fee. There are two main types of organizations—religious and secular—although there are rarely restrictions on participation for either. Websites like **www.volunteerabroad.com, www.servenet.org,** and **www.idealist.org** allow you to search for volunteer openings both in your country and abroad.

I HAVE TO PAY TO VOLUNTEER? Many volunteers are surprised to learn that some organizations require large fees or "donations," but don't go calling them scams just yet. While such fees may seem ridiculous at first, they often keep the organization afloat, covering airfare, room, board, and administrative expenses for the volunteers. (Other organizations must rely on private donations and government subsidies.) If you're concerned about how a program spends its fees, request an annual report or finance account. A reputable organization won't refuse to inform you of how volunteer money is spent. Pay-to-volunteer programs might be a good idea for young travelers who are looking for more support and structure (such as pre-arranged transportation and housing) or anyone who would rather not deal with the uncertainty of creating a volunteer experience from scratch.

ENVIRONMENTAL CONSERVATION

Germans are wild about their wilderness and work hard to preserve its splendor. As "ecotourism" becomes a household term around the globe, local and international organizations alike offer the chance to escape into nature and to improve the already immaculate landscape.

Agriventure, Lerchenborg Gods, 4400 Kalunborg, Denmark (☎45 59 51 15 25; www.iaea.de or www.agriventure.com). Organizes agricultural exchanges and homestays at farms throughout Europe. Prices vary by program.

Biosphere Expeditions, PO Box 11297, Marina del Ray, CA 90295, USA (☎+1-800-407-5761; www.biosphere-expeditions.org). Provides a menu of eco-friendly getaways to the Bavarian Alps. Organizes large-scale projects ad hoc and also offers pre-arranged "Taster Weekends" (€195).

Bund Jugend, Am Köllnischer Park 1A, 10179 Berlin, Germany (☎030 27 58 65 84; www.bundjugend.de). This eco-friendly group provides information and organizes events for youth in Germany, including volunteer and internship opportunities.

Earthwatch, 3 Clocktower Pl. Ste. 100, Box 75, Maynard, MA 01754, USA (☎+1 800-776-0188 or 978-461-0081; www.earthwatch.org). Arranges 1- to 3-week programs in Europe (occasionally Germany) to promote conservation of natural resources. Fees vary based on location and duration; costs average US$1700 plus airfare.

Willing Workers on Organic Farms (WWOOF), Postfach 210259, 01263 Dresden, Germany (www.wwoof.de). Membership (€20) in WWOOF offers room and board at a variety of organic farms in Germany in exchange for work.

RESTORATION AND ARCHAEOLOGY

One result of the prolonged occupation of Germany after WWII was the haphazard care afforded to the country's war-ravaged historical sights. As money flows into former East Germany, new projects seem to sprout daily. No experience needed to participate in archaeological digs and restoration projects.

Archaeological Institute of America, 656 Beacon St., Boston, MA 02215, USA (☎+1 617-353-9361; www.archaeological.org). The Archaeological Fieldwork Opportunities Bulletin, on the website, lists field sites throughout Europe.

Open Houses Network, Goethepl. 9B, D-99423 Weimar, Germany (☎036 43 50 23 90; www.openhouses.de). A group dedicated to restoring and sharing public space (mostly in the former DDR); offers lodging in return for work. 18+ only.

Pro International, Bahnhofstr. 26A, 35037 Marburg, Germany (☎0642 16 52 77; www.pro-international.de). Since 1949, this volunteer organization has brought together youth from around the world to help reconstruct and preserve sites in Germany. Many of their projects also serve local children and the environment. Ages 16-26.

YOUTH AND THE COMMMUNITY

AFS Interkulturelle Begegnungen e.V. (AFS Intercultural Programs), Postfach 50 01 42, 22701 Hamburg, Germany (☎040 399 2220; www.afs.de). In the US, 71 West 23rd St., New York, NY 10010 (☎+1 212-807-8686; www.afs.org). 6- to 12-month volunteer opportunities to serve local communities available for 18+ travelers. Student exchanges available for high schoolers over the summer and during the school year.

Big Friends for Youngsters, Tempelhofer Ufer 11, D-10963 Berlin (☎030 25 76 76 12; www.biffy.de). The German arm of the Big Brothers Big Sisters program; provides mentoring for young kids on a longer term basis.

Canadian Alliance for Development Initiatives and Projects, 129-1271 Howe St., Vancouver, BC V62 1R3, Canada (☎+1 604-628-7400; www. cadip.org). Offers diverse 2- to 3-week programs in Germany, with the aims of peace, tolerance, and community. Program fee roughly US$280, including accommodation and food.

Camp Adventure Youth Services, 1223 W. 22nd Street, Cedar Falls, IA 50614, USA (☎+1 319-273-5960). Sends college students to 118 camps in 16 countries to serve as counselors for children of US military. Airfare, housing, travel, food stipend of $22 per day, and 12 units of undegraduate credit provided. Participation fee of US$285.

Habitat for Humanity International, 121 Habitat St., Americus, GA 31709, USA (☎+1 800-422-4828; www.habitat.org). Volunteers build houses in over 83 countries. Periods of involvement range from 2 weeks to 3 years. Short-term programs US$1200-4000.

United Planet, 11 Arlington St., Boston, MA 02116 USA (☎+1 617-267-7763; www.unitedplanet.org). Sends volunteers 18-30 to perform a wide range of community service work. Short-term (up to 12 weeks) and long-term (6-12 months) for individuals and groups. 6 months US$4695, 1 year US$7195.

Service Civil International Voluntary Service (SCI-IVS), SCI Deutscher Zweig e.V., Blücherstr. 14, D-53115 Bonn, Germany (☎0228 21 20 86; www.sci-d.de). In the US, SCI USA, 5474 Walnut Level Rd., Crozet, VA 22932 (☎+1 206 350 6585; www.sci-ivs.org). Arranges work experience in German civil service camps from 2 weeks to 12 months for individuals over 18. Program fee US$250.

Freunde der Erziehungskunst Rudolf Steiners e.V. (Friends of Waldorf Education, Neisser Str. 10, D-76139 Karlsruhe, Germany (☎0721 35 48 06 17; www.freunde-waldorf.de/en/voluntary-services/in-germany). 75 placements for 7-12 months and 1-2 years to volunteer with disabled or elderly people. Group housing included, no program fee, stipend of €150 per month. Must be over 18 and have basic German language skills.

Volunteers for Peace, 1034 Tiffany Rd., Belmont, VT 05730, USA (☎+1 802-259-2759; www.vpf.org). Grassroots organization arranges 1-12 week or 3-12 month programs for individuals or groups to volunteer in low-income housing, environmental projects, social services, and historic preservation. Registration fee US$250. Typically 18+.

SOCIAL AND POLITICAL ACTIVISM

This category has a lot of overlap; for instance, political parties often do work relating to (and hopefully helping) the environment or providing aid to health organizations. Although we like to think that our blessing is the holy grail of German politics, it is important to remember that Let's Go does not endorse any of the organizations listed here.

Amnesty International, Sektion der Bundesrepublik Deutschland e.V., 53108 Bonn, Germany (☎0228 98 37 30; www.amnesty.de). Human rights organization with various internship and volunteer positions available.

Internationale Begegnung in Gemeinschartsdiensten, e.V., Schlossertstr. 28, 70819 Stuttgart, Germany (☎0711 649 0263; www.ibg-workcamps.org). Bring together Germans and foreigners to promote mutual understanding while working on projects 30hr. per week. to serve local communities. Fee of about US$90 in Germany and Austria.

ICJA Freiwilligenaustausch weltweit, e.V., Stralauer Allee 20E, 10245 Berlin, Germany (☎030 21 23 82 52; www.icja.de). Non-profit that promotes sociopolitical commitment by organizing practical peace work for volunteers for 2-12 months.

Service Civil International (SCI), Blücherstr. 14, 53115 Bonn (☎0228 21 20 86; www.sci-d.de). Non-profit, international organization sends volunteers to work for peace, force-free conflict resolution, social justice, lasting development, and intercultural exchange. There are over 35 national branches on five continents and cooperates with approximately 80 partner organizations.

Mobility International USA, 132 E. Broadway St., Suite 343, Eugene, OR 97401, USA (☎+1 541-343-1284; www.miusa.org). Joins people with and without disabilities to staff international community service projects and to champion disability rights.

STUDYING

> **VISA INFORMATION. Residence permits** are necessary for all foreign citizens to study in Germany. For information on obtaining one, see **Essentials** (p. 8).

It's difficult to dread the first day of school when Munich is your campus and your meal plan consists of exotic restaurants and sunny beer gardens. A growing number of students report that studying abroad is the highlight of their learning careers. If you've never studied abroad, you don't know what you're missing—and if you have studied abroad, you do know what you're missing. Either way, let's go back to school!

Study-abroad programs range from basic language and culture courses to university-level classes, often for college credit (it's legit, Mom and Dad). In order to choose a program that best fits your needs, research as much as you can before making your decision—determine costs and duration, as well as the types of students that participate in the program and what sorts of accommodations are provided. Although universities are not officially ranked in Germany, there are some major differences in areas of study or campus size and layout that distinguish German universities.

In programs that have large groups of students who speak the same language, there is a trade-off. You may feel more comfortable in the community, but you will not have the same opportunity to practice a foreign language or to befriend other international students. For accommodations, dorm life provides a better opportunity to mingle with fellow students, but there is less of a chance to experience the local scene. If you live with a family, you could potentially build lifelong friendships with natives and experience day-to-day life in more depth, but you might also get stuck sharing a room with their pet iguana. Conditions can vary greatly from family to family.

UNIVERSITIES

Most university-level study-abroad programs are conducted in German, although many programs offer classes in English as well as lower-level language courses. Savvy linguists may find it cheaper to enroll directly in a university abroad, although this may make getting college credit more difficult. Your local Goethe Institute branch may be able to help you with direct enrollment (p. 66). You can search **www.studyabroad.com** for various semester-abroad programs that meet your criteria, including your desired location and focus of study. If you're a college student, your friendly neighborhood study-abroad office is often the best place to start.

GERMAN PROGRAMS

Germany is famous for a fantastic student life and for good reason. Whether you're in the being rowdy in the medieval university town of Heidelberg, profiting from the grandeur of Munich's many schools, living it up in Hamburg's vast student universe, or experiencing the edgy urban-campus life in Berlin, you will be grateful that you decided on Germany. Whether you stay for a summer or a year, you will undoubtedly improve your German skills, gain a new perspective on the country and the people, and learn every kind of beer by tongue.

Council on International Educational Exchange (CIEE), 300 Fore St., Portland, ME 04101, USA (☎+1-207-553-4000 or 800-40-STUDY/407-8839; www.ciee.org). One of the most comprehensive resources for work, academic, and internship programs around the world, including in Germany.

International Association for the Exchange of Students for Technical Experience (IAESTE), Referat 225, Kennedyallee 50 D-53175 Bonn Germany (☎0228 88 22 31; www.iaeste.org). Chances are that your home country has a local office, too; contact it to apply for hands-on technical internships in Germany. You must be a college student studying science, technology, or engineering. "Cost of living allowance" covers most non-travel expenses. Most programs last 8-12 weeks.

Congress-Bundestag Youth Exchange for Young Professionals, 81 United Nations Plaza, New York, NY 10017, USA (☎+1 212-497-3500; www.cdsintl.org/cbyx/cbyxfromusa.htm). Co-sponsored by the German and US governments, this year-long cultural exchange is geared toward 18-24 year-old young professionals. 75 people are chosen to participate in language immersion, classes, and an internship in Germany; airfare and accommodations are provided. Application deadline Dec. 1.

Deutscher Akademischer Austauschdienst (DAAD), 871 United Nations Plaza, New York, NY 10017, USA (☎ 212-758-3223; www.daad.org). In Germany, Kennedyallee 50, 53175 Bonn; mailing address Postfach 200404, 53134 Bonn. Information on language instruction, exchanges, and scholarships for study in Germany. Processes foreign enrollement in German universities. Also distributes applications and information brochures.

LANGUAGE SCHOOLS

Enrolling at a language school has two major perks: a slightly less rigorous courseload and the security of knowing exactly what those kids in Bonn are calling you under their breath. There is a broad spectrum of language schools—independently run, affiliated with a larger university, local, international—but one thing is constant: they rarely offer college credit. Their programs are also good for younger high-school students who might not feel comfortable with older students in a university program. Fortunately for you, German has a variety of options to offer you. Some worthwhile organizations include:

Goethe-Institut, Dachauer Str. 122, 80637 Munich, Germany; mailing address Postfach 190419, 80604 München (☎89 159 212 00, toll-free from North America 1-888-446-3843; www.goethe.de). Look on the web, contact your local branch, or write to the main office. Runs German language programs in 14 German cities and abroad, as well as high school exchange programs in Germany. 8-week intensive summer course from about US$2980, with room from US$3990 (prices vary by course and city).

German Language School (GLS), Kastanienallee 82, 10435 Berlin (☎030 780089 11; www.gls-berlin.de). Berlin-based language school offers variety of language courses with on-site accommodation or homestays, internships, high school exchanges, and

A CLOSER LOOK

Women and Science in Germany

When did you last use your computer? Did you use a car today? Did you listen to an mp3? If so, you were benefiting from the German innovative spirit. The car was invented by Karl Benz and Gottlieb Daimler in Stuttgart, 1886; the computer by Konrad Zuse in Berlin, 1941; the mp3 format by the Fraunhofer Research Institute in Erlangen, 1987.

Germany's science industry is one of the most powerful and productive in the world and has generated 79 Nobel Prize Laureates. One of them is Christiane Nüsslein – Volhard, who was awarded the prize in 1995, together with two colleagues, for "their discoveries concerning the genetic control of early embryonic development." Christiane? A woman wins the Noble Prize? Nothing unusual, one would hope to say, but unfortunately, the statistics speak a different language. To date, Dr. Nüsslein—Volhard, is the first and only German women to receive this honor. So why does a cutting-edge country like Germany have one of the lowest rates of women researchers across Europe, even accounting for the overall gender gap?

One reason might be that German society tends to favor a conservative family model. It is not uncommon for a woman to be confronted with the belief that she must decide between having a family with children and having a successful career. Politics support this family model by providing benefits for stay-at-home parents. According to German law, one parent can stop working for as much as three years after having a child, and the employer is obligated to keep the position available. For the first year, the state awards Elterngeld, compensating the parenting partner by 67% of his or her last income. Though this initially seems to provide an ideal environment for having children, it actually puts pressure on parents—especially on women—to spend this time entirely with their child. If they prefer to start working earlier, using one of the rare state-run day-care facilities, they are labeled a *Rabenmutter* (cruel mother).

For researchers, this system plays out even more dramatically. Most academic positions in science have contracts that last for only a couple of years, giving little security to young parents. At the same time, Germany is slowly building up a tenure-track system that replaces *Habilitiation*, a system introduced into German science by Alexander von Humboldt in 1819. After six years, a scientist can receive a *Habilitation* on the basis of teaching ability and academic merit. This is the highest German academic degree and it enables a scientist to apply for permanent positions and professorships. The system puts female German scientists in a precarious situation, filled with opposing expectations.

Consider the example of a friend of mine, Isabel. She is pursuing her *Habilitation*, studying how the brain processes information from sensory organs. She did her PhD in the laboratory of a Nobel Prize winner, and after post-doctoral work in the US, she returned to Germany in order to work with her own research group. Recently, she gave birth to her second child, a son named Moritz. A couple of days after the delivery, her group had a meeting and decided—in her absence—that she would no longer to be part of the group. The decision was perhaps influenced by the belief that she would need to spend more time with her children and would not be as good a researcher as before. It was an enormous professional disappointment for the successful scientist—and a difficult set-back for the young mother. Women in academia tend either to change careers before starting a family, since industry offers more money and security, or to have children later or not at all.

Luckily, this climate is slowly improving. When Moritz was 4 months old, Isabel was back in the laboratory, with her little boy on her knees, performing experiments. After securing him a daycare spot, she got back on track, producing important data that might be the basis for one of the next ground-breaking German inventions.

Dr. Angelika Lampert *is a German neuroscientist studying the role of sodium channels in pain. She spent three years of postdoctoral training at Yale University, and now works at the University of Erlangen-Nuremberg, Germany.*

summer camps in Berlin and Munich for 18+. Standard 5-week course roughly US$810, 5-week accommodation US$2,160.

Eurocentres, 56 Eccleston Sq., London SW1V 1PH, UK (☎020 7963 8450; www.eurocentres.com). Language programs for beginning to advanced students with homestays in Berlin for 2-12 weeks. Must be 16+. Prices begin at roughly US$550 for 2 weeks. (regular session) and US$690 for two weeks (intensive session).

BWS Germalingua, Bayerstr. 13, 80335 Munich, Germany (☎089 599 892 00; www.germalingua.com). Full- and part-time language classes in Munich and Berlin for up to 1 year. Standard 6-week courses from about US$1,625 with a single room in a dorm or a homestay for an additional US$277 per week.

Deutschkurse für Ausländer bei der Universität München e.V., Adelheidstraße 13b, 80798 Munich, Germany (☎089 271 26 42; www.dkfa.de). Offers courses for foreigners studying or applying to study in Germany. 8-week day course US$1,111. 25% off course fee for students enrolled in Munich universities.

WORKING

Nowhere does money grow on trees (though *Let's Go*'s researchers aren't done looking), but there are still some pretty good opportunities to earn a living and travel at the same time. As with volunteering, work opportunities tend to fall into two categories. Some travelers want long-term jobs that allow them to integrate into a community, while others seek out short-term jobs to finance the next leg of their travels. English-speakers can be a prized commodity in the tourism industry and can find all types of work in bars, hotels, and restaurants. For more long-term employment, you can find unique opportunities in anything from organic farming to scientific research. Specific skill sets, especially in the field of computer science, will work to your advantage. **Transitions Abroad** (www.transitionsabroad.com) also offers updated online listings in a wide range of fields for work over any time span.

The recruitment of non-EU workers is strictly regulated in Germany. You can consult local, federally run employment offices. These fall under the umbrella of **Bundesanstalt für Arbeit** (Federal Employment Service), through which you can find local agencies (www.arbeitsagentur.de). The best tips on jobs for foreigners often come from other travelers or resources at hostels and tourist offices; newspaper and web listings are another start. Online search engines are also increasingly useful. While big job sites like **Monster** (www.monster.de) and **JobSafari** (www.jobsafari.de) have loads of listings, travelers might have more luck with local, user-driven sites like the popular **Kijiji** (www.kijiji.de). Note that working abroad often requires a special work visa.

LONG-TERM WORK

If you're planning on spending a substantial amount of time (more than three months) working in Germany, search for a job well in advance. International placement agencies are often the easiest way to find employment abroad, especially for those interested in teaching. Although they are often only available to college students, **internships** are a good way to ease into working abroad. Many say the interning experience is well worth it, despite low pay (if you're lucky enough to be paid at all). Be wary of advertisements for companies claiming to be able get you a job abroad for a fee—often the same listings are available for free online or in newspapers. Some reputable organizations include:

CA Education Programs (CAEP), 112 E. Lincoln Ave., Fergus Falls, MN 56538. (☎+1 218-739-3241; www.caepinc.org). Coordinates educational experiences with agricultural organizations in over 40 countries. Jobs range from farming to wine-making. Pay and/or college credit available.

Carl Duisberg Gesellschaft e.V. (CDG), Weyerstr. 79-83, 50676 Cologne, Germany (☎0221 209 80; www.cdg.de). Professional training for students and young people from Germany and abroad.

CDS International, 871 United Nations Plaza, New York, NY 10017, USA (☎+1 212-497-3500). Arranges 6- to 12-month paid internships for students and recent graduates of accredited US colleges and universities.

Internatinal Association for the Exchange of Students for Technical Experience (IAESTES), 10400 Little Patuxent Pkwy., Ste. 250 Columbia, MD 21044, USA (☎410-997-3069; www.iaesteunitedstates.org). 8- to 12-week internships in Germany for college students with 2 years of technical study. US$50 application fee.

International Cooperative Education, 15 Spiros Way, Menlo Park, CA 94025, USA (☎+1-650-323-4944; www.icemenlo.com). Finds summer jobs for students in Germany. Semester- and year-long commitments also available. Costs include a US$250 application fee and a US$700 fee for placement.

Research Internships in Science and Engineering (RISE), Deutscher Akademischer Austausch Dienst (DAAD), Michaela Gottschling, Referat 315, Kennedyallee 50, D-53175 Bonn, Germany (☎0228 882 567; www.daad.de/rise). Pairs German PhD candidates with North American undergraduates. Stipend provided.

MORE VISA INFORMATION. To work in Germany, non-European Union citizens will need a **residence permit** and, in many cases, a work permit. Work permits are difficult to acquire unless you have a specialization in high demand. The other exception is non-EU workers employed by a European Economic Area (EEA) company. In this case, workers can qualify for a "Van der Elst" visa and work without a work permit. For more instructions on securing work and residence permits, see **Essentials** (p. 10).

TEACHING ENGLISH

While some elite private American schools offer competitive salaries, it's safe to say that teaching jobs abroad pay more in personal satisfaction and emotional fulfillment than in actual cash. Perhaps this is why volunteering as a teacher instead of getting paid is a popular option. Even then, teachers often receive some sort of a daily stipend to help with living expenses. In certain parts of Germany, especially Berlin, a low cost of living means that even meagre stipends afford a comfortable quality of life. In almost all cases, you must have at least a bachelor's degree to be a full-fledged teacher, although college undergraduates can often get summer positions teaching or tutoring. Due to a high demand for native English-speaking teachers, a bachelor's degree serves as a sufficient qualification for teaching in Germany. Freelancing is a quick and popular option for recent college graduates.

Many schools require teachers to have a **Teaching English as a Foreign Language (TEFL)** certificate. You may still be able to find a teaching job without one, but certified teachers often find higher-paying jobs. The German-impaired don't have to give up their dream of teaching, either. Private schools usually hire native English speakers for English-immersion classrooms where no German is spoken. (Teachers in public schools will more likely work in both English and German.) Placement agencies or university fellowship programs are the best resources for finding teaching jobs. The alternative is to contact schools directly or to try your luck once you arrive in Germany. In the latter case, the best time to look is several weeks before the start of the school year. The following organizations are extremely helpful in placing teachers in Germany.

International Schools Services (ISS), 15 Roszel Rd., P.O. Box 5910, Princeton, NJ 08543, USA (☎+1 609-452-0990; www.iss.edu). Hires teachers for more than 200 overseas schools, including in Germany. Candidates should have teaching experience and a bachelor's degree. 2-year commitment is the norm.

Fulbright English Teaching Assistantship, US Student Programs Division, Institute of International Education, 809 United Nations Plaza, New York, NY 10017, USA (☎212-984-5400; www.iie.org). This highly competitive program sends college graduates to teach in Germany.

Oxford Seminars, 244 5th Ave., Ste. J262, New York, NY 10001, USA (☎+1 212-213-8978; www.oxfordseminars.com). Offers TEFL programs and job placement in Europe.

TESall.com, (www.tesall.com). The original search engine for jobs abroad maintains the most extensive, if hard-to-navigate, database. Site also features other jobs in Germany.

AU PAIR WORK

Au pairs are typically women aged 18-27 who work as live-in nannies, caring for children and doing light housework in foreign countries in exchange for room, board, and a small stipend. One perk of the job is that it allows you to get to know Germany without the high expenses of traveling. Drawbacks, however, can include mediocre pay and long hours. While salaries and stipends can vary greatly, expect to earn around €250 per month. Much of the au pair experience depends on the family with which you are placed. The agencies below are good starting points for looking for employment.

Au Pair Worldwide, Lückenweg 18, 64743 Beerfelden, Germany (☎06068 91 21 68; www.aupair-worldwide.de). Matches international au pairs with German families.

InterExchange, 161 6th Ave., New York City, NY 10013, USA (☎+1 212-924-0446 or 800-AU-PAIRS/287-2477; www.interexchange.org).

Childcare International, Trafalgar House, Grenville Pl., London NW7 3SA, UK (☎+44 20 8906 3116; www.childint.co.uk).

SHORT-TERM WORK

Traveling for long periods of time can be hard on the wallet. Many travelers try their hand at odd jobs for a few weeks at a time to help pay for another month or two of touring around. Finding these jobs takes some creativity and cajones, since most work would be under-the-table work and potentially illegal in Germany. If you know some guitar chords and a couple Dylan songs, try busking in the Altstadt. Otherwise, making friends with a local cafe owner is a good idea. Another popular option is to work several hours a day at a hostel in exchange for free or discounted room and/or board. Most often, these short-term jobs are found by word of mouth or by expressing interest to the owner of a hostel or restaurant. Due to high turnover in the tourism industry, many places are eager for help, even if it is only temporary. If you are at all bilingual, you might also find temporary work as a translator in any given sector. *Let's Go* lists temporary jobs of this nature whenever possible; look in the **Practical Information** sections of larger cities or see below.

FURTHER READING ON BEYOND TOURISM

Alternatives to the Peace Corps: A Guide of Global Volunteer Opportunities, edited by Paul Backhurst. Food First, 2005 (US$12).

The Back Door Guide to Short-Term Job Adventures: Internships, Summer Jobs, Seasonal Work, Volunteer Vacations, and Transitions Abroad, by Michael Landes. Ten Speed Press, 2005 (US$22).

Green Volunteers: The World Guide to Voluntary Work in Nature Conservation, by Fabio Ausenda. Universe, 2007 (US$15).

How to Get a Job in Europe, by Cheryl Matherly and Robert Sanborn. Planning Communications, 2003 (US$23).

How to Live Your Dream of Volunteering Overseas, by Joseph Collins, Stefano DeZerega, and Zahara Heckscher. Penguin Books, 2001 (US$20).

International Job Finder: Where the Jobs Are Worldwide, by Daniel Lauber and Kraig Rice. Planning Communications, 2002 (US$20).

Live and Work Abroad: A Guide for Modern Nomads, by Huw Francis and Michelyne Callan. Vacation Work Publications, 2001 (US$20).

Live and Work in Germany, by Ian Collier. Vacation Work Publications, 2002 (US$20).

Study Away: The Unauthorized Guide to College Abroad, by Mariah Balaban and Jennifer Shields. Anchor, 2003 (US$14).

Volunteer Vacations: Short-Term Adventures That Will Benefit You and Others, by Doug Cutchins, Anne Geissinger, and Bill McMillon. Chicago Review Press, 2006 (US$18).

Work Abroad: The Complete Guide to Finding a Job Overseas, edited by Clayton A. Hubbs. Transitions Abroad, 2002 (US$16).

Work Your Way Around the World, by Susan Griffith. Vacation Work Publications, 2007 (US$22).

BERLIN

Berlin is bigger than Paris, up later than New York, wilder than Amsterdam, and more eclectic than London. Simultaneously cosmopolitan, dynamic, and in some regards oblivious, the city is in the midst of a profound transition from a reunited post-Cold War metropolis into the thriving center of an eastward-expanding European Union. Everything in this city of 3.4 million is changing, from the demographics of the diverse population to which *Bezirk* (neighborhood) is currently "in." The long, agonizing period of division and the unanticipated and abrupt reunification in 1989—which saw the Berlin Wall literally shattered at the hands of eager civilians—resulted in a turbulent decade filled with euphoria, disillusionment, wild despair, and even wilder optimism. In 1999, the unified federal government moved from Bonn to Berlin, throwing the new capital back into chaos as construction sites sprang up everywhere and droves of bureaucrats provided a sudden contrast to the wayward artists and nihilistic punks that had freely ruled the city streets. Amid lingering turmoil, ambitious plans for the city's renovation now speed toward completion. The glass and steel Potsdamer Platz now towers where the *Mauer* used to stand and the new Hauptbahnhof, Europe's largest train station, connects Berlin to the rest of the continent without the blockades that once marred its path. But while Berlin surges ahead, memories of a long and complicated past remain etched into the city's geography, its architecture, and the texture of its daily life.

Many Berliners remain strikingly ambivalent to the sweeping transformation taking place all around them. The problem of *Mauer im Kopf* (literally translated as "wall in the head") seems more prevalent here than anywhere else in the country and feelings of division persist. *Wessis* (West Berliners) resent spending so much in taxes to prop up their less-affluent eastern neighbors. *Ossis* (East Berliners) disdain the West's corporate demeanor and air of superiority. Conflicted yet brilliant, the resulting city exudes a creative vibrancy that has established Berlin as an epicenter of global culture.

HIGHLIGHTS OF BERLIN

ABANDON MODESTY AND MODERATION while diving in Berlin's notorious **nightlife** (p. 123) in the districts of Mitte, Kreuzberg, Prenzlauer Berg, and Friedrichshain, or while experiencing the unparalleled **gay scene** in Schöneberg.

CHECK OUT CUTTING-EDGE ARCHITECTURE that is among the best in Europe, on a walking tour that includes an aquarium-cum-elevator (p. 114).

ASCEND the sleek spiraling glass dome atop the **Reichstag** (p. 108) and wonder how many other countries have a **solar-powered parliament.**

ABSORB OBSCENE AMOUNTS OF ART by Old Masters and contemporary renegades alike in **Museumsinsel** (p. 116) and **Kulturforum** (p. 116).

MINGLE WITH THE HIPSTERS in **Hackescher Markt** before relaxing with a foaming *Milchkaffee* at one of the many cafes in the **Hackesche Höfe** (p. 110).

RELIVE THE COLD WAR at **Checkpoint Charlie** (p. 118) or at the longest surviving stretch of the Berlin Wall, now the canvas for the **East Side Gallery** (p. 111).

Unlike most major capitals, Berlin does not have a traditional "downtown" area; instead, the city is composed of many *Bezirke.* These neighborhoods began as individual settlements on the Spree River, growing together over generations into a city with a surface area ten times the size of Paris. Neighborhoods struggle to maintain their individuality in the face of increasing integration. Areas that no one would have dreamed of visiting five years ago are now nightlife hotspots, and districts where everyone wanted to live last week will be passé tomorrow. Berlin is the most tolerant Germany city, with a world-famous gay and lesbian scene. The city's progressiveness extends even into its urban development scheme. But, as Berlin rushes into the future, this very dynamism could endanger the preservation of its rich history. In Mitte, controversy rages over plans to tear down the DDR-era Palast der Republik, while the longest remaining portion of the Berlin Wall is rapidly being defaced by tourist scribblings. Come watch Berlin change before your very eyes; as an old German song goes, *"Es gibt nur einmal, und kommt nicht wieder"* ("It will only happen once, and never again"). Neighborhoods of Berlin

The **River Spree** snakes west to east through Berlin, north of the narrower **Landwehrkanal** that flows into it. The vast **Tiergarten,** Berlin's beloved park, lies between the waterways at the city's center. If you see a radio tower, it's either the **Funkturm** (pointed and Eiffel-like) in the west or the **Fernsehturm** (with the globe) in the east at **Alexanderplatz.** Major streets include **Kurfürstendamm** (nicknamed the Ku'damm), lined with department stores and running into the **Bahnhof Zoo,** the regional transit hub of West Berlin. The eloquent ruins of the **Kaiser-Wilhelm Gedächtniskirche** are near Bahnhof Zoo, as is the **Europacenter,** one of Berlin's few real skyscrapers.

FACTS AND FIGURES

METRO AREA POPULATION: 3,416,255

TOTAL AREA: 892 sq. km

OFFICIAL CURRENCY: the Euro (€)

NUMBER OF DOGS: 108,509

TURKISH CITIZENS LIVING IN BERLIN: 117,624.

NUMBER OF REGISTERED TAXIS: 6800

UNEMPLOYMENT RATE: 15.5%.

NUMBER OF DENTISTS: 3162

NUMBER OF MUSEUMS: 170

TOTAL LENGTH OF SUBWAY, SUBURBAN RAIL, STREETCAR, AND BUS LINES: 2368 km

NUMBER OF TRAFFIC ACCIDENTS ANNUALLY: 123, 592

AVERAGE MALE LIFE EXPECTANCY: 77

AVERAGE FEMALE LIFE EXPECTANCY: 82

NUMBER OF PLAYGROUNDS: 1824

PERCENTAGE OF POPULATION AGED 18-25: 9

APPROXIMATE NUMBER OF JOBS IN BERLIN'S TOURIST INDUSTRY: 170,000

NUMBER OF SWIMMING POOLS: 101

NUMBER OF PUBLIC LIBRARIES: 108

STUDENTS IN BERLIN'S UNIVERSITY SYSTEM: 141,010

HIGHEST ELEVATION: The Müggelberge and Teufelsberg hills at a staggering 115m.

The grand, tree-lined **Straße des 17 Juni** runs east-west through the Tiergarten, ending at the triumphant **Brandenburger Tor** at the park's eastern border. From here it becomes **Unter den Linden,** flanked by the bulk of Berlin's imperial architecture (**Sights,** p. 102). Next to the Brandenburger Tor is the **Reichstag,** and several blocks south, **Potsdamer Platz** is shadowed by the glittering **Sony Center** and the Deutsche Bahn headquarters. Streets in Berlin are short and frequently change names. Street numbers often climb to the end of the street and wrap around to the other side, (not so) conveniently making the highest- and lowest-numbered buildings opposite one another. A map with an index is invaluable. The former West, including **Charlottenburg** and **Schöneberg,** is still the commercial heart of Berlin. The former East holds the most happening neighborhoods: swanky **Mitte,** hipster-populated **Prenzlauer Berg,** and the newest scene,

Friedrichshain. Counter-culture-heavy **Kreuzberg** was part of West Berlin, but falls in the east geographically. Berlin is rightly called a collection of towns, not a homogeneous city: each *Bezirk* maintains an individual history and identity. Every year, for example, citizens of Kreuzberg and Friedrichshain battle with vegetables for possession of the **Oberbaumbrücke** on the border between them.

CHARLOTTENBURG

S3, S5, S7, S9, or S75 to Bahnof Zoo, Charlottenburg, Pichelsburg, Savigny Platz, or Zoologischer Garten. U1, U2, U5, or U7 to Ernst-Reuter Platz, Konstanzer Str., Sophie-Charlotte Platz, or Uhlandstr. *See also: Accommodations (p. 87), Food (p. 98), and Sights (p. 102).*

Like any good hipster, Berlin does its best to steer clear of the European mainstream: it buys all of its clothes at flea markets, it drinks PBR on the weekends, and it eschews Camel Lights in favor of hand-rolled. Should you forget you're in an old-school European capital, Charlottenburg will quickly remind you. Originally a separate town founded around the grounds of Friedrich I's imperial palace, Charlottenburg became an affluent cultural center during the Weimar years, home to dozens of fashionable cabarets. Today the neighborhood maintains its bougie, old-world feel with upscale Beaux-Arts apartments that house a quiet, somewhat older crowd. Nightlife options are few and far between, but there is no shortage of yuppy couples walking silly little dogs in Charlottenburg's well manicured (and beautiful) **Tiergarten.** The area around the **Bahnof Zoo,** which includes Berlin's main shopping strip, the **Kurfürstendamm,** is slightly more lively than the rest of the neighborhood—but not by much. Ku'Damm, as the locals know it, is home to department stores, street performers, teenagers darting in and out of H&M, and enough hot-dog stands to give midtown Manhattan a run for its money. Charlottenburg is also home to Europe's largest department store, **KaDeWe** (p. 120). Five massive floors keep the neighbors outfitted in Prada and Chanel, while the gourmet floor up top keeps their pantries well-stocked with truffle oils, chichi mustards, and over 1300 varieties of smelly cheese.

SCHÖNEBERG AND WILMERSDORF

S1 to Julius-Leber-Brücke. U1, U2, U3, U4, U7, U9, or U15 to Bülowstr., Eisenacher Str., Fehrbelliner Platz, Guntzelstr., Nollendorfplatz, Rathaus Schöneberg, Wittenbergplatz, or Yorckstr. *See also: Accommodations (p. 88), Food (p. 98), and Sights (p. 104).*

South of the Ku'damm, Schöneberg and Wilmersdorf are middle-class residential districts noted for their world-class restaurants and shopping. The area around Nollendorfpl., where even the military store is draped with rainbow flags, is the nexus of Berlin's gay and lesbian community, and the streets surrounding Hauptstr. are home to a sizable Turkish population. The birthplace of Marlene Dietrich and former stomping grounds of Christopher Isherwood, Schöneberg maintains a decidedly mellow mood.

MITTE

S1, S2, S3, S5, S7, S9, S25, or S75 to Alexanderplatz, Anhalter Bahnhof, Bellevue, Hackescher Markt, Oranienburger Str., or Unter den Linden. U2, U5, U6, or U8 to Französische Str., Oranienburger Tor, Potsdamer Platz, Rosa-Luxemburg-Platz, Rosenthaler Platz, Stadmitte, Weinmeisterstr., or Zinnowitzer Str. *See also: Accommodations (p. 90), Food (p. 99), and Sights (p. 104).*

If you spend one day in Berlin, spend it in Mitte. It is in Mitte, once the heart of Berlin, that the contrast between East and West is most palpable and alive. The district was once split down the middle by the wall, and much of the Eastern segment languished in disrepair, but the wave of revitalization that swept post-wall Berlin hit Mitte first. Today, monstrous relics of the DDR era, including the enormous **Fernsehturm** (TV tower) and colossal statues of Marx and Engels, compete for attention with spruced-up Imperial architecture. Tourists spend most of their time in Mitte, hitting major sights like the **Museumsinsel** (Museum Island), **Brandenburg Gate,** and the recently renovated **Reichstag. Unter din Linden,** Mitte's elegant, tree-lined boulevard, is also a must for any visit to Berlin. When you tire of museum-going, hop in line at the famous **Cafe Einstein** (p. 99) for an elegant, Viennese pastry pick-me-up. Though Mitte is still home to first-rate nightlife, the best clubs have closed—they were the illegal ones, as every good Berliner knows—as the city's nightlife culture swept farther East. Mitte may have received a final coat of polish, but you can still find devastated war wrecks squeezed in among grandiose Prussian palaces, glittering modern constructions, and swank galleries.

LET'S GO PICKS

BEST WAY TO CURE A HANGOVER: A smorgasbord buffet brunch at **Cafe Morgenland** (p. 101) in Kreuzberg.

BEST PLACE (OR MAYBE THE ONLY PLACE) TO SPOT CELEBRITIES AND POLITICIANS: Paris Bar (p. 98) in Charlottenburg.

BEST DRUNK MUNCHIES: The chicken shawarma at **Maroush** (p. 101) in Kreuzberg.

BEST REINVENTED CURRYWURST: Friederichshain's **Frittiersalon** (p. 100)–a "frying salon" with an organic twist.

BEST BATHROOMS: Check out the bathroom "art" at the **Schwarzes Cafe** (p. 98)–it's like peeing in a Prince video.

BEST PLACE TO WEIN: the Weinerei (p. 126) in Prenzlauer Berg.

BEST PLACE TO SIT ON KARL MARX'S LAP: Get up close and personal at the **Marx Engels forum** (p. 107).

BEST PLACE TO WRITE YOUR EX-PAT NOVEL: In the midst of Schöneberg's cafe culture at **Cafe Bilderbuch** (p. 98).

BEST PLACE TO DINE: For an authentic German feast, head to **Schwarzwaldstuben** (p. 99) in Mitte.

BEST U-BAHN: all of them, because you can drink beer on the subway and it never ever gets old.

BEST PLACE TO SPOT NUDE SUNBATHERS: around the **Victory Column** (p. 108) in the Tiergarten.

BEST POLAR BEAR AND WHERE TO FIND HIM: His name is **Knut** and he lives in the **Zoologischer Garten** (p. 102) in Charlottenburg.

PRENZLAUER BERG

S8, S41, or S42 to Prenzlauer Allee or Schönhauser Allee. U2 or U8 to Bernhauer Str., Eberswalder Str., Rosenthaler Platz, Senefelderplatz, or Voltastr. See also: Accommodations (p. 92), Food (p. 100), and Sights (p. 110).

Though largely overlooked during post-war reconstruction efforts, Prenzlberg (as locals call it) has been transformed in recent years from a heap of crumbling, graffiti-covered buildings into perhaps the trendiest of Berlin's *Bezirke*. Attracted by low rents, students and artists stormed the neighborhood after reunification. Today, the streets are owned by well-dressed first graders and their young, effortlessly hip parents and studded with cool, costly second-hand clothing stores. In Prenzlauer Berg, everything used to be something else, including the expats dropping English phrases in neighborhood cafes. Scrumptious brunches unfold every Sunday in what were once butcher shops, a former power plant stages thoughtful furniture exhibitions, and students cavort in breweries-turned-nightclubs. Relics of Prenzlberg's past life are disappearing, but cafe-bar owners know shabby-chic when they see it: mismatched sofas and painted advertisements for cabbage remain the decorating standard. Though by now you've probably missed the boat, you can still find traces of

Prenzlberg's graffitied past among the strollers and baby bjorns of **Mauerpark** (literally, Wall Park). Also check out **Kasthanianallee** and **Oderbergerstrasse,** where you can still find pockets of young and hip in the form of cheaper vintage stores and trendy bars. In general, Prenzlberg is the bar scene to Friedrischain's club culture—if you prefer drinking against a backdrop of studied cool to gyrating in the dark, this is the neighborhood for you.

FRIEDRICHSHAIN

S3, S5, S6, S7, S9, or S75 to Ostbahnhof or Warschauer Str. U5 or U15 to Frankfurter Tor, Magdalenenstr., Samariter Str., or Strausberger Platz. *See also: Accommodations (p. 94), Food (p. 100), and Sights (p. 111).*

As the avant-garde crowd follows low rents ever eastward and farther from the geographical center of the city, Friedrichshain is becoming a new temple of bohemian—make that punk-rock—living. While this *Bezirk* still retains much of its DDR atmosphere, from the pre-fab apartment houses and gray concrete to the massive remains of the Wall, some of its long-standing proponents complain that gentrification has found its way even here. The oppressive architecture of central axis **Frankfurter Allee** is overtaken by more traditional residential areas, while the main drag for the young populace is **Simon-Dach-Strasse** and **Boxhagenerplatz,** covered with sun-soaked outdoor seating and crowds of chic 20-somethings. Farther north, **Rigaerstrasse** is a stronghold of Berlin's legendary underground, home to squatter bars, make-shift clubs, and sidewalk punks. Friedrichshain is definitely the place to be for hardcore shows in someone's basement or radical, anarchist actions, just keep an eye out at night, as Friederichshain is still a little rough around the edges, and can be desolate in some spots.

BERLIN

KREUZBERG

U1, U2, U6, U7, or U15 to Gleisdreieck, Gneisenaustr., Görlitzer Bahnhof, Kochstr., Kottbusser Tor, Mehringdamm, Möckernbrücke, Platz der Luftbrücke, Prinzenstr., Schlesisches Tor., or Yorckstr. *See also: Accommodations (p. 94), Food (p. 101), and Sights (p. 112).*

If Prenzlberg is too bougie and Friederichshain too punk-rock, then Kreuzberg may be just right. Across the Spree and over the wall from Freidrichshain, Kreuzberg ladles out West Germany's dose of counter-culture. A center of Berlin's alternative scene, Kreuzberg's only certainty is unpredictability. In the 1960s and 70s, much of the area was occupied by *Hausbesetzer* (squatters) until a conservative city government forcibly evicted most of them in the early 80s. The ensuing riots threw the city into chaos; during President Reagan's 1985 visit to Berlin, authorities so feared protests from Kreuzberg that they cordoned off the entire district. This *Bezirk*'s anti-establishment reputation exists alongside an incredibly diverse demographic. Home to an especially large number of the city's immigrants, Kreuzberg is a neighborhood of sidewalk food stands, fruit vendors, and cafes. Much of Kreuzberg's immigrant population is Turkish, which means Turkish bakeries, Turkish grocery stores, and the famous **Türkische Markt** every Tuesday and Friday. Its increasing trendiness has attracted a wave of gentrification in the form of yuppies and sober government workers, particularly in the western half; farther east, the neighborhood remains as forward-looking as ever. Kreuzberg defiantly rejects stereotypes, presenting instead a kaleidoscopic mix of people who keep the dynamic scene alive with a tireless supply of partiers.

LIFE AND TIMES

HISTORY

THE BEGINNING: LOTS OF WAR. Berlin, now Germany's most populous city, was originally the site of small Slavic settlements in the marshlands along the Havel and Spree Rivers during the early Middle Ages. Berlin takes its name from the Slavonic word *birl* (swamp). The Saxon duke **Albrecht der Bär** (Albert the Bear) came to power in Brandenburg during the 12th century and removed the Slavs from the region, resettling with immigrants from the west. By the 13th century, the trading posts Cölln and Berlin were founded, and in 1307 the two formally united. The electors of Brandenburg seized control in 1411 and built a capital to match their dreams of glory. With the Edict of Potsdam (1685), **Friedrich Wilhelm** bolstered the city's population by accepting Huguenot and Jewish refugees from newly intolerant France, and in 1701 Berlin became the capital of the Kingdom of Prussia. Berlin flourished as an intellectual hotspot thanks to thinkers like dramatist **Gotthold Ephraim Lessing,** educators like the **Humboldt brothers,** and the ruler **Friedrich II**—whose penchant for martial pomp and circumstance turned the city into an assortment of broad avenues and grandiose parade grounds. Conquered by **Napoleon** in 1806 and beset by revolution in 1848, the city fell into a decline until **Otto von Bismarck** unified Germany in 1871. Though Berlin was made capital of the fledgling empire, it never became the center of the new nation, and most Germans felt little affection for the capital.

BETWEEN WARS: REBELLION AND POVERTY. WWI and the Allied blockade reduced Berlin to poverty. A popular uprising led to Kaiser Wilhelm II's abdication and **Karl Liebknecht's** declaration of a socialist republic with Berlin as its capital on November 9, 1918. Locally, the revolt, led by Liebknecht and **Rosa Luxemburg,** turned into a full-fledged workers' revolution that controlled the city for several days. The rival Social Democratic government lead by **Philipp Scheidemann** enlisted the aid of right-wing mercenaries, **the Freikorps,** to suppress the rebellion and murder Liebknecht and Luxemburg. As Berlin recovered from economic and political instability, it grew into one of the major cultural centers of Europe. Expressionist painting flourished, Bertolt Brecht (p. 110) revolutionized theater, and artists and writers from all over the world flocked to the city. The city's "Golden Twenties" ended abruptly with the 1929 economic collapse, when the city erupted with bloody riots and political chaos.

WAR AGAIN: A CITY DIVIDED. With economic woes came a rise in the popularity of the extremist Nazi party. When Hitler took power on January 30, 1933, traditionally left-wing "Red Berlin" was not one of his strongholds. Furious at the radical city, Hitler famously declared: "Berliners are not fit to be German!" He finally consolidated control over the city through economic improvements and totalitarian measures, marshalling support for the savage anti-Semitic pogrom of November 9, 1938, known as **Kristallnacht.** Only 7000 members of Berlin's once-thriving Jewish community of 160,000 survived the Holocaust. Allied bombing and the Battle of Berlin leveled one-fifth of the city, killing 80,000 citizens. The pre-war population of 4.3 million was reduced to a mere 2.8 million by 1945. With nearly all healthy men dead or gone, it was Berlin's **Trümmerfrauen** (rubble women) who literally picked up the pieces of the city. The Allies divided post-war Germany into American, British, French, and Soviet sectors, controlled by a joint **Allied Command.** On June 16, 1948, the Soviets

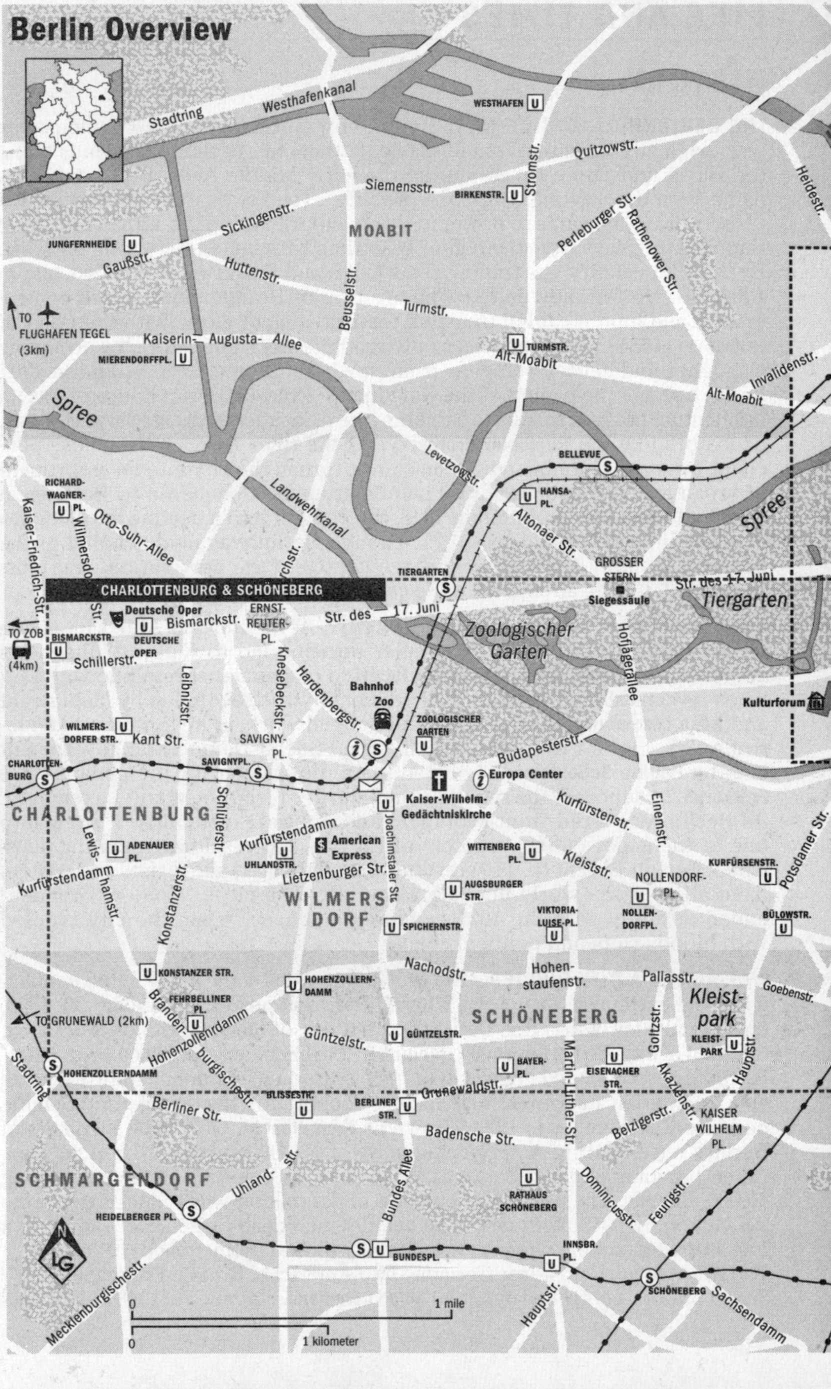
Berlin Overview
Stadtring
Westhafenkanal
WESTHAFEN
Quitzowstr.
Heidestr.
Siemensstr.
BIRKENSTR.
Stromstr.
Sickingenstr.
MOABIT
Perleburger Str.
Rathenower Str.
JUNGFERNHEIDE
Gaußstr.
Huttenstr.
Beusselstr.
Turmstr.
TO FLUGHAFEN TEGEL (3km)
Kaiserin- Augusta- Allee
MIERENDORFFPL.
TURMSTR.
Alt-Moabit
Invalidenstr.
Spree
Levetzowstr.
BELLEVUE
HANSA-PL.
RICHARD-WAGNER-PL.
Landwehrkanal
Altonaer Str.
Kaiser-Friedrich-Str.
Otto-Suhr-Allee
GROSSER STERN
TIERGARTEN
Str. des 17. Juni
CHARLOTTENBURG & SCHÖNEBERG
Deutsche Oper
Siegessäule
Tiergarten
TO ZOB (4km)
Bismarckstr.
ERNST-REUTER-PL.
Zoologischer Garten
BISMARCKSTR.
DEUTSCHE OPER
Schillerstr.
Hofjägerallee
Leibnizstr.
Knesebeckstr.
Hardenbergstr.
Bahnhof Zoo
Kulturforum
WILMERS-DORFER STR.
Kant Str.
SAVIGNY-PL.
ZOOLOGISCHER GARTEN
Budapesterstr.
CHARLOTTEN-BURG
SAVIGNYPL.
Europa Center
Kaiser-Wilhelm-Gedächtniskirche
CHARLOTTENBURG
Schlüterstr.
Joachimstaler Str.
Kurfürstenstr.
Einemstr.
Potsdamer Str.
Lewis-hamstr.
ADENAUER PL.
Kurfürstendamm
American Express
UHLANDSTR.
WITTENBERG PL.
Kleiststr.
KURFÜRSENSTR.
Lietzenburger Str.
NOLLENDORF-PL.
AUGSBURGER STR.
WILMERSDORF
VIKTORIA-LUISE-PL.
NOLLEN-DORFPL.
BÜLOWSTR.
Konstanzerstr.
SPICHERNSTR.
Nachodstr.
Hohen-staufenstr.
Pallasstr.
Goebenstr.
KONSTANZER STR.
HOHENZOLLERN-DAMM
Kleist-park
FEHRBELLINER PL.
Branden-burgischestr.
TO GRUNEWALD (2km)
Hohenzollerndamm
SCHÖNEBERG
Güntzelstr.
GÜNTZELSTR.
Goltzstr.
KLEIST-PARK
Martin-Luther-Str.
Hauptstr.
BAYER-PL.
EISENACHER STR.
Akazienstr.
HOHENZOLLERNDAMM
Grunewaldstr.
BLISSESTR.
BERLINER STR.
Berliner Str.
Belzigerstr.
KAISER WILHELM PL.
Badensche Str.
Uhland-str.
SCHMARGENDORF
RATHAUS SCHÖNEBERG
Dominicusstr.
Feurigstr.
Bundes Allee
HEIDELBERGER PL.
BUNDESPL.
INNSBR. PL.
SCHÖNEBERG
Sachsendamm
Mecklenburgischestr.
0
1 mile
1 kilometer

BERLIN

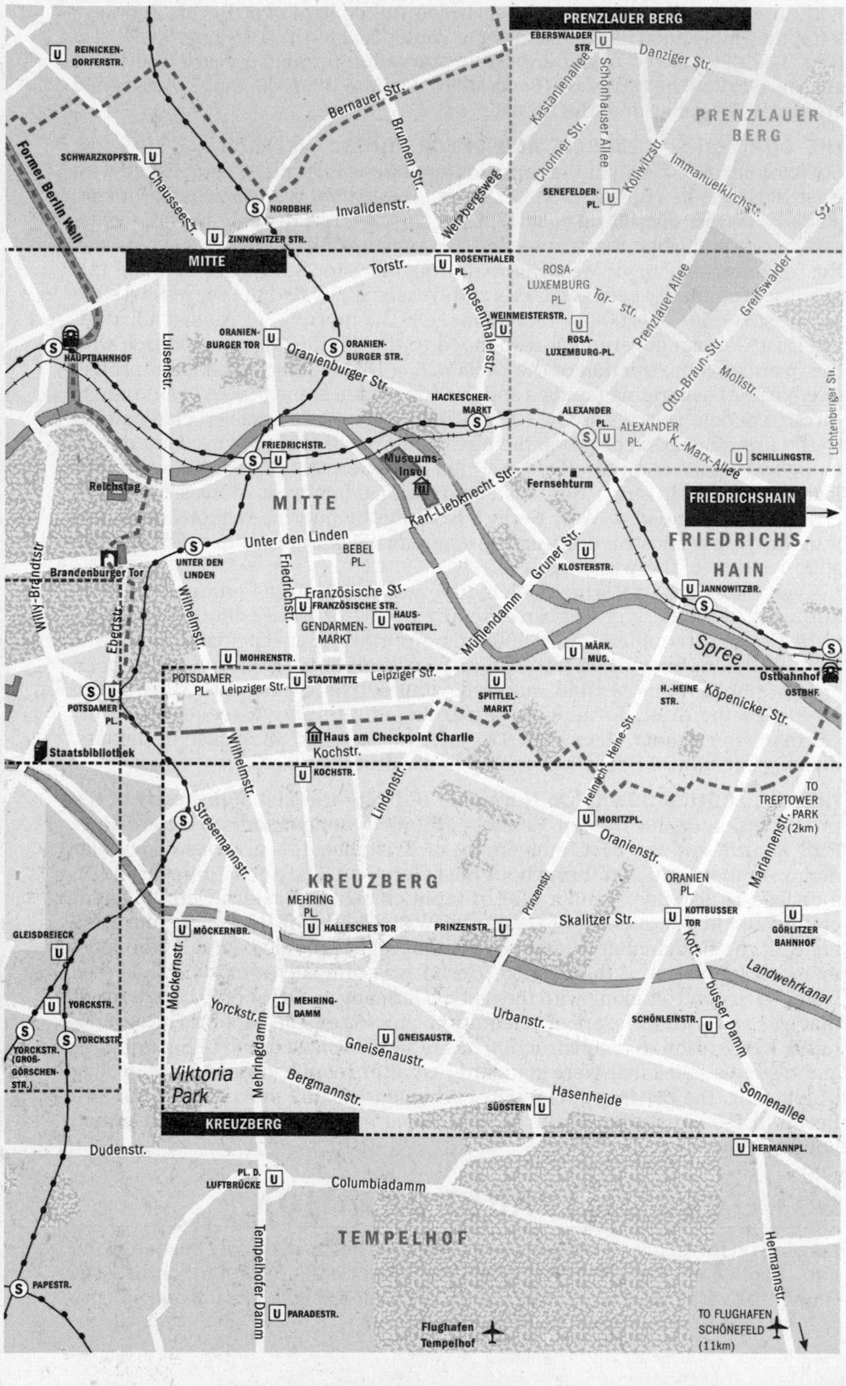
PRENZLAUER BERG
MITTE
FRIEDRICHSHAIN
KREUZBERG
REINICKEN-DORFERSTR.
SCHWARZKOPFSTR.
Former Berlin Wall
Chausseestr.
NORDBHF.
ZINNOWITZER STR.
Bernauer Str.
Brunnen Str.
Invalidenstr.
Wer bergsweg
EBERSWALDER STR.
Danziger Str.
Kastanienallee
Schönhauser Allee
Choriner Str.
SENEFELDER-PL.
Kollwitzstr.
Immanuelkirchstr.
PRENZLAUER BERG
Torstr.
ROSENTHALER PL.
ROSA-LUXEMBURG PL.
Tor-str.
Prenzlauer Allee
Greifswalder
Rosenthalerstr.
WEINMEISTERSTR.
ROSA-LUXEMBURG-PL.
Otto-Braun-Str.
Mollstr.
Lichtenberger Str.
ORANIEN-BURGER TOR
ORANIEN-BURGER STR.
Oranienburger Str.
HAUPTBAHNHOF
Luisenstr.
HACKESCHER-MARKT
ALEXANDER PL.
ALEXANDER PL.
K.-Marx-Allee
SCHILLINGSTR.
FRIEDRICHSTR.
Museums-insel
Reichstag
MITTE
Karl-Liebknecht Str.
Fernsehturm
FRIEDRICHSHAIN
FRIEDRICHS-HAIN
Unter den Linden
UNTER DEN LINDEN
BEBEL PL.
Brandenburger Tor
Willy-Brandtstr.
Wilhelmstr.
Friedrichstr.
Gruner Str.
KLOSTERSTR.
Französische Str.
FRANZÖSISCHE STR.
HAUS-VOGTEIPL.
GENDARMEN-MARKT
Mühlendamm
JANNOWITZBR.
Ebertstr.
MOHRENSTR.
MÄRK. MUS.
Spree
POTSDAMER PL.
Leipziger Str.
STADTMITTE
Leipziger Str.
SPITTEL-MARKT
H.-HEINE STR.
Köpenicker Str.
Ostbahnhof
OSTBHF.
POTSDAMER PL.
Haus am Checkpoint Charlie
Kochstr.
Staatsbibliothek
KOCHSTR.
Lindenstr.
Heinrich-Heine-Str.
TO TREPTOWER PARK (2km)
Stresemannstr.
MORITZPL.
Oranienstr.
Mariannenstr.
KREUZBERG
ORANIEN PL.
MEHRING PL.
Prinzenstr.
Skalitzer Str.
MÖCKERNBR.
HALLESCHES TOR
PRINZENSTR.
KOTTBUSSER TOR
GÖRLITZER BAHNHOF
GLEISDREIECK
Kottbusser Damm
Landwehrkanal
Möckernstr.
YORCKSTR.
MEHRING-DAMM
Yorckstr.
Urbanstr.
SCHÖNLEINSTR.
YORCKSTR.
YORCKSTR. (GROß-GÖRSCHEN-STR.)
GNEISAUSTR.
Gneisenaustr.
Viktoria Park
Mehringdamm
Bergmannstr.
Hasenheide
Sonnenallee
SÜDSTERN
KREUZBERG
Dudenstr.
HERMANNPL.
PL. D. LUFTBRÜCKE
Columbiadamm
TEMPELHOF
Hermannstr.
PAPESTR.
Tempelhofer Damm
PARADESTR.
Flughafen Tempelhof
TO FLUGHAFEN SCHÖNEFELD (11km)

withdrew from the alliance and demanded full control over Berlin. Ten days later, they blockaded the land and water routes that led into the non-Soviet sectors. The Allies saved West Berlin from starvation through a massive airlift of supplies, called the **Luftbrücke (Berlin Airlift).** On May 12, 1949, the Soviets ceded control of West Berlin to the Allies.

THE DDR YEARS: CONCRETE AND CHECKPOINTS. On October 5, 1949, the Soviet-controlled German Democratic Republic was formally established with East Berlin as its capital. East Berliners, dissatisfied with their government, staged a **workers' uprising** on June 17, 1953. Soviet tanks overwhelmed the demonstrators, and when the dust settled, the only upshot of the day's events was the renaming of a major West Berlin thoroughfare to "Straße des 17. Juni" in a gesture of solidarity between *Ossis* and *Wessis*. Many fled the repressive state for West Berlin—200,000 in 1960 alone. On the morning of August 13, 1961, the East German government responded to the exodus of its workforce with the overnight construction of the **Berlin Wall,** a 165km-long "anti-fascist protective barrier," separating families and friends, and in some places even running through people's homes. In the early 1970s, a second wall was erected parallel to the first; the space between them was filled with barbed wire, land mines, and glass shards and patrolled by armed East German guards. Known as the **Todesstreifen** (death strip), this wasteland claimed hundreds of lives. The Western Allies responded to West Berlin's isolation by pouring millions of dollars into the city's reconstruction, turning it into *das Schaufenster des Westens* (the shop-window of the West).

Even though West Berliners elected a mayor, the Allies retained ultimate authority over the city—never officially a part of the Federal Republic—until German reunification in 1990. One perk of this "special status" was West Berliners' exemption from military conscription. Thousands of German artists, punks, homosexuals, and left-wing activists moved to West Berlin to escape the draft, forming an unparalleled alternative scene. The West German government, determined to make a Cold War showcase of the city, directly subsidized Berlin's economy and cultural scene.

THE WALL COMES DOWN. On November 9, 1989—the 71st anniversary of the proclamation of the Weimar Republic, the 66th anniversary of Hitler's Beer Hall Putsch, and the 51st anniversary of Kristallnacht—a series of popular demonstrations erupted throughout East Germany. The public unrest rode on a decade of discontent and a year of rapid change in Eastern Europe, and it culminated in the opening of the Berlin Wall. Photos of Berliners embracing beneath the Brandenburg Gate (p. 104) that night provided some of the most memorable images of the century. Berlin was officially reunited (and freed from Allied control) along with the rest of Germany on October 3, 1990, a result that was met with widespread celebration. Since then, the euphoria has evaporated. Resignation to reconstruction has taken the place of the biting criticism and tasteless jokes that were standard just after reunification. After a decade of planning, the **Bundestag** (German Parliament) finally moved from Bonn to Berlin in 1999, restoring Berlin to its pre-war status as the locus of German political power.

INTERCITY TRANSPORTATION

Located on the plains of northeastern Germany, Berlin is rapidly becoming the hub of both domestic and international rail networks. Three hours southeast of Hamburg by train and seven hours north of Munich, Berlin has rail and air connections to most European capitals, including those in Eastern Europe. Nearly all European airlines have frequent service to one of Berlin's airports.

Flights: For information on Berlin's airports, call ☎0180 500 0186 or visit www.berlin-airport.de. Berlin is currently restructuring its airport system to send all travelers through the state-of-the-art **Capital Airport Berlin Brandenburg International (BBI),** an expansion of the current **Flughafen Schönefeld Airport.** As part of this process, Tempelhof Airport was closed on Oct. 30, 2008, and in 2011, **Tegel Airport** will be closed in preparation for BBI's big debut. To get to Tegel, take express bus #X9 or #109 from "Jakob-Kaiser-Pl." on U7, bus #128 from "Kurt-Schumacher-Pl." on U6, or bus TXL from "Beusselstr." on S42 and S41. Follow signs in the airport for ground transportation. To get to Flughafen Schönefeld, take S9 or S45 to "Flughafen Berlin Schönefeld" or the Schönefeld Express train, which runs every 30min. through most major S-Bahn stations, including Alexanderpl., Friedrichstr. Hauptbahnhof, and Ostbahnhof.

Train Stations: Berlin's massive new **Hauptbahnhof,** which opened just in time for the World Cup in 2006, is now the city's major transit hub, with some international and national trains continuing on to **Ostbahnhof** in Friedrichshain. **Zoologischer Garten** (almost always called **Bahnhof Zoo**), formerly West Berlin's main station, connects to regional destinations and offers S-bahn service. Many trains also connect to **Schönefeld** airport. A number of S-Bahn lines make stops at **Oranienburg, Spandau,** and **Potsdam.** Trains in the Brandenburg regional transit system tend to stop at all major stations, as well as Friedrichstr. and Alexanderpl.

Trains: Every hr. to: **Cologne** (4¾hr., €122); **Frankfurt** (4½hr., €129); **Hamburg** (2hr., €81); **Leipzig** (1¼hr., €46). Every 2hr. to: **Dresden** (2½hr., €46); **Munich** (7-8hr., €130); **Rostock** (2¾hr., €49). International connections to: **Amsterdam, NTH** (6½hr.); **Brussels, BEL** (7hr.); **Budapest, HUN** (13hr.); **Copenhagen, DNK** (7hr.); **Kraków, POL** (10hr.); **Paris, FRA** (9hr.); **Prague, CZR** (5hr.); **Stockholm, SWE** (13½hr.); **Vienna, AUS** (9½hr.); **Warsaw, POL** (6hr.); **Zurich, CHE** (11hr.). Times and prices change frequently—check at the computers located in the train stations. Prices depend on when you book—save 25-50% by booking **3 weeks to 3 days in advance.**

Rail Information: Deutsche Bahn Information (☎0180 599 6633; www.bahn.de). Long lines snake out the door of the **Reisezentrum** (Travel Center) in the Hauptbahnhof (open daily 6am-10pm), Bahnhof Zoo, and Ostbahnhof.

Buses: ZOB, Masurenallee 4, the central bus station (☎030 301 0380), by the Funkturm near Kaiserdamm. U2 to "Kaiserdamm" or S4, S45, or S46 to "Messe Nord/ICC" Open M-F 6am-9pm, Sa-Su and holidays 6am-8pm. To **Paris, FRA** (15hr., €85), **Prague, CZR** (5hr.; €40), and **Budapest, HUN** (14½hr.; €76). **Gullivers,** at ZOB (☎030 31 10 21 10; www.gullivers.de) often has good deals on buses.

Mitfahrzentralen (Ride Share): Mitfahrzentrale, Theaterstr. 22, D-53111 Bonn (☎228 410 110; www.mitfahrzentrale.de). Rideshare in Germany is a popular, relatively affordable way to get around. Mitfahrzentrale is one of the largest and most popular websites; it allows you to search for and map rides and calculate fares. Rates vary; prices listed are approximate. To: **Hamburg** (€16); **Hannover** (€16); **Frankfurt** (€30).

Hitchhiking: *Let's Go* does not recommend hitchhiking as a safe mode of transportation. Hitching is rare in Berlin and also illegal at rest stops or anywhere along the highway.

LOCAL TRANSPORTATION

SCOOP **INSIDE SCOOP.** If you feel like splurging on a cab but don't want pay the hefty metered rates, ask the driver for a *Kurzstrecke*—a special deal whereby, for only €3, you can travel 2km in any given direction. You probably won't get all the way to your doorstep, but you may get close. The *Kurzstrecke* applies only for cabs that you hail, not those you call.

Berlin may be the second largest city in Europe, but with a train pass and a city map, it's yours. Maps cost €1 at any tourist office and include a **transit map** of S-Bahn and U-Bahn lines, enough to get you almost anywhere. Make sure to pick up a *Nachtnetz* (night bus map) if you plan to be out past midnight on weeknights, as most U-Bahn and several S-Bahn lines shut down until 4am.

Public Transportation: The **BVG** (Berliner Verkehrsbetriebe; www.bvg.de) is one of the most efficient transportation systems in the world. Disruptions in service are rare.

Orientation and Basic Fares: It is futile to try to see all of Berlin on foot. Fortunately, the extensive **Bus, Straßenbahn** (streetcar or tram), **U-Bahn** (subway), and **S-Bahn** (surface rail) systems will get you to your destination safely and relatively quickly. Berlin is divided into 3 transit zones. **Zone A** encompasses central Berlin. The rest of Berlin, including Tegel Airport, is in **Zone B.** Those looking to explore Berlin's great outdoors should visit **Zone C,** which covers the outlying areas. (Zones AB €2.10, BC €2.50, ABC €2.80. Children under 6 free with an adult, under 14 reduced fare.) Tickets are valid for 2hr. **Within the validation period, they may be used on any S-Bahn, U-Bahn, bus, or tram.**

BERLIN

Special Passes: Single tickets are seldom worth purchasing during a visit to Berlin. A day pass (AB €6.10, BC €6.30, ABC €6.50) is good from the time of validation until 3am the next day. The **WelcomeCard** (sold at tourist offices) is valid on all lines for 48hr. (€16.50 for AB, €21.50 for ABC), 72hr. (€18/24.50) or 5 days (€29.50/34.50) and includes discounts on select tours. The **CityTourCard** is good for 48hr. (€15.90 for AB, €17.90 for ABC), 72hr. (€20.90/22.90), or 5 days (€28.90/33.90) and offers discounts at over 50 attractions. The **7-Tages-Karte** (AB €26.20, BC €27, ABC €32.30) is good for 7 days of travel. A **VBB Umweltkarte** (AB €72, BC €73, ABC €88.50) is valid for 1 month. **Bikes** require a supplemental ticket (AB €1.50 per trip, BC €1.70, ABC €2), and are permitted on the U-Bahn, S-Bahn, and select trams.

Purchasing Tickets: Buy tickets, including monthly passes, from **Automaten** (machines), bus drivers, or ticket windows in the U- and S-Bahn stations. When using an *Automat,* make your selection before inserting money. Machines will not give more than €10 change. Also, many machines do not take bills—save coins or use a ticket window to buy more expensive day or week passes. Some machines accept credit cards. **Validate your ticket** by inserting it into the machines marked *hier entwerfen* **before boarding!**

THERE ARE NO FREE RIDES. You may have noticed that getting on and off the U-Bahn, S-Bahn, tram, or bus doesn't involve that ticket that you just bought. Does Berlin public transportation work on the honor system? No way! Every so often, plainclothes officials will board your car and ask to see your ticket once the doors close. They accept no excuses for *Schwarzfahren* (riding without paying), and if you fail to produce a validated ticket you'll be slapped with a €40 fine, due on the spot if you can't provide identification.

Maps and Information: The BVG's numerous **Fahrscheine und Mehr** (tickets and more) stations have tons of maps. They can be found in most major transfer stations (e.g.,

Alexanderpl.). Liniennetz maps of the U-Bahn, S-Bahn, bus lines, and night bus lines are free. BVG information line: ☎030 194 49, open 24hr.; www.bvg.de.

Night Transport: U- and S-Bahn lines generally do not run M-F 1:30-4am. On F-Sa nights, S-Bahn and U-Bahn lines continue to run, though less frequently. An extensive system of just under 100 **night buses** runs every 20-30min. and tends to follow major transit lines; pick up the free Nachtliniennetz map at a Fahrscheine und Mehr office. The **letter "N"** precedes night bus numbers. Some trams also continue to run at night.

Ferries: Stern und Kreis Schifffahrt, Puschkinallee 15 (☎030 5363 6026; www.sternundkreis.de), in Treptower Park. Operates along the Spree Apr.-Oct. Ferries leave from locations daily 10am-4:20pm throughout the city, including Friedrichstr., Jannowitzbrucke, and the Nikolaiviertel. Fares (€7.50-16) depend on distance traveled. Pleasure cruises available. *Fahrscheine und Mehr* counters offer information. Advance sale at their office at the Treptow S-Bahn Station (M-F 9am-6pm, Sa 9am-2pm).

Taxis: (☎030 26 10 26, toll-free 0800 263 0000). Call 15min. in advance. Women can request female drivers. Trips within the city cost up to €21.

Car Rental: Most companies have counters at the airports and around Bahnhof Zoo, Ostbahnhof, and Friedrichstr. stations. Offices are also in the Europa Center with entrances at Budapester Str. 39-41. Rates average around €65 for a small car. 19+. Try **Avis,** Budapesterstr. 41 (☎030 230 9370; open daily 24hr.) or **Hertz,** Budapesterstr. 39 (☎030 261 1053; open M-F 7am-7pm, Sa 8am-2pm, Su 9am-1:30pm).

Bike Rental: Fat Tire Bike Rental (☎030 24 04 79 91; www.berlinfahrradverleih.com) has 2 locations in Berlin: one in the East directly under the TV Tower in Alexanderplatz (U2 to Alexanderplatz), and one in the West at the Zoologischer Garten (Zoo Station). €12 per day, €7 for half-day (up to 4hr.). Rates decrease with longer rental periods.Open daily Mar. 1-Apr. 9 and Oct. 1-Nov 30 (9:30am-6pm), Apr. 10-Sept. 30 (9:30am-8pm). **Velomondo,** Motzstr. 12 (☎030 21 75 30 46; www.velomondo.de), U1-U4 to "Nollendorfpl." €10 per day, €49 per week. Open M-F 10am-7pm, Sa 10am-2pm. Deutsche Bahn **Call-A-Bike** (☎0700 522 5522; www.callabike.de) are parked all over the city. €0.08 per min. (up to €9 per 24hr.) or €36 per week.

PRACTICAL INFORMATION

CITY CODE: The city code for all of Berlin is **☎030.**

TOURIST OFFICES

Now privately owned, tourist offices provide a narrower range of free services and information than they once did. They still sell a useful **city map** (€1) on which sights and transit stations are clearly marked, and book same-day **hotel rooms** for a €3 fee—room prices start around €30. The monthly *Berlin Programm* (€1.75) lists museums, sights, restaurants, and hotels, and opera, theater, and classical music performances. German speakers should get *Tip* (€2.70) or *Zitty* (€2.70) for full listings of film, theater, concerts, and clubs. *Siegessäule*, *Sergej*, and *Gay-Yellowpages* have gay and lesbian event and club listings. English-language movie and theater reviews are in the *Ex-Berliner* (€2), and www.berlin.de has quality information on all aspects of the city.

EurAide (☎1781 828 2488), in the Hauptbahnhof, across from the McDonald's. Sells rail tickets, maps, phone cards, and walking tour tickets.

Tourist Info Centers, Berlin Tourismus Marketing GmbH, Am Karlsbad 11, 10785 (☎030 25 00 25; www.berlin-tourist-information.de) reserve rooms for a €3-6 fee, with friendly service in English. A list of campgrounds and pensions is available. Transit maps (free) and city maps (€1). There's an office located on the ground fl. of the **Hauptbahnof.** The entrance is on Europlatz. Open daily 8am-10pm. Another is located near the **Brandenburger Tor,** S1, S2, or S25 or bus #100 to "Unter den Linden," on your left as you face the pillars from the Unter den Linden side. Open daily 10am-6pm.

CITY TOURS

Unless otherwise noted, the tours listed below are conducted in English.

Terry Brewer's Best of Berlin (☎0177 388 1537; www.brewersberlintours.com). Terry and his guides are legendary for vast knowledge and engaging personalities, making the 6hr.+ walk well worth it. Tours leave daily from in front of the Bandy Brooks shop on Friedrichstr. (S5, S7, S9, S75, or U6 to "Friedrichstr.") at 10:30am. €12. Not exactly a family affair, the **Sinful Berlin** tour meets Th and Sa at 8pm, and includes entrance into Europe's largest erotic museum.elehner@fas.harvard.edu

Insider Tour (☎030 692 3149; www.insidertour.com) offers a variety of fun, erudite tours that hit all the major sights. More importantly, the guides' enthusiasm for Berlin is contagious and their accents span the English-speaking world. The **Famous Insider Walk** picks up daily from Apr. 1 to Oct. 31 10am and 2:30pm at the McDonald's outside the Zoo Station, 30min. later from the Coffeemamas at "Hackescher Markt"; from Nov. 1 to Mar. 30 10am from the Zoo Station and 10:30am at "Hackescher Markt" only. Tours last 4hr. €12, under 26 or with WelcomeCard or ISIC €10. **Bike tours** (4hr.) meet by the Coffee Mamas at "Hackescher Markt." From June 1 to Sept. 15 at 10:30am and 3pm, from Apr. 1 to Nov. 15 10:30am only. €20/18. Offers tours of Nazi Berlin, Cold War Berlin, Potsdam, and a Berlin Pub Crawl as well as daytrip tours to Dresden.

Original Berlin Walks (☎030 301 9194; www.berlinwalks.de) offers a range of English-language walking tours, including "Infamous Third Reich Sites," "Jewish Life in Berlin," "Nest of Spies," and "Discover Potsdam." Their **Discover Berlin Walk** (4hr.; €12, under 26 €10, WelcomeCard and ISIC €9) is a great way to get acquainted with the city. Guides' knowledge complements their eager attitude. Tours meet Apr.-Oct. at 10am and 2:30pm at the taxi stand in front of Bahnhof Zoo and at 10:30am and 3pm at the Hackescher Markt Häagen-Dazs. Nov.-Mar. 10am and 10:30am only.

New Berlin (☎030 51 05 00 30; www.newberlintours.com) offers free tours (on a tips only basis, which means some pandering from the guides) of Berlin's biggest sights, and special tours (Sachsenhausen, Third Reich tour, pub crawl, etc.) for a fee. Backpackers with little cash are encouraged to take the tour, but occasionally dislike the cursory nature of the set-up. Tours leave every day from the Brandenburg Gate Starbucks (11am, 1, 4pm) and the Zoologischer Garten Dunkin' Donuts (10:30am, 12:30, and 3:30pm). A new **bike tour** (€15 with bike, €12 without) meets daily at 11am and 2pm in front of the Postfuhramt, on the corner of Oranienburgerstr. and Tucholskystr., S-Bahn to "Oranienburger Straße."

TRAVEL AGENCIES

STA: Books flights and hotels and sells ISIC cards. Branches at: **Dorotheenstr. 30** (☎030 20 16 50 63). S3, S5, S7, S9, S75, or U6 to "Friedrichstr." Open M-F 10am-7pm, Sa 11am-3pm. **Gleimstraße 28.** S4, S8, S85, or U2 to "Schönhauser Allee." Open M-F 10am-7pm, Sa 11am-4pm. **Hardenbergerstraße 9.** U2 to "Ernst-Reuter-Pl." Open M-F 10am-7pm, Sa 11am-3pm. **Takustraße 47.** Open M-F 10am-7pm, Sa 10am-2pm.

EMBASSIES AND CONSULATES

Berlin's construction plans include a new complex to house foreign dignitaries. Though most have moved to their new homes, the locations of some embassies and consulates remain in a state of flux. For the latest information, call the **Auswärtiges Amt Dienststelle Berlin** (☎030 500 00; www.auswaertiges-amt.de) or visit their office on the Werderscher Markt (U2 to "Hausvogteipl."). See **Consular Services Abroad,** p. 8, for embassy and consulate contact information.

FINANCIAL SERVICES

Currency Exchange: The best rates are usually found at exchange offices with *Wechselstube* signs outside, at most major train stations, and in large squares. **ReiseBank,** at the Hauptbahnhof (☎030 20 45 37 61; M-Sa 8am-10pm), at **Bahnhof Zoo** (☎030 881 7117), and at **Ostbahnhof** (☎030 296 4393), is conveniently located, but has poor rates.

Bank and ATM: ATMs are labeled *Geldautomat.* **Berliner Sparkasse** and **Deutsche Bank** have branches everywhere; their ATMs usually accept MC/V. **Citibank** has 23 branches in Berlin with **24hr. ATMs,** including Friedrichstr. 194-99 (U-Bahn to "Stadmitte").

American Express: Main Office, Bayreuther Str. 37-38 (☎030 21 47 62 92). U1 or U2 to "Wittenbergpl." Holds mail and offers banking services. No commission for cashing American Express Traveler's Cheques. Expect out-the-door lines F-Sa. Open M-F 9am-7pm, Sa 10am-2pm. **Branch,** Friedrichstr. 172 (☎030 201 7400). U6 to "Französische Str." Same services and hours.

LOCAL SERVICES

Luggage Storage: In the **Hauptbahnhof,** in "DB Gepack Center," 1st fl., East side. €4 per day. In **Bahnhof Zoo,** lockers €3-5 per day, depending on size. Max. 2hr. Open daily 6:15am-10:30pm. 24hr. lockers are also at **Ostbahnhof** and **Alexanderplatz.**

Bookstores:

Marga Schöller Bücherstube, Knesebeckstr. 33 (☎030 881 1112). S5, S7, S9, or S75 to "Savignypl." Off-beat and contemporary reading material in English. Open M-W 9:30am-7pm, Th-F 9:30am-8pm, Sa 9:30am-4pm.

Hugendubel is a massive chain-store. Branches at Tauentzienstr. 13 (☎030 48 44 84; www.hugendubel.de) by the Ku'damm; Karl-Marx-Str. 66; Alte Potsdamer Str. 7; Wilmersdorfer Str. 121. Open M-Sa 10am-8pm.

Libraries: Staatsbibliothek Preußischer Kulturbesitz, Potsdamer Str. 33 (☎030 26 60). A book for every Berliner; 3.5 million in all. Lots of English-language newspapers. Built for West Berlin in the 1960s, after the Iron Curtain cut off the original *Staabi* at Unter den Linden 8, next to the Humboldt-Universität (p. 105). Now you can choose between them. Both open M-F 9am-9pm, Sa 9am-5pm; Potsdamer Str. also Sa until 7pm. Day pass (€0.50) required for entry.

EMERGENCY AND COMMUNICATIONS

Police: Pl. der Luftbrücke 6. U6 to "Pl. der Luftbrücke." **Emergency** ☎110. **Ambulance** and **Fire** ☎112. **Non-emergency advice hotline** ☎030 46 64 46 64.

SAFETY PRECAUTION. Berlin is by far the most tolerant city in Germany, and, among major cities, Berlin has the fewest hate crimes per capita and very few neo-Nazi skinheads. However, minorities, gays, and lesbians should exercise caution in the outlying eastern suburbs at night. If you see skinheads wearing dark combat boots (especially with white laces), proceed with caution, but do not panic, and avoid drawing attention to yourself.

CRISIS LINES: ENGLISH SPOKEN AT MOST CRISIS LINES.

American Hotline (☎0177 814 15 10). Crisis and referral service.

Poison Control (☎030 192 40).

Berliner Behindertenverband, Jägerstr. 63d (☎030 204 38 47; www.bbv-ev.de). Advice for the handicapped. Open W noon-5pm and by appointment.

Deutsche AIDS-Hilfe, Wilhelmstr. 138 (☎030 690 0870; www.aidshilfe.de).

Drug Crisis (☎030 192 37) 24hr.

Women's Resources: Frauenkrisentelefon (☎030 615 4243; www.frauenkrisentelefon.de). Women's crisis line. Open M and Th 10am-noon; Tu-W, F 7pm-9pm; Sa-Su 5pm-7pm.

Lesbenberatung, Kulmer Str. 20 (☎030 215 2000; www.lesbenberatung-berlin.de). Lesbian counseling.

Schwulenberatung, Mommsenstr. 45 (☎030 194 46; www.schwulenberatungberlin.de). Gay men's counseling.

Maneo (☎030 216 3336; www.maneo.de). Legal help for gay violence victims. Daily 5pm-7pm.

LARA, Fuggerstr. 19 (☎030 216 8888; www.lara-berlin.de) Sexual assault help. M-F 9am-6pm.

Pharmacies: Ubiquitous in Berlin. **Apotheke im Bahnhof Zoo** (☎030 31 50 33 61) located within Bahnhof Zoologischer Garten. Open M-F 7am-8pm, Sa 8am-8pm, Su 11am-6pm. Pharmacies list a rotating schedule of 24hr. service.

Medical Services: The American and British embassies list English-speaking doctors. **Emergency doctor** (☎030 31 00 31); **Emergency dentist** (☎030 89 00 43 33).

Internet Access: Free internet with admission to the **Staatsbibliothek** (see **Libraries**). Also try: **Netlounge,** Auguststr. 89 (☎030 24 34 25 97; www.netlounge-berlin.de). U-Bahn to "Oranienburger Str." €2.50 per hr. Open daily noon-midnight. **Easy Internet** has several locations throughout Berlin: Karl-Marx-Str. 78, Ku'damm 224, Schloßstr. 102, Sony Center, and Rathausstr. 5. **Wi-Fi** can be found throughout Berlin, both free and charge-based services (see **Essentials,**).

Post Offices: Joachimstaler Str. 7 (☎030 88 70 86 11), down Joachimstaler Str. from Bahnhof Zoo and near Kantstr. Open M-Sa 9am-8pm. Branches: **Tegel Airport,** open M-F 8am-6pm, Sa 8am-noon; **Ostbahnhof,** open M-F 8am-8pm, Sa-Su 10am-6pm. Most branches open M-F 9am-7pm, Sa 9am-1pm. **Postal Code:** 10706.

ACCOMMODATIONS

Same-day accommodations in Berlin aren't impossible to find, but you may need to wait until late in the day when establishments have vacancies due to cancellations. If you want to stay in the same place longer than a couple of days or on weekends, reservations are essential. Book a week ahead to get a room and a month ahead to have a selection. For a €3-6 fee, **tourist offices** will find you a room in a hostel, pension, or hotel. Be prepared to pay at least €30 for a single and €50 for a double. Some tourist offices also have the pamphlet *Hotels und Pensionen*, listing accommodations across the price spectrum.

For longer stays, **Mitwohnzentrale** (home share companies) find rooms in *Wohngemeinschäfte* ("WGs," shared apartments). Leases typically require a passport and payment up front for those without a German bank account. Rooms start at €250 per month. Private apartments run at least €350 per month. *Mitwohnzentralen* charge commission on the monthly rent; the longer the stay, the lower the percentage. **Home Company Mitwohnzentrale,** Bundesallee 39-40A, is the biggest. Commission is 25% for stays up to one month. (U7 to "Berlinerstr." ☎030 194 45; www.berlin.homecompany.de. Open M-Th 9am-6pm, F 9am-5pm, Sa 10am-1pm.) Located in Mitte, **City-Wohnen,** Linienstr. 111, has pictures of the rooms it rents. Commission starts at 25%. (S1 to "Oranienburgerstr." ☎030 194

30; www.city-wohnen.de. Open M-F 10am-6pm, Sa 10am-3pm.) **Erste,** Sybelstr. 53, charges 29% commission, but adds a personal touch. (U7 to "Adenauerpl." ☎030 324 3031; www.mitwohn.com. Open M-F 9am-7pm, Sa 10am-3pm.) **Fine+Mine,** Neue Schönhauser Str. 20, is in the Hackescher Markt. (☎235 51 20; www.fineandmine.de. Open M-F 9am-7pm, Sa 10am-6pm.)

Another long-term option is to live in a **Wohnheim** (residential hostel). **Studentenwerk** (www.studentenwerk-berlin.de) manages over 40 of these apartments, limited to students studying in Berlin. For long-term stays like internships, **Wohnheim Berlin Junge Politik** in Charlottenburg offers single rooms from €180 per month and apartments from €230 (www.wohnheim-berlin.de).

HOSTELS AND DORMITORIES

HI hostels in Berlin are state-owned and usually clean, reliable, and filled with German school groups. Some impose a curfew or require an access code for late entry. Most require a membership card and charge an extra €3 per night without one. Purchase an **HI membership card** at any HI hostel. For a more party-ready crew, crash at a **private hostel,** popular among international travelers. These epicenters for the hip are often located near train stations and nightlife areas and have a turnover rate of two days—you'll never be bored.

PENSIONS

Pensions are generally smaller and shabbier than hotels, but way cheaper. Most are also amenable to *Mehrbettzimmer*, where extra beds are moved into a large double or triple. Most affordable hotels are in western Berlin, though inexpensive options are beginning to appear in the east, notably around Mitte's **Oranienburger Strasse** Find cheap rooms is Charlottenburg, especially around **Savignyplatz** and **Wilmersdorfer Strasse.**

CAMPING

Deutscher Camping-Club runs campgrounds in Wannsee, Spandau, and Köpenick. Reservations are recommended; write to Deutscher Camping-Club Berlin, Geisbergstr. 11, 10777 Berlin, or call in advance. (☎030 218 6071; www.dccberlin.de. Sites charge €5.60 per person, €2.50 per child, €4 per tent.) One convenient campground is **Kladow 1 ❶,** Krampnitzer Weg 111-117 (☎030 365 2797). Take U7 to "Rathaus Spandau," then bus #135 (dir.: Alt-Kladow) to the end. Switch to bus #234 to "Krampnitzer Weg/Selbitzerstr.," then follow Krampnitzer Weg 500m. This far-off suburban locale rewards with a store, restaurant, and swimmable lake. (Open year-round. €5.60 per person. Cash only.)

CHARLOTTENBURG

Hotels and hostels tend to be quieter and slightly more upscale here than in other parts of the city. While central locations listed below may be in the center of Charlottenburg, Zoologischer Garten is a solid 20min. Ubahn ride away from the tourist stretch along Unter den Linden.

Berolina Backpacker, Stuttgarter Pl. 17 (☎030 32 70 90 72; www.berolinabackpacker.de). S3, S5, S7, S9, or S75 to "Charlottenburg." This quiet hostel with an ivy-laced facade keeps things elegant with print art in the bunk-free dorms and daisies on the breakfast table. Surrounding cafes and proximity to the S-Bahn make up for its distance from the rush of the city. Communal and private kitchens (communal €1 per day, private €9.50) available for use. Breakfast buffet €7; "backpackers' breakfast" (a roll with cheese and coffee) €3.50. Internet €0.50 per 15min. Reception 24hr. Check-out 11am.

Charlottenburg and Schöneberg

ACCOMMODATIONS

A&O Hostel, **34**
Art Hotel Connection, **25**
Berolina Backpacker, **10**
CVJM-Haus, **21**
Frauenhotel Artemisia, **18**
JetPAK, **23**
Jugendhotel Berlincity, **42**
Meininger City Hostel, **36**

BARS & NIGHTLIFE

Connection, **24**
Hafen, **28**
Heile Welt, **26**
Neue Ufer, **41**
Quasimodo, **49**
Salz, **37**
Slumberland, **31**
Trane, **48**

FOOD & DRINK

Am Nil, **44**
Baharat Falafel, **32**
Bar Tolucci, **38**
Cafe Berio, **30**
Cafe Einstein, **20**
Cafe Bilderbuch, **43**
Die Feinbeckerei, **40**
Kuchi, **45**
Mensa TU, **47**
Paris Bar, **39**
Schwarzes Cafe, **29**
Seidles Gotenstraße, **46**
Vegetables and Fish, **33**

SIGHTS

Aquarium, **15**
Elefantententor, **14**
Gay Memorial, **27**
Kaiser-Wilhelm-Gedächtiskirche, **13**
Olympia-Stadion, **35**
Schloss Charlottenburg, **9**
Siegessäule, **5**

MUSEUMS

Akademie der Künste, **3**
Bauhaus-Archiv, **16**
Bröhanmuseum, **1**
Brücke Museum, **22**
Erotik Museum, **12**
Gemäldegalerie, **8**
Käthe-Kollwitz Museum, **19**
Kunstgewerbemuseum, **7**
Neue Nationalgalerie, **17**
Museum Berggruen, **2**
Museum Für Fotografie, **6**
Schloß Bellevue, **4**

5-bed dorms €10-13.50; singles €29.50-35.50; doubles €37-47; triples €39-64; quads €46-60. AmEx/MC/V. ❶

Frauenhotel Artemisia, Brandenburgische Str. 18 (☎030 873 89 05; www.frauenhotel-berlin.de). U7 to "Konstanzer Str." Pricey but rare—an elegant hotel for women only, the 1st of its kind in Germany. Outdoor terrace provides a sweeping view of Berlin. Named after Italian painter Artemisia Gentileschi, the hotel hosts rotating art exhibitions. Phone and TV by request. Breakfast buffet €7. Free Wi-Fi. Reception 7am-9:30pm. Singles €49-54, with bath €64-79; doubles €78/78-108. Additional beds €20. Ages 3-8 €10 per night, under 3 one-time €10 fee. Discounts for longer stays. AmEx/MC/V. ❺

A&O Hostel, Joachimstaler Str. 1-3 (☎030 809 47 53 00; www.aohostels.com), 30m from Bahnhof Zoo. Reliable dorms right on Zoo. Lobby, bar, and rooftop terrace stay packed at night. Private rooms include linens, bath, and breakfast. Breakfast buffet €6. Linens €3. Internet €5 per day. Bike rental €12 1st day, less each additional day. Reception 24hr. 8- to 10-bed dorms from €8; smaller dorms from €10.50; singles from €25; doubles from €30. Prices fluctuate with season and availability. Branches in Mitte and Friedrichshain. MC/V. ❶

SCHÖNEBERG AND WILMERSDORF

Jugendhotel Berlincity, Crellestr. 22 (☎030 7870 2130; www.jugendhotel-berlin.de). U7 to "Kleistpark" or "Yorckstr." The high ceilings and enormous windows in this former factory provide guests with spacious, airy rooms. Funky light fixtures shaped like fried eggs illuminate the hallways, which are lined with dark hard wood. Request a room with a view of the TV tower. Breakfast and linens included. Wi-Fi €1 per 20min., €5 per day. Reception 24hr. Singles €38, with bath €52; doubles €60/79; triples €87/102; quads €112/126; quints €124/150; 6-person room €146/168. MC/V. ❺

JetPAK, Pücklerstr. 54, Dahlem (☎030 8325 011; www.jetpak.de). U3 to "Fehrbelliner Pl." or U9 to "Güntzelstr.," then bus #115 (dir.: Neuruppiner Str.) to "Pücklerstr." Follow sign to Grunewald and turn left on Pücklerstr. Turn left again when the JetPAK sign directs you at the edge of the forest. Hidden in an old *Wehrmacht* military complex in the Grunewald forest, this casual hostel has a summer-camp feel that belies its history and makes up for the distance. Ping-pong table and basketball hoop outside. Common

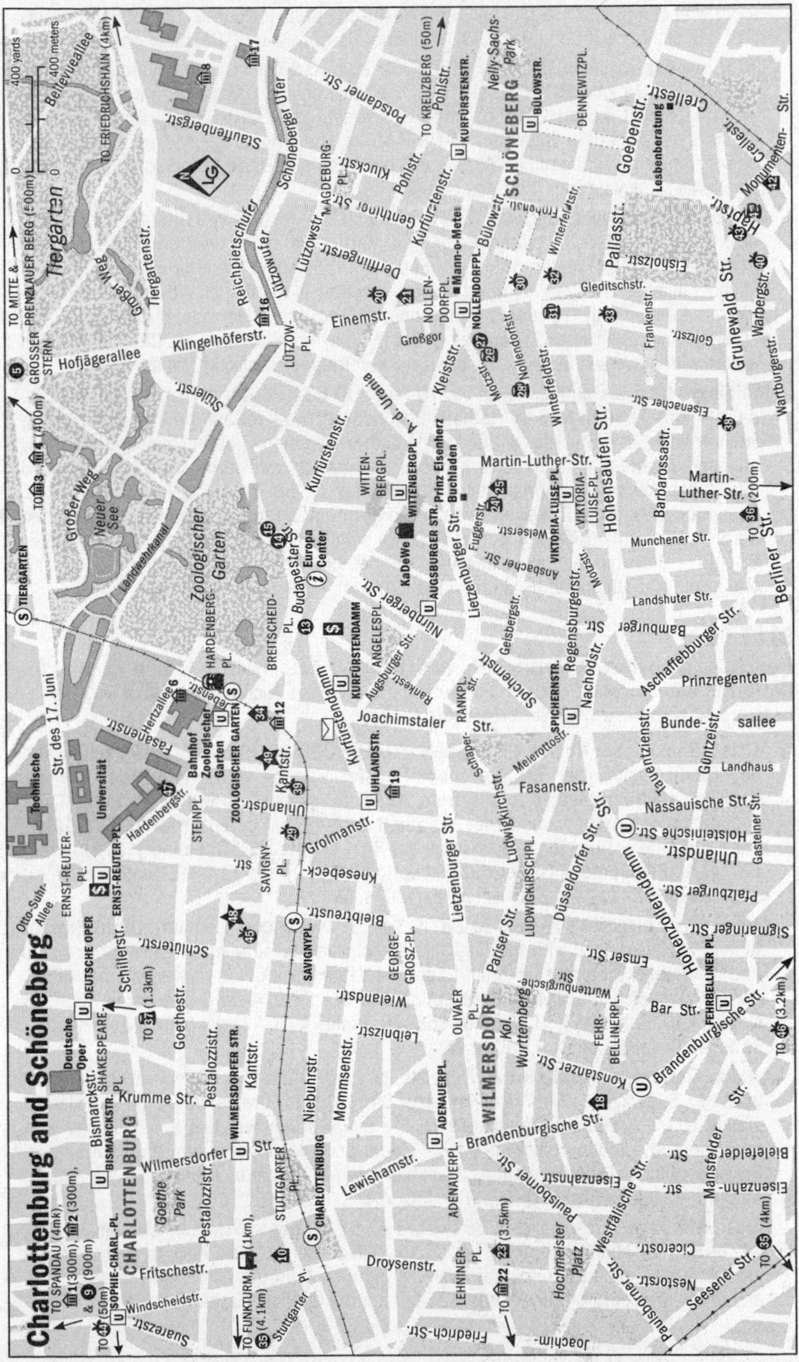

Charlottenburg and Schöneberg
CHARLOTTENBURG
SCHÖNEBERG
WILMERSDORF
Tiergarten
Zoologischer Garten
Neuer See
Landwehrkanal
Großer Weg
Hofjägerallee
Klingelhöferstr.
Stülerstr.
Tiergartenstr.
Stauffenbergstr.
Reichpietschufer
Schöneberger Ufer
Lützowufer
Potsdamer Str.
Kurfürstenstr.
Kurfürstendamm
Budapester Str.
Europa Center
Joachimstaler Str.
Kantstr.
Hardenbergstr.
Str. des 17. Juni
Bismarckstr.
Kaiserdamm
Wilmersdorfer Str.
Lewishamstr.
Brandenburgische Str.
Hohenzollerndamm
Uhlandstr.
Nürnberger Str.
Lietzenburger Str.
Martin-Luther-Str.
Hohenstaufen Str.
Grunewald Str.
Hauptstr.
Goebenstr.
Pallasstr.
Bülowstr.
Kleiststr.
Motzstr.
Nollendorfstr.
Winterfeldtstr.
Bundesallee
Prinzregenten Str.
Aschaffenburger Str.
Bamberger Str.
Landshuter Str.
Regensburger Str.
Nachodstr.
Düsseldorfer Str.
Pariser Str.
Ludwigkirchstr.
Fasanenstr.
Berliner Str.
Westfälische Str.
Konstanzer Str.
Paulsborner Str.
Seesener Str.
Joachim-Friedrich-Str.
Droysenstr.
Suarezstr.
Windscheidstr.
Fritschestr.
Pestalozzistr.
Goethestr.
Schillerstr.
Schlüterstr.
Bleibtreustr.
Knesebeckstr.
Grolmanstr.
Wielandstr.
Leibnizstr.
Mommsenstr.
Niebuhrstr.
Goethe Park
Hochmeister Platz
Technische Universität
Deutsche Oper
Bahnhof Zoologischer Garten
KaDeWe
Prinz Eisenherz Buchladen
Mann-o-Meter
Lesbenberatung
Nelly-Sachs-Park
TO MITTE & PRENZLAUER BERG (1500m)
TO FRIEDRICHSHAIN (4km)
TO KREUZBERG (50m)
TO SPANDAU (4km)
TO FUNKTURM (1km)
400 yards
400 meters

BERLIN

room with computers and foosball. Breakfast and linens included. Free internet. Dorms €14-18; singles €30; doubles €50. Additional €1 charge on F-Sa. Cash only. ❷

CVJM Jugendgastehaus, Einemstr. 10 (☎030 264 10 88; www.cvjm-jugendgaestehaus.de). U1, U2, U4, or U15 to "Nollendorfpl." An inexpensive, basic alternative to a dorm. Breakfast buffet included and packed lunch available (€3.20-€3.50). Linens €4, free for stays of over 3 days. Reception M-F 8am-5pm. Quiet hours 11pm-7am. Reserve well ahead. Singles €37; doubles €45; 4- to 6-bed rooms €23.50 per person. €3 per night surcharge for guests over 27. Cash only. ❸

Art-Hotel Connection, Fuggerstr. 33 (☎030 210 21 88 00; www.arthotel-connection.de). U1, U2, or U15 to "Wittenbergpl.," off Martin-Luther-Str. Located above the club Connection (p. 124) on the 3rd fl. of an apartment building. The airbrushed imitation of Michaelangelo's *The Creation of Adam* on the ceiling is the first clue that this establishment is for men only. 17 rooms with phone, TV, and bath. "Playrooms" have slings and other sex toys. Singles €59; doubles €79-110; playrooms €103-130. Cheaper M-Th, in winter, with advanced booking, or for stays over 3 nights. AmEx/MC/V. ❺

Meininger City Hostel, Meininger Str. 10 (☎0800 634 64 64; www.meininger-hostels.de). U4, bus #146 or N46 to "Rathaus Schöneberg." Walk toward the Rathaus tower on Freiherr-vom-Stein-Str., turn left on Martin-Luther-Str., then right on Meininger Str. Lively atmosphere and superb value in a hostel that has its own terrace, beer garden, and pool table. All-female dorms available. Breakfast €3.50. Linens included. Free Wi-Fi. Reception 24hr. Door locked at midnight; ring to enter. Book in advance. 5- to 6- bed dorms €18-26; 4- to 6- bed dorms €20-36; singles €49-69; doubles €66-98; triples €81-117. Branches at Hallesches Ufer, Tempelhofer Ufer, Senefelderplatz and a new one at the Hauptbahnhof (main train station) with same rates. MC/V. ❸

MITTE

For those who stay in Berlin only one night, it makes sense to find accommodation in sightseeing central. Those here longer or looking to party would do better in Kreuzberg or Friedrichshain.

Mitte's Backpacker Hostel, Chausseestr. 102 (☎030 28 39 09 65; www.backpacker.de). U6 to "Zinnowitzer Str." The apex of hostel hipness, with a gregarious English-speaking staff and themed rooms, from "Aztec" to "skyline" (of Berlin, of course). The social common room is lined with antique theater sets. A pickup spot for Terry Brewer's Tours and Insider Tours bike tours (p. 84). Sheets €2.50. Laundry €7. Internet €3 per hr. Bike rental €10 per day. Reception 24hr. Dorms €14-19; singles €30-34; doubles €48-54; quads €80-84. AmEx/MC/V. ❷

Circus, Weinbergersweg 1A (☎030 28 39 14 33; www.circus-berlin.de). U8 to "Rosenthaler Platz." Designed with the English-speaking traveler in mind. Nightly happy hours and W karaoke. Breakfast €2-5 until 1pm. Free laundry. Wi-Fi in rooms; internet €0.05 per min. Wheelchair-accessible. Reception and bar 24hr. 4- to 8-bed dorms €19-23; singles €40, with bath €50; doubles €56/70; triples €75. A larger branch at Rosenthaler Pl. on Rosenthaler Str. 1. MC/V. ❷

BaxPax Downtown Hostel/Hotel, Ziegelstr. 28 (☎030 251 52 02; www.baxpax-downtown.de). S1, S2, or S25 to "Oranienburger Str." or U6 to "Oranienbuger Tor." The sleeker sibling of the Kreuzberg branch has all the usual amenities plus a bar/lounge with fireplace and a rooftop bar with a huge kiddie pool. All-female dorm rooms available. Breakfast €5.50. Laundry facilities available. Internet €3 per hr. Dorms €13-17; singles €29-45; doubles €60-65; triples €70. MC/V. ❷

Three Little Pigs, Stresemannstr. 66 (☎030 32 66 29 55; www.three-little-pigs.de). S1, S2, or S25 to "Anhalter Bahnhof" or U2 to "Potsdamer Pl." Next door to a church and itself a former nunnery, this quiet hostel is minutes from the glitzy Potsdamer Pl. Free city tours. Breakfast €4.50. Linens €2.50. Laundry service €5. Internet €1 per 30min.

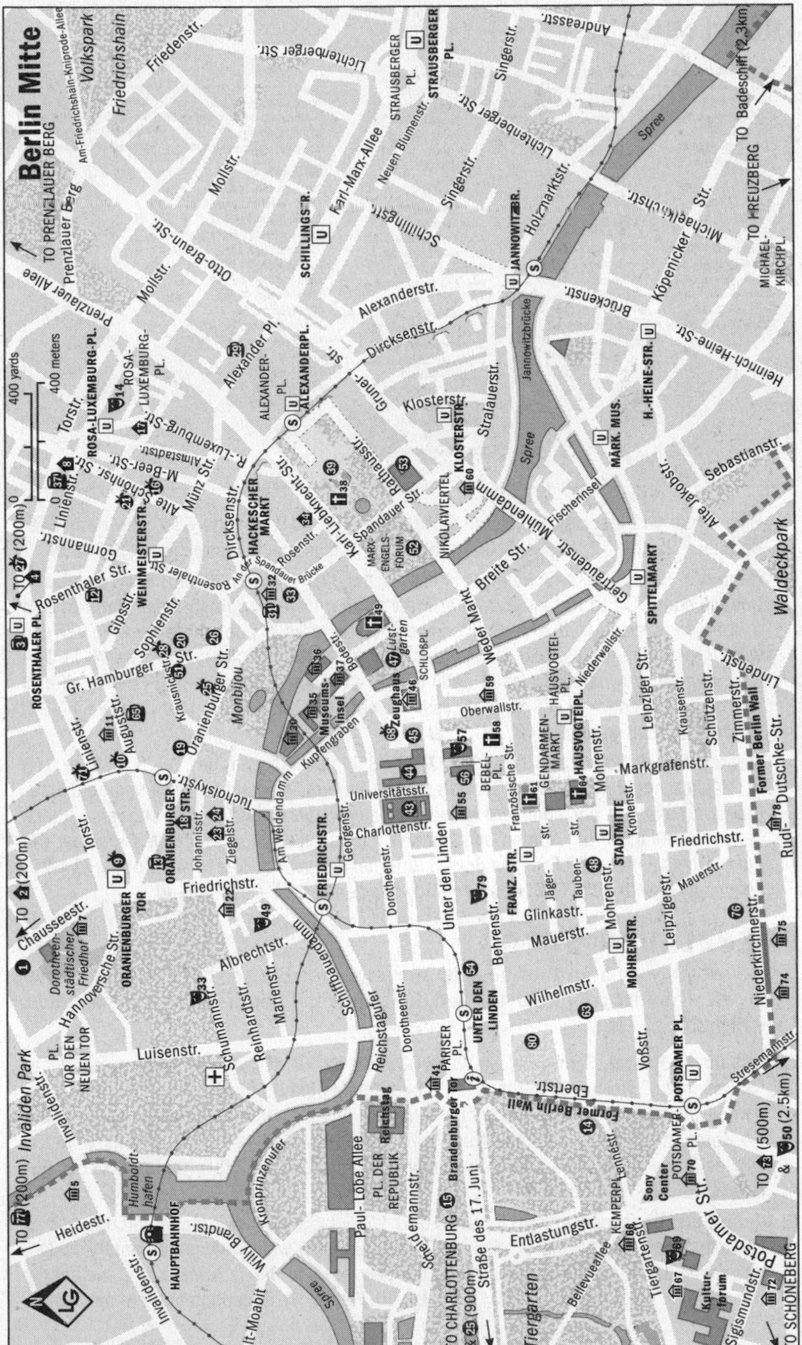
Berlin Mitte
TO PRENZLAUER BERG
Prenzlauer Berg
Prenzlauer Allee
Friedrichshain
Volkspark
Am-Friedrichshain-Kniprode-Allee
Friedenstr.
Mollstr.
Otto-Braun-Str.
Lichtenberger Str.
STRAUSBERGER PL.
Karl-Marx-Allee
Neuen Blumenstr.
Singerstr.
Schillingstr.
SCHILLINGSTR.
Alexanderstr.
ALEXANDERPL.
Alexander Pl.
Grunerstr.
Dircksenstr.
Klosterstr.
KLOSTERSTR.
Stralauerstr.
Spree
Jannowitzbrücke
JANNOWITZBR.
Holzmarktstr.
Brückenstr.
Köpenicker Str.
Michaelkirchstr.
MICHAEL-KIRCHPL.
TO KREUZBERG
TO Badeschiff (2.3km)
Heinrich-Heine-Str.
H.-HEINE-STR.
MÄRK. MUS.
Sebastianstr.
Alte Jakobstr.
Waldeckpark
Lindenstr.
SPITTELMARKT
Gertraudenstr.
Fischerinsel
Mühlendamm
NIKOLAIVIERTEL
Rathausstr.
Spandauer Str.
MARX-ENGELS-FORUM
Karl-Liebknecht-Str.
HACKESCHER MARKT
Rosenstr.
An der Spandauer Brücke
Rosenthaler Str.
Gormannstr.
WEINMEISTERSTR.
Alte Schönhauser Str.
Münz Str.
M.-Beer-Str.
Almstadtstr.
R.-Luxemburg-Str.
ROSA-LUXEMBURG-PL.
Torstr.
Linienstr.
400 yards
400 meters
ROSENTHALER PL.
Gipsstr.
Sophienstr.
Gr. Hamburger Str.
Krausnickstr.
Auguststr.
Oranienburger Str.
Monbijou
Museumsinsel
Lustgarten
Bodestr.
Zeughaus
SCHLOSSPL.
Breite Str.
Werder Markt
Oberwallstr.
Niederwallstr.
HAUSVOGTEIPL.
GENDARMENMARKT
Leipziger Str.
Krausenstr.
Schützenstr.
Zimmerstr.
Former Berlin Wall
Rudi-Dutschke-Str.
Markgrafenstr.
Mohrenstr.
Französische Str.
BEBELPL.
Kupfergraben
Universitätsstr.
Charlottenstr.
Tucholskystr.
ORANIENBURGER STR.
Johannisstr.
Ziegelstr.
Am Weidendamm
FRIEDRICHSTR.
Georgenstr.
Dorotheenstr.
Unter den Linden
FRANZ. STR.
Jägerstr.
Taubenstr.
STADTMITTE
Kronenstr.
Friedrichstr.
Mauerstr.
Glinkastr.
Behrenstr.
MOHRENSTR.
Wilhelmstr.
Niederkirchnerstr.
Voßstr.
POTSDAMER PL.
Stresemannstr.
Chausseestr.
Dorotheenstädtischer Friedhof
ORANIENBURGER TOR
Hannoversche Str.
Albrechtstr.
Schumannstr.
Reinhardtstr.
Marienstr.
Schiffbauerdamm
Reichstagufer
UNTER DEN LINDEN
PARISER PL.
Brandenburger Tor
Ebertstr.
Luisenstr.
VOR DEN NEUEN TOR PL.
Invalidenstr.
Invaliden Park
Heidestr.
Humboldthafen
HAUPTBAHNHOF
Willy Brandtstr.
Kronprinzenufer
Reichstag
PL. DER REPUBLIK
Paul-Löbe Allee
Scheidemannstr.
Alt-Moabit
TO CHARLOTTENBURG
Straße des 17. Juni
Entlastungstr.
Tiergarten
Bellevueallee
Tiergartenstr.
KEMPERPL.
Lennéstr.
Sony Center
POTSDAMER PL.
Potsdamer Str.
Kulturforum
Sigismundstr.
TO SCHÖNEBERG

BERLIN

Berlin Mitte

ACCOMMODATIONS
BaxPax Downtown Hostel, **24**
Circus, **4** & **17**
CityStay Hostel, **34**
Mitte's Backpacker Hostel, **2**
Three Little Pigs, **73**
Wombat's Hostel, **8**

FOOD & DRINK
Beth Cafe, **10**
Cafe Fleury, **27**
Dada Falafel, **9**
Maedchenitaliener, **21**
Monsieur Vuong, **21**
Schokogalerie, **28**
Schwarzwaldstuben, **71**
Sophien 11, **15**
Tadshickishe Teestube, **68**

BARS & NIGHTLIFE
Bang Bang Club, **31**
Clärchen's Ballhouse, **65**
Cookies, **42**
Delicious Doughnuts, **12**
Kaffee Burger, **37**
Tacheles, **13**
Tape, **20**
Week-End, **29**
CCCP, **3**

ENTERTAINMENT
Berliner Ensemble, **49**
Deutsche Staatsoper, **57**
Deutsches Theater, **33**
English Theater Berlin, **50**
Komische Oper, **45**
Konzerthaus, **62**
Philharmonie, **69**
Volksbühne, **14**

CHURCHES
Berliner Dom, **49**
Deutscher Dom, **64**
Französischer Dom, **61**
Marienkirche, **38**
St.-Hedwigs-Kathedrale, **58**

MUSEUMS
Alte Nationalgalerie, **36**
Altes Museum, **48**
Anne Frank Zentrum, **32**
Art Center Berlin, **22**
Bodemuseum, **30**
Deutsche Guggenheim Berlin, **55**
Deutsches Hist. Museum, **46**
Filmmuseum Berlin, **70**
Gemäldegalerie, **67**
Hamburger Bahnhof, **5**
Hanfmuseum, **60**
Haus am Checkpoint Charlie, **23**
Kunst-Werke Berlin, **11**
Martin-Gropius-Bau, **74**
Neue Nationalgalerie, **72**
Neuer Berliner Kunstverein, **7**
Pergamonmuseum, **35**
Musikinstrumenten Museum, **66**
Schinkelmuseum, **59**
Topographie des Terrors, **75**

SIGHTS
Alte Bibliothek, **56**
Alter-Jüdischer Friedhof, **26**
Bertolt-Brecht-Haus, **1**
Denkam Für Die Ermordeten Juden Europas, **18**
Fernsehturm, **39**
Französischer Dom, **48**
Führerbunker, **63**
Gay Memorial, **15**
Hi-Flyer Balloon, **76**
Humboldt-Universität, **44**
Lustgarten, **47**
Marx-Engels-Forum, **52**
Missing House, **51**
Neue Synagoge, **19**
Russian Embassy, **54**
Siegessäule, **25**
Sowjetisches Ehrenmal, **15**
Staatsbibliothek zu Berlin, **43**
The Kennedys Museum, **41**

Bike rental €12 per day. Reception 24hr. Dorms €13-16; singles €35, with bath €45; doubles €22-23/32; triples €20; quads €18. €1 discount in winter. AmEx/MC/V. ❷

Wombat's Hostel, Alte Schönhauser Str. 2 (☎030 84 71 08 20; www.wombats-hostels.com). U2 to Rosa-Luxemburg-Platz. With an eye-poppingly bright interior and a space-age exterior, this year-old newcomer features a pool table, rooftop terrace with a view of the TV tower, a cheap breakfast buffet (€3.50), and free Wi-Fi. The chic womBar downstairs is open daily 6pm-2am. Happy hour 6-8pm. Free drink and city map with check-in. Kitchen access. Reception 24hr. 4- to 6-bed dorms €17-21, 2-bed €25-29; doubles €40. MC/V. ❷

CityStay Hostel, Rosenstr. 16 (☎030 23 62 40 31; www.citystay.de). S5, S7, S9, or S75 to "Hackescher Markt" or U2, U5, or U8 to "Alexanderpl." A social hostel with ample amenities—an all-night bar, courtyard barbecues, clean dorms, and private showers—smack in the middle of Berlin. Women-only dorms on request. Kitchen available. Breakfast €4. Free lockers. Linens €2.50. Laundry €5. Internet €3 per hr.; free Wi-Fi. Dorms €14-20; singles €40, with bath €55; doubles €50/64; quads €84. Cash only. ❷

BERLIN

PRENZLAUER BERG

There are only a handful of hostels in Prenzlauer Berg, where students have been priced out by yuppies in the bed department, if not in the beer department (see **Nightlife**, p. 126).

East Seven Hostel, Schwedter Str. 7 (☎030 93 62 22 40; www.eastseven.de). U2 to "Senefelderpl." No bunks in the well-lit, beautifully painted dorms. The grill area in the garden out back is friendly and social. Kitchen available. Linens €3. Towels €1. Laundry €4. Internet €0.50 per 20min; free Wi-Fi. Reception 7am-midnight. Dorms €13-17; singles in low-season €30, in high season €37; doubles €42/50; triples €52.50/63; quads €66/76. Cash only. ❷

Pfefferbett, Christinenstraße 18-19 (☎030 93 93 58 58; www.pfefferbett.de). U2 to "Senefelderpl." Juxtaposing its original 19th-century brick walls with contemporary design, this hostel has a roof deck and some of the best deals in Berlin. Named after the nearby beer garden. Breakfast buffet €4. Linens €2.50. Free Wi-Fi. Reception and bar open 24hr.

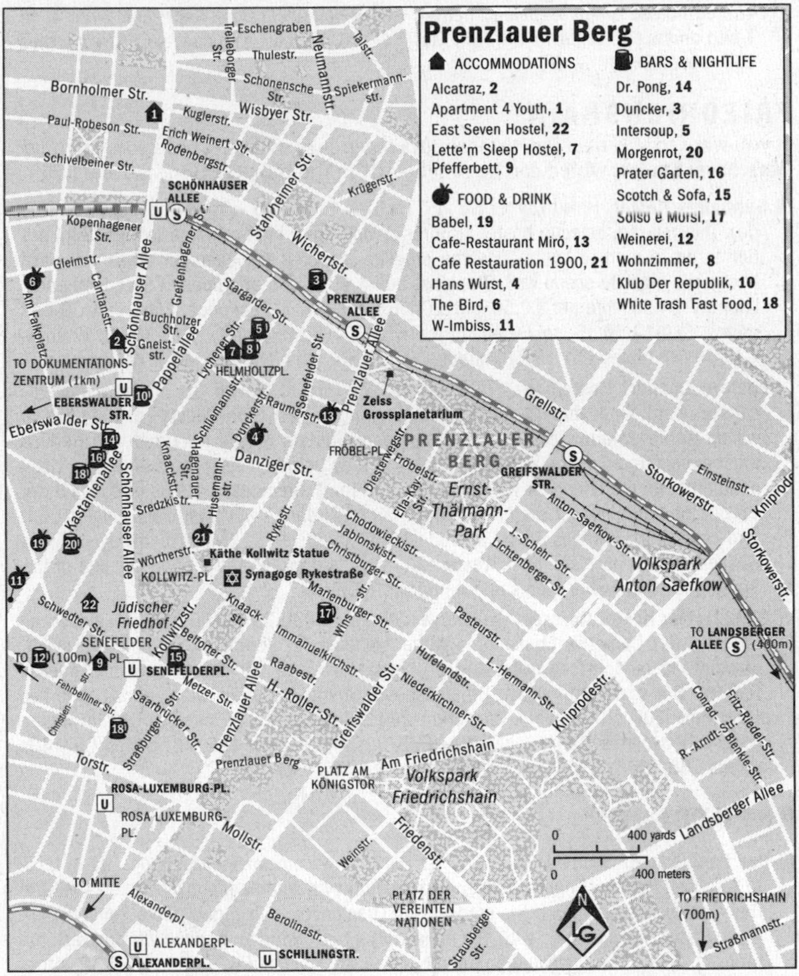

6- to 8-bed dorms with shared bath from €12; 4- to 6-bed dorms with private bath from €17.50. Doubles with private bath, TV, and telephone €27. Cash only. ❶

Alcatraz, Schönhauser Allee 133A (☎030 48 49 68 15; www.alcatraz-backpacker.de). U2 to "Eberswalder Str." Tucked away in a spray-painted courtyard. 80 beds in small but carefully decorated rooms. The "chill out room" is quite the hangout after dark. Kitchen facilities. Linens €2. Free internet and Wi-Fi. Bike rental €5. Reception 24hr. 8-bed dorms in summer €16, in winter €13; singles €40/30; doubles €50/42; triples €66/54; quads €72/60. 5% discount per night with ISIC Card. MC/V. ❷

Lette'm Sleep Hostel, Lettestr. 7 (☎030 44 73 36 23; www.backpackers.de). U2 to "Eberswalder Str." If it weren't for the bright paint job, you could mistake the hostel for one of the cafes and bars lining Helmholtzpl., one of the neighborhood's most lively areas. The big kitchen, complete with comfy red couches, is the social nexus of this

48-bed hostel. Linens €2. Free internet. Wheelchair-accessible. Reception 24hr. 4- to 7-bed dorms Apr.-Oct. €17-23, Nov.-Mar. €11-20; doubles with sheets €55/40; triples €68/60. AmEx/MC/V. ❷

FRIEDRICHSHAIN

If you want to stay near Friedrichshain's legendary nightlife, base yourself near **Warschauer Strasse,** which can be reached from the U15, S3, S5-7, S9, and S75.

Sunflower Hostel, Helsingforser Str. 17 (☎030 44 04 42 50; www.sunflower-hostel.de). This relaxed, eclectic hostel features a vine-hung bright orange lounge. Spotless dorms are a marked contrast to the studied chaos of the common areas. The staff knows the nightlife scene well. Breakfast buffet €3. Locks and linens €3 deposit each. Laundry €4.50. Internet €0.50 per 10min.; free Wi-Fi. Reception 24hr. 7- to 8-bed dorms €10-14.50; 5- to 6-bed dorms €12.50-16.50; singles €30-36.50; doubles €38-46.50; triples €51-61.50; quads €60-79.50. 7th night free. MC/V. ❶

Eastern Comfort Hostelboat, Mühlenstr. 73-77 (☎030 66 76 38 06; www.eastern-comfort.com). Enter through the first opening in the East Side Gallery (p. 111). Those willing to brave narrow corridors and cramped quarters will be rewarded with Berlin's most adventurous hostel: a docked boat. The truly bold can sleep outside on the deck in summer for the cheapest view of the river in town. Breakfast €4. Linens €5. Laundry €5 per load. Internet €2 per hr. Tent/open-air €12; dorms €16; 1st-class singles €64, 2nd-class €50; doubles €78/58; triples €69; quads €76. 2-night bookings only on weekends. The new sister ship, Western Comfort, is docked on the opposite side of the Spree and rents pricier rooms and no dorms. MC/V. ❶

Globetrotter Hostel Odyssee, Grünberger Str. 23 (☎030 29 00 00 81; www.globetrotterhostel.de). Convenient base for nightlife "sightseeing." Rooms with psychedelic swirls of paint, an outdoor courtyard, and a pool table by the bar make this a backpacker favorite. Bar open until dawn. Breakfast €3. Sheets included with deposit. Internet €0.50 per 10min; free Wi-Fi. Reception 24hr. 8-bed dorms in summer €13, in winter €10; 6-bed dorms €15/12; doubles €45/39, with shower €52/46; triples €57/48; quads €68/56. 7th, 13th, and 14th nights free. MC/V. ❶

KREUZBERG

Bax Pax, Skalitzer Str. 104 (☎030 69 51 83 22; www.baxpax-kreuzberg.de). U1 or U15 to "Görlitzer Bahnhof," right across the street. Run by the same friendly people as Mitte's Backpacker Hostel. Around the corner from Oranienstr., with a pool table, roomy common spaces, walls painted with film reels, and a bed inside an antique VW Bug (ask for room 3). Kitchen facilities and an outdoor terrace. Breakfast €4.50. Linens €2.50. Internet €2 per 30min. Bike rental 1st day for €12, 2nd €10, additional days €5. Reception 24hr. Big dorms in high season €16, in low season €15; 7- to 8-bed dorms €17/15; 5- to 6-bed rooms €18/17; singles €31/30; doubles €48/46, with bath €60/56; triples €63/60; quads €76/72. AmEx/MC/V. ❷

Hostel X Berger, Schlesische Str. 22 (☎030 69 53 18 63; www.hostelxberger.com). U1 or U15 to "Schlesisches Tor," or night bus #N65 to "Taborstr." This social hostel is a good launching pad for the one Kreuzberg area that might be more fun at night than Oranienstr. The colorful graffiti outside is more exciting than the basic, roomy dorms. Female-only dorms available. Sheets €2, towel €1. Free internet. Reception 24hr. Dorms €11-15; singles €28-32; doubles €36-40; triples €36-38. Cash only. ❶

Berlin Boutique Hostel, Gneisenaustr. 109 (☎030 69 81 923). U6, U7, or night bus #N19 to "Mehringdamm." The name refers to pleasant details like chiffon curtains, plants, and beautiful pillows in the otherwise standard dorms. On the quieter side of

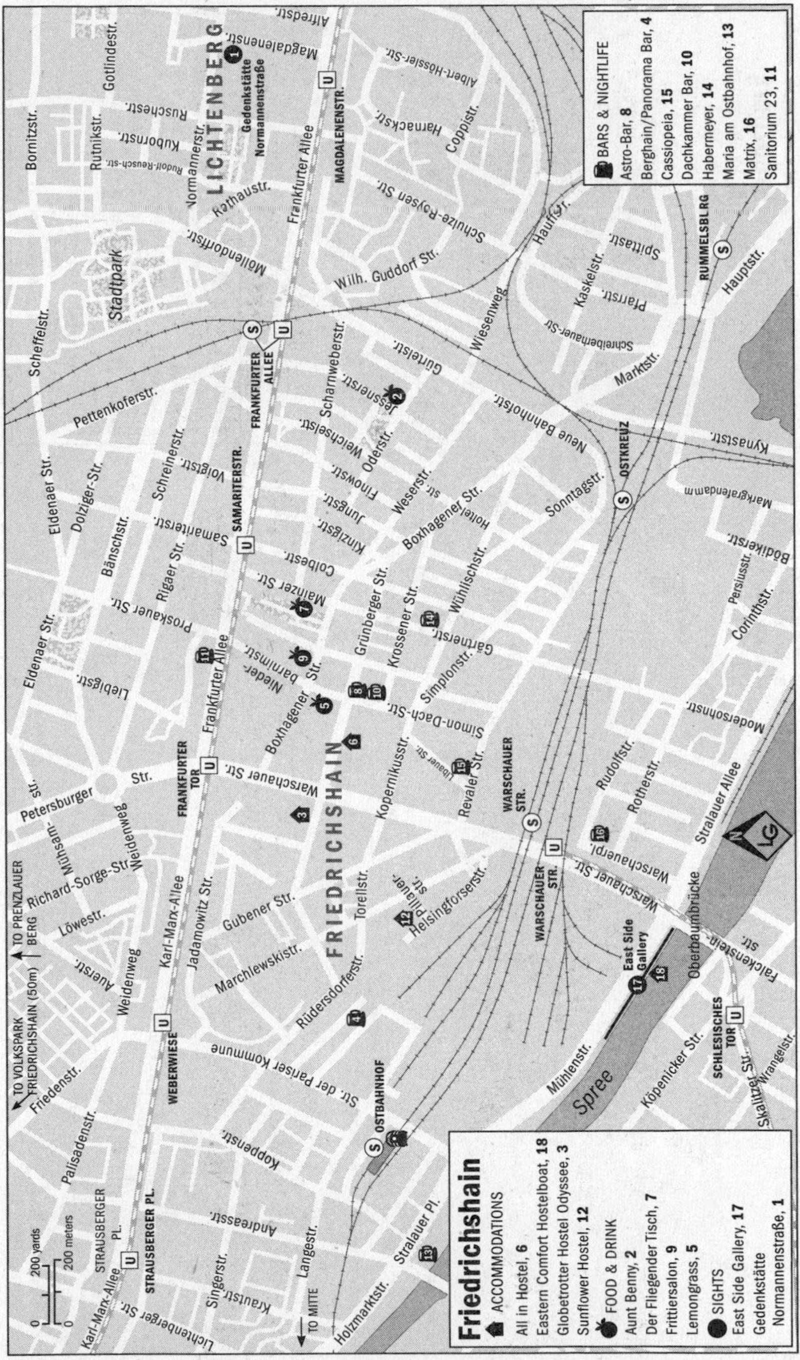
Friedrichshain
ACCOMMODATIONS
All in Hostel, 6
Eastern Comfort Hostelboat, 18
Globetrotter Hostel Odyssee, 3
Sunflower Hostel, 12
FOOD & DRINK
Aunt Benny, 2
Der Fliegender Tisch, 7
Frittiersalon, 9
Lemongrass, 5
SIGHTS
East Side Gallery, 17
Gedenkstätte Normannenstraße, 1
BARS & NIGHTLIFE
Astro-Bar, 8
Berghain/Panorama Bar, 4
Cassiopeia, 15
Dachkammer Bar, 10
Habermeyer, 14
Maria am Ostbahnhof, 13
Matrix, 16
Sanitorium 23, 11
FRIEDRICHSHAIN
LICHTENBERG
Stadtpark
Spree
East Side Gallery
TO VOLKSPARK FRIEDRICHSHAIN (50m)
TO PRENZLAUER BERG
TO MITTE
200 yards
200 meters
OSTBAHNHOF
WARSCHAUER STR.
OSTKREUZ
FRANKFURTER ALLEE
FRANKFURTER TOR
SAMARITERSTR.
WEBERWIESE
STRAUSBERGER PL.
SCHLESISCHES TOR
MAGDALENENSTR.
RUMMELSBURG
Karl-Marx-Allee
Frankfurter Allee
Warschauer Str.
Boxhagener Str.
Str. der Pariser Kommune
Stralauer Allee
Mühlenstr.
Köpenicker Str.
Revaler Str.
Simon-Dach-Str.
Petersburger Str.
Neue Bahnhofstr.

BERLIN

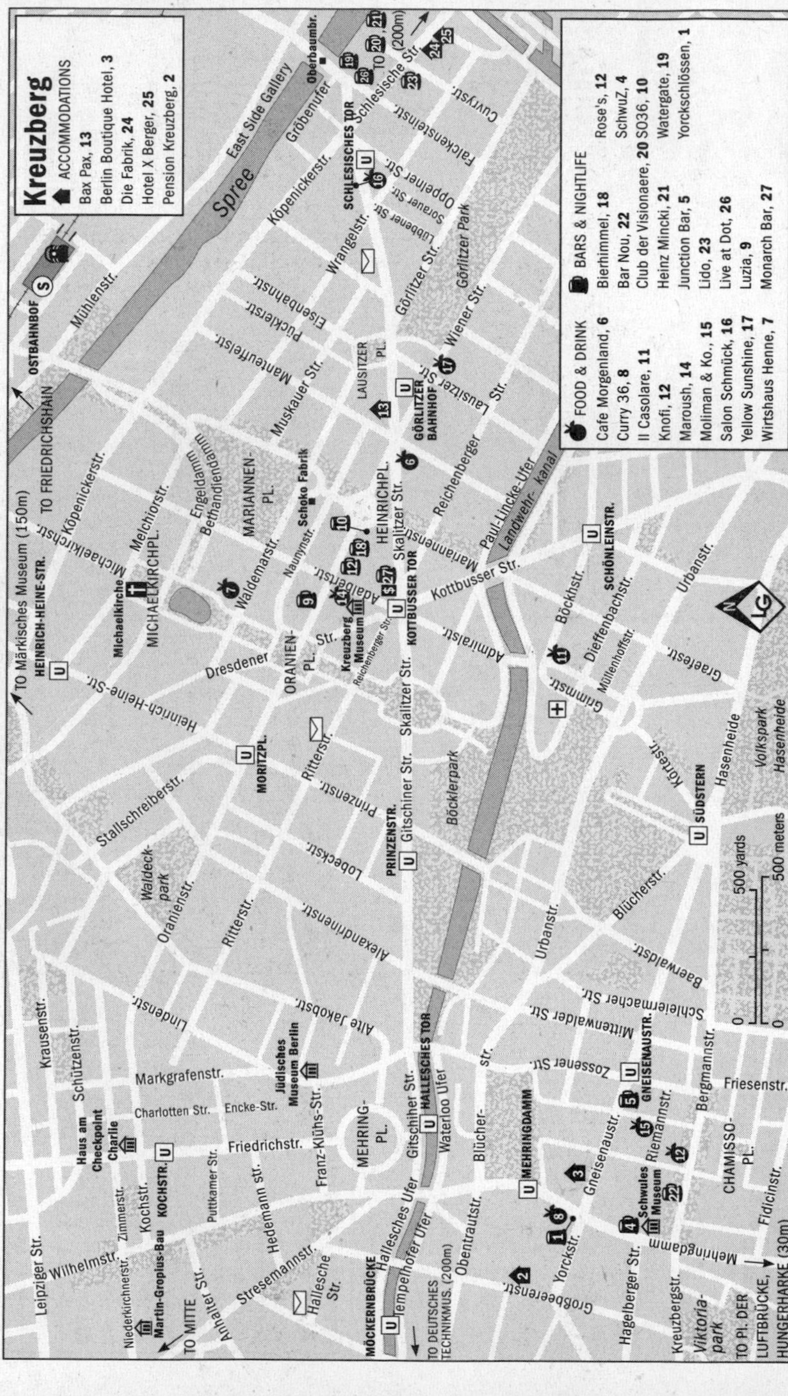
Kreuzberg
ACCOMMODATIONS
Bax Pax, 13
Berlin Boutique Hotel, 3
Die Fabrik, 24
Hotel X Berger, 25
Pension Kreuzberg, 2
FOOD & DRINK
Cafe Morgenland, 6
Curry 36, 8
Il Casolare, 11
Knofi, 12
Maroush, 14
Moliman & Ko., 15
Salon Schmück, 16
Yellow Sunshine, 17
Wirtshaus Henne, 7
BARS & NIGHTLIFE
Bierhimmel, 18
Bar Nou, 22
Club der Visionaere, 20
Heinz Minck, 21
Junction Bar, 5
Lido, 23
Live at Dot, 26
Luzia, 9
Monarch Bar, 27
Rose's, 12
SchwuZ, 4
SO36, 10
Watergate, 19
Yorckschlössen, 1
TO Märkisches Museum (150m)
TO FRIEDRICHSHAIN
OSTBAHNHOF
Spree
East Side Gallery
Mühlenstr.
Gröbenufer
Oberbaumbr.
Köpenickerstr.
SCHLESISCHES TOR
Schlesische Str.
TO (200m)
Falckensteinstr.
Cuvrystr.
Oppelner Str.
Sorauer Str.
Lübbener Str.
Görlitzer Park
Görlitzer Str.
Wiener Str.
Wrangelstr.
Eisenbahnstr.
Pücklerstr.
Manteuffelstr.
Muskauer Str.
LAUSITZER PL.
GÖRLITZER BAHNHOF
Lausitzer Str.
Reichenberger Str.
Paul-Lincke-Ufer
Landwehr- kanal
HEINRICH-HEINE-STR.
Michaelkirchstr.
Köpenickerstr.
Melchiorstr.
Engeldamm
Bethaniendamm
MARIANNEN- PL.
Schoko Fabrik
Michaelkirche
MICHAELKIRCHPL.
Waldemarstr.
Naunynstr.
HEINRICHPL.
Skalitzer Str.
Mariannenstr.
Adalbertstr.
Kreuzberg Museum
Reichenberger Str.
KOTTBUSSER TOR
Kottbusser Str.
SCHÖNLEINSTR.
Dresdener Str.
ORANIEN- PL.
Heinrich-Heine-Str.
Admiralstr.
Böckhstr.
Dieffenbachstr.
Müllenhoffstr.
Urbanstr.
Grimmstr.
Graefestr.
MORITZPL.
Ritterstr.
Prinzenstr.
Stallschreiberstr.
Skalitzer Str.
Gitschiner Str.
PRINZENSTR.
Böcklerpark
Körtestr.
SÜDSTERN
Hasenheide
Volkspark Hasenheide
Waldeck- park
Oranienstr.
Lobeckstr.
Alexandrinenstr.
Blücherstr.
Urbanstr.
Baerwaldstr.
500 yards
500 meters
Lindenstr.
Alte Jakobstr.
Schleiermacher Str.
Mittenwalder Str.
Krausenstr.
Schützenstr.
Markgrafenstr.
Jüdisches Museum Berlin
Zossener Str.
GNEISENAUSTR.
Bergmannstr.
Friesenstr.
Haus am Checkpoint Charlie
Charlotten Str.
Encke-Str.
HALLESCHES TOR
KOCHSTR.
Friedrichstr.
MEHRING- PL.
Gitschiner Str.
Waterloo Ufer
Blücher- str.
MEHRINGDAMM
Gneisenaustr.
Riemannstr.
CHAMISSO- PL.
Puttkamer Str.
Hedemann str.
Franz-Klühs-Str.
Leipziger Str.
Zimmerstr.
Kochstr.
Wilhelmstr.
Niederkirchnerstr.
Martin-Gropius-Bau
Hallesches Ufer
Tempelhofer Ufer
Obentrautstr.
Yorckstr.
Schwules Museum
Mehringdamm
Fidicinstr.
TO MITTE
Anhalter Str.
Stresemannstr.
Hallesche Str.
MÖCKERNBRÜCKE
TO DEUTSCHES TECHNIKMUS. (200m)
Großbeerenstr.
Hagelberger Str.
Kreuzbergstr.
Viktoria- park
TO PL. DER LUFTBRÜCKE, HUNGERHARKE (30m)

Kreuzberg. Continental breakfast and linens included. Free internet. 12- to 8-bed dorms €12-15; 4- to 5-bed dorms €14-16. AmEx/MC/V. ❷

Pension Kreuzberg, Großbeerenstr. 64 (☎030 251 1362; www.pension-kreuzberg.de). U6, U7, or night bus #N19 to "Mehringdamm." Elegant, old-fashioned staircases, a cheery yellow breakfast room, and antique iron stoves. The neighborhood is lively, even by Kreuzberg standards. Breakfast included. Reception 8am-9pm. 3- to 5-bed dorms €25, with bath €27; singles €42/60; doubles €58/69. AmEx/MC/V. ❸

Die Fabrik, Schlesische Str. 18 (☎030 611 7116; www.diefabrik.com), next to Hostel X Berger. U1 to "Schlesische Tor." S1, S5, S7, S9 to "Warschauerstr." Despite the party location, a slightly older, calmer clientele gathers at this former factory. Light-filled rooms, some with carpets, leather furniture, and oriental carpets. Breakfast €3.50-6.50. Internet €1 per 20min; free Wi-Fi. Reception 24hr. Dorms €18; singles €38; doubles €46-58; triples €60-78; quads €75-90. Cash only. ❷

OUTER DISTRICTS

TEGEL

Two hostels are north of the city, near the beautiful Tegeler See lake.

Backpacker's Paradise, Ziekowstr. 161 (☎030 433 86 40; www.backpackersparadise.de). Take the U6 to "Alt-Tegel," and then bus #222 or night bus #N22 (dir.: Alt-Lübars) to "Titusweg." Alternatively, take the S25 to "Tegel," take a right out of the station, and walk 20m to catch the #222. Nightly campfires, hot showers, and a free-spirited vibe in a little yard behind the Jugendgästehaus. Cheapest overnight stays in Berlin. Space is nearly always available, except when overrun by school groups. Breakfast buffet €2.50. Laundry €4. Free internet. Bike rental €4. Reception 24hr. Open May 15 to Sept. 1. €8.50 gets you a blanket and foam pad in a 20-person tent, €1 more buys a cot to put them on. Bring a sleeping bag. Cash only. ❶

Jugendgästehaus Tegel, Ziekowstr. 161 (☎030 433 30 46; www.jugendgaestehaus-tegel.de). A dignified red brick building with an institutional, boarding-school feel. Breakfast included. Linens €3. Free internet. Reception 7:30am-midnight. €20 per person. Under 27 only. Cash only. ❷

FOOD

Food in Berlin is less German than it is cosmopolitan. Besides a variety of tasty local options, terrific ethnic food abounds thanks to the Turkish, Indian, Italian, and Thai populations. There are, however, a number of traditional German restaurants; in early summer, expect an onslaught of the popular *Spargel* (asparagus). Fall is pumpkin season, and pumpkin soup is everywhere. Berlin's dearest culinary tradition, however, is breakfast, a gloriously civilized institution often served in cafes well into the afternoon. Relax over a leisurely *Milchkaffee*, a bowl of coffee foaming with milk.

Almost every street in Berlin has its own Turkish restaurant and *Imbiß* (snack bar). Most are open ridiculously late, some 24hr. The *döner kebap* (shaved roast lamb or chicken in a toasted flatbread and topped with vegetables and garlic sauce) has cornered the fast-food market, with falafel running a close second. Another budget option for travelers is to buy *belegte Brötchen*, or stuffed baguettes, at a local *Bäckerei* or *Konditorei* (€2.50-3.50). Quality Indian and Italian eateries are everywhere, and the city of course has its fair share of *Currywurst* and *Bratwurst*. **Aldi, Plus, Spar, Edeka,** and **Penny Markt** are the cheapest supermarket chains, followed by **Bolle, Reichelt,** and the ubiquitous **Kaisers.** Supermarkets are usually open M-F 9am-6pm and Sa 9am-4pm, though some are open as late as 8pm on weekdays. **Ullrich** at Bahnhof Zoo is open M-Sa 9am-10pm, Sa 11am-10pm. Bahnhof Zoo's open-air market fires up Saturday mornings on **Winterfeldtplatz,** and almost every neighborhood has its own market. For cheap veggies and huge wheels of *Fladenbrot* (pita bread), hit the kaleidoscopic **Turkish market** in Kreuzberg, along Maybachufer on the Landwehrkanal (U1 or U8 to "Kottbusser Tor." Open Tu and F 10am-6pm.)

CHARLOTTENBURG

Schwarzes Cafe, Kantstr. 148 (☎030 313 8038). S3, S5, S7, S9, or S75 to "Savignypl." The most popular boho cafe in the area for a reason: absinthe all night in the dimly lit, frescoed space, followed by delicious breakfast when the sun comes up. Weekly specials served 11:30am-8pm (€7-10). Breakfast always available (€5-8.50). Open 24hr., (except Tu 3am-11am). Cash only. ❸

Am Nil, Kaiserdamm 114 (☎30 321 44 06) U2 to "Sophie-Charlotte Platz." Recline on the Oriental carpets and enjoy platters of spiced Egyptian food (€7-14). Belly dancer F and Sa 9pm. Open Tu-Su 3pm-1am. Cash only. ❸

Kuchi, Kochstr. 30 (☎030 31 50 78 15). S5, S7, S9 or S75 to "Savignypl." A bit more pricey than the sushi *Imbisse,* but you can be sure you are eating real fish in this trendy little restaurant. Sushi rolls from €4. Hot Japanese entrees. Open M-Th noon-midnight, F-Su 12:30pm-1am. Cash only. ❷

Mensa TU, Hardenbergstr. 34 (☎030 939 39 7439). U2 to "Ernst-Reuter Pl.," bus #245 to "Steinpl.," a 10min. walk from Bahnhof Zoo. You'll find the cheapest hot meal around in this cafeteria. 3 entree choices as well as vegetarian options. Meals €2-4, students €2-3. Cafeteria downstairs has slightly higher prices. Open M-F 11am-2:30pm. Cafeteria open M-F 11am-3:30pm, coffee bar M-F 11am-6pm, and cake shop M-F 7:30am-2:30pm. Cash only. ❶

Paris Bar, Kantstrasse 152 (☎030 313 8052) U1 to "Uhlandstr." One of the most popular restaurants of the former West Berlin is still a gathering point for hot artists, popular politicians, uber-celebs who enjoy the bistro food, and students who can only afford the desserts. Entrees €10-25. Open daily noon-2am. AmEx/MC/V. ❺

SCHÖNEBERG AND WILMERSDORF

To experience Schöneberg's relaxed cafe culture look no farther than the intersection of **Maaßenstraße** and **Winterfeldstraße.**

Cafe Bilderbuch, Akazienstr. 28 (☎030 78 70 60 57; www.cafe-bilderbuch.de). U7 to "Eisenacher Str." Fringed lamps, oak bookcases, and velvety couches give this cafe the feel of a Venetian library. The tasty brunch baskets, served around the clock, reach their pinnacle in a sumptuous Sunday buffet (€8). Dinner specials €5-8.50. Open M-Th 9am-1am, F-Sa 9am-2am, Su 10am-1am. Kitchen open 9am-11pm. Cash only. ❷

Seidls Gotenstraße 1 (030 78 09 79 97; www.seidls-berlin.de). S1 to "Julius-Leber-Brücke." This airy, out-of-the-way restaurant with artwork and tablecloths is the best splurge in the area. Entrees €9-17. Open M-Sa noon-1am, Su 9-1am. Cash only. ❷

Baharat Falafel, Winterfeldtstr. 37 (☎030 216 8301). U1-U4 to "Nollendorfpl." This isn't your average *Döner* stand—it's all about falafel fried to order and a place to sit down. Get your choice of 3 or 5 chickpea balls in a fluffy pita with veggies and tahini mango, or chili sauce (€3/4). Plates €6-8, with hummus, tabouleh, and salad. Wash it down with fresh-squeezed *Gute Laune Saft* (good-mood juice; €1-2). Open M-Sa 11am-2am, Su noon-2am. MC/V. ❷

Cafe Berio, Maaßenstr. 7 (☎030 216 1946; www.cafe-berio.de). U1, U2, U4, or U15 to "Nollendorfpl." Always jam-packed with (mostly gay) locals, this 2-floor Viennese-style cafe tempts passersby off the street with its unbeatable breakfast menu (€3-11). The place to go before clubbing. Entrees €5-9. Happy hour mixed drinks 2-for-1 M-Th and Su 7pm-midnight and F-Sa 7-9pm. Open M-Th and Su 8am-midnight, F-Sa 8am-1am. Kitchen open daily 8am-11pm. Cash only. ❸

Cafe Einstein, Kurfurstenstr. 58 (☎030 261 5096; www.cafeeinstein.com). U1, U2, U3, or U4 to "Nollendorf Pl." An obligatory stop (yes, for the other tourists, too). Berlin's premier Viennese coffee shop will make you drool for the apple strudel and home-roasted coffee. Elegant wood-panneled interior and outdoor garden. Entrees €15-19. Open daily 8am-1am. The bar **Lebensstern** is open 7pm-1am, all mixed drinks €9. AmEx/MC/V. ❹

Bar Tolucci, Eisenacher Str. 86 (☎030 214 1607; www.bar-tolucci.de). U7 to "Eisenacher Str." This tastefully understated Tuscan restaurant pays homage to the Italian filmmaker Bertolluci by decorating the walls with images from his films. The small garden is a perfect place to enjoy a leisurely meal (entrees €6-9). Stone-oven pizza served 5pm-midnight (€4-8), just one option on the exhaustive menu. Open daily 10am-1am, garden 10am-midnight. MC/V. ❷

MITTE

Steer clear of the enormous tourist-trap restaurants along Oranienburger Str. The best bet for a moderately-priced sit-down meal is one of the small restaurants in the **Scheunenviertel,** p. 107.

Schwarzwaldstuben, Tucholskystr. 48, (☎030 28 09 80 84). S-Bahn to "Oranienburger Str." Fitted out like a rustic southern German restaurant with sofas between the tables and stuffed boar heads on the wall, this is the best place for a schnitzel and Rothaus beer, made in the only state brewery left in Germany. Reserve on weekends, or drop by during the day for a *Flammkuchen* (€4.50-8), a sort of German pizza, and to read by the light of the fringed lamps. Entrees €8-18. ❹

Tadshickische Teestube, Am Festungsgraben 1, (☎030 204 1112). S3, 5, 7, 9, or 75 to "Hackescher Markt." Dating back to the Soviet days, this Tajik teahouse is a hidden haven of oriental carpets, tea served in samovars (€2-6), and sour cream covered meat pierogi (€5). Take off your shoes before settling cross-legged onto the cushions around the low tables. Open M-F 5pm-midnight, Sa-Su 3pm-midnight. Cash only. ❷

Monsieur Vuong, Alte Schönhauser Str. 46 (☎030 99 29 69 24; www.monsieurvuong.de). U8 to "Weinmeisterstr." or U2 to "Rosa Luxembourg Pl." Gallerists, artists, and, yes, tourists (the word is out) perch on the red cube seats in this trendy, extremely popular Vietnamese restaurant. Fresh fruit drinks €3.40. Entrees €6-9. Open daily noon-midnight. Cash only. ❷

Cafe Fleury, Weinbergsweg 20 (☎030 044 03 41 44). U8 to Rosenthaler Platz. One Berlin-dweller imported some blue-and-white wallpaper, photographs, and knicknacks from her native France and turned her hobby into a job, opening this gorgeous cafe. Unbeatable croque monsieur and fresh soups and snacks. Entrees €5-6. Open M-F 8am-10pm, Sa-Su 10am-10pm. Cash only. ❷

Dada Falafel, Linienstr. 132 (☎030 27 59 69 27). U6 to "Oranienburger Tor." Located just off of Oranienburger Str. Lebanese *Imbiss.* Caters to executives during the day and clubgoers at night. Though seating in this cubbyhole is limited, take your meal next door to Dada's Galerie and eat while enjoying rotating art exhibitions and the occasional live music. Spicy falafel or beef shawarma sandwich (€3.50), platter (€4.50), vegetarian platter for 2 (€6.50). Open daily 10am-2am; F-Sa until 3am. Cash only. ❶

Beth Cafe, Tucholskystr. 40 (☎030 281 3135), just off Auguststr. S-Bahn to "Oranienburger Str." A favorite of the local Jewish community, Beth Cafe sports an "I Love Kosher" bumper sticker in its window and offers a menu with Hebrew translations. The restaurant serves quality classics like bagels with lox and cream cheese (€2.50). Other dishes €3-8. Open M-Th and Sa-Su 11am-6:30pm. AmEx/MC/V. ❷

Maedchenitaliener, Alte Schönhauser Str. 12. (☎030 40 04 17 87) U8 to "Weinmeisterstr.' or U2 to "Rosa Luxembourg Pl." It may not look like much, it may not even look like a restaurant given the lack of signage—but this is the best inexpensive Italian food in town. Settle in at your candlelit table and order ½-L of wine (€6-12) and one of the 3 dishes on the chalkboard menu. Pasta with fresh figs, fennel, and parmesan (€12), one of the few menu regulars, is always a good bet. Entrees €8-15. Open daily 5pm-late. Cash only. ❸

PRENZLAUER BERG

Prenzlauer Berg is flooded with all manner of restaurants, particularly at the borders of **Helmholzplatz** and **Kollwitzplatz.** The little streets around **Kastanienallee** are also good places to explore. On most Sundays, when virtually every restaurant serves brunch, you'll be hard-pressed to find a free table outside unless you get an early start.

Hans Wurst, Dunckerstr. 2A (☎030 41 71 78 22). U2 to "Eberswalderstr.," M10 to "Husemannstr." This cafe/restaurant-on-a-mission serves only organic, vegan foods with no flavor enhancers. Readings, DJs, and acoustic concerts in the evenings. The menu changes daily, with seasonal offerings and fresh creations (€3.70-8). Free Wi-Fi. Brunch Sa-Su 11am-5pm. Open Tu-Th noon-midnight, F-Sa noon-late. ❷

Cafe-Restaurant Miró, Raumerstr. 29 (☎030 44 73 30 13; www.miro-restaurant.de). U2 to "Eberswalder Str." A Mediterranean cafe whose candelit, pillowed back room and fresh entrees (€8-11) capture the region's essence perfectly. Breakfast €4.50-8.25. Soups €3.20-3.70. Large appetizers and salads €4-9. Open daily 10am-late. Kitchen closes at midnight. ❸

The Bird, Am Falkplatz 5 (☎0305 105 3283). U8 to "Voltastr." One of the few, if not the only, places to get an honest-to-goodness burger in Berlin, cooked by 2 gruff New York transplants in their exposed-brick restaurant. Everything is made from scratch daily, including the sauce for the aptly named "napalm wings" (€6). Burgers €9-12. Angry hour (buy 1 beer get 1 free) 6-8pm. Open M-Sa 6pm-late, Su noon-late. Cash only. ❸

W-Imbiss, Kastanienallee 49 (☎030 4849 2657). U8 to "Rosenthaler Pl." Look for the upside-down McDonald's sign and crowded outdoor seating at this casual spot. Naan cooked fresh to order and covered with your choice of toppings to make a sort of Indian pizza. Entrees €2.50-6. Open daily in summer noon-midnight, in winter 12:30-11:30pm. Cash only. ❷

Babel, Kastanienalle 33 (☎030 44 03 13 18). U8 to "Bernauer Str." Locals obsessed with Babel's falafel (€3-6) keep this neighborhood Middle Eastern joint busy at all hours. Grab your food to go, or lap up the large portions under the garlic dangling from the ceiling. Open daily 11am-2am. Cash only. ❷

FRIEDRICHSHAIN

Most come to Friedrichshain for the techtonic dancing, but that can make you hungry. The areas around **Simon-Dach-Strrasse** and before the bridge over the **Spree** are full of late-night options.

Frittiersalon, Boxhagener Straße 104 (☎030 25 93 39 06). U5 to "Frankfurter Tor." Multicultural, all-organic "frying salon" serves french fries and organic burgers with all kinds of fusion twists, including a meatless currywurst. The cheery place has won prizes for Berlin's best currywurst and best hangover breakfast, among other honors. Everything €2.20-9. Open M 6pm-late, Tu-F noon-late, Sa-Su 1pm-late. Cash only. ❷

Der Fliegender Tisch, Mainzer Strasse 10 (☎030297 7648). U5 to "Samariter Str." A cozy candelit spot serves inexpensive Italian food to its local devotees. The pizza is good but the pasta and risotto are better. Entrees €6-7. Open M-F and Su noon-midnight, Sa 5pm-midnight. Cash only. ❷

Lemongrass, Simon-Dach-Str. 2 (☎030 20 05 69 75). Laid-back decor and classic Thai specialties cooked within view make this a neighborhood favorite. Entrees €5.50-8. Open daily noon-midnight. Cash only. ❷

Aunt Benny, Oderstr. 7 (☎030 66 40 53 00). The love is in the details at this new cafe: check out the gorgeous lamps and little rock garden set into the wall. Everything from the lemon squares to the chickpea chili salad is made by hand. Free Wi-Fi. Everything under €10. Open M-F 8:30am-7:30pm, Sa-Su 10am-late. Cash only. ❷

KREUZBERG

Kreuzberg is packed with small restaurants, cafes, and no shortage of kebab stands. You'll find most eateries along Bergmannst. and Oranienstr., and cheaper places on the sidestreets off of them. But if you're looking for the best deal, the **Turkish market** along Maybachufer (Tu and F 11am-6:30pm) should not be missed. Rings of sesame bread, all kinds of spreads, cheeses, and cured olives make great sandwiches.

Maroush, Adalbertstr. 93 (☎030 69 53 61 71). U1 or U15 to "Kotbusser Tor." Tourists flock to Turkish Hasir, across the street, which claims to have invented the *Döner* kebab, but this Lebanese *Imbiss* is cosier and much cheaper. Favorite choices from the menu, handwritten in Arabic and German, are chicken shawarma wrap (€2.50) and a vegetarian platter with falafel and salads (€6). Open 11am-2am. Cash only. ❷

Wirtshaus Henne, Leuschnerdamm 25 (☎030 614 7730; www.henne-berlin.de). U1, or U15 to "Kottbusser Tor." Though this slightly out-of-the-way German restaurant does serve other dishes (€2.50-6), virtually everyone orders the famous *Brathähnchen* (fried chicken), arguably the best in Berlin. It has a small beer garden, but the real charm is in its dark wood interior, with plaid tablecloths and antique lanterns. Always packed, so reserve in advance. Open Tu-Sa from 7pm, Su from 5pm. Cash only. ❷

Curry 36, Mehringdamm 36. U7 or U8 to "Mehringdamm." A Berlin instutitution, currywurst is sliced sausage with ketchup and curry powder, served with fries and eaten with a miniature plastic fork. Connoisseurs say this stand is the best in the city. Non-connoisseurs say it is a convenient location for a post-clubbing or drinking snack, the only time they can stomach the stuff. "Red and white meal" (sausage with curry ketchup, mayonnaise, and fries; €2.40). Open M-F 9am-4am, Sa 10am-4am, Su 11am-3am. Cash only. ❶

Molinari & Ko., Riemannstr. 13 (☎030 691 3903). U7 to "Gneisenaustr." Students come here in 2 waves each day, mornings to enjoy Italian coffee (€1.80-2.80) with their newspaper and evenings to share large Italian entrees with friends (€5-14). The interior has a rustic feel, with wooden school desks, checked tablecloths, and the obligatory dripping candles. Open M-F 8am-1am, Sa-Su 9am-1am. Cash only. ❸

Salon Schmück, Skalitzer Str. 80 (☎030 69 00 47 75). U1 to Schlesisches Tor. The coffee, cakes, and snacks are good, but the real draw is the soft armchairs and sofas and secondhand clothing store in the back of the cafe. The place morphs into a bar at night, with a DJ on W and living-room style concerts on Su in a range of genres. Food €2-8. Beer €2.20. Open M-F 9am-late, Sa-Su 10am-late. Cash only. ❷

Cafe Morgenland, Skalitzer Str. 35 (☎030611 3291). U1 or U15 to "Görlitzer Bahnhof." Morgenland deserves its reputation as Kreuzberg's best brunch spot with its varied spread of seafood salads, rice dishes, and rich desserts alongside more traditional offerings like rolls, cheese, and sausage. Unfortunately, the secret is out, so make a reservation, avoid Sundays, arrive early—or, better, all three. All-you-can-eat brunch €9. Entrees €5-16. Open M-F 9am-1am, Sa-Su 10am-1am. Cash only. ❸

PASTRY OR PRESIDENT?

On June 26, 1963, President John F. Kennedy ended his speech to the citizens of Berlin with the words *"Ich bin ein Berliner"* in a declaration of international solidarity against the encroachments of the Soviet Union. After he spoke these words, the American media claimed that he should have said *"Ich bin Berliner,"* and that by adding the indefinite article *ein,* he actually spoke the words "I am a jelly donut." On June 27, 1963, newspapers from Tulsa to Tokyo were plastered with caricatures of talking pastries.

But the notion that Kennedy committed a major faux pas is more myth than reality. A "Berliner" is indeed a common name for a type of donut that originated in Berlin. And indeed, by adding *ein* to his statement, Kennedy's words could have been interpreted as a declaration of solidarity with fried dough. Nevertheless, nobody in Berlin would have misunderstood his words. For, though "Berliner" is a common term in the rest of Germany, Berliners themselves refer to the donut as a *Krapfen.* And though *ein* is often omitted when speaking of a particular individual, it is grammatically necessary when speaking figuratively, as Kennedy was doing.

Whatever the grammar police say, it's also possible that Kennedy was just taking the saying "You are what you eat" a bit too literally.

Yellow Sunshine, Wiener Str. 19 (☎030 69 59 87 20; www.yellow-sunshine.com). U1 or U15 to "Görlitzter Bahnhof." This is the spot to meet dreadlocked German 20-somethings indulging in organic vegetarian and vegan "burgers" at tables overlooking the park. The burgers are a little tasteless, but the variety of sauces makes up for it and the fries are delicious. Burger with fries and salad €6.65. Open M-Th and Su noon-midnight. F-Sa noon-1am. AmEx/MC/V. ❷

Knofi, Bergmannstr. 98 and Bergmannstr. 11 (☎030 494 5807). U6 or U7 to "Mehringdamm." You aren't seeing double. One Knofi (north side) sells nuts, spreads, pastas, fine olive oil, and more, while the Knofi on the other side of the street (south) is a Mediterranean cafe that doubles as a bakery. Outdoor seating and one of the few reasonably priced meals on Bergmannstr. are available at both. Entrees including filled crepes, meat dishes, and salad plates €2.50-10. Glass of wine €2.50. Open daily 9am-9pm. Cash only. ❷

SIGHTS

Most of central Berlin's major sights are along the route of **bus #100,** which travels from Bahnhof Zoo to Alexanderpl., passing the Siegessäule, Brandenburg Gate, Unter den Linden, and the Berliner Dom, among others. Tickets for individual bus rides quickly add up—buy a day pass to save money (see **Local Transportation,** p. 82). There are only a few places to see **remnants of the Berlin Wall:** a narrow band stands in Potsdamer Pl.; the touristed **Haus Am Checkpoint Charlie** guards another piece (p. 118); the sobering **Documentation Center** in Prenzlauer Berg has preserved an entire city block (p. 110); and a much-embellished section of the wall in Friedrichshain has become the **East Side Gallery** (p. 111). A line of double bricks in the pavement (usually unmarked) traces the former location of the wall; if you're interested, you can hoof the whole thing.

CHARLOTTENBURG

During the city's division, West Berlin centered around Bahnhof Zoo, the station that inspired U2's "Zoo TV" tour. The area around the station is dominated by department stores and peep shows intermingled with souvenir shops and more G-rated attractions.

ZOOLOGISCHER GARTEN. Germany's oldest zoo houses around 14,000 animals of 1500 species, most in open-air habitats. The southern entrance is the famous **Elefantentor** (across from Europa-Center), a decorated elephant pagoda standing at

Budapester Str. 34. You had better visit the world-famous polar bear **Knut;** otherwise he might go berserk. Originally deemed the cutest polar bear alive, Knut has been diagnosed by animal specialists as a psychopath who is addicted to human attention. *(☎030 25 40 10; www.zoo-berlin.de. Park open daily 9am-7:30pm, animal houses open 9am-6pm; entrance closes at 6:30pm. €12, students €9, children €6. Combination ticket to zoo and aquarium €18/14/9.)*

AQUARIUM. Within the walls of the zoo, but independently accessible, is an aquarium, with three floors of fish, reptiles, amphibians, and insects. Highlights include the psychedelic jellyfish, freaky eels, and carp petting zoo. *(Budapester Str. 32. ☎030 25 40 10; www.aquarium-berlin.de. Open daily 9am-6pm. €12, students €9, children €6. See above for Aquarium-Zoo combo tickets.)*

KAISER-WILHELM-GEDÄCHTNISKIRCH (MEMORIAL CHURCH). Berliners nicknamed the older part of the complex **Hohler Zahn** (hollow tooth) for its jagged steeple, left bombed out after WWII as a testament to warfare. Finished in 1895 in a neo-Romanesque/Byzantine style, the church has a striking interior lined with cracked, colorful mosaics. Inside is a small exhibit showing what the church used to look like, as well as horrific photos of the city in the wake of WWII. The other part of the complex is the **New Church,** a separate nave and tower with a blue stained glass-interior, consecrated in 1992. Together they are nicknamed the "lipstick and case." *(☎030 218 5023. Exhibit open M-Sa 10am-4pm. Church open daily 9am-7pm.)*

SCHLOSS CHARLOTTENBURG (CHARLOTTENBURG PALACE). The broad Baroque palace, which was commissioned by Friedrich I in the 17th century for his second wife, Sophie-Charlotte, stands impassively at the end of a beautiful, tree-lined esplanade in northern Charlottenburg. The *Schloß*'s extensive grounds include the **Altes Schloß,** underneath the iconic dome topped with a stature of Fortuna; the **Große Orangerie,** which contains rooms filled with historic furnishings (much of it reconstructed as a result of war damage) and gratuitous gilding; the **Neuer Flügel,** which includes the marble receiving rooms and the more sober royal chambers; the **Neuer Pavillon,** a museum dedicated to Prussian architect Karl Friedrich Schinkel; the **Belvedere,** a small building housing the royal family's porcelain collection; and the **Mausoleum,** the final resting place for most of the family. Stroll the **Schloßgarten** behind the main buildings, an elysium of small lakes, footbridges, fountains, and meticulously manicured trees. *(Spandauer Damm 10-22. Take bus #M45 from Bahnhof Zoo to "Luisenpl./Schloß Charlottenburg" or U2 to "Sophie-Charlotte Pl." ☎030 320 9275. Altes Schloß open Tu-Su Apr.-Oct. 10am-6pm, Nov.-Mar. 10am-5pm. Neuer Flügel open M and W-Su Apr.-Oct. 10am-6pm, Nov.-Mar. 10am-5pm. Belvedere and Mausoleum open daily Apr.-Oct. 10am-6pm, Nov.-Mar. noon-5pm. Altes Schloß €10, students €7; Neuer Flügel €6/5; Belvedere €2/1.50; Mausoleum €2/1.50. Audio tours, available in English, are included.)*

BERLIN

OLYMPIA-STADION. This massive Nazi-built stadium comes in a close second after Tempelhof Airport in the list of monumental Third Reich buildings in Berlin. It was erected for the infamous 1936 Olympic Games, in which African-American Jesse Owens won four gold medals. Hitler refused to congratulate Owens, a legendary runner who now has a Berlin street (Jesse-Owens-Allee) named after him. Film buffs will recognize the complex from Leni Riefenstahl's terrifying film *Olympia* (1938) while others will recognize it as the sight of the 2006 World Cup final. The **Glockenturm** (bell tower) provides a great lookout point and houses an exhibit on the history of German athletics. *(S5, S7, or U2 to "Olympia-Stadion." For Glockenturm, S5 or S7 to "Pichelsburg." ☎030 25 00 23 22; www.olympiastadion-berlin.de. Open daily Mar. 20-May 9am-7pm, Jun.-Sept. 15 9am-8pm, Sept. 16-Oct.*

31 9am-7pm, Nov.-Mar. 19 9am-4pm. €4, students €3. Tour with guide €8, students €7; children under 6 free. Audio tour €2.50.)

SCHÖNEBERG AND WILMERSDORF

Schoeneberg sights are a mix of gorgeous park and whatever cultural bits and pieces ended up in this largely residential neighborhood.

GRUNEWALD. In summer, this 3 sq. km birch forest, the dog-walking turf of many a Berliner, provides an ideal retreat from the heat and chaos of the city. About 1km into the woods, the **Jagdschloß,** a restored royal hunting lodge, houses paintings by German artists like Graff and Cranach. The one-room hunting museum is worth skipping. Instead, walk around the grounds, or take a hike north in the forest to **Teufelsberg** ("devil's mountain"), the highest point in Berlin, made of overgrown rubble from WWII piled over a Nazi military school. *(Am Grunewaldsee 29. U3 or U7 to "Fehrbelliner Pl.," or S45 or S46 to "Hohenzollerndamm," then bus #115 (dir.: Neuruppiner Str. or Spanische Alle/Potsdamer) to "Pücklerstr." Turn left on Pücklerstr. following the signs and continue straight into the forest to reach the lodge. ☎ 030 813 3597; www.spsg.de. Open Tu-Su 10am-6pm. €4, students €3; with tour €5/4.)*

BRÜCKE MUSEUM. This museum features four rooms of bright, fierce paintings from Die Brücke (The Bridge), a short-lived component of German Expressionism. *(Bussardsteig 9. U3 or U7 to "Fehrbelliner Pl." then bus #115 (dir.: Neuruppiner Str. or Spanische Allee/Potsdamer) to "Pücklerstr." ☎ 030 831 2029; www.bruecke-museum.de. Open M and W-Su 11am-5pm. €4, students €2.)*

GAY MEMORIAL. Just outside the Nollendorfpl. U-Bahn station, heading in the Motzstr. direction, stands an unassuming and unmarked memorial to gay victims of the Holocaust.

MITTE

The sights of Mitte alone could keep a tourist busy for weeks. The most efficient approach is to start at the Brandenburg Gate and either walk due east on Unter den Linden or take the #100 bus to do a drive-by of Imperial Berlin.

UNTER DEN LINDEN

This famous street was named "under the linden trees" for the 18th-century specimens that still line what was the spine of Imperial Berlin and what has become the nerve center of tourist Berlin. During the DDR days, it was known as the "idiot's mile," because it was often all that visitors saw, giving them little idea of what the eastern part of the city was really like. Originating in Pariser Platz, dominated by Brandenburger Tor, the street runs east through Bebelpl. and the Lustgarten, passing most of what remains of the city's still-impressive imperial architecture. *(S1, S2, or S25 to "Unter den Linden." Bus #100 runs the length of the street every 4-6min.)*

BRANDENBURGER TOR (BRANDENBURG GATE). Don't deny yourself the obligatory photo op. Berlin's only remaining city gate and and most recognizable symbol was built by Friedrich Wilhelm II in the 18th century as a symbol of victory, although in recent years this has been rephrased as "The Victory of Peace" in a fit of political correctness. During the Cold War, when it sat along the wall and served as a barricaded gateway, it became the symbol of a divided Berlin. Today, it is the most powerful emblem of reunited Germany—in 1987, Reagan chose this spot to make his "Tear down this wall" speech. The **Room of Silence** in the northern end of the gate provides a non-denominational place for meditation and reflection. *(Open daily 11am-6pm.)*

NEUE WACHE. The combination of Prussian Neoclassicism and a copy of an Expressionist statue by Käthe Kollwitz, *Mutter mit totem Sohn* (*Mother with Dead Son*), makes for an oddly moving memorial to "the victims of war and tyranny." The "New Guardhouse" was designed by architect Karl Friedrich Schinkel, turned into a memorial to victims of "fascism and militarism," and closed after reunification. Now the remains of an unknown soldier and an unknown concentration camp victim are buried inside with earth from the camps at Buchenwald and Mauthausen and from the battlefields of Stalingrad, El Alamein, and Normandy. *(Unter den Linden 4. Open daily 10am-6pm.)*

PARISER PLATZ. Why is Berlin's most historic square named after its nemesis city? The 1814 Prussian overthrow of Napoleon was apparently reason enough. Arguably the most spectacular post WWII renovation in the square is the **Hotel Adlon,** once the premier address for visiting dignitaries and, more recently, the site of the infamous Michael Jackson baby-dangling incident. *(The square is in front of the Brandenburger Tor.)*

THE KENNEDYS. His "Ich bin ein Berliner" speech reserved JFK a special place in Berliners' hearts and their most important square, now home to one of the world's most extensive compilations of the family's photographs, official documents, private letters, and memorabilia. *(Pariser Platz 4A. Take S-Bahn to "Unter den Linden." ☎ 030 20 65 35 70; www.thekennedys.de. Open daily 10am-6pm. €7, students €3.50.)*

RUSSIAN EMBASSY. Rebuilding the edifices of the rich and famous wasn't a major priority in the workers' state of the DDR. The exception was Berlin's largest embassy, which covers almost an entire city block. The quiet removal of the enormous Lenin bust at the end of the Cold War completed its transformation into just another embassy. *(Unter den Linden 65.)*

STAATSBIBLIOTHEK ZU BERLIN (BERLIN STATE LIBRARY). The stately library features an ivy-covered courtyard filled with lounging intellectuals. It was founded in 1661, making it one of the oldest buildings in all of Berlin. Inside are over 10 million books along with an endless list of cultural assets. *(Unter den Linden 8. ☎ 030 26 60. Open M-F 9am-9pm, Sa 9am-5pm. Free internet with admission. €0.50.)*

HUMBOLDT-UNIVERSITÄT (HUMBOLDT UNIVERSITY). Just beyond the Staatsbibliothek lies the H-shaped main building of Humboldt University, whose hallowed halls have been paced by the likes of Hegel, Einstein, Bismarck, the Brothers Grimm, and Karl Marx. In the wake of post-1989 academic warfare, in which many departments were purged of Marxist leanings, international scholars have descended upon the university to take part in its dynamic renewal. Budding socialists can peruse the works of Marx and Lenin at the book vendors outside under the statue of a triumphant **Frederick the Great.** *(Unter den Linden 6.)*

POTSDAMER PLATZ

POTSDAMER PLATZ. Both Berlin's shiniest commercial center and the site of its most high-profile architectural failures, Potsdamer Platz is amazing for the sheer speed of its construction. Built under Friedrich Wilhelm I (in imitation of Parisian boulevards) as a launch pad for troops, the area became the commercial and transportation hub of pre-war Berlin, regulated by Europe's first traffic lights (the massive clock is set into a replica of what they looked like). But the square was flattened by bombers in WWII and caught in the death strip between East and West during the Cold War. In the decade that followed reunification, a number of commercial buildings sprouted up, the most recognizable being an off-kilter glass recreation of Mt. Fuji. *(U2, or S1, S2, or S25 to "Potsdamer Pl.")*

FÜHRERBUNKER. Near Potsdamer Pl., unmarked and inconspicuous, is the site of the bunker where Hitler married Eva Braun and then shot himself. During WWII, it held 32 rooms including private apartments and was connected to Hitler's chancellery building (since destroyed). Plans to restore the bunker were shelved for fear that the site would become a pilgrimage spot for neo-Nazis; all that remains is a dirt expanse and the occasional tourist. *(Under the parking lot at the corner of In den Ministergärten and Gertrud-Kolmar-Str.)*

GENDARMENMARKT

Several blocks south of Unter den Linden, Berlin's most typically Old Europe square became the French quarter in the 18th century after the arrival of an influx of Huguenots fleeing persecution by Louis XIV. During the last week of June and the first week of July, the square becomes an outdoor stage for open-air classical concerts. *(U6 to "Französische Str." or U2 or U6 to "Stadtmitte.")*

DEUTSCHER DOM. Though destroyed during WWII, the cathedral was rebuilt to its Renaissance glory in the 1970s. Once again gracing the southern end of the square, the Dom is not currently used as a church but instead houses **Wege Irrwege Umwege** ("Milestones, Setbacks, Sidetracks"), a humble exhibit tracing German political history from despotism to democracy. *(Gendarmenmarkt 1. ☎030 22 73 04 31. Open Tu-Su and holidays 10am-6pm. Free.)*

FRANZÖSISCHER DOM. Built in the early 18th century by French Huguenots, the Dom now holds a restaurant and small museum on the Huguenot diaspora. The tower commands a sweeping view of the city. *(Gendarmenmarkt 5. ☎030 229 17 60; www.franzoesischer-dom.de. Open Tu-Su noon-5pm. Tower open daily 9am-7pm. Museum €2, students €1. Tower €2/1.50.)*

FASSBENDER & RAUCH CHOCOLATIERS. This fancy chocolate store provides the perfect opportunity to review or preview your Berlin sightseeing with enormous models of the **Kaiser Wilhelm Memorial Church** (p. 103), **Reichstag** (p. 108), and the **Brandenburg Gate** (p. 104), all rendered in chocolate and wafers. *(Charlottenstr. 60. ☎030 20 45 84 40. Open M-Sa 10am-8pm, Su 11am-8pm.)*

BERLIN

MUSEUMSINSEL (MUSEUM ISLAND)

There are more than a handful of reasons to set aside a good chunk of time for Museum Island, the entirety of which is a **UNESCO World Heritage Sight.** After crossing the Schloßbrücke over the Spree, Unter den Linden becomes Karl-Liebknecht-Str. and cuts through the Museumsinsel, which is home to five major museums (p. 106) and the **Berliner Dom.** *(Take S3, S5, S7, S9, or S75 to "Hackescher Markt" and walk toward the Dom. Alternatively, pick up bus #100 along Unter den Linden and get off at "Lustgarten." For information on the Altes Museum, Pergamon, Bodemuseum, and Alte Nationalgalerie, see Museums, p. 113.)*

BERLINER DOM. One of Berlin's most recognizable landmarks, this elegantly bulky, multiple-domed cathedral proves that Protestants can design buildings as dramatically as Catholics. Built during the reign of Kaiser Wilhelm II in a faux-Renaissance style, the cathedral suffered severe damage in a 1944 air raid and took 20 years to fully reconstruct. Look for the Protestant icons (Calvin, Zwingli, and Luther) that adorn the decadent interior, or soak up the glorious view of Berlin from the top of the cupola. *(☎030 20 26 91 19; www.berlinerdom.de. Open M-Sa 9am-8pm, Su noon-8pm, closed during services 6:30-7:30pm. Free organ recitals W-F 3pm. Frequent concerts in summer; buy tickets in the church or call ahead. Combined admission to Dom, crypt, tower, and galleries €5, students €3. Audio tour €3.)*

LUSTGARTEN. The "pleasure garden," is bounded by the Karl Friedrich Schinkel-designed Altes Museum to the north and the Berliner Dom to the east. The massive granite bowl in front of the museum was meant to adorn the main hall but didn't fit through the door.

SCHLOSSPLATZ. Known as Marx-Engels-Pl. during the days of the DDR, the "palace square" is at the heart of Berlin's biggest architectural and urban-planning controversy. The Berliner Schloß, the Hohenzollern Imperial palace, used to stand here, but was torn down in 1950 by the East German authorities to overwhelming (mostly West Berliner) protest. The Schloß was replaced by the concrete Palast der Republik, where the East German parliament met. After reunification, the Palast was knocked down to make way for a replica of, you guessed it, the Schloß, to enormous (mostly East Berliner) protest. *(Across the street from the Lustgarten.)*

ALEXANDERPLATZ AND NIKOLAIVIERTEL

Formerly the heart of Weimar Berlin, **Alexanderplatz** became the center of East Berlin, an urban wasteland of fountains, pre-fab concrete apartment buildings, and—more recently—chain stores and malls. **Karl-Liebknecht-Strrasse,** which divides the Museuminsel, leads into the monolithic Alexanderplatz, a former cattle market. Behind the Marx-Engels-Forum, the preserved cobblestone streets of **Nikolaiviertel** (Nicholas' Quarter) stretch toward Mühlendamm. *(Take U2, U5, or U8, or S3, S5, S7, S9, or S75 to "Alexanderpl.")*

FERNSEHTURM (TV TOWER). The tremendous and bizarre tower, the tallest structure in Berlin (368m0, was originally intended to prove East Germany's technological capabilities, though Swedish engineers were ultimately brought in when construction faltered. As a result, the tower has acquired some colorful, politically infused nicknames, among them "Walter Ulbricht's Last Erection." Look at the windows when the sun is out to see the cross-shaped glint pattern known as the *Papsts Rache* (Pope's Revenge), so named because it defied the Communist government's attempt to rid the city of religious symbols. An elevator whisks tourists up to the magnificent view from the spherical node (203m) and a slowly rotating cafe one floor up serves international meals for €8-16. *(☎030 242 3333; www.berlinerfernsehturm.de. Open daily Mar.-Oct. 9am-midnight, Nov.-Feb. 10am-midnight. €10, under 16 €4.50.)*

MARIENKIRCHE. The non-bombed and non-reconstructed church (Berlin's second oldest) is Gothic, the altar and pulpit Rococo, and the tower Neo-Romantic thanks to centuries of additions to the original structure. Knowledgeable guides explain the artifacts as well as the painting collection, which features works from the Dürer and Cranach schools. *(☎030 242 4467. Open daily in summer 10am-9pm, in winter 10am-6pm.)*

ROTES RATHAUS (RED TOWN HALL). The name of the high-Italian Renaissance-style city hall refers to its gorgeous brick facade, not its politics—although it was the city hall of communist East Berlin. Since 1991 it has served as the city hall for the reunified Berlin. *(Closed to the public.)*

MARX-ENGELS FORUM. Across the river from Museumsinsel on the south side of Karl-Liebknecht-Str. is this rectangular park with a memorial of imprinted steel tablets dedicated to the worldwide workers' struggle against fascism and imperialism. Somber statues of Marx and Engels preside over the oft-graffitied tablets. Tourists jump into Marx's lap for a popular photo-op—we won't judge you if you join in.

SCHEUNENVIERTEL AND ORANIENBURGER STRASSE

Northwest of Alexanderpl., near Oranienburger Str. and Große Hamburger Str., is the **Scheunenviertel** (Barn Quarter), once the center of Berlin's Orthodox

BERLIN

Jewish community. Prior to WWII, wealthier and more assimilated Jews tended to live in Western Berlin, while Orthodox Jews from Eastern Europe settled in the Scheunenviertel (originally a derogatory term coined by Nazis). Full of cobblestone streets, Judaica-oriented bookstores and art galleries, this is one of the most pleasant strolls in all of Berlin. *(S1, S2, or S25 to "Oranienburger Str." or U6 to "Oranienburger Tor.")*

NEUE SYNAGOGE. This huge building, modeled after the Alhambra, was designed by Berlin architect Eduard Knoblauch in the 1850s. The synagogue, which seated 3200, was used for worship until 1940, when the Nazis occupied it and used it for storage. Amazingly, the building survived *Kristallnacht*—the SS torched it, but a local police chief bluffed his way past SS officers to order the fire extinguished. The synagogue was later destroyed by bombing, but its restoration, largely financed by international Jewish organizations, began in 1988 and was completed in 1995. Too big for Berlin's remaining Jewish community, the striking building is no longer used for services and instead houses an exhibit chronicling its history as well as that of the Jewish community that once thrived in the surrounding neighborhood. *(Oranienburger Str. 29. ☎030 88 02 83 00; www.cjudaicum.de. Open Apr.-Sept. M and Su 10am-5pm, Tu-Th 10am-6pm, F 10am-5pm; Mar. and Oct. M and Su 10am-2pm, Tu-Th 10am-8pm, F 10am-6pm; Nov.-Feb. M and Su 10am-2pm, Tu-F 10am-6pm. Last entry 30min. before closing. Permanent exhibition "Open Ye the Gates" €3, students €2. Dome €1.50/1. Temporary exhibition €3/2.)*

ALTER JÜDISCHER FRIEDHOF (OLD JEWISH CEMETERY). Obliterated by the Nazis, the cemetery now contains only the restored gravestone of Enlightenment philosopher and scholar Moses Mendelssohn; the rest is a quiet park. In front, a prominent plaque marks the site of the **Jüdisches Altersheim** (Jewish Old-age Home), which served as a holding place for Jews before their deportation to concentration camps. *(At the end of Große Hamburger Str., near Oranienburger Str.)*

BERLIN

THE MISSING HOUSE. Across the street from the Jewish Cemetery is a 1990 art installation by Christian Boltanski in the space where a house was bombed during WWII. Boltanski researched the apartment's earlier inhabitants—Jews and non-Jews alike—and put plaques on the walls of the surrounding buildings at the approximate height of their apartment floors with their names, dates of birth and death, and professions. *(Große Hamburger Strasse.)*

TIERGARTEN

Stretching from Bahnhof Zoo in the west to the Brandenburg Gate in the east, this vast landscaped park was formerly used by Prussian monarchs as a hunting and parade ground. Today, it is frequented by strolling families, elderly couples. **Straße des 17. Juni** bisects the park from west to east, connecting Ernst-Reuter-Pl. to the Brandenburg Gate. The street is the site of many demonstrations and parades, including Barack Obama's 2008 speech, which attracted over 200,000 viewers.

THE REICHSTAG. The current home of Germany's governing body, the **Bundestag,** the Reichstag has seen some critical historical moments in its day. Philipp Scheidemann proclaimed *"Es lebe die Deutsche Republik"* ("Long live the German Republic") here in 1918. In 1933 Adolf Hitler used a fire at the Reichstag as an excuse to declare a state of emergency and seize power. In 1997, a glass dome was added to the top, built around the upside-down solar cone that powers the building. A walkway spirals up the inside of the dome, providing visitors with information about the building, panoramic views of the city, and a view of the parliament meeting inside—a powerful symbol of government transparency. Braving the line is worth it. *(☎030 22 73 21 52; www.bundestag.de. Open daily 8am-midnight. Last entry 10pm. Free.)*

DENKMAL FÜR DIE ERMORDETEN JUDEN EUROPAS (MEMORIAL FOR THE MURDERED JEWS OF EUROPE). Just looking at the block of concrete stelae—large rectangular columns of concrete varying in height—it is hard to know what this prominent memorial, opened in the spring of 2005 and designed by architect Peter Eisenman, represents. Most agree, however, that it is quite moving. An underground information center tells the stories of specific families murdered during the Holocaust. *(Cora-Berliner-Str. 1, at the corner of Behrenstr. and Ebertstr. near the Brandenburg Gate. ☎030 26 39 43 36; www.stiftung-denkmal.de. Open daily 10am-8pm. Last entry Apr.-Sept. 7:15pm, Oct.-Mar. 6:15pm. Free audio tour. Guided public tours Sa-Su 11am and 2pm in German and Su 4pm in English. Admission €3, students €2.50.)*

AROUND THE REICHSTAG. Also known as the *Kohllosseum* for its size and first resident (Helmut Kohl), the huge white and blue **Chancellory** was reportedly a source of embarrassment to former Chancellor Gerhard Schröder, who wished to keep a low profile. Tourists aren't permitted inside. The **Palais am Pariser Platz,** directly north of the Brandenburg Gate, was once the site of a castle; enter the courtyard to find Stephen Balkenhol's startling 1998 statue *Großer Mann mit kleinem Mann* (Big Man with Little Man).

SIEGESSÄULE (VICTORY COLUMN). In the heart of the Tiergarten, this slender 70m monument commemorates Prussia's victory over France in 1870. The statue at the top—Victoria, the goddess of victory—is made of melted-down French cannons. In a less-than-subtle affront to the French, the Nazis moved the monument here in 1938 from its former spot in front of the Reichstag in order to increase its visibility. Climb the monument's 285 steps for a panorama of the city. *(Großer Stern. Take bus #100 or 187 to "Großer Stern" or S5, S7, or S9 to "Tiergarten." Accessible via the stairs at the west corner around the traffic circle. ☎030 391 2961. Open Apr.-Nov. M-F 9:30am-6:30pm, Sa-Su 9:30am-7pm; Dec.-Mar. M-F 10am-5pm, Sa-Su 10am-5:30pm. €2.20, students €1.50.)*

SOWJETISCHES EHRENMAL (SOVIET CENOTAPH). At the eastern end of the Tiergarten, a Soviet memorial rises (yes, in western Berlin) above a pair of red star-emblazoned tanks, the first two to enter Berlin in 1945. The position of the soldier's hand is an inverted Nazi salute. *(Bus #100 to "Pl. der Republik.")*

WALKING ON HISTORY. It is possible to literally trip over Berlin's most pervasive memorial. Small plaques are set into the sidewalk outside apartment buildings from which Jews were deported and murdered during WWII with their names. German artist Gunther Demnig started installing the "stumbling blocks" in 1993.

GAY MEMORIAL. Berlin's mayor unveiled a memorial to homosexuals persecuted by the Nazis on the eastern end of the Tiergarten in 2008. Peer into the 4m concrete block to see a video of two men kissing on continuous loop. *(Bus #100 to "Pl. der Republik.")*

FISCHERINSEL

The other half of the island that holds Museum Island, "Fisher Island" was the first part of Berlin to be settled, back when the city was called Cölln. It is well off the tourist track but worth a stop if only visit the two special Berliners living in the Köllnischen Park. *(U2 to "Klosterstr.")*

KÖLLNISCHEN PARK. The most memorable part of this rambling park is the "bear pit," surrounded by a moat and containing Schnute and Maxi, two live brown bears. Living versions of the city mascot have lived in the park for centuries, and were among the casualties during bombings in WWII. The only other attraction is a nice statue of artist Heinrich Zille. *(Open dawn to dusk.)*

FRANZISKANER-KLOSTERKIRCHE (FRANCISCAN CLOISTERS). What used to be a working monastery beginning in the 14th century is now a stunning shell of a building, bombed during WWII. An experimental theater groups stages performances here in the summer. *(Dawn to dusk)*

OTHER SIGHTS IN MITTE

DIE HACKESCHE HÖFE. Built in the early 1900s, this gorgeous series of Art Deco courtyards house a combination of theaters, art galleries, bars and offices. Just to the right as you enter is Berlin's best arthouse cinema. *(Rosenthaler Str. 40/41. www.hackesche-hoefe.com.)*

BERTOLT-BRECHT-HAUS. If any one man personifies the maelstrom of Berlin's political and aesthetic contradictions, it is the playwright Bertolt Brecht, who lived and worked in this house from 1953 to 1956. "There is a reason to prefer Berlin to other cities," the playwright once said, "because it is constantly changing. What is bad today can be improved tomorrow." The **Literaturforum im Brecht-Haus** on the second floor sponsors exhibits and lectures. *(Chausseestr. 125. U6 to "Oranienburger Tor" or "Zinnowitzer Str." ☎ 030 28 22 003. Obligatory German tours every 30min. Tu, W, F 10-11:30am; Th 10-11:30am and 5-6:30pm; Sa 9:30am-1:30pm; Su 11am-6pm. Max. 8 people. €5, students €2.50.)*

DOROTHEENSTÄDTISCHER FRIEDHOF (DOROTHEEN MUNICIPAL CEMETERY). Attached to Brecht's house is the cemetery where he and his wife, Helene Weigel, are buried in simple graves. Other famous personages interred in the cemetery include Karl Friedrich Schinkel, Heinrich Mann, and Georg Hegel and Johann Fichte, who lie side-by-side in the middle of the yard. A map near the entrance points out locations of notable graves. *(Open daily 8am-dusk.)*

HI-FLYER BALLOON. Tethered to the ground near Potsdamer Platz, this hot-air balloon rises 150m into the air every 15min. for a bird's-eye view of the surrounding area. *(At the corner of Wilhelmstr. and Niederkirchnerstr. ☎ 030 226 67 88 11; www.air-service-berlin.de. Open in summer M-Th and Su 10am-10pm, F-Sa 10am-12:30am; in winter M-Th abd Sy 11am-6pm, F-Sa 11am-7pm. €19, students €13.*

BERLIN

PRENZLAUER BERG

BERLINER MAUER DOKUMENTATIONZENTRUM (BERLIN WALL DOCUMENTATION CENTER). A museum, a chapel, and an entire city block of the preserved Berlin Wall—two concrete barriers separated by the open *Todesstreife* (death strip)—come together in a memorial to "victims of the communist tyranny." The museum has assembled a comprehensive collection of all things Wall. Exhibits include photos, film clips, and sound bites. The collection here is both cheaper and more informative than the private museum at Checkpoint Charlie covering similar material. *(Bernauer Str. 111; www.berliner-mauer-dokumentationszentrum.de. ☎ 030 464 1030. U8 to "Bernauer Str.", switch to S1 or S2 to "Nordbahnhof." Open Apr.-Oct. Tu-Su 10am-6pm, Nov.-Mar. Tu-Su 10am-5pm. Free.)*

JÜDISCHER FRIEDHOF (JEWISH CEMETERY). Prenzlauer Berg was one of the major centers of Jewish Berlin during the 19th and early 20th centuries. The ivy-covered Jewish cemetery on Schönhauser Allee contains the graves of composer Giacomo Meyerbeer and painter Max Liebermann. *(Enter by the "Lapi-*

darium." Open M-Th 8am-4pm, F 8am-1pm. Men must cover their heads.) Nearby, **Synagoge Rykestraße,** Rykestr. 53, is one of Berlin's loveliest synagogues. It was spared on *Kristallnacht* thanks to its inconspicuous location. Unfortunately, visitors are currently not allowed in, as the synagogue is a still-operational school.

KOLLWITZPLATZ. This little triangle of greenery is one big playground, with toddlers climbing even on the statue of Käthe Kollwitz, the renowned painter. Non-parents are drawn by the upscale **market** on Saturdays where vendors sell everything from boar meat sausage to handmade ravioli. *(U2 to "Senefelderpl.")*

ZEISS-GROSSPLANETARIUM. In 1987 this planetarium opened as the most modern facility of its kind in the DDR. Compared to its peers in the West, it seems about as technologically advanced as a Trabi, the East German car and butt of many jokes, but it can still show you the stars. Call or check the website for showtimes and special events. *(Prenzlauer Allee 80. S8, S41, S42, or tram M2 to "Prenzlauer Allee"; the planetarium is across the bridge. ☎ 030 421 8450; www.astw.de. Open Tu and Th 9am-noon, W 9am-noon and 1:30-3pm, F 7-9pm, Sa 2:30-9pm, Su 1:30-5pm. €5, students €4.)*

FRIEDRICHSHAIN

EAST SIDE GALLERY. The longest remaining portion of the Berlin Wall, this 1.3km stretch of cement slabs also serves as the world's largest open-air art gallery. The murals are not remnants of Cold War graffiti, but rather the organized efforts of an international group of artists who gathered here in 1989 to celebrate the end of the city's division. One of the most famous is artist Dmitri Vrubel's depiction of a wet kiss between Leonid Brezhnev and East German leader Eric Honecker. The stretch of street remains unsupervised and, on the Warschauer Str. side, open at all hours. *(Along Mühlenstr. Take U1 or U15 or S3, S5-S7, S9, or S75 to "Warschauer Str." or S5, S7, S9, or S75 to "Ostbahnhof" and walk back toward the river. www.eastsidegallery.com.)*

STASI MUSEUM. The Lichtenberg suburb harbors perhaps the most hated and feared building of the DDR regime: the headquarters of the East German secret police, the *Staatssicherheit* or Stasi. During the Cold War, the Stasi kept dossiers on some six million of East Germany's own citizens, an amazing feat and a testament to the huge number of civilian informers in a country of only 16 million people. On January 15, 1990, a crowd of 100,000 Berliners stormed and vandalized the building to celebrate the demise of the police state. Since a 1991 law returned the records to the people, the "Horror Files" have rocked Germany, exposing millions of informants—and wrecking careers, marriages, and friendships—at every level of German society. Officially known today as the **Forschungs- und Gedenkstätte Normannenstraße,** the building maintains its oppressive Orwellian gloom and much of its worn 1970s aesthetic. The exhibit displays the extensive offices of Erich Mielke, the loathed Minister for State Security from 1957 to 1989, a large collection of tiny microphones and hidden cameras used for surveillance by the Stasi, and a replica of a Stasi prison cell. *(Ruschestr. 103, Haus 1. U5 to "Magdalenenstr." ☎ 030 553 6854; www.stasimuseum.de. Exhibits in German. English info booklet €3. Open M-F 11am-6pm, Sa-Su 2-6pm. €4, students €3.)*

CONFRONTING THE PAST. Files housed in the Stasi Museum are now officially open to the public, but privacy rules dictate that you can only look up the name of informants if they were informing on you. A beautiful German film addressing this topic is Florian Henckel von Donnersmarck's **Das Leben der Anderen** *(The Lives of Others)*.

KARL-MARX-ALLEE. Formerly known as Stalinallee, this was the main drag of the East German Potempkin Village, where party members staged elaborate military parades. Built in the early 1950s and widened in the 1960s, it is flanked by hideous gray pre-fab buildings that give way to the wedding-cake style "people's palaces" at Strausberger Pl. *(U5 to "Strausberger Pl.")*

KREUZBERG

Kreuzberg sights are mostly devoted to the area's hybrid history as a hub for both punks and immigrants.

SOUTHERN KREUZBERG. The cobblestone streets and pre-war ornamented apartment blocks just east of Mehringdamm form the most gentrified area of Kreuzberg—witness the outdoor organic food market on Saturdays in Chamissopl. The spine of of the area is **Bergmannstraße,** a stretch of cafes, secondhand clothing and record stores, and bookshops. West of Mehringdamm, forested Viktoria Park is the highest natural point in Berlin at 66m. A huge neo-Gothic memorial commemorating the Napoleonic Wars provides a great view of Berlin. Vineyards first planted by the Knights Templar and a number of small restaurants and beer gardens—including philosopher Georg Friedrich Hegel's favorite watering hole—are tucked away in the park near the artificial waterfall. Farther south down Mehringdamm is **Tempelhof Airport,** built by Nazi architect Albrecht Speer but most famous as the site of the Berlin Airlift, 1948-1949, one of the most dramatic crises of the Cold War. The German government closed the airport in 2008, but still visible in a flower-ringed field is a monument known as the **Hungerharke** (hunger rake) representing the three air corridors and dedicated to the 78 pilots who lost their lives in the 328 days of the airlift. *(U6 to "Platz der Luftbrücke" or U6 or U7 to "Mehringdamm.")*

EASTERN KREUZBERG. The **Landwehrkanal,** a channel bisecting Kreuzberg, is a lovely place to take a stroll, with moored boats doubling as on-the-water cafes. Its history is less pleasant: it is where the conservative, nationalist Freikorps threw the body of left-wing activist and communist revolutionary Rosa Luxemburg after murdering her in 1919. The Berlin Wall once ran near **Schlesisches Tor,** a nightlife hotspot with a huge Turkish and Balkan influence and arguably the best street art and graffiti in the city—especially around Wrangelstraße. The **Oberbaumbrücke,** an iconic double-decker brick bridge, spans the Spree River. It was once a border crossing into East Berlin, and now connects Kreuzberg to Friedrichshain. Residents of the rival neighborhoods duke it out in a "water fight" on the bridge each July 27, with up to a thousand people throwing water and rotten vegetables at one another. *(U1 or U15 to "Schlesisches Tor.")*

ORANIENSTRASSE. This strip's colorful mix of cafes, bars, and stores is home to the city's punk and radical elements. May Day parades, which start on Oranienpl., were the scene of violent riots in the 1980s, although May 1 has since become a family holiday complete with a big block party. The street's **Heinrichplatz** boasts, in addition to great cafes, a women-only Turkish-style bath, **Schoko Fabrik,** which doubles as a community center (www.schokofabrik.de; open M 3-11pm, Tu-Su noon-11pm). Squatters still occupy the **Bethanien Kunsthaus** in Marienplatz (www.bethanien.de), which hosts frequent exhibitions and an open-air cinema in summer. *(U1 or U15 to "Kottbusser Tor" or "Görlitzer Bahnhof.")*

GÖRLITZER PARK. Built on the ruins of an old train station, Görlitzer Park is a bizarre landscape of graffitied ruins, freestanding sculpture, and—in summer—neighborhood hipsters playing frisbee and families grilling on portable barbecues. In the center, you'll find a basin, marked by a large iron sculpture; to the northeast is a small playground and petting zoo. What remains of the old station building is now a Heidi-in-the-Alps-themed cafe, **Das Edelweiß,** complete with beach chairs and outdoor screenings of soccer games in summer. *(Cafe open 11am-late.)*

MUSEUMS

Berlin is one of the world's great museum cities, with collections of art and artifacts encompassing all subjects and eras. The **Staatliche Museen zu Berlin** (**Stiftung Preußischer Kulturbesitz** or **SPK,** or simply **SMB**) runs over 20 museums in four major regions—**Museumsinsel** (an island of historic museums in the middle of the Spree), **Kulturforum, Charlottenburg, and Dahlem**—as well as elsewhere in Mitte and around the Tiergarten. Prices are generally standardized: €8, students €4 for Hamburger Bahnhof, Charlottenburg, the KulturForum, and Museumsinsel houses. Dahlem museums are €6, students 3. Tickets are valid for all SMB-PK museums in a given complex on the day of purchase. The **Drei-Tage-Karte** (€19, students €9.50) is valid for three consecutive days. Buy either card at any SMB-PK museum. Admission is free the first Sunday of every month. Non-SMB-PK-affiliated museums tend to be smaller and more specialized, dealing with everything from Käthe Kollwitz to the cultural history of marijuana. *Berlin Programm* (€1.75) lists museums and galleries. Most state museums close on Mondays and are free Thursday nights 6-10pm. Twice every year, all state museums stay open all night on the **Long Night of the Museums.** Check online for more information (www.smb.museum).

CHARLOTTENBURG

Charlottenburg's museums range from high culture to smut and house one of the strongest collections of Picasso outside of Barcelona.

MUSEUM BERGGRUEN. This intimate three-floor museum exhibits some wonderful Picassos alongside works that influenced the artist, including African masks and late French Impressionist paintings by Matisse. The top floor showcases paintings by Bauhaus teacher Paul Klee and Alberto Giacometti's surreally elongated sculptures. *(Schloßstr. 1. Near the Schloß Charlottenburg. Take bus #M45 from "Bahnhof Zoo" to "Luisenpl./Schloß Charlottenburg" or U2 to "Sophie-Charlotte-Pl." ☎030 3269 580. Open Tu-Su 10am-6pm. €6, students €3, children free. Audio guide free.)*

KÄTHE-KOLLWITZ-MUSEUM. Through both World Wars, Käthe Kollwitz, a member of the Berlin *Sezession* (Secession) movement and one of Germany's most prominent 20th-century artists, protested war and the condition of the working class through her haunting depictions of death, poverty, and suffering. The artist's biographical details—her son died in World War II and she withdrew into so-called inner migration during the DDR—provide context for her depictions of death, pregnancy, and starvation and for her somber self-portraits shown in what used to be a private home. *(Fasanenstr. 24. U1 to "Uhlandstr." ☎030 882 5210; www.kaethe-kollwitz.de. Open daily 11am-6pm. €5, students €2.50. Audio guide €3.)*

BRÖHANMUSEUM. This sleek building is full of Jugendstil (a.k.a Art Nouveau) and Art Deco paintings, houseware, and furniture. The ground floor consists of several ensembles of furniture, complete with accompanying paintings from the same time period (1889-1939). The first floor is a small gallery dedicated to the Modernist Berlin *Sezession* painters and the top floor houses special exhibitions. *(Schloßstr. 1A, next to the Berggruen, across from the Schloß. ☎030 32 69 06 00; www.broehan-museum.de. Open Tu-Su 10am-6pm. €5, students €4.)*

BEATE UHSE EROTIK MUSEUM. The world's largest sex museum contains over 5000 sex artifacts from around the world. Attracting a quarter of a mil-

BERLIN

ARCHITECTURE OF MITTE

START: Radisson Hotel on Karl-Liebnecht-Str.

FINISH: Sony Center on Potsdamer Pl.

DURATION: 1½-3hr.

WHEN TO GO: Late afternoon.

If there is anything that single-handedly embodies the strange spirit of Berlin's weighty history and forward-thinking hyper-modernity, it's the city's architecture. Although remnants of its imperial past still line Unter den Linden, a stroll through the heart of the city shows that Berlin's reputation for edginess and artistry is well deserved. The construction cranes puncturing the skyline mean that while the buildings listed here may represent some of the greatest feats in contemporary architecture, they are in fact only the beginning of Berlin's steamroll toward a new kind of cosmopolitan future.

1. AQUADOM. In the lobby of the Radisson Hotel, built in a square formation around a central courtyard, towers a massive elevator shaft. And not just any elevator shaft: a roughly five-story cylindrical aquarium on a concrete foundation, with thousands of colorful fish swirling about in sparkly blue water. While you have to pay entrance to the neighboring aquarium to ride up the "AquaDom," simply ask the concierge's permission to enter the building and get a glimpse.

2. LUSTGARTEN. This is a typical Berlin contrast between the formidably old and jarringly new. You'll find yourself surrounded on one side by the **Altes Museum** (p. 116), designed by imperial architect Karl Friedrich Schinkel, and the towering **Berliner Dom** (p. 106). On the other, Schloßplatz holds the modern **Staatsrat,** a federal government building, which incorporates a fragment of the old facade. Decide for yourself why the park is called Lustgarten (Pleasure Garden).

3. DEUTSCHES HISTORY MUSEUM. One of the newest additions to Berlin's trove of cultural treasures, I.M. Pei's 2004 masterpiece stands hidden behind the **Zeughaus** on Unter den Linden and houses the temporary exhibits of the German History Museum. The building, however, tends to outdo its contents. A conical glass structure with a spiraling staircase links the different floors. The new marble supports blend into the more traditional segments of the old building, framing the glass entrance hall. The interior, largely visible from outside, contains crisscrossed, multi-tiered walkways leading to different floors of the museum. In back, imposing marble is interrupted by a triangular balcony with a window overlooking a single tree, while the front contains an indentation resembling a half-column, perhaps a contemporary reference to the imperial structures along neighboring Unter den Linden.

4. INTERNATIONALES HANDELSZENTRUM, FRIEDRICHSTRAβE., AND SCHIFFBAUERDAMM. From the museum, continue away from Under den Linden and turn left on Dorotheenstr. As you follow this to Friedrichstr., you'll pass the **Internationales Handelszentrum** (Trade Center), built in 1978 and a very prominent feature of the Berlin skyline. Heading right on Friedrichstr., take in the wavy glass-plated facade at **#148** before crossing the Spree and heading left on Schiffbauerdamm, which is lined with a mish-mash of modern buildings.

5. GOVERNMENT COMPLEX. Schiffbauerdamm will lead you to some of Berlin's most unusual architectural marvels. Opposite the glass-domed **Reichstag** (p. 108) spans a stretch of government buildings dating from 1997-2003: they begin with the **Marie-Elisabeth Lüders Building,** designed by Stephan Braunfels and home to the Bundestag's library; cross over the river to Braunfels' **Paul Löbe Building,** which holds the Bundestag's many committees; and continue to the **Federal Chancellery,** the hyper-modern structure imagined by Axel Schultes and Charlotte Frank and best known for the huge circular windows on its sides. The contrast between fluid shapes and sharp angles in these buildings make them totally unlike normal bureaucratic architecture, with its habitual stiffness. The walkway over the Spree, an area once located in the death strip, symbolizes a newly reunified Germany. To the northwest, you can spot the shimmering Hauptbahnhof, the largest train station in Europe.

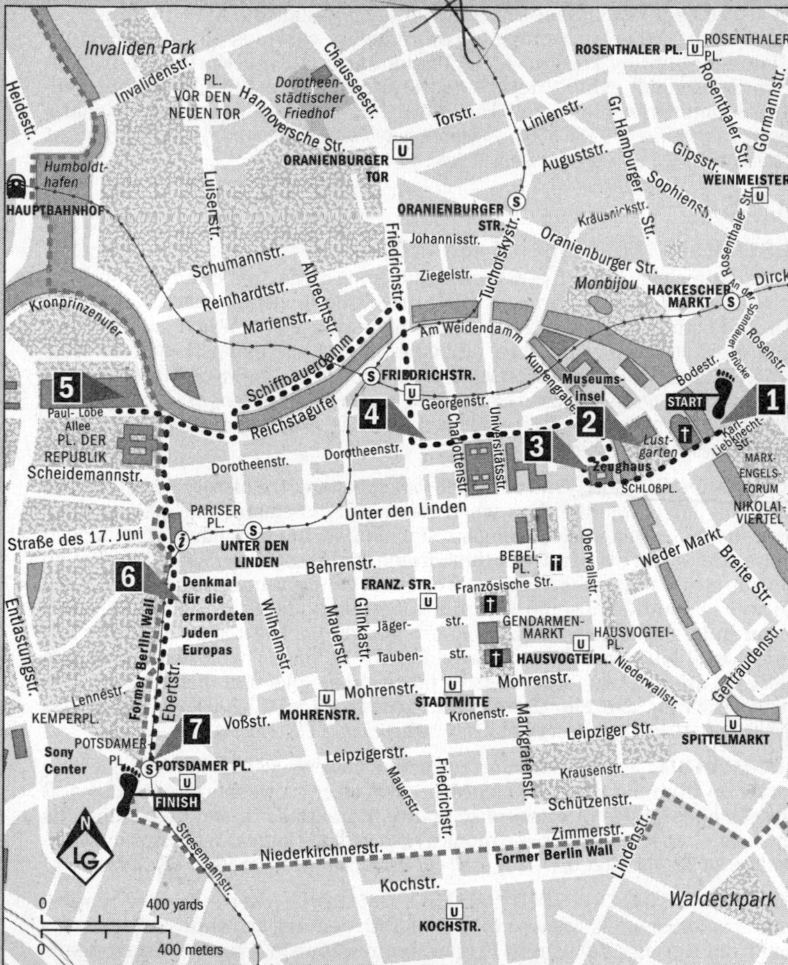

6. DENKMAL FÜR DIE ERMORDETEN JUDEN EUROPAS (MEMORIAL FOR THE MURDERED JEWS OF EUROPE). Cutting across the top of the Tiergarten, you'll reach this new memorial, opened in 2005. Designed by Peter Eisenman, it spans 19,000 sq. meters and allows you to walk unsteadily on the wavy ground between slabs of concrete. Their varying heights, coupled with the uneven walkways, will leave you feeling (appropriately) unsettled.

7. POTSDAMER PLATZ. Welcome to the glittering hub of modern Berlin, surrounded by an array of towering contemporary buildings, with more on the way. None is more striking than the **Deutsche Bahn Tower,** which commands attention with its curved glass front, jutting upward at an abrupt angle. Next door, the triangular Sony Center (p. 105) lures in spectators with its courtyard arena, which is covered in a strangely asymmetrical structure resembling a circus tent.

lion visitors per year, it is Berlin's fifth-most popular tourist attraction. Visitors come to see erotica ranging from naughty carvings on a 17th-century Italian deer-hunting knife to a 1955 calendar featuring Marilyn Monroe in the nude. A small exhibit describes the life of Beate Uhse, a pilot-turned-entrepreneur who pioneered Europe's first and largest sex shop chain. *(Joachimstalerstr. 4. ☎ 030 886 0666; www.erotikmuseum.de. Museum open daily 9am-midnight. €6, students €5. Gift store open M-Sa 9am-9pm, Su 1-10pm.)*

MITTE

MUSEUMSINSEL (MUSEUM ISLAND)

The Museumsinsel holds five separate museums on an area cordoned off from the rest of Mitte by two arms of the Spree. The museums were built in the 19th- and 20th centuries, suffered bombing during World War II and isolation and neglect afterwards, but have all been recently and extensively renovated. *(S3, S5, S7, S9, or S75 to "Hackescher Markt" or bus #100 to "Lustgarten." ☎ 030 266 3666. All national museums, unless otherwise noted, open Tu-W and F-Su 10am-6pm, Th 10am-10pm. Free audio tours in English. Admission to each €8, students €4. All sell a 3-day card good for admission to every museum; €14, students €7.)*

PERGAMONMUSEUM. One of the world's great ancient history museums, the Pergamon dates from the days when Heinrich Schliemann and other zealous 19th-century German archaeologists dismantled the remnants of collapsed empires the world over and sent them home for reassembly. Named for Pergamon, the city in present-day Turkey from which the enormous **Altar of Zeus** (180 BC) was taken, the museum features gargantuan pieces of ancient Mediterranean and Near Eastern civilizations from as far back as the 10th century BC. The colossal blue **Ishtar Gate** of Babylon (575 BC) and the **Roman Market Gate** of Miletus are just two more massive pieces in a collection that also includes Greek, Assyrian, and Far Eastern art. *(Bodestr. 1-3. ☎ 030 2090 5577. Open M-Su 10am-6pm, Th 10am-10pm. Last entry 30min. before closing. €8, students €4.)*

BODE-MUSEUM. The island's most attractive museum, which looks like it rises straight up from the water, reopened in 2006 after six years of renovations. It houses a hodgepodge of classical sculpture, Byzantine art, and oil painting. Its numismatic collection (coins and monies) is one of the largest in the world. *(Monbijoubrücke. ☎ 030 266 3666. Open Tu-W and F-Su 10am-6pm. Th 10am-10pm. €8, students €4.)*

ALTE NATIONALGALERIE (OLD NATIONAL GALLERY). After extensive renovations, this museum is open to lovers of 19th-century art, showcasing everything from German Realism to French Impressionism. Camille Pisarro leads the all-star cast of featured artists. *(Am Lustgarten. ☎ 030 2090 5577. Open Tu-W and F-Su 10am-6pm. Th 10am-10pm. €8, students €4.)*

ALTES MUSEUM. At the far end of the Lustgarten, the museum in the stately columned building designed by Karl Friedrich Schinkel is surprisingly untouristed. The lower level contains a permanent collection of ancient Greco-Roman (especially Etruscan) decorative art. The highlight of the upstairs Egyptian collection, and probably the whole museum, is the amazingly realistic bust of Nefertiti. *(AmLustgarten. ☎ 030 266 3660. Open M-W and F-Su 10am-6pm. Th 10am-10pm. €8, students €4. Free audio tour.)*

KULTURFORUM

The Kulturforum is a cluster of museums, concert halls, and libraries right off Potsdamer Platz. Two of its most recognizable buildings are the twin **Philharmonie** (p. 121) and the **Neue Staatsbibliothek** (new state library), both a warm honey color. *(S1, S2, S25 or U2 to "Potsdamer Pl." and walk down Potsdamer Str.; the museums will be on your right on Matthäikirchpl. www.kulturforum-berlin.com. Full day ticket to the entire Kulturforum €8, students €4. Opening times vary; all free Th 6-10pm.)*

GEMÄLDEGALERIE (PICTURE GALLERY). This is the place to come in Berlin, and arguably in Germany, for painting. The city's most famous museum houses a collection of 2700 13th- to 18th-century masterpieces by Dutch, Flemish, German, and Italian masters, including works by Botticelli, Bruegel, Dürer, Gainsborough, Raphael, Rembrandt, Rubens, Titian, Velazquez, and many, many others. *(Matthäikirchplatz 4-6. ☎ 030 266 2951. Open Tu-W and F-Su 10am-6pm, Th 10am-10pm.)*

NEUE NATIONALGALERIE (NEW NATIONAL GALLERY). This sleek building, designed by **Mies van der Rohe** at the height of 1960s Minimalism, contains often wacky temporary exhibits in the glass entrance hall and gallery downstairs. The real draw is its formidable permanent collection of 20th-century art, including works by Warhol, Munch, Kirchner, and Beckmann. *(Potsdamer Str. 50. ☎ 030 266 2651. Open Tu-W and F 10am-6pm, Th 10am-10pm, Sa-Su 11am-6pm.€8, students €4.)*

KUPFERSTICHKABINETT (MUSEUM OF PRINTS AND DRAWINGS). Sketches by everyone from Botticelli to Picasso to Warhol show that sometimes it is more thrilling to see genius' works-in-progress than it is to see the "finished" product. *(Matthäikirchplatz 8. ☎ 030 266 2002. Open Tu-F 10am-6pm, Sa-Su 11am-6pm.)*

MUSIKINSTRUMENTEN-MUSEUM (MUSICAL INSTRUMENT MUSEUM). Benjamin Franklin's design for a glass harmonica, J.S. Bach's *cembalo*, and a few of King Friedrich II's old flutes are just some of the instruments on display here. It is worth taking the tour to hear the "Mighty Wurlitzer," a monstruous organ, played live. *(Tiergartenstr. 1. ☎ 030 25 48 11 78. Open Tu-F 9am-5pm, Th 9am-8pm, Sa-Su 10am-5pm. Tours Th 6pm and Sa 11am, €2.)*

OTHER MUSEUMS IN MITTE AND TIERGARTEN

HAMBURGER BAHNHOF: MUSEUM FÜR GEGENWART (MUSEUM FOR THE PRESENT). With a colossal 10,000 sq. m of exhibition space, this converted train station houses Berlin's foremost collection of contemporary art. The museum features several whimsical works by Warhol, as well as pieces by Twombly and Kiefer and some more puzzling exhibits in its vast white spaces. *(Invalidenstr. 50-51. S3, S5, S7, S9, or S75 to "Hauptbahnhof" or U6 to "Zinnowitzer Str." ☎ 030 3978 3411; www.hamburgerbahnhof.de. Open Tu-F 10am-6pm, Sa 11am-8pm, Su 11am-6pm. €8, students €4; Th 2-6pm free.)*

DEUTSCHE HISTORISCHES MUSEUM (GERMAN HISTORY MUSEUM). The oldest building on Unter den Linden, a baroque former military arsenal dating to 1730, the museum now houses a thorough exploration of German history, from Neanderthals to the Nazis to the fall of the Wall. Temporary exhibitions focus on the last 50 years, with plenty of depictions of smiling workers from the DDR era. Behind the main building stands its modern counterpart, a new wing designed by I. M. Pei that further bolster Berlin's reputation for cutting-edge architecture. *(Unter den Linden 2. S3, 5, 7, 9, or 75 to "Hackescher Markt." ☎ 030 2030 4444; www.dhm.de. Open daily 10am-6pm. €5, 18 and under free. Audio tour €3.)*

KUNST-WERKE BERLIN (INSTITUTE OF CONTEMPORARY ART). MoMA curator Klaus Biesnbach transformed this former margarine factory into a non-profit "art laboratory," with constantly chainging exhibitions, an open library of art magazines and journals, and a number of artists' *ateliers*. It is perhaps best known as the home of the **Berlin Biennale**, a contemporary art fair, when the normally tranquil garden cafe is overrun. *(Auguststr. 69. U6 to "Oranienburger Tor." ☎ 030*

243 4590; www.kw-berlin.de. Open Tu-W and F-Su noon-7pm, Th noon-9pm. Check the website for current shows. €6, students €4. Garden and cafe open daily 9am-8pm. Free.)

DEUTSCHE KINEMATHEK. The museum chronicles the development of German film with a special focus on older works like Fritz Lang's *Metropolis* (1927), but for non-film buffs, the best part is the futuristic mirrored entrance. There is a mix of old film (whole rooms are devoted to such icons as Marlene Dietrich) and new, with a permanent display on television that was unveiled in 2006. Captions are in English. *(Potsdamer Str. 2; 3rd and 4th fl. of the Sony Center. S1, S2, S25 or U2 to "Potsdamer Pl." ☎030 300 9030; www.filmmuseum-berlin.de. Tickets sold on ground fl. Open Tu-W and F-Su 10am-6pm, Th 10am-8pm. €6, students €4.50, children €2.)*

BAUHAUS-ARCHIV MUSEUM FÜR GESTALTUNG (BAUHAUS ARCHIVE MUSEUM FOR DESIGN). A must-visit for design fans, this building was conceived by Bauhaus founder **Walter Gropius** and houses rotating exhibits of paintings, sculptures, and of course, the famous furniture. *(Klingelhöferstr. 14. Bus #100, 187, 200, or 341 to "Nordische Botschaften/Adenauer-Stifteng" or U1, U2, U3, or U4 to "Nollendorfpl." ☎030 254 0020; www.bauhaus.de. Open M and W-Su 10am-5pm. M-Tu and Sa-Su €7, students €4; W-F €6/3. Audio tour free.)*

KREUZBERG

Museums in Kreuzberg are a grab-bag. This area has one must-see (the Jewish Museum). You can see the rest if it's raining out or you're feeling especially ambitious.

JÜDISCHES MUSEM (JEWISH MUSEUM). Architect Daniel Libeskind's design for the zinc-plated Jewish Museum is fascinating even as an architectural experience. No two walls are parallel, creating a sensation of perpetual discomfort. Underground, three symbolic hallways—the **Axis of the Holocaust,** the **Axis of Exile,** and the **Axis of Continuity**—are intended to represent the trials of death, escape, and survival. The labyrinthine "Garden of Exile" replicates the dizzying effects of dislocation and the eerie "Holocaust Tower," a giant, asymmetrical concrete room nearly devoid of light and sound, encourages reflection. Exhibits feature works by contemporary artists, memorials to victims of the Holocaust, and a history of Jews in Germany. Enter at the top of the stairs from the Axis of Continuity. *(Lindenstr. 9-14. U6 to "Kochstr.," or U1, U6, or U15 to "Prinzenstr." ☎030 25 99 33 00. Open M 10am-10pm, Tu-Su 10am-8pm. Last entry 1hr. before closing. €5, students €2.50. Special exhibits €4. Audio tour €2.)*

BERLIN

MARTIN-GROPIUS-BAU. After standing for years in the shadow of the Wall, Martin-Gropius-Bau has returned to its rightful place as the city's most beautiful and important exhibition space. Bauhaus founder Walter Gropius' great-uncle designed the building, which houses temporary exhibits of photography, painting, and decorative art. *(Niederkirchnerstr. 7. U6 to "Kochstr." ☎030 254 860; www.gropiusbau.de. Open M and W-Su 10am-8pm. Price varies by exhibition. Free tours of the space once per month; check the website.)*

HAUS AM CHECKPOINT CHARLIE. Checkpoint Charlie, the border crossing between former East and West Berlin has become one of Berlin's most popular attractions, with tour buses, stands selling DDR memorabilia, actors clad as soldiers, and a table where you can get your passport "stamped." Perhaps the biggest rip off (those actors only charge €1 per photo) in the area is the **Haus am Checkpoint Charlie,** a two-bedroom apartment turned private museum. The exhibits detail how women curled up in loudspeakers, students dug tunnels with their fingers, and others found ingenious ways of getting into the West. Much of the same information can be gleaned for free by reading the placards along **Kochstraße,** where the wall used to run. *(Friedrichstr. 43-45. U6 to "Kochstr." ☎030 253 7250; www.mauer-museum.de. Museum open daily 9am-10pm. German-language films with English subtitles every 2hr. from 9:30am. €12.50, students €9.50. Audio tour €3.)*

DEUTSCHES TECHNIKMUSEUM. The airplane on the roof is a C-47, one of the original fleet of "raisin bombers" that kept West Berlin fed during the airlift. Inside, a colossal museum features aged trains, a history of film technology, and full-size model ships through which you're free to wander. Across the parking lot, another building features a collection of classic cars, music-makers, a plethora of science experiments involving optical illusions, and—best of all—a revolving playhouse. The new aeronautical wing documents the history of flight; its displays range from life-size planes to a whole room full of engines. Some exhibits are in English. *(Trebbiner Str. 9. U1, U2, or U15 to "Gleisdreieck," or U1, U7, or U15 to "Möckernbrücke." ☎030 902 540; www.stdb.de. Open Tu-F 9am-6pm, Sa-Su 10am-6pm. Last entry 30min. before closing. €4.50, students €2.50. Audio guides €2. Some special exhibits cost extra. 1st Su of the month free.)*

SCHWULES MUSEUM (GAY MUSEUM). Tucked into a courtyard off Mehringdamm, the only federally funded museum focused on gay culture in the world recounts on the history of homosexuals in Germany from 1800 to 1970, with a focus on persecution under the Nazis. A lending library contains thousands of periodicals, books, and films. *(Mehringdamm 61. ☎030 6959 9050. Open Tu-F 2-6pm, Sa 2-7pm. €5, students €3.).*

GALLERIES

Berlin has an extremely well-funded art scene, with many first-rate galleries. The work is as diverse as Berlin's cultural landscape and includes everything from early Christian antiques in Charlottenburg to conceptual installations in Mitte. A few good pamphlets, all with maps and available just about anywhere in the city, are: *ARTery Berlin* (€2.50), with complete show listings in English and German; *Berliner Kunst Kalender* (€2); and *Berliner Galerien* (free). The normal city guide, *Zitty*, also lists the major openings.

The center of Berlin's gallery world is Mitte, which has more contemporary work than classics; the *Berlin Mitte* pamphlet provides listings and a map. Five times a year, Mitte offers a *Galerienrundgang* tour of the galleries (dates are listed in the pamphlets). On nearby **Sophienstaße, Gipsstraße, Auguststraße,** and **Linienstraße,** galleries

SAMMLUNG HOFFMANN

From the gallery-filled streets of Mitte to the state-curated collections at the Kulturforum, it's almost impossible to visit Berlin without taking in some of its masterpieces. While everyone knows that museums show some of the city's most cutting-edge work, most tourists miss the major exhibition of modern art that lies hidden in, of all places, a private residence on Sophienstr.

In 1968, Rolf and Erika Hoffmann began to purchase contemporary art and have since amassed an impressive collection. The Hoffmanns have turned their Mitte home into a veritable museum—which the[redacted]call "an experiment in living a[redacted]g art."

Every Saturday, the family opens up their home in order to share their love of art. They rotate the works on display every summer, but the living room, with a large Frank Stella piece permanently on the wall, marks the heart of the collection. The space features everything from neon installations to video art to painting. Tours are required, so if you are planning to spend a Saturday roaming between the galleries along Sophienstrasse, Augustr., and Linienstr., remember to call ahead: it's not every day that you get to see great art and great real estate all rolled into one[redacted]

Sophienstr. 21 ([redacted]0 28 49 91 21; www.sophie-g[redacted].de). Open Sa 11am-4pm. German only, but guides can speak English. €6.

TOP TEN TASKS FOR THE MOVIE BUFF IN BERLIN

Run across the **Oberbaumbrücke,** where *Run Lola Run* (1998) shot some of its most beautiful footage. Meander along the scenic routes Lola takes to collect the money that will save her boyfriend. (Or, if you're truly hardcore, take the *Lola Rennt* running tour.)

Come to the *Cabaret* (1972) and look for Sally Bowles at the **KitKatClub**. Although the present fetish incarnation is a far cry from the interwar nightclub of the film, your chances of seeing someone dressed as the Emcee are fairly good. N[redacted]t for the faint of heart, though[redacted] patrons are allowed to have s[redacted] on the dance floor.

Take a bunch of pictures in the **Alexanderplatz.** When you get home, Photoshop out all the Westernized billboards in homage to Alex in *Good-Bye, Lenin* (2003) and his desperate attempt to protect his sickly mother from the reality of the fall of the Berlin Wall.

Since you're already in "der Alex," arrange a meeting with someone mysterious at the **World Clock.** You probably know who you are, but why not take in the city à la Jason Bourne in *The Bourne Supremacy* (2004).

Have a drink at **Cafe Adler** and ta[redacted] a look at **Checkpoint Charlie**[redacted]hen imagine the diggers of *Der Tunnel* (2001) burrowing beneath you to save their families stranded in East Berlin

pack the streets and *Hinterhöfe* (courtyards hidden behind building facades). Charlottenburg also has a large selection of galleries, many of which are more upscale. Kreuzberg hosts a handful of galleries, many with a political focus, and there's a new, small scene in Prenzlauer Berg off **Danziger Straße.** Be sure to pick up some **free wine** at many of the openings.

The galleries below are some of the more prominent ones; all are located in Mitte.

AKADEMIE DER KUNST. This 300-year-old institution has been the core of Berlin's art community for years, with students and artists working in every medium from film to painting to music and more. The Akademie sponsors a variety of prizes and hosts exhibitions in its Hanseatenweg location. A futuristic branch, at Pariser Pl. 4, houses the Akademie archives and five additional exhibition halls. *(Hanseatenweg 10. S3, S5, S7, S9, or S75 to "Bellevue," or U9 to "Hansapl." ☎030 390 760; www.adk.de. Open Tu-Su 11am-8pm. Exhibitions range from free to €12, students €10. Last Su of the month free.)*

NEUER BERLINER KUNSTVEREIN. Besides hosting a gallery space, Berlin's most democratic art organization sponsors the weekly "Treffpunkt NBK," a series of lectures, discussions with artists, performances, and more. It also lends reproductions of masterpieces to Berlin residents for €0.50 per month through the **Artothek** and has thousands of videos available to the public via the **Video-Forum.** *(Chausseestr. 128-129. ☎030 280 7020; www.nbk.org. Artothek ☎0881 927 0400. Gallery open Tu-F noon-6pm, Sa-Su 2-6pm. Video-Forum www.nbk.org. Open Tu and Th 2-6pm, W and F noon-5pm.)*

ENTERTAINMENT

Berlin's vibrant cultural scene is bustling with exhibitions, concerts, plays, and dance performances. The city generously subsidizes its artists despite recent cutbacks, and tickets are usually reasonable, especially with student discounts. Reservations can be made through the box office. Most theaters and concert halls offer up to 50% discounts for students who buy at the *Abendkasse* (evening box office), which generally opens 1hr. before shows. Other ticket outlets charge 15-18% commissions and do not offer student discounts. There is also a ticket counter on the sixth floor of the **KaDeWe.** (☎030 217 7754; www.showtimetickets.de. Open M-F 10am-8pm, Sa 10am-4pm.) Theaters generally accept credit cards, but many ticket outlets do not.

Most theaters and operas close from mid-July to late August.

Hekticket, Hardenbergpl. (☎030 230 9930; www.hekticket.de), near the Cineplex. 2nd branch at Alexanderpl., Karl-Liebknecht-Str. 12.Last-minute tickets up to 50% off. Open M-Sa 10am-8pm, Su 2-6pm; closed July to mid-Aug.

Berlin Ticket (☎030 2309 9333; www.berlin-ticket.de). Tickets for everything from sporting events and club parties to classical music concerts. *Klassik Kard* (€20) allows under 25 patrons to buy last minute €10 tickets for the opera or ballet.

CONCERTS, DANCE, AND OPERA

Berlin reaches its musical zenith in September during the fabulous **Berliner Festwochen,** which draws the world's best orchestras and soloists. The **Berliner Jazztage** in November, featuring top jazz musicians, also brings in the crowds. For tickets (which sell out months in advance) and more information for both festivals, call or write to **Berliner Festspiele** (☎030 25 48 90; www.berlinerfestspiele.de). In mid-July, the **Bachtage** feature an intense week of classical music, while every Saturday night in August the **Sommer Festspiele** turns the Ku'damm into a concert hall with genres from punk to folk competing for attention.

The monthly pamphlets *Konzerte und Theater* in Berlin und Brandenburg (free) and *Berlin Programm* (€1.75) list concerts, as do the biweekly *Zitty* and *Tip.* Tickets for the Philharmonie and the Oper are nearly impossible to get without writing months in advance, except by standing outside before performances with a small sign saying *"Suche Karte"* (seeking ticket)—people often try to unload tickets at the last moment, usually at outrageous prices.

Berliner Philharmonisches Orchester, Herbert-von-Karajan-Str. 1 (☎030 25 48 89 99; www.berlin-philharmonic.com). S1, S2, or S25 or U2 to "Potsdamer Pl." and walk up Potsdamer Str. It may look bizarre, but this yellow building, designed by Scharoun in 1963, is acoustically perfect: every audience member hears the music exactly as it is meant to sound. The Berliner Philharmoniker, led by the eminent Sir Simon Rattle, is one of the world's finest orchestras. It's tough to get a seat; check 1hr. before concert time or write at least 8 weeks in advance. Closed from late June to early Sept. Box office open M-F 3-6pm, Sa-Su 11am-2pm. Tickets from €7 for standing room, from €13 for seats.

Konzerthaus (Schauspielhaus am Gendarmenmarkt), Gendarmenmarkt 2 (☎030 203 092 101; www.kon-

or James Bond sneaking through in search of *Octopussy* (1983).

Boogie-woogie all night at the **Rock'n'Roll Club Spreeathen** and try to pick up one of the *Swing Kids* (1993).

Pop by the **Gendarmen Market.** Get a snack and have a flashback to the *V for Vendetta* (2005) Norsefire rally.

Stroll around the **Charlottenburg Palace** and pretend you're in Paris, like Jackie Chan in *Around the World in 80 Days* (2004). Marvel at the idea that someone who can't even tell Paris from Berlin would try to travel around the world via hot air balloon.

Walk through the **Brandenburg Gate,** like the actors in Billy Wilder's *One, Two, Three* (1961). Ponder the fact that the gate closed during the filming, and nobody made that trip again until the Wall fell. Ponder further whether the closing was due to the Communism=bad, Coca-Cola=awesome plot of the movie.

Find a smoky jazz club, order something made with blue gin, and dream of another Lola—Marlene Dietrich as the sexy cabaret singer who causes the downfall of a university professor in *The Blue Angel* (1930).

zerthaus.de). U2 or U6 to "Stadtmitte." The opulent home of Berlin's symphony orchestra. Last-minute tickets are somewhat easier to come by. No performances from mid-July to Aug. Box office open M-Sa noon-7pm, Su noon-4pm. Open in July M-Sa noon-6pm.

Deutsche Staatsoper, Unter den Linden 7 (☎030 2035 4555; www.staatsoper-berlin.de). U6 to "Französische Str." or bus #100, 157, or 348 to "Deutsche Staatsoper." Eastern Berlin's leading opera company. Box office open M-F 11am-7pm, Sa-Su 2-7pm, and 1hr. before performances. Closed from mid-July to Aug. Tickets €5-160; students €12, if purchased 30min. before shows and ½-price on cheaper seats for certain performances.

Deutsche Oper Berlin, Bismarckstr. 35 (tickets ☎030 34 38 43 43; www.deutscheoperberlin.de). U2 to "Deutsche Oper." Berlin's best and youngest opera. Box office open M-Sa 11am until 1hr. before performance (11am-7pm on days without performances), Su 10am-2pm. Evening tickets available 1hr. before performances. Closed July-Aug. Tickets €12-118. 25% student discounts.

THEATER

Theater listings, found on the yellow and blue posters in most U-Bahn stations, are available in the monthly pamphlets *Kultur!news* and *Berlin Programm*, as well as in *030*, *Zitty*, and *Tip*. In addition to the world's best German-language theater, Berlin also has a lively English-language scene; look for listings in *Zitty* or *Tip* that say "*in englischer Sprache*" (in English). A number of privately run companies called **Off-Theaters** also occasionally feature English-language plays. As with concert halls, virtually all theaters are closed in July and August (closings are indicated by the words *Theaterferien* or *Sommerpause*).

Deutsches Theater, Schumannstr. 13A (☎030 2844 1225; www.deutschestheater.de). U6, S1, S2, S5, S7, S9, S25, or S75 to "Friedrichstr." Even western Berlin admits it: this is the best theater in Germany. The **Kammerspiele** stages smaller, provocative productions. Box office open July M-F 1-7pm; Aug.-June M-Sa 11am-6:30pm, Su 3pm-6:30pm. Tickets for Deutsches Theater €5-43, for Kammerspiel €14-30; students €6-10.

Berliner Ensemble, Bertolt-Brecht-Pl. 1 (☎030 28 40 81 55; www.berliner-ensemble.de). U6 or S1, S2, S5, S7, S9, S25, or S75 to "Friedrichstr." The theater, established by Brecht, is enjoying a renaissance under the leadership of Claus Peymann. Hip repertoire with Heiner Müller, young American playwrights, and Brecht. Box office open M-F 8am-6pm, Sa-Su 11am-6pm, and 1hr. before shows. Tickets €2-30, students €7.

Volksbühne, Am Rosa-Luxemburg-Pl. (☎030 24 06 55; www.volksbuehne-berlin.de). U2 to "Rosa-Luxemburg-Pl." High on shock value, low on name recognition. Box office open daily noon-6pm. Tickets €10-30, students €6-15. The Volksbühne also features 2 nightclubs for the proletariat: the Roter Salon and Grüner Salon. Ask permission to eat downstairs with the actors in the cantina.

English Theater Berlin, Fidicinstr. 40 (☎030 691 1211; www.etberlin.de). U6 to "Pl. der Luftbrücke." This smaller, less well-funded stage produces new, experimental works and old favorites by the likes of Samuel Beckett and Tennessee Williams. Box office opens 1hr. prior to showtime. Most shows at 8pm. Tickets €8-15.

FILM

On any night in Berlin you can choose from over 150 different films. **O.F.** or **O.V.** next to a movie listing means original version (i.e., not dubbed in German); **O.m.U.** means original version with German subtitles; **O.m.e. U.** means original with English subtitles. Check *Tip*, *Zitty*, or *030* for theater schedules. Monday through Wednesday are Kinotage at most theaters, with reduced prices and further discounts for those with a student ID. The city also hosts the international **Berlinale film festival** (early February).

Arsenal, (☎030 26 95 51 00; www.fdk-berlin.de), in the Filmhaus at Potsdamer Pl. U2, S1, S2, or S25 to "Potsdamer Pl." Run by the founders of the Berlinale, Arsenal showcases indie films and some classics (€6.50). Frequent appearances by guest directors make the theater a popular meeting place for Berlin's filmmakers.

Filmkunsthaus Babylon, Rosa-Luxemburg-Str. 30 (☎030 242 59 69; www.babylon-berlin.de). U2 to "Rosa-Luxemburg-Pl." Shows classics like *Goodfellas* in the main theater and art films from around the world in the intellectual **Studiokino** (entrance on Hirtenstr.). Most English-language films not dubbed in German. Main theater M-W €5.50, Th-Su €6.50.

Odeon, Hauptstr. 116 (☎030 7870 4019; www.yorck.de). U4 to "Innsbrucker Pl." One of the 1st English-language theaters in Berlin, Odeon shows mainstream American and British flicks, sometimes dubbed in German and sometimes with subtitles. €7.50, students €7; M €5, Tu-W €6.

CineStar, in the Sony Center, Potsdamer Pl. 4 (☎030 2606 6260; www.cinestar.de). S1, S2, or U2 to "Potsdamer Pl." English-language blockbusters in a huge theater with stadium seating so steep you'll fear for your life. Last showing around 11pm, M no late show. M and W €6.50, Tu €4.50, F-Sa €7.50; students M and W-Th €5.50, F-Su €6.

NIGHTLIFE

Berlin's nightlife is world-renowned absolute madness—a teeming cauldron of debauchery that bubbles around the clock. Bars typically open at 6pm and get crowded around 10pm, just as the clubs open their doors. Bar scenes wind down anywhere between midnight and 6am; meanwhile, around 1am, dance floors fill up and the lights flash at clubs that keep pumping beats until dawn, when a variety of after-parties keep up the perpetual motion. In summer months it's only dark from 10:30pm to 4am, so it's easy to be unintentionally included in the early morning crowd, watching the sun rise on Berlin's landmarks and waiting for the cafes to open. From 1-4am on weekdays, 70 night buses operate throughout the city, and on Friday and Saturday nights the U- and S-Bahn run on a limited schedule throughout the night. The best sources of information about bands and dance venues are the bi-weekly magazines *Tip* (€2.70) and the superior *Zitty* (€2.70), available at all newsstands, or the free *030*, distributed in hostels, cafes, shops, and bars.

CHARLOTTENBURG

Charlottenburg's quiet cafes and music venues cater to the 30-something set. It's a nice place for a mellow evening or to hear the city's best jazz, but the real parties are eastward. **The Ku'damm** is best avoided at night, unless you enjoy fraternizing with drunk businessmen.

Trane, Bleibtreustr. 1 (☎030 313 2550; www.a-trane.de). S3, S5, S7, S9, or S75 to "Savignypl." Cozy tables litter the floor of this comfortably sized club for serious jazz fans. Classic black and white photographs adorn walls, and a small chalkboard next to the stage lists the night's performers. Herbie Hancock, Wynton Marsalis—all the classics have played here. Late-night jam with no cover Sa from 12:30am. Cover €7-15, students €5-13. Open M-Th and Su 9pm-2am, F-Sa 9pm-late. Reserve a table online in advance. Cash only.

Salz, Salzufer 20 (☎01702 833504; www.salz-club.de). U2 to "Ernst-Reuter-Platz." Exposed brick walls keep the disco-ball-lit dance floor looking classy at this salt warehouse turned techno club. The 2 real prizes: a gorgeous patio with tiki lamps and never, ever a cover. Check the website for music schedule. Open F-Sa 8pm-late.

BERLIN

Quasimodo, Kantstr. 12A (☎030 312 8086; www.quasimodo.de). U2, S5, S7, S9, or S75 to "Zoologischer Garten." Beneath a huge cafe, this grownup, spacious venue showcases soul, R&B, and jazz. Drinks €2.50-4.50. Cover for concerts €8-30. Tickets available F from 4:30pm or Sa-Su from 11am at the cafe upstairs or from KonzertKasse ticket service (☎030 61 10 13 13); cheaper if reserved in advance. Check website for schedule. Open daily 9pm-late. Cash only.

SCHÖNEBERG AND WILMERSDORF

BARS AND CLUBS

Slumberland, Goltzstr. 24 (☎030 216 5349). U1-U4 to "Nollendorfpl." Palm trees, rotating art from Africa and, yes, a real sand floor that transports you to the Bahamas in what is otherwise a standard looking pub. Listen to reggae while sipping a mixed drink (€5). The secret to the frappés (€2.30) is coffee crystals. Most drinks €2-5. Open M-Th and Su 6pm-2am, F 6pm-4am, Sa 11am-4am. Cash only.

Alt Berliner Biersalon, Ku'damm 225 (☎030 88 43 990). Go for a taste of the former West Berlin opulence at this spacious pub-like bar. For all the gorgeous wooden paneling the atmosphere is far from stuffy: locals gather to watch German league (Bundesliga) soccer games here on Sa. (Hint: root for Hertha and you will make friends.) Beer €3-4.50. Open 24hr.

GAY AND LESBIAN

Schöneberg is Berlin's unofficial "gay district" and teems with GLBT nightlife.

Hafen, Motzstr. 19 (☎030 211 4118; www.hafen-berlin.de). U1-U4 to "Nollendorfpl." Nearly 20 years old, this bar has become a landmark for Berlin's gay community. The sign outside specifically invites in "drop dead gorgeous looking tourists," but there are plenty of locals here, too. The mostly male crowd jams the surrounding sidewalk in summer. Weekly pub quiz M 8pm (1st M of the month in English). New DJs W. Open daily 8am-4am. Cash only.

Connection, Fuggerstr. 33 (☎030 218 1432; www.connection-berlin.de). U1 or U2 to "Wittenbergpl." The name says it all. Find your soulmate (or one-night stand) in the disco, then go next door to the labyrinthine **Connection Garage** to get acquainted. First F of the month mixed; otherwise, men only. Cover €7, includes 1st drink. Club open F-Sa 11pm-late; Garage open M-Sa 10am-1am, Su and holidays 2pm-1am. AmEx/MC/V.

Begine, Potsdamer Str. 139 (☎030 215 1414; www.begine.de). U2 to "Bülowstr." In a neighborhood dominated by sceney gay clubs, this is a welcome retreat for women. Named after a now-defunct lesbian squat, Berlin's biggest lesbian community center has a popular, low-key cafe/bar with live music and readings at night. No cover. Open M-F 6pm-late, Sa-Su 9:30pm-late.

Heile Welt, Motzstr. 5 (☎030 2191 7507). U1-U4 to "Nollendorfpl." Despite the addition of 2 enormous, quiet inner sitting rooms, the 20-something clientele still pack the bar and spill into the street. Aside from a fur-covered wall and single tiara hanging above the bar, both the decor and mood are reserved. Mostly male crowd during "prime time;" more women in the early evening, on weekdays, and in the early morning. Open daily 6pm-4am, sometimes later. Cash only.

Neue Ufer, Hauptstr. 157 (☎030 7895 7900). U7 to "Kleistpark." Formerly Anderes Ufer (The Other Shore), this long-running cafe has become "the new shore," abandoning the rainbow ship that once decorated the interior. A photo of David Bowie commemorates the many hours he spent drinking here. The beer (€2.80-3.80) and coffee (€2.20-2.80) flow and the mood is still mellow. Open daily 11am-2am. Cash only.

MITTE

The Mitte nightlife scene centers on **Hackescher Markt** and **Oranienburger Straße** (also, incidentally, the city's most conspicuous prostitution drag). The pricey, packed strip offers a mixture of both world-renowned and touristy bars and clubs. If you'd prefer to get off the beaten track, head to the outskirts of Mitte or its eastern neighborhoods.

Week-End, Alexanderpl. 5 (☎030 24 63 16 76; www.week-end-berlin.de), on the 12th and 15th fl. of the building with the "Sharp" sign overlooking the city. A staple of the Berlin club scene, where minimal techno fuels the floor until the sun rises over the block-housing of East Berlin. Wheelchair-accessible. Cover €8-12. Open F-Su 11pm-late. Cash only.

Tape, Heidestr. 14 (☎030 848 4873; www.tapeberlin.de), near a few art galleries along a strip close to the Hauptbahnhof. This converted warehouse is worth the trip. The walls, the entrance, and ravers' hands are all stamped with images of cassette tapes, the club's symbol. An artsy crowd dances in the enormous main room and hangs out on couches in the silver lounge. Cover varies. Open F-Sa 11pm-late.

Clärchen's Ballhouse, Auguststr. 24 (☎030 282 92 95; www.ballhaus.de). This odd-looking building was a ballroom before WWI, and now it is again. Older couples gather to tango and swing, while younger groups attempt to join in or enjoy beer in the flower-filled courtyard. Free introductory "swing tease" lesson W. Classical concerts and chacha brunch W. Open daily noon-late.

Bang Bang Club, Neue Promenade 10 (☎030 60 40 53 10; www.bangbang-club.de). Twiggy look-alikes run around a dance floor while guys in fedoras nod and smile. Grab your best tight jeans and ankle boots for "Death by Britpop" on F. Opening days and times vary. Check website or show up after midnight.

CCCP Klub, Torstr. 136 (☎0179 69 29 13). The only marker is the red star above the rusty iron door. Inside, this bar looks like your crazy aunt's closet—in a good way. There's a skeleton on one wall and a bearskin rug on another. Listen for the old Russian pop music or seek out indie and electro. Open Tu-Sa 11pm-late. Cash only.

Kaffee Burger, Torstr. 60 (☎030 28 04 64 95; www.kaffeeburger.de). U2 to "Rosa-Luxemburg-Pl." Iconic retro DDR-style bar draws huge crowds for twice monthly "Russian disco" night. Connected to the more laid-back **Burger Bar** (Torstr. 58) through a cloakroom guarded by a life-size statue of a Russian soldier. Live bands Th 10pm. Cover M-Th €1, F-Sa €5-6. Open M-Sa 10pm-late, Su 7pm-late. Cash only.

Cookies, Friedrichstr. at Unter den Linden (☎030 27 49 29 40; www.cookies-berlin.de). U6 to "Französiche Str." Once a mobile weekly dance party among a group of friends, the party is now open to the public, as is the hip restaurant, **Cookies Cream.** Go dancing Tu and Th 11pm-6am. Restaurant open Tu-Sa from 8pm. The affiliated **Crush** party happens Sa at Behrenstr. 55. Open midnight-late. Cash only.

Tacheles, Oranienburger Str. 54-56 (☎030 282 6185; www.tacheles.de). U6 to "Oranienburger Tor" or S1, S2, or S25 to "Oranienburger Str." or night buses N6 or N84. Housed in a bombed-out former department store and the adjacent courtyard, this edgy complex boasts a motif of graffiti and scrap metal artwork. A playground for artists, punks, and curious tourists, the labyrinth leads into several art galleries, movie theaters, and balcony bars. Opening times for the theater and galleries vary, as do party dates—check the website. For theater tickets, call ☎030 28 09 68 35.

Delicious Doughnuts, Rosenthaler Str. 9 (☎030 28 09 92 74; www.delicious-doughnuts.de). U8 to "Rosenthaler Pl." This backpacker hangout's curved design draws you into one of the loungeable booths. Other facilities include pinball and a pocket-sized dance floor. Shades keep early-morning stragglers protected from the sun. Cover M-Th and Su €3, F-Sa €5. Open daily 10pm-late. Cash only.

BERLIN

TROPICAL BERLIN. Berliners like to do everything outside in summer: grill meat in the parks, attend outdoor cinemas (www.freiluft-kino.de), and play on tropical beaches—manmade tropical beaches, that is, with sand and deck chairs laid out to make temporary bars. One of the most popular is along **Monbjou Park** (SBahn "Hackescher Markt") but they're everywhere along the Spree.

PRENZLAUER BERG

Prenzlauer Berg is the place to go for a slightly more relaxed, less techno oriented scene than the elsewhere in Berlin. Trendy bars and late-night cafes cluster around **Kastanienallee** (U2 to "Eberswalder Str.") while the areas around **Helmholtzplatz** (SBahn to "Prenzlauer Allee") are your best bet for the neighborhood's trademark shabby chic.

The Weinerei, Veteranenstr. 14 (☎030 440 6983). The unmarked wine bar has gone from local secret to local legend, based on comfortable elegance and a strange pricin-system. Pay €1 for a glass, sample all of the wines, sample again, and again, and before leaving pay however much you think you owe. Open 10am-very late. Cash only.

Klub Der Republik (KDR Bar), Pappelallee 81. U2 to "Eberswalderstr.," M10, N2, N42. Turn into what looks like a deserted parking lot and climb the stairs of a dance studio to find a totally preserved DDR ballroom turned favorite post-wall watering hole. Cheap drinks for the neighborhood (€2-4). Open in summer from 9pm, in winter from 8pm. Cash only.

Wohnzimmer, Lettestr. 6 (☎030 445 5458). U2 to "Eberswalder Str." The name means living room, and they aren't kidding. With wood-beam floors, the bar resembles an old-fashioned kitchen, and glassware cabinets line the walls. You'll feel right at home as you settle into a velvet armchair with a matching mixed drink. Damn good mojito €5. Open daily 9am-4am. Cash only.

Solsi e Morsi, Marienburger Str. 10. Owner Johnny Petrongolo flits around his always packed familial wine bar opening bottles and bestowing plates of free *parma* ham, cheese, and olives. The young clientele love their Galouises: Solsi e Morsi is not for the faint of lung. Open 6pm-late.

Dr. Pong, Eberswalder Str. 21. U2 to "Eberswalder Str." The centerpiece at this minimalist bar is a ping-pong table, ringed with intense hipsters gripping their paddles. Beginners and the severely intoxicated are both equally welcome. Drinks €2-5.50. Open M-Sa 8pm-late, Su from 2pm. Cash only.

Prater Garten, Kastanienallee 7-9 (☎030 448 5688; www.pratergarten.de). U2 to "Eberswalder Str." Giant chestnut trees hung with lanterns overhang sprawling picnic tables and umbrellas at what is arguably Berlin's most pleasant beer garden. Outdoor theater and TV. Bratwurst €2.50. Beer €2.50-3.50. Open in good weather Apr.-Sept. daily from noon until late. Cash only.

White Trash Fast Food, Schönhauser Alle 6-7 (☎030 50 34 86 67; www.whitetrash-fastfood.com). Guarded by 2 gilded lions out front, 4 levels of kitsch and irony provide endless eye-candy inside. Fish tanks, rabbit skins, and movie memorabilia abound. Drinks come with honest, English explanations. Try a "Zombie" (€8): "blast your head into 1000 pieces!" There's also a pinball machine. Open daily 6pm-late. Cash only.

Intersoup, Schliemannstr. 31 (☎030 23 27 30 45; www.intersoup.de). U2 to "Eberswalder Str." Named after DDR-era general stores (Intershop), this shabby bar eschews fancy designer drinks and popular music in favor of worn 70s furniture, soup specials (€4.50-5), and retro floral wallpaper. Downstairs, the small club **undersoup** keeps things wild with live music (most W and Sa nights), karaoke, occasional films, and a puppet theater (M and Tu). DJs most nights. Club cover €5 and under. Free Wi-Fi. Open M-Sa 6pm-3am, Su 5pm-2am. Cash only.

Morgenrot, Kastanienallee 85 (☎030 44 31 78 44; www.cafe-morgenrot.de). U2 to "Eberswalder Str." Candy-print wallpaper and abrupt art lure hipsters off the Kastanienallee strip. By day, it's a vegan hangout with a great brunch—by night, there are frosty vodka shots (€2). Open Tu-Th 10am-1am, F 10am-3am, Sa 11am-3am, Su 11am-1am. Cash only.

Duncker, Dunckerstr. 64 (☎030 445 9509; www.dunckerclub.de). S8, S41, or S85 to "Prenzlauer Allee." This intense club draws crowds with its insider vibe. Grill in back. Ring the bell for entry. M and Su goth, Tu hippie, Th live bands. Cover €1.50-4, Th often free. Open M-Tu and Th-Su 8pm-late. Heats up around 1am. On F and Sa, all drinks €2 max. Cash only.

Scotch & Sofa, Kollwitzstr. 18 (☎030 44 04 23 71). U2 to "Senefelderpl." Exactly what the name promises, (and a very comfortable sofa at that). Hangout of intellectual types who spill over from the nearby bookstores to enjoy the good music, which often includes some soul. Smoking downstairs, banned upstairs. Open daily 2pm-very late. Cash only.

FRIEDRICHSHAIN

When people think of Berlin techno clubs, they're thinking of Friedrichshain. There are more legendary converted factory or warehouse clubs in this neighborhood than you can shake a stick at. The more low-key bars cluster around **Simon-Dach-Strrasse** Raging dance venues are scattered between the car dealerships and empty lots on **Mühlenstrasse.**

Berghain/Panorama Bar, Am Wriezener Bahnhof (☎030 29 00 05 97; www.berghain.de). S3, S5, S7, S9, or S75 to "Ostbahnhof." Heading up Str. der Pariser Kommune, take the 3rd right into what looks like a parking lot. The granddaddy of Berlin's "it" clubs deserves its reputation as a must-visit. Beneath the towering ceilings of this former power plant, spaced-out techno-fiends pulse to the reverberating music. Cover generally €12. Open F-Sa and occasionally W from midnight. Cash only.

Maria am Ostbahnhof, Am der Schillingbrücke (☎030 21 23 81 90; www.clubmaria.de). S-Bahn to "Ostbahnhof." From Stralauer Pl. exit, take Str. der Pariser Kommune to Stralauer Pl., follow it right along the wall, turn left at the bridge, and look for the red lights by the water. Tucked away by the river in an old factory, this club embodies the industrial legacy of Friedrichshain's scene. Sizable—and usually full—dance floor. Mostly electronic music, occasional punk, and reggae. Beer €2.50-3.50. Cover €10-12. Open F-Sa 11pm-late, weekdays for concerts and events only. Cash only.

Sanitorium 23, Frankfurter Allee 23 (☎030 42 02 11 93; www.sanatorium23.de). Large windows look into a sterile yet hip interior of this sleek break from converted warehouses. Hang your coat on the overturned gurney and try the "Moscow Mule" (€5). Open daily 2pm-late. Chic rooms available above. Singles €40; doubles €55. Cash only.

Häbermeyer, Gärtnerstr. 6 (☎030 29 77 18 87). U5 to "Samariterstr." Retro stylings and soft red lighting from funky lamps complement the New Wave DJ sessions. Foosball table in back lends a competitive edge to the otherwise relaxed atmosphere. Mixed drinks €5.90-7.40. Open daily 7pm-late. Cash only.

Dachkammer Bar (DK), Simon-Dach-Str. 39 (☎030 296 1673). U5 to "Frankfurter Tor." Draped vines give this bar a rustic feel, along with plenty of brick, wood, and comfy nooks adorned with vintage furniture. Quieter than its neighbors, DK is the place for conversation along with mixed drinks (€5-8), snacks (from €3.50), and a huge variety of beer on tap. Breakfast buffet 1am-3pm (€6.50). Open daily noon-late. Cash only.

Matrix, Warschauer Pl. 18 (☎030 29 36 99 90). S3, S5, S7, S9, S75, or U1 to "Warschauer Str." No, you aren't imagining the pounding bass coming from under the station—4 dance floors and multiple bars extend under the tracks. The stylish can opt for a mixed drink (€4.50-7.50) in the VIP lounge. No sneakers. Cover €3-6. 18+ (bring ID). Open daily 10pm-late. Cash only.

Astro-Bar, Simon-Dach-Str. 40 (www.astro-bar.de). U5 to "Frankfurter Tor." Gritty retro-galactic bar with plastic robots in action poses proves yet again that Berlin is anything but normal. DJs play everything from R&B to electronica. Mixed drinks €3-5.50. Open daily from 6pm. Cash only.

Cassiopeia, Revaler Str. 99 (☎030 29 36 29 66). U- or S-Bahn to "Warschauer Str." A sprawling nightlife oasis in an abandoned train repairs factory, this club/beer garden/restaurant/theater has outdoor couches that provide relief from the packed dance floor. Beer €2-3. Movies €5-6. Cover €3-10. Open F-Sa from 11pm; check website for weekdays. Cash only.

KREUZBERG

Although clubs are emerging throughout the rest of eastern Berlin (especially Friedrichshain), Kreuzberg is still a nightlife stronghold, full of options for virtually every demographic. Although there is no shortage of bars, **Oranienstraße** has the densest and coolest stretches of nightlife offerings. A unique row of bars along the water on **Schlesisches Straße** allow travelers to watch the sun set and then sip drinks until it rises again.

Club der Visionaere, Am Flutgraben 1 (☎030 69 51 89 42; www.clubdervisionaererecords.com). U1 or U15 to "Schlesisches Tor" or night bus #N65 to "Heckmannufer." Lounging around on their torch-lit raft in the canal in summer is the single most pleasant bar experience in Berlin. Legend has it that bargoers occasionally fall into the water, but more common activities include dancing to house music or downing a pizza (€5-8) along with your drink. Beer €3. Open M-F 2pm-late, Sa-Su noon-late. Cash only.

Monarch Bar, Skalitzer Str. 134. U1 or U15 to "Kotbusser Tor." Don't be put off by the urine smell in the staircase that leads up to this small, unmarked bar above Kaiser's supermarket. Some of the cheapest beer (€1 and up) around, a panoramic view of the raised S-Bahn thundering by, and a nightly DJ spinning electronica. Open 10pm-late. Cover €1.

Watergate, Falckensteinstr. 49 (☎030 61 28 03 96; www.water-gate.de). U1 or U15 to "Schlesisches Tor." Depending on who is spinning, this can be the best party in the city on any given night. 2 constants: the polka-dot light show on the ceiling and the unbeatable view of the Spree from the "Water Floor" lounge and terrace. Crowds pick up at 2am. Cover W €6, F-Sa €10. Open W and F 11pm-late and Sa midnight-late. Cash only.

Live At Dot, Falckensteinstr. (☎030 76 76 62 67; www.liveatdot.com) U1 or U15 to "Schlesisches Tor." This new 2-story bar and alternative live music venue is slicker than most places in the neighborhood. Skip the downstairs restaurant and head straight for the concert above, where the acoustics are so good there are often live recordings taking place. Cover €5-10. Hours vary, open most nights; check the website for a schedule. Cash only.

Luzia, Oranienstr. 34 (☎030 81 79 99 58; www.luzia.tc). U1 or U15 to "Kotbusser Tor." Movie theater chairs, dark gold walls, and lofts accessible by ladders make Luzia the darling of a young, international crowd. That guy ordering a Krusovice on tap (€3) next to you at the bar is probably a freelance video artist. No cover. Open daily 9pm-late

Lido, Cuvrystr. 7 (☎030 81 79 99 58; www.lido-berlin.de). U1 or U15 to "Schlesisches Tor." Despite its unassuming exterior plastered with peeling posters, this former cinema provides Kreuzberg and greater Berlin with parties (cover €3-6) and concerts (€12-15) that feature internationally popular indie and rock groups.

Bar Nou, Bergmannstr. 104 (☎030 74 07 30 50). U7 to "Gneisenaustr.," or night bus #N4 or N19 to "Zossener Str." Bartenders joke about a 1 guest, 1 drink rule, but should think about enforcing it for real—these are some strong, strong drinks. Between the booze, the sexy red lighting, and communal sofa seating, more pickups happen here than at most German bars. Mixed drinks €7.50-9.50. Open daily 8pm-4am.

Yorckschlösschen, Yorckstr.15 (☎030 215 80 70; www.yorckschloesschen.de). U7 or S1 to "Yorckstr." Local radicals mix with international students in the "small castle," which opened as a corner pub at the turn of the century. These days, it is Berlin's most relaxed jazz club. Live jazz, blues, and funk W and Sa (9pm-midnight) and Su (2-6pm). Cover €4. Open M-F 5pm-3am, Su 10am-3am.

Junction Bar, Gneisenaustr. 18 (☎030 694 6602; www.junction-bar.de). U7 to "Gneisenaustr.," or night bus #N4 or N19 to "Zossener Str." Small but energetic venue for classic and pop rock, with nightly shows on an intimate subterranean stage. Can be packed or oddly empty depending on the night. Take a break at **Junction Cafe** upstairs (open 11am-2am). Live rock, soul, funk, jazz, or blues M-Th and Su from 9pm, F-Sa from 10pm. DJs start M-Th and Su 11:30pm, F-Sa 12:30am. Cover €5-8 for live music. Cover for DJs M-Th and Su €3, women free; F-Sa €4. Open daily 8pm-5am. Cash only.

Heinz Minki, Vor dem Schlesischen Tor 3 (☎030 69 53 37 66; www.heinzminki.de). U1 or U15 to "Schlesisches Tor" or night bus #N65 to "Heckmannufer." A beer garden that (shockingly) is actually a garden. Plush drapery lines the small interior, but the real fun is outside. Patrons pound beers (½L €3.10) at long tables under hanging colored lights and surrounded by greenery. Gourmet pizza €2.60-2.90. Grilled bratwurst €2. Foosball tournament last Su of every month. Open daily noon-late; check website for winter hours. Cash only.

GAY AND LESBIAN

GLBT-friendly nightlife in Keuzberg is clustered around **Oranienstraße** between Lausitzer Pl. and Oranienpl. and **Mehringdamm** north of the Platz der Luftbrücke.

Rose's, Oranienstr. 187 (☎615 65 70). U1 to "Görlitzer Bahnhof." Marked only by "Bar" over the door. It's Liberace meets Cupid meets Satan. A friendly, gay and lesbian clientele packs this intense and claustrophobic party spot all night. The voluptuous dark-red interior is accessorized madness, boasting hearts, glowing lips, furry ceilings, feathers, and glitter. The small menu covers the basics with whiskey (€5) and schnapps (€2). Open M-Th and Su 11pm-6am, F-Sa 11pm-8am. Cash only.

SchwuZ, Mehringdamm 61 (☎030 629 0880; www.schwuz.de). U6 or U7 to "Mehringdamm." Enter through Melitta Sundström, a popular gay and lesbian cafe. The city's longest-running gay bar features 2 dance floors and a loungy underground area lined with pipes and its own DJ and disco lights. Music varies from alternative to house depending on the night, and the crowd varies from young to very young. Lesbian night every 2nd F of the month. Cover F €5 before midnight, €6 after; Sa €6/7. Open F-Sa 11pm-late. Cash only.

SO36, Oranienstr. 190 (☎030 61 40 13 06; www.so36.de). U1 to "Görlitzer Bahnhof." One of Kreuzberg's oldest, grungiest, and best punk venues, named after the neighborhood's postal code, doubles as a gay nightclub. "Gayhane," Berlin's only Turkish gay night, is especially popular. Cover €3-10. Open 10pm-late. Cash only.

Bierhimmel, Oranienstr. 183 (☎030 61 53 122). U1 to "Görlitzer Bahnhof." Translating to "beer heaven," this place is also a heaven of good coffee and homemade cake during the day and a heaven of handsome men in the very dark back lounge at night. Mixed crowd uses it as a stop on the way to SO36. Open 11am-3am. Cash only.

BRANDENBURG

Completely surrounding Berlin, the Land of Brandenburg is a perfect escape from the sprawling urban behemoth resting at its center. The infamous Hohenzollern family emerged from the province's forests to become the rulers of Prussia, leaving their mark on the region in the shape of more than 30 stunning palaces. The castles attract their share of visitors to Brandenburg, especially the sprawling Sanssouci, only a 30min. train trip from the nation's capital making this Prussian take on Versailles a favorite jaunt for native Berliners.

HIGHLIGHTS OF BRANDENBURG

RINSE AWAY the (figurative) grit of Berlin with a visit to the refreshingly lavish Park **Sanssouci** (p. 132) in regal **Potsdam** (p. 130).

LOUNGE in a gondola on the winding canals near tiny **Lübbenau** (p. 137), under the trees and among the ghosts of the swampy **Spreewald** (p. 136).

POTSDAM ☎0331

Visitors disappointed by Berlin's distinctly unroyal demeanor can get their Kaiserly fix by taking the S-Bahn to Potsdam (pop. 146,000), the glittering city of Friedrich II (the Great). While his father, Friedrich Wilhelm I (the "Soldier King"), wanted to turn Potsdam into a huge garrison of the tall, tall men he had kidnapped to serve as his toy soldiers, the more aesthetically-minded Friedrich II beautified the city. His additions include Schloß Sanssouci and the surrounding park, and the nearby Neues Garten with its Marmorpalais. Potsdam was Germany's "Little Hollywood" in the 1920s and 30s, when the suburb of Babelsberg played a critical role in the early film industry. A 20min. air raid in April 1945 brought Potsdam's cinematic glory days to an end. As the site of the 1945 Potsdam Conference, in which the Allies divvied up the country, Potsdam's name became synonymous with German defeat. After hosting Communist Party fat cats for 45 years, the 1000-year-old city gained independence from Berlin in 1991, recovering its eminent status as capital of the Land. Much of the residential city has been renovated to create long boulevards adorned with gateways and historic buildings. Today, the city moves at a leisurely pace, its palaces and avenues swelling with curious visitors.

TRANSPORTATION

Trains: S7 runs to Potsdam's Hauptbahnhof, as does the RE1 from Berlin's Friedrichstr., Alexanderpl., and other major stations (40min. or 25min., €2.80). Trains every hr. to: **Dessau** (2hr., €32); **Leipzig** (1¾hr., €44); **Magdeburg** (1¼hr., €19.20).

Public Transportation: Potsdam is in Zone C of Berlin's BVG transit network. It is also divided into its own subdivisions of A, B, and C; special Potsdam-only tickets can be purchased on any bus or tram (€1.20, valid 1hr.; all-day €3.70-5.50). The **Berlin Welcome Card** (€18-24.50) is also valid in Potsdam.

Bike Rental and Tours: Potsdam is best seen by bike, and bike rental places often map out the best way to see all the sights. **Potsdam Per Pedales** (☎0331 748 0057; www.

pedales.de) rents them out from their main location at Rudolf-Breitscheid-Str. 201, in the "Griebnitzsee" S-Bahn station or on the S-Bahn platform at Potsdam Hauptbahnhof. From the former, pay to take your bike on the S-Bahn (special bike pass €1.20-1.80 at any BVG ticket office). Bike tours in English (reserve ahead) and German (€10.50, students €8.50; €6 audio guide.) **Canoe** and **kayak** rental €28-30 per day. Griebnitzsee Station open Good Friday-Oct. daily 9am-6:30pm; Potsdam Hauptbahnhof open May-Sept. daily 9am-7pm. **Cityrad** rents **bikes** right across from the Babelsbergerstr. exit of the Hauptbahnhof. (☎0177 825 4746; www.cityrad-rebhan.de. €11 per day. Open Apr. 1-Oct. 31 M-F 9am-7pm, Sa-Su 9am-8pm).

PRACTICAL INFORMATION

Tourist Office: Brandenburger Str. 3 (☎0331 27 55 80; www.potsdamtourismus.de) by Brandenburg Gate. Buy city maps and book a room (from €15). Open Apr.-Oct. M-F 9:30am-6pm Sa-Su 9:30am-4pm; Nov.-Mar. M-F 10am-6pm, Sa-Su 9:30am-2pm.

Tours: The tourist office runs 2hr. tours of the city; inquire at the office (€8, departs May-Sept. daily 3pm). Original Berlin Walks has 5-6hr. walking tours that leave from the taxi stand outside Berlin's Bahnhof Zoo Apr.-Oct., Th and Su 9:50am. €15, under age 26 €11.50. Double-decker buses from **Potsdam City Tours** leave daily on the hour from Hauptbahnhof 10:45am-3:45pm. €14, students €11.

Post Office: Pl. der Einheit. Open M-F 9am-6:30pm, Sa 9am-1pm. **Postal Code:** 14476.

ACCOMMODATIONS AND CAMPING

Budget options are limited in Potsdam. The tourist office finds private rooms and has a list of campgrounds in the area.

Jugendherberge Potsdam (HI), Schulstr. 9 (☎030 264 9520; www.jh-potsdam.de), located in Babelsberg just one S-Bahn stop from the Potsdam Hauptbahnhof. Head left out of the S-Bahn station and take the 1st left. Breakfast and sheets included. Internet €0.50 for 10min. Dorms €15, over 27 €18; singles €31.50/34.50; doubles €26.50/29.50. Nov.-Feb. all rooms €15 per person. Cash only. ❷

Campingplatz Sanssouci-Gaisberg, An der Pirschheide 41 (☎0331 951 0988; www.campingpark-sanssouci-potsdam.com) on the scenic banks of the Templiner See. Take S7 to Potsdam Hauptbahnof, then tram #91 to "Bahnhof Pirschheide." Call 8:45am-9pm for free shuttle to campsite. Phone reception 8am-1pm and 3-8pm. €10.50 per person. Internet available for €2 per day. Laundry €4. ❶

FOOD

Bright, renovated **Brandenburger Str.,** the local pedestrian zone, encompasses many of the city's restaurants, fast-food stands, and markets. The dozens of cafes near Brandenburger Tor are lovely but pricey, as are the cafes and restaurants along parts of Friedrich-Ebert-Str. and the **Holländisches Viertel.** Head to the **flea market** on Bassinpl. for fresh produce. (Open M-F 9am-6pm.) In the Hauptbahnhof is a massive **Kaufland** grocery store. (Open daily 6am-8pm.)

Siam, Friedrich-Ebert-Str. 13 (☎0311 200 9292), prepares tasty Thai food (€5-8) right before your eyes in a bamboo-laden interior. Open daily 11:30am-11pm. Cash only. ❷

Kashmir Haus, Jägerstr. 1 (☎0331 870 9580), offers Indian food in a trapestry-draped setting removed from the tourist bustle. The weekday lunch special (€4.50-6.50, 11am-4pm) includes vegetarian options and is an unbeatable deal. Open M-F 11am-11pm, Sa-Su 11am-midnight. Cash only. ❸

Cafe Heider, Friedrich-Ebert-Str. 29 (☎0331 270 5596). Heider is a beautiful outdoor cafe, located right on the border of the Hollandisches Viertel. Entrees €8-12. Open M-F from 8am, Sa from 9am, Su from 10am. ❸

SIGHTS

A **Premium Day Ticket** (€15, students €10) is a good investment for anyone interested in serious sightseeing. It is valid and available at all castles in Potsdam, including Sanssouci, which requires separate admission.

PARK AND SCHLOSS SANSSOUCI

PARK SANSSOUCI. Schloß Sanssouci's 600-acre "backyard," a testament to the size of Friedrich II's treasury and the diversity of his aesthetic tastes, has two distinct areas to explore. Half of the park is done in the Baroque style, with straight paths intersecting at topiaries and statues of nude nymphs arranged in geometrically pleasing patterns. The other half is in the rambling, rolling style of English landscape gardens. The sheer magnitude of the park—encompassing wheat fields, rose trellises, and lush, immaculate gardens—makes it a compelling place to spend an afternoon. For information on the park's many attractions, from Rococo sculptures to beautiful fountains, head to the visitors center next to the windmill, behind the *Schloß*. *(☎0331 969 4200. Open daily Mar.-Oct. 8am-10pm; Nov.-Feb. 9am-8pm.)*

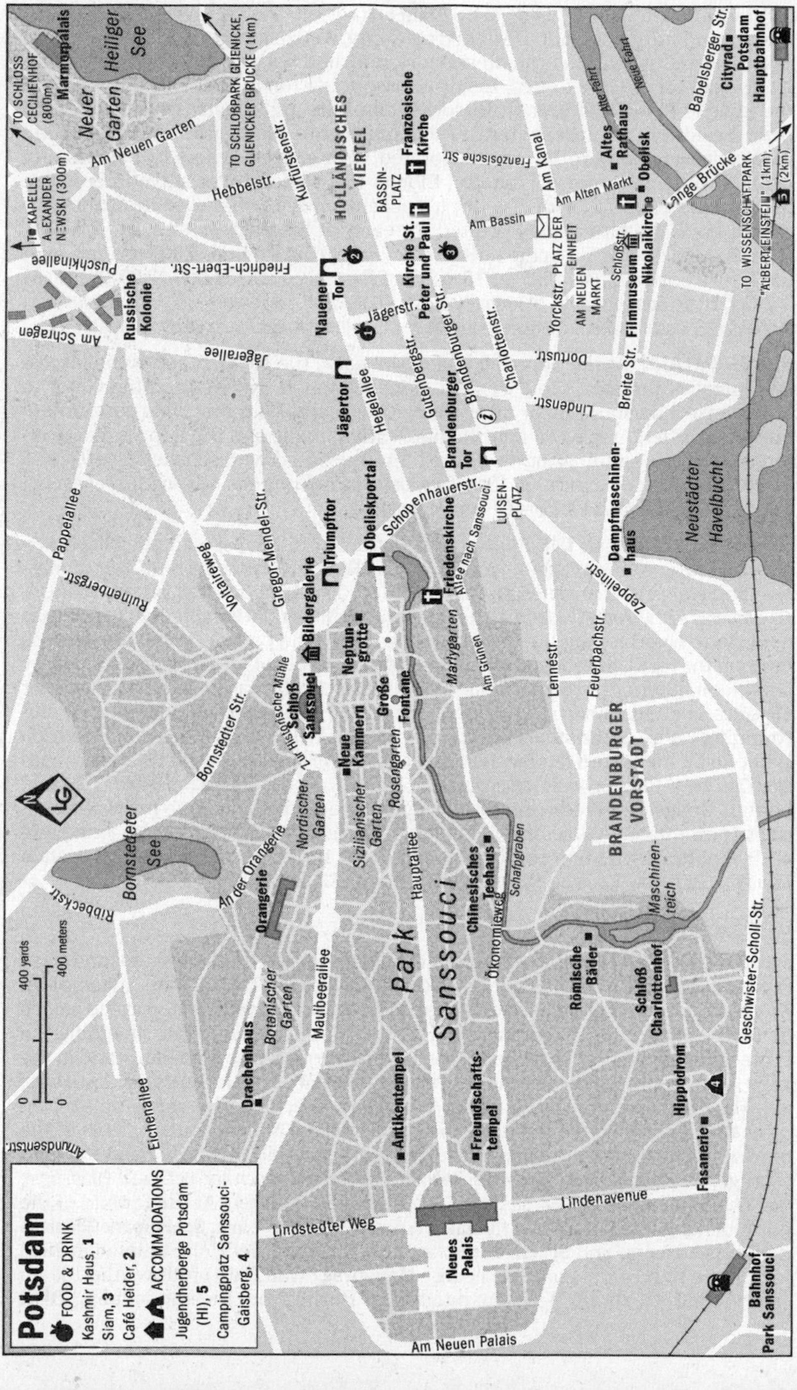

BRANDENBURG

SCHLOSS SANSSOUCI. The park's main attraction, the very-Versailles *Schloß*, sits atop a landscaped hill. Designed by Georg Wenzeslaus von Knobelsdorff in 1747, the yellow palace is small and airy, adorned with rich depictions of Dionysus and other Greek gods. Inside Sanssouci (French for "without worry"), the style is cloud-like French Rococo—all pinks and greens with gaudy gold trim. Friedrich, an unrepentant Francophile until his death, built the exotic **Voltairezimmer** (Voltaire Room), decorated with carved reliefs of parrots and tropical fruit, in honor of Voltaire, though the writer never stayed here. The library reveals another of Friedrich's eccentricities: whenever he wanted to read a book, he had a copy printed for each of his palaces—*en français*, of course. Also on display in the palace is Andy Warhol's modern interpretation of the king's portrait. *(Bus #695 or X15 to "Schloß Sanssouci." ☎ 0331 969 42 00. Open Tu-Su Apr.-Oct. 10am-6pm, last entry 5:30pm; Nov.-Mar. 10am-5pm, last entry 4:30. Price of admission for Schloß Sanssouci and Buldergalerie together: €12, students €8. Audio guide included.)*

NEUES PALAIS. At the opposite end of the park, the New Palace is the largest and latest of the park's four castles. Commissioned by Friedrich the Great to emphasize Prussia's power after the Seven Years' War, this 200-room ornate pink *Schloß* features royal apartments, festival halls, and the impressive Grottensaal, whose shimmering walls are literally coated with seashells. *(☎ 0331 96 94 361. Open Apr.-Oct. M and W-Su 10am-6pm, last entry 5:30pm; Nov.-Mar. and 10am-5pm, last entry 4:30.. €5, students €4. Tours €1 extra in summer.)*

OTHER BUILDINGS IN THE PARK. Next to the Schloß Sanssouci, the **Bildergalerie's** collection of Caravaggio, van Dyck, and Reubens crowd a long hall of massive and elaborate canvases. *(☎ 0331 969 4181. Open Apr. 1-Oct. 31. Tu-Su 10am-5:30pm. €3, students €2.50. Audio Guide €1.)* The stunning **Sizilianer Garten** (Sicilian Garden) is next door. Overlooking the park from the north, the pseudo-Italian **Orangerie** is famous for its 67 dubious Raphael imitations that replace originals swiped by Napoleon. *(Open from mid-May to mid-Oct. Tu-Su 10am-12:30pm and 1-5pm. Mandatory tours €3, students €2.50. Tower only €2.)* Romantic **Schloß Charlottenhof,** whose park surroundings were a Christmas gift from Friedrich Wilhelm III to his son Friedrich Wilhelm IV, melts into landscaped gardens and grape arbors to the south. *(Open May-Oct. Tu-Su 10am-6pm. €4, students €3.)* Nearby are the **Römische Bäder** (Roman baths), alongside a reedy pond with a miniature bridge. Meant to provide a contrast to the Italian villas, the gold-plated **Chinesisches Teehaus** stands complete with a parasol-wielding rooftop Buddha and 18th-century *chinois* porcelain inside. *(Open May-Oct. Tu-Su 10am-6pm. €3, students €2.50)*

OTHER SIGHTS

NEUER GARTEN. Running alongside the Heiliger See, Potsdam's second park contains several royal residences. **Schloß Cecilienhof,** built in the image of an English Tudor manor, houses exhibits on the **Potsdam Treaty,** signed at the palace in 1945. Visitors can see numerous Potsdam Conference items, including the table at which the Big Three bargained over Europe's fate, and can stand in the very room Stalin used as his study. *(☎ 0331 969 4244. Open Tu-Su Apr.-Oct. 10am-6pm; Nov.-Mar. 10am-5pm. €5, students €4. Tours in summer €1 extra.)* The garden also contains the centerpiece of the park, the **Marmorpalais** (Marble Palace). One of the quirkier buildings is a replica of an Egyptian pyramid formerly used for food storage. *(Take bus #692 to "Schloß Cecilienhof." Marmorpalais open Apr.-Oct. Tu-Su 10am-6pm; Nov.-Mar. Sa-Su 10am-5pm. €4, students €3. Tour extra €1 in summer.)* At the far end of the park, beachgoers bare all by the lake. Another palace-park, **Schloßpark Glienicke** contains a casino and **Schloß Glienicke,** built by Karl Friedrich Schinkel in 1828 for Prince Karl of Prussia. The nearby **Mauerweg** (Wall Path) follows the 160km route along which the Wall separated West Berlin from the surrounding DDR territory. *(Take tram #93 to "Glienicker Brücke" and continue along Berliner Str. to the bridge; the castle is just on the other side to the left. Open from mid-May to mid-Oct. Sa-Su 10am-5pm).*

FILMMUSEUM. Housed in an old orangerie that once held Friedrich's stables, this museum documents Potsdam's days as a film mecca, with artifacts like Marlene Dietrich's costumes, as well as a silent film archive and a small **movie theater.** *(On the corner of Breite Str. and Schloßstr. ☎0331 271 8112; www.filmmuseum-potsdam.de. Open daily 10am-6pm. €3.50, students €2.50. Movies from M-W 6 and 8pm, Th-Su 6pm, 8pm, and 10pm. Theater open daily noon-1am. €5, students €4. €3 on M.)*

BRANDENBURG AN DER HAVEL ☎03381

When Albert the Bear chose Brandenburg (pop. 74,000) "on the Havel" for the site of his cathedral in 1165, the small, unpretentious town had to deal with sudden prominence, reluctantly assuming a central political role in the region. In the end, Brandenburg's slow pace triumphed over the commercial demands imposed by its key river-side location. These days, the town has reclaimed its more peaceful past, cultivating an atmosphere lightyears away from its urbane neighbor.

TRANSPORTATION AND PRACTICAL INFORMATION. Brandenburg is on the Magdeburg-Berlin regional express line, the RE1, with frequent **trains** to Berlin (45min., €7.60) and Magdeburg (45min, €18.40). Visitors from Berlin should consider buying a day ticket valid on all Berlin and Brandenburg public transportation (€19). The **tourist office,** Steinstr. 66/67, is at the tram stop "Neustädtischer Markt." From the station, cross Am Hauptbahnhof, walk along Große Gartenstr., and follow it right onto Jakobstr., which becomes Steinstr. The staff books rooms for free, distributes English maps and brochures, and leads **walking tours** (1hr., May-Sept. Sa-Su at 11am, €3) and **boat tours,** which leave several times per day from near the Jahrtausendbrücke at the end of Hauptstr. (☎03381 20 87 69; www.stadt-brandenburg.de. Boat tours €5-6. Open M-F 9am-7pm, May 1-Sept. 30 Sa-Su 10am-3pm; Oct. 1-Apr. 30 Sa 10am-2pm.) The **Steinstr.** and **Neustädtischer Markt** areas are the town's main thoroughfare, while **Hauptstr.** offers more commercial shopping and chain stores.

ACCOMMODATIONS AND FOOD. There aren't any youth hostels in Brandenburg, but private rooms are abundant and cheap—ask at the tourist office for a brochure or look for *Zimmer frei* signs. Hidden behind a cafe directly on Steinstr. is the **Pension Blaudruck ❷,** Steinstr. 21, with six small, charming rooms adorned with paintings and stray ivy creeping in from the windows. The proprietors dress in the same homemade blue fabric that adorns the rooms. Enter through the passage into the courtyard at #21. (☎03381 22 57 34; www.blaudruck-design.de. Breakfast €3.85. Reserve ahead. Singles €21; doubles €42. Cash only.) By a quiet canal between the Altstadt and the train station, **Pension "Haus am Jungfernsteig" ❸,** Kirchhofstr. 9 Jungfernsteig 6a, run by two kindly violinists, has spacious rooms with TV, skylights, and shared bathrooms. (☎03381 20 15 11; www.pension-haus-am-jungfernsteig.de.) Wi-Fi available Breakfast included. Singles €28-32; doubles €49-52; triples €65-72. AmEx/MC/V.)

The main cafe and *Imbiß* scenes are on Steinstr. and perpendicular to Hauptstr., which also features an open-air **farmer's market** behind the Katharinenkirche. Along Mühlendamm, dockside cafes and snack stands let you sample the region's freshly-caught fish. (Open M-F 7am-5pm, Sa 7am-noon.) **Nummer 31 ❷,** Steinstr. 31, offers tasty gourmet pizzas in a traditional German setting for €3-6. (☎03381 22 44 73; www.nummer31.de. Open M-Sa from 11am, Su from 5pm. Cash only.) The **Kartoffelkäfer ❷,** Steinstr. 56, serves delicious meals that take advantage of every possible variation of the potato. The outdoor cafe is a short walk from Neustädtischerer Markt. (☎03381 22 41 18;

www.derkartoffelkaefer.de. Entrees €5-9. Open daily 11am-midnight. Cash only.) **Bismarck Terrassen ❸,** Bergstr. 20, is located at on the corner of Bergstr. and Am Marienburg, right at the base of the hill on which the Friedenswarte tower sits. Try authentic, traditional German fare (€6-10) in a room devoted to Otto von Bismarck. (☎03381 30 09 39. Open daily. Cash only.)

SIGHTS. Brandenburg's sights can be found along Steinstr. and its extension. Begin your tour of the Neustadt at the end of Steinstr. with the 14th-century **Steintorturm** (Stone Gate Tower), which holds a maritime history museum with displays on each level of the tower. Brave the steep, narrow spiral staircase for a view of the Havel and pedestrian Brandenburg. And you can ring a big bell. (☎03381 20 02 65. Tower open Tu-F 9am-5pm and Sa-Su 10am-5pm. €3, students €1, families €5, children under 6 free.) Work your way up the street to the cluttered rooms of DDR paraphenalia at the **Nostalgie-Museum,** Steinstr. 52. (☎03381 22 52 39; www.nostalgie.de. Open Tu-Su 10am-noon and 1-4pm. €1.50.) Walking through Molkenmarkt, across the river and along St. Petri will bring you to the famed **Dom St. Peter und Paul,** Burghof 11, a cathedral currently housing a rotating exhibition. Artwork is placed in the aisles with surprising abandon. The church is also adorned with its own art; architect Friedrich Schinkel couldn't resist adding a few touches like the "Schinkel-Rosette" and the window over the entrance. (☎03381 211 2221. Open M-Tu and Th-Sa 10am-5pm, W 10am-noon, Su 11:30am-5pm. Last entry for museum 4:30pm. €3, students €2.) Across the street, the **Petrikapelle** has gone from church to contemporary art gallery. (☎03381 20 03 25. Open M-Tu and Th-F 10am-4pm, W 10am-noon, Sa 10am-5pm, Su 11am-5pm.)

SPREEWALD (SPREE FOREST)

The Spree River splits apart 100km southeast of Berlin and branches out over the countryside in an intricate maze of streams, canals, meadows, and primeval forests stretching over 1000 sq. km. The Spree Forest's tiny villages were first settled in the Middle Ages, and the folklore is an especially rich tradition. The **Sorbs,** Germany's native Slavic minority, originally settled the region and continue to influence its cultural identity.

Webbed by shaded canals, this popular vacation destination for Berliners is known as the "Venice of the North." Farmers row to their fields, and children paddle home from school. The fields and forests teem with owls, otter, and foxes, so that even a fleeting walk through the woods becomes strikingly idyllic. Now recognized as a biosphere nature reserve by the UN, some sections of the forest are off-limits to the public and others close during mating and breeding seasons. Tourist season bears its own fruit—campgrounds abound, bike paths proliferate, and excellent hiking trails weave through the trees. Bearing in mind the fragile state of the ecosystem, visit local tourist offices for advice on how to be environmentally responsible in protected areas.

Lübben and Lübbenau, two tiny towns that open into labyrinths of canals, are popular destinations within daytrip-range of Berlin, while nearby Cottbus is the area's largest transporation hub. The forest is divided into two sections. The Unterspreewald is a mountain biker's dream, while the Oberspreewald, surrounding Lübben and Lübbenau, is best explored by boat.

LÜBBENAU ☎03542

Tiny Lübbenau (pop. 7000) is the most famous of the Spreewald towns and deservedly so—its interwoven canals and roads seem worlds away from the modern cities around it. For tourists, the village serves as a springboard for trips into the kingdom of the *Irrlichter* (will o' the wisp). The landscape here is dense with waterways, and has more gondolas than houses. Buried in the forest, the neighboring village Lehde has tiny houses with straw roofs and a museum that recreates life as it once was for the Spreewald Sorbs.

TRANSPORTATION AND PRACTICAL INFORMATION. **Trains** go to: Berlin (1hr., 2 per hr., €10.40); Cottbus (25min., every hr., €5.10); Lübben (10min., 2 per hr., €2.00). For a **taxi** call ☎03542 31 53. **Kowalsky's,** near the station at Poststr. 6, rents **bikes.** (☎03542 28 35. €7 per day. Open M-F 9am-12:30pm and 2-6pm, Sa 9am-noon, Su call in advance.) Rent a **kayak** at the campsite (below) or at **Franke,** Dammstr. 72., down the walkway over the bridge. From the station, turn right down Bahnhofstr. and left at Dammstr. (☎03542 27 22. Paddleboats €3-8per hr. Open Apr.-Oct. daily 8am-7pm.) **Hannemann,** Am Wasser 1, rents **boats** at the other port. Follow Spreestr. to the end, cross the bridge, and continue to the next bridge. (☎03542 36 47. 1-seaters €3-4 per hr. Call ahead to reserve a boat. Open daily Apr.-Oct. 8am-7pm.) The **tourist office**, Ehm-Welk-Str. 15, at the end of Poststr., has maps and finds rooms for a €3 fee. (☎03542 36 68; www.spreewald-online.de. Open Nov.-Mar. M-F 10am-4pm; Apr.-Oct. M-F 9am-7pm; Sa 9am-4pm; May-June Su 11am-3pm, Jul.-Sept 11am-4pm.) The **post office** is at Kirchpl. 6. (Open M-F 9am-6pm, Sa 9am-noon.) **Postal Code:** 03222.

ACCOMMODATIONS AND FOOD. Though the closest hostel is in Lübben, 10min. away by train (p. 138), finding a room isn't a problem in friendly Lübbenau. Check for *Zimmer frei* signs, particularly common along **Poststr.,** or ask for the *Gastgeberverzeichnis* brochure at the tourist office. Otherwise, **Pension Am Alten Bauernhafen ❸**, Stottoff 5 (☎03542 29 30; www.am-alten-bauernhafen.de), between the train station and the center of town. From Poststr., take a left onto Ehm-Welk-Str., which eventually becomes Karl-Marx-Str. Take a left on Stottoff. (Single €30-35; doubles €42-49; triples €65; quads €50-80. Bikes €7 per day; paddleboats €17 per day or €3.50 per person per hr. On the road to Lehde and surrounded by water, **Campingplatz "Am Schloßpark" ❶** has 125 tent plots with cooking and bathing facilities on-site, as well as a convenience store. (☎03542 35 33; www.spreewaldcamping.de. Bikes €8 per day; paddleboats €15 per day. Reception 7:30am-12:30pm and 2-10pm. €6 per person, €6 per child, 5-6 per tent. 2- to 4-person bungalows €20-50. Cash only.)

For cheap food—and pickles, beets, and beans by the barrel—check out the *Imbiße* (snack bars) and stands along the **Großer Hafen.** Cheerful yellow **Cafe Fontane ❸** dishes out delicious local cuisine just behind the church at Ehm-Wehk-Str. 42; try a salad with baguette (€9-10) or one of the homemade cakes. (Open daily from 11:30am. Cash only.) **Spreewald Idyll ❸,** Spreestr. 13, serves regional specialties like *Grützwurst* with potatoes (€7), fish dishes (€7-14), and salads (€2.60-6.60) within spitting distance of the Kleiner Hafen on an outdoor patio. (☎03542 22 51. Open M-Sa 10am-10pm, Su 10am-8:30pm. Cash only.)

SIGHTS AND HIKING. The Altstadt is a 10min. walk from the station. Go straight on Poststr. until you reach the marketplace and the Baroque **Nikolaikirche.** (Kirchplatz 3. ☎03542 27 78; www.kirche-luebbenau.de. Open May-Oct. M-Sa 2-4pm.) The requisite **Schloß** is now a handsome, pricy hotel and restaurant with lush grounds open to the public. Across the marketplace in the gatehouse (a prison until 1985) is the **Spreewaldmuseum,** Topfmarkt 12, which gives a historical overview of the Spreewald and its customs. (☎03542 24 72; www.spreewald-web.de. Open from Apr. to mid-Oct. Tu-Su 10am-6pm. €3, students €2.) The **Haus für Mensch und Natur** (House for Man and Nature), Schulstr. 9, has a free exhibit on the local ecosystem. (Open Apr.-Oct. Tu-Su 10am-5pm.)

Gondola tours of the forest depart from the **Großer Hafen** and the **Kleiner Hafen** (larger and smaller ports, respectively). The Großer Hafen, along Dammstr. behind the church, offers a wider variety of tours, including 2-3hr. trips to Lehde. The boats take on customers starting at 9-10am and depart when full (about 20 passengers) throughout the day. **Genossenschaft der Kahnfährleute,** Dammstr. 77a, is the biggest company. (☎03542 22 25; www.grosser-hafen.de. Open Mar.-Oct. daily 9:30am-6pm. 2hr. round-trips to Lehde €8.50, children €4.25; 3hr. €10/5; 5hr. tour of the forest €13/6.50.) From the Kleiner Hafen, less-touristed but nearly identical wilderness trips are run by the **Kahnfährmannsverein der Spreewaldfreunde,** Spreestr. 10a. (☎03542 40 37 10. Open Apr.-Oct. daily 9am-6pm. Tours 2-10hr.; 4-5hr. tours recommended. €8-20, children €4-10.)

It's only a hop and a paddle from Lübbenau to the haystacks and thatched-roof houses of **Lehde,** a UNESCO-protected landmark that is accessible by foot (15min.), bike, or boat. Follow the signs from the Altstadt or Großer Hafen, or take a boat from the harbor. The **Freilandmuseum** (Open-Air Museum), a recreated 19th-century village, portrays a time when entire Spreewalder families slept in the same room and newlyweds literally went for a "romp in the hay." Follow the signs to Lehde; it's just behind the aquarium and over the bridge. (☎03542 24 72. Open daily Apr.-Sept. 10am-6pm, Oct. 10am-5pm. Last entry 5:30pm. €3, students and seniors €2, children €1.) Just before the bridge to the museum lies the **Fröhlichen Hecht ❷**, Dorfstr. 1, a large cafe, restaurant, and Biergarten with a patio right on a river. Enjoy a *Kartoffel mit Quark* (potatoes with curd cheese) in a special Spreewald sauce (€6.50) as gondolas drift. (☎03542 27 82; www.zumhecht.com. Open daily 11am-7pm.)

LÜBBEN ☎03546

With canals and trails fanning out from all ends, little Lübben (pop. 15,000) fills with German tourists milling around the colorful Altstadt and gliding by in kayaks, canoes, and gondolas. Lübben offers easy access to wooded bike paths and hiking trails, as well as a ceaseless supply of juicy *Gurken* (pickles, the region's specialty) and fresh fish that make for a woodland picnic.

TRANSPORTATION AND PRACTICAL INFORMATION. **Trains** go to: Berlin Ostbahnhof and other major stations (1hr., 2 per hr., €9); Cottbus (45min., every hr., €6.30); Lübbenau (10min., 2 per hr., €2). For a **taxi** call ☎403546 812 or 30 39. Rent **bikes** at the tourist office (€6 per day, €25 per week). The **tourist office** is at Ernst-von-Houwald-Damm 15. From the station, head right on Bahnhofstr., make a left on Logenstr., which becomes Lindenstr., and cross the two bridges; the office will be to the right, on the *Schloßinsel*. The staff finds private rooms (€15-40) for a €3 fee. After hours, they post a list of private rooms outside the entrance. (☎03546 30 90 or 24 33. Open Apr.-Oct. daily 10am-6pm; Nov.-Mar. M-F 10am-4pm.) The **post office,** Poststr. 4, has a 24hr. ATM. (Open M-F 9am-6pm, Sa 9am-noon.) **Postal Code:** 15907.

ACCOMMODATIONS AND FOOD. The **Jugendherberge Lübben (HI) ❶,** Zum Wendenfürsten 8, is in a field at the edge of town. Follow Bahnhofstr. to its end, turn left on Luckauer Str. and then right on Burglehnstr. before the big crossing.

Go right again on Puschkinstr., which becomes Cottbuser Str., then left on Dorfaue and follow signs from there. Though remote, the hostel is dreamily flanked by a river and a stretch of hayfields and offers easy access to wilderness paths. Playground, ping-pong, and canoes available. (☎03546 30 46; www.jh-luebben.de. Breakfast and Sheets included. Reception 9am-7pm. Dorms €14.50. Campsites €10. Cash only.) For convenience, **Pension am Markt ❸,** Hauptstr. 5, can't be beat. Each large room has a kitchen and fold-out couches. (☎03546 32 72; pension-am-markt@gmx.net. Breakfast included. Doubles €54-60; 2-4 person apartments €65-95. To get to **Spreewald-Camping Lübben ❶,** follow the directions to the Jugendherberge until Puschkinstr., and then turn left at the sign, where Puschkinstr. becomes Cottbusserstr, aross the street from the sign for Burglehnstr. (☎03546 70 53; www.spreewald-camping-luebben.de. Boat rental €3.50 per hr., €20 per day; for campers €2.70/16. Reception 8am-noon and 3pm-9pm. Open from mid-Mar. to Oct. €6.50per person, €3.50-4.50 per tent.)

Don't even think about leaving Lübben without sampling the Spreewald's pickled delicacies, famous throughout Germany. **Gurken Paule ❶,** at the entrance to the tourist office plaza on the *Schloßinsel,* is an outdoor stand offering the freshest of the Spreewald's unique pickle assortment: *Salzdillgurken* (dill), *Senfgurken* (mustard), and *Gewürzgurken* (spicy). They're sold by weight, averaging €0.50 per pickle and €2.50 per jar. (Open daily 9am-6pm.) Varied local cuisine and music ranging from *Schlager* to country can be found at **Bubak ❸,** Ernst-von-Houwald-Damm 9, named after the Sorbian bogeyman who carries naughty children off into the forest. Sample the *Gurken-Kartoffelsuppe* (pickle-potato soup; €3) with local entrees (€5.50-15). (☎03546 18 61 44; www.bubak.de. Open M-F 11:30am-3pm and 5:30-10:30pm, Sa-Su 11:30am-10:30pm.)

SIGHTS AND OUTDOOR ACTIVITIES. Der Hain, Lübben's forested park, lies at the end of Breite Str., a continuation of Haupstr. To the south, the **Schloßinsel,** an island whose park is more impressive than its namesake palace, houses the tourist office, docks, and pricey cafes. The **Schloß** contains an exhibit on Lübben's history and culture. (Ernst-von-Houwald-Damm 14. ☎03546 18 74 78; www.schloss-luebben.de. Open Apr.-Oct Tu-Su 10am-5pm; Nov-Mar W-F 10am-4pm, Sa-Su 1pm-4pm. €4, students €2.) Most of Lübben's attractions are in the forests surrounding the town. The **Fährmannsverein "Lustige Gurken" Lübben/Spreewald,** Ernst-von-Houwald-Damm 15 on the Schloßinsel, offers boat trips exploring the Spreewald. (☎03546 71 22; www.lustige-gurken.de. Open daily 9am-4pm. 1½-7hr., €8-18.) The **Fährmannsverein "Flottes Rudel,"** at the end of the parking lot across Lindenstr. from Am Spreeufer, offers boat and barge trips with picnics starting daily at 10am. (Eisenbahnstr. 9. ☎03546 82 69; www.flottes-rudel.de. 1½-8hr. tours €8-22.) Rent kayaks or canoes at **Bootsverleih Gebauer,** Lindenstr. 18. From Luckauer Str., turn right on Lindenstr. before the tourist office. (☎03546 71 94; ID required. Open daily Apr.-Oct. 9am-7pm. M-F 1-person kayaks €8 for first 2hr., €2.50 per additional hr., €16 per day. Sa-Su €9 for first 2hr., €3 per additional hr., €19 per day.)

MECKLENBURG-VORPOMMERN

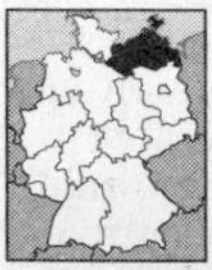

Nature takes center stage in sparsely populated Mecklenburg-Vorpommern. Over 1700 lakes scoop out oases amid thickly-forested parkland and peaceful towns, stretching northward to spectacular cliffs and sandy beaches along the Baltic Sea coast. A popular tourist destination for the Berlin elite at the turn of the 20th century, Mecklenburg-Vorpommern (especially the islands of Rügen and Usedom) has been rediscovered in the wake of reunification. Dramatic Hanseatic architecture emerges from rubble as restoration renews Germany's poorest *Land.*

HIGHLIGHTS OF MECKLENBURG-VORPOMMERN

SUN YOURSELF as you revel in nature on the car-less island of **Hiddensee** (p. 160).

HIKE the white chalk cliffs of **Jasmund National Park** (p. 156).

ENJOY student-based nightlife at the Baltic's oldest university in **Rostock** (p. 152).

SCHWERIN ☎0385

Founded in 1018, Schwerin (pop. 96,000) is the great-grandfather of Mecklenburg-Vorpommern's cities, and the capital of the province. Encircled by lakes and largely free of communist "architectural innovations," Schwerin's *Schloß* and well-preserved townhouses lend the town a regal flair. The undeniable cultural center of Mecklenburg, Schwerin hosts dozens of art festivals and concerts every year, and is home to some of the region's finest traditional cuisine.

TRANSPORTATION

Trains: Every hr. to **Berlin** (2½hr., €34); **Lübeck** (1hr., €12); and **Rostock** (1hr., €14).

Public Transportation: A frustratingly slow system of buses and trams covers the city and outlying areas (single ride €1.30, day pass €4). The **Schwerin-Ticket,** available through the tourist office, grants free **tram** and **ferry** rides as well as reduced entrance to many attractions, including museums and tours. (Day ticket €5, children under 14 €3.)

Bikes: The city's **Räder Center** shop in the train station rents **bikes,** recommends trails, and leads **tours.** (☎0385 500 76 30. M-F €6 per day, Sa-Su €7, €50 deposit required. Rentals from mid-Apr. to Oct. daily 9am-6pm.).

PRACTICAL INFORMATION

Tourist office: Am Markt 14, books hotel rooms for free and leads 1½hr. German-language walking tours (daily 11am, €4.50). From the train station, go right on Grundthalpl. and continue as it turns into Wismarsche Str., with the river to your left; go left on Arse-

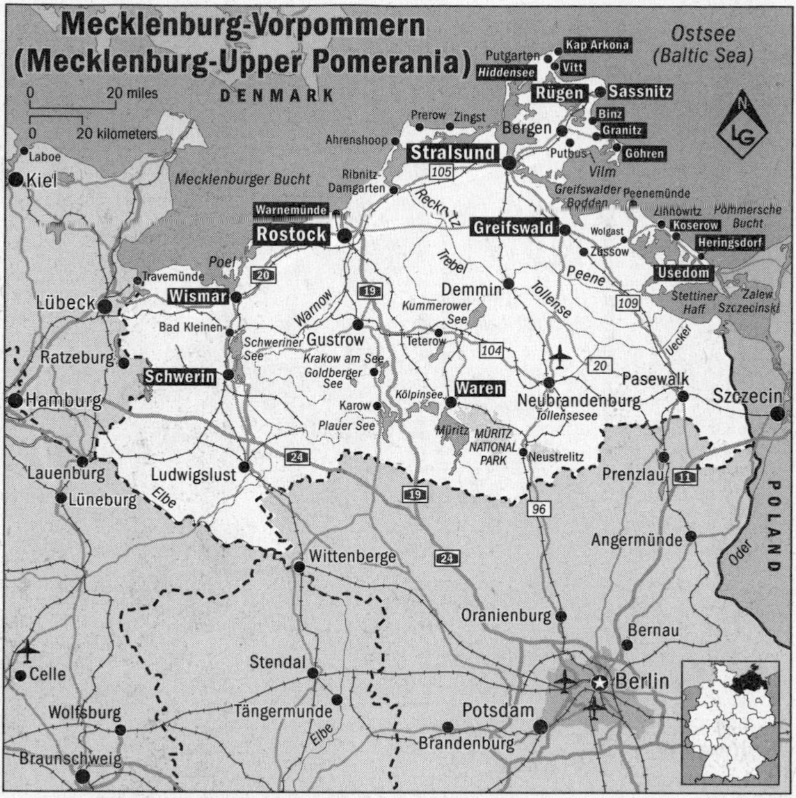

nal Str., and a right on Puschkinstr. (☎0385 592 5212; www.schwerin.com. Open Apr.-Sept. M-F 9am-7pm, Sa-Su 10am-6pm; Oct.-Mar. M-F 9am-6pm, Sa-Su 10am-4pm.)

Laundry: Schnell & Sauber, on Pl. der Freiheit near the train station. (Wash €3 per 6kg. Dry €0.50 per 12min. Open daily 6am-11pm.)

Pharmacy: Apotheke, Puschkinstr. 61-65, is just off the Markt. (☎0385 59 37 90. Open M-F 8am-6pm, Sa 9am-12:30pm.)

Internet access: Check email at **Internet Cafe,** Lubeckerstr. (€1 per hr. Open M-F 10am-10pm, Sa 10:30am-9pm.)

Post office: Mecklenburgstr. 4-6. From the Markt, go down Schmiedestr. and turn right. (Open M-F 8am-6pm, Sa 9:30am-12:30pm.) **Postal Code:** 19053.

ACCOMMODATIONS

Zimmervermietung Familie Kuhnert, Voßstr. 44 (☎0385 79 79 79), is in the blue house next to the easily spottable yellow Cafe Bernstein (p. 143). Take bus #10 or 11 from the train station to "Alter Friedhof" and cross the street at the intersection. While the back facade of the building is still pocked from WWII grenades, the inside is all comfort, with bright rooms, cheerful bedspreads, TVs, and friendly proprieters. Breakfast €5. Singles €20-30; doubles €35-45. Cash only. ❷

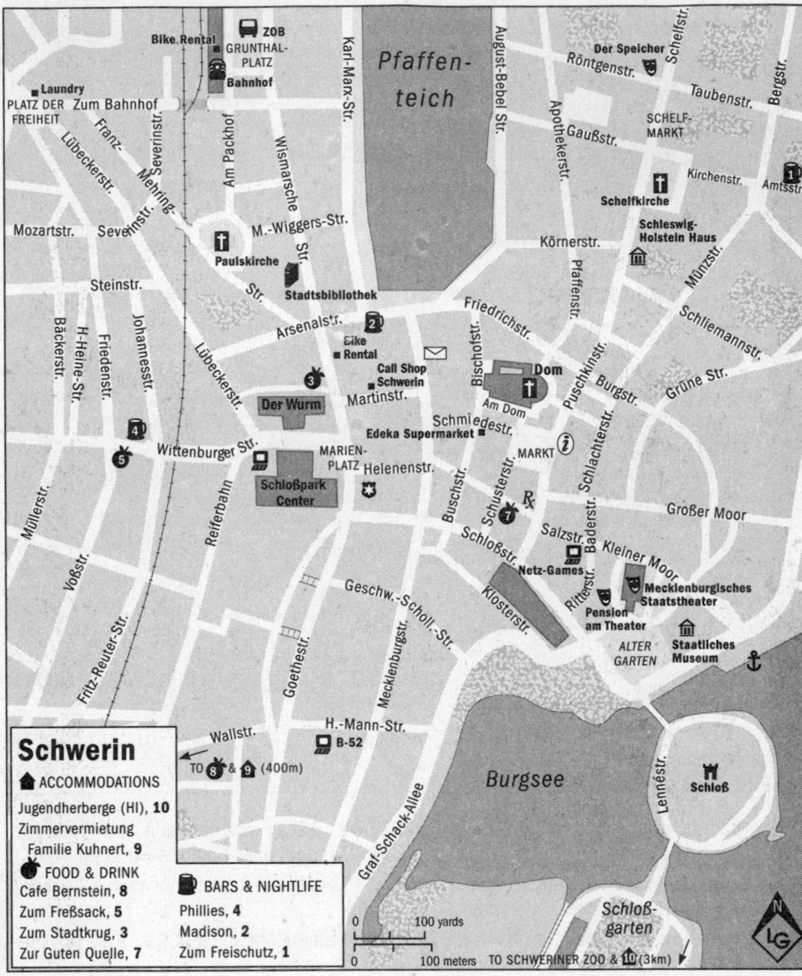

Jugendherberge (HI), Waldschulweg 3 (☎0385 326 0006). The hostel is 3km south of town in the woods by the lake, complete with a small ropes course. From the station, take a right on Wismarschestr. to Marienpl. Take bus #14 to the end of the line at "Jugendherberge" and follow the road into the woods. The hostel will be on your left. Breakfast and sheets included. Reception 8am-8pm. Curfew midnight. Full board packages available. Dorms €19, under 27 €16. Cash only. ❷

FOOD

Fast food joints proliferate in the **Schloßpark Center,** a modern shopping mall with chain-caliber staples. Buy groceries at **Edeka,** Schmiedestr. 10, just off the Markt. (Open M-F 8am-8pm, Sa 8am-6pm.)

Zum Stadtkrug, Wismarschestr. 126 (☎0385 593 6693; www.altstadtbrauhaus.de). Schwerin's cozy micro-brewery serves German specialties and award-winning beer in the company of quaint brewery machinery. The local brew, Schweriner Altstadtbräu (€1.70 for 0.25L), complements a hearty spiced blood sausage with sauerkraut, potatoes, and onions, served in an iron pan; €10). Beware of expensive tap water. Open daily 11am-1am, kitchen closes M and Su 10pm, Tu-Th 11pm, F-Sa midnight. Cash only. ❸

Zur Guten Quelle, Schusterstr. 12 (☎0385 56 59 85; www.m-vp.de). Dark wood, red vinyl, and DDR-style furniture reign at this homely guesthouse (singles from €53). Locals dig into *Matjes* (herring; €7-8.65), the restaurant's specialty. Entrees €8-13. ❸

Zum Freßsack, Wittenburgerstr. 52 (☎0385 760 71 72), at the corner of Voßstr., serves delicate local specialties like *gepökeltes Eisbein* (pickled pig's knuckles on sauerkraut €8.50). Wimps and potato lovers may opt for the gigantic stuffed potatoes (€3.30-6.50). M-Th and Su 11:30am-10pm, F-Sa 11:30am-midnight. AmEx/MC/V. ❸

Cafe Bernstein, Voßstr. 44. Take bus #10 or 11 from the train station to "Alter Friedhof" and cross the street at the intersection. Busy for its semi-remote location, Bernstein stays full of people sipping iced drinks and delicious *Milchkaffee* (coffee with cream; €2.40) served in giant bowls. Open daily 9am-2am. Cash only. ❷

SIGHTS

SCHLOSS. Schwerin's fairy-tale **Schloß,** on an island south of the city center, is a grandiose amalgamation of building styles. Begun in the 16th century and expanded for several hundred years, the castle now serves as the seat of State Government in Mecklenburg-Western Pomerania. The Schloßmuseum's tortoise shell-inlaid floors lead through ornate chambers to the throne room, where not a square inch of space goes undecorated. A hill at the far side of the adjoining **Schloßgarten** affords a sweeping view of the castle grounds. *(☎0385 525 2920. Open from mid-Apr. to mid-Oct. daily 10am-6pm, from mid-Oct. to mid-Apr. Tu-Su 10am-5pm. €4, students €2.50, families €7.)* Now used for outdoor concerts, the **Alter Garten,** was the site of mass demonstrations preceding the DDR's 1989 downfall.

STAATLICHES MUSEUM (STATE MUSEUM). The castle's neighbor may suffer a bit of *Schloß* envy, but this museum is no rinky-dink collection. Housing a remarkable assortment of 15th- to 19th-century Dutch and German art, including works by Rembrandt, Rubens, and Brueghel. A room full of Barlach statues and extensive Duchamp holdings will please fans of modernism. *(☎0385 595 8237. Open Apr. 15-Oct. 14 daily 10am-6pm, Oct. 15-Apr. 14 Tu-Su 10am-5pm. Temporary exhibit €8, permanent exhibit €5, combo €10; students €6/4/8, families €12/6/16. Enter through the side doors, not up the sweeping front steps. Tours in German W 3pm and Su 11am and 3pm.)*

DOM. Uphill from the Alter Garden, the 13th century Dom's spires survey the city from one of its highest vantage points. Many of the church's treasures, including its 42 altars, were lost when the Dom was redecorated in the Neo-Gothic style at the beginning of the 19th century, though it has since undergone restoration to its old Gothic style, retaining its elaborate organ and stained glass. The church's striking Gothic triumphal cross comes from Wismar's Marienkirche, which was demolished in 1961. *(Open M-Sa 10am-4:30pm, Su noon-4:30pm. 117m high tower €1.50, children €0.50.)*

ENTERTAINMENT AND NIGHTLIFE

The cream-pillared building next door to the Staatliches Museum is the **Mecklenburgisches Staatstheater Schwerin,** which puts on the most highly regarded plays, ballets, and symphonies in town. (Alter Garten 2. ☎0385 530 0123. Tickets €4-49.) Buy tickets for most shows through **Ticketservice am Markt** in the tourist office. (☎0385 56 05 00. Open M-F 9am-7pm, Sa 10am-noon.) Schwerin's most famous sights pull double duty as performance spaces in the summer as the famed **Schlossfestspiele** transforms the steps of the museum into an opera stage. (Tickets €51-64. Reduced student prices. Call ☎0385 530 0123 or visit www.theater-schwerin.de.) **Der Speicher,** Röntgenstr. 20-22, airs cult films and hosts book readings and folk music shows. (Entrance on Schelfstr. ☎0385 51 21 05.) New releases screen at **Das Capitol,** Wismarsche Str. 127, daily from 2:30pm. (☎0385 591 8018. www.das-capitol.de. Tickets €5-7.) *Piste,* a monthly guide to local clubs and parties, is available for free from the tourist office.

Zum Freischutz, Am Ziegenmarkt 11 (☎0385 56 86 55). This popular bar near the Speicher covers its dimly lit walls with a peculiar combination of Beethoven portraits, puffer fish, mounted antlers, and mannequin legs. The beer (€1-2.50) attracts young crowds at night while daytime crowds come for the lunchtime favorite: *Flandenbrot* stuffed with sandwich toppings of choice (€7-7.40). Open daily from 9am. Cash only.

Phillies, Wittenburgerstr. 51 (☎0385 71 31 01). Schwerin's glamorous and those seeking to emulate them gather here for mixed drinks (€5.50-7) and Cuban cigars (€4.50) from an extensive list. Exotic fish swim in a corner fish tank while the bar glows amber. Open daily from 8pm. Free outdoor movies in summer Su 10pm. Cash only.

Madison, Arsenalstr. 16 (☎0385 572 7904). Neon straws and sleek leather chairs exemplify the struggle between crazy and classy here. Themed nights include Fr night club with dance floor and DJ, W night movie screenings, and the Gay Party on the first Sa of every month. Open M-F 6pm-midnight, Sa-Su 6pm-3am. Cash only.

MECKLENBURGISCHE SEENPLATTE (MECKLENBURG LAKE PLAIN)

When things got hectic in Berlin, Chancellor Otto von Bismarck found refuge in the beauty of the Mecklenburgische Seenplatte, the lowland lake district of southern Mecklenburg-Vorpommern. The region's landscapes are a product of Ice Age glacial activity—hundreds of lakes speckle the Seenplatte, surrounded by wetlands and deciduous forests. A popular destination for the past century, the area fills with hikers, bikers, and paddlers during the summer.

MÜRITZ NATIONAL PARK

Some 20,000 years ago, enormous glaciers covered the landmass that is now Müritz. Torrents of melting ice deposited mounds of sand in their wake, making pebbles of the boulders planted in the middle of otherwise undisturbed fields. Though the thousands of years represent a more complex process, simply put, glacial runoff gradually filled basins in the sand, creating the crystalline lakes now celebrated by kayakers and fish alike. With 103 lakes bigger than one hectare and countless smaller ponds, Müritz is home to the largest network of connected, navigable water in Central Europe, from the gurgling headwaters of the Havel River to the sprawling waters of the Müritzsee.

ORIENTATION

The two separate regions of Müritz National Park are west and east of **Neustrelitz.** The much larger western area is bordered by **Lake Müritz,** Germany's largest freshwater lake. At the northwestern corner, the port town of **Waren** (p. 147) is a major jumping-off point for tourists. The park's southwestern quarter, mostly wetland, is home to much of its wildlife. The remainder of the western portion is forest interspersed with expansive fields and sparkling lakes. Müritz's eastern region has more hills and is thickly forested, but is also dotted with lakes and brooks. The **Hirschberg,** not exactly looming at a mere 143.5m, is the highest point in the park. Other major towns around the park are **Kratzeburg,** in the center of the western region; **Speck,** west of Kratzeburg; **Federow,** on the north edge of the park southeast of Waren; and **Serrahn,** somewhat west of center in the eastern region. Maps of the park (€6) are highly recommended and available at all national park information offices and local tourist offices.

MÜRITZ NATIONAL PARK AT A GLANCE

AREA: 322 sq. km.

CLIMATE: Relatively dry weather and mild temperatures year-round.

FEATURES: Largely flat, forested terrain dotted with lakes, meadows, and bogs.

GATEWAYS: Waren (p. 147) and Neustrelitz act as good starting points.

HIGHLIGHTS: Imposing oak and endangered beech forests, scores of rare birds, and Germany's largest freshwater lake.

CAMPING: Only in designated campsites, most outside the park.

FEES AND RESERVATIONS: Free entry to park. Camping fees vary.

TRANSPORTATION

Nearly everyone gets to the park through Neustrelitz or Waren, both of which are on the Berlin-Rostock rail line. **Trains** shuttle between Waren and Neustrelitz every hour, some direct, some stopping in Kargow, Klockow, and Kratzeburg (€5.70). The **Müritz-Nationalpark-Ticket** runs **buses** every hour 9am-4pm (July-Aug. until 5pm) from Waren to Federow, Speck, and Boek. The line also includes a **boat** that connects Waren, Klink, Röbel, and Bolter Kanal on the Müritz lake. Most park rangers recommend the bus as the prime means of visiting the park's depths. Buy tickets on board buses or boats or at tourist information centers. (Buses run 9am-5:40pm. Day ticket €7, students and children €3.50, families €14; with unlimited boat travel €14/7/28. 3- and 7-day passes also available. Check the schedule: many tours are free with purchase of these passes.) Renting a **bike** is an efficient way to be mobile within the park, as many trails are simply too long to conquer on foot. For all the talk of rolling hills, very few are steep climbs, so inexperienced riders need not be intimidated. Rental stores are ubiquitous, even in the smaller towns.

PRACTICAL INFORMATION

National Park Information Centers: Start any trip into the park with a visit to *Nationalparkinformation* offices for hiking maps (€6), brochures, and advice.

Waren, Am Teufelsbruch (☎03991 66 27 86). Follow the directions to Ecktannen Campingplatz (p. 148) but stay on Am Seeufer as it becomes Specker Str., then turn left on Am Teufelsbruch at the park sign. Or, take Waren's bus #1 to "Schabernack." Open May-Sept. daily 9:30am-5pm.

Neustrelitz, Am Tiergarten (☎03981 20 32 84). Take Marienstr. from the train station past the Opfern des Faschismus monument. Veer left onto Friedrich-Wilhelm-Str. Go past the traffic circle and follow signs. The office is upstairs. Wheelchair-accessible. Open May-Oct. daily 10am-5pm.

Nationalparkamt Müritz, Schloßpl. 3, 17237 Hohenzieritz (☎039824 25 20; www.nationalpark-mueritz.de), is the office to contact for information before you arrive.

Nationalpark-Service Müritz, Informationhaus 17192 Federow (☎03991 66 88 49; www.nationalpark-service.de), leads daily nature tours (€5-7.50) and sells maps (€6-12).

Branches are located in Boek, Federow, Kratzeburg, Schwarzenhof, Serrahn, Speck, and other locations throughout the region. Check www.nationalpark-mueritz.de for more information.

Tours: Free themed walking and biking tours of the park, including family tours, are available May-Oct. Tours last 3-6hr., most around 4hr., and depart several times a day. For a list of dates, durations, and meeting points, visit the park website or any park center.

Emergency: Police ☎110. **Fire** and **Ambulance** ☎112.

CAMPING

Camping is permitted only in designated campgrounds. *Camping im Land der Tausend Seen*, a detailed brochure available at most tourist offices, lists campgrounds within and near the park. Waren (p. 147) offers visitors several options that balance the adventure of wilderness and the comfort of town life. Travelers interested in Müritz East should contact the **Neustrelitz tourist office,** Strelitzer Str. 1. (☎03981 25 31 19. Open May-Sept. M-F 9am-6pm, Sa-Su 9:30am-1pm; Oct.-Apr. M-Th 9am-noon and 1-4pm, F 9am-noon.) Within the park itself, signs lead from the Kratzeburg train station to **Campingplatz "Naturfreund" am Käbelicksee,** Dorfstr. 3, on a secluded lake shore. (☎039822 202 85. Reception 8:30am-8pm. Open year-round. €5 per person, €4.50 under 18. €2-8 per tent, €2 per car. Showers €0.50 for 3min. Boat rental €18-20 per half-day.)

OUTDOOR ACTIVITIES

HIKING. Trails in Müritz are marked by colored images; many trails share similar symbols, so be wary of small differences. Grünow is the best starting point for trails in the east, while the trails in the west begin in many different towns, notably Kargow, Speck, Groß Datow, and Kratzeburg. The extensive booklet *Wandern im Müritz-Nationalpark*, available at park information centers, describes all the trails and has handy color maps to save you from unfolding the enormous trail map (€12). Some recommended trails include:

Rotes Eichhörnchen (Red Squirrel; 11km). To reach the trailhead, leave Kratzeburg on the road leading to highway B-193 (dir.: Neustrelitz); the beginning of the trail will appear on your left, across from a small parking area. A local favorite that passes several of Müritz's lakes, the trail has a closed loop in the north: 2hr. takes you around the lily-padded **Wienpletschsee** and then by the banks of the Müritz and Binnenmuritz, where the *Strandpromenade* (boardwalk) is scalloped with tiny beach alcoves.

Violetter Pilz (Purple Mushroom; 6km). Follows the coastline of the Müritzsee from starting point Boek, providing good opportunities to spot wildlife, including white-tailed eagles, beavers, and the occasional fox. In fall, wild swans are everywhere, while in summer, fish-hawks hunt for lunch on the water.

Gelber Schmetterling (Yellow Butterfly; 8.5km). Follow Strandstr. past site of the Waren Jugendherberge to reach the trailhead. In the north near Waren, this trail makes a circuit around the Feisnecksee, with grassy fields and views of the lake. The small *Burgwallinsel* in the middle of the lake is a remnant of a former Slavic settlement.

Grünes Blatt (Green Leaf; 10km). Beginning from Grünow in Müritz East, this path meanders through rolling country hills, forests, and along lakeside paths.

TIP **OF MOORS AND MOSQUITOS.** Müritz's location amid swampy lakes may be pleasant for you, but it's even more exciting for mosquitoes. Use bug spray and wear long pants while hiking to avoid a day of futile swatting.

BIKING. Bike routes are nearly as common as hiking trails. Circling the Müritzsee, the 106km **Müritz-Radrundweg** is the park's most popular bike trail. The trail begins in Waren and passes through Boek, stopping near two of the park's tallest watchtowers. Other recommended trails include the **Gelber Vögel** (Yellow Bird) near Grünow, the **Violette Blüme** (Purple Flower) south of Waren, and the comprehensive 159km **Radrundweg Blaues Müritzband.** The road to Federow is beautiful, but bikes must yield to frequent buses on Federower Weg. From Neustrelitz, there are several ways to enter the park's western section. To get to the heart of Müritz West, bike on road B-193 in the direction of Penzlin (signs indicating this road begin at the town's main traffic circle on Strelitzer Str.) and then fork left to Kratzeburg, as indicated by road signs. The road to Userin, on the southern border of the park (in the opposite direction of Penzlin), leads to a number of trails that veer north into Müritz West. Follow the signs to Grünow, another springboard for trips in the park's east. Though most roads in and around the park are stunning, but it is never a bad idea to check with a park ranger to ensure that there is no better alternative to your chosen route.

WATERSPORTS. The stretch of the Havel River between the Käbelicksee and the Granzinersee has the most spectacular canoeing in Müritz. Rent boats at several locations on the coast including **Bootsvermietung Hecht,** Dalmsdorf 6, just outside of Kratzeburg, which rents canoes, kayaks, and rowboats. (☎039822 202 41; www.kanu-hecht.de. Boats €15-25 per half-day.) Sailing and windsurfing are popular on the Müritzsee, and rentals are readily available in Boek.

WAREN ☎03991

Waren is always abuzz with vacationers eager to explore Müritz National Park. Between its beautiful marina, cheerful atmosphere, and abundance of accommodations, the town (pop. 22,400) makes an ideal base.

TRANSPORTATION AND PRACTICAL INFORMATION. **Trains** head to Berlin (1¾hr., every hr., €24.70) and Rostock (1hr., every 2hr., €14.60). For a **taxi,** call ☎03991 12 22 55. To get to the park, ride the bus operated by **Personenverkehr Müritz,** accessible every hr. from the harbor, across from the Müritzeum (☎03991 64 50; www.pvm-waren.de). **Bikes** can be rented at **Zweirad Karberg,** off the Neuer Markt at Lange Str. 46. (☎03991 66 60 80. €4-7 per day.) **Sport-Assmuß,** Friedensstr. 17, sells other outdoor gear. (☎03991 66 52 33. Open M-F 9am-6pm, Sa 9am-4pm.) Waren's **tourist office,** Neuer Markt 21, books rooms (from €25) for free. From the train station, turn right onto the footpath next to the tracks and follow it under the overpass at Schweriner Damm; go left on Friedensstr. which becomes Mühlenstr. and left again on Langestr. (☎03991 66 61 83; www.waren-tourismus.de. Open daily May-Sept. 9am-8pm; Oct.-Apr. M-F 9am-6pm, Sa-Su 10am-3pm.) All accommodations in Müritz charge a daily *Kurtaxe* (€1), entitling travelers to discounts on local attractions and services. A **pharmacy, Löwen-Apotheke,** Neuer Markt 21, is next to the tourist office. (☎03991 66 61 53. Open May-Oct. M-F 8am-6:30pm, Sa 8am-1pm; Nov.-Apr. M-F 8am-6pm, Sa 8am-1pm.) Do **laundry** at **Waschsalon Wirbelwind,** Strandstr. 1. (66 26 63. Wash and dry €8. Open M-F 9am-6pm, Sa 9am-2pm.) **Internet** is available at **Am Yachthafen Hotel Garni,** Sandstr. 2. (€1.50 per 30min. or Wi-Fi, €1 per hr. Open to non-guests daily 7am-8pm.) The **post office** is at Neuer Markt 19. (☎03991 67 39 30. Open M-Sa 9am-noon, M-F 2pm-6pm.) **Postal Code:** 17192.

ACCOMMODATIONS AND FOOD. The most convenient campground is **Ecktannen Campingplatz ❶,** Fontanestr. 66, near the lake. Take bus #3 (dir.: Ecktannen) to the last stop. (☎03991 66 85 13. www.camping-ecktannen.de. Reception daily May-Sept. 8am-10pm, Apr. and Oct. 8am-6pm; if you arrive later, camp outside the gate and check in the next day. Showers included. Snack shop 8am-8pm. Open Apr.-Oct. €5.10 per person, €3-4 per tent. Small houses available. Cash only.) At the north of the park, the **Pension Zur Fledermaus ❸,** Am Teufelsbruch 1, has brightly decorated rooms with a meadow view unadulterated by the bustle of downtown Waren, a full 3km away. Follow the directions to Waren's National Park Information Center, and continue another 1½km along the dirt road. (☎03991 66 32 93; www.pension-fledermaus.de. Breakfast included. Singles €28-33; doubles €50-62; triples €75. Bath €3 extra; add €3 for 1-night stays. Reception 10am-6pm. AmEx/MC/V.) To get to **Waren's Jugendherberge (HI) ❷,** An der Feisneck 1a, follow Am Seeufer out of the center of town. The hostel is on the left immediately before the intersection with An der Feisneck. (☎03991 77 66 70. Breakfast and sheets included. TV and game room. €22.15 per night, under 27 €19.15. Half board add €2.50, full board add €3.50. Jul. and Aug. add €0.50. Cash only.)

Buy groceries at **Frischemarkt,** Neuer Markt 23. (Open M-F 8am-7pm, Sa 8am-2pm.) On Tuesdays, Fridays, and Saturdays, vendors gather in the **Markt** to sell a mouthwatering array of food (10am-5pm). **Langestraße** and **Neuer Markt** in Waren's Altstadt are crammed with bakeries and *Imbiße*. For seafood in the harbor, **Windfang ❸,** Müritzstr. 19 offers a wide selection (fish entrees €9-16.30) in a classy, unrushed atmosphere. Customers sit outside in all weather under the yellow-striped awning, or inside in the cozy, nautically inspired dining room. (☎03991 66 84 65. www.restaurant-windfang.de. Open daily from 10am. MC/V.) Budget-conscious diners can enjoy a waterfront view at **Schnitzel-König ❷,** Strandstr. 3. Tasty schnitzel dishes (€6.60-7.50) can all be supersized and complement live music. Vegetarian options are largely limited to baked potatoes for €3.30-5. (☎03991 66 90 11. Open daily 11am-11pm. Cash only.)

SIGHTS AND OUTDOOR ACTIVITIES. The **Müritzeum,** Friedensstr. 5, has been presenting the natural history of the area through 1866. Enjoy the how-to on stuffing birds and small mammals and visit the aquarium showcasing local fish. (☎03991 63 36 80; www.mueritzeum.de. Open daily Apr.-Oct. 10am-7pm, Nov.-Mar. 10am-6pm. Admission €7.50, students €5, children €3, families €17.) **Boat tours** of the lake are available through **Warener Schifffahrtsgesellschaft,** Am

Stadthafen (☎03991 12 56 24; www.warener-schifffahrt.de), **Müritzwind Personenschifffahrt,** on Strandstr. (☎03991 66 66 64; www.schifffahrt-mueritzwind.de), and the **Weiße Flotte Müritz,** Kietzstr. 17 (☎03991 12 26 68; www.mueritz-schifffahrt.de). Tours run 1-7hr. (€7-20, children ½-price). To tackle the waters yourself, visit **Eastside** (☎03991 73 50 61), next to Campingplatz Ecktannen, which rents kayaks, small dinghies, catamarans, and windsurf boards. Follow Strandstr. as it becomes Kietzstr. and then Gerhart-Hauptmann-Allee, to get to the **Volksbad,** a grassy beach with a dock where swimming is permitted. (Windsurfers €8 per hr, two man kayaks €6 per hr., solo kayaks €4 per hr., sailboats €15 per hr.). For a more revved-up experience closer to town, try **Bootscharter Jörg Malow,** right on the harbor. (☎03991 66 23 94; www.bootscharter-malow.de. Motorboats €7-27 per hr., many including a skipper.)

ROSTOCK ☎0381

A victim of socialist industrial ambitions after WWII, the port city of Rostock (pop. 200,000), the largest in sparsely populated Mecklenburg, has been reconstructed but never fully restored. Fortunately, most of the concrete eyesores erected during the DDR-era are relegated to the city's suburbs, and hints of Rostock's glorious past as a member of the Hanseatic League can still be glimpsed downtown. Rostock's university, the oldest in the Baltic region, infuses the city with youthful energy, contributing to a thriving nightlife a safe distance from typical tourist haunts. Tourists flock to the charming resort town of Warnemünde, whose wide, sandy beaches are just minutes away.

TRANSPORTATION

Trains: To: **Berlin** (2½hr., every 2hr., €33.80); **Dresden** (5¼hr., every 2hr., €51-70); **Hamburg** (2½hr., every hr., €29.70-38); **Schwerin** (1hr., every hr., €14.60-18.50); **Stralsund** (1hr., every hr., €12); **Wismar** (1¼hr., every hr., €9.90).

Public Transportation: Trams #5 and 6 run from the train station to the Altstadt. Single bus/tram ticket €1.70, *Tageskarte* (day ticket) €4.30. To get to the bus station for lines to smaller towns, leave the train station through the Südstadt exit. Bus service slows after 10pm; after midnight, *Fledermaus* (bat) buses run to some central stops every hr.

Ferries: Boats for Scandinavia leave from the Überseehafen docks. **TT-Line** runs ferries to Trelleborg, Sweden. (☎04502 81 03 48; www.TTLine.com. 5hr.; 2-3 per day; round-trip from €60, children and students from €30, bicycles €10.) **Scandlines** sends boats to Gedser, Denmark. (☎03831 207 3317; www.scandlines.de. 2hr.; 3 per day; 1-way June-Sept. €10, children €11; Oct.-May €6/5.)

ORIENTATION AND PRACTICAL INFORMATION

Rostock lies on the Warnow River, just over 10km inland from the Baltic Sea. The city's main attractions are within the **Altstadt,** which is bordered to the north by the Warnow, and encircled on the other three sides by segments of the old city wall. Stretching across the Altstadt from **Kröpeliner Tor** in the west to the Rathaus in the east is **Kröpeliner Straße,** the city's main pedestrian zone and shopping district, also home to the city's university. As many tourists tend to stick to the big attractions in the east, many of the city's cafes and bars are to the west of the Altstadt in the lively student quarter near **Doberaner Platz** The **Hauptbahnhof** is south of the Altstadt. The beaches of **Warnemünde** lie 11km to the northwest of Rostock, where the Warnow river meets the Baltic Sea.

Tourist Office: Neuer Markt 3 (☎0381 22 22), in the post office building. From the train station, take tram #5 or 6 to "Neuer Markt." The staff books rooms for €3 and leads **tours.** (May-Oct. M-Sa 2pm, Su 11am. Apr.-Oct. also Th 6pm. €4. Available in English for groups on request.) Open June-Aug. M-F 10am-7pm, Sa-Su 10am-4pm; May and Sept. M-F 10am-6pm, Sa-Su 10am-4pm; Oct.-Apr. M-F 10am-6pm, Sa-Su 10am-3pm.

Currency Exchange: Deutsche Bank, Kröpeliner Str. 84 (☎0381 456 50), changes traveler's checks and has **ATMs.** Open M-Tu and Th 9am-6pm, W 9am-1pm, F 9am-3pm.

Gay and Lesbian Resources: rat + tat, Leonhardstr. 20, focuses on sexuality and AIDS prevention. (☎0381 45 31 56; www.schwules-rostock.de). Open Tu 10am-6pm, Th 1-6pm, and by appointment. Monthly program announces gay parties and events while Rostock's *Gay City Map* helps locate them. Both available at tourist office.

Emergency: Police ☎110. **Ambulance** and **Fire** ☎112.

Pharmacy: Rats Apotheke, Neuer Markt 13 (☎0381 493 4747). www.ratsapotheke-rostock.de. Open M-F 8am-6pm, Sa 8am-1pm.

Internet Access: Find free **Internet** at the library. Kröpeliner Str. 82. Open M-Tu and Th-F 10am-6pm, W noon-6pm, Sa 9am-1pm. **Treffpunkt,** Am Vögenteich 23 (☎0381 643 8067), inside the Ostseesparkasse building. €1.50 per 30min. Open 9am-7pm.

Post Office: Neuer Markt 3-8. Open M-F 9am-6pm, Sa 9am-12:30pm. **Postal Code:** 18055.

ACCOMMODATIONS

Hanse-Hostel Rostock, Doberaner Str. 136 (☎0381 128 6006; www.hanse-hostel.de). Tram #5 to "Volkstheater." A 15min. walk from the Altstadt but right on the doorstop of the hip Doberaner Platz, this hostel has a lively kitchen and a TV lounge stocked with board games. The friendly owners happily give great advice on navigating the city's sights. Breakfast €4. Sheets €2. Laundry €2.50 wash, €1.50 dry. Internet €0.50 per 30min. Check-out 11am. Reception 8am-10pm. 8-bed dorms €14; 6-bed dorms €16; quads €18; triples €19; doubles €22; singles €24. ISIC discount 10%. MC/V. ❶

Jugendgästeschiff Rostock: MS Georg Büchner (HI), Am Stadthafen 72 (☎0381 670 0320). Take tram #5 to "Kabutzenhof," turn right onto Am Kabutzenhof, walk until you reach the water (5min.). A converted cargo ship, now permanently docked in Rostock's harbor, successfully breaks up hostel monotony. Beautiful waterfront views outside and a wood-paneled officers' mess hall make up for the distance from town and small porthole windows. Breakfast included. Sheets €6. Dorms €16.50, over 27 €19.50. ❷

Jugendherberge Warnemünde (HI), Parkstr. 47 (☎0381 54 81 70), 1km west of the Warnemünde harbor; take bus #36 or 37 to "Warnemünde Strand." Right across the street from the beach, a former water tower's bottom floors hold 40 rooms with bath and 20 with hallway facilities that fill up quickly in summer. Internet €1 per 10min. Breakfast included. Dorms €23.15, over 27 €27.15. ❷

FOOD

Neuer Markt, on Steinstr. across from the Rathaus, fills with produce, spices, meat, and clothing vendors. (Open M-F 8am-5pm, Sa 8am-1pm.) For groceries, try **Rewe,** on on Friedhofsweg 3. (Open M-Sa 7am-10pm.) The bakeries on Kröpeliner Straße sell cheap sandwiches and pastries.

Cafe Central, Leonhardstr. 22 (☎0381 490 4648), fills with a 20-something crowd that spills out into the street. Despite cutesy flowers sprouting from the ceiling, it is clear that the cafe takes its food seriously, presenting light pasta dishes (€6-8), salads (€7.50),

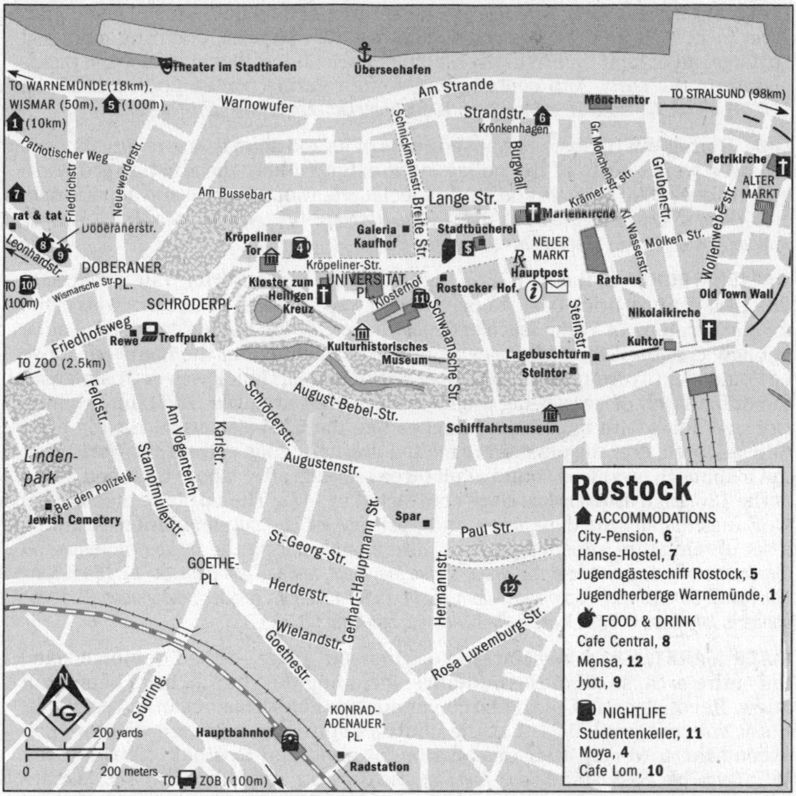

soups (€3.60-4.30), and wraps (€5.20-5.90). Come back at night for a drink (€2-4). Open M-Sa 9am-2am, Su 10am-2am with brunch 10am-3pm. Cash only. ❷

Jyoti, Leonhardstr. 23 (☎0381 459 0485). Silk pillows and flower garlands set the mood for hearty Indian dishes. A lengthy list of meat dishes (€7-9) and many vegetarian options (€6.50). Exquisite fresh bread comes with every entree. Open 9:30am-late. ❷

Mensa, St.-Georg-Str. 104-107, near the Leibnizpl. tram stop, in the basement of the cream stucco Studentenwerk building. Super-cheap cafeteria lunches (€1-4) feed a university crowd. Open M-F 11:15am-2pm, Sa noon-1:30pm. Cash only. ❶

SIGHTS

KRÖPELINER STRASSE. Rostock's main pedestrian mall runs west from the Rathaus to 12th-century **Kröpeliner Tor,** the former town gate. This lively nucleus is the place to take care of any shopping, snacking, or gawking at passersby. Although much of the city was destroyed in WWII, many of the half-timbered and glazed-brick houses along this stretch have been restored. The main buildings of **Rostock University,** one of the oldest in Northern Europe, are located near the middle of Kröpeliner Str., surrounding the massive Rococo fountain at Universitätspl. Next to the university, along the remains of the city wall, is the

Kloster zum heiligen Kreuz, a restored cloister founded by the Danish Queen Margaret in 1270. It now houses the **Kulturhistorisches Museum,** featuring medieval artifacts, an exhibit on life in the cloister, a selection of local landscape paintings from the early 20th century, and some rotating contemporary exhibits. *(☎0381 45 41 77. Open Tu-Su May-Sept. 10am-6pm; Oct.-Apr. 11am-5pm. Free entry.)*

ZOO. During WWII, Rostock housed some of its zoo animals in public offices—the apes were guests of the police station. Since then, the zoo has grown to include over 2000 animals and lends special attention to arctic and aquatic species. *(Tram #3 or 6 to "Zoo." ☎0381 208 20. Open daily Apr.-Oct. 9am-7pm; Nov.-Mar. 9am-5pm. www.zoo-rostock.de. €11, students €9, children €6.)*

MARIENKIRCHE. In the final days before the fall of the Berlin Wall, services at this 13th-century brick basilica overflowed with political protesters who came for the sermons of **Pastor Joachim Gauck.** In one of his bolder gestures, Gauck publicly chastised the *Stasi* (secret police) by calling out the names of those he could identify from the pulpit. After reunification, Gauck was entrusted with the difficult job of overseeing the fate of the Stasi archives. The church's interior overflows with impressive touches like the **5704-pipe organ.** Having been fully restored after the pipes were melted down for guns in the First World War, the mammoth produces sound a full three seconds after a note is played. Gape at the 12m high **astronomical clock** contracted in 1472. The intricate mechanical workings display the date, time, and positions of the sun and moon. At noon, a set of miniature apostles pop out, circumambulating the figure of Jesus. *(At the end of Kröpeliner Str. near the Neuer Markt. May-Sept. M-Sa 10am-6pm, Su 11:15am-5pm; Oct.-Apr. M-Sa 10am-12:15pm and 2-4pm, Su 11:15am-12:15pm. Requested donation €1. Organ concerts July-Sept. W 8pm. Tours daily 11am. €1, students €0.50.)*

ALTER MARKT. The Alter Markt is old in name alone—Allied bombs leveled the entire area, so all of the buildings, including the church, have been built anew. Reconstruction of the large yet austere **Petrikirche** began in the 1950s, but it was not until 1994 that the church's spire was restored. Visitors can ascend the tower by stair or elevator for a view of Rostock. *(Open June-Aug. M-F 10am-7pm, Sa-Su 10am-5pm; Apr.-May and Sept.-Oct. daily 10am-5pm; Nov.-Mar. M-F 10am-4pm, Sa-Su 10am-5pm. Tower €2, reduced price €1.50.)*

SCHIFFAHRTSMUSEUM (NAVIGATION MUSEUM). Paintings, photographs, and models tell the story of Rostock's maritime past from the Vikings to the present day, with special exhibits on aviation and trade. *(August-Bebel-Str. 1. ☎0381 857 9711. Open Tu-Su May-Sept. 10am-6pm, Oct.-Apr. 11am-5pm. €3, students €1.)*

JEWISH ROSTOCK. Nazi storm troopers burned the synagogue on Augustenstr. on Kristallnacht and, in the following months, deported Rostock's once substantial Jewish population. Of the 175 sent to concentration camps, only two survived. The town's small **Jewish cemetery** was damaged in the war, and in the 1970s, the government turned the remaining gravestones face-down to create the city's **Lindenpark.** Pressure from the international community convinced the city to right most of the stones and add a memorial in 1988, though gravestones are still scattered in the underbrush on the park's fringes. *(Take tram #3 or 6 or bus #24 to "Saarpl.," then walk south through the park.)*

FESTIVALS AND NIGHTLIFE

Every August, the extravagant **Hanse Sail** festival attracts over a million visitors to ogle at tall ships, dance, and drink. Rostock also hosts the largest **Christmas market** in the north of Germany (annually Nov. 22-Dec. 22). At night, Rostock's students come out to play, congregating along Kröpeliner Str., Wismarische

Str., and Barnstorfer Weg. Check out *Piste* and *Rostock Szene*, which lists local clubs and performances, in addition to *Nordost Eventguide*, which covers clubs across Mecklenburg-Vorpommern. All are free at the tourist office.

Studentenkeller, Universitätspl. 5 (☎0381 45 59 28; www.studentenkeller.de). Entrance on Schwaansche Str., across from the Parka Hotel. The nexus of Rostock's university crowd, which fills the cavernous brick cellar and attached garden. The *Keller* hosts DJs, parties, and movies. Open Tu-Th from 9pm, F-Sa from 10pm. Cover Tu-Th €1, F-Sa €1.50; €3 for non-students. Free entry 10-11pm. Cash only.

Cafe Lom, Barnstorfer Weg 19 (☎0381 364 4587). Patrons chat while draped over cushy, candle-lit benches or couches under paper lanterns. The decor is colorful without being frenetic, and the drinks are cheap. Beer €1.50-2.20. Pan-Asian dishes €5-7.50. Come early for the lunch special (€4; 11am-3pm). Open daily from 9am. Cash only.

Moya, Kröpeliner Str. 56 (☎0381 375 4619; www.moya.ro), hosts frequent themed parties on its enormous darkened dance floor and under flashing lights. The bar's location near the university attracts a student crowd. Check website for a schedule. Entry €2.50-6, students €4 before 11pm. Open Tu and Th-Su from 8pm.

DAYTRIP FROM ROSTOCK: WARNEMÜNDE

S-Bahn or Fledermaus bus to "Warnemünde." (20min., 4 per hr. 4:45am-8:30pm.) Less frequent service at night. Rostock day ticket is valid for the ferry across Warnemünde harbor.

The beach town of Warnemünde sits a tempting 18min. north of Rostock. Warnemünde's **Alter Strom** (Old Harbor) bustles with the sounds of fishing boats and clicking cameras. Across the bridge from the Bahnhof, stands sell snacks and trinkets to eager tourists along the waterfront promenade. Tourist information is at Am Strom 59. *(☎0381 54 08 00. Open Jun.-Aug. M-F 9am-6pm, Sa-Su 10am-4pm; Sept.-Oct. and Mar.-May M-F 10am-6pm, Sa-Su 10am-4pm; Nov.-Feb. M-F 10am-5pm, Sa 10am-3pm.)* Climb the lighthouse by the Alter Strom for a view of shores stretching far into the distance. *(Open daily May-Sept. 10am-7pm. €2, students €1, families €4.)* Walk long enough, and you can disrobe at the town's nude beaches (look for FKK signs at beach entrances, or mass nudity).

STRALSUND ☎03831

Stralsund (pop. 58,000) is famous for the distinctive red brick Gothic architecture pervading its lively Altstadt. Founded in 1234, the city amassed great wealth as an instrumental member of the Hanseatic League. Stralsund came under Swedish rule after the Thirty Years' War before a short occupation by France and eventual annexation by Prussia in 1815. Although the city was heavily damaged in WWII, reconstruction efforts have maintained the architectural integrity of the Altstadt. In 2002, Stralsund and nearby Wismar were recognized as a UNESCO World Heritage Site. Sadly, a slumping economy in the wake of reunification has left many of the city's historic buildings to decay. Nevertheless, tourism is now blossoming thanks to its lively atmosphere, fueled by its progressive student population and its proximity to pristine Hiddensee.

TRANSPORTATION

Trains: To: **Berlin** (3½hr., 2 per hr., €26-33); **Binz** and **Sassnitz** on Rügen (both 1hr., every hr., €7.40); **Hamburg** (3hr., every hr., €28-35); **Rostock** (1hr., every hr., €12).

Buses: Intercity buses depart from the **ZOB** at Frankenwall, in the south of the Altstadt. Take Tribseer Damm right from the train station and then another right at the split onto

Frankenwall. Within Stralsund, bus #1 circles the Altstadt. Lines #2-6 serve the Altstadt and the outskirts of town. Single ride €1.70, 9hr. day pass €4.20.

Taxis: Call ☎03831 39 49 09, or find one outside of the train station.

Ferries: Reederei Hiddensee (☎0180 321 21 50) runs 3 times per day to **Kloster, Vitte,** and **Hiddensee** (round-trip €17.80, €9.70 for children under 14; bikes €7.50).

Bike Rental: Fahrradverleih, Tribseer Damm 75 (☎03831 30 61 58). To your right as you exit the train station. From €5 per day. Open M-F 8am-6pm, Sa 10am-2pm.

ORIENTATION AND PRACTICAL INFORMATION

Stralsund's historic **Altstadt** sits on a small island, bordered to the south and west by the **Frankenteich** and **Knieperteich,** two large natural ponds, and to the east by the Strelasund, a strait separating Rügen Island from the mainland. Two of 11 city gates in the city's now defunct wall remain: the **Kütertor** in the west and the **Kniepertor** to the north, though a segment of wall stretches between them. Stralsund's main pedestrian zone, **Ossenreyerstraße,** runs north-south through the center of the Altstadt from the **Alter Markt** to the **Neuer Markt.** The distinctive spires of the town's three main churches are landmarks that simplify navigation within the Altstadt. Stralsund's train station lies near the Altstadt's southwest corner across the Tribseer Damm.

Tourist Office: Alter Markt 9 (☎03831 246 90). From the train station, turn right on Tribseer Damm and follow the signs just past the Rathaus (10min.). Or take bus #4 to "Kütertor." Distributes free maps, finds rooms for €3, and rents audio guides (€5) of the Altstadt in English, German, and Swedish. Walking tours depart May-Sept. daily 11am and 2pm, and F at 9pm. (€4-6, students €2.50-4). Open May-Sept. M-F 9am-7pm, Sa 9am-2pm, Su 10am-2pm; Oct.-Apr. M-F 10am-5pm, Sa 10am-2pm.

Emergency: Police ☎110. **Fire** and **Ambulance** ☎112.

Pharmacy: Tribseer Damm 6 (☎03831 29 23 28), across the street from the train station. Open M-F 8am-6pm, Sa 8am-noon.

Internet Access: One terminal in the tourist office. €0.50 per 10min., €2.50 per hr. Free Wi-Fi. **EisCafe MATRIX,** Wasserstr. 8-9. €0.07 per min. Open daily 1-10pm.

Post Office: Neuer Markt 4. Open M-F 9am-6pm, Sa 9am-noon. **Postal Code:** 18439.

MECKLENBURG-VORPOMMERN

ACCOMMODATIONS

Younior-Hotel, Tibseer Damm 78 (☎0800 233 38 82 34; www.younior-hotel.de). With a life-size chess board, an outdoor fire pit, and tennis courts, this brand-new hostel, right on the water, is built for fun. Breakfast and sheets included. Dorms €18-25. Half pension €21-30. Full pension €25-35. Cash only. ❷

Hostel Stralsund, Reiferbahn 11 (☎03831 28 47 40; www.hostel-stralsund.com). In this giant orange box of opportunities, find everything from a fitness room equipped with ping-pong tables to bike rentals (€10 per day). Sparkling new facilities. Kitchen access. Free Wi-Fi. Breakfast €4. Dorms €16-20; 2-bed room €23; singles €35. Cash only. ❷

Jugendherberge Stralsund-Devin (HI), Strandstr. 21 (☎03831 49 02 89). From the station, take bus #3 to the end of the line at "Devin" (20min., €1.70). Continue on the trail to the left of the Kurhaus-Devin, and turn left when you hit Strandstr. Located in the seaside village of Devin, this older (though clean and well-organized) hostel occupies 20 buildings near the beach. Breakfast included. Reception 7:30am-10:30pm. Check-in 3-7pm. Dorms €20.50, over 27 €24.50. Add €2-4 for private shower. MC. ❷

FOOD

Buy groceries in the Alstadt at **Susanne Neubauer,** in the Ostwest Passage off Ossenreyer Str. 49. (☎03831 28 17 55. Open M-F 8am-7pm, Sa 8am-6pm.) The restaurants near the harbor serve fresh seafood late into the night, while cheap bakeries and sidewalk cafes line **Ossenreyerstr.** and both **Neuer** and **Alter Markt.**

Fischermann's, An der Fährbrücke 3 (☎03831 29 23 22). This massive, entertainingly social restaurant and bar sprawls onto the pier. Prepare to share your meal with a crowd Fish dishes €8.50-16. Open daily 10am-11pm. MC/V. ❸

Hansekeller, Mönchstr. 48 (☎03831 70 38 40), occupies a Renaissance-era brick cellar. From the privacy of leather booths, customers relish regional dishes like duck and *Sauerfleisch* (sour-cured meat; €9.50-14). Open daily 11am-11pm. AmEx/MC/V. ❸

Salsarico, Frankenstr. 7 (☎03831 66 60 50). While serving the German take on Mexican (entrees €8.20-13.30), south-of-the-border decor and imported Mexican beers (€2-3) provide a complete change of atmosphere from surrounding Stralsund. Popular bar for a young, boisterous crowd at night. Open daily 11am-1am. Cash only. ❸

SIGHTS

DEUTSCHES MUSEUM FÜR MEERESKUNDE UND FISCHEREI (GERMAN MUSEUM FOR OCEANOGRAPHY AND FISHING). At Germany's largest oceanographic museum, located in the former St. Katharinen monastery between Alter and Neuer Markt, mackerel and mussels have replaced monks and manuscripts. The museum is home to four aquariums, including a display of the Baltic and North Sea fishes and a tide pool environment, but not before leading through room after room of fake fish in glass showcases. *(On the corner of Mönchstr. and Böltcherstr. ☎03831 26 52 10; www.meeresmuseum.de. Open daily June-Sept. 10am-6pm; Oct.-May 10am-5pm. Feedings Sa-Su 11am. €7.50, students €5, families €17. Audio guides €2.)*

KULTURHISTORISCHES MUSEUM (CULTURAL HISTORY MUSEUM). Sharing St. Katharinen with the Meeresmuseum, this wide-ranging collection, the oldest in Mecklenburg-Vorpomern, follows Stralsund's history from stone-age spears to luxuriously painted playing cards. Guests wander straight from museum exhibitions into a series of historically furnished rooms, including a DDR-style living room. Highlights range from the luxurious—the spectacular Goldschatz von Hiddensee, 596 grams of intricate pure gold jewelry created by the Vikings.

RÜGEN ISLAND

In the Baltic Sea northeast of Stralsund, Germany's largest island is a natural paradise of white beaches, rugged chalk cliffs, beech forests, and sprawling meadows. Ancient stone burial sites and monuments scattered about the island bear witness to Rügen's stone age past. In the 5th century, the Slavs pushed out the Teutonic tribes inhabiting the island, only to be converted to Christianity by the Danes 500 years later. Briefly under Swedish control, Rügen eventually became part of Prussia. Prince Wilhelm Malte I was the precursor to bikinis, introducing bathing tourism to the island in the early 1800s, and by the beginning of the 20th century, the island had established itself as a favorite destination for nobility. The fall of the Berlin Wall opened Rügen to a flood of westerners, and the island now draws throngs of rugged bikers, backpacking hikers, relaxed beachgoers, and armies of bedazzled pint-sized dogs.

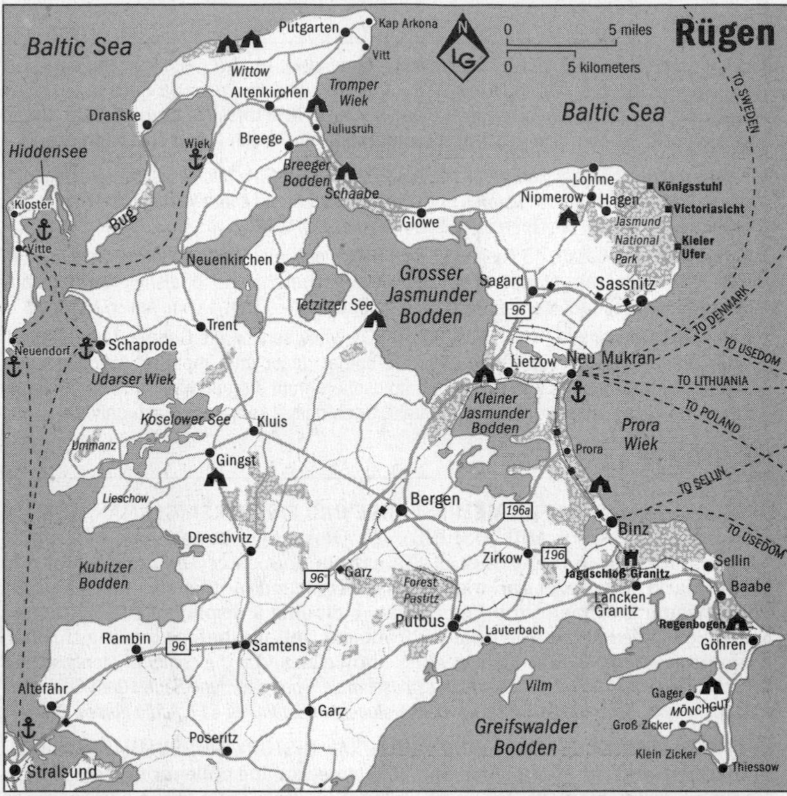

Trains leave Stralsund, the mainland gateway to Rügen, for Binz and Sassnitz (1hr., every hr., €9) via Bergen, an unattractive transportation hub in the center of the island. **Buses** connect Stralsund with Rügen's largest towns, and a ferry runs from Stralsund to Schaprode, near Hiddensee, on Rügen's west coast. Most visitors drive onto the island, and public transportation tends to be expensive. To get to Kap Arkona in the north or Göhren in the south, you'll have to take an **RPNV** bus from Bergen or Sassnitz. (☎03838 194 49. Every hr., €3-7, day pass €10.) The efficient RPNV also connects nearby towns like Binz and Sellin. The **Rasender Roland,** a narrow-gauge rail line with historic steam locomotives, runs every 2hr. from Putbus to Göhren (€8) with stops in many spa towns. However, with a top speed of 30kph, the railway is more of a tourist attraction than an efficient means of transportation. The best way to appreciate Rügen's stunning scenery and picturesque towns is by hiking and biking. Although the whole island is criss-crossed by trails, the best are found along the eastern coast in **Nationalpark Jasmund, NSG Granitz,** the **Mönchgut Peninsula,** and on **Hiddensee Island** to the west. There are 21 campgrounds in Rügen, with the majority to the southeast on the Mönchgut Peninsula.

JASMUND NATIONAL PARK

Carved out by massive glaciers 12,000 years ago, Jasmund's jagged, white *Kreideklippen* (chalk cliffs) drop into an emerald-green sea. Thanks to erosion, the sheer faces of the tooth-like cliffs hang precariously over the stormy coast, receding 2-5cm each year. Fortunately, the roots of the red beech trees above the cliffs help the chalk to weather fierce Baltic winds, although nature can at times overpower these safeguards, sending sections of chalky rock into the sea. These 5000-year-old groves, as well as miles of canopied forest (the Baltic's largest), and the highest cliffs on the German coast make Jasmund Rügen's most attractive landscape.

TRANSPORTATION

Rügen is small enough that no matter where you stay, getting to the park will not take long. Unfortunately, public transportation runs sporadically, often turning back before reaching more distant park attractions. Trains run from Stralsund to Sassnitz, the gateway to the park. Since trails are plentiful and well-marked, bikes and feet are the best modes of transportation once in Jasmund. Many of the more scenic coastline trails are off-limits to bikes because of numerous winding stairways. Buses #20 and 23 run from the Sassnitz train station to the **Königsstuhl** (King's Throne), the park's most famous site (1-2 per hr. in summer, until 5:40pm; €1.55.) Plan well—there are often gaps of 2hr. between buses. Private cars are not permitted on the 3km stretch of road leading to the Königsstuhl. Drivers must park in Hagen and take the #19 "Pendelbus" shuttle to the Königsstuhl (every 10min. in summer, €2.40) or walk the trail.

JASMUND NATIONAL PARK AT A GLANCE

AREA: 30 sq. km

CLIMATE: Frequent alternation between sun and rain. Warm, sunny summers; wet and windy winters.

FEATURES: Chalk cliffs, beech forests, wet grasslands, sandy beaches.

GATEWAY: Sassnitz.

HIGHLIGHTS: Imposing cliff formations, like the arresting Königsstuhl (118m).

CAMPING: Forbidden within the park.

FEES AND RESERVATIONS: Admission fee at selected sights. Reserve nearby campsites in advance for summer months. Parking €1.50-8.

ORIENTATION AND PRACTICAL INFORMATION

Jasmund is a peninsula of Rügen that is nearly an island itself, flanked by the Großer Jasmunder Bodden on the west and the Baltic Sea on the east. The national park is at the easternmost tip of the peninsula, stretching between the towns of Sassnitz in the south and Lohme in the north. Twelve kilometers of chalk cliffs descend over 100m into the sea along the coast and Stubnitz plateau, while beech forests, orchids, springs, lakes, moors, and ancient gravesites fill the areas inland. Hiking and biking trails run throughout the park.

Emergency: Police ☎110. **Fire** and **Ambulance** ☎112.

Climate: Summer is the best time to come, as temperatures are generally warm enough for hikers to wear shorts and T-shirts. Surprise rain showers spring up year-round.

Ranger Stations: The brand-new **Nationalpark-Zentrum am Königsstuhl** (☎038392 66 17 66; www.koenigsstuhl.com), by the entrance to the Königsstuhl lookout point, has maps and park information on hand. Exhaustive multimedia exhibits popular with children highlight the history and ecology of the park. Open daily Easter-Oct. 9am-7pm; Nov.-Easter 10am-5pm. Exhibits €6, children €3. Because the station is flooded with instant-gratification tourists, consider skipping the bigger attractions. The #6 ("Wedding") parking lot in Sassnitz is also staffed daily 9am-6pm.

CAMPING

The closest campsite to the park is **Wald-Camping-Nipmerow ❶**, 4km west of Königsstuhl. Take bus #20 or 23 from the Sassnitz station (dir.: Königsstuhl) to "Nipmerow." Most buses do not make the complete trip; be sure to ask before boarding. (☎038302 92 44. Bike rental €3 per day. Tent rental €8 per night. Camping fee €6 per night per person. Reception 7am-6pm, summer 7am-9pm; arrive anytime and check in the next morning. Closed from late-Oct. to Apr.)

HIKING

KÖNIGSSTUHL HOCHUFERWEG. The park's signature trail is an 8.1km, 3hr. hike that starts in the #6 ("Wedding") parking lot in Sassnitz at the end of Weddingstr. and runs the length of the park's coastline from atop the cliffs. When hiking, you can follow the white blazes with blue horizontal stripes painted on trees, but the signs at trail crossings or maps from the ranger station are more reliable. Six hundred meters into the trail, the **Piratenschlucht** leads down to the beach, perfect for those who would rather look up at the cliffs than down from them, but the trail continues on to the Kieler Bach lookout several kilometers farther. From there, you can walk the next stretch along the rocky water's edge or head back up the trail to the **Victoriasicht** lookout, offering a dramatic view with fewer tourists than the famous **Königsstuhl** 0.5km farther. Following the mob might mean paying the cost of admission to the Nationalpark-Zentrum (above), and the view is only slightly better than what you can see from Victoriasicht for free. According to local legend, the inhabitants of Rügen once elected as their king anyone who could climb the crumbling chalk cliff face from the seaside, hence the name Königsstuhl, or "king's throne."

HERTHASEE. Running from the Hagen parking lot to the Königsstuhl beneath the shelter of red beech trees, this 3km trail offers an alternative to the shuttle bus. Two kilometers into the walk is the Herthasee, a lake named after the German harvest goddess. The **Herthaburg,** a U-shaped earth wall built by the Slavs in the 7th century, still stands near the shore.

BINZ ☎038393

Blindingly white seaside villas with frilly gables and wide balconies embody the *Bäderarchitecktur* (spa architecture) of Rügen's largest, liveliest, and most elegant resort town (pop. 5500). Nudists bare all at Binz's clothing-optional *FKK* (Free Body Culture) beaches, tastefully situated at either end of town. Jazz crooners make frequent appearances on the stage by the Kurplatz pier.

TRANSPORTATION AND PRACTICAL INFORMATION. **Trains** arrive from Stralsund (1hr., every hr., €10). RPNV **Buses** #20, 23, and 28 make multiple stops in Binz (every 20min., €1.30). **Pauli's Radshop,** just down the alleyway at Hauptstr. 9a, rents **bikes** from €5.50 per day. (☎038393 669 24. Open daily 9am-6pm.) The **Rügener Reiselotse Zimmervermittlung & Touristinformation,** Proraer Chaussee 3g, books rooms and provides local information. Head right out of the station and veer right onto Proraer Chaussee. (☎038393 337 89; www.reiselotse.com. Open M-F 9am-6pm, Sa noon-5pm, Su noon-4pm.) For a **taxi,** call ☎038393 24 24. **Internet** is available for a whopping €1 per 10min. at **Easy@Internet,** in the Loev Passage off of Hauptstr. (Open daily 7am-11pm.) A **laundromat, SB Waschsalon,** is at Proraer Chaussee 3c. (Wash €4 for 8kg. Dry €1 per 13min. Open daily 6am-11pm.) The **post office,** Proraer Chaussee 2, is in the Netto shopping complex. (Open M-F 9am-6pm, Sa 9am-noon.) **Postal Code:** 18609.

ACCOMMODATIONS AND FOOD. Accommodations in Binz fill up quickly and run €5-10 more than those on other parts of the island. *Ferienwohnungen* (vacation apartments) are the best options, but only for couples or groups staying for a minimum of three days. The most cost-effective accommodations (doubles €40-70 per night) line the narrow alley at the eastern edge of Binz that climbs the Klünderberg. Judging by its location and gourmet breakfast, one could mistake the **Jugendherberge Binz (HI) ❷,** Strandpromenade 35, for a luxurious beach hotel. (☎038393 325 97; www.jugendherberge-binz.de. Breakfast included. Curfew 11pm but access code available. Dorms €21, over 27 €25. Internet €1 per 20min. Reception daily 7am-9pm.) If the hostel in Binz is full, try the larger yet more distant **Jugendherberge Sellin (HI) ❷,** Kiefernweg 4, a block away from the train station in the neighboring resort town of Sellin, accessible via RPNV bus #20. (☎038303 950 99. "Selin Ost" bus stop. Breakfast included. Dorms €23.50, over 27 years €27.50. Members only. Check-in 3-6pm. Reception 7-9:15am, 9:45am-1pm, 1:30-7:30pm, and 8-10pm. Cash only.) At the end of Zepplinstr., **Edeka Neukauf,** Schillerstr. 5, sells groceries. (Open M-Sa 8am-8pm, Su noon-6:30pm.) Binz also teems with restaurants, bars, and ice cream stands. To get your fill of fresh fish, try **Poseidon ❸,** opposite the Jugendherberge, teeming with regional specialties for €8-15. (Open daily 11:30am-10pm. AmEx/MC/V) **Taverne "Minos" ❸,** Strandpromenade 38, oozes *ouzo*, Greek music, and tantalizing food, including gyros (€10.40), moussaka (€9.70), and grilled specialties. (☎038393 148 88. Open M-F from 4pm, Sa-Su noon-3pm and 5pm-late.)

DAYTRIP FROM BINZ: JAGDSCHLOSS GRANITZ. The **Jagdschloß Granitz,** commands the dense Granitz forest from atop its Temeplberg hill, a testament to the lodge's history of aristocratic hunting parties that transformed the wilderness into a managed preseve for guests of the Potbus family, once owners of a third of Rügen. An exhibit inside pays tribute to the castle's history, annotating everything from Prussian architect Friedrich Shinkel's 1836 design to the extensive art collection. Through the magnificent wrought iron staircase, the 38m tower offers an unmatched view of the forest and surrounding areas. Faint of heart, beware: 164 animal heads are mounted in the **Jagdmuseum** (Hunting Museum), and antlers have been crafted into chairs and chandeliers. (☎038391 22 63. Open May-Sept. daily 9am-6pm, Oct.-Apr. Tu-Su 10am-4pm. €3, students €2.50.) The **Roland rail line** stops in the woods at "Jagdschloß," 15min. down the hill from the lodge, while the **Jagdschloßexpress** leaves from the *Seebrücke* in Binz or the Jagdschloß parking lot. Call for times and reservations. (☎038391 338 80; www.jagdschlossexpress.de. One-way €3.50.) To reach the castle from the Roland "Jagdschloß" stop, head uphill on the trail to the right. To walk or bike from Binz (5km), take the red-striped trail near the top of the Klünderberg hill in eastern Binz or walk down Zum Jagdschloß, following the signs 2km down the road. South of the "Jagdschloß" stop, the village of Lancken-Granitz displays **prehistoric graves** from 2300 BC—larger ones lie southwest of town.

KAP ARKONA AND VITT ☎038391

At Rügen's northernmost extreme, the dramatic Kap Arkona—Germany's only cape—lies on the charming half-island of Wittow (in the local Plattdeutsch, or Low German, it means "land of the wind"). Quieter and less accessible than Rügen's southern regions, Wittow is carpeted with wildflowers and yawning fields. Near Kap Arkona is the tiny fishing village of Vitt, with 13 reed homes.

TRANSPORTATION AND PRACTICAL INFORMATION. **Buses** run every hr. from Sassnitz (#13, 40min., €4.85) to Altenkirchen, where you can transfer to bus #11 to "Putgarten" (15min., €1.40), 1.5km away from the cape and its lighthouses. The 1km walk along the coast between Kap Arkona and Vitt is jaw-dropping—in spring, flowering bushes and brilliant red poppies carpet the hills. The gorgeous 4.6km loop between Putgarten, Kap Arkona, and Vitt is ideal for **biking.** You may prefer the painfully slow **Arkonabahn,** a tourist train that connects these destinations for a modest fee. (30min. round-trip; 2 per hr.; €2 one-way to either Kap Arkona or Vitt from Putgarten, or €3 round-trip to both, children 6-13 €0.50/1.50.) **Horse-drawn carts** also make the loop at a leisurely pace (1½hr.; 2 per hr.; €10, children €4). The tourist office, in Putgarten's parking lot, 300m down the road from the bus stop in the direction of Altenkirchen, sells maps, souvenirs, and answers the occasional question. (☎038391 41 90; www.kap-arkona.de. Open M-F 9am-5pm, Sa 10am-5pm, Su 11am-5pm.)

CAMPING. Putgarten is sorely lacking in affordable accomodations, but if you fall under Kap Arkona's spell, the nearby **Campingplatz "Drewoldke" ❶,** Zittkower Weg 27, is 2km east of the Altenkirchen bus stop. (☎038391 129 65; www.camping-auf-ruegen.de. Reception 9am-noon and 3-6pm. Open Apr.-Oct. €3-5 per adult, €2-3 per child. Tents €3.50-8. Bungalows €30-120.)

SIGHTS. Before reunification, the three "lighthouses" on Kap Arkona were part of a restricted area belonging to the DDR's National People's Army. The short, rectangular **Schinkelturm** (Schinkel Tower), designed in 1827 by architect Karl Friedrich Schinkel, guarded the DDR's sea borders, but has been open to the public since 1993. Next door, the **Neuer Leuchtturm** (New Lighthouse) towers above the other two lighthouses, offering the best views. (Schinkelturm open daily 10am-7pm. Neuer Leuchturm open daily 11am-6pm. Neuer Leuchtturm €3, Schinkelturm €2.) From the two lighthouses, you can make the steep descent to the beach via the wooden steps of the Königstreppe. The nearby **Marinepeilturm** (Naval Pinpointing Tower), often mistaken for a lighthouse, was rigged to spy on British radio communications. The tower now houses art exhibits along the stairway spiraling up to an observation deck. (Open daily 10am-6pm. €2, students €1.50.) Next to the Marinepeilturm is the **Slawischer Burgwall,** the remains of an old Slavic fortification. (Open daily 10am-5:45pm. €1.)

HIDDENSEE ☎038300

Planted in the Baltic just west of Rügen is the elusive island of Hiddensee, called *"das söte Länneken"* (the sweet little island) in Plattdeutsch. Hidden as it may be, the sliver of land has drawn the likes of Sigmund Freud, Albert Einstein, and Thomas Mann with its natural beauty, and several ill-fated (read: soon-to-be shipwrecked) schooners with its wild waters.

TRANSPORTATION AND PRACTICAL INFORMATION. You can easily see the entire island in a day on bike, making the island a superb daytrip from Stralsund or Rügen. **Reederei Hiddensee** (☎0180 321 21 50. www.reederei-hiddensee.de) operates **ferries** from Stralsund to Hiddensee's three towns: Neuendorf, Vitte, and Kloster (1½-3hr.; round-trip €17.80, €9.70 for children 14 and under including Hiddensee *Kurkarte*; bikes €8), as well as ferries from Schaprode, on Rügen. (Round-trip to Vitte €16, ages 4-14 €9.30, families €45.70.) To get to Schaprode, take bus #410 from Bergen. (30min., €3.40.) Round-trip tickets are much cheaper than separate one-way tickets. Plan ahead to avoid the potentially long waits between ferries. **Fahrradverleih** (bike rentals) are hard to miss;

the standard rate is €6 for a 5-speed. Since the island's more remote roads are either muddy country trails or sandy beach paths, a mountain bike with fat tires and plenty of gears is best, though main roads are paved or brick.

ACCOMMODATION AND FOOD. As Hiddensee has neither a hostel nor a campground, visit the **tourist office,** Norderende 162, in Vitte's Rathaus, to book a room. (☎038300 642 26; www.seebad-insel-hiddensee.de. Open May-Sept. M-F 8:30am-5pm, Sa-Su 10am-noon; Oct. M-F 8:30am-4pm; Nov.-Mar. M-F 9am-3pm.) In Vitte, **Hotel Godewind ❹,** Süderende 53, serves up the freshest pre-exploration lunches and liveliest dinners in a nightlife-hungry town. Try the fresh fish (€9-21.50), with a glass of *Sanddornsaft*, a rust-colored, honey-like local specialty (€3.50), also available in stores for €3-6 per bottle and €2.30-13 for an alcoholic variant. (☎038300 6600; www.hotelgodewind.de. Restaurant open daily noon-5pm. Rooms €39-165. Cash only). Escape from Vitte's hoardes of cycling tourists in **Kloster's Zum Kleinen Inselblick ❸,** set at the foot of several paths leading up into the wild, overgrown hills. Inside, the restaurant is decorated with Rolling Stones posters, colorful furniture, and a nutcracker collection. (At the corner of Mühlberg and Birkenweg. Open M and W-Su noon-11pm, kitchen until 9:30pm. Most entrees €8-14. MC.) Choose from a large selection of groceries at **Edeka Markt,** Wallweg 1, a block from the Vitte Harbor. (☎038300 05 01 47. Open M-F 8am-7pm, Sa 8am-6pm, Su 8am-1pm.)

BEACHES. The majority of the island is part of the protected **Nationalpark Vorpommersche Boddenlandschaft** (Vorpommern Lagoon National Park), and automobiles are prohibited, allowing bikes and horse-drawn carriages to rule the island. Without the constant hum of car engines, there is not a point on the narrow island from which the crash of waves cannot be heard on a windy day. **Vitte** (pop. 650) is Hiddensee's main town and home to the island's best beaches. Pay attention to the flag system, though—while Binz is like a bathtub, the waves on Hiddensee mean business. The **National Park Information Center,** Norderende 2, at the northern edge of Vitte on the way to Kloster, offers maps of the island and free guided **nature tours** of the Dünenheide (Tu 10am) or north hills (W 3pm). (☎038300 680 41. Open daily in summer 10am-4pm; in winter 10am-3pm.)

SCHLESWIG-HOLSTEIN

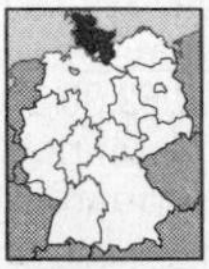

The only *Land* to border two seas, Schleswig-Holstein bases its livelihood on the trade generated by its bustling port towns. Between the western coast of the North Sea and the eastern coast of the Baltic, the velvety plains are populated primarily by sheep and bales of hay. Although Schleswig-Holstein became a Prussian province in 1867 following Bismarck's defeat of Denmark, the region retains close cultural and commercial ties with Scandinavia. Linguistically, Schleswig-Holstein is also isolated from its southern neighbors by its various dialects of *Plattdeutsch* (literally, "low German") and, to a lesser extent, the Dutch-like Frisian spoken throughout the *Land*. The most noticeable difference is the greeting *Moin* or *Moin moin*, a Plattdeutsch salutation used all day.

HIGHLIGHTS OF SCHLESWIG-HOLSTEIN

BARE ALL on the barren dunes of the island **Sylt** (p. 173), Germany's favorite beach.

BIKE along the extensive trails of **Wattenmeer National Park** (p. 170).

SAVOR legendary marzipan from Lübeck's **I.G. Niederegger Marzipan Cafe** (p. 164) while listening to the strains of the world's largest mechanical organ echo through the magnificent **Marienkirche** (p. 166).

LÜBECK ☎0451

A medieval aura lingers in the shadowy facades of Lübeck's old homes and around the steeples of its many churches. In its heyday, the city was capital of the Hanseatic League, controlling trade across Northern Europe. Later it was home to literary giants Heinrich and Thomas Mann, who had a tempestuous relationship with the local bourgeoisie. The city still has a tendency to rest on its glorious past, as meticulous post-WWII reconstruction has refashioned Lübeck into an engaging medieval town. It may no longer be a center of political and commercial influence, but tourists still flock to Lübeck (pop. 214,000) for its history, famous marzipan, and red-blonde *Duckstein* beer.

TRANSPORTATION

Trains: Every hr. to: **Berlin** (3½hr., €39.40-57); **Hamburg** (45min., €11-15.50); **Kiel** (1hr., €13); **Rostock** (2hr., €22-24.50); **Schwerin** (1¼hr., €12.50).

Taxis: Catch a taxi just outside the train station or call ☎0451 811 22.

Ferries: Many ferries run tours out of the waterfront on An der Obertrave and An der Untertrave. **Quandt-Linie,** An der Obertrave (☎0451 777 99; www.quandt-linie.de), cruises around the Altstadt and harbor from the bridge in front of the Holstentor. €8, students €6.50. May-Oct. daily every 30min. 10am-4pm; less frequent in the low season.

Public Transportation: The Altstadt is easily seen on foot, though Lübeck also has an excellent bus network. The **ZOB** (central bus station) is across from the train station. Single ride €1.40-2.10, children €0.85-1.20; day pass €7. To reach the Lübeck airport,

take bus #6 (dir.: Blankenese/Seekamp) to "Flughafen." Direct questions to the **LVG Service Center,** am ZOB (☎0451 888 2828). Open M-F 5am-8pm, Sa-Su 9am-4pm.

Car Rental: Hertz, Willy-Brandt-Allee 1 (☎0451 70 22 50), near the train station. From €52 per day. 2-passenger cars €30 per day. Cheaper prices online at www.hertz-miera.de. Open M-F 7am-6pm, Sa 7am-1pm, Su 9-10am. AmEx/MC/V.

PRACTICAL INFORMATION

Tourist Office: Holstentorpl. 1 (☎0451 88 22 33), next to the Holstentor. The informed staff books rooms for free, dispenses city maps (€0.90), offers internet access (€3 per hr.), and sells the **Happy Day Card** (€6), which provides unlimited access to public transportation and discounted admission to many of Lübeck's museums. Open June-Sept. M-F 9:30am-7pm, Sa 10am-3pm, Su 10am-2pm; Oct.-Nov. and Jan.-May M-F 9:30am-6pm, Sa 10am-3pm; Dec. M-F 9:30am-6pm, Sa 10am-3pm.

Tours: Red LVG Open-Air-Stadtrundfahrt buses embark on city tours every 30min. from the "Untertrave" and "Holstentorbrüke" stops. ☎04502 86 16 44. July-Aug. daily 11am-4pm, June and Sept. W and Sa-Su only, May Sa-Su only. €5.50, children €3.80, families €14.50.

Laundromat: McWash, on the corner of An der Mauer and Hüxterdamm (☎0451 702 0357). Wash €4.20 per 7kg, soap included. Dry €1 per 15min. Open M-Sa 6am-9pm.

Emergency: Police, Mengstr. 18-20 (☎110). **Fire** ☎112. **Ambulance** ☎0451 192 22.

Women's Resources: Rape Crisis Center, Musterbahn 3 (☎0451 70 46 40). Open M 9am-1pm, Tu and Th 4-6pm. Hotline available M and W-F 9am-1pm, Tu and Th 4-6pm.

Pharmacy: Adler-Apotheke, Breite Str. 71 (☎0451 798 8515, after hours 710 81). Open M-F 8:30am-7pm, Sa 9am-6pm.

Internet Access: Handy-Shop Lübeck, Königstr. 111 (☎0451 409 9770). €1 per hr. Open M-F 10am-6pm, Sa 10am-4pm.

Post Office: Königstr. 44-46. **24hr. ATM.** Open M-F 8:30am-6:30pm, Sa 8:30am-1pm. **Postal Code:** 23552.

ACCOMMODATIONS AND CAMPING

Rucksack Hotel, Kanalstr. 70 (☎0451 70 68 92; www.rucksackhotel-luebeck.de). Take bus #1, 11, 21, or 31 to "Katharineum." This popular hostel, a member of a collective of communalist, eco-friendly shops, attracts gregarious guests with brightly colored rooms, a quirky library of board games, and a kitchen in a former glass factory. Breakfast €3. Sheets €3. Free Wi-Fi. Reception 10am-1pm and 5-9pm. 6- to 10-bed dorms €13, singles €35, doubles with bath €34-40, quads €60-68, bungalows for 6 available. Offers a student discount in winter. Cash only. ❶

Jugendherberge Lübeck-Altstadt (HI), Mengstr. 33 (☎0451 702 0399). Excepting the unusually thoughtful decorative touches, this is a typical hostel in an unbeatable location. Breakfast included. Reception 7am-midnight. Lockout midnight; guests 18+ can get a key. Dorms €18.70, over 27 €21.70; singles and doubles from €24-27. €1 discount for stays of 3+ nights. Non DJH members add €3.10 per night. MC/V. ❷

Jugendherberge Lübeck "Vor dem Burgtor" (HI), Am Gertrudenkirchhof 4 (☎0451 334 33; www.djh-ris.de), off Travemünder Allee. This recently renovated hostel 15min. from the town center offers standard hostel rooms but brims with activity. Breakfast included. Internet €0.50 per 5min. Laundry €2.60. Dorm beds €17.60, over 27 €20.60. Non DJH members add €3.10 per night. AmEx/MC/V. ❷

Sleep-In (CVJM), Große Petersgrube 11 (☎0451 719 20; www.cvjm-luebeck.de). This cozy lodge, run by a Christian organization, has a tame pub downstairs that echoes with jazz on weekdays. Breakfast €4. Key with €10 deposit. Check-in before 7pm. Reception open daily 8am-8pm. 4- to 8-bed dorms €16.50 (includes sheets), doubles €20-40, 2-person apartments from €50. Cash only. ❶

Campingplatz Lübeck-Schönböcken, Steinrader Damm 12 (☎0451 89 30 90), 3km west of the city. From the ZOB, take bus #7 to "Schönböckener Hauptstr." Showers, washing machines (€3), and cooking facilities. Reception 7am-10:30pm. €5 per person, €2 per child, €4-5 per tent, €6 per RV. Electricity €2.50 per day. Pets €1 per day. ❶

FOOD

While the rest of Germany dog-paddles through beer, Lübeck swims in coffee. The city's cafes stay open into the wee hours of the morning and become the nightlife venue of choice. The hippest cafes line **Mühlenstraße,** while **Huxstraße** squeezes tons of tiny restaurants and cafes between independent boutiques and artists' ateliers. The king of sweets is *Lübecker Marzipan*, a sweet almond paste enjoyed raw in molded shapes, covered in chocolate, or creatively stuffed into baked goods. Buy groceries at **Aldi,** just south of Glockengießerstr. on Kanalstr. (Open M-F 8am-8pm, Sa 8am-5pm.)

I.G. Niederegger Marzipan Cafe, Breitestr. 89 (☎0751 530 11 26). This famous confectionery shop and cafe is the place to eat marzipan cake (€1.75-2.15), sample marzipan-flavored ice cream, or buy candies shaped like pigs, jellyfish, or the town

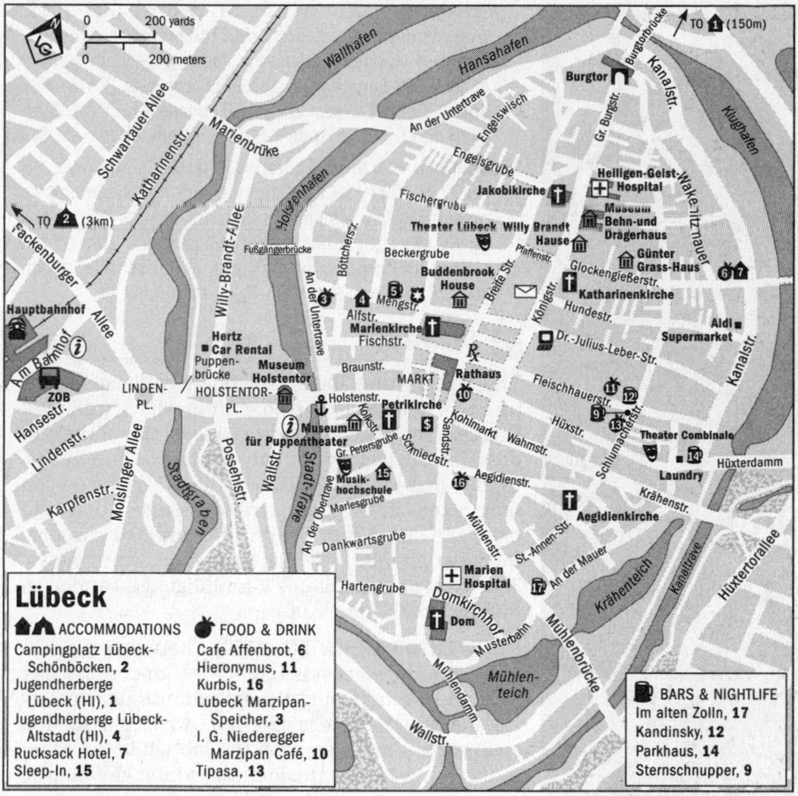

gate (all cheaper at the counter than in the cafe). Niederegger's nougat is an equally sweet treat. The **Marzipan Salon,** a free upstairs exhibit dedicated to the history and preparation of the almond-sweet displays sculptures fashioned out of several tons of the paste and often features a live marzipan artist at work. Cafe and Salon both open M-F 9am-7pm, Sa 9am-6pm, Su 10am-6pm. AmEx/MC/V. ❷

Cafe Affenbrot, Kanalstr. 70 (☎0751 721 93), on the corner of Glockengießerstr. A vegetarian cafe and *Biergarten, Affenbrot* (literally, "monkey bread") is part of the same co-op as Rucksack Hostel. Buy indulgences for your marzipan sins from €4.50-8.50 surrounded by students with style as unique as the bright purple and neon green decor. Breakfast €3.50-9. Open daily 9am-midnight. Kitchen closes at 11pm. Cash only. ❷

Kurbis, Mühlenstr. 9 (☎0751 707 0126). Though a *Kurbis* (pumpkin) theme pervades the decor in this dimly lit, casual restaraunt, no gourds are on the menu. Pastas and *Pfanne* (enormous pan-cooked meals served piping hot and topped with melted €7-9. Many creative vegetarian options. Open M-Tu and Th 11am-1am, F-Sa 11am-2am. Kitchen closes 30min. earlier. AmEx/MC/V. ❸

Tipasa, Schlumacherstr. 12-14 (☎0751 706 0451). Cave art on the walls adds neolithic charm to this sprawling student haunt. The *Tipasa-Topf* (€6.60) is a zesty tomato, beef, mushroom, and pepper stew. Beer garden out back. Pizza €4-6.50, Open M-Th and Su noon-1am, F-Sa noon-2am. Kitchen closes 30min. earlier. MC/V. ❸

LOCAL LEGEND

MEDICATED MARZIPAN

Trips to the doctor would surely be in higher demand if physicians still medicated with marzipan. Believing in its fortifying and healing properties, doctors in the middle-ages recommended the treat in a prescription exceeded in popularity only by "more cowbell." Lübeck's official pharmacist in 1575, David Schellenberger, supplied the Fishermen's Guild with marzipan in diamond shape molds, easily divisible into 85 grams each for treatment.

Monks in the middle ages got their share of the substance too; chefs in monasteries put the confection into various dishes, as its was one of few ingredients approved for Lent.

Of course, individuals hoping to get their hands on the confection could not simply skip off to the candy store. Confectioners in Lübeck were not licensed to produce the substance until 1714, centuries after chemists had begun to freely manufacture it.

Today, world-famous Lübecker marzipan is lawfully required to have a minimum of 2 parts almond paste to 1 part sugar. The all-killer, no filler law owes its stringency to Lübecker marzipan's status as a Protected Geographical Indication, a marking established to protect regional foods, preserving their reputation, avoiding both unfair competition and deception of the customer, and perhaps in middle-age terms, to avoid medical malpractice.

Hieronymus, Fleischhauerstr. 81 (☎0751 706 3017; www.hieronymus-restaurant.de). The fireplace, dim lighting, and wooden beams are thoroughly 15th-century at this pan-European treat. Lunch specials (€5-8) M-F before 5pm. Entrees €9-14.50, pizzas €5.50-8. Open M-Th and Su noon-1am, F-Sa noon-2am. Cash only. ❸

Lübecker Marzipan-Speicher, An der Untertrave 98 (☎0751 897 3939). Though lacking Niederegger's prestige, offers similar confections. Purists buy it raw for €1 per 100g. Shows daily at 11am and 2pm on the history and process of marzipan manufacturing. Open M-Sa 9am-6pm, Su 10am-6pm. Cash only. ❶

SIGHTS

The streets of Lübeck are filled with small surprises. Hundreds of transparent signs (all with English translations) scattered throughout the city describe the history of many of Lübeck's buildings. In the northeastern section of the Altstadt, you can find dozens of *Gänge* (narrow passages) that lead from the street into beautiful courtyard gardens, the most popular of which appear on tourist maps. The town also maintains a multiligual information hotline (☎0751 92 92 00).

HOLSTENTOR (HOLSTEN GATE). Between the Altstadt and the station is Lübeck's 15th-century city symbol, the imposing though admittedly droopy Holstentor. The gate is guarded by two playful lion sculptures—one sleeps on the job while the other looks on in horror. Inside, an exhibit details the city's rise to prominence while exploring the tower's massive walls (over 3m thick on the defensive side), gun bays, and limestone troughs for dumping hot tar on enemies. Ironically, the tower was never engaged in active defense, as Napoleon—the only invader since its construction—bypassed the gate entirely by entering the city from the north. *(☎0751 122 4129. Open Apr.-Dec. daily 10am-6pm, Jan.-Mar. Tu-Su 11am-5pm. €5, students and seniors €2, families €6.)*

MARIENKIRCHE. The Marienkirche's two brick towers dominate Lübeck's skyline. Construction of the church began around 1200 in the Romanesque style, but it was completed as a Gothic cathedral in 1350. The gigantic building sustained heavy damage during WWII—a giant bronze bell, warped and splintered, lies embedded in the shattered marble floor where it fell during the air raids of 1942. Pictures of the church's famous **Totentanzbild,** an intricate mural depicting the "dance of the dead," hang in the left apse, where the original, lost in the fires that followed the attacks, once stood. To the left of the pews is the church's newly restored astronomical clock. On your way out, take a peek at the little devil sitting just outside the main door. Legend has it that the devil helped build the church, thinking it was to be a bar. When he realized his mistake, locals only prevented him from destroying the church with the very boulder on which the sculpture now sits by building a bar across the street, in the Rathauskeller. *(Open daily in summer 10am-6pm, in winter 10am-4pm. Suggested donation €1. Brief organ showcases daily at 12:05pm. Free tours in German daily June-Sept. at 12:15pm. Tower tours June-Sept. W and Sa 3:15, Apr.-Oct. Sa only. €4, students €3, families €10.)*

THEATERFIGURENMUSEUM (THEATER FIGURE MUSEUM). Exquisitely detailed hand, string, shadow, and stick puppets from across the globe pack the museum's five floors, forming the largest such collection in the world. Video presentations reveal puppeteers in action. These are no muppets, however; small children are likely to be frightened of the figures. *(Kolk 14. Just below the Petrikirche. ☎0751 786 26. www.tfm-luebeck.com. Open daily Apr.-Sept. 10am-6pm; Oct. 10am-4pm; Nov.-Mar. 10am-3pm. €4, students €3, children €2.)* Across the street, the **puppet theater** puts on daily performances. *(3pm, €4. Sa also at 6 and 7:30pm €8; students €6.50)*

RATHAUS. Lübeck's beloved city hall, at the center of the Altstadt, is a somewhat wild conglomeration of three starkly contrasting architectural styles. The original building, constructed in the 13th century, is the portion with the striking glazed black and red brick. New wings were added in the 14th and 15th centuries. *(Admission with tour only. In German. M-F 11am, noon, and 3pm. €2.60, students €1.50.)* The complex's courtyard now encloses vendors and spillover seating from its many neighboring cafes.

BUDDENBROOKHAUS. Author **Thomas Mann,** who won the Nobel Prize in 1929, set his novel *Buddenbrooks* in this house, where he and his brother Heinrich were raised. It now houses a sleek, citrus-colored museum dedicated to the life and works of the brothers, drawing upon their family members and contemporaries. Watch for special events during the summer. *(Mengstr. 4, beside the Marienkirche. ☎0751 122 4192; www.buddenbrookhaus.de. Open daily 10am-6pm; Jan. 11am-5pm. Some exhibits captioned in English. Walks last 2hr., €8. "Literary Walk" June-Aug. Su 11am. Admission €7, students €3.50; combo ticket with Günter Grass-Haus €7/4.)*

DOM. Founded by Henry the Lion in 1173, Lübeck's oldest church is guarded by a distinctive lion statue. Approach the church from the north on Fegefeuer and you'll be able to say you walked through Purgatory (the literal translation of the street's name) to reach the cathedral. Inside, tangled iron grates and baroque clocks stand out against huge expanses of whitewashed walls. *(Domkirchhof, at the southernmost end of the inner island. ☎0751 747 04. Open daily 10am-6pm. Free. Organ concerts July-Aug. F 5pm; €6, students €4.)*

PETRIKIRCHE. An elevator rises 50.5m to the viewing platform inside the 13th-century steeple for a sweeping, windy view of the Altstadt and Lübeck's many spires. The nave of the church occasionally exhibits modern art—check website for details. *(East of the Rathaus at Schüsselbuden 13. www.st-petri-luebeck.de Church open Tu-Su 11am-4pm. Tower open daily Apr.-Oct. 9am-9pm; Mar. and Nov. 11am-5pm; Dec. 9am-7pm. Requested donation €1. Tower €2.50, students €1.50.)*

MUSEUM BEHN-UND DRÄGERHAUS. This 18th-century house exhibits furnishings from the early 19th century and a unique display of historical musical instruments. Still, the art takes center stage, with locally focused selections of Expressionist, Impressionist, Nazarene, Classical, and Realist art, featuring portraits by Edvard Munch, and statues by Ernst Barlach. The **sculpture garden** outside showcases local artists. *(Königstr. 9-11. ☎0751 122 4148. Open Apr.-Dec. Tu-Su 10am-5pm, Jan.-Mar. Tu-Su 11am-5pm. €5, students €2.50, ages 6-18 €2, families €6.)*

WILLY BRANDT HAUS. This newly opened museum houses an impressively multimedia presentation on Germany's history from the years before WWII to the present. Though the exhibit clearly appeals to fans of the former Chancellor, the billingual museum is a must-see for anyone interested in the history of German socialism, fascism, and unification. *(Königstr. 21. ☎0751 122 4050. Open daily 10am-5pm. Entry €5, students €2.50, ages 6-18 €2, families €6.)*

GÜNTER GRASS-HAUS. The cousin of the Buddenbrookhaus, this museum contains a visually enticing presentation of symbolically loaded bronze sculpture, sketches, and watercolors created by acclaimed author and Nobel laureate **Günter Grass,** who lived in Lübeck for many years. There is also an exhibit on Grass's political activity. *(Glockengießerstr. 21. Open daily Apr.-Dec. 10am-5pm; Jan.-Mar. 11am-5pm. Admission €5, students €2.50; combo ticket with Buddenbrookhaus €7/4.)*

ENTERTAINMENT

Lübeck is world-famous for its Saturday **organ concerts** at the Jakobikirche (5pm) and the Marienkirche. (6:30pm. €8, students €5. See *Musik in Lübeck's Kirchen*, available at both churches, for full schedule.) The city's music academy, the **Musikhochschule,** Gr. Petersgrube 17-29, plays frequent free concerts, often of professional caliber. (☎0751 150 50; www.mh-luebeck.de.) For entertainment listings (in German), pick up *Heute*, *Piste*, *Szene*, or *Ultimo* at the tourist office. Lübeck's two main theaters offer student discounts, but are closed from July to August. The huge **Theater Lübeck,** Beckergrube 16, puts up operas, symphonies, and plays. (☎0751 745 52; www.theaterluebeck.de. Tickets €10-42; students half-price. Box office open Tu-F 10am-6:30pm, Sa 10am-1pm, and 30min. before shows.) The **Theater Combinale,** Hüxstr. 115, shows avant-garde works. (☎0751 788 17. Tickets €8-14.)

NIGHTLIFE

Most of the better *Diskotheken* (dance clubs) are scattered around the perimeter of the **Altstadt.** Avoid the northwestern part of the island along the waterfront late at night, when drug dealers and addicts frequent the area.

Parkhaus, Hüxterdamm at Kanalstr. (☎0751 707 2557; www.parkhaus.tv). This 3-story club boasts 2 dance floors, a classy lounge, and enough smoking areas to compete with Mt. Vesuvius. From May to September, affiliated **Roof Pirates** operate a rooftop beach club, complete with cabanas, sand, and planked boardwalk. Beer €2-2.50, mixed drinks €4.20-8. Th ladies' night (€1 drinks for women). 21+. Open Tu and Th-Sa 10pm-late. Beach Club open from 5pm. Cover €3-5. Check website for schedule. Cash only.

Sternschnuppe, Fleischhauerst. 88 (☎0751 759 60). Pinpricks of light form constellations on the ceiling of this celestial bar. Young, hip groups of friends come for drinks or for Monday TV night (*Simpsons* and *Futurama* on a big screen from 8-9pm) followed by a laid-back DJ set. Open daily 7pm-late. MC/V.

Kandinsky, Fleischhauerstr. 89 (☎0751 702 0661). Tables explode into the street, while students choose from a mile-long drink list of teas, coffees, and beer (€2-3). Jazz every Tu night (except in summer). Open M-Th and Su noon-1am, F-Sa noon-2am.

Im alten Zolln, Mühlenstr. 93 (☎0751 723 95). Don't come here for a visa: the "old customs office" is now decked out with classy wood paneling and an old upright piano. Beer €2.60-3.50. Food €5.50-13 Open daily noon-1am. Cash only.

PLÖN ☎04522

Amid the glacial moraines of wooded Holsteinische Schweiz, Plön (pop. 13,000) balances on a land bridge between the Kleiner Plöner See and the Großer Plöner See. Sparkling waters and the chance to paddle, sail, and fish lure school groups and nature lovers alike. The red brick steeple of Plön's central church and the white facade of its castle dominate the pleasant town.

TRANSPORTATION AND PRACTICAL INFORMATION. **Trains** run every hr to Kiel (30min., €5.60) and Lübeck (40min., €7.70). Rent **bikes** at **Wittich,** Lange Str. 39. (☎04522 27 48. €6 per day, €30 per week. Open M-F 9am-6pm, Sa 9am-2pm.) **Bike trails** loop around the lakes, including a daytrip-appropriate 40km circuit around the Großer Plöner See, with stops in Dersau and Bosau. The leisurely ride to Prinzeninsel (10km) is perfect for beginners. Rent **boats** at the **Kanuvermietung Plön,** Ascheberger Str. 70, right next to the Jugendherberge. (☎04522 41 11; www.kanuvermietungploen.de. Canoes €8 per day or €5 per 2hr., childen under 13 €6 per day. Open May-Sept. daily 9am-7pm.) **Großer Plöner Seerundfahrt** chugs around the lake from the dock on Strandweg. (Daily 10am-5pm. Round-trip €9, students €8.) The swanky **tourist office,** inside the train station, distributes maps, and books rooms for free. (☎04522 509 50; www.ploen.de. Open M-F 9am-6pm, Sa-Su 10am-1pm; shorter hours in winter.) Check email at the town library, which has **internet** for €1.50 per 30min. (Open M-F 9:30am-1:30pm and 3-6pm). Open M-Sa 9am-11pm, Su noon-11pm.) The **post office,** Lange Str. 18, is near the square. (Open M-F 9am-1pm and 2:20-6pm, Sa 9am-12:30pm.) **Postal Code:** 24306.

ACCOMMODATIONS AND FOOD. Plön's **Jugendherberge (HI)** ❶, Ascheberger Str. 67, is 2km outside of town. Take bus #360 (every hr.) to "Spitzenort." Enjoy your vacation with a beach volleyball court, a soccer field, and ping-pong on the shores of the Großer Plöner See. (☎04522 25 76. Breakfast included. Lockout 10pm-7am, but key available. Dorms €16.20, over 27 €19.20; 2 or more nights €15/16.30; singles €23.30-26.) Just before the hostel, **Naturcamping Spitzenort** ❶, Ascheberger Str. 76, claims waterside real estate for its grassy plots. (☎04522 27 69; www.spitzenort.de. €5.20 per person, €2.40 per child age 4-14; €5-7.30 per tent, low season €4.50-6.20. Laundry €1. Kitchen available. AmEx/MC/V.) **Lange Straße** is full of cafes and bakery chains. **Eisenpfanne** ❸, Lange Str. 47, serves the colossal *Plöner Teller* (€12.50), a feat of digestive heroicism with three kinds of fried fish. (☎04522 22 90. Entrees €6.80-14.50. Pizza €4-6.80. Open daily 11am-11pm. Kitchen open 11am-10:30pm. Cash only.) **Antalya-Grill** ❷, Lange Str. 36, offers a solid range of grill platters (€7), spicy Turkish pizzas (€4.70-7.80), and *Döner kebap* (€2.70-5). (☎04522 39 82. Open M-F 11am-1am, Sa-Su 11am-2am. Cash only.) **Sky,** Markt 31, sells groceries. (☎04522 74 47 30. Open M-Sa 8am-8pm, Su 11am-6pm.)

SIGHTS. Now a private school, Plön's late **Renaissance Schloß** is the most noticeable building in town, and arguably its biggest tourist attraction. The path in front of the very sprawling building affords a spectacular view of the lake. (Enter the *Schloß* Tu-W, Sa, and Su 4:30-6:30pm on a guided tour; call ahead at ☎04522 80 10). Wooded trails lead away from the *Schloß* to the stately brick **Prinzenhaus,** with its athletic-complex backyard and the **Schloßgarten.** Built in 1744, the Prinzenhaus is now a museum detailing the history of the *Schloß*. (☎04522 509 50. Admission only with a tour May-Sept. W 11:30am, Sa-Su 3, 4pm; Nov.-Apr. Su 11:30am. €3, children €2, families €6.50.) To the southwest, the **Prinzeninsel,** an island in the Großer Plöner See, is connected to the mainland by a small footbridge stretching across the tiny canal.

WATTENMEER NATIONAL PARK (SCHLESWIG HOLSTEIN)

Schleswig-Holstein's Wattenmeer National Park is part of an expansive network that stretches down the coast into Hamburg and Lower Saxony. The Watt refers to the mud—miles and miles of it—that sustains a wide variety of unique plant and animal life. Walking across the flats is surreal. Twice daily, the ocean retreats, exposing miles and miles of walkable sea floor to the open air. The region is filled to the brim with small town "health resorts" that capitalize on the invigorating salt-laden air circulating through the region and the supposed curative properties of the mud. The park is full of distinctive features, like the tiny Halligen islands, where houses built on mounds become their own tiny islands when the island floods (up to 20 times per year.) Below ground, the tidal flats contain a higher animal biomass than tropical forests. The Wattenmeer National Park witnesses a seasonal migration of birds and tourists alike, with resort towns more than tripling in population during the summer.

WATTENMEER NATIONAL PARK AT A GLANCE

AREA: 4400 sq. km

CLIMATE: Mild, yet often relatively chilly summers, wet winters. Windy year-round.

FEATURES: Sandy beaches, the wild Wattenmeer mud flats, grassy dunes, historical towns, health spas.

HIGHLIGHTS: Free guided Watt hikes, extensive network of bicycle paths, incredible birdwatching, and endless beaches.

GATEWAYS: Tönning, St. Peter-Ording.

CAMPING: Not allowed within the park, but common on its fringes.

ORIENTATION

Wattenmeer National Park stretches along Schleswig Holstein's western coast, situated on the North Sea. **Tönning** (p. 172), in the central region of the park, is a good place to collect information before you begin exploring. To the northwest, the North Frisian Islands including **Sylt** and **Amrum** peek out of the sea, with beautiful white sand beaches on their western shores and wide stretches of Wattenmeer tidal flats on their sheltered eastern sides.

WHAT IS THE WATT? Created by the radical fluctuation of tides, the Wattenmeer is an area of mudflats stretching along the North Sea from the Dutch to the Danish coasts. The Watt is classified into three unique bands: the Sandwatt, as its name suggests, includes the sandy part of the shore where sea worms burrow to hide from predatory birds. Farther inland, the Mischwatt, a bank of mixed sand and mud, teems with species from bacteria to mussels. Extending to the highest water line is the charcoal-black Schlickwatt, where only the most resilient organisms live in the oxygen-poor mud that is marketed to health-seekers as a nutrient-rich skin treatment. A relatively rare ecosystem, the Wattenmeer habitat supports some 3200 different types of animals. Among the most visible are the mussels that filter the ocean water, the fish that stock the plankton-rich waters with their eggs, the birds that feast at low tide on creatures trapped in shallow pools, and the seals that frolic on sandbanks just offshore.

TRANSPORTATION AND PRACTICAL INFORMATION

Trains provide easy access to nearly all towns and sights along the coast. Most trains within the greater Wattenmeer National Park area are **NOB** (Nord-Ostsee-Bahn) regional trains; tickets for these can be purchased onboard. Hourly trains shuttle between St. Peter Ording and Husum, stopping in Tönning. **Bus** connections are less frequent and less extensive than train connections. Though most tourist offices address transportation, the region's bus terminals often lack information centers, so plan ahead and inquire about bus routes in town or decipher the posted schedules on your own.

Emergency: Police ☎110. **Fire** ☎112.

Information Centers: Schutzstationen (protection stations) are on each of the islands and in major mainland coastal towns. The staff offer guided tours of the Watt and information on local plant and animal life, including extensive brochures on the how-tos of birdwatching. (See city listings for locations and contact info.) Additionally, information pavilions—part of the **Besucherinformationenssystem (BIS)**—are at the beginning of many paths in the region. Contact the **Wattenmeer Information Line** (☎04681 962 00; www.wattenmeer-nationalpark.de) for further details.

Boat Tours: Adler-Schiffe (☎04842 90 00 30; www.adler-schiffe.de) leads 2½hr. seal bank trips (€12-17.50), while **Reederei Rahder** (☎04834 36 12; www.rahder.de), conducts 2½hr. tours from Ankerplatz in Büsum to the seal habitat in Dithmarschen (Adults €16, children €9.50. Open Mar.-Oct. 9am-6pm. Tours at 10:30am, 2pm, and 5:30pm.)

ACCOMMODATIONS

Youth hostels dot the North Sea coast. In addition to the hostels described in the city listings, other HI hostels in the region are listed here (prices are per night and exclude *Kurkarte;* over age 26 add €3-4):

Büsum, Dr.-Martin-Bahr-Str. 1, Büsum (☎04834 933 71). €17.35.

Heide, Poststr. 4, Heide, on Holstein Island (☎0481 715 75). €15.85.

Husum, Schobüller Str. 34, Husum (☎04841 27 14). €16.85.

Niebüll-Deezbüll, Deezbüll Deich 2, Niebüll (☎04661 93 78 90). €17.35.

Niebüll-Mühlenstraße, Mühlenstr. 65, Niebüll (☎04661 93 78 90). €17.35.

> **WATT SAFETY.** *Let's Go* does not recommend hiking the Watt without a guide. Tour guides are familiar with tidal patterns, and can steer you away from dangerous quicksand. Always heed markings: orange balls forbid entrance, yellow flags warn that a sandbank will be submerged at high water, and green flags encourage caution at high tide. Watch for protected sanctuaries, and be alert to changing tides. Many seemingly benign activities like shell collecting are legal only extremely close to shore. Though much of the Schleswig-Holstein Wattenmeer is barefoot-friendly during the summer, sharp mussels proliferate Lower Saxony, so select footwear appropriately.

OUTDOOR ACTIVITIES

WATTWANDERN (WATT HIKES). When the tides ebb, the mud flats of the Watt become exposed, making it possible to walk across areas usually populated by fish. To arrange a tour, call the **National Park Service** (☎04681 962 00) or a nearby *Schutzstation.* Private companies also offer tours. **Adler-Schiffe** leads walks across the Watt between the islands of Amrum and Föhr. The 2hr. trip departs from Nordstrand, near Husum, and includes the cost of ferry rides to and from the islands. (☎04842 900 00 or pick up a brochure to see the schedule. www.adler-schiffe.de. €18, children €12.50.) **Reederei Rahder** (see **Boat Tours,** p. 171) offers 1½-2hr. guided hikes of the Watt in the vicinity of Büsum, leaving from Ankerplatz. (€6, children €3, families €15. Ask the tourist office for a schedule.) If you insist on striking out independently, pick up a tide chart and seek advice from one of the information centers to avoid racing a rising tide.

BEACHES AND SWIMMING. Most costal towns levy fees called *Kurtaxe* for beach access. The cost varies, but is generally €1.50-3 per day, €0.50-1 for children. Hotels and pensions in the area automatically add the cost of the *Kurkarte* to your bill. Guests not staying overnight can purchase day cards granting beach access for roughly the same cost. Swimming is allowed at all beaches in the park not reserved for surfing, although the water can be uncomfortably cool year-round. The plentiful nude beaches are labeled *FKK Strand,* denoting the *Freier Körper Kultur* (Free Body Culture) association.

HIKING AND BIKING. Biking is an incredibly popular and effective way to explore the park, both on the mainland and the islands. The park has a broad network of paved and gravel trails, and the powerful North Sea wind can send you flying along at exhilarating speeds or slow your progress to a painful crawl. For information on renting bikes, see individual town listings. Hiking trails crisscross the park and environs—visit local information centers for maps.

TÖNNING ☎04681

The charming little town of Tönning (pop. 5000) is an easily accessible gateway to the Wattenmeer. From the town square, white fish painted on the sidewalk lead past the harbor to the **Multimar Wattforum,** Am Robbenberg, a combined museum, aquarium, and national park office. (☎04681 96 20 38; www.multimar-wattforum.de. Open daily Apr.-Oct. 9am-7pm, Nov.-Mar. 10am-5pm. €8, children €5.50. €7.50/5 with *Kurtaxe.*) Tönning is also home to a pleasant though tiny **Schloßgarten,** which faces the market square.

To reach the hunting lodge style **Jugendherberge Tönning ❶,** Badallee 28, turn left from the train station and follow Badallee for 15min. The building doubles as an environmental center and offers programs on Watt biology. (☎04861 12 80. Breakfast included. €18.10, over 27 €21.10.) Halfway to the hostel, **Camping Eiderblick ❶,** Strandweg 19, is an enormous complex with a swimming pool and tennis courts nearby, and minigolf on site. (☎04861 15 69. Reception 8am-1pm and 2:30-8pm. Laundry €3.50. Dry €3.50. Bike Rental €5-7 per day. €3 per adult, €2 per child, €5 per tent. Small singles with shared bath and TV from €20 per night. AmEx/MC/V.) Restaurants near the **market** are generally less expensive and offer more variety than those along the harbor. Near the train station, **Restaurant Nordfriesland ❸,** Westerstr. 24, serves fresh local fish within china plate-studded walls. (☎04681 318. Entrees €8-14. Open daily 8am-9:30pm. Cash only.) **Fischimbiß ❷,** am Hafen 33, serves scrumptious fish sandwiches (€1.30-3.50) and plates (€4-10.70). (☎04681 740. Open daily in summer 9am-7pm; in winter 9am-5pm. Cash only.) For groceries, visit the **Edeka,** Am Markt 8. (Open M-F 7:30am-6pm, Sa 7:30am-12:30pm, in summer also Su 9am-noon.)

NOB regional **trains** run every hour to St. Peter-Ording (25min., €4.20) and Husum (30min., €5.10). The city center is a 5min. walk directly out the front door of the train station. Across the square near the St. Laurentis church is the **tourist office,** Am Markt 1. (☎04681 614 20. Open May 15-Sept. 30 M-F 9am-noon and 2-5pm, Sa 10am-noon; Oct.-May 14 M-Th 9am-noon and 2-3pm, F 9am-noon.)

Accommodations listings are outside the office door. In the side entrance of the same building, the **Stadtbibliothek** offers **Internet** for €1 per 30min. The main **National Park Information Center,** at Schloßgarten 1, is an administrative center; direct questions about park visits to the **Multimar Wattforum** or the **National Park Hotline.** (☎04681 96200; www.wattenmeer-nationalpark.de.)

SYLT ISLAND ☎04651

The windswept island of Sylt—with miles of trails, white sand beaches, and traditional thatched-roof Frisian houses—has long been Germany's favorite vacation spot, drawing in families looking for a little beach time, hikers and cyclists hoping to hit the trail, and shoppers armed with little more than credit cards and directions to the spa. **Westerland,** the island's largest city and transportation hub, was founded as a resort town in the middle of the 19th century. Long regarded as a playground for the rich, the island is now the destination of choice for everyone from the biggest German celebrities to the nation's vacationing families. Wealthy vacationers schmooze in **Kampen,** just north of Westerland, while everyone else spreads out along the island's beaches in wicker *Strandkorbs* or "beach baskets" to shield them from the stiff North Sea breeze as they watch windsurfers battle the gale.

TRANSPORTATION. **Trains** run from Westerland to: Flensburg (2hr., €19); Hamburg (3¼hr., €30); Hanover (5½hr., €66); Tönning (1½hr., €14.70). Crowded buses with bike racks circuit the island, leaving the **ZOB** terminal immediately next to the train station. (Every 20min. Single trips €1.55-6.20, day card €12.80, families €18, 3-day pass €20.50.) **Ferries** run from List harbor to Havneby on the Danish island of Rømø. Call **Rømø-Sylt Linie** in List for reservations. (☎0180 310 30 30; www.sylt-faehre.de. 2hr.; depart at noon or 1:30pm, return at 4:45-5:20pm; €9, children €5.50.) **Adler-Schiffe** at Boysenstr. 13, Westerland, runs daytrips to Amrum or Fohr. Buy tickets 30min. in advance at the ticket booth at the Hörnum harbor (☎04651 88 12 97) or in the tourist office. (☎04651 987 00; www.adler-schiffe.de. Open daily 9am-5:30pm; round-trip €22.50, children €13. 2 ferries per day.) Sylt's **bus** company **SVG** offers a variety of tours around the island and its neighbors. (☎04651 83 61 00. Departs Apr.-Nov. M-F from the Westerland ZOB.) The most convenient **bike** rentals is **Fahrrad am Bahnhof,** across from track 1 at the station (around the left side). (☎04651 58 03. €5.70-8 per day, €27-42 per week; tandems €13.40/66.50. Open daily 7am-7pm.)

ORIENTATION AND PRACTICAL INFORMATION. Visitors pour in from trains crossing the 10km long Hindenburgdamm as well as ferries docking in southern **Hörnum** and **List,** Germany's northernmost town. North of List, the dunes of the slender **Ellenbogen peninsula** separate the Wattenmeer from the open ocean. The ritzy **Kampen** lies just north of Westerland; tiny **Tinnum** is just east. The poetically named **L24 road** and corresponding **bike path** connect all of Sylt's towns. Other paths snake through the dunes, many of which must be explored on foot. The **tourist office** in the train station books rooms for a €16 fee plus an exorbitant deposit, and a big bulletin board in front of the station also list available rooms (☎04651 99 88). Consider grabbing a listing of all accommodations, or peruse pamphlets like *Reiten Auf Sylt* (lists horseback riding opportunities, mostly in Tinnum) or *Wassersport Auf Sylt,* which details the best places to windsurf, kitesurf, or sail. There is another **branch** in Hörnum. (Strandweg 2. ☎04651 962 60; www.hoernum.de. Open M-F 9am-5pm, Sa-Su 9am-1pm; in winter M-Th 9am-4pm, F 9am-1pm.) There is yet another **branch** in Kampen. (Hauptstr 12. ☎04651 46 98. www.kampen.de. Open Easter-Oct. M-F 10am-5pm, Sa 10am-1pm;

Jul.-Aug. Sa-Su 10am-1pm; Nov.-Easter M-F 9am-4pm.) **Nordsee Apotheke** is at Sandstr 22. (☎04651 92 90 00. Open M-F 8:30am-6:30pm, Sa 8:30am-1pm.) Find **internet** at **Stadtbücherei Westerland,** Alte Post, Stephanstr. 6b, across from the Rathaus. (☎04651 227 10. €1 per 20min. Open M-Tu 10am-noon and 3-6pm, Th 10am-8pm, F 10am-noon, Sa 8:30am-noon.) The **post office,** Kampende 11, has a **24hr. ATM.** (Open M-F 7am-6pm, Sa 7am-1pm.) **Postal Code:** 25980.

FOOD. Dining options on Sylt cater to the luxury crowd that frequents the island, though Westerland has cheaper choices. Kampen is home to the famous **Whiskey Alley,** lined with posh bars and cafes. **Friedrichstr.** in Westerland is the lively main drag between the train station and the beach, and caters to every purchasing need on the spectrum from errand to extravagance. Near the train station in Westerland is the grocery store **Edeka,** Wilhelmstr. 6. (Open M-F 8:30am-7pm, Sa 8:30am-6pm, Su 11am-1:30pm and 3:30-6pm.) Cash-conscious diners head to **Toni's Restaurant ❸,** Norderstr. 3 in Westerland (☎04651 258 10; open daily 11:30am-midnight), serving well-priced examples of traditional German cuisine (€7.80-13.80) in a quiet, candle-lit atmosphere. If you're sick of the waves, surf the web instead from comfy armchairs at **Woyton ❶,** Friedrichstr 44, which offers free Wi-Fi. Downstairs, tasty sandwiches (€2.60-3.90) and baked goods won't break the bank. (Open 8am-9pm.) Prices rise with the killer view from **Badezeit Strand Restaurant ❸,** Dünenstr 3. The menu is limited, but the food is appetizing and the proximity to the beach unbeatable. Warm barrel tables behind glass protect diners from the fierce wind. (☎04651 83 40 20. www.badezeit.de. Lunch entrees €6.50-11.50, dinner €7.50-21.50. Open M-F 11:30am-10pm, Sa-Su 10am-10pm.)

SIGHTS AND OUTDOOR ACTIVITIES. Once you've gotten rid of your luggage, the best way to explore the 39km-long island is by bicycle. The main **bike path** hugs the highway, making it perfect for inter-town travel. Smaller dirt and gravel paths meander through the dunes, with views of the ocean, flowering hills, and dense heath below. The most spectacular view is from atop **Uwedüne,** the island's highest point, located near Kampen. Western Sylt offers the wildest wave-beaten beaches, including the nude beach **Bühne 16,** though most detailed maps reveal several more FKK (Free Body Culture) beaches. The island's eastern side looks out onto its mudflats and water smooth enough to be a giant bathtub. Beginning **windsurfers** flop around on the eastern side of the island, while the more experienced brace themselves against the cold, turbulent waters of the unprotected western side at **Wenningstedt, Hörnum,** and **List,** with the most popular haunts marked by "Surfgebiet" on maps. *Kurtaxe* for most beaches are €2-3, though children under 18 are often free. List is also an excellent base for hikers and bikers hoping to explore the trails leading into the remote dunes of **Ellenbogen,** 8km north of town. The Wattenmeer National Park's **Schutzstation Hörnum,** 100m south of bus stop "Steintal," offers information about the region and leads a variety of Watt-related activities. Look out for themed 2-2½hr. tours in German, exploring the island's plant and animal life or its unique geography. (Free; €4 suggested donation for adults, €2.50 for children. ☎04651 88 10 93. www.schutzstation-wattenmeer.de. Open daily Apr. 1-Oct. 31 10am-noon and 3-6pm; Dec. 23-Jan. 6 10am-noon and 2-4pm.) The brand new **Westerland Aquarium,** Gaadt 33, is filled with fish from the North Sea and more tropical locales. (☎04651 836 2522. Walk south 15min. along the coast from the town's center. Open daily 10am-7pm. €11, children €7.) Next to the aquarium, and up a long flight of stairs, an **Aussichtspunkt** (outlook point), provides a panoramic view of both the beach and the city.

AMRUM ISLAND ☎04682

The smallest of the North Frisian Islands, Amrum manages to pack in all of Sylt's beauty and charm in a quieter, more personal environment, though often at the expense of the larger island's excitement and diversity. The island's main attractions are, naturally, nautical: a lighthouse and pristine beaches.

TRANSPORTATION. **Ferries** to the town of Wittdün, run by **Adler-Schiffe,** leave from Hörnum on Sylt and Nordstrand, near Husum. (☎04842 900 00; www.adler-schiffe.de. Hörnum to Wittdün 50min. on the **Adler-Express,** 1¾hr. on the Adler IV. 10 and 11:55am from Sylt, 4:10 and 5:25pm from Wittdün on Amrum. Round-trip €22.50, children €13.) For more frequent service, the **Wyker Dampfschiffs-Reederei** goes to Wittdün from Dagebüll harbor on the mainland, near Dagebüll's train station. (☎01805 08 01 40, €0.14 per min., or the Wittdün office 04842 94 92 11; www.faehre.de. From Dagebüll 10 per day 6:15am-8pm, from Amrum 10 per day 5:00am-5:30pm; €8.50, round-trip €10.60, children €4.25/5) Amrum's **bus lines** connect the towns from 9am-6:30pm. (Apr.-Nov. single rides €1.40-2.20, day ticket €8, with *Kurkarte* €4.80.) **Bikes** are available for rent all over the island, but prices increase with convenience. Distance yourself from Wittdün for the best prices (around €3 per ½-day, €5 per day.)

ORIENTATION AND PRACTICAL INFORMATION. At the southern end of the island, the town of **Wittdün** is home to Amrum's **ferry terminal.** The island's four other towns, **Steenodde, Süddorf Nebel,** and **Noddorf,** straddle the main road, Inselstr., as it heads north. Amrum is small enough to be comfortably covered with a bike in one day. **Island tours** leave from the ferry terminal's parking lot, whether on the red double-decker bus or the tiny train, the **Amrumer Inselbahn** (☎04842 949 70. Adults €8, children 3-12 €3.50. 70min. tours leave at 11am, noon, 12:45, and 2:15pm.) The **tourist office,** Am Fähranleger, is just across the parking lot from the ferry terminal. (☎04842 940 30; www.amrum.de. Open M-F 9am-5pm, Sa 9:30am-12:30pm.) The Wattenmeer National Park's **Schutzstation Wittdün** (☎04842 27 18), Mittelstr. 34, is near the hostel and offers guided tours of the Watt (€4, children €2. www.schutzstation-wattenmeer.de. Look for signs for the Nordseehall Diele Naturschutzzentrum.) Find a **pharmacy, Louisen Apotheke,** on Inselstr 19. (☎04682 15 50. Open M-F 8:30am-12:30pm and 3-6pm, Sa 8:30am-12:30pm.) **Laundry** facilities are at **Marlene's Münz Wasch,** Inselstr. 56, about 700m from the ferry landing. (Wash €3. Dry €2. Look for "Kiosk Moin Moin" to give yourself a prayer of finding the tiny place. Open daily 8am-8pm.) The **post office** is on Inselstr. 30. (Open M-Tu and Th-F 9am-noon and 2:30-6pm, W and Sa 9am-noon.) **Postal Code:** 25046.

ACCOMMODATIONS AND CAMPING. Book a room by early spring to stay anywhere on the island during the summer—you'll be out of luck by June and possibly May. To get to **Haus Eckart ❷,** Mittelstr. 20, walk away from the ferry dock past Inselstr. on Quedens-Str., then turn right on Mittelstr. Family-run since 1902, this retreat offers thoughtfully decorated rooms, easy beach access, a garden perfect for picnicking, a sunroom thick with tropical plants, and in-house yoga and meditation seminars. (☎04842 20 56; www.haus-eckart.de. Breakfast included. Dorms €16, singles €27-30, doubles €44.) **Jugendherberge Wittdün ❷,** Mittelstr. 1, 100 yards before Eckart, has large, clean rooms, some with beach views, all with easy beach and town access. (☎04842 20 10. Breakfast included. Internet access €1 per 10min. Reception 7am-1pm and 5-10pm. Check-in from 5pm. Dorms €18, multiple nights €16.70; singles €26/24.70; over 27 add €3 per night. *Kurtaxe* €2.50.) **Campingplatz Amrum ❶,** Inselstr. 125,

Wittdün, sits at the foot of the dunes with its own restaurant and *Biergarten*. (☎04842 22 54; www.amrum-camping.de. Check-in 9:30am-12:30pm and 4:30-6pm. Tents €5-9, €6.50, ages 12-18 €3.50-5.50, plus *Kurtaxe*. Cash only.)

FOOD. Restaurants in Wittdün tend to be fairly expensive, but there are two **Edeka** supermarkets on Inselstr. 18 and 26-28, close to the docks. Find a bigger selection at 26-28. (Open M-Sa 7:45am-7pm.) Plenty of intimate cafes line **Nebel's Uasterstigh.** Travelers with insatiable sweet teeth should head to **Nebel's Friesen Cafe,** Vasterstigh 7, for a leisurely break from their bike routes. Try the dainty *Friesenwaffeln* (wafers with plum sauce and whipped cream; €3.40) and invigorating *Eiergrog* (egg, sugar, and hot rum; €5), though the cozy cafe is sure to please with any of its cakes, soups, or gourmet drinks. (☎04842 966 20. Open daily 11:30am-6pm.) A few blocks west of Wittdün's ferry dock, the aggressively nautical **Restaurant Klabautermann ❹,** Inselstr. 13, serves big portions of reasonably priced fish and meat (€8.80-17), next door to the restaurant's private bowling alley. (☎04842 21 39. Open daily 11am-1:30pm and 5-9:30pm. €15 per hr. for a lane.) For a more casual bite in Wittdün, **Kaffeeflut ❷,** Inselstr. 24, serves crepes and waffles (€3.10-4.50) and light lunches (€3.40-8.90) along with plenty of coffee to wash it down. Eat inside in a casual cafe setting under huge paper lanterns, or outside in the shade of a *Strandkorb*. (☎04842 96 88 65. M-Sa 9am-6pm. Cash only.) In the evening, crowds fill **Die Blaue Maus ❸,** Inselstr. 107, on the fringes of Wittdün. This plaid-happy pub is Amrum's most beloved bar, festooned with strands of buoys and shells. (☎04842 20 40. Open M-Tu and F-Su 8pm-3am, W 8pm-2am, kitchen open until 1am. Beer €1.80-4.20. MC/V.)

SIGHTS AND HIKING. Wittdün revolves around the quiet but commercial main street, Inselstr., which it shares with most other towns on the island, as well as a souvenir- and *Imbiß*-free **Strandpromenade** (beach walk). To the west lies the **Kniepsand,** a surprisingly wide, refreshingly wild stretch of North Sea beach. Between the Kniepsand and the towns, hiking trails crisscross a strip of grassy dunes crowned by the candy-cane-striped **Amrumer Leuchtturm,** the tallest lighthouse on Germany's North Sea coast. (Open Apr.-Oct. M-F 8:30am-12:30pm. €5, with *Gastkarte* €2, children €0.50.) The **Aussichtsdünen** (lookout dunes) along the island's trails offer similar king-of-the mountain views of the island. **Nebel,** a village of traditional thatch-roof Frisian houses even quieter than Wittdün, is the cultural center of the island, admittedly not a difficult title to claim. The **Mühlenmuseum** (Windmill Museum), in an old thatched windmill, contains a small exhibit on the history of Amrum. (☎04842 872. Open Mar.-Oct. daily 11am-5pm, donations happily accepted.) The nearby **Ömrang Hüüs,** Waaswai 1, highlights the island's Frisian culture, capturing the harshness of life in austere Nordfriesland in an 18th-century captain's home. Rooms have been restored with authentic furnishings, including a tiny closet bedroom in which the whole family slept sitting up to keep from freezing during the night. (☎04842 10 11. Open M-Sa 3-5pm, early May to late Oct. also M-F 10:30am-12:30pm. Donations accepted.) **St. Clemens,** Nebel's tiny church, is ringed by a small, well-landscaped graveyard with a WWII memorial. Outside Nebel, three **trails** run to **Norddorf.** The middle trail, following Inselstr., is not much to look at, but is the quickest route with the smallest possibility of getting lost. The occasionally confusing forest trail (7.9km, marked by green triangles) cuts through the western portion of the island, offering plenty of chances to abscond to the beach via smaller paths. The last path, **Wattenmeer trail** (7.4km, marked by yellow dots), cuts through villages and open pastures on the eastern shore of the island. Go left on the smaller paths that branch off the green triangle path to reach the 2km wide *Kniepsand* beaches. Some hikers cross the Wattenmeer to Amrum's neighboring island, **Föhr,** at low tide, though it is advisable to take a guided tour due to the danger of quicksand pits. Check the tourist office for more information.

HAMBURG

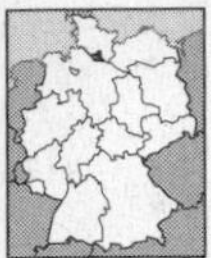

Water shapes every aspect of life in the harbor city of Hamburg, Germany's second-largest. Joggers and walkers flock to the Alster lakes to enjoy the area's beauty, while the bustling port on the Elbe floods the city with new people, ideas, and trade. Hamburg's many canals reflect images of spectacular church steeples alongside modern facades. A walk through the city is a walk over water—with a grand total of 2479 bridges, Hamburg has more than Venice.

A hub for commerce since its early history, Hamburg was a founding member of the Hanseatic trade league in the 13th century. Overland trade from the Baltic Sea brought prosperity in the 16th century, leading to the establishment of the first German stock exchange here in 1558. By the 17th century, Hamburg's influence had spread, and it gained the title of "Free Imperial City" in 1618. Along with Berlin and Bremen, it is one of the three remaining city-states among Germany's 16 states. Hamburg still values its autonomy, which, along with great sea-trade wealth, has seen the city through many hardships.

The Great Fire of 1842 leveled the entire downtown, but a massive rebuilding effort resurrected the city as an industrial-age powerhouse in naval construction and home of the Hamburg-America Line, then the world's largest shipping firm. In WWII, a series of air raids once again turned the downtown to rubble. Over 50,000 tenants of the crowded buildings on the waterfront were killed in a single strike in July of 1943. Thanks to a massive reconstruction effort begun in the 1960s, Hamburg has restored many of its most beloved buildings.

Today's Hamburg is both cosmopolitan and progressive. With large ethnic populations, including many Turkish and Portuguese residents, the city is one of Germany's most diverse. The district of St. Georg is also home to a flourishing gay scene. As the unassuming cultural mecca of Germany, Hamburg houses world-renowned opera and theater companies and many of the country's finest museums. Hamburg's venues hosted The Beatles before they were famous, and a thriving independent music scene exists today. At night, tens of thousands of revelers flock to the infamous red-light district of the Reeperbahn, and bars throughout the city fill up nearly every night of the week.

HIGHLIGHTS OF HAMBURG

DANCE until dawn in the midst of Hamburg's spectacular **nightlife** (p. 194).

BARGAIN for the freshest fish in the land while listening to local rock bands play on Sunday morning at the **Fischmarkt** (p. 190).

MARVEL at the works of the Old Masters and contemporary artists in the museums along the **Kunstmeile** (p. 192).

INTERCITY TRANSPORTATION

Flights: Air France (☎01805 83 08 30) and **Lufthansa** (☎01803 80 38 03), among other airlines, service Hamburg's **Fuhlsbüttel Airport** (☎040 507 50). **Jasper Airport Express** buses (☎040 22 71 06 10, www.jasper.de) run from the Kirchenallee exit of the Hauptbahnhof directly to the airport (25min.; every 10-15min. 4:45am-7pm, every 20min. 7:00-9:20pm; €5, under 12 €2, group discounts). Alternatively, you can take U1 or S1/S11 to "Ohlsdorf," and then an **express bus** to the airport (every 10min.

4:30am-11pm, every 30min. 11pm-1am; €2.60, children 6-14 €0.90). The same modes of transportation are available from the airport into the center of the city.

Trains: The **Hauptbahnhof,** Hamburg's central station, has connections to: **Berlin** (1½hr., €52); **Copenhagen,** Denmark (5hr., €76); **Frankfurt** (5hr., €81); **Hanover** (1½hr., €34); **Munich** (7hr., €108), though prices may vary with day of travel, time of year, and proximity of purchase date to travel date. The efficient staff at the DB Reisezentrum sells tickets. Open M-F 5:30am-10pm, Sa-Su 7am-10pm. Or, purchase them online at www.bahn.de. **Dammtor** station is near the university to the west of the Außenalster; **Harburg** station is south of the Elbe; **Altona** station is to the west of the city's center; and **Bergedorf** is to the southeast. Most trains to and from Schleswig-Holstein stop only at Altona, while most trains towards Lübeck stop only in the Hauptbahnhof. Frequent local trains and the S-Bahn connect the stations. Lockers are available for €2-6 per day.

Buses: The **ZOB** is across Steintorpl. from the Hauptbahnhof. Terminal open M-Th 5am-10pm, F-Sa 5am-midnight, Su 5am-10pm. **Autokraft** (☎040 280 8660) goes to **Berlin** (3hr., every 2hr. 7am-9pm). **Touring Eurolines** (☎040 20 90 99 97) goes to **Amsterdam,** Netherlands (8hr., M-Sa, €39); **London,** England (daily, connecting in Brussels, €89); **Paris,** France (11hr., daily, €69); **Copenhagen,** Denmark (6hr., daily, €62). Dicount rates for students, children, and seniors.

Ride Share: Mitfahrzentrale Citynetz, Ernst-Merck-Str. 12-14 (☎040 194 44; www.citynetz-mitfahrzentrale.de). To: **Berlin** (€18.50); **Cologne** (€28); **Frankfurt** (€27.50); **Munich** (€42). Open M-F 9:30am-6:30pm, Sa 10am-2pm.

ORIENTATION

Hamburg lies on the northern bank of the Elbe river, 100km from the North Sea. The ideally situated harbor has shaped the city's growth. Hamburg's center is between the Elbe and the nearby Alster lakes, **Außenalster** and **Binnenalster,** which are formed by the confluence of the Alster, Bille, and Elbe rivers. Lush parks, including the beautiful Planten un Blomen (p. 190), skirt the western boundary of downtown and arch northward from the *Landungsbrücken* (piers) of **Sankt Pauli** all the way to the western shore of the Alster lakes. The **Hauptbahnhof** lies at the eastern edge of the city center, along Steintorwall. Bisecting the downtown, the **Alsterfleet** canal separates the Altstadt on the eastern bank from the **Neustadt** on the west. The city's best museums, galleries, and theaters are located within these two districts.

Extending from the Kirchenallee exit of the Hauptbahnhof, the predominantly gay district of **Sankt Georg** follows the Außenalster's east bank. Here, the seediness of the Hansapl. area near the station falls away to a quiet cafe scene along the Lange Reihe. Outside the Hauptbahnhof's main exit on Steintorwall is the **Kunstmeile** (Art Mile), a row of museums extending from the Alster Lakes to the banks of the Elbe. Perpendicular to Steintorwall, **Mönckebergstraße,** Hamburg's most famous shopping street, runs westward to the **Rathausmarkt.** The Neustadt's **Hanseviertel,** nestled between Rathausmarkt and Gänsemarkt, is crammed with banks, shops, galleries, and auction houses. The area's glamor turns window-shopping into high art, while the nearby *Fleete* (canals) give the quarter a Venetian charm. To the north, students and intellectuals command the university's **Dammtor** district, duking it out with the city's wealthiest neighborhoods, including **Winterhude** and **Harvesthude** on the shores of the lake. Both enjoy the trendy stores and young designers of the **Karoviertel,** just to the west.

Farther west, the **Schanzenviertel** is a politically active community inhabited by artists, students, and a sizable Turkish population. Here, row after row of street-art-covered restaurants, shops, and a bustling late-night bar scene reflect the quarter's newfound hipness. Even farther west, the **Altona** district feels like

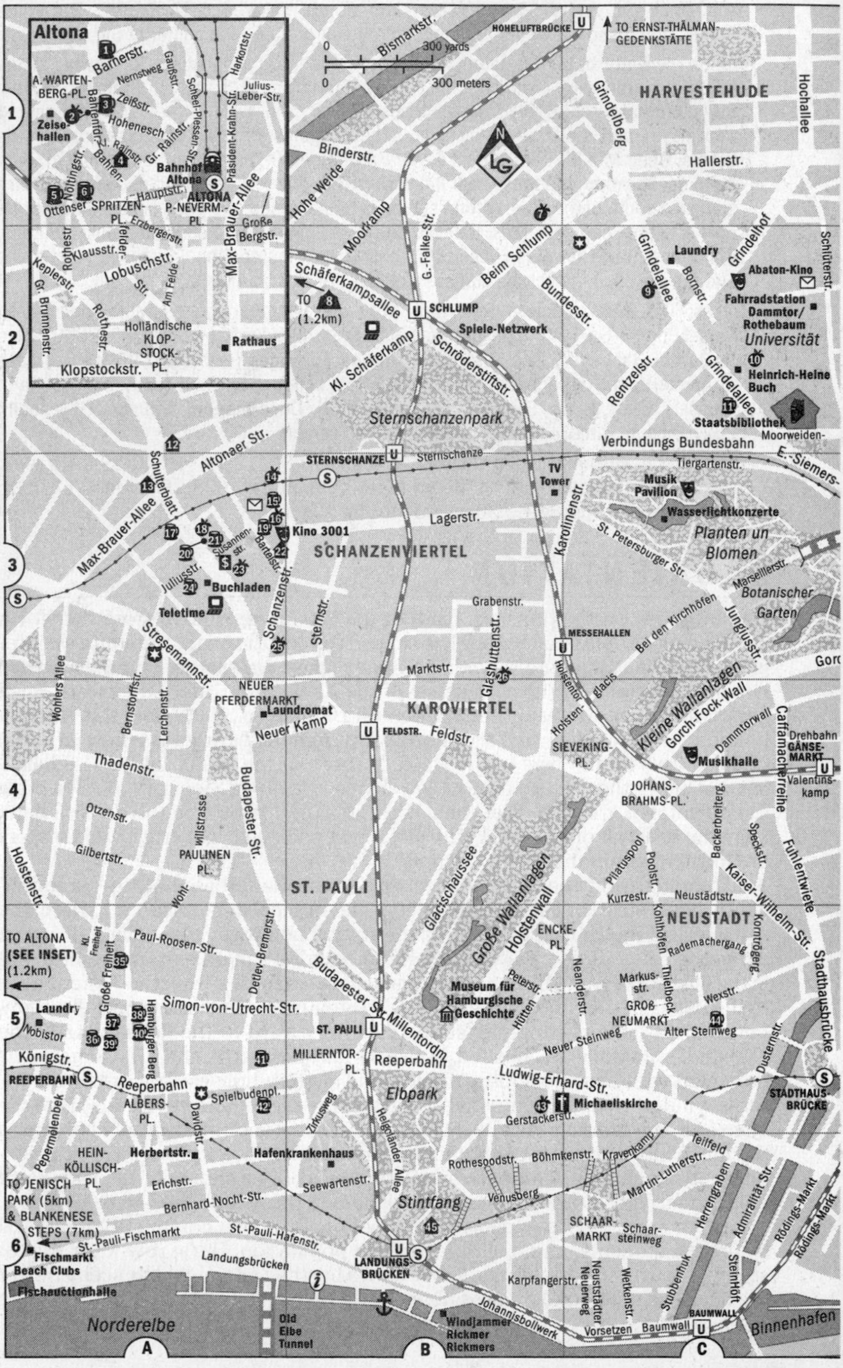
Altona
A. WARTEN-BERG-PL.
Zeise-hallen
Bahnhof Altona
ALTONA
P.-NEVERM.-PL.
SPRITZEN-PL.
Rathaus
Holländische KLOP-STOCK-PL.
Klopstockstr.
Max-Brauer-Allee
HOHELUFTBRÜCKE
TO ERNST-THÄLMAN-GEDENKSTÄTTE
300 yards
300 meters
HARVESTEHUDE
Binderstr.
Hallerstr.
Hohe Weide
Moorkamp
Beim Schlump
Laundry
Abaton-Kino
Fahrradstation Dammtor/ Rothebaum
Universität
Heinrich-Heine Buch
Staatsbibliothek
Schäferkampsallee
TO (1.2km)
SCHLUMP
Spiele-Netzwerk
Schröderstiftstr.
Kl. Schäferkamp
Sternschanzenpark
Verbindungs Bundesbahn
STERNSCHANZE
Altonaer Str.
TV Tower
Musik Pavilion
Wasserlichtkonzerte
Planten un Blomen
Botanischer Garten
Kino 3001
SCHANZENVIERTEL
Lagerstr.
Buchladen
Teletime
MESSEHALLEN
Kleine Wallanlagen
Gorch-Fock-Wall
NEUER PFERDERMARKT
Laundromat
Neuer Kamp
KAROVIERTEL
FELDSTR.
Feldstr.
SIEVEKING-PL.
Musikhalle
GÄNSE-MARKT
JOHANNES-BRAHMS-PL.
Thadenstr.
Budapester Str.
PAULINEN PL.
ST. PAULI
Große Wallanlagen
Holstenwall
NEUSTADT
TO ALTONA (SEE INSET) (1.2km)
Museum für Hamburgische Geschichte
Simon-von-Utrecht-Str.
Laundry
ST. PAULI
Millerntordm
MILLERNTOR-PL.
Reeperbahn
Ludwig-Erhard-Str.
REEPERBAHN
Spielbudenpl.
ALBERS-PL.
Elbpark
Michaeliskirche
STADTHAUSBRÜCKE
HEIN-KÖLLISCH-PL.
Herbertstr.
Hafenkrankenhaus
TO JENISCH PARK (5km) & BLANKENESE STEPS (7km)
Stintfang
St.-Pauli-Fischmarkt
St.-Pauli-Hafenstr.
Fischmarkt Beach Clubs
Fischauctionhalle
LANDUNGSBRÜCKEN
Norderelbe
Old Elbe Tunnel
Windjammer Rickmer Rickmers
Johannisbollwerk
Vorsetzen
Baumwall
BAUMWALL
Binnenhafen
A
B
C
1
2
3
4
5
6

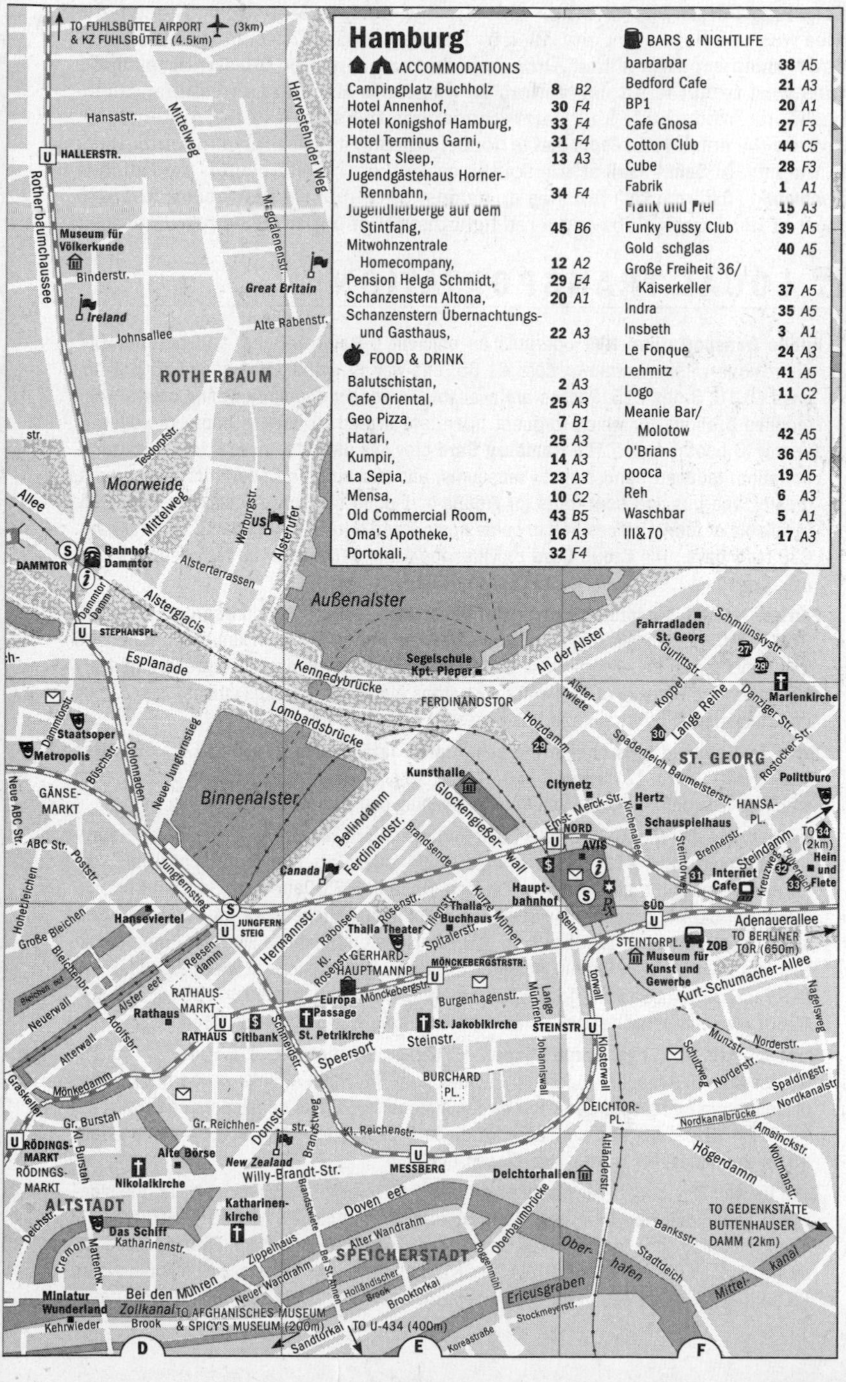
Hamburg
ACCOMMODATIONS
Campingplatz Buchholz 8 B2
Hotel Annenhof, 30 F4
Hotel Konigshof Hamburg, 33 F4
Hotel Terminus Garni, 31 F4
Instant Sleep, 13 A3
Jugendgästehaus Horner-Rennbahn, 34 F4
Jugendherberge auf dem Stintfang, 45 B6
Mitwohnzentrale Homecompany, 12 A2
Pension Helga Schmidt, 29 E4
Schanzenstern Altona, 20 A1
Schanzenstern Übernachtungs- und Gasthaus, 22 A3
FOOD & DRINK
Balutschistan, 2 A3
Cafe Oriental, 25 A3
Geo Pizza, 7 B1
Hatari, 25 A3
Kumpir, 14 A3
La Sepia, 23 A3
Mensa, 10 C2
Old Commercial Room, 43 B5
Oma's Apotheke, 16 A3
Portokali, 32 F4
BARS & NIGHTLIFE
barbarbar 38 A5
Bedford Cafe 21 A3
BP1 20 A1
Cafe Gnosa 27 F3
Cotton Club 44 C5
Cube 28 F3
Fabrik 1 A1
Frank und Frei 15 A3
Funky Pussy Club 39 A5
Gold schglas 40 A5
Große Freiheit 36/ Kaiserkeller 37 A5
Indra 35 A5
Insbeth 3 A1
Le Fonque 24 A3
Lehmitz 41 A5
Logo 11 C2
Meanie Bar/ Molotow 42 A5
O'Brians 36 A5
pooca 19 A5
Reh 6 A3
Waschbar 5 A1
III&70 17 A3
TO FUHLSBÜTTEL AIRPORT (3km) & KZ FUHLSBÜTTEL (4.5km)
HALLERSTR.
Museum für Völkerkunde
Ireland
Great Britain
ROTHERBAUM
Moorweide
US
DAMMTOR
Bahnhof Dammtor
STEPHANSPL.
Außenalster
Segelschule Kpt. Pieper
Fahrradladen St. Georg
Marienkirche
ST. GEORG
Staatsoper
Metropolis
GÄNSEMARKT
Binnenalster
Kunsthalle
Citynetz
Hertz
Schauspielhaus
Politbüro
Canada
NORD
AVIS
Hauptbahnhof
Internet Cafe
Hein und Flete
TO 34 (2km)
SÜD
Hanseviertel
JUNGFERNSTEIG
Thalia Theater
Thalia Buchhaus
GERHARD-HAUPTMANNPL.
MÖNCKEBERGSTR.
STEINTORPL.
ZOB
Museum für Kunst und Gewerbe
TO BERLINER TOR (650m)
Adenauerallee
Kurt-Schumacher-Allee
Europa Passage
RATHAUSMARKT
Rathaus
RATHAUS
Citibank
St. Petrikirche
St. Jakobikirche
STEINSTR.
BURCHARD PL.
DEICHTOR-PL.
RÖDINGSMARKT
Alte Börse
New Zealand
MESSBERG
Deichtorhallen
Nikolaikirche
ALTSTADT
Katharinenkirche
Das Schiff
SPEICHERSTADT
TO GEDENKSTÄTTE BUTTENHAUSER DAMM (2km)
Miniatur Wunderland
Zollkanal
TO AFGHANISCHES MUSEUM & SPICY'S MUSEUM (200m)
TO U-434 (400m)
Oberhafen
Mittelkanal
D
E
F

Schanzenviertel's baby brother with an edgy, independent streak. Indeed, the area was an independent city ruled by Denmark in the 17th century before several formative power shifts. Altona's pedestrian zone, the **Ottenser Hauptstraße,** runs west from the Altona station. To the north, Hamburg's wealthier neighborhoods, Winterhude and Harvesthude, line the shores of the Außenalster. Toward the northwest, **Eppendorf** is home to the most beautiful outdoor markets in the city. In **Sankt Pauli** at the southwest end of the city center, the raucous **Fischmarkt** (fish market) brushes up against the infamous **Reeperbahn,** home to most of Hamburg's clubs and a red light district of unparalleled rowdiness.

LOCAL TRANSPORTATION

Public Transportation: HVV operates an efficient U-Bahn, S-Bahn, and bus network. Short rides within downtown cost €1.65, one-way in greater Hamburg €260; 1-day pass €5.10, 3-day €15. Passes are available for longer, though anything over a week requires a photo, for which frequent riders are invited to bring a photo or vogue in nearby ID booths for €5. The **Hamburg Card** provides unlimited access to public transportation, reduced admission to museums, and discounts on souvenirs, restaurants, theater, and bus and boat tours for groups of 1 adult and up to 3 children under 15. (Available at tourist offices and in some hostels and hotels. €8 per day, €18 for 3 days, €33 for 5 days.) The **Group Card** provides the same benefits for up to 5 people of any age. (1-day €11.80, 3-day €29.80, 5-day €51.)

Ferries: HADAG Seetouristik und Fährdienst AG, St. Pauli Landungsbrücken (☎040 311 7070). Most locals suggest taking the HVV-affiliated ferries in lieu of the expensive tour boats for an equally up-close and personal view of the river Elbe. Departing every 15min. from the docks at St. Pauli to 21 stops along the river. Full circuit lasts 75min. Price included in HVV train and bus passes; €2.60 for a new ticket.

Taxis: All Hamburg taxis charge the same rates. **Taxi Hamburg,** ☎040 666 666. **Das Taxi,** ☎040 22 11 22. **Autoruf,** ☎040 44 10 11. Normally about €2.40 to start, then €1.68 or less per additional km. Price bargaining can sometimes be useful.

Car Rental: Avis (☎040 32 87 38 00, international ☎018 05 55 77 55), in the Hauptbahnhof near track #12 on the Spitalerstraße side. Cars from €242 per week, with insurance and 24hr. emergency assistance. Open M-F 7:30am-9pm, Sa 8am-6pm, Su 10am-6pm. Lower prices online at www.avis.de. **Hertz,** Kirchenallee 34-36 (☎040 280 1202, international ☎01805 33 35 35), is across the Kirchenallee from Ernst-Merck-Str. Cars from €243 per week, including insurance. Lower prices at www.hertz.de. Open M-F 7am-7:30pm, Sa 8am-4pm, Su 10am-4pm. **Europcar**, Holstenstr. 156 (☎040 306 8260; www.europecar.de), U3 to "Feldstr." Cars from €245 per week. Open daily 24hr.

Boat Rental: Die Segelschule Pieper, An der Alster/Atlantikstieg (☎040 24 75 78; www.segelschule-pieper.de), directly across from the Hotel Atlantic at the intersection of Holzdamm and the An der Alster on the Außenalster. Rents pedalboats and rowboats for €12-€13 per hr., and sailboats for up to 6 people for €16-19 per hr. Open daily 10am-9pm. Must be 14+ to rent. Closed Oct.-Apr.

Bike Rental: Hamburg is extremely bike-friendly, with wide bike lanes built into the sidewalks. **Fahrradstation Dammtor/Rotherbaum,** Schlüterstr. 11 (☎040 41 46 82 77), offers the best price in Hamburg. €3 per day. Open M-F 9am-6pm. **Fahrradladen St. Georg,** Schmilinskystr. 6 (☎040 24 39 08), is off the Lange Reihe near the Außenalster. €8 per day; €56 per week with a €50 deposit. Open M-F 10am-7pm, Sa 10am-1pm.

PRACTICAL INFORMATION

CITY CODE: The city code for all of Hamburg is ☎040.

TOURIST AND FINANCIAL SERVICES

Tourist Offices: Hamburg's main tourist offices supply free English language maps and pamphlets. All sell the **Hamburg Card** (p. 182). The **Hauptbahnhof office,** in the Wandelhalle (the station's main shopping plaza) near the Kirchenallee exit (☎040 30 05 12 01; www.hamburg-tourism.de), books rooms for a €4 fee and shares a space with the local transportation resource (HVV). Open M-Sa 8am-9pm, Su 10am-6pm. The **Sankt Pauli Landungsbrücken office** (☎040 30 05 12 03), between piers 4 and 5, is often less crowded than the Hauptbahnhof office. Open Oct.-Mar. daily 10am-5:30pm; Apr.-Sept. M, W, Su 8am-6pm, Tu and Th-Sa 8am-7pm. The English-speakers on the **Hamburg Hotline** (☎040 30 05 13 00) book rooms (€4 fee), sell event tickets, and answer questions. Open daily 8am-8pm.

Tours: Information booths for many tours are located at the **Sankt Pauli Landungsbrücken** and in the **Hauptbahnhof.**

Top-Tour Hamburg (☎040 641 3731; www.top-tour-hamburg.de). Double-decker buses leave from the Kirchenallee exit of the Hauptbahnhof for landlubbers (Top-Tour) and the St. Pauli Landungsbrücken for the nautically inclined (Maritim-Tour). The ambitious may combine the two in the all-encompassing Gala Tour. Buses leave every 30min. daily Apr.-Oct. 9:30am-5pm; fall and winter tours every hr. 10am-3pm. If a sight seems intriguing, you can hop off anytime for a look and catch the next bus. English-language tours upon request. €14, students €11.50, children free.

Stattreisen Hamburg, Kuhberg 2 (☎040 430 3481; www.stattreisen-hamburg.de). Offbeat 1-2hr. themed walks, with titles like "Reeperbahn by Night," "Merchants and Catastrophes Downtown," and "Neon-lights, Seedy Bars, and Catholics in St. Pauli." Most tours are given in German; however, English-language tours are offered on a less frequent basis. Call for times and locations. €7-46.

Alster-Touristik (☎040 357 4240; www.alstertouristik.de), on Jungfernstieg by the Außenalster. See Hamburg as the swans do. Walk to the Außenalster or take the U1 or U2, or S1 or S3 to "Jungfernstieg" and follow the swan signs. 50min. boat rides around the lakes. Tours leave daily late Mar.-Oct. every 30min. 10am-6pm, €10, under 16 €5. Winter tour with cocoa through Nov. Group discounts. Also offers more expensive trips through the city's canals as well as a 3hr. tour to Bergedorf.

Consulates: Most consulates flank the ritzy neighborhoods on the western shore of Außenalster, Harvestehuder Weg, and smaller streets branching off of them. **Canada:** Ballindamm 35 (☎040 460 0270), between Alestertor and Bergstr. U1 or S1-3 to "Jungfernstieg." Open M-F 9:30am-12:30pm. **Ireland:** Feldbrunnenstr. 43 (☎040 44 18 61 13). U1 to "Hallerstr." Open M-F 9am-1pm. **New Zealand:** Domstr. 19 (☎040 442 5550), on the 2nd fl. of block C of of Zürich-Haus. U1 to "Messberg." Open M-Th 9am-1pm and 2-5:30pm, F 9am-1pm and 2-4:30pm. **UK:** Harvestehuder Weg 8a (☎040 448 0320). U1 to "Hallerstr." Open M-Th 9am-4pm, F 9am-3pm. **US:** Alsterufer 27/28. (☎040 41 17 11 00). S11, S21, or S31 to "Dammtor." Open M-F 9am-noon.

Currency Exchange: ReiseBank (☎040 32 34 83), 2nd fl. of the Hauptbahnhof near the Kirchenallee exit, arranges money transfers for Western Union, cashes traveler's checks (1.5% commission, charges €6.50 to cash 1-9 checks, €10 for 10 checks, and €25 for 25 checks, and exchanges currency for a fixed charge of €3-5. Open daily 7:30am-10pm. ReiseBank also has branches in the Altona and Dammtor train stations as well as in the Flughafen. **Citibank,** Rathausstr. 2 (☎040 30 29 62 02), U3 to "Rathaus." Cashes traveler's checks, including AmEx. Open M-F 9am-1pm and 2-6pm. For better rates, try one of the dozens of exchanges and banks (most of which are open M-F 9am-5pm) near the Hauptbahnhof or downtown.

LOCAL SERVICES

Home Share: Mitwohnzentrale Homecompany, Schulterblatt 112 (☎040 194 45; www.hamburg.homecompany.de). U3, S21, or S31 to "Sternschanze" then follow the Schulterblatt under the bridge. Apartments available for 1 month or more. Passport and deposit of 1-2 months' rent required. Open M-F 9am-1pm and 2-6pm, Sa 9am-1pm.

Bookstores: Thalia-Buchhandlungen, Spitalerstr. 8 (☎040 48 50 11 22; www.thalia.de), U2 to Mönckebergstr., is one of the city's largest bookstores. **Europa Passage,** Ballindamm 40 (☎309 54 980), U1, U2, S1, or S3 to "Jungfernstieg," offers the city's biggest English language selection. **Heinrich-Heine Buchhandlung,** Grindelallee 26-28 (☎040 441 13 30; www.heinebuch.des), has an excellent travel section and a decent selection of English-language novels. Open M-F 9:30am-7pm, Sa 10am-4pm. MC/V.

Library: Staats- und Universitätsbibliothek, Von-Melle-Park 3 (☎040 428 38 22 33; www.sub.uni-hamburg.de). Open to the public M-F; hours vary by department, but generally 10am-6pm. Computers on the 2nd fl., but internet access is limited to library cardholders. Some temporary internet access for non-cardholders may be arranged. Library card €5 per month or €15 per 6 months.

Gay and Lesbian Resources: St. Georg is the center of the gay community. **Cafe Gnosa,** Lange Reihe 93, offers delicious refreshments and several free publications regarding Germany's gay community. To get to **Hein und Fiete,** Pulverteich 21 (☎040 24 03 33), walk down Steindamm away from the Hauptbahnhof, turn right on Pulverteich and look for a rainbow-striped flag on the left. Open M-F 4-9pm, Sa 4-7pm. A self-described switchboard, the center gives advice on doctors, disease prevention, and tips on the social scene. **Magnus-Hirschfeld-Centrum,** Borgweg 8 (☎040 27 87 78 00). U3 to "Borgweg." Daily films and counseling sessions, and a gay-friendly evening cafe, **Dementy** (☎040 27 87 78 01). Open M-Th 5-11pm, F 5pm-late, Su 3-10pm. The center operates hotlines for gays (☎040 279 0069, M-F 2-6pm, Tu-W also 7-10pm) and lesbians (☎040 279 0049, W 7-9pm).

Laundromat: Schnell und Sauber, Neuer Pferdemarkt 27. U3 to Feldstr. Wash €3.50 for 6kg or €7 for 12kg. Dry €0.50 per 10min. Open daily 7am-10:30pm. Other locations at Grindelallee 158 (S21 or S31 to "Dammtor," then bus #5or walk) and Nobistor 34 have similar prices and hours. Sip a beer while laundering at **Waschbar** (p. 196).

EMERGENCY AND COMMUNICATIONS

Emergency: Police, ☎110. From the Kirchenallee exit of the Hauptbahnhof, turn left and follow signs for "BGS/Bahnpolizei/Bundespolizei." Another **branch** is located on the Reeperbahn at the corner of Davidstr. and Spielbudenpl. and in the courtyard of the Rathaus. **Fire** and **Ambulance:** ☎112.

Pharmacy: Senator-Apotheke, Hachmannpl. 14 (☎040 32 75 27). English-speaking staff. Open M-F 8am-6:30pm, Sa 9am-1pm. Also, try the **Hauptbahnhof-Apotheke Wandelhalle,** (☎040 32 52 73 83), in the station's upper shopping gallery. Open M-F 7am-8pm, Th-F 7am-10pm, and Sa-Su 8am-9pm.

Internet Access: Internet Cafe, Adenauerallee 10 (☎040 28 00 38 98), directly across from the ZOB, offers one of the best deals in town. €0.75 per 30min. Open daily 10am-11:55pm. **Teletime,** Schulterblatt 39 (☎040 41 30 47 30), in the heart of the Sternschanze district, doubles as a hookah bar at night. €0.50 per 15min. Open M-F 10am-10pm, Sa-Su 10am-7pm. Free Wi-Fi available in **Wildwechsel,** Beim Grünen Jäger 25. The cafe, with its forest-chic decor, is open daily from 4pm. Just a few steps farther down the road at 23 is Altan Hotel, another source of free wireless. Open 24hr.

Post Office: At the Kirchenallee exit of the Hauptbahnhof. Open M-F 8am-6pm, Sa 8:30am-12:30pm. **Postal Code:** 20099.

ACCOMMODATIONS

The vibrant **Schanzenviertel** area, filled with students, leftist dissidents, and a large ethnic community, houses two of the city's best backpacker hostels near many excellent, inexpensive cafes and shops. More expensive hotels cluster around the **Binnenalster** and eastern **Außenalster.** A slew of small, relatively cheap pensions (often renting by the hour) line **Steindamm, Steintorweg, Bremer Weg,** and **Bremer Reihe,** around the Hauptbahnhof, where several safe hotels provide respite from some the area's several unsavory characters. There are nicer budget options north of the Bahnhof around **Ernst-Merck-Straße, Holzdamm,** and **Lange Reihe.** The tourist office's *Hotelführer* can help direct you for free.

HOSTELS AND CAMPING

Schanzenstern Übernachtungs- und Gasthaus, Bartelsstr. 12 (☎040 439 84 41; www.schanzenstern.de). U3, S21, or S31 to "Sternschanze." In the middle of the electrifying Schanzenviertel, this guesthouse offers bright, hotel-like rooms on the upper floors of a renovated pen factory and shares a block with an independent film theater. Wheelchair-accessible. Breakfast €4-6. Laundry €4.50. Free internet kiosk for guests. Reception 6:30am-2am. Reserve ahead in summer. Dorms €19, singles €37.50, doubles €53, triples €63, quads €77, quints €95. Cash only. ❷

Instant Sleep, Max-Brauer-Allee 277 (☎040 43 18 23 10; www.instantsleep.de). U3, S21, or S31 to "Sternschanze." Follow the Schulterblatt under the bridge, enter the building on its left side, and find reception on the 2nd fl. With its improvised library and communal kitchen, Instant Sleep caters to younger travelers who want a social homebase. Helpful, bilingual staff. Sheets €3. Towels €0.50. Internet access €1 per 30min. Lockers €5 deposit. Reception 8am-2am. Check-in 3pm-midnight. Dorms €15.50, singles €30, doubles €44, triples €60. Cash only. ❷

Schanzenstern Altona, Kleiner Rainstr. 24-26. (☎040 39 91 91 91; www.schanzenstern-altona.de), close to Altona Station. Just as hospitable as its Schanzenviertel counterpart in terms of professional staff and quality of rooms but located in a quiet residential neighborhood with plenty of cafes and restaurants. Breakfast €6.30. Common room downstairs. Private bath in all rooms. Apartments available. Dorms €19, singles €43, doubles €58-68, triples €73, quads €83. Cash only. ❷

Campingplatz Buchholz, Kieler Str. 374 (☎040 540 45 32; www.camping-buchholz.de). From Altona station, take bus #183 to "Basselweg" (20min., 2-3 per hr. 5am-midnight), then walk 100m farther. This parking area is packed with RVs, surrounded by houses, and just off a busy road. Breakfast €4. Showers €1. Reception M-Th and Su 8am-noon and 3-7pm. F-Sa 8am-noon and 2-7pm. Quiet hours 10pm-7am. €5.50 per tent. No tent rental. Bed & breakfast singles with bath €50-60; doubles €65-75. ❶

HOTELS AND PENSIONS

Hotel Annenhof, Lange Reihe 23 (☎040 24 34 26; www.hotelannenhof.de). Brightly colored walls offset striking moldings, making these well-priced rooms feel like a rainbow during the Gilded Age. The hotel's location in St. Georg provides a comfortable yet exciting vibe. Singles €40, doubles €70, triples €100, quads €130. Cash only. ❹

Hotel Konigshof Hamburg, Pulverteich 18 (☎040 284 0740; www.koenigshof-hamburg.de). Walk down Steindamm from the Hauptbahnhof and turn right on Pulverteich. This snappily decorated hotel mixes modern Mediterranean with traditional. The rooms are large, with TV, radio, and phone. Some private bathrooms. Free WLAN internet in the rooms. Breakfast included. GLBT-friendly neighborhood. Reception M-Sa 7am-10pm, Su 8am-10pm. Singles €45, doubles €85. Check the website for deals. AmEx/MC/V. ❹

FOOD

While traditional German beer, bread, cheese, and wurst are still staples here, Hamburg's harbor brings in a daily catch of fresh seafood, while the city's diverse population cooks up a unique set of specialties. The king of fish here is herring, grilled as *Brathering* or pickled as *Matjes* and served on a sandwich bun. The Portuguese community of Hamburg serves its own seafood dishes in the area between the Michaeliskirche and the river, among other places, while ubiquitous Turkish *Imbiße* (snack bars) serve cheap *Döner Kebaps* and falafel wraps. In early spring when asparagus is in season, it's hard to find a restaurant that doesn't serve *Spargelcremesuppe* (asparagus cream soup), and late summer sees a similar burst in *Blumenkohl* (cauliflower) dishes. For the sweet tooth, *Rote Grütze* is a beloved pudding made of red berries, usually served with vanilla sauce. Small markets selling cheap fresh fruit and Persian flatbread line Suzannestr. in the Schanzenviertel.

SCHANZENVIERTEL

The Schanzenviertel overflows with fruit stands, Asian *Imbiße*, and avant-garde cafes. **Schulterblatt, Susannenstraße,** and **Schanzenstraße** host a slew of inexpensive yet tasty restaurants with an eccentric kick. **Real,** Neuer Kamp 31 (M-Sa 7am-8pm), has a huge selection of groceries and many international brands.

La Sepia, Schulterblatt 36 (☎040 432 2484; www.la-sepia.de). This Spanish and Portuguese restaurant prepares some of the city's tastiest and most affordable seafood. From 11am-5pm, the lunch menu (€4-6) is a steal. Fill up on the grilled salmon, served with potato soup and a hearty side of potatoes and vegetables (€5). For dinner, try a heaping paella (€12-14). Dinner €7.50-22. Open daily noon-3am. AmEx/MC/V. ❸

Hatari Pfälzer Cantina, Schanzenstr. 2 (☎040 43 20 88 66). Hatari offers an impressive array of typical German food from *bratwurst* to *flammekuchen,* a sort of flatbread topped with savory cheeses, meats, and vegetables (€8-12). Decorated like a hip hunting lodge. A young crowd flocks here for hamburgers (€7.30-7.80) and people-watching on the busy street corner. Cash only. ❸

Omas Apotheke, Schanzenstr. 87 (☎040 43 66 20). With its retro wall decorations, pub-like atmosphere, and namesake apothecary drawers, Omas draws a mixed casual crowd. The food is an appetizingly priced mixture of German, Italian, and American cuisine. *Schnitzel* platter €7.50; hamburger with 1 lb. of fries €6.60. Open daily 9am-1am, F-Sa until 2am or later. Cash only. ❷

Cafe Oriental, Markstr. 21a (☎040 42 10 29 95). Transport yourself to the markets of Marrakesh with this moody cafe's dark wood, woven carpets, and hanging lamps. Go for the *Yogitee,* honey tea with cinnamon-dusted mountains of milk foam (€2.50-3). Also offers breakfast and a variety of entrees, including wraps (€3.50) and pastas (€4.50-5). Open daily 10am-1am, later on weekends. Cash only. ❷

Kumpir, Schanzenstr. 95 (☎040 43 09 76 04). Baked potatoes in all possible incarnations. Be prepared to shovel through the generous toppings before hitting your spud foundation (€2.90-3.90). Many vegetarian options in this simple but popular joint. Open M-Th and Su noon-midnight, F-Sa until 1am. Cash only. ❶

UNIVERSITY

Slightly cheaper establishments can be found in the university area, especially along **Rentzelstraße, Grindelhof,** and **Grindelallee.**

Mensa, Von-Melle-Park 5. S21 or S31 to "Dammtor," then bus #4 or 5 to "Staatsbiliothek" (1 stop). Turn right into the courtyard past the bookstore, Heinrich-Heine Buchhandlung, on Grindelallee. Student crowd, massive plates of cafeteria food, and a bulletin board of events listings. Meals €2-2.50 with student ID. Non-students add up to €1. Open M-Th 10am-4pm, F 10am-3:30pm. Limited summer hours. Cash only; ATM in building. ❶

Geo Pizza aus dem Holzbackofen, Beim Schlump 53 (☎040 45 79 29). U2 or U3 to "Schlump." Diners linger over their deep wood tables at this relaxed pizza joint. While there are plenty of vegetarian options, carnivorous diners will melt for the Inferno Pizza's blend of jalapeños, red peppers, beef, onions, salsa, and corn (€7.30). Pizzas €4-8. Open M-Th 11am-midnight, F 11am-1am, Sa-Su noon-1am. The branch at Beim Schlump 27 has a slightly smaller menu. Open daily 11:30am-midnight. Cash only. ❷

ELSEWHERE IN HAMBURG

In Altona, the pedestrian zone along Ottenserstr. next to the train station is packed with ethnic food stands and produce shops. A decidedly younger and more boisterous crowd eats and drinks at Altona's **Alma-Wartenberg-Platz.** In a pinch, the shopping arcade at the **Hauptbahnhof** has about a dozen fast-food joints (open daily 6am-11pm). **Lange Reihe,** in the heart of **St. Georg,** as well as the **Elbe's bank** between the Fischmarkt and Landungsbrüken, offer good but overpriced Portuguese, Italian, and Spanish restaurants. **Gänsemarkt** and **Gerhard-Hauptmann-Platz** have decent options near the city center.

Balutschistan, Bahrenfelderstr. 169 (☎040 390 2229) on A.-Wartenberg-Pl. in Altona, at the corner of Friedensallee. In a sea of ethnic food options, Balutschistan stands out with its beautifully prepared Pakistani food served in a quiet, elaborately decorated interior accented with peaked archways, delicate light fixtures, and tapestries. Enjoy the Kofta curry lichi (vegetable balls in curry with sweet lichee fruit and almonds; €9.50) and the pink, nutty doodh soda (€3). Entrees €8-15, lunch plates €5-6. Open daily noon-midnight. Additional **locations** at Schulterblatt 88 (☎040 43 36 61) and Grindelallee 91 (☎040 41 28 02 46). Cash only. ❸

Portokali Afghanische Spezialitäten (☎040 280 2758), on the corner of Keuzweg and Pulverteich. This *Imbiß*-style Afghan grill serves creative kebabs and rice dishes to guests seated on metal stools at the bar. The strong of heart wash down the huge Kabeli Osbaki (brown rice with raisins, lamb, and meat sauce; €6) with thick *Dogh* (bitter buttermilk laced with mint and pickle bits; €1). Open daily 10am-10pm. Cash only. ❷

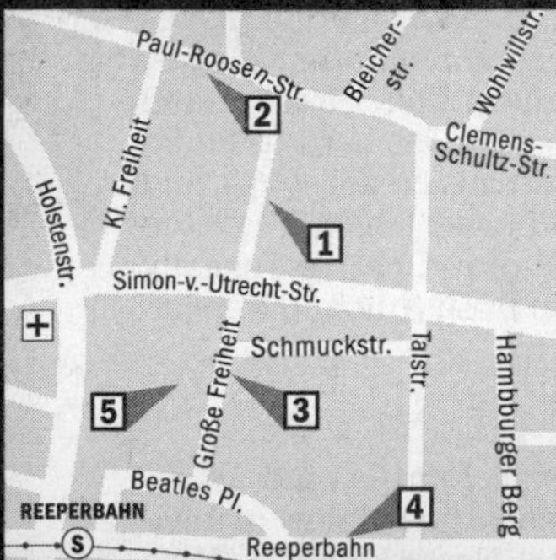

ACROSS THE UNIVERSE: THE BEATLES IN HAMBURG

The Beatles got their first break when a promoter landed them a gig in Hamburg. The experience they gained performing in clubs here played an integral part in shaping the group, and by the time they returned to England they were well on their way to stardom. The boisterous St. Pauli district proudly displays its history as the Beatles' incubator on the way to world stardom—look for a monument at the intersection of the Reeperbahn and Große Freiheit.

1. Indra (64 Große Freiheit): John, Paul, George, and Pete Best played their first Hamburg shows at the Indra, beginning August 17, 1960. The 8hr. gigs were grueling and the pay was poor, but the group learned a bit about working a crowd. A plaque at the front of the building commemorates the group's performances.

2. Bambi Kino (33 Paul-Roosen-Str.): while playing at the Indra, the Beatles slept in tiny quarters

SIGHTS

ALTSTADT

RATHAUS. With more rooms than Buckingham Palace, the 1897 Hamburg Rathaus, which replaced the one destroyed in the Great Fire of 1842, towers extravagantly over its surroundings. Its lavishly furnished chambers, accessible only through a worthwhile guided tour, contain intricate carvings, gigantic murals, and spectacular chandeliers. The building still serves as the seat of both city and state government, while the Rathausmarkt out front hosts constant festivities, from political demonstrations to medieval fairs. *(☎040 428 31 24 70. Tours of the Rathaus in German every 30min. M-Th 10am-3pm, F 10am-1pm, Sa 10am-5pm, Su 10am-4pm. Tours in English every 2hr. M-Th 10:15am-3:15pm, F 10:15am-1:15pm, Sa 10:15am-5:15pm, Su 10:15am-4:15pm. €3, with Hamburg Card €2.)*

GROSSE MICHAELISKIRCHE. The tower of the gargantuan 18th-century Michaeliskirche is one of the most salient features of the city's skyline. The church has had a tumultuous past, having been destroyed by lightning, fire, and Allied bombs. Guarded by a dashing, Satan-crushing St. Michael, the newly renovated church's wide nave and scalloped walls often function as a venue for evening concerts and performances. But don't expect to get much praying done among the throngs of tourists rushing up the tower for the best view of Hamburg. Use the elevator (€3) to cut the 462-stair climb to only three flights. A small exhibition about the history of the church is housed in the crypt. *(☎040 37 67 81 00. Open daily May-Oct. 9am-8pm, Nov.-Apr. 10am-5pm. Church €2 suggested donation, tower €2.50. Organ music daily Apr.-Aug. at noon. Movie on the history of the church every hr. M-Sa 12:30-3:30pm, every 30min. Su 11:30am-3:30pm; €2.50. Crypt open June-Oct. daily 11am-4:30pm, Nov.-May Sa-Su 11am-4:30pm. €1.50, discounts with Hamburg Card.)*

MÖNCKEBERGSTRASSE. Hamburg's glossiest shopping zone stretches from the Rathaus to the Hauptbahnhof. Along the water sits the famed **Europa Passage,** jewel of Germany's shopping malls with over 120 stores and regular events that range from Buddha exhibitions to dance parties.. *(Ballindamm 40. ☎040 36 17 44 44; www.europa-passage.de. Open M-Sa 10am-8pm.)*

NIKOLAIKIRCHE. The blackened spire of this neo-Gothic ruin, destroyed during air raids in July of 1943, has been preserved as a memorial to the victims of war and persecution. Empty frames for

upstairs at the Bambi Kino, the blue-gray house. Look for the small plaque on the door.

3. Kaiserkeller (36 Große Freiheit): After the police shut down the rough-and-tumble Indra, the Beatles moved down the street to the **Kaiserkeller**, where they played shows from Oct. 4 to Nov. 30, 1960. It was here that the group first met drummer Ringo Starr, who joined them when Pete Best fell ill. A sign on a pillar outside the door marks this bit of history.

4. Top-Ten-Club (136 Reeperbahn): After spending time in Liverpool, the Beatles returned to Hamburg to perform at the **Top-Ten-Club.** They lived upstairs while playing the gigs, which lasted from April 1 to July 1, 1961. The club has since changed its name to moon δoo.

5. Star Club (39 Große Freiheit): The Beatles played their final Hamburg show on New Year's Eve, 1962 at the Star Club. The recordings were later released as the famous "Star Club Tapes." Directly across from the Kaiserkeller, go through the archway and look to the left, immediately inside the arch. A guitar-shaped marker denotes the site where the building housing the Star stood until a 1987 fire destroyed it.

stained-glass windows and half-ruined walls face visitors as they ride the elevator to the top of this skeleton. An exhibition underneath the glass pyramid behind the mostly intact spire displays chilling photos of Hamburg and other cities bombed during WWII. *(Exhibition open M-F 10:30am-5:30pm. Elevator open Jan.-Mar. 10am-5:30pm, Apr. 10am-7pm, May-Aug. 10:30am-8pm, Sept.-Oct 10am-7pm, Nov.-Dec. 10:30am-5:30pm. €3.50, students €2.80, children €2.)*

ELSEWHERE IN CENTRAL HAMBURG

PLANTEN UN BLOMEN. This large expanse of gardens is one of a crescent of parks that arcs from the futuristic TV tower to the Dammtor station and south to St. Pauli. The stunning flower displays and relative quiet lure families and romantics to the park, where they can wander for miles on scenic paths. *(S21 or S31 to "Dammtor." Open May-Sept. 7am-11pm, Oct.-Apr. 7am-8pm.)* The park houses the largest **Japanese garden** in Europe, a rose garden featuring over 300 breeds, and a botanical garden with an array of exotic plants. *(Open Mar.-Oct. M-F 9am-4:45pm, Sa-Su 10am-5:45pm; Nov.-Feb. M-F 9am-3:45pm, Sa-Su 10am-3:45pm.)* Children can enjoy three playgrounds, a water slide, giant chess sets, water-jet soccer, a minigolf course, and a trampoline while adults admire the famed rose garden. Daily performances by groups ranging from Irish step dancers to Hamburg's police choir fill the outdoor **Musikpavillion** at 3pm from May to September. The nightly **Wasserlichtkonzerte** draws crowds to the lake with choreographed fountains and underwater lights. *(May-Aug. 10pm, Sept. 9pm. Visit www.plantenunblomen.hamburg.de or a tourist office for a full schedule of events.)*

FISCHMARKT. A Hamburg tradition since 1703, the Sunday morning Fishmarkt is an anarchic mass of vocal vendors hawking fish, produce, flowers, and clothing. Early risers mix with Reeperbahn partyers fresh out of last night's party. Whether you like fruit, pastries, fish sandwiches, or beer for breakfast, this is the perfect place to find them delicious and cheap. Bands of all genres entertain shoppers with loud rock music from the stages of the fish auction hall, though the real action happens outside. *(www.fischmarkt-hamburg.de. S1, S3, or U3 to "Landungsbrücken" or S1 or S3 to "Königstr." or "Reeperbahn." Open Su Apr.-Oct. 5-9:30am; Nov.-Mar. 7-9:30am.)*

ST. PAULI LANDUNGSBRÜCKEN. Hamburg's harbor, the second largest port in Europe, lights up at night with ships from all over the world. Although crowded with tourists, the piers provide an exceptional view of the Hamburg harbor, and are a starting point for most cruises and tours. **Kapitän Prüsse** gives tours of the harbor departing every 30min. from Pier 3 as well as Blankenese and night tours. *(S1, S3, or U1 to "Landungsbrücken." ☎ 040 31 31 30; www.hafenrundfahrt-classic.de. 1hr.; daily in summer 9am-5pm, in winter 9am-4pm; in German only; €10, ages 5-14 €5.)* **HADAG** offers elaborate cruises of outlying areas from Pier 2. *(☎ 040 311 7070. Times and prices vary by cruise.)* **Rainer Abicht** offers similar tours from Pier 1, departing every 30min. *(☎ 040 317 8220; www.abicht.de. Starting at €10, €5 for children. Daily 10am-6pm.)* Docked at Pier 1 is the tri-masted, 97m long **Windjammer Rickmer Rickmers.** Constructed in 1896, the ship has been renamed five times and served many different roles before finally coming to rest in the harbor as the green-hulled museum. All quarters have been painstakingly restored to the original 1890s decor. The ship houses a large special exhibit space, an account of the vessel's unique history, as well as a cafe. *(☎ 040 319 5959. Open daily 10am-5:30pm. €3, students €2.50, families €7. Discounts with Hamburg card.)*

ALSTER LAKES. Just north of downtown, the Alster river flowing from Schleswig-Holstein expands into the two Alster lakes before converging with the Elbe. Follow the elegant promenades around the **Binnenalster** *(U1, U2, S1 or S3 to "Jungfernstieg")*, or join the joggers and bikers near the larger Außenalster *(S21* *or S31 to "Dammtor").* Rent a sailboat, row boat, or windsurf board and enjoy the water on sunny days. **ATG Alster-Touristik GmbH** leads 50min. tours of the lakes. *(☎040 357 4240; www.alstertouristik.de. Tours every 30min. Mar.-Oct. 10am-6pm; Oct.-Nov. 10am, every 30min. 11am-4pm, 5pm. Adults €10, children under 16, €5.)* On the far northeastern shore of the Außenalster, the brilliant blue **Imam Ali Mosque** is home to the world's largest circular rug. *(www.izhamburg.com. Open M-F 9am-5pm.)*

BEYOND THE CENTER

KZ NEUENGAMME. Built in a once idyllic agricultural village east of Hamburg, this concentration camp held 110,000 people as forced laborers between 1938 and 1945. Close to half of its inhabitants died from overwork or execution. After the war, some of the buildings were cleared to make way for a new German prison, now closed. Several paths lead from the meticulously multilingual main exhibition, **Zeitspuren,** which features artifacts from the camp, recorded testimony from survivors, and a detailed history. The paths skirt the remains of the camp's brick-making factory, passes labor barracks, and wanders through powerful memorials. *(Jean-Dolidier-Weg 75. S21 to "Bergedorf," then bus #327 to KZ--Gedenkstätte, Aussellung or #227 to "Jean-Dolidier-Weg or KZ-Gedenkstätte, Aussellung." Bus runs from Bergedorf M-Sa every hr., Su every 2hr. ☎040 428 13 15 00; www.kz-gedenkstaette-neuengamme.de. Museum and memorial open Apr.-Sept. M-F 9:30am-4pm, Sa-Su noon-7pm; Oct.-Mar. M-F 9:30am-4pm, Sa-Su noon-5pm. Path open 24hr. Tours Su noon and 2pm.)*

JENISCH PARK. This park and its museums sit upon a beautiful swath of green running up from the Elbe. **Ernst-Barlach-Haus,** the plain, white building, contains many of the Expressionist artist's most esteemed wood-carvings. It also hosts changing exhibits from other artists and occasional concerts. *(☎040 82 60 85. S-Bahn to "Klein-Plottbek," go left on Jürgensallee, then right on Baron-Vought-Str. The park is on the left side 5min. down. Or, take a ferry to Teufelsbrück. Open Tu-Su 11am-6pm. Free tour in German Su 11am. €6, students €4, families €7.)* Directly across from the S-Bahn station near the Universität Hamburg complex, you can also visit a beautiful **Botanical Garden,** whose grounds radiate from a large pond. *(Open daily 9am-8pm. Free.)*

GEDENKSTÄTTE BULLENHUSER DAMM. The Janusz-Korczak School and its adjoining rose garden serve as a memorial to the 20 Jewish children who underwent "medical testing" at KZ Neuengamme and were murdered on April 20, 1945, at the school only hours before Allied troops arrived in Hamburg. Visitors are invited to plant a rose in memory of the victims, whose photographs line the fence of the flower garden. Inside the school, a small exhibition tells the victims' story. *(Bullenhuser Damm 92. S21 to "Rothenburgsort." Follow the signs to Bullenhuser Damm along Ausschläger Billdeich, over the bridge. The garden is on the left side of the intersection with Grossmannstr.; the school is through the garden's leftmost gate, 200m farther. ☎040 428 1310; www.www.kz-gedenkstaette-neuengamme.de. Rose garden open 24hr. Exhibition open Th 2-8pm, Su 10am-5pm. Free.)*

U-434. After being decommissioned in 2002, the world's largest non-nuclear sub was purchased from the Russian navy and towed to a remote Hamburg harbor. Here, this piece of Cold War history is now open to curious tourists. The 90m long ship and its 84-man crew were stationed off the American coast on reconnaissance missions from 1976-1978, after which the ship served on patrols of the North Sea. The maze of pipes and instruments will fascinate the mechanically-inclined and terrify the claustrophobic. Prepare to squeeze through small hatches and wait in narrow halls behind tourist traffic. Tours in German only. *(Vermannstr. 23c. Hitch a ride with the red double-decker Stadt Rundfahrt tour bus (€2.50 each way) from the St. Pauli Landungsbrücken; call ☎040 792 8979 for details. Otherwise, the 25min. walk from "Messberg" (U1) along pedestrian-unfriendly streets is not recom-*

mended. If you dare, head toward St. Katharinenkirche, turn left over the 1st bridge, and continue over 3 more until you reach Booktor, which becomes Versmannstr. Continue walking for 15min.; the museum will be on your right. www.u-434.de. Open Apr. 1-Oct. 3 M-Th 10am-6pm, F-Su 9am-7pm; Oct. 4-Mar. 31 daily 10am-6pm. €8, students €6, families €18. Tour €3.)

HAGENBECK'S TIERPARK. Founded in 1907 by the enthusiastic and slightly eccentric collector of exotic animals, Carl Hagenbeck, Hamburg's zoo maintains its quirky character. Animals wander about the park freely, while children clamber up to the elephants to feed them fresh vegetables. *(U2 to "Hagenbecks Tierpark." ☎ 040 540 0010; www.hagenbeck.de. Open daily 9am-6pm. €15, ages 4-16 €10. Separate aquarium €13/9. Combined €25/16. Group discounts.)*

MUSEUMS

Many of Hamburg's finest museums are located along the Kunstmeile, running from from the Alster Lakes to the Elbe. The Hamburg Card provides discounted admission to most museums. With new galleries populating many neighborhoods, Hamburg's contemporary art scene is currently thriving—pick up a list of current gallery exhibits at any tourist office. The free newspaper **Museumswelt Hamburg,** available at tourist offices, lists museum exhibitions and events. Unless specified, museums are closed on Mondays and open 10am-6pm the rest of the week, and until 9pm on Thursdays.

MUSEUM FÜR KUNST UND GEWERBE (MUSEUM OF ART AND INDUSTRY). The exhibitions at Hamburg's applied arts museum span nations and centuries as a bridge between cultures and a monument to the lost art of exquisite craftsmanship. A huge exhibit containing over 430 historical keyboard instruments including harpsichords, clavichords, and hammer-klaviers illustrates the development of the modern piano, while another exhibit views history through the lens of porcelain. The museum also has an extensive photography collection, an impressive Art Nouveau display, and a treasure trove of antique gold jewelry. *(Steintorpl. 1. 1 block south of the Hauptbahnhof. ☎ 040 42 81 34; www.mkg-hamburg.de. €8; students, Hamburg Card holders, and seniors €5; under 18 free.)*

HAMBURGER KUNSTHALLE (HALL OF ART). It would take days to fully appreciate this expansive art museum, regarded as one of the finest in Germany. Luckily, the collection is logically organized into chronological categories: Old Masters and 19th-century work on the upper levels, prints and drawings downstairs, and an adjoining four-story contemporary art collection in the adjacent **Galerie der Gegenwart** just through the museum shop and marble-pillared cafe. Highlights include a set of medieval altars, works by 17th-century Dutch painters including a number of Rembrandts, the dynamic new media wing, and a large Impressionist gallery. The impressive rotating temporary exhibits in the Galerie der Gegenwart should not be missed. *(Glockengießerwall. Turn right from the "Spitalerstr./City" exit of the Hauptbahnhof and cross the street. ☎ 040 428 13 12 00; www.hamburger-kunsthalle.de. €8.50, students €5, families €14.)*

DEICHTORHALLEN HAMBURG. Hamburg's contemporary art scene thrives inside these two hangar-sized former fruit markets, which house rotating photography, paintings, and sculpture and film installations. Each season brings new exhibits to the vaulted halls. Though both are worth the trip, the south hall features photography while the north hall divides its attention among several creative media, taking advantage of the phenomenal space for installations. *(Deichtorstr. 1-2. U1 to "Steinstr." Follow signs from the U-Bahn station. ☎ 040 32 10 30; www.deichtorhallen.de. Open Tu-Su 11am-6pm. Each building €7, students €5, families €9.50. Combination ticket to both halls €12/8/16.50. Combined ticket €4.50 Tu after 4pm. Under 18 free.)*

HAMBURGER MUSEUM FÜR VÖLKERKUNDE (ETHNOGRAPHY MUSEUM). From African masks to an entire Maori house, this museum of world cultures is an anthropologist's paradise. The exhibit on nationalism and the creation of a European culture is especially interesting in light of contemporary European politics. Along with impressive English documentation, the museum's geographic and thematic organization makes browsing a breeze. *(Rothenbaumchaussee 64. U1 to "Hallerstr." ☎01805 30 88 88, €0.12 per min.; www.voelkerkundemuseum.com. €7, with Hamburg Card €3, students €3.50, under 18 free. Open Tu-Su 10am-5pm.)*

MUSEUM FÜR HAMBURGISCHE GESCHICHTE (HISTORY MUSEUM). On the edge of the Große Wallanlagen gardens near St. Pauli, this four-story complex provides a thorough, well-translated overview of Hamburg's history. The museum features everything from the largest model train display in Western Europe to time-capsule rooms with authentic 1950s furniture to the side of a ship open for exploring. *(Holstenwall 24. U3 to "St. Pauli." ☎040 4281 32 23 80. €7.50, with Hamburg Card €5, students €4, families €12. F €4, families €6. Open Tu-Su 10am-5pm.)*

ENTERTAINMENT

In addition to the regular offerings of music, theater, and film, Hamburg's Rathausmarkt and other locations often host lively street fairs, especially during the summer. Hamburg owes its prosperity to Friedrich Barbarossa, who granted the town the right to open a port on May 7, 1189. The city still celebrates with the **Hafengeburtstag** (Harbor Birthday) every May, which attracts 1.5 million people to party onshore against a backdrop of ships parading, a tugboat ballet, the Hamburg Philharmonic, and fireworks. (www.hafengeburtstag.de.) During April, August, and November, the **Heiligengeistfeld** north of the Reeperbahn transforms into the **"Dom,"** a titanic amusement park bursting with beer and wild partying. Enthusiastic cultural consumers can learn about listening and viewing opportunities at the tourist office and larger box offices. Students should ask about significant discounts.

MUSIC

The **Staatsoper,** Große Theaterstr. 36, houses one of the best **opera** companies in Germany as well as the national dance powerhouse, the **John Neumeier Ballet Company.** (☎040 35 68 68. U2 to "Gänsemarkt." Open M-Sa 10am-6:30pm and 90min. before performance.) **Orchestras** abound: the Philharmonie, the Norddeutscher Rundfunk Symphony, and Hamburg Symphonia all perform at the Musikhalle on Johannes-Brahms-Pl., formally called the Laeiszhalle. (U2 to "Gänsemarkt.") The **Musikhalle** (☎040 34 69 20; www.musikhalle-hamburg.de) also hosts **chamber music,** orchestras, concerts, and the occasional jazz performance. Hamburg's churches (see **Sights,** p. 189) offer a wide variety of classical and organ concerts, often free of charge.

Live music of all genres thrives in Hamburg. Superb traditional jazz swings at the **Cotton Club** and **Indra** (see **Nightlife,** p. 194). On Sunday mornings, musicians talented and otherwise play at the **Fischmarkt.** The magazine *Szene* (€3) has an exhaustive listing of events. During the summer, big-name bands come to the **Stadtpark** (☎040 41 80 68; www.karsten-jahnke.de, a generally useful website for big-name concerts). The **West Port Jazz Festival,** Germany's largest, runs in mid-July. Call the Konzertkasse (☎040 32 87 38 54) for information. Casual listeners can find smaller acts keeping the dream alive in bars across the city.

THEATER AND FILM

Most theaters sell reduced-price tickets to students at the evening box office, generally open 1hr. before performances, if not at the regular box office. In July and August, many theaters close down only to make way for the summer arts festivals. Pick up a schedule of programs at one of the tourist offices.

The acclaimed **Deutsches Schauspielhaus,** Kirchenallee 39, is diagonally across from the Hauptbahnhof. The theater presents contemporary international works interspersed with Shakespeare and Sophocles. (☎040 24 87 13; www.schauspielhaus.de. Box office open M-Sa 10am-7pm or showtime. Student tickets from €7.50.) The satellite **Polittbüro,** Steindamm 45, puts on more experimental performances for an intellectual crowd. (☎040 28 05 54 67. Open 1hr. before showtime. Tickets also available at the **Deutsches Schauspielhaus.** €5-20.) The **English Theater,** Lerchenfeld 14, entertains natives and tourists alike with its English-language productions. (U2 to "Mundsgurg." ☎040 227 7089. Performances M-Sa 7:30pm, matinees Tu and F 11am. Box office open M-F 10am-2pm and 3:30-7:30pm, Sa 3:30-7:30pm, and 1hr. before show. Tickets €23-28, matinees €15.) **Thalia,** Alstertor 1, sets up avant-garde musicals, plays, and readings, mostly in German. (S21 or S31 to "Mönckebergstr." ☎040 32 81 44 44. www.thalia-theater.de.) The German **cabaret** tradition lives on at several venues, including **Das Schiff,** at Holzbrückestr. 2. (U3 to Rödingsmarkt. Head east 1 block on Ost-Weststr. then turn right—the boat is docked at the bridge, unless it's off touring. ☎040 69 65 05 60; www.theaterschiff.de.)

Kino 3001, Schanzenstr. 75, shows indie and international flicks (☎040 43 76 79), and viewers often linger in the courtyard to discuss. The university crowd packs **Abaton-Kino,** Allendepl., and its adjoining cafe for classics and new releases in English and German. (☎040 41 32 03 20; www.abaton.de. Weekend reservations recommended.) In Altona, the **Zeise Kinos,** Friedensalle 7-9, offers themed film festivals and projects movies in the open-air courtyard of Altona's Rathaus on warm summer evenings (☎040 39 90 76 37; www.zeise.de).

NIGHTLIFE

St. Pauli, the Schanzenviertel, and Altona host Hamburg's unrepressed nightlife scene. The infamous **Reeperbahn,** a long boulevard that makes Las Vegas look like the Vatican, is the backbone of St. Pauli. Sex shops, strip joints, peep shows, and other establishments seeking to satisfy every lust compete for space with fast-food stands and regular theaters. This area is also home to many of the city's best clubs and bars, so don't let its reputed seediness scare you away from the party. On weekends, this street doesn't sleep, as discos and bars stay open nearly through the night. Though the Reeperbahn itself is reasonably safe for both men and women, it is not recommended for women to venture onto some of the less populated side streets alone. **Herbertstraße,** Hamburg's "official" prostitution strip, runs parallel to the Reeperbahn; its bright red barrier opens only to men 18+, but prostitutes patrol the area and nearby Davidstr. The industry is legal and regulated: all the prostitutes on Herbertstr. are licensed and required to have health inspections. If you attract unwanted attention, simply ignore it or respond with a firm *"Nein."*

Those who would rather avoid the hypersexed Reeperbahn should head north to the trendy streets of the **Schanzenviertel,** where students drink beers in cafes and enjoy the outdoors. Splattered with spectacular street art and wallpapered in posters that could be the products of high-end design schools, the neighborhood is steeped in creative energy. Much of Hamburg's **gay scene** is located in the **St. Georg** area, near **Berliner Tor** and along **Lange Reihe.** Gay and straight bars in this area are more welcoming and classier than those in the Reeperbahn, though larger parties spill back to St. Pauli. *Szene*, available at newsstands (€2.50), lists events, while the German-language gay magazines *hinnerk*, *Blu*, or *Schwulissimo*, and the more condensed *Gay Map*, list gay and lesbian events. In general, clubs open late and close late, with some techno and trance clubs remaining open past daybreak—consider napping before going out. Though bars are not as picky, you must be 18+ to enter most clubs.

ST. PAULI

If Hamburg is a party, Reeperbahn is the sweaty, scantily clad girl whom everyone wants to dance with. Take U3 to "St. Pauli" or S1 or S3 to "Reeperbahn."

Große Freiheit 36/Kaiserkeller, Große Freiheit 36 (☎040 317 7780; www.grosse-freiheit36.de). The Beatles played here during their early years. Today, young people pour in to hear everyone from Radiohead to the Roots. Though they fly under the same flag, Kaiserkeller caters to the rock and metal contingent in glamorously gothic-inspired, dungeon-like quarters, while Große Freiheit 36 attracts a more mainstream clubbing crowd. Cover €5-6, live bands €10-30. Live music or DJ usually 10:30pm-5am. Frequent free entry until 11pm. Cash only.

Docks, Spielbudenpl. 19 (☎040 317 8830; www.docks.de). Off the Reeperbahn, between Davidstr. and Taubenstr. A massive dancefloor, oil drum tables, and a movie theater alter ego make the Docks unique with the same throbbing electronica you've come to know and love. Drinks €1.50-8. Cover €4-8, sometimes €1 or free for students and women. Open F-Sa from 10 or 11pm. Cash only.

Meanie Bar/Molotow, Spielbudenpl. 5 (☎040 31 08 45; www.molotowclub.com). A basement club, Molotow takes pains to keep it hip with 70s decor and music, live bands, and horn-rimmed glasses. Upstairs, the nature-themed Meanie Bar (open daily 9pm-late) is more relaxed. Molotow cover €3-4, live bands €8-15. Open F-Sa 11pm-late, from 8pm for concerts. Cash only.

barbarabar (☎0160 9036 1519; www.barbarabar.de). Hamburger Berg 11. Like an inside-out party, an outdoor living room complete with sofas and armchairs on the sidewalk makes room for dancing. Casual barhoppers float in and out for beer (around €2.40) and mixed drinks (around €5). Open daily 8pm-late. Cash only.

Indra, Große Freiheit 64 (☎0174 49 74 61 23; www.indramusikclub.com). The newly formed Beatles played here in 1960, as ubiquitous photos attest. The club now draws younger crowds, but don't expect any ragers in this lounge-like atmosphere. Cover only for concerts. Open summer W-Su 6pm-2am or later. Cash only.

Cotton Club, Alter Steinweg 10 (☎040 34 38 78; www.cotton-club.de). U3 to "Rödingsmarkt." A Hamburg institution for over 45 years, this intimate club draws an older crowd for boisterous jazz, dixie, and swing. Cover from €5. Open M-Th 8pm-midnight, F-Sa 8pm-1am, Su 11am-3pm. Shows at 8:30pm. AmEx/MC/V.

SCHANZENVTIERTEL

Student cafes and bars fill the colorful and hip Schanzenviertel. Take U3, S21, or S31 to "Sternschanze."

Bedford Cafe, Schulterblatt 72 (☎040 43 18 83 32), on the corner of Schulterblatt and Susannesstr. Students and 20-somethings pack one of the trendiest bars in the Schanzenviertel inside and out. Salads and sandwiches €3.30-4.80. Beer €2-3.40. Mixed drinks €5-6. Open daily 10am-late. Cash only.

BP1, Schulterblatt 74 (☎040 432 2996). The fashionable and social of the Schanzenviertel float between the casual BP1 and its neighboring Bedford Cafe. It's all about new music and good company here, with experimental DJs supplying the soundtrack every night. Check the website for a performance schedule. Open daily 9pm-late. Cash only.

Goldfischglas, Bartelstr. 30. While some bars are stops along the way, Goldfischglas is a destination. Metallic fish swim across the walls and electronic aquarium while young guests lounge around the perimeter on low leather couches. Downstairs, a dance floor opens on weekends, with a DJ Th-Sa. Cocktails around €6. Open Su-W noon-2am, Th noon-3am, F-Sa noon-5am. Cash only.

III&70, Schulterblatt 73 (www.dreiundsiebzig.de). This all-purpose cultural center puts on several wildly popular faces: a popular cafe breakfast until 3pm, a happy hour from 5pm, and a night menu at 7pm. This is a province of partiers, feisty foosballers, and music heads. Check website for a schedule of short films, language roundtables, concerts, etc. €5 cover for shows. Wi-Fi. Open M-Sa 9am-late, Su 10am-late. Cash only

ALTONA

With lively but less rowdy cafes and bars, Altona is a calmer alternative to the craziness of St. Pauli. Take S1, S3, or S31 to "Altona."

Fabrik, Barnerstr. 36 (☎040 39 10 70; www.fabrik.de). This former weapons factory, complete with a rusted-out crane on top, now cranks out beats instead. For years, crowds have packed the 2-level club to hear big-name rock acts and an eclectic mix of other bands, with styles ranging from Latin to punk. Music nearly every day, beginning at 9pm. Every 2nd Sa of the month "Gay Factory" attracts a mixed crowd. Tickets €18-30. Live DJ most Sa nights at 10pm, cover €7-8. Cash only.

Waschbar, Ottenser Hauptstr. 56. (☎0179 232 5918). Gleaming, state-of-the-art machines and well-stocked bar make this not your usual laundromat. Residents crowd Waschbar to start the evening off with a beer (€2-2.90), hot chocolate (€2), or light fare (€4-7) while their clothes go for a spin (€3 per 6kg, soap €0.50, dryers €0.50 per 15min.). Happy hour M-Th and Su 7-10pm (mixed drinks €4) and F-Sa 8-11pm (mixed drinks €4.50-8.50). Live DJ 4 nights per week. Open daily 9am-late.

Insbeth, Bahrenfelder Str. 176 (☎040 390 1924). The over-the-top decor can only be described as celestial. Nevertheless, the 3-room cafe makes for a comfy hangout spot. The cheap, tasty breakfast is especially popular (1 *brötchen* with cold cuts €2, 1st cup of coffee included), served daily 10am-2:30pm. Sunday brunch also available (€6.50). Open M-Sa from 9am, Su from 10am, closes 2-4am. Cash only.

Reh, Nöltingstr. 84 (☎040 99 99 22 09). This elegant green-and-gold bar is well loved by Altona locals looking for a scene. Serves a variety of exotic mixed drinks (€6-8) and beer (€1.80-3.50) to a mixed clientele. Open daily 9:30am-2am. Cash only.

Imoto, Bahrenfelder Str. 206. A collage of colorful geometric shapes, Imoto personifies Altona's relaxed character. A young crowd enjoys the nightly DJ and relaxes on the wraparound couch and windowsill benches with beer (€2-3) or mixed drinks (€5.50-7, €4.50 until 10pm). Open daily 7pm-late. Cash only.

ST. GEORG

Hamburg's daytime gay scene can be reached by following Ernst-Merck-Str., which runs along the Hauptbahnhof's northern facade, to Lange Reihe.

Cube, Lange Reihe 88 (☎0173 313 6632). Mixed bar in the heart of St. Georg provides a relaxed yet vivacious alternative to the raucous pubs near the Reeperbahn. Mixed drinks €2-8. Happy hour until 10pm. Open daily from 7pm. Cash only.

Cafe Gnosa, Lange Reihe 93 (☎040 24 30 34; www.gnosa.de). A social nucleus for the gay community of St. Georg. Serves drinks (€2-5), appetizing desserts (€3-5), and tasty entrees (€5-9) in a bright, comfortable atmosphere to 20-somethings of mixed orientation. Free gay publications like *hinnerk* and *Hamburg's Gay Map* available. Open M-Th and Su 10am-1am, F-Sa 10am-2am. Cash only.

NIEDERSACHSEN AND BREMEN

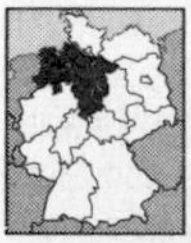

Niedersachsen (Lower Saxony) extends from the Ems River in the west to the Harz Mountains in the east, and from the North Sea down to the hills of central Germany. The deep forest around the Weser that inspired Grimm Brothers' fairy tales has retreated in the face of agriculture—a train ride through the region is a blur of corn and barley fields, windmills, and languid cows. In the remote East Frisian islands, fishermen still cling to their traditional language and culture, while the cities to the south constantly strive to outdo one another with new subway lines, shopping centers, and skyscrapers. The sea-faring cities of Bremen and Bremerhaven have united to make up Germany's smallest *Land*, a popular summertime destination.

HIGHLIGHTS OF NIEDERSACHSEN AND BREMEN

EXPLORE the independent *Land* of **Bremen** (p. 212) and its feisty residents, liberal political climate, and uncontainable **nightlife** in the student-dominated **Viertel.**

PEDAL along beautifully barren island trails in the **East Frisian Islands** (p. 220) before hitting the **superb beaches.**

SUBLATE THE PSYCHOLOGICAL IMMEDIACY OF ABSTRACT EXPRESSIONISM and other complicated things with the art at the **Sprengel Museum** in Hanover (p. 202).

SMELL THE ROSES in the **Herrenhausen** gardens, the wild animals at the **Erlebnis-Zoo Hannover** (p. 202), or **Hanover's** sweaty nightlife scene (p. 203).

WALK ON WATER along the mud flats in the **Wattenmeer National Park** (p. 220).

HANNOVER (HANOVER) ☎0511

Hanoverian George I ascended the British throne in the 18th century, making the successive three centuries of "English" royals *Deutsch* by lineage. The German-British connection endowed Hanover (pop. 523,000) with prominent status and numerous English gardens. Today, the city is a center of economic, social, and political activity. Broad avenues, pedestrian zones, and parks make the city a model of effective urban planning. Hanover is also home to a famous opera house, expansive museums, numerous summer outdoor festivals, and a vibrant nightlife, all of which contribute to making the city a cosmopolitan dreamboat on the river Leine. The 2000 World's Fair left a shining exhibition hall, new municipal facilities, and improved tourist services in its wake, and the city, saturated with modern art, remains abuzz at all hours.

TRANSPORTATION

Available at the tourist office and hostel, the **Hannover Card** (the budget traveler's lifesaver) provides public transportation within the city and to the airport, as well as free admission or discounts at several museums (1 day €9; 3 days €15; group ticket for up to 5 people €17/29). The card is valid from 7pm the day before use and the entire 24hr. of the day of use, so plan ahead and buy your ticket one day early to score some bonus hours.

Flights: Hanover's airport (☎0511 977 1223) is 30min. from the Altstadt. Schnellbuslinie (express bus) #60 and the S-Bahn run from the Hauptbahnhof to the airport. M-F every 20min. 5am-10:30pm, Sa-Su every 30min. 5:30am-10:30pm. €5.

Trains: Trains leave at least every hr. to: **Berlin** (2hr., €49-57); **Frankfurt** (2hr., €65); **Hamburg** (1hr., €29-34); and **Amsterdam, Netherlands** (4-5hr., €56-61).

Public Transportation: ÜSTRA, Hanover's mass-transit system, is extremely efficient. Pick up a free map of the U-Bahn and bus lines at the tourist office or the aluminum stand at the "Raschpl." bus stop behind the station. Stand open M-W and F 8am-6pm, Th 8am-7pm, Sa 9am-2pm. Buy tickets at machines or from drivers. Hanover has 3 zones with varying prices. **Kurzstrecke** (3 stops) €1; single ride €2-3.30, ages 6-11 €1; day ticket €3.90-6.30; group ticket for up to 5 people €7.80-12.60. The Altstadt and Mitte are both in Zone 1. **If your ticket does not have the date printed on it, you must punch it in a blue machine or risk a €40 fine.** For more information and maps, call or stop by the ÜSTRA customer service booth (☎0511 16 68 22 38) in the Kröpcke station. Open M-W and F 8am-6pm, Th 8am-7pm, Sa 9am-2pm.

Taxis: Taxi Ruf (☎0511 214 10), or **Funk Taxi Zentrale** (☎0511 38 11).

Bike Rental: Fahrradstation, Fernroderstr. 2 (☎0511 353 9640; www.fahrradstation.de), to your left as you exit the train station. €7.50 per day, €45 per week, €25 deposit. Open M-F 6am-11pm, Sa-Su 8am-11pm.

ORIENTATION AND PRACTICAL INFORMATION

In Old Saxon, *Hon overe* meant "high bank," referring to the city's position on the river Leine. The Hauptbahnhof is in **Mitte,** the heart of Hanover. **Bahnhofstraße** leads to the landmark **Kröpcke Cafe** and eventually south into the Altstadt. Below sprawls the underground **Passerelle,** a mall-like cave of cheap diners and souvenir shops. Behind the station is **Raschplatz,** home to a disco, film, and club scene. A pedestrian zone connects most of the center, including the shopping districts along **Georgstraße** and the **Altstadt.** The vibrant student quarter surrounding the university to the northwest of the city center is often overlooked. West of Mitte and just south of the university, **Limmerstraße** runs through **Linden,** historically a working-class area and now home to many artists, immigrants, and a burgeoning nightlife scene.

Tourist Office: Hanover Information, Ernst-August-Pl. 8 (☎0511 12 34 51 11). Across the street from the station, in the Spardabank building. Friendly staff finds rooms for a €2.50-6.50 fee (free by phone ☎0511 12 34 55 55), provides maps (€0.30) and information on cultural events, sells tickets to concerts and exhibits, and runs a full travel agency. Free hotel list available. Open M-F 9am-7pm, Sa 9am-2pm; Apr.-Sept. also Su 9am-2pm. The tourist office offers 12 themed **tours** (€3-15), including "Hanover's Cemeteries" and "Animal Magic." (☎0511 16 84 97 34.) To experience Hanover fully, follow the **Red Thread,** a 4km walking tour along a painted red line connecting all the sites. The Red Thread Guide (€2), available from the tourist office, details the tour in English.

Budget Travel: STA, Callinstr. 23 (☎0511 131 8531), in the same building as the Mensa. Open M-Th 9am-5pm, F 9am-4pm, Sa 10am-1pm.

Currency Exchange: ReiseBank, to the left just before the main exit of the train station. Open M-Sa 8am-10pm, Su 9am-10pm.

American Express: Georgstr. 54 (☎0511 368 1003), near the opera house in ReiseLand. Travel agency and card member services. Mail held up to 4 weeks for card members and Traveler's Cheque clients. Open M-F 9am-noon and 1-6pm, Sa 10am-1pm.

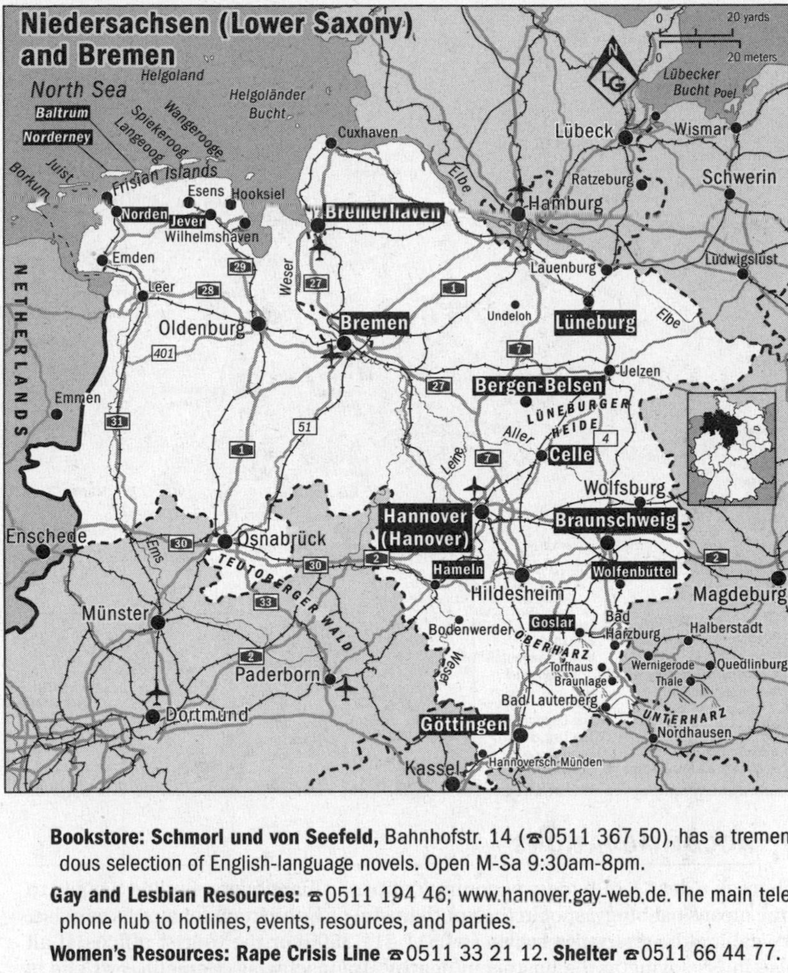

Bookstore: Schmorl und von Seefeld, Bahnhofstr. 14 (☎0511 367 50), has a tremendous selection of English-language novels. Open M-Sa 9:30am-8pm.

Gay and Lesbian Resources: ☎0511 194 46; www.hanover.gay-web.de. The main telephone hub to hotlines, events, resources, and parties.

Women's Resources: Rape Crisis Line ☎0511 33 21 12. **Shelter** ☎0511 66 44 77.

Laundromat: Münz Waschcenter, at Hildesheimer Str. and Siemensstr. From the station take U1, U2, or U8 (dir.: Ägidientorpl.) to "Altenbekener Damm." Backtrack 1 block; it's on the left. Wash €3.50. Dry €1 per 15min. Open daily 6am-11pm, last wash 10pm.

Emergency: Police ☎110. **Fire** ☎112. **Ambulance** ☎0511 192 22.

Pharmacy: Europa Apotheke, Georgstr. 16 (☎0511 32 66 18). Walk down Bahnhofstr. and turn right on Georgstr.; it's 150m down on the left. Assistance available in several languages. Open M-Sa 8am-8pm.

Internet Access: Weltcafe Telefon & Internet Cafe, on Kanalstr. (☎0511 21 35 91 01) off the Georgstr. pedestrian zone near Steintor. Internet (€1.25 per 30min.) or call home for cheap (€0.10 per min. to US/Canada/UK). Open M-Sa 9am-midnight.

Post Office: Right of the train station exit. Open M-F 9am-7pm, Sa 9:30am-2pm. **Postal Code:** 30159.

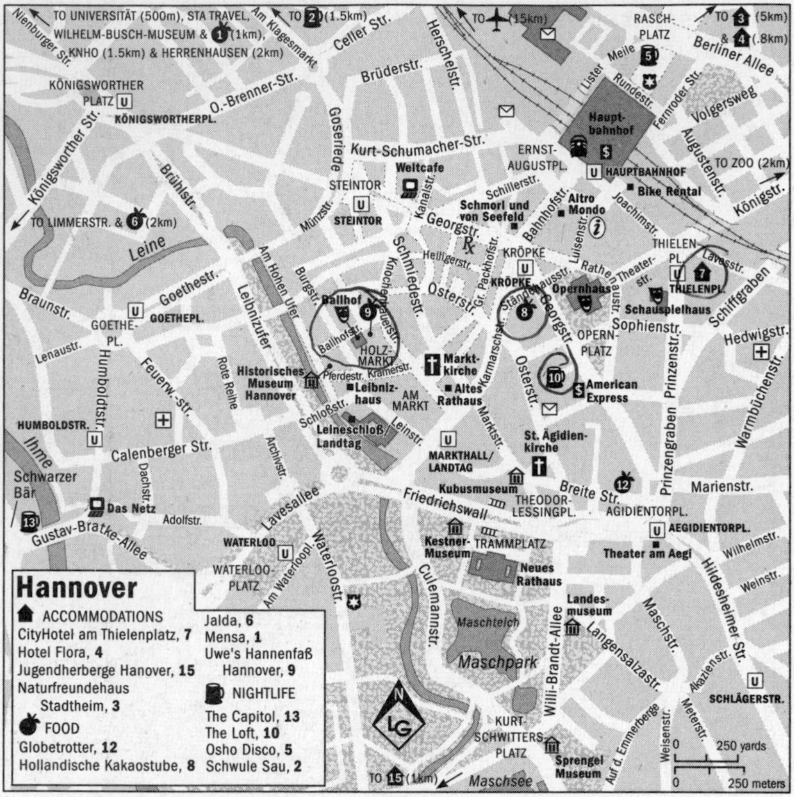

ACCOMMODATIONS

There is a dearth of budget accommodations in Hannover—finding a place to stay means nabbing a spot in the youth hostel or Naturfreundehaus. Otherwise, try calling the **reservation hotline** (☎0511 811 3500) or the tourist offices. If all else fails, staying in the hostels in nearby Braunschweig, Hamelin, or Celle is cheaper than settling for one of Hanover's royally priced hotels.

CityHotel am Thielenplatz, Thielenpl. 2 (☎0511 32 76 91). From the station, turn left onto Joachimstr. and go 1 block to Thielenpl. Prime location a few hundred yards behind the Opernhaus. Luxurious lobby and 150 beds in well-maintained, furnished rooms, all with TV and bath, some with panoramic views of the city. Glamorous, moderately priced hotel bar on a busy street. Breakfast €5. Check-out 11:30am. Singles from €55, doubles with shower from €62. MC/V. ❹

Naturfreundehaus Stadtheim, Hermann-Bahlsen-Allee 8 (☎0511 69 14 93). U3 (dir.: Lahe) or U7 (dir.: Fasanenkrug) to "Spannhagengarten." Walk back to the intersection and follow Hermann-Bahlsen-Allee to the left for 5min.; follow sign to your right into the narrow path. An environmentally friendly hostel with economical rooms far from town. Breakfast included. Reception 8am-noon and 3-10pm. Singles €20, over 27 €22. ❸

Jugendherberge Hannover (HI), Ferdinand-Wilhelm-Fricke-Weg 1 (☎0511 131 7674). Located near the Maschsee and 500m from the soccer stadium but far from nightlife options. U3 or U7 (dir.: Wettbergen) to "Fischerhof/Fachhochschule." From the stop, walk 10m back, turn right, cross the tracks, follow the path as it curves, and cross Stammestr. Go over the enormous red footbridge and turn right. Hostel is 50m down the road on the right. The Cadillac of youth hostels–spacious rooms with balconies, an airy dining room, and a fully stocked bar. 6-, 4-, and 2-bed, and single rooms available. Internet access €0.10 per min. Breakfast included. Reception 7:30am-1am. After 1am, doors open every hr. on the hr. €19.70 35.30. MC/V. ❷

FOOD

Hanover offers plenty in high culture, and growing options in cuisine. The pedestrian zone's expensive cafes cater to tourists—even the beloved Kröpcke diner, a favorite local meeting place for the last 50 years, has been bought out by ice cream czar Mövenpick. Find **groceries** at **Euro-Spar** by the Kröpcke U-Bahn stop (open M-Sa 7am-8pm) or walk from the Hauptbahnhof to the lively, clean, and well-decorated **Markthalle,** affectionately known as "the belly of Hanover," a food court where snacks, meals, and booze await. (Open M-W 7am-8pm, Th-F 7am-9pm, Sa 8am-5pm.) Along **Limmerstraße,** restaurants and *Imbiße* (snack bars) serve up cheap international flavors.

Uwe's Hannenfaß Hannover, Knochenhauerstr. 36 (☎0511 32 16 16), in the timber-framed house once home to Hanover's master brewer. Decor as heavy and dark as the vittles. The house-brewed Hannen Alt (€3.65 for 0.5L) accompanies steaming potato casserole Niedersachsenschmaus (€5), Jägerschnitzel (€6.50), and other specialties. Open M-Th and Su 4pm-2am, F 4pm-4am, Sa noon-4am. AmEx/MC/V min. €25. ❷

Hollandische Kakaostube, Standehausstr. 2-3 (☎0511 30 41 00). This hugely popular cafe features a dozen awe-inspiring hot chocolates (€3-6) and a truly decadent assortment of cakes. Try the *Mohrenkof* (merengue filled with hazelnuts and enrobed in chocolate; €1.85), or the rich marzipan cake (€2.20). The classy gold-accented dining room features a Titanic-esque winding staircase. Outdoor seating also available. Open M-Sa 9am-7:30pm and Su 9am-6pm. Cash only. ❷

Jalda, Limmerstr. 97 (☎0511 212 3261). Take U10 (dir.: Ahlem) to "Ungerstr." With Mediterranean-inspired cuisine, this restaurant serves popular Italian, Greek, and Arabic dishes, soups, pizza, and salads (€5-10). Weekdays bring 3-course lunch specials (€7). Eat dinner by candlelight to the sweet sound of funk. Open M-Th and Su 11:30am-12pm, F-Sa 11:30am-1am. Cash only. ❷

SIGHTS

HERRENHAUSEN GARDENS. In 1714, the crown of the United Kingdom was handed to George I, son of Hanover's Princess Sophie, in order to maintain Protestant rule in Britain. His descendants reigned over both Hanover and the UK until 1837, when the Hanoverians refused to accept the rule of Queen Victoria. The city owes much to Princess Sophie, who built the three Herrenhausen gardens. Here, the Princess waited to inherit the crown from Queen Anne, only to die just weeks too soon. The Baroque centerpiece of the gardens is the **Großer Garten,** where the striking geometry of the intricately laid paths in the landscaping manifests itself in square trees and spiral bushes, all overseen by godly statues. The **Große Fontäne,** one of Europe's highest fountains, builds to an astounding 80m and sprays unwitting downwind bystanders with cool mist. At the end of August, a dazzling fireworks contest adds to the spray in the sky. *(Fountain spurts Apr.-Oct. M-F 11am-noon and 3-5pm, Sa-Su 11am-noon and 2-5pm.*

Garden open daily Apr. to mid-Oct. 9am-8pm; mid-Oct. to Mar. 8am-dusk. Entrance €3, €4 including admission to Berggarten. Concerts and performances June-Aug.; ☎0511 16 84 12 22.) The wide-open meadows and broad, tree-lined paths—perfect for running or biking—of the **Georgengarten** might convince you that you are hundreds of kilometers from anything resembling a city. *Open 24hr. Free.)* The **Berggarten** has an indoor rainforest with a winding path ascending through the canopy amid tropical birds and butterflies. *(Berggarten open same hours as Großer Garten. €2. Rainforest open June-Aug. M-Th 10am-6pm, F 10am-10pm, Sa-Su 10am-8pm; Sept.-Oct. and Apr.-May M-Th 10am-5pm, F-Su 10am-8pm; Nov.-Mar. M-Th 10am-4pm, F-Su 10am-6pm. €8.50, students €5.50. Combination ticket €10, students €7.50, children €5.)*

NEUES RATHAUS. On the outskirts of the Altstadt, built over swampland and filled in with beech trees, is the spectacular Neues Rathaus. Don't be fooled by the palatial turn-of-the-century style—this beauty is indeed the new city hall, painstakingly recreated by Hanoverians after WWII. Inside, models depict the city in 1689, 1939, 1945, and today. Take the famous slanted elevator up the tower and see the city from 98m. *(Open May-Sept. M-F 9am-6pm, Sa-Su 10am-6pm. Elevator runs M-F 9:30am-6pm, Sa-Su 10am-6pm; ticket sales until 5:30pm. €2.50, students €2.)*

ERLEBNIS-ZOO HANOVER. More than 2500 animals live in this self-explanatory "experience zoo," specially designed to give visitors the sensation of observing wildlife in nature. Themed areas include the African Zambezi, the Indian Jungle Palace, and Gorilla Mountain. The swift lory, a colorful tropical bird, might decide to perch on your head inside the Tropical House. Swarms of people, dogs, and strollers fill the zoo on sunny afternoons. All shows free with admission. *(Adenauerallee 3. ☎0511 28 07 41 63; www.zoo-hannover.de. Take U11 to "Zoo." Open daily Mar.-Oct. 9am-6pm, Nov.-Feb. 10am-4pm. €19.50, children €13.50, under 4 free; dogs €8.)*

MUSEUMS

SPRENGEL MUSEUM. A 20th-century art lover's dream, with works by Beckmann, Dalí, Chagall, Klee, Magritte, Moore, Picasso, Turrel, and hometown hero Kurt Schwitters. One modernist installation holds you in a pitch-dark space for 5min. so your mind can become attuned to the light that is actually there. *(Kurt-Schwitters-Pl. At the corner of the Maschsee and Maschpark, near the Neues Rathaus. ☎0511 16 84 38 75; www.sprengel-museum.de. Open Tu 10am-8pm, W-Su 10am-6pm. Permanent collection €3.50, students €2; with special exhibits €7/4.)*

KESTNER-MUSEUM. August Kestner, Hanover's emissary to Rome, began this immensely entertaining collection with Egyptian and Greco-Roman artifacts he picked up abroad: miniature figurines, ancient Mediterranean glassware, and a sofa shaped like enormous lips. You need not be a chair enthusiast—but who isn't?—to appreciate the intriguingly large and terrific chair collection. *(Trampl. 3. Next to the Neues Rathaus. ☎0511 16 84 21 20; www.kestner-museum.de. Open Tu-Su 11am-6pm, W until 8pm. €5, students €4; F free.)*

LANDESMUSEUM (MUNICIPAL MUSEUM). The playful displays inside this child-friendly cultural museum include a vivarium of exotic lizards and fish, a non-European ethnology exhibit (jumbles of African masks, Oceanic weaponry, and Inuit huts), Neanderthal skulls, and paintings by Lieberman, Rubens, and Monet. *(Willy-Brandt-Allee 5. ☎0511 980 75; www.nlmh.de. Open Tu-Su 10am-5pm, Th 10am-7pm. €4, students €3, children €1.50, free F 2-5pm.)*

KUBUSMUSEUM. This Hanoverian artists' co-op shows contemporary art with origins ranging from local to international in a large one-room gallery on the second floor. *(Theodor-Lessing-Pl. 2, near the Ägidienkirche. ☎0511 16 84 57 90. Open Tu-F 11am-6pm, Sa-Su 11am-4pm. €3, students €2.)*

FESTIVALS

If you're within a 100km radius of Hanover the first week in July, detour to its **Schützenfest** (marksmanship festival), the largest such fête in the world. Every summer since 1539, Hanoverians have congregated—weapons in hand—to test their marksmanship before retreating to the beer gardens. The 10-day festival in early July comes complete with parade, fireworks, and amusement park rides, but its main attraction is the **Lüttje Lage,** a feisty traditional drink: you down the contents of two shot glasses simultaneously, holding them side by side in one hand and trying not to spill. One glass contains *Weißbier*, the other schnapps. This party is a mere warm-up for the **Maschseefest** (late July to early Aug.), which provides another wild mix of concerts, masked balls, and street performances. Hanoverians let loose at the **Altstadtfest** the first or second weekend in August. The annual international **Feuerwerk** (Fireworks) competition in the Herrenhausen Gardens also lights the skies in August. The **Flohmarkt** (flea market) on the **Leibnizufer** hits town every Saturday 7am-2pm.

ENTERTAINMENT AND NIGHTLIFE

More than 20 theaters supply Hanover with ballet, opera, and theater. The four largest are the **Opernhaus,** Opernpl. 1; the **Ballhof,** Ballhofstr. 5; the **Schauspielhaus,** on Theaterpl.; and the **Theater am Ägi,** on Ägidientorpl. Tickets for most shows (from €10) are sold at the tourist office (ticket line ☎0511 30 14 30). The monthly *Hannover Vorschau* and *Hannover Live*, free at the tourist office, list cultural events, and the Opernhaus provides a free guide to opera and ballet. **KNHO,** Schaufelder Str. 30 (☎0511 70 38 14; www.kino-im-sprengel.de), near the university, shows art-house flicks. Take U6 or 11 to "Kopernikusstr."

When the sun goes down, Hanover lights up with an array of packed cafes, *Kneipen*, and sweaty discos. The university crowds swarm Linden-Nord, the area beginning at Goethepl. and running along Limmerstr. For parties, snoop around the Mensa for signs, or check *Prinz* (€1) or *Schädelspalter* (€2.50), both available at the tourist office and newsstands. The free *MagaScene* (www.magascene.de) lists clubs and concerts. For live music, check out *The Capitol* or **Altro Mondo,** Bahnhofstr. 8 (☎0511 32 33 27), in the City-Passage. (Tickets can be purchased at ☎0511 41 99 99 40.)

The Loft, Georgstr. 50a (☎0511 473 93 10), near Kröpcke. The mood-lighting at this hip spot draws packs of students on weekends. Go down alleyway to enter this bar or its companion bistro **Masa.** Enjoy falafel (€3.50) and milkshakes (€3) next to the waterfall in the garden. Happy hour M-Th and Su 9-10pm, F-Sa 1-2am. Masa open daily noon-1am. Loft open daily 8pm-2am, F-Sa 8pm-4am. Cash only.

The Capitol, Schwarzer Bär 2 (☎0511 304 49). U9 to "Schwarzer Bär," and walk back toward the river. Loosen up in a sea of bumping bodies. F nights "Dancing Queen" or "Destiny's Child" (discount with student ID). Sa nights the disco moves to the main hall to make way for live indie rock bands. Cover €2-5. Open F 10pm-3am, Sa 10pm-6am.

Osho Disco, Raschpl. 7L (☎0511 34 22 17; www.osho-disco.de). At the round, banner-covered building just behind the train station, DJs spin everything from house to Frank Sinatra. Rest your feet upstairs with the dolphins. Lots of themed parties and a long drink list. Every W is "Forever Young"—ages 30+ no cover. 18+. Cover €5-10, including one drink. F cover €2, Sa €2.50. Open W-Su from 10pm. Cash only.

Schwule Sau, Schaufeldstr. 30 (☎0511 700 05 25). U6 or U11 to "Kopernikusstr.," exit left on An der Lutherkirche and turn right on Schaufeldstr. It's on the left, entrance on the far side of building. Popular gay and lesbian bar in the university district. Weekly themed parties. Tu ladies only 10pm-2am. W men only 8pm-2am. Tea and cake Su afternoons. Open Tu-Sa from 9pm, Su from 2pm. Cash only.

GÖTTINGEN ☎0551

Home to Europe's first free university, Göttingen (pop. 129,000) is a college town to the core. Although the university counts Otto von Bismarck, J.P. Morgan, and the Brothers Grimm among its alumni, Göttingen's real fame comes from the sciences. Over 40 Nobel laureates have studied or worked here, including Max Planck (the father of quantum mechanics) and Werner Heisenberg (the head of the Nazi atomic bomb project and its alleged saboteur). Completely independent of the German government since its inception, the university has historically taken extreme political positions—far left in 1734, reactionary right in the 1920s, and back again to the left in the 1950s, earning its reputation as a *rote Uni* (red university).

TRANSPORTATION

Trains: 2 per hr. to: **Berlin** (2hr., €45.20); **Frankfurt** (2hr., €34.30); **Hamburg** (2hr., €49.40); **Hanover** (1hr., €18.30).

Public Transportation: Most **GöBV** buses stop at the central "Markt" in 1 direction and "Kornmarkt" in the other. Single ride good for 1hr. (€1.80). Day tickets (€4) good until buses stop running, usually 11pm. For schedule and info, visit www.goevb.de.

Taxis: Hallo Taxi ☎0551 340 34. 24hr. Also offers night taxis for women.

Car Rental: Europcar, Groner Landstr. 27 (☎0551 54 71 90). Open daily 7:30am-midnight. Prices from €69 a day.

Bike Rental: Fahrrad-Parkhaus (☎0551 599 94), to the left facing the station's main exit. From €11 per day. Open M-Sa 5:30am-10pm, Su 8am-11pm.

ORIENTATION AND PRACTICAL INFORMATION

The Altstadt, encircled by an ancient wall, is bisected along a north-south axis by Weender Str., which becomes Kornmarkt south of the Markt. At the center are the **Altes Rathaus** and **Wilhelmsplatz,** the original site of the university.

Tourist Office: Markt 9 (☎0551 49 98 00; www.goettingen-tourismus.de), in the Altes Rathaus. From the station, walk straight across the green and follow Goetheallee into the Altstadt. Turn right onto Weender Str.; it's up the stairs on the right side of the Markt. Free maps and room booking, along with city **tours** (1½hr., €5.50). Open Apr.-Oct. M-F 9:30am-6pm, Sa-Su 10am-4pm; Nov.-Mar. closed Su.

Currency Exchange: Commerzbank, Prinzenstr. 2 (☎0551 40 80), has the best rates in town. Open M-W 9am-4pm, Th 9am-6pm, F 9am-5:30pm.

Laundromat: Wasch-Salon, Ritterplan 4 (www.derwaschsalon.de), opposite the Städtisches Museum. Wash €3. Soap €0.50. Dry €0.70. Open M-Sa 7am-10pm.

Bookstore: Deuerlich, Weender Str. 33 (☎0551 495 00 0). Across from the Jakobikirche; stocks English-language books with gusto. Open M-F 9am-7pm, Sa 9am-6pm.

Emergency: ☎110. **Police station** (☎0551 49 10), Groner Landstr. 51. **Fire** ☎112.

Pharmacy: Universitäts-Apotheke, Markt 6 (☎0551 588 49). Helping students cure headaches and "other illnesses" since 1734. Open M-F 8:30am-7pm, Sa 9am-4pm.

Internet Access: Media-Room Service, Kurze-Geismar-Str. 45 (☎0551 488 28 56). €1 per hr. Open M-F 9am-10pm, Sa 10am-10pm, Su noon-8pm.

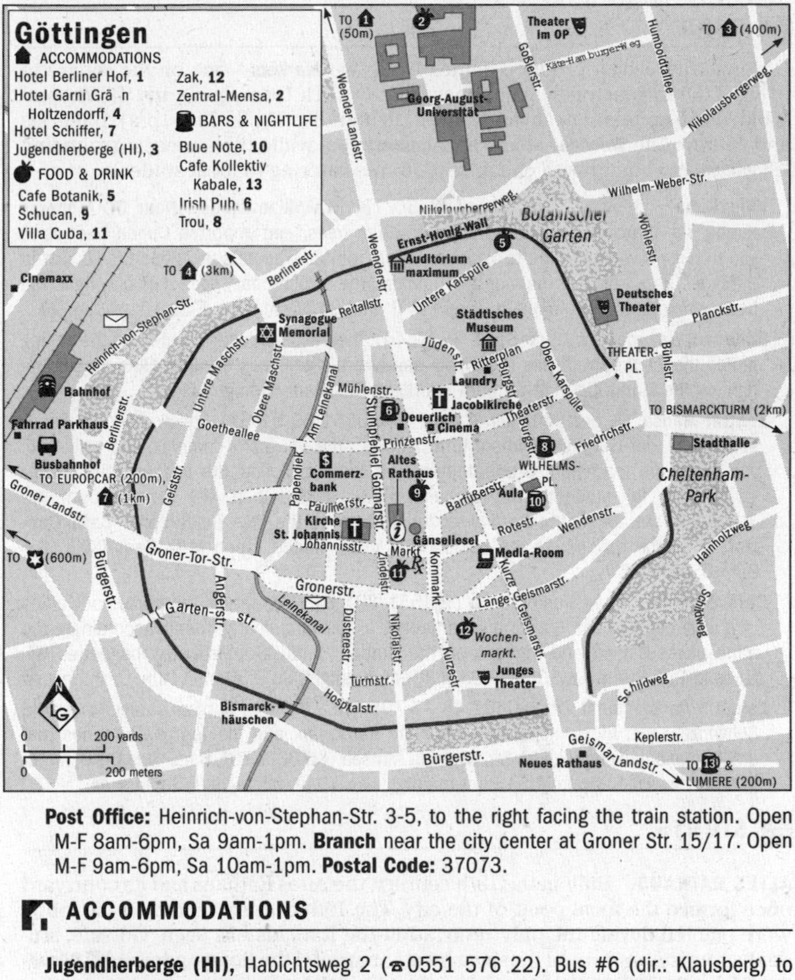

Post Office: Heinrich-von-Stephan-Str. 3-5, to the right facing the train station. Open M-F 8am-6pm, Sa 9am-1pm. **Branch** near the city center at Groner Str. 15/17. Open M-F 9am-6pm, Sa 10am-1pm. **Postal Code:** 37073.

ACCOMMODATIONS

Jugendherberge (HI), Habichtsweg 2 (☎0551 576 22). Bus #6 (dir.: Klausberg) to "Jugendherberge," across the street and down the path. Helpful staff and a pool table and volleyball court. Breakfast and sheets included. Internet €3 per hr.; Wi-Fi available. Reception 6:30am-midnight. Curfew midnight; keys available. Check-out 9am. Dorms €24.50, under 27 €21.50; doubles €51/45, singles €26.50/23.50. MC/V. ❷

Hotel Berliner Hof, Weender Landstr. 43 (☎0551 38 33 20; www.berlinerhof.de). Bus #10 from the station (dir.: Herberhausen) to "Auditorium"and walk up Weender Landstr. toward the university. Simply decorated rooms with TV and phone. Large 3-bedroom suites (€77) are ideal for groups. Free Wi-Fi. Breakfast included. Reception 8am-11pm. Singles €34, with shower €40-44; doubles with showers €65-75. AmEx/MC/V. ❸

Hotel Garni Gräfin Holtzendorff, Ernst-Ruhstrat-Str. 4 (☎0551 639 87). From the station, take bus #13 (dir.: Esebeck) to "Florenz-Sartorius-Str." Continue in the direction of the bus and take the 1st left. Though somewhat distant, the leafy courtyard garden feels like a retreat. Breakfast included. Singles €32, with bath €50; doubles €58/65-72. ❸

FOOD

Göttingen's freshest produce comes from two **markets**—one on the square in front of the **Rathaus,** open in summer (Apr.-Oct. Th 10am-8pm), and the **Wochenmarkt,** off Hospitalstr. near the Junges Theater (Tu, Th, Sa 7am-1pm). Bakeries and *Imbiße* line **Weender Straße** and **Jüdenstraße,** while the streets surrounding **Wilhelmsplatz** abound with cheap restaurants catering to local students.

Villa Cuba, Zindelstr. 2 (☎0551 488 66 78; www.villacuba.de). Near St. Johannis Kirche. The thatched roof above the bar, palm trees, and imported Cuban beer send you through a vacuum-tube to Havana. Tapas from €5, Creole specialties €5-10. Eat in the *Fidel Garten* or near the fountain upstairs. The revolutionary speeches playing in the bathroom impart an epic quality. Open M-Th and Su 10am-2am, F-Sa 10am-3am. ❷

Schucan, Weender Str. 11 (☎0551 48 62 44). The pastel toucans painted on the ceiling match the ice cream dishes (€2-5) by day, and the cocktails at night. Outdoor seating right on the Markt. Open M-Sa 9am-midnight, Su 10am-midnight. ❷

Zentral-Mensa, Pl. der Göttinger Sieben 4 (☎0551 39 51 51). Follow Weender Landstr. onto Pl. der Göttinger Sieben, turn right into the university complex, and walk until you reach the mammoth Studentenwerk on the left. Follow the line upstairs. Meals €1.80-3.80 for students, non-students €2.20-4.30. Open M-F 9am-3:30pm, Sa 10am-2:40pm. Avoid the hordes at lunch time at the less institutional **Cafe Central,** down the hall, where the selection is more limited. Open M-Th 9am-7:30pm, F 9am-6:30pm. ❶

Cafe Botanik, Untere Karspüle 1b (☎0551 391 31 00), serves botanical specialties in a cozy bend by the Stadtmauer adjacent to the botanical gardens. Accordingly, the atmosphere is lush and fragrant on the outdoor patio. Sophisticated baguettes €4. Open M-Th 9:30am-11:30pm, F-Sa 9:30am-midnight, Su 9:30am-11pm. Cash only. ❷

Zak, Am Wochenmarkt 22 (☎0551 48 77 70), has a menu of burgers named for Arnold Schwarzenegger films, including *Conan the Barbarian,* and the *Terminator* series that are lean and juicy enough for Mr. Olympia himself (€6.60-8.70). Baguettes €4-5, Arnie-free entrees €5-8. Open M-Sa 9am-midnight, Sa 10am-midnight. F-Sa later. ❷

SIGHTS

ALTES RATHAUS. Built in the 13th century, the Altes Rathaus and its courtyard once formed the focal point of the city. The 19th-century murals in the lobby were painted during the only renovation the Rathaus has seen. Outside, students, tourists, and street musicians gather around the flower-adorned **Gänseliesel fountain.** It is customary for graduates of the university, upon completing their degree, to kiss the innocent maiden on the cheek.

BISMARCK SIGHTS. The **Bismarckhäuschen,** built into the city wall in 1459, is a tiny stone cottage. Here, the 17-year-old law student Otto von Bismarck took up residence after authorities expelled him from the inner city for overzealous partying. On display is his 1832-1833 class schedule, as well as his wooden student ID. *(From behind the Rathaus, walk down Zindelstr. and follow it as it becomes Nikolaistr.; just before the intersection with Bürgerstr., turn right by the bus stop onto the footpath on top of the wall; the house is on your left. ☎0551 48 62 47. Open Tu 10am-1pm, W-Th and Sa 3-5pm. Free.)* The **Bismarckturm** (Bismarck Tower) in the Hainberg forest east of town affords a great view of the city. *(Im Hainberg. Bus #9 to "Hainbundstr.," then continue up the hill, following Bismarckstr. as it winds into the woods. After about 1km, watch for signs pointing to the tower, on your left. ☎0551 561 28. Open Apr.-Oct. Sa-Su 11am-6pm. Free.)*

MEDIEVAL CHURCHES. Göttingen is home to several notable churches. Inside the **Jacobikirche,** the modern and the ecclesiastical collide. In 1480, artists who had just discovered the secrets to perspective had a field day checkering the columns with patterns that create ambiguous, illusory contours, vacillating between concave and convex. Other, cylindrical columns are made to appear octagonal. *(Corner of Prinzenstr. and Weender Str. ☎0551 575 96. Open daily 11am-3pm. Free. Tower open Sa from 11am. €2. Services Su 10am; organ music F 6pm.)* Behind the Altes Rathaus stands the fortress-like **Sankt Johannis-Kirche,** whose 301-step tower housed students for 80 years. Without toilets or running water in the church, the students were evicted for sanitary reasons in 2001. *(Am Johanniskirchhof 2. ☎0551 48 62 41. Open daily 11am-1pm and 4-6pm. Tower open Sa 2-4pm.)*

SYNAGOGUE MEMORIAL SCULPTURE. On Untere Maschstr., this sculpture stands on the former site of a Göttingen synagogue, razed in 1938. Steel triangles of steadily decreasing size twist back and forth, forming a spiraling tree. Plaques list the names of Jews from the synagogue who died during WWII. Viewed from above, the memorial forms a Star of David.

ENTERTAINMENT

Deutsches Theater, Theaterpl. 11 (☎0551 49 69 11; www.dt-goettingen.de), presents classics, contemporary plays, and improv. Tickets €8-21.50, students €5-12. Box office open M-F 10am-1:30pm and 5-8pm, Sa 11am-2pm, and 1hr. before shows.

Junges Theater, Hospitalstr. 6 (☎0551 49 50 15; www.junges-theater.de). This edgy but top-notch theater presents a new outlook on both classic and innovative works. Box office open Tu-Sa 11am-2pm and 30min. before shows. Tickets €13, students €9.

Theater im OP, Käthe-Hamburger-Weg 3 (☎0551 39 70 77; www.thop.uni-goettingen.de). Where doctors used to make a spectacle out of tinkering with organs, students now tinker with scripts: the university operating theater. Box office open Tu and Th 2-4pm. Tickets €9, students €6; can also be purchased at the tourist office.

Cinema: The cosmopolitan **Lumière,** Geismarer Landstr. 19 (☎0551 48 45 23), housed in Cafe Kollektiv Kabale (p. 207), plays art-house films daily and also hosts open-air cinema Jul.-Aug. at the Freibad am Brauweg swimming pool, south of the city. Shows Th-Sa, usually 10pm. Tickets €6.50/6, includes swimming pool admission.

NIGHTLIFE

University students maintain a traditional hardy pub scene. Check out the bars on **Wilhelmsplatz,** or along **Hospitalstraße,** near the southern edge of the city.

Trou, Burgstr. 20 (☎0551 439 71; www.trou.de). This 500-year-old, candlelit cellar has been Göttingen's most intimate watering hole for 45 years. People cluster around barrels amid light jazz. A specialty is *Altbierbowle mit Erdbeeren* (strawberries in a 0.3L-bowl of Diebels beer; €2.70). Open M-Th 7:30pm-2am, F-Su until 3am.

Irish Pub, Mühlenstr. 4 (☎0551 456 64; www.irishpub-goettingen.de.), winner of Guinness' "Most Entertaining Pub" award. Popular student bar with lots of Guinness (€3.90 a pint) and live Irish music nightly at 10pm (summer 3 times per week). 0.5L beer on tap €2. M-Th and Su special offers on beer. Open daily 3pm-3am.

Blue Note, Wilhelmspl. 3 (☎0551 469 07), in the corner, under the Aula. The most diverse venue for music in the Altstadt features a different theme every day (jazz, reggae, and African pop are favorites). W and Su salsa dancing (€2.50 includes €1.50 drink credit). F-Sa discos €3. Open W and F-Su 10pm-4am.

Cafe Kollektiv Kabale, Geismarlandstr. 19 (☎0551 48 58 30; www.cafe-kabale.de). Head past the Neues Rathaus (5min.) and watch for the sign on your left. Hidden behind a stone wall, this progressive cafe oozes culture. Liberal socio-political slogans scrawled on the walls. Call for schedule of theme parties, art exhibitions, and poetry readings. Tu Lesbian bar 8:30pm. Open M-F 4pm-1am, Sa 2pm-1am, Su 10am-1am.

GOSLAR ☎05321

Tiny Goslar (pop. 45,700) is one of Niedersachsen's most historic and culturally prominent cities. Spared from WWII air raids by proclaiming neutrality, and home to an avant-garde art institution, the *Mönchehaus*, historic Goslar holds a fluid mixture of half-timbered homes and modern sculptures. The town's beauty and proximity to the Harz Mountains draw intimidating crowds of tourists, but the town retains the charm that once lured Goethe and Henry Moore.

TRANSPORTATION AND PRACTICAL INFORMATION

Trains roll to: Brunswick (45min., every hr., €6.60); Göttingen (1hr., every hr., €14.60); Hanover (1hr., 2 per hr., €16.60). A hub for the extensive RBB **bus** network, Goslar is a convenient gateway to the region (www.rbb-bus.de; tickets €1.70, *Tageskarte* €5). For a good price on **bike** rental, head to **Hans Speed,** Kuhlenkamp 1c. (☎05321 68 57 34; www.hans-speed.de. Open M-F 10am-1pm and 2:30-6pm, Sa 10am-2pm. 3hr. rental €4, 5hr. €8, 8hr €13.) The **tourist office,** Markt 7, across from the Rathaus, books rooms (from €20) for free and sells maps (€1.50). The free museum guide contains a useful map of the city center, with major sights marked. (☎05321 780 60; www.goslar.de. Open May-Oct. M-F 9:15am-6pm, Sa 9:30am-4pm, Su 9:30am-2pm; Nov.-Apr. M-F 9:15am-5pm, Sa 9:30am-2pm.) **Tours** of the Altstadt depart from the Markt daily at 10am (2hr.; €5.60) and May-Oct. and Dec. M-Sa 1:30pm (1½hr., €4). **GE Money Bank,** Shuhhof 6-8, has a **24hr. ATM** near the Rathaus. (Open M-Th 9am-1pm and 2-6pm, F 9am-1pm and 2-4pm.) Get **internet** access at **Telecenter,** Breitestr. 79. (☎05321 381 80. Open M-Sa 10:30am-8pm. €1.80 per hr.) The **post office** is at Klubgartenstr. 10. (Open M-F 8:30am-6pm, Sa 9am-12:30pm.) **Postal Code:** 38640.

ACCOMMODATIONS AND FOOD

The half-timbered **Jugendherberge (HI) ❷,** Rammelsberger Str. 25, is a bit of a hike; it's best to take bus #803 from the train station (dir.: Bergbaumuseum) to "Theresienhof." (10min., every hr. until 8pm; €1.70). Continue along in the same direction, and take a sharp left up the hill at the white "Jugendherberge" sign. The small rooms provide a stunning view of the mountains and farmland. (☎05321 222 40. Breakfast and sheets included. Reception 8am-10pm, call if arriving later. Curfew 10pm, keys available. Dorms €19, over 27 €22; singles €24/27, with bath €25.80/28.80.) For something closer and cozier, try **Gästehaus Schmitz ❸.** Bright second-floor rooms ring the courtyard of this darling half-timbered house near the Markt. All rooms with bath. Kitchen access. Facing the Glockenspiel, take Kornstr. straight ahead on the right. The pension comes up on the second corner with Domstr. (☎05321 234 45. Singles €39, doubles €50. Breakfast included. Single-night stays add €2. Cash only.)

The town has a weekday **market** (Tu and F 8am-1pm) on **Jakobikirchhof,** while cheap *Imbiße* (snack bars) abound along **Hokenstrasse** On the Markt, pricey restaurants poach tourists. Head to nearby **Markt Treff ❷,** Fleischscharren 6, for fast, cheap German favorites for €2.50-7.50. (☎05321 30 67 61. Open daily 10am-8pm. Cash only.) At the rustic **Paulaner ❸,** Gemeindehof 3-5, busty barmaids and knickered men serve refined deer goulash (€11.80) and Bavarian specialties (€9) inside a creaky half-timbered cabin. A full gamut of Munich beers complements the hearty fare, and outdoor seating abounds between a lazy watermill and a castle-like music school. (☎05321 260 70; www.paulaner-an-der-lohmuehle.de. Open daily 11am-10pm. Entrees €7-14. MC/V, €15 min.) Find festive pub fare at **Brauhaus Wolpertinger ❷,** Martallstr. 1, a *Biergarten* in a 16th-century courtyard. (☎05321 221 55; www.wolpertinger-brauhaus.de. Entrees €6-9. Open M-F noon-2pm and 5pm-midnight, Sa noon-2am, Su 10am-midnight; closing times approximate. MC/V.) Music, beer, and the local 20-something crowd converge at **Kö Musik-Kneipe,** Marktstr. 30, which also keeps free internet on tap. (☎05321 268 10; www.musikkneipe-koe.de. Open M-Th 4pm-2am, F-Sa 4pm-3am. Live music takes a pause in summer. MC/V.)

SIGHTS

RAMMELSBERG. The sprawling 1000-year-old mine complex that made Goslar prosperous welcomes visitors into its bowels and refineries, now a giant museum. The **Magazine building** surveys the mine's history, dating back to the Dukes of Brunswick, and glorifies the trade with exhibits on miner culture, including music, sports, and garb. The ore-processing facility is now a dark maze of industrial machinery, showcasing lunar-looking minerals under glowing lights. The **Power Plant building** shows special mine-related exhibits and art amid bizarre nozzled tanks and old wagons. In addition to the museum, the mine offers two 1hr. excursions into the mountain. The **"Roeder Stollen" tour** journeys on foot into an 18th-century mine, while the **"Train Ride" tour** displays more modern techniques from aboard an underground locomotive. *(Bergtal 19. Catch bus #803 from the "Brusttuch" stop behind the Marktkirche and ride until "Bergbaumuseum" (7min., every hr. until 8pm, €1.70). Or, make the 800m walk down Rammelsberger Str. from the Jugendherberge. ☎05321 75 01 22; www.rammelsberg.de. Open daily 9am-6pm. Tours leave every hr. 9:30am-4:30pm. Museum €6, tours €5 each. Under 16 €3.50/3. Call for English tours.)*

MUSIKINSTRUMENTEN- UND PUPPENMUSEUM. Owned by a former musical clown in a traveling circus, the museum retains a certain sideshow flair. Germany's largest private instrument collection gives Leipzig's Grassi museum a run for its money. See violins of all shapes and sizes: double-sided, pocket violins, and even one made of Meißen porcelain, as well as multi-belled trumpets, meter-long harmonicas, and other freaks of sound. Upstairs, a village of dolls gazes back at you—it's a little bit creepy. *(Hoher Weg 5. ☎05321 269 45. Open daily 11am-5pm. €3, children €1.50.)*

KAISERPFALZ. Guarded by a pair of bronze Brunswick lions, this austere Romanesque palace served as a summer residence for 11th- and 12th-century emperors. Its glory was short-lived, however, as the palace was abandoned and subsequently converted into a prison. By the 19th century it had fallen into disrepair, but a romantic infatuation with the Middle Ages led a group of Prussian aristocrats to restore it to its prior majesty. The **Reichssaal** (Imperial Hall) is plastered with jaw-dropping murals, painted over 18 years, depicting fairy tales and emperors. In the palace's **Ulrichskapelle,** Heinrich III lies inside a massive sarcophagus, while the stone entrance still bears evidence of its stint as the town jail. *(Kaiserbleek 6. ☎05321 311 9693. Open daily Apr.-Oct. 10am-5pm, Nov.-Mar. 10am-4pm. Last entry 30min. before closing. €4.50, under 18 €2.50. Ask for an English guide.)*

GLOCKEN-UND-FIGURENSPIEL. The clocktower rings four times each day as a sea of tourists looks on, necks craned and cameras poised for the next perfect shot. At each performance, figures of nobles and miners emerge from the former treasury roof and dance to songs once sung in the Rammelsberg mine shafts. *(Chimes at 9am, noon, 3, and 6pm.)*

MÖNCHEHAUS. This media-drenched museum houses racy video displays and cutting-edge modern art exhibitions in a half-timbered home. The museum annually awards the prestigious **Kaiserring** prize to a modern artist based on a vote by the townspeople. Recipients include Henry Moore, Willem de Kooning, and Cindy Sherman. *(Mönchestr. 1. ☎05321 295 70; www.moenchehaus.de. Open Tu-Su 10am-5pm. €5, students €1.50.)*

HAMELN (HAMELIN) ☎05151

In the 700 years since the Rattenfänger (Pied Piper) last strolled out of town, his talents have kept this once-obscure German village in the limelight. On June 26, 1284, after Hamelin (pop. 59,000) failed to pay the piper his rat-removal fee, he walked off with 130 children in thrall. Today, tourists still flock to the charming town. In addition to the day's worth of sights in the city itself, Hamelin is a gateway to the region; buses connect nearby countryside castles and the villages tucked between them.

TRANSPORTATION AND PRACTICAL INFORMATION

Hamelin bridges the Weser River and is 45min. from Hanover by **train** (2 per hr., €9.10). **Flotteweser,** Deisterallee 1 (in the same building at the tourist office), runs **ferries** up and down the Weser to Bodenwerder, Holzminden, and Hannoversch Münden. (☎05151 93 99 99; www.flotte-weser.de. Operates May-Oct. Call for schedule. 1hr. trip €6.50, children €3.50; 2hr. €10.50/5.) For a **taxi,** call ☎05151 74 77, 33 38, or 122 00. Rent **bikes** from **Troche Fahrrad-Shop,** Kreuzstr. 7. (☎05151 136 70. www.trochebike.de. €10 per day; €45 per week. Open M-F 9:30am-1pm and 2:30-6pm, Sa 9:30am-1pm.) The **tourist office,** Deisterallee 1, on the Bürgergarten, books rooms (from €20) for free and lists hotels and pensions. From the station, cross Bahnhofpl., make a right on Bahnhofstr., and turn left on Deisterstr., which becomes Deisterallee. (☎05151 95 78 23; www.hameln.de. Open May-Sept. M-F 9am-6:30pm, Sa 9:30am-4pm, Su 9:30am-1pm; Oct.-Apr. M-F 9am-6pm, Sa 9:30am-1pm.) **Tours** leave from the tourist office. (M-Sa 2:30pm, Su 10:15am. €4, children €2.) To reach the Altstadt, cross the road just past the tourist office. **Matthias Buchhandlung,** Bäckerstr. 56, has English paperbacks. (☎05151 947 00. Open M-F 9am-7pm, Sa 9am-6pm). Access the **internet** at **Witte: Bürotechnik,** Kopmanshof 69. (☎05151 994 40. Open M-F 9am-6pm, Sa 10am-2pm. €2 per 30min.) The **post office** is at Ostertorwall 22a. Walk along Ostertorwall so that the Altstadt is to the right. (Open M-F 9am-6pm, Sa 9am-1pm.) **Postal Code:** 31785.

ACCOMMODATIONS

Hamelin's tourism boom has spawned a large number of pensions, listed in a detailed free brochure provided by the tourist office. The best deal is **Gästehaus Alte Post ❷,** Hummenstr. 23, in the Altstadt, offering colorful rooms complete with Picasso prints, TV, phone, and clock radio. (☎05151 434 44; ottokater@aol.com. Breakfast included. Reception 11:30am-2:30pm and 5pm-midnight; call ahead to arrange other times. Check-out 11am. Singles €25-35; doubles €50-65. Cash only.) The scenic **Jugendherberge (HI) ❶,** Fischbeckerstr. 33, sits on a bend in the Weser River, a 20min. walk north of the Altstadt. From the station, take bus #2 to "Wehler Weg" and make a right on Fischbecker Str. To get there on foot, cross the street north of Altstadt and walk down Erichstr. Make a left onto Fischbeckerstr. at Mertens-Platz. (☎05151 34 25. Breakfast included. Reception 12:30-1:30pm (if you call ahead) and 5-9pm. Curfew 10pm, key available with €15 deposit. €15.20, over 27 €18. MC/V.) Southeast of the city center on the shores of Tönebon Lake, **Campground Jugendzeltplatz ❶**, Tönebonweg 8, has warm showers and a sauna. Take bus #44 or 51 (only runs a few times per day) to "Südbad." It's 30min. by foot from the city center. (☎05151 262 23. Reception 8am-8pm. Open May-Sept. €3 per person.)

FOOD

Hamelliners stock up on fruit, vegetables, and other treats at the open-air market on the **Bürgergarten** (W and Sa 8am-1pm.) The streets of the Altstadt around **Osterstraße** and **Pferdemarkt** are lined with restaurants and cafes, but the chances of finding a bargain are slim, particularly on Osterstr. Some good deals await along Bäckerstr. near the Münster or in the alleys branching off from the touristy cafe area. **Mexcal ❸**, Osterstr. 15, serves excellent, if unexpected, German-Mexican meals and inexpensive lunch specials (noon-3pm; burritos, rice, and drink €5). (☎05151 428 06. Dinners €6-10. Happy hour 3-6pm and 11pm-close mixed drinks €4. Open M-Th noon-midnight, F and Sa until 11pm. Cash only.) For traditional German dishes in the Altstadt, try the popular **Zur Krone ❸**, Osterstr. 30. From the tourist office, cross the street and enter the Altstadt through Osterstr. It's on the left. Try one of the six creative Schnitzel dishes, including "Schnitzel Cordon Bleu" or "Schnitzel Hawaii" (€11.40). They also serves steak, pasta, soup, and salad. (☎05151 90 70. Children's menu items all under €7.)

SIGHTS

If you want to make your own escape from rats, you may have to venture out of the compact Altstadt: the Piper motif is ubiquitous. A small exception is the **Bürgergarten,** near the tourist office, where the locals relax and play life-size chess. (Open daily 7am-10pm.) At Rathauspl. is the **Theater Hameln,** featuring a musical about the Piper and other theater, opera, and dance. (Information and tickets ☎05151 91 62 20 and the tourist office. Box office open Tu-F 10am-2pm.) One hundred meters away, the Leisthaus, Osterstr. 8-9, is where the **Museum Hameln** exhibits an eclectic collection of pieces from Hamelin's history, among them some fossils, 1960s rock albums with the Piper theme, and a cane with a hidden erotic skeleton—use your imagination. (☎05151 20 22 15. Open Tu-Su 10am-4:30pm. €3, students and children €1.50.) The Rattenfänger tale is enacted zealously by the community theater every Sunday at noon in a *Freilichtspiel* (open-air play) outside the 17th-century

The Chronicle

IN RECENT NEWS

RAUCHEN VERBOTEN!

In a country that touts its fresh sea air so fervently, it may seem surpising that fully one third of German adults regularly fill their lungs with tobacco smoke instead. Though initially slow to jump on the anti-smoking bandwagon, Germany finally joined its peers in January 2008 in an attempt to reduce public smoking.

Proud signs trumpeting "rauch frei!" decorate storefronts, hotels, and restaurants, belying the frustration of business owners, who claim revenue losses of 30 to 50 percent as a result of the new laws. Bars complain that former patrons now meet in more private locations to drink and smoke, putting many establishments out of business.

Sly businesses have found clever ways to thwart the new legislations. Some have gone the privatizing route, implementing a nominal charge enough to deem the bars "private clubs." This nominal shift makes them impervious to the the smoking ban. Other businesses simply fly in the face of legislation, such as the devious Goslar restaurant in Lower Saxony, where owner Michael Windisch devised a system of holes in the walls through which smokers may put their heads and hands. Though perhaps a bit awkward, patrons can technically "smoke outside" without ever leaving their seats.

Hochzeithaus (Wedding House) on Osterstr., as well as in **RATS: Das Musical,** every Wednesday, 4:30pm, in the same place. (May-Sept., weather permitting. Free.) At 9:35am, the *Glockenspiel* (bell routine) on the **Hochzeithaus** (Wedding House) plays the haunting *Rattenfängerlied* (Pied Piper song); at 11:45am the Weserlied; and at 1:05, 3:35, and 5:35pm, a tiny stage emerges from the Hochzeithaus and "rats" circle around a wooden flautist. The **Glashütten Hameln** (Glassworks), Pulverturm 1, provides respite from the ubiquitous piper obsession with a glass-blower's workshop upstairs. (☎05151 272 39; www.gladblaeserei.de. Open M-Sa 10am-1pm and 2-6pm, Su 10am-5pm. Workstation entrance €3, students €2. Removed from Piperville, the **Schloß Hämelschenburg** 12km to the south comes with horses, brooks, a waterwheel, and a pond full of huge goldfish. To get there, take bus #40 from "Münster" on the south edge of the Altstadt toward Emmerthal (30min., every hr., €2). This Renaissance-style moated castle, built in 1588, shelters gargoyles next to a trail with panoramic views of the countryside. (☎05151 95 16 90. Open Apr.-Oct. Tours every hr. Tu-Su 10am-noon and 2-5pm. €5, students €2.50. Admission only with tour.) For hiking, try one of the trails that laces the woods, meadows, and hills of the area surrounding the castle. For routes ranging from 5-14km, check out the map next to the bus stop or pick up a hiking map at the tourist office (€7).

BREMEN ☎0421

Bremen (pop. 550,000)—the surly, leather-jacketed rebel of the Hanseatic League—was expelled from the trading conglomerate after citizens made a bonfire of Hanseatic documents. Despite its rebellious flair, the city has done an exceptional job of preserving the relics of its past, including its medieval architecture, fortunately spared from much WWII damage. The historic Rathaus and Dom dominate the city's public image, and the Schnoorviertel, with its winding alleyways and tiny brick homes, provides a fascinating (if touristy) glimpse into its medieval heart. At its fringes, a sizable student population keeps the atmosphere lively. Though relatively small, Bremen's renowned cultural institutions and busy bar scene rival those of cities several times its size.

TRANSPORTATION

Flights: Flughafen Bremen (☎0421 559 50) is 3km from city center; take S6 (15min.). Frequent flights to East Frisian Islands and major German and international cities.

Trains: 2 per hr. to **Bremerhaven** (1hr., €10); 1 per hr. to **Hamburg** (1hr., €24), **Hanover** (1hr., €25), and **Osnabrück** (45-75min., €20).

Public Transportation: VBN runs an integrated system of trams and buses across the city. 1 ride €2.15, day pass €5.70, week pass €15.50. A night bus with limited stops (1-2 per hr.) runs throughout the night. More frequent on weekends. In the round building opposite the Hauptbahnhof, an **information center** has tickets, schedules, transportation maps. Open M-F 7am-7pm, Sa 8am-6pm.

Ferries: Hal Över, Schlachte 2 (☎0421 33 89 89; www.hal-oever.com), runs boats to suburbs and towns on the Weser, ending in Bremerhaven. (3½hr. May-Sept. Sa 8:30am, Su 9:30am; June-Aug. also W and Th 8:30am. €13.80, round-trip €21.80, students and children ½-price.) Also offers 75min. harbor tours May-Oct. 5 times daily; Nov.-Apr M-F 3 per day, Sa-Su 5 per day. (€9, students €7, children €5.)

Taxis: ☎0421 140 14. **Frauen Nachttaxi** (☎0421 133 34) is for women (6pm-6am).

Bike Rental: Radstation (☎0421 301 56 09), between the Hauptbahnhof and Übersee Museum. €9.50 per day, €39 per week. Open M-F 8am-8pm, Sa-Su 9am-8pm.

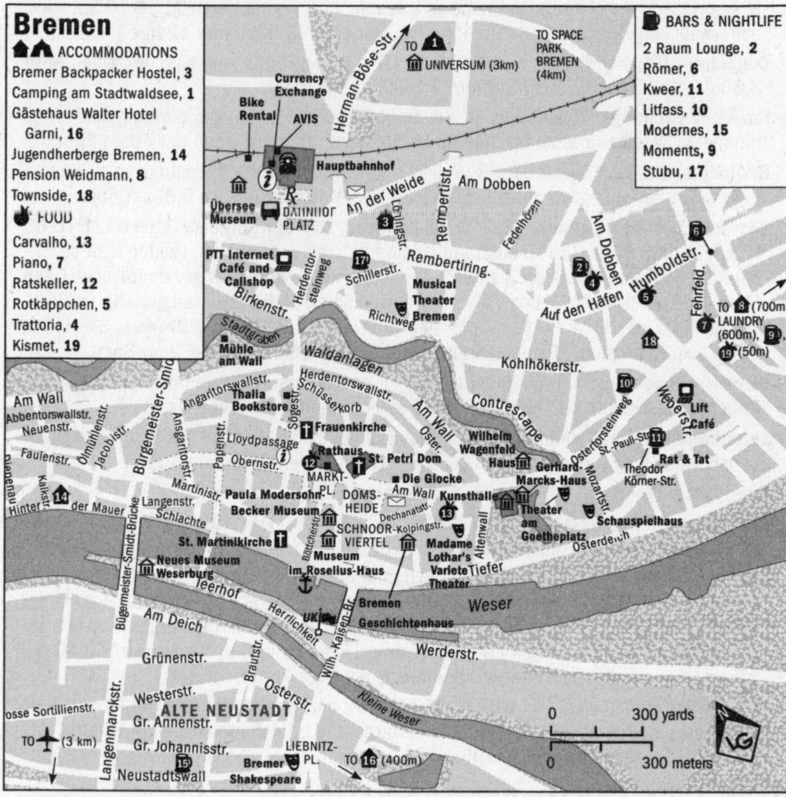

ORIENTATION AND PRACTICAL INFORMATION

Where the Weser River meets the North Sea, Bremen's four neighborhoods have developed unique personalities: the tourist-filled **Altstadt,** flaunting the most sights and the oldest architecture; the **Alte Neustadt,** a residential neighborhood south of the Weser; the **Schnoor,** an old neighborhood-turned-shopping-village; and the **Viertel,** a student quarter filled with stylish college kids, clubs, and cheap food. Exercise caution in the area around Ostertorsteinweg and Am Dobben late at night. An **ErlebnisCARD Bremen,** available at the tourist office, offers free entrance to several attractions in Bremen as well as free public transportation within Bremen, and on certain regional train segments. (1-day card €7.90, 2-day card €9.90. Group cards provide the same services for up to 5 people; 1 day €16, 2 days €20.)

Tourist Office: The central office (☎0180 510 1030, €0.12 per min.; www.bremen-tourismus.de) in the Altstadt on Obernstr. at the Liebfraukirchenhof, facing the Rathaus. Tram #2 or 3 to "Obernstr." Provides free maps of the city center, books rooms, and sells tickets. Open M-F 10am-6:30pm, Sa-Su 10am-4pm. **Branch** in the Hauptbahnhof. Open M-F 9am-7pm, Sa-Su 9:30am-6pm. **Walking tours** of the Altstadt leave daily from the central office. (2hr.; 2pm, Apr.-Oct. also Sa 11am; €5.40.) The **Astro Walk**

Bremen leads visitors through Bremen's scientific high points. (☎0421 10 10 30; www.astro-walk.com. 90min., Tu-Su 2pm. €7.50, students €6.50, under 12 free.)

Consulate: UK, Herrlichkeit 6 (☎0421 59 07 01; www.britishembassy.de). Open M-Th 8:30am-12:30pm and 2:30-3:30pm, F 8:30am-12:30pm.

Currency Exchange: Reisebank, in the Hauptbahnhof. Exchanges currency and wires money via **Western Union;** accepts **AmEx** Traveler's Cheques. Open daily 8am-8pm.

Bookstore: Thalia, Sögestr. 36-38 (☎0421 30 29 20), in the pedestrian zone, has an large selection of English paperbacks. Open M-F 9:30am-8pm, Sa 9:30am-6pm.

Gay and Lesbian Resources: Rat- & Tat-Zentrum, Theodor Körnerstr. 1 (☎0421 70 00 07). Take tram #2 or 3 to "Theater am Goethepl.," and continue on, veering right on St.-Pauli-Str. Provides advice on Bremen's gay scene with a library of gay periodicals. Open M, W, F 11am-1pm; Tu 3-6pm. Also in the building is **AIDS Beratungsstelle** (☎0421 70 41 70). Open M, W, F 11am-1pm; Tu and Th 3-6pm. **AIDS-Help Bremen,** Sielwall 3, offers help to those of all orientations. (☎0421 719 25). Open M-F 9am-3pm.

Women's Resources: Info pertinent to women travelers is available on the web at www.frauenseiten.bremen.de. The tourist office sells women's city maps for €1.

Laundromat: Schnell und Sauber, Vor dem Steintor 105. Take tram #2, 3, or 10 to Brunnenstr. Wash €3.50 per 7kg. Dry €0.75 per 15min. Open daily 6am-11pm.

Emergency: Police ☎110. **Fire** and **Ambulance** ☎112.

Pharmacy: Ginkgo Apotheke, Bahnhofspl. 5-7 (☎0421 169 1994). Straight from the Hauptbahnhof's main exit, on the right side of the Platz. M-F 8am-7pm, Sa 8am-6pm.

Internet Access: Cheap internet cafes proliferate across from the Bahnhof, including **PTT Callshop and Internet Cafe,** Bahnhofstr. 10. (☎0421 153 8939. €0.50 per 30min. Open daily 9:30am-midnight.) Across town is the **Lift Internetcafe,** Weberstr. 18 (☎0421 774 50), just off Ostertorsteinweg. Tram #2 or 3 to "Wulwesstr." €0.40 per 15min. plus a one-time €1 registration fee. Open daily 2pm-midnight.

Post Office: Domsheide 15 (☎0421 367 3366), near the Markt. Open M-F 8am-7pm, Sa 9am-1pm. Branch, Bahnhofspl. 21, left out of the train station. Open M-F 9am-7pm, Sa 9am-1pm. **Postal Code:** 28195.

ACCOMMODATIONS AND CAMPING

Townside Hostel Bremen, Am Dobben 62 (☎0421 780 15; www.townside.de). Tram #10 to "Humboldstr." and contine down Am Dobben. A hip, young hostel, with high-ceilinged rooms and cozy lofts for additional beds. Wi-Fi. Bike rental available (€2 per hr. €8 per day). Laundry €5 to wash and dry. Breakfast available. 6- to 7-bed dorms €20, 4- to 5-bed dorms €23, Doubles €56, singles €35. Sheets €2. Cash only. ❷

Bremer Backpacker Hostel, Emil-Waldmann-Str. 5-6 (☎0421 223 8057; www.bremer-backpacker-hostel.de). From the Hauptbahnhof, go left on An der Weide, right onto Löningstr., and right again onto Emil-Waldmann-Str. Simple, spacious rooms in an unbeatable location. Internet access. Linen €3. 5- to 7-bed dorms €17; 4-bed dorms €19; 3-bed dorms €21; singles €28; doubles €45; triples €61; quads €76. Cash only. ❷

Jugendherberge Bremen (HI), Kalkstr. 6 (☎0421 16 38 20). Bus #26 or 27 or Tram #1 to "Am Brill." Perched on the the river in the center of town, this orange and yellow glass house is a recently renovated gem. Game room, terrace, and panoramic dining hall. Reception 24hr. Wi-Fi. Breakfast included. Dorms €22.20, over 26 €25.20. MC/V. ❷

Gästehaus Walter Hotel Garni, Buntentorsteinweg 86-88 (☎0421 55 80 27; www.hotel-walter.de). Tram #4-6 to "Theater am Leibnizpl." Left onto Buntentorsteinweg. Large rooms with hardwood floors and cheerful decorative touches in a quiet neighborhood. Breakfast included. Singles €35-55, doubles €55-75. AmEx/MC/V. ❹

Camping: Camping an Stadtwaldsee Bremen, Hochschulring 1 (☎0421 841 0748; www.camping-stadtwaldsee.de). Tram #6 to "Universität/NW1," then bus #28 to "Campingpl." Shaded campground on the water near the university. Showers included. Cafe on site. €4-5.50 per site, €7.50 per adult, €4.50 per child. Lower prices in winter. ❶

FOOD

For cheap eats, try the open-air **market** in front of the Rathaus (M-Sa 6am-2pm) or follow the bronze pig statues to the cafes on **Sögerstraße** in the Marktpl. Cheap bakeries and *Imbiße* (snack bars) crowd around the **Hauptbahnhof.** To escape the tourist mob, head to **Auf den Häfen,** where even locals get lost in cobblestone alleys crammed with gourmet restaurants and trendy bars. Student pubs proliferate farther east in the **Viertel** around **Ostertorsteinweg** (see **Nightlife,** p. 207). The popular **Schlachte,** on the banks of the Weser, is home to bars and restaurants with huge outdoor seating areas. For groceries, head to **Extra,** Vor dem Steintor 74. (☎0421 780 47. Open M-F 8am-10pm, Sa 7am-10pm.)

Piano, Fehrfeldstr. 64 (☎0421 785 46). Take tram #2, 3, or 10 to "Sielwall" and walk a block toward the Altstadt; it's on your right. Students and locals flock to this neighborhood eatery for coffee, conversation, and delicious, surprisingly well-priced pasta dishes (€5.80-8.20) and overstuffed baguettes (€3.60-4.80). Open daily 9am-late, kitchen closes at midnight. Breakfast M-F until 4pm, Sa-Su until 5pm. Cash only. ❷

Trattoria, Auf den Häfen 12-15 (☎0421 70 03 35). Take tram #10 to "Humboldtstr." and turn right on Auf den Häfen and then right again down the corridor under the neon sign. Ideal for a warm summer evening, this unadorned Italian bistro has excellent pastas (€5.40-9.60) and appetizing meat dishes (€10-17). Cash only. ❸

Rotkäppchen, Am Dobben 97 (☎0421 754 46). Tram #10 to "Humboldtstr." Heaping lunch specials (€5-7), weekend breakfast buffets (€5.50-8.50), and light salads, crêpes (3.10-6.20), veggie meals (€7-10.70), and magazines to read (free) near the bustle of the Ostertorsteinweg. Open daily 10am-2am, kitchen 11:30am-1am. Cash only. ❷

Carvalho, Kolpingstr. 14 (☎0421 336 5080). Tram #2-6 or 8 to "Domsheide," 2 blocks behind the post office. The easily missed basement restaurant combines colorful tapas (€4-12) and specialty dishes (€9.50-17) with good sangria and a decorative style halfway between Art Deco and 1950s Cuba. Open daily from 6pm. ❸

SIGHTS

ST. PETRI-DOM. A survivor of WWII, the 1200-year-old St. Petri Dom was excavated from 1973 to 1976 and subsequently restored to its prior medieval glory. The interior now explodes with color, its canopied vaults embellished by wall paintings. If you look closely, you can see the "Bremen Church Mouse," a tiny rodent carved into a pillar near the south entrance to the choir. *(Sandstr. 10-12. ☎0421 36 50 40. Cathedral open M-F 10am-5pm, Sa 10am-2pm, Su 2-5pm. Free. Tower, a nosebleed-inducing 265 steps, open Easter-Oct. €1, children €0.70.)* Inside the cathedral, the **Dom Museum** houses original 15th-century paintings and the remains of 900-year-old silk attire, recovered from the bodies of entombed archbishops unearthed during the archaeological dig. English-language guides at the door help make the most of the impressive holdings. *(☎0421 334 71 42; www.stpetridom.de. Open May-Oct. M-F 10am-4:45pm, Sa 10am-1:30pm, Su 2-4:45pm; Nov.-Apr. M-F 11am-4pm, Sa 10am-1pm, Su 2-5pm. Call in advance for English tours. Free.)* Behind the church, the **Bibelgarten** provides access to the macabre **Bleikeller** in the Dom's basement. Here, the assortment of mummified corpses is just as gruesome as it sounds. *(Open M-F 10am-5pm, Sa 10am-2pm, Su 2-5pm. €1.40, children €0.70.)* Just past the Domshof, turn left on Domsheide to reach the **Schnoorviertel,** Bremen's historic district filled with charming shops and restaurants in tiny red-brick houses.

RATHAUS. Bremen's Altstadt radiates from the striking Renaissance-era Rathaus, a UNESCO World Heritage Site since July 2004. The hall and surrounding square are largely preserved in their original states, since the English WWII bomber assigned to obliterate the area deliberately missed his target. On the west side of the Rathaus is Gerhard Marcks's famous 1951 sculpture **Die Musikanten,** the town's symbol, which portrays the Grimms' famed donkey, dog, cat, and rooster. *(Tram #3 or 4 to "Obernstr." Rathaus accessible only with 45min. tour M-Sa 11am, noon, 3, 4pm. €5, children €2.50. English tours available. Buy tickets at tourist office.)*

BECK'S BREWERY. Guides usher wide-eyed beer-drinkers through this giant brewery, explaining the drink's Sumerian origins and imparting mind-boggling statistics (e.g., Beck's annual export of 320 million liters). The 2½hr. tour ends with a tasting challenge and two free rounds of beer. Don't miss the bitter regional specialty, Haake Beck, announced by a 10min. introductory film. *(Am Deich 18-19. Tram #1-3 or 8, or bus #25, 26, or 27 to "Am Brill." Cross the Bürgermeister-Smidt-Brücke, then turn right on Am Deich. Walk toward the Stephan Bridge to get to the visitors center. ☎0421 50 94 55 55; www.becks.de. Tours F-Sa; English tours 2pm; German tours more frequent, normally Jan-Mar 12:30, 2, 3:30, 5pm; Apr.-Dec. 11am, 12:30, 2, 3:30, 5pm, additional tour Sa 9:30am, but call to verify variable times. €8. 16+.)*

BÖTTCHERSTRASSE. The pet project of Ludwig Roselius, millionaire inventor of decaffeinated coffee, this street was transformed from a cramped artisans' quarter to a graceful concert of Art Nouveau and Expressionist architectural elements. The street houses two worthwhile museums: the **Museum im Roselius-Haus** (p. 217) and the **Paula Modersohn-Becker Haus** (p. 217), alongside several cafes and shops. Tourists huddle every day at noon, 3, and 6pm awaiting the bell routine, several minutes of orchestrated bell music chiming from the array of bells between two buildings' gables.

MUSEUMS

KUNSTHALLE. Bremen's respectable art collection includes paintings and sculptures dating from the 15th century to the present. Modern interpretations of old classics are playfully interspersed throughout the galleries. The museum's best holdings are of the German Expressionist and French Impressionist persuasions, although the temporary exhibitions are carefully selected as well. An exhibit on the second floor showcases achievements in sound, video, photography, and installation art. *(Am Wall 207. Tram #2 or 3 to Theater am Goethepl. ☎0421 32 90 80. Open Tu 10am-9pm, W-Su 10am-6pm. €8, students €5, children €3.)*

NEUES MUSEUM WESERBURG BREMEN. Almost all of this refurbished coffee factory's collection is privately owned, creating a quirky, evolving array of works by contemporary artists from across the globe. Many captions in both English and German. *(Teerhof 20. Off the Bürgermeister-Smidt-Brücke on an island in the Weser River. Tram #1-3, 8, or bus #25, 26, or 27 to "Am Brill." ☎0421 59 83 90. Open Tu-W and F 10am-6pm, Th 10am-9pm, Sa-Su 11am-6pm. €7, students and children €5, families €14. Tours daily in German; €10, students and children €8.)*

UNIVERSUM BREMEN. Visitors explore scientific phenomena through sleekly designed interactive exhibits. Travel through the womb to examine the body's display of emotion, or fight the urge to run Baywatch-style in front of a green screen. An attached building houses rotating exhibits most recently showcasing an in-depth look at the history of chocolate. *(Wiener Str. 1a. ☎0421 334 60;*

www.universum-bremen.de. Tram 6 to "Universität/NW1." Open M-F 9am-6pm, Sa-Su 10am-7pm. Explorer's park open until 10pm in summer. €9.50, reduced €7, families €25.50.)

WILHELM WAGENFELD HAUS, DESIGN IM ZENTRUM. This museum celebrates all things design with a series of visually appealing exhibits. Past exhibits have featured old versus new design, juxtaposing blocky mobile phones with modern touch screen devices. Other holdings include the smallest computer you're ever seen and an exhibit on gold. *(Am Wall 209, near the Kunsthalle. ☎0421 38 81 16. www.wwh-bremen.de. €3, reduced 1.50. Open Tu 3-9pm, W-Su 10am-6pm. Tours Su 1pm.)*

GERHARD-MARCKS-HAUS. This elegant sanctuary of contemporary sculpture displays rotating exhibits inside and a peaceful sculpture garden alongside works by Marcks (1889-1981), creator of Bremen's famous **Musikanten.** *(Am Wall 208, next to the Kunsthalle. ☎0421 32 72 00. Open Tu-Su 10am-6pm. German language tours Th 5pm, Su noon. €3.50, students and children €2.50.)*

MUSEUM IM ROSELIUS-HAUS. Tapestries, pious icons, carved wooden furniture, and a killer collection of compasses and pocketwatches complete this showcase of medieval upper middle class life with a religious bent. *(Böttcherstr. 6-10. Tram #2-6 or 8 to "Domsheide." ☎0421 336 5077. Open Tu-Su 11am-6pm. €5, students and children €3. Includes admission to Paula Modersohn-Becker Haus.)*

ÜBERSEE MUSEUM. This museum saves visitors big bucks on airfare with its *Weltreise im Minutentakt* (quick trip around the world), displaying a huge range of exhibits from a Shinto garden to a South Sea fishing village. When you're finished with the life-size wildlife dioramas and artifacts, head upstairs for a polished exhibit on the history of Bremen, Bremerhaven, and the container shipping business. *(Bahnhofspl. 13, a right outside the train station's front doors. ☎0421 61 03 81 01. Open Tu-F 9am-6pm, Sa-Su 10am-6pm. €6.50, students €4.50, children €2.50, families €13.50. Audio guides €2.)*

PAULA MODERSOHN-BECKER HAUS. Celebrating the work of the early Expresionist, this museum is the first to be dedicated solely to a female artist. Her pre-Expressionist paintings are accompanied by works of varying styles from both traditional and contemporary artist. *(Böttcherstr. 6-10. Tram #2-6 or 8 to "Domsheide." ☎0421 336 5077. www.pmbh.de. Open Tu-Su 11am-6pm. Tours Su 11:30am and W 6pm. €5, students €3. Includes admission to Roselius Haus.)*

ENTERTAINMENT AND FESTIVALS

Known for operas, musicals, and dance, the 900-seat **Theater am Goetheplatz,** Am Goethepl. 1-3, is the city's largest. Take tram #2 or 3 to "Theater am Goethepl." Its sister, the **Schauspielhaus,** Ostertorsteinweg 57a, behind the Theater am Goethepl., presents new drama. Tickets for both range €15-54 with significant student discounts and must be purchased at the Theater am Goethepl. (☎0421 365 3333. Open M-F 11am-6pm, Sa 11am-2pm.) The **Musical Theater Bremen,** Richtweg 7-13, favors musicals. Take tram #4, 6, or 8 to "Herdentor." Purchase tickets by phone. (☎0421 35 36 37; www.musicaltheater-bremen.de. Open M-F 8am-10pm, Sa 9am-6pm, Su 10am-6pm.) The **Bremer Shakespeare Company,** in the Theater am Leibnizplatz, enjoys an unrivaled national reputation for its productions of the English playwright. Take tram #4-6 to "Theater am Leibnizpl." (☎0421 50 03 33. www.shakespeare-company.com. Box office open Tu-Sa 3-6pm. Tickets€8-16.) For slightly less intellectual fun, **Madame Lothar's** drag queen shows draw the curious into the Schnoor. (Kolpingstr. 9. ☎0421 337 9191; www.madamelothar.de. W-Sa shows begin at 10:30pm.)

The last two weeks of October find Bremen residents drinking beer and eating tubs of lard cakes during the colorful **Freimarkt Fair,** an annual event dating from 1035. Bremen also hosts concerts in the **Stadthalle** (☎0421 35 36 37. Box office open M-F 8am-6pm, Sa 9:30am-1pm), behind the train station, and in the **Weserstadion** (☎0421 491 31 10). Summertime brings performances to parks around the city, though most big theater companies go on summer holiday; a children's production of Bremen's famous fairy tale takes place on the main Platz every Sunday at noon. Many magazines list upcoming events in German. *Foyer*, free at many museums, details theater, music, film, and art events. *Belladonna* lists cultural events of special interest to women. The indispensable *Prinz* provides monthly party listings and the lowdown on the Bremen scene (€1 at the tourist office and newsstands), as does the popular *Mix* (Free). *Partysan*, a Hamburg magazine free at many cafes, also lists parties in Bremen.

NIGHTLIFE

To experience Bremen's raucous pub culture, head for the Viertel. For wild, multi-floor clubs where the tourist population is swallowed by hordes of dancing locals, hit the **Rebertiring,** across from the Hauptbahnhof.

Modernes, Neustadtswall 28 (☎0421 50 55 53; www.modernes.de). Tram #1 or 8, or bus #26 or 27 to "Hochschule Bremen," backtrack 1 block, and turn right on Neustadtswall. In a gutted movie theater, this popular club hosts events from Sugar Hill Gang concerts to Studio 54 parties for a mostly student crowd. Retractable roof cools things down on steamy nights. Cover €3-5. Disco open F-Sa 11pm-4am. Cash only.

Stubu Dancehouse, Rembertiering 21 (☎0421 32 14 23; www.stubu.de). Across from the Hauptbahnhof, partiers dressed to kill squeeze themselves into this multi-floored club with separate rooms for hip hop, latin, techno/dance/trance, 60s, and mainstream hits. Delightfully difficult to move or breathe on weekends. Cover Tu-Th €2, F-Sa €5. Open Tu-Th 10pm-3am, F-Sa 11pm-9am. Cash only.

Litfass, Ostertorsteinweg 22 (☎0421 70 32 92). Tram #2 or 3 to "Wulwesstr." A late-night bastion of alternative chic in bar form, with a big outdoor terrace and open facade that make for Litfass equally popular as a daytime cafe. Open M-Th and Su 10am-2am, F-Sa 10am-4am. Beer €2.30-3.30. Cash only.

2 Raum Lounge, Auf den Häfen 12-15 (☎0421 745 77). Next to Trattoria, this flamboyantly lit bar offers a huge variety of mixed drinks (€5.50-7.50) and beer (€2.30-3.20) from its mod-inspired digs. Think Zenon meets Twiggy. Cash only.

Moments, Vor dem Steintor 65 (☎0421 792 6633; www.club-moments.de). Tram #2 or 3 to "Sielwall," and another block farther. An unpretentious mixture of live music and dance-hall fun. Hosts events like Turkish music nights and reggae concerts the third Sa of each month (€8 to enter, €4 after first set). Jazz concerts during the week. Th 10pm-1:30pm happy hour; Beck's €1.50, mixed drinks €2. Open Tu-Sa 10pm-late.

Kweer, Theodor-Körner-Str. 1 (☎0421 70 00 08). Tram #2 or 3 to "Theater am Goethepl.," and right onto St.-Pauli-Str. The relaxed atmosphere of this intimate cafe and bar attracts a crowd of regulars. All proceeds go to AIDS education. Open 1st and 3rd Tu of the month and every W 8pm-midnight, F 8pm-1am, Su 3-6pm.

OSTFRIESLAND (EAST FRISIA)

Germany's North Sea shoreline and the seven sandy islands strung like pearls a few kilometers off its coast conceal some of the most rewarding natural and cultural wonders of western Germany. The flat landscape of the mainland that unfolds into the North Sea is dotted with windmills, clusters of idle cows, and asymmetrical clouds—a stunning visual wonder that throws into sharp relief the neighboring bustle of river valleys and modern skylines. The seafaring

Frisians, whose dialect is a close linguistic relative to English, treasure their strong tea, which is customarily served in elaborate porcelain sets over sugar candies called *Kluntje*, and is often spiked. Try some *Ostfriesische Rosinenstütten*, a sweet raisin loaf on display in every bakery, or the unforgettable *Bohnensuppe* (literally, bean soup), which has nothing to do with beans, and is in fact a sweet delight made with raisins, brandy, and sugar. Though buses and trains in the area are often inconvenient, miles of unspoiled and uncrowded beaches, green fields, and rolling dunes compensate for the planning required. Travel to Baltrum and Norderney is relatively manageable, while buses to Borkum are still infrequent.

JEVER ☎04461

Jever received city rights 450 years ago from its patroness, Lady Mary, who commissioned art and built fortifications and a school. The town's modern patron is the nationally famous local brewery, which serves up some of the most refreshing beer in Germany. A regional **rail line** runs to Jever from Oldenburg and Osnabrück (1hr., one train change, every hr., €10). For a **taxi** call ☎04461 30 30. The hidden-away **tourist office,** Alter Markt 18, across from the *Schloß*, books rooms for free. From the train station, follow Anton-Günther-Str. to the right, turn left at Mühlenstr., and it will be near the Schloßpl. on the left. (☎04461 710 10; www.stadt-jever.de. Open Mar.-Oct. M-F 9am-6pm, Sa 9am-1pm; Nov.-Feb. M-F 9am-5pm.) From the office, signs indicate the way to major sights. Brick **post office,** Schlosserstr. 45. **Postal Code:** 26441.

Im Schmidz Pension ❹, Alter Markt 2, matches convenient location with snug comfort and personal touches in the center of town. (☎04461 75 90 36. Breakfast included. Singles €38; doubles €70; 10-15% discount for multiple nights. Cash only.) The **Jugendherberge Jever (HI) ❶,** at Dr. Fritz-Blume-Weg 4, is relatively near both the train station and the Altstadt. From the train station, go straight down Bahnhofstr. and turn left onto Wittmunder Str., right onto Jahnstr., and then left onto Dr. Fritz-Blume-Weg. (☎04461 33 33. Breakfast and sheets included. Check-in M-F and Su 5-5:30pm, Sa 5:30-6pm; late check-in 9:45pm or call from the front desk. Curfew 10pm, key available. Open Apr.-Oct. €18-20.20, over 27 €20.20-26.90. Cash only.) **Balu ❸,** Kattrepel 1a, tucked into a quiet courtyard off the Altstadt, cooks African specialties like yam wings and plantains, as well as a range of other distinctive finger food (€10-13). Salat à la Rosemarie (€10), with chicken, avocado, orange slices, and warm pita bread, is life-affirmingly good and draws a loyal local following. (☎04461 70 07 09. Open Apr.-Oct.daily noon-3pm and 5pm-midnight, Nov.-Mar. M and W-Su 6pm-midnight and F-Su noon-3pm and 5pm-midnight. Cash only.) A rare late-night option in Jever is the popular **La Casetta Pizzeria ❷,** Bahnhofstr. 44. If the selection of 34 pizzas doesn't satisfy your tastes, try the pasta (€6.70). (☎04461 725 89. Entrees €3-8. Open daily noon-3pm and 5pm-midnight. Cash only.)

North of the Altstadt, the **Frieisisches Brauhaus,** Elisabethufer, is a futuristic glass brewing complex that puts Jever on the map—and on tap—all over northern Germany. To reserve tour tickets or purchase the essential Jever survival gear (sweatshirt, sun visor, watch, and beer mug), head for the eye-catching **Der Jever-Shop,** Elisabethufer 18. (☎04461 137 11; www.jever.de. Open M-F 10am-6pm, Sa 10am-2pm. 45min. German tours begin at half past every hr. €6.50, including a souvenir mug and 2 glasses of beer. Sa tours go to museum only.) Most Jeverische dismiss Pilsner as their claim to fame by insisting that the town's castle is its most prized and noteworthy possession. Each room in the beautiful, salmon-colored, 15th-century **Schloß** details a facet of East Frisian heritage, from intricate traditional tea sets to 18th-century clothing. (☎04461 96 93 50; www.schlossmuseum.de. Open Tu-Su 10am-6pm; July and

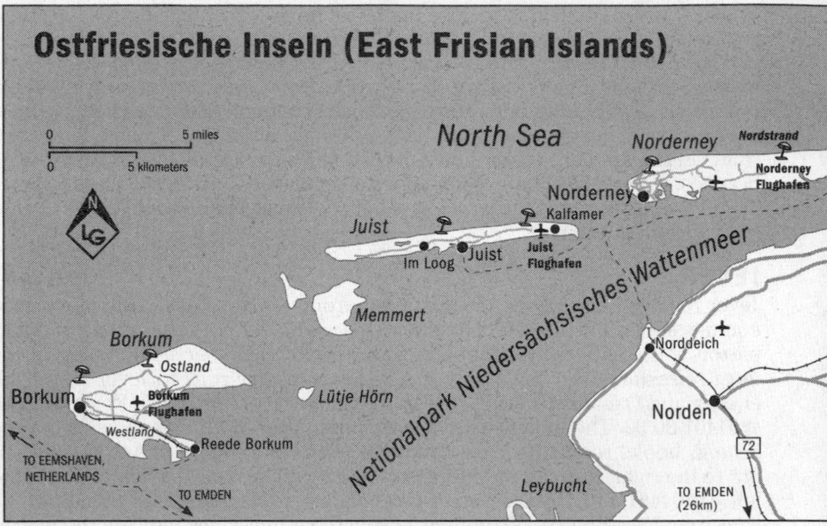

Aug. also open M. €3, students €1.50, children €1. Tower €1.) Nestled between the tourist office and the *Schloß* is the **Lady Mary Statue,** the city's enduring monument to its beloved patroness. Just outside the castle entrance and facing the tourist office at the Hof von Oldenburg is a **Glockenspiel,** which goes off every hr. from 11am-noon and 3-6pm, releasing figurines from Jever's history through its trap doors. The cheerful characters, among them Lady Mary and a Russian Empress, extend their hands in greeting. On Kirchpl., the **Stadtkirche** is a product of the citizens' dedication—after it burned down, they reconstructed and modernized it. The ornate brick facade of the Renaissance **Rathaus** is a few blocks away from the main square.

WATTENMEER NATIONAL PARK

Twice daily, tides rush out of the Wattenmeer National Park, laying kilometers of the ocean floor completely exposed. The Frisian Islands make up one component of a much large, and ecologically diverse wonder. The delicately sloping continental shelf along the coast that creates this dramatic ebb and flow sustains a unique ecology at Wattenmeer, the westernmost of Germany's three Wattenmeer parks. Dunes formed here millions of years ago, protecting the islands from erosion and the flora and fauna from salt water. Hundreds of local plant and insect species interact in the protected island interiors, while various fish, birds, and invertebrates have evolved to thrive on the surrounding ocean floor **mudflats.** Familiar with the intricacies of the Watt terrain and timing of the tides, local experts lead popular **Wattwanderung** (Watt walk) groups out onto the flats during low tides, describing this specialized ecosystem as everyone enjoys a romp in the mud.

ORIENTATION

The National Park stretches along the coast from the **Ems** to the **Weser Rivers.** It includes the coastline as well as the seven **East Frisian Islands.**

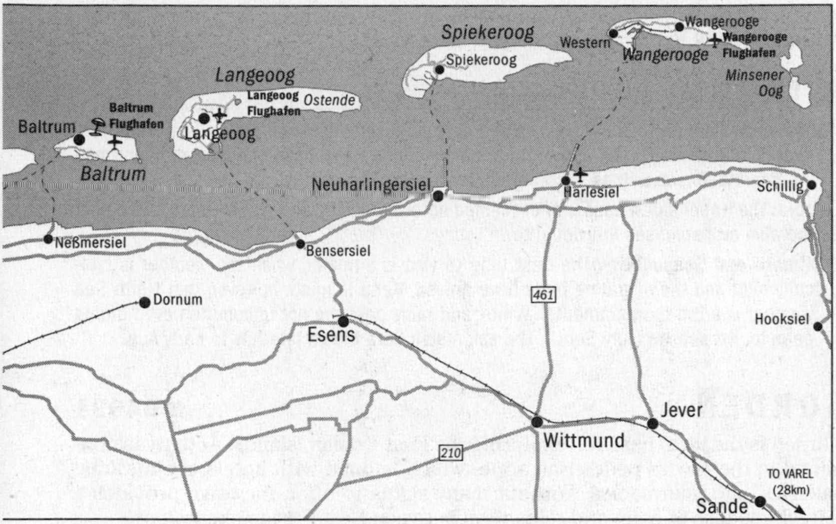

WATT NOT TO DO. A few rules apply throughout the park. First, **always keep at least 500m from seals.** Your approach will frighten them and as they flee they are likely to hurt their sensitive underbellies. Second, **do not venture off marked trails within the park** between April and July—you'll disturbed protected bird nesting areas. Third, in areas labeled "Schutzzone I: Ruhezone," **never leave the marked trails at any time of year.** These areas, which make up more than 60% of the park, are especially protected, and you will be **fined** if a ranger catches you anywhere in these areas. Venturing indepedently across the mudflats is generally ill-advised, as the tide rushes in all at once and you can easily get caught in a tidal channel. Let a guide lead you through the intricacies of the unique ecosystem.

TRANSPORTATION

Trains run to Norden and Norddeich from Bremen (2-3hr., every hr., €26) and Oldenburg (1-2hr., every hr., €16). Only two mainland ports are accessible by train: **Emden,** the ferry port for Borkum, and Norddeich, the ferry port for Norderney and Juist. The departure points for all other islands lie in a string of tiny ports on the coast, all connected by the costly **Bäderbus,** which runs on a sparse schedule from Norden to Carolinensiel. Be advised: the Bäderbus is not scheduled to connect with departing ferries. The ferry companies servicing **Baltrum** run a separate bus from the Norden train station which is conveniently timed with the ship. Pick up a bus schedule from the train station in Norden and **plan at least a day ahead,** or you may get stuck waiting for hours with no bus or ferry. Watch for new ferry services; companies sometimes run inter-island trips. In general, unless you want to take a tiny, vibrating **plane** for €40-150 (which can get you to all islands except Spiekeroog), you can't travel between islands—you must return to the mainland. To learn all the ins and outs of your chosen island, buy its brochure (in German only) at a regional tourist office. These handy pamphlets contain extensive accommodations listings and full explanations of local attractions.

PRACTICAL INFORMATION

Information Centers: A series of Nationalparkhäuser offer information and tours; the best is in **Baltrum** (p. 223). Town information centers also have transportation and hiking information, as well as accommodations listings.

Tours: The Nationalparkhäuser offer themed nature tours. Private guided tours of the Watt are also available; see individual town listings.

Climate and Seasonality: The best time to visit is summer, when the weather is typically mild and the migrating birds have arrived. Keep in mind, however, that North Sea weather is a tad temperamental. Windy and rainy days are not uncommon even during peak tourist season (July-Sept.). The salt marsh flora bloom late July to early Aug.

NORDEN ☎04931

Norden is the ideal base for exploring the East Frisian Islands. Activity is contained in the town's pedestrian zone, which is lined with hotels, restaurants, bakeries, and pharmacies. Without many sights to offer, the town provides a refreshing dose of calm and relaxation between East Frisian excursions.

TRANSPORTATION AND PRACTICAL INFORMATION. **Trains** travel to Emden (every hr., € 6) and Norddeich (2 per hr., €2), and the **Bäderbus** provides easy access to most other port towns. The train station is 2km from the city center. From the station follow Bahnhofstr. to the right and veer right at the fork onto Neuer Weg. At the pedestrian zone, turn left on Osterstr. to the main market square. The **tourist office** is a kiosk in the middle of the square opposite the Rathaus. Go transportation information or free room reservations. (☎04931 98 62 01. Open M-F 9am-12:30pm and 2-5pm, Sa 9am- 1:30pm and 2-4pm.) Access the **Internet** at **Spiel Center,** Osterstr., (€2 for 50min., M-Sa 9am-noon, Su 10am-noon.) Find a **post office** at Am Markt 4-6. **Postal Code:** 26506.

NORDDEICH ☎04931

The busy port of Norddeich, 3km north of sister city Norden, is a logical base for budget travelers. The town offers affordable accommodations, easy access to the ferry network, and spectacular seascapes along a string of beaches.

TRANSPORTATION AND PRACTICAL INFORMATION. The convenient **train station** is Norddeich-Mole, which is the end of the line. To reach town, follow the pathway uphill and over the dike to the right. Badestr. runs parallel to the dike and intersects Dörper Weg after 800m. **Ferries** leave Norddeich 2-3 times daily for Norderney and Juist. Pick up schedules in the ferry ticket offices outside of the train station. **Bike** rental shops line Dörper Weg; many also rent popular go-carts from €3 per hr. (Bikes about €7 per day, €25 per week; ID required.) The patient staff at the out-of-the-way Norddeich **tourist office,** Dörper Weg 22, finds rooms for free, hands out ferry schedules, gives information about Watt tours, and offers the only **Internet** access (€4.50 per hr.; €10 deposit) for miles. (☎04461 837 5200; www.norddeich.de. Open M-F 9am-5pm, Sa 10am-5pm, Su 10am-1pm.) For a **taxi,** call ☎04461 80 00. The **post office** is in the Fernseh Hemken building on Frisiastr., which intersects Badestr. near the train station. **Postal Code:** 26506.

ACCOMMODATIONS AND FOOD. The town's **Jugendherberge (HI) ❶,** Strandstr. 1, is excellent for those lucky enough to snatch a reservation: it's affordable and conveniently located between the train station and the tourist attractions. From Badestr., turn left just past the Hotel Regina Maris; the hostel is on the next corner on the left. The main hostel compound is generally filled with school groups, but the adjacent *Blockhütten* (pine cabins) provide some escape. (☎04461 80 64. Breakfast included. Reception 8am-7pm. Book weeks, if not months, in advance. €21.55-25. €5.80 to pitch your own tent in the backyard. MC/V.) **Hotel Seeblick ❸,** Badestr. 11, provides snug rooms in an ideal location near the beach at unbeatable prices. (☎04461 80 86. Breakfast included. Reception 8am-10pm in the restaurant below. June-Sept. singles €22-31; doubles €25-34. Cash only.) **Gästehaus Merlan ❷,** Kakteenweg 7, just off of Deichstr., has spacious and airy doubles and red-bricked apartments, each equipped with cable TV, radio, and private bath. (☎04461 816 30. Reservations strongly recommended. Doubles €48, including breakfast; 2- to 6-person apartments €23 per person. Cash only.) **Nordsee-Camp ❶,** Deichstr. 21, is 20min. farther down Badestr., which becomes Deichstr. It has impressive views of the sea (though dike-side camping gets very chilly), a cheap bar, and a moderately priced grocery store on the grounds. (☎04461 80 73. Reception until 10pm. Open mid-Mar. to Oct. €2.60 per person, €6.80 per day. *Kurtaxe* €1.50.) **Diekster Köken ❸,** Deichstr. 6 (☎04461 822 42), serves fresh regional fare. Specialties include delicious potato pancakes (€3-15), served with almost anything, and fresh seafood (€12-20). (Open daily 10:30am-10pm. MC/V.)

SIGHTS. **Seehundstation,** Dörper Weg 22. Follow signs behind the waterpark to get to the park behind the tourist office. Here, injured North Sea seals are rehabilitated before their return to the wild. Get up close and personal with the playful sea critters, who entertain with their underwater acrobatics on the other side of a glass wall. (☎04461 89 19; www.seehundstation-norddeich.de. Open daily 10am-5pm. €5, children €4, family €14.) For an *Erlebnisbad* (adventure pool) and saunas, visit the island's waterpark **Ocean Wave,** Dörper Weg 23. Female-only saunas every Wednesday. (☎04931 98 63 00; www.ocean-wave.de. Open M-F 10am-9pm, bathing until 8:30pm, Sa and Su 10am-8pm, bathing until 7:30pm. Open July-Aug. 9am. Pool: 90min. €6.50, 4hr. €8.50, day pass €9.50; Sauna: 4hr. €13, day pass €15. Reductions for groups of 15+.)

BALTRUM ISLAND ☎04939

The smallest of the Frisian Islands with only 500 residents, Baltrum is dominated by bold wildlife—rabbits and pheasants regularly emerge from the brush to size you up. A ban on motor vehicles creates a much-treasured silence, broken only by the occasional animal call or clopping of horse hooves. Baltrum is a scenic escape from the mainland, promising calming views of flat grasslands and sandy dunes. Houses are numbered in the order they were built, which seems charming until you have to find one.

TRANSPORTATION AND PRACTICAL INFORMATION. To reach Baltrum, take the **Ferry Company Frisia** bus from the Norden train station to Neßmersiel. Ferry times vary greatly, as the boats can only travel this route close to low tide. The first **ferry** leaves for Baltrum anywhere between 6am and 2:30pm, the last ferry returns between 2 and 9:30pm. (June-Nov. 2-3 per day. Open-ended return €21, children €10. Daytrip €16/7.50.) **Buses** leave Norden about 1hr. before the ferry (€6 round-trip). Check the schedule at the information signs at the market square in Norden or www.wattfuehrer.com. For more information, call the ferry company, **Reederei Baltrum Linie** (☎04939 913 00.) The **tourist office,** in the Rathaus, Nr. 130, books private rooms and helps coordinate transportation to the island. It's a bit far to get there and no motor vehicles are allowed. Hotels pick up their guests with either horse-drawn carriages or with bikes that have a big wagon attached to hold luggage and passengers. Turn right at the harbor exit and then take the third left; it's near the end of the road on the left. (☎04939 800; www.baltrum.de. Open M-F 9am-noon, Sa-Su 10am-noon.) For essential hiking tips and bird-call lessons, head to the quiet **National Park Haus,** Nr. 177, to your right as you leave the harbor. (☎04939 469. Open Tu-F 10am-noon and 3-7pm, Sa-Su 3-7pm.) Seek out and plan well in advance for **Watt tours** between the island and the mainland during low tide. For tour times, call a local Wattführer or look for signs at the tourist office. Family Ortelt runs tours for Baltrum, Norderney, Langeoog, and Spiekeroog in German supplemented with some English. (☎04933 17 06; www.wattfuehrer.com. 2hr. €12.50, children €6.) The unlabeled **post office** is across the street, Nr. 43., next door to the Hotel zur Post. (Open M-F 9am-noon and 3-5pm, Sa 9am-noon.) **Postal Code:** 26579.

ACCOMMODATIONS AND FOOD. The island feels like every house could be a quiet bed and breakfast. For unbeatable prices, try the **Haus Störtebeker ❷,** Nr. 167. From the National Park Haus, turn right and take the second left, between two brick walls. Take the next right; it will be on your right, overlooking the water. All rooms have full-size beds and huge windows. (☎04939 295; www.stoertebeker-baltrum.de. Kitchen available. Singles €19, doubles €18 per person, apartment €78 per person. Call in advance as reception times vary. Cash only.) **Jugendbildungsstätte ❶** lets you camp within the national park. Baltrum might be a good option for camping because it feels safer and warmer than the other islands. Turn right immediately after the harbor and continue for 1.5km along the bike path. (☎04941 99 11 64. Cot and tent included. Open June-Sept. €7.40 per person, €4.50 per child. Mar.-May €6.15 per person, €4 per child. Cash only.) For cheap eats, the popular **Strandcafe ❷,** Kleine Düne 70, serves pizza, salads, pasta, sausages, and potatoes (all items under €10) cafeteria-style and is apparently staffed by every teenager on the island. Go past Haus Störtebeker until the road forks, stay left, and continue until the sand dunes at the end of the road. (☎04939 200. Open daily 10am-midnight. Closed M in off-season.) Where the road splits after Haus Störtebeker, **Kiek Musikkneipe,** Nr. 123, lights up with late entertainment, a respectable head count, and occasional live music. (☎04939 89 60. Open F and Sa from 10pm. Must be 16 to enter, 18+ after midnight. Cash only.) Enjoy theater, cinema, and concerts at **Turnhalle.** To get there, start with Haus Störtebeker to your left, and take the first right. It's on the right at the end of the street. (Entrance €6.50, shows from 4-9pm.)

HIKING. The island map from the tourist office shows the marked trails. To get to the trailhead from the National Park Haus, take a right and continue for 600m. Take the fourth left (just past the pond on your right) and then the first right. Follow the path as it curves to the right before a large off-white house. From there take an immediate left and then the following left; take the stairs over the large sand dune with its peak enclosed by faded green fences and continue east on the middle path for 400m. Stay left when the path merges as you enter the *Ruhezone* (quiet zone) after another 300m. From here, there are two hiking options options. For a short hike (1hr.), continue straight for 500m and make a right onto the riding and hiking path marked alternately with red and green markers. The trail eventually brings you back to the road from which you began. For a long hike (3hr.), go left toward the beach. From there you can walk through the sand dunes or parallel to the dunes along the beach.

For the dunes, take the first right. For the beach, walk until you hit the sand, then turn right. Both paths head east to the end of the island. Once there, you can either double back the way you came or take the Watt Trail; which is only accessible within 1hr. of the tide. Check with the National Park Haus. Taking this trail adds at least 1hr. to the long hike; make sure you budget enough time to emerge before the tide rushes in. If you hike the Watt trail in the other direction, be careful not to miss the trailhead coming back into town. To enter the Watt trail eastward, go to the Jugendstätte campground, then fork right, curving around to the south. When you hit the Watt, lose your shoes, roll up your pant legs, and enjoy the 1hr. slosh east through the mud.

NORDRHEIN-WESTFALEN

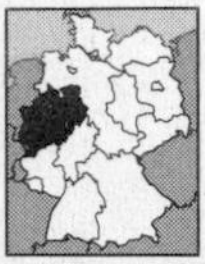

In 1946, the victorious Allies attempted to expedite Germany's recovery by merging the traditionally distinct regions of Westphalia, Lippe, and the Rheinland in order to expand and strengten the industrial nucleus of post-war Germany. The resulting *Land*, Nordrhein-Westfalen, defies all German stereotypes. A dense concentration of highways and rail lines forms the infrastructure of the most heavily populated and economically powerful region in Germany. An industrial boom that happened here during the late 19th century sparked social democracy, trade unionism, and revolutionary communism. The enormous wealth of the regiou continues to support a multitude of cultural offerings for the citizens and visitors. While industrial squalor may have inspired the philosophy of Karl Marx and Friedrich Engels, the natural beauty of the Teutoburg mountains and Rhein River, coupled with the intellectual energy of Cologne and Düsseldorf, have influenced writers from Goethe to Heine.

HIGHLIGHTS OF NORDRHEIN-WESTFALEN

INDULGE IN CHOCOLATE from a special fountain in **Köln** (Cologne), internationally renowned for its striking Dom.

PAY YOUR RESPECTS at Beethoven's birthplace in **Bonn** (p. 236) and **Aachen's** (p. 241) collection of Charlemagne's body parts. Despite the body count, these hip university towns are alive and well.

STRUT WITH STYLE down the **"Kö"**—a glitzy strip of designer boutiques in **Düsseldorf** (p. 245), the nation's undisputed center of high fashion. By night, its citizens head out to the 500+ *Kneipen* (the "longest bar in the world") lining the city's Alstadt.

KÖLN (COLOGNE) ☎0221

Founded as a Roman colony (*colonia*, hence Köln) in 32 BC by Agrippina, wife of Roman Emperor Claudius, Cologne (pop. 991,400) was Petrarch's "city of dreams" when the rest of Germany was primarily wilderness. Cologne's modern prosperity camouflages the staggering damage it sustained in WWII, when relentless air raids crumbled 90% of the city center, though miraculously leaving the city's magnificant Dom intact. Looming over the city skyline, the legendary Dom serves as a reminder of a turbulent past with discolored stones marking old war wounds. Today, Cologne is North Rhein-Westphalia's largest city and cultural center, with a wide range of world-class museums and theatrical offerings. The city's long history also includes a variety of traditionally extravagant festivals and celebrations. Each year, *Karneval* plunges Cologne into a frenzy of parades, costume balls, and intoxication for the week before Lent. Meanwhile, locally brewed *Kölsch* beer helps to instill a festive mentality all year, and the city's expanding nightlife indulges the eclectic tastes of the university crowd, whose presence keeps the city buzzing around the clock.

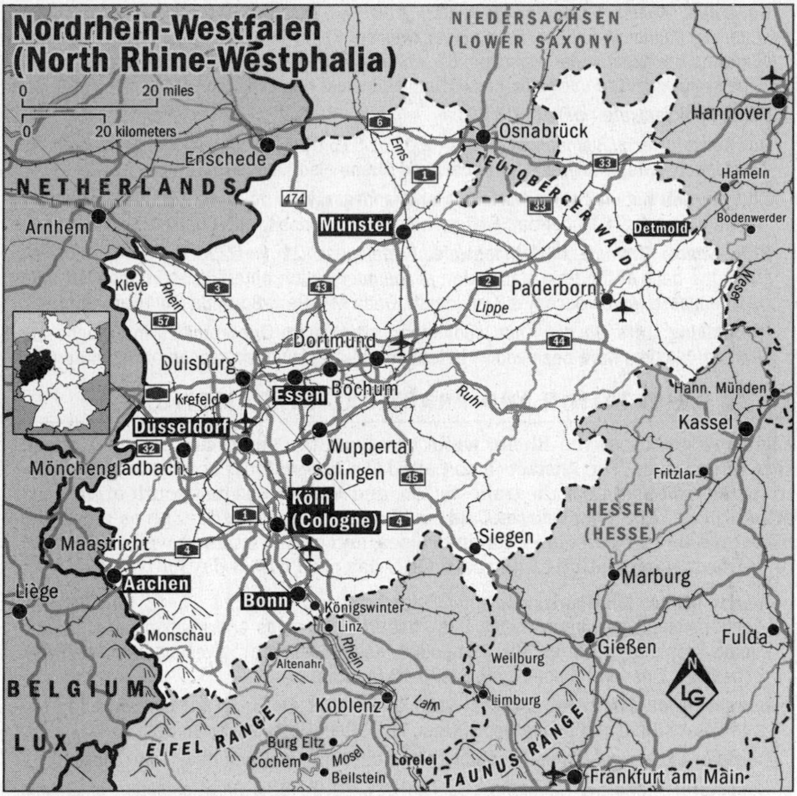

TRANSPORTATION

Flights: Flights depart from **Köln-Bonn Flughafen.** Flight information ☎0221 18 03 80 38 03; www.koeln-bonn-airport.de. S13 leaves the train station M-F every 20min., Sa-Su every 30min. Shuttle to Berlin 24 per day 6:30am-8:30pm.

Trains: Berlin (4hr., 1-2 per hr., €86-104); **Düsseldorf** (½-1hr., 5-7 per hr., €10-18); **Frankfurt** (1-2hr., 2 per hr., €34-63); **Hamburg** (4hr., 2-3 per hr., €74-86); **Munich** (4-5hr., 2-3 per hr., €91-124). International Service to **Amsterdam, Netherlands** (2-3hr., 1-3 per hr., €40-56) and **Paris, France** (4hr., every 3 hr., €87-120).**Ferries: Köln-Düsseldorfer** (☎0221 208 8318; www.k-d.com) begins its popular Rhein cruises here, at the end of Salzgosse Sail to Koblenz (€37.40, €41 round-trip) or see the castles along the Rhein to Mainz (€49/55.60). Ships to Bonn (€27/29) offer a scenic alternative to trains. Children ages 4-13 travel for €3.50 on cruises, seniors half-price M and F. Many trips are covered by Eurail and German railpasses.

Public Transportation: VRS offices have free maps of the **S-Bahn, bus,** and **tram** lines; one office is downstairs in the Hauptbahnhof, at the U-Bahn station. Major terminals include the Hauptbahnhof, Neumarkt, and Appellhofpl. Single ride from €1.50, depending on distance. Day pass from €5.20. Week ticket from €13.70. The **Minigruppen-Ticket** (from €5.60) allows up to 4 people to ride M-F 9am-midnight and all day Sa-Su.

Gondolas: Kölner Seilbahn, Rhiehlerstr. 180 (☎0221 547 41 84), U17-U19 (dir.: Ebertpl./Mülheim) to "Zoo/Flora." Float over the Rhein from the Zoo to the Rheinpark, enjoying the spectacular cityscape. €4, children ages 4-12 €2.40; round-trip €6/3.50. Open mid-March to early Nov. daily 10am-6pm, last ride 5:45pm.

Taxis: Funkzentrale (☎0221 28 82).

Car Rental: Hertz, Bismarckstr. 19-21 (☎0221 515 08 47). Open M-F 7:30am-6pm, Sa 8am-noon. **Avis, InterRent, Europcar,** and **Alamo** also have airport offices.

Bike Rental: Kölner Fahrradverleih, Markmannsgasse (☎0171 629 87 96), in the Altstadt. €2 per hr., €10 per day, €40 per week; €25 deposit. Open daily 10am-6pm.

Ride Share: Citynetz Mitfahrzentrale, Krefelderstr. 21 (☎0221 194 44). Turn left from the back of the train station, left at the intersection onto Eigelstein, then left onto Weidengasse, which becomes Krefelderstr. Open M-F 9am-8pm, Sa-Su 10am-6pm.

Hitchhiking: *Let's Go* does not recommend hitchhiking. Opportunities in Cologne are limited; hitchers have been known to look for rides at the train station or the airport.

ORIENTATION AND PRACTICAL INFORMATION

Eight bridges cross the Rhein, while nearly all the sights are on the western side of the river. The **Altstadt** (also called the Innenstadt) is split into two districts: **Altstadt-Nord** near the train station, and **Altstadt-Süd** just south of the Severinsbrücke. The **Köln WelcomeCard,** sold at the tourist office, gives generous discounts on city museums, Rhein cruises, and bike rentals as well as free use of public transportation (1-day card €9, 2-day card €14, 3-day card €19).

Tourist Office: KölnTourismus, Unter Fettenhennen 19 ☎0221 22 13 04 10; www.koelntourismus.de), opposite the Dom, has free city maps and multilingual staff, and books rooms for a €3 fee. The €1 booklet "Köln im [month]" gives city info and event schedules. Open M-F 9am-10pm, Sa-Su 10am-5pm.

Budget Travel: STA Travel, Zülpicher Str. 178 (☎0221 44 20 11). U8 or U9 to "Universität." Sells ISICs and books flights. Open M-F 10am-6pm, Sa 11am-3pm.

Currency Exchange: At the **Reisebank** in the train station. Open daily 7am-10pm.

Bookstore: Thalia.de, Neumarkt 18a (☎0221 20 90 90). Great selection of English bestsellers and classics on the 5th fl. Open M-Sa 9:30am-8pm.

Women's Resources: Frauenamt, Markmannsgasse 7 (☎0221 22 12 64 82), has a friendly staff to field questions. Open M and W-Th 8am-4pm, Tu to 6pm, F to midnight.

Room Share: Mitwohnzentrale, Im Ferkulum 4, (☎0221 194 45) finds apartments for long stays. Open daily 8am-8pm.)

Laundromat: Eco-Express Waschsalon, at the corner of Richard-Wagner-Str. and Händelstr. Wash 6-10am €1.90, 10am-11pm €2.50. Soap €0.50. Dry €0.50 per 10min. Open M-Sa 6am-11pm.

Gay and Lesbian Resources: SchwIPS Checkpoint, Pipinstr. 7, just around the corner from Hotel Timp (☎0221 92 57 68 11; www.checkpoint-koeln.de). **Emergency helpline** ☎0221 192 28.

Emergency: Police ☎110. **Fire** and **Ambulance** ☎112. A police station is located at Maximinenstr. 6 (☎0221 299 6130), behind the train station.

Pharmacy: Apotheke im Hauptbahnhof, at the back of the train station, near platform 11 (☎0221 139 1112). Open M-F 6am-10pm, Sa 8am-10pm.

Internet Access: Telepoint Callshop & Internet C@fe, Komödenstr. 19 (☎0221 250 9930), by the Dom. €1.50 per hr. Open M-F 9am-10pm, Sa-Su 10am-10pm.

Post Office: At the corner of Breite Str. and Tunisstr. in the WDR-Arkaden shopping gallery. Open M-F 9am-7pm, Sa 9am-2pm. **Postal Code:** 50667.

ACCOMMODATIONS

Cologne's hotels raise rates from March to October, when trade winds blow conventioners into town. The hotel haven is **Brandenburger Straße,** on the less busy side of the train station. Looking for last-minute rooms during **Karneval** is foolish—book up to a year ahead and expect to pay a premium.

Station Hostel for Backpackers, Marzellenstr. 44-56 (☎0221 912 5301; www.hostel-cologne.de). Abuzz with backpackers. Relaxed in-house bar (*Kölsch* €2) with reggae. Breakfast €3. Towels €1 with €5 deposit. Locker key with €5 deposit. Laundry €4. Free Wi-Fi. Kitchen. Reception 24hr. Check-in 2pm. Check-out noon. 4- to 6-bed dorms €17-21; singles €30, with bath €37; doubles €45-52, triples €63. Cash only. ❷

Meininger City Hostel, Engelbertstr. 33-35 (☎0221 355 33 2014; www.meininger-hostels.com). U1, U7, U12, or U15 to Rudolfpl. Exit station, then turn left on Habsburgerst., right on Lindenstr., and left on Engelbertstr. This trendy hostel boasts a game room, lounge, cinema, and bar. Reception 24hr. Breakfast included. Free Wi-Fi, lockers, towels, and linen. Dorms (max. 8) €17-22, small dorms (max. 6) €20-24, 4- to 6-bed rooms €24-32, triples €28-36, doubles €34-44, singles €43-56. Cash only. ❷

Pension Jansen, Richard-Wagner-Str. 18 (☎0221 25 18 75), on the 3rd fl. U1, U6, U7, U12, or U15 to "Rudolfpl." Close to nightlife hotspots and shopping. Chic pension with a social atmosphere, sky-high ceilings, bright color-themed rooms, and spacious shared bathrooms. The resident pet bunny befriends all. Breakfast included. Singles €45-80, doubles €65-90. Discount for longer stays. Cash only. ❹

Jugendherberge Köln-Deutz (HI), Siegesstr. 5 (☎0221 81 47 11; www.koeln-deutz.jugendherberge.de), just over the Hohenzollernbrücke. U1 or 7-9 to "Deutzer Freiheit." Exit the station toward Siegesstr.; the hostel is 100m ahead. This massive, newly built, family-oriented hostel with minishop offers clean rooms, all with shower and bath. Disco in the basement offers a no-nonsense way to bond with fellow travelers. Breakfast and sheets included. Laundry €1. Internet access €4 per hr. Reception 24hr. Dorms €24.80, singles €42, doubles €62. MC/V. ❸

FOOD

Cologne's local cuisine centers on sausage and **Rievkooche**—slabs of fried potato to dunk in *Apfelmus* (apple sauce). Don't pass through without sampling the city's smooth *Kölsch* beer, a local favorite whose shield adorns most bars. Local brews include *Sion*, *Küppers*, *Früh*, *Gaffel*, and the devout *Dom*. Cheap restaurants and cafes packed with students line the trendy **Zülpicher Str.** Take U8 or U9 to "Zülpicher Pl." Mid-priced ethnic restaurants are concentrated around the perimeter of the Altstadt, particularly from **Hohenzollernring** to **Hohenstaufenring.** The city's best deals are found in the Turkish district on **Weidengasse** north of Ebertpl., and an open-air **market** on Wilhelmsplatz takes over the Nippes neighborhood. (Open M-Sa 8am-1pm.) **Aldi,** Richmodstr. 31, is a no-frills supermarket. (Open M-Sa 8am-8pm.)

Päffgen-Brauerei, Friesenstr. 64-66 (☎0221 13 54 61). U3-U6, U12, or U15 to "Friesenplatz." A must-see local favorite since 1883. Legendary *Kölsch* (€1.40) brewed on the premises is enjoyed in cavernous halls. Room seats 600. Meals €2-20. Open daily 10am-midnight. F-Sa until 12:30am. Kitchen open 11:30am-11pm. Cash only. ❸

Engel Bät, Engelbertstr. 7 (☎0221 24 69 14). U8 or U9 to "Zülpicher Pl." In this darkwood restaurant, enjoy scrumptious sweet and savory crepes (€5-8) with endless vegetarian and dessert options. Anything that can fit in a crepe will be added upon request. Open daily 11am-midnight. Cash only. ❷

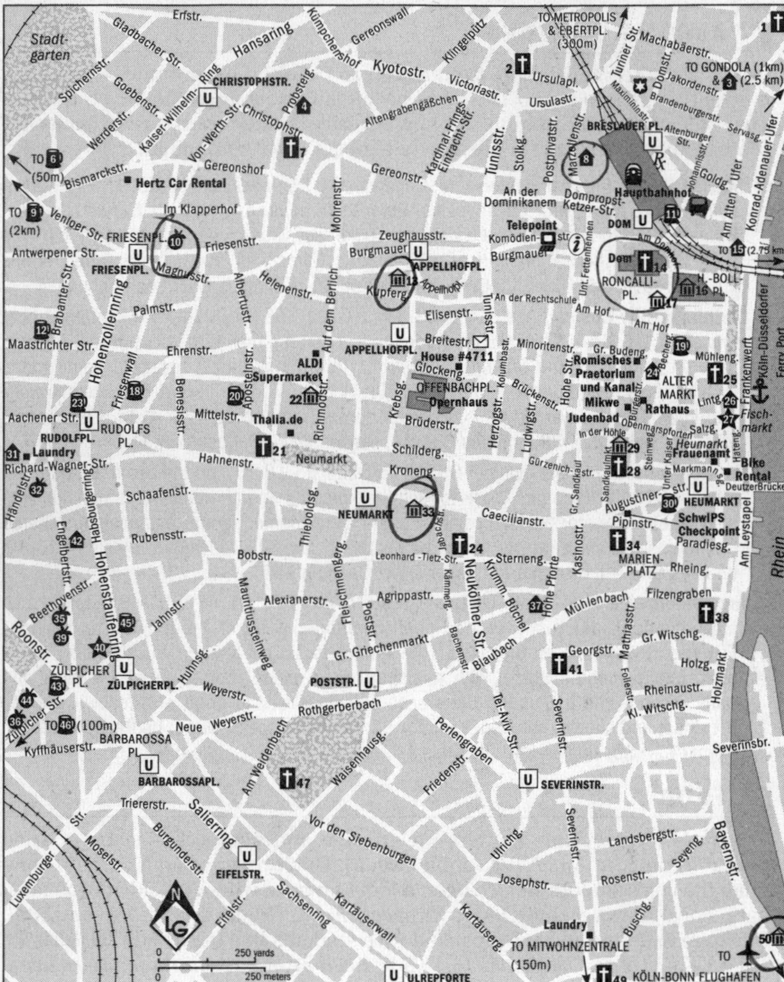

Köln (Cologne)

ACCOMMODATIONS
- Das Kleine Stapelhäus'chen, **26**
- Hotel Am Rathaus, **24**
- Hotel Heinzelmännchen, **37**
- Hotel Im Kupferkessel, **4**
- Jugendgästehaus Köln-Riehl, **3**
- Jugendherberge Köln-Deutz, **15**
- Meininger City Hostel, **42**
- Pension Jansen, **31**
- Station Hostel for Backpackers, **8**

FOOD & DRINK
- Café Magnus, **36**
- Café Orlando, **35**
- Engel Bät, **39**
- Feynsinn, **44**
- Ganesha, **32**
- Päffgen-Brauerei, **10**

BARS & NIGHTLIFE
- Alter Wartesaal, **11**
- Bar o, **18**
- Cent Club, **40**
- Cuba Bar, **46**
- Das Ding, **45**
- Gloria, **20**
- Hotel Timp, **30**
- M20, **12**
- MTC, **43**
- Papa Joe's Jazzlokal, **27**
- Stadtgarten, **6**
- Teatro am Rudolfplatz, **23**
- Underground, **9**
- Zum Pitter, **19**

CHURCHES
- Alt St. Alban, **28**
- Dom, **14**
- Groß St. Martin, **25**
- St. Aposteln, **21**
- St. Cäcilien, **24**
- St. Georg, **41**
- St. Gereon, **7**
- St. Kunibert, **1**
- St. Maria im Kapitol, **34**
- St. Maria Lyskirchen, **38**
- St. Pantaleon, **47**
- St. Severin, **49**
- St. Ursula, **2**

MUSEUMS
- Imhoff-Stollwerck-Museum, **50**
- Käthe-Kollwitz-Museum, **22**
- Museum Ludwig, **16**
- Museum Schnütgen, **33**
- NS-Dokumentations-Zentrum, **13**
- Römisch-Germanisches Museum, **17**
- Wallraf-Richartz Museum, **29**

Cafe Orlando, Engelbertstr. 9 (☎0221 23 75 23; www.cafeorlando.de). U8 or U9 to "Zülpicher Pl." With tapestry-covered benches and jovial music. Breakfasts from €3.10, salads (€5.50-6.80), and mixed drinks (€3.50-4.80) draw a devoted following of students who squeeze in at all hours. Free Wi-Fi. Open daily 9am-midnight. Cash only. ❷

Cafe Magnus, Zülpicherstr. 48 (☎0221 24 16 14 69). U8 or U9 to "Zülpicher Pl." Though students dominate the night scene, locals of all ages come for artfully prepared meals (from €4) and the vegetarian options (€5-7). Open daily 8pm-3am. Cash only. ❷

Ganocha, Händelstr. 26 (☎0221 21 31 65), at the corner of Richard-Wagner-Str. U1, U6, U7, U12, or U15 to "Rudolfpl." A favorite with curry-obsessed Germans, this elaborately draped restaurant offers a range of authentic Indian specialties, including chicken vindaloo (€9.50) and a plethora of Naan bread options. Entrees €7-12. Open daily 6pm-midnight, Tu-Su also noon-3pm for lunch. AmEx/MC/V. ❸

SIGHTS

DOM

Across from the train station. ☎0221 52 19 77; www.koelner-dom.de. Open daily 6am-7:30pm. Tours in German M-Sa 11am, 12:30, 2, and 3:30pm; Su 2 and 3:30pm; in English M-Sa 10:30am and 2:30pm, Su 2:30pm. €6, children €4. Tower open daily May-Sept. 9am-6pm; Mar.-Apr. and Oct. 9am-5pm; Nov.-Feb. 9am-4pm. €3.50, students €1. Domschatzkammer open daily 10am-6pm; €4, students €2. Diözesanmuseum open Tu-Su 10am-5pm. €4, students €2, under 18 free.

This structure has defined Cologne since its erection in 1880. With its colossal spires, a canopied ceiling towering 44m above the floor, and 1350 sq. m of exquisite stained glass casting a harlequin display of colored light, the cathedral is the perfect realization of High Gothic style. Evidence of the Cologne Bishopric reaches back to the 4th century, suggesting that multiple structures have existed at the site of current cathedral. Today, construction continues to repair the damage wrought by WWII and centuries of pollution, pigeons, and acid rain. Beneath the scaffolding affixed to its spires, the body of the cathedral is being meticulously replaced with new stone.

Inside, a chapel to the right of the choir houses a **15th-century triptych** painted by Stephen Lochner to represent the city's five patron saints. St. Ursula and her bevy of female attendants (a whopping 10,000 virgins, according to legend) dominate the left wing, St. Gereon the right, and in the center, the Three Kings pay tribute to a newborn Christ. Silver, gold, and thousands of encrusted jewels ornament the **Shrine of the Magi,** which reportedly holds the remains of the Three Kings. Transplanted to Cologne by an archbishop in 1164, the reliquary demanded an appropriately opulent building to house this treasure. Construction began on the cathedral in 1248 to heed the request. The **Chapel of the Cross** holds the world-famous, 10th-century **Gero Crucifix,** the oldest intact sculpture of *Christus patiens* (a crucified and deceased Christ with eyes shut). Nearby, a doorway leads into the **Domschatzkammer** (treasury), which holds the requisite clerical reliquaries: thorn, cross, and nail bits, as well as pieces of 18 saints. Back at the entrance, 15min. and 509 steps (100m) are all it takes to scale the **Südturm** (south tower) and catch an impresive view of the city and river below. Catch your breath at the **Glockenstube** (about ¾ of the way up), a chamber for the tower's nine bells. Four of the bells date from the Middle Ages, but the 19th-century upstart known affectionately as **Der Große Peter** (at 24 tons, the world's heaviest swinging bell) is loudest. Those who prefer the view from below can attain a sense of the tower's immenseness. The plant-like statue located directly opposite the front door is a scale replica of the cathedral's crowning pinnacles. Find more ecclesiastic treasures in the **Diözesanmuseum,** just outside the south portal in the red building. The allure of the cathedral illuminated from dusk to midnight is irresistible, drawing natives and tourists to the expansive Domvorplatz to admire it.

INNENSTADT

In the shadow of the cathedral, the Hohenzollern bridge empties out onto a promenade flanked by equestrian statues of the imperial family. A monumental flight of stairs leads from the Rhein to Heinrich-Böll-Pl. and its cultural center (see **Museums,** p. 233), a complex of modern architecture that complements the Dom. Farther on, the squares and crooked streets of the Altstadt and old Fischmarkt district open onto paths along the Rhein and gives way to an expanse of grass along the river.

HOUSE #4711. In the 18th century, Goethe noted "How grateful the women are for the fragrance of **Eau de Cologne.**" Hard to avoid, the scent dominates all department store, boutique, and tourist shop perfume displays. The recipe for this revolutionary water was presented to its first manufacturer, Wilhelm Mühlens, on his wedding day in 1792. Though it was once prescribed as a potable curative containing 80% alcohol, today it is treasured merely for its scent, which is supposed to heighten one's senses. Genuine bottles read *Echt kölnisch Wasser* (real Cologne water) and have a "4711" label. The name comes from Mühlens's residence, called House #4711 under a Napoleonic system that abolished house names because it confused soldiers. The home now functions as a boutique, where a corner fountain bubbles with the scented water and elegantly attired attendants dole out small samples. The free upstairs museum has a full history of the famous fragrance. (*Glockengasse, at the intersection with Tunisstr. Open M-F 9am-7pm, Sa 9am-6pm.*)

CHURCHES

The Romanesque period saw the construction of 12 churches in a semi-circle around the Altstadt, each containing the holy bones of saints to protect the city. Though dwarfed by the splendor of the Dom, these churches attest to the glory and immense wealth of what was once the most important city north of the Alps. In addition to those below, other Romanesque churches include **Alt St. Alban** (Martinstr. 39), **St. Maria** (An Lyskirchen 10), **St. Georg** (Georgspl. 17), **St. Pantaleon** (An Pantaleonsberg 2), **St. Severin** (Im Ferkulum 29), **St. Kunibert** (Kunibertsklosterg. 2), and **St. Aposteln** (Neumarkt 30).

ST. GEREON. This magnificent rose-colored medieval church was constructed in the 11th century over the remains of its patron St. Gereon, a Roman soldier canonized for refusing to kill fellow Christians. Its decagon structure contains a gilt mosaic of a sword-wielding David tackling an oafish Goliath. (*Gereonsdriesch 2-4. ☎0221 13 49 22. Open daily 10am-6pm, Su closed for 10am and 11:30am mass. Free.*)

ST. URSULA. North of the Dom, this church commemorates Ursula's attempts to maintain celibacy despite her betrothal. This was easier after she was struck by an arrow in 383 during an untimely attack put her and 11,000 of her chaste companions in the midst of a Hunnish siege. Relics and more than 700 skulls line the walls of the Goldene Kammer. (*Ursulapl. 24. ☎0221 13 34 00. Open M-Sa 10am-noon and 3-5pm, Su 3-4:30pm. Church free. Kammer €1, children €0.50.*)

GROSS ST. MARTIN. Along with the Dom, Groß St. Martin defines Cologne's skyline. Near the Rathaus in the Altstadt, the church was reopened in 1985 after near destruction in WWII. The interior is tiled with mosaics from the Middle Ages, and crypts downstairs house an esoteric collection of stones and diagrams. *(An Groß St. Martin 9. ☎ 0221 257 79 24. Open Tu-F 10am-noon and 3-5pm, Sa 10am-12:30pm and 1:30-5pm, Su 2-4pm. Church free. Crypt €0.50.)*

MUSEUMS

NEAR THE DOM

MUSEUM LUDWIG. This attractive museum, the pride of the city, features works by virtually every big-name artist of the 20th century, including displays of pop art, photography, and one of the world's largest Picasso collections. American artists featured include Andy Warhol, Roy Lichtenstein, and George Segal. *(Bischofsgartenstr. 1, behind the Römisch-Germanisches Museum. ☎ 0221 22 12 61 65. Open Tu-Su 10am-6pm, first F of the month 10am-10pm. €9, students €6.)*

WALLRAF-RICHARTZ MUSEUM. Cologne's oldest museum was recently relocated to accommodate its growing collection. Now, the pastel galleries are filled with masterpieces dating from the Middle Ages through Post-Impressionism. Featured artists include Monet, Renoir, and Van Gogh. *(Martinstr. 39. ☎ 0221 211 19. Open Tu-W and F 10am-6pm, Th 10am-10pm, Sa-Su 11am-6pm. Free German tours W 4:30pm, Su 11:30am and 3:30pm. Call ahead for English-language tours, min. 10 people. €7.50, students and children €5, children under 7 free. Special exhibitions €1.)*

RÖMISCH-GERMANISCHES MUSEUM (ROMAN-GERMANIC MUSEUM). Discovered in 1941 during the excavation of an air raid shelter, a 3rd-century Dionysus Mosaic is the foundation for this extensive collection. Three floors of artifacts including ancient toys, gambling dice, and Roman statues illuminate Cologne's history as a Roman colony. *(Roncallipl. 4, next to the Dom. ☎ 0221 244 38. Open Tu-Su 10am-5pm. German tours Su 11:30am. €6, students and children €3.50.)*

ELSEWHERE IN COLOGNE

IMHOFF-STOLLWERCK-MUSEUM (CHOCOLATE MUSEUM). This museum not only demonstrates how to make hollow chocolate soccer balls but also displays artifacts from the first cultures who cultivated (and revered) the cocoa bean in Central and South America. Salivate at every step of production, from rainforests of cocoa trees to the gold fountain that spurts a stream of free chocolate samples. *(Rheinauhafen 1a. Near the Severinsbrücke. Proceed under the Deutzer Brücke and take the 1st footbridge. ☎ 0221 931 8880. Open Tu-Sa 10am-7pm, Su 11am-7pm. Last entry 1hr. before closing. Museum €6.50; students, seniors, and children €4.)*

KEBAP 101

If there's one thing [redacted] every German town can pr[redacted], it's a kebap stand with de[redacted]cious, inexpensive street fare. As the name suggests, kebap was brought to Germany by the millions of Turkish guest workers in the 1970s. But for many first-time visitors, the kebap stands—and their offerings—are something of a mystery.

Döner: a sandwich with thinly sliced, spiced lamb carved from a vertical rotating spit. The meat—with lettuce, tomato, and a yogurt-based sauce—is stuffed into a pocket of thick pita bread.

Yufka Kebap (also called a **Dürüm**) is like a *Döner* rolled in Turkish flatbread—something like a Mexican tortilla.

Pide: the Turkish term for the leavened flat bread (otherwise known as a pita) can[redacted]ean a few different things. The[redacted]egetarian Pide is served with spinach and feta cheese; the non-vegetarian with lamb meat either placed on top of or stuffed inside a warm slice of bread.

Lahmacun: a Turkish pizza topped with minced beef and lamb and sprinkled with lemon juice. Served rolled up to-go or flat with a fork and knife.

To get a fresh meal, try to detect whether baking is done on location. (Let your nose lead you.) If you do happen upon such a stand—which are becoming increasingly rare—don't pass up the chance. Order a *Döner mit alles* (with everything on top).

KÄTHE-KOLLWITZ-MUSEUM. Holding the world's largest collection of the brilliant activist, the museum contains over 270 of Kollwitz's drawings, 500 of her prints, and all of her posters and sculptures. Dark and deeply moving images chronicle the struggle of daily life and pains of personal loss against the stark black and white landscape of early 20th-century Berlin. *(Neumarkt 18-24. Take U1, U3, U7-U9, U16, or U18 to "Neumarkt." On the top floor of the Neumarkt Passage. ☎0221 227 2363. Open Tu-F 10am-6pm, Sa-Su 11am-6pm. German tours Su at 3pm. €3, students €1.50.)*

NS-DOKUMENTATIONS-ZENTRUM. Cologne's former Gestapo headquarters, now houses exhibits on the city under Nazi rule. The **Mutterkreuz,** an award given to mothers of three or more children for doing their part to help build a strong Nazi state, is on display. Explore prison cells in the basement, where political prisoners memorialized themselves in over 1200 wall inscriptions, including poems of protest, simple calendars, love letters, and self-portraits. English translations are available. *(Am Appellhofpl. 23-25. ☎0221 263 32. Open Tu-W and F 10am-4pm, Th 10am-6pm, Sa-Su 11am-4pm. €3.60, students €1.50. Audio tour €2.)*

MUSEUM SCHNÜTGEN. This museum showcases one of the world's largest collections of medieval art from the early Middle Ages to the end of the Baroque period. With over 5000 Romanesque and Gothic stone sculptures and 2000 works in silver, gold, ivory, and bronze, this museum is a bastion of ecclesiastical art from its very beginnings. Also included is an extensive collection of stained glass windows, tapestries, and priestly fashions. *(Cäcilienstr. 29. ☎0221 223 10. Open Tu-F 10am-5pm, Sa-Su 11am-5pm. €3.20, students €1.90. Guided tours W 2:30pm and Su 11am.)*

FESTIVALS AND ENTERTAINMENT

Cologne explodes with festivity during **Karneval** (late Jan. to early Feb.): a week-long pre-Lenten "farewell to flesh." Celebrated in the hedonistic spirit of the city's Roman past, Karneval is made up of 50 neighborhood processions in the weeks before Ash Wednesday. **Weiberfastnacht** (Feb. 19, 2009; Feb. 11, 2010), is the first major to-do. The mayor mounts the platform at Alter Markt and abdicates leadership of the city to the city's **Weiber** (a regional, untranslatable, and unabashedly politically incorrect term for women). In a demonstration of power, the women then traditionally find their husbands at work and chop their ties off. In the afternoon, the first of the big parades begins at Severinstor. The weekend builds up to the out-of-control parade on **Rosenmontag,** the last Monday before **Lent** (Feb. 25, 2009; Feb. 17, 2010). Everyone dresses in costume and gets and gives a couple dozen *Bützchen* (*Kölsch* dialect for a kiss on the cheek). While most revelers nurse their hangovers on **Shrove Tuesday,** pubs and restaurants set fire to the straw scarecrows hanging out of their windows.

Cologne has more than 30 theaters, including the **Oper der Stadt Köln** and **Kölner Schauspielhaus** near Schildergasse on Offenbachpl. (☎0221 22 12 84 00. Open M-F 10am-7:30pm, Sa 11am-7:30pm. Tickets €8-55.) KölnTicket, in the same building as the Römisch-Germanisches Museum (p. 233), sells tickets for the opera as well as other venues, from Cologne's world-class Philharmonie to open-air rock concerts. (☎0221 28 01; www.koelnticket.de. Open M-F 10am-7pm, Sa 10am-4pm. Tickets €30-150.) **Metropolis,** Ebertpl. 19, plays new releases in their original language, and children's movies dubbed in German. (☎0221 739 1245. Shows daily from 2:15pm. Last screenings start around 10pm. €4-8, children €2.50-3.50, all shows €4 on Th.)

NIGHTLIFE

Roman mosaics dating back to the AD 3rd century record the wild excesses of the city's early residents, but Cologne has come a long way. Pick up *Kölner* (€1) from newsstands or ask the reception at your hostel or hotel. The closer to the Rhein or Dom you venture, the more quickly your wallet will empty. After dark, in **Hohenzollernring,** crowds of people move from theaters to clubs and finally to cafes in the early hours of the morning. Students congregate in the **Bermuda-Dreieck** (Bermuda Triangle), bounded by **Zülpicherplatz, Roonstraße,** and **Luxemburgstraße** The center of gay nightlife runs up **Matthiasstraße** to **Mühlenbach, Hohe Pforte, Marienplatz,** and up to the **Heumarkt** area by **Deutzer Brücke.** Radiating westward from Friesenplatz, the **Belgisches Viertel** (Belgian Quarter) is dotted with more expensive bars and cafes.

> TIP **INSIDE SCOOP.** At the various *Brauhäuser*, where original *Kölsch* is brewed, servers greet you with "Kölsch?" and bring glass after glass until you cover your glass with a coaster.

Papa Joe's Jazzlokal, Buttermarkt 37 (☎0221 257 7931; www.papajoes.de). Papa Joe's has a legendary reputation, drawing locals and expats alike. Local groups play traditional jazz 6 days per week. Drinks are pricey, but a 0.4L *Kölsch* (€3.60) goes a long way. Add your business card or expired ID to the informal collage that adorns the perimeter of the bar. Open daily 8pm-3am. Live jazz M-Sa 10:30pm-12:30am, Su "4 o'clock Jazz" is 8hr. of nonstop jazz from 3:30pm (except June-Sept.). Cash only.

Cent Club, Hohenstaufenring 25-27 (www.centclub.de), near Zülpicher Pl. U8 or U9 to "Zülpicher Pl." Just next to the the Zulpicher U-bahn stop. A student disco, the bar features more dance (to hip hop, pop, dance classics) and less talk, with the appeal of enticingly inexpensive drinks (€0.50 shooters, €3 mixed drinks, €1-1.80 beers). Open W-Sa from 9pm. Cover €5. Cash only.

Stadtgarten, Venloerstr. 40 (☎0221 952 9940; www.stadtgarten.de). From Friesenpl. follow Venloerstr. for several blocks. 2 clubs in 1 location: the downstairs **Studio 672** plays techno and house, while the upstairs concert hall hosts live jazz. Cover €6-15, depending on event. Open M-Th 9pm-1am, F-Sa 9pm-3am. Cash only.

Das Ding, Hohenstaufenring 30-32 (☎0221 24 63 48). Smoky and dedicated to drinking, this eclectic student bar and disco has dirt-cheap specials (€1 and under) and themed parties. W German music. Sa 9-11pm drinks €0.80. Open Tu, Th, Su 9pm-3am; W 9pm-2am; F-Sa 9pm-4am. Cover €5. Student ID required. Cash only.

Alter Wartesaal, Johannisstr. 11 (☎0221 912 8850; www.wartesaal.de). In the basement of the train station, this enormous dance floor fills with pierced 20-somethings. Cover €8. Disco open 10pm-5am most nights. Parties can last until 6am. AmEx/MC/V.

M20, Maastrichter Str. 20 (☎0221 51 96 66). Distinguished DJs deliver drum'n'bass, rock, and punk at this mellow lounge. Cocktails €5. Open daily from 8pm. Cash only.

MTC, Zülpicherstr. 10 (☎0221 240 4188). Take U8 or U9 to "Zülpicher Pl." Frequent live bands, generally of the rock and indie-pop persuasion in a lively area. Cover €5, includes 1 drink; on concert night €5-15. Open daily from 10pm-late. Cash only.

GAY- AND LESBIAN-FRIENDLY

Hotel Timp, Heumarkt 25 (☎0221 258 1409; www.timp.de), opposite the "Heumarkt" U-Bahn stop. This outrageous club and hotel is an institution for transvestite theater. A mixed crowd comes nightly for gaudy, glitter-filled cabarets. No cover, but your 1st drink is €8, weekends €13. Open daily from 10pm. Shows daily from 1-4am. AmEx/MC/V.

Zum Pitter, Alter Markt 58-60 (☎0221 258 3122). Warm evenings bring a primarily gay crowd to the outside patio of this easygoing pub. Open daily noon-1am. Cash only.

Gloria, Apostelnstr. 11 (☎0221 25 44 33; www.gloria-theater.com). A former movie theater, this popular local cafe, theater, and occasional club is at the nexus of Cologne's trendy gay and lesbian scene. Call for a schedule of themed parties. Cover €7-30, may include show ticket. Open M-Sa 10am-11pm, until 5am on party nights. General ticket office open M-F noon-6pm. MC/V.

BONN ☎0228

Known derisively for the past 50 years as the *Hauptdorf* (capital village), Bonn (pop. 314,300) was basically a non-entity before falling into the limelight by chance. Konrad Adenauer, the Federal Republic's first chancellor, resided in the suburbs, and the occupying Allied powers made Bonn the "provisional capital" of the Western Occupation Zone before naming it capital of the fledgling Republic. Today, the Bundestag stands as a vestige of bygone years. The summer of 1991 brought headlines of "Chaos in Bonn" as Berlin fought to reclaim the seat of government. By the narrowest of margins, Berlin won, and in 1999, the Bundestag packed up and moved east. Though Berliners joke that Bonn is "half the size of a Berlin cemetery and twice as dead," it has the perfect combination of a forward-thinking university and a sparkling, historical Altstadt.

TRANSPORTATION

Flights: Köln-Bonn Flughafen (☎02203 40 40 01 02). Bus #670 runs from the train station (every 30min. 5am-10pm; €3, children €1.50).

Trains: To: **Cologne** (30min., 5 per hr., €9-12); **Frankfurt** (1½-3hr., 5 per hr., €30-70); **Koblenz** (45min., 4 per hr., €9-20).

Public Transportation: Bonn is linked to Cologne and other riverside cities by the **VRS** S-Bahn and U-Bahn network. Areas are divided into zones; the farther you go, the more you pay. Single tickets (€1.50-9.30) and day tickets (€7.60-26) are available at Automaten. With the *Minigruppenkarte* (€9.60-32.80 per day), 5 people can ride M-F after 9am and all day on weekends. Stop by the Reisezentrum in the train station or go to the tourist office to pick up a free transit map. Open M-F 6:30am-9pm, Sa 7am-8pm, Su 8am-8pm. The **Bonn RegioWelcome Card** covers public transportation.

Taxis: Funkzentrale ☎0228 55 55 55.

Bike Rental: Radstation, Quantiusstr. 26 (☎0228 981 4636), behind the train station. €6 per day, €35 per week. €30 deposit. Open M-F 6am-10:30pm, Sa 7am-10:30pm, Su 8am-10pm.

Car rental: Avis, Römerstr. 4 (☎0228 22 80 20). Open M-F 7:30am-6pm, Sa 8am-noon.

PRACTICAL INFORMATION

Tourist Office: Windeckstr. 1 (☎0228 77 50 00; www.bonn.de), off Münsterpl. near the cathedral. Staff doles out free maps, offers sightseeing bus tours (2½hr.; daily at 2pm; €14, students €7), runs walking tours (Sa 11am, free), and books rooms via phone for a €2 fee or online for free (☎0228 910 4170). Open M-F 9am-6:30pm, Sa 9am-4pm, Su 10am-2pm. Bonn RegioWelcomeCard, available at the tourist office, covers public transportation into the Cologne area (M-F after 9am; all day Sa-Su), admission to more than 20 museums in Bonn and the surrounding area, and reduced city-tour rates (1-day €9, 2-day €14, 3-day €19; family €18/28/38).

Bookstore: The mammoth **Bouvier,** Am Hof 28-32 (☎0228 72 90 10), has a wide range of foreign books, many in English, on the top floor. Open M-F 9:30am-8pm, Sa 10am-8pm. MC/V.

Gay and Lesbian Resources: Schwulen- und Lesbenzentrum, Am Frankenbad 5 (☎0228 63 00 39; www.zentrumbonn.de), at the far left corner of the Mobil parking lot. From Münsterpl., follow Windeckstr., which becomes Sternstr. Walk across Berliner Pl. to Bornheimer Str. and take a right on Adolfstr.; Am Frankenbad is down the street on the left. Counseling and gay assault hotline (☎0228 63 00 39) open M 1:30-4pm and 10pm-1am, W 1:30-4pm.

Women's Resources: Frauenberatungsstelle, Kölnstr. 69 (☎0228 65 95 00). Open M and Th 5-7:30pm, W and F 10am-noon. Emergency hotline (☎0228 63 53 69). Pick up *Frauen in Bonn* at the tourist office.

Laundromat: Eco-Express Waschsalon, Bornheimer Str. 56 (☎0228 560 26 03). Wash 6-10am €1.90, 10am-11pm €2.50. Dry €0.50 per 10min. Open M-Sa 6am-11pm.

Emergency: Police (☎110), inside the train station. **Fire** and **Ambulance** ☎112.

Pharmacy: Bahnhof-Apotheke, Poststr. 19 (☎0228 65 30 66). Open M-W and F 8am-7pm, Th 8am-8pm, Sa 9am-6pm.

Internet Access: Bonner Internet Cafe & Tele-Service, Am Hauptbahnhof 8. €0.60 per 30min. Open M-Th 8am-1am, F-Sa 8am-2am, Su 9am-1am.

Post Office: Münsterpl. 17. Open M-F 9am-8pm, Sa 9am-4pm. **Postal Code:** 53111.

ACCOMMODATIONS AND CAMPING

Deutsches Haus, Kasernenstr. 19-21 (☎0228 63 37 77; www.hotel-deutscheshaus.net). On a quiet residential street connecting busy squares (Münsterpl. and Berlinerpl.), this value hotel offers lightly furnished rooms with TV. Complimentary breakfast in a tulip-filled room. Reception 6am-11pm. Singles €35-38, with bath €65-75; doubles €65-67/83-90; triples €110-118. MC/V. ❸

Hotel Bergmann, Kasernenstr. 13 (☎0228 63 38 91). Next to Deutsches Haus, this hotel offers elegant accommodation. Well-decorated rooms in a Victorian home. Call ahead for reservations. Breakfast included. Singles €35, doubles €50. Cash only. ❸

Jugendgästehaus Bonn-Venusberg (HI), Haager Weg 42 (☎0228 28 99 70). Take bus #621 (dir.: Ippendorf Altenheim) to "Jugendgästehaus," or bus #620 (dir.: Venusberg) to "Sertürnerstr." Turn left on Haager Weg and walk 10min. A modern hostel in the suburbs with a bar and standard rooms with bath. Wheelchair-accessible. Breakfast included. Laundry €4. Reception 7am-1am. Dorms €24, singles €40, doubles €60. MC/V. ❷

Campingplatz Genienaue, Im Frankenkeller 49 (☎0228 34 49 49). U16 to "Bad Godesberg," then bus #613 (dir.: Giselherstr.) to "Guntherstr." Turn left on Guntherstr. and right on Frankenkeller. Rhein-side camping in suburban Mehlem, 40min. from the city. Reception 9am-noon and 3-10pm. €5 per person, €3-5 per tent. Cash only. ❶

FOOD

The **market** on Münsterplatz teems with haggling vendors and determined customers. At the end of the day, voices rise and prices plummet. (Open M-Sa 8am-6pm.) **Plus** supermarket is on Oxfordstr. 26. (Open M-Sa 8am-8pm.) There is a food court, **Dinea,** on the fourth floor in the Kaufhof on Münsterpl. (Open M-F 9:30am-8pm, Sa 9am-4pm.)

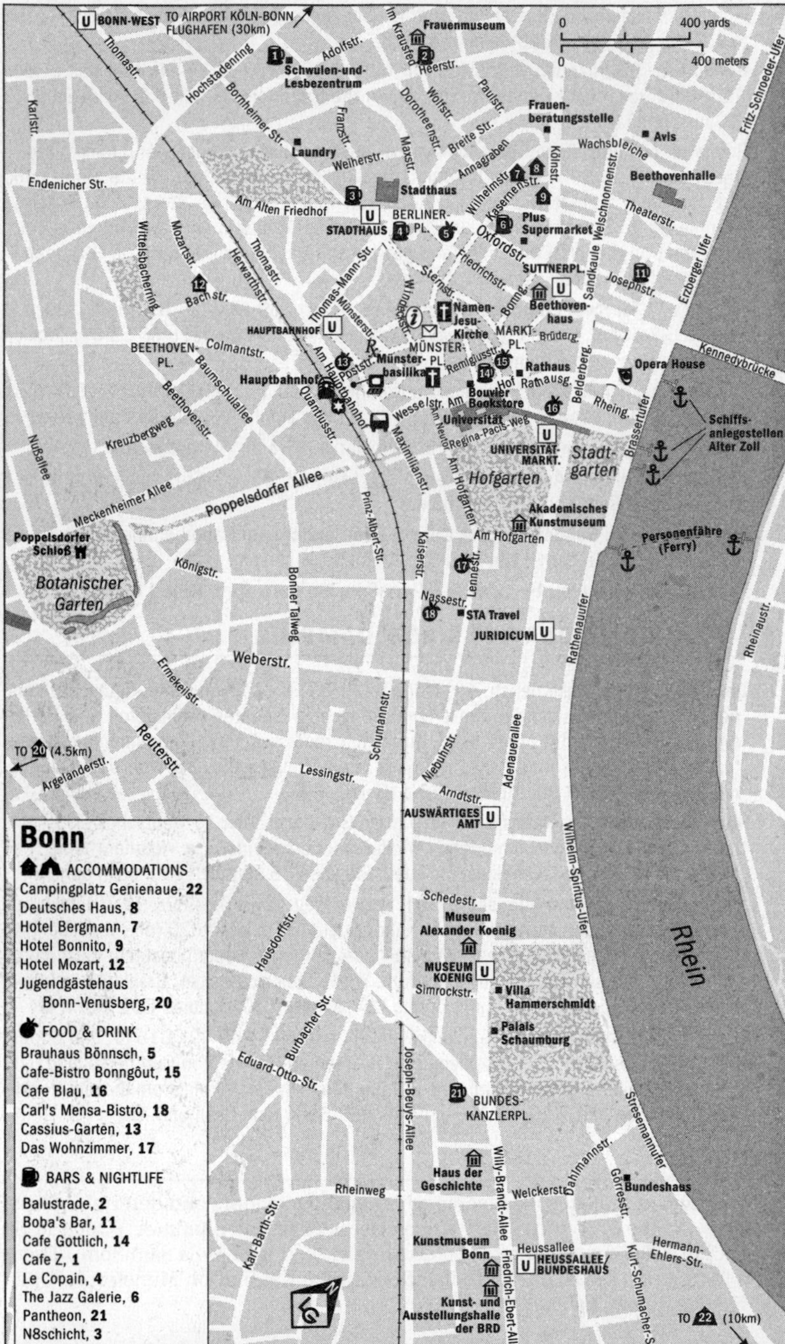
Bonn
ACCOMMODATIONS
Campingplatz Genienaue, 22
Deutsches Haus, 8
Hotel Bergmann, 7
Hotel Bonnito, 9
Hotel Mozart, 12
Jugendgästehaus Bonn-Venusberg, 20
FOOD & DRINK
Brauhaus Bönnsch, 5
Cafe-Bistro Bonngôut, 15
Cafe Blau, 16
Carl's Mensa-Bistro, 18
Cassius-Garten, 13
Das Wohnzimmer, 17
BARS & NIGHTLIFE
Balustrade, 2
Boba's Bar, 11
Cafe Gottlich, 14
Cafe Z, 1
Le Copain, 4
The Jazz Galerie, 6
Pantheon, 21
N8schicht, 3
BONN-WEST
TO AIRPORT KÖLN-BONN FLUGHAFEN (30km)
0 400 yards
0 400 meters
Frauenmuseum
Schwulen-und-Lesbezentrum
Frauen-beratungsstelle
Avis
Laundry
Beethovenhalle
Stadthaus
STADTHAUS
BERLINER-PL.
Plus Supermarket
SUTTNERPL.
Beethoven-haus
Namen-Jesu-Kirche
HAUPTBAHNHOF
MARKT-PL.
MÜNSTER-PL.
Münster-basilika
Rathaus
Opera House
Hauptbahnhof
Bouvier Bookstore
Universität
UNIVERSITÄT-MARKT.
Schiffs-anlegestellen Alter Zoll
Stadt-garten
Hofgarten
Akademisches Kunstmuseum
Personenfähre (Ferry)
Poppelsdorfer Schloß
Botanischer Garten
STA Travel
JURIDICUM
TO 20 (4.5km)
AUSWÄRTIGES AMT
Museum Alexander Koenig
MUSEUM KOENIG
Villa Hammerschmidt
Palais Schaumburg
Rhein
BUNDES-KANZLERPL.
Haus der Geschichte
Bundeshaus
Kunstmuseum Bonn
HEUSSALLEE/ BUNDESHAUS
Kunst- und Ausstellungshalle der BRD
TO 22 (10km)
Thomastr.
Hochstadenring
Adolfstr.
Im Krausfeld
Heerstr.
Karlstr.
Bornheimer Str.
Franzstr.
Dorotheenstr.
Wolfstr.
Paulstr.
Breite Str.
Fritz-Schroeder-Ufer
Wachsbleiche
Endenicher Str.
Weiherstr.
Maxstr.
Annagraben
Kölnstr.
Am Alten Friedhof
Wilhelmstr.
Kasernenstr.
Theaterstr.
Oxfordstr.
Welschnonnenstr.
Wittelsbacherring
Mozartstr.
Herwarthstr.
Friedrichstr.
Sandkaule
Josephstr.
Erzberger Ufer
Sternstr.
Bachstr.
Thomas-Mann-Str.
Bonng.
Windeckstr.
Münsterstr.
Brüderg.
Kennedybrücke
BEETHOVEN-PL.
Colmantstr.
Remigiusstr.
Belderberg
Baumschulallee
Poststr.
Rathausg.
Beethovenstr.
Am Hauptbahnhof
Rheing.
Quantiusstr.
Wesselstr.
Am Neutor
Regina-Pacis-Weg
Brassertufer
Kreuzbergweg
Maximilianstr.
Nußallee
Am Hofgarten
Meckenheimer Allee
Poppelsdorfer Allee
Prinz-Albert-Str.
Königstr.
Bonner Talweg
Kaiserstr.
Lennéstr.
Nassestr.
Rathenauufer
Rheinaustr.
Weberstr.
Ermekeilstr.
Schumannstr.
Reuterstr.
Argelanderstr.
Lessingstr.
Niebuhrstr.
Adenauerallee
Arndtstr.
Wilhelm-Spiritus-Ufer
Schedestr.
Hausdorffstr.
Simrockstr.
Burbacher Str.
Eduard-Otto-Str.
Joseph-Beuys-Allee
Stresemannufer
Dahlmannstr.
Görresstr.
Rheinweg
Welckerstr.
Willy-Brandt-Allee
Karl-Barth-Str.
Heussallee
Hermann-Ehlers-Str.
Friedrich-Ebert-Allee
Kurt-Schumacher-Str.

Cassius-Garten, Maximilianstr. 28d (☎0228 65 24 29; www.cassiusgarten.de), at the edge of the Altstadt facing the station. Take a break from meaty German specialties at this fresh veggie bar. 50 kinds of salads, noodles, hot entrees, soups, desserts, and whole-grain baked goods, all €1.60 per 100g. Sunny terrace, booth, and rear garden seating. Open M-Sa 8am-8pm. MC. ❷

Das Wohnzimmer, Lennestr. 6 (☎0228 209 4972; www.clios.de). This casual and intimate bookstore-cafe. Inside, comfortable booth and bar seating, and walls lined with shelves filled with philosophy, literature, and social science texts for students to catch up on their reading over cappuccinos (€0.90) and beers (€1.50). Open M-F 10:30am-6:30pm, Sa 10:30am-3pm. Cash only. ❷

Cafe-Bistro Bonngôut, Remigiuspl. 2-4 (☎0228 65 89 88) on Blumenmarkt. A chic atmosphere without the pretense. Indulge in meaty entrees (€10-15) or dessert crepes (€3.50-4.50). Huge breakfasts (€5-10) M-F until noon, Sa until 1pm, Su until 3pm. Open M-Sa 9am-1am, Su 10am-midnight. Kitchen open until 11:30pm. MC/V. ❸

Carl's Mensa-Bistro, Nassestr. 15, has cheap restaurant-quality meals (i.e., lots of pasta) served cafeteria-style to a multitude of students. Catch a quick bite for €3 on M, €2.60 on Tu, €4.30 on W, and €3.30 on Th. Salad €0.75 per 100g. Open M-Th 10:30am-4:30pm, F 10:30am-3pm. Cash only. ❷

NORDRHEIN-WESTFALEN

SIGHTS

While most of Bonn's bureaucracy has been packed up and shipped out, these erstwhile seats of power have a historical novelty factor. Bonn's more interesting sights include its many museums and castles.

BEETHOVENHAUS. Attracting music aficionados of all sorts, Beethoven's birthplace hosts a fantastic collection of the composer's personal effects, with over 1000 manuscripts, primitive hearing aids, and his first violin. The *Haus* also hosts the annual **Beethoven Festival** (mid-Sept. to mid-Oct.). The first fête, in 1845, was a riot—Franz Liszt brawled with French nationalist Louis Berlioz while King Ludwig's mistress Lola Montez table-danced. This historic 18th-century residence is one of the few preserved from its era. *(Bonngasse 20. ☎0228 981 7525; www.beethoven-haus-bonn.de. Open Apr.-Oct. M-Sa 10am-6pm, Su 11am-6pm; Nov.-Mar. M-Sa 10am-5pm, Su 11am-5pm. Last entry 30min. before closing. €5, students €4.)*

RATHAUS. This voluptuous birthday cake of a Baroque building is frosted with pastel pink, blue, and gold trim, providing a backdrop for countless celebrity photo-ops. From these very steps Charles de Gaulle, John F. Kennedy, and Elizabeth II charmed the crowds. In the absence of foreign dignitaries, the scenic Rathaus now provides a performance space for concerts and town presentations. Located straight past the university building to the right. *(Reception room open first Saturday of the month May-Oct. noon-4pm.)*

MÜNSTERBASILIKA. Three stories of arches within arches yield to a gorgeous gold-leaf mosaic inside this impressive basilica. A 12th-century cloister laced with crossways and passages branches off under the doorway labeled *Kreuzgang*. Keep an eye out for the incongruous blue-red windows, designed by Expressionist Heinrich Campendonk. *(Münsterpl., or Gerhard-von-Are-Str. 5. ☎0228 985 8810. Open daily 7am-7pm. Cloister open daily 9am-5pm. Free.)*

DEUTSCHLANDBUNDESHAUS (FORMER GERMAN PARLIAMENT). In its heyday, this Bauhaus-inspired structure earned the title of "Least Prepossessing Parliament Building." Its transparent walls were meant to mark a new German democracy where the governors acknowledged their responsibility to the people. *(Take U16, U63, or U66 to "Heussallee" or bus #610 to "Bundeshaus." Mandatory tour Sa-Su 2 and 3pm; free tickets in tourist office.)*

MUSEUMS

The "Museum Mile" begins at the Museum Alexander Koenig. Take U16, U63, or U66 to "Heussallee" or "Museum Koenig." The **WelcomeCard** (p. 236) gives free admission to all museums listed below.

HAUS DER GESCHICHTE (MUSEUM OF HISTORY). Beginning in the broken landscape of 1945 and culminating in a chronicle of modern issues, this museum studies a nation grappling with its past and future. Along the way, enjoy the artful exhibits, including Konrad Adenauer's first Mercedes, rubble from the Berlin Wall, the first German green card granted to a foreigner, and a genuine moon rock. *(Willy-Brandt-Allee 14. ☎0228 916 50. Open Tu-Su 9am-7pm. Free.)*

KUNSTMUSEUM BONN (ART MUSEUM OF BONN). Unveiled in 1992, this immense building designed by Berlin architect Axel Schultes houses an impressive collection of 20th-century German art. Highlights include the genre-defying canvases by Richter, cameo works by Warhol and Duchamp, and an extensive selection of oils and sketches by local Expressionist August Macke. *(Friedrich-Ebert-Allee 2. ☎0228 77 62 60. Open Tu-Su 11am-6pm, W 11am-9pm. €5, students €2.50. With Kunstmuseum Bonn and Ausstellungshalle €10/5.)*

KUNST- UND AUSSTELLUNGSHALLE DER BRD (ART AND EXHIBITION HALL OF THE FEDERAL REPUBLIC OF GERMANY). This modern hall has no permanent art collection. Scheduled shows vary widely, and the hall hosts films, concerts, and theatrical performances. The striking building is a defining element of the Bonn skyline with its three sharp cone spires and 16 columns flanking the **Ausstellungshalle,** designed to represent Germany's federal states. *(Friedrich-Ebert-Allee 4. ☎0228 917 1200; www.bundeskunsthalle.de. Open Tu-W 10am-9pm, Th-Su 10am-7pm. €8, students €5. F 9am-7pm free for students. See website for rotating exhibition info.)*

MUSEUM ALEXANDER KÖNIG. If taxidermy had a Louvre, this would be it. The recently renovated zoology museum displays superb specimens in natural poses amid detailed dioramas, with a focus on conservation and revival. A vivarium has live lizards in the basement. *(Adenauerallee 160. ☎0228 912 20. Open Tu-Su 10am-6pm, W until 9pm. €3, students €1.50.)*

FRAUENMUSEUM (WOMEN'S MUSEUM). This museum is the first of its kind in the world and currently the only one in Germany. The museum appreciates and promotes women's cultural contributions to society, featuring over 700 works by female artists, including Yoko Ono. *(Im Krausfeld 10. ☎0228 69 13 44. U61 to "Rosental/Herrstr." Open Tu-Sa 2-6pm, Su 11am-6pm. €4.50, students €3.50. Tours Su 3pm.)*

NIGHTLIFE

Of Bonn's monthly nightlife glossies, *Schnüss* (€1), available at all newsstands, is unbeatable and more complete than the free *Szene Bonn.* The tourist office sells tickets to most of Bonn's theater offerings through *BonnTicket.*

The Jazz Galerie, Oxfordstr. 24 (☎0228 65 06 62). There's no jazz to be found at this rowdy bar and disco, popular with swank youths. Dance classics on F or catch disco fever on Sa. If you're over 30, you're invited to the "ab 30!" bash on Th. Cover €8.50, includes 2 drinks. Open Th 9pm-late, F-Sa 10pm-late. Cash only.

Pantheon, Bundeskanzlerpl. 2-10 (☎0228 21 25 21; www.pantheon.de), in the shadow of the enormous Mercedes logo. Follow Adenauerdlee out of the city until you reach Bundeskanzlerpl. This popular club also hosts concerts, stand-up comedy, and art exhibits. Website lists shows and events. Cover €6.50-8. Disco open 11pm-late. MC/V.

Cafe Gottlich, Fürstenstr. 4 (☎0228 65 99 69). Modern decor and casual atmosphere rule at this popular student scene. Serves mixed drinks (€2-5) and beer (€2-4). Do your stomach a favor and munch on *Fladenbrot* (€3.20), filled liberally with an assortment of condiments. Open M-Th 9am-2am, F-Sa 9am-4am, Su 10am-2am. Cash only.

N8schicht, Bornheimer Str. 20-22 (☎0228 963 8308). This quirky Bonn standby rocks with a different kind of party every night. Tu theme nights (such as karaoke), Th ladies night (free entry before midnight and ½-price drinks for women). Cover Th-Sa €4. Open W-Th and Su 10pm-4am, F-Sa 10pm-5am. Cash only.

Balustrade, Heerstr. 52 ☎0228 63 95 96). Enjoy a beer (2.30) or *caipirinha* (Brazilian mixed drink; €4.50) at this hip bar. Monthly theme nights include beach, snowball, and jungle parties—breakfast buffet follows. Open daily 7pm-late. Cash only.

GAY AND LESBIAN

Cafe Z, Am Frankenbad 5, in the Schwulen- und Lesbenzentrum (p. 228). This upstairs bar with colorful wall art is the center of gay and lesbian life in Bonn. M gay night, Tu lesbian party, W youth group (ages 16-27), and Th mixed. Open M-Th 8pm-midnight. Closed in July and August. Cash only.

Boba's Bar, Josephstr. 17 (☎0228 65 06 85; www.bobasbar.de). A relaxed bar drawing a lively crowd of mostly gay men. Open daily 8pm-3am. Cash only.

AACHEN ☎0241

Aachen (pop. 259,000) bustles day and night in four different languages, exuding a youthful internationalism in spite of its age—it was founded in Neolithic times. Bordering Belgium and the Dutch town of Maastricht, Aachen has been tossed between empires for centuries. The Romans took advantage of the city's hot springs and turned the town into a recreational center by building thermal mineral baths. The ruins of the baths have long since been built over, but visitors can still relax as the Romans did at Aachen's modern spa **Carolus Thermen,** Passstr. 79. The capital of Charlemagne's Frankish empire in the eighth century, Aachen has preserved his palace and cathedral—and fragments of his body. Today, this thriving university town is a nexus for research.

YUMMI GUMMI

Forget Knut, Germany's most famous bears are two centimeters tall, jewel toned, and delicious. Though they may be found in candy stores worldwide, Gummi bears still call Germany home. Here, the treats are known as *Gummibären* (rubber bears) or *Gummibärchen*, (little rubber bears).

These sweet bears, originally tall and thin, were first made by candy giant Haribo, based in Bonn. Company founder Hans Riegel dreamed up the "dancing bear" in 1922. The bears were poured into plaster molds and coated in a thin layer of beeswax to ensure shinyness and prevent stickiness.

In 1925, at the height of the bears' popularity, the flavor of choice was black licorice. Today, bears comes in pineapple, lemon, orange, raspberry, and the curiously green strawberry.

Even though several imitation companies have emerged to capitalize off of the chewy treats' success, Germans still swear by their Haribo Goldbears. The company's first slogan—which has been translated into every language—preserves a piece of cheery history, insisting, *"Haribo macht Kinder froh und Erwachsene ebenso,"* (the English slogan preserved the rhyme: Kids and grown-ups love it so, the happy world of Haribo.)

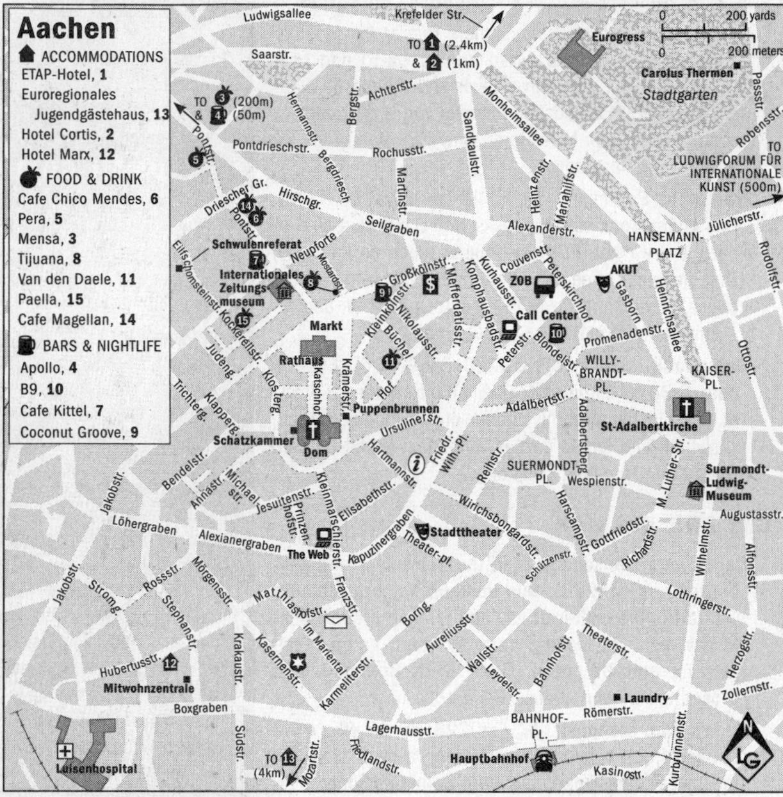

TRANSPORTATION

Trains: To **Cologne** (1hr., 2-3 per hr., €14). The Airport Aixpress **shuttle** stops at Elisenbrunnen en route to the **Düsseldorf** and **Köln/Bonn** airports. Daily every 60-90min. 3:30am-7pm.

Public Transportation: The **bus station** is at Peterskirchhof and Peterstr. Tickets are priced by distance; 1-way trips run €1-6. 24-hr. tickets provide a full day of unlimited travel within Aachen (€6), though most attractions are within easy walking distance.

PRACTICAL INFORMATION

Tourist Office: (☎0211 180 2960). From the train station, cross the street and head up Bahnhofstr., turn left on Theaterstr., which becomes Theaterpl., then right on Kapuzinergraben, which becomes Friedrich-Wilhelm-Pl. The office is in the Atrium Elisenbrunnen on your left. Staff dispenses free maps of the Altstadt, runs playful tours in English, and finds rooms for free. Open M-F 9am-6pm, Sa 9am-2pm; Apr.-Dec. also Su 10am-2pm. **Altstadt tours** in German Apr.-Oct. Sa 11am and 2pm, Su 11am; Nov.-Mar. Sa and Su 11am (€4, students €2.50). Tours in English Apr.-Oct. Sa 11am (€6, students 4.50).

Currency Exchange: Citibank, Großkölnstr. 64-66 (☎0211 470 3480), near Rathaus. €3 fee and 3.5% commission. Open M-Tu and Th 9am-1pm and 2-6pm, W and F 9am-1pm and 2-4pm.

Room Share: Mitwohnzentrale, Stefanstr. 56 (☎0211 194 45). Finds lodging for extended stays. Open M-F 9am-5pm.

Gay and Lesbian Resources: Schwulenreferat Aachen, Eilfschornsteinstr. 12 (www.knutschfleck-online.de). Office open Th from 7:30pm, Coffee hour Tu-Th noon-1pm.

Laundromat: Eco-Express, Römerstr. 31. Wash €2.30. Dry €0.50 per 10min. Open M-Sa 6am-11:40pm.

Emergency: Police, Kasernenstr. 23 (☎110). **Fire** and **Ambulance** ☎112.

Internet Access: The Web, Kleinmarschierstr. 74-76. €0.50 per hr. Open M-W 11am-11pm, Th 11am-midnight, F-Sa 11am-3am, Su noon-10pm.

Post Office: An den Frauenbrüdern 1. Open M-F 9am-6pm, Sa 9am-1pm. **Postal Code:** 52062.

ACCOMMODATIONS

Many hotels close in January; check with the **Mitwohnzentrale** (see above).

Euroregionales Jugendgästehaus (HI), Maria-Theresia-Allee 260 (☎0211 71 10 10). From the "Misereorstr." stop on Lagerhausstr. From the train station, cross the street and make a left, walk until you see the Misereorstr. stop on your right, and take bus #2 (dir.: Preusswald) to "Ronheide." Pristine rooms atop a steep hill, next to a cow pasture. Reservations recommended. Breakfast and sheets included. Curfew 1am. Dorms €23.20, singles €37, doubles €57.40. Cash only. ❷

Hotel Marx, Hubertusstr. 33-35 (☎0211 375 41; www.hotel-marx.de). Nicely decorated rooms near the Altstadt, and a quiet duck pond in back. Breakfast included. Free Wi-Fi. Rooms with TV and telephone. Check-out noon. Singles €37-50, with bath €54-75; doubles €70-90; triples €99-115. MC/V. ❸

Hotel Cortis, Krefelderstr. 52 (☎0211 997 41 10; www.hotel-cortis.de). Bus #51 to Rolandstr. Walk to the end of the street and turn left. Hotel is next to the gas station. Comfortable B&B near the Aachener Stadtgarten, a 20-25min. walk to the Dom and Rathaus. Taxis run €5-8. Cable TV in every room. Reception until midnight. Singles €28, with shower and bath €35; doubles €50/61. MC/V. ❸

FOOD

Food in Aachen has a distinctly international character. Here, quiche and crepes meet wurst and *Kartoffeln* (potatoes). Aachen's specialties include popular desserts *Reisfladen*, a rice pudding cake often served with strawberries or cherries and *Printen*, spicy gingerbread biscuits from an old Belgian recipe.

Tijuana, Markt 45-47 (☎0211 40 19 37). This Mexican bar and restaurant is a popular haunt for the young and hip, with red lighting and leather booths in a central location. The gigantic bar, occupying an entire wall, serves jumbo drinks like "Killer Cool Aid" (€8.40) and "Mega Mojito" (€11) as well as the best enchiladas, tacos, quesadillas, and burritos for miles (€7-13). Open daily noon-1am, F-Sa until 2am. MC/V. ❸

Cafe Magellan, Pontstr. 78 (☎0211 401 6440). Enjoy a Sunday brunch (€10) or split a breakfast platter (€15.70) at this huge cafe. Fish, pasta, pizza, soup, and salads. Mixed drinks (€4.50) during cocktail hour at 7:30pm. Open Su-Th 10am-1am, F-Sa 10am-2am. Kitchen open until 11:30pm. ❸

Van den Daele, Büchel 18 (☎0211 357 24), just off the Markt past the left of the Rathaus. Occupying the oldest house in the city, built in 1655, is this self-proclaimed "most famous cafe and bakery in Aachen." Enjoy a homemade selection of Aachen's famed local delicacies (€2.50). Customized English, French, and Dutch breakfasts €5-11. Open M-Sa 9am-6:30pm, Su 11am-6:30pm. MC/V. ❷

Cafe Chico Mendes, Pontstr. 74-76 (☎0211 470 0141), located inside the Katakomben Studentenzentrum, is a lively cafe (food €4-6). Neon green bar and over 80 board games accompany finger food and free W-Fi. Cheap beer F-Su 6-8pm and all night M. Open M-F 9am-1am, Sa and Su 6pm-1am. Kitchen open 6-10pm. Cash only. ❷

Paella, Kockerellstr. 22 (☎0211 401 0757; www.restaurant-paella.de). This Spanish-inspired restaurant stays true to its name, stirring up an impressive paella for €9 (each additional person €8). The restaurant also serves tapas (€2) and vegetarian dishes (from €6.50) on clay plates. Lunch specials run for €5.30 each and include a side of soup. Legendary cocktails from 6pm for only €4. Open M-Th and Su 11:30am-1:30am, Su 11:30am-2:30am. Lunch specials served noon-4pm. ❸

SIGHTS

In AD 765, the Frankish King Pepin the Short liked to unwind at the hot springs north of Aachen's city center. After assuming power, his son **Charlemagne** (Karl der Große) made the family's former vacation spot the capital of a rapidly expanding kingdom, casting a long shadow of Carolingian influence.

DOM. With its three-tiered dome, intricate marble inlays, and dazzling blue-gold mosaics, the Aachen city cathedral echoes of Charlemagne's "second Rome." Inaugurated in AD 805 as his palace chapel, the magnificent Dom is said to be protected by the emperor to this day—in WWII, a bomb aimed at the cathedral was apparently deflected by a statue of Charlemagne. For 700 years after his death, new Holy Roman Emperors would travel to this cathedral to be crowned on the simple throne still displayed upstairs in order to link themselves to the greatest king Europe had ever known. The ornate gold filigree and Gothic stained glass are the modest attempts of these rulers to join in his glory. Though Charlemagne was originally buried in the **Proserpina Sarcophagus** in the Schatzkammer, today his remains reside in the jewelled reliquary behind the altar. *(☎0211 470 9127. Visiting hours M-F 11am-7pm, Sa-Su 1-7pm, except during services. Services M-F 7 and 10am; Sa-Su 7, 8, 10am; Su also 11:30am. Guided tours Sa and Su 2pm. Call ahead to book group tours. Access above the 1st fl. by guided tour only.)*

SCHATZKAMMER (CATHEDRAL TREASURY). Regarded as the most important ecclesiastical treasury north of the Alps, it contains one of the largest collections of late antique and early medieval devotional art. The Schatzkammer's reliquaries are said to contain everything from John the Baptist's hair to nails and splinters from the true cross and Christ's scourging rope. Charlemagne himself is also divided among numerous containers. The most famous likeness of him, a gold-plated silver bust, was made in Aachen in 1349 and donated by Emperor Charles IV. *(Klosterpl. 2. ☎0211 47 70 91 27. Open M 10am-1pm, Tu-Su 10am-10pm. Last entry 30min. before closing. €4; students, seniors, and children €3. Tours €3/2.50.)*

MARKTPLATZ. Built on the ruins of Charlemagne's palace, the 14th-century stone Rathaus on the Marktplatz offers a great view of the Dom. The upstairs Coronation Hall contains his saber, and is garnished with 19th-century frescoes of military scenes. On the facade stand 50 statues of German sovereigns, 31 of whom were crowned in Aachen. *(☎0211 432 17 10. Open daily 10am-1pm and 2-5pm. Last entrance 30min. before closing. €2, students and children €1.)* The **Puppenbrunnen,** a fountain of bronze figures with movable joints inviting passersby to interact, portrays Aachen's townspeople. *(At the intersection of Krämerstr. and Hofstr.)*

MUSEUMS

LUDWIGFORUM FÜR INTERNATIONALE KUNST (FORUM FOR INTERNATIONAL ART). Aachen has recently focused its cultural energies on acquiring cutting-edge visual art, with the Ludwigforum at the center of this endeavor. In addition to hosting impressive international exhibits, the museum explores artistic expression in all media. Exhibits from the permanent collection rotate monthly. **Space,** underneath the museum, is a forum for modern dance, music, and theater. *(Jülicher Str. 97-109. Bus # 1, 16, or 52 to "Lombardenstr." ☎0211 180 70. Open Tu-W and F noon-6pm, Th noon-8pm, Sa-Su 11am-6pm. Last entry 30min. before closing. Free German tours Su noon. €5, students €2.50. Events at Space €7-18.)*

INTFRNATIONALES ZEITUNGSMUSEUM (INTERNATIONAL NEWSPAPER MUSUEM). Housed in a 15th-century building and the registry office of the world press since its founding in 1886, this museum stores more than 165,000 different international newspapers from the 17th century to the present, covering the revolutions of 1848, the World Wars, the day Hitler died, and the fall of the Berlin Wall in 1989. The museum also has a reading room of current papers. *(Pontstr. 13. Up the street from the Markt. ☎0211 432 4508. Open Tu-F 9:30am-6pm. Call ahead for free tours.)*

ENTERTAINMENT AND NIGHTLIFE

Aachen has a lively theater scene, led by the **Stadttheater,** on Theaterpl. in the central city. (☎0211 478 4244; www.theater-aachen.de. Box office open M-Sa 11am-7pm and before performances. Tickets €8-20; up to 40% discount for students.) A small strip of newer, edgier theaters lines Gasborn, spearheaded by the **Theater 99/Aachener Kultur- und Theaterinitiative (AKuT),** Gasborn 9-11 (☎0211 274 58/02 41). **Apollo,** Pontstr. 141-149, has a multi-screen cinema, mellow terrace cafe, space-age underground club, and a grab-and-go bar outside for premovie beer runs. The wide range of themed events includes gay and lesbian nights, Britpop parties, and salsa dancing. Drinks €3. (☎0211 900 8484; www.apollo-aachen.de. Cafe open Tu-F noon-8pm, Sa 9am-2pm. *Kneipe* open M-Th and Su noon-midnight, F-Sa noon-1am. Cash only.)

Most nightlife in Aachen centers on **Pontstraße** and **Pontwall.** The free *Klenkes Magazin*, available at newsstands, has movies and music listings. The thorough *Stonewall TAC*, available in cafes and at newsstands, lists gay and lesbian events. The trendy **Cafe Kittel,** Pontstr. 39, maintains a dedicated student following with a leafy beer garden accross the street and a hip waitstaff. Come early and score a student breakfast for only €4. Posters smother the door with announcements for live music and parties. (☎0211 365 60. Open M-Th and Su 10am-2am, F-Sa 10am-3am. Cash only.) **B9,** Blondelstr. 9, is crowded even mid-week, and spins Top 40 for dance-happy 20-somethings. (☎0211 26304; www.b9-aachen.de. Drinks €2-3.50. €1 Party on Th, Ladies Night F, Free Beer Tu—€4.50 cover for all you can drink 10pm-midnight. Cover weekdays €2-5, weekends €4. Open M-Th 10pm-4am, F-Sa 10pm-6am. Cash only.) Just off the Markt, **Coconut Groove,** Kleinkölnstr. 3 (☎0211 929 0609; www.coconut-groove-club.de), offers a trip to the tropics and all inclusive karaoke on Fridays. (Open from Tu and Th from 11pm; W, F, Sa from 10pm.)

DÜSSELDORF ☎0211

The capital of densely populated North Rhine-Westphalia crawls with German businessmen and fashionistas. Founded in the 13th century, Düsseldorf (pop. 582,000) has thrice rebounded after pummelings in the Thirty Years' War, the War of Spanish Succession, and WWII. Today, the city is Germany's *Hautstadt*—a pun on Hauptstadt (capital) and the French *haute*. The Altstadt in the modern metropolis features graceful promenades and a boisterous nightlife along the Rhein. Just beyond the riverbank is the *Königsallee* ("the Kö"), a kilometer-long catwalk that sweeps down both sides of the old town moat. By day, the social scene revolves around browsing the racks at chic boutiques or sitting in one of the many busy cafes along the Rhein. By night, cast-away remnants of propriety (and sobriety) litter the streets as thousands of Düsseldorfers flock to the 500 pubs lining the laid-back Altstadt for glasses of local *Altbier*.

> **SUMMERTIME** is low season for Düsseldorf's tourist industry. From August to April, the city swarms with trade fairs, and hotels often double prices. If planning an autumn visit, reserve accommodations at least a month in advance and confirm the room price upon arrival.

TRANSPORTATION

Flights: S7 and a Lufthansa shuttle travel from main train station to Flughafen Düsseldorf (approx. 10min.). Call ☎0211 421 2223 for flight information. Open 5am-12:30am.

Trains: To: **Berlin** (4hr., 2 per hr., €100); **Frankfurt** (2hr., 4 per hr., €70); **Hamburg** (4hr., 4 per hr., €80); **Munich** (5-6hr., 3-4 per hr., €100-122). It's cheaper to take the **S-Bahn** to **Aachen, Cologne,** and **Dortmund.**

Public Transportation: The **Rheinbahn** (☎0211 582 28) includes U-Bahn, trams, buses, and S-Bahn. Single tickets €1.20-10 depending on distance. A **Tagesticket** (€5-21.20) is the best value—up to 5 people can travel for 24hr. on any line. Düsseldorf's S-Bahn is integrated into regional **VRR system,** connecting most surrounding cities.

Taxi: ☎0211 333 33, 0211 999 99, or 0211 21 21 21.

Car Rental: Hertz, Immermannstr. 65 (☎0211 35 70 25). Open M-F 7am-6pm, Sa 8am-noon. **Avis,** Berliner Allee 26 (☎0211 865 6220) and Kreuzstr. 55-57. Open M-F 7:30am-6pm, Sa 8am-noon.

Ride Share: Mitfahrzentrale, Bismarckstr. 88 (☎0211 194 40) and Graf-Adolf-Str. 80. Open daily 9am-7pm.

Bike Rental: Zweirad Egert, Ackerstr. 143 (☎0211 66 21 34). S6 (dir.: Essen) to "Wehrbahn." Turn right from the exit on Birkenstr., then right on Ackerstr. and walk 10min. Call ahead to check availability. Bikes €7.50 per day, €12 per weekend. €35 deposit and ID required. Open M-F 10am-6:30pm, Sa 10am-2pm.

PRACTICAL INFORMATION

Tourist Office: Immermannstr. 65 (☎0211 172 0228; www.duesseldorf-tourismus.de). Walk to the right from the train station and look for the Immermannhof building. Free German monthly *In Düsseldorfer* details local goings-on. Open for event ticket sales (their 12% fee is better than a 20% surcharge at the door) and information M-F 8:30am-6pm, Sa 9am-12:30pm. Books rooms for free (€5 during fairs) M-F 9:30am-1pm and 1:30-5:30pm, Sa 10am-1pm. Branch office, Berliner Allee 33 (☎0211 300 48 97), inside the Kö-Gallerie shopping mall. Open M-F 10am-6pm.

Consulates: Canada and **UK,** Yorckstr. 19 (☎0211 944 80). Open M-F 8:30am-12:30pm, F also 1:30-4:30pm; **US,** Willi-Becker-Allee 10 (☎0211 788 89 27). Open M-F 9am-5pm.

Currency Exchange: ReiseBank, in the station. Open M-Sa 7am-10pm, Su 8am-9pm.

American Express: Inside the main tourist office. Open M-F 9:30am-1pm and 1:30-5:30pm, Sa 10am-1pm.

Room Share: Mitwohnzentrale, Immermannstr. 24 (☎0211 194 45).

Bookstore: Stern-Verlag, Friedrichstr. 24-28 (☎0211 388 10). Paperbacks in many languages plus internet access (€3 per hr.). Open M-F 9:30am-8pm, Sa 9:30am-6pm.

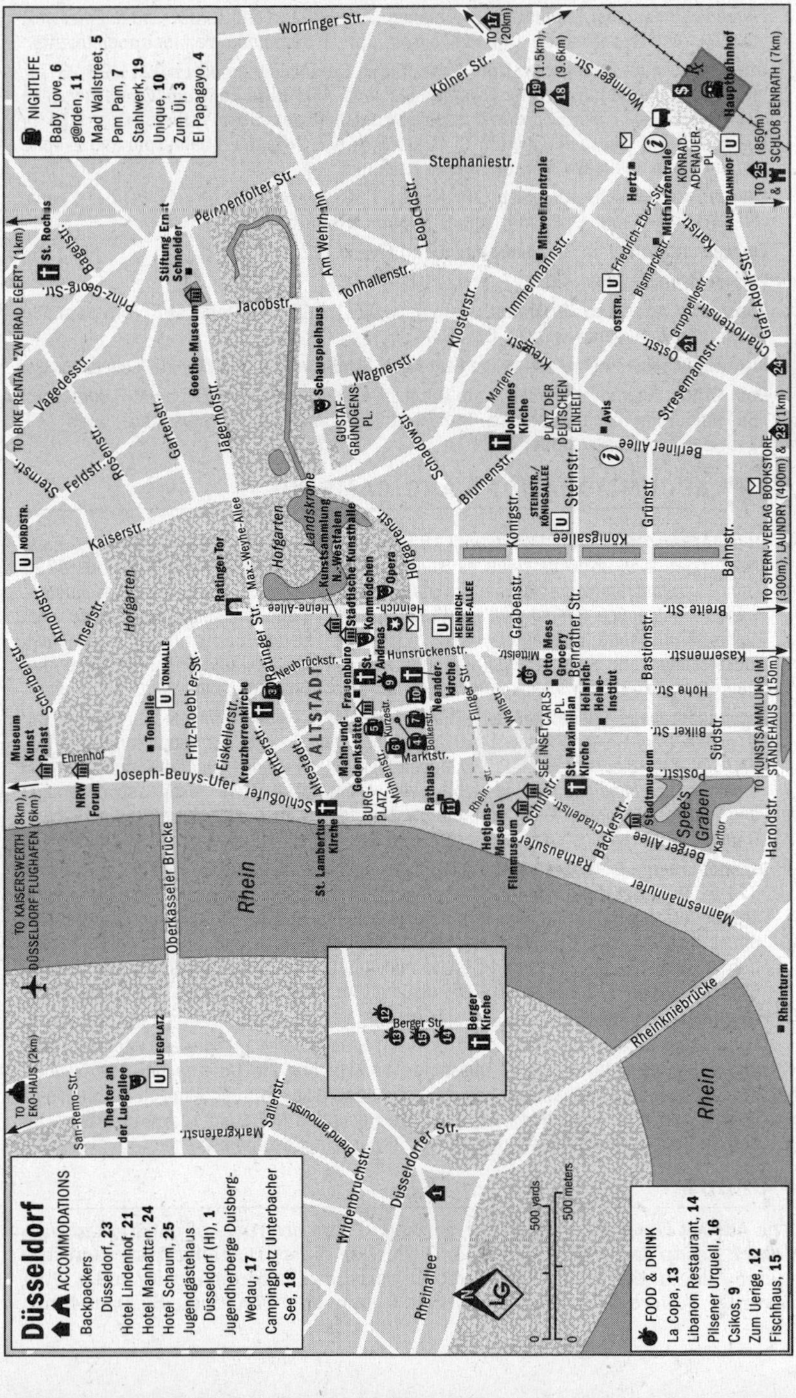
Düsseldorf
ACCOMMODATIONS
Backpackers Düsseldorf, 23
Hotel Lindenhof, 21
Hotel Manhattan, 24
Hotel Schaum, 25
Jugendgästehaus Düsseldorf (HI), 1
Jugendherberge Duisberg-Wedau, 17
Campingplatz Unterbacher See, 18
FOOD & DRINK
La Copa, 13
Libanon Restaurant, 14
Pilsener Urquell, 16
Csikos, 9
Zum Uerige, 12
Fischhaus, 15
NIGHTLIFE
Baby Love, 6
g@rden, 11
Mad Wallstreet, 5
Pam Pam, 7
Stahlwerk, 19
Unique, 10
Zum Ül, 3
El Papagayo, 4
500 yards
500 meters
Rhein
ALTSTADT
Hofgarten
Königsallee
Hauptbahnhof
Spee's Graben
Rheinkniebrücke
Oberkasseler Brücke
Joseph-Beuys-Ufer
TO KAISERSWERTH (8km), DÜSSELDORF FLUGHAFEN (6km)
TO BIKE RENTAL "ZWEIRAD EGERT" (1km)
TO EKO-HAUS (2km)
TO KUNSTSAMMLUNG IM STÄNDEHAUS (150m)
TO STERN-VERLAG BOOKSTORE (300m), LAUNDRY (400m) & 23 (1km)
TO 25 (850m) & SCHLOß BENRATH (7km)
TO 17 (20km)
TO 19 (1.5km), 18 (9.6km)
SEE INSET
Berger Str.
Berger Kirche
St. Lambertus Kirche
Rathaus
Schauspielhaus
Goethe-Museum
Kunstsammlung N. Westfalen
Städtische Kunsthalle
Opera
Tonhalle
Museum Kunst Palast
Ehrenhof
NRW Forum
Stadtmuseum
Hetjens-Museum
Filmmuseum
Heinrich-Heine-Institut
Johannes Kirche
St. Maximilian Kirche
St. Rochus
Rheinturm
Hertz
Avis
Mitfahrzentrale
Mitwohnzentrale
Theater an der Luegallee

Women's Resources: Frauenbüro, Mühlenstr. 29 (☎0211 899 36 03), 3rd fl. Enter next to Mahn-und-Gedenkstätte. Open M-Th 8am-4pm, F 8am-noon; call for appointments.

Gay and Lesbian Resources: Cafe Rosa Mund, Lierenfelderstr. 39 (☎0211 99 23 77; www.rosamund.de). Events for gays and lesbians. **Aids-Hilfe Zentrum,** Oberbilker Allee 310 (☎0211 77 09 50; www.duesseldorf.aidshilfe.de). S6 to "Oberbilk" or U74 or U77 to "S-Bhf. Oberbilk." Open M-Th 10am-1pm and 2-6pm, F 10am-1pm and 2-4pm. Hotline open weekdays 9am-6pm. €0.12 per min.

Laundromat: Waschwerk, Talstr. 10. Wash €3.50. Soap €0.50. Dry €0.50 per 11min. Free Wi-Fi available. Open M-F 7am-8:30pm, Sa 8am-6pm.

Emergency: Police ☎110. **Ambulance** and **Fire** ☎112.

Police: Heinrich-Heine-Allee 17 (☎0211 870 9113).

Pharmacy: Apotheke im Hauptbahnhof, ☎0211 115 00. Open M-F 7am-8pm, Sa 8am-8pm. Emergency ☎0211 01 15 00.

Internet Access: Internet shops line **Graf-Adolf-Straße,** and **g@rden** (p. 252) offers access.

Post Office: Konrad-Adenauer-Pl., to the right of the tourist office. Open M-F 8am-6pm, Sa 9am-2pm. Limited service M-F 6-8pm. **Branch** in Hauptbahnhof open M-F 7am-6:30pm. **Postal Code:** 40210.

NORDRHEIN-WESTFALEN

ACCOMMODATIONS AND CAMPING

Backpackers Düsseldorf, Fürstenwall 180 (☎0211 302 0848; www.backpackers-duesseldorf.de), lives up to its claim as "the cleanest hostel in the world." Take bus #725 (dir.: Lausward/Franziusstr.) from the station to "Cornelius-St." and walk down Fürstenwall in the direction of Kirchpl. It's to the right. Fully equipped kitchen, proximity to most sights, and a youthful clientele make this a rare find in Düsseldorf. Light breakfast, lockers, linen, and Wi-Fi access (computer stations also available) included. Reception 8am-9pm. Reservations recommended for summer weekends. Dorms €22. MC/V. ❷

Jugendgästehaus Düsseldorf (HI), Düsseldorfer Str. 1 (☎0211 55 73 10). Take U70 or U74-U77 (dir.: Heinrich-Heine-Allee) to "Lügpl.," then walk to "Belsenpl." and take bus #835 or 836 (dir.: Graf-Adolf-Pl.) to "Jugendherberge." Providing standard rooms, a hefty breakfast, and handicapped-accessible facilities, this hostel caters mostly to school groups and families. Reception 6am-1am. Curfew 1am; doors open every hr. on the hr. 2-6am. Dorms €24.80, singles €42, doubles €62. HI discount €3.10 per night. Cash only. ❸

Jugendherberge Duisburg-Wedau (HI), Kalkweg 148e (☎0211 203 72 41 64). S1 or S21 to "Duisburg Hauptbahnhof," then bus #934 to "Jugendherberge." These dorm beds are too far from the city to accommodate wild nights. But the reliability and inexpensive prices justify a visit. Breakfast and sheets included. Wash and dry €2 each. Reception 7:30am-11pm. Closed mid-Dec. to mid-Jan. Curfew 1am. Dorms €17.50, over 27 €20.50; singles €25.20/28.20. 10% discount for stays over 2 nights. Cash only. ❷

Campingplatz Unterbacher See, Kleiner Torfbruch 31 (☎0211 899 2038). S-Bahn to "Düsseldorf Geresheim," then bus #735 (dir.: Stamesberg) to "Seeweg." Pitch your tent and enjoy the natural side of Düsseldorf by exploring the Unterbacher See by foot, bike, or boat. Paddleboats, canoes, sailboats, and bikes for rent. Minigolf on premises. Washer and dryer available. Open Apr.-Oct. Reception M-F 9am-1pm and 3-8pm, Sa and Su 9am-8pm. €5.50 per person, €6.60 per tent. Cash only. ❶

FOOD

The **Altstadt** is a gastronomic wonderland. There are rows of cheap pizzerias, *Döner Kebap* and waffle stands, and Chinese diners reaching from Heinrich-Heine-Allee to the Rhein. The **Markt** on Carlspl. sells foreign fruits and a local favorite, *Sauerbraten* (pickled beef). (Open M-F 9am-6pm, Sa 9am-4pm.)

Groceries can be found in the grocery store in the basement of the **Galeria Kaufhof,** Königsallee 1-9.

La Copa, Bergerstr. 4 (☎0211 323 8858). Traditional Spanish restaurant serving 50 tasty types of tapas (€2-9) and the popular paella (€15.50). Bring friends or the whole family along to reach the bottom of the paella pan. Rinse with a refreshingly sweet sangria (€7 per L). Open daily 11am-midnight. MC/V. ❷

Fischhaus, Bergestr. 3-7 (☎0211 854 9864). Amidst jovial Bergestr.'s many cafes and bars, the one at Fischhalle stands out. Every kind of fish can be found here—oysters, salmon, haddock, lobster, and even octopus (€11-25). Fischhaus' relentless patrons flock for a strategic outdoor seat in the center of the Altstadt. ❸

Zum Uerige, Bergerstr. 1 (☎0211 86 69 90). This heavy-wood, heavy-food restaurant competes with Im Füchschen for the best beer in town. Savor breezy Rheinisch nights over a *Schlößer Alt* or one of their *Uerige* beers (€1.65, *Uerige Weizen* €2.40). Meals from €2. Open daily 10am-midnight. Kitchen open M-F 6-9pm, Sa 11am-4pm. ❷

Csikós, Andreasstr. 7-9 (☎0211 32 97 71; www.csikos.de). This colorful little *Kneipe* bursts with unique character and Hungarian cuisine. Though some brave the bear meat and Viennese apple strudel, less experimental taste buds will revel in the tasty *Gulyassuppe* (Hungarian stew; €5). Open M 6pm-3am, Tu-Th and Su 6pm-midnight, F-Sa 6pm-1am.Closed Aug. Cash only. ❷

Libanon Restaurant, Bergerstr. 19-21 (☎0211 13 49 17). For a gastronomic trip into the exotic, enjoy the Middle Eastern specialities, including falafel and humus. Splurge on the *Masa* (5-course menu; €29). Early birds eat half price. Meals €8-20. W-Sa belly dancing from 9pm. Open daily noon-midnight. AmEx/MC/V. ❹

SIGHTS

KÖNIGSALLEE (KING'S AVENUE). The glitzy Königsallee just outside the Altstadt epitomizes the vitality and glamour of wealthy Düsseldorf. Though lacking the fashion-center status of Milan or New York, it packs in enough boutiques and pretension to fill Fifth Avenue. The name originates from the town's attempt to quell the anger of King Wilhelm IV after he was hit with a piece of manure. The calm, green-tinted river down the middle trickles to a halt at the toes of an ornate statue of the sea god Triton. Midway up the street is the highbrow Kö-Galerie, a marble-and-copper shopping mall showcasing one sleek store after another. *(Head 10min. down Graf-Adolf-Str. from the train station.)*

SCHLOSS BENRATH. Originally built as a retreat and hunting lodge for Elector Karl Theodor, this 18th-century palace is one of the latest examples of Rococo architecture in western Europe. The architect used strategically placed mirrors and false exterior windows to make the pink castle appear larger. The vast French gardens and central fountain put the building in perspective. Walk along the reflecting pool behind the castle or explore the tree-lined paths in the park. *(Benrather Schloßallee 100-106. S6 (dir.: Köln) to "Benrath." ☎0211 899 3832. Castle open Tu-Su mid-Apr. to Oct. 10am-6pm, Nov. to mid-Apr. 11am-5pm. Tours on the hr., last one at 5pm, in English if requested. €7, students and children €4.)*

HEINRICH-HEINE-INSTITUT. Beloved poet Heinrich Heine is Düsseldorf's melancholy son. His birthplace and homestead are marked by plaques, and every third restaurant and fast-food stand bears his name. This institute is the official shrine—the only Heine musuem in the world—housing a collection of manuscripts, Lorelei paraphernalia, and an unsettling death mask. Going south on Königsallee, turn right on Benrather Str., walk two blocks, and turn left on

Bilker Str. *(Bilker Str. 12-14. ☎0211 89 99 29 02; www.duesseldorf.de/kultur/heineinstitut. Open Tu-F and Su 11am-5pm, Sa 2-5pm. €3, students €1.50.)*

HOFGARTEN. At the upper end of the Kö, the Hofgarten park—the oldest public park in Germany—is an oasis of lush green. Stroll to the eastern end of the garden, where the 18th-century **Schloß Jägerhof** houses the **Goethe-Museum** (p. 251) behind white iron gates. The Neoclassical **Ratinger Tor** gatehouse leads into the garden from Heinrich-Heine-Allee. *(From the train station, follow Immermannstr. until it becomes Kaiserstr. The garden will emerge on both sides after 2 blocks of walking.)*

MUSEUMS

Düsseldorf takes pride in its supply of museums, especially the collections of contemporary art from the last century. Museums cluster around **Ehrenhof** above the Altstadt and **Grabbeplatz** near the center. The **Düsseldorf WelcomeCard** (available at the tourist office) includes entrance to major museums, free public transportation, and other discounts. (Day card €9; 2-day card €14; 3-day card €19.)

FILMMUSEUM. Generations of movie madness are chronicled through demonstrations of early animation, dubbed clips from notable directors, dioramas, and lots of Greta Garbo. Impress your friends with excellent shadow puppets or transport yourself using blue screen technology. The **Black Box theater** (p. 251), in the same complex, specializes in recent cult flicks. *(Schulstr. 4. between Carlspl. and the Rhein. ☎0211 899 2232. Open Tu-Su 11am-5pm, W until 9pm. €3, students €1.50.)*

K21: KUNSTSAMMLUNG IM STÄNDEHAUS (ART COLLECTION IN THE ESTATE HOUSE). Once home to the *Land*'s parliament, this enormous building reopened in April 2002 as the companion museum to the Kunstsammlung Nordrhein-Westfalen, focusing on experimental art from the late 20th century onward. A box fan swinging like an erratic pendulum greets you as you prepare to delve into the most progressive styles the art world has to offer. The museum features prolific modern artists such as Sigmar Polke and Katharina Fritsch, and each exhibit has German and English captions. *(Ständehausstr. 1. Take tram #704, 709, or 719 to "Graf-Adolf-Pl." Walk 1 block down Elisabethstr. and turn right on Ständehausstr. ☎0211 838 16 00; www.kunstsammlung.de. Open Tu-F 10am-6pm, Sa-Su 11am-6pm, 1st W of month 10am-10pm. €6.50, students €4.50; combined K21/K20 ticket €10/8. German and English audio tours €1.)*

K20: THE KUNSTSAMMLUNG NORDRHEIN-WESTFALEN (THE REGIONAL ART COLLECTION). Within this black glass edifice, skylights pour sunshine on Matisse, Picasso, Surrealists, and Expressionists. The collection of works by Düsseldorfer Paul Klee is one of the most extensive in the world. The museum hosts rotating exhibits of modern art and film. *(Grabbepl. 5. U70, U74-U79 or tram #706, 713, or 715 to "Heinrich-Heine-Allee." ☎0211 838 1130. Open Tu-F 10am-6pm, Sa-Su 11am-6pm, 1st W of month 11am-10pm. Tours W 3:30pm, Su 11:30am. €3, students €1.50.)*

HETJENS-MUSEUM. Connected to the **Filmmuseum,** the Hetjens-Museum fills four floors with 8000 years of ceramics, including intricate Islamic tilework, African and South African antiques, 19th-century porcelain pets, and pre-Columbian relics. *(Schulstr. 4, directly next to the Filmmuseum. ☎0211 899 4210. Open Tu and Th-Su 11am-5pm, W until 9pm. €3, students €1.50; exhibitions €1 extra.)*

STÄDTISCHE KUNSTHALLE (MUNICIPAL ART GALLERY). Across the square from K20 is a gallery of rotating modern art exhibits. The stove-pipe on the museum is a piece by Joseph Beuys meant to symbolize the link between art and the real world. *(Grabbepl. 4. ☎0211 899 62 43; www.kunsthalle-duesseldorf.de. Open Tu-Sa noon-7pm, Su 11am-6pm. Admission depends on exhibit; usually €5, students €4.)*

MUSEUM KUNST PALAST (PALACE OF ART). This dizzying display mingles masterworks of antiquity with modern creations. On the ground floor, glassware, tapestries, and some astonishingly intricate locks memorialize 11 centuries of aristocratic decor. The museum's rotating contemporary exhibits lie beyond stained-glass windows. The newly designed Robert-Schumann-Saal complex features theatrical and musical performances. *(Ehrenhof 4-5. ☎0211 899 2460; www.museum-kunst-palast.de. Open Tu-Su 11am-6pm. Tours Th and Su 3pm. €10, students €4.)*

MAHN- UND GEDENKSTÄTTE (JEWISH MEMORIAL). Through photographs, videotapes, and recorded interviews, the Gedenkstätte documents the persecution of Jews during the Nazi era. Established as a memorial in 1987, this museum addresses the workers' movement and racial persecution. Be sure to check out the permanent exhibition on Düsseldorf WWII resistance. *(Mühlenstr. 29. ☎0211 899 6205. Open Tu-F and Su 11am-5pm, Sa 1-5pm. Free.)*

GOETHE-MUSEUM. Though Goethe only visited Düsseldorf for four weeks in 1792, this museum has the world's largest collection of artifacts related to his life with 1000 exhibits from a collection of 50,000 original testimonials. *(Jakobistr. 2. In Schloß Jägerhof. Tram #707 or bus #752 to "Schloß Jägerhof." ☎0211 899 6262. Open Tu-F and Su 11am-5pm, Sa 1-5pm. Library open Tu-F 10am-noon and 2-4pm. €3, students €1.50.)*

NORDRHEIN-WESTFALEN

ENTERTAINMENT AND NIGHTLIFE

Folklore holds that Düsseldorf's 500 pubs make up "the longest bar in the world." Every night, pubs in the Altstadt fill to the brim by 6pm, and foot traffic is shoulder-to-shoulder by nightfall. The tourist-friendly **Bolkerstraße** and **Flingerstraße** are littered with street performers of the musical and beer-Olympics varieties, while locals head to **Ratingerstraße.** Though the Altstadt is a casual setting for all ages, the city's debutantes flaunt their designer purchases in upscale bars and clubs—don't expect to mingle if you don't dress the part. Pick up *Prinz* (€3), Düsseldorf's fashion bible, often free at youth hostels. *Facolte* (€2), a gay and lesbian nightlife magazine, is available at most newsstands. Clubbers should watch their valuables around **Charlottenstraße** at night.

Kommödchen is a tiny, extraordinarily popular theater behind the Kunsthalle on Kay-und-Lore-Lorentz-Pl. (☎0211 32 94 43. Box office open M-Sa 11:30am-8pm, Su 5-8pm.) To avoid a service charge, purchase ballet and opera tickets at the **Opernhaus,** Heinrich-Heine-Allee 16a. (☎0211 890 82 11. Box office open M-F 10am-8pm, Sa 10am-6pm, and 1hr. before each performance. Tickets €8-59.) In the Filmmuseum, the wildly popular **Black Box,** Schulstr. 4 (☎0211 899 24 90), off Rathausufer along the Rhein, serves art-film aficionados with foreign flicks in the original format (€5, students €4). Tickets for all events are available by phone, at the box office, or from the tourist office. (Tickets ☎0180 564 4322.)

Mad Wallstreet, Kurzestr. 6 (www.madwallstreet.de). An economist's vision of heaven, this bar is a play on the market economy, showing fluctuating drink prices every 300 seconds throughout the night on flatscreens. The law of drunken supply and demand means prices of popular drinks soar as others plummet. Prices crash to historical lows on Black Fridays (beer €0.90, shooters €1.90, mixed drinks €2.90). Expect a loyal crowd of trendy youths every weekend. Open W-Sa 10pm-5am. Cash only.

Unique, Bolkerstr. 30 (☎0211 323 0990). Instead of joining the endless beerfest with neighboring bars, this aptly named club focuses on the music, which is house, electro, funk, breakbeat, and freestyle. Draws a trendy yet diverse young crowd with deeper pockets. Cover €5-10 depending on the event. Open W-Sa from 11pm. MC/V.

Pam-Pam, Bolkerstr. 32 (☎0211 854 9394). This minimally lit basement disco is overflowing by midnight, but the crowds keep coming. Dance the night away to house,

ON THE MENU

BATTLING BEERS

Drinking beer is generally a simple af[redacted] When indulging in Düsseldor[redacted]however, it is important to remember one rule of thumb: never, under any circumstances, order a *Kölsch*. The rationale behin[redacted]this is twofold. Legally, accor[redacted]g to the 1985 Kölsch Convention, this special beer can only be served within a 20-mile radius of Cologne. More important, though, is the long-standing rivalry between Düsseldorf and its upstream neighbor Cologne.

Historians date the rift back to 1288 when Count Adolf vom Berg (of what was then Duseldorp) led 6000 troops into battle against the Archbishop of Cologne in one of the bloodiest spectacles of the Middle Ages. Locals say that mere jealousy fuels the hatred: Cologne resents the fact that its protégé has become an international corporate and fashion h[redacted]rters, while Düsseldorf rema[redacted]ous of the art, history, and [redacted] will never have.

Others argue that the fierce compe[redacted]on is founded on more serious[redacted]grounds: beer. Nothing elicits town pride more than the local brew: Cologne boasts a gold fountain of *Kölsch* (known by its gold color and subtle, fruity flavor), while Düsseldorf prides itself on its coppery reservoirs of *Altbier* (bitter and thick). Fortunately, travelers can experience (and taste) the charms of both cities, which are less than an hour of train travel apart. Just keep your preferences to yourself.

rock, pop, and plenty of American music. Open daily 9pm-5am. Cash only.

Zum Ül, Ratinger Str. 16 (☎0211 32 53 69). A huge crowd congregates out front, while inside people of all ages down glasses of *Füchschenbier* (€1.60 for 0.2L). Open M-Sa 9am-4am, Su 10am-1am. Food served M-Sa until 3pm, Su until 4pm. Cash only.

El Papagayo, Mertensgasse 2 (☎0211 13 33 30; www.elpapagayo.de). Whether you're hungry (for tapas) or thirsty (for alcohol), El Papagayo caters to your mood. Show up early (8-10pm) to enter free and enjoy €4 cocktails. M night karaoke, Mexican Nights doused in tequila and nachos, and Freaky Fridays with R&B and hip-hop beats. Hormone-driven Singles' Nights are sure to provide you with a good time. Open daily 10pm-late.

Baby Love, Kurzerstr. 2 (☎0211 828 4345). This favorite booms with dancing and music. W reggae and R&B, Th punk, F-Sa techno. Open Tu-Th 10pm-4am, F-Sa 10pm-5am, happy hour M-Sa 10pm-midnight. Cash only.

g@rden, Rathausufer 8 (☎0211 86 61 60). This futuristic cafe has internet access (€2 per 30min., €3 per hr.), a beautiful view of the Rhein, and DJs playing everything from hip hop to techno by request. Checking email never felt so cool. Open Mar.-Sept. Cafe open 11am-1am. Club open from 9pm on 1st and 3rd Sa of the month. MC.

HESSEN

Prior to the 20th century, Hessen was known for exporting mercenary soldiers to rulers like King George III, who enlisted them to control an unruly gang of colonials across the Atlantic in 1776. Today, Hessen's ivy clad castles and immense steeples find their modern analog in the region's skyscrapers. Hessen is the busiest economic center in the country, led by the unsparing financial behemoth of Frankfurt. Overshadowed by its capital, the rest of understated Hessen attracts little tourist attention, leaving the medieval charisma of Marburg and the artistic offerings of Kassel blessedly secluded.

HIGHLIGHTS OF HESSEN

LAND at **Frankfurt's** busy airport, and stick around for fast-paced **Römerberg** nightlife (p. 262) and superb museums (p. 260) .

PARTY ALL NIGHT LONG in the hip university town of **Marburg** (p. 263), which influenced the writings of the **Brothers Grimm** and has spawned a racy youth culture.

SEE IT TO BELIEVE IT in **Wilhelmshöhe Park,** where waterfalls and castles complement the curious cosmopolitanism of **Kassel** (p. 266).

FRANKFURT AM MAIN ☎069

Though Frankfurt may lack some of the traditional architecture of other German cities, its modern buildings perfectly complement the older cathedrals and half-timbered houses. It is said that while fleeing the Saxons, Charlemagne and his Franks saw a deer crossing the Main River in a shallow *Furt* (ford) and followed the animal to safety on the opposite bank, where Charlemagne proceeded to found a city. In 1356, Frankfurt rose to prominence when the Golden Bull of imperial law made it the site of emperors' elections and coronations until the Holy Roman Empire dissolved.

Ten years after Allied bombers destroyed much of the city in March 1944, Frankfurt received a concrete makeover paid for by the countries that ruined it. Today, skyscrapers loom over crowded streets and dark-suited stock traders scurry about. It's easy to see how Frankfurt acquired the nicknames "Bankfurt" and "Mainhattan"—the EU's bank is based here. Frankfurt has a reputation for being the most Americanized city in Europe, but the government works to preserve the city's rich history. Though a transportation blip for many travelers, Frankfurt spends more on cultural attractions than any other German city.

TRANSPORTATION

Flights: The largest and busiest airport in Germany, Frankfurt's **Flughafen Rhein-Main** (☎01805 372 46 36) is the gateway to Germany for thousands of travelers from all over the world. From the airport, Schnellbahn (S-Bahn) trains S8 and S9 travel to the Frankfurt Hauptbahnhof every 15min. Buy tickets (€3.60) from green ticket machines marked *Fahrkarten* before boarding. Most public transportation and trains to major cities depart from Airport Terminal 1. Take the free bus (every 15min.), or walk through the skyway to reach the terminal from the main airport. Taxis to the city center (around €20) can be found outside any terminal.

Trains: ☎0180 519 4195; www.bahn.de for reservations and information. Trains from Frankfurt's **Hauptbahnhof** to: **Amsterdam, Netherlands** (4hr., every 2hr., €150); **Berlin**

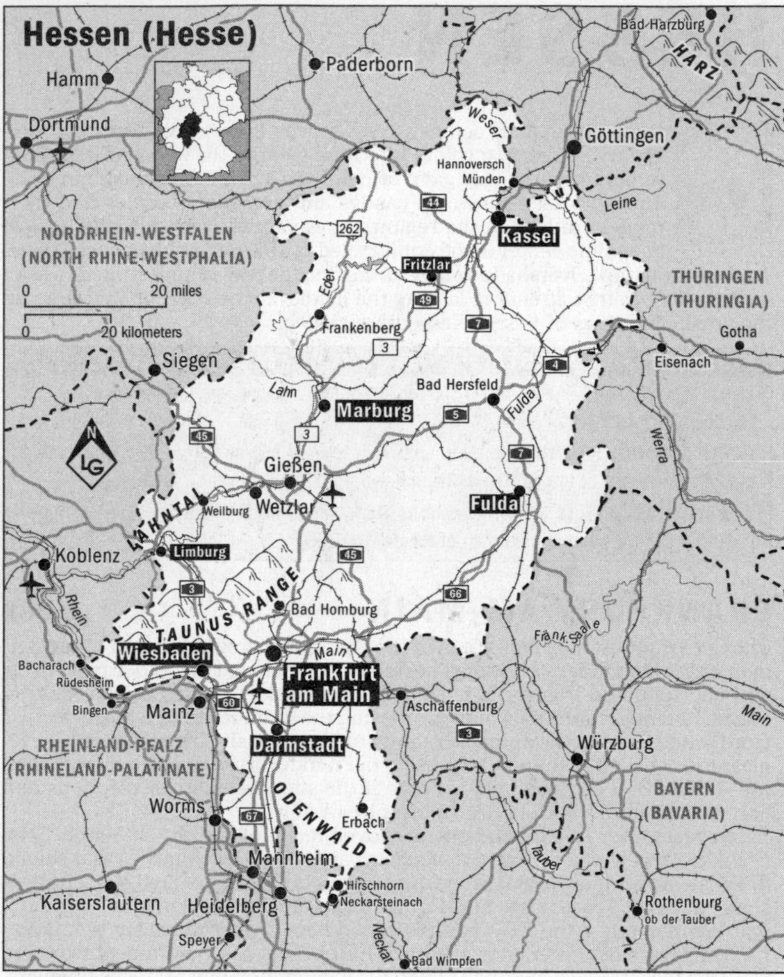

(5-6hr., 2 per hr., €90-105); **Cologne** (2hr., every hr., 38-60); **Hamburg** (3-5hr., 2 per hr., €93); **Munich** (3-4hr., 3 per hr., €55); **Paris, France** (6-8hr., 4 per day, €82.60).

Ride Share: Mitfahrenzentrale, Stuttgarter Str. 12 (☎069 23 64 44). Take a right on Baseler Str. at the side exit of the Hauptbahnhof (track 1) and walk 2 blocks toward the river. Arranges rides to **Berlin** (€20), **München** (€15), and elsewhere. Open M-F 8am-6:30pm, Sa 8am-4pm, Su 10am-4pm.

Public Transportation: Single-ride tickets valid for 1hr. in 1 direction, transfers permitted (€2.10; 6-9am and after 4pm €2.20). Eurail passes valid only on S-Bahn trains. For unlimited access to the S- and U-Bahn, trams, and buses, the *Tageskarte* is valid until midnight the day of purchase. (€5.60, children €3.35.) **Passengers without tickets face an immediate €40 fine.** At the Hauptbahnhof, long-distance trains depart from the main level, while the S-Bahn leaves from the lower level. Escalators to the U-Bahn are in the **Einkaufspassage** (shopping passage). Trams #11, 16, 17, 20, and 21 pass by the island platform outside the entrance, while buses #35, 37, and 46 leave to the right of the main entrance.

Taxis: ☎069 23 00 01, 069 23 00 33, or 069 25 00 01. €1.38-1.53 per km.

Boat Rides: Several companies offer Main tours, departing from the Mainkai near the Römerberg (M-Sa 1 tour per hr.; Su 2 per hr.; 50min. tour €6.95, 100min. tour €8.95). **Primus Linie** also cruises to wine towns along the Main, including Rüdesheim and Loreley (☎069 13 38 37 10; www.primus-linie.de).

Bike Rental: Deutsche Bahn (DB) runs the citywide bike rental, **Call a Bike.** Look for bright red bikes with the DB logo on street corners throughout the city. Retrieve unlocking code by phone or online (☎0700 05 22 55 22; www.callabike.de). €0.10 per min., max. €15 per day. Credit cards only.

Hitchhiking: *Let's Go* does not recommend hitchhiking as a safe mode of transport and it is not encouraged in Germany. However, hitchers reportedly wait near the Festhalle/Messe in the city, near the entrance to the Autobahn.

TIP

HIGH CULTURE, LOW BUDGET. The **Frankfurt Card,** available at tourist offices and travel agencies, allows unlimited travel on trains and buses including the airport line. It also gives discounts on 20 museums, the Palmengarten, zoo, city tours, river cruises, and **free drinks** with meals at selected restaurants. (1-day €8.70, 2-day €12.50.) The **Museumsufer Ticket** gets you in to 26 museums for 2 days (€12, students €6, family €20). See **Museums,** p. 260, for more info.

ORIENTATION

A sprawling collage of steel, concrete, glass, and scaffolding, Germany's fifth-largest city bridges the **Main** (pronounced "mine") 35km east of its confluence with the Rhein. The Main runs east-west, separating the functional downtown area north of the river from the more residential Sachsenhausen district to the south. Most travelers arrive at Frankfurt's Hauptbahnhof, which sits at the western end of **Kaiserstraße,** the main boulevard in Frankfurt's red-light district. Due east of Kaiserstr. lies the heart of downtown Frankfurt, home to designer boutiques, enormous department stores, and the reconstructed old city, or Altstadt. Naturally, these neighborhoods have both the highest concentration of prominent sights and the highest concentration of tourists. To get a better feel for Frankfurt's urban culture, venture northwest to the Frankfurter **Westend,** home of the Johann Wolfgang Goethe Universität. The large student population in this affluent neighborhood keeps prices down and bars open late. But for the neighborhood that has it all, travel south across the Main to **Sachsenhausen.** Here you'll find traditional German restaurants specializing in *Äpfelwein* (apple wine) and other regional delicacies, a riverside drive lined with an array of intriguing museums, and some of the city's best bars and nighclubs.

PRACTICAL INFORMATION

TOURIST AND FINANCIAL SERVICES

Tourist Office (☎069 21 23 88 00; www.frankfurt-tourismus.de), in the Hauptbahnhof, next to the main exit. Brochures, tours, and free maps. Books rooms for a €3 fee; free if you call or email ahead. Open M-F 8am-9pm, Sa-Su and holidays 9am-6pm. A **branch,** at Römerberg 27, also books rooms. Open M-F 9:30am-5:30pm, Sa-Su 10am-4pm.

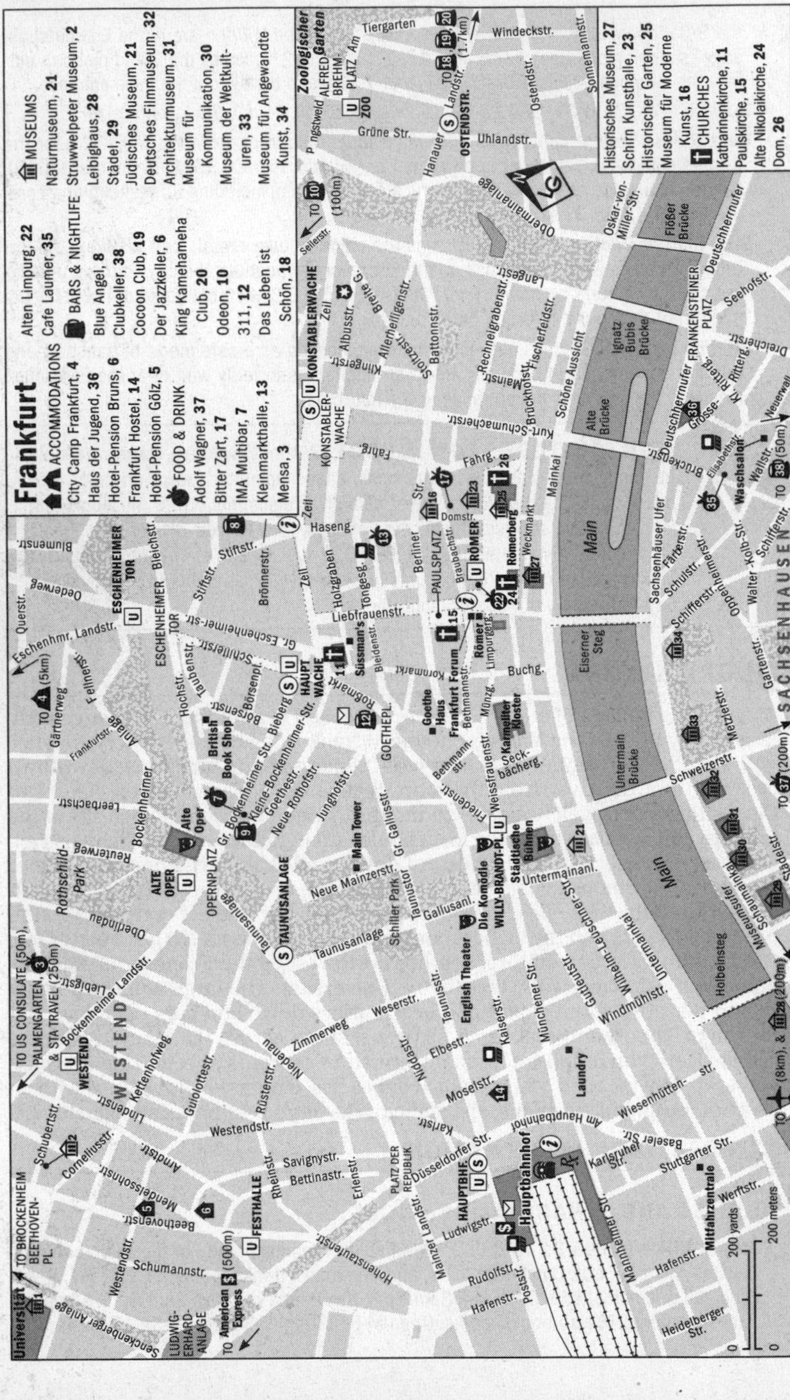
Frankfurt
ACCOMMODATIONS
City Camp Frankfurt, 4
Haus der Jugend, 36
Hotel-Pension Bruns, 6
Frankfurt Hostel, 14
Hotel-Pension Gölz, 5
FOOD & DRINK
Adolf Wagner, 37
Bitter Zart, 17
IMA Multibar, 7
Kleinmarkthalle, 13
Mensa, 3
Alten Limpurg, 22
Cafe Laumer, 35
BARS & NIGHTLIFE
Blue Angel, 8
Clubkeller, 38
Cocoon Club, 19
Der Jazzkeller, 6
King Kamehameha Club, 20
Odeon, 10
311, 12
Das Leben ist Schön, 18
MUSEUMS
Naturmuseum, 21
Struwwelpeter Museum, 2
Leibighaus, 28
Städel, 29
Jüdisches Museum, 21
Deutsches Filmmuseum, 32
Architekturmuseum, 31
Museum für Kommunikation, 30
Museum der Weltkulturen, 33
Museum für Angewandte Kunst, 34
Historisches Museum, 27
Schirn Kunsthalle, 23
Historischer Garten, 25
Museum für Moderne Kunst, 16
CHURCHES
Katharinenkirche, 11
Paulskirche, 15
Alte Nikolaikirche, 24
Dom, 26
WESTEND
SACHSENHAUSEN
Main
Hauptbahnhof
200 yards
200 meters

Tours: Depart daily 10am and 2pm (in winter only 2pm) from the Römerberg tourist office, and 15min. later from the Hauptbahnhof tourist office. Tours available in 14 foreign languages and last 2½hr. €26, students €21, under 12 €10. 25% discount with a Frankfurt-Card. Evening tours lasting 1½hr. depart from the Hauptbahnhof at 5:45pm. €16, students €12, under 12 €5.

Budget Travel: STA Travel, Bockenheimer Landstr. 133 (☎069 70 30 35; www.statravel.de), near the university. U-Bahn to "Bockenheimer Warte," turn left after leaving the U exit on Bockenheimer Landstr. Books national and international flights and sells ISICs. Open M-F 10am-6pm, Sa 11am-2pm.

Consulates: Australia, Neue Mainzer Str. 52-58, 28th fl. (☎069 90 55 80). Open M-Th 9am-4:30pm, F 9am-4pm. **US:** Gießener Str. 30 (☎069 753 50). Open M-F 8am-4pm, closed holidays and last Th of every month.

Currency Exchange: At any bank. Banks in the airport and the Reise Bank (open daily 7:30am-10:30pm) in the station have slightly worse rates, but, unlike most banks, stay open during the weekend.

American Express: Kaiserstr. 10 (☎069 210 5111). Exchanges currency, handles traveler's checks, and arranges hotel and rental car reservations. Open M-F 9:30am-6pm, Sa 10am-2pm.

LOCAL SERVICES

Bookstore: British Book Shop, Börsenstr. 17 (☎069 28 04 92). Classics, Shakespeare, popular novels, and nonfiction in English. Also a good selection of magazines and a bargain bin with paperbacks (€2). Open M-F 9:30am-7pm, Sa 9:30am-6pm.

Gay and Lesbian Resources: The **Switchboard,** Alte Gasse 36 (☎069 283 53; www.ag36.de), contains a gay info desk, as well as the **Cafe der AIDS-Hilfe Frankfurt,** a popular bar/cafe run by the local AIDS foundation. Take the U- or S-Bahn to "Konstablerwache." Open Tu-Th 7pm-midnight, F-Sa 7pm-1am, Su 7-11pm. Another solid resource is the **AIDS Anonyme Beratungsstelle** (Aids Anonymous Information Center; ☎069 21 24 32 70; www.gesundheitsamt.stadt-frankfurt.de).

Laundromat: SB Waschsalon, Wallstr. 8, near Haus der Jugend in Sachsenhausen. Wash €3.50 for a small machine (6kg) or €5 for a large machine (12kg). Soap €0.50. Dry €0.50 per 15min. Open M-Sa 6am-11pm.

EMERGENCY AND COMMUNICATIONS

Emergency: ☎110. **Fire** and **Ambulance:** ☎112.

Women's Helpline: ☎069 70 94 94. More information at Frankfurt Forum (see below).

AIDS hotline: ☎069 405 8680.

Disabled Travelers: Frankfurt Forum, Römerberg 32 (☎069 21 24 00 00; www.vgf.ffm.de), publishes a guide to accessible locations in Frankfurt. Open M-W 10am-4:30pm, Th 10am-6pm, F 10am-2pm. Call-in hours daily from 8am-close.

Pharmacy: Apotheke im Hauptbahnhof is in the train station's **Einkaufspassage** (☎069 23 30 47). Open M-F 6:30am-9pm, Sa 8am-9pm, Su 9am-8pm.

Internet Access: Alpha, in the Hauptbahnhof's gambling salon, past track 24 on the north side. €2.50 per hr. Open M-Sa 8:30am-1am. **CybeRyder,** Tongesgasse 31, offers a more comfortable cafe setting, though internet is more costly. €1.60 per 15 min. during peak hours (M-F 9:30am-7pm, Sa 10am-7pm), €1.30 on Su (noon-10pm), €1 during happy hours (M-Sa after 7pm). Elizabethstr., directly behind the Haus der Jugend, and Kaiserstr., across from the Haupbahnhof, have plenty of Internet-Telefon stores.

Post Office: Goethe Platz 7, walk 10min. down Taunusstr. from the Hauptbahnhof, or take the U- or S-Bahn to "Hauptwache" and walk south to the square. Open M-F 7am-8pm,

Sa 8am-2pm. **Filiale Frankfurt 2,** Zeil 90/Schäfergasse. (☎069 13 81 26 21), inside the Karstadt on the pedestrian-only Ziel. U- or S-Bahn to "Hauptwache." or "Konstablerwache." Open M-W 9:30am-8pm, Th-Sa 9:30am-9pm. **Postal Code:** 60313.

ACCOMMODATIONS AND CAMPING

In the financial center of Europe, deals are rare, and trade fairs make rooms scarce, so book in advance. The **Westend/University** area has affordable options in a quiet setting, though nighlife is more accessible from the accommodations near **Sachsenhausen** and the **Hauptbahnhof.**

Haus der Jugend (HI), Deutschherrnufer 12 (☎069 610 0150; www.jugendherberge-frankfurt.de). Bus #46 from the station to "Frankensteiner Pl." Located along the Main and in front of the pubs and cafes of the old Sachsenhausen district, this popular hostel attracts student groups and young travelers. Large groups of schoolchildren crowd the halls, but the price and location compensate. Breakfast (7-9am) and sheets included. Check-in 1pm. Check-out 9:30am. Curfew 2am. Locks available for €5 deposit. Some private bathrooms. Dorms from €21.50, under 27 from €17. MC/V. ❷

Frankfurt Hostel, Kaiserstr. 74 (☎069 247 5130; www.frankfurt-hostel.de). Walk straight down Kaiserstr. from the Hauptbahnhof, and the hostel is on your left. A convenient location and great prices attract an young international crowd to this bustling hostel, located only 1 block from the Hauptbahnhof. Inclusive breakfasts, frequent free dinners, and free Wi-Fi compensate for its location in the red light district. Internet €1 per hr. Free bag storage. Reception 24hr. Dorms €17-20, singles €50, doubles €60, triples €66. Prices rise during trade fairs. MC/V. ❷

City Camp Frankfurt, An der Sandelmühle 35b (☎069 57 03 32; www.city-camp-frankfurt.de). U1-U3 to "Heddernheim," leave through the unmarked exit, take a left at the Kleingartnerverein sign and continue down the road until you reach the Sandelmühle sign. Cross the stream and turn left, following the signs until you reach the campground. Reception M-F 9am-1pm and 4-8pm, Sa-Su 10am-1pm and 5-8pm. €6 per person, €2.50 per child under 14, €4 per tent. Showers €1 per 4min. Cash only. ❶

HESSEN

FOOD

Frankfurters love sausages and beer, but they have their own regional specialties as well. Feast on *Handkaese mit Musik* (cheese curd with raw onions; Goethe's favorite), *grüne Sosse* (a white sauce with various green herbs, usually served over boiled eggs and potatoes), and *Äpfelwein* (apple wine). Large mugs (0.3L) of apple wine should never top €2 and are regularly enjoyed in Sachsenhausen, one of the old districts in Frankfurt.

Two grocery stores, **Tengelmann Supermarkt** and **HL-Markt,** can be found in virtually every neighborhood, including near the Hauptbahnhof, at Karlstr. 4, and in Westend, at Arntstr. 22. (Open M-F 7am-9pm, Sa 8am-9pm.) The most reasonably priced meals are around the university in **Bockenheim** and nearby **Westend** (U6 or U7 to "Bockenheimer Warte"), and many pubs in Sachsenhausen serve food at a decent price (U1-3 to "Schweizer Pl."). A number of inexpensive food carts and stands populate the **Zeil.**

Cafe Laumer, Bockenheimer Landstr. 67 (☎069 72 79 12). U6 or U7 to "Westend." Dine like a local on the outdoor patio or the backyard garden of this celebrated cafe in the Westend, only blocks from the university. Young businessmen on their lunch break enjoy the hearty special of the day (€6.70), while neighborhood residents read the newspaper, drink a cup of coffee (€2.20) and eat generous slices of cake (from €2.40). Open M-F 8am-7pm, Sa 8:30am-7pm, Su 9:30am-7pm. AmEx/V/MC. ❷

Kleinmarkthalle, on Hasengasse between Berliner Str. and Töngesg. U4 or 5 to "Dom/Römer," U6 or U7 to "Hauptwache." Make your own lunch in this 3-story warehouse of bakeries, butchers, and produce stands. Cutthroat competition among the many vendors pushes prices down. Enough meat to feed a small nation (possibly Monaco), though most of it is raw. Open M-F 8am-6pm, Sa 8am-4pm. Cash only. ❶

Adolf Wagner, Schweizer Str. 71 (☎069 61 25 65). Saucy German dishes (€5-17) and some of the region's most renowned *Äpfelwein* (€1.40 per 0.3L) keep the patrons of this famous corner of old Sachsenhausen jolly. Sit with storied regulars and try some of the *Grüne Sosse* that you keep hearing about. Open daily 11am-midnight. Cash only. ❸

IMA Multibar, Kleine Bockenheimer Str. 14 (☎069 90 02 56 65). This fast-paced and hip bar/cafe combo on the back streets off of Zeil offers delicious smoothies (€3.50), and wraps (€4-7.30) by day, and a great selection of beer, wine, and long drinks by night. Drinks from €7. Open M-W 11am-10:30pm, Th-Sa 11am-1:30am. MC/V. ❸

SIGHTS

Beneath the daunting skyscrapers that define the Frankfurt landscape are several historic sights, all of which have undergone some degree of reconstruction since the Altstadt's destruction in 1944. Old and new come to a head in the conflicted metropolis—some attractions reflect the city's increasingly contemporary identity for itself and others remain as relics of a foregone Frankfurt. The city's museums are its most prized cultural possessions. Over a dozen well-funded museums feature everything from sculpture to film to Frankfurt history, catering to the diverse interests of residents and tourists alike.

RÖMERBERG. A voyage through Frankfurt should begin in this central area of the Altstadt, among the half-timbered architecture and medieval-looking fountains that appear on postcards of the city. To celebrate the 13 coronations of German emperors held in the city, the **Statue of Justice** in the center of the square once spouted wine. Today, she only offers pigeons some refreshment.

RÖMER. At the west end of the Römerberg, the gables of Römer have marked the site of Frankfurt's city hall since 1405. It was also the original stop on the Main for the merchants who began

THE BEST WURST

So you're finally in Germany and itching to sink your teeth into your first authentic German wurst. With over 1500 varieties, you'll have plenty of choices. All have one thing in common: German law mandates that sausages can only be made of meat and spices. If it has cereal filling, it's not wurst.

Bockwurst: This tasty sausage is commonly roasted or grilled at street stands, and is served dripping with ketchup and mustard in a *Brötchen* (roll). Although Bock means billygoat, this wurst is made of ground veal with parsley and chives. Complement your Bockwurst with some Bock beer.

Thüringer Bratwurst: Similar to the Bockwurst, the Bratwurst has a little pork too, plus ginger and nutmeg.

Frankfurter: Unlike the American variety, the German Frankfurter can only have this name if made in Frankfurt. It's made of lean pork ground into a paste and then cold smoked, which gives it that orange-yellow coloring.

Knockwurst: Short and plump, this sausage is served with sauerkraut. It's made of lean pork and beef, with a healthy dose of garlic.

Weißwurst: Cream and eggs give this "white sausage" its pale coloring. *Weißwurst* goes with rye bread and mustard.

Currywurst: A great late-ni snack, this pork bratwu smothered in a tomato s sprinkled with paprik the city's long trade tradition. Today, the building's upper floors are open to the public. Visit the **Kaisersaal,** a former imperial banquet hall adorned with portraits of 52 German emperors, from Charlemagne to Franz II. Be forewarned, however, that private events are occasionally held in the Römer, closing it to the public entirely. *(Entrance from Limpurgergasse. Open daily 10am-1pm and 2-5pm. German tours every hr. €2.)*

ARCHÄOLOGISCHEN GARTEN. Between the Dom and the rest of the Römerberg are the Schirn Kunsthalle and a plantless "garden" of crumbled building foundations dating back to the 2000-year-old Roman settlement. Three sets of ruins, one from the first century BC, another from the AD ninth century, and a third from the AD 15th century were uncovered when the Altstadt was destroyed. The specimens are preserved in a well-maintained garden landscape.

DOM. East of the Archäologischen Garten stands the only major historical building in the city center that escaped complete destruction in WWII. The red sandstone Gothic church is nevertheless in a process of almost incessant renovation. The seven electors of the Holy Roman Empire chose emperors here, and the Dom served as the site of coronation ceremonies from 1562 to 1792. The Dom Museum inside the main entrance has architectural studies of the Dom, intricate chalices, and the ceremonial robes of imperial electors. The Haus am Dom, across the couryard from the church itself, houses artifacts from the Limburg cathedral. *(☎069 13 37 61 86. Open Tu-F 10am-5pm, Sa-Su 11am-5pm. German tours Tu-Su 3pm; €3, students €2. Museum admission €3/2.)*

HESSEN

GOETHEHAUS. The house in which the father of Faust was born is preserved as a relic (read: shrine) to the author, with all his family's fine furnishings on display. Wind your way up the four stories of sitting rooms, bedrooms, and writing chambers and learn more than you ever thought possible about the childhood of this literary giant. The memorable writing chamber, puppet-show room, and personal library should not be missed. For those who want still more, the neighboring **Goethe Museum** traces the progression of Goethe's portraits, artistic tastes, and sensibilities throughout his life. *(Großer Hirschgraben 23-25, northwest of the Römer. ☎069 13 88 00. Open M-Sa 10am-6pm, Su 10am-5:30pm; last Sa of the month 10am-8pm. Tours in German daily 2 and 4pm. €5, students €2.50, families €8.)*

MAIN TOWER OBSERVATION DECK. For anyone who loves a good view, taking the 250m trip to the top of the Main Tower is a must. Take the elevator to the 54th floor and then walk three floors to the outdoor observation deck, where you can see for miles. Feel larger than life as you sip a cocktail (from €4) in the bar just one floor below. *(Neue Mainzer Str. 52-58. ☎069 36 50 47 77. Open Mar.-Oct. M-Th and Su 10am-9pm, F-Sa 10am-11pm; Nov.-Feb. M-Th and Su 10am-7pm, F-Sa 10am-9pm. Observation deck €4.60, students €3.10.)*

MUSEUMS

Pick up a **Frankfurt Card** or a **Museumsufer Ticket** (p. 255) for museum savings, or go on the last Saturday of the month, when public museums are free.

MUSEUMSUFER

The Museumsufer, also known as Schaumainkai, hosts an eclectic range of museums housed in opulent 19th-century mansions and more contemporary buildings on the south bank of the Main between the Eiserner Steg and the Holbeinsteg. The sheer diversity of topics covered in the museums along the Schaumainkai means that there's something for everyone, from film to anthropology to impressionist art. The Museumsufer is also home to Frankfurt's **Museumsuferfest,** a huge cultural celebration thrown every July with art showings, music, and general revelry along the Main. Frankfurt also has nearly 50 commercial art galleries clustered around Braubachstr. and Saalgasse.

STÄDEL. The crown jewel of the Museumsufer presents seven centuries of art, from Old Masters, like Botticelli, Rembrandt, and Vermeer, to the godfathers of modern art including Monet, Renoir, and Picasso. Start your day at the museum with breakfast (from €4) at **Holbein's,** the celebrated restaurant and cafe on the ground floor. *(Schaumainkai 63, between Dürerstr. and Holbeinstr. ☎ 069 605 0980. Open Tu and F-Su 10am-6pm, W-Th 10am-9pm. Audio tours available in English and German €4. €10, students €8, family €16, under 12 free.)*

LIEBIEGHAUS. The impressive building and gardens contain antique, medieval, Renaissance, Baroque, Rococo, and Classical statues, friezes, and other sculptures. *(Schaumainkai 71. ☎ 069 21 23 86 15. Open Tu and Th-Su 10am-5pm, W 10am-8pm. Call ☎ 069 21 23 86 15 for tour information. €7, students €5. Last Sa of the month free.)*

DEUTSCHES FILMMUSEUM. Observe the progression of film from a 19th-century obsession with optical illusions to the first pictures of the Lumière Brothers. On the first floor, rotating exhibits focus on contemporary phenomena in film, while a nickelodeon plays silent comedy classics on the second. Regular themed screenings highlight specific directors, localities, and genres and attract a large arts crowd. All captions are in German. *(Schaumainkai 41. ☎ 069 21 23 88 30; www.deutsches-filmmuseum.de. Open Tu, Th-F, and Su 10am-5pm; W 10am-9pm; Sa 2-9pm. Tours Su 3pm. €2.80, students €1.30. Last Sa of the month free. Films €5.50/4.50.)*

MUSEUM FÜR KOMMUNIKATION. Guarded by a mounted knight made of old radios and TVs, this museum focuses on the importance of communication technology. Go behind the scenes at the post office, learn how telegraphs and telephones work, and trace the rise of radio, television, and the internet. Interactive displays are in German. English audio tours are available. *(Schaumainkai 53. ☎ 069 606 00. Open Tu-F 9am-5pm, Sa-Su and holidays 11am-7pm. €2.50, children €2. Guided tours Su 2pm and W 3pm.)*

HESSEN

ELSEWHERE IN FRANKFURT

MUSEUM FÜR MODERNE KUNST (MUSEUM OF MODERN ART). Blocks from the Dom, this highly stylized postmodern "slice of cake" building provides an ideal setting for the modern art within. The museum rotates through its permanent collection of European and American art from the 1960s to the present, and prides itself on special exhibits of new and unknown artists and forms. *(Domstr. 10. ☎ 069 21 23 04 47; www.mmk-frankfurt.de. Open Tu and Th-Su 10am-5pm, W 10am-8pm. €7, students €3.50.)*

SCHIRN KUNSTHALLE. With no permanent exhibits, the Schirn morphs up to 10 times a year to accommodate every imaginable genre—from sedate Baroque painting to experimental photodocumentary. The museum's objective remains the same: to create an array of art experiences for the masses. Accordingly, the Schirn holds a variety of art classes for children of all ages, adults, and families. *(Next to the Dom. ☎ 069 299 8820; www.schirn.de. Open Tu and F-Su 10am-7pm, W-Th 10am-10pm. €8; students €6. Audio guides for most exhibits €8.)*

HISTORISCHES MUSEUM. Perched at the southern end of the Römerberg, Frankfurt's most historic plaza, the Historisches Museum seeks to preserve the city's long and storied past. See treasures from Old Frankfurt, learn about life in the city during the Middle Ages, and visit more contemporary exhibitions on the ground floor. *(Saalgasse 19. ☎ 069 21 23 55 99; www.historisches-museum.frankfurt.de. Open Tu and Th-Su 10am-6pm, W 10am-9pm. €4, students €2.)*

ENTERTAINMENT AND NIGHTLIFE

When it comes to culturally or intellectually enriching entertainment, Frankfurt features first-rate ballet, theater, and opera heavily subsidized by the city. There are two major theaters. The **Alte Oper,** Opernpl. (U6 or U7 to "Alte Oper;" ☎069 134 0400; www.alteoper.de), a magnificent classical building rebuilt in the 1980s, offers a full range of classical music, while the **Oper Frankfurt** (☎069 212 02; www.oper-frankfurt.de) displays premier German opera. The **Städtische Bühne,** Untermainanlage 11 (U1-4 to "Willy-Brandt-Pl"; ☎069 21 23 71 33), stages ballets, operas, and experimental renditions of traditional German plays. For productions in English, the **English Theater,** Kaiserstr. 34 (☎069 24 23 16 20; www.english-theatre.org), near the Hauptbahnhof, puts on comedies and musicals. **Die Komoedie,** Neuer Mainzerstr. 14-18 (U1-4 to "Willy-Brandt-Pl"; ☎069 28 45 80; www.diekomoedie.de), produces lighter theatrical fare. Shows and schedules of the city's stages are detailed in several publications, including *Fritz* and *Strandgut* (free at the tourist office), and the *Journal Frankfurt* (€2), available at any newsstand and online at www.journal-frankfurt.de. Students can often buy tickets at reduced prices (from €10) 1hr. before a show. For ticket information, call **Frankfurt Ticket** (☎069 134 0400).

For drinks, head to the **Sachsenhausen** district between **Brückenstr.** and **Dreieichstr.** for rowdy pubs and taverns specializing in local *Äpfelwein.* The complex of cobblestone streets centering on **Grosse** and **Kleine Rittergasse** teems with cafes, bars, restaurants, and Irish pubs. While nightlife can be fickle, Frankfurt has thriving clubs and prominent DJs, mostly between **Zeil** and **Bleichstraße,** and near **Hanauer Landstraße.** In general, things don't heat up until after midnight. Wear something dressier than jeans—unless they're really sweet jeans—if you plan to get past picky bouncers. Most clubs are 18+; covers run €5-16.

Odeon, Seilerstr. 34 (☎069 28 50 55). Look for the whitewashed medieval villa with cut-out octopi on the door and ornate pillars. The party changes daily, with M night hip hop, and Th-Sa deep house music. F 27+, Sa Wild Card. M and Th-F drinks ½-price until midnight. Cover starts at €5, students €3 on Th. Open M-Sa from 10pm. Cash only.

King Kamehameha Club, Hanauer Landstr. 192 (☎069 480 0370; www.king-kamehameha.de). Take the U6 to "Ostbahnhof" and walk down Hanauer Landstr. With intricate timber rafters, gritty exposed brick, and a raging dance floor, this club lures Frankfurt's hip 20-somethings to its weekend parties to drink vodka cocktails (€8) and dance to house music. Watch your step around the indoor stream. Open Th-Sa from 10pm. Cover from €10. Cash only.

Cocoon Club, Carl-Benz-Str. 21 (☎069 90 02 05 90; www.cocoonclub.net). This popular club epitomizes ultra-hip German nightlife and features star DJs, actual cocoons for socializing, vaguely intergalactic decor, and a green foam VIP pod. Dress to kill. Open F-Sa 9am-6am. Cover €10-15. AmEx/MC/V.

Der Jazzkeller, Kleine Bockenheimer Str. 18a (☎069 28 85 37; www.jazzkeller.com). U6 or U7 to Alte Oper. Founded in Sept. 1952, the oldest jazz club in Germany has hosted many masters, including Dizzy Gillespie. The mature clientele enjoys the W night jazz and F night Latin. Cover €15-45. Open W-Sa 9pm-late, Su 8pm-late. Cash only.

Blue Angel, Brönnerstr. 17 (☎069 28 27 72; www.blueangel-online.de). Techno music and flashing lights dominate the interior of the liveliest gay club around, a Frankfurt institution for 30 years. Ring the bell to enter. Crowds arrive after 1am. Cover €5. Usually open daily 11pm-late, 24hr. starting 2am Sa. Cash only.

LAHNTAL (LAHN VALLEY)

The peaceful Lahn River flows through this verdant valley, and the hills on either side of it are dappled with vineyards, quiet hamlets, and German families in search of outdoor fun. Every spring and summer, campgrounds and hostels fill with people who have come to take advantage of the hiking, biking, and kayaking available along the Lahn. Rail service runs regularly between Koblenz in the west and Gießen at the eastern end of the valley, as well as between Frankfurt and Limburg. Visit local bookstores to pick up hiking maps, and inquire at town tourist offices for locations of bike and boat rentals.

MARBURG ☎06421

In 1527, Landgrave Philip founded the world's first Protestant university in Marburg (pop. 79,100), an isolated town on the banks of the Lahn River. The university has produced an illustrious list of alumni, including Martin Heidegger, T.S. Eliot, Richard Bunsen (of burner fame), and the Brothers Grimm. It seems that nothing here is at a right angle—teetering rows of *Fachwerkhäuser* (half-timbered houses) look as though they will topple into the Lahn at any moment. Fast-paced student culture in a rich historical setting will win over visitors and satisfy a variety of interests. The city's snug perch between mountains and river provides a dramatic setting where tourists and students play watersports, and enjoy the scenery at local cafes.

TRANSPORTATION AND PRACTICAL INFORMATION

Trains: To **Cologne** (3hr., 2 per hr., €34-41); **Frankfurt** (1hr., every hr., €12-15); **Hamburg** (3hr., 6 per day, €60-68); **Kassel** (1hr., 2 per hr., €15-20).

Public Transportation: Buses run throughout the city. Single tickets €1.50.

Taxis: Funkzentrale (☎06421 477 77).

Tourist Office: Pilgrimstein 26 (☎06421 991 20; www.marburg.de). Bus #1, 2, 3, 5 or 6 to "Rudolphspl.," and exit to the north along Pilgrimstein; the office is on the left. Or, walk across the bridge straight out of the train station, turn left on Elisabethstr. right after you pass the post office, and continue straight (10min.). Do not follow the tourist information sign pointing in the direction of a parking garage; instead, continue straight. Provides maps, books rooms for free, sells theater tickets, and offers a variety of city **tours** in German, no reservation required (€3). English tours available if arranged 2 weeks in advance. Open M-F 9am-6pm, Sa 10am-2pm.

Banks: Deutschebank, at the corner of Pilgrimstein and Biegenstr., has a **24hr. ATM.**

Women's Resources: Autonomes Frauenhaus, Alter Kirchhainer Weg 5 (☎06421 16 15 16). Open M and W 10am-1pm, Th 4-7pm.

Laundromat: Waschcenter, at the corner of Gutenbergstr. and Jägerstr. From the HI hostel, cross the wooden bridge, then another bridge, turn left on Frankfurterstr. and quickly hang a right on Gutenbergstr. Wash €3. Soap €0.50. Dry €0.50 per 15min. Open daily 8am-midnight, closed Su and school holidays.

Emergency: Police ☎110. **Fire** ☎112.

Internet access: Internet Treff, Pilgrimstein 27 (☎06421 92 47 05), right across from the tourist office. Choose from a variety of hot and cold drinks (€1.50-3) while surfing the web (€1.50 per 30min.). Open M-Sa 10am-2am, Su noon-1am.

Post Office: Bahnhofstr. 6. A 5min. walk from the train station. Open M-F 9am-6pm, Sa 9am-12:30pm. **Postal Code:** 35037.

ACCOMMODATIONS AND CAMPING

Marburg offers more than 30 hotels and pensions, but competition hasn't done much to keep prices down. Plan ahead if you intend to spend less than €30.

Jugendherberge (HI), Jahnstr. 1 (☎06421 234 61). Bus C (dir.: Marburg Stadtwerke P+R) to "Auf der Weide," backtrack and turn right into a street that becomes 2 bridges (one metal, one wooden). From the tourist office, go to Rudolphspl., cross the bridge and turn right on the river path; the hostel is on the left (40min.). Scenic location, close to town. Large rooms, some with bath. Breakfast included. Reception 7:30am-11:30pm. Keys available with ID or €25 deposit. Dorms €21.50. Cash only. ❷

Tusculum-Art-Hotel, Gutenbergstr. 25 (☎06421 227 78; www.tusculum.de). Follow Universitätsstr. from Rudolphspl. and take the 1st left on Gutenbergstr. Many tourists visit modern art museums, but here you can feel like you're staying in one. Each room is decorated with a different theme—bathroom fixtures can get pretty creative. Reception 4-9pm, call ahead to arrange other times. Singles €38-54, doubles €68-76. Online booking with PayPal available. AmEx/MC/V. ❹

Camping: Lahnaue, Trojedamm 47 (☎06421 213 31; www.lahnaue.de), on the Lahn River and close to the city center. Follow directions to the hostel and continue downriver another 5min. €5 deposit for use of electricity and showers. Laundry €3 for wash and €3 for dry. The Terrassencafe has moderately priced food and drink near the minigolf course. Open Apr.-Oct. €4 per person, €4 per tent. Cash only. ❶

HESSEN

FOOD

Marburg's cuisine caters to its students, with wurst, pizza, kebaps, and the omnipresent Marburger beer. The streets around the Markt are full of cafes serving inexpensive sandwiches. **Aldi** has groceries; from Rudolphpl. take Universitätstr. and turn left on Gutenbergstr. (Open M-F 9am-7pm, Sa 8am-4pm.)

Bückingsgarten: Restaurant am Schloss, 6 Landgraf-Philipp-St. (☎064 21 136 10). Conveniently located just before the Landgrafenschloss and right after a short, daunting vertical trek, this restaurant with stunning views offers appetizers for under €10 and entrees for €10-16. Treat yourself to a glass of beer as you overlook the city of Marburg. Gladly hosts large parties and family picnics. Open daily from 11:30am. ❸

Café Barfuß, Barfüßerstr. 33 (☎06421 253 49), is packed with locals and students. Big breakfast menu (€3-8) served until 3pm, and the unique (if slightly intimidating) *Fladenbrot*-meets-pizza 'Fetizza.' The booths and picnic tables, as well as the laid-back staff, make this the kind of place to sit all afternoon. Open daily 10am-1am. Cash only. ❷

Café Vetter, Reitg 4 (☎06421 258 88). A century-old cake shop proud of its terrace on the edge of the Oberstadt. Take advantage of the student breakfast (€5.60), complete with bread, wurst, cheese, ham, eggs, jam, orange juice, coffee or tea, and chocolate and butter spreads. Cake and coffee €5. Chocolates, marzipan, and gourmet tea for sale. Open M and W-Su 9am-6pm, Tu 11am-6pm. Cash only. ❷

SIGHTS

UNIVERSITÄTSMUSEUM FÜR BILDENDE KUNST (UNIVERSITY MUSEUM FOR VISUAL ARTS). The university's impressive collection of 19th- and 20th-century German painting and sculpture is housed in a modest building. Pieces by Paul Klee and Otto Dix compete with temporary exhibits of provocative modern work and a section on Expressive Realism and the lost generation of artists who matured during the Nazi period. *(Biegenstr. 11. ☎06421 2 82 23 55. Open Tu-Su 11am-1pm and 2-5pm. €2, students €1.)*

LANDGRAFENSCHLOSS (DUKE'S PALACE). The exterior of this castle, which sits on the Gison cliffs, looks almost as it did in 1500 when it was a haunt of infamous Teutonic knights. In 1529, Count Philip brought rival Protestant reformers Martin Luther and Ulrich Zwingli to his court to convince them to reconcile. Inside, the *Schloß* has been completely remade into the **Museum für Kulturgeschichte** (Museum for Cultural History), which exhibits Hessian history and art, including shields and ornate crosses. The basement holds a 7th-century skeleton and recently unearthed 9th-century wall remnants. The *Landesherrschaft* (Provincial Rule) floor is a war buff's dream come true. Behind the *Schloß* is a quiet garden that provides views in all directions. *(From Rudolphspl. or Markt, take bus #16 (dir.: Schloß) to the end, or hike up from the Markt. ☎06421 282 2355. Open Tu-Su Apr.-Sept. 10am-6pm, Oct.-Mar. 10am-4pm. Last entry 30min. before close. €4, students €2.)*

ELISABETHKIRCHE. Save some ecclesiastic awe for the oldest Gothic church in Germany, modeled on the French cathedral at Reims. The name of the church honors the town patroness, a widowed child-bride (engaged at 4, married at 14, dead by her 20s) who took refuge in Marburg, founded a hospital, and snagged sainthood four years after her death. The reliquary for her bones is the centerpiece for the elaborate choir, which is like a church-within-a-church, so overdone it's glorious. The somber brown interior is illuminated by glowing stained-glass windows. *(Elisabethstr. 3. With your back to the train station, walk down Bahnhofstr. 10min. and turn left on Elisabethstr. ☎06421 655 73. Open Apr.-Oct. M-Sa 9am-6pm, Nov.-Mar. daily 10am-4pm. Church free; reliquary €2.50, students €1.50.)*

HESSEN

ALTE UNIVERSITÄT. The modern university building was erected in 1871, but the original Alte Universität on Rudolphspl. was built on the rubble of a monastery conveniently empty after Reformation-minded Marburgers ejected the resident monks. The enormous stone building stands at the foot of the big hill, anchoring the Altstadt that spreads up and out behind it. The **Aula,** or main hall, bears frescoes illuminating Marburg's history, but you can see it only by reservation (☎06421 991 20). The nearby houses are former fraternities, and the topsy-turvy state of their frames attest to a proud, beer-soaked tradition. *(Pass the tourist office on Pilgrimstein until it becomes Rudolphspl. The building is on the right.)*

ENTERTAINMENT AND NIGHTLIFE

Marburg's upper village alone has over 60 bars and clubs. Live music, concert, theater, and movie options appear in the weekly *Marburger Express,* available at bars and pubs. Posters plaster the main streets to announce larger events. The **Hessisches Landestheater** hosts an array of theatrical and dance productions. Ask for a program of upcoming performances at the tourist office, and buy tickets at the Stadthalle, Biegenstr. 15. (☎06421 256 08; www.hlth.de. Open M-F 9am-12:30pm and 4:30-6pm.) There are a number of movie theaters. **Marburger Filmkunsttheater,** Steinweg 4, shows old American hits and more unusual recent releases. One movie per week is not dubbed. Check out the website or posters by the door. (☎06 42 16 72 69 or 626 77; www.marburgerfilmkunst.de.) The first Sunday in July, costumed citizens parade onto the Markt for the rowdy **Frühschoppenfest** (Morning Beer Festival). Drinking officially kicks off at 11am when the brass rooster on top of the Rathaus flaps its wings. Unofficially, the barrels of Alt Marburger Pils are tapped at 10am when the ribald old *Trinklieder* (drinking ballads) commence.

Bolschoi Café, Zwischenhausen 22 (☎06421 622 24). From Rudolfspl. walk up Pilgrimstein to the Elisabethkirche and turn left on Ketzerbach; it's at the end of the block. The tavern's decor is pure communist kitsch: red candles, walls, and ceiling, and 20 kinds of vodka (€1.50-3). You might find some comrades in debauchery. Open M-Sa 8pm-2am. Cash only.

Kult Halle Marburg, Temmlerstr. 7 (☎06421 601 3520; www.kult-hallen.de). Bus #A1 (dir.: Pommernweg) or A2 (dir.: Cappeler Gleiche) to "Stadtbüro." This warehouse is the place to dance with Marburg's teens on one of 3 dance floors, to bass-throbbing techno and hip-hop, or join the 20-somethings at any of the 4 bars. Lots of different theme nights; call for schedule. Cover €2-4. Open Tu-W 9pm-3am, F-Sa 9pm-4am. Cash only.

Hinkelstein, Markt 18 (☎06421 242 10). This medieval cellar now features tunes from the Kinks and the Stones. A blue jeans-friendly pub with a sturdy cast of regulars at the bar sipping beer (€3 for 0.5L). Walking uphill from the Markt, and it's on the left. Open M-Th and Su 7pm-3am, F-Sa 7pm-5am. Cash only.

FULDA ☎0661

Only 30km from the former East-West border, Fulda (pop. 64,590) gained notoriety during the Cold War as the most likely target for a Warsaw Pact invasion, earning it the undesirable nickname "Fulda Gap." The city's central location changed from burden to asset as reunification turned Fulda into a transportation hub, ultimately transforming it into an economic center of East Hessen. Its palace and castle do not draw overwhelming crowds, leaving the beautiful Baroque quarter and gardens refreshingly free of tourist clichés. In the summer, the relaxed picnic atmosphere is an inviting setting for sunbathers.

TRANSPORTATION AND PRACTICAL INFORMATION. Fulda offers a selection of rail connections from a strategic location. Trains to: Frankfurt (1hr., 2-4 per hr., €25-31); Hamburg (3hr., 2 per hr., €67-77); Kassel (1hr., 2 per hr., €17); Nuremberg (1hr., every hr., €35); Weimar (2hr., every hr., €40). **Public transit** consists of two bus fleets, with the hub upstairs to your left as you leave the train station. The **tourist office** (☎0661 102 18 14; www.tourismus-fulda.de) is a 200m walk from across the intersection from the *Schloß*. It distributes) maps and tour booklets and books rooms for free. (Open M-F 8:30am-6pm, Sa 9:30am-4pm, Su and public holidays 10am-2pm. **Tours** begin at the tourist office, Apr.-Oct. daily 11:30am and 3pm, Nov.-Mar. Sa-Su 11:30am; call ahead for English. €2.75, children and students €1.75.) Find an **ATM** at the **Sparkasse** on Rabanusstr. Do **laundry** at **Wash n' Dry,** Florengassesse 18. From behind Stadpfarrkirche, take Steinweg, which becomes Florengasse. (Wash €4-7.50, dry €1-1.50. Open daily 7am-10pm.) The **post office** (☎0661 92 13 30) is on Heinrich-von-Bibra-Pl. 5-9. (Open M-F 9am-6pm, Sa 9am-1pm.) **Postal Code:** 36043.

ACCOMMODATIONS AND FOOD. Fulda's **Jugendherberge (HI) ❷,** Schirmannstr. 31, can be reached from the train station by bus #5052 or 1B to "Stadion." Proceed 5min. up the hill; it's on the left. Its small size, purple halls, and attentive staff make for a restful experience. (☎0661 733 89. Breakfast included. Curfew 11:30pm. Dorms €17.50, singles €24, doubles €44. Cash only.) The ebullient Frau Kremer maintains technicolor accommodations at the **Gasthaus Kronhof ❸,** Am Dronhof 2, behind the Dom just outside the old city walls. Take bus #7, AS 5, or AS 12 to "Hinterburg/Am Kronhof" and continue down Kronhofstr. Ask for one of the top floor singles that open onto the roof deck, complete with flowers and lawn furniture. (☎0661 741 47. Breakfast included. Singles €23-41, doubles €55-75. Cash only.) For something a bit more upscale, try the family-run **Hotel Garni Peterchens Mondfahrt ❺,** Rabnusstr. 7. Equipped rooms include cable TV, phone, modem connection, and cosmically decorated bed linens. (☎0661 90 23 50. Breakfast included. Singles €58-68, F-Sa €48-58; doubles €78-98/58-78; family suites €88-108. MC/V.)

Mercado ❷, Gemüsemarkt 15, offers a different vegetarian meal every day, as well as staples like veggie burgers, all for €3-5. To get there from the Stadtschloß, follow Friedrichstr. past the Stadtpfarrkirche and down Mittelstr. and take a right into Gemüsemarkt. (☎0661 229 88. Open M-F 9am-6pm, Sa 9am-4pm. Cash only.) **Vini & Panini ❸,** Steinweg 2-4, is a Italian delicatessen tucked between Karstadt and Pfarrkirche. Enjoy gourmet pasta, crostini, or risotto (€7-14) or sip fine wine (from €4) among innumerable bottles of olive oil. Indulge in tiramisu for dessert. (☎0661 774 93. Open M-Sa noon-2am, kitchen until 11pm. MC/V.) Taking a left past the church down Marktstr. brings you to the **Buttermarkt,** where cheap dinner options abound.

SIGHTS. Prince-abbots reigned in Fulda for 700 years, leaving behind a glorious, if small, **Residenz palace.** As an extension to an earlier Renaissance palace, the **Stadtschloss** (city palace) is a baroque masterpiece designed by Johann Dientzenhofer in 1706 as the centerpiece of the town. The Stadtschloß now contains offices and a one-room exhibit on Fulda's Nobel Prize-winning Carl Braun, inventor of the television tube. Particularly striking are the **Spiegelsäule** (mirror rooms) and the **Fürstensaal** (Hall of Princes), ringed with paintings from Greek mythology. One corner room has 420 mirrors and 46 tiny paintings. Every Friday morning the castle closes for Fulda's wedding ceremonies, held here because the *Schloß* serves as the de facto city hall. Entrance to the castle also includes access to the **Schloßturm** (tower), where you can look out over the town. To reach this yellow behemoth from the train station, head down Bahnhofstr. and turn right onto Rabnusstr. Enter across from the tourist office. (Castle open M-Th and Sa-Su 10am-6pm, F 2-6pm; last tower entrance 5:30pm. Castle and tower €2.50, students €1.50. Tower only €1/0.50.) Behind the palace is the luxurious **Schloßpark** lined with terraces. Just beyond the fountain sits the 18th-century Orangerie, topped with golden pineapples and originally built to house the royal garden of imported lemon trees, now a ritzy cafe and convention center. The Baroque **Floravase** sculpture graces the steps of the Orangerie.

Across the street from the is the stunning 18th-century **Dom,** which houses the tomb of St. Boniface. An 8th-century English monk and missionary known as "the apostle of Germany," Boniface founded the Fulda abbey in 744. Dozens of alabaster saints and cherubs are scattered among marble pillars and gilded alcoves, including a skeleton posing near the pulpit. (Open daily 8am-7pm. Free.) To the left of the cathedral is the **Dommuseum,** with an array of Baroque relics and sacred items. (Open Apr.-Oct. Tu-Sa 10am-5:30pm, Su and public holidays 12:30-5:30pm; Nov.-Mar. Tu-Sa 10am-12:30pm and 1:30-4pm, Su and public holidays 12:30-4pm. €2.10, students €1.30.) To the right of the Dom is the **Kupferstich Schloß,** one of Germany's oldest and most unusual churches, which dates back to 822. Take the stairs to the right of the circular sanctuary to enter the twisting crypt. (Open daily Apr.-Oct. 10am-6pm, Nov.-Mar. 2-4pm. Free).

KASSEL ☎0561

After Napoleon III and his soldiers were captured in the Battle of Sedan in 1870, the Aacheners jeered "Ab nach Kassel" ("Off to Kassel") at the crestfallen monarch as he was marched into Kassel's Schloß Wilhelmshöhe. Since then, Kassel (pop. 198,000) has developed into a city of modern architecture, unique museums, and artsy citizens. From bizarre castles and monuments to sweeping vistas, Kassel offers plenty to draw the curious in search of an unusual locale. Documenta, an international exhibition of contemporary art held every five

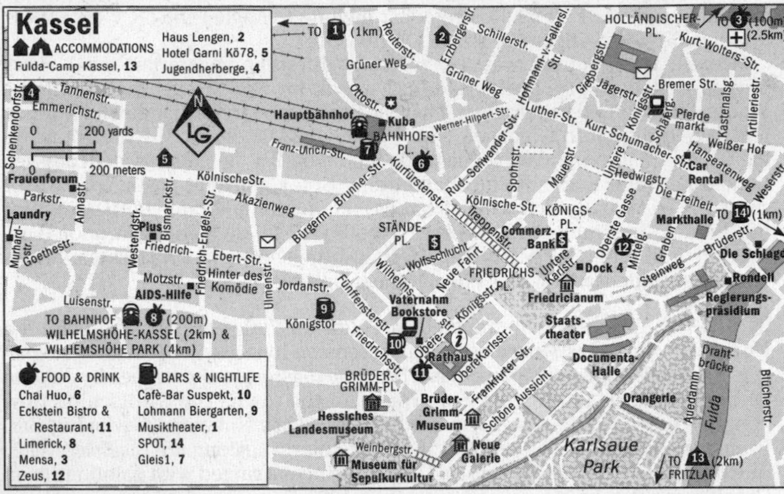

years, will again bring Kassel into the limelight from June to September, 2012. The project is designed to reconcile the German public with modernity after years of Nazi barbarism and Germany's failed Enlightenment-era revolution.

TRANSPORTATION

Trains: From Bahnhof Wilhelmshöhe-Kassel to: **Berlin** (3hr., 2 per hr., €74); **Düsseldorf** (3hr., every hr., €38-45); **Frankfurt** (2hr., 2 per hr., €36-49); **Hamburg** (2hr., 2 per hr., €57-65); **Munich** (4hr., every hr., €78-87).

Ferries: Personenschifffahrt Söllner, Die Schlagd/Rondell (☎0561 77 46 70; www.personenschifffahrt.com), offers daily 3hr. Fulda Valley tours May to mid-Sept. 2pm and W, Su, and holidays 9:30am (leaves Hannoversch Münden at 3pm). 1-way to Hannoversch Münden €11, children €6; round-trip €17/8.

Public Transportation: Kassel is a very walkable city. Nevertheless, the sophisticated system of **buses** and **trams** is integrated into the NVV. Tickets are priced by distance and single rides range from €1.25 (up to 4 stops) to €2.50 (anywhere in Kassel). The Multiticket (€5) is valid for 2 adults and 3 children throughout Kassel. The **Kassel Card,** available at the tourist office, gives free public transportation and tours as well as museum discounts. 1-day card €7, 3-day €10; 2 people €10/13; 4 people €15/19.

Taxis: ☎0561 66 18 81 11.

Bike Rental: FahrradHof, Bahnhof Wilhelmshöhe (☎0561 31 30 83). €10 per day, €40 per wk. Open M-Sa 9am-1pm and 2-6:30pm, Apr.-Oct. Sa 9am-3pm.

ORIENTATION AND PRACTICAL INFORMATION

When Deutsche Bahn chose Kassel to be an **InterCity Express connection,** they rebuilt Bahnhof Wilhelmshöhe-Kassel to its current streamlined contemporary specs. While the new station elevated Kassel's status as a connected urban hub, it also had the effect of taking a lot of the action away from the old city center, since it is at the far western end of Wilhelmshöhe Allee at the edge of an enormous park (see **Sights,** p. 270). The **old Hauptbahnhof** overlooks the economically depressed downtown area, which is probably not a safe place to be at night. Now marketed as more of a cultural center than a train station, it has been outfitted with postmodern adornments, including the popular Gleis 1 restaurant and bar and one of the documenta exhibitions, the **Caricatura** (p. 271). IC, ICE, and some IR trains stop only at Wilhelmshöhe, but frequent trains and tram #7 shuttle between the stations. Trams #1-4 run between the Altstadt and the Wilhelmshöhe areas. Be careful walking along the underground walkway in the tram station alone after dark. Treppenstr., Kassel's original pedestrian zone (the first in all of Germany), takes you from the hill where Kurfürstenstr. ends from the front of the station and to Obere Königsstr., the main pedestrian zone and condensed site of major shops and eateries.

Tourist Office: Main office is in the Rathaus, Obere Königstr. 8 (☎0561 70 77 07; www.kassel.de). The hip, young staff book rooms for a €2.50 fee and offer free maps. Smaller **branch** in the the Kassel-Wilhelmshöhe Allee station provides the same services (☎056 13 40 54). Ask about the Kassel Card (€10-19), which gives free public transportation and **tours,** and museum discounts. Both offices open M-F 9am-6pm, Sa 9am-2pm.

Currency Exchange: Commerzbank, Königspl. 32-24 (☎0561 66 17 89 90). **24hr. ATM.** Open M and W 9am-4pm, Tu and Th 9am-6pm, F 9am-2pm.

Bookstore: Buchhandlung Vaternahm, Obere Königsstr. 7 (☎0561 78 98 40). Broad selection of English paperbacks. Open M-Su 9am-7pm. Women's Resources: **Frauenforum,** Annastr. 9 (☎0561 77 05 87). **Mädchenhaus,** Annastr. 9 (☎0661 717 83).

Laundromat: Wasch-Treff, Friedrich-Ebert-Str. 83, near the HI hostel. Wash €3.50-7. Dry €0.50 per 12min. Open M-Sa 5am-midnight.

Emergency: Police ☎110. **Fire** and **Ambulance** ☎112.

AIDS-Hilfe: Motzstr. 4 (☎05 61 97 97 5910; www.kassel.aidshilfe.de), in a small complex of medical facilities. Open M-W and F 10am-1pm, Th 1-4pm.

Hospital: Klinikum Kassel, Mönchebergstr. 41-43 (☎0561 98 00).

Internet Access: Red Sea Telecafe, Fünffensterstr. 9 (☎0561 70 33 40), has computers and comfy office chairs around the corner from the Rathaus. €1.50 per hr. Open M-F 9am-11pm, Sa-Su 10am-11pm.

Post Office: Untere Königsstr. 95, between Königspl. and the university. Open M-F 8am-6pm, Sa 8am-1pm. **Branch** at the corner of Friedrich-Ebert-Str. and Bürgermeister-Brunner-Str. with the same hours. **Postal Code:** 34117.

ACCOMMODATIONS AND CAMPING

Jugendherberge am Tannenwäldchen (HI), Schenkendorfstr. 18 (☎0561 77 64 55). From Bahnhof Wilhelmshöhe, take tram #4 (dir.: Lindenberg) to "Annastr." or the bus to "Jugendherberge." Spacious cafeteria, clean rooms, and a good location. Breakfast included (7-8:30am). Internet €2 per hr. Reception 9am-11:30pm. Curfew 12:30am, but code available. Dorms €20, singles €35, doubles €44. Cash only. ❷

Hotel Garni Kö78, Kölnische Str. 78 (☎0561 716 14; www.koe78.de). From the Hauptbahnhof, exit through the Südausgang, walk up the stairs, and turn right on Kölnische Str. Coming from Bahnhof Wilhelmshöhe, follow the directions to the Jugendherberge (above), and walk up Annastr. from the tram stop. Turn right onto Kölnische Str. and cross the street. Handsome brick townhouse with several spacious rooms, many with balconies overlooking a garden behind the building. Good location. Most rooms have cable TV and phone. Breakfast included. Reception 7am-10pm. Singles €32, with bathroom and shower €41-51; doubles €51/61-75. MC/V. ❸

Haus Lengen, Erzberger Str. 23-25 (☎0561 188 01). Lengen features quiet, cozy rooms in a home a mere 10min. from the city center and a 5min. walk from the Hauptbahnhof.

HESSEN

Breakfast €4. Reception located through right door; open 11am-1pm and sporadically after 3:30pm. Singles €28, doubles €38; all with shared bath and sauna room. ❸

Camping: Fulda-Camp Kassel, Giesenallee 7 (☎0561 224 33; www.fulda-camp.de). Bus #16 (dir.: Auestadion) from Königspl. or #25 (dir.: Lindenberg) from Kirchweg on Wilhelmshöher Allee to "Damaschkebrücke." Located on the Fulda. Reception 8am-1pm and 3-10pm. Open Mar.-Oct. €4.50 per person, €2.50, €6.50 per tent. Cash only. ❶

FOOD

Friedrich-Ebert-Str., the upper part of Wilhelmshöher Allee, and the area around Königspl. all have supermarkets, bakeries, *Imbiße* (snack bars), and cafes sprinkled among department stores and fashion boutiques. **Plus** is a cheap supermarket at the corner of Friedrich-Ebert Str. and Bismarckstr. (Open M-Sa 8am-8pm.) The **Markthalle,** a block from the Fulda off Brüderstr. hosts an indoor and outdoor **market** with goods from local farms, many proudly claiming "bio" (organic) quality. (Open Th-F 7am-6pm, Sa 7am-1pm.)

Limerick, Wilhelmshöher Allee 116 (☎0561 77 66 49), proves that the jack of all trades can be master of many. Pan-European menu boasting 237 appetizers and entrees. The pizza list alone (60 in total, €2.60-6.70) is broken down by meat, vegetarian, poultry, and seafood categories. 25 beers on tap and a variety of fixed 4-course lunches (€5-8) attract loyal crowds. Open M-Th 11am-1am, F-Sa 11am-2am, Su 11am-midnight. ❷

Eckstein Bistro & Restaurant, Obere Königsstr. 4 (☎0561 71 33 00; www.ecksteinbistro.de), at the corner of Fünffensterstr. Pizzas and veggie meals (€5-9). Well known for its steak specials (€12.70). Lunch €5.10. Open daily 11am-midnight. AmEx/MC/V. ❷

Zeus, Entenanger 4 (☎0561 173 53), works wonders with the pita (€6-12). Try their zucchini and calamari omelette (€7) amid the plaster busts and stained glass windows. Leave room for the baklava (€3.33). Open daily noon-1am. Cash only. ❸

Chai Huo, Kurfürstenstr. 8 (☎0561 739 8853), downhill from the Hauptbahnhof. Lavish, crimson decor and a laughing Buddha at the entrance sets the mood for Chinese specialties served near a goldfish pond. Though main courses cost €7-12, the lunch (€5.40) or dinner buffets (€8.80) are excellent ways to fill up for less. Try the lychee wine (€2.60). Open Tu-Su 11:30am-3pm and 5:30-11pm. AmEx/MC/V. ❸

Mensa (☎0561 804 3132) on Arnold-Bode-Str. Walk down Unter-Königsstr. from the pedestrian zone or take tram #1 to "Holländischer Pl." Cross through the underground passage and veer right on Diagonale, which cuts through campus. €2.50-4, students €1.10 off. Lunch M-F 11:15am-2pm. The **Moritz-Restaurant** (☎0661 804 33 90), in the same building as the *Mensa,* serves a more elaborate lunch with much shorter lines. open M-F 11am-2:30pm. Students €1.10 off. **Studentenwerke-Pavillon** is a cheap cafe just around the corner on Diagonale. Open M-F 8am-6:30pm. ❶

HESSEN

SIGHTS

The Rathaus area is home to various museums, many of which are devoted to Kassel's pride and joy: **documenta** (held every 5 years; June 6-Sept. 19, 2012). During this three-month summer event, the area around the Schloß Wilhelmshöhe offers an adventurous jaunt into German history. The **Staatliche Museen Kassel**—Schloß Wilhelmshöhe, Ballhaus, Hessisches Landesmuseum, Neue Galerie, and Orangerie—are covered by the Tageskarte (day card), for sale at any of the museums and tourist offices (€7, students €5).

DOCUMENTA AND RATHAUS AREA

For the past 50 years, documenta has showcased cutting-edge art in a festival that takes over the town. Exhibitions explore the role of contemporary art within global culture, often with an emphasis on politics and social conscience; the projects ask whether art can help us gain access to what is essential in contemporary life. Though it only happens every five years, the international event leaves indelible marks on Kassel. Several works from past documentas have become permanent exhibitions: visit Claus Oldenburg's *Pick-axe* and Joseph Beuys's *7,000 Oak Trees*, both from documenta VII in 1982. Many of the permanent exhibitions are found in the Neue Gallery. The 13th documenta is expected to take place from June 9-Sept. 19, 2012.

WILHELMSHÖHE (WILHELM HEIGHTS). The Wilhelmshöhe area is a hillside park that must be seen to believed. Impeccably manicured gardens and emerald lawns surround one enormous castle, while another sits crumbling on a wooded hill above. Towering over both castles by a few hundred meters is the Greek titan Herkules, visible from miles away. To fully experience this escape from the city, allow yourself a full afternoon, good walking shoes, and willingness to wander off the paved paths. *(From Bahnhof Wilhelmshöhe, take tram #1 to Wilhelmshöhe, at the eastern end of the park.)*

MUSEUM FÜR SEPULKRALKULTUR (SEPULCHRAL MUSEUM). An ultramodern structure houses death ritual-related paraphernalia. The museum strives to "arrest the taboo process which surrounds the subject of 'death and dying' in today's world, and open it to public discussion." Painted skulls, mourning garb, elaborate crucifixes, spliced organs in plexiglass, and monuments are sure to satisfy anyone's morbid curiosity. *(Weinbergstr. 25-27. ☎0561 91 89 30. Open Tu-Su 10am-5pm, W until 8pm. €4, students €2.50.)*

HESSEN

MUSEUM FRIDRICIANUM. The large yellow Fridricianum is the oldest public museum on the continent. During documenta years, it functions as the central exhibition hall. Otherwise it houses work from past festivals, as well as other exhibitions of modern art. *(Friedrichspl. 18. ☎0561 707 2720; www.fridricianum-kassel.de. Tu, F-Su 10am-6pm, W 8am-6pm. €6, students €3.*

NEUE GALERIE (NEW GALLERY). Whatever the documenta leaves in its wake, the Neue Galerie picks up and puts on display. Their well-rounded collection also includes paintings dating back to the 1700s and important works from the "Neue Sachlichkeit" movement. *(Schöne Aussicht 1. ☎0561 31 68 04 00. Open Tu-Su 10am-5pm. €3.50, students €2.50. F free.)*

BRÜDER-GRIMM-MUSEUM (BROTHERS GRIMM MUSEUM). Rooms are filled with drawings and cutouts of characters from the famous tales, as well as large busts and personal effects bringing to life the men who wrote down blithesome, if frightening, German folktales. *(Schöne Aussicht 2, across from the Neue Galerie. ☎0561 787 2033; www.grimms.de. Open M-Su 10am-5pm, W 10am-8pm. €1.50, students €1.)*

KUBA. Short for KulturBahnhof, it houses Caricatura, the self-proclaimed "gallery for bizarre art." Nothing is off-limits—missing limbs and scatological humor are the main currency at this off-color museum. *(Bahnhofspl. 1. ☎0561 77 64 99; www.caricatura.de. During exhibitions, Caricatura open Tu-F 2-8pm, Sa-Su noon-8pm. Bar open from 7pm. €3, students €2.)*

AMKARLSAUE. This English garden has sprawling lawns along the Fulda. At its southern tip is the **Insel Siebenbergen,** Karlsaue's unique "Island of Flowers." *(From Königspl., hop on bus #16 (dir.: Auestadion) to "Siebenbergen.")* The **Orangerie,** in a yellow manor house at the north end of the park, contains the mechanical and optical marvels and a planetarium of the Astronomy and Technology Museum. *(Karlsaue 20c. ☎0561 7 15 43. Open Tu-Su 10am-5pm. €3, students €2, under 18 free. Planetarium shows in German Tu, Th, Sa 2pm; W and F 3pm. €3, students €2.)*

HESSISCHES LANDESMUSEUM (HESSIAN REGIONAL MUSEUM). Surprises include 16th-century leather-and-gold Spanish hangings, a rare depiction of the Battle of Austerlitz, a wallpaper printer, and a letter from Goethe to Schiller mentioning a wallpaper order. The museum houses several other collections, including prehistoric artifacts. *(Brüder-Grimm-Pl. 5. In the yellow building near the Rathaus. ☎0561 31 68 03 00. Open Tu-Su 10am-5pm. €3, students €2, under 18 free.)*

SCHLOSS WILHELMSHÖHE. The rulers of Kassel once called this mammoth building home. Napoleon III was imprisoned here after the Battle of Sedan. Although the main wing was rebuilt in the aftermath of WWII, the museums inside continue to impress. The **Antikensammlung und Gemäldegalerie Alte Meister** (Antique Collection and Picture Gallery of Old Masters) collection includes works by Rembrandt, Rubens, and the pride of the town—Dürer's *Elsbeth Tucher*, featured on the former 20-Deutschmark bill. A tour through the **Museumsschloß** reveals the palace's extravagant rooms. *(From the tram stop, follow the path under the overpass. ☎0561 31 68 00. Gemäldegalerie open Tu-Su 10am-5pm. Museumsschloß open Tu-Su Mar.-Oct. 10am-5pm and Nov.-Feb. 10am-4pm; Sa-Su Dec. 10am-4pm. Obligatory tours every hr., last tour 1hr. before closing. Each museum €6, students €2, under 18 free.)*

ENTERTAINMENT AND NIGHTLIFE

The stretch along Friedrich-Ebert-Str. and Obere Königsstr., between Bebelpl. and Königspl., is home to numerous bars and clubs; the free monthly magazines *Fritz* and *Xcentric* list schedules of parties at most of the city's clubs. **Bali** (☎0561 71 05 50; www.balikinos.de) is an open-air theater in the Hauptbahnhof and shows movies in their original language. Kassel hosts an **outdoor film festival** every summer behind the Museum Friedricianum at the **Dock 4 theater** (www.filmladen.de; info and ticket sales at the Bali). Shows €6.50, students €6; all tickets €4.50 on Monday. The **Staatstheater** (☎0561 109 4333; www.staatstheater-kassel.de) on Friedrichspl. hosts plays, musicals, concerts, operas, and ballet from mid-Sept. to early July. Entrance to shows runs at about €5.

Lohmann Biergarten, Königstor 8 (☎0561 701 6875; www.lohmann-kassel.de). One of Kassel's oldest beer gardens, and the only one open late. Serves beer (€3 for 0.5L) and Äpfelwein (€1.70), and some highly creative variations on schnitzel (€5-6.50). Open M-F noon-3pm and 6pm-11pm; Sa-Su 6pm-11pm. Cash only.

Café-Bar Suspekt, Fünffensterstr. 14 (☎0561 10 45 22). A popular hangout where 20-somethings linger over drinks and enjoy the laid-back ambience. Perpetually dim lighting, even by day, overpowers even the most insistent clock. By day a laid-back cafe (Tu-Su 1-8pm), at night a bar (Tu-Su 8pm-1am, F-Sa 8pm-2am). Cash only.

SPOT, Ölmühlenweg 10-14 (☎0561 562 09; www.spot-kassel.de). Take tram #4 or 8 (dir.: Kaufungen Papierfabrik) to "Hallenbad Ost," backtrack 10m toward the city, and turn right on the path through the parking lot. Move to techno and hip hop on 3 dance floors, or hit the quieter front bar. Event programs change weekly and are available online. Cover €3-6. Most nights open 9pm-early morning. Cash only.

Musiktheater, Angersbachstr. 10 (☎0561 840 44; www.musiktheater-kassel.de). Bus #14 or 18 to "Drei Brücken," or #27 to "Naumburgerstr.," or follow Schenkendorfstr. as it curves left and over the tracks. A party mecca where eternal 20-somethings congregate. 3 massive dance floors fill 2 city blocks. Theme areas include "Hell's Kitchen" (heavy metal) and the Gothic "Dark Place." Weekly event information available online. The area is dimly lit and sparsely traveled; use caution or take public transportation. Cover €2-7. Open W 8:30pm-3am, F-Sa 11pm-5am. Cash only.

Gleis1, Hauptbahnhof 1 (☎0561 786 4240; www.gleis1.eu). Located in the Hauptbahnhof, Gleis1 serves both as a restaurant and a nightclub/bar. Hosts various themed events, including the weekly "Swing Sunday." The restaurant, open for lunch noon-2pm, boasts delectable dishes, including its "Ofenkartoffel" (€6.80), an open potato topped with condiments of your choice. Salads €3-6, appetizers €4-7, and entrees €7-14. Indulge in crème bruleé (€3.80) or a mojito (€6.60).

DAYTRIP FROM KASSEL

FRITZLAR

An ideal jaunt from Kassel, accessible from either station by train (40min., 3-4 per day, €1.70), or by bus #50 (45-60min.; M-F 1 per hr., Sa-Su 3 per day; €12.70). Treasury, Dom, museum, and crypt open May-Oct. M 2-5pm, Tu-F 10am-noon and 2-5pm, Sa 10-11:30am and 1:30-4:30pm, Su 1:30-4:30pm; Nov.-Apr. M 2-4pm, Tu-F 10am-noon and 2-4pm, Sa 10-11:30am and 1:30-4:30pm, Su 1:30-4:30pm. €2, students €1. Grauer Turm open Apr.-Oct. daily 9am-noon and 2-5pm. €0.25. Tourist office ☎ 0561 98 86 43; www.fritzlar.de. Open M 10am-6pm, Tu-Th 10am-5pm, F 10am-4pm, Sa-Su 10am-noon.

Fritzlar was named **Frideslar** (Place of Peace) in 723, when St. Boniface chopped down the huge Donar's Oak, the pagan religious symbol of the Thor-worshipping Chatti tribe. The "Apostle of Germany" used the timber to build his own wooden church, which today is the Petersdom. Heinrich I was proclaimed king here in 915, inaugurating the medieval Holy Roman Empire. Since then, this miniature medieval town (pop. 14,800) has become happily isolated from the main routes of commerce. Fritzlar is content as a town of half-timbered houses, cobbled streets, and slow-gaited ambience on the Märchenstraße, the German **Fairy Tale Road.** The gem of Fritzlar is the 12th-century **Petersdom,** with its golden altar, stained-glass windows, and sizable treasury, which includes the 11th-century diamond- and pearl-covered **Heinrichkreuz** (Cross of Heinrich) and precious robes and relics. A statue of the axe-toting Boniface stands in the square just outside the Dom. On the western end of the medieval city wall, the austere 39m **Grauer Turm** (Grey Tower) is the tallest defense tower in Germany. On the way to the tower from the Markt you'll pass the **Hochzeitshaus** (Wedding House), which has hosted weddings and festivals since the 16th century. Fritzlar also spawns big festivals. The **Pferdemarkt** (Horse Market) happens from the second Tuesday to the following Sunday every July, and the **Altstadtfest** (Old Town Festival) occurs the third weekend of every other August (Aug. 14-15, 2009). Both inspire a mad array of Lederhosen, traditional music, and steins.

The **tourist office,** Zwischen den Krämen 5, next to Fritzlar's **Rathaus,** built in 1109, is the oldest official building in Germany. Make a left out of the train station and a quick right on Gießener Str., following it up the hill until it reaches Marktpl., then go left on Zwischen den Krämen. Town **tours** in German (min. 5 people) leave from the Rathaus. (1hr. Mid-Apr. to mid-Oct. Tu-Sa 10:30am, Su 11am. €2.50, under 15 free.)

RHEINLAND-PFALZ AND SAARLAND

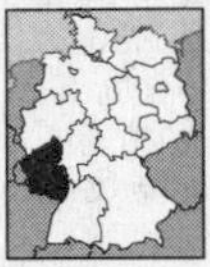

With plunging hills, adorable hamlets, and a surfeit of worn castle ruins, Rheinland-Pfalz is speckled with historically rich remnants of the Middle Ages. The fatal call of Lorelei sirens and the fireside folklore of Nibelung treasure echo across the dramatic landscape. The region is not without actual nourishment—the vineyards of the Rhein and Mosel valleys produce world-famous wines. The Rheinland electors once chose the kings of the Holy Roman Empire, and the Saarland's minerals have been coveted by Germany and France for centuries.

HIGHLIGHTS OF RHEINLAND-PFALZ

BIKE along the Rhein (p. 282), beginning in the charming town of Bacharach.

SAMPLE every wine produced along the cliffs of the lush Rhein Valley (p. 278).

KOBLENZ ☎0261

Beautiful, quiet Koblenz (pop. 105,900) sits at the point where the Rhein and Mosel rivers meet, an occasion which led the Romans to name the city *confluentes* (confluence) or *Deutsches Eck* (German Corner). The city has been strategically coveted by every empire seeking to conquer Europe in the last two millenia. Before reunification, Koblenz was West Germany's largest munitions dump, but the blasts that light up the city now are decorative—Koblenz turns into a flaming spectacle during **Rhein in Flammen** (August 8, 2009).

TRANSPORTATION

Trains: Koblenz is on the line connecting Frankfurt to Cologne. To: **Bonn** (45min., 4 per hr., €9-20); **Cologne** 1-1½hr., 4 per hr., €16-21); **Frankfurt** (2hr., 2-3 per hr., €20-24); **Mainz** (50min., 3 per hr., €15-19); **Trier** (1-2hr., 2-3 per hr., €18-22).

Public Transportation: 10 main bus lines cruise around the city and suburbs for €1.25-3 per ride. Zentralpl., serviced by all bus lines, offers the most convenient access to the Altstadt. Purchase tickets from the driver.

Taxis: Taxi Koblenz (☎0261 330 55) or **Funk Taxi** (☎0261 12 150.

Bike Rental: Biking the Rhein and Mosel valleys is an excellent way to take in the sights. **Fahrradhaus Zangmeister,** Am Löhrrondell (☎0261 323 63), rents bikes for €8-10 per day, depending how long you plan to rent. Open M-F 9am-6:30pm, Sa 10am-4pm.

ORIENTATION AND PRACTICAL INFORMATION

Koblenz's sights are clustered in the Altstadt between the **Deutsches Eck** (a spit of land jutting into the Mosel and Rhein) and the **Markt.** The train station lies farther inland—busy **Löhrstraße** runs from there to the Markt.

Tourist Offices: Bahnhofpl. 17 (☎0261 100 43 99; www.koblenz.de), across from the train station. Boat schedules and maps, and free hotel booking. Open May-Oct. M-Su 9am-7pm, Nov.-Apr. until 6pm. Another **branch** in the Rathaus (at the entrance to Jesuitenpl.) offers the exact same services. Open M-F 9am-7pm, Sa-Su 10am-7pm.

Rheinland-Pfalz (Rhineland-Palatinate) and Saarland

Bookstore: Reuffel, Löhrstr. 62, fills 3 stories on Koblenz's main shopping street. Current mainstream English books on the top floor. Open M-Sa 9:30am-7pm.

Laundromat: Eco-Express Waschsalon, Bahnhofstr. 22. Wash €2.50. Dry €0.50 per 10min. Soap €0.50. Open daily 6am-11pm, last wash 10pm.

Emergency: Police, Moselring 10-12 (☎110). **Fire** and **Ambulance,** ☎112.

Pharmacy: Medico Apotheke, Bahnhofpl. 6 (☎0261 91 46 60), is directly in front of the train station, a short walk past the buses. Open M-F 8am-6:30pm, Sa 9am-1pm.

Internet Access: Chatpoint, Am Plan 10. Palm trees, funky booths, and plastic dolphins. Baguettes (€2-4), and pizza (€4). Internet and Wi-Fi €0.04/min. Open M 10am-10pm, Tu-Th 10am-midnight, F-Sa 10am-2am, Su noon-midnight.

Post Office: To the right of the train station exit. Open M-F 8-6:30pm, Sa 8:30am-1:30pm. **Postal Code:** 56068.

ACCOMMODATIONS AND CAMPING

Rooms in Koblenz are expensive, so if you want to avoid the long, dreary hike to the outer reaches of town, make reservations early.

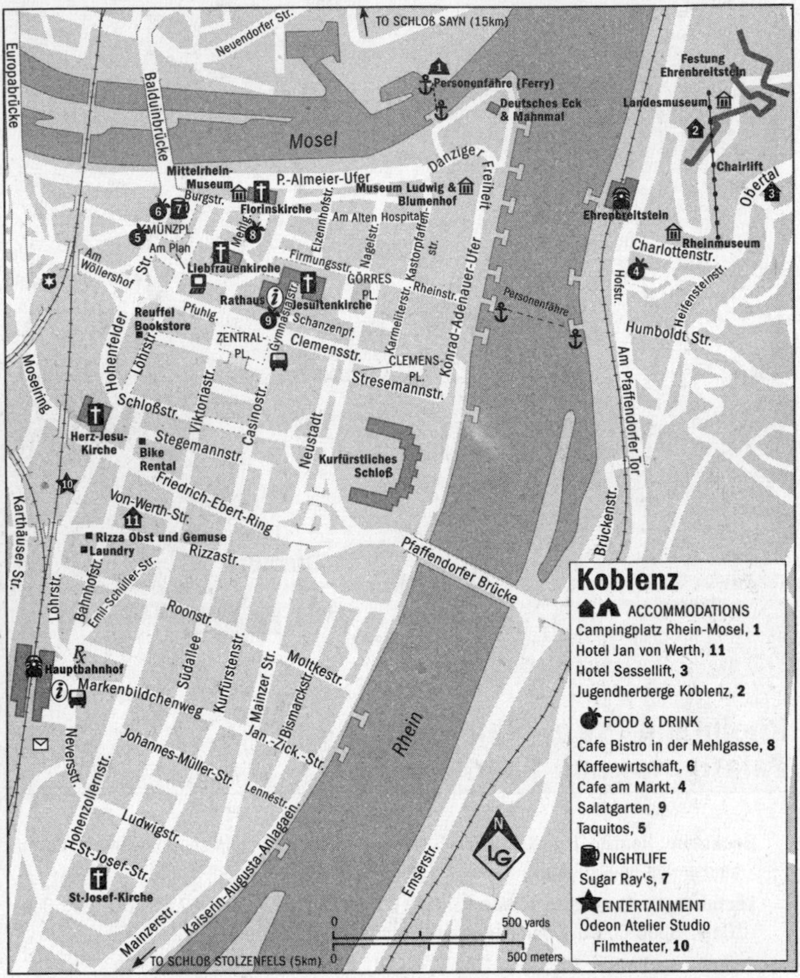

Hotel Jan von Werth, Von-Werth-Str. 9 (☎0261 365 00). This classy family-run establishment is inexpensive living with a touch of elegance—and one of the best values in Koblenz. Large breakfast included. Reception 6:30am-9pm. Check-out 10am. Singles from €24, with shower and toilet €43; doubles from €50/64; triples €65-73. MC/V. ❸

Hotel Sessellift, Obertal 22 (☎0261 752 56), next to the "Obertal" bus stop; take bus #8 or 9. Though a bit far from town, this hotel offers basic, functional rooms with showers. Breakfast included. Singles €20-40, doubles €42, triples €60. Cash only. ❷

Jugendherberge Koblenz (HI) (☎0261 97 28 70), is in the fortress Festung Ehrenbreitstein (p. 277) 118m above the Rhein. Short on amenities and far-flung, but has great views of the valley. Take bus #8 or 9 from the bus station to "Ehrenbreitstein." To hike there, follow the main road along the Rhein side of the mountain, following the DJH signs. Take the path leading to the Festung (20min. steep uphill walk); after dark, the hike can be tricky. The **Sessellift** (chairlift) is a block farther. (Easter-May and Oct. 10am-4:50pm, June-Sept. 9am-5:50pm. €4.50, round-trip €6.20; students and hostel guests €2.70/3.70.) Breakfast included. Reception 7am-10pm. Curfew 11:30pm. Dorms €17.40, doubles €23. MC/V. ❷

Campingplatz Rhein-Mosel, Am Neuendorfer Eck (☎0261 827 19), across the Mosel from the Deutsches Eck. Cross the river by ferry (€0.80). Reception daily 8am-10pm. Open Apr.-Oct. 15. €4.50 per person, €2.50-3.50 per site. Cash only. ❶

FOOD AND NIGHTLIFE

The **Rizza Obst und Gemüse** grocery store, Rizzastr. 49, provides an assortment of fruit and necessities. (Open M-F Sa 7am-7pm, Su 7am-2pm.)

Taquitos, Münzpl. 6 (☎0261 973 46 94; www.taquitos.de), has a Latin American menu with a variety of cheap tasty tapas (€2-3.50). Try the shrimp with olive oil and garlic (€2.50), and wash it down with your favorite tropical mixed drink (€7). ½price mixed drinks 5-7pm daily. Margaritas ½-price after 11pm. Open daily noon-late. MC. ❷

Kaffeewirtschaft, Münzpl. 14 (☎0261 914 47 02). Crimson and navy walls, candlelight, and fresh roses set the scene at this hip bar and cafe. Local seasonal entrees (€8-14). Open M-Th 9am-midnight, F-Sa 9am-2am, Su 10am-midnight. MC/V. ❸

Cafe am Markt, Am Markt 222 (☎0261 261 76151), down the hill from the hostel, a block from the chairlift. Sit back and enjoy the slow-paced Markt with seasonal specials. Open M-Sa 6am-6pm, Su 8am-6pm.

Cafe Bistro in der Mehlgasse, Mehlgasse 12 (☎0261 144 57). Sandwiches on tasty ciabatta bread (€4.50-6), fresh salads (€3.50-7), rotating soup menu (€3.40-5.50), and a relaxed pace. Open daily 9:30am-11pm, F-Sa until midnight. Cash only. ❷

SIGHTS

FESTUNG EHRENBREITSTEIN. Towering over the town, this 12th-century fortress, completed in 1828, offers a bird's-eye view of the clear Mosel as it blends into the muddy Rhein. Constructed over settlements from AD 4000, the fortress is an excavation site. Stay at the Jugendherberge Koblenz, located inside the fortress (p. 276), or pop up for to marvel at the defensive pits and portcullises on the grounds. *(45min., tours from tourist office every hr. Apr.-Oct. 10am-5pm; €1.10. English translation sheet free. Fortress €1, students €0.60, hostel guests free.)*

DEUTSCHES ECK (GERMAN CORNER). The Rhein, the Mosel, and German nationalism converge at the Deutsches Eck, 100m from the pier where ships leave for Rhein or Mosel cruises. This area allegedly witnessed the first stirrings of the German nation in 1216, when the Teutonic Knights settled here. Erected in 1897, the large monument at the top of the steps stands in tribute to Kaiser Wilhelm I for his forced resolution of the internal conflicts of the German Empire. The 14m equestrian statue of the Kaiser that once topped the monument was destroyed in 1945 and replaced by a duplicate in 1993. Beginning in 1953, the corner also became known as *Mahnmal der Deutschen Einheit* (Monument of German Unity) as a reminder of the bonds still shared by a divided East and West Germany.

CHURCHES. Koblenz's Altstadt is dotted with churches, many of which received post-WWII facelifts. The 12th-century **Florinskirche** was used as a slaughterhouse during the Thirty Years' War. *(Open daily 11am-5pm. Free.)* Nearby, Baroque towers rise above the intricate latticework of the Liebfrauenkirche, whose choir windows depict women's roles in the Passion of Christ. *(Open M-Sa 8am-7pm, Su 9am-8pm. Free.)* More stained-glass windows hide behind a masterful Rheinisch facade in the modern interior of the **Jesuitenkirche** on the Marktpl. *(Open daily 7am-6pm. Free.)* The

19th-century **Herz-Jesu-Kirche** dominates the city center and looks down upon the Schängelbrunnen, where a statue of a young boy spits water on passersby every two minutes. *(Church open daily 7:30am-7pm. Free.)* On the other side of the train station, **St.-Josef-Kirche** is awash in yet more stained glass. *(Open daily 9am-6pm. Free.)*

MUSEUMS

Koblenz's Museums are outstanding and diverse, and a 4-day pass (€5.10), available at tourist offices and museums, gets you into all those listed below, as well as the **Festung Ehrenbreitstein, Schloß Stolzenfels,** and the **Wehrtechnische Studiensammlung** (Military Technology Museum).

MUSEUM LUDWIG IM DEUTSCHHERRENHAUS. Just behind the Deutsches Eck, this art museum showcases modern French artists and presents high-caliber exhibitions every six to eight weeks. The original building was erected by the Teutonic Knights who settled in Koblenz in 1212. The permanent collection is on the second floor. *(Danziger Freiheit 1. Behind the Mahnmal. ☎0261 30 40 40. Open Tu-Sa 10:30am-5pm, Su 11am-6pm. €2.50, students €1.50.)*

MITTELRHEINMUSEUM (CENTRAL RHINE MUSEUM). This museum's floors of art are devoted to religious sculpture and romantic landscapes depicting the Rhein Valley, through Gothic, Renaissance, and contemporary periods. The 2nd floor holds rotating exhibits. *(Florinsmarkt 15-17, next door to the Florinskirche. ☎0261 129 2520. Open Tu-Sa 10:30am-5pm, Su 11am-6pm. €2.50, students €1.50, children free.)*

LANDESMUSEUM KOBLENZ (KOBLENZ STATE MUSEUM). A collection of shiny antique automobiles and regional artifacts, including huge wooden winepresses. *(Hohe Ostfront, in Festung Ehrenbreitstein. ☎0261 970 30. Open daily Easter to mid-Nov. 9:30am-5pm. Last entry 30min. before closing. €2.90, students €2.50.)*

DAYTRIPS FROM KOBLENZ

SCHLOSS STOLZENFELS

Take bus #650 (dir.: Boppard) from the train station to "Stolzenfels Mitte" (10min., 2 per hr., €2), then walk 10min. up the winding Schloßweg. Information ☎01805 22 13 60. Koblenz tourist office ☎0261 100 4399. Obligatory 45min. tours in German (English translation sheet €0.50). Open daily Apr.-Sept. 10am-6pm; Jan.-Mar. and Oct.-Nov. 10am-5pm. Last entry 1hr. before closing. €2.60, students €1.30, children €1.

Five kilometers south of Koblenz, the elegant, orange Schloß Stolzenfels gleams with the typical decadence of a Prussian royal residence. Once a 13th-century stronghold, the palace became a summer home for the Prussian royal family until being destroyed during a 19th-century French siege. Since King Wilhelm IV died in 1863, the only people to stay in the castle have been refugees from Koblenz during WWII. Glossy imported fabrics, paneled ceilings, intricate antiques, and mirrors adorn every room. See the merging of medieval and Romantic styles inside the chapel in the cast-iron staircase. The garden, with dangling flowerpots, rose-shaded trellises and languishing statues, has the feel of an Italian villa.

RHEINTAL (RHINE VALLEY)

Though the Rhein River runs from Switzerland all the way up to the North Sea, the Rhein of the poetic imagination exists in the 80km gorge from Bonn to just north of Mainz. Here, 12th- and 16th-century castles crown steep bluffs overlooking the river, and minor estuaries cut through the hills in search of larger waters. Of all places along the Rhein, none has captured the imaginations of poets and artists like the Lorelei Cliffs. Towering above some of the narrowest plunges of the river, these cliffs are home to the golden-haired siren immortalized in Heinrich Heine's 1823 poem "Die Lorelei." Heine, however, cannot claim sole credit for the river's resonance: Wagner paid homage to the mythical legacy in his *Der Ring des Nibelungen* opera cycle, and British Romantic artists captured its jagged beauty in violent brushstrokes. In 2002, UNESCO echoed these praises by naming the Rheintal a World Heritage Sight.

Two different train lines (one on each bank) plod along this stretch of the Rhein. The line on the west bank runs between Koblenz and Mainz and hugs the water's edge, providing superior views. Many choose to skip the large tourist crowds and experience the landscape by boat. The **Köln-Düsseldorfer (KD) Line** and **Bingen Rüdesheim Line** cover the stretch up to five times per day.

ST. GOARHAUSEN AND THE LORELEY CLIFFS ☎06771

Though it was the Lorelei maiden who once drew sailors to the shores of this rugged region, her hypnotic song is now unnecessary; today, hordes of travelers are seduced by scenery alone. Hillsides rise from the Rhein, cloaked in slanting vineyards, romantic villages, and restored medieval castles. **Trains** run to St. Goarshausen from Cologne (1hr., €24.50) and Wiesbaden (1 hr., €9.90) The **Loreley VI ferry,** the oldest family-run ferry in Germany, crosses the river to and from St. Goar every 15min. (Ferries M-F 6am-11pm, Sa-Su from 7am. €1.30.) These two towns host the spectacular **Rhein in Flammen** (Rhine in Flames) fireworks celebration in mid-September.

The St. Goarshausen **tourist office,** Bahnhofstr. 8, hands out free maps and local listings. (☎06771 91 00; www.loreley-touristik.de. Open M-F 9am-1pm and 2-5pm, Sa 10am-noon.) The **police** station, Bahnhofstr. 12 (☎06771 932 70), is a few doors down. Thirty minutes up the Lorelei Cliffs, the hostel **Jugendheim Loreley ❶** lures travelers with its spectacular location, only to drown them in crashing waves of schoolchildren. From Rheinstr., make a left at the Marktpl. and head under the bridge. Follow the signs for the Jugendheim up into the hills. (☎06771 26 19; www.loreley-herberge.de. Sheets included. Breakfast buffet €4.50. Curfew 10pm. €12 per person for the first night, subsequent nights €9. Tent space €4.50. Singles add €5 and doubles add €3 per person; call ahead to reserve. Cash only.) To overnight close to the famed cliffs, try **Campingplatz Auf der Loreley ❶.** Follow signs from the Lorelei statue. (☎06771 430; www.loreley-camping.de. Warm showers included. €5 per person, €5 per tent. €3 per car, €5 per RV. Cash only.) Directly above St. Goarshausen, the dark **Burg Katz** (Cat Castle) stands just a few kilometers downstream from its nephew **Burg Maus** (Mouse Castle). Though all of Burg Katz is privately-owned and closed to sightseers, Burg Maus, at the end of a very strenuous 1hr. hike, contains an eagle and falcon court with demonstrations daily at 11am and 2:30pm (also at 4:30pm on public holidays and Su) from May to the beginning of October. If you're lucky, you can watch falcons snatch rats off the heads of small children. (☎06771 76 69; www.burg-maus.de. €8, children €6.)

ST. GOAR ☎06741

Across the river from St. Goarhausen, St. Goar sits in the shadow of the Rhein's largest castle. Alledgedly the site of a church built by Charlemagne, the village provides a good base for excursions to the Loreley cliffs and nearby wineries.

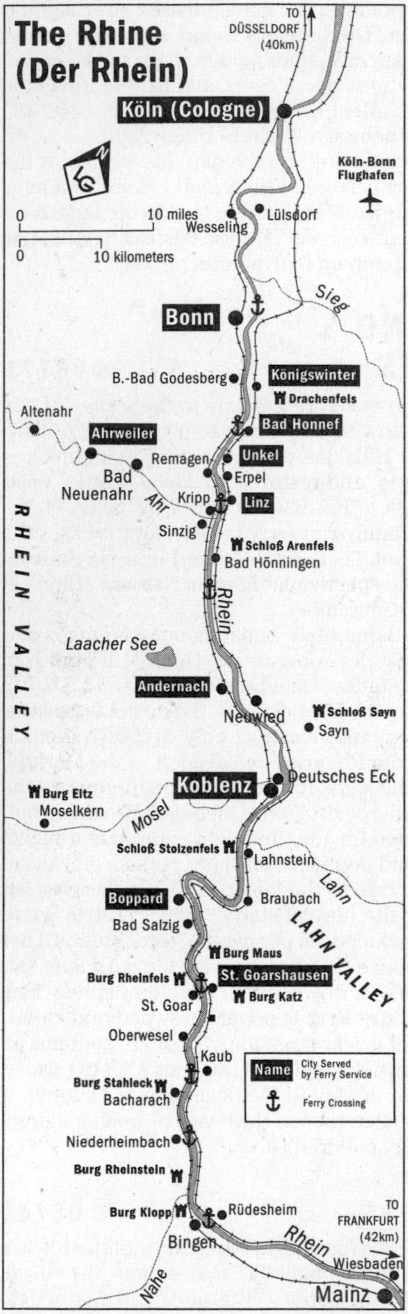

TRANSPORTATION AND PRACTICAL INFORMATION. St. Goar is accessible by **train** from Cologne (1½hr., every hr., €24.50) and Mainz (1hr., 2 per hr., €9.90). The **tourist office,** at Heerstr. 86, sells regional hiking and biking maps, distributes free town maps, and helps find rooms in town. (☎06741 383; www.st-goar.de. Open May-Sept. M-F 9am-12:30pm and 1:30-6pm, Apr. and Oct. M-F 9am-12:30pm and 1:30-5pm, Nov.-Mar. M-Th 9am-12:30pm and 1:30-5pm, F 9am-2pm.) **Bike** rentals are available outside the train station at Oberstr. 44. Bikes cost €11.50 per day, and there are discounts for consecutive days. (Open May-Oct. daily 9am-1pm and 6-8pm. €50 or ID deposit required.) Check your email at **Hotel Montag,** Heerstr. 128, for €2 per 20min. There's a **pharmacy,** the **Rheinfels Apotheke,** at Heerstr. 91. (Open M-F 8am-12:30pm and 2:30-6:30pm, Sa 8am-noon.) The **post office** is inside the Präsent-Galerie store at Heerstr. 102. (Open M-F 9am-1pm and 2-6pm, Sa 9am-1pm.) **Postal Code:** 56329.

ACCOMMODATIONS AND FOOD. Conveniently located between the heart of town and Burg Rheinfels, the **Jugendherberge (HI) ❷,** Bismarckweg 17, is a 10min. walk from the train station and the harbor. Follow Oberstr. to the end and make a left under the bridge. Bismarckweg is the next right. Though space can be tight, the staff is friendly and the beds are cheap. (☎06741 388. Breakfast and sheets included. Reception 8am-8pm. Curfew 10pm, but keys available. Rooms, including some singles and doubles, €17.90 per person. MC/V.) With a fantastic view of the Rhein, the **Hotel an der Fähre ❸,** Heerstr. 47, offers romantic rooms at the right price. (☎06741 980 577; www.hotel-stgoar.de. Breakfast included. Singles with bath €25; doubles €40-50.

Cash only.) In and around the Marktpl., several sit-down restaurants sell German fare for around €10 per entree. For a piping-hot pizza (€4.50-7) or a bowl of pasta (€4.80-7.50), try **Alla Fontana ❷**, Pumpengasse 5. Tucked away on a side street, this Italian restaurant is a local favorite. (☎06741 96 117. Open Tu 5:30-10pm, W-Su 11:30am-2pm and 5:30-10pm.) Grab dessert at **Eis Café Milano,** Heerstr. 103, where a jovial Italian man named Rocco serves excellent homemade gelato for €0.70 per scoop. (Open daily 11am-10pm.)

SIGHTS. High above town, the beautiful, age-worn **Burg Rheinfels** is a sprawling, half-ruined castle with underground passages—it doesn't get more *romantisch* than this (☎06741 383; www.burg-rheinfels.de). Castle visitors are provided with a detailed map of the castle that plots two excellent walking tours through the ruins. Choose a path and wind through either the old castle defenses or the large banquet halls and courtyards. (Open daily from mid-Mar. to mid-Oct. 9am-6pm, from mid-Oct. to Nov. 9am-5pm, from Dec. to mid-Mar. Sa-Su 11am-5pm. €5, children €2.50. Bring a flashlight, or buy a candle in the museum for €0.30.) The castle is a 20min. walk from the center of town; follow signs for **Fußweg Burg Rheinfels.** Or, hop on the **Rheinfels Express,** a trolley to the castle that leaves every 25min. from the Marktpl. in the center of town. (Trolley runs Apr.-Oct. 9am-6pm. One-way €2, round-trip €3. Children €1.50/2.)

BACHARACH ☎06743

Bounded by a lush river promenade, a resilient town wall, and dramatically sloping vineyards, Bacharach retains an irrepressible sense of identity in the face of increasing tourist traffic. Renovated Tudor-style houses surround the popular market square, and narrow alleyways contain wine cellars and taverns alike. Once home to a stone altar to Bacchus (hence the town name), today Bacharach fills with pilgrims journeying to worship at the town's numerous *Weinkeller* and *Weinstuben* (wine cellars and pubs), tucked between, and sometimes directly within, historic half-timbered houses.

TRANSPORTATION AND PRACTICAL INFORMATION. Due to a lack of bridges, **ferries** provide the most efficient transport to Bacharach. The **Köln-Düsseldorfer** line (☎0221 208 8318; www.k-d.com) stops at most towns on the Rhein. Ferries run from Bacharach to Bingen (1½hr., 5 per day, €7). The **tourist office,** Oberstr. 45, sells excellent hiking and biking maps of the region (€2-8.50) and books rooms for free. (☎06743 91 93 03. Open Apr.-Oct. M-F 9am-5pm, Sa-Su 10am-3pm; Nov.-Mar. M-F 9am-noon.) In this largely cash-only town, an **ATM** and **currency exchange** can be found at the **Volksbank,** Blücherstr. 19. (M-Tu and Th 8:30am-noon and 1-4:30pm, W and F 8:30am-1pm.) Take the first left off Oberstr. after the tourist office.

ACCOMMODATIONS. Every budget accommodation in Bacharach—and maybe Germany—pales in comparison to the **Jugendgästehaus Burg Stahleck (HI).** This 12th century castle was converted into a youth hostel in the early 20th century. The experience is worth every step of the 15min. trek uphill for the amazing view, bargain beds, and lively bistro. (☎06743 12 66. Breakfast included. Many rooms have bath. Reception 7:30am-8pm. Check-in at the bar until midnight. Check-out 9:30am. Curfew 10pm. Reservations recommended. Dorms €17.40. MC/V.) Closer to town, **Hotel Am Markt ❹,** Oberstr. 64, maintains quaint yet spacious rooms in a family-owned environment. (☎06743 17 15; www.hotel-dettmar.de. Singles €25-30; doubles €50-60. Cash only.) Pitch a tent by the water at **Campingplatz Bacharach ❶,** directly on the Rhein. Walk south for

A RIDE DOWN THE RHEIN

Start and Finish: Bacharach

Total Distance: 13km 1-way, 26km round-trip

Time: 5hr.; 7hr. with a stop at Burg Rheinfels and a hike up to the Loreley Cliffs.

In 2002, UNESCO declared the Upper Middle Rhein Valley a World Heritage Site, with the explanation that the 65km stretch of the river "graphically illustrates the long history of human involvement with a dramatic and varied natural landscape." What they really meant to say was: these castles are sweet. The Rheintal is a lush valley lined with vineyards, hotels, wine taverns, and of course, medieval castles. It is a traveler's paradise, and there's no better way to experience it than on a bike: cruising up and down the banks of the Rhine on two wheels puts you in contact with the landscape in a way that a train, a car, or even a boat simply cannot. The best part of all is that you can hop off your bike at your leisure and really take the opportunity to explore the amazing sights along the way.

1. BACHARACH. Start your tour in the little town of Bacharach, which is remarkably uncorrupted by tourism despite the large number of visitors that flood through each day. If you're in need of a bike, stop in the tourist information office and ask for assistance. The office keeps a list of local hotels and stores that rent bikes for €8-10 per day. When you're fully equipped, hop on the bike and set out north, following the bike path along the river. Your destination is the town of St. Goar, about 13km downstream from Bacharach. The path is flat and paved the entire way—it generally takes casual riders between 1 and 1½hr.

2. OBERWESEL. You'll know you've reached the halfway point of your ride when you pass the town of Oberwesel. Once you've passed Oberwesel, keep your eyes peeled for the wild blackberry bushes that grow along the bike path. If you're there at the right time (mid-July to late Aug.), stop and pick some of the fresh, delicious fruit.

3. BURG RHEINFELS. Once you get to St. Goar, lock your bike in town and head out on foot. Follow the signs for Fußweg Burg Rheinfels, which is the largest castle overlooking the Rhine. Today, the ruins of this massive 13th-century structure are open for visitors to explore. The view from within the castle walls is stunning. A self-guided walking tour, which costs €5, winds you through the old fortifications and banquet rooms. The walk to the castle takes about 20min., and there is also a trolley car (€2 one-way, €3 round-trip) that leaves every 25min. from the Markpl and brings you to the ruins.

4. ST. GOAR. After taking in the view from Burg Rheinfels, head back into the town of St. Goar and stop for an otherworldly ice cream cone at Eis Café Milano, where Rocco Calabrese serves up scoops of his homemade Italian gelato for €0.70.

5. ST. GOARSHAUSEN. Refreshed and ready to go, walk to the harbor and hop on the Loreley VI, the ferry that will take you from St. Goar to St. Goarshausen, just across the river. The oldest family-run ferry in Germany, the Loreley VI leaves every 15min. and takes about 8min. for the river crossing. (Ferries M-F 6am-11pm, Sa-Su from 7am. €1.30.)

6. LORELEY CLIFFS. When you hit shore, make a right out of the ferry docks and follow Rheinstr. until you come to the Marktpl. Make a left at the Marktpl., cross under the bridge, and head straight uphill for about 40min. to the famed Loreley Cliff. This cliff, at the narrowest part of the Rhine, overlooks the site of many mysterious boating tragedies, and lovely Loreley is often said to be to blame. The view is breathtaking and the hike is invigorating. As you make your way down from the cliff and board the ferry back to St. Goar (where your bike awaits),

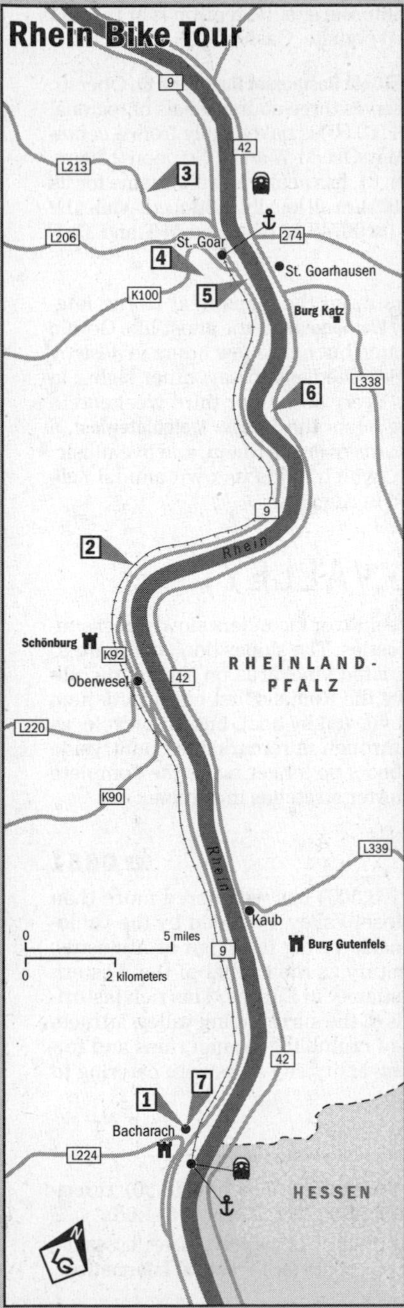

start thinking about how you want to get home. Biking is of course an option, but if you're worn out from the day's adventures, there's also a train that runs from St. Goar to Bacharach every 30min. (€3), as well as a boat, the Köln-Düsseldorfer, which sails between the two. Boat service is much more sporadic and a bit more expensive, but floating down the Rhine would definitely contribute to the day's mystique.

7. BACHARACH. Hold off to eat until you're back in Bacharach. You'll understand why when you sit down for dinner at Cafe Restaurant Rusticana, where a warm, welcoming elderly couple serves you a 3-course meal of homemade German fare for €7-12. Between the two of them, this impressive duo speaks eight or nine foreign languages, and they're happy to share their amazing life stories with diners. Don't leave without having a slice of the legendary apple strudel (€3.50), made fresh daily from a recipe passed down from the owner's Romanian grandmother.

Tired, full, and happy, retire to bed in the Jugendgästehaus Burg Stahleck. There's perhaps no hostel more spectacular than this one, which is located in a castle perched high upon the hill above Bacharach. The walk to the castle will get your heart rate going, but the view from the top just might make it stop. You won't believe that beds in this surreal location cost only €17.40. Follow the signs from the center of town for Jugendherberge/Burg Stahleck.

10min. along the water and you'll run right into the site. Reception is at the bar. (☎06743 17 52. €5 per person, €3 per tent, €6 per site. Cash only.)

FOOD. Have the best meal of your life at **Café Restaurant Rusticana ❸,** Oberstr. 40, where a welcoming, very elderly couple serves three-course meals of regional dishes for €7-12. The legendary apple strudel (€3.50) is baked daily from a centuries-old family recipe. (☎06743 17 41. Open May-Oct. M-W and F-Su noon-9:30pm. Cash only.) The **Weinhaus Altes Haus ❸,** Oberstr. 61, has achieved minor fame for its half-timbered perfection. The wines (€2.10-2.90) are all locally produced, while the entrees (€5-15) feature Rheintal specialties. (☎06743 12 08. Open M-T and Th-F 1-11pm, Sa-Su from noon. Cash only.)

SIGHTS AND FESTIVALS. On Oberstr., up the steps next to the late-Romanesque **Peterskirche,** is the 14th-century **Wernerkapelle,** the ghost-like Gothic skeleton of a chapel that took 140 years to build but only a few hours to destroy in the Palatinate War of Succession of 1689. Needless to say, other sights in Bacharach revolve around food and drink. Every second or third weekend in June, the nearby town of Bacharach-Steeg hosts the **Steeger Weinblütenfest,** a festival replete with free wine tasting, firewords over the Rhein, and live music. Festivities inevitably spread to Bacharach, which holds its own annual **Kulinarische Sommernacht** on the fourth weekend in August.

MOSELTAL (MOSEL VALLEY)

Before joining the Rhein at Koblenz, the Mosel River meanders slowly past sun-drenched hills, scenic towns, and ancient castles. The slopes don't compare to the Rhein's narrow gorge, but the less-touristed vineyards on the gentle hill-sides have been pressing quality wines since the Romans first cultivated them 2000 years ago. The valley's scenery is best viewed by boat, bus, or bicycle, as the train between Koblenz and Trier cuts through unremarkable countryside rather than following the river. Passenger boats no longer make the complete run, but companies run daily trips along shorter stretches in summer.

TRIER ☎0651

The oldest town in Germany, Trier (pop. 103,500) has weathered more than two millennia in the western end of the Mosel Valley. Founded by the Gallo-Celtic Treveri tribe and seized by the Romans during the reign of Augustus, Trier reached its zenith in the early 4th century as the capital of the Western Roman Empire and a major center for Christianity in Europe. This rich historical legacy, coupled with the tiered vineyards of the surrounding valley, attracts throngs of tourists. Unfazed by the surfeit of crumbling Roman ruins and foreign flash bulbs, Trier remains a bustling university city at its core catering to a large and highly visible student population.

TRANSPORTATION

Trains: To: **Cologne** (3hr., 2-4 per hr., €27-35); **Koblenz** (2hr., 2 per hr., €18.50); **Luxembourg** (50min., every hr., €14.40-17.40); **Saarbrücken** (1hr., 2 per hr., €14.60).

Buses: Although most sights are within walking distance of the town center, buses run everywhere. Prices vary. A **Trier Card** may save you money (see **Practical Information**).

Taxis: Taxi-Funk ☎0651 120 12.

Bike Rental: Zweirad-Werkstatt (☎0651 825 00), in the main train station building on track 11. From €9 per day, €42 per week. €30 deposit. Open M-F 9am-4pm, Sa 9am-noon. Reservations recommended for groups.

ORIENTATION AND PRACTICAL INFORMATION

Trier lies on the Mosel River fewer than 50km from the Luxembourg border. The entrance to the Altstadt, the **Porta Nigra** (Black Gate) is a 5min. walk from the train station down Theodor-Heuss-Allee or Christophstr. A **Trier Card,** available at the tourist office, provides unlimited inner-city bus fare and discounts on museums and Roman sites over a three-day period (€9, family card €15).

Tourist Office (☎0651 97 80 80; www.trier.de), right in the shadow of the Porta Nigra, runs English tours Sa at 1:30pm (€6, students €5). Open May-Oct. M-Th. 9am-6pm, F-Sa 9am-7pm, Su 10am-5pm; Nov.-Dec. M-Sa 9am-6pm, Su 10am-3pm; Jan.-Feb. M-Sa 10am-5pm, Su 10am-1pm.

Bookstore: Interbook Akademische Buchhandlung, Kornmarkt 3 (☎0651 97 99 01). Small selection of English paperbacks. Open M-F 9am-7pm, Sa 9am-6pm.

Laundry: Wasch Salon, Brückenstr. 19-21, down the street from Karl Marx's old house. Wash €5. Dry €2 per 30min. Open daily 8am-10pm.

Emergency: ☎110. **Police Station,** Salvianstr. 9 (☎0651 977 90).

Internet Access: Arcor Shop, Theodor-Heuss-Allee at Porta-Nigra-Platz 4 (☎0651 145 5462). €1.50 per hr. Open M-F and Su 11am-10pm.

Post Office: On Bahnhofpl. Open M-F 8:30am-6pm, Sa 8:30am-1pm. **Postal Code:** 54292.

ACCOMMODATIONS AND CAMPING

Hilles Hostel, Gartenfeldstr. 7 (☎0651 710 2785; www.hilles-hostel-trier.de). This family-run hostel offers bright, festive decor and the opportunity to leave your photo on the wall. All rooms with bath. Fully stocked kitchen. Dorms from €15, doubles €32-38, quads €64, homestays from €400 a month. Laundry €2. Free internet. MC/V. ❷

Jugendgästehaus Trier (HI), An der Jugendherberge 4 (☎0651 292 92). Bus #2, 8, 12, or 87 (dir.: Trierweilerweg or Pfalzel/Quint) to "Zur Laubener Ufer," and walk 10min. downstream along the embankment. Or, from the station, follow Theodor-Heuss-Allee as it becomes Nordallee and forks right onto Lindenstr.; at the bank of the Mosel, turn right and follow the path along the river (30min.). Festive riverside rooms with bath. Breakfast and sheets included. Reception 7am-10pm. Doubles €40, dorms €18. MC/V. ❸

Jugendhotel/Jugendgästehaus Warsberger Hof im Kolpinghaus, Dietrichstr. 42 (☎0651 97 52 50). Slightly hidden in a corner building. Unbeatable location, with halls crowded with boisterous students until late. Internet €5 per hr. Breakfast €5.50. Reception 8am-11pm. Reserve ahead. Dorms €22.50, sheets €2.50; singles €27.50, doubles €24.50, sheets included. Cash only. ❷

Casa Chiara, Engelstr. 8 (☎0651 27 07 30; www.casa-chiara.de), a modern hotel featuring soft-colored, well-furnished rooms with private bath and cable TV. Young gregarious staff. Generous brunch included. Internet €2 per hr. Reception from 6:30am. Singles €48-78, doubles €78-108, triples €113-135. Cash only. ❺

Treviris: Trier City Campingplatz, Luxemburger Str. 81 (☎0651 869 21). From Hauptmarkt, follow Fleischstr. to Brückenstr. to Karl-Marx-Str. to the Römerbrücke. Cross the bridge, head left on Luxemburger Str., and then left at the camping sign. Standard grounds. Showers available. Open Apr.-Oct. Reception M and Sa-Su 8-11am and 4-6pm, Tu-F 8-11am and 4-8pm. €4.50 per person, €4.30-5.30 per tent. Cash only. ❶

FOOD

For groceries, head to the well-stocked **Nahkauf,** at the corner of Brückenstr. and Stresemannstr. (Open M-F 8am-8pm, Sa 8am-4pm.)

Astarix, Karl-Marx-Str. 11 (☎0651 722 39). Squeezed in a passageway, Astarix can be reached from the Trier Theater area or by walking down Brückenstr. toward the river and making a left into the passageway. Customers spill out onto the terrace of this laid-back restaurant to enjoy heaping portions of Italian staples at great prices, served by a hip waitstaff. Salads and baguettes €2.60-6.40; pastas and pizzas €2.50-4.90. Open daily 11am-11:30pm. Cash only. ❷

Cafe Lecca, Bahnhofspl. 7 (☎0651 994 98 30; www.cafe-lecca.de). Steamed milk with honey €1.40, cappuccino €1.40-2.80. Quick service and a laid-back atmosphere. Lecca is a coffeehouse by day and trendy bar by night with booth, bar, and outdoor terrace seating. Flatscreen TVs and free Wi-Fi. Beers €2. Sandwiches and desserts €1.50-3.30, mixed drinks €5-7. Open daily 9am-late. Cash only. ❸

Domstein, Hauptmarkt 5 (☎0651 744 90; www.domstein.de). A decadent option with unbeatable views of the Dom. Inside, the rich mahogany walls are decorated with oil paintings of Trier. Menu offers several cheese plates (€8.80) and wine flights (€5.50-7.50), with a sampling of five local Rieslings. Try the salmon in Riesling sauce with leafy spinach and pine kernels (€15.30). Open daily 11:30am-9:30pm. MC. ❹

Italienisches Restaurant Fornelli, Jakobstr. 34 (☎0651 433 85), serves up large, scrumptious pizza (€5-9), pasta dishes (€7-11), and gelato (€1.40-3.50) for lunch and dinner crowds. Open daily 11:30am-11pm. Cash only. ❸

SIGHTS

History enthusiasts will want to pick up a one-day combination ticket valid at all Roman monuments (€6.20, students €3.10).

PORTA NIGRA (BLACK GATE). Trier is full of Roman history, the most impressive remnant of which is the Porta Nigra. This massive sandstone construction, held together only by iron clamps, was originally light yellow, but now stands tarnished by years of weathering and pollution. Built in the AD 2nd century, the gate was an entrance to the city until a local archbishop named it a church and pilgrimage site in the 11th century. It has survived relatively unscathed, though Napoleon's troops melted the metal roof into bullets. Climb to the top for a great view of Trier. *(☎0651 754 24. Open daily Apr.-Sept. 9am-6pm; Oct.-Mar. 9am-5pm; Nov.-Feb. 9am-4pm. Last entry 30min. before closing. €2.10, students €1.60.)*

DOM. This cloister-complex 11th-century cathedral shelters the tombs of archbishops. The **Tunica Christi** (Holy Robe of Christ) is enshrined at the eastern end of the cathedral. Tradition holds that this relic was brought to Trier from Jerusalem around AD 300 by St. Helena, mother of Emperor Constantine. The Tunica is shown to the public only on rare occasions, usually once every 30 years. Near the south end of the cathedral, outside the doorway, stands a fractured granite pillar supposedly cracked by the devil himself. Also within the Dom, the **Schatzkammer** holds a treasury of holy relics. Behind the cathedral is the **Bischöfliches Dom- und Diözesanmuseum,** a surprisingly modern building showcasing large archaeological collections and restored frescoes. *(☎0651 710 52 55. Dom open daily Apr.-Oct. 6:30am-6pm; Nov.-Mar. 6:30am-5:30pm. Admission free. Tour €3, children €1. Schatzkammer open Apr.-Oct. M-Sa 10am-5pm, Su 12:30-5pm; Nov.-Mar. M 1:30-4pm, Tu-Sa 11am-4pm, Su 12:30-4pm. €1.50, children €0.50. Diözesanmuseum, Windstr. 6-8. Open M-Sa 9am-5pm, Su 1-5pm; Nov.-Mar. closed M. €2, students €1.)*

AMPHITHEATER. A short walk from the city center, the Trier Amphitheater dates from the 2nd century and bears witness to the famed Roman tradition of gladiatorial games. Seating 20,000, this venue would have hosted shows with jesters, exotic animals, and gladiators. The amphitheater is now a stage for city productions; check *Theater Trier* for listings. *(The signs will lead you to a 10min. walk uphill from the Kaiserthermen along Olewiger Str. Open daily Apr.-Sept. 9am-6pm; Oct. and Mar. 9am-5pm; Nov.-Feb. 9am-4:30. Last entry 30min. before closing. €2.10, students €1.60.)*

KAISERTHERMEN (IMPERIAL BATHS). Though vivid when viewed from above, the ruins of 4th-century Roman baths are most memorable for gloomy, underground passages remaining from the ancient sewer network. Paths intersect often, making it easy to get lost. *(Enter through the Palastgarten. Open daily Apr.-Sept. 9am-6pm, Oct. and Mar. 9am-5pm, Nov.-Feb. 9am-4pm; last entry 30min. before closing. €2.)*

LIEBFRAUENKIRCHE. Adjacent to the Dom is the magnificent Gothic Liebfrauenkirche, one of the earliest Gothic church in Germany, built over the foundations of a Roman basilica. Angular red- and blue-patterned stained-glass windows dominate the plain interior. *(Liebfrauenstr. 2. ☎0651 425 54. Open daily Apr.-Oct. 7:30am-6pm, Nov.-Mar. 7:30am-5:30pm; tour available with purchase of Dom tour.)*

KARL-MARX-HAUS. The walls of Karl's humble birthplace are plastered with articles, photographs, and other memorabilia interesting to die-hard Marxists and social scientists. Copies of the *Communist Manifesto* abound. *(Brückenstr. 10. ☎0651 430 11. Open Apr.-Oct. M 1-6pm, Tu-Su 10am-6pm; Nov.-Mar. M 2-5pm, Tu-Su 10am-1pm and 2-5pm. Audio tours available in English €3, students €2.)*

AROUND THE BASILIKA. Built as a throne room for Emperor Constantine, the-Basilika is the only remaining Roman brick structure in Trier. This towering building served as a palace and church before it was heavily damaged by bombing during WWII. Unadorned walls and simple wood benches reveal little of its former splendor. *(Open Apr.-Oct. M-Sa 10am-6pm, Su noon-6pm; Nov.-Mar. Tu-Sa 11am-noon and 3-4pm, Su noon-1pm. Free.)* Next door is the bubble-gum-pink **Kurfürstliches Palais,** a former residence of the archbishops and electors of Trier that today houses municipal government offices. The lavish landscaping of the Palastgarten completes the Rococo motif. On the eastern edge of the garden lies the **Rheinisches Landesmuseum** (Roman Archaeological Museum), a terrific collection of Roman sculpture, mosaics, and even an Egyptian mummy. Check out the meticulous model of 4th-century Trier. *(Weimarer Allee 1. Open M-F 9:30am-5pm, Sa-Su 10:30am-5pm; Nov.-Apr. closed M. Audio tours available in English. €3, students €2)*

SIMEONSTIFT. An 11th-century monastery inside the Porta Nigra's courtyard, the Simeonstift holds the **Städtisches Museum,** renovated in 2007 to include a comprehensive and interactive summary of 2000 years of Trier history. Temporary exhibits continue to display ancient artifacts. *(☎0651 718 14 59. Open Tu-Su 10am-6pm, 1st M of the month until 9pm. €5, students €3.60, 1st Su of the month free.)*

ENTERTAINMENT AND NIGHTLIFE

Several annual festivals spice up Trier's atmosphere. The **Altstadtfest** brings live music, wine, and beer to the streets during the fourth weekend in June. The second weekend in July brings the **Moselfest** with Saturday night fireworks over the water, and the first weekend in August welcomes the **Weinfest** in the nearby town of Olewig. The **Weihnachtsmarkt,** in late November through Christmas, is also known as **Glühweinmarkt** to the local college students because of the featured spiced wine version of the local vintage. The **Theater Trier,** Am Augustinerhof, has three stages and a wide variety of shows. (☎0651 718 1818; www.theater-trier.de. Tickets €8-28. Box office open Tu-F 9:30am-2pm and 3:30-8pm,

Sa 10am-12:30pm.) Pubs and clubs of all flavors fan out from the Hauptmarkt, with dense collections on Judengasse and the **Pferdemarkt.** Check out *Lifestyle* magazine online (www.lifestyle-tr.de) for party and concert information.

Walderdorff's (☎0651 994 4412; www.walderdorffs.de), across from the Dom. At night, the mellow cafe surrenders to throngs of dancers crowding the hip, young underground disco. Beer €2. Mixed drinks €5.50-9. Cover €5. Cafe/bar open M-Th and Su 10am-1am, F-Sa 10am-2am. Disco open Tu and F-Sa. Themes include Tu Live Bar Jazz and Sa Sex and the City party. Dancing starts around 12:30am; crowds pack in around 2am. Website lists additional events. MC.

Barocco, Viehmarktpl. 10 (www.barocco.de). For unremitting partiers, this chic, relaxed bar and club combo offers decadent velvet couches, enormous works of art, and Romanesque pillars. ½-price mixed drinks 6-9pm. Friday Salsa night 10pm-2am, Sa hip hop. F-Sa cover €3. Open daily 10:30am-1am, F-Sa until 4am. MC.

O'Dwyer's Irish Pub, Jakobstr. 10 (☎0651 495 39; www.irish-pub.de), fills up with American and British crowds on regular theme nights, including "U2 Tuesdays" (free Guinness or Bailey's every time a U2 song is played). M karaoke at 9pm (€2, students €1.50), Su trivia at 9pm. Su and Th cheaper drinks (€0.50 less) for students. Live sports on TV. Free Wi-Fi. Open M-Th and Su 11am-1am, F-Sa 11am-2am. AmEx/MC/V.

Bierakademie, Bahnhofstr. 28 (☎0651 994 3195). With 100 beers and numerous local wines, Bierakademie is all about the drinks—just ask the local regulars. Foosball, billiards, and darts in back. Open M-Sa noon-1am, Su 3pm-midnight. Cash only.

WORMS ☎06241

Worms (pop. 82,000) was immortalized as the city whose imperial council, the Diet of Worms, sent Martin Luther into exile for refusing to renounce his heretical doctrine that religious truth existed only in scripture. Numerous Jewish memorials and synagogues are scattered throughout the city, which served as a cultural center before the Holocaust. A town with a crowded pedestrian zone by day, Worms quiets down at night in the shadow of its stately monuments.

TRANSPORTATION AND PRACTICAL INFORMATION. Frequent **trains** run to Mainz from Worms (1hr., 3 per hr., €7.60-11.70) and to Frankfurt (€15.50-29). The **tourist office,** Neumarkt 14, is located in the Rathaus, two blocks away from the Dom St. Peter. From the train station, head straight down Wilhelm-Leuschner-Str. and follow the signs. (☎06241 250 45; www.worms.de. Open M-F 9am-6pm, Sa 9:30am-1:30pm. Nov.-Mar. closed Sa.) A variety of walking **tours** (in German) are available from March to October. Ask at the tourist office for details. **Exchange money** at the **Deutsche Bank** down Wilhelm-Leuschner-Str. from the station. (Open M-W, F 9am-1pm and 2-4pm, Th 9am-1pm and 2-6pm. **24hr. ATM.**) The **police station,** Hagenstr. 5, is near the city council building. (☎06241 85 20; emergency ☎110. Open 24hr.) **TeleBistro,** Kämmererstr. 50, has **Internet** access for €1 per hour. (Open M-Sa 9:30am-11pm, Su 10am-11pm.) To reach the **post office,** continue along Neumarkt from the tourist office and take a right 2 blocks into the Kaiser Passage shopping center in Marktpl. (Open M-F 9am-8pm, Sa 9am-4pm.) **Postal Code:** 67547.

ACCOMMODATIONS AND FOOD. To get to the centrally located **Jugendgästehaus (HI) ❷,** Dechaneigasse 1, follow Bahnhofstr. right from the station to Andreasstr., and turn left. The hostel will be to your left across from the Dom. A pink staircase spirals upward to yellow hallways and bright three- to six-bed rooms, each with bath. (☎06241 257 80. Breakfast and sheets included. Reception 7am-11pm. Doors lock at 10pm. Dorms €18.40; singles

€28.40; doubles €46.80. MC/V.) Though many believe the famous Nibelungen treasure is lost forever under the Rhein, the friendly family that owns **Hotel Boos ❸,** Mainzer Str. 5, claims to have found it. From the train station, walk down Siegfriedstr. and turn left. Pastel rooms have private bath and cable TV in this pleasant hotel. The stained-glass windows of the breakfast room, pieced together by the owner and his son, chronicle the *Nibelungenlied* for which the town is famous. (☎06241 94 76 39; www.hotel-boos.de. Singles €44; doubles €65-72; triples €81; quads €98. Discounts available for weekend stays or stays longer than one night. Cash only.) *Imbiße* and bakeries line **Wilhelm-Leuschner-Str.** on the way from the train station to the center of town. The pedestrian zone is packed with sit-down Italian and German restaurants, though many charge €7 or more for mediocre fare. A better meal is a better deal at **Café im Affenhaus ❷,** Judengasse 17, where homemade *Pfannkuchen* come with an array of fillings for €5.30-6.10. This tiny spot on a tiny street is great for a cup of coffee, breakfast, or a hot meal. Another good option is **Pubjabi-Haus ❷,** Petersstr. 27, which serves Indian and Pakistani specialties, including chicken curry (€6), samosas (€3.50 for 2), and an array of vegetarian dishes. (Open M-Sa 11:30am-10:30pm, Su noon-10:30pm.)

SIGHTS. With its Romanesque towers soaring above the rest of Worms' skyline, the **Dom St. Peter** rises from ancient Celtic foundations. The Dom has been destroyed and rebuilt several times, but the renovations have been thorough. The stained glass window to the right of the altar depicts the town's history, including a Jewish rabbi in one pane and Martin Luther in another—perhaps Luther's only likeness in a Catholic church. (Open daily Apr.-Oct. 9am-5:45pm; Nov.-Mar. until 4:45pm. Donation requested.) The site of Luther's confrontation with the Diet is memorialized at the **Lutherdenkmal.** The 1868 statue, three blocks southeast of the station along Wilhelm-Leuschner-Str., is inscribed with the words, "Here I stand. I have no choice. May God help me. Amen." Luther never actually said these words; after leaving the trial, he said, "I am finished!" He was then "kidnapped" by friends who knew that he was an open target for murder and escaped safely. Across the walkway toward the Dom, the **Kunsthaus Heylshof** showcases 15th-century glass paintings, Rococo porcelain, and tortoiseshell furniture. Renaissance German and Dutch paintings include Rubens' *Madonna with Child.* Contemporary works are in the basement. (Open May-Sept. Tu-Su 11am-5pm; Oct.-Apr. Tu-Sa 2-5pm. €2.50, students €1.)

The legendary *Nibelungenlied*, a German myth primarily associated with Worms, is the focus of the modern **Nibelungen Museum.** Without any artifacts or rare text, the museum emphasizes the continued importance of storytelling. An audio tour delves into the many intricacies, ambiguities, and misinterpretations of the bloody legend, exploited by German rulers from the Kaiser to Hitler. Follow Petersstr. until you reach the town wall and turn right. (☎06241 20 21 20. Open Tu-F 10am-5pm, Sa-Su 10am-6pm. €5.50, students €4.50; price includes mandatory headset available in multiple languages.)

Long known as "Little Jerusalem," Worms was once home to one of Germany's first, largest, and best-established Jewish communities. Formerly the hub of the Jewish culture, the small cobbled streets around **Judengasse** are now lined with monuments and museums. Start at the **Jüdisches Museum** in the Raschi-Haus for a chronological history of Worms's Jewish population. The museum houses an 11th-century letter in which the King commends "the Jews of Worms," as well as charred sections of the Torah burned on Kristallnacht (Nov. 9-10, 1938). A 10min. video is available in English upon request. (☎06241 853 47 01. Open Tu-Su 10am-12:30pm and 1:30-5pm. €1.50, students €0.80.) Next to the museum, the old **Mikwa** (ritual bath) and **Synagoge** are both technically still in use, though turnout at weekly services is always low. The Synagoge traces its foundations back to 1175, when it was rebuilt after the First Crusade. It remained the spiritual and cultural center of Jewish learning north of the Alps until it was burned on Kristallnacht. In 1961 it was rebuilt, and houses a small commemorative hall in honor of the Jews of Worms lost in the Holocaust. (Open daily Apr.-Oct. 10am-12:30pm and 1:30-5pm; Nov.-Mar. 10am-12:30pm and 1:30-4pm. Required head coverings available at the door.)

ENTERTAINMENT. **80's Club,** Judengasse 11-13, lies in the historic area around Worms's erstwhile Jewish community. The only true nightclub in Worms, it pounds disco for a big crowd on F and Sa nights. (☎06241 238 5019. Open M-Th 7pm-2am, F 7pm-5am, Sa 8-5am, Su 8-2am. Cash only.) Facing the large memorial to Ludwig., **Cocktail's,** Ludwigspl. 5, predictably serves cocktails (€6) on the first floor and becomes a hookah lounge on the second. Daily happy hours until 10pm mean that all cocktails are €5. (☎06241 503 9624; www.diebar-ma.de. Open M-Th 2pm-2am, F-Su 2pm-3am.) The open-air Worms **Jazz and Joy Festival** takes place annually in early June, while the **Backfischfest** brings a wine-soaked party of 70,000 people to Worms for nine days starting the last weekend in August. Preparations begin a month in advance for the **Nibelungen-Festspiele,** held the first two weeks of August. Theatrical interpretations of the Nibelungenlied are almost as important as the food and drink that accompany them. Two weeks later, the **Backfischfest** takes over showcasing a Worms delicacy during the first week of September for 75 years in a row.

BADEN-WÜRTTEMBERG

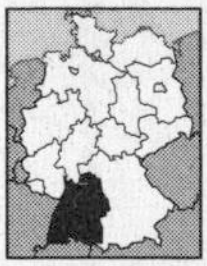

Once upon a time, the states of Baden, Württemberg-Hohenzollern, and Württemberg-Baden were all independent. When the Federal Republic was founded in 1951, the Allies combined the states into Baden-Württemberg. However, the Badeners and the Swabians (never "Württembergers") still proudly proclaim their distinct regional identities. Today, two powerful German stereotypes—the brooding romantic of the Brothers Grimm and the modern *homo economicus* exemplified by Mercedes-Benz—battle it out in Baden-Württemberg. Pretzels, cuckoo clocks, and cars were all pioneered here, and the region is as diverse as its exports. Rural customs live on in the bucolic hinterlands of the Schwarzwald (Black Forest) and the Schwäbische Alb, while the modern capital city of Stuttgart celebrates the ascendancy of the German industrial machine. The province also plays home to the ritzy resort of Baden-Baden, the Bodensee (Lake Constance, a.k.a. Germany's Riviera), and the historic university towns of Freiburg, Tübingen, and Heidelberg, each with a distinctive youthful flair.

HIGHLIGHTS OF BADEN-WÜRTTEMBERG

SPOT THE ALPS or roam among the manicured gardens of **Mainau,** on the **Bodensee** (p. 322), tropical for Germany, with wind-swept beaches and turquoise waters.

HIKE through thick stretches of spruce forest in the **Schwarzwald** (p. 318).

SOAP UP in the indulgent mineral baths and lush Schloßgarten of **Stuttgart** (see this page), sleek corporate home of Mercedes and Porsche.

SCRAMBLE OVER CASTLE RUINS with local brew in hand at Heidelberg's (p. 300) crumbling yet still imposing *Schloß*.

PUNT ALONG THE LAZY NECKAR in Tübingen (p. 306), an exquisite university town home to centuries of world-class intellectual achievement.

STUTTGART ☎0711

It would be a mistake to take the sleek modern buildings and speeding sportcars of Stuttgart (pop. 591,000) at face value. Though Porsche, Daimler-Benz, and a slew of other corporate powerhouses keep the city rich, fast-paced, and sparkling, thoroughfares and shopping streets are never more than a stone's throw from manicured gardens and ornate fountains. The city's famous mineral baths draw old and young alike to their healing waters, and the Ludwigsburg palaces, bucolic forests, and lush vineyards are just a short train ride away.

TRANSPORTATION

Flights: Flughafen Stuttgart (☎01805 94 84 44; flight information 0711 948 3388). Take S2 or S3 (30min., €3.10).

Trains: Stuttgart is the transportation hub of southwestern Germany. To: **Berlin** (6hr., 2 per hr., €122); **Frankfurt** (1-2hr., 2 per hr., €38-55); **Munich** (2-3hr., 2 per hr., €34-50).

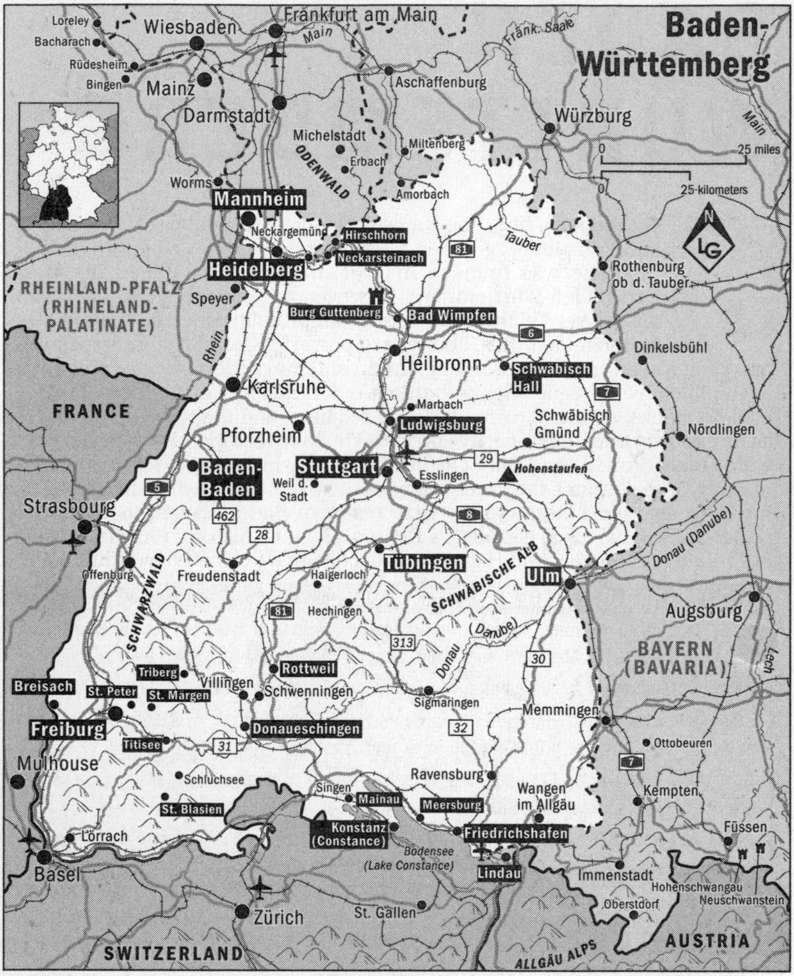

International Service to: **Basel, Switzerland** (3hr., 2-4 per hr., €42-55); **Paris, France** (8hr., 4 per day, €95-111); **Prague, Czech Rep.** (8½hr., 1-3 per hr., €127).

Ferries: Neckar-Personen-Schifffahrt (☎0711 54 99 70 60; www.neckar-kaeptn.de). Boats leave the Bad Cannstatt dock by Wilhelma Zoo. Take U14 (dir.: Remseck) to "Wilhelma." Ships cruise the Neckar Easter-Oct. 3-4 times daily €8-25. Return trip add €5.

Public Transportation: Single ride €1.90. If traveling 3 stops or fewer, a Kurzcard is available for €1. A 4-ride Mehrfahrkarte is €6.70 within city limits; a **Tageskarte,** valid 24hr. on all trains and buses, is €5.50 and up. A 3-day tourist pass is available at the tourist office and most hotels for a paltry €9.90.

Car Rental: Offices in the station at track 16 for: **Avis** (☎0711 223 7258); **Hertz** (☎0711 226 29 21); **Sixt/Budget** (☎0711 223 7822). At least 1 office open M-F 7am-9pm, Sa

7:30am-9pm, Su 7:30am-9pm. There's also a **EuropCar** just outside track 16; follow the signs for the U- and S-Bahn. (☎0711 954 6960. Open M-Sa 7:30am-9pm, Sa 8:30am-9pm.)

Bike Rental: Deutsche Bahn (DB) runs the citywide bike rental, **Call a Bike.** Look for bright red bikes with the DB logo on street corners throughout the city. Retrieve unlocking code by phone or online (☎0700 05 22 55 22; www.callabike.de). €0.08 per min. or €15 per day. Credit cards only. Bikes can go on the U- and S-Bahn for the price of a children's ticket except M-F 6-8:30am and 4-6:30pm; never on buses.

Ride Share: Mitfahrzentrale Stuttgart West, Lerchenstr. 65 (☎0711 194 48). Bus #42 to "Rosenberg/Johannesstr." Open M-F 9am-6pm, Sa 10am-1pm.

ORIENTATION AND PRACTICAL INFORMATION

The heart of Stuttgart is an enormous pedestrian zone cluttered with shops and restaurants running south from the Hauptbahnhof. **Königstraße** and the smaller **Calwerstraße** are the main pedestrian thoroughfares; from the train station, Königstr., along with a host of other streets and squares, is accessible by the underground **Arnulf-Klett-Passage.** The always vibrant **Calwerstraße** picks up steam after the **Schloßplatz,** an expanse of green lined with sidewalk cafes that extends behind the **Neues Schloß.** To the left sprawls the tranquil **Schloßgarten;** to the right, the thriving business sector, including **Rotebühlplatz,** two blocks right from the end of Königstr. The **Stuttcard** (€18, without transportation €12) offers three days of unlimited city transportation, admission to many museums, and discounts for guided tours, theaters, mineral baths, the zoo, and other sights.

Tourist Offices: I-Punkt, Königstr. 1A (☎0711 222 80; www.stuttgart-tourist.de), in front of the escalator leading to the Klett-Passage. Daily tours of the city in German or English (11am-12:30pm; €6). Contains an **ATM.** Open M-F 9am-8pm, Sa 9am-6pm, Su 11am-6pm. **Tips'n'trips,** Lautenschlagerstr. 22 (☎0711 222 2730; www.tips-n-trips.de), hands out youth-oriented pamphlets on the hottest clubs, affordable lodgings, and popular cafes. Open M-F noon-7pm, Sa 10am-2pm.

American Express: Arnulf-Klett-Pl. 1 (☎0711 226 9267). Cashes checks. Open M-F 9:30am-noon and 1-6pm, Sa 10am-1pm.

Gay and Lesbian Resources: Weißenburg, Weißenburgstr. 28a (☎0711 640 4494; www.zentrum-weissenburg.de). Open M-W and F 7-10pm, Th 5-10pm, Su 3-10pm.

Women's Resources: Fraueninformationszentrum (FIZ), Moserstr. 10 (☎0711 239 4124). Open M-F 9am-1pm.

English Bookstore: Piccadilly English Shop, Schellingstr. 11 (☎0711 226 0906) carries mostly paperbacks but will place orders upon request. Open M-Sa 10am-8pm.

Laundromat: Lavo'Magic, Katharinenstr. 21d (☎0711 259 9848). U-Bahn to "Rathaus." Wash €3.50. Dry €0.50 per 10min. Open M-F 9am-8pm, Sa 9am-10pm.

Emergency: ☎110. Police, Hauptstätterstr. 34 (☎0711 89 90 31 00). Fire ☎112.

Pharmacy: Bahnhof, Königstr. 4 (☎0711 29 02 14). Open M-F 8am-8pm, Sa 9am-8pm.

Hospital: Katharinenhospital, Kriegsbergstr. 60 (☎0711 27 80), near the train station.

Internet Access: Cafe Naser, Arnuff-Klett-Pl. 2 (☎0711 29 27 43) located in the Hauptbahnhof. Has 17 internet terminals available with purchase (coffee from €1.10).

Post Office: Inside the train station, Arnulf-Klett-Pl. 2. Open M-F 8:30am-6pm, Sa 8:30am-12:30pm. **Postal Code:** 70173.

ACCOMMODATIONS AND CAMPING

Hotels around the pedestrian zone and train station cater to customers paying top euro—call ahead for better deals. The best budget beds in Stuttgart are along the two ridges surrounding the city and are easily accessible with

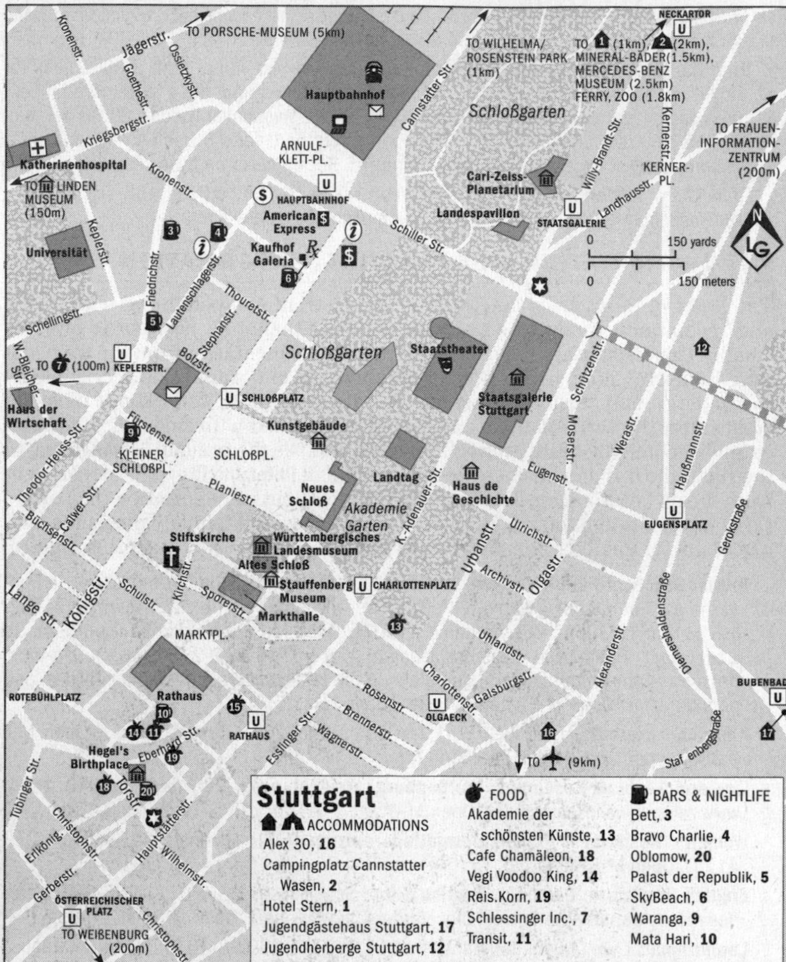

the S- or U-Bahn. **Tips'n'trips** (see **Tourist Offices**) can help you find affordable accommodations. In general, the best deals are easily reached by the S-Bahn. Try the **Jugendherberge Ludwigsburg ❷**, Gemsenbergstr. 21 (☎07141 515 64; dorms €17.40-20 for first night, €14.30-17 thereafter).

Jugendgästehaus Stuttgart (IB), Richard-Wagner-Str. 2 (☎0711 24 11 32; www.hostel-stuttgart.de). Tram #15 (dir.: Ruhbank) or night bus #N8 to "Bubenbad." The hostel is behind the tram stop on the right. Perched on a hill overlooking the city, this hostel offers the most comfortable and affordable beds in town. Breakfast and sheets included. Dinner M-Th €7. Laundry facilities €1.50. Key deposit €20. Reception 24hr. Dorms €16.50, singles €21.50, doubles €19 per person. With bath add €5. 1-night stays add €2.50. Show your *Let's Go* for a 10% discount! AmEx/MC/V. ❷

Alex 30, Alexanderstr. 30 (☎0711 838 8950; www.alex30-hostel.de). Tram #15 (dir.: Ruhbank) to "Eugenspl." 5min from the Schloßpl and walk down Alexanderstr. back towards town. Spacious, clean rooms and a location within walking distance of downtown make this hostel an attractice place to base out of. Backyard *Biergarten* open noon-10pm. Reception 24hr. Breakfast €6. Sheets €3. TV €2. 3- to 5-bed dorms €22, singles €34, doubles €54-64. MC/V. ❷

Jugendherberge Stuttgart (HI), Haußmannstr. 27 (☎0711 664 7470; www.jugendherberge-stuttgart.de). Take U15 (dir.: Ruhbank) to "Eugenspl." Walk uphill and follow the street as it bears left. The entrance is through the glass tower, attached by a bridge to the hillside; take the elevator down to the 5th fl. Recently renovated, this enormous, impeccable hostel has endless amenities: bistro, internet cafe, tourist info center, etc. Reserve more than a week ahead by email, otherwise by phone. Internet access €3 per 30min. Breakfast and sheets included. Locks €5. Reception 24hr. Use bell at back door 1-5am. Dorms €22.80, over 27 €26.30; additional nights €19/23.70. Cash only. ❷

Campingplatz Cannstatter Wasen, Mercedesstr. 40 (☎0711 55 66 96; www.campingplatz-stuttgart.de), in Bad Cannstatt. S1 (dir.: Daimler-Stadion) to "Cannstatter Wasen." Cross the large parking lot towards the river. Reception daily Apr.-Oct. 7am-noon and 2-10pm, Nov.-Mar. 8-10am and 5-7pm. Wash €4.50, dry €2.80. Shower €2. €5 per person, €2.20 per child, €2.20 per car, €3.10-6.50 per campsite. AmEx/MC/V. ❶

FOOD

> TIP **EATING DEPARTMENT.** In Germany, large department stores are almost guaranteed to have two things: a grocery in the basement and a cafe on top. If you're wandering a big city and don't know where to find an inexpensive bite to eat, check out the department store. You can't go wrong.

Fast-paced and cosmopolitan, Stuttgart is known for its excellent international cuisine. While a number of Swabian restaurants serve up *Spätzle* (thick egg noodles) and *Maultaschen* (pasta pockets filled with meat and spinach), some of the best dinners might be a little less traditional. Reasonably priced restaurants lie along the pedestrian zone between **Pfarrstraße** and **Charlottenstraße,** while **Rotebühlplatz** and **Kronenstraße** have *Imbiße* (snack bars). More stylish but inexpensive options for fresh sandwiches and vegetarian wraps can be found in the **Eberhardstraße** area near Hegel's birthplace. The basement of the **Kaufhof Galeria** at Königstr. 6 has a supermarket (open M-F 9:30am-8pm, Sa 9am-8pm).

Reis.Korn, Torstr. 27 (☎0711 664 76 33). This centrally located trendy Thai restaurant features a caliber of atmosphere and cuisine seldom found at budget prices. Heaping plates of noodles or curries with rice start at €7. Open M-Sa 11:30am-1am, Su 5pm-1am. Cash only. ❷

Schlesinger Int., Schlosstr. 28 (☎0711 29 65 25; www.schlesinger-int.de) is the place to go for regional specialties at the right price (from €6), locally brewed beers, and great atmosphere. Only blocks from the university, this student favorite attracts a vibrant young crowd. Open M-Th 5pm-1am, F 5pm-2am, Sa 6pm-2am. Cash only. ❸

Vegi Voodoo King, Steinstr., serves up vegetarian and vegan falafel sandwiches (€3), soups, and delicious hand-cut french fries in a semi-psychedelic, *Imbiß*-style eatery. Don't miss the "Freedom Fries." Open M-W 11:30am-12:30am, Th 11:30am-2am, F 11:30am-4am, Su 1pm-12:30am. Cash only. ❷

Akademie der schönsten Künste, Charlottenstr. 5 (☎0711 24 24 36; www.academie-der-schoensten-kuenste.de). U-Bahn to "Charlottenpl." High ceilings, art-decked walls, and a shaded garden draw packs of visitors of all ages to this restaurant-bar. Entrees €3.50-7.50. Open M-Th 6am-midnight, F 6am-1am, Sa 9am-1am, Su 9am-6pm. Kitchen closes 10pm. Cash only. ❷

Transit, Geissstr. 7 (www.transitbar.de) is an unassuming sandwich counter and cafe by day and a thumping bar by night. Enjoy your sandwich (€2.50-3) and cup of coffee (€2) or glass of wine (€2) in one of Stuttgart's most beautiful and most secluded plazas. Return later in the evening for cocktails and dancing; the place heats up F-Sa nights, when the DJs bring in the dance crowd. Opens daily noon-2am. ❶

SIGHTS

SCHLOSSGARTEN. Because almost 20% of Stuttgart is under a land preservation order, the city is known for its urban green spaces, the crown jewel of which is the palatial Schloßgarten. At the northern end of the gardens is **Rosensteinpark,** home to the **Wilhelma,** a zoo and botanical garden housed in the ornate buildings constructed by King Wilhelm as a summer retreat. The zoo keeps more than 8000 different animals, including a polar bear named **Wilbär** who draws thousands of visitors per day. Over 6000 plant species make up the manicured gardens. It is unlike any other zoo in the world. *(Take U14 (dir.: Remseck) to "Wilhelma." ☎0711 540 20; www.wilhelma.de. Open daily 8:15am-dusk. €11.40, after 4pm and Nov-Feb. €8; ages 6-17 €5.70/4. German guidebooks €3.30.)*

SCHLOSSPLATZ. The Schloßgarten extends down to this plaza, off Königstr., just north of the elegant Baroque **Neues Schloß,** where the mythological figures guard the bureaucrats working inside. Local professional and amateur orchestras often hold free performances in the graceful, colonnaded Renaissance courtyard of the 16th-century **Altes Schloß.** The **Württembergisches Landesmuseum** (p. 297) is inside.

MINERALBÄDER (MINERAL BATHS). Join geriatric Germans as they soak in Stuttgart's renowned mineral baths, filled from Western Europe's most active mineral springs. The 40 million liters of spring water pumped out every day are said to have curative powers, and bathers flock from far and wide to soak in pools, saunas, and showers supplied by the stuff. Loll in the **Mineralbad Leuze,** an official healthcare facility. *(Am Leuzebad 2-6. U1 to "Mineralbäder." Past the volcano-like geyser-fountains. ☎0711 216 4210. Open daily 6am-9pm. Day card €14, students €10. 2hr. soak €7.30, ages 14-18 €5.60; 3hr. €9.50/7.20.)* **Mineralbad Berg** is less expensive and less luxurious. *(Am Schwanenpl. 9. U1 or U14 or tram #2 to "Mineralbäder." ☎0711 923 6516. Open M-Th 6am-8pm, F-Sa 6am-9pm, Su 6am-5pm. Day card €6.50, under 16 €5.30. Last entry in both baths 1hr. before closing.)*

CARL ZEISS PLANETARIUM. Stuttgarters stargaze at the city's planetarium, named after one of the most famous telescope manufacturers in the entire galaxy. Enjoy shows with German voiceovers, visual effects, and spacey background music. *(Willy-Brandt-Str. 25. U1, U4, U9, or U14 or tram #2 to "Staatsgalerie." ☎0711 162 9215. Shows Tu and Th 10am and 3pm; W and F 10am, 3, 8pm; Sa-Su 2, 4, 6pm. Sa night laser show at 7:15. €6, students €4.)*

HEGEL'S BIRTHPLACE. Like a shrine of sorts, the first and second floors of this unassuming house give insight to the great thinker's life and work. Familiarity with Hegel, the "European Phenomenon," is probably useful in order to fully appreciate the display, all of which is in German. *(Eberhardstr. 53, a couple blocks east from the end of Königstr. Take S1-6, U14, or tram #2 or 4 to "Rotebühlpl. (Stadtmitte)." ☎0711 216 6733. Open M-W and F 10am-5:30pm, Th 10am-6:30pm, Sa 10am-4pm. Free.)*

MUSEUMS

STAATSGALERIE STUTTGART (NATIONAL GALLERY). A superb collection in two wings: the stately paintings in the old wing date from the Middle Ages to the 19th century, while the new wing has a first-rate collection of moderns including works by Picasso, Kandinsky, and Dalí. An amazing collection of German Expressionists has particular relevance in its home country. *(Konrad-Adenauer-Str. 30-32. ☎0711 47 04 00; www.staatsgalerie.de. Open Tu-W and F-Su 10am-86pm, Th 10am-9pm; 1st Sa of the month 10am-midnight. €8, ages 13-20 €2, under 13 free. Tours €3/1.50. Permanent exhibits free W. Audio tour €4, students €3, with €10 deposit.)*

MERCEDES-BENZ MUSEUM. Visitors are led on a comprehensive journey through automotive history in this sleek museum. A century's worth of gleaming automobiles—from Gottlieb Daimler's and Karl Benz's first experiments to the showy prototypes of tomorrow—will make even the most lukewarm car enthusiast drool. *(Mercedesstr. 100. S1 (dir.: Plochingen) to "Gottlieb-Daimler-Stadion." Continue on Mercedesstr. past the stadium and look for signs. ☎0711 173 0000; www.mercedes-benz.com/museum. Open Tu-Su 9am-6pm, ticket counter closes at 5pm. €8, students €4, under 15 free. Free audio tour available. Free factory tour daily 2pm.)*

WÜRTTEMBERGISCHES LANDESMUSEUM. Fittingly situated in the Altes Schloß, this amazing collection of artifacts charts the history of the Swabian region and people from the stone age to today. Excellent exhibits on Bronze Age Celtic metalwork, along with well-worn weaponry and crown jewels. Don't miss the stunning exhibit on the history of glass in the basement. The ticket also allows entry to a musical instrument collection at Schillerpl. 1. *(Schillerpl. 6. ☎0711 279 3498; www.landesmuseum-stuttgart.de. Open Tu-Su 10am-5pm. €4.50, students €3, under 14 free. Free audio tour available.)*

HAUS DER GESCHICHTE. More than 1400 artifacts and 1000 photos give shrewd insight into the fate of the Kingdom of Württemberg from the 1790s to today. *(Konrad-Adenauer-Str. 16. ☎0799 212 3989; www.hdgbw.de. Open Tu-W, F-Su 10am-6pm, Th 10am-9pm. €3, students €2.)* Small but mighty, the affiliated **Stauffenberg Memorial** is in the basement of the Altes Schloß. This museum honors the lives of Berthold and Claus von Stauffenberg, the two brothers responsible for the July 20, 1944 attempt on Hitler's life. The boys were raised in the *Schloß* above as members of the German elite. The gripping exhibits detail their development from Nazi youth to leaders of

WHAT'S THE PUNKT?

Germany has a well-earned reputation as one of the world's most environmentally friendly countries, and its system of charging *Pfand*, a monetary deposit on glass and plastic bottles—which applies not only at *Biergarten* but also in grocery stores and vending machines throughout the country—is only one manifestation of this heightened awareness.

In 1990, Germany instituted a system called *Der Grüne Punkt* (The Green Dot), which has become the most widely used recycling program in Europe. The system created incentives for manufacturers to use less packaging on all their materials. Basically, retailers have to pay for a "Green Dot" on products: the more packaging, the higher the fee. The system has led to about one million tons less garbage being processed annually.

As of 2002, the German recycling initiative was expanded and deposits were added to many plastic and glass bottles sold in grocery and convenience stores. Don't just thrown your bottle away when you've finished. Instead, do your part to help the environment (and your wallet), by returning your bottle to one of the big machines in the supermarket and get your euros back.

the 1944 plot to assasinate Hitler. *(In the Altes Schloß across from Karlspl. ☎0711 212 3989; www.stauffenberg-museum.de. Open Tu-Su 10am-6pm. €1.50, students €1. Combined admission with the Haus der Geschichte €3.50/2.50.)*

PORSCHEMUSEUM. In 2009, Porsche unveils its long-awaited and much-expanded museum, a futuristic bastion of polished metal. The new space is nearly ten times larger than the original museum, really just a glorified show-room, and provides a behind-the-scenes look at maintaining the museum's 80+ vintage automobiles. *(Original musuem, Porschestr. 42, in Stuttgart-Zuffauhausen. S6 (dir.: Weil der Stadt/Leonberg) to "Neuwirtshaus (Porschepl.)"; exit the station to the right; cross the intersection and take a left on Moritz-Horkheimer-Str. ☎0711 911 56 85. Open M-F 9am-4pm, Sa-Su 9am-5pm. Free. The new museum is also on Porchestr., just outside the S-Bahn station.)*

ENTERTAINMENT AND NIGHTLIFE

The **Staatstheater,** across the plaza from the Neues Schloß, is one of Germany's most impressive theaters and the heart of the city's cultural vibrancy. (Reservations ☎0711 20 20 90; www.staatstheater-stuttgart.de. Box office open M-F 10am-6pm, Sa 10am-2pm, and 1hr. before performances. Tickets €8-155; students €8-12.)

The **Stuttgarter Weindorf** (Wine Village) is the largest wine festival in Germany. From late August to early September, wine lovers descend upon Schillerpl., Marktpl., and Kirchstr. to sample Swabian specialties and 350 kinds of wine. Beer gets two weeks in the spotlight during the 160-year-old **Cannstatter Volksfest,** Germany's second largest beer fesival, held annualy on the Cannstatter Wasen (last week of Sept. and first week of Oct.). The **Christopher Street Day** gay and lesbian festival occurs the last week in July (☎0179 464 4694).

Stuttgart's nightlife runs the gamut from calm lounges to techno-filled clubs. The somewhat pricey sit-down cafes along **Königstraße** and **Calwerstraße** are packed in the early evening, while the real nightlife follows a chic, Benz-driving crowd to the innumerable sidewalk lounges on **Theodor-Heuss-Str.** The club scene doesn't pick up until after midnight—when it does, **Rotebühlplatz** and **Eberhardstraße** are the most popular areas. **Tips'n'trips** (see **Tourist Offices,** p. 293) publishes comprehensive guides to nightlife in German and English. For more on current events, buy a copy of *Lift* (www.lift-online.de), also available at Tips'n'trips (€1.70). For gay nightlife, check *Schwulst* (www.schwulst.de).

Bravo Charlie, Lautenschlagerstr. 14 (☎0711 231 6882; www.bravo-charlie.de), a trendy cafe and restaurant by day and Stuttgart's most popular nightclub after dark. A hip crowd of students and young professionals arrive in flocks. DJs hit the turntables on F and Sa nights. Open M 8:30am-1am, Tu-W 8:30am-2am, Th 8:30am-3am, F 8:30am-5am, Sa 10am-5am, Su noon-1am. Cash only.

Suite 212, Theodor-Heuss-Str. 15 (☎0711 253 6113; www.suite212.org). The streets and couches in front of this simple bar-lounge stay packed with beer-guzzling and martini-sipping hipsters. Relax with a quieter crowd sitting outside during the day. Art films play above the bar. The open spaces both inside and out provide a welcome respite from your typical crowded bar. DJ and VJ on weekends. Beer €2.50-3, mixed drinks €6.50-8. Open M-W 11am-2am, Th 11am-3am, F-Sa 11am-5am, Su 2pm-2am. Cash only.

SkyBeach, Königstr. 6 (www.skybeach.de). On the newly sand-covered roof of the Kaufhof Galleria on Königstr. In good weather, young Germans flock to this club to lounge in bikinis, drink mojitos, and watch the occasional live fire show in a faux-tropical atmosphere. Open daily 11am-late. Cash only.

Bett, Friedrichstr. 23a (☎0711 284 1667; www.bett-lounge.de). Jungle-deco walls surround a 20-something and younger crowd filling the dance floor of this bar/club late into the night. The canopied beds out back are crowded with perennial late-night loungers. Bar area open daily 3pm-1am, while the club pulses F-Sa 11pm-late. Cash only.

Palast der Republik, Friedrichstr. 27 (☎0711 226 4887). A circular wooden pavilion with a bar blasts music for fresh-air fans and after-hours aficionados. On weekends, the crowd overflows onto the sidewalk with alarming density. Beer €2-3. Open M-W 11am-2am, Th-Sa 11am-3am, Su 3pm-1am. Cash only.

Oblomow, Torstr. 20 (☎0711 236 7924). The best seats in the house in this downtown bar are at the top of a ladder in a cushioned loft. The pounding bass and occasional live DJs play more to seated guests than hardcore dancers, but the atmosphere is convivial. Come early and climb the ladder to grab seats in the cushioned loft. Snacks €3-6 (served 3pm-4am); drinks €3-8. Live DJs Sa 11pm. Open daily 3pm-7am. Cash only.

Waranga, Kleiner Schloßpl. 13-15 (☎0711 99 79 92 66; www.waranga.de), overlooks the expansive Schloßpl. Grab a drink and sit on the famous steps leading down to Königstr. Open weekdays 11am-1am, weekends until 3am. MC/V.

DAYTRIP FROM STUTTGART

LUDWIGSBURG

From Stuttgart, take S4 (dir.: Marbach) or S5 (dir.: Bietigheim; 15min., 6 per hr., €2.90) to "Ludwigsburg."

Just 15min. outside of Stuttgart lies the town of Ludwigsburg and its jaw-dropping palace. Construction on the *Schloß* began in 1704, when Duke Eberhard Ludwig of Württemberg decided to expand his hunting lodge into a full-blown estate to spend more time with his mistress. Though Eberhard, poor dear, died during the 30-year-long construction of the enormous Baroque palace, a town sprung up in the decades following its completion. **Residenzschloß,** the largest and most impressive of the three palaces now in Ludwigsburg, can only be seen on a guided tour (1½hr.). Well-versed tour guides lead groups through a mere 60 of the palace's 452 rooms, explaining every lavish detail from gifts from Napoleon to Ludwig's 3m long bed. From the train station, head down Myliusstr. until you pass the statue of Schiller on your right. Make a right onto Mathildenstr. and follow it until you come to Schloßstr. (☎07141 18 64 40. Open mid-Mar. to Oct. daily 10am-6:30pm, last entry 5pm; Nov. to mid-Mar. 10am-noon and 1-4pm. German-language tours in summer daily every 30min.; in winter M-F 4 per day, Sa-Su 8 per day. English-language tours in summer M-F 1:30pm, Sa-Su 11am, 1:30, 3:15pm. €6, students €3; combined ticket with gardens and Schloß Favorite €15/7.50)

The *Schloß* sits on the **Blühendes Barock,** more than 70 acres of gardens so ornate that the palace is often called "the Swabian Versailles." (☎07141 97 56 50. Open Mar.-Oct. daily 7:30am-8:30pm. €7.50, students €3.60.) Inside, a perennial **Märchengarten** features scenes from major fairy tales in a large park of wild vegetation. The **Schloß Favorite,** behind the Residenzschloß garden, is an excellent destination for a stroll or picnic. (☎07141 18 64 40. Open mid-Mar. to Oct. daily 10am-12:30pm (last entry noon) and 1:30-5pm; Nov. to mid-Mar. 10am-12:30pm (last entry noon) and 1:30-4pm. Guided tours in German every 30min. €3, students €1.50.) If you're not *Schloß*-ed out, stop to pet the wild deer (at your own risk) as you continue through the **Favoritenpark.** (Open daily Apr.-Aug. 8am-7pm, Sept.-Oct. 9am-6pm, Nov.-Jan. 9am-4pm, Feb.-Mar. 9am-5pm. Free.) The third Ludwig palace, the Rococo **Monrepos,** is privately owned and contains a hotel. (1hr. from entrance.)

Ludwigsburg's **tourist office,** Marktpl. 6, has free maps and guides. (☎07141 91 75 55. Open M-F 9am-6pm, Sa 9am-2pm.) From the Bahnhof, head down Myliusstr. until it becomes Arsenalstr. Bear left on Arsenalstr. and make the next right onto Wilhelmstr. The Marktpl. is on the left.

HEIDELBERG ☎06221

Over the years, this sun-drenched town on the Neckar and its crumbling *Schloß* have called to scores of writers and artists: Mark Twain, Wolfgang von Goethe, Friedrich Hölderlin, Victor Hugo, and Robert Schumann, to name a few. During the summer, roughly 32,000 tourists answer the call every day. Even in the off season, legions of camera-toting fannypackers swell Hauptstr., where postcards and T-shirts sell like hotcakes and every sign is posted in four languages. The incessant buzz of tourism, however, does little to detract from Heidelberg's beautiful hillside setting, bustling waterfront, and legendary nightlife in student-packed, pub-lined streets and gritty clubs. In many ways, Heidelberg (pop. 142,000) epitomizes the enigmatic German university town, reckoning with the crushing weight of history, the fun-loving disaffection of students, and the ever-evolving effort to market itself in souvenir-size to foreigners.

TRANSPORTATION

Trains: To **Frankfurt** (50min., 2 per hr., €15-25), **Mannheim** (16-20min., 2 per. hr., €6), and **Stuttgart** (40min., every hr., €23-34).

Ferries: Rhein-Neckar-Fahrgastschifffahrt (☎06221 201 81), on the southern bank in front of the Kongresshaus, runs up the Neckar to Neckarsteinach and back (3hr., Easter-Oct. 19 every hr. 9:30am-4:50pm; €10.50, children €6), and all over Germany. For an eco-friendly trip, take a ride with **Heidelberger Solarschifffahrts,** Willy-Brandt-Pl. 1 (☎06221 19 433) on the world's largest (yet entirely silent) solar-powered boat.

Public Transportation: Single bus ride prices vary with destination (around €2). Day passes (€5, €8 for 2-5 people) valid on all trams and buses for 24hr. from the time stamped. 3-day passes €12.50. Tickets purchased on Sa are valid until Su midnight.

Taxis: ☎06221 30 20 30.

Bike Rental: Eldorado, Neckarstaden 52 (☎06221 654 44 60; www.eldorado-hd.de). €15 per day or €5 per hr. Open Tu-F 9am-noon and 2-6pm, Sa 10am-6pm, Su 2-6pm. Discounts available for longer rentals.

Boat Rental: Bootsverleih Simon (☎06221 41 19 25; www.bootsverleih-heidelberg.de). On the north shore of the Neckar by Theodor-Heuss-Brücke. 30min. rentals. 3- or 4-person paddle boat €7/8. 3- or 4-person motorboat €13/15.

Hitchhiking: *Let's Go* does not recommend hitchhiking as a safe mode of transportation. Those who do hitch reportedly wait at the western end of Bergheimer Str.

ORIENTATION AND PRACTICAL INFORMATION

About 20km east of the Neckar's confluence with the Rhein, Heidelberg stretches along the river for several kilometers, with almost all of the city's attractions in the eastern quarter of the southern bank. To get to the Altstadt from the Hauptbahnhof, take any bus or tram to "Bismarckpl.," where Hauptstraße leads into the city's heart. Heidelberg has a huge population of fierce bicyclists—stay out of the red bike lanes. A **Heidelberg Card** grants free or reduced-price admission to major attractions and can be purchased at the tourist office. One-, two-, and four-day cards available for €10, 14, or 20 per person.

Tourist Office (☎06221 138 8121; www.cvb-heidelberg.de), in front of the Haputbahnhof. Books rooms for €3 plus a small deposit, and sells maps (€1) and hotel/sights info pamphlets (€1). Pick up copies of the magazines *Meier* (€1) and *Heidelberg Aktuell* (€1) to see what's up. Open M-Sa 9am-6pm. Additional **branches** in the Rathaus (open

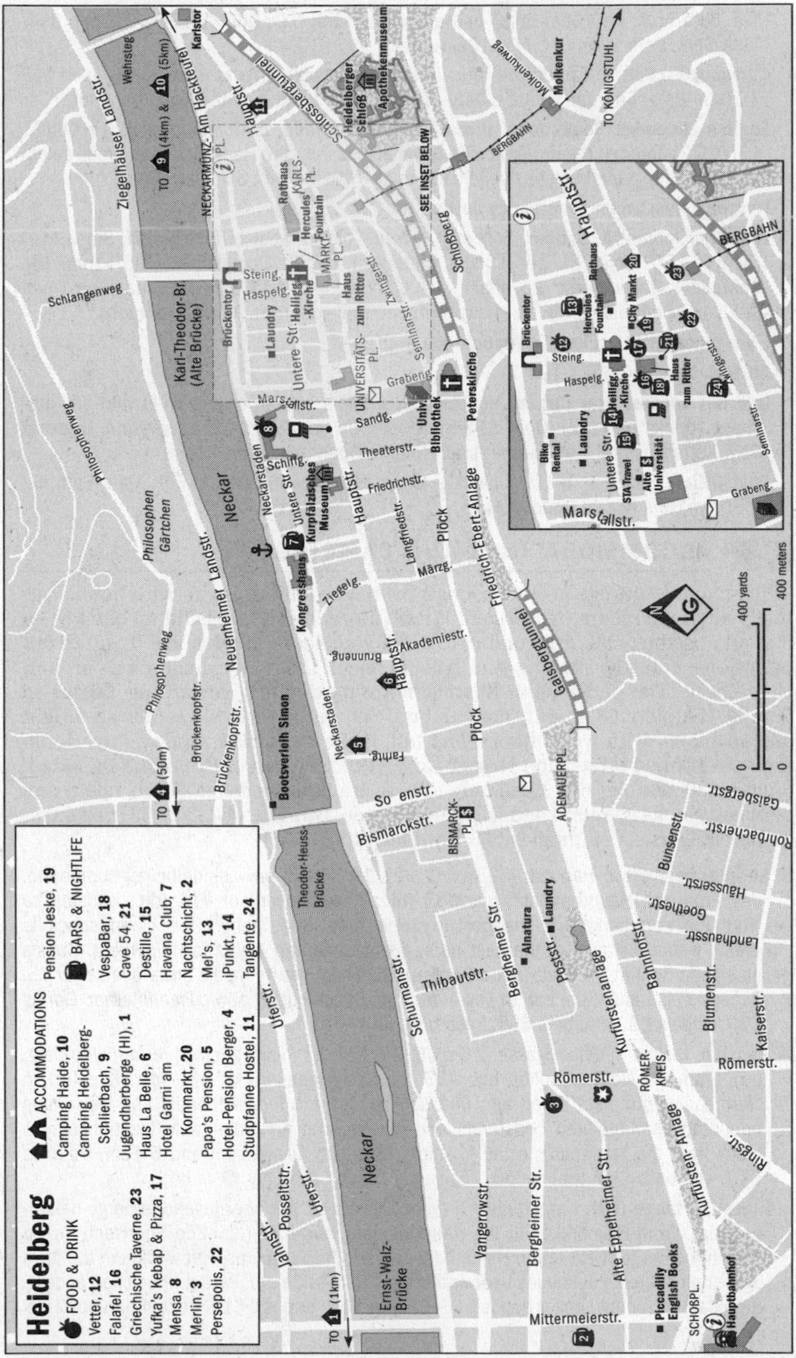
Heidelberg
FOOD & DRINK
Vetter, 12
Falafel, 16
Griechische Taverne, 23
Yufka's Kebap & Pizza, 17
Mensa, 8
Merlin, 3
Persepolis, 22
ACCOMMODATIONS
Camping Haide, 10
Camping Heidelberg-Schlierbach, 9
Jugendherberge (HI), 1
Haus La Belle, 6
Hotel Garni am Kornmarkt, 20
Papa's Pension, 5
Hotel-Pension Berger, 4
Studpfanne Hostel, 11
Pension Jeske, 19
BARS & NIGHTLIFE
VespaBar, 18
Cave 54, 21
Destille, 15
Havana Club, 7
Nachtschicht, 2
Mel's, 13
iPunkt, 14
Tangente, 24
Neckar
Karl-Theodor-Br (Alte Brücke)
Theodor-Heuss-Brücke
Ernst-Walz-Brücke
Heidelberger Schloß
Apothekenmuseum
Hauptstr.
Bismarckstr.
Friedrich-Ebert-Anlage
Kurfürstenanlage
Hauptbahnhof
SEE INSET BELOW
TO KÖNIGSTUHL
BERGBAHN
400 yards
400 meters

BADEN-WÜRTTEMBERG

M-F 8am-5pm, Sa 10am-5pm) and at Neckarmünzpl. (☎06221 137 40. Open daily June-Sept. 9am-6pm, Oct.-May 10am-4pm.)

Currency Exchange: Sparkasse branches on Universitätspl. and Bismarckpl. Open M-F 7:30am-8pm, Sa 9am-5pm, Su 9am-1pm. A **Reise Bank** is in the Hauptbahnhof.

English-Language Bookstores: Piccadilly English Shop, Kurfürstenlage 62 (☎06221 16 77 72), through the Kurfürsten-Passage across from the Hauptbahnhof. Small selection of mostly paperback bestsellers. Open M-F 10am-7pm, Sa 10am-6pm.

Women's Resources: Emergency hotline ☎06221 582 54.

Laundry: Schnell & Sauber, Poststr. 45, a few blocks west of Bismarckpl. Small load (3kg) €3.50, dryer €1 per 10min., detergent €0.50. Open daily 6am-11pm. **Die Schleuder,** Dreikoenigstr. 25, offers wash and dry for €7, with a 2-3hr. turnaround. Open M-F noon-6pm during the university term and M-F noon-4pm during vacations.

Emergency: ☎110. **Fire** and **Ambulance** ☎112.

AIDS Hotline: ☎06221 194 11.

Internet Access: Star Coffee, Hauptstr. 129, offers 30min. of free Wi-Fi with any purchase (drinks from €2). Open M-F 8am-9pm, Sa 9am-9pm, Su 11am-8pm. **Internet City,** Kettengasse 8, has internet for €1 per hr. Open daily 9am-11pm.

Post Office: Sofienstr. 8-10, 1 block south of Bismarckpl. Open M-F 9:30am-6pm, Sa 9:30am-1pm. **Postal Code:** 69115.

ACCOMMODATIONS AND CAMPING

With so many tourists in such a small town, Heidelberg is rife with hotels, virtually all of which are overpriced. What's more, these hotels fill up quickly, so if at all possible, call or go online to book your room in advance. If you're out of options, consider making your base in one of the many small towns around Heidelberg. The pensions at **Hirschhorn** are particularly rewarding. **Haus La Belle ❸**, Hauptstr. 38, is aptly named: Frau Schernthaner's two rooms are bright and spacious, with wood floors, and tall, white-curtained windows overlooking the crooked street one story below. (☎06221 14 00. Breakfast included. Singles €30, doubles €60. Cash only.) There is a **Jugendherberge** 20min. upstream, between Neckargemünd and Dilsberg. (Untere Str. 1. ☎06223 21 33. Breakfast included. Dorms €18, singles €28, doubles €46. MC/V.)

Sudpfanne Hostel, Haputstr. 223 (☎06221 16 36 36; www.heidelberger-sudpfanne.de). From the Hauptbahnhof, bus #33 (dir.: Ziegelhausen) or #11 (dir.: Karlstor) to "Rathaus/Kornmarkt." The cheapest hostel in town, Sudpfanne offers clean, spacious rooms within distance of the best bars, restaurants, and sights in Heidelberg. Guests also get a deal at the **Sudpfanne Restaurant,** where hearty meals are available for €5. Reception is behind the bar. Check-in at 3pm. Check-out by noon. Free internet. Dorms €20, singles €30, doubles €60. Cash only. ❸

Pension Jeske, Mittelbadgasse 2 (☎06221 237 33; www.pension-jeske-heidelberg.de). From the Hauptbahnhof, bus #33 (dir.: Ziegelhausen) or #11 (dir.: Karlstor) to "Rathaus/Kornmarkt." Small and unassuming, Jeske offers a friendly and welcoming prioprietor, handpainted bedstands and closets, and an unbeatable location only 1 block from the Marktplatz in the Altstadt. Reception 11am-1pm and 5-7pm. Doubles €40, with bath €60; triples €60/75; quints €100. Cash only. ❹

Jugendherberge (HI), Tiergartenstr. 5 (☎06221 65 11 90; www.jugendherberge-heidelberg.de). From Bismarckpl. or the Hauptbahnhof, bus #23 (dir.: Zoo-Sportzentrum) to "Jugendherberge." Next to the Heidelberg Zoo, this hostel teems with wildlife in the form of schoolchildren. Pub serves beer and snacks 6pm-midnight. Partial wheelchair access. Breakfast included. Locker deposit €2. Required key deposit €10. Reception until 2am.

Check-out 10am. Reserve at least 1 week ahead. Dorms €20.30, over 27 €23.30; singles add €10 per person, doubles add €5. Discount for longer stays. MC/V. ❷

Hotel-Pension Berger, Erwin-Rohde-Str. 8 (☎06221 40 16 08). Take bus #12 to "Mönchhofstr." Located in the upscale residential neighborhood just across the Theodor-Heuss-Brücke from the center of town, this beautiful hotel is well worth the somewhat distant location and swimming pool. Singles €40-75, doubles €75-95. Cash only. ❹

Papa's Pension, Fahrtgasse 1 (☎06221 16 50 33). This little hostel is in the center of the action, but it's also above a loud bar that's open until 2am. Singles €35, doubles €65; add €20 for each additional person. Cash only.

Camping: Haide (☎06223 21 11; camping-haide.de), on the northern bank of the Neckar. Bus #35 (dir.: Neckargmünd) to "Orthopädisches Klinik," then cross the river, turn right, and walk 20min. Bike rental €8 per day. Wash €3, dry €2. Reception 8-11am and 4-8pm. Open mid-April to Oct. 31 €5.30 per person, €3.50 per tent, €5 per RV, €1 per car. Cabins €13. Showers €0.50 per 5min. Electricity €2 per night. Cash only. ❶

FOOD

Most of the restaurants around Hauptstr. are geared toward the tourists that frequent them, which means that prices are high and quality is not. *Imbiße* (snack bars) and bakeries abound, however, offering cheaper options. Outside the central area, historic student pubs offer good values. **City-Markt Ruedinger,** at Hauptstr. 198, is one of several grocery stores around the Martkpl. (Open M-F 8am-8pm, Sa 8am-7pm.) **Alnatura,** Bergheimer 59-63, has a selection of organic foods. (☎06221 61 86 34. Open M-W 9am-7pm, Th-Fr 9am-8pm, Sa 9am-6pm.)

Falafel, Heugasse 1 (☎06221 21 61 03 03). Tucked away from the busy Hauptstr., this tiny Lebanese falafel shop offers delicious and affordable meals. Get a piping hot falafel or spicy chicken rolled into bread with fresh mint leaves, lettuce, tomato, and sauce (€3). The storefront is usually packed, but the service is friendly. ❶

Merlin, Bergheimer Str. 85 (☎06221 65 78 56). The tables of this calm cafe spill out onto an untouristed sidewalk away from the rush of Hauptstr. The sorcery-themed breakfast menu (€4-10.20) includes the Harry Potter and the Merlin (served M-F 10-11:30am, Sa-Su 10am-3pm). Lunch M-F 11:30am-3pm (daily special €6.50). In good weather, have your meal outside on a cushioned sofa. Open M-Th and Su 10am-1am, F-Sa 10am-3:30am. AmEx/MC/V. ❷

Persepolis, Zwingstr. 21 (☎06221 65 78 56), serves up Persian food at prices impossible to find anywhere else in the Altstadt. The rotating menu always offers 5 delicious dishes, including 1 vegetarian option. Regular portion from €3.30, large portions from €5. Show your student ID for a €0.50 discount on all meals. Open M-F 11am-5pm, Sa-Su noon-8pm. Cash only. ❷

Vetter, Steingasse 9 (☎06221 16 58 50; www.brauhaus-vetter.de). Don't miss Vetter's homemade beer. The restaurant specializes in German food, offering individual plates (from €7) as well as enormous platters (€24-59) that could easily feed a group of 6. Open M-Th and Su 11:30am-midnight, F-Sa 11:30am-2am. Cash only. ❸

Yufka's Kebap and Pizza, Haputstr. 182 (☎06221 48 59 30; www.yufka.de), serves up the best Turkish food in town. Though its location right in the Marktpl. might make you wary, locals unanimously recommend this spot for lunch, dinner, late-night snacks, or all of the above. Open daily 11am-3am. Cash only. ❶

SIGHTS

HEIDELBERGER SCHLOSS. Heidelberg owes its existance to the *Schloß*, the enormous castle that towers over the city below. Construction on the *Schloß* began in the 14th century, but it was expanded, destroyed, and expanded again over a period of almost 400 years. As a result, the *Schloß* that you see today is an enormous conglomeration of architectural styles including crumbled Gothic and recently refurbished High Renaissance. In nice weather, almost 7000 tourists make the trip to the *Schloß* daily, so if hordes of foreign tourists aren't your thing, dress for the elements and go in the rain. Once there, be sure to check out the **Großes Faß**—it's the largest wine barrel ever used, holding nearly 220,000L and topped with a dance floor. The measly **Kleines Faß** holds a mere 125,000L. Walk through the impressive gardens around the castle, which provide the best views of Heidelberg below. Also, stop in the **Apotheken-Museum** (Pharmacy Museum) to learn more than you ever thought possible about the history of modern medicine. The *Schloß* is accessible by a 10min. walk up a winding path or by the **Bergbahn**, one of Germany's oldest cable cars, which runs from the "Bergbahn/Rathaus" bus stop to the castle. *(Trams depart from the parking lot next to the bus stop every 10min. Mar.-Oct. daily 9am-8pm, every 20min. Nov.-Feb. daily 9am-6pm. Take bus #11 (dir.: Karlstor) or #33 (dir.: Ziegelhausen) to "Rathaus/Bergbahn." Cable car round-trip €5 (free for Heidelberg Card-holders). Castle ☎06221 53 84 21. Grounds open daily 8am-6pm, last entry 5:30pm. Guided tours every hr. M-F 11:15am-4:15pm, Sa-Su also 10:15am; in English every hr. M-F 11:15am-4:15pm, Sa-Su also 10:15am; €4, students €2. Schloß, Großes Faß, and Apotheken-Museum €3, students €1.50. English audio tours €3.50.)*

UNIVERSITÄT. Heidelberg is home to Germany's oldest (established 1386) and most prestigious university. The oldest remaining buildings border the stone lion fountain of the Universitätspl. Other university buildings dot the western Altstadt. The **Museum der Universität Heidelberg** traces the university's long history; in the same building is the magnificent **Alte Aula,** Heidelberg's oldest auditorium. *(Grabengasse 1. ☎06221 54 21 52. Open Apr.-Sept. Tu-Su 10am-6pm, Oct. Tu-Su 10am-4pm, Nov.-Mar. Tu-Sa 10am-4pm. €3, students €2.50; also includes Studentenkarzer.)* Don't even think about skipping out on the so-called **Studentenkarzer,** a prison used until 1914 for jailing university students who had committed infractions of the rules. *(Augustinergasse 2. ☎06221 54 35 54.)* The **Bibliothek** (Library) has a collection of medieval manuscripts. *(Plöck 107-109. ☎06221 54 23 80. Open M-W 9am-5pm, Th 9am-6pm, Sa 9am-1pm. Free.)*

PHILOSOPHENWEG (PHILOSOPHER'S PATH). This favorite stroll of famed thinkers Goethe, Lugwig Feuerbach, and Ernst Jünger stretches along the Neckar, high on the side of the **Heiligenberg,** and offers views of the city. On top of the Berg are the ruins of the 9th-century **St. Michael Basilika,** the 13th-century **Stefanskloster,** and an **amphitheater** built under Hitler on the site of an ancient Celtic gathering place. *(To the west of the Karl-Theodor-Brücke, in the direction of the Theodor-Heuss-Brücke. Take tram #1 or 3 to "Tiefburg," for the longer route. Or use the steep, stone-walled footpath 10m west of the Karl-Theodor-Brücke, across from the bus #34 or 734 stop "Alte Brücke Nord.")*

KARL-THEODOR-BRÜCKE. On your requisite (and worthwhile) trip from the *Schloß* to the Philosophenweg, you'll cross this bridge, also known as the Alte Brücke. After all, no trip to Heidelberg would be complete without a walk along the northern bank of the Neckar. On both sides of the Karl-Theodor-Brücke, plump statues of the bridge's namesake, the prince who commissioned the bridge in 1786 as a symbol of his modesty, stand guard. At night, the bridge provides a view of the illuminated *Schloß*.

KURPFÄLZISCHES MUSEUM. Built for Palatinate Germany fanatics, this large museum features an extensive collection of oil paintings by local and regional artists from the 18th and 19th centuries, as well as an archaeology exhibit in its bottom levels. You'll be amazed when you see just how many portraits of Renaissance-era German nobility can fit in a single room. *(Hauptstr. 97, near Universitätspl. ☎06211 583 4000. Open Tu-Su 10am-6pm. €3, students €1.80; Su €1.80/1.20.)*

ENTERTAINMENT

Small though it is, there's always something going on in Heidelberg, from a dense bar scene and raging dance parties to annual festivals that attract a more family-oriented crowd. Winter visitors should see the **Faschingsparade** (Mardi Gras Parade) cavort through the city on Shrove Tuesday (Feb. 24, 2009; Feb. 16, 2010). In warmer weather, the first Saturdays in June and September and the second Saturday in July draw giant crowds to fireworks in front of the *Schloß*. The **Handschuhsheim Fest** lures revelers the third weekend in June, while the **Schloßfestspiele Heidelberg** features a series of concerts and plays at the castle from late June to early August. (☎06221 582 0000 or www.heidelberger-schlossfestspiele.de for tickets.) For the last weekend in September, the **Heidelberger Herbst** brings a medieval market to the Altstadt, which later hosts the **Weihnachtsmarkt** during the month before Christmas.

NIGHTLIFE

The **Marktpl.** is the hub of the action—most nightspots fan out from here. After 11pm, **Untere Straße,** on the Neckar side of the Heiliggeistkirche, boasts the densest conglomeration of bars in the city. During fair weather, drunken revelers fill the narrow way until 1 or 2am. **Steingasse,** off the Marktpl. to the Neckar, is a bit less rambunctious but equally lively earlier in the evening. Nightclubs are not as concentrated geographically, but with the sheer variety of parties thrown every night of the week, you're guaranteed a good time.

Destille, Unterstr. 16 (☎06221 228 08). A tree (fake, but you'd never guess it) grows out of this forest-themed bar, one of the few spots in town that's lively every night of the week. Students drink themselves silly with quirky shots, including vodka with Pop Rocks (from €2). Open M-Th and Su noon-2am, F-Sa noon-3am. Cash only.

Nachtschicht (☎06221 43 85 50; www.nachtschicht.com), in Landfried-Komplex. Walk through the Kurfürstenlage-Passage opposite the Hauptbahnhof, cross the street, and walk through the parking lot past the abandoned factory. Look for the white tent with a bar inside. Universally recognized as the most popular club in Heidelberg, Nachtschicht is the place to be for the under-30 crowd. Th nights are all hip hop, F and Sa house. If you last through early Sunday morning, free breakfast starts at 3am. Cover €8, M and F students €4. Open Th-F 10pm-4am, Sa 10pm-5am. Cash only.

Mel's, Heiliggeiststr. 1 (☎06221 657 7447). This small bar nestled between the Marktpl. and the Neckar fills quickly with young partygoers. German kids sing along to loud American pop tracks and dance on the tables for lack of floorspace. Tu night beer €1 and cocktails €3; F Cuban theme, Havanas €3.50. Open M and Tu-Th 10pm-2am, Sa 10pm-3am.

Tangente, Kettengasse 23 (☎06221 16 94 45; www.t-club-hd.de). This club 1 block south of Hauptstr. fills quickly, so come early if you want to get in. The sound system blasts techno and electro on one of the only dance floors in the Altstadt. Popular parties include the enigmatic Th night "Orange Obsession" and the Sa night "Sound Deluxe." Beer from €3, cocktails from €6. Open Tu-Sa 10pm-3am. Cash only.

Havana Club, Neckarstaden 24 (☎06221 94 15 92 30; www.havana-salsa.de), is a busy club near the Neckar. From Th-Sa, the basement of the historic Kongresshalle heats up with salsa, merengue, and other Latin beats. Open Th-Sa 10pm-late. Cash only.

Cave54, Krämergasse 2 (☎06221 278 40). This jazz club's cavernous dungeon, connected to the tiny entry by a tight, spiraling steel staircase, fills with students during jam sessions. Cover €3. Open daily 10pm-3am, from 8:30pm during live shows. Cash only.

NECKARTAL (NECKAR VALLEY)

The Neckar Valley—a swath of the Oden Forest sliced by the Neckar—reaches from Heilbronn to Heidelberg. Centuries ago, a series of enterprising royals built castles to "protect merchants from pirates," and reaped hefty tolls for their services. Today, their castles dot the hilltops of the Neckartal, forming part of the **Burgenstraße** (Castle Road) that stretches from Mannheim to Prague.

Two train lines connect Heidelberg and Heilbronn, with stops in the small towns along both sides of the valley. Local buses also traverse the Neckar Valley, but one- and three-day train passes from Heidelberg are also valid for bus connections in the valley. Check at the train station in Heidelberg for details. One of the best and most popular ways to explore the valley is by biking along the many well-maintained routes or hopping a ferry up the Neckar. The **Rhein-Neckar Fahrgastschifffahrt** runs **boat tours** from Easter to Oct. 19 between Heidelberg, Neckargemünd, Neckarsteinach, Hirschhorn, and Eberbach.

TÜBINGEN ☎07071

The smiling punters along the Neckar River along the old town's edge hint at Tübingen's unique vibrancy. Famous for its river promenades and pristine hilltop *Schloß*, Tübingen is young and energetic—naturally, since half the town's residents are affiliated with the 500-year-old university. Even the Altstadt is more students' lair than austere historic center in the city awarded the title of "highest quality of life in Germany."

TRANSPORTATION

Trains and buses: Tübingen is well connected to Stuttgart (by bus or train, 1hr., 2 per hr., €11) and many small towns in the Schwäbische Alb.

Taxis: ☎07071 92 05 55 and 07071 243 01.

Bike Rental: Radlager, Lazarettgasse 19-21 (☎07071 55 16 51; www.radlager-tuebingen.de). €10 per day. Open M, W, F 9:30am-6:30pm; Tu and Th 2-6:30pm; Sa 9:30am-2:30pm; in winter Sa until 1pm.

TAP THAT

Although droves of tourists visit Germany to guzzle its renowned beer, few understand the intricacies of German *Bierkultur*. Beer is typically served by the quart (*Maß*, ask for *"Ein Maß, bitte,"*) and sometimes by the pint (Halb-Maß). A *Helles* is a pale, often Bavarian, lager. Those looking for a bitter, less malty beer with more alcohol order the foam-crowned *Pilsener*, and often search far and wide for the perfect head.

A *Radler* (bikers' brew)–called an *Alster* in the north–is a 50-50 blend of *Helles* and sparkling lemonade, so named because the inventor sought to mitigate the inebriation of the crazed cyclists passing through his pub. In the north, this beverage is called an *Alster* after the river. *Weißbier* is a cloudy, strong beer made with malted wheat (*Weizen*), while *Rauchbier* acquires its distinctive smoky taste from malted barley.

Even the toasted, malty lager, *Dunkeles*, is not the strongest beer. If you're in the mood for severe inebriation, try a Bock (strong beer) or a *Doppelbock* (even stronger). These potent beers are often brewed by monks, as they are rich enough to sustain them through religious fasts. Piety has never looked so enticing.

There are over 1000 German breweries producing thousands more brands of German beer each year. With a liquor pool that big, you'll have more than enough opportunities to lift a glass and shout *"Prost!"*

Boat Rental: Bootsverleih Märkle (☎07071 315 29), on river under tourist office. Rowboats from €7.50 per hr., paddleboats from €10. Open Apr.-Sept. daily 11am-dusk.

PRACTICAL INFORMATION

Tourist Office: An der Neckarbrücke 1 (☎07071 913 60; www.tuebingen-info.de), on the Neckarbrücke. From the front of the station, turn right, walk to Karlstr., turn left, and walk to the river. City maps available. **Tours** (in German) €5.50, children under 14 €2.50. Ask for a schedule. Call ahead for English tours. Open M-F 9am-7pm, Sa 9am-5pm.

Women's Resources: Frauencafe, Karlstr. 13 (☎07071 328 62), in the magenta house 1 block from the station, has a women-only night spot on the 2nd fl. Call for hours.

Bookstores: The 400-year-old **Osianderische Buchhandlung,** Wilhelmstr. 12 (☎07071 920 1118; www.osiander.de), has an impressive collection of English-language books and occasionally hosts English-language authors. Open M-F 9am-8pm, Sa 9am-6pm.

Laundromat: Wash & Chat, Mühlstr. 20 (☎07071 36 08 41). Wash €3.90 per 6kg, €6.20 per 10kg. Dry €1 per 10min. Coffee €0.80 Open M-Sa 8am-10pm.

Emergency: Police ☎110. **Fire** and **Ambulance** ☎112.

Pharmacy: Apotheke, Am Lustnauer Tor 4, in the Altstadt, (☎07071 510 30). Open M-F 8am-6:30pm, Sa 9am-2pm.

Internet Access: Three internet cafes line Mühlstr. **Wash & Chat,** Mühlstr. 20, offers the best price (€1.50 per hour); a slightly quieter environment can be found at Mühlstr. 13, €2 per hr. Open M-Sa 10am-10pm, Su noon-10pm.

Post Office: Europapl. 2, 100m to the right of the station. Open M-F 8am-6:30pm, Sa 8:30am-1pm. Also on Neue Str. 7 in the Altstadt. Open M-F 9am-6pm and Sa 9am-1pm. **Postal Code:** 72072.

ACCOMMODATIONS AND CAMPING

Jugendherberge (HI), Gartenstr. 22/2 (☎07071 230 02; www.jugendherberge-tuebingen.de). From the Hauptbahnhof, walk towards the Neckar, cross the bridge and make an immediate right; the hostel is a 5-10min. walk down the river, or take bus #22 (dir.: Neuhaldenstr.) to "Jugendherberge." A rare hostel that fills with more prospective university students than schoolchildren, with a breakfast terrace overlooking the lively riverbanks. Breakfast included. Lockers €2 deposit. Internet €1 per 10min. Reception M-Sa 7am-noon, 1-3:30pm, 4:30-7pm and 7:30pm-midnight; Su from 4pm. Curfew midnight, but key is available for a €15 deposit. Dorms 1st night €21.30, 27+ €24.30; thereafter €18/21. Singles and doubles, some with shower, add at least €5. MC/V. ❷

Hotel Meteora, Weizsäckerstr. 1 (☎07071 227 35; www.hotel-meteora.de). Follow Wilhelmstr. past the university and turn right on Weizsäckerstr. Or take bus #1 or 7 to "Pauline-Krone-Heim" and walk back 1 block. Friendly management and spotless rooms compensate for the 1km distance from the Altstadt; Greek/Swabian restaurant downstairs. All rooms with phone and TV. Breakfast included. Free Wi-Fi. Singles €33, with shower €38-52; doubles €62-83; triples €78-102. MC/V. ❸

Camping: Neckarcamping Tübingen (☎07071 431 45; www.neckarcamping.de). Follow Neckarhalde away from town until Hirschauerstr. and finally Rappenberghalde (25min.). Or take bus #9 to "Rappenberg" and follow the river to your left. Bike rental €4.50 per day. Wash €2.10. Dry €2.10. Reception daily 8am-12:30pm and 2:30-10pm. Open Easter to Nov. €5.50 per person, €3.70 per child, €4.20 per tent, €7.80 per caravan, €2.70 per car. Cash only. ❶

FOOD

Tübingen's superb restaurants seduce students and tourists alike. Most inexpensive eating establishments are clustered around **Metzgergasse** and **Am Lustnauer Tor.** Modern *Imbiße* (snack bars) crowd along **Kornhausgasse,** and there is a **market** on Am Markt (M, W, F 7am-1pm). Buy groceries at **Markt Am Nonnenhaus** at the bottom of Neue Str.

Wurstküche, Am Lustnauer Tor 8 (☎07071 927 50). Nestled into a steep hillside in the Altstadt, this traditional German restaurant prides itself on its use of fresh local ingredients. Enjoy *Kasespätzle* and other traditional Swabian dishes (from €9). Open daily 11am-midnight. MC/V. ❸

El Chico, Gartenstr. 4 (☎07071 55 02 56). Along the Neckar near the winding pedestrian district, this Mexican cafe promises diners "a fiesta in every bite." Daily happy hour with ½-price cocktails 5-8pm; all margaritas €3.30 11pm-midnight. Open daily noon-late. AmEx/MC/V; €20 min. ❷

Kalender, Gardenstr. 1 (☎07071 96 99 72). A constant line of hungry locals fills the doorway at Kalender, the hottest kebap stand in town. Open M-W 11:30am-midnight, Th-Sa 11:30-12:30am, Su 11:30am-10:30pm. ❶

Kamla's, Lange Gasse 5, serves up piping hot plates of spicy Indian food (€3-6). The menu is mostly vegetarian, though some dishes include chicken and beef. Try the homemade specials. Open M-F noon-7pm, Sa noon-4pm. Cash only. ❷

Mensa, Wilhelmstr., and the nearby **Cafe Clubhouse,** offer sandwiches and hot dishes from €1.50. No student ID required. (*Mensa* open M-Th 8am-8pm, F 8am-6:30pm; cafe open M-Th 8am-7pm, F 8am-5:30pm. Shorter hours during university holidays.) ❶

SIGHTS

Anyone with even a casual interest in history will go wild for Tübingen's **Altstadt** (old city). The city was largely spared destruction in WWII, allowing visitors today to see remnants of more than 1500 years of a rich past.

WURMLINGER KAPELLE. This modest, sunbleached chapel crowns a hill wrapped in grapevines and offers sweeping views of the surrounding countryside. Its naked simplicity is as moving as some of the most imposing cathedrals of Germany. Don't forget your camera, and consider packing a picnic lunch to enjoy at the top. *(Follow Kapellenweg to the hill from the Schloß, then continue up the hill through the vineyards; at the 1st fork take a left, then a right at the 2nd fork (6km); ask at the tourist office for the walking map "Tübingen Promenades 2." Or, take bus #18 (dir.: Rottenburg) to "Hirschau Kirchpl." (10min., 2 per hr. M-F, every 2hr. Sa-Su, €1.50.) Chapel open May-Oct. Su 10am-4pm; Nov.-Apr. call ☎07071 221 22.)*

SCHLOSS HOHENTÜBINGEN. This 11th-century castle stands atop the hill in the center of town. A dark tunnel and staircase on the far side of the courtyard lead through the castle wall to a view of the surrounding valley second only to that of the Wurmlinger Kapelle. *(Accessible from Am Markt. Castle grounds open daily 7am-8pm. Free.)* Occupied by various university institutes, the Schloß is also home to the excellent **Museum Schloß Hohentübingen,** the largest university museum in Germany and, at 2000 sq. meters, one of the largest collections of archaeological artifacts in Europe. Egyptian and East Asian coins, crafts, and curiosities figure as prominently as remnants of Europe's primeval and early modern past. A notable collection of about 350 replicas of Greek statues fills the bottom level. *(Enter at Burgsteig inside courtyard. ☎07071 297 7384. Open W-Su May-Sept. 10am-6pm; Oct.-Apr. 10am-5pm. Classical casts open until 4pm. €4, students €3. Tours Su 3pm; €2.)*

STIFTSKIRCHE. The Gothic 15th-century church serves as the focal point of the Altstadt's winding alleys. Medieval statues stand on display in the foyer as reminders of the church's history. Behind the pulpit in the chancel lie the tombs of 14 members of the House of Württemberg, topped with life-size stone sculptures of the deceased and illuminated with magnificent stained glass windows. The church tower offers a rewarding view after the steep climb. *(☎07071 431 51. Open daily in summer 9am-5pm, in winter 9am-4pm. Chancel and tower open Easter through November W, Sa, Su 11am-5pm. €1, students €0.50. Free tours every W at 4pm.)*

HÖLDERLINTURM (HÖLDERLIN TOWER). After being told in 1806 that hospitalization would not help his madness, poet Friedrich Hölderlin retreated to a room in this tower, which sits along the Neckar in the shadow of of the Protestant Seminary where young Friedrich had studied. Only 36 years old at the time, Hölderlin lived out the rest of the remaining 36 years of his life in this tower. Today, the tower houses a museum describing his impact on German literature and an extensive collection of his original compositions, viewable upon request. *(Below Bursagasse on the river. ☎07071 220 40. Museum tours Sa and Su 5pm. Open Tu-F 10am-noon and 3-5pm, Sa-Su 2-5pm. €2.50, students €1.50.)*

PLATANENALLEE (SYCAMORE ALLEY). The buildings of the Neckarfront are best viewed from this quiet tree-lined avenue that runs the length of the man-made island on the Neckar. **Punting trips** down the Neckar are available from university students; inquire at the tourist office. *(Boats seat 12-16. M-F and Su €60 per hr., Sa €60. 2hr. punting lessons also available from €28 per person.)*

OTHER SIGHTS. Across from the Stiftskirche is the unassuming **Buchhandlung Heckenhauer Antiquariat** (Heckenhauer Antique Bookstore), where Hermann Hesse worked from 1895 until 1899. The old-fashioned store sells rare books. *(Holzmarkt 5. ☎07071 230 18; www.heckenhauer.de. Open M-F 2-6pm, Sa 11am-3pm.)* On the way from the church to the castle, don't miss the gilded rostrum of the **Rathaus,** Am Markt. The nearby Kornhaus contains the **Stadtmuseum** (Municipal Museum), with exhibits on the city's history from the 15th to 20th centuries. *(Kornhausstr. 10. ☎07071 204 17 11. Open Tu-Su 11am-5pm. €2.50, students and children €1.50, group tours €35.)* Above the river is the **Evangelisches Stift** (Evangelist monastery), Klosterberg 2. This theology dorm once housed such luminaries as Kepler, Hölderlin, and Hegel.

UNIVERSITÄTSKARZER (STUDENT PRISON). Use of the Tübingen Karzer dates back to 1515, making it the oldest known facility of its kind in Germany. Until 1845 when it closed for good, anyone affiliated with the University was imprisoned here for infractions of the rules. Unsurprisingly, students generally filled the cells. The walls are covered with intricate paintings of Biblical scenes, commissioned by the University to combat student graffiti. *(Münzgasse 20. ☎07071 913 60. Accessible only via guided tours, offered Apr-Oct. Sa and Su at 2pm. Contact the tourist office for more information. €1, students €0.50.)*

ENTERTAINMENT AND NIGHTLIFE

Tübingen's laid-back nightlife befits its tranquil location along the Neckar. A walk along its streets at night yields not pulsing house music, but the sounds of intense conversations over coffee and beer. On weekends, the scene heats up, with popular clubs hosting regular dance parties. Look for posters around town. For after-hours transportation, take the **Nachtbus** from Lustnauer Tor (Th-Sa 12:45-2:45am), or call **Nacht-SAM** to pick you up (☎07071 340 00).

Tübingen also has two major theaters: the progressive **Zimmertheater,** Bursagasse 16 (☎07071 927 30; open M-F 10am-5:30pm, Sa 10am-12:30pm, and 1hr. before shows; tickets also available at **Buchhandlung Osiander,** Wilhemstr. 12, and **Verkehrsverein,** Ander Neckarbrücke 1), and the **Landestheater,** Eberhardstr. 6. (☎07071 931 3149; www.landestheater-tuebingen.de. Open Tu-F 2-7pm, Sa 10am-1pm. Tickets available by phone or online.)

BADEN-WÜRTTEMBERG

Liquid, Schmiedtorstr. 17 (☎07071 55 11 96; www.liquid-bar.de), is a hopping bar tucked away in the back of Altstadt. Replete with dim lighting and high slick barstools, the chic atmosphere comes at a reasonable price. Beer and wine from €2.50. Open M-Sa 11am-2am, Su 6pm-1am. Cash only.

Schloß Cafe, Burgsteige 7 (☎07071 96 51 53; www.schlosscafe-tuebingen.de), near the Schloß. This retro-fitted student lair is decorated with an eclectic mix of couches, old church pews, and other slapdash furnishings. Live music on weekends, poetry readings, jam sessions, open mics, and more. Beer €2.40-2.70. Mixed drinks from €5.20. Open M-Th 11am-2am, F and Sa 11am-3am, Su 10am-1pm. Cash only.

Sudhaus, Hechinger Str. 203 (☎07071 746 96; www.sudhaus-tuebingen.de). Bus #3 or 5 or night bus #N95 to "Fuchsstr.," then go under the busy road. This "socio-cultural center" in a former brewery hosts wacky art films, dance parties, and live acts. Schedules are plastered all over town. Cover €5-16. In the summer, the outdoor **Takco Biergarten** serves drinks and has a small dance floor. Open May-Aug. 11:30am-11pm. **Tacko Bar,** Sudhaus' weekend incarnation, opens F and Sa nights 10pm-3am. Cash only.

Tangente-Night, Pfleghofstr. 10 (☎07071 230 07), at the corner of Lustnauer Tor. A popular student hangout. Beer from €2. Mixed drinks €6. Come on M for karaoke or W for techno with live DJs. Open M-Sa noon-3am, Su 4pm-1am. Cash only.

Foyer Blaue Brücke, Friedrichstr. 12 (☎07071 53 82 44). Take bus #3 or night bus N87 to "Blaue Brücke." This 2-fl. disco, which once housed French officers, now attracts an even more party-oriented crowd. Beer €2.10-3.30. Mixed drinks €4.50-5. Cover €5. Open F-Sa 10pm-3am. Cash only.

Marktschenke, Am Markt 11 (☎07071 220 35) is a small bar that attracts a young, clean-cut crowd. Wine is the drink of choice (€3 for 0.2L). Open M-Th 9am-1am, F-Sa 9am-2am, Su 10am-1am. Cash only.

MANNHEIM ☎0621

The alphanumeric street names of Mannheim (pop. 327,000) are straight out of a game of Battleship, and its historic treasures are undergoing extensive renovation. However, the tangled web of tram cables above Mannheim's cobbled streets typify the cultural and physical anachronisms of modern German cities. This commercial powerhouse is a convenient, if slightly less picturesque, base for visiting Heidelberg while avoiding crowds of tourists.

TRANSPORTATION AND PRACTICAL INFORMATION

Trains run to Frankfurt (1hr., 2 per hr., €13.40) and Stuttgart (40min., every hr., €20). Trams cost €2.10; 24-hour Tagesticket €5. The **tourist office,** Willy-Brandt-Pl. 3, on your left across from the station, distributes free maps and info on accommodations and cultural events. (☎0621 10 10 11; www.tourist-mannheim.de. Open M-F 9am-7pm, Sa 10am-1pm.) A **laundromat, Waschinsel,** is on Seckenheimer Str. 8, 2 blocks northeast of the station. (Wash €3.50. Dry €2. Detergent €0.40. Open M-F and Su 8am-8pm, Sa 9am-4pm.) A **pharmacy, Bahnhof-Apotheke,** is at block L15, across from the station and to the left. (☎0621 12 01 80. Open M-F 7am-10pm, Sa 8am-10pm.) Use the **Internet** at **Chat Corner,** #16-17 L14, two blocks from the train station. Start an account on the machine near the doors. (€1 per 30min. 1 free cup of coffee. Open daily 9am-3am.) **Star Coffee,** Sofienstr. 33, has free **Wi-Fi** with any purchase. (Open M-W 7am-9pm, Th-F 7am-11pm, Sa 8am-11pm, Su 9am-9pm.) The **post office,** Willy-Brandt-Pl. 13, is a block east of the station. (Open M-F 9am-6pm, Sa 9am-noon.) **Postal Code:** 68161.

ORIENTATION

Mannheim sits on a peninsula at the junction of the Rhein and Neckar. The bustling Innenstadt is at the tip of this peninsula and is surrounded by the **Kaiserring,** a large boulevard in a ring shape along which street cars run. The train station is outside the southeast corner of the ring. **Kurpfalzstraße** and **Breite Straße** (also called *Planken*) bisect the ring road, divided into a grid of 144 blocks. Each block is named by a letter and number. Blocks along Kurpfalzstr. have increasing numbers as they move farther away from the central axis. Blocks to the west of Kurpfalzstr. are named south to north by letters A through K, and streets to the east are lettered L through U. Again, think Battleship, and the layout will make sense. East of Kaiserring, streets assume regular names.

ACCOMMODATIONS AND FOOD

Mannheim's Jugendherberge (HI) ❷, Rheinpromenade 21, has small rooms and aging facilities, but compensates with low prices and a convenient location

10min. from the station. Walk through the underground passage from the tracks at the east end of the station and take a left up the stairs at the very end. Cross the street, walk left past the big glass building, cross the tracks, and continue down Rennershofstr. with the park on your right. Turn right onto Rheinpromenade; the hostel is in a small enclave one block up. Tram #7 (dir.: Neckarau) to "Lindenhofpl." stops in front of the glass building. (☎0621 82 27 18; www.jugendherberge-mannheim.de. Breakfast 7:30-8:30am included. Key deposit €10. Reception 7-9:30am and 4-10pm. Strictly enforced check-out 9am. Dorms €17.50, over 27 €20.50 additional nights €14.30/17.30. Singles add €10; doubles add €5. MC/V.) Two blocks north of the train station, **City Hotel Mannheim ❹**, Tattersallstr. 20, offers 40 clean rooms at half the price of nearby hotels. (☎0621 44 99 48; www.city-hotel-mannheim.de. Singles €35-60, doubles €50-80.)

Bakers and grocers gather at the **market** in the square at the intersection of **Kurpfalzstraße** and **Kirchstraße** in the center of the city grid. (Open Tu, Th, Sa 7am-1:30pm.) Fresh vegetables and fruit can be found in the area even outside of market hours. Blocks **G2** through **J6** also have a dense array of *Imbiße* and ethnic restaurants, where meals are generally €3-7. For delicious, organic, all-vegetarian meals at low prices, head to **Heller's Vegetarisches Restaurant and Cafe ❷**, N7 #13-15. The restaurant has a buffet with both hot and cold selections priced by weight (€1.49 per 100g) as well as a rotating menu of entrees priced per dish (about €5). (☎0621 12 07 20; www.hellers-restaurant.de. Open M-F 11am-8pm, Sa 11am-4:30pm, Su 11:30am-3:30pm.) Nothing beats the bewitching decor of **Zur Hexe ❸**, F2 #4A, home to hearty German and Polish specialties (€4.50-12.50) and a variety of beers (€2.10-2.80) in a bar covered in witches. Witches hang from the ceiling, poke their heads out of the walls, and greet you at the entryway. (☎0621 10 25 17. Open Su-Th 11am-2am, F-Sa 11am-3am.) The cheapest meals in town (€4.70-5) are at the **Studentenwerk Mannheim Mensa ❶**, behind the Residenzschloß (open M-F 11:30am-2pm), and the adjacent cafeteria. (Sandwiches €1-1.80. Open M-Th 8:30am-4pm, F 8:30am-3:45pm.) **Flic Flac,** #12 B2, is a favorite student night spot. Decorated as a 1920s zeppelin, this bar has a daily happy hour after 9pm, Monday €5.90 pasta buffet, and Thursday live bands. (☎0621 225 53. Open M-Th and Su 9am-1am, F-Sa until 2am. MC/V.)

SIGHTS

The bustling **Paradeplatz,** with its Baroque fountain, is the heart of Mannheim. Restaurants, department stores, cafes, and movie theaters surround the square and extend along the pedestrian zones on **Breite Straße** and **Planken.** At the east end of Planken is the city's emblematic masterpiece, the elegant sandstone **Wasserturm**—said to be "the most beautiful water tower in the world"—and the surrounding gardens on **Friedrichsplatz** South of Friedrichspl. is the excellent **Kunsthalle,** Friedrichspl. 4, a museum surveying art from the mid-19th century to today. The permanent collection includes works by Manet, Van Gogh, and Beckmann, and also showcases more contemporary works in a variety of media. The museum is laid out thematically rather than chronologically, so a room entirely devoted to florals might include a pastel Monet, a vibrant Expressionist work, and a 21st-century painting so formless that it's virtually unidentifiable. (☎0621 293 6450. Open Tu-Su 11am-6pm. €7, students €5.) The giant **Kurfürstliches Residenzschloß,** the largest Baroque palace in Germany. The palace was reduced to next to nothing during WWII, but years of reconstruction have restored the facade to its original condition. Some of the palace's interior has been similarly restored, but most rooms look like the museum space that they are. (☎0621 213 63. Open Apr.-Oct. Tu-Su 10am-5pm. €5, students €2.50.) A few blocks north, the many buildings of the **Reiss-Engelhorn-Museen** house some of Mannheim's finest treasures. The **Museum Weltkulturen** is an anthropology and natural history museum, the **Museum Zeughaus** displays applied arts, and the **Schillerhaus** serves as a shrine of sorts to the great poet and philosopher, who lived in Mannheim for two whole years. (☎0621 293 3150; www.rem-mannheim.de. Open Tu-Su 11am-6pm. €5, students €2.50.) On the other side of the Innenstadt, several blocks northeast of the Wasserturm, lies the 100-acre **Luisenpark.** The greenhouses, flower gardens, aviary, zoo, water sports, afternoon concerts, and boat rides provide a welcome diversion from the gritty city outside the park's gates. (☎0621 127 090. Open daily Nov.-Feb. 9am-9pm; Mar.-Oct. 9am-sunset. Mar-Oct €5, Nov-Feb €2.50; students €3.50/1.80; after 6pm in summer and 5pm in winter €1.50; students €1.)

SCHWÄBISCHE ALP (SWABIAN JURA)

The limestone plateaus, sharp ridges, and pine-forested valleys of the Schwäbische Alp, or Swabian Jura, are secluded between the Neckar and the Danube. Grab a one-way ticket to Schwäbisch Hall to travel back in time and relax in some of Germany's most picturesque villages. The region can be difficult to navigate, since train lines wind curiously through the hills and valleys, but it's well worth the ride to see what these remote towns have to offer: a unique glimpse into Swabian culture along with the opportunity to experience misplaced bits of medieval history and the humble yet breathtaking outdoors. Lofty ruins crowning the peaks are all that remain of fortifications erected by the once powerful dynasties that held the region. The Schwäbische Albstr. (Swabian Jura Road) bisects the plateau, crossing the Romantic Road at Nördlingen. A web of trails serves hikers and maps are available at regional tourist offices in most towns.

FREIBURG IM BREISGAU ☎0761

Tucked in the western edge of the Black Forest, Freiburg (pop. 214,000) hums with activity at all hours. Home to a renowned jazz house as well as a large university population, this metropolis is the darling child of Baden-Württemburg. Chairs spill out of boisterous cafes onto medieval cobblestones, and a web of streams trickle through the city. Complementing the urban din, untouched countryside lies minutes from town, where hiking trails crisscross the rippled forest floor and cow pastures stretch across the horizon.

TRANSPORTATION

Trains: To **Basel, Switzerland** (1hr., 2 per hr., €13.70-21.30), **Karlsruhe** (1hr., every hr., €22-32), and **Stuttgart** (2hr., every hr., €29-57).

Public Transportation: Single fare on Freiburg's bus and tram lines €2-4.80. Regio24 day pass €5; up to 5 people €8. Most transportation stops at 12:30am, but a system of night buses covers major stops through the night (€4 per ride; €2 with day pass; F-Su every hr. 1:30-4:30am). Trams stop at the train station, on the overpass to the right.

Taxis: ☎0761 55 55 55.

Bike Rental: Mobile, Wentzingerstr. 15 (☎0761 292 7998), is in the the round wooden structure just under the overpass behind the train station. €7.50 per 4hr., €15 per day. Reduced fares for consecutive days. Open daily 8am-8pm.

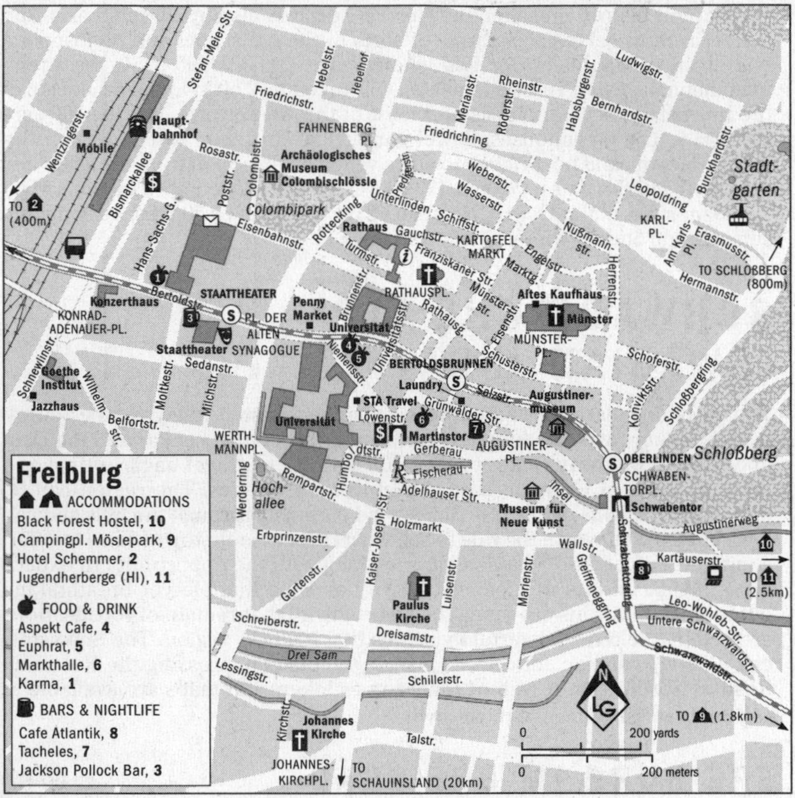

ORIENTATION AND PRACTICAL INFORMATION

The city's sights and restaurants are concentrated in the Altstadt, a 10min. walk from the Hauptbahnhof down tree-lined Eisenbahnstr. to Rathauspl.

Tourist Office: Rathauspl. 2-4 (☎0761 388 1880; www.freiburg.de), in the Altes Rathaus. Take the underpass from the station, then walk down Eisenbahnstr. until it runs into Rotteckring. Cross this busy road or take the underpass and head down Rathausgasse until you reach Rathauspl. (5-10min.). Books rooms for a €3 fee and has free city maps. 24hr. automated displays in front of the office and the train station can help you find lodging as well. Open June-Sept. M-F 8am-8pm, Sa 9:30am-5pm, Su 10am-noon; Oct.-May M-F 9:30am-6pm, Sa 9:30am-2pm, Su 10am-noon. The tourist office also offers two types of city **tours** in English. From Apr.-Oct., a guide leads a 1½-2hr. tour of the Altstadt and the Münster every Sa at noon (€7, students €6).

Currency Exchange: The closest to the Hauptbahnhof is the Volksbank across from the main entrance. 24hr. **ATM.** Open M-W and F 8:30am-4pm, Th 8:30am-6pm. Volksbank at the Martinstor has an exchange machine and ATMs. Open 24hr.

Laundromat: WashTours, Salzstr. 22 (☎0761 288 8666), is a laundromat and internet cafe two blocks from the Schwabentor. The entrance is in through a narrow passageway. Wash €4.50 including soap. Dry €2. Internet €0.50 per 15min. Open M-Sa 9am-7pm.

Emergency: Police: ☎110. **Fire** and **Ambulance:** ☎112.

Rape Crisis Hotline: ☎0761 285 8585.

Pharmacy: Apotheke, Bertoldstr. 8 (☎0761 07 61), is near Kaiser-Joseph-Str. Open M-F 8:30-7pm, Sa 9am-6pm.

English Bookstore: Walthari, Bertoldstr. 28 (☎0761 38 77 70; www.bookworld.de). This university bookstore has an impressive selection of English books. Open M-F 9am-7pm, Sa 9:30am-6pm.

Internet Access: Planet Internetcafe, Kartäuserstr. 3 7, near the Schwabentor. €1.80 per hr. Open M-Sa 9am-midnight, Su 11am-midnight. Several spots in town, including the university library and the plaza in front of the Rathaus, have free **Wi-Fi,** as do some of the upscale hotels. Free internet access is available in the university library.

Post Office: Eisenbahnstr. 56-58, 1 block straight ahead from the train station. Open M-F 8:30am-6:30pm, Sa 9am-2pm. **Postal Code:** 79098.

ACCOMMODATIONS AND CAMPING

Black Forest Hostel, Kartäuserstr. 33 (☎0761 881 78 70; www.blackforest-hostel.de). Take tram #1 (dir. Littenweiler) to "Oberlinden," walk through the medieval city gate, and turn left down Kartäuserstr. Look for the anchor, inner-tube, and signs to the hostel. This congenial and wacky hostel is a rare find in the Black Forest. Kitchen, comfy common room, and piano ensure entertainment into the early morning. Bike rental €5 per day. Linen €3, sleeping bags are encouraged. Internet access €1 per 30min. Reception 7am-1am. Check-out 11am. Dorms €13-21; singles €28; doubles €46. Cash only. ❶

Jugendherberge Freiburg (HI), Kartäuserstr. 151 (☎0761 676 56; www.jugendherberge-freiburg.de). Bus #1 to "Lassbergstr." Take a left and then a right on Fritz-Geiges-Str. Its location at the far end of town and somewhat sterile atmosphere make this a less than homey place to stay, but beds are clean and cheap. Breakfast and sheets included. Reception every hr. on the hr. Check-in 1-10pm. Curfew 2am. Dorms €21.30, over 27 €24.30; subsequent nights €18/21. Cash only. ❷

Hotel Schemmer, Eschholzstr. 63 (☎0761 20 74 90; www.hotel-schemmer.de). Behind the Hauptbahnhof; cross the overpass, and make a left after the church. The hotel is two blocks down on the left. Elegant rooms, some with balconies. Breakfast included. Reception M-F 7am-7pm, Sa-Su 7-11am and 4-7pm. Singles €34-39, with shower €39-45; doubles €51-62; triples €65-78; quads €85. AmEx/MC/V. ❸

Campingplatz am Möslepark, Waldeseestr. 77 (☎0761 767 9333; www.camping-freiburg.com). Tram #1 (dir. Littenweiler) to "Stadthalle." Head south on Möslestr., cross the tracks, and keep going straight on Waldseestr. past the park (about 15min.). Ideally situated near hiking trails and the Waldkurbad (M-Sa 9:30am-11pm, Su 9:30am-10pm). Wash and dry €6.65. Internet access €2.50 per 30min., €3.50 per hr. Open mid-Mar-Oct. only. Reception 8am-noon and 2:30-10pm. €6 per person, €2-2.60 per child. €5.90 per plot, add €2.50 for a car. Electricity €2. MC/V. ❶

FOOD

With more than 23,000 university students to feed, Freiburg overflows with budget options. Typical *Imbiße* and bakeries are hardly in short supply, but plenty of sit-down restaurants lining the side streets in the western corner of the Altstadt serve full meals for under €8. The cheapest groceries in town are at **Pennymarkt,** Bertoldstr. 25, though the selection is pretty standard. (Open M-Sa 8am-10pm.) Head to the grocery store in the basement of the **Karstadt,** Kaiser-Joseph-Str., for an impressive variety. (☎0761 282 40. Open M-F 9:30am-8pm, Sa 9am-8pm.) An outdoor farmer's **market** pops up in front of the Münster on F and Sa mornings, with vendors selling everything from fruits and veggies to scrumptious homemade pickles.

Markthalle, on Grünwälderstr next to the Martinstor (☎0761 38 11 11). This indoor marketplace is home to over a dozen different stands serving both prepared foods and groceries. Vendors sell heaping plates of delicious ethnic foods (€3-7), including Asian, Mediterranean, and South American fare. Open M-F 7am-7pm, Sa 7am-4pm.

Euphrat, Niemensstr. 13. A never-ending stream of hungry customers flows into this Turkish restaurant near the University. Delicious chicken, lamb, or vegetarian sandwiches and wraps rolled in homemade breads make any meal here a steal. All dishes €3.20-6.50. Open M-F 11am-midnight, Sa 11am-1am, Su noon-midnight. Cash only. ❶

Karma, Bertholdstr. 51 (☎0761 20 74 50; www.karma-freiburg.de), is a cafe by day and bar by night, with a fantastically inexpensive menu of salads (around €3), pizza (€2.40-3.90), and create-your-own pasta. Choose the type of pasta (€1.90-2.40) and then select the sauce (€1.40-4.90). Options are diverse and range from marinara to spicy chicken curry. Open M-F 11am-midnight. Cash only. ❷

SIGHTS

In only one night in 1944, the Allies finished a bombing job that the *Luftwaffe* had mistakenly started four years earlier, obliterating most of the Altstadt. Since then, the citizens of Freiburg have painstakingly recreated the city's architecture and public spaces. The results are convincing—Freiburg's beautiful town center displays weathered cobblestone streets and tilting 16th-century houses that just happen to have been rebuilt a few decades ago.

MÜNSTER. Freiburg's pride and joy is its stunning cathedral, which towers 116m over an expansive plaza below. With sections constructed between the 13th and 16th centuries, this architectural melange immortalizes in stained glass the different medieval guilds that financed its construction. Check out the gargoyles on the outside and then, for a stunning view of the surrounding city, climb up 209 steps to the ticket counter—the windows on the way up afford a free view. The top of the tower is only 126 more stairs. The cathedral is worth a second visit at night, when the bell tower and haunting spires loom half-illuminated over the square below. *(☎0761 298 5963. Open M-Sa 9:30am-5pm, Su 1-5pm. Tours M-F 2-3pm, Sa-Su 2:30-3:30pm. Tour €2. Tower open M-F 9:30am-5pm, Su 1-5pm. €1.50, students €1, under 12 €0.50.)*

BADEN-WÜRTTEMBERG

ARCHÄOLOGISCHES MUSEUM COLOMBISCHLÖSSLE (ARCHAEOLOGICAL MUSEUM). Stunning early Victorian Colombischlößle overlooks vineyards and a lush park. Inside, artifacts track the history of the South Baden region from the Stone Age to medieval times, with English translations. Don't miss the 500-year-old jewelry in the basement. *(Rotteckring 5. In Colombipark; enter from Eisenbahnstr. ☎0761 201 2571. Open Tu-Su 10am-5pm. €3, student €1.50. English guide €2.)*

AUGUSTINERMUSEUM. Offering a comprehensive cultural history of the Upper Rhine, the Augustiner impresses with medieval sculpture, paintings, and tapestries, and numerous depictions of 18th-century Schwarzwald life. Unfortunately, the Augustiner has been undergoing extensive renovations since early 2008 that are slated to take 5-6 years. The museum plans to remain open despite the construction. *(Augustinerpl. in an old monastery 2 blocks south of the Münster. ☎0761 201 25 21 or 0761 201 25 31. Open Tu-Su 10am-5pm. Free.)*

SCHLOSSBERG. From the Schwabentor, take the overpass across the busy Schloßbergring and climb the Schloßberg for a superb view of the city. Or, reach the Oberer Schloßberg on the **cable car** from the Stadtgarten at Leopoldring. *(Cable car open Apr.-Oct. daily 11am-7pm, closed first M of every month; Nov.-Mar. W-Su 11am-5pm. €2.10, round-trip €3.60; ages 4-14 €1.60/2.60.)* To get to the top on foot, start at Schloßbergring across from Hermannstr. (20min.).

ENTERTAINMENT AND NIGHTLIFE

Traditional Freiburg nightlife centers around good wine and good music. No matter where you find yourself in town, you're never far from a *Weinstube* (wine tavern) or *Kneipe* (pub). For current events listings, drop by the **Badische Zeitung** office, Bertoldstr. 7, off Universitätstr., where you can buy tickets for upcoming events. (☎0761 555 6656. Open M-F 9am-7pm, Sa 9am-2pm.) The **Freiburger Theater,** Bertholdstr. 46, presents plays, ballets, musicals, and concerts. (☎0761 201 2853; www.theaterfreiburg.de. Student tickets from €7. Ticket office open Tu-F 10am-6pm, Sa 10am-1pm.) The annual **Freiburger Weinfest** is held on Münsterpl. the first weekend in July. Sample some 400 different vintages (€1.50-3 per glass) to live swing music and take home a bottle (€4.50 and up). The two-week international **Zelt-Musik-Festival** (late June to early July) brings big-name classical, rock, and jazz acts to two circus tents at the city's edge. Tickets (€15-30) sell fast and can be bought over the phone (☎0761 50 40 30), online (www.zmf.de), or through the Badische Zeitung office.

Freiburg's student population keeps the city alive at all hours of day and night. The small streets around the university provide the densest conglomeration of bars and clubs, but some of the better parties require a slighly longer commute. When the weather's right, huge crowds gather outside on **Augustinerplatz.** People bring drinks, guitars, and blankets and settle in until at least midnight or 1am. From there, they start filling the clubs.

Jackson Pollock Bar, Bertholdstr. 46 (☎0761 28 15 94; www.jacksonpollockbar.de). A hip but unpretentious crowd—mostly students from the nearby Uni—flocks to this nightclub, which sits just behing the Staattheater. Come on F nights for a 50s, 60s, or 70s throwback party. Open M-Th 11pm-2am, F-Sa 11pm-3am. Cash only.

Cafe Atlantik, Schwabentorring 7 (☎0761 27 83 94; www.cafe-atlantic.de). A casual and congenial atmosphere just outside the Altstadt. Cheap food (think €2.90 spaghetti), more than 20 beers on tap, and indie rock music humming in the background complement intense games of foosball. Happy hour daily 7-10pm, drinks from €1. Beer €1.70 and up. Open M-Th 11am-2am, F-Sa 11am-3am.

Tacheles, Grünwälderstr. 17 (☎0761 319 6669; www.tacheles-freiburg.de). Take the winding stairs down into this expansive bar and nightclub in the heart of town. Pop music and popular long drinks are never in short supply. Come before 11pm to beat the crowd of students and 20-somethings. Open Su-Th 10am-midnight, F-Sa 10am-5am.

HIKING

Freiburg's plentiful accommodations and accessibility by train make it a great base for hikes in the Black Forest. **Mountain biking** trails also traverse the hills; look for symbols with bicycles (maps €3.50-6 at tourist office). The **Schwarzwaldverein** office, Schloßbergring 15, provides trail information. (☎0761 38 05 30; www.schwarzwaldverein.de. Open M-Th 9am-noon and 2-4pm, F 9am-noon.)

A good starting spot in Freiburg is Schauinsland, the region surrounding a 1220m mountain by the same name. Take tram #2 (dir.: Dorfstr.) to the end. (15min. from Hauptbahnhof; 1 per 10min.), then bus #21 to "Talstation" (7min., 2 per hr.). From the station, take the red circle trail to the top (3hr.), or ride the spectacular 3.6km **Schauinslandbahn.** (20min.; €8, students €7.50; round-trip fare is €11.50/10.50. Open July-Sept. 9am-6pm, Oct.-June 9am-5pm.) Once on the mountain, choose from many well-marked hikes. (Maps are for sale at the base of the mountain, €2-6.) The trail marked with a yellow circle that starts at the top of the mountain connects "Schauinsland Gipfel," "Rappeneck," and "Kappel." When you're done with the hike (approx. 4hr.), take the bus #17 back to Freiburg. A Rundweg also takes you from the top station in a panoramic circle around the top of the mountain (1hr.). On top, find the **Bergwelt Schauinsland,** with a wildlife park and the **Museums-Bergwerk** (Mining Museum), where visitors don helmets, head lanterns, and working gloves before descending slippery metal ladders into the mountain. The guided tour explores 800 years of mining history with demonstrations and plenty of muddy, narrow passages, huge caverns, and harrowing drops. Wear closed-toe shoes that can get wet and dirty. (☎0761 264 68; 45min. family tour €4.50, children €3.50; 1½hr. tour, €12; 2½hr. tour venturing 50m into the mountain, €18; May-Oct only. Family tours every hr. W, Sa, Su 11:30am-3:30pm. July and Aug. also M, Tu, Th at the same times. Longer tours W, Sa, Su 11am and 2pm.) Adventurous travelers should try the **roller ride,** an 8km downhill path on a device that looks like a giant push scooter. While a helmet and some padding are provided, recognize that this activity is at your own risk—check your brakes before picking up too much speed. (☎0761 264 68. Ride only €18; roller ride plus cable car to the top, €23. W evenings from 5pm to dusk, €14 without cable car.)

SCHWARZWALD (BLACK FOREST)

The Black Forest comprises the famous and mysterious tangled expanse of evergreen covering the southwest corner of Baden-Württemberg. It is no wonder that the Schwarzwald—so named for the eerily pervasive darkness under its leafy canopy—inspired so many of the macabre German fairy tales still popular today. Its murky caves, impenetrable thickets, and clever squirrels assume an unsettling quality even in daylight, or at least whatever light makes it to the needled ground. Today, many of the region's erstwhile authentic specialties, from cuckoo clocks to *Lederhosen*, have become kitsch, thanks to the ubiquitous kiosks and souvenir shops lining the streets and otherwise scenic trails.

Myriad trails wind through the hills, leading willing hikers into secluded parts of the forest. Skiing is wildly popular, and the longest slope is at Feldberg, near Titisee. The main entry points to the Schwarzwald are Freiburg, in the center; Baden-Baden to the northwest; Stuttgart to the east; and Basel, Switzerland to the southwest. Several rail lines encircle the perimeter, while only two cut through. The best way to access more towns without train service is to take the train to the closest station and then hop a bus to your destination.

ST. BLASIEN ☎07672

St. Blasien (pop. 4000) at first seems to be just one of many sleepy towns tucked into the forested hills around the twin lakes of Schluchsee and Titisee. While the mountainous region surrounding the town has always been a hiker's paradise, St. Blasien itself is famous for a monumental cathedral, or Dom, third only in size to St. Peter's in Rome and Les Invalides in Paris.

TRANSPORTATION AND PRACTICAL INFORMATION. To get to St. Blasien, take the **train** to nearby Seebrugg and then bus #7319 into town (20min., €1.90). If you plan to use the bus three or more times, consider buying a 24hr. **Tagesticket** (€5.50). The **tourist office,** Am Kurgarten 1-3, has hiking maps (€5), a free town map, and a room catalog. From the main bus station, cross Umgehungsstr., turn right, and head for the "Haus des Gastes"; the tourist

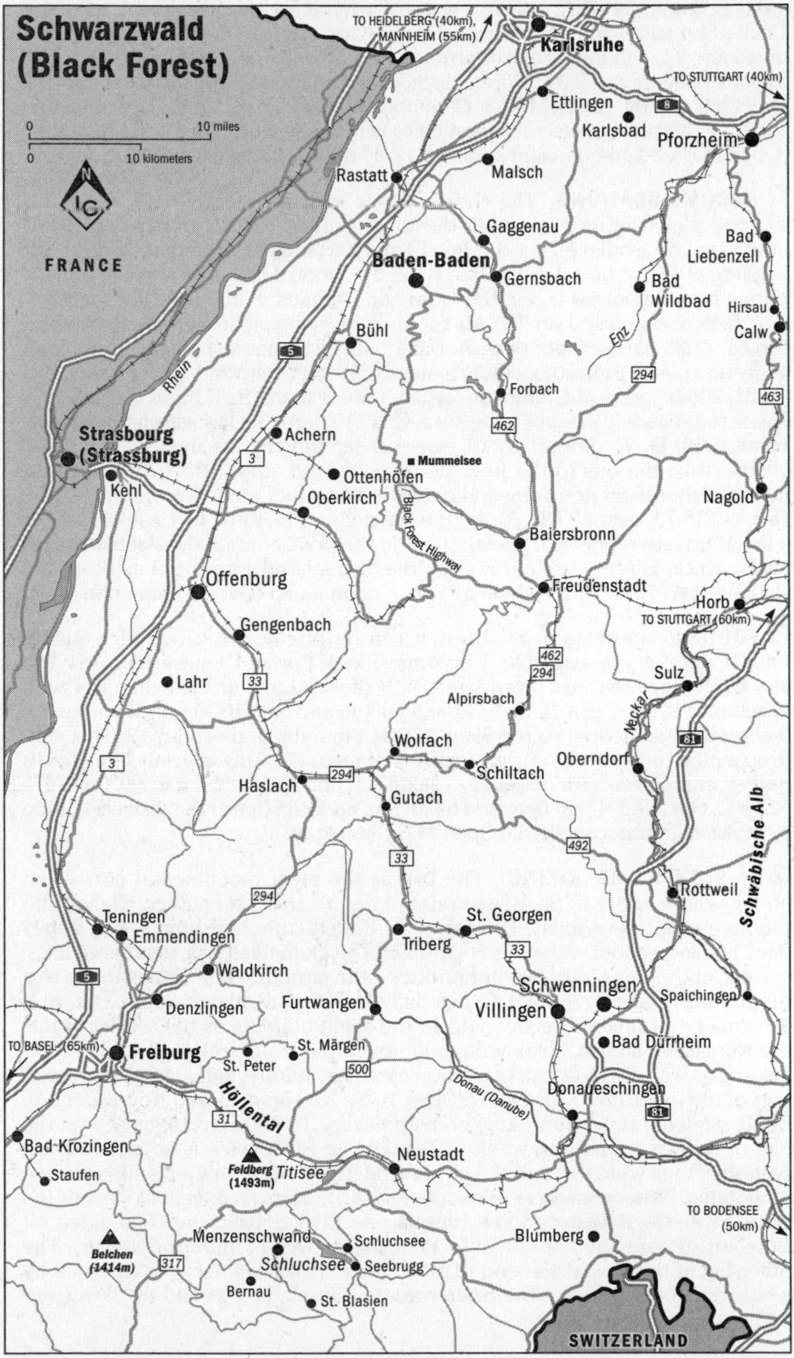
Schwarzwald (Black Forest)
0 10 miles
0 10 kilometers
N
FRANCE
TO HEIDELBERG (40km), MANNHEIM (55km)
Karlsruhe
TO STUTTGART (40km)
Ettlingen
Karlsbad
Pforzheim
Rastatt
Malsch
Gaggenau
Baden-Baden
Gernsbach
Bad Liebenzell
Bad Wildbad
Hirsau
Calw
Bühl
Rhein
Enz
Forbach
Strasbourg (Strassburg)
Achern
Mummelsee
Ottenhöfen
Kehl
Oberkirch
Black Forest Highway
Nagold
Baiersbronn
Offenburg
Freudenstadt
Horb
TO STUTTGART (60km)
Gengenbach
Lahr
Sulz
Alpirsbach
Neckar
Wolfach
Schiltach
Oberndorf
Haslach
Gutach
Rottweil
Schwäbische Alp
Teningen
Emmendingen
St. Georgen
Triberg
Waldkirch
Schwenningen
Villingen
Spaichingen
Denzlingen
Furtwangen
TO BASEL (65km)
Freiburg
St. Märgen
St. Peter
Bad Dürrheim
Höllental
Donau (Danube)
Donaueschingen
Bad Krozingen
Feldberg (1493m)
Titisee
Neustadt
Staufen
TO BODENSEE (50km)
Belchen (1414m)
Menzenschwand
Schluchsee
Seebrugg
Blumberg
Bernau
St. Blasien
SWITZERLAND
8
5
3
33
294
462
463
81
492
500
31
317

BADEN-WÜRTTEMBERG

office is inside. (☎07672 414 30; www.st-blasien-menzenschwand.de. Open M-F 10am-noon and 3-5pm; May-Sept. also Sa 10am-noon.) The **Dom Apotheke,** Todtmoserstr. 11, will keep your pharmaceutical needs under control. (Open M-F 8:30am-12:30pm and 2:30-6:30pm, Sa 8:30am-12:30pm. The **Sparkasse** across the street has an **ATM.** (Open M-W 8:30am-noon and 2-4:30pm, Th 8:30am-noon and 2-6pm, F 8:30am-4:30pm.) The **post office** is in the Quelle shop on Hauptstr. 45. (Open M-F 8:30am-noon and 2-5pm, Sa 8:30-noon.) **Postal Code:** 79837.

ACCOMMODATIONS. The cheapest way to spend a night in St. Blasien is to book a private room through the tourist office (from €19 per person). If no rooms are available, try the **Hotel Garni Kurgarten ❷,** Fürstabt-Gerbert-Str. 12, across from the tourist office near the Dom. Most of the snug, well-lit rooms have balconies facing the Dom and Rathaus. Some have TV. (☎07672 527. Reception closed on Th. All rooms with showers. Singles €23, doubles €46-58. €1.35 *Kurtaxe* per person. Cash only.) The nearest hostel, along with many inexpensive guesthouses, is in nearby Menzenschwand. (10km away. Bus #7321, 20min., runs M-F almost every hr. until 6:45pm, Sa 6:15pm, Su 5pm, but check the schedule plaques to be sure. €2.25.) There, the **Jugendherberge Menzenschwand (HI) ❷,** Vorderdorfstr. 10, offers cheap lodgings in an authentic wood chalet. Take the bus to the first Menzenschwand stop. (☎07675 326; www.jugendherberge-menzenschwand.de. Breakfast included. Reception 5-9pm. Dorms €18.70, over 27 €21.70. Additional nights €15.40/18.40. Cash only.) For a list of private rooms and guesthouses in the area, contact the **Menzenschwand tourist office,** Hinterdorfstr. 15, near the "Hirschen/Hintertor" bus stop and Rathaus. (☎07675 930 90. Open M-F 9am-noon and 3-6pm, Sa 9am-noon.)

FOOD. Restaurants in St. Blasien can be pricey, but a few high-quality budget options are available. For some Black Forest Chinese food, try **Hoa May ❷,** Bernau-Menzenschwanderstr. 6. (Chicken Lo Mein €6, beef curry with vegetables €7.50. Open Tu-Su 11:30am-2:30pm and 5:30-10:30pm.) If you're not feeling the Asian vibe, go for **Bistro "S" ❶,** Fürstabt-Gerbert-Str. 10. This self-proclaimed "unique" restaurant features homemade daily specials like *Maultaschen* or moussaka for under €5, a salad bar, and spaghetti for €2.90. (☎07675 922 962. Open M-F 11am-5pm and 6-9:30pm, Sa 11am-3pm.) For groceries, stop in **Neukauf,** Todtmooserstr. 8. (Open M-Sa 8am-8pm.)

SIGHTS AND HIKING. The **Dom** is the most monumental part of an abbey whose roots in St. Blasien date back to the 9th century. Though no monks reside there today, the formerly Benedictine and now Jesuit abbey does house a school with over 800 pupils. The Dom itself has weathered fires, revolts, and vicious intra-cloister politics—the structure that stands today was rebuilt most recently in 1883. (Open daily May-Sept. 8:30am-6:30pm, Oct.-Apr. 8:30am-5pm. Donation requested.) In the same building as the tourist office, the **Museum St. Blasien,** hosts with exhibits on the Dom's religious and secular history, as well as the distinctive wood carvings, culture, and natural surroundings of the town. (☎07672 414 37. Open Tu-Su 2:30-5pm; closed Nov. 2-Dec. 25. €1.60, students €0.50. June-Aug. concerts every Tu and Sa 8:15pm.) From the end of August to the first week of September, St. Blasien hosts **wood-carving contests.** Trails wind through the virgin wilderness of St. Blasien's surrounding mountains. **Philosophenweg** (Philosopher's Path) offers an excellent view of the Dom. From the Rathaus, follow Hauptstr. to Friedrichstr., then take a left on Bötzbergstr. and another left onto Philosophenweg (45min. round-trip). The other leg of the fork at the end of Bötzbergstr., Blasiwälder Weg (marked by a blue diamond), leads to the *Kletteranlage* climbing rocks and the *Windberg* creek (1hr. round-trip). On the other side of town, more hiking trails scale the idyllic **Holzberg.** From the **Kurgarten** next to the Dom, take **Tuskulumweg** and head through the tunnel, following the blue diamond markers.

CENTRAL BLACK FOREST

TRIBERG ☎07722

Tucked in a lofty valley 670m above sea level, the tiny but heavily touristed village of Triberg (pop. 5100) is known best for its waterfalls, the highest in Germany. Spruce forests cover the steep hills around the town, and a well-marked series of trails provide a comprehensive, if cardiovascularly taxing, cross-section of the Central Black Forest. The town has also worked hard to cultivate an image as the quintessential Schwarzwald town, with nearly every storefront displaying either a cuckoo clock or a slice of Black Forest cake.

TRANSPORTATION AND PRACTICAL INFORMATION. **Trains** travel from Triberg to Freiburg (€18-26) and Donaueschingen (€6). Call ☎0772 55 33 for a **taxi.** To get into the center of town from the train station, turn right on Bahnhofstr. and follow the signs: cross the bridge, go under it, and take the steep, strenuous hike up Frejusstr., which turns into Hauptstr. Or, take any **bus** to Marktpl. (€2). The **tourist office,** Wallfahrtstr. 4, is opposite the entrance to the waterfalls. Walk to the end of Hauptstr. and go right; the tourist office and the Schwarzwald Museum are on the right. (☎0772 86 64 94; www.triberg.de. Open daily 10am-5pm.) **Sparkasse** at Marktpl. has an **ATM.** The **Stadt-Apotheke pharmacy,** Am Marktpl., is right next to the Rathaus. (☎45 37. Open M-F 8:30am-12:30pm and 2:30-6:30pm, Sa 8:30am-12:30pm.) The **post office** is at Hauptstr. 41. (Open M-F 8:30am-12:30pm and 2-5:30pm, Sa 9am-noon.) **Postal Code:** 78098.

ACCOMMODATIONS AND FOOD. Many private rooms and holiday apartments are available for €15-25—ask for a list at the tourist office. A stay in any hotel in the Triberg area will get you the **Schwarzwald Gästekarte,** providing free bus and train transportation within 50km of the city for the duration of your stay as well as free or reduced admission to almost every sight in town. Check into your hotel first to reap maximum benefits. Close to the center, the friendly family who runs **Hotel Zum Bären ❸,** Hauptstr. 10 (on the way into town from the station), goes far out of their way to make guests feel comfortable and cared for. Rooms are clean and most have showers. (☎07722 44 93. Breakfast included. Singles €24-27.50, doubles €52, triples €69. Cash only.) The town's **Jugendherberge (HI) ❷,** Rohrbacher Str. 35, sits (far) up a (steep) mountain and offers plunging views of two valleys, although the staff is inattentive. Climb straight up Friedrichstr. (which turns into Rohrbacher Str.) from the tourist office (30min.). A taxi from the station costs about €7. (☎07722 41 10; www.jugendherberge-triberg.de. Internet €0.10 per min. Breakfast included. Reception 5-7pm and 9:45pm. Curfew 10pm, key available. €20.30, over 27 €23.30; additional nights €17.30/20.30. Mostly 4- or 6-bed dorms, but some doubles available at no extra charge. Cash only.)

Imbiße (snack bars) around the entrance to the Wasserfall park or down Hauptstr. toward the train station offer cheap food. Many sit-down restaurants in town seem to serve the same mediocre dishes at the same inflated prices. Locals flock to **Bergseestüble ❷,** Clemens-Maria-Hofbauer-Str. 19, 10min. down the Kulturweg in the waterfall park. The traditional menu includes *Wurstsalat*

(€6.20) and schnitzel (€7.50), but the patio overlooking the Bergsee can't be beat. (☎07722 91 64 45. Open M-W and Th-Su 11:30am-11pm.)

SIGHTS. The **Gutacher Wasserfal** is technically the highest waterfall in Germany; in reality, it is more a inclined stream, bubbling over smooth, green-velvet rocks broken into relatively small vertical drops. Within the park surrounding the waterfalls are three hiking trails. The steep **Kaskadenweg** ("Cascade Trail," 1hr. round-trip, marked with a squirrel symbol) draws fewer noisy family groups than the longer, less strenuous **Kulturweg** (Culture Trail). The **Naturweg** (Nature Trail) features signs with information about local flora and fauna. (Park lit until midnight. Admission 9am-7pm. €1.50, under 18 €0.50, families €3.50.) Signs along the Kulturweg point to the **Wallfahrtskirche Maria in der Tanne,** a small Pilgrimage church where, according to legend, the pious have been miraculously healed since the 17th century. (☎07722 45 66. Closes around 7pm.) At the tiny Bergsee (mountain lake) uphill from the church, rent rowboats (€1.50 per 30min., under 14 €1.20) or paddleboats (€4.50 per 30min.) from the kiosk. (Usually open M-W and F-Su 8:30am-7pm.) Cross the main road onto Kroneckweg and follow the "Panoramaweg" signs for hiking trails with a view of the valley. The town's surrounding region offers even more rewarding hikes. Numerous trail signs on the outskirts of town point the way to a portion of the **Pforzheim-Basel Westweg** (red diamond trail markers; access via blue diamond markers). The tourist office sells maps for hiking (€6-8), biking (€4-6), and mountain biking (€4-6).

Back in town, visit the **Schwarzwald Museum,** Wallfahrtstr. 4, just across the street and left from the waterfalls. This museum is packed with Black Forest history and culture, including nearly 100 mechanical musical instruments, wood carvings, and, of course, more Black Forest cuckoo clocks than you could possibly need to see. (☎07722 44 34; www.schwarzwaldmuseum.de. Open daily 10am-5pm. Closed Nov. 15-Dec. 15. €4, students and ages 14-18 €2.50, ages 5-13 €2.) There is a certain laissez-faire attitude surrounding the superlative "biggest." The "world's biggest cuckoo clock" of Wiesbaden lives in peaceful harmony with the "world's biggest cuckoo clock" in St. Goar, just as the "world's biggest cuckoo clock" on the one side of Triberg is at ease with the "world's biggest cuckoo clock" on the other. The first and the oldest is a bit out of town toward Schonach on L109. (☎07722 46 89. Open daily 9am-noon and 1-6pm.) Another is 15min. away from the train station and accompanied by a **museum:** turn left on Bahnhofstr. and then continue on Franz-Göttler-Weg. After the road below enters a tunnel, take the next right to the clock park. (☎07722 962 20. Clock is outside the building. Museum is open Easter-Oct. Sa 9am-6pm, Su 10am-6pm; Nov.-Easter M-Sa 9am-6pm. €1.50. Audio tour €1.)

BODENSEE (LAKE CONSTANCE)

As the pine thatching of the Black Forest thins, the German landscape opens into the Bodensee, a strikingly beautiful and expansive crystalline lake. In this stretch of southern Baden-Württemberg, the so-called "German Riviera," potted palms line the streets, public beaches are filled with sunbathers tanning to a melanomic crisp, and business is conducted with profoundly un-German casualness. Set against snow-capped Alps, the Bodensee is a must-see.

Getting to the region by **train** is easy. Both Constance and Friedrichshafen have direct connections to many cities in southern Germany. Rail transport within the region requires long rides and occasionally tricky connections because no single route encircles the lake. The bright white boats of the **BSB**

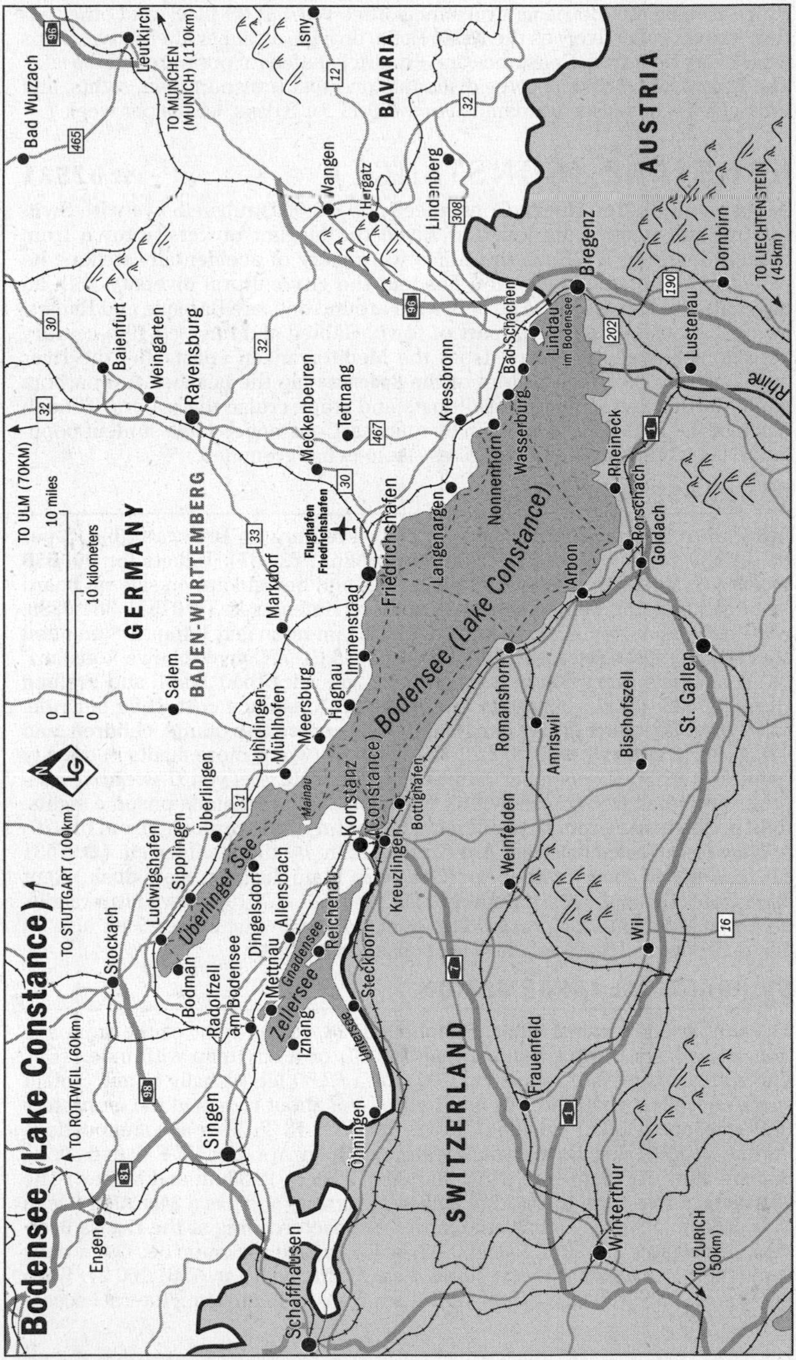

BADEN-WÜRTTEMBERG

(Bodensee-Schiffs-Betriebe; Constance office ☎07531 28 13 98) and other ferries, known collectively as the **Weiße Flotte,** provide a calmer alternative. Ships leave every hour from Constance and Friedrichshafen for ports around the lake. The **BodenseeErlebniskarte** gives discounts on most transportation, sights, and tours. (www.bodensee-tourismus.com. €39-71 for 3 days, €49-89 per week.)

KONSTANZ (CONSTANCE) ☎07531

At the mouth of the Rhein, Constance (pop. 82,000) rubs elbows with Switzerland and Austria. Its location saved the elegant university town from bombardment in WWII, as the Allies were leery of accidentally striking its neighbors. The unique location has lent the city cultural diversity with an international flair. Crooked streets wind around delicate Baroque and Renaissance facades in the central part of town. Gabled and turreted 19th-century houses, seemingly imported from the Mediterranean coast, line the river promenades. The green waters of the **Bodensee** lap the beaches and harbors while, farther out, countless sailboats and ships cruise the waters. Though much of the Bodensee is overrun by tourists, Constance's large student population keeps the city—and its prices—somewhat grounded.

TRANSPORTATION

Trains go to Singen (20min., 3 per hr., €9), Freiburg im Breisgau (3hr., 3 per hr., €25.30-42), and Stuttgart (2-3hr., every 2hr., €29-37). Tickets for the **BSB ship line** to Meersburg (€4.30), Mainau (€6), and beyond are on sale on board or in the building behind the train station, Hafenstr. 6. (☎07531 364 0389; www.bsb-online.com. Open Apr.-Oct. M-Th 8am-noon and 1-4pm, F 8am-noon and 1-5pm.) **Giess Personenschifffahrt** (☎07533 21 77; www.moewe-konstanz.de) runs boats every 40min. from Dock 2 to Freizeitbad Jakob and Freibad Horn (p. 326; €2.50, round-trip €6). **Buses** in Constance cost €1.90 per ride, €3.70 for a **Tageskarte** (1-day card), and €6.20 covers two adults, children, and a dog. For a **taxi,** call ☎07531 222 22. A stay of two or more nights in the city requires a €1.50 *Kurtaxe* per adult per night. This gets you *Gästekarte* coupons, providing free transit within Constance and discounts onsome sights. Rent paddleboats (from €5 per 30min., €8 per hr.) or motorboats (from €16/26) at **Marc Fluck Bootsvermietung,** Am Gondelhafen, by the Stadtgarten. (☎07531 218 81. Open in good weather Apr.-Oct. M-Sa 11am-dusk, Su 10am-dusk.) Rent **bikes** from *Kultur-Rädle*, Bahnhofpl. 29. (☎07531 273 10; www.kultur-raedle.de. Open M-F 9am-12:30pm and 2:30-6pm, Sa 10am-4pm. Easter-Sept. also Su 10am-12:30pm. €10 per day, less for consecutive days.)

PRACTICAL INFORMATION

The tiny, friendly **tourist office,** Bahnhofspl. 13, to the right of the train station, provides a helpful walking map (€0.50) or a city map with index (€1). The staff finds private rooms (€21-30) for a €2.50 fee (usually a min. 3-night stay), as well as youth hostels and hotels. Ask about rooms in the monastery in Hegne, about 12km outside of town. (☎07531 13 30 30 or accommodations hotline ☎07531 194 12; www.konstanz.de. Open Apr.-Oct. M-F 9am-6:30pm, Sa 9am-4pm, Su 10am-1pm; Nov.-Mar. M-F 9:30am-12:30pm and 2-6pm.) The **Sparkasse** across from the station **exchanges currency** and has a **24hr. ATM.** (Open M-W 8:30am-4:30pm, Th 8:30am-6pm.) Get beach reading at the **English Bookshop,** Münzgasse 10. (☎07531 150 63; www.englishbookshop.de. Open daily 9am-6pm.) Do **laundry** at **Waschsalon & Mehr,** Hofhalde 3. (☎07531 160 27. Wash €4.50, soap €0.60, dry €3.50. Open M-F 10am-7pm, Sa 10am-4pm.) Internet access is at the **TelCenter,** Bahnhofpl. 6, across from the station. (☎07531 28 42 66. €4.20 per hr. Open daily 9am-10pm.) The **post office,** Marktstätte 4, is up the stairs from the station, away from the harbor. It also has an ATM and offers Western Union services. (Open M-F 8:30am-6pm, Sa 9am-noon.) **Postal Code:** 78462.

ACCOMMODATIONS

Searching for last-minute lodging in Constance can prove to be a significant strain on the nerves and the purse. Hostels and guesthouses fill up fast in this popular summer getaway, and most budget options are to be found in smaller villages (from Tägerwilen to Güttingen) 20-30min. away by train. Most private rooms require a minimum 2- or 3-night stay—the tourist office is an invaluable resource for finding both private rooms and hotel or hostel accommodations.

Jugendherberge Kreuzlingen (HI), Promenadenstr. 7 (from Germany ☎+41 71 688 2663; from Switzerland 071 688 2663). South of the Swiss border in Kreuzlingen, but closer to downtown than the Constance hostel, this beautiful, wood-panelled hostel commands the tip of a lakefront hill and features plush furniture. From the train station, head to the harbor, turn right, and walk along Seestr. through the border checkpoint "Klein Venedig" until the road curves under the bridge. Instead of following the street, take the gravel path that veers slightly to the right. The hostel is about 500m ahead in an old gray building on the left. The hostel rents kayaks for €8 per hr. Delicious breakfast of local breads and cheeses included. Reception 8-10am and 5-9pm. Closed Dec.-Feb. €20 per person per room. AmEx/MC/V. ❷

Pension Gretel, Zollernstr. 6-8 (☎07531 45 58 25; www.hotel-gretel.de). Offers bright, pine-trimmed rooms at prices that belies their superb location. Breakfast included. Call at least a month ahead in summer. Singles €35, doubles €50-68, triples €84, quads €92; extra bed €18. Apr.-Oct. around €10 more per person. Cash only. ❸

Jugendherberge Otto-Möricke-Turm (HI), Zur Allmannshöhe 18 (☎07531 322 62; www.jugendherberge-konstanz.de). If you call well in advance, you might be able to spend the night in this former water tower on a hill overlooking the lake. At least a 45min. walk, but an easy bus or bike ride from town. Beware of school children running up and down the tower stairs. Take bus #4 from the train station to "Jugendherberge," then turn back and head uphill on Zur Allmannshöhe. Breakfast included. Sheets €3.10. Reception Apr.-Oct. 8am-noon and 3-10pm, Nov.-Mar. 8am-noon and 5-10pm. Lockout 9:30am-noon. Curfew 10pm, housekey for €20 deposit. Call at least 2 months ahead. €21.30, over 27 €24.30; additional nights €18/21. MC/V min. €50. ❷

Campingplatz Brudehofer, Fohrenbühlweg 50 (☎07531 313 88; www.campingkonstanz.de). Take bus #1 to "Staad," and walk for 10min. with the lake to your left. The packed campground is on the waterfront. Reception closed 1-3pm. €4 per person, €2.30 per child, €3.80-5.80 per tent, €6-8 per RV, €0.50 per bike, €2.80 per car. Warm showers €1. Electricity €2. Cash only. ❶

FOOD

Many of the best and most affordable restaurants serve ethnic fare and cluster around Kreuzlingerstr. or the narrow, winding streets north of the Münster. Pick up a copy of Dining Out's *Gastronomie Guide* for a full listing of restaurants in Konstanz, organized by type. Find groceries in the basement of the **Karstadt** department store, on Augustinerpl. and Blätzlepl. (☎12 31 58; open M-F 9:30am-8pm, Sa 9:30am-7pm) and slightly pricier organic foods at **Alnatura,** Münzgasse 4. (Open M-F 9am-8pm, Sa 9am-7pm.)

Radieschen, Hohenhausgasse 1 (☎07531 228 87; www.radieschen-konstanz.de). The heaping bowls at this authentic Turkish restaurant are an affordable reminder that Turkish cuisine is more than the kebap. Try the *Ali Nazik,* a hearty beef stew (€6.80 small, €9.60 large) or the *Kartoffelgratin Rahm,* a vegetarian-friendly casserole (€7.40). The less adventuresome will love the pizza (€6). Open daily 11:30am-11:30pm. ❷

Hafenhalle, Hafenstr. 10. (☎07531 211 26). In an unbeatable location overlooking the harbor, this huge Biergarten offers hearty portions. Two wursts (€4.80) will certainly fill you up, and the steak dinner (€6.70) is a steal. Get your greens at the fresh salad bar (€3.80-4.80). Open daily 11am-11pm or midnight. ❷

Cafe Zeitlos, St.-Stephans-Pl. 25 (☎07531 18 93 84; www.cafe-zeitlos.net). Cooks all meals (€5.10-7.70) with local ingredients. All-you-can-eat brunch buffet Su 10am €12.50. Weekly beer specials. Snacks €2.50-3.60. Open daily 10am-1am, kitchen 10am-3pm and 6-10pm. Cash only. ❷

Fachhochschule Mensa, stands in a modern building on Webersteig, overlooking the Rhein. An ISIC is required for a meal card; ask in the cafeteria downstairs. The hassle is worth it—meals cost only €4.70-5.30. Open M-F 11am-1:45pm. Cafeteria open M-Th 7:30am-4pm, F 7:30am-2pm. Cash only. ❶

SIGHTS AND BEACHES

The first must-see sight in Constance's Altstadt is the **Münster,** built over the course of 600 years. Its 76m soaring Gothic spire and display of ancient religious objects are almost as cool as the *Kreuzgang* (cloister) frescoes, downstairs to the left of the crypt. Climb the **Münsterturm** for an excellent view of the city, Bodensee, and distant Alps. *(Church open daily 8am-6pm; tower open M-F 10am-5pm, Sa-Su 12:30-5pm. Münsterturm €2.)*

From there, head to the **Rathaus,** Kanzleistr. 15, whose late 16th-century frescoes illustrate the religious and martial history of the city. Farther south, off Bodanstr., the 13th-century **Schnetztor** shows off proud layers of battlements, guarding a network of busy shopping streets. For the obligatory walk along the **Lake Konstanz**, choose from two idyllic promenades: **Rheinsteig,** along the Rhein, or **Seestraße,** on the lake across the bridge. The tree-filled **Stadtgarten,** next to Constance's main harbor, provides a panoramic view of the harbor. Across the Rhein from the Altstadt, near the "Sternenpl." bus stop, is the **Archäologisches Landesmuseum,** Benediktinerpl. 5, an assemblage of ancient things from Baden-Württemberg's long-lost past, from old town walls and pots to reassembled skeletons and spearheads. *(☎07531 980 40. Open Tu-Su 10am-6pm. Tours Su 11am and 3pm. €4, students €3, families €6. Special exhibitions add €1. First Sa of the month free.)* Visit the aquatic critters of the Rhein at the **Sea-Life Museum,** Hafenstr. 9, on the way to the Swiss border. Beginning with an ice cave, the museum traces the history of sea life, with a special focus on the Bodensee region. Exhibits include a large trout tank and a walk-though shark tunnel. *(☎07531 12 82 70. Open July-Sept. daily 10am-7pm; May-June and Oct. daily 10am-6pm; Nov.-Apr. M-F 10am-5pm, Sa-Su 10am-6pm. Last entry 1hr. before closing. €13.95, students €11.95, ages 3-14 €8.50.)*

After sightseeing, kick back on one of Constance's public beaches, all of which are free and open May to September. Though the price can't be beat, these beaches are generally narrow strips of gravel or concrete, with the occasional patch of grass. This is not the case at **Freibad Horn,** a grassy park with a volleyball nets, a playground, and plenty of open beach. Be forewarned: Horn is the largest and most crowded public beach in town. There is also an FKK corner (nude section) enclosed by hedges. In inclement weather, immerse yourself in **Bodensee Therme Konstanz,** Wilhelm-von-Scholz-Weg 2, a slick, modern pool complex with thermal baths, saunas, and sun lamps. *(Take bus #5 to "Bodensee Therme Konstanz." (☎07531 611 63. Open daily 9am-9pm. Swimming pool €5, students €3.50; thermal bath €6.50/4.60.)*

DAYTRIPS FROM CONSTANCE

MAINAU. The island of Mainau is all one richly manicured garden, the result of the horticultural prowess of generations of Baden princes and the Swedish royal family. A lush arboretum, exotic birds, and huge flower animals surround the pink 13th-century Baroque palace and church built by the Teutonic Knights. Now tourists scamper across the footbridge from Constance to pose with the peacocks and take in an unparalleled view of the Bodensee amid 25 varieties of butterflies. *(Take bus #4 (dir.: Bettingen) to "Mainau" (20min., 1-2 per hr., €2), or a boat from behind the train station (1hr., every 1-2hr., €6). Island (www.mainau.de) open daily Apr.-Oct. 7am-8pm, Nov.-Mar. 9am-6pm. Apr.-Oct. €13.90, students and children ages 13-18 €7.50, children 12 and under free; half price after 5pm, free after 7pm; Nov.-Mar. €6.50, students €3.20.)*

MEERSBURG. Glowering over the Bodensee, the medieval fortress **Burg Meersburg** is the centerpiece of this town and was formerly displayed on the 20-Deutschmark bill. The first watchman moved into Germany's oldest inhabited castle in 628. Today, staffers dressed in less-than-authentic medieval garb welcome you to the fortress, which displays fully furnished chambers and dungeons from the 16th-18th centuries. Also on display are the living quarters of Annette von Droste-Hülshoff, generally recognized as Germany's greatest female poet. Keep an ear out for traditional folk music concerts in the summer months. *(☎07532 800 00. Open daily Mar.-Oct. 9am-6pm, Nov.-Feb. 10am-6pm; last entry 30min. before closing. €6, students €5.10, children €3; with a tour of the tower Apr.-Nov. 1 €8/6.80/5.)* In the 18th century, a prince bishop rejected King Dagobert's Altes Schloß and commissioned the sherbert-pink Baroque **Neues Schloß** up the hill on Schloßpl., which now houses the town's art collection in the **Schloßmuseum.** The **Dorniermuseum** has models of Dornier airplanes, while the **Stadtische Galerie** (Municipal Gallery) has a collection of Romantic paintings, many detailing the beauty of the Burg. *(☎07532 440 49 00. Open Apr.-Oct. daily 10am-1pm and 2-6pm. €4, students and Guest Card holders €3, families €8/6, children €1. Combo card with entrance to the Weinbaummuseum and the Stadtmuseum €5/4.)*

For most visitors, particularly the German ones, the main attraction in Meersburg is the fantastic **wine.** In the town's neighboring countryside, the vineyards lining the hillsides produce some of southern Germany's most celebrated varietals. The **Weinbaumuseum,** Vorburggasse 11, situated in an old cellar, focuses on regional winemaking. (☎08382 44 04 00. Open Apr-Oct. Th-F and Su 2-6pm. €2, under 6 free.) The **Staatsweingut,** Seminarstr. 6, sells regional wines (from €6 per bottle) and offers 2hr. tastings. *(☎08382 44 64 44. Open M-F 9am-6pm, Sa 9am-4pm. Wine tastings Apr.-Oct. F 7pm. €10.)*

Amidst an endless sea of pricey options, stop by **Ins Fischernetz ❶,** Unterstadtstr. 32, for terrific ambience and a budget-friendly bite. A small restaurant overflowing with anchors, ropes, and other maritime knick-knacks, they serve up quick meals for less than €5. If you're daring, ask about the super spicy wurst (€3.50) or the XXL burger (€4.60). *(☎08382 58 45. Open Mar-Oct daily 10am-midnight.)* On Fridays, an outdoor **market** takes over the Rathauspl. from 6am-noon.

Reach Meersburg by boat *(30min.; 1-2 per hr., last boat around 6:30pm; €4.30),* or by bus #7395 from Friedrichshafen *(30min.; 2 per hr., last return around 10pm; €2.80).* If you decide to stay the night, an accommodation service is available at ☎07532 440 4100, or at the tourist office, Kirchstr. 4. *(☎07532 44 04 00; www.meersburg.de. Open M-F 9am-12:30pm and 2-6pm, Sa 10am-1pm.)*

LINDAU IM BODENSEE ☎08382

More in the Bodensee (Lake Constance) than on it, the tiny island of Lindau (pop. 24,000) embodies everything that this region has to offer, and does so to the extreme. The Alps loom large across the waters, and Switzerland and Austria are both visible and readily accessible from the shoreline. The innumerable cafes, souvenir shops, and harbor promenades, charming and calm in the early morning and late evening, are otherwise overrun by tourists rushing to catch the last boat back to Constance in the evening.

TRANSPORTATION

Trains: To **Friedrichshafen** (20-30min., €5), **Constance** (1-2hr., every hr., €15.70), **Munich** (2-3hr.; €30-36), and **Stuttgart** (3hr.; €29-43).

Bus: Public transport in Lindau costs €1.80 per ride or €4.50 for a 24hr. ticket. There is also a direct line to Friedrichshafen (30min., €2.50).

Ferries: Several lines link Lindau with Constance, usually stopping at Friedrichshafen, Mainau, and Meersburg along the way (3hr.; 3-6 per day; €12 to Constance). Inquire at the tourist office for more information.

Bikes: Unger's Fahhradverleih, Inselgraben 14, 1 block down Ludwigstr. from the tourist office. (☎08382 94 36 88; www.fahrrad-unger.de. Bikes €6-12 per day, helmets €2. Open M-F 9am-1pm and 2-6pm, Sa-Su 9am-1pm.)

Boats: A string shops renting out **boats** line the shore on the Kleiner See between the island and the mainland. (☎08382 29 77 71; www.bootsverleih-lindau.de. Row- and paddleboats from €9 per hr. Open late Mar. to Oct. 9am-9pm.)

PRACTICAL INFORMATION

Tourist Office: Ludwigstr. 68, across from the station, has an excellent telephone system to find rooms, though most options top €35 per person per night. (☎08382 26 00 30; www.lindau-tourismus.de. Open mid-June to mid-Sept. M-F 9am-6pm, Sa-Su 10am-2pm; Apr. to mid-June and early Sept. to Oct. M-F 9am-1pm and 2-6pm, Sa 10am-2pm; Nov.-Mar. M-F 9am-noon and 2-5pm.)

Currency Exchange: The **Bodenseebank,** across the street at Maximilianstr. 27, also has an **ATM.** (Open M-W and F 9am-noon and 2-4pm, Th 9am-noon and 2-5:30pm.)

Internet Access: MarMorSaal, Bahnhofspl. 1, a bar and restaurant on the Seepromenade with a view of the harbor, offers free **Wi-Fi.** (☎08382 934 07. Open daily 11am-midnight.)

Post Office: Located 50m to the left of the station. (Open M-F 8am-noon and 1:30-5:30pm, Sa 9am-noon.) **Postal Code:** 88131.

ACCOMMODATIONS AND CAMPING

All accommodations in Lindau charge a *Kurtaxe* of €1.40 per person per night (children €0.85).

Jugendherberge (HI), Herbergsweg 11 (☎08362 967 10; www.lindau.jugendherberge.de), lies across the Seebrücke. Cross the bridge, turn right onto Bregenzer Str., right again on Kolpingstr., and left onto Herbergsweg after the Limare indoor swimming pool (20min.). Or, take bus #1 or 2 from the train station to "Anheggerstr./ZUP," then bus #3 (dir.: Zech) to "Jugendherberge." Spacious, modern post-and-beam dorms fill up fast in the summer months, so call well in advance. Breakfast included. Wash €1.50. Dry €1.50. Reception 7am-10pm. Curfew midnight, door code available. Prices rise in the summer. Apr-Oct. dorms €21.90, Nov-Mar. €18.40. Private rooms add €4-6. MC/V. ❷

Hotel Pension Noris, Brettermarkt 13 (☎08362 36 45). This pension has white-walled rooms right off the promenade. Large, delicious breakfast included. All rooms with bath. Singles €35-40, doubles €75-80. ❸

Park-Camping Lindau Am See, Frauenhofer Str. 20 (☎08362 722 36; www.park-camping.de), is 3km to the east on the mainland, within spitting distance of the Austrian border. *Let's Go* does not recommend spitting at Austria. Take bus #1 or 2 to "Anheggerstr./ZUP," then bus #3 (dir.: Zech) to the next-to-last stop, "Laiblachstr." Exit the bus and turn right, then left onto the large Bregenzer Str., where the campground is marked. Reception 8am-noon and 2-8pm. €5.50-6.50 per adult, €2.10-2.60 per child, €2.50 per tent, €5.50-8.50 for vehicle. Electricity €3. Hot showers included. Grocery store and restaurant open daily 7am-9pm. ❶

FOOD

In Lindau, finding a good meal at the right price can be a bit of a challenge. A dense conglomeration of cheap, *Imbiß*-style food lies along **In Der Grub.**

Patio, Eat & Art Gallery (☎08362 943 0789), off of Maximilianstr. toward the harbor on Krumgasse, is a chic restaurant that doubles as an art gallery. A young crowd frequents the glossy bar. Daily specials €7.80-9. Open Tu-Su noon-10pm. Cash only. ❸

MarMorSaal, Bahnhofspl. 1 (☎08382 93 407). Come for the view and the summer drinks. Stay for the free Wi-Fi and shisha. Open daily 11am-midnight. ❸

SIGHTS AND BEACHES

The 14th-century gabled houses on **Maximilianstraße** form the center of town. On Maximilianstr., the **Altes Rathaus** is a blend of stylized frescoes, completed in 1456. The muraled **Cavazzen-Haus** in the Marktpl. houses the **Stadtmuseum** (Municipal Museum), which displays a collection of furniture and art, ranging from French porcelain and bureaus to portraits of pompous-looking nobles. *(☎08382 94 40 73. Open Apr.-Oct. Tu-F and Su 11am-5pm, Sa 2-5pm. €2.50, students €1, families €5. Tours Apr.-Oct. 2:15 and 3pm €2.50, students €1.50. Combined ticket €4/2, families €5.)* A walk down In der Grub leads to the Rapunzel-esque **Diebsturm** (Thieves' Tower), the former town jail. The medieval **Peterskirche** next door, now a memorial to all victims of the World Wars, contains the only surviving murals by Hans Holbein the Elder. A walk along the waterfront from the Mangturm leads to unobstructed views of the lake, and to the **Pulverschanze** (Gun Powder Tower), an erstwhile military fortification. If you're in the Lindau area from late July to late August, ask about the **Bregenzer Festspiele,** an extravagant opera over the Austrian border in Bregenz. Huge crowds have gathered in past years to see *Die Zauberflöte*, *Tosca*, and *La Bohème* staged on a platform over the Bodensee. *(☎55 74 40 76; www.bregenzerfestspiele.com. Tickets from €26-280, and sell quickly.)*

Lindau has two public beaches, the bigger and busier of which is **Eichwald,** with three heated pools and a slide. Walk to the east along Uferweg for 30min. or take bus #1 or 2 to "Anheggerstr./ZUP," then bus #3 to "Kamelbuckel." (☎08382 55 39. Open June-Aug daily 9am-8pm, Sep-May M-F 9:30am-8pm, Sa-Su 9am-8pm. Last entry 1hr. before closing. €3, ages 6-18 €2.) To reach the quieter **Lindenhofbad,** take bus #1 or 2 to "Anheggerstr./ZUP" and then bus #4 to the end; take the hedged road uphill and look for signs. *(☎08362 66 37; www.seebad-lindenhof.de. Open June to mid-Aug. daily 10:30am-8pm; May-Sept. M-F 10:30am-7:30pm, Sa-Su 10am-8pm. Last entry 1hr. before closing. €2.50, ages 6-18 €2. Warm showers €0.50.)* Inside the Lindenhofpark, the **Strandbad Bad Schachen** boasts a luxurious heated pool. *(Open May-Aug. daily 9am-7pm.)*

BAYERN (BAVARIA)

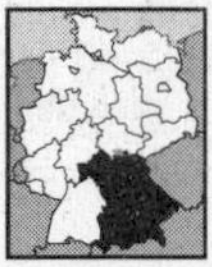

Bavaria is the Germany of Wagnerian opera, medieval fairy tales, and Teutonic myth. From tiny forest villages to stately Baroque cities along the Danube and castles perched high in the Alps, the region attracts more visitors than any other part of the country. When foreigners conjure up images of Germany, they are thinking of Bavaria: land of beer gardens, sausage, and *Lederhosen*. But tourists soon discover that there is much more to Germany's largest federal state than the clichés it indulges. From international powerhouses like BMW and Audi to thriving university towns, Bavaria is too dynamic to be regarded as an open-air museum. The region's residents will be the first to say they are Bavarians first and Germans second. Bavaria was a sovereign kingdom for ages, after all. Through wars with France and Austria, Otto von Bismarck pulled Bavaria into his orbit, but it remained its own kingdom until 1918. Local authorities still insist upon using the Land's proper name: *Freistaat Bayern* (Free State of Bavaria). Despite such long-standing cultural identities, modern cosmopolitanism combines with historical preservation to animate the truly individual character of Germany's southernmost state.

HIGHLIGHTS OF BAVARIA

ABSORB the culture, and the *Bier*, of **Munich** during **Oktoberfest** (Sept. 19-Oct. 4, 2010; p. 353), or check out the city's sleek bars, lively museums, and garden three times the size of New York's Central Park.

BEAR WITNESS to Germany's Nazi past at the **Dachau** memorial and **Nuremberg's** Nazi ruins (p. 405).

CHUG extra-strength monks' brew at **Andechs,** a hilltop monastery still serving the 12% alcohol beer it has produced since the 16th century (p. 356).

DISCOVER the medieval splendor of the **Romantic Road** (p. 389).

DRINK milk practically straight from the cow in the spectacular **Berchtesgaden National Park** (p. 362), a stunning setting for hikes and other outdoor activities.

REALIZE YOUR CINDERELLA FANTASIES on a visit to King Ludwig II's extravagant **Königsschlößer** (p. 360) or at his "cozy" **hunting lodge** on the Chiemsee (p. 368).

MÜNCHEN (MUNICH) ☎089

Tourists who step past the stereotypes of *Lederhosen* and pot-bellied curmudgeons will be pleasantly surprised to discover that Munich (pop. 1,248,000) is both the sleek southern capital of German affluence and the leafy home of true German merriment. The city's cosmopolitan attractions and its long-standing tradition of enjoying beer, life, and nature (in that order) make it both a relaxing and a stimulating place. World-class museums, handsome parks, unforgettable architecture, and a rowdy art scene combine to create a city of astonishing vitality.

INTERCITY TRANSPORTATION

Flights: Flughafen München (☎97 52 13 13; www.munich-airport.de). S1 and S8 trains run between the airport and the Hauptbahnhof (45min., every 10min., €8.80, sit in the rear half of the S1 train). Group tickets cover 2-5 adults for €21 (see **Public Transportation,** p. 332).

Trains: Munich's **Hauptbahnhof** is the transportation hub of southern Germany, with connections to: **Berlin** (6hr., 2 per hr., €110); **Cologne** (4½hr., 2 per hr., €122); **Frankfurt** (3hr., 2 per hr., €85); **Füssen** (2hr., every 2hr., €20); **Hamburg** (6hr., every hr., €115); **Amsterdam, NTH** (7-9hr., every hr., €140); **Innsbruck, AUT** (2hr., every 2hr., €35); **Paris, FRA** (8-10hr., 6 per day, €129); **Prague, CZR** (6-7hr., 4 per day, €55); **Salzburg, AUT** (2hr., 1 per hr., €29); **Vienna, AUT** (5hr., 1 per hr., €73); **Zürich, CHE** (4hr., 4-5 per day, €70). For 24hr. schedules, fare information, and reservations (in German), call ☎01805 99 66 33 (€0.12 per min.) from outside of Germany or ☎089 118 61 (€0.39 per min.) from within. The **Bayern-Ticket** (single €21, 2-5 people €29) is valid for all train transit from 9am-3am, and can take you all the way to Salzburg; a night Bayern-Ticket valid after 6pm is available for €21. **EurAide** (see **Tourist Offices,** p. 333) provides free information in English and books train tickets. The Hauptbahnhof's **Reisezentrum** (travel center), directly across from track 20, is open daily 7am-9:30pm, and **DER Reisebüro** (☎55 14 02 00; www.der.de), located at the main entrance to the Hauptbahnhof, sells train tickets and railpasses M-F 9:30am-6pm, Sa 10am-1pm.

Ride Share: Mitfahrzentrale, Lämmerstr. 6 (☎194 40). Arranges intercity transportation with drivers going the same way. Around €30. Open M-F 9am-1pm and 2-6pm.

Hitchhiking: *Let's Go* does not recommend hitchhiking as a safe mode of transportation. Those who choose to hitch often can check the bulletin boards in the **Mensa.** Otherwise, hitchers have been known to try Autobahn on-ramps; those who stand beyond the blue and white Autobahn signs may be fined. Hitchers going to Salzburg take U1 or U2 to "Karl-Preis-Pl." Those heading to Nuremberg and Berlin take U6 to "Studentenstadt" and walk 500m to the Frankfurter Ring. Those heading to the Bodensee and Switzerland take U4 or U5 to "Heimeranpl.," then bus #133 to "Siegenburger Str."

ORIENTATION

Munich rests on the banks of the Isar in the middle of south-central Bavaria, with King Ludwig's castles and the Alps only a short trip past its outskirts. **Marienplatz** is the center of Munich's sight-strewn **Altstadt.** To get there from the **Hauptbahnhof,** take any S-Bahn to "Marienpl.," or head out the main entrance and across Bahnhofpl. Continue east on Prielmayerstr. past the fountain at **Karlsplatz** (called **Stachus** by locals) and through the **Karlstor;** Marienpl. is another 10min. straight ahead down the pedestrian mall. The huge **Deutsches Museum** lies on the well-named **Museumsinsel** (Museum Island) in the middle of the Isar river. North of the Altstadt is the **Residenz,** the former home of the Wittelsbach rulers; the **Hofgarten** beyond stretches to the corner of the **Englischer Garten,** which in turn sprawls toward the northeast reaches of the city.

On the other side of town, the grand **Schloß Nymphenburg** rests beside the manicured Botanischer Garten. Sports fans head north of town to the Olympiapark, built for the 1972 Olympic Games. The **University of Munich** (a.k.a. **Ludwig-Maximilians Universität**) is north, next to **Schwabing's** student-friendly restaurants and bookstores. The **Technical University** is north of the city near the museums of the **Königspl.** area. South of town is the **Glockenbachviertel,** filled with nightspots, including many gay bars. The area around the **Hauptbahnhof,** formerly dominated by sex shops, is getting nicer and now houses many hotels. The large, open **Theresienwiese,** southeast of the Hauptbahnhof on the U4 and U5 lines, hosts **Oktoberfest.** Several publications help visitors navigate Munich—the most comprehensive (in English) is the monthly *Munich Found* (€3 at newsstands).

BAYERN

LOCAL TRANSPORTATION

Public Transportation: MVV, Munich's public transport system (☎089 41 42 43 44, www.mvv-muenchen.de), runs M-Th and Su 5am-12:30am, F-Sa 5am-2am. S-Bahn to the airport starts running at 3:30am. **Eurail, InterRail,** and **German railpasses** are valid on the S-Bahn but not on the U-Bahn, trams, or buses. Buy tickets at the blue MVV-Fahrausweise vending machines and validate them in the blue boxes marked with an "E" before entering the platform. Disguised agents sometimes check for tickets, levying a €40 fine on those who haven't validated them correctly. Always descend from the right-hand side of the S-Bahn. Transit maps and maps of wheelchair-accessible stations are at tourist offices and at MVV counters in U-Bahn and train stations. *Fahrpläne* (schedules) cost €1 at newsstands, but are free online.

Prices: Single-ride tickets €2.20 (valid for 2hr.). *Kurzstrecke* (short trip) tickets €1.10 (1hr. or 2 stops on the U- or S-Bahn, or 4 stops on a tram or bus). A *Streifenkarte*

(10-strip ticket) costs €10.50 and can be used by more than 1 person. Cancel 2 strips per person for a normal ride, or 1 strip for a *Kurzstrecke.* Beyond the city center, cancel 2 strips per zone. A *Single-Tageskarte* (1-day ticket; €5) is valid until 6am the day after purchase. At €12.30, the 3-Day Pass is a great deal. Alternatively, a *Partner-Tageskarte* (€9) can be used by up to 5 people. The *München XXL Ticket* offers day-long transit on almost all transportation in and around Munich (€6.70 single, €11.80 for up to 5 individuals), and can be used to reach Dachau (p. 355). If you're coming from the airport, consider getting an all-access *Gesamtnetz Tageskarte* (€9.60).

TIP **TRAVEL CHEAP.** Unless you're traveling with 3 or more people (up to 5) and going to at least 5 of the sites for which the card gives you a discount, it's **not** worth purchasing **Das München Ticket.** In addition, the sights it gives discounts on are not the best or most popular attractions.

Taxis: Taxi-München-Zentrale (☎089 216 10 or 194 10; www.taxizentrale-muenchen.de). Located immediately outside the Hauptbahnhof. Women can ask for female drivers. Call ahead to make special requests such as pet-friendly or large-capacity cabs.

Car Rental: Upstairs at the Hauptbahnhof are **Avis** (☎01805 55 77 55; open M-F 7am-9pm, Sa-Su 8am-5pm), **Europcar** (☎01805 8000; open M-F 7:30am-8pm, Sa-Su 8am-12pm), **Hertz** (☎1805 33 35 35; open M-Sa 24hr.), and **Sixt** (☎1805 26 02 50; open daily 6am-9pm).

Bike Rental: Radius Bikes (☎089 59 61 13), in the Hauptbahnhof opposite tracks 30-36. €3 per hr.; €14.50 per day for 3-speed, €18 for 21-speed. Deposit €50, passport, or credit card. 10% discount for students. Open from May to mid-Oct. daily 10am-6pm.

Mike's Bike Tours (☎089 25 54 39 87), across from the back entrance of the Hofbräuhaus, on Hochbreukenstr. All day €12, overnight €18, €9 per day for subsequent rentals. ½-off with a tour (see below).

DB Call a Bike (☎0700 05 22 55 22; www.callabike.de) is a Deutsche Bahn service, available by phone after registering online. Also located in front of the Hauptbahnhof. Rental €0.08 per min. €15 max. €5 deposit.

Bike Sale: Second Hand Sports, Nymphenburgerstr. 29 (☎089 59 70 74). U1 or U7 to "Stiglmaierpl." Used bikes €50+; buyback options. Good selection of outdoor and adventure gear, snowboards, skis, and helmets. English-speaking staff also services bikes. Open M 12:30-7pm, Tu-F 10:30am-7pm, Sa 10:30am-3:30pm. Cash only.

PRACTICAL INFORMATION

TOURIST OFFICES

EurAide in English (☎59 38 89; www.euraide.com). Counter in the Reisezentrum, Hauptbahnhof. Main office located next door to Subway sandwich shop. Deutsche Bahn's English-speaking office books train tickets for all European destinations for free. Tickets for public transit (at standard prices), maps of Munich (€0.50), and discounted tickets for English-language walking, bus, and bike tours are also available. Drop in for sound advice from the manager and pick up a free copy of the helpful and informative brochure *Inside Track.* Open M-Sa 8am-noon and 2-4pm, Su 8am-noon. Extended hours in the summer.

Main Office (☎23 39 65 00; www.muenchen-tourist.de). Take a right out of the main Hauptbahnhof entrance. English-speaking staff gives advice about sights as well as tour info, though EurAide (see above) is a better resource for in-depth train and travel-related questions. The tourist office books rooms (for free with 10% deposit)

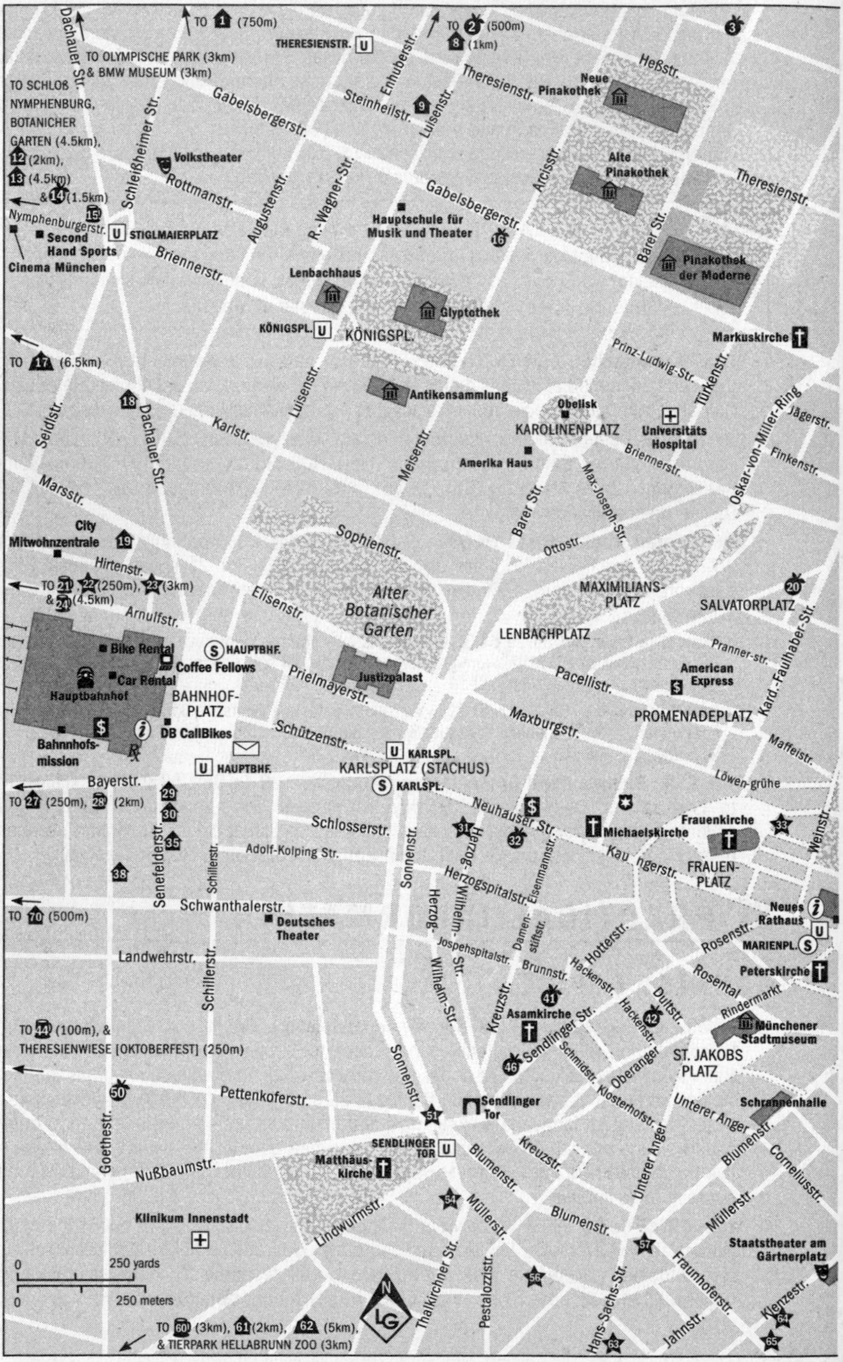
TO 1 (750m)
TO 2 (500m)
8 (1km)
TO OLYMPISCHE PARK (3km) & BMW MUSEUM (3km)
TO SCHLOß NYMPHENBURG, BOTANICHER GARTEN (4.5km), 12 (2km), 13 (4.5km) & 14 (1.5km)
THERESIENSTR.
Neue Pinakothek
Alte Pinakothek
Pinakothek der Moderne
Volkstheater
Hauptschule für Musik und Theater
STIGLMAIERPLATZ
Second Hand Sports
Cinema München
Lenbachhaus
Glyptothek
KÖNIGSPL.
TO 17 (6.5km)
Markuskirche
Antikensammlung
Obelisk
KAROLINENPLATZ
Universitäts Hospital
Amerika Haus
City Mitwohnzentrale
TO 21, 22 (250m), 23 (3km) & 24 (4.5km)
Alter Botanischer Garten
MAXIMILIANSPLATZ
SALVATORPLATZ
LENBACHPLATZ
Bike Rental
HAUPTBHF.
Coffee Fellows
Car Rental
Hauptbahnhof
Justizpalast
BAHNHOFPLATZ
American Express
PROMENADEPLATZ
DB CallBikes
Bahnnhofsmission
KARLSPL.
KARLSPLATZ (STACHUS)
TO 27 (250m), 28 (2km)
Michaelskirche
Frauenkirche
FRAUENPLATZ
Deutsches Theater
Neues Rathaus
MARIENPL.
Peterskirche
TO 70 (500m)
Asamkirche
Münchener Stadtmuseum
ST. JAKOBS PLATZ
TO 44 (100m), & THERESIENWIESE [OKTOBERFEST] (250m)
Schrannenhalle
Sendlinger Tor
SENDLINGER TOR
Matthäuskirche
Klinikum Innenstadt
Staatstheater am Gärtnerplatz
0 250 yards
0 250 meters
TO 60 (3km), 61 (2km), 62 (5km), & TIERPARK HELLABRUNN ZOO (3km)
Dachauer Str.
Schleißheimer Str.
Gabelsbergerstr.
Theresienstr.
Heßstr.
Steinheilstr.
Enhuberstr.
Luisenstr.
Arcisstr.
Barer Str.
Rottmanstr.
Augustenstr.
R.-Wagner-Str.
Nymphenburgerstr.
Briennerstr.
Prinz-Ludwig-Str.
Türkenstr.
Karlstr.
Meiserstr.
Max-Joseph-Str.
Oskar-von-Miller-Ring
Jägerstr.
Finkenstr.
Seidlstr.
Marsstr.
Sophienstr.
Ottostr.
Hirtenstr.
Elisenstr.
Arnulfstr.
Prielmayerstr.
Pranner-str.
Pacellistr.
Kard.-Faulhaber-Str.
Maxburgstr.
Schützenstr.
Maffeistr.
Löwen-grühe
Bayerstr.
Neuhauser Str.
Schlosserstr.
Adolf-Kolping Str.
Senefelderstr.
Schillerstr.
Sonnenstr.
Herzog-Wilhelm-Str.
Eisenmannstr.
Herzogspitalstr.
Weinstr.
Schwanthalerstr.
Josephspitalstr.
Damenstiftstr.
Brunnstr.
Hotterstr.
Rosenstr.
Rosental
Landwehrstr.
Hackenstr.
Dultstr.
Rindermarkt
Kreuzstr.
Sendlinger Str.
Schmidstr.
Oberanger
Klosterhofstr.
Pettenkoferstr.
Unterer Anger
Blumenstr.
Corneliusstr.
Goethestr.
Nußbaumstr.
Lindwurmstr.
Müllerstr.
Thalkirchner Str.
Pestalozzistr.
Hans-Sachs-Str.
Fraunhoferstr.
Jahnstr.
Klenzestr.
BAYERN

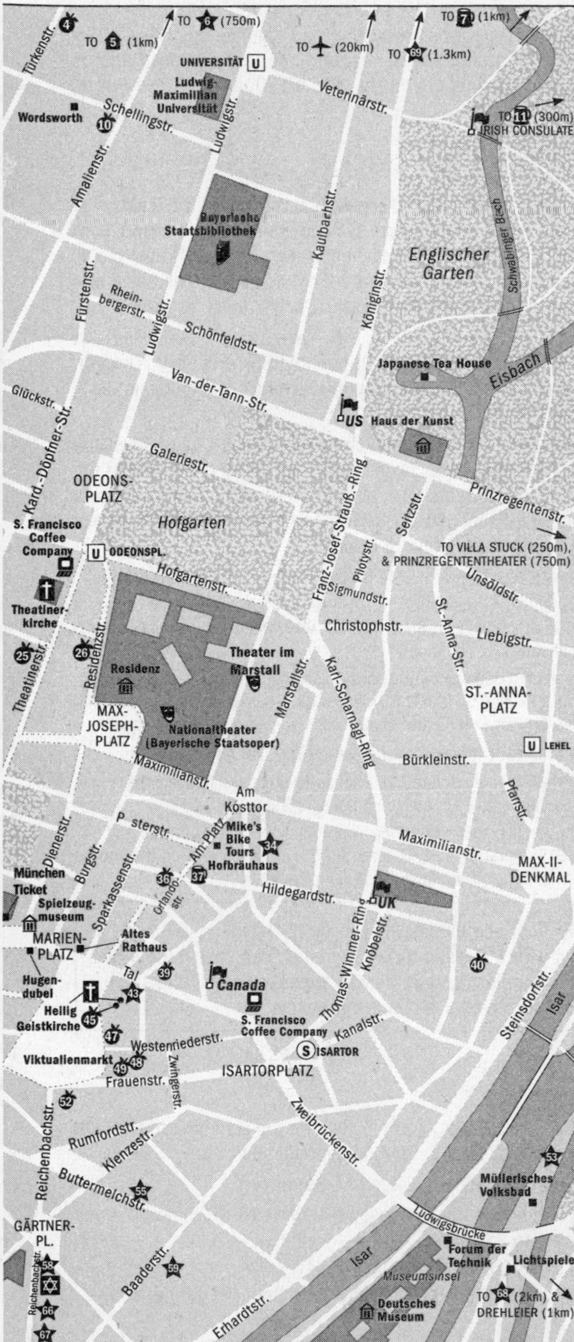

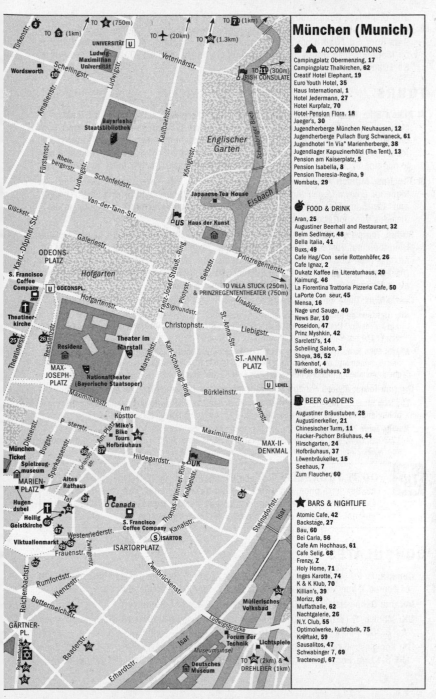

München (Munich)

ACCOMMODATIONS

Campingplatz Obermenzing, **17**
Campingplatz Thalkirchen, **62**
Creatif Hotel Elephant, **19**
Euro Youth Hotel, **35**
Haus International, **1**
Hotel Jedermann, **27**
Hotel Kurpfalz, **70**
Hotel-Pension Flora, **18**
Jaeger's, **30**
Jugendherberge München Neuhausen, **12**
Jugendherberge Pullach Burg Schwaneck, **61**
Jugendhotel "In Via" Marienherberge, **38**
Jugendlager Kapuzinerhölzl (The Tent), **13**
Pension am Kaiserplatz, **5**
Pension Isabella, **8**
Pension Theresia-Regina, **9**
Wombats, **29**

FOOD & DRINK

Aran, **25**
Augustiner Beerhall and Restaurant, **32**
Beim Sedlmayr, **48**
Bella Italia, **41**
Buxs, **49**
Cafe Hag/Con serie Rottenhöfer, **26**
Cafe Ignaz, **2**
Dukatz Kaffee im Literaturhaus, **20**
Kaimung, **46**
La Fiorentina Trattoria Pizzeria Cafe, **50**
LaPorte Con seur, **45**
Mensa, **16**
Nage und Sauge, **40**
News Bar, **10**
Poseidon, **47**
Prinz Myshkin, **42**
Sarcletti's, **14**
Schelling Salon, **3**
Shoya, **36, 52**
Türkenhof, **4**
Weißes Bräuhaus, **39**

BEER GARDENS

Augustiner Bräustuben, **28**
Augustinerkeller, **21**
Chinesischer Turm, **11**
Hacker-Pschorr Bräuhaus, **44**
Hirschgarten, **24**
Hofbräuhaus, **37**
Löwenbräukeller, **15**
Seehaus, **7**
Zum Flaucher, **60**

BARS & NIGHTLIFE

Atomic Cafe, **42**
Backstage, **27**
Bau, **60**
Bei Carla, **56**
Cafe Am Hochhaus, **61**
Cafe Selig, **68**
Frenzy, **Z**
Holy Home, **71**
Inges Karotte, **74**
K & K Klub, **70**
Killian's, **39**
Morizz, **69**
Muffathalle, **62**
Nachtgalerie, **26**
N.Y. Club, **55**
Optimolwerke, Kultfabrik, **75**
Kr@ftakt, **59**
Sausalitos, **47**
Schwabinger 7, **69**
Tractenvogl, **67**

and dispenses English city maps (€0.30). The free English guide *Young and About in Munich* lists beer gardens and gives tips on cycling and sightseeing. Open M-Sa 9am-8pm, Su 10am-6pm. Another branch inside the entrance to the Neues Rathaus on Marienpl. also books rooms and sells city maps (€0.30). Open M-F 10am-8pm, Sa 10am-4pm, Su noon-4pm.

TOURS

Mike's Bike Tours (☎089 25 54 39 87; www.mikesbiketours.com), at Altes Rathaus in Marienpl. Pedal, laugh, and down a few beers as you pick up some creative history from English-speaking guides. 4hr. tours (6.5km, €24) include bike rental and *Biergarten* break. Tours daily from mid-Apr. to Aug. 11:30am and 4pm; from Sept. to mid-Nov. and from Mar to mid-Apr. 12:30pm. Combo tickets available for castle and Dachau tours (p. 336).

The New Munich Free Tour (☎089 30 51 05 00 30; www.neweuropetours.eu), at Marienpl. Enjoy a free, highly entertaining, young adult-oriented 3hr. tour daily 10:45am and 11:45am. Tips highly encouraged. Tours covering Dachau €19, students €17, includes transportation costs; 10:45am.

Radius Tours (☎089 55 02 93 74; www.radiusmunich.com), opposite track 32 of the Hauptbahnhof. Historical walking tours of the city in English, including a 2hr. tour of the Altstadt (Apr.-Oct. daily 10am; €12, students €10, under 6 free) and a Third Reich tour (Apr.-Oct. daily 3pm; Nov.-Mar. Tu, F, and Su 11:30am; same prices). Combo tickets available for both walking tours and guided tour of Dachau.

Castle Tours: There are many ways to be guided into the magical realm of mad King Ludwig II.

City Sightseeing Tours offers a 10½hr. bus excursion (in English) to Neuschwanstein and Linderhof that leaves Apr.-Oct. daily at 8:30am, Nov.-Mar. Tu-Su at 8:30am. €49, children €24; castle admission (€15) not included. Book ahead.

Mike's Bike Tours (p. 336) offers guided daytrips in English that include a visit to Neuschwanstein, biking, swimming, and a stop at an Alpine slide (€1.30). Tours leave during summer at 8:30am; check website for meeting places. By bus €49, by train €39; castle admission (€8) not included.

Dachau Tours: Always confirm that your guide is qualified by The Dachau Memorial.

The New Munich Free Tour (above) offers a guided tour of Dachau Tu-Su. In Dachau, meet at noon; at Marienplatz, at 10:45am. €19, students €15, including transportation.

Radius Tours (above) gives a 5hr. English tour of Dachau. Tours Apr.-Oct. 15th Tu-Su at 9:15am, 12:30pm; Nov.-Mar. at 11am. €19, students €21, children €9.50. All prices include transportation. Meet 20min. before start time across from Track 32 of Hauptbahnhof.

TIP **DO IT YOURSELF.** Tour companies will get you to Dachau and Bavaria's castles for a price, but with a **Bayern ticket,** 5 friends can save quite a bit. Even if you can't get 5 people together, an **XXL tageskarte** still offers substantial savings for one person over two one-way tickets.

CONSULATES

Canada: Tal 29 (☎089 219 9570). S1-S8 to "Isartor"; look for the gold door to the right of Conrad. Open M-Th 9am-noon; also from 2-5pm by appointment only.

Ireland: Dennigerstr. 15 (☎089 20 80 59 90). Open M-F 9am-noon.

UK: Möhlstr. 5 (☎089 21 10 90; www.britishembassy.de). Tram 18 to "Effnerpl." Open M-F 8:30am-noon and 1-5pm (F to 3:30pm).

US: Königinstr. 5 (☎08 92 88 80; munich.usconsulate.gov). U3-U6 to "Odeonspl." Open M-F 8-11am. For visa info, call ☎090 01 85 00 55 M-F 7am-8pm (€1.86 per min.).

FINANCIAL SERVICES

Currency Exchange: ReiseBank (☎089 551 0837; www.reisebank.de), at the front of the Hauptbahnhof, has decent rates. Open M-Su 7am-11pm.

American Express: Reisebüro, Promenadepl. 6 (☎089 290 90 145; 24hr. hotline ☎0800 185 3100), to the left of the Hotel Bayerischer Hof. Cashes traveler's checks. Open M-Sa 9:15-12:30pm and 1-4:15pm.

LOCAL SERVICES

Luggage Storage: At the airport (☎089 97 52 13 75). 24hr. staffed storage room in the main hall of the Hauptbahnhof (☎089 13 08 50 36). Lockers in main hall and opposite tracks 16, 24, and 28-36. €3-5 per 24hr. for up to 3 days. Open M-F 8am-8pm and Sa-Su 8am-6pm.

Lost Property: Hauptbahnhof (☎089 13 08 66 64), by track 26. Open M-F 7am-11pm, Sa-Su 7:30am-10:30pm.

Home Share:

Mitwohnzentrale Wolfgang Sigg GmbH/An der Uni, Fendstr. 6 (☎08 93 30 37 40; www.mrliving.de). U3 or U6 to "Munchener Freiheit." Walk south on Leopoldstr., make a left on Fendstr. At #6, ring buzzer, and go through the corridor to 2nd building. Apartments available by the month. Open M-F 9am-1pm and 2-6pm.

City Mitwohnzentrale, Lämmerstr. 6 (☎08 91 94 30; www.mitwohnzentrale.de), by the Arnulfstr. exit of the Hauptbahnhof also rents apartments. Open 24h.

Studentenwerk, Leopoldstr. 15 (☎089 38 19 60; www.studentenwerk.mhn.de). U3 or U6 to "Giselastr." Inexpensive housing for students and the general public. Thorough English-language website. Open M-Th 8:30am-5pm and F 8:30am-2pm. They also provide info for students on classes, medical care, and other miscellaneous student needs.

Bookstores:

Hugendubel, Marienpl. 22 (☎01 801 48 44 84; www.hugendubel.de). U3 or S1-S8 to "Marienpl." A 6-story bookstore and cafe offering hundreds of English-language titles. Enjoy books before purchase (rare in Germany) in cabbage-shaped alcoves. Open M-F 9:30am-8pm, Sa 9:30am-8pm.

The Munich Readery, Augustenstr. 104 (☎089 12 19 24 03; www.readery.de). U2 to "Theresienstr." A small, spiffy secondhand bookshop with a bizarre but very good selection. Poster series of "Famous Literary Cottages" on the wall. Open M-F 11am-8pm and Sa 10am-6pm.

Words Worth, Schellingstr. 3 (☎08 92 80 91 41). U3 or U6 to "Universität." An orderly array of English-language titles in a quiet niche off the main street. Open M-F 9am-8pm, Sa 10am-4pm.

Library: Bayerische Staatsbibliothek, Ludwigstr. 16 (☎089 28 63 80; www.bsb-muenchen.de), U6 to "Universität." A large library with over 8.3 million books, magazines, and newspapers. Reading room open until midnight. Open 24hr.; closes earlier Aug.-Sept.

Visitor Publications: New In the City (www.newinthecity.de). Extremely thorough yearly publication in German and English (€6.90) covering everything from apartment registration to popular nightlife, local universities, and cultural venues. Available at newsstands. **SZ Woche,** the *Süddeutsche Zeitung*'s Th supplement with cultural listings about events in and around Munich (in German).

Gay and Lesbian Resources: Gay Services Information (☎089 260 3056), open 1pm-midnight. Another point of reference is the 24hr. reception of **Hotel Deutsche Eiche,** Reichenbachstr. 13 (☎089 231 1660). Resources for lesbians at the **LeTRa Lesbenberatungsstelle,** Angertorstr. 3 (☎089 725 4272). Hotlines open M and W 2:30-5pm; Tu 11:30am-1pm. Office open M-W 3-6pm and Th 5-8pm. Also see **Gay and Lesbian Munich,** p. 352.

Women's Resources:

Kofra Kommunikationszentrum für Frauen, Baaderstr. 30 (☎089 201 0450). Job advice, magazines, lesbian politics, books, and a small cafe. Open M-Th 4-10pm, F 2-6pm.

Frauentreffpunkt Neuperlach, Oskar-Maria-Graf-Ring 20-22 (☎089 670 6463; www.frauentreffpunkt-neuperlach.de). Services and venues for women, including an international coffeehouse. English conversation nights; check website or call for dates and times.

Lillemor's Frauenbuchladen, Barer Str. 70 (☎089 272 1205), is a women's bookstore. Open M-F 10am-7pm, Sa 10am-2pm.

Disabled Resources: Info Center für Behinderte, Schellingstr. 31 (☎089 211 70; www.vdk.de/bayern), lists Munich's resources for disabled persons. Open M-Sa 9am-8pm and Su 10am-6pm.

Ticket Agencies: To order event tickets by phone call **München Ticket** (☎0180 54 81 81 81, €0.14 per min.; www.muenchenticket.de). Advance tickets are available at München Ticket's retail locations in the Rathaus in Marienpl. (open M-F 10am-8pm, Sa 10am-4pm) and at the Hauptbahnhof's main tourist office (open M-Sa 10am-6:30pm).

Laundromats: SB-Waschcenter, Lindwurmstr. 124. U1 to "Sendlinger Tor." Wonderfully modern large-capacity washers and dryers. Vending machines with coffee available. Free Wi-Fi. Wash €3.50 (soap €0.30), dry €0.60 per 10min. Open daily 7am-11pm. **Branch** at Untersbergstr. 8. U2, U7, or U8 to "Untersbergstr." Same prices and hours.

Swimming Pools: The city's 8 outdoor pools are open May to mid-Sept., but you can enjoy 11 adjacent indoor pools year-round. Pick up *Münchener Bäder* at the tourist office for full listings (in German). Swim in the wake of the greats at the Olympic Pool (☎089 30 67 22 90) in Olympiapark. U3 to "Olympiazentrum." Open daily 7am-11pm.

EMERGENCY AND COMMUNICATIONS

Emergency: Police ☎110. **Ambulance** and **Fire** ☎112. **Emergency medical service** ☎08 91 92 22, home service 089 55 17 71. Emergency road service ☎089 0180 222 22 22. Free of charge only for ADAC (Allgemeiner Deutscher Automobil-Club e.V.) members.

Bahnhofsmission: Near track 11 at the Bayerstr. exit. The experienced staff at this 24hr. walk-in center help in non-medical emergencies that occur at or near the Hauptbahnhof.

Rape Crisis Line: Frauennotruf München, Güllstr. 3 (☎089 76 37 37; www.frauennotrufmuenchen.de). Available 6pm-midnight.

AIDS Hotline: ☎089 194 11 or 089 23 32 33 33. In German. M-F 7-9pm.

Pharmacy: Bahnhofpl. 2 (☎089 59 41 19 or 59 81 19), on the corner outside the Hauptbahnhof. Open M-F 8am-8pm, Sa 8am-2pm.

Medical Services: Klinikum Rechts der Isar, across the river on Ismaninger Str. U4 or U5 to "Max-Weber-Pl." Open 24hr. for emergency. **Münchener AIDS-Hilfe,** Lindwurmstr. 71 (☎089 544 6470). Free and anonymous **STI/AIDS tests.** Open M-Th 9:30am-6pm, F 9:30am-2pm. UK and US consulates carry lists of English-speaking doctors.

Internet Access:

Coffee Fellows Cafe, Bahnhofpl. 7 (☎089 51 50 46 88; www.coffee-fellows.de), located on the corner of Bahnhofpl. and Arnulfstr., immediately left as you exit the main entrance to the Bahnhof. €2.50 per hr., €3 per day. Open 6am-11pm. Branches all over Munich; check the website for locations and hours.

MISC24 Internetcafe, Sonnenstr. 8. From the Bahnhof, head down Schillerstr. take a left on Schwanthalerstr. and look for the passage on the left side. Offers over 60 work stations in addition to copy, print, fax, telephone, and laptop services. €1 per 30min., €20 per day. Open 24hr.

San Francisco Coffee Company, Im Tal 15 (☎089 995 2973), near the Isartor (open M-F 7:30am-11pm, Sa 8am-11pm, Su 9am-9pm), or in Theatinerstr. 23/Odeonspl. (Open M-F 6:30am-11pm, Sa 7am-11pm and Su 8am-11pm.) Wi-Fi vouchers available €3 per hr. €4.90 per day, €26 per month.

Post Office: (☎0180 300 3008). The yellow building opposite the Hauptbahnhof. Open M-F 7:30am-8pm, Sa 9am-4pm. **Postal Code:** 80335.

ACCOMMODATIONS AND CAMPING

The constant appearance of new hostels and the wide availability of public transportation in Munich make it an easy place to stay as long as you plan ahead. During Oktoberfest, rooms are in short supply—begin your search for accommodations up to a year in advance. Be forewarned that **rates increase by 10-20% during Oktoberfest** for all types of accommodations. In summer, it's best to call before noon or book a few weeks in advance. For extended stays, call the **Mitwohnzentrale** (p. 337) or try bargaining with a pension owner. Munich has a vibrant hostel scene and many recent additions, with options to suit all tastes and budgets. Many only admit guests under 26 or families with children, or they may charge a small fee for older guests. At most of Munich's hostels you can check in all day, but start your search before 5pm. Don't plan on sleeping in a public area; police patrol all night long.

HOSTELS

NEAR THE HAUPTBAHNHOF

Euro Youth Hotel, Senefelderstr. 5 (☎089 59 90 88 11; www.euro-youth-hotel.de). Friendly, well-informed staff offers helpful info and spotless rooms. Fun and noisy travelers' bar serves *Augustinerbräu* (€2.90) daily 6pm-4am, lending this alpine lodge a frat-house atmosphere. Happy hour 6-9pm, beer €2. Breakfast €3.90. Free storage lockers (€10 deposit). Larger lockers available; locks €1.50 or bring your own. Laundry: wash €3, dry €1.50. Internet €1 per 30min. Free Wi-Fi. Reception and security 24hr. Large dorms €17.50; 3- to 5-person dorms €21.50; singles €35; doubles €60-70; quads €84. AmEx/MC/V. ❷

Wombat's, Senefelderstr. 1 (☎089 59 98 91 80; www.wombats-hostels.com). Sleek, modern, and surprisingly sophisticated. Enjoy your free welcome drink in the ultra-cool glassed-in lounge with beanbags and lounge chairs. Swanky colored walls complement the large rooms, lending this relaxed hostel a cool, laid-back feel. Breakfast buffet €3.70. Laundry: wash €2, dry €2.50. Internet €0.50 per 20min. Free Wi-Fi. Reception 24hr. Dorms from €18; singles and doubles from €35 per person. MC/V. ❷

Jugendhotel "In Via" Marienherberge, Goethestr. 9 (☎089 55 58 05). An unmarked yellow building with a black door. Rooms are cheery and spotless, and the atmosphere is peaceful. Kitchen and TV. Breakfast included. Laundry €3. Reception M-Th 8am-midnight, F 9am-3pm, Su 6pm-11pm. Check-out 9am. Lockout midnight-6am. 4-bed dorms €25; singles €30; doubles €50; triples €75. Women under 28 only. Cash only. ❷

ELSEWHERE IN MUNICH

Jugendlager Kapuzinerhölzl (The Tent), In den Kirschen 30 (☎089 141 4300; www.the-tent.com). Tram #17 (dir.: Amalienburgstr.) to "Botanischer Garten" (15min.). Follow the signs on Franz-Schrank-Str. and turn left on In den Kirschen. Join 250 international "campers" under a gigantic tent in a series of bunk beds or on the wood floor. Join this alternative backpacking community at evening campfires. Organic breakfast €2. Free lockers. Wash €2.50, dry €2. Internet access €0.50 per 15min. Free city tours in German and English on W mornings. Free kitchen facilities. Passport or €25 required as deposit. Reception 24hr. Open June to mid-Oct. €7.50 gets you a foam pad, wool blankets, and shower facilities. Beds €10.50; camping €5.50 per site plus €5.50 per person. Cash only; MC/V if you book online. ❶

Jugendherberge München Neuhausen (HI), Wendl-Dietrich-Str. 20 (☎089 20 24 44 90; www.muenchen-neuhausen.jugendherberge.de). U1 (dir.: Westfriedhof) to "Rotkreuzpl." Go past the Galeria Kaufhof and down Wendl-Dietrich-Str.; the entrance is

BAYERN

2 blocks ahead on the right. The most "central" of the HI hostels offers simple but exceptionally bright rooms on a quiet side street. Kitchen access. Free luggage storage. Breakfast and linens included. Lunch or dinner €5.40. Bike rental €10. Reception 24hr. 33-bed co-ed dorm €21-25; 4-to 6-bed dorms €28; doubles €46. MC/V. ❷

Haus International, Elisabethstr. 87 (☎089 12 00 60; www.haus-international.de). U2 (dir.: Feldmoching) to "Hohenzollernpl.," then tram #12 (dir.: Romanpl.) or bus #53 (dir.: Aidenbachstr.) to "Barbarastr." With billiards, ping pong, a small Biergarten, TV room, cafeteria, a disco with bar, and over 600 beds. Reception 24hr. Singles €32, with bath €48; doubles €28/38; triples €28; quads €27; quints €25. AmEx/MC/V. ❸

CAMPING

Munich's campgrounds are open from mid-March to late October and provide cheaper alternatives to the city's pricey hostels. A first rate public transit system means that camping is a viable alternative for those who want to see the city center without paying city-center prices.

Campingplatz Thalkirchen, Zentralländstr. 49 (☎089 723 1707). U3 (dir.: Fürstenried West) to "Thalkirchen," change to bus #135, and get off at the "Campingplatz" (20min.). The surrounding woods and meandering paths give the site a rural feel. TV lounge and supermarket. Showers €1 per 6min. Laundry: wash €5, dry €0.50 per 10min. Reception open 7am-11pm. €4.70 per person, under 14 €1.50; €3-8 per tent; €4.50 per car. RVs €11.50 per person. Cash only. ❶

Campingplatz Obermenzing, Lochhausener Str. 59 (☎089 811 2235; www.campingplatz-muenchen.de). Hedge-lined plots and lots of trees. Showers €1. Laundry: wash €4, dry €0.50 per 9min. Reception 7am-10pm. €4.70 per person, under 14 €2; €3.50 per tent, with car €7.50. Cash only. ❶

HOTELS AND PENSIONS

Although most will find Munich's hostels perfect for a short stay, hotels are abundant, particularly near the Hauptbahnhof, and they provide a welcome respite from the nonstop partying of some of the hostels. Although hotels are slightly pricier in Munich, they are no less busy than the hostels and fill up on most weekends. Be sure to reserve weeks ahead as tour groups often make massive bookings.

NEAR THE HAUPTBAHNHOF

Creatif Hotel Elephant, Lämmerstr. 6 (☎089 55 57 85; www.creatif-hotel-elephant.com). Located just around a quiet corner from the Bahnhof, this funky, modern hotel offers a circus-inspired ambience with modern furniture and an accommodating staff. Newly renovated rooms with playful decor, private bath, phone, and TV. Breakfast included. Free Wi-Fi and 1 computer for guest use. Reception 24hr. Singles from €39; doubles from €59. Extra beds €15. Book well in advance. Best rates through the website. AmEx/MC/V. ❹

Hotel Westend, Schwanthaler Str. 121 (☎089 540 9860; www.kurpfalz-hotel.de). Tram #18 or 19 to "Holzapfelstr." Each trendy, colorful room includes phone, private bath, and satellite TV. Swanky bar. Breakfast included. Free Wi-Fi. Reception 24hr. Singles from €45; doubles from €59. Extra bed €15. Book early. AmEx/MC/V. ❹

Hotel Jedermann, Bayerstr. 95 (☎089 54 32 40; www.westend-hotel.de/indexe.htm). Tram #18 or 19 (dir.: Freiham Süd) to "Hermann-Lingg-Str." Nice, carpeted rooms with large windows, avant-garde photographs instead of room numbers, a chic reception, and a central location, albeit with a little street noise. Satellite TV and phones available. A/C in some rooms. Breakfast buffet included. Free Wi-Fi and 1 computer for guest use. Singles from €35; doubles from €49. Extra bed €30. Book in advance for best rates. MC/V. ❹

ELSEWHERE IN MUNICH

Pension am Kaiserplatz, Kaiserpl. 12 (☎089 34 91 90). U3 or U6 to "Münchener Freiheit." With the Karstadt on your right, turn left on Herzogstr. and again on Viktoriastr.; the pension is on the right at the end of the street (10min.). Each elegant room is in its own period style, from Victorian to Baroque. The quiet neighborhood is somewhat removed from the city center. Breakfast (served in-room) included. Reception 8am-8pm. Singles from €31, with shower €47; doubles €49; triples €72; quads €92; quints €110; 6-bed rooms €138. Cash only. ❸

Pension Isabella, Isabellastr. 35 (☎089 271 3503; www.pensionisabella.de). U2 (dir.: Feldmoching) to "Hohenzollernpl." Walk west on Hohenzollernpl. and turn left on Isabellastr.; it's on the right. Each room offers plenty of space and unique (if somewhat old-fashioned) decor with large, clean bathrooms. Breakfast included. Reception 8am-8pm. Singles €37-42; doubles €68-58; triples €75-90; quads €84-104. Cash only. ❹

FOOD

Throughout the city, ubiquitous *Biergärten* (beer gardens) serve savory snacks and booze. For an authentic Bavarian lunch, spread some *Brezeln* (pretzels) with *Leberwurst* (liverwurst) or cheese. *Weißwürste* (white veal sausages) are another favorite, served with sweet mustard and a soft pretzel on the side; real Müncheners only eat them before 11am. Slice the skin open and devour their tender meat. *Leberkäse*, a local lunch, is a pinkish mix of ground beef and bacon which contains neither liver nor cheese. *Leberknödel* are liver dumplings served in soup or with *Kraut* (cabbage). *Kartoffelknödel* (potato dumplings) and *Semmelknödel* (bread and egg dumplings) should be eaten with a hearty chunk of meat. Herbivorous travelers can enjoy *Käsespätzle* (egg noodles baked with cheese) or a plate of *Spargel* (asparagus) with a *Germknödel* (a sweet, jelly-filled dumpling topped with vanilla sauce) for dessert. Travelers looking for traditional brews should simply ask for "*ein Bier*" to get the house specialty on tap. You can also specify the type of beer you want (as opposed to the brand) such as *Weiß* (white), *Dunkel* (dark), or *Hell* (bright) to get the house version of that. The quarter of Munich's population born outside of Germany supplies the city with diverse ethnic offerings, including Turkish, Pakistani, Ethiopian, and Japanese cuisines.

The vibrant **Viktualienmarkt,** south of Marienpl., offers everything from basic to exotic, but prices can be steep. (Open M-Sa 7am-8pm, in summer M-F 7am-8pm, Sa until 7am-4pm.) Many eateries change character as the day wears on, doubling as bars in the evening. For those looking to eat for cheap, supermarkets can be found throughout the city at most major subway stops. They're often underground, sharing space with the station, so keep an eye out.

TRADITIONAL GERMAN

Weißes Bräuhaus, Tal 7 (☎089 290 1380; www.weisses-brauhaus.de). Founded in 1490, this traditional restaurant cooks up dishes like the *Münchener Voressen* (€6.50) made of calf and pig lungs. Choose from 40-50 options on the daily menu (€3-17) served by waitresses in classic Bavarian garb. Open daily 8am-12:30am. MC/V. ❸

Augustiner Beerhall and Restaurant, Neuhauser Str. 27 (☎089 23 18 32 57), between Marienpl. and the Hauptbahnhof. Reasonable Bavarian specialties and Augustiner brew (*Maß* €7.20). English, French, and Italian menus as well. Entrees €4-13.50. Open daily 9am-midnight. AmEx/MC/V. ❸

Beim Sedlmayr, Westenriederstr. 14 (☎089 22 62 19), off the Viktualienmarkt. This authentic *Weißwurst* joint, frequented almost exclusively by locals, serves only Bavarian meat. Not much English here, but that just adds to the experience. Specials €7-16.50. Open M-F 10am-11pm, Sa 9am-5pm. Kitchen open M-F 10am-9:30pm, Sa 8am-4pm. Cash only. ❸

CAFES

Schelling Salon, Schellingstr. 54 (☎089 272 0788), U3 or U6 to "Universität." Bavarian *Knödel* and billiards since 1872. Rack up at tables where Lenin, Rilke, and Hitler once played (€7 per hr.). A great spot to unwind with a beer and friends after a hectic week of drinking. Breakfast €3-5. German entrees €4-11. Open M and Th-Su 6:30am-1am. Cash only. ❸

Dukatz Kaffee, Maffeistr. 3a (☎089 710 40 73 73; www.dukatz.de). The center of literary events in Munich since 1997. Gourmet food (€7-12) and creative drinks (€2-4) in this modern glass and steel triangle. Sip a coffee and people-watch—you'll be observing the city's trendiest writers. Open M-Sa 8:30am-1am, Su 9:30am-7pm. Cafe cash only; restaurant MC/V. ❸

Aran, Theatinerstr. 12 (☎089 25 54 69 82; www.aran.coop). This upscale chain of bakeries has a location serving fresh goods next to the Theatinerkirche. Pick a loaf of bread and have it toasted with cream cheese spread, the house favorite (€4-5.50). Also serves strong coffee. Open M-Sa 10am-8pm. Cash only. ❷

Türkenhof, Türkenstr. 78 (☎089 280 0235), U3 or U6 to "Universität." Huge portions of delicious global cuisine, from Mexican to Thai, along with traditional German fare. Popular among the hipster student crowd. Smoky and buzzing from noon until late. Variable daily menu with numerous veggie options. Entrees €5-9. Open M-Th and Su 11am-1am, F-Sa 11am-2am. Cash only. ❷

INTERNATIONAL

Kaimug, Sendlingerstr. 42 (☎089 20 60 33 27; www.kaimug.de), just down the street from the Asamkirche. A little gem with excellent curry and dirt cheap stir-fry that doesn't sacrifice atmosphere. Desserts, especially those with coconut or mango, are excellent. The curb-side to-go offers pad thai and chicken satay. Generous portions. Plenty of vegetarian entrees. Menu changes daily. Entrees €5-9; smaller portions available for €3-7. Open M-Sa 11am-10pm. Kitchen closes at 9pm. Cash only. ❷

Nage und Sauge, Mariennenstr. 2 (☎089 29 88 03; www.nageundsauge.de). S1-S8 to "Isartor." Golden walls, old wooden floors, and dim lighting set off this cool Italian restaurant. The extremely tasty focaccia salads (€9-11) keep a hip, local crowd coming back for more, despite slightly slow service. Outdoor seating available in the summer. Open daily 5pm-1am. Cash only. ❸

Bella Italia, Sendlingerstr. 28 (☎089 260 9377). Facing Sendlingertor, turn right just before the Asamkirche into the "Asamhof Passage" and look for the large signs. A casual blend of German and authentic Italian tastes in a quiet courtyard off the busy street. Fresh pizza (€4.50-6.50) and delicious pasta (€8-13) in addition to hearty German dishes (€7-14). Open daily 11am-midnight. AmEx/MC/V. ❸

La Fiorentina Trattoria Pizzeria Cafe, Goethestr. 41 (☎089 53 41 85), a few blocks from the Hauptbahnhof. A quiet haven serving a daily menu of large pasta dishes (€6-12). Main courses €7-17. Pizzas €5-13. Open M-F 11:30am-11:30pm, Sa 12:30-3pm and 6-11pm. AmEx/MC/V. ❸

VEGETARIAN

Cafe Ignaz, Georgenstr. 67 (☎089 27 16 093; www.ignaz-cafe.de). U2 to "Josephspl." Take Adelheidstr. 1 block north and turn right on Georgenstr. Have a heart-healthy dinner of anything from crepes to stir-fry dishes (€5-9) at this rockin' eco-friendly cafe, before diving into one of its many desserts. Breakfast buffet (€7) M and W-F 8-11:30am.

Lunch buffet (€7.50) M-F noon-2pm. Brunch buffet (€9) Sa-Su 9am-1:30pm. Open M and W-F 8am-10pm, Tu 11am-11pm, Sa-Su 8am-11pm. AmEx/MC/V. ❷

Prinz Myshkin, Hackenstr. 2 (☎089 26 55 96; www.prinzmyshkin.com). U3 or U6, S1-S8 to "Marienpl." This upscale restaurant, decorated with tapestries and elegant chairs, is worth the splurge. Asian-influenced cuisine featuring luscious paneers. Main courses €9.50-16. Open daily 11am-12:30am. AmEx/MC/V. ❹

OTHER

Mensa, Arcisstr. 17 (☎089 86 46 62 51; www.studentenwerk.mhn.de), to the left of the Pinakothek just below Gabelsbergstr. on Arcisstr. U2 or U8 to "Königspl." Students hit the cafeteria on the ground fl. for light meals (€1-4). The massive Mensa upstairs serves large portions of cheap food (€2-4), with at least 1 vegetarian dish and views of the main museums. To eat there, get a *Legic-Karte* in the main office (€6 deposit and student ID required, or simply shell out the extra €0.50-1 for the guest price). Open M-Th 11am-2:30pm; limited hours during vacations. 7 other cafeterias throughout the city; call or check online for info. ❶

Poseidon, Westenriederstr. 13 (☎089 29 92 96; www.fisch-poseidon.de), off the Viktualienmarkt. Bowls of bouillabaisse with bread (€11) in a bustling fish-market atmosphere. Other fish and tasty seafood dishes (€4-13). Join locals for the sushi menu on Th (€21.50) or pick out your own fresh fish from the small market they have. Open M-F 8am-6:30pm, Sa 8am-4pm. Cash only. ❸

DESSERT

LaPorte Confiseur, Heiliggeiststr. 1 (☎089 29 16 21 12), on the Viktualienmarkt. The LaPortes have made delicious truffles and chocolates in the back of this boutique for over 15 years. Check out the sugar cube cathedrals; it took the proprietor over 400 hours to create each one. Most items €5.60 per 100g. The French couple also makes crepes (€2.30-2.70) and hot chocolate. Open M-F 10am-6:30pm, Sa 10am-5pm. Cash only. ❶

Sarcletti's, Nymphenburgerstr. 155 (☎089 15 53 14; www.sarcletti.de). U1 to "Rotkreuzpl." Over 50 flavors of ice cream and more than 75 specialties. Well worth the trek to Rotkreuzplatz. Cones €0.80 per scoop. Mouthwatering specialties €5-12. Soy and diabetic varieties available. Open M-F Apr.-Sept. 8am-11:30pm, Oct.-Mar. 8am-11pm. Cash only. ❸

SIGHTS

Munich is often described as a serious city lacking character, but its rich tradition as the "Athens of the Isar" and a number of opulent monarchs have left the city with a number of sights that will stun even the most jaded backpacker. Although most sights are within the city center and can be enjoyed at a leisurely pace, some require using Munich's excellent public transit system. Don't let a short trip on the U-bahn deter you from taking in Munich's sights.

CENTRAL MUNICH

RESIDENZ. The richly decorated Residenz is the most visible presence of the Wittelsbach dynasty, whose state rooms now make up the **Residenzmuseum.** The luxurious apartments reflect the Renaissance, Baroque, Rococo, and Neoclassical styles. Also on display are collections of porcelain, gold and silverware, and a 17th-century court chapel. Highlights include the Rococo **Ahnengalerie,** hung with over 100 family portraits tracing the royal lineage, and the spectacular **Renaissance Antiquarium,** the oldest room in the palace, replete with stun-

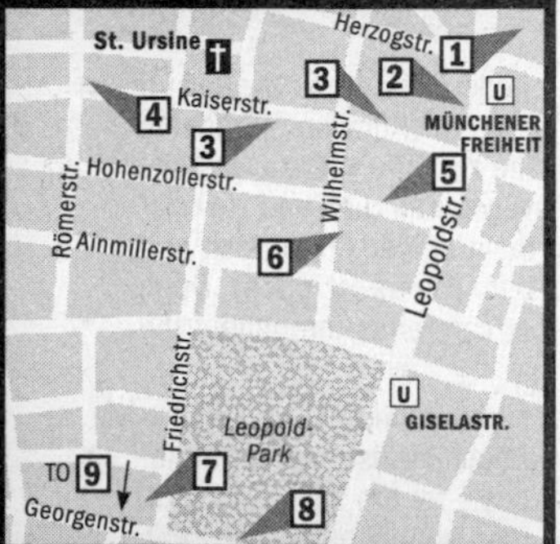

YOUNG SCHWABING: THE MUNICH BOHÈME

In 1900, the Schwabing quarter of Munich was home to the blossoming community of artists and writers who developed Jugendsti[redacted]entral Europe's version of Ar[redacted]ouveau. Leaving ornate and classical styles behind, this revolutionary movement—headlined by Vassily Kandinsky and Paul Klee—was the first of the 20th century to break completely with tradition. Named after Munich's bohemian magazine *Die Jugend (The Youth)*, the style celebrated the curvilinear floral motifs and bright colors that can still be spotted on Schwabing's facades.

1. Erlöserkirche, Ungererstr 13. The first Jugendstil church, built 1899-1901, has green ceiling decor, a baptismal font, Jugendstil column-tops, a clock, and a cock on the roof. (U3 or 6 to "Münchener Freiheit." Open M-Th and Sa 8am-5pm.)

[redacted]**eopoldstr. 77** has a floral facade that's worth checking out.

ning frescoes and statuary. *(Max-Joseph-Pl. 3. U3-6 to "Odeonspl." ☎089 29 06 71; www.residenz-muenchen.de. Open daily from Apr. to mid-Oct. 9am-6pm; from late Oct. to Mar. 10am-4pm. Last admission 30min. before closing. German-language tours meet outside the museum entrance Su at 11am. €6, students €5, under 18 free.)*

HOFGARTEN. Behind the Residenz, the beautifully landscaped Hofgarten shelters a small temple where couples gather on Sunday afternoons for free swing dancing. The **Schatzkammer** (treasury), which shares the same entrance as the Residenz, contains the most precious religious and secular symbols of Wittelsbach power: crowns, swords, crosses, and reliquaries collected during the Counter-Reformation to increase the dynasty's Catholic prestige. A comprehensive free audio tour of both the Schatzkammer and the Residenz is available in five languages. A collection of **Egyptian art** is also housed on the premises. *(Treasury open same hours as Residenzmuseum. €6; students, seniors, and group members €5; under 18 free. Combination ticket to Schatzkammer and Residenzmuseum €9, students and seniors €8. Art collection ☎089 28 92 76 30. Open Tu-F 9am-5pm, Sa-Su 10am-5pm. €5, students and seniors €4, under 18 free, Su €1.)*

ENGLISCHER GARTEN. Stretching majestically along the city's western border, the Englischer Garten (English Garden) is the largest metropolitan public park in the world, dwarfing both New York's Central Park and London's Hyde Park, offering everything from nude sunbathing and bustling beer gardens to pick-up soccer games and shaded bike paths. On sunny days, all of Munich turns out to fly kites, ride horses, and tan. Nude sunbathing areas are designated **FKK** (Frei Körper Kultur, or Free Body Culture) on signs and park maps. The main park ends with the **Kleinhesseloher See,** a large artificial lake, but the park extends much further and becomes ever more wild. If you look carefully you might see a roaming flock of sheep. There are several beer gardens on the grounds as well as a Japanese tea house, a Chinese pagoda, and a Greek temple. Daring Müncheners surf the white-water rapids of the Eisbach, the artificial river that flows through the park.

FRAUENKIRCHE. A vestige of the city's Catholic past and a symbol of Munich, the Frauenkirche towers were topped with their now-iconic domes in the mid-16th century. See the final resting place of Kaiser Ludwig der Bayer and take a German-language tour (€5) or ride the elevator to the top of the tower for the highest vantage point in the old city. *(Frauenplatz 1. Church open daily 7am-7pm. Free. Towers* *open Apr.-Oct. M-Sa 10am-5pm. Tours Apr.-Oct. Tu, Th, Su 2pm, €3.50, students €1.50, under 6 free.)*

ASAMKIRCHE. This small Rococo masterpiece commemorates Prague's patron saint, **John of Nepomuk,** who was thrown in the Moldau River on the orders of the Emperor for allegedly refusing to violate the confidentiality of confession. Gold, silver, and rich marble glimmer on almost every surface of this tiny, 11-pew marvel. Mesmerizing ceiling frescoes narrate the story in detail. To either side of the church stand the residences of the two Asam brothers, Cosmas Damian and Egid Quirin, who financed its construction. Their houses are still connected to the church balcony. *(Sendlinger Str. 32; 4 blocks down Sendlinger Str. from the Marienpl. Open daily 9am-5:30pm.)*

MARIENPLATZ. Sacred stone spires tower above the Marienpl., a major S- and U-Bahn junction and the social nexus of the city at the center of Munich's large pedestrian zone. The plaza, formerly known as Marktplatz, takes its name from the ornate 17th-century monument to the Virgin Mary at its center, the **Mariensäule,** which was built in 1638 and restored in 1970 to celebrate the city's near-miraculous survival of both the Swedish invasion and the plague. At the neo-Gothic **Neues Rathaus** (built in medieval style at the dawn of the 20th century), a **Glockenspiel** chimes with a display of a victorious Bavarian jouster. (Chimes daily 11am and noon; summer also 5pm.) At 9pm a mechanical watchman marches out and the Guardian Angel escorts the *Münchner Kindl* ("Munich Child," a symbol of the city) to bed. All of Munich's coats of arms are on the face of the **Altes Rathaus** tower, to the right of the Neues Rathaus, with the notable exception of the Nazi swastika-bearing shield. Hitler commemorated his failed 1923 Putsch in the ballroom, which is still in use for official functions. *(Tower open daily 10am-7pm. €2, under 18 €1, under 6 free.)*

TRACES OF MUNICH'S NAZI PAST. Amid Munich's Baroque elegance are visible signs of the Third Reich. Buildings erected by Hitler's regime stand as grim reminders of Munich's role as the ideological **Hauptstadt der Bewegung** (capital of the movement). The **Haus der Kunst,** built to enshrine Nazi principles of art, serves as a modern art museum (p. 348); swastika patterns have been left on the roof as a reminder of its origins. The gloomy limestone building now housing the **Hauptschule für Musik und Theater** was built under Hitler's auspices and functioned as the Führerbau, his Munich headquarters. The Munich Pact was signed here in 1938.

3. Bayrischer Revisionsverein, Kaiserstr. 14 and 29, display fruit and children, two typical elements of the Jugendstil style.

4. Römerstr 26 and 28 display cherubs and water, other common themes of Jugendstil.

5. Hohenzollernstr. 10 is pink, pink, pink.

6. Adam and Eve lie under a tree at Ainmillerstraße 22[redacted]he best-preserved Jugendstil [redacted]ding. Bourgeois contemporaries condemned the bright colors and threatening medusas when it appeared in 1899.

7. The floral motifs on **Friedrichstr. 3** imitate nearby Leopoldpark.

8. Georgenstr. 10, brightly decorated with medallions of artists, sits on a street named after Schwabing poet Stefan George, next door to the neo-Baroque **Pacelli-Palais** (Georgenstr. 8).

9. Founded in 1903, the pub **Alter Simpl,** Türkenstr. 57 (☎089 272 3083), was named after *Simplizissimus*, a Munich satirical review, which (together with *Die Jugend*) was the Schwabing crowd's newspaper of choice. *Weißbier* €3.10. Open Su-Th 11am-3am[redacted]-Sa 11am-4am. Cash only.

10. Villa Stuck museum (p. 348, not on map), a former Jugendstil mansion, displays the art of the movement and is a great way to cap off a Bohemian day.

At the Königsplatz, one block away from the Führerbau between the Antikensammlung and the Glyptothek Museums, thousands of books were burned on the night of May 10, 1933. Memorials dedicated to the **Weiße Rose** student movement, whose leaders were executed in Munich in 1943 for speaking out against the Third Reich, stand at the Ludwig-Maximilians-Universität and in the Hofgarten past the Staatskanzlei.

ON THE PERIPHERY

SCHLOSS NYMPHENBURG. Breathtaking Schloß Nymphenburg, modeled after Versailles, was built in 1662 and expanded upon in the two centuries that France dominated Europe. Now a museum chronicling the lives of Munich's rich and famous, the extravagant Rococo decor and the Neoclassical themes in the lavish two-story stone hall are reminiscent of Louis XIV's France, while the empire-style furniture in the electors' apartments is Napoleonic. The **Gallery of Beauties** is a fascinating collection of portraits of both noblewomen and commoners whom the king fancied (or slept with). Situated in the expansive landscaped gardens, the **Amalienburg,** the **Badenburg,** and the oriental **Pagodenburg**—all richly decorated, intimate manors— once held exclusive parties. *(Tram #17 (dir.: Amalienburgstr.) to "Schloß Nymphenburg." 15min. ☎089 17 90 80. Entire complex open daily Apr.-Oct. 15 9am-6pm, Oct. 16-Mar. 10am-4pm. Badenburg, Pagodenburg, and Magdalen hermitage closed in winter. Schloß €5, students €4. Manors €2/1. Entire complex €10/8; in winter €8/6. Under 18 free. English audio tours €3.50. Reduced prices for groups of 15 or more.)*

BOTANISCHER GARTEN. Next door to Schloß Nymphenburg, the immense Botanischer Garten sports rare and wonderful flora from around the world. Be sure to visit the greenhouses bursting with palms and orchids, an alpine lake, and other exotic landscapes. *(Tram #17 (dir.: Amalienburgstr.) to "Botanischer Garten." ☎089 17 86 13 12; www.botmuc.de. Open daily May-Aug. 9am-7pm; Apr. and Sept. 9am-6pm; Feb.-Mar. and Oct. 9am-5pm; Nov.-Jan. 9am-4:30pm. €4, students €2.50.)*

BMW-MUSEUM. A marvel of architectural daring, the enormous steel and glass spiral of the BMW museum houses state-of-the-art interactive exhibits detailing the history, development, and design of Bavaria's second-favorite export. Illuminated frosted glass walls and touch-sensitive projections lead visitors past engines, chassis, and concept vehicles with exhibits in both English and German. Visitors can also tour the adjacent production factory with a tunnel that runs through the entire production line, or enjoy the video games and customizable test cars in the **BMW Welt** building. *(Petuelring 130. U3 to "Olympiazentrum"; take the "Olympiaturm" exit and walk a block up Lerchenauer Str. The museum will be on your left. ☎089 18 02 11 88 22; www.bmw-museum.de. Open Tu-F 9am-6pm, Sa-Su 10am-8pm. Museum €12, students €6. Museum tours Tu-F 9am-4pm, Sa-Su 10am-6pm; €15, students €7.50. 2½hr. tours of the production facility €6, students €3.)*

OLYMPIAPARK. Built for the 1972 Olympic Games, the lush, green Olympiapark offsets the curved steel and transparent spires of the impressive Olympia-Zentrum complex as well as the 290m tall **Olympiaturm,** the tallest building in Munich. Three tours in English are available: the "Adventure Tour," an introduction to the history and construction of the entire park, leaves from April to October daily at 2pm from the Info-Pavilion, while a soccer stadium tour meets from mid-March to October daily at 11am. For more adventurous spirits, the **Roof Climb,** daily at 2:30pm, is a daring two-hour exploration of the Olympiastadion with a rope and hook. Tourists can also marvel at the view from the top of the Turm or attend outdoor events all summer, from flea markets (on Sa) to concerts, in the park itself. *(All tours meet at the north box office of the Olympic Stadium. Adventure tours €8, students and ages 6-15 €5.50. Soccer Stadium tour €6/4. Roof climb*

€39/29. Reserve ahead as tours may be cancelled due to events. For tower, take U3 to "Olympiazentrum." Tower open daily 9am-midnight. €4.50, ages 6-15 €2.80. Info pavilion ("Besucherservice") at skating rink ☎ 089 30 67 24 14. Open M-F 10am-6pm, Sa 10am-5pm.)

MUSEUMS

Munich has been a superb museum city ever since Ludwig I decided to make it into an "Athens on the Isar" in the 19th century. The **Münchner Volkshochschule** (☎089 48 00 62 29) offers many museum tours for €6. State-run museums (including the three *Pinakotheken*) are €1 on Sunday.

KÖNIGSPLATZ

This somewhat quiet neighborhood is home to a veritable buffet of art streching from antiquity to the present. Like all buffets, you can get too much of a good thing and be left feeling nauseated, so try to take in a few each day rather than all of them at once to truly appreciate Munich's vast artistic offerings. The three *Pinakotheken* have free detailed audio guides available in English; be sure to pick one up by the entrance.

PINAKOTHEK DER MODERNE. In a sleek metal and concrete museum designed by Munich's own Stephan Braunfels, this Pinakothek displays a rich collection of 20th-century art, particularly strong in "classical" modernism. Seminal works of Expressionism, Surrealism, Futurism, and Cubism share space with Jasper Johns, Gerhard Richter, Pablo Picasso, and engaging contemporary sculpture and video installations. The design section has something for everyone, tracing the development of design through history with innovative exhibits displaying everyday objects in a giant conveyer belt. The museum's two other departments feature graphic art and architecture. *(Barer Str. 40. U2 to "Königspl." Go right at Königspl. and left after 1 block onto Meiserstr. Walk 1 block to the museum. ☎089 23 80 53 60. Open Tu-W and F-Su 10am-6pm, Th 10am-8pm. €10, students €7.)*

NEUE PINAKOTHEK. Built by Ludwig I to house his private collection, the Neue Pinakothek is devoted entirely to 19th-century art. Special attention is given to German art and "overlooked" movements, with excellent Impressionist collections. It also features renowned Monet waterlilies and Van Gogh sunflowers. Look for the iconic portrait of Goethe by Joseph Karl Stieler. Follow the room numbers to get a sense of the progression of art during this period. *(Barer Str. 29, next to the Alte Pinakothek. ☎089 23 80 51 95. Open M and Th-Su 10am-5pm, W 10am-8pm. Tour M noon. €5.50, students €4.)*

ALTE PINAKOTHEK. Munich's finest 14th- to 18th-century art is on display at this world-renowned museum. Northern European artists are well represented, including Dürer, Cranach, Brueghel, Rembrandt, and Rubens. Look for Rubens' gigantic *The Last Judgment*—the museum's galleries were sized to accommodate this canvas. French, Italian, and Spanish masterpieces are also on display. *(Barer Str. 27. ☎089 23 80 52 16. Open Tu 10am-8pm, W-Su 10am-6pm. €7, students €5.)*

NEAR THE CITY CENTER

DEUTSCHES MUSEUM. The Deutsches Museum is one of the world's most comprehensive museums of science and technology. Exhibits include an early telephone, the work bench on which Otto Hahn first split an atom, and a recreated subterranean labyrinth of mining tunnels. The museum's 50+ departments cover over 17km. An English guidebook (€4) thoroughly explains all exhibits, though many signs have English translations. The **planetarium** shows educational films (4 shows per day; €2). Don't miss the aviation display featuring full-sized prop-planes and Leonardo da Vinci-esque flying machines, or the over 50 try-it-yourself (but not at home) experiments in the physics department. Finally, stroll through the fascinating sundial garden with a panoramic city view on the roof next to the planetarium. The museum also maintains an impressive **flight museum** in a WWI hangar in Schleißheim and a **transportation museum.** *(Museumsinsel 1. S1-S8 to "Isartor" or tram #18 to "Deutsches Museum." ☎089 21 791; www.deutsches-museum.de. Open daily 9am-5pm. €8.50, students €3, under 6 free. Flight museum: Effnerstr. 18. ☎089 315 71 40. S-Bahn to "Oberschleißheim," then follow signs. Open daily 9am-5pm. €5, students and seniors €3. Transportation museum: Theresienhöhe 14a. ☎089 500 8067 62. U4-5 to "Schwanthalerhöhe." Open daily 9am-5pm. €5, students and seniors €3. Combined admission to flight, transportation, and science museums €17.)*

VILLA STUCK. This elegant villa, designed by Munich artist Franz von Stuck, provides a sophisticated backdrop for paintings, design, and graphic art of the early 20th-century German **Jugendstil,** a movement that celebrated nature and the smooth lines of the body. Gold mosaic arches, marbled fireplaces, and recessed black ceilings offset the colorful landscapes and still lifes. *(Just over the bridge from the Englischer Garden. From Hauptbahnhof Nord, bus #100 (dir. Ostbahnhof) to Friedensengel. ☎089 45 55 510; www.villastuck.de. Open Tu-Su 11am-6pm. €9, students €4.50.)*

HAUS DER KUNST (HOUSE OF ART). Originally built by the Nazis as a "Hall of German Art" and a center for visual propaganda, this enormous building somehow survived the Allied bombing unscathed. Bucking the hyper-nationalism of its creators, the enormous blank walls now play host to the the many world-class, temporary exhibitions that pass through Munich. *(Prinzregentenstr. 1. U4 or U5 to "Lehel," then tram #17 for 1 stop (dir.: Effnerpl.) ☎089 21 12 71 13; www.hausderkunst.de. English tours Sa at 4pm. Open M-W and F-Su 10am-8pm, Th 10am-10pm. €7-8, depending on exhibit; students €5-6; ages 12-18 €2; under 12 free.)*

ENTERTAINMENT

THEATER AND OPERA

At the turn of the century, theater and opera were at the center of European intellectual life, and Munich was home to luminaries like Bertolt Brech. Today, 60 theaters speckle the city, putting on everything from the classics at the **Residenztheater** and **Volkstheater** to comic opera at the **Staatstheater am Gärtnerplatz** and experimental works at the **Theater im Marstall** in Nymphenburg. Standing room and student tickets run about €8. The **Hochschule für Music** on Arcisstr. also offers an unconventional assortment of free performances by the latest generation of German music. In **Schwabing,** Munich shows its bohemian face with scores of small fringe theaters, cabarets, and art cinemas. Munich's opera festival (usually in July) is held in the **Bayerische Staatsoper,** accompanied by a concert series in the Nymphenburg and Schließheim palaces. Don't miss the annual **Opera für Alle** (Opera for All), a free performance series conducted every year in mid-June as part of the opera festival. Each theater publishes its own *Monatsprogramm* (monthly program) detailing current performances, while *Munich Found* (in English, €3) lists schedules for Munich's stages, museums, and festivals. Look for student deals that provide a chance for even the most budget-wary backpacker to enjoy the same shows as Munich's monarchs.

Bayerische Staatsoper (National Theater), Max-Joseph-Pl. 2 (tickets ☎089 21 85 19 20; www.staatsoper.de). U3-U6 to "Odeonspl." or tram #19 to "Nationaltheater." Built by Max Joseph to bring opera to the people, this magnificent theater has soaring white balustrades, an enormous chandelier, and rich red velvet seating. Student tickets (€8) sold 1hr. before shows at the entrance on Maximilianstrand; 2 weeks in advance from the box office. Bring student ID and another form of ID—they do not accept ISICs. Box office, Marstallpl. 5, open M-Sa 10am-7pm and 1hr. before shows. Tickets can also be purchased online. No performances Aug.-Sept.

Gasteig Kulturzentrum, Rosenheimer Str. 5 (☎089 48 09 80; www.gasteig.de). S1-S8 to "Rosenheimerpl." or tram #18 to "Am Gasteig." The complex's 3 concert halls (and black box theater) rest on the former site of the Bürgerbräukeller—where Adolf Hitler launched his failed Beer Hall Putsch (p. 345)—and house a conservatory, music school, and the **Munich Philharmonic.** The complex also hosts the Munich Film Festival. Buy tickets online or in the Glass Hall of the Gasteig (open M-Sa 7am-11pm).

Staatstheater am Gärtnerplatz, Gärtnerpl. 3 (☎089 20 24 11, box office 089 21 85 19 60; www.staatstheater-am-gaertnerplatz.de). U1 or U2 to "Fraunhoferstr.," then follow Reichenbachstr. to Gärtnerpl. Stages everything from comic opera to jazz concerts. €8 student tickets must be purchased 2 weeks in advance. Standing room tickets available. Box office open M-F 10am-6pm, Sa 10am-1pm, and 1hr. before performances.

FILM

English films are usually dubbed in German—look for "OV" (original language) or "OmU" (subtitled) on the poster or in the listings. Munich's **Internationales Dokumentarfilmfestival** (www.dokfest-muenchen.de), an international documentary competition, takes place every year in early May. The broader **Filmfest München** (☎089 381 90 40; www.filmfest-muenchen.de) takes place in the summer. *In München* (see **Nightlife,** p. 350) and other publications list movie screenings.

Museum Lichtspiele, Lilienstr. 2 (tickets ☎089 48 24 03; www.museum-lichtspiele.de). 4 small theaters show an eclectic mix of small, independent films, old classics, and new Hollywood releases (most in English). Rocky Horror Picture Show screenings F-Sa at 11pm. Admission €6.50-7.50, M-Th students €5.50.

Cinema München, Nymphenburgerstr. 31 (☎089 55 52 55; www.cinema-muenchen.com). U1 to "Stiglmaierpl.," then 2 blocks west on Nymphenburgerstr. Plays English-language films almost exclusively; most are current and American. Sip a *Bier* (€2.50) during the movie to remember you're in Munich. Reserve tickets early online, as movies do sell out. €7-9, students €6-7. M-Tu and before 5pm W-Th €5.50.

MUSIC

Big-name pop stars perform at the **Olympiahalle** and the **Olympia-Stadion.** Follow the rest of the city to the Olympiapark on concert nights; you can relax on the grass and enjoy major artists for free.

Tollwood Festival (☎089 700 38 38 50 24; www.tollwood.de). Every year from mid-June to mid-July and from late Nov. to Dec., Munich's culture festival attracts a young German audience. Hundreds of concerts, theatrical productions, and circus performances compete for attention amid Oktoberfest-style tents serving delicacies, including Munich's own sweet nectar (beer). *Tollwood Magazine,* available from the tourist office, lists performances, many of which are free. U3 to "Olympiazentrum." Shuttle buses depart from "Westfriedhof" (U1) and "Scheidplatz" (U2 or U3). Open M-F 2pm-1am, Sa-Su 11am-1am.

Feierwerk, Hansastr. 39-41 (☎089 72 488 0; www.feierwerk.de). U4, U5, or S7 to "Heimeranpl." and left down Hansastr. (10min.) The center of Munich's concert scene, with 7 stages and huge tents. The buildings host indie rock, reggae, hip-hop, and electronica acts. Beer gardens open at 6pm. Box office open M-F 10am-1pm and 2-6pm.

NIGHTLIFE

In keeping with its penchant for breaking the mold, Munich's nightlife runs the gamut from exclusive, trend-defining clubs to underground caverns of alternative rebellion. You won't have to go far in Munich to find *Schicki-Mickis*—beautiful, expensively dressed, and coiffed specimens of both sexes. The city's streets bustle with raucous beer halls, loud discos, and outdoor cafes, particularly during the weekend when hard-working Germans let loose. Most locals begin their nights at a *Biergarten*, which generally close before midnight and are most crowded in the early evening. Alcohol keeps flowing at cafes and bars, which close their taps at 1am during the week. **Münchener Freiheit** (on the U3 and U6 lines) is the city's most famous (and most touristed) bar district. The bars, cafes, cabarets, and discos along **Leopoldstraße** in **Schwabing** attract tourists from all over Europe, though student-friendly prices and relaxed crowds lend the southwestern section of Schwabing, behind the university on **Amalienstraße** and **Türkenstraße,** a more low-key feel. High-end venues dot **Maximilianstraße** in the city's theater district. The old town center is filled with tourists and caters to a more international crowd, while the eastern edge of the **Glockenbachviertel** hosts a treasure trove of undiscovered spots. Dress well for the city's more exclusive clubs (leave the shorts and flip-flops at home). Otherwise, try less central venues such as **Kultfabrik** (p. 352), **Muffathalle** (p. 352), and **Backstage** (p. 352). Pick up *Munich Found*, *In München*, or *Prinz* at newsstands to help you sort out the scene.

BEER HALLS AND GARDENS

Bavaria agreed to become a part of a larger Germany on one condition: that it be allowed to maintain its beer purity laws. Since then, Munich has remained loyal to six great labels: **Augustiner, Hacker-Pschorr, Hofbräu, Löwenbräu, Paulaner,** and **Spaten-Franziskaner,** which together provide Müncheners and tourists alike with all the fuel they need for late-night revelry. Four main types of beer are served in Munich: *Helles* (standard light beer with a crisp, sharp taste); *Dunkles* (dark beer with a heavier, fuller flavor); *Weißbier* (smooth, cloudy blond beer made from wheat instead of barley); and *Radler* or *Russ'n* ("shandy" or "cyclist's brew": half beer and half lemon soda with a light, fruity taste). Munich's beer is typically 5% alcohol, though in **Starkbierzeit** (the first two weeks of Lent), Müncheners traditionally drink *Starkbier*, a dark beer that is 8-10% alcohol. Daring travelers can go for a full liter of beer, known as a **Maß** (€5-7). Specify if you want a *halb-Maß* (.5L, €3-4); Weißbier is almost exclusively served in 0.5L sizes. While some beer gardens offer veggie dishes, vegetarians may wish to eat elsewhere before a post-meal swig. It's traditional to bring your own food to outdoor beer halls—drinks, however, must be bought at the *Biergarten*. Bare tables usually indicate cafeteria-style *Selbstbedienung* (self-service).

BAYERN

Augustiner Bräustuben, Landsberger Str. 19 (☎089 50 70 47; www.augustiner-braustuben.de). S1-S8 to "Hackerbrücke." Walk to the far side of the bridge to Landsberger Str. and take a right. In the Augustiner brewery's former horse stalls. With a candlelit interior and some of the cheapest beer in the city (*Maß*; €5.10), this relatively undiscovered beer hall is the perfect place to share laughs over heaps of Bavarian food at great prices (€5-9) either inside or on the recently completed roof terrace. Devoted carnivores should try the *Bräustüberl* (duck, two cuts of pork, *Kraut,* and two types of dumplings; €10). Open daily 10am-midnight; kitchen open daily 11am-11pm. MC/V.

Hirschgarten, Hirschgarten 1 (☎089 17 999 119, www. hirschgarten.de). Tram #17 (dir.: Amalienburgstr.) to "Romanpl." Walk south to the end of Guntherstr. The largest *Biergarten* in Europe (seating 8000), tucked away in a small park just outside the city center, is boisterous and always crowded. Families come for the grassy park and carousel, and to see the deer still kept on the premises. Entrees €6-18. *Maß* €6. Open daily 9am-midnight; kitchen open until 10:30pm. MC/V.

Zum Flaucher, Isarauen 8 (☎089 723 2677; www.zum-flaucher.de), U3 to "Brudermühlstr." Walk down Brudermühlstr, follow street signs to "Nürnberg," and take a right just over the bridge onto the wooded path. At the next bridge, turn left and follow signs to "Zum Flaucher"; it's on the right. Gorgeous 2000-seat *Biergarten* near the banks of the Isar and riverside bike path. Lift a *Maß* (€6.50-6.80) with locals relaxing near the water, or join one of the pickup soccer games. Try the individually made *Leberkäse* (€3.80). Open May-Oct. daily 10am-midnight, Nov.-Apr. Sa-Su 10am-9pm. Cash only.

Chinesischer Turm (☎089 38 38 73 19, www.chinaturm.de), in the Englischer Garten right next to the pagoda. U3 or U6 to "Giselastr." or bus #54 from Südbahnhof to "Chinesischer Turm." A fair-weather tourist favorite with bustling tables, massive pretzels, and plenty of Bavarian charm. Live brass band music drifts from the pagoda throughout the park. *Maß* €6.80. Open daily in balmy weather 10am-midnight. MC/V above €20.

Augustinerkeller, Arnulfstr. 52 (☎089 59 43 93, www.augustineerkeller.de), at Zirkus-Krone-Str. S1-S8 to "Hackerbrücke." From the Hauptbahnhof, make a right on Arnulfstr. Founded in 1824, Augustiner is widely viewed as the finest *Biergarten* in town, with enormous pretzels and dim lighting beneath 100-year-old chestnut trees. Clinking beer glasses resound as early as 11am at this local favorite. The real attraction in the more expensive restaurant at the entrance is the sharp Augustiner beer (*Maß*; €6.70). Bavarian specialties €7-19. Open daily 10am-1am; hot food served until 10pm. *Biergarten* cash only. Restaurant AmEx/MC/V.

BARS

Many of the cafes in Munich double as night spots, serving drinks after dark.

K & K Klub, Reichenbachstr. 22 (☎089 20 20 74 63; www.kuk-club.de). U1-U2 to "Frauenhoferstr." Subdued walls, cube seats, and a large projection screen playing art films attract a young, artsy crowd. Sip a beer (€3.40) or slam a shot (€2.50) against the orange glow of the illuminated tribal symbols and retro video games (€0.50). Local DJs play electro, indie, and house M-Sa. Open M-W and Su 8pm-2am, Th-Sa 8pm-5am. Cash only.

Cafe Am Hochhaus, Blumenstr. 29 (☎089 058 152, www.cafeamhochhaus.de). U1-U3 or U6 to "Sendlinger Tor." Sometimes a dance party, sometimes a relaxed cafe with quirky wallpaper, the mood at this popular bar changes nightly with the crowd. Live DJs spin everything from funk to house starting at 10pm. Open daily 8pm-3am or even later. Cash only.

Killian's Irish Pub and Ned Kelly's Australian Bar, Frauenpl. 11 (☎089 24 21 98 99 and 24 21 99 10). U3 or S1-S8 to "Marienpl."; behind the Frauenkirche. 2 venues in 1, with live music daily, Irish and Australian fare, and live sports. Low-key, mostly international travelers come to hang out in the relaxed atmosphere amid crocodile-head stools and Celtic patterns. Come sample the best Guiness in Munich (€4.40) or some of the cheap lunch options inside (€4-5.50). Open M-Sa 11am-late, Su noon-late. AmEx/MC/V.

Holy Home, Reichenbachstr. 21 (☎089 201 45 46), U1-U2 to "Sendlinger Tor." Throw back a beer (€3.20) or mixed drink (€7.50) with Munich's up-and-coming artists and musicians in a sea of red and gold. DJs play everything from jazz to electro. Open M-W and Su 7pm-1am, Th-Sa 7pm-3am. Cash only.

Frenzy, Frauenhoferstr. 20 (☎089 20 23 26 86; www.frenzy-family.de). U1-U2 to "Frauenhoferstr." The funky pink and green interior serves breakfast (€3-9), pan-Asian specialties (€7-9), and coffee to visitors during the day. At night, the turquoise stools accommodate a crowd of young locals casually sipping beer (€3.20) beneath the Munich night sky. Open M-Sa 9am-1am, Su 9am-midnight. Cash only.

CLUBS

In adjacent lots lie **Kultfabrik,** Grafinger Str. 6 (☎089 49 00 90 70; www.kultfabrik.info), and **Optimolwerke,** Friedenstr. 10 (☎089 45 06 920; www.optimolwerke.de), two massive complexes that provide nocturnal venues of all kinds. Take U5 or S1-S8 to "Ostbahnhof," then follow the constant stream of people onto Friedenstr. and Grafingerstr. Hours, covers, and themes vary. All clubs have relaxed door policies, particularly in the summer. Optimolwerke, with 15 clubs, is smaller and caters to a slightly older crowd (mid-20s to early 30s). **Club Duo** (☎089 40 28 73; www.clubduo.de) is one of the best-established and hippest venues, playing 70s disco music and house as partiers surround an abandoned cop car. (Open M-Sa.) Kultfabrik features 21 clubs and attracts a crowd in its late teens and mid-20s. Party the Russian way at **Kalinka** (☎089 40 90 72 60; www.clubkalinka.tk), recognizable by its 7 ft. bust of Lenin. Choose from 100 types of vodka and dance to techno under the hammer and sickle. (Open F-Sa.)

Muffathalle, Zellstr. 4 (☎089 45 87 50 10; www.muffathalle.de), in Haidhausen. Tram #18 (dir.: St. Emmeram) to "Deutsches Museum." This former power plant is the venue for techno, hip-hop, spoken word, jazz, and dance performances. The massive performance hall hosts international DJs and artists, while the attached beer garden and cafe provide a more relaxed venue for enjoying the evening. Cover from €5, though many events are free. Check the website for aschedule. Buy tickets online or through München Ticket. Open M-Sa 8pm-3am, Su 4pm-1am.

Backstage, Wilhelm-Hale Str. 38 (☎089 126 6100; www.backstage089.de). Tram #16 or 17 to "Steubenpl." or bus #132 to Wilhelm-Hale Str. Underground scene, playing hardcore, rock, and electronica. Local crowd reflects the evening's act. The best beer deal in town: *Maß* €2 from 7-11pm. *Biergarten* also shows movies and soccer games. Check online for concert listings. Open M-Th and Su 7pm-3am, F-Sa 7pm-5am.

Atomic Cafe, Neuturmstr. 5 (☎089 228 3052; www.atomic.de). The Bavarian take on mod glory. Sticks to 60s and 70s beats, avoiding disco. Young audiences come for live Britpop, R&B, ska, and reggae. Beer €4 for ½L. Cover €3-7. Happy hour 10-11pm, 9-10pm on concert nights, mixed drinks €6. Open W-Th 10pm-3am, F-Sa 10pm-4am. Cash only.

GAY AND LESBIAN MUNICH

Although Bavaria has a reputation for traditionalism, gay nightlife thrives in Munich, centering around **Müllerstraße** and **Gärtnerplatz** in the **Glockenbachviertel,** and stretching from south of Sendlinger Tor through the Viktualienmarkt/Gärtnerpl. area to the Isartor. The crowd is mostly late 20s to 40s. Pick up *Sergej*, Munich's "scene magazine," at **Max&Milian Bookstore,** Ickstattstr. 2 (☎089 260 3320; open M-Tu and Th-F 10:30am-8pm, W 10:30am-2pm and 3:30-8pm, Sa 11am-4pm) for listings of gay hot spots. Also try *Our Munich*, available at the tourist office (see **Practical Information,** p. 333). **Schwules Kommunikations und Kulturzentrum,** Müllerstr. 43 (www.subonline.org), offers an array of services as well as a cafe and library for gay men. (Info ☎089 260 3056, staffed daily 7-11pm; **violence hotline** ☎089 192 28, daily 10am-7pm. Some English spoken. Center open M-Th and Su 7-11pm, F-Sa 7pm-midnight.) For resources for lesbians, call **Lesbentelefon.** (☎089 725 42 72. Open M and W 2:30-5pm, Tu 10:30am-1pm, Th 7-9pm.)

Morizz, Klenzestr. 43 (☎089 201 6776). U1 or U2 to "Frauenhofer Str." Subdued ambient lighting and stylish decor create an intimate interior that attracts a mixed crowd. Settle into the chic low chairs for a mixed drink (€7.60-8.50) and upscale Thai dishes (€6-15), served until 12:30am. Open M-Th and Su 7pm-2am, F-Sa 7pm-3am. MC/V.

Bau, Müllerstr. 41 (☎089 26 92 08; www.bau-munich.de). U1 or U2 to "Fraunhoferstr." Broad rainbow stripes on the door and posters of leather-clad men on the walls suit the heavy-duty construction theme of this gay club and bar. No mixed drinks—only beer (€2.70) and liquor (€2.50). Drinks buy 1 get 1 free M 8-10pm; €1 shots every Th 8-10pm and 1-3am. Open daily 8pm-4am. AmEx/MC/V.

Cafe Selig, Hans-Sachs Str. 3 (☎089 23 88 88 78; www.einfachselig.de). U1 or U2 to "Fraunhoferstr." Sleek wooden tables and striking red contemporary art attract a diverse crowd (all sexual orientations by day, mostly gay Sa-Su and at night) to this chic locale. The modern cafe and bar also serves international coffees, homemade cakes, and strudel (€3-7). Open M and W-Sa 9am-late. AmEx/MC/V.

Inges Karotte, Baaderstr. 13 (☎089 201 06 69). U1 or U2 to "Frauenhoferstr." or S1-S8 to "Isartor." This small lesbian bar attracts an eclectic, friendly crowd with *Schlager* set to techno beats and carousel horses suspended from the ceiling. Open M-Sa 6pm-1am, Su 4pm-1am. Cash only.

Kr@ftakt, Thalkirchenstr. 4 (☎089 21 58 88 81; www.kraftakt.de). Munich's only gay internet cafe features a bar and a street cafe, popular for breakfast (3-9am) and brunch. The simple but stylish cafe with minimal black tables and airy windows attracts a mixed clientele who come here more to socialize than to check email. Internet €1 per 30 min. Free Wi-Fi. Happy hour W-Th 7-9pm (beer €1); all mixed drinks €4 Th 7-10pm. Open M-Th and Su 10am-1am, F-Sa 10am-3am. MC/V.

OKTOBERFEST

Every fall, colonies of tourists make an unholy pilgrimage to Munich to drink and be merry in true Bavarian form. From noon on the penultimate Saturday of September through early October, participants chug five million liters of beer after eating 200,000 Würste. Oktoberfest is the world's largest folk festival—in fact, it has gotten so large (and sometimes out of hand) that the city of Munich has stopped advertising it. Those who plan on attending better have some close Bavarian friends with extra beds, as most budget accommodations are booked up to a year in advance and prices can double or triple depending on the venue.

Oktoberfest began on October 12, 1810, to celebrate the wedding of the future king Ludwig I of Bavaria. Representatives from all over Bavaria met outside the city gates, celebrating with a week of horse racing on fields they named **Theresienwiese** in honor of the bride (U4 or U5 to "Theresienwiese"). The bash was so much fun that Munich's citizens have repeated the revelry (minus the horses) ever since. An agricultural show, inaugurated in 1811, is still held every three years, and a panoply of carousels, carnival rides, and touristy souvenirs continues to amuse beer-guzzling participants.

The festivities begin with the **Grand Entry of the Oktoberfest Landlords and Breweries,** a parade that ends around noon with the ceremonial drinking of the first keg, to the cry of *O'zapft is!*, or "it's tapped," by the Lord Mayor of Munich. Other special events include international folklore presentations, a costume and rifleman's parade, and an open-air concert. Each of Munich's breweries set up tents in the Theresienwiese. The **Hofbräu tent** is the rowdiest. Arrive early (by 4:30pm) to get a table. You must have a seat to be served alcohol. Drinking hours are relatively short, about 10am to 10:30pm, depending on the day; fairground attractions and sideshows are open slightly later. Those who share a love of alcohol with their kin will appreciate the reduced prices on family days every Tu from noon-6pm.

DAYTRIPS FROM MUNICH

STARNBERG AM STARNBERGER SEE

From Munich, take S6 (dir: Tutzing) to "Starnberg" (30min., every 20min., €6.70 with Munich XXL card). The train stops right in the center of town. Tourist office Wittelsbacherstr. 2c (☎08151 90600; www.sta5.de). Open May-Oct. M-F 8am-6pm, Sa 9am-1pm.

The beautiful small town of Starnberg (pop. 16,000), situated at the northern end of the Stanberger See just 20km south of Munich, has been a favorite vacation spot for Germans since the Wittelsbach family named the city its summer destination of choice in the 16th and 17th centuries. Today, leafy forests and the shimmering waters of the pristine Sternberger See, capped by the magnificent Alps to the south, draw visitors to this oasis of quiet beauty.

The stunning **Saint Joseph Kirche,** Schlossbergstr. 3, is a short walk (5min.) uphill from the train station. Completed in 1770, the church's unique interior blends the styles of Baroque, Rococo, and Classical. Yellow arches and rainbow pastel columns support a frescoed ceiling. The white marble altar, designed by famed Rococo master Franz Ignaz Günther, epitomizes the ornate detail and penchant for precious metals that characterized the opulent movement. Outside, the meticulously manicured garden offers a breathtaking view of the city and lake below. (Free. Open 9am-6pm.) Just off the lake shore, three minutes west of the train station is the **Heimat Museum** (Local History Museum), Possenhofener Str. 5, which has fascinating exhibits that chronicle the city's maritime history. The museum leads visitors between the modern main building and the ancient **Lochmann-Haus** next door, where the floorboards date back to 1474. Also on display is the "Delphin," the last ship to be commissioned by Ludwig I, complete with glass cabin. The museum also displays a collection of local landscapes and still lifes and ancient religious artifacts and medical instruments. *(☎08151 44 77 570; www.museum-stanberger-see.de. €3, students €2. Open Tu-Su 10am-5pm. Cash only.)*

The **See Promenade,** stretching along the northwestern coast of the lake, is dotted with cafes, restaurants, and playgrounds. Visitors can join locals dipping their feet in the water along the boardwalk, or stretch out and soak up the sun on one of the many public docks in the area. **Bootverleih Schroop,** Seepromenade 4, offers the best value for renting boats in town. (☎08151 162 52. Motorboats from €17 per hr., rowboats from €9 per hr. Open daily 10am-7pm.) For more fun in the sun, head to the **Starnberger Wasserpark,** Strandbadstr. 5. From the station, head right on Bahnhofpl. Turn right under the train tracks onto Nepomukweg. Follow the signs to "Wasserpark" at the water's edge. With an outdoor beach and small playground, this complex is the perfect place to enjoy the fresh air and cool waters of the Starnberger See. The park also features an indoor pool, waterslide, and sauna. (☎0815 11 26 66; www.wasserpark-starnberg.de. Outdoor beach €3, students €2; indoor complex €4/2.50. Open M 10am-5pm, Tu-F 1-9pm, Sa-Su 8am-8pm.) Adventurous weekenders enjoy **balloon rides** (breathtaking in winter) from **Landstettener-Ballonfahrten,** Klosterholzweg 1. (☎0815 791 04; www.landstettener-ballonfahrten.de. From €180.) **Action & Funtours** organizes canoe, rafting, and biking trips. (☎0850 59 04; www.action-funtours.de. From €35.)

Cafes and restaurants dot the lakeshore, while more traditional beer gardens can be found up the hill in the town itself. For a quick bite, try the small, shaded eaves of **Cafe Restaurant City** ❷, Zweigerstr. 2. Generous portions of seafood, grilled specialties, and traditional Bavarian fare start at €5. (☎08151 64 10. Open daily 11am-11pm. Cash only.) **Undosa** ❹, Seepromenade 1, serves rich Italian and Bavarian fare (€11-16) on a Mediterranean-inspired terrace at the water's edge. Live music and a marble dance floor make it worth the splurge. (☎0815 199 8930; www.undosa.de. Open daily 10am-midnight. Cash only.)

DACHAU

From Munich, take S2 (dir.: Petershausen) to "Dachau" (20min., 4 stripes on the Streifenkarte or €6.70 with Munich XXL ticket), then bus #724 (dir.: Krautgarten) or #726 (dir.: Kopernikusstr.) from in front of the station to "KZ-Gedenkstätte" (10min., €1.10 or 1 stripe on the Streifenkarte; look for the red signs). Camp open Tu-Su 9am-5pm. Informative 2hr. English tours leave from the museum May-Sept. M-F 1:30pm, Sa-Su and holidays additional tours at noon; Oct.-Apr. Th, Sa-Su, and holidays at 1:30pm (€3). Basic 30min. introduction to the camp daily at 12:30pm, Sa-Su also at 11am; Oct.-Apr. only on Th, Sa-Su, and holidays (€1.50). Audio headsets in English, French, German, Hebrew, Italian, and Spanish are available inside the entrance to the camp for self-guided tours (€3, students €2). Small museum guides available in Dutch, English, French, German, Hebrew, Hungarian, Polish, Russian, and Spanish €0.50; call ☎08131 66 99 70 for more info. Commercial tours also available (p. 336).

TIP **BRING WATER.** Food and beverages are not available at Dachau. Pack water and a snack to prevent dehydration and stay energized.

The first thing prisoners saw as they entered Dachau was the inscription *Arbeit Macht Frei* (work will set you free) on the iron gate of the **Jourhaus,** the only entry to the camp. Dachau was the Third Reich's first concentration camp, opened in 1933 to house political prisoners on the former grounds of a WWI munitions factory. After Hitler visited the camp in 1937, it became a model for the construction of the more than 30 other camps throughout Nazi-occupied Europe and a training ground for the SS officers who would work at them. Dachau was primarily a work camp, as opposed to extermination camps like Auschwitz; during the war, prisoners made armaments and were hired out to work sites in the area. Many prisoners were worked to death. Those who volunteered for medical experiments in hopes of release were frozen to death or infected with malaria in the name of science. The barracks, designed for 6000 prisoners, once held 30,000 men—two of the buildings have been reconstructed for purposes of remembrance, but the rest have been destroyed. Walls, gates, and the camp's crematorium have also been restored in a chillingly sparse memorial to the camp's victims. On the site of the memorial are Jewish, Catholic, Lutheran, and Russian Orthodox prayer spaces. The **Museum at the Dachau Memorial Site,** in the former administrative buildings, examines pre-1930s anti-Semitism, the rise of Nazism, the establishment of the concentration camp system, and the lives of prisoners through photographs, documents, videos, interactive exhibits and artifacts. Most exhibits have captions in English. A short, particularly graphic film (22min.) shows in English at 11:30am, 2, and 3:30pm. An additional display in the bunker chronicles the lives and experiences of the camp's prominent prisoners, including Georg Elser, the SS officer who attempted to assassinate Hitler in 1939.

ANDECHS MONASTERY AND BREWERY

From Munich, take S5 (dir.: Herrsching) to "Herrsching" (45min., use a €10 Gesamtnetz Tageskarte). Once in Herrsching, you have a number of options: the MVV bus runs only a few times a day, but there is also a private bus that runs every 30min. (10min., €2.20). You can also bike the 3.5km to Andechs, or take the picturesque hiking path, following the brown signs through the town along the stream. Keep following the stream along Kienbachstr., then Andechstr., at the end of which, opposite a golden Madonna on a column, you can turn left onto the Kientalstr., a path that follows the river Kien through a wooded valley, or turn right and follow the (harder to find) scenic route. About 50min.

Andechs, atop Heiligenberg hill on the Ammersee, has been a pilgrimage destination since the Middle Ages, due in part to its valuable collection of reliquaries. Its first cloister dates to 1392, but it gained notoriety in 1455, when Albrecht III founded a Benedictine monastery here. Albrecht is buried at Andechs, along with a number of 20th-century Wittelsbachs. Shut down during the 1803 secularization of all church property, Andechs was bought back by Ludwig I for an outrageous sum and reopened in 1843. Twenty-three monks are current members of the monastery; seven of them live on the hill. Guided tours of the sanctuary run M-F at noon. (Free. Group tours in English (min. 10 people) available by advance request; €4.50 per person.) The beautiful sundial and onion-topped domes of the pink and white **Andechs Church** sit stately atop the steep hill leading up to the monastery. The church was built after a fire in the 17th century destroyed its predecessor and refurbished in spectacular, full-blown Rococo for the 1755 tercentenary. The sprawling ceiling frescoes and gold accents complement the mural above the altar by Johann Baptist Zimmermann. (Free. Tower with panoramic view open M-Sa 9am-5pm, Su 12:15-5pm. €1.)

Modern-day pilgrims are motivated by the monks' famous **Andechs brew,** whose sale has financed the Benedictines' good works since 1455. German-language tours of the brewery, which produces 100,000 hectoliters of beer a year, take place Tu-Th at noon (€3.50). Andechs beer is delicious but uniquely strong: the *Helles* has an alcoholic content of 11.5%, and *Doppelbock Dunkles* reaches a dizzy 18.5%. Join the imbibing crowds of locals at the boisterous atmosphere and panoramic views of **Bräustüberl ❷**, featuring a terrace and savory pork cuts from €1.75 per 100g. The beer (*Maß* €5.20) is cheaper than in Munich, and the fresh-baked pretzels with butter from the monks' dairy farm are delicious. (☎081 52 37 62 61. Enormous pretzels €2.70, butter €0.70. Open daily 10am-8pm; hot dishes 11am-6:30pm. AmEx/MC/V.) If you prefer seated service, the Klostergasthof 4, offers entrees for €10-16 or a *Maß* €3.60. (☎08152 930 90. Open 10am-11pm; kitchen open until 10pm. MC/V.) The monks also make their own spirits, in four varieties (herbs, apples and pears, berries, and honey; €13.75 each). They're available at the **Klosterladen,** open Feb.-Dec. M-F 10am-5:30pm, Sa-Su 10am-6:30pm. Mind the Kien river on your way back. If you are still on your feet, gaze at the Ammersee from one of the ferries departing from Herrsching or take the bus to the **Starnberger See** (p. 353), home to the highest per capita income in the whole Federal Republic.

BAYERISCHE ALPEN (BAVARIAN ALPS)

On a clear Munich day, you can see a series of snow-covered peaks and forested slopes, a rugged terrain spanning from southeast Germany across Austria and into Italy. Ludwig II of Bavaria, the mad "Fairy-Tale King," built his idyllic palaces here, among mountain villages, glacial lakes, icy waterfalls, and world-class ski slopes. Castles, cows, and Christianity are some of the major players in the region—you'll see crucifixes high on mountaintops and hear the rattling of cowbells from across the valley. People still wear *Lederhosen*, and everyone seems to be on the way to a hike. Rail lines are sparse, but buses cover the gaps. For travel information, contact **Fremdenverkehrsverband Oberbayern,** Bodenseestr. 113, in Munich. (☎089 829 21 80. Open M-Th 9am-4pm, F 9am-12:30pm.)

FÜSSEN ☎08362

The word Füssen means "feet," an apt name for this little town (pop. 14,500) nestled in the foothills of the towering Bavarian Alps. Füssen's proximity to Ludwig's famed **Königsschlößer** (p. 360) draws hordes of English-speaking, camera-toting tourists, but Germans also vacation here to take advantage of the area's excellent hiking, biking, and watersports. Füssen's own castle, the **Hohes Schloß,** overlooks a sea of red-tiled roofs and the Lech River. Each night, its ghostly illumination is visible from the outdoor cafes of the Altstadt.

TRANSPORTATION AND PRACTICAL INFORMATION. **Trains** travel to: Augsburg (2hr., every hr., €17.10) and Munich (2hr., every hr., €21.40). Bus #9606 runs to Oberammergau (1hr.; M-F 5-8 per day, Sa-Su 3-6 per day; €7.60 with Tagesticket) and Garmisch-Partenkirchen (2hr., €7.60 with Tagesticket). For a **taxi,** call ☎08362 77 00 or 08362 62 22. Rent **bikes** at **Ski Sport Luggi,** to the left of the station. (☎08362 505 9155. First day €8, second day €7, subsequent days €6. Open Easter.-Oct. M-F 9am-6pm, Sa 9am-2pm.)

The **tourist office** is at Kaiser-Maximilian-Pl. 1. From the station, turn left and head into town. Cross the roundabout to the yellow building on the left behind the large stone fountain. The staff finds rooms for free, sells hiking maps (€3.30-7), and organizes guided hikes of the area (Sa mornings, only with *Kurkarte*). (☎08362 938 50; www.fuessen.de. As a designated *Kurort*, or "spa area," overnights in Füssen require a *Kurkarte* (€1.60). Though it seems an additional expense, the *Kurkarte* grants free admission or reduced prices at many tours, museums, and hikes in town. Open M-F 9am-6pm, Sa 10am-2pm, Su 10am-noon. The **police** station is at Herkomerstr. 17 (☎110), around the corner from the hostel. The **Bahnhof-Apotheke,** Bahnhofstr. 8, has a bell for night **pharmacy** service. (☎08362 918 10. Open M-F 8:30am-1pm and 2-6:30pm, Sa 8:30am-12:30pm.) Access the **Internet,** rent DVDs, and drink free coffee at **Videoland@Internet,** Luitpoldstr. 11. (€2 per 30min., €3 per hr. Open M-Sa 4-10pm, Su 4-8pm.) The **post office** is at the corner of Bahnhofstr. and Rupprechtstr. (Open M-F 8:30am-5:15pm, Sa 8:30am-noon.) **Postal Code:** 87629.

ACCOMMODATIONS AND FOOD. Füssen's **Jugendherberge (HI) ❷,** Mariahilfer Str. 5, shares a neighborhood with local homes, vacation condos, and some intrepid sheep and goats unaffected by the passing trains. Turn right from the station and follow the tracks for 15min. (☎08362 77 54. Laundry €1.60. Reception daily Mar.-Sept. 7am-noon and 5-10pm; Oct.-Apr. 5-10pm. Closed Nov. Lock-out 11pm-6:30am, access code available. Lockers require €1-2 deposit. €17.50, 2nd and 3rd nights €17, additional nights €16.50. Private rooms available; add €5 per person. MC/V.) **Pension Haslach ❷,** Mariahilfer Str. 1b, is only a few doors down from the youth hostel. Give the bell a ring and Grandma Haslach will poke her head out of the second-floor window to say whether her three small rooms with sinks and quaintly quilted beds are *frei* (free) or *belegt* (occupied). (☎08362 24 26. Singles €25; doubles €45. Cash only.)

Reasonably priced bakeries, butcher shops, and *Imbiße* (snack bars) stand among the pricier cafes on **Reichenstraße,** particularly off the **Luitpold Passage.** Be wary of establishments touting their "regional cuisine," which more often than not means wurst and french fries for €7. If you're trailbound, head to the **Plus** supermarket, on the right toward the rotary from the station. (Open

BAYERN

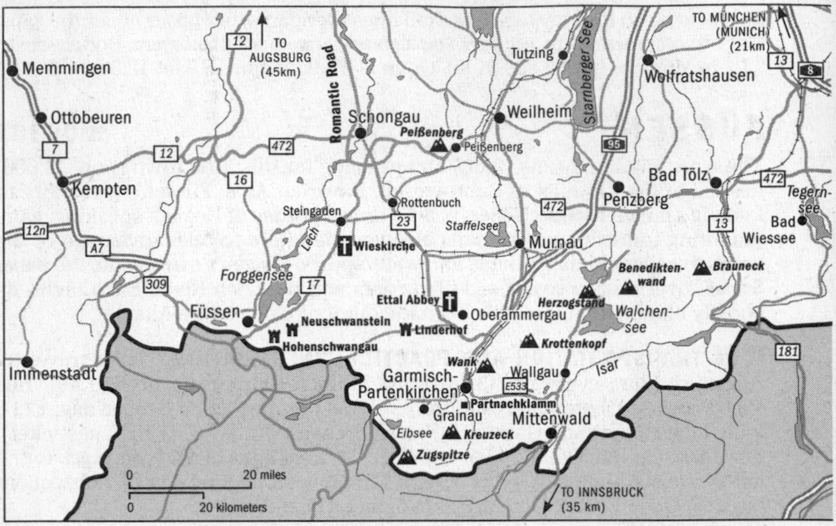

M-Sa 8am-8pm.) For lunch, stop at the **Markthalle ❶**, Schrannenpl. 1, an indoor marketplace in the town's old granary with stands selling fresh bread, fish, cheese, and wine. (Hot dishes from €3.50. Beer and wine from €2. Open M-F 9am-6:30pm, Sa 9am-2pm). Generous bowls of pasta and delicious pizzas can be found at **Il Pescatore ❸**, Franziskanergasse 13. Though the menu features pricier items, a wide variety of dishes are available for under €8. (Open M-Tu and Th-Su 11:30am-2:30am and 5pm-midnight.

SIGHTS. Füssen's very own castle, the **Hohes Schloß,** is the former home of the local prince-bishop, whose wealth and power left an indelible mark on the town and its architecture. Today, much of the *Schloß* is used for municipal offices, but visitors can enter the compound and see the castle from the exterior at no charge. The only way to enter the *Schloß* is by paying for admission to the **Staatsgalerie** (municipal gallery), which displays mostly religious art from the 15th-19th centuries. (☎08362 90 31 46. Open Tu-Su Apr.-Oct. 11am-54pm; Nov.-Mar. 1-4pm. €2.50, students €2, under 14 free. Tours in German W 2:30pm.) Down the hill from the castle is the Baroque **Sankt Mangkirche,** dating from the 9th century. An ancient fresco discovered during renovations in 1950 lights up the church's 10th-century subterranean crypt. The abbey hosts an 18th-century Baroque library. (☎08362 48 44. Tours year-round after Su services; Jan.-Oct. also Sa 10:30am; May-Oct. also Tu 4pm; July and Aug. also Tu and Th 4pm. Tours on demand Nov.-Dec.) The **Museum der Stadt** (City Museum) in the St. Mang's monastery details Füssen's history as a manufacturing center struck by flood, plague, and war. Walk through the museum to find the **Annakapelle,** a chapel devoted to commemorating victims of the bubonic plague, in which 20 macabre skeleton-decked panels depict everyone from the Pope and Emperor to the smallest child engaged in the *Totentanz* (dance of death). (☎08362 90 31 46. Open Tu-Su Apr.-Oct. 11am-5pm; Nov.-Mar. 1-4pm. €2.50, students and children €2. Tours in German Tu and Th 2:30pm.) A combined ticket to the Stadtmuseum and the Staatsgalerie (€3) can be purchased at either museum, except during special summer exhibitions.

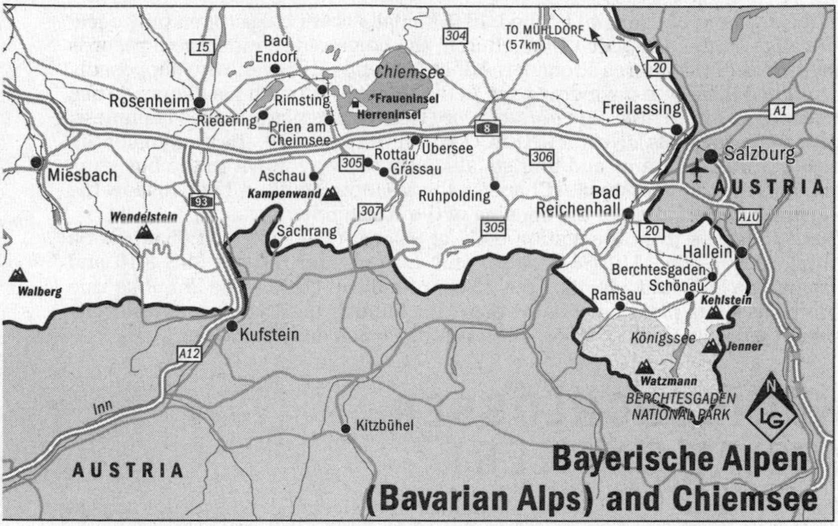

Bayerische Alpen (Bavarian Alps) and Chiemsee

OUTDOOR ACTIVITIES. The soaring mountains and alpine lakes that surround Füssen create some of the most beautiful terrain imaginable for biking, hiking, skiing, and boating. A popular excursion from Füssen is a 23km bike ride around the **Forggensee.** The ride takes you past kiosks selling snacks, farmers tilling their fields, and calm beaches where a few brave souls go for a dip in the cold Alpine water. For those who want to cycle halfway, a ferry, the **Forggensee Schifffahrt,** Weidachstr. 80, runs return trips to Füssen from 5 different spots on the far side. (☎08362 92 13 63; www.schifffahrt.fuessen.de. 11:15am to 5pm daily.) Boat rentals are also available on the numerous lakes surrounding Füssen—to take a canoe or kayak tour of the region, head to **Kanu Kini,** Weidachstr. 71. (☎08362 939 6969; www.kanu-kini.de. 2hr. tours €8. 5-hr. €20. Open May-Oct daily 9am-dusk.) Ride the **Tegelbergbahn** to the top of the 2000m peak in any season for a breathtaking view of the surrounding Alps. In summer, ride down the mountain on your own luge (€2.50). Weather permitting, rent skis or a snowboard (€14-16 for first day, €11-13 thereafter) and hit the slopes (€21 per day, students €19). (☎08362 983 60; www.tegelbergbahn is 15 min. away via bus 73 or 78 to "Tegelbergbahn." Buses leave M-F every hour from 8:15am-6pm. Open daily in summer 9am-5:30pm; in winter 9am-4:30pm. €9, students €8.50, children €4.50; round-trip €15/14/7.50.)

DAYTRIP FROM FÜSSEN: WIESKIRCHE. Count yourself lucky if your bus ride from Füssen or Oberammergau to the Ammergau Alps includes a brief stop at the **Wieskirche** (Church in the Meadows), a small gem set in the midst of yellow wildflowers. The Rococo pilgrimage church houses a relic from the Miracle of Wies in 1738, when the wood-and-cloth likeness of the Scourged Savior began to cry. The interior of the church is breathtaking, with a *troupe l'oeil* ceiling. The painter and sculptor collaborated to blend the gold-gilded ornaments into the frescoed walls and ceiling, blurring the line between the two- and three-dimensional worlds—see if you can spot the mischievous cherub poking his foot through the ceiling. Dominikus Zimmermann, the architect who built the church from 1746 to 1754, was so devoted to his work that he lived in the adjacent house until he died. In the small **Abbot's Lodge** (open only occasionally) on the east side of the church, the balustrade's monogram records the words of the church's founder, Abbot Marianus II Mayer, who supposedly scratched them into a window pane in the Prelate Hall with his diamond ring: *Hoc loco habit fortuna, hic quiescit cor* (Here in this place abides happiness; here the heart rests). Now a UNESCO World Heritage site, the church continues to attract pilgrams and tourists alike. On the way down to the bus stop, pop into the tiny **Wieskapelle** (Chapel in the Meadow), built in 1738, to view the illustrated celebration of the opening of the Wieskirche.

Bus #73 leaves from the station daily at 9:45am (M-F only), 11:05am (M-Sa only), 12:35, 1:05, 2:10 (M-F only), and 4:05pm, and returns M-F 3:10 and 3:50pm, Sa-Su 2 and 3:50pm. (1hr. €2.80, round-trip €5.60.) The 2hr. bike ride from Füssen is pleasant. Follow signs for Munich until you see Wieskirche signs. (☎08862 93 29 30; www.wieskirche.de. Open daily 8am-7pm.)

KÖNIGSSCHLÖSSER (ROYAL CASTLES)

Perhaps it was to his credit that Maximilian II neglected to educate his sons in the mundane affairs of government, allowing them to cultivate a taste for literature and the arts instead. With Max's untimely death, the royal line was left in the hands of his naïve 18-year-old son Ludwig II, a tragic figure often dismissed as a whimsical, but insane, boy-child. In truth, Ludwig was incurably isolated from those around him, burying his despair of modernity in castle plans and reading Schiller until the day before his death. A frenzied visionary and fervent Wagner fan, Ludwig created fantastic castles soaring into the alpine skies, a veritable fantasia inspired by scenes from the opera *Lohengrin*. Whether the king was actually crazy has never been determined—some claim that his detractors fabricated medical evidence—but in 1886 a band of upstart nobles and bureaucrats deposed Ludwig in a coup d'etat, had him declared insane, and imprisoned him in Schloß Berg on the Starnberger See, outside of Munich. Three days later, the king and his psychiatrist were discovered dead in the lake under mysterious circumstances—murder, suicide or a failed escape attempt, perhaps. The young King remains an adored Bavarian icon, his portrait still hanging proudly in the foyers of more traditional family homes. Thousands of tourists flock to his castles daily to explore the captivating enigma of Ludwig's life, death, and self-fashioned dream-world. As over-touristed and over-priced as they may seem, the castles are worth the trip.

HOHENSCHWANGAU AND NEUSCHWANSTEIN CASTLES

From the Füssen train station, bus #73 or 78 to "Königsschlößer" (10min.; 2 per hr.; €1.60, round-trip €3.10) stops in front of the information booth. (☎08362 81 97 65. Open daily 9am-6pm.) The Ticket-Service Center, Alpseestr. 12, is a short walk uphill on Alpseestr. A less-touristed path to Hohenschwangau starts from the left side of the information booth and meanders through the forest (10min.). Horse-drawn carriages run to Car Park D and Hotel Müller (uphill €3.50, downhill €1.50), and to Neuschwanstein (€5/2.50). To Neuschwanstein from Car Park D is the shortest but steepest trail to the top (20-40min.). After exiting Neuschwanstein, continue past the castle for Pöllat gorge and the Marienbrücke. The trail on the other side of the bridge winds through the gorge and back to the base of the hill (20min.; only in summer). Private buses run from Hotel Lisl to a point 5min. below Marienbrücke and 600m above Neuschwanstein (round-trip €2.60). A Tagesticket (€7.60) entitles castle-hoppers to unlimited regional bus use (not including the bus to Bleckenau); buy it on the bus. (☎08362 93 08 30; www.ticket-center-hohenschwangau.

de.) Both castles open daily Apr.-Sept. 9am-6pm; Oct.-Mar. 10am-4pm. Required tours, available in 10 languages, included in entrance fee. Apr.-Sept. Tours in German and English of each castle every 20min.; Oct.-Mar. every 30min. Ticket sales for Neuschwanstein Apr.-Sept. 8am-5pm; Oct.-Mar. 9am-3pm. Hohenschwangau ticket sales close 30min. later. Tickets for both may be purchased at the Ticket-Service Center. Arrive early in the morning, or you may wait many hours for your ticket and tour. Tickets can be reserved in advance for a €1.60 fee per ticket; call ☎08362 93 08 30. Each castle €9, under 18 free with an adult; students and seniors €8. Combination ticket €17/15.

Ludwig II spent childhood summers at **Schloß Hohenschwangau,** the bright yellow neo-Gothic castle rebuilt by his father on the site of a crumbling medieval fortress. It was no doubt within these frescoed walls that he acquired a taste for the romantic German mythology of the Middle Ages. After Maximilian II died, nocturnal Ludwig ordered servants to paint a night sky upon the royal bedroom ceiling. The vast constellations were inlaid with crystals so that the "stars" would twinkle when lit from above with oil lamps. The castle also houses the piano and bed that Richard Wagner used during his visits. Today, a 175-year-old loaf of bread survives, as well as a network of secret passageways.

Ludwig's desperate building spree across Bavaria peaked with the construction of glitzy **Schloß Neuschwanstein,** begun in 1869 to create jobs in a period of rising unemployment. Germany's most clichéd tourist attraction and the inspiration for Disney's Cinderella's Castle is as mysterious and paradoxical as Ludwig himself. The first sketches of the *Schloß* were reportedly drawn by a set designer, not an architect, and young Ludwig II lived to spend a mere 173 days in the extravagant edifice before he was betrayed by a servant and imprisoned. The palace mirrors Ludwig's untimely death; 63 rooms are unfinished, and the platform in the lavish throne room is eerily lacking a throne. Completed chambers include a neo-Gothic Tristan-and-Isolde bedroom, an artificial grotto, and an immense **Sängersaal** (Singers' Hall), an acoustic masterpiece built expressly for Wagnerian opera performances. Though the hall was never used in Ludwig's lifetime, concerts have taken place here since 1969, always in September (for more info, contact the Schwangau tourist office, ☎08362 819 80; www.schwangau.de). Almost all the castle walls are painted with scenes from Wagnerian operas; the king and composer were united in affection for Teutonic myth and tragic heroes, and Wagner acted as a confidante during the king's spells of uncertainty and abdication.

For the fairy godmother of all views, hike up to the **Marienbrücke,** spanning the **Pöllat Gorge** behind Neuschwanstein (10min.). Though some may flinch at crossing the circa-1860 bridge over a 149 ft. waterfall, those with stout hearts and legs can continue uphill from here for a view of the castle and nearby lake (1hr.). In the opposite direction, descend the mountain from Schloß Hohenschwangau to the lilypad-topped **Schwansee** (Swan Lake), the ballet's namesake. Follow the Schwansee-Bundweg path through fields of flowers to a beach and secluded swimming hole. The **Alpseebad,** the famous lake in the background of most Neuschwanstein publicity shots, is closer and more crowded, but still picturesque. Hang-gliders preparing for a jump and sane people alike ride the Tegelbergbahn cable car 1720m up to the top of the Tegelberg. The valley station is to the left of the castles as you face the mountain; some buses continue on from the castle stop. (☎08362 983 60. Open daily in summer 9am-5:30pm; in winter 9am-4:30pm. €9, students €8.50, children €4.50; round-trip €15/14/7.50.)

SCHLOSS LINDERHOF

Bus #9622 runs between Oberammergau and the park (9:50am-4:55pm). The last bus leaves Linderhof at 6:40pm (20min., every hr., €5.40 round-trip), but check the schedule. Hikers and cyclists can follow the path along the Ammer river to Linderhof (10km). From the Oberammergau tourist office head left on Eugen-Papst-Str.; when the road forks at the bridge, select the gravel bike path and follow signs to Linderhof. ☎08822 920 30; www.schlosslinderhof.de. Open daily Apr.-Sept. 9am-6pm; Oct.-Mar. 10am-4pm. Obligatory castle tours €7, students and seniors €6; Oct. 13.-Mar. only the palace is open. €6/5; under 18 free with an adult. Park open all day Apr.-Sept. Free. Lockers available to the left of the ticket office (€1).

Halfway between Füssen and Oberammergau is the exquisite **Schloß Linderhof,** Ludwig II's compact hunting palace, surrounded by a meticulously manicured park. Like Herrenchiemsee Palace, Linderhof's intricate design reflects Ludwig's admiration for the French Bourbon kings, in particular Louis XIV. Though it lacks Neuschwanstein's pristine exterior, the decadent interior is filled with royal goodies like **Meißen porcelain** and **Gobelin chairs.** The entire castle is slathered in 5kg of 24-carat gold leaf, except for the servants' room—they had to settle for silver. Across the ceiling in the entrance stretches the French Bourbon affirmation *Nec pluribus impar,* which loosely translates to "I'm too sexy for democracy." Living up to this motto, the royal bedchamber is unbelievably lush, with gold leaf and a crystal chandelier that weighs half a ton. Dark blue (the king's favorite color) velvet encases the bed, specially made to fit the 6'4" king. Ludwig, "the Dream King," was almost entirely nocturnal, waking at dusk and returning to bed after his breakfast, because he strongly disliked sunlight. He was also known for sequestering himself, fueling the myth that he had his dining table raised and lowered on a lift from the servants' quarters. The malachite tables were gifts from Russian Tsarina Marie Alexandrovna, who tried to match Ludwig (a "confirmed bachelor" to his death) with one of her daughters. Ludwig kept the tables and rejected the girls. The final room of the tour is the irregularly shaped **Spiegelsaal.** Mirrors cover the walls, making the elaborate ivory-chandeliered room appear to stretch into infinity.

More impressive than the palace itself is the magnificent park surrounding it. The force of water cascading down steps behind the palace mechanically powers the fountain in front. Once an hour, the dam is opened, and water shoots higher than the top of the building. To the right of the palace is an artificial grotto; red and blue floodlights illuminate trellises and stalagmites. A subterranean lake and floating lettuce-leaf boat complete Ludwig's personal 19th-century Disney ride. There are brilliant red-and-blue stained-glass windows on the **Maurischer Kiosk,** an elaborate, mosque-inspired building and the only sight on the grounds not built expressly for Ludwig. He saw it at the 1867 World Exposition in Paris and liked it so much that he had it brought home. Within these walls, Ludwig would sit on the peacock throne, smoke his water pipe, and order his servants to dress up in costumes and read him tales from *1001 Nights.* Under the right moon, Ludwig the Sultan would even throw midnight Turkish orgies. The path down the hill to the left (20min.) leads to the reconstructed **Hunding-Hütte,** modeled after a scene in Wagner's *Die Walküre* from *Der Ring des Nibelungen.* In another of Ludwig's flights of fancy, bearskin-covered log benches surround a tree that is—surprise—artificial.

BERCHTESGADEN NATIONAL PARK

The paintings of Romantic artist Caspar David Friedrich have impressed the iconic image of the Watzmann peak upon every German's mind. For centuries, the mountain—and the sparkling blue lakes and deep forests surrounding it—was dominated by herdsmen and shepherds. Soon artists, then tourists, flocked to these mountains, and the herdsmen became pension owners and guides. The park now hosts multitudes of weekend adventurers in addition to seasoned outdoor explorers, who are offered everything from mountain biking and hiking to skiing, rafting, bobsledding, and paragliding. The park accommodates the seemingly endless number of activities and trails through high alpine pastures and the forest areas designated to remain untouched by human hands.

BERCHTESGADEN NATIONAL PARK AT A GLANCE

AREA: 210 sq. km. Lowest point 413m at the bottom of the Königssee, highest point 2713m at the summit of Mt. Watzmann.

CLIMATE: Snowy winters, rainy springs, cool (16°C/60°F) summers. Cold at higher elevations, temperate in valleys.

CAMPING: Strictly forbidden. A system of alpine huts accommodates outdoor enthusiasts within the park.

FEATURES: Extensive forest, steep rock faces, sparkling glacial lakes.

FEES AND RESERVATIONS: There are no entrance or trail fees. Parking starts at €2 per day. Reservations not usually needed for huts, are wise in summer.

HIGHLIGHTS: Hiking through the Magic Forest, breathtaking views of the Königssee, the summit of the Watzmann.

ORIENTATION

Berchtesgaden National Park is a German peninsula jutting into a sea of Austrian Alps. To the north, it borders the towns of Berchtesgaden, Ramsau, and Schönau. The park and its environs extend along three valleys. The fjord-like **Königssee valley** holds the ski-friendly Jenner and the notoriously challenging Kehlstein to the east. The mighty **Watzmann,** the highest peak in the park and second-highest in the country (2713m), sits along the valley's western edge. According to legend, the cruel King Watzmann was turned into stone, and now looks down on Berchtesgaden with his wife and seven children—the **Kleiner Watzmann** and Watzmann Kinder peaks—by his side. On the far side of the Watzmann range is the **Wimbach valley,** overlooked by the **Hochkalter** on the west. The third valley contains the alpine **Hintersee,** starting above Ramsau and cutting its way through the Klausbach valley, where the only public bus in the park circulates. At the convergence of the three valleys in the south lie the Steinernes Meer massif and a number of Austrian peaks, with the Austrian town of Maria Alm in the valley on the south side of the peaks. The park's major rivers, ideal for rafting, are the **Königsseer Ache** and the **Ramsauer Ache,** which combine at the city's edge to form the Berchtesgadener Ache.

TRANSPORTATION

Cars are not allowed into the park, with the exception of those bringing supplies to the many *Alpenhütte* (huts) scattered throughout. Several roads on the park's outskirts lead to trailheads and nearby villages. The **boat** across the Königssee or the **bus** along the Klausbachtal are your best bet to penetrate the depths of the park. Good bases outside the park include **Berchtesgaden, Ramsau,** and **Schönau.** Berchtesgaden can be reached by bus and train, and offers bus connections to both Ramsau and Schönau. Once within the park, more than 200km of well-marked hiking trails extend along the reserve's glacial-cut valleys and jagged moutain peaks. Some are navigable by **mountain bike** in the summer, others by **touring skis** in the winter. You can start a hike from just about anywhere—trails run from every town, crisscrossing each other. If arriving by car, the parking lot at the end of Königsseerstr. in Schönau (€3 per day, €2 with

Kurkarte) or one of the many smaller trailhead parking lots (€1-3 per day) are ideal starting points for hikes.

PRACTICAL INFORMATION

Emergency: Police ☎110. **Fire** and **ambulance** ☎112. For a hiking accident, you can also call ☎08652 192 22. If you have hiked into Austria, call ☎144. To send a distress signal, repeat a loud noise or visual signal 6 times in 1min., followed by a 1min. pause, then repeat. The response is a signal 3 times per min. Official visual signals include flashing a red scarf or raising both arms above your head in a Y formation. Standing with 1 arm raised and the other at your side signifies that you do not need assistance.

National Park Information Centers: While the main National Park info center in Berchtesgaden offers the best starting point for serious adventures, tourist offices in towns bordering the reserve are also well versed in the area's geography and distribute free maps. In addition, unmanned information centers located at many of the trailheads throughout the park offer maps as well as exhibits on the park's flora and fauna. Hikers will appreciate the green *Berchtesgadener Alpen für Wanderer und Bergsteiger* map (€6.50), which labels all hiking routes with numbers corresponding to signposts throughout the park, and shows the location of all of the *Alpenhütte* (alpine huts; see **Accommodations**) and *Gaststätte* (restaurants). The free brochure **Berg und Tal,** at the tourist office, offers extensive descriptions of hiking trails for every difficulty level including elevation maps, points of interest, and info about accommodations (in German).

Nationalpark-Haus, Franziskanerpl. 7, Berchtesgaden (☎08652 643 43; www.nationalpark-berchtesgaden.de). From the main train station, turn right and follow the "Zum Markt" signs up the stairs, across the bridge, and up the small gravel path to Maximilianstr., which runs through Franziskanerpl. The info center is on the right overlooking the Bahnhof. A must for anyone interested in outdoor activities—the well-informed staff offers personalized recommendations on excursions into the park speckled with insider secrets and local knowledge. Check out the interactive exhibits, including a 3D map of the reserve and a panoramic picture of the park. Open daily 9am-5pm.

Deutscher Alpenverein (German Alpine Club), Maximilianstr. 1, Berchtesgaden (☎08652 22 07; www.DAV-Berchtesgaden.de). From the Nationalpark-Haus, turn right and follow the street for about 500m; look for the small, wooden building on the right at the edge of the Kurgarten. Exceptionally friendly mountain veterans offer advice on outings into the park and sell memberships that get you discounts on many of the *Alpenhütte* within the park. Open Tu and Th-F 3-5:30pm.

Hintersee, Hirschbichlstr. 26 (☎08657 14 31), at the foot of the Klausbach valley. Offers info on hiking trails and weather updates as well as rotating exhibits on wildlife and the forest ecosystem. Open daily 9am-5pm.

Tours: The park service leads free **Wanderführungen** (guided nature hikes) in German throughout the year. Check the *Wandern Sommerprogramm* brochure at the Nationalpark-Haus for days, times, and meeting points. Tours in English sometimes available for groups of 7 or more for a fee; advance notice required.

Fees and Reservations: Entrance to the park and all hikes are free. Camping within the park is forbidden, along with all forms of fire, including campfires and camp stoves. Reservations are helpful but usually not required for the *Alpenhütte.*

Parking: Available in the lot at the end of Königsseerstr. in Schönau (€3 per day) and at trailheads throughout the park (around €2 per day; check map for locations).

Gear: Sport M+R Brandner in Berchtesgaden or Ramsau. Both rent **bikes** and stock hiking boots and other equipment. Rent **skis** at the **M+R Brandner, Intersport** in Berchtesgaden, or the **Ski School Berchtesgaden-Jenner** (☎086 52 66 710). A listing of 15+ additional rental locations servicing all of the major ski areas is also available at the Berchtesgaden, Ramsau, or Schönau tourist offices (ask for the *Winter activ* brochure).

Climate and Seasonality: During winter, the park sleeps under many feet of snow. In early summer it rains almost every day. Summer brings the warmest weather; average July temperature is around 16°C (60°F) and about 4°C warmer in valleys. Autumn is also beautiful, with forests ablaze in color. For current weather information, call ☎08652 96 72 97 or check www.dwd.de.

ACCOMMODATIONS

The National Park is an easy day trip from the bordering towns. If you want to try longer routes or stay up in the high country, 21 *Alpenhütte*—simple cabins offering food and a bed for €10-20—are scattered throughout the park. These are the only authorized accommodations within the park boundaries and are usually open from the end of May until October. Don't expect many comforts; you'll be squished next to others on mattresses on the floor, or in a bed for more money. Sheets are an unreliable luxury—bring your own. The food is standard Bavarian *Gaststätte* (tavern) fare with plenty of meat and potatoes.

Reservations are typically not necessary, although weekends in June, July, and September do get busy. If you're staying more than five nights, the 50% discount that comes with membership to the German Alpine Club (€48; ages 19-25 €24; under 18 €15) might be worthwhile. Camping within the reserve is strictly forbidden. The free *Berghütten und Almen* brochure available at the Nationalpark-Haus has detailed information on all the huts in the park.

Blaueishütte, 1685m (☎08657 271 or 546). Wood beams and breathtaking views on a rugged overlook on the north face of Hochkalter. 2-3hr. from Ramsau or Hintersee. 20 beds, 63 mattresses. Bed €20, mattress €15, under 18 €8. Open mid-May to mid-Oct.

Carl-von-Stahl-Haus, 1734m (☎08652 27 52; www.carl-von-stahl-haus.com). Abutting the German-Austria border on the southern face of Hohes Brett, this cabin squeeze mattresses onto bunks rather than the floor. About 2hr. from the Hinterbrand parking lot. 24 beds, 70 mattresses. Bed €20, mattress €14, under 18 €8. Open year-round.

Kärlingerhaus am Funtensee, 1633m (☎08652 609 1010; www.kaerlingerhaus.de). This simple cabin, located in a shaded valley above an alpine lake, offers the perfect place to repose after a long day of hiking. 48 beds, 182 mattresses. Bed €20, matress €15, under 18 €8. Open June to mid-Oct. Reservations recommended in summer.

Wasseralm in der Röth, 1416m (☎08652 98 58 02). Perched atop a wide meadow above the Röthbach waterfall overlooking the Obersee, this hut offers very basic accommodations for the night. 3hr. from Salet, off the Königssee. 40 mattresses. €13, under 18 €8. Open year-round.

HIKING

Literally thousands of hikes can be put together from the network of marked trails that snake through the park; the **Nationalpark-Haus** can help you plan a trip based on your preferences, time contraints, and level of fitness. Most trail signs give the length and an estimated time for each section. The dotted lines on maps are routes for experienced hikers only. Those planning a substantial hike might want to consider renting poles, available at **Bergsport Geistaller,** Griesstätterstr. 8 (☎08652 31 86) in Berchtesgaden. Poles are €2 per day, €13 per week. A few of the more popular, scenic hikes include:

Watzmannhaus (15km, full day). The iconic Watzmann, the park's most recognizable peak, was first conquered in 1799 and challenges trekkers with a strenuous hike and a spectacular view of the entire northern valley and the top. From Berchtesgaden, take bus #846 to "Wimbachbrücke" (20min., every hr. 7:30am-7:15pm; limited weekend service; €3), where there is an Information Center. Then follow signs through the parking lot and onto trail 441. Most hikers take 5-5½hr. to reach Watzmannhaus—the cow pasture is halfway up. The ascent to the peak is for experienced hikers only; the National Park helicopter has to fly out daily to this route to rescue hikers who overestimated their ability. Proper layered clothing (including a good rain jacket), robust hiking shoes, food, and plenty of water are essential for this ambitious hike. 1300m elevation gain.

Blaueishütte (10km, 5-6hr. round-trip). Start from the "Pfeiffensmacherbrücke" parking lot in Ramsau, where there will be signs for the Blaueishütte. Then, turn left 20min. into the hike onto trail 482. This strenuous but manageable hike heads up the side of Mt. Hochkalter to the Blaueishütte, 1680m over Ramsau. The incline steepens as you approach the outcropping, but the view of the valley against the sheer rock edge is incredible. 820m elevation gain.

Obersee (4km, 3-3½hr. round-trip, not including ferry). Take the ferry (1hr.) to Salet at the far end of the Königssee. Follow signs for the 15min. walk to the Obersee. From here, a flat, counterclockwise route leads, in under 1hr., along the shimmering lake to the Fischunkelalm, which dispenses milk and butter in summer. Another 30min. of hiking leads to the stunning Röthbach waterfall. On the return trip, overheated hikers splash in the refreshing Obersee. Be sure to check the departure time for the last ferry to avoid spending the night on the wrong end of the lake.

Wimbachtal (17km; 4½-5hr. round-trip). Visitors looking for a more relaxed hike can enjoy this lengthy but mild route that winds along the western valley below Watzmann. Take bus #846 (see Watzmannhaus, above) to "Wimbachbrücke" and follow the signs to Wimbachklamm gorge to see the rock formations. Head up trail 421 and stroll along the Wimbach stream's striking valley to Wimbachschloß, built in 1784, which serves refreshments in the summer. You can turn around at this halfway point, or continue to the Wimbachgrieshütte for striking views of the Hochkalter. 700m elevation gain.

St. Bartholomä and Eiskapelle (6km; 2-3hr. round-trip, not including ferry). This short moderately challenging Königssee hike starts from the beautiful St. Bartholomä church, now a restaurant (p. 367). After a visit to the National Park Information Center, follow signs past the St. Johann and Paul Chapel into the shadow of Watzmann to the gorgeous **Eiskapelle** (Ice Chapel), a dome formed at the front edge of the glacier by the river of melted snow running underneath. The trail's location below the sheltered rock face keeps things cold; be sure to bring a jacket.

BIKING

Mountain bikes are permitted on a limited number of routes around the edges of the national park, although the rest of the Berchtesgaden area there contains plenty to keep cyclists busy. From long, paved routes winding their way into Salzburg to short, challenging climbs up the park's formidable peaks, thoroughfares throughout the parkare always buzzing with bikers. Cycling maps trail guides, and the free brochure, *Bike Berchtesgaden* are available from the Berchtesgaden tourist office (p. 365).

"Radler" along the Klausbachtal. Easily one of the park's most popular bike routes, this path leads bikes along the steep path in the Klausbachtal valley to Hirschbichl. Once there, bikers can turn around and enjoy the downhill journey back to the Hintersee or follow the trail east into Austria as it loops around the Reiter Alps following the Saalach river before heading back to the Taubensee along the base of the Lattengebirge. 20km round-trip along Hirschbichl, 55km with loop. 1½hr./4-5hr. riding time for each route respectively. Recommended for intermediate bikers. 868m elevation gain for both.

"Rad und Kultur" from Berchtesgaden to Salzburg. A flat, paved loop that begins at the tourist office in Berchtesgaden before heading north along the Berchtesgadener Ache. The path continues along the river's edge as it joins with the Salzbach before circling back through the center of Salzburg. A great ride for families. Cyclists can enjoy the calm beauty of the hills at the park's northern edge before indulging in the bustle of Salzburg's downtown pedestrian zone. 61.7km, 3-4hr. riding time. 165m elevation gain.

"Echo" Berchtesgaden to Gotzenalm. Beginning at the tourist office, this route is a rugged mountain biker's dream. The steep path leads up to the mid-way station of the Jennerbahn. From there, a relatively flat trek around the mountain before a leg-pumping, switchback-laden final climb up to Gotzenalm with a breathtaking view of the Königssee and Waltzmann to the west. 36.8km, 3-4hr. riding time. This challenging ride is for **experienced cyclists only.** 1200m elevation gain.

BAYERN

OTHER OUTDOOR ACTIVITIES

Treff Aktiv, Jennerbahnstr. 19 (☎08652 667 10; www.treffaktiv.de), just below the Jennerbahn base station, offers various outdoor adventure trips, including **rafting, paragliding, mountain bike tours,** and **canyoning,** starting at around €30. They also offer ski weekends, climbing, bobsledding, rappelling, and guided hikes. To try out everything from rafting (from €39) to paragliding (from €180) to hot air ballooning from €155 for 4½hr.), contact the **Berchtesgaden Outdoor Club** (☎08652 977 60; www.outdoor-club.de), with 13 locations in the area.

The **Jenner,** serviced by the Jennerbahn, is the largest **ski** slope around with several intermediate ski runs open in winter. (☎08652 958 10. Day pass €25, ages 6-15 €13.50.) The **Berchtesgaden tourist office** and most ticket counters also sell a five-day pass good for all eight ski areas in the region (only available with Kurkarte €110, ages 6-14 €60). For the **Ski School Berchtesgaden-Jenner,** call ☎08652 66 710. Ask at the tourist office in Berchtesgaden for a list of ski and snowboard schools in the area, most of which also rent equipment. You can also get a trip down the **Kunsteisbahn bobsledding** track with **Rennbob-Taxi** from mid-October to February for €85, including all insurance and a "Bobsled Diploma." (☎08652 97 60 69; www.rennbob-taxi.de.)

CHIEMSEE

The original inhabitants of these picturesque islands, meadows, and marshlands, located between Munich and Salzburg, built the famed 9th-century island monasteries. Later, King Ludwig II chose the Herreninsel as the site for his last and most extravagant fairy-tale château. This "Bavarian Ocean" has been overrun by resorts and rising prices. Much of the lake is now a *Naturschutzgebiet* (Nature Preserve) and its waters remain relatively pristine. Chiemsee also attracts a younger, more active audience, thanks to the variety of sports on tap, from wind-surfing and sailing to hiking and mountain biking. Prien, the largest lake town, functions as a hub for the other towns around the lake, including Aschau, resort paradise Bad Endorf, and the ski areas of Kampenwand.

PRIEN AM CHIEMSEE ☎08051

Tranquil Prien's best qualities are its proximity to the Chiemsee and its hub train station. A particularly popular summer destination for German travelers, this pleasant town surrounded by sheep pastures and *Wanderwege* (hiking trails) serves as a base for adventures on the lake and in the mountains.

TRANSPORTATION AND PRACTICAL INFORMATION

BAYERN

Trains: To: **Munich** (1hr., 1-2 per hr., €14.60) and **Salzburg, Austria** (50min., 1-2 per hr., €10.90-14.50). The train station is a couple of blocks from the city center and a 20min. walk north of the lake. To reach the Marktpl. from the station, turn right on Hochriesstr. and then left at the end of the road on to Seestr., which becomes Alte Rathausstr.

Buses: Buses to nearby towns leave from the parking lot to the left as you exit the train station (every 1-2hr., €1.50-6).

Bike Rental: Chiemgauer Radhaus, Bahnhofpl. 6 (☎08051 46 31; www.chiemgauer-radhaus.de). €9 per day. Deposit required. Open M 7:30am-12:30pm and 1:30-8pm, Tu-F 8:30am-12:30pm and 1:30-6pm, Sa 8:30am-1pm.

Tourist office: Alte Rathausstr. 11. Free maps, a list of private rooms, and free **internet** access. (☎08051 690 50; www.tourismus.prien.de. Open May-Oct. M-F 8:30am-6pm, Sa 8:30am-4pm, Nov.-Apr. M-F 8:30am-5pm.)

Bank: There is a 24hr. **ATM** at **Sparkasse,** Hochreisstr. 7.

Post Office: 400m to the left of the train station at Hochreisstr. 21. (Open M-F 8am-12:30pm and 2-5:30pm, Sa 9am-12:30pm.) **Postal Code:** 83209.

ACCOMMODATIONS AND CAMPING

Though the city abounds with hotels, rooms are notoriously difficult to find in the summer. Be sure to book at least two weeks in advance for the best price.

Jugendherberge (HI), Carl-Braun-Str. 66 (☎08051 687 70; www.prien.jugendherberge.de), 20min. from the station and 5min. from the lake. From the station, turn right, then right on Seestr., and continue straight under the train overpass. After 2 blocks, go left on Staudenstr., which curves right and turns into Carl Braun Str. The cheapest bed in town. Breakfast included. Reception 8am-noon and 5-7pm. Curfew 10pm; door code available. Open early Feb-Nov. 4- to 6-bed dorms €19 including *Kurtaxe.* MC/V. ❷

Haus Lüdke-Süß, Birkenweg 78 (☎08051 34 65; www.zimmer.skyline.de), is 15min. from the station and 5min. from the lake. From the Bahnhof, take a right, then another onto Seestr. Follow the road for 10min. before turning left onto Birkenweg. Look for building number 66; it's in the second complex in the corner near the garage. Tucked away in a quiet residential neighborhood, rooms here are minimal but homey. Singles and doubles €25 per person. Breakfast included. Cash only. ❷

Schmiedhof, Ludwigstr. 119 (☎08051 18 41), often has room when everything else is full. Take bus #9494 from the first platform at the bus stop (1 every 2-4hr., €1.50) to "Bacham." Although remote, wide hallways lead to simple but spacious rooms in this converted barn. Breakfast included. Singles €30, doubles €60. Cash only. ❷

Campingplatz Hofbauer , Bernauer Str. 110 (☎08051 41 36), is a 25min. stroll from the center of town. From the station, turn left at Seestr., and left again at the next intersection following Bernauer Str. out of town past 3 gas stations and a McDonald's; the campsite is on the right just before the traffic circle. Though far from rustic, this small site offers green grass and great prices. Reception 7:30-11am and 2-8pm. Open Apr.-Oct. €6.20 per adult, €3.10 per child, €5.40 per site. Free showers. MC/V. ❶

FOOD AND NIGHTLIFE

Prien offers a surprisingly robust range of restaurants and cafes. **Lidl,** at the corner of Seestr. and Franziska-Hager-Str., has groceries and is open daily 8am-8pm. Every F 8am-2pm, join a crowd of locals buying fresh local produce at the **farmer's market** behind the church.

Wieninger Bräu, Bernauer Str. 13b (☎08051 610 90). Descend into this bustling beer cellar for delicious *Schweinbraten* with *Semmel* and *Krautsalat* (broiled pork filet with dumplings and sauerkraut; €10) and *Lederhosen*-clad waitstaff. Entrees from €6. Open M and W-F 10am-midnight, Su 9am-midnight. ❸

Kur-Cafe Heider, Marktpl. 6 (☎08051 15 34), is in the pedestrian zone behind the church. Enjoy your coffee under the shadow of the town's church steeple. Various light entrees from €4. Open Tu-Su 8am-6pm. Cash only. ❷

Cafe Neuer am See, Seestr. 104 (☎08051 60 99 60). At the end of the lakefront promenade, this cafe serves unique dishes like zucchini baked gnocchi (€8.90) or *Hirschgulasch* (€10.20), a dish of red deer served with flour dumplings. Finish off with a slice from one of the incredible assorted cakes (€2). Open daily 8am-11pm. MC/V. ❸

Cafe del Sol, Seestr. 7 (☎08051 18 28; www.cafe-sol.net). A cozy bar in a sleepy town. Spanish name. Italian owners. Asian decor. Open Tu-Su noon-4am. Cash only.

SIGHTS

HIMMELFAHRT KIRCHE. The red-and-blue marble interior of this church boasts beautiful 18th-century chandeliers, paintings, statues, and an enormous ceiling **frescoes** by Johann Baptist Zimmermann, of Wieskirche fame. On the square behind the church, the **Heimatmuseum** (Local History Museum) tells the story of distinctive local Bavarian culture through exhibits of life-like stuffed falcons, religious relics, century-old postcards, and a traditional candle factory. *(☎08051 927 10. Open Apr.-Oct. W-Sa 10am-noon and 2-5pm. €2, students and seniors €1.50.)*

OUTDOOR ACTIVITIES

Bootsverleih Stöffl rents the cheapest boats in town. From the train station, turn left and walk the 20min. to the end of Seestr. Turn left before the ferry dock. (☎08051 20 00. Open Apr.-Oct. daily 9am-dusk. Pedal boats €5.50-7 per hr.; rowing boats €6 per hr.; electric 11-22. Cash only.) The massive glass and steel **Prienavera Erlebnisbad,** Seestr. 120, just along the lakefront from the ferry wharf, houses a sauna, fun pool, 25m pool, 70m slide, and an outdoor heated pool with view of the Chiemsee. (☎08051 60 95 70; www.prienavera.de. Open M-F 10am-9pm, Sa-Su 9am-9pm. Beach pool open in summer 9am-8pm. Full-day admission €12, with Sauna €15; students and with *Kurkarte* €11, with sauna €14; children under 15 €6.50. Cash only.) **Chiemgau Biking,** Bahnhofstr. 4 in Bernau, offers a variety of guided mountain bike tours in the area (☎08051 96 17 613; www.chiemgau-biking.de). Ask about the **Naturerlebnistouren** (nature tours), at the tourist office. Experts lead visitors to the delta of the **Tiroler Achen,** around remote areas of the lake, and along the Alz river for dawn and sunset trips on a wooden raft. (All tours take place regularly in summer; most €8-16.) For information on whitewater rafting, contact **Sport Lukas,** in Schleching. Trips start at €30 per person. (☎08051 864 92 43; www.sportlukas.de).

ISLANDS ON THE CHIEMSEE

Chiemsee Schifffahrt, Seestr. 108, ferries float across the waters of the Chiemsee from Prien to **Herreninsel** (Gentlemen's Island), **Fraueninsel** (Ladies' Island), and towns on the other side of the lake. Both islands are extremely popular, so take a ferry before 10am to avoid crowds. (Departs from the Prien dock roughly every 30min. in summer and every hr. in winter, 7:15am-7:30pm. Last ferry from the islands to Prien leaves Fraueninsel 7pm, Herreninsel 7:10pm. Round-trip to Herreninsel €6.30, under 15 €3.10; to Fraueninsel or both islands €7.40/3.70.) An **Augustinian monastery** on Herreninsel once complemented the still-extant **Benedictine nunnery** on Fraueninsel in religious isolation. Supposedly, mischievous members of the cloth met up on **Krautinsel** (Herb Island) and engaged in a scandalous practice: gardening. For more information on getting to the islands, call **Chiemsee Schifffahrt** (☎08051 60 90; www.chiemsee-schifffahrt.de). To get to the dock, hang a right from the Prien train station and follow Seestr. for 15min. Or, take the **Chiemseebahn,** a slow, green 19th-century steam train, from the train station to the dock. (Every hr. 10am-6pm. €2.10, round-trip €3.30; under 15 €1/1.60. Tickets available from the booth next to the tracks or on the train. Combination train/ferry ticket available at the train station.

HERRENINSEL. Though the island's lush wooded landscape is certainly picturesque, the real reason to come to Herreninsel, the largest island on the Chiemsee, is the sprawling **Schloß Herrenchiemsee** whose lavish rooms and stately grounds mark the last of King Ludwig II's attempts to create a lasting legacy for himself. Throughout the year, tourists pack the palace's marble walls and overpriced museum shop for the short (30min.), entertaining tours of the palace interior. A monument to the "Sun King," Louis XIV of France, the ornate temple is a temple to Ludwig's admiration for his omnipotent 17th-century namesake (Ludwig is the German equivalent of Louis). Unfortunately, Ludwig's death in 1886 left the dream incomplete and the family coffers empty; the jarring disparity between fantasticaly opulent chambers and barren, uncompleted rooms in the palace betray the sudden halt in construction. The entire palace is an unparalleled extravagance, shamelessly copying Versailles, with a **Hall of Mirrors,** replicas of furnishings and artwork, and a lavish golden bed chamber. Ludwig II's private chambers include the most expensive chandelier ever produced by the famed Meißen porcelain factory (Ludwig had the blueprint destroyed to ensure the piece's uniqueness) and a dining room table that rose up through the floor on a specially designed dumbwaiter that allowed the King to dine in complete isolation without ever having to see his servants. To get to the palace from the ferry landing, walk along the paved footpath (20min.) or ride in true kingly fashion with a horse-drawn carriage. (Apr.-Oct. every 15min.; €3, ages 6-17 €1.) The attached **Ludwig II Museum,** in the same building, documents the King's life and notable obsession with the composer Richard Wagner. (☎08051 688 70. Open daily Apr. to mid-Oct. 9am-6pm, last tour 5pm; mid-Oct. to mid-Dec. and Jan.-Mar. 9:40am-4:15pm, last tour 3:40pm. German-language tours every 10min., English-language tours every hr. 10:15am-4:15pm. Admission and obligatory tour €7; seniors, students, and disabled persons €6; under 18 free with ID.) Halfway down the path back to the dock is the former monastery, known as **Altes Schloß** becuase of Ludwig's short stay there during the construction of his new palace. Herreninsel came to the fore in the 1940s, when the Federal Republic's constitution was drafted here; an exhibit explains the event. (Open daily Apr.-Oct. 9am-6pm, Oct. 10am-4:45pm. Free with admission to palace.) On select Thursdays and Sundays in the summer (May-Oct.), two local storytelling grandmothers lead an evocative **fairy-tale walk** around the Herreninsel. (☎08667 71 99; www.maerchenwanderung.de. 2½hr. €9, children €6. In German. Check website for dates.

BAYERISCHER WALD (BAVARIAN FOREST)

Sun-speckled forest paths weave by cold natural streams and lush foliage in central Europe's largest range of wooded land. Germany's national treasure has peaks (60 of which are over 1km high) that cover 6000 sq. km, and numerous creeks and rivers that stretch from the Danube to the Austrian and Czech borders. In recent years, an insect known as the *Buchdrucker* (bark beetle) has attacked thousands of trees—be careful of falling branches—but has also allowed new mountain spruce forest to regenerate. The remoteness of the towns discourages most non-German visitors from visiting this year-round paradise of hiking, camping, and cross-country skiing. A dozen HI youth hostels dot the forest, many around the reserve's edge.

Palaces, churches, and castle ruins hide among the rolling green hills of the forest, tucked away in tiny villages. The region is famous for its crafts, particularly glass-blowing. The glass produced here is prized throughout the world, especially the dark green *Waldglas* (forest glass). Every forest town seems to have its own *Glashütte*, and Bavarian tourist officials have designated a 250km long route from Passau through the park as the *Glasstraße* (Glass Road).

BAYERISCHER WALD NATIONAL PARK

Founded in 1970, the Bayerischer Wald National Park was the first national park in Germany. Clearly marked trails lace 59,900 acres of forest in this hiking mecca. The park strictly prohibits any activities that might alter the ecosystem, including camping and building fires, but there are many campsites at the park's edge. The newspaper *Informationsblatt Nationalpark Bayerischer Wald* gives the latest forest news, *Grenzenlose Waldwildnis* is a free park map, and *Ihre Gastgeber* lists accommodations in towns within the park and on its borders. All brochures are available in park centers and area tourist offices.

BAYERISCHER WALD NATIONAL PARK AT A GLANCE

AREA: 240 sq. km.

CLIMATE: Snowy winters; warm, sunny springs and autumns; cool summers. Light precipitation year-round.

HIGHLIGHTS: Extensive, well-kept hiking and biking trails; vivid fall foliage; excellent cross-country skiing.

FEATURES: Lush forests, dramatic mountain peaks.

GATEWAYS: Grafenau (p. 375) and Zwiesel (p. 376).

CAMPING: Strictly forbidden within the park, but available along the park's border.

FEES: None.

TRANSPORTATION AND ORIENTATION

A series of open roadways run through the southern half of the park and along the northwestern border; many of the trailheads can be reached by car. Public transportation within the park is also very good. The biofuel-powered **Igelbusse** (hedgehog buses) of **RBO** (Regionalbus Ostbayern) run from Grafenau, Neuschönau, Spiegelau, and Zwiesel to the interior of the park. The **Bayerwald Ticket** (€6) allows unlimited travel on buses and trains within the forest and along its border for one day. Your best bet is to pick the trails you want to cover and have one of the tourist offices tell you the precise connections to take. The park is located in along the eastern border of central Bavaria, neighboring the Czech Republic's Bohemian Forest National Park to the east. It stretches from Mauth in the south to Bayerisch Eisenstein in the north. Zwiesel is outside the western border of the park in the north, while Grafenau lies to the south. Ninety-eight percent of the park is forested, and the three most important (and hike-able) peaks within its borders are the **Lusen** (1373m), on the Czech border directly north of Neuschönau; the park's highest peak, **Großer Rachel** (1453m), in the middle of the park; and the **Großer Falkenstein** (1315m), in the northernmost section of the park. The entire area is etched with extensive hiking and cycling trails, though biking is more common in the northern regions.

PRACTICAL INFORMATION

Emergency: Police ☎110. **Ambulance** ☎192 22.

Information Offices: There are 4 within the park, in addition to the administrative offices located in Grafenau.

Informationszentrum Hans-Eisenmann-Haus, Böhmstr. 35 (☎08558 961 50; www.nationalpark-bayerischer-wald.de). From Grafenau (p. 376), take Igelbus #7594 (Lusen-Bus) from stop 4 in front of the station to "Nationalpark Infozentrum" (approx. every hr. 8am-5pm). The Hans-Eisenmann-Haus is up the hill across the street. Rotating exhibits, free pamphlets, a 20min. film (in English upon request), and *Wanderkarten* (hiking maps; €5.85). Information on the **Süd Teil** (south part) of the park is located in Hans-Eisenmann Haus, while information on the **Nördl Teil** (north part) is situated in the Haus zur Wildnis (listed below). Open daily mid-Jan. to mid-Mar. 9am-4pm, mid-Mar. to Oct. 9am-5pm. Buses run mid-May to Oct.

Erlebniszentrum Haus zur Wildnis, Ludwigsthal, 94227 Lindberg (☎09922 500 20). Built in 2006 and responsible for north of the Großer Rachel, this center offers exhibits, maps (€5.85), and pamphlets. Open late Dec.-Oct. daily 9:30am-6pm.

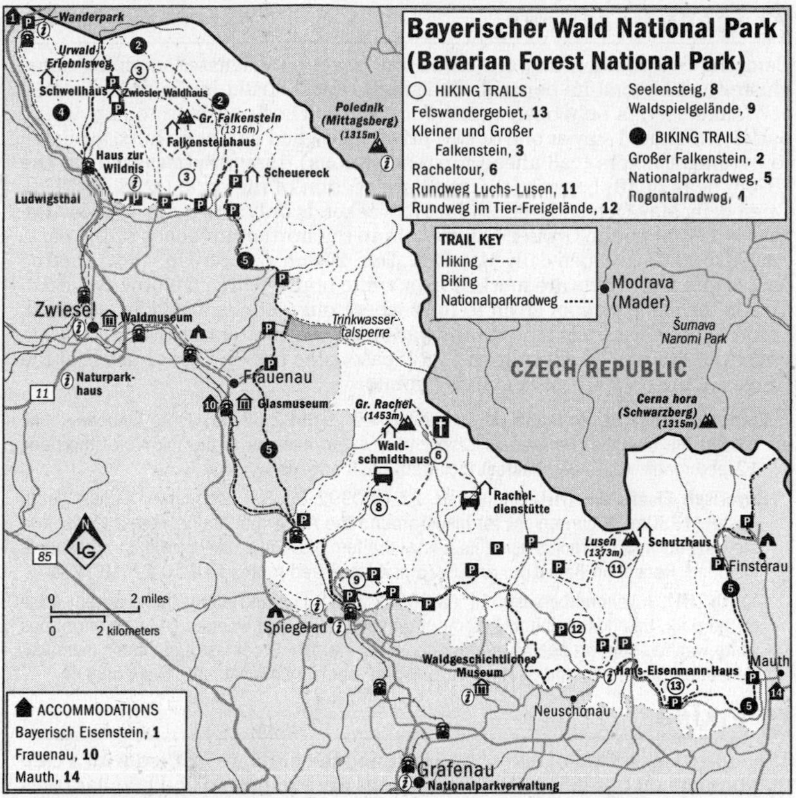

Infostelle Spiegelau, Konrad-Wilsdorf-Str. 1, 94518 Spiegelau (☎08553 960 017). Open Jan.-Oct. M-Th 8am-5pm, F 8am-3:30pm; Jul. to mid-Oct. also Sa 9-11am.

Infostelle Mauth, Mühlweg 2, 94151 Mauth (☎08557 97 38 38). Open Jan.-Oct. M-F 9am-5pm, Su 9am-noon.

Nationalparkverwaltung Bayerischer Wald, Freyunger Str. 2, 94481 Grafenau (☎08552 960 00). Park's administrative offices. Open M-Th 8am-noon and 1-4pm, F 8am-noon.

Tours: Guided hikes geared towards conservation and eco-awareness leave daily from the Hans-Eisenmann-Haus (see above); contact them a day in advance to book a tour (€3-5 per person, under 18 free). The free seasonal *Führungen und Veranstaltungen* brochure at park info centers lists tour times and themes. Most tours in German, with some in English. Prices vary by duration and type.

Gear: Rent **bikes** from **Radsport Leitl** (p. 377) in Zwiesel or from **Radsportshop de Graaf** (p. 376) in Grafenau. **Intersport Fuchs** (p. 376) in Grafenau rents **skis.**

Climate and Seasonality: The park is open and accessible year-round. Precipitation is generally light, though winter can be snowy; only select trails are cleared by the park service for cross-country skiing. Summer is relatively cool and moist, with occasional thunderstorms. Spring, which starts in May (snow remains until Apr.), and autumn are warm and sunny. Sept. and Oct. are ideal times to visit. Vegetation is primarily coniferous forest at higher elevations, mixed forest and bogs at lower elevations.

ACCOMMODATIONS

Camping is forbidden on park lands, but several designated camping areas cluster just beyond its borders. The single youth hostel in the park, located at Waldhäuser, is only open to school groups. Those wishing to stay in the park itself should stay at one of two privately owned mountain huts, available to overnight hikers (call ahead for reservations). **Lusenschutzhaus** is near the 1373m peak of Mt. Lusen in the southern section of the park. (☎08553 12 12. Open daily May-Oct. and Dec. 25-Jan. 6, weekends only Jan. 6-Apr.) **Falkenstein-haus** is 1315m up the Großer Falkenstein in the northern reaches of the park. (☎09925 90 33 66. Open daily May-Oct., Dec. 26-Jan. 6, F-Su Jan.-May.) On free park maps, these huts are marked by a white house with a window and door. This is the same symbol given to huts where only food is available, so check beforehand. Most trails through the park pass a restaurant or *Gaststätte* (tavern) every hour or so with surprisingly reasonable prices. Other hostels at the fringes of the park are great starting points.

Frauenau, Haus St. Hermann (HI), Hauptstr. 29 (☎0992 67 35). From Frauenau, hike around the beautiful *Trinkwassertalsperre,* a water reservoir in the middle of the park. 12-bed rooms €14.10, breakfast included. Cash only. ❶

Bayerisch Eisenstein (HI), Brennesstr. 23 (☎0992 53 37). Germany's highest youth hostel (1330m) is convenient for hikes around the Arber mountains. Forest views, iron stoves, and wood in rooms give this hostel the feel of a log cabin. Breakfast and sheets included. Reception 8am-1pm and 5-7pm. 4- to 6-bed rooms €14.40-17. MC/V. ❶

Mauth (HI), Jugendherbergestr. 11 (☎08557 289). Located along the southern edge of the park, this hostel epitomizes mountain ski-lodge with wooden ceilings, enormous white-washed support beams, and plenty of ski storage. Breakfast and sheets included. Reception 8am-noon and 5-7pm. 4- to 6-bed rooms €14.40-17.20. Cash only. ❶

HIKING

The more than 300km of hiking trails around the park are marked with a care that borders on obsession. All intersections are signposted and popular trails have inlaid wooden maps every 500m and color-coded signs every 100m. Trails with yellow signs are loops, and those with white markers lead from one trail-head to another. Guided hikes leave daily from the **Hans-Eisenmann-Haus** (p. 373). To explore the park on foot, pick up a park-wide *Wanderkarte* (hiking map) or look for the small gray brochures detailing specific routes.

Kleiner und Großer Falkenstein (10km, 4-5hr. round-trip). In the northern section; take the bus from Zwiesel or Ludwigsthal to "Zwieslerwaldhaus." From the Falkenstein parking lot, follow the white signs of a branch adorned with 2 bells for a 2½hr. climb past a lovely waterfall, then over Kleiner Falkenstein (with the hike's best view) and on to the top of its larger brother. Return via the same route or via another trail; buses also run from Lindbergmühle and Spiegelhütte; the Waldbahn (p. 376) runs to Ludwigsthal. Steep in places; not recommended for novice hikers. 600m elevation gain.

Rundweg im Tier-Freigelände (7km loop, 3-4hr.). A fun hike perfect for beginners from the Hans-Eisenmann-Haus. Yellow signs mark this flat loop leading through a unique zoo: along the trail, brown bears, bison, lynx, and wolves roam enclosures resembling their natural habitat. Carved wooden signs clarify unusual German animal names. In the wild swine quarters, piglets and their mothers overrun the trail alongside the tourists.

Racheltour (4hr. round-trip). From Spiegelau, take the Rachel Bus to "Gfäll." Follow the marked bird symbols past the Liesl fountain and the Waldschmidthaus (which serves beer). From there, it's a short final uphill trek to the highest peak in the entire park.

Descent passes the Rachelkapelle, with views of the Rachelsee (with a 100m spur leading to the water's edge), and a branch that leads to Racheldiesthütte, which offers food and a bus back down. 500m elevation gain.

Felswandergebiet (1½hr. round-trip). From the Hans-Eisenmann-Haus, take the Finsterau Bus to "Jugendwaldheim." Cross the street and follow the yellow signs depicting a bird with a spotted chest. Hike curves up through the rocky hilltops to outlook points on top of the Kanzel mountains. On a clear day, see the Alps or peer west into the Czech Republic. Can also be reached via a pleasant hike by following the white signs with 3 trees on them and arrows to "Felswandergebiet" from the Hans-Eisenmann-Haus parking lot. Good for novice hikers. 190m elevation gain.

Rundweg Luchs-Lusen (4km loop, 2½hr.). Lace up your boots and climb one of the highest peaks in the park. From Grafenau, take the bus past the Hans-Eisenmann-Haus to the end of the line at the Lusen parking lot. From there, follow the yellow signs with the lynx picture. About 300m past the gorgeous view from granite outcroppings, the Lusenschutzhaus serves food to hungry hikers. 250m elevation gain.

Waldspielgelände (2km, 1hr. round-trip, plus playtime on the ziplines and see-saws). Take the Waldbahn to "Spiegelau," head across the tracks away from town, and take a left towards the Kurpark. Then, take a right towards the parking lot where the trail begins. A non-looping trail with a series of playgrounds and physical challenges every 100m, starting in Spiegelau. Family-friendly and stroller-accessible.

BIKING

More than 200km of trails are also accesible by bike; signs at the start indicate whether or not wheels are allowed. Pick the *Radwander- und Mountainbikekarte* in tourist offices in neighboring towns for park bike trails. Routes marked in purple are recommended only for fit folks with mountain bikes.

Nationalparkradweg (86km) is the main trail through the forest, running southeast from Zwiesel and curving up to cross the Czech border before merging with the Donau-Wald-Radweg back in Germany. The incline is generally mild, and the route is recommended for familes and chidren. Accessible from Waldbahn-linked towns Bayerisch Eisenstein, Zwiesel, and Spiegelau, as well as towns on the Finsterau Igelbus line between Spiegelau and Finsterau. Though it's probably too long for most beginners to do in a single day, it's a very popular route and is generally not too difficult.

Regentalradweg (162km), accessible from Bayerische Eisenstein and good for leisurely biking, follows the course of the Regen west from the Czech border to Regensburg. Recommended for more experienced cyclists, especially through the National Park.

Großer Falkenstein is crisscrossed by more than 50km of trails. The outer loop is recommended for beginners; peak climb suggested only for fit bikers. Good beginning and/or endpoints are the train stations in Zwieselau, Zwiesel, or Ludwigsthal.

GRAFENAU ☎08552

Just west of the national park, easily accessible Grafenau (pop. 9000) is an ideal place to begin excursions on the web of hiking trails that laces the park's southern half. The *Kurgarten*, behind the Rathaus, reflects the pastoral elegance of a city just inches away from adventures in the Bayerischer Wald.

The simple rooms at **Pension Tauscher ❷**, Stifterstr. 22, come with private baths and sun-soaked atriums overlooking the garden and river valley. Take a right out of the tourist office, an immediate right on Freyunger Str., and a left when it forks onto Stifterstr. (☎08552 626; www.pension-tauscher.de. Breakfast included. Singles €22, doubles €40; less after 3 nights. Cash only.) Located just downhill from the Bahnhof, **Rewe,** Bahnhofstr. 12, is a **grocery store** of American proportions. (Open M-Sa 7am-8pm. AmEx/MC/V.) Enjoy enormous portions of pizza (€6-9), salad (€5-9), and pasta (€7-10) at **La Luigi ❸**, Stadtpl. 2. (☎08552 97 58 62. Beer €2.50. Open M-Sa 11am-2pm and 5pm-midnight.) **Cafe-Restaurant Fox ❸**, Stadtpl. 3, offers a sophisticated selection of meat and seafood dishes (€8-12). (☎08552 92 03 77; www.cafe-fox.de. Open daily M-F 8am-midnight, Sa 9am-midnight, Su 10am-midnight. Cash only.)

The village is the last stop on the special **Waldbahn** (forest train) line from Zwiesel (50min., every 2-3hr., €6 with the Bayerwald ticket) and can also be reached from Munich (4hr., €21 with the Bayern ticket) or Passau (3hr., €21). Although traveling from Passau to Zwiesel is cheaper with just a straight ticket, adding the trip down to Grafenau makes it worth buying the Bayern ticket. Within Grafenau, the city bus runs from the train station to town (€1.50, ages 5-15 €0.50). **Radsportshop de Graaf,** Rosenauerstr. 20, Grafenau, rents bikes 15min. from Stadtpl. Head uphill from Stadtpl.; it will be on the right, at the top of a hill. (☎08552 36 04. €8-12 per day. Open M-F 9am-12:30pm and 2-6pm, Sa 9am-1pm.) **Intersport Fuchs,** Hauptstr. 16, Grafenau, rents skis and snowshoes at great prices. (☎08552 14 36. Skis €9-12.50 per day, less for multiple days. Snowshoes €7 per day. Open M-F 9am-6pm, Sa 9am-4pm.) Once in Grafenau, walk left off the train until you reach the Stadtpl. (200m). Walk across the square bearing left and follow the signs to the right to reach the friendly **tourist office** in the back of the Rathaus, which books rooms for free and conducts free guided hikes every Tuesday at 11am. A computer outside lists available rooms and contacts prospective hosts for late arrivals. (☎08552 96 23 43; www.grafenau.de. Open year-round M-Th 8:30am-4:30pm, F 8:30am-1pm, Sa 10-11:30am; extended hours Jul-Oct. and Dec.-Feb.) **Internet** is available for €4 per hr. at the **Wunder Bar,** Kröllstr. 2. Open M-Th 6pm-midnight, F-Su 1pm-midnight. Other services include: **VR-Bank,** between the train station and Stadtpl., with a **24hr. ATM** (open M-F 8am-12:30pm and 2-4:30pm); the **Marien-Apotheke pharmacy,** Stadtpl. 10 (☎08552 35 38; open M-F 8am-6pm, Sa 8am-noon); and the **post office,** Spitalstr. 7. (☎08552 97 43 81. Open M-F 8:30am-noon and 2-5pm, closed W afternoon, Sa 9-11:30am.) **Postal Code:** 94481.

ZWIESEL ☎09922

An abundance of train connections and a proximity to the park make Zwiesel (pop. 10,500) an excellent gateway to the Bavarian Forest. A skier's paradise in winter, the town highlights its 600-year glass-making history in summer. Summer nights heat up with the *Grenzlandfest* (Frontier Fest), held in mid-July.

TRANSPORTATION AND PRACTICAL INFORMATION. Trains run every hour to **Munich** (3hr., €30) and **Plattling** (1hr., €10). Note that if you're paying more than €21 for a single ticket, it's cheaper to buy a Bayern Ticket, which costs €21 and covers all of Bavaria. Ticket machines will gladly sell you the more expensive option without ever mentioning the Bayern Ticket. City buses run one per hour. M-F 7:58am-5:58pm, Sa 7:58-11:58am. The **Stadtlinie bus** runs to the Stadtpl. from just outside the station. Call at **taxi** at ☎09922 15 45 or 12 70. Rent **bikes** at **Radsport Leitl,** Theresienthaler Str. 25, around the corner and across the river from the Bahnhof. (☎09922 80 21 57. Touring bikes €5 per day, mountain bikes €10. Open M-F 8am-noon and 2-6pm, Sa 8am-noon.) The **tourist office,** Stadtpl. 27, in the Rathaus, is an ideal place to start a visit to the forest or the Glas Park. Provides maps and information on hiking and biking tours and finds private rooms for free. To get there from the train station, turn right and walk downhill on Dr.-Schott-Str. Bear left, cross the bridge, turn left after the Greek restaurant and head up through the Stadtpl. (10min.); the

Rathaus is on the left. (☎0992 284 05 23; www.zwiesel-tourismus.de. Open M-F 8:30am-5pm, Sa 10am-noon, Nov.-Christmas M-F 9am-5pm. Find **internet** access at **Cafe Flair,** Dr.-Schott-Str. 18 (see **Food,** below). **Sparkasse,** Stadtpl. 7 to the left of the Rathaus, has two **24hr. ATMs.** (Open M-F 8:25am-12:30pm and 1:30-5pm.) The **post office,** Stadtpl. 18-20, is across from the tourist office in the **Edeka** complex. (Open M-F 8am-6pm, Sa 8am-1pm). **Postal Code:** 94227.

ACCOMMODATIONS. Zwiesel has no youth hostel, but groups can opt for **Arbeiterwohlfahrt (AWO) ❶,** Karl-Herold-Str. 9, which offers fully furnished apartments and spacious cabins, complete with living room and kitchen, 15min. from the town center. Walk left from the train station and make a left at the pedestrian walkway. Cross under the tracks and head straight on Waldesruhweg; where it curves left, go straight onto Karl-Herold-Str.; AWO is on the left. (☎09922 91 75; www.awo-zwiesel.de. Reception daily 7am-5pm. Apartments with 7 beds €49 per night. *Kurtaxe* and additional cleaning charges not included. Cash only.) Located between the train station and Stadtpl., **Haus Lederer ❷,** Jägergasse 4, is a bed and breakfast with three beautiful rooms, wood-paneled ceilings, and a lovely veranda. Make a right out of the train station and a left on nearby Holzweberstr. Cross Fachschulstr. and cross the pedestrian bridge over the river. Continue onto Jagergasse; the pension is on the left. It's unmarked; knock to ask about availability. (☎09922 92 46. Breakfast included. Singles €17; doubles €30-34. Cash only.)

FOOD. A year-round open-air **market** convenes in the parking lot behind the Rathaus (Sa 6am-noon). **Edeka,** at Stadtpl. 18-20, sells groceries. (Open M-F 8am-7pm, Sa 8am-6pm. Cash only.) For Bavarian meals, try **Gasthaus zum Kirchenwirt ❸,** Bergstr. 1, for their *Schweinbraten* (pig roast with sauerkraut; €5-12), and free folk music Tu and Th at 8pm. (☎09922 25 70. Open daily 11am-1am. Cash only. Zwiesel's 18+ crowd heads to **Cafe Flair ❷,** Dr.-Schott-Str. 18, where every salad (€6-8) comes with its own flaming sparkler. Faux leather chairs mix well with mirrored pillars and rainbow-striped tablecloths. (☎09922 50 07 98. Internet access €3 per hr. Open daily 10am-1am. Cash only.)

SIGHTS. Just north of town, the **Glas Park Theresienthal** features a museum of minutely decorated glass objects and several shops. The real reason to go is to peer behind-the-scenes into the factory. After getting a ticket at the museum, turn left, head down the road, and take the stairs down to the big yellow house to see glass-blowers at work: no fences, no signs. (€2, students and children €1. Open M-F 10am-2pm. Buses shuttle to the Glas Park from the Stadtpl. M-F 11 per day from 8:30am, last return 6:30pm. €1.70.) The **Waldmuseum** (Forest Museum), Stadtpl. 27, behind the Rathaus, tells the tinkly tale of glass-making and teaches about everyday life in the forest through 17 exhibits and 3 impressive dioramas. (☎09922 608 88. Open mid-May to mid-Oct. M-F 9am-5pm, Sa-Su 10am-noon and 2-4pm; mid-Oct. to mid-May M-F 10am-noon and 2-5pm, Sa-Su 10am-noon; closed Nov. €2.50, students €1.) For more information on happenings around town, pick up a free copy of *Mein Urlaub* from the tourist office.

PASSAU ☎0851

Baroque arches cast long shadows across the cobblestone alleys of Passau (pop. 50,800), a 2000-year-old city situated at the confluence of the Danube, Inn, and Ilz rivers. The splendor of the peninsular Altstadt recalls the era when Passau controlled lands in Austria, Bavaria, and the Czech Republic. The heavily fortified castle, glorious cathedral, and patricians' palaces stand alongside modern shops, cafes, and museums. This **Dreiflüssestadt** (three-river city) and university town, inspiration for the 12th-century epic poem the *Nibelungenlied,* hosts the summer-long art, music, theater, and film **European Festival,** held every year since 1952 in support of a peaceful and unified Europe.

TRANSPORTATION

Trains: Every hr. to: **Munich** (2½hr., €29-45); **Nuremberg** (2-3hr., €32-41); **Regensburg** (1½hr., €20-25); **Vienna, Austria** (3hr., €43.20). Ticket counter open M-F 5:50am-6:35pm, Sa 6am-6:25pm, Su 8:50am-7:25pm. Lockers €2-3.

Buses: Regionalbus Ostbayern (☎0851 75 63 70) provides service from the train station to cities throughout eastern Bavaria. SWP Passau buses make a number of stops within the city and in neighboring towns. Maps at the tourist office. Single ticket €1.50.

Ferries: Donau Schifffahrt (☎0851 92 92 92), ticket booth across from main tourist office. Sails to Linz, Austria (5hr.; May-Sept. Tu-Su 9am and noon, departs Linz 9:45am and 2:20pm; €22, round-trip €25). The 45min. "Three Rivers" tour of the city leaves daily from docks 7 and 8, Mar.-Oct. every 30min. 10am-5pm and Nov.-Dec. at 11am, noon, 1, 2, 3pm (€7.50, under 15 €3.75). Though there are many alternative ferry services, this one is the most conveniently located from the tourist office.

Taxis: Call ☎0851 88 700 or catch a cab at Ludwigspl.

Bike Rental: Rent a Bike (☎0800 460 2460), in the Bahnhof on track 1. €12 per day. Open daily 9am-noon and 3-5pm. **Fahrrad Klinik,** Bräugasse 10 directly across from the suspension bridge below the Veste Oberhaus (☎0851 334 11; www.fahrradklinik-passau.de) charges €11 per day, less for longer rentals. Open M-F 9-noon and 1-6pm, Sa 9-noon. The stunning **Donau Radweg bike path** begins in Donaueschingen and continues through Passau into Austria—ask for a map at the tourist office.

ORIENTATION AND PRACTICAL INFORMATION

To get to the tourist office from the station, head across the street and down the stairs to the edge of the Danube river. Take a right and follow the path all the way to the Altstadt. The tourist office is located on the right, across from docks 7 and 8 (25min.). Uphill lies the **Veste Oberhaus** fortress. Farther east, the three rivers converge. The Inn is on the right; to the left is the Danube, and the third and smallest river, the Ilz. East of the Altstadt, **Innstraße** runs along the Inn to the university. Bridges span the Danube towards nightlife hotspot **Innstadt,** a German enclave on the Austrian side of the rivers.

Tourist Office: Rathauspl. 3 (☎0851 95 59 80; www.tourismus.passau.de), on the Danube next to the Rathaus. Free brochures, schedules, tour information, cycling map. English city guides €5. The staff books rooms (€3 deposit) and provides info on hotels and pensions (€18-52) in the area. *WasWannWo,* a free monthly pamphlet in German, chronicles happenings in Passau. Office open Easter-Nov. M-F 8:30am-6pm, Sa-Su 9am-4pm; Nov. to Easter M-Th 8:30am-5pm, F 8:30am-4pm. **Branch** at Bahnhofstr. 36, across from the train station and to the left (☎0851 95 59 80). Free maps and brochures available outside after hours. Open Easter-Sept. M-F 9am-noon and 12:30-5pm; Oct.-Easter M-Th 9am-noon and 12:30-5pm, F 9am-noon and 12:30-4pm.

Tours: German-language walking tours (1hr.) May-Oct. M-Sa 10:30am and 2:30pm, Su 2:30pm. €4, children €2. Meet at the front entrance of the Stephansdom. English group tours available with advance request.

Currency Exchange: Go right out of the train station and walk 5min. down Bahnhofstr. to reach **Volksbank-Raiffeisenbank,** Ludwigspl. 1 (☎0851 335 30). **24hr. ATM.** €1 fee per traveler's check cashed. Open M-W and F 8:30am-4:15pm, Th until 5pm.

Laundromat: Waschtreff, Neuburger Str. 21 (☎0851 459 91). From Ludwigspl., walk up Dr.-Hans-Kapfinger-Str., follow it to the end as it curves right and becomes Neuburger Str., then bear left. Wash €2.80, soap €0.50. Dry €1.50. Open daily 7am-11pm.

Emergency: Police, Nibelungenstr. 17 (☎110, non-emergency 0851 50 30). **Fire** ☎112. **Ambulance** ☎0851 192 22.

Pharmacy: Apotheke, Bahnhofstr. 17 (☎0851 513 01). Open M-Sa 8am-6pm.

Internet Access: Screenpark Media Services, Kl. Exerzierpl. 14a (☎0851 75 67 611). €2 per hr. Open M-Sa 10am-8pm. Free access at **Cafe Unterhaus,** Höllgasse 12 (☎0851 989 04 64), a trendy art gallery, bookshop, and cafe, a few blocks from the Rathaus. (Open Apr.-Sept. M and W-Su 10am-1pm, Tu 7pm-1am; Oct.-Mar. M and W-Su noon-1am, Tu 7pm-1am.) Free Wi-Fi at **Coffee Fellows,** Schrottgasse 12 (☎0851 756 8674). Open M-Th 9am-1am, F 9am-3am, Sa 10am-3am, Su 10am-midnight.

Post Office: Bahnhofstr. 27, to the right as you exit the station. Open M-F 8am-6pm, Sa 9am-12:30pm. **Postal Code:** 94032.

ACCOMMODATIONS AND CAMPING

Most pensions in downtown Passau start at €30, while those in the surrounding area run €15-35. The city's youth hostel is usually swarming with German schoolchildren, especially during June and July.

Fahrrad Pension, Bahnhofstr. 33 (☎0851 34 784; www.fahrrad-pension.com). Bright rooms with colorful bedding, hardwood floors, and a prime location above an aromatic bakery. Try a *Teeblatt,* a decadent German adaptation of s'mores, for less than a euro. Exit the train station and walk 200m to the left; look for the "Bäckerei" sign. €18 for singles, less for more people and longer stays. Reservations recommended. Cash only. ❶

Jugendherberge (HI), Veste Oberhaus 125 (☎0851 49 37 80). Perched high above the Danube, the hostel's ancient walls, conceal a modern interior and rooms with impressive sink vanities. Take the suspension bridge over the river downstream from the Rathaus and turn right through the tunnel. Take the steep cobblestone road on the left about 100m and turn left when the road splits. Then turn right at the *Kasse und Museumsshop* sign; the hostel is 20m up on the right (25min.). Or, hop on the *Pendelbus* (shuttle) from Rathauspl. bound for the museum adjacent to the hostel (Easter to mid-Oct. every 30min. M-F 10:30am-5pm, Sa-Su 11:30am-6pm; €2, same-day round-trip €2.50). Breakfast included. Reception 7:30am-11am, 5-10pm. Curfew 10pm, access code available. Dorms €19.80, slightly lower in winter. AmEx/MC/V. ❷

Pension Rößner, Bräugasse 19 (☎0851 93 13 50; www.pension-roessner.de). The quaint rooms, with very low, arched ceilings, are suited to the building's 1000-year history. To get there from the Rathaus, walk downstream along the Danube. Directly on the river, these pleasant rooms are low-priced for the Altstadt. Call upstairs if no one is at the reception. All rooms with bath, radio, and TV. Breakfast included. Singles €35; doubles €60; panorama suite with river-view balcony, €80. Cash only. ❸

Rotel Inn, Hauptbahnhof/Donauufer (☎0851 951 60; www.rotel-inn.de). From the train station, walk straight ahead down the steps, down Haissengasse, and through the tunnel to this outlandish hotel right on the river. Built in 1993 in the shape of a sleeping man to protest Europe's decade-long economic slumber, this "Hotel of the Future" packs travelers into closet-sized rooms bedecked with primary-color plastics. Breakfast €5.50. Reception 24hr. Open May-Sept. Rooms €25 for 1 person, €40 for 2. Cash only. ❷

Campingplatz Faltbootabteilung, Halser Str. 34 (☎0851 414 57). This gorgeous campsite, situated just feet from the banks of the Ilz and surrounded by sloping green hills, offers a quiet refuge from the tumult of the city. Follow directions to the hostel but continue along the right side of the road following the camping signs through the residential neighborhood along the river bank. Or, take bus #12 or 4 from "Exerzierpl." to "Ilzbrücke," cross back over the river, and turn right following the camping signs. Open May-Oct. Breakfast €3-4. Reception 7:30am-11pm; you can pitch your tent any time. €8, ages 5-17 €6.50, under 4 free. Hot showers included, pay phone available. Cash only. ❶

FOOD

The student district centers on **Innstraße** near the university. From Ludwigspl., head down Nikolastr. and turn right on Innstr., which runs parallel to the Inn River; the street is dotted with cheap restaurants and buzzing cafes. **Norma** is a supermarket at Bahnhofstr. 16b. (Open M-F 8:30am-7pm, Sa 8am-4pm. Cash only.) There is an open air **market** in Domplatz Tuesday and Friday mornings.

Cafe Innsteg, Innstr. 15 (☎0851 512 57), 1 block from Nikolastr. Bizarre modern art, wooden floors, and a large terrace overlooking the river round out this low-key restaurant offering generous portions of fresh, gourmet food at unbelievably cheap prices. Fascinating conversations and wonderfully welcoming waitresses. Sandwiches €5-6. Pastas €7. Daily menu (€5) 11:30am-2pm. Beer (0.5L) €2.60. Open M-Sa 8:30am-1am (hot food 11:30am-midnight), Su 8:30am-7pm (hot food 11:30am-6pm). Cash only. ❷

Cafe Kowalski, Oberer Sand 1 (☎0851 24 87). Students and hip locals head to this swanky cafe for breakfast (€4-6), salads, and pasta (€6-8). Cafe Kowalski also serves the largest schnitzel in Passau, at a whopping 20cm in diameter (€8). Specials almost every night. Student's Night Tu (€1 beer and schnitzel happy hour) and Mojito Weekends (cocktails €3.80). From Ludwigspl., head down Ludwigstr. and take a right onto Theresienstr.; the cafe is by the river on the right. Open daily 10am-1am. AmEx/MC/V. ❷

Sensasian, Heuwinkel 9 (☎0851 989 0152). An upscale restaurant at downscale prices. Sit in the outside courtyward, the sleek interior, or the glamorous upstairs lounge. Delicious pan-Asian specialties (sushi, pad thai) with plenty of vegetarian options. Weekly menu €6.80. Open M-Sa 10am-11pm, Su from 11am. Cash only. ❷

Ganesha, Dr. Hans-Kapfinger-Str. 28 (☎0851 966 7677). If the overdone faux-opulence of the restaurant's blue and white interior doesn't win you over, the delicious lunch buffet (€6, M-F 11:30am-3pm) just might. Spicy entrees €7-10. Plenty of vegetarian options. From Ludwigspl., head down Dr.-Hans-Kapfinger-Str. and follow it as it curves to the right. Open daily 11:30am-3pm, 5-11pm. ❸

SIGHTS

STEPHANSDOM. When a fire devastated Passau, Italian artists were brought in to rebuild the city. This spectacular cathedral, the largest Baroque structure north of the Alps, is the centerpiece, despite its few Gothic remnants. Hand-carved pillars and breath-taking frescos cover the ceiling in this towering masterpiece. The world's largest church organ stands above the choir loft. Up to five organists can play its 17,774 pipes and multiple keyboards. *(Open daily in summer 6:30am-7pm, in winter 6:30am-6pm. No entrance during concerts. Organ concerts May-Oct. and Christmas week M-Sa at noon; €4, students and children €2. €5 students, seniors, and children €3. Daily German-language tours May-Oct. and Christmas week M-F 12:30pm, meet in front of the side aisle. €3, children €1.50.)*

VESTE OBERHAUS. Over the Luitpoldbrücke and up the footpath is the former palace of the bishop. The complex was once a prison for the bishops' enemies and a fortress with control over the city and the rivers below. It now houses the exciting **Kulturhistorisches Museum** (Cultural History Museum), with interactive rotating exhibits and 54 rooms of art and artifacts that chronicle 2000 years of Passau's history, thorough English commentary, and great views of the city from the tower. Look out for the 16th-century Luther Bible and the colorful Turkish tent, equipped with an intercom that streams stories from *1001 Ara-*

bian Nights. (Oberhaus 125. Shuttle bus from the Rathaus stops here every 30min. Last bus back leaves Oberhaus at 5:15pm. ☎0851 493 3512; www.oberhausmuseum.de. Open mid-Mar. to mid-Nov. M-F 9am-5pm, Sa-Su 10am-6pm. €5, students €4. Tower €1, under 16 €0.50.)

GLASMUSEUM. This huge collection of fancy glasswork celebrates Bohemian production from the Baroque era to the present, including an elaborate glass birdcage, a copy of da Vinci's *Last Supper* engraved on a chalice, and various fluorescent Jugendstil experiments. Two rooms in which Austrian Empress Elisabeth lived have been preserved, complete with her gloves, socks, and toiletries. *(Am Rathauspl. ☎0851 350 71; www.glasmuseum.com. Open daily 1-5pm. €5, students €4, under 12 free with parents. Get a 20% discount by showing your Passau boat tour ticket.)*

ALTSTADT. Behind the cathedral is the **Residenzplatz,** lined with former patrician dwellings, and the **Residenz,** past home of Passau's bishops. The **Domschatz** (cathedral treasury) within the Residenz has an extravagant collection of the bishops' most precious items in its old library. Weird contemporary art exhibits contrast with aged volumes of Papal decrees. *(Residenzpl. 8. ☎0851 39 33 74). Enter through the back of the Stephansdom, to the right of the altar. Open May-Oct. M-Sa 10am-4pm. €2, students and children €1, families €2.50.)* The less opulent 13th-century Gothic **Rathaus** was appropriated from a wealthy merchant in 1298 to house the city government. The impressive high water marks from past floods (the last big one was in 2002) are marked on the outside wall beneath the clock. Inside, the **Prunksaal** (Great Hall) is a masterpiece of rich wooden paneling and dark marble. *(Open daily Apr.-Dec. 10am-4pm. €2, children €1.50.)* The **Glockenspiel** plays over eighty tunes, according to time, day, and season. *(Daily 10:30am, 2, 7:25, and 9pm.)* Across Rathauspl. and down Bräugasse, just past the Altes Brauhaus stands the **Museum Moderner Kunst** (Museum of Modern Art), a small collection of paintings, sculpture, photography, and video installations with an emphasis toward Expressionist works and local artists. *(Bräugasse 17. ☎0851 383 87 90; www.mmk-passau.de. Open Tu-Su 10am-6pm. €5, students and children €3.)*

ENTERTAINMENT AND NIGHTLIFE

Thespian Passau is centered on **Theater-Opernhaus Passau,** Gottfried Schäfferstr. 2-4 (☎0851 929 1913; www.sudostbayerisches-staedtetheater.de). From Ludwigspl. walk down Nikolastr. to the river and go left; the theater is just before the bridge. Repertoire spans from Beckett to Wagner. (Box office open Tu-F 10am-12:30pm and 4-5:30pm. Tickets from €10, reduced rates available 1hr. before showtime, usually 7:30pm. Closed early July to mid-Sept.)

Passau's students and young professionals party at the many bars and clubs on Innstr. by the university, or across the footbridge in the Innstadt. Although all beer gardens close at 11pm, the city still manages to stay out late. The best way to keep abreast of the nightlife scene is to read *Pasta,* a free monthly magazine available at most bars, clubs, and cafes. *Innside,* available at the tourist office, lists events in the Innstadt. Both publications are in German.

Bluenotes, Ledererg. 50 (☎0851 343 77). Cross over the Innbrücke and make a right onto Lederergasse. Enjoy your beer or mixed drink outside in the super popular *Biergarten,* next to the live events of the *Scheune* (inquire for details), or inside on plush white furniture set against blue ambient lighting. The place for good, laid-back fun in Passau. Happy hour every night 8-9pm and midnight-1am and all night W (mixed drinks €4.50). Bring your own grill items May-Sept. Open daily 6pm-1am. Cash only.

Colors, Mariahilfstr. 8 (☎0851 322 20). Right across the Innbrücke in Innstadt, past the Kirchenpl. Gulp down a Helles (€2.70) as you throw darts, shoot pool, or relax in the *Biergarten* or intimate glass bar. Tu night happy hour, mixed drinks €3-5. DJs spin everything from reggae to easy listening. Open daily 7pm-1:30am. Cash only.

GO, Kl. Klingergasse 7 (www.go-danceclub.de). A trendy, young crowd packs the large dance floor in Passau's upscale club for rap, R&B, and house. Beer €2.80. Mixed drinks €6.80-8. Dress to impress. Open W and F-Sa 10pm-4am. Cover F-Sa €3. Cash only.

Camera, Am Ludwigspl. (☎0851 343 20), around the corner from the McDonald's. Stark black exterior foreshadows an underground cavern of student angst and inebriation. Plays everything from electro to pop. Beer €2.20 (0.3L). Open daily 10pm-3am, weekends and holidays until 5am. €4 cover for special events gets you drink coupons (drink €4 worth of booze and you'll have earned it back). Cash only.

Cafe Aquarium, Unterer Sand 2 (☎0851 25 90). Students chill out next to the aquariums with a mixed drink (€5.80-6.80) or ice cream, and capitalize on free Wi-Fi. Beer €2.60. W karaoke nights (from 8:30pm). Open Su-Th 10am-1am, F-Sa 10am-2am.

Selly's, Bratfischwinkel 5 (☎0851 711 30). The place to go for gay and lesbian nightlife. Small, Italian-themed bar with nude sculptures, potted plants, and a xylophone of colored water-filled bottles behind the bar. Open M, W-Th 6pm-1am. F 7pm-3am, Sa 2pm-3am,Su 2pm-midnight. Cash only.

REGENSBURG ☎0941

When Goethe first visited Regensburg (pop. 145,000), he wrote: "Regensburg is beautifully situated; the area couldn't help but attract a city." Nearly two millennia ago in AD 179, Roman emperor Marcus Aurelius laid the city's foundations by building the Castra Regina fortress where the Naab and Regen Rivers flow into the Danube. It was the first capital of Bavaria, the seat of the Perpetual Imperial Diet, and the site of the first German parliament. Regensburg was one of the few Bavarian cities to escape major bombing in WWII, and its historic sites are remarkably intact. Today, the city is alive with young people and a surprisingly vibrant nightlife. Indeed, Regensburg is said by many to have more cafes and bars by area than any other city on the entire European continent.

TRANSPORTATION

Trains: Every hr. to: **Munich** (2hr., €22); **Nuremberg** (1hr., €17); **Passau** (1hr., €20).

Ferries: Regensburger Personenschifffahrt, (☎0941 521 40; www.schifffahrtklinger.de), on Thunerdorfstr. next to the Steinerne Brücke. Ferries tourists to Walhalla (p. 386) with commentary in German and English. (45min., May.-Oct. daily 10:30am and 2pm, round-trip €10, students €6.50, children €4.50, families €23). Also offers a **city tour** in German (50min., May-Oct. daily every hr. 10am-4pm, €7.50/4.50/3/16).

Public Transportation: Routes, schedules, and fares for Regensburg's bus system are available at the Presse & Buch store in the Hauptbahnhof, or at the tourist office. Bus map (no fares or times) free. City info €0.50, area bus schedule €1.50. The transport hub is "Bustreff Albertstr.," to the right from the train station. Single ride within zone 1 €1.80; **Tageskarte** for zones 1 and 2 €3.80 (Sa-Su and holidays up to 5 people zones 1-3). Buy tickets at the *Automaten* in bus shelters or from the driver (sometimes more expensive) and validate your ticket on the bus. Buses run until midnight.

Taxis: Taxi Funk Vermittlung Regensburg ☎0941 27 27 70.

Bike Rental: Bike Haus, Bahnhofstr. 17 (☎0941 599 8194; www.bikeproject.de), near the Hauptbahnhof. Offers mountain bikes and 4-person bikes. Also provides route suggestions. €7 for 4hr., €9.50 per day, children €6. Open daily 10am-1pm and 2-7pm.

ORIENTATION AND PRACTICAL INFORMATION

Surrounded by parks, the concentrated Altstadt sits on the southern bank of the Danube, opposite its confluence with the Regen. To the south of the Altstadt

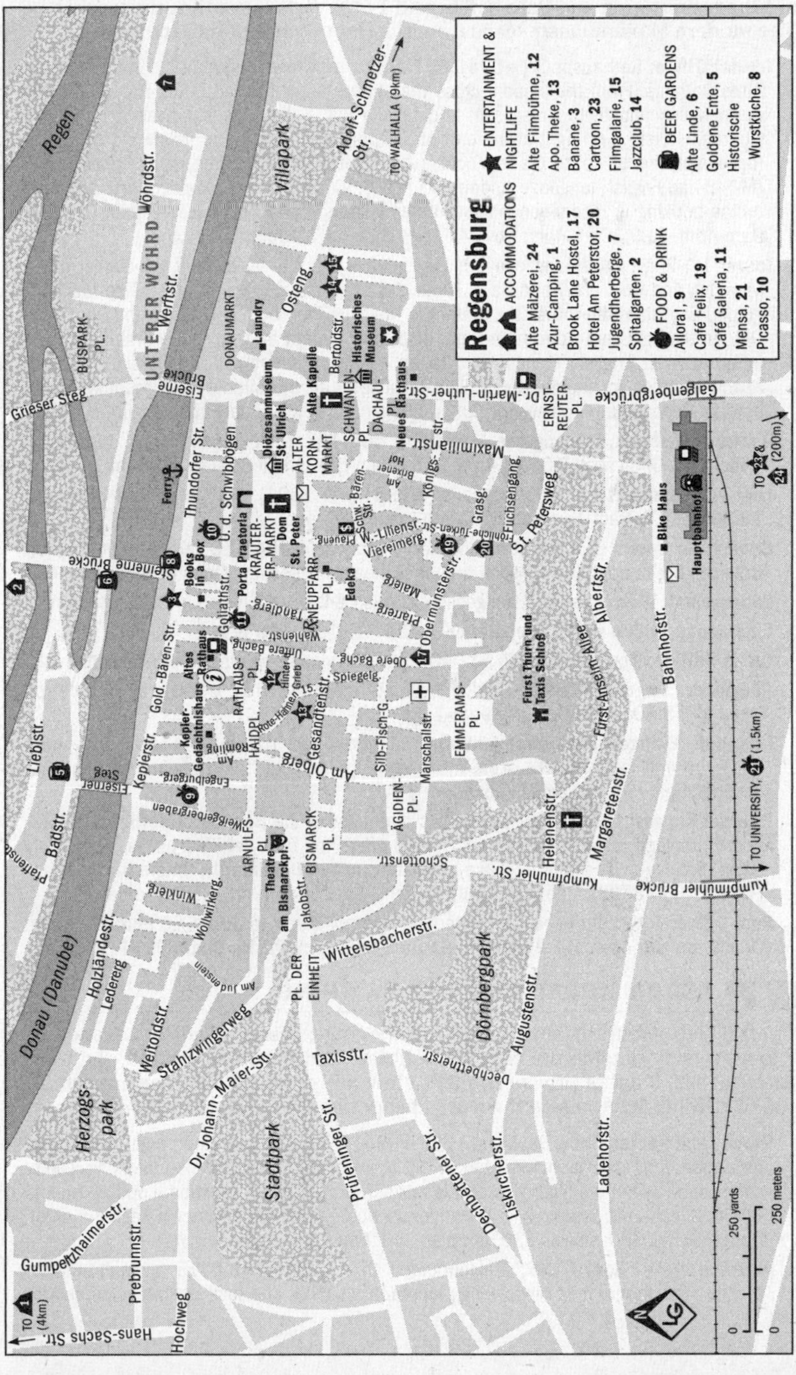
Regensburg
ACCOMMODATIONS
Alte Mälzerei, 24
Azur-Camping, 1
Brook Lane Hostel, 17
Hotel Am Peterstor, 20
Jugendherberge, 7
Spitalgarten, 2
FOOD & DRINK
Allora!, 9
Café Felix, 19
Café Galeria, 11
Mensa, 21
Picasso, 10
ENTERTAINMENT & NIGHTLIFE
Alte Filmbühne, 12
Apo. Theke, 13
Banane, 3
Cartoon, 23
Filmgalarie, 15
Jazzclub, 14
BEER GARDENS
Alte Linde, 6
Goldene Ente, 5
Historische Wurstküche, 8

are the train station and Bahnhofstr, and 1.5km farther south is the university. The modern Maximilianstr. leads from the Hauptbahnhof into the city.

Tourist Office: Rathauspl. 3 (☎0941 507 4410; www.regensburg.de), to the left of the Altes Rathaus. From the station, cross the street, follow the red "Altes Rathaus" signs down Maximilianstr. to Grasgasse, and take a left. Follow the street as it turns into Obermünsterstr., turn right at the end onto Obere Bachgasse and follow it 5 blocks to Rathauspl. The office, to the left across the square, provides free maps, sells tickets (M-Sa) and English-language guidebooks (€6-6.50), and books rooms for free, although online booking is recommended for foreign visitors. Open Apr.-Oct M-F 9am-6pm, Sa 9am-4pm, Su 9:30am-4pm; Nov.-Mar. also Su until 2:30pm.

Tours: 1½-2hr. English-language walking tours of the city leave from the tourist office May-Oct. and Dec. on W and Sa 1:30pm. €8, students €5. Tourist office also has self-guided English **audio tours.** 3hr. rental €8. The "City Tour" bus leaves from the Dom May-Oct. on the hr. 10am-4pm; June-Sept. also 5pm, except at 1pm tour, 45min. recorded information in English, French, and Italian. €7.50, students €6, families €17. Check at tourist office for themed tours, like Regensburg in the Middle Ages (complete with actors), Regensburg for Teens, or Cultural Regensburg. Many have multilingual options.

Banks: Volksbank, Pfauengasse 1 (☎0941 584 70), 1 block south from the Dompl. **24hr. ATM.** Open M-W 8:30am-4pm, Th 8:30am-5:30pm, F 8:30am-3:30pm.

Lost and Found: In the Neues Rathaus (☎0941 507 1196). Open M-W 8am-noon and 12:30-4pm, Th 8am-1pm and 1:30-5:30pm, F 8am-noon.

Bookstore: Books in a Box, Goldene-Bären-Str. 12 (☎0941 56 70 14). Entrance on Brückstr. Dig through their English-language clearance section. Open M-Sa 9am-8pm.

Laundromat: Wasch-Salon, Ostengasse 4a. Wash €4. Dry €2. Open M-Sa 6am-10pm.

Emergency: Police ☎110. **Ambulance** ☎0941 192 22. **Fire** ☎112.

Crisis Hotline: Caritas (☎0941 502 10) counsels victims of rape or other trauma.

Pharmacy: Engel-Apotheke, Tändlergasse 24 (☎0941 567 4850), at Neupfarrpl. Open M-F 8:30am-6:30pm, Sa 9am-2pm.

Hospital: Evangelisches Krankenhaus, Emmeramspl. 10 (☎0941 504 00), near the Thurn und Taxis Schloß, is the most centrally located. It is a private hospital that accepts most forms of foreign insurance plans.

Internet Access: Located just two blocks northeast of the Bahnhof, **Internetcafe Runway,** Luitpoldstr. 2 (☎0941 504 08 00 00) offers the best deal. €1 per hr. Open daily 9am-1am. Free Wi-Fi with purchase at **Boston Coffee Community,** Untere Bachgasse 1 (☎0941 630 8593). Open M-F 7:30am-9pm, Sa 8:30am-9pm, Su 9:30am-6pm.

Post Office: Across from the Hauptbahnhof. Open M-F 8am-6:30pm, Sa 8am-12:30pm. Dompl. **branch** open M-F 9am-6pm, Sa 9am-12:30pm. **Postal Code:** 93047.

ACCOMMODATIONS AND CAMPING

Central Regensburg is short on cheap lodgings; reserve well in advance or expect to stay outside the city. If the hotels and pensions are full, the tourist office has a list of private rooms (a few are in the €22-30 range; most are €35-65). Hotels just outside town are cheaper and accessible by bus.

Brook Lane Hostel, Obere Bachgasse 21 (☎0941 690 0966; www.herberge-regensburg.de). Apartment-style rooms located in the heart of the old city. Small kitchens, comfy sofas, and TVs are the highlights of this rather bare but highly functional option. Sheets €2.50. Check-in at supermarket or call for service. Reserve in advance. Check-out noon. Dorms €15-17.50, singles €30, doubles €40. AmEx/MC/V. ❶

Alte Mälzerei's "Rent A Bed," Galgenbergstr. 20 (☎0941 788 8115; www.alte-maelzerei.de). This former malt processing plant features a bar and rock-bottom accommodations. Expect noise from concerts in the basement during the school year. Check-in M-F 10am-4pm. 4- to 6-bed dorms €12.50, students €10. Cash only. ❶

Jugendherberge (HI), Wöhrdstr. 60 (☎0941 574 02), on an island in the Danube. Bus #3, 8, or 9 from the station to "Wöhrdstr." Sloped ceilings, tile mosaics, and graffiti depicting the city's sights lend character to otherwise typical rooms 20min. from the station. Breakfast included. Reception 7-10am and 3pm-midnight. Doors lock at midnight; access code available. Dorms €19.40, less for longer stays. AmEx/MC/V. ❷

Spitalgarten, St.-Katharinen-Pl. 1 (☎0941 847 74; www.spitalgarten.de), inside a 13th-century hospital with a river view. Bus #17 from the station to "Stadtamhof." Enter by the pink Biergarten. Spacious rooms and sparkling new bathrooms despite not fully modern interior design. Breakfast included. Reception until 6pm, midnight if you call ahead. Reserve well in advance. Singles €30, doubles €54. Cash only. ❷

Hotel Am Peterstor, Fröhliche-Türken-Str. 12 (☎0941 545 45), 5min. from the station. Bare but comfortable rooms with shower, toilet, and TV, on city center's edge. Breakfast €5. Reception 7-10:30am and 4-11pm. Singles €38, doubles €48. MC/V. ❸

Azur-Camping, Am Weinweg 40 (☎0941 27 00 25; www.azur-camping.de). Bus #6 (dir.: Wernerwerkstr.) to "Westheim." Conveniently located right next to the bus stop. Reception 8am-1pm and 3-10pm. €5.50-7.50 per person, €3-4 per child, €6.50-8.50 per site. Small tent site without car €4.50-6.50. Prices higher in summer and during holiday season. Shower and bathroom facilities included in price. Cash only. ❶

FOOD

The 17th-century English dramatist Sir George Etherege noted that Regensburg's "noble, serene air makes us hungry as hawks." To satisfy that hunger, every other doorway is a cafe. Breakfast is an institution. You can't walk two blocks without seeing a supermarket—there's an **Edeka** in the basement of Galeria Kaufhof, Neupfarrpl. 8 (☎0941 533 61; open M-Sa 9am-8pm; cash only), and a **Norma's** inside the Hauptbahnhof (open M-Sa 7am-8pm, Su 10am-8pm).

Cafe Felix, Fröhliche-Türken-Str. 6 (☎0941 590 59; www.cafefelix.de). This lively cafe with classy decor specializes in gigantic salads with ingredients from pineapple to prawns (€8-13). Beer €2.50 (0.5L). Happy hour drinks €3.50. Balcony seating. Open M-Th and Su 9am-2am, F-Sa 9am-3am. Kitchen open until midnight. Cash only. ❸

Cafe Galerie, Kohlenmarkt 6 (☎0941 56 14 08; www.cafe-galerie.de), near the Rathaus. The wonderful "small" breakfast of mixed wurst and cheese, fresh fruit, and a huge basket of rolls and croissants is just €4.80. Fills with a hip, young crowd at night. Free coffee and tea for students. Open daily 9am-2am. AmEx/MC/V. ❸

Allora!, Engelburgerg. 18 (☎0941 584 0783; www.allora-regensburg.de), near Arnulfspl. in the alley between Engelburgergasse and Weißgerbergraben. Colorful wall paintings, bright windows, and a rotating menu with a vegetarian bent. Tasty homemade soup €3.20. Pastas and gnocchi €6.50-8.20. Fish €8-9.50. Open Tu-Su 10am-2pm and 6pm-1am. Kitchen open until midnight. Cash only. ❷

Picasso, Unter den Schwibbögen 1 (☎0941 536 57), down Goliathstr. from the Altes Rathaus. Former Gothic chapel now features pasta instead of prayers under its awe-inspiring yellow vaulted ceiling. 17 varieties of pasta (lunch €4). Mixed drinks €5-7. Open M-Th and Su 10am-2am, F-Sa 10am-3am. Cash only. ❷

Mensa, on Albertus-Magnus-Str., in the park on the university campus. Bus #6 (dir.: Klinikum) or #11 (dir.: Burgweinting) to "Universität Mensa." Plenty of open space, foosball tables, and a ton of students makes for a lively, conversation-rich atmosphere. *Mensa* card available from office on the ground floor near the reading room, open M-F 8:30am-10:45am and 11:45am-2pm; student ID and €10 deposit required. Meals

€2-4. Open M-F 11am-2pm, M-Th also 5pm-7pm.; Nov.-Feb. and May-July also open Sa 11:30am-1:30pm. No evening meals mid-Aug. to mid-Sept. ❶

SIGHTS

DOM ST. PETER. The soaring high-Gothic **Dom St. Peter** and adjacent **Diözesanmuseum St. Ulrich** (St. Ulrich Diocesan Museum) are situated on the city's Dompl. Begun in 1276, the cathedral was completed in 1486, but the delicate 105m twin spires were finished under King Ludwig I in the 19th century. Rich stained-glass windows date from the 13th and 14th centuries. Inside the cathedral is the Domschatz, an impressive collection of gold and jewels. Underneath the Dom is the resting place for many of Regensburg's bishops and recently unearthed Roman ruins. *(Dompl. 1. Dom Information ☎0941 298 6278. Open daily Apr.-Oct. 6:30am-6pm, Nov.-Mar. 6:30am-5pm. Tower closed to the public. German-language tours daily at 2pm, May-Oct. also 10:30am. Meet at info center, Dompl. 5. €3, students and children €1.50. English-language group tours available on advance request. Church choir sings for Solemn Mass Su at 10am. Dom entry free. Domschatz ☎0941 576 45. Open Apr.-Oct. Tu-Sa 10am-5pm, Su noon-5pm; Nov.-Mar. F-Sa 10am-4pm, Su noon-4pm. €2, students €1, families €4. Combination ticket for the Domschatz and Diözesanmuseum €3. Wheelchair access via the Eselturm.)*

WALHALLA. Down the river from Regensburg, this faux-Greek temple, modeled after the Parthenon and named for the mythic resting place of Norse heroes, is poised dramatically on the northern bank of the Danube. **Ludwig I** built the monument of ancient Germanic *Nibelungen* lore between 1830 and 1842 to honor everyone from German kings and generals to poets and scientists. The plaques above the busts honor those whose faces are unknown, such as the author of the *Nibelungenlied.* Albert Einstein is just one of the new members added since Ludwig's time: the Bavarian ministry of culture adds a bust every five or six years. Most recently, they chose **Sophie Scholl,** a young Munich student who was executed for leading the **Weiße Rose** resistance against Hitler in 1942. In summer, students gather on the hallowed steps for picnics and guitar-playing. The bus drops you off at the bottom. After hiking for about 30min. on the trail that winds quickly up past an abandoned house, turn a corner, and bam: a Greek temple right in the middle of the Bavarian forest. *(Take the ferry from Regensburg or bus #5 from the Albertspl. bus station to "Donaustauf Walhallastr." for €2.70, then look for the white signs to "Walhalla" and bear right onto the dirt hiking path (10min.). By bike, take the Donau Radweg. ☎0941 69 16 80. Open Apr.-Sept. daily 9am-5:45pm; Oct. 9am-4:45pm; Nov.-Mar. 10-11:45am and 1-3:45pm. €4, students €3, under 18 free. Guide books and audio tours €4.)*

DOKUMENT NEUPFARRPLATZ. Ten years ago, archaeological excavations revealed the remains of a Gothic synagogue destroyed in 1519 under Regensburg's first Lutheran church (founded 1542). Regenburg's Jews were expelled in the 16th century from the last surviving Jewish community in a German city. The 624 gold coins from the 14th century found at the Neupfarrpl. dig bear witness to its wealth. Beneath the Jewish quarter are vestiges of ancient Roman constructions. A circular Nazi-era bunker is also on display. *(Located beneath Neupfarrpl. Look for the glass and steel triangle. ☎0941 507 1452. Obligatory 1hr. German-language tour Th-Sa 2:30pm; July-Aug. also M and Su. Includes film presentation. Buy tickets at Tabak Götz, Neupfarrpl. 3. €5, students and seniors €2.50.)*

FÜRST THURN UND TAXIS SCHLOSS. Across from the station, this 11th-century Benedictine cloister became the 500-room residence of the Prince of Thurn und Taxis in 1812. The family was originally Italian: *Thurn und Taxis* is the Germanized version of *Torriani e Tassi* (which translates as "towers and badgers," two symbols that are featured prominently on their coat of arms). The house earned its title in 1695, in recognition of its booming business: the first Europe-wide postal service of the modern era. The Thurn clan ran the mail service until it was taken over by Prussia in 1867. In 1991, when the latest Fürst died, the surviving Fürstin opened 25 rooms of the palace to public tours. *(Emeramspl. 5. ☎0941 504 82 42. Open Apr.-Oct. M-F 10:30am-5pm, Sa-Su 9:30am-5pm; Nov.-Mar. Sa-Su 9:30am-4pm. Thorough 1hr. tours Apr.-Oct. daily at 11am, 2, 3, and 4pm, Sa-Su additional tour at 10am and 1pm; Nov.-Mar. Sa-Su at 10, 11am, 2, and 3pm; English-language tours available by advance request and Jul.-Sept. daily at 1:30pm. €11.50, students with ID €9. English audio tour included.)*

ALTES RATHAUS. A few blocks away from the cathedral is the yellow Gothic town hall, which served as the capitol building of the Holy Roman Empire from 1663-1803. The town council is now housed in the adjacent "Neues Rathaus." The permanent meeting of the **Imperial Diet** made Regensburg home to a German parliament of sorts, though it did not bring the city much wealth, since the Imperial delegation did not pay taxes on their imports. The town hall also houses a **Reichstagsmuseum** (Diet Museum). Chair heights reflect the legislators' political ranks: four steps high for the emperor, two for the electors (among them the Wittelsbachs), one for the 100 *Fürsten* (princes). The 50-odd free city representatives sat on ground level. *(1hr. obligatory German tours Apr.-Oct. every 30min. M-Sa 9:30am-noon and 2-4pm, Su 10am-noon and 2-4pm; Nov.-Mar. every hr. English tours May-Sept. M-Sa 3pm. €7.50, students €4. Buy tickets at the tourist office next door.)*

PORTA PRAETORIA. A Roman gateway, the Porta Praetoria is one of only two standing Roman ruins in Germany. (The other is the Porta Nigra in Trier). One of the earliest documents of Regensburg's past can be seen on the front wall of a house built into the ruins of an accompanying wall—a flat foundation stone from the fort of Castra Regina, inscribed with the date AD 179. It's a quick stop but also an incredible historical experience. *(Open 24hr. Free.)*

HISTORISCHES MUSEUM (HISTORICAL MUSEUM). In a former Franciscan monastery, the museum chronicles the city's history from its time as one of the most imporant military strongholds on the Roman border from the 1st to the 5th century to the rich cultural and artistic center it became in the Middle Ages. **St. Salvator,** the massive Franciscan church, is also open to the public. *(Dachaupl. 2-4. ☎0941 507 24 48, www.regensburg.de. Open Tu-W and F-Su 10am-4pm, Th 10am-8pm. €2.20, students €1.10, families €4.40. Audio tours in Czech, English, German, and Italian €2.)*

ENTERTAINMENT AND NIGHTLIFE

Many of the cafes and beer gardens listed under **Food** double as nighttime haunts. Ask at the tourist office for a free copy of *Logo* or *Filter*, or pick up *Stadtzeitung*—these publications list events at bars and cafes in German. Beyond the bar and club scene, Regensburg is a fabulous city for movie- and theatergoers. Stop by the central box office in the **Theater am Bismarckplplatz,** Bismarckpl. 7 (☎0941 507 2424; www.theaterregensburg.de), to inquire about theater, ballet, and opera performances. Discounted "Last Minute Tickets" (€7.50) are available for students 15min. before performances begin. (Open M-F 10am-6pm, Sa 10am-2pm.) This fantastic deal can literally save students up to 86% on tickets to high-end shows, and the box office claims that they rarely run out of them. Kick back to sophisticated live jazz performances at the **Jazzclub,** Bertoldstr. 9. (☎0941 56 33 75; www.jazzclub-regensburg.de. Most performances Th or Su at 8pm. About 60 shows a year, with many Jul.-Aug. Show and dinner events available. Tickets €15-20, students €10-12. Call or check online for upcoming events.)

Students and the local intelligentsia head to **Filmgalarie,** Bertoldstr. 9, next to the jazz club, to enjoy foreign and independent films in their original languages, usually with German subtitles. (☎0941 56 09 01. Tickets €6, students €5. Office open M-F 10am-4pm and in the evening before shows.)

BEER GARDENS

Historische Wurstküche, Thundorfer Str. 3 (☎0941 46 62 10; www.wurstkuchl.de), next to the Steinerne Brücke, with a view of the river. Having recently celebrated its 850th birthday, the local favorite Wurstküche is the oldest operating fast-food joint in Europe—workers who built the nearby bridge in the 12th century broke for lunch here. 6 *Würste* with sauerkraut and bread €7. Beer €3.20 (0.5L). Open daily Apr.-Oct. 8am-7pm; Nov.-Mar. Su 8am-3pm. Cash only.

Alte Linde, Müllerstr. 1 (☎0941 880 80), just over the Steinerne Brücke from the Wurstküche, to the left on the island. Serves students and professors delicious food (entrees €5-10) inside a glass atrium overlooking the river. Exceptionally good selection of salads. Beer €6.20 (1L). Open daily 11am-midnight. AmEx/MC/V.

Goldene Ente, Badstr. 32 (☎0941 854 55). Under chestnut trees on the banks of the Danube, just across the Eiserner Steg footbridge. During summer this centrally located Biergarten, part of the oldest inn in Regensburg, serves steaks, *Würstchen,* and *Wiener Schnitzel* (€5-8). *Helles* (wheat beer) €5.40 (1L). Open daily 11am-1am. Cash only.

BARS AND CLUBS

Alte Filmbühne, Hinter der Grieb 8 (☎0941 579 26). Take the staircase down to the green gate. Regensburg's coolest scene attracts tons of students with its arched stone ceilings, red Chinese laterns, pinball machines, and film posters. Features indie on W and electro on F, soul and hits on Sa, and reggae the first Tu of the month. Beer €2.80. Mixed drinks €4.80, M €3. 18+. Open June-Sept. daily 9pm-2am, Oct.-May 8pm-2am.

Cartoon, Galgenbergstr. 20 (☎0941 78 88 10). Regensburg's lively "Art and Culture Factory," an old malt processing plant, is a hopping student hangout (☎0941 757 38; small meals €4-6.50) playing pop, jazz, funk, reggae, and blues. Bar open daily 5pm-1am. Check website for event dates and prices. Cash only.

Apo.Theke, Rote Hahnengasse 8 (☎0941 584 3999). Candles on bare wood tables and a laid-back bohemian crowd sipping wine (€2-3.50) and beer (€2.70). DJs spin electro, funk, and jazz M and F-Sa. Open M-Sa 10am-2am, Su 10am-1am. Cash only.

Banane, Goldene-Bären-Str. 3 (☎0941 529 70), upstairs from the **Orange Bar,** is the place for hard rock music. Turns into a smoking bar after midnight. Sharks, plastic women, and other oddities hang from the ceiling and walls. Eclectic mix of seating. Beer €2.70, mixed drinks €3-5. Open M-Th and Su 8pm-1am, F-Sa 8pm-3am. Cash only

ROMANTISCHE STRASSE AND BURGEN STRASSE (ROMANTIC ROAD AND CASTLE ROAD)

Vineyards, groomed fields of sunflowers and wheat, rolling hills, and dense forests checker the landscape between Würzburg and Füssen. Officially dubbed the Romantic Road in 1950, the area has become the most heavily touristed part of Germany. In 1954, Bavaria christened the Castle Road, which runs east-west through the region. Both routes have breathed new life into the region, though some towns have preserved their authentic appeal more than others. Every day, Deutsche Bahn's **Europabus** shuttles throngs of tourists from Frankfurt to Füssen and back on the Romantic Road. The Castle Road runs from Mannheim to Prague, although Europabus only services the route from Mannheim to Nuremberg. Europabus's Castle Road bus service is timed to allow a transfer to the Romantic Road bus at Rothenberg. Travelers then head on the Romantic Road bus in the direction of Füssen. Tickets between consecutive towns on the two routes are usually more affordable than the train and are almost certainly more direct. Traveling through each stop also affords a closer look at towns that would typically blur by the window of an ICE.

For those without the railpass discount—or those who prefer to travel on their own schedule without a disembodied voice describing the view from the bus window—a more economical way to see both routes is (paradoxically) to use the faster and more frequent trains, which run to every town except Dinkelsbühl. If you plan to travel by train or local bus, take into account that both run less frequently (or sometimes not at all) on weekends. Those traveling by car may have to park in lots outside the old city walls of some towns, but will have easy access to many suburban budget hotels, private rooms, and campgrounds that lie outside the reach of bus or train. The Romantic Road is an excellent opportunity for a leisurely bike journey, with campgrounds 10-20km apart. Hardcore cyclists could finish the 350km route in a few days, but at a more modest pace you'll be on the road a week or two. Tourist offices offer excellent cycling maps and information on campgrounds along the road. Deutsche Touring also operates regular bus lines between select domestic and international destinations, often at rock bottom prices. For information or reservations, call Deutsche Touring, Am Römerhof 17, 60486 Frankfurt (☎069 790 30; www.touring.de). For more information on the Romantic Road, contact the Romantische Straße Arbeitsgemeinschaft, Waaggässlein 1, 91550 Dinkelsbühl (☎09851 55 13 87; www.romantischestrasse.de). For more info on the Castle Road, contact the Burgen Straße Arbeitsgemeinschaft, Rathaus, 74072 Heilbronn (☎07131 56 22 83). Even better, contact Munich's Euraide office (p. 333); they specialize in information and travel bookings for English-speaking tourists. All Euraide services are free.

AUGSBURG ☎0821

Unlike the many eternally medieval and Baroque cities in Bavaria, Augsburg peaked during the Renaissance. Founded in 15 BC by the Roman emperor Augustus, this town (pop. 272,000) likes to consider itself the northernmost city of Italy. The second-oldest city in Germany, Augsburg was the financial center of the Holy Roman Empire and a major commercial hotspot by the end of the 15th century. The town owes its success in great part to the Fuggers, an Augsburg family that virtually monopolized the banking industry. After the Thirty Years' War, however, Munich eclipsed Augsburg as Bavaria's most important area. WWII destroyed most of the city, and while much of Augsburg was built anew, major historical buildings have been carefully reconstructed in their original style. Today the town exudes an easy-going nonchalance towards its rich history from its cobblestoned streets and inspiring church towers to its lush greenery and endearing backstreet architecture. Mozart's father was born in Augsburg, Mozart himself probably had his first love affair here during a 1777 trip, and the German Mozart Society *(Deutsche Mozart-Gesellschaft)* was founded in Augsburg in 1951. Home to the world's oldest stained glass windows and the birthplace of German playwright and critic

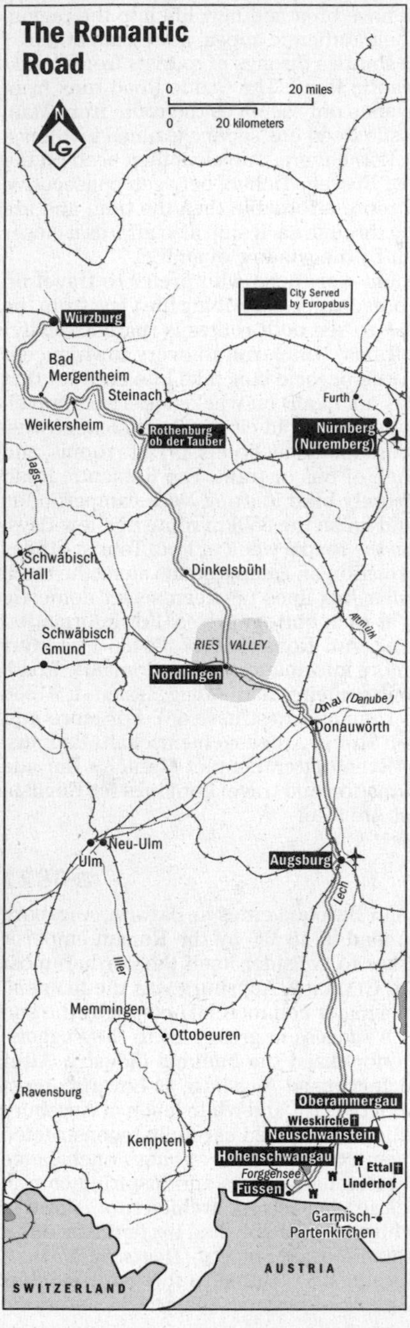

Bertold Brecht, Augsburg today is a small, picturesque city with many tourist attractions to offer.

TRANSPORTATION. Augsburg is connected by **train** to: Berlin (6hr., 2 per hr., €101); Frankfurt (3hr., every hr., €69); Füssen (2hr., 2 per hr., €17); Munich (45min., 3-5 per hr., €10-18); Nuremberg (1-2hr., 2 per hr., €22-32). Augsburg's **public transportation** hub is at Königspl., two blocks down Bahnhofstr. from the station (single ride €1.10, *Tageskarte* (daypass) €5); for transit information, head to the **Stadtwerke Augsburg Bus and Tram Info Center** there, which distributes free maps and schedules. (☎08 21 65 00 58 88. Open M-F 7am-6pm, Sa 9am-1pm.) For a **taxi,** call ☎082 13 50 25 or 363 33. **Rent bikes** at **Rent A Bike,** Maximilianstr. 57, right next to the **tourist office** (☎082 15 02 07 24; open M-F 9am-6pm, Sa 10am-5pm, Su 10am-2pm; from €10 per day, €30 deposit).

PRACTICAL INFORMATION. The **tourist office,** Maximilianstr. 57 (☎082 15 02 07 24, 50 20 72 00 for reservations; www.augsburg-tourismus.de), offers €0.50 city maps and books rooms for a €2 fee. From the station, keep to the right as you follow Halderstr. toward the city center passing the transportation hub on your left. Continue straight onto Katharinen Schätzlerpalais until you reach Maximilianstr. (Open Apr.-Oct. M-F 9am-6pm, Sa 10am-5pm, Su 10am-2pm; Nov.-Mar. M-F 9am-5pm, Sa 10am-2pm.) **Bilingual walking tours** of the city leave from the Rathaus (Apr.-Oct. daily 2pm, Nov.-Mar. Sa 2pm; €7, students €5), and cover the Fuggerei and or the Mozarthaus. From April to October, bus tours of the city in German and English leave from the same place and cover the Goldener Saal, Kurhaustheater, and Schäzlerpalais (Th-Su at

10am; €9, students €7). Other services include: **Sparkasse,** Halderstr. 3, two blocks east of the station (open M and Th 8:30am-6pm, Tu-W 8:30am-4pm, F 8:30am-3pm); **Bücher Pustet,** Karolinenstr. 12 (☎08 21 50 22 40; open M-F 9am-8pm, Sa 9am-6pm); **laundromat,** Heilig-Kreuz-Str. 32; enter on Klinkertorstr. (wash and dry €6-7; open M-Th 7:30am-5pm, F 7:30am-1pm). The **police station** is at Frolichstr. 2 (☎110, non-emergency 082 13 23 21 10). For a **pharmacy,** head to **Stern-Apotheke,** Maximilianstr. 27 on Moritzpl. (☎08 21 82 13 08 38; open M-Tu and Th-F 8:30am-6:30pm, W 8:30am-6pm, Sa 8am-1pm) or check out **DM drug store,** Burgermeister-Fisderstr. 5. Head straight down Bahnhofstr. and bear right onto Burgermeister-Fisderstr. at Königspl. (☎08 21 56 76 202. Open M-Su 9am-8pm.) **Internet access** can be found at **TeleCafe,** Jakoberstr. 1 (☎08 21 45 40 393. €1 per hr. Open M-F 10am-11pm, Sa-Su noon-11pm. **EasyInternet,** Bahnhofstr. 29, across from the train station, offers reasonable rates for internet access. (€1 per hr. ☎082 15 08 18 78; open daily 9am-11pm.) Augsburg's **post office,** Halderstr. 29, is on the right as you exit the Bahnhof. (Open M-F 8am-6:30pm, Sa 9am-1pm.) **Postal Code:** 86150.

ACCOMMODATIONS AND FOOD. Augsburg's new **"Living Cube" Jugendherberge (HI) ❷,** Unterer Graben 6, has better-than-standard HI rooms behind its sleek reception. Large, sparse rooms come with sinks, spacious storage closets, and extra bright reading lights in a central location. Linoleum floors, wooden bunks, and yellow sheets provided. €1 or 2 coin operates closet lock. Floor showers private and clean. From Königspl., take bus #23 (dir: Firnhaberau) to "Pilgerhausstr." (M-Sa until 6pm), or tram #1 (dir: Neuer Ostfriedhof) to "Barfüsserbrücke," walk to the end of Am Perlachbergstr. and turn left onto Mittlerer Graben; follow the street until it becomes Unterer Graben. (☎082 17 80 88 90; www.augsburg-jugendherberge.de. Internet €1 per hr. Breakfast included. Reception 3-10pm, call ahead for later check-in. 4-bed dorm €19.40; 2-bed €24; over 26 €4 extra. Single rooms with shower and toilet €40; doubles €55.40. MC/V.) The cheapest privacy you'll find in a central location is at **Jakober Hof ❸,** Jakoberstr. 39-41, 20min. from the station, across from the Fuggerei. Follow the directions to Rathauspl., then head downhill on Perlachberg, which becomes Barfüsserstr. and eventually Jakoberstr., or take tram 1 or Bus 23 to "Fuggerei." The rooms are spacious and tastefully designed with cable TV. (☎08 21 51 00 30; www.jakoberhof.de. Breakfast and parking included. Singles €26, with bath and TV €49; doubles €39, with shower €54, with bath €64. AmEx/MC/V.) The small **Pension Herrenhäuser ❸,** Georgenstr. 6, has a friendly owner and bright rooms with bathroom and TV. Elegant and still cozy, this pension combines taste with thoughtful decoration. From the Hauptbahnhof, take tram #2 to "Fischertor" and walk straight on Herrenhäuserstr. and walk to Georgenstr. (☎082 13 46 31 73. www.pensionherrenhaeuser.online.de. Breakfast included. Singles €36; doubles €51-56. Cash only.)

Bahnhofstraße, Annastraße, Karolinenstraße, and **Maximilianstraße** are lined with food stands in the summer; some of the *Imbiß* (snack bar) fare can be surprisingly pricey. A **Plus supermarket** is at the corner of Halderstr. and Hermannstr., at the southeast corner of the Königspl. park. (Open M-Sa 8am-8pm.) Try the **König von Flandern ❸,** Karolinenstr. 12, under the bookstore. Augsburg's first brewery smells of yeast and barley. Large portions of soup, salad, and meat entrees (€3-12) are served in a well-decorated basement, and satisfy even the most ravenous Bavarians. (☎08 21 15 80 50; www.koenigvonflandern.de. Beer €2.50 (0.3L), €1 daily 4-6pm. Open daily 11am-1am. Cash only.) The ever-popular **Capitol Cafe ❷,** Maximilianstr. 25, serves breakfast until 5pm, large salads, and a wide variety of meat (€8-13) and vegetarian (€6-10) options. Very popular with the locals after 6pm, the cafe also includes an ice cream bar. The food is fresh and well prepared. (☎082 13 49 72 82; www.capitol-augsburg.com. Beer €3 0.5L. Mixed drinks from 6pm €6-7. Open M-Th and Su 9am-1am, F-Sa 9am-2am; food until 11pm. Cash only.)

SIGHTS. Overlooking the broad Rathauspl. in the city center is the huge **Rathaus,** which encloses the impressive **Goldener Saal** (Gilded Hall), with reconstructed frescoes surrounded by gold centerpieces of the Augsburg Renaissance. (☎082 13 49 63 98. Open daily 10am-6pm. €2, students and children €1.) Those willing to climb 258 narrow steps can catch a view of Augsburg from the **Perlachturm,** next to the Rathaus; enter at Am Perlachberg and Karolinenstr. (Open Apr.-Oct. daily 10am-6pm. €1, children €0.50. Technically open Easter Sunday.) Behind the Rathaus is the former artisans' quarter, a maze of small lanes laced with canals. Up **Hoher Weg** to the left is the **Hoher Dom,** the regional bishop's seat. Built in the 9th century, the cathedral was renovated in the 14th century in Gothic style, and later restored after WWII. The stained glass windows reportedly date from 1140, making them the oldest in the world (though many were bombed in WWII). Impressive frescoe include four panel paintings by **Hans Holbein the Elder.** There's a beautiful garden in front. (Open daily in summer 6am-6:30pm, in winter 6am-5:30pm. German-language tours available M-Sa 10:15am-4pm.) The **Augsburg Puppenkiste** (Puppet Theater) Spitalgasse 15, has a museum of the ornate marionettes that still bring fame to the city with annual productions of The Little Prince, The Ugly Duckling, Aladdin, and, of course, Hansel and Gretel. (www.diekiste.net. Open Tu-Su 10am-7pm, ticket sales until 6pm. €4.20, ages 4-12 €2.70.) The striking **Synagogue** serves as a testament to the 2000 Jews who lived in Augsburg until the 1930s. Turn right from the station on Halderstr.; the synagogue is on the left. Inside, the **Jewish Cultural Museum** has sophisticated, detailed exhibits displaying valuable ritual objects. (☎08 21 51 36 11. Open Tu-F 9am-4pm and Su 10am-5pm. €4, students and children €2. Guided visits in English, German, or Russian can be arranged.) **Bertolt Brecht's birthplace,** next to a stream in a serene old neighborhood, was renovated in 1998 on the 100th anniversary of his birth. Brecht said the house "left us cold, looked very old, very gloomy and shabby (poor, destitute)." The museum, however, is quite warm and welcoming. The museum chronicles the life of the influential 20th-century playwright and poet through photographs, letters, and poetry. From Rathauspl., head downhill on Perlachberg and take the 3rd left onto Auf dem Rain 7. (Open Tu-Su 10am-5pm. €3, students and children €2.) In addition, little red man statues all over the city guide you on a walking tour of various Brecht-related sights.

The new **Maximilianmuseum,** Philippine-Welser-Str. 24, displays remarkable Renaissance sculptures and historical exhibits. Walk through the garden of the Baroque Schaezler Palace to reach the Staatsgalerie (State Gallery), Maximilianstr. 46, a collection of religious art including works by Cranach, Holbein, and Dürer. (☎082 13 24 41 02. Both museums open Tu-Su 10am-5pm. Each €7, students and children €5.50.)

ROTHENBURG OB DER TAUBER ☎09861

As the crossroads of the Romantic and Castle Roads, Rothenburg ob der Tauber (pop. 12,000) caters to tourists seeking an authentic medieval experience. Don't let the hordes of camera-wielding foreigners scare you away. This town, which originally blossomed around 1500, is rife with moody side streets and picturesque parks largely untouched by the tourist deluge. Carefully preserved, pastel-colored Rothenburg may seem more medieval than the Middle Ages themselves, but the town's charm—even if slightly affected—is undeniable.

TRANSPORTATION AND PRACTICAL INFORMATION

Trains: Run to: **Steinach** (15min., every hr., €1.90), where you can transfer to trains for Munich and Würzburg.

Buses: Also serve the train route, sometimes in place of the train in the evening. The **Europabus** (p. 389) leaves from the Busbahnhof, right next to the train station.

Taxi: Call ☎09851 44 05 or 09851 72 27.

Bikes: Rent at **Fahrradhaus Krauss,** Wenggasse 42. From Marktpl. head south on Schmiedgasse and take a left on Wenggasse. (☎09851 34 95; www.fahrradhaus-krauss.de. Open Tu-F 9am-6pm, Sa 9am-1pm. €5 per ½-day, €10 per day. Cash only.)

Tourist office: Marktpl. 2, books rooms and supplies free maps. Free 15min. internet access. Walk left from the station, bear right on Ansbacherstr., and follow it straight to the Marktpl. (15min.); the office is on your right, across the square in the pink building. (☎09851 40 48 00; www.rothenburg.de. Open May-Oct. M-F 9am-6pm, Sa-Su 10am-3pm; Nov.-Apr. M-F 9am-noon and 1-5pm, Sa 10am-1pm.)

Laundromat: Johannitergasse 9 (☎09851 27 75; wash and dry €5.50; open M-F 8am-6pm, Sa 8am-2pm).

Police: Ansbacherstr. 72 (☎110, **non-emergency** ☎09851 97 10).

Pharmacy: Löwen-Apotheke, Marktpl. 3, posting 24hr. pharmacy information (☎09851 93 51 90). Open M-F 8am-6pm, Sa 8:30am-12:30pm.

Internet: Inter@Play, Milchmarkt 3, 2 blocks from Marktpl. (☎09851 93 55 99. €3 per hr. Open daily 8am-2am; closed holidays.)

Post office is at Bahnhofstr. 15, across from the station in the Zentro mall. (Open M-F 9:30am-5pm, Sa 9:30am-noon.) **Postal Code:** 91541.

ACCOMMODATIONS

An incredible number of private rooms (singles €15-30; doubles €28-45) not registered with the tourist office are available; look for *Zimmer frei* (free room) signs in the areas outside the city walls. Despite the abundance of rooms, reservations are recommended in the summer and around Christmas. There are also many pensions in town, some cheaper than others.

Pension Becker, Rosengasse 23 (☎09851 35 60). In the Altstadt, this pension is centrally located and has a friendly owner. Small, bright rooms are well lais out with private shower and toilet. Singles €31, doubles €50, triples €90. MC/V. ❸

Pension Pöschel, Wenggasse 22 (☎09851 34 30). The small, welcoming guesthouse across the street has clean, standard rooms. Breakfast included. Singles €22, doubles €45, triples €55. Cash only. ❷

Pension Raidel, Wenggasse 3 (☎09851 31 15; www.romanticroad.com). A charming budget option in the Altstadt, this 500-year-old half-timbered house has rooms built by the owner. From Marktpl., go down Obere Schmiedgasse and make a left on Wenggasse. Breakfast included. Singles €24, with bath €49; doubles €42/59. Cash only. ❷

Jugendherberge Rossmühle (HI), Mühlacker 1 (☎09851 941 60). This inexpensive hostel was a horse-powered mill in the 16th century, but now features ping-pong and pool tables, a TV room, internet access (€2.40 per 30min.), and an English-speaking staff. Extremely clean, near a park with walking paths. From the tourist office, take a left down Obere Schmiedgasse, and continue until you see the small, white Jugendherberge sign on the right. Breakfast included. Wash €2.50. Dry €2.50. Reception 7am-10:30pm. Curfew 10pm; doorcode available. Dorms €19.70, doubles €25.70 per person. ❷

Gasthof Goldene Rose, Spitalgasse 28 (☎09851 46 38; www.zur-goldenen-rose). This family-run guesthouse on the main street has cheery, spacious rooms with English-language books. Ask for a double (€46-50) in the blue house at the end of the garden. Breakfast included. Singles €24; doubles €38, with bath €70; triples €85. MC/V. ❸

FOOD

Rothenburg's festive *Schneeballen* (snowballs)—thin layers of fried dough rolled into large balls—are available all year. Their traditional powdered sugar coating is now often replaced by elaborate and messy guises involving chocolate, coconut, cointreau, marzipan, and amaretto. Buy them fresh at a *Bäckerei*, such as **Diller's** (the "*Schneeball* king"), which has six locations around town, including one at Obere Schmiedgasse 7, and offers these doughy concoctions for €1-3. (Open in summer M-Th and Su 9am-9pm, F-Sa 9am-10pm; in winter daily 11am-6pm. Cash only.) **Lidl,** Ehrlbacherstr. 48, is a cheap supermarket located just opposite Rad und Tat. (Open M-Sa 8am-8pm. Cash only.) The international tourist traffic supports scores of overpriced restaurants near the **Marktplatz,** but it's not impossible to find good food at budget prices.

Molkerei, Schweinsdorfer Str. 25b (www.molkerei.rothenburg.de). Young locals head outside the city walls to this warehouse-like restaurant to have beer (€2.50 for 0.5L), mixed drinks (€5-7), or some good food, including fresh seafood, from a rotating menu (€4-12). Su brunch 10am-2pm. Open M-Th 5pm-midnight, F-Sa 3pm-2am, Su 10am-midnight. Kitchen open M-Su 6pm-11pm. Cash only. ❸

Zur Höll, Burggasse 8 (☎09851 42 29; www.rothenburg-hoell.de). Those looking for bygone days with their bread will enjoy dining in the oldest house (AD 980) in town. Franconian food (€4-18) in dim candlelight. Open daily 5pm-1am. Cash only. ❸

Pizzeria Roma, Galgengasse 19 (☎09851 45 40), serves large portions of pasta, pizzas, and fresh salads (€4-7) at affordable prices. Open Th-Tu 11:30am-midnight. MC/V. ❷

Gasthof Rödertor, Ansbacherstr. 7 (☎09851 20 22), by the Rödertor, has a *Biergarten* (beer €2.60 for 0.4L) and potato-centric entrees (€4-11). Open daily 11:30am-2pm and 5:30-10:30pm. Cash only. ❸

SIGHTS

MEDIEVAL CRIME MUSEUM. The macabre exhibits in the Medieval Crime Museum present the creative ways in which Europeans have punished one another. The rigidity of medieval law is evidenced in such grim instruments as chastity belts, iron maidens, gag bonnets, the stocks, and the pillory. Downstairs, exhibits detail ancient tortures. Upstairs focuses on death and shaming devices. All displays explained in English. *(Burggasse 3-5. ☎09851 53 59. Open daily Apr.-Oct. 9:30am-6pm, Dec. and Mar. 10am-4pm, Nov. and Jan.-Feb. 2-4pm. Last entry 45min. before closing. €3.80, students €2.60, children €1.70.)*

RATHAUS. The Renaissance Rathaus stands on the Marktpl. Climb the claustrophobia-inducing 60m tower and pay at the top to ascend the last few stairs for a panoramic view. *(Open Apr.-Oct. daily 9:30am-12:30pm and 1-5pm; Nov. and Jan.-Mar. Sa-Su noon-3pm; Dec. daily noon-3pm. €2, children €0.50.)* For a free view of the city and its surrounding countryside, climb atop the medieval **town wall,** accessible at points around the city's inner perimeter. Inside the courtyard behind the Rathaus are the **Historical Vaults,** once a medieval bakery and now a depiction of Rothenburg during the Thirty Years' War, the conflict that destroyed the wealth and prestige of both the city and the Holy Roman Empire. The first floor presents military and social history, while torture instruments lurk in the gloomy stone cells of the dungeon. *(☎09851 867 51. Open Apr.-Oct. daily 9:30am-5:30pm, during Christmas market, 1-4pm. €2, students €1.50, ages 6-10 €0.50, under 6 free.)*

MEISTERTRUNK (MASTER DRAUGHT). According to local lore, during the Thirty Years' War, the conquering Catholic general Johann Tilly offered to spare the town from destruction if any local could chug a cask containing 3.25L (almost a gallon) of wine. Mayor Nusch successfully met the challenge, passed out for several days, then lived to a ripe old age. His saving *Meistertrunk* is reenacted with great fanfare each year (May 29-June 1, 2009). Hang around with all the other tourists for an anti-climactic version of the episode acted out by the clock over the Marktpl. in the pink building (every hr. 11am-3pm and 8-10pm).

JAKOBSKIRCHE. This church is famed for its Altar of the Holy Blood, a beautifully carved wooden Last Supper by Würzburg master Tilman Riemenschneider, who idiosyncratically placed Judas at the center. A former pilgrimage site, the church holds a famous reliquary: three drops of Jesus' blood. The **Altar of the Twelve Apostles** is also a masterpiece, with paintings by Nördlingen artist Friedrich Herlin. *(Klostergasse 15. ☎09851 70 06 20. Open Apr.-Oct. M-Sa 9am-5:15pm, Su 10:45am-5:15pm; Dec. daily 10am-5pm; Nov. and Jan.-Mar. daily 10am-noon and 2-4pm. €2, students €0.50. Free German-language tours May-Sept. and Dec. 11am and 2pm. Free English-language tours Sa 3pm. Free 30min. organ concerts July-Aug. W 5pm.)*

WÜRZBURG ☎0931

Sweeping vistas of the Main River, striking Baroque churches, and the 13th-century Marienburg fortress form the perfect setting to sample famous local white wines, a Würzburg (pop. 134,000) passion every bit as strong as any Bavarian fondness for *Bier*. The fortress and flamboyantly Rococo Residenz, now host to museums and festivals, are symbols of the past power of Würzburg's prince-bishops. These sovereigns, who governed this part of Franconia from 1168 until 1802, steered the region back to Catholicism even as its citizens longed to adhere to the principles of the Reformation. Today, the city is known for Julius-Maximilians-Universität, a hub for science which counts 13 Nobel Prize winners among its faculty. Over 80% of the city was destroyed by bombings in the last days of WWII, but most of the historic buildings have been restored or rebuilt, making Würzburg a scenic gateway to the Romantic and Castle Roads. A kind of "little Munich," the town offers an array of history, nightlife, attractions, festivals, and funny local traditions.

TRANSPORTATION

Trains: To: **Bamberg** (1hr., 2 per hr., €17); **Frankfurt** (2hr., 2 per hr., €22.40); **Munich** (3hr., 3 per hr., €61); and **Rothenburg ob der Tauber** (1hr., 1 per hr., €11).

Buses: Europabus (p. 389) traces the Romantic Road to Füssen and Munich daily starting at 10am. The bus station is to the right of the Hauptbahnhof.

Ferries: Personenschifffahrt (☎0931 556 33; www.vpsherbert.de) ferries tourists to **Veitschöchheim** (one-way 40min.), leaving from Alter Kranen (near the Congress Center) at the white kiosk, every hr. 10am-4pm. €6, round-trip €9. The rival company next door is similar, but generally attracts an older crowd.

Public Transportation: Trams are the most efficient way around, but large sections outside the downtown are not covered. The **bus** network is comprehensive, but most routes do not run nights or weekends. Ask for **night bus** schedules at the **Reisezentrum**

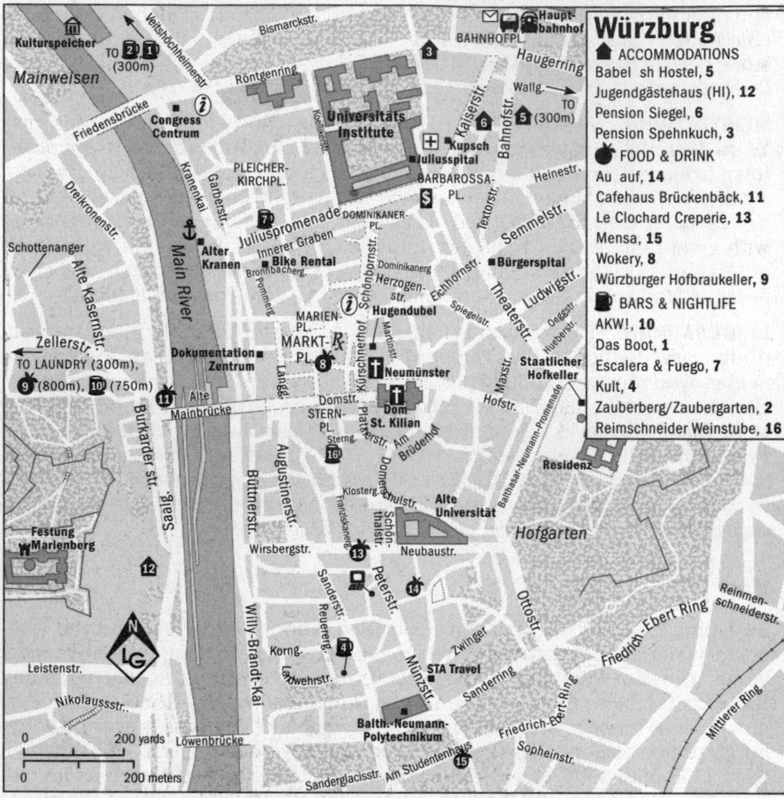

in the Hauptbahnhof (open M-F 6am-8pm, Sa 8am-7pm, Su 8am-8pm) or the info booth located right across the hall (open daily 6am-10:30pm) or at the **WVV Center,** Juliuspromenade 64 (open M-F 9am-5:30pm, Sa 9am-1:30pm). Single fare €2. 6 trips €7.95. Day ticket €4.10, families €8.30. Sa-Su day ticket covers both days.

Taxi: ☎0931 194 10.

Bike Rental: Ludwig Korner, Bronnbachergasse 3 (☎0931 53 340), just north of Marktpl. €12 per day, €50 per week. Open M-F 9am-6pm, Sa 9am-2pm.

ORIENTATION AND PRACTICAL INFORMATION

To get to the city's center at Marktplatz, follow the pedestrian zone all the way to the city center. Head straight across the street from the Bahnhof onto Kaiserstr. and follow it for two blocks, then take a right on Juliuspromenade, and hang a left on Schönbornstraße, the main pedestrian and tram road; the Markt is a few blocks down and to the right. Trams #1, 3, and 5 run from the station to the Markt. The Main River separates the rest of the city from the steep surrounding hills. The **Festung Marienberg** (p. 399) lies in the West; its ubiquitous visibility makes it a good point of reference.

Tourist Office (☎09851 37 23 98) in Haus zum Falken, a yellow Rococo building on the Marktpl. right next to the big church (the Marienkapelle). Provides free city maps, lists hotels, and books rooms for free. Open Apr.-Dec. M-F 10am-6pm, Sa 10am-2pm; May-Oct. also Su 10am-2pm; Jan.-Mar. M-F 10am-4pm, Sa 10am-1pm. The **main office,** Am Congress Centrum (☎09851 37 23 35; www.wuerzburg.de), offers the same services. Near the Friedensbrücke, where Röntgenring intersects the Main, accessible by tram #2 or 4. Open M-Th 8:30am-5pm, F 8:30am-1pm. After hours, there's a map and hotel information on the board just outside the Hauptbahnhof.

Tours: German language tours of the city depart mid-Mar. to Oct. daily at 10:30am. (€6, students €4.) English-language tours daily 6:30pm; meet in front of the tourist office (€6, students €4). For nocturnal adventures, join the (German-speaking) night watchman, with lantern and spear, on his rounds of the Altstadt. W-Sa Apr.-Dec. 8 and 9pm; Feb.-Mar. 8pm only. Meet at the fountain across from the Rathaus. (€4, children free.)

Bus tours: Leave the bus station and return 2hr. later. In German. Apr. to Oct. M-Sa 2pm, Su 10:30am. (☎0931 36 23 20. €8.90, students €7.90.) For a comprehensive list of tours (in German), ask at the tourist office for the brochure *Führungen & Ausflüge*.

Budget Travel: STA, Zwinger 6. (☎0931 521 76). Open M-F 9:30am-6pm and Sa 9:30am-1pm.

Currency Exchange: Sparkasse, Barbarossapl. 2 (☎0931 304 8910). Open M-W and F 8:30am-4:30pm, Th 8:30am-6:30pm.

Laundromat: Waschhaus, Frankfurterstr. 13a. Wash €3. Dry €0.50 per 10min. Open M-Sa 7am-10pm. Located at a tram stop.

Emergency: Police ☎110. **Fire** and **Ambulance** ☎112.

Pharmacy: Engel Apotheke, Marktpl. 36 (☎0931 32 13 40), posts 24hr. pharmacy information. Open M-F 8:30am-6:30pm, Sa 8:30am-4pm.

Internet Access: Rolan Telecommunications, Peterstr. 10 (☎0931 404 72 75) offers clean stations, leather chairs, and printing, scanning, and copying facilities. €1.50 per hr., €10 per day, €6 access from 5-11pm. Open M-F 9am-midnight, Sa 10am-midnight, Su 1pm-midnight.

Post Office: Bahnhofpl. 2. Open M-F 8am-6pm, Sa 9am-noon. **Postal Code:** 97070.

ACCOMMODATIONS

Würzburg's accommodations are surprisingly pricey. The least expensive beds can be found near the Hauptbahnhof, around Kaiserstr. and Bahnhofstr. Bright streetlights and fairly continuous foot traffic at night make this neighborhood feel more safe despite its proximity to the downtown area.

Babelfish Hostel, Prymstr. 3 (☎0931 304 0430; www.babelfish-hostel.de), 500m from the Hauptbahnhof. From the station, cross over to the far side of Haugerring and turn left. Walk about 7min. and look for the green, yellow, and red sign on the 3rd fl. just before the rotary. This funky, space-themed hostel comes complete with free coffee from its large kitchen, hand-painted murals, and flowers hanging from the ceiling above the showers. Wheelchair-accessible. Sheets €2.50. Free internet. Wash and dry €4. 10-bed dorms €16, 6- to 8-bed €17, 4-bed €18, 2-bed €22. Cash only. ❷

Jugendgästehaus (HI), Burkarderstr. 44 (☎0931 425 90). Tram #3 (dir.: Heidingsfeld) or #5 (dir.: Heuchelhof-Rottenbauer) to "Löwenbrücke," then backtrack 300m. Follow the Jugendherberge sign down the stairs, turn right, and walk through the tunnel; it's on the left. Enormous villa with big lockers, heavy wooden doors, and great views. Wheelchair-accessible. Breakfast included. Reception from 8am. Check-in 2-10pm. Curfew 1am; door code available. 4- to 8-bed dorms €21.50, singles €25.50. Cash only. ❷

Pension Spehnkuch, Röntgenring 7 (☎0931 547 52). Turn right after leaving the station and walk 1min. down Röntgenring. Renovated rooms are small and basic, but conveniently located. Breakfast included. Free Wi-Fi. Singles €31-33, doubles €56-62, triples €78-81. Call ahead Dec.-Feb. Cash only. ❸

Pension Siegel, Reisgrubengasse 7 (☎0931 529 41), features a vast mural in the stairwell and basic rooms situated just off Bahnhofstr. Breakfast included. No reception M-Sa 2-5pm, Su 12:30-6:30pm. Singles €33, doubles €62. Cash only. ❸

FOOD

Würzburg's distinctive wines are sold in equally distinctive bottles, known as *Bocksbeutel* (goat bags; locals claim that they emulate the shape of goats' testicles). To sample the wine, **Juliusspital,** Juliuspromenade 19 (Apr. to mid-Nov. F-Sa 5pm), **Bürgerspital,** Semmelstr. 2 (Apr.-Oct. Sa 2pm), and **Staatlicher Hofkeller,** next to the Residenz (Mar.-Nov. Sa-Su every hr. 10am-noon and 2-5pm; Su no 5pm tour) all offer 1hr. **Kellerführungen** (cellar tours; €6), which include a glass of wine. Ask at the tourist office. For groceries, try **Kupsch,** Kaiserstr. 5, near Barbarossapl. (Open M-F 8am-8pm, Sa 8am-6pm. Cash only.) **Killian's Bäckerei,** Domstr. 7, is a bakery with seating, sandwiches, and ice cream in addition to a wide array of freshly baked goods. (☎0931 120 51. Open M-F 7am-7pm, Sa 7am-5pm, Oct.-May also Su 1-5pm. Cash only.)

Le Clochard Creperie/Bistro, Neubaustr. 20 (☎0931 129 07, www.leclochard.de). Hearty crepes, sandwiches, and vegetarian dishes (€4-8) on a quiet street. Crepe of the day and coffee €3.50, daily 3-5pm. Open M-Tu 5pm-1am, W-Su 10am-1am. MC/V. ❷

Auflauf, Peterpl 5 (☎0931 57 13 43). Generous portions of delicious *Auflauf* (casseroles) with ingredients ranging from shittake mushrooms to spicy shrimp and pineapple (€8-10). Lunch specials M-F noon-2:30pm €5.60. Open M-F noon-2:30pm and 5:30pm-midnight, Sa-Su noon-midnight. Kitchen open until 11:30pm. MC/V. ❸

Riemenschneider Weinstube, Franziskanerg. 1a (☎0931 57 14 87). Enjoy traditional Bavarian specialities and delectable seafood entrees (€5-10) in the wine cellar of the famous sculptor's former residence. Stone walls, wooden chandeliers, and candlelight. Open Tu-Sa 5pm-midnight, Su 11am-midnight. Cash only. ❷

Wokery, Schmalzmarkt 5 (☎0931 04 19 22; www.wokery.de). Chinese buffet with many vegetarian options. Pay by plate size, not weight. W-Sa from 6pm, all you can eat €7.77; arrive by 6pm for full selection. Open Tu 11am-8pm, W-Sa 11am-9pm. Cash only. ❷

Cafehaus Brückenbäck, Zellerstr. 2, by the Alte Mainbrücke (☎0931 41 45 45). Large windows overlooking the river. Salads, sandwiches, and rice dishes €4-8.50. Daily lunch special €5 for *Flammkuchen* noon-2pm. Open Tu-W and Su 8am-midnight, Th-Sa 8am-1am. Kitchen closes 11pm. Cash only. ❷

Würzburger Hofbraukeller, Höchbergerstr. 28 (☎0931 429 70). Biergarten serving local brew (€3, 0.5L). Frankish specialties €6-18 are worth a splurge. Open daily 11am-midnight; garden closes daily at 11:30pm, food until 10pm. MC/V. ❸

Mensa, Am Studentenhaus, 1 block from Sanderring. University dining hall serving international cuisine to local students. Attractive indoor and outdoor seating. Discount with student ID. Entrees €4-6. Open M-Th 7:30am-7pm, F 7:30am-2pm, Sa 11am-2pm. Breakfast from 7:30am. Lunch 11am-2pm, dinner (M-Th only) 4:30-7pm. ❷

SIGHTS

RESIDENZ. Visit the town's most glorious sight for free. Johannes Zick's **ceiling fresco** in the first-floor garden room epitomizes the extravagance of the 18th-century Residenz. The work is so bright that it has never needed to be restored, although the artist's use of such extravagant colors got him fired. The Italian painter Giovanni Tiepolo replaced him, creating the largest frescoed ceiling in the world, above the grand staircases. Now that restoration on Tiepolo's masterpiece is complete, his work in the **Kaisersaal,** which combines painting, sculpture, and stucco for stunning depth. Then-unknown architect Balthasar Neumann made the Residenz's shallow dome so sturdy that it withstood Allied bombings. His glass room and gaudy pink marble **Residenzhofkirche** also deserve careful attention. The university's **Martin-von-Wagner-Museum,** in a wing of the Residenz, displays Greek antiques that belonged to the collector, whom Ludwig commissioned to create the Glyptothek and the Antikensammlung in Munich. A number of pieces, including early Italian and fleshy Baroque paintings, ended up in the intermediary's house. Behind the complex, the **Hofgarten** is trisected into an Italian amphitheater, a geometric Austrian garden with cone-shaped evergreens, and a faux-wild English garden (all the rage after 1780). *(From the station, walk down Kaiserstr., and veer right onto Theaterstr. ☎0931 35 51 70; www.residenz-wuerzburg.de. Open daily Apr.-Oct. 9am-6pm, Nov.-Mar. 10am-4:30pm. Last entry 30min. before closing. Exceptionally informative tours in English depart daily at 11am and 3pm. €5, students and seniors €4. Martin-von-Wagner-Museum's painting gallery. ☎0931 31 22 88; www.uni-wuerzburg.de/museum. Open Tu-Sa 10am-1:30pm. Greek collection open 1:30-5pm. The 2 galleries alternate being open Su 9:30am-12:30pm. Both free. Church open the same times as the Residenz. Free. Gardens open in summer dawn-8pm, in winter dawn-6pm. Free.)*

FESTUNG MARIENBERG (MARIENBERG FORTRESS). This striking fortress has been holding vigil over the Main since the 12th century, when the prince-bishops lived here before the Residenz was built. The **Fußweg** (footpath) to the fortress starts a short distance from the Medieval **Alte Mainbrücke,** lined with Baroque statues of saints and figures, and built to exalt the prince-bishops' prestige during the Counter-Reformation. The strenuous climb to the Festung reveals the strategic value of its lofty location. Within the fortress compound, you'll find the 11th-century **Marienkirche,** the 40m high 12th-century Bergfried watchtower under which lies the **Hole of Fear** (a dungeon), the Fürstengarten rose garden, and the 104m deep Brunnentempel well. *(Garden open M until 4pm, Tu-Su until 5:30pm. Well open M 9am-3:30pm, Tu-F 9am-5:30pm, Sa-Su only by guided tour.)* Artifacts from the lives of the prince-bishops, scale-models of Würzburg at both its ancient splendor and post-WWII deprivation, and *objets d'art* cluster in the **Fürstenbaumuseum** (Princes' Building Museum). *(☎0931 55 17 53. Open Tu-Su Apr. to mid-Oct. 9am-6pm; mid-Oct. to Mar. 10am-4pm; last entry 30min. before closing. €4, students €3.)* Outside the walls of the main fortress, the long hallways of the **Mainfränkisches Museum** (Main-Frankish Museum), a former arsenal, are lined with religious statues featuring the expressive wooden sculptures of Tilman Riemenschneider (1460-1531), the "Master of Würzburg." Legend holds that the "Master" paid dearly for siding with the peasants in their 16th-century revolts: when the insurrection was suppressed, the bishop Julius Echter allegedly had the sculptor's fingers broken to prevent him from working again. Riemenschneider's house is now a restaurant on Franziskanergasse. *(Take bus #9 from the Residenzpl. to "Festung," or a 30min. walk. Tours in German depart from the courtyard Apr.-Oct. Tu-F 11am, 2, 3pm. Sa-Su every hr. 10am-4pm, except noon. €3, seniors and students €2. English-language guidebooks at museum shop or kiosks, €2.60. Mainfränkisches Museum ☎0931 20 59 40. Open Tu-Su Apr.-Oct. 10am-5pm, Nov.-Mar. 10am-4pm; last entry 30min. before closing. €4, students €2, under 14 free. Audio tour in English €3. Pass to both museums €5.)*

DOM ST. KILIAN. The 950-year-old Catholic cathedral was rebuilt in the 1960s after destruction in WWII. The interior's modern design represents the passage of time, from the menorah symbolizing the Old Testament to the white Christ emerging from a golden medallion at the altar. *(☎0931 21 18 30; www.dom-wuerzburg.de. Open Easter-Oct. M-Sa 10am-7pm, Su 1-6pm; Oct.-Easter M-Sa 10am-noon and 2-5pm,*

Su 12:30-1:30pm and 2:30-6pm. Free. Tours M-Sa 12:20pm, Su 12:30pm and include the otherwise inaccessible Schönbornkappelle. €2.50, students €2. Organ concerts M-Sa at 12:05pm.)

DOKUMENTATION ZENTRUM (DOCUMENTATION CENTER). On March 16, 1945, the Allies dropped 300,000 firebombs on Würzburg, obliterating the city. This small exhibit has photographs, a startling diorama of the city after the bombing, and names of the some of the victims on the ceiling. A rare look at what it really means to live in a city that was 80% destroyed. *(At the town hall by the Alte Mainbrücke, face the "Ratskeller" restaurant, and head into the small alley just to the left. The entrance is on the right just before the arch. Open daily 9am-11pm. Free.)*

ENTERTAINMENT AND NIGHTLIFE

In summer, Würzburg finds a reason to party almost every weekend, with the largest **African festival** in Europe (Africa-Festival, May 29-June 1, 2009), the lively **Kiliani-Volksfest** (July 3-19, 2009; take tram #4 to "Talavera")—dedicated to the patron saint Killian, an Irish bishop who died a martyr's death in Würzburg—and the **Mozartfest** (May 29-July 5, 2009, www.mozartfest-wuerzburg.de), with many concerts in the beautiful Residenz gardens. Würzburg's young and beautiful party around **Sanderstraße,** a pedestrian street packed with bars and clubs, and along **Juluispromenade;** the streets near the **Marktplatz** offer a number of outdoor cafes. For a list of concerts, events, and club parties, check out the free German magazine *Frizz*.

Das Boot, Veithöchheimerstr. 14 (☎0931 593 53; www.das-boot.com). Large fishing ship anchored in the Main with wildly cool lighting and decoration. Join rowdy students dancing to all genres of music. Cover Th €3, F €3-8, Sa €5. Beer €2.80 (0.5L). Th 2 beers €2.50, mixed drinks €4 (€4.50 all night F and until midnight Sa). Open Th 8pm-4am, F-Sa 8pm-5am. Cash only.

Kult, Landwehrstr. 10 (☎0931 531 43), right off Sanderstr. toward the Ludwigsbrücke, is a mellow bar and cafe run as a co-op catering to students. A solid hang-out joint for young people who like rolling their own cigarettes and reading poetry. Sa-Su create-your-own breakfast menu until 3pm. Entrees €4-8. Beer €2.50 (0.5L). Open M-F 9am-1am, Sa-Su 10am-1am or later. Cash only.

AKW!, Frankfurterstr. 87 (☎0931 41 78 00; www.akw-info.de). Take tram #2 or 4 to "Siebold Museum," walk 50m away from city, and look for the small blue sign on the left. A bistro, beer garden, and club that attracts indie and reggae crowds on alternating nights. Cover €3-14; many events free. Beer €2.70 (0.5L). Bistro and Biergarten open daily 3pm-2am. Food (€3-6) until midnight. Disco open F-Sa 11pm-5am. Cash only.

Zauberberg/Zaubergarten, Veithöchheimerstr 20 (☎0931 329 2680; www.zauberberg.info). Club with blacklight, loud music, lounge, and cozy beer garden that becomes a hookah tent in winter. Beer €3.80 (0.5L). Th student night (drinks 2 for 1). 3rd F of the month gay night. Sa 30+. Cover Th €3-4, F-Sa €5, before 11pm €2.50; more for special events. Club open Th 9pm-4am, F-Sa 9pm-5am. Garden open M-Sa 4pm-1am, Su 1pm-1am. Cash only.

Escalera & Fuego, Juliuspromenade 7 (☎0931 359 8306). This touristed restaurant and bar takes its Caribbean theme seriously, with a rainforest upstairs (including tropical salt water aquarium). Pricey mixed drinks €6-8, M-W €3.90. Happy hour daily 6-8pm and 1-2am. Open M-Th and Su 5pm-2am, F-Sa until 3am or later. Cash only.

NÜRNBERG (NUREMBERG) ☎0911

Before the names Berlin or Munich meant anything, Nuremberg (pop. 500,000) was one of the most important cities in the German Reich. Albrecht Dürer, the foremost German Renaissance painter, worked here, part of a wider Nuremberg arts community that bloomed during the 14th-16th centuries. Although the Holy Roman Empire was a loose confederation with no true capital, the free city of Nuremberg considered itself the unofficial one, holding Imperial Diets at the Kaiserburg. Drawing on tradition, Hitler chose the city for his massive rallies, held each September from 1933 to 1938, and proclaimed his 1935 Racial Purity Laws here as well. Accordingly, the Allies took aim and by 1945 reduced 90% of the city's historical buildings to rubble. Because of Nuremberg's Nazi ties, the Allies also selected this city to host the war crimes tribunals of 1945.

Apart from the rally site and other Nazi relics, the city is famous for its toy fair and *Weihnachtsmarkt* (Nov. 11-Dec. 24, 2009 and 2010), for its sausages and gingerbread, and as the birthplace of composer Johann Pachelbel. The city's gritty rock vibe, boisterous shopping district, open-air markets, and raging nightlife is punctuated by quaint medieval cobblestone streets. Today, the city's Renaissance buildings are not the only things being reconstructed—every other year since the early nineties, the city has given out a human rights award as part of the attempt by Nurembergers to refashion their city as the *Stadt der Menschenrechte* (City of Human Rights).

TRANSPORTATION

Flights: The airport, Flughafenstr. 100 (☎0911 937 00) is 7km north of Nuremberg. U2 connects the airport to the city (15min., €1.80).

Trains: To: **Berlin** (4½hr., every hr., €86); **Frankfurt** (2hr., 2 per hr., €46); **Munich** (1hr., 2 per hr., €47); **Prague, Czech Republic** (6-7hr., 1 per hr., €45-84); **Regensburg** (1hr., 2 per hr., €17); and **Stuttgart** (2-3hr., every hr., €30-36).

Public Transportation: U-Bahn, trams, buses, regional trains (R-Bahn), and S-Bahn. Single ride within the city €1.90. *Kurzstrecke* (short distance) €1.50. 10-stripe *Streifenkarte* €8.60. Day or weekend card €3.80. The **Tagesticket Plus** day card covers 2 adults and 4 children for €6.40. The **Nürnberg Card,** available at the tourist office, covers 2 consecutive days of public transportation and entrance to all museums, as well as other discounts, for €19. Further information on the public transit system is available at the VGA office in the Königspl. underpass. Open M-F 7am-8pm, Sa 9am-2pm.

Taxis: Taxizentrale ☎0911 194 10 or **City Taxi** 0911 27 27 70.

Bike Rental: Ride on a Rainbow, Adam-Kraft-Str. 55 (☎0911 39 73 37; www.ride-on-a-rainbow.de), northwest of the Altstadt. Take Johannisstr. to Frauenholzstr. and turn right, then another right onto Adam-Kraft-Str. Bikes (not actually rainbow-colored) €8-10 per day. Open M-Tu and Th-F 10am-7pm, W 2:14-7:19pm, Sa 10am-3pm.

Ride Share: Mitfahrzentrale, Hummelsteiner Weg 12 (☎0911 194 40; www.citytocity.de). 100m from the southern exit of the Hauptbahnhof. Open M-F 9am-6pm, Sa 9am-1:30pm, Su 10am-1pm.

ORIENTATION AND PRACTICAL INFORMATION

Nuremberg's old city wall encloses the worthwhile central district. From the Hauptbahnhof, follow the "Ausgang City" signs down into the tunnel and the "Altstadt" signs out the other side to reach the main thoroughfare, Königsstr. From there, head north to Lorenzerpl. and the pedestrian zone that straddles the river. Modern cafes, shopping centers, and Nuremberg's red light district cover the southern half on the city near the Bahnhof, while open squares, museums, and the city's 11th-century Kaiserberg hold watch over the north.

Tourist Offices: Königstr. 93 (☎0911 233 61 31; www.tourismus-nuernberg.de). Walk through the tunnel from the train station to the Altstadt and take a right; it will be on your left. The staff books rooms and distributes English maps for free. They also sell

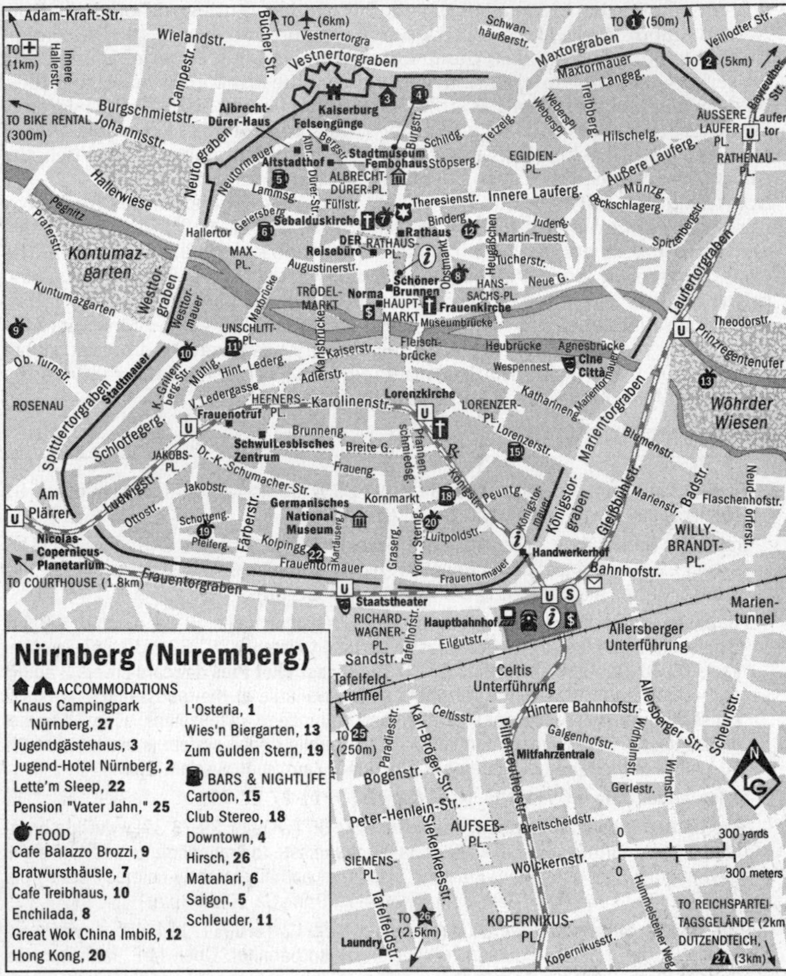

city guides (€4-8.50) and event schedules. Open M-Sa 9am-7pm and Su 10am-4pm. **Branch** (☎091 12 33 61 35) on the Hauptmarkt near the fountain. Open May-Oct. M-Sa 9am-6pm, Su 10am-4pm; Nov.-Apr. M-Sa 9am-6pm.

Tours: 2½hr. English tours depart from the Hauptmarkt tourist office May-Oct. and Dec. daily at 1pm. €9, under 14 free. A bilingual 2½hr. combo bus and walking tour leaves from the Hallpl. (Mauthalle) May-Oct. and Dec. daily 9:30am. €13, students €9, under 12 €6.50 (☎0911 202 29 10). Additionally, a Nightwatchman tour leaves from Hauptmarktpl. Apr-Sept. F at 7pm. €9, students €6. The tourist office rents self-guided English-language audio tours. (www.cityaudiotours.de. €5 per 3hr.)

Currency Exchange: Reisebank (☎0911 22 67 78; www.reisebank.de), in the central hall of the train station. €3-5 commission for currency exchange. Traveler's checks €6, AmEx free. Open M-Sa 7:30am-7:45pm, Su 8am-12:30pm and 1:15-4pm.

Luggage Storage: In the Hauptbahnhof. Several different locker clusters in the various station halls. Up to 72hr. €2-8.

Lost and Found: Fundbüro, Siebenkeesstr. 6 (☎0911 431 76 24). Open M-W 9:30am-4pm, Th 9:30am-6pm, F 9:30am-12:30pm. For items lost on trains, go to DB Fundstelle (☎091 12 19 20 21) in the Hauptbahnhof. Open M-F 7:30am-7pm, Sa 8-11:30am and 12:15-6pm.

Gay and Lesbian Resources: Fliederlich e.V. SchwulLesbisches Zentrum, Breite G.76 (☎0911 423 45 70; www.fliederlich.de), on the 2nd fl. (German 1st fl.). Open M noon-2pm and W 11am-2pm. Additionally, gay men can call **Rosa Hilfe** ☎0911 194 46; open W 7-9pm), and lesbians can call **Lesben-Beratung** (☎0911 42 34 57 25; open 1st and 3rd M of the month 7-9pm).

Laundromat: SB Waschsalon, Tafelfeldstr. 42 (☎0911 598 59 25). Wash €3.50. Dry €0.50 per 12min. Open M-Sa 7am-11pm.

Emergency: Police, Theresienstr. 3 (☎110). **Fire** ☎112. **Ambulance** ☎0911 192 22.

Rape Crisis: Frauennotruf, Ludwigspl. 7 (☎0911 28 44 00; www.frauennotruf.info).

Pharmacy: Königstr. 31 (☎0911 22 45 51). Open M-F 8:30am-6:30pm, Sa 9am-4pm.

Hospital: Städtisches Klinikum Nord, Prof.-Ernst-Nathan-Str. 1 (☎0911 389 25 22); Städtisches Klinikum Süd, Breslauer Str. 201 (39 80).

Internet Access: Tele Point, Königstorpassage 20, in the underground level of the train station. When you descend, at the city mosaic head left toward the U-Bahn. €1.50 per hr. Leather seats and rather clean workstations. Open daily 8am-midnight.

Post Office: Bahnhofpl. 1. Open M-F 8am-7pm, Sa 9am-2pm. **Postal Code:** 90402.

ACCOMMODATIONS AND CAMPING

Nuremberg's budget options can fill quickly in summer; reserve in advance.

Jugendgästehaus (HI), Burg 2 (☎0911 230 93 60). From the Hauptmarkt, head toward the golden fountain on the far left and bear right on Burgstr. Walk toward the castle and follow the sign (20min.). A 15th-century stable for the imperial castle, the hostel has Romanesque arches, a dizzying view of the city, and friendly multilingual staff. Basic rooms, linoleum floors, 2-6 bunk beds. June and July define the phrase "overrun with schoolchildren;" reserve at least 3wk. in advance. Internet €3 per hr. Reception 7am-1am. Staffed 24hr. Curfew 1am, ask ahead for flexibility. 4- to 6-bed dorms €21.40, 4+ nights €20.30; singles €39.50. AmEx/MC/V. ❷

Lette'm Sleep, Frauentormauer 42 (☎0911 99 28 128; www.backpackers.de). U2 to "Opernhaus"; look for the bright yellow building across the street. Incredibly friendly bilingual staff, social atmosphere, and big, colorful kitchen. Rooms are bohemian, with names like "The Italian Embassy" and "Viva La Trance." Free internet. Sheets (optional) €3. Reception 24hr. Check-out noon. Reservations recommended. 8-bed women-only dorms and 12-bed dorms €16; 5- and 6-bed dorms €16; 3- and 4-bed dorms €20; doubles €49; private apartments from €65. AmEx/MC/V. ❷

Jugend-Hotel Nürnberg, Rathsbergstr. 300 (☎0911 521 60 92). From the station, take U2 (dir.: Flughafen) to "Ziegelstein," then bus #21 (dir.: Buchenbühl) to "Zum Felsenkeller." This cheerful hostel gently blends Victorian and Bavarian aesthetics. However, it's about 45min. outside of the city via public transportation. All large, very basic dorm rooms with shower and WC. Breakfast €5.50. Internet €1 per 30min. Reception M-F 8am-9pm, Sa-Su 8-11am and 7-9pm. Check out 10am. Dorms €16; singles €25.50-30; doubles €39-49. €2.50 surcharge for 1-night stays. Cash only. ❶

Knaus Camping Park Nürnberg, Hans-Kalb-Str. 56 (☎0911 981 27 17; www.knaus-camp.de), in Volkspark Dutzendteich. S2 (dir.: Feucht/Altdorf) to "Frankenstadion." After exiting the station, turn away from the intersection towards the gray and blue stadium. Follow Hans-Kalbstr. as it turns left at the stadium and eventually right 10min.

later by the small blue camping sign (25min. from the station). Tent rental available (6-person tent €35-41, depending on season). Reception 8am-1pm and 3-10pm. €10.50 per person; more for cars and/or RVs. Electricity and shower included. Internet and washing facilities available. Cash only. ❷

FOOD

Nuremberg is famous for its *Rostbratwurst* (small, delectable grilled pork sausage), boiled *Sauere Zipfel* (sausage cooked in vinegar, salt, and spices), and *Lebkuchen*, a candied gingerbread traditionally devoured at Christmas. **Norma,** Hauptmarkt 11, across from the Frauenkirche, has cheap groceries. (Open M-F 8am-8pm, Sa 8am-6pm. Cash only.) The **Hauptmarkt** fills up with vendors selling fresh fruits and veggies in the mornings and afternoons (M-Sa).

Cafe Treibhaus, Karl-Grillenberger-Str. 28 (☎0911 22 30 41), in the Altstadt south of Westtor. Serves snacks (€2-6), salads and pasta (€5-7), and breakfast (€3-7) in a greenhouse-inspired interior. Their large Milchkaffee (€3.10) raises foam to new heights. Open M-W 8am-1am, Th-F 8am-2am, Sa 9am-2am, Su 9:30am-1am. Kitchen open until 10:30pm. Cash only. ❷

L'Osteria, Pirckheimerstr. 116 (☎0911 55 82 83; www.losteria.info), northeast of the Altstadt just outside Maxtor. About a 10min. walk from the Kaiserberg. At this busy local favorite, boisterous waiters serve gigantic pizzas and authentic pasta dishes(€5.50-9). Limited seating. Open M-Sa 11am-midnight, Su 5pm-midnight. Cash only. ❷

Wies'n Biergarten, Johann Sörgel Weg (☎0911 240 66 88), in the Wöhrder Wiese. U2 to "Wöhrder Wiese," a park in the middle of the Altstadt. Biergarten popular with families and students playing pick-up soccer games. *Maß* €5.40. Bratwurst with sauerkraut €5.40. Open May-Sept. M-F 10am-10pm Sa 1-10pm. Cash only. ❷

Cafe Balazzo Brozzi, Hochstr. 2 (☎0911 28 84 82), outside the Rosenau park. Airy cafe with glass and steel floor and a private patio. Order at the counter. Breakfast €3-8, baguettes €2.40-4, salads €2-6, veggie options €4.50-8. Su breakfast buffets and winter concerts (call for details). Open M-Sa 9am-11pm, Su 9am-9pm. Cash only. ❷

Hong Kong Store, Vordere Sterngasse 3 (☎0911 24 30 28). *Imbiß*-style Thai-influenced food at deliciously cheap prices (€2.60-5). Standing room only. Attached grocery sells Asian goodies. Open M-F 10am-7pm, Sa 10am-4pm. Cash only. ❶

Zum Gulden Stern, Zirkelschmiedgasse 26 (☎0911 205 92 88; www.bratwurstkueche.de), in the Altstadt. Best approached from the pedestrian zone from the North. Though the restaurant is in a safe neighborhood, it lies just west of the heart of the red light district. The oldest bratwurst kitchen in the world roasts sausages over an open fire. 6 Bratwurst with sauerkraut €7.20. Open daily 11am-10pm. AmEx/MC/V. ❸

SIGHTS

After WWII, Nuremberg rose from the ashes of Allied bombing, rebuilding the *Handwerkerhof*, a tourist trap disguised as a history lesson, in faux-medieval style. The real sights lie farther up Königstr., in the northwest of the Altstadt.

AROUND THE ALTSTADT AND KAISERBURG

KAISERBURG. Atop the hill, this symbolic structure offers the best vantage point for views of the city. The castle, originally erected in the 11th century and expanded significantly by Holy Roman Emperor Friedrich Barbarossa, is known as a *Pfalz* (Palatinate), a hotel for the Emperor's frequent visits to the city. The original castle was almost completely destroyed in the 14th century during a war with the Hohenzollern family, whose own *Burg* was next door. The aristocratic family left for Brandenburg, and the Kaiserburg was rebuilt in 15th- and 16th-century Gothic style. The spartan chambers housed every Holy Roman Emperor after Konrad III—it was law that every German Kaiser spend at least his first day in office in Nuremberg, a testament to its prominence. Massive stone walls (13m tall and 7m thick) surround the castle and manicured gardens, and a 40m deep well once provided water during sieges. The castle can only be visited by tour, conducted in English through the tourist office and in German at the castle, though the museum can be viewed by itself. *(☎0911 244 65 90. From the Hauptmarkt, head up Burgstr. until you see the castle to the left. Burg open daily Apr.-Sept. 9am-6pm; Oct.-Mar. 10am-4pm. Garden open daily in summer, 8am-8pm. Obligatory 1½hr. German tours every 30min.; last tour Apr.-Sept. 4:30pm; Oct.-Mar. 3:30pm. Admission to both Burg and museum €6, students €5.)*

LORENZKIRCHE. Destroyed in WWII, this 13th-century Gothic church has been carefully restored, though some damage is still visible. Located near the town center, the church houses gifts from various provinces throughout Germany and the greater Roman empire and chronicles the shifting alliance between Nuremberg and its neighbors. Of particular interest is the 20m tall tabernacle, built by Adam Kraft, whose self-portrait is one of the supports at the base of this stone masterpiece. Veit Stoß's 1517 wooden carving *Engelsgruß* (Annunciation) hangs in front of the altar. *(On Lorenzpl. ☎0911 24 46 99 14; www.lorenzkirche.de. From the Hauptbahnhof, head through the tunnel straight down Königsstr. until you see the church on the right. Open M-Sa 9am-5pm, Su noon-4pm. Free German-language tours meet at the entrance in summer M-Sa 11am and 2pm, Su 2pm; in winter M-F 2pm; call ahead for English-language tours. Suggested donation €1, students €0.50.)*

RUINS OF THE THIRD REICH

REICHSPARTEITAGSGELÄNDE (NAZI RALLYING GROUNDS). The site of the Nazi Party Congress rallies of 1933 to 1938, which drew more than a half million people each year, now hosts a park, a storage area, and the Nürnberg Symphony Orchestra. The planned Nazi compound, which Hitler proudly declared "the largest building site in the world," was to become much larger than the city of Nuremberg. Here, tourists can explore still-extant parts of the grounds, witness the construction relics, and visit the thorough **Dokumentationszentrum** (Documentation Center). The center explores the overwhelming emotional power of Nazi events—achieved by injecting strains of Wagnerian theater and Catholic ritual into fascist grandiosity—through exhibits covering the rise of the Third Reich, Nuremberg's role in the growth of Nazism, and the tribunals of 1946. The museum is in the **Kongresshalle** (Congress Hall), a prime example of Nazi architecture—massive, harsh, mixing Modernist straight lines with Neoclassical pretension, constructed with the intent to make the individual feel powerless. Intended to host the Nazi Party headquarters, the building was begun in 1935, but its construction was stalled by the onset of war. The 2km long Große Str., leading across the **Volkspark,** was a symbolic link between Hitler and the German Kaisers, providing a view of Nazi headquarters at one end and the Kaiserburg at the other. The **Zeppelinwiese,** a field across the **Großer Dutzendteich** lake from the Kongresshalle where Hitler addressed more than 100,000 spectators at a time, was made infamous by Leni Riefenstahl's striking film *Triumph of the Will.* Today, the Zeppelin field hosts concerts, and the Kongresshalle houses practice halls for the Nuremberg Symphony Orchestra. *(Bayernstr. 110.Take bus #36 or tram #9 to "Doku-Zentrum." For the Zeppelinwiese, walk around the lake from the Kongresshalle or take S2 (dir.: Feucht/Altdorf) to "Dutzendteich," then take the middle of 3 exits, head down the stairs, and turn left. Follow the paved path from the museum to reach other sections of the complex. ☎0911 231 56 66; www.museen.nuernberg.de. Open M-F 9am-6pm, Sa-Su 10am-6pm. Last entry 5pm. €5, students €2.50. Free multilingual audio tours.)*

JUSTIZGEBÄUDE (COURTHOUSE). In Courtroom 600, Nazi leaders faced Allied judges during the infamous Nuremberg war crimes trials. Spanning 218 days, more than 360 witnesses were called and over 1000 people were directly involved in the court proceedings. A total of 24 Nazi leaders were charged with war crimes, waging wars of aggression, conspiracy to commit crimes against the peace, and committing crimes against humanity. Soon after the trials, in October 1946, 10 men were hanged for their crimes against humanity, the first ever to be punished for wartime human rights violations. The building is still an active courthouse, but on weekends visitors can watch a short film in the room where the trials were held. *(Bärenschanzstr. 72. Take U1 (dir.: Fürth Klinikum) to "Bärenschanze" and continue away from the Altstadt on Fürtherstr. ☎ 0911 231 5421; www.olg-nuernberg.bayern.de. Entry on the hr., with bilingual commentary and a video with English subtitles: Sa-Su 1-4pm. €2.50, students and children €1.25.)*

MUSEUMS

GERMANISCHES NATIONAL MUSEUM (NATIONAL GERMANIC MUSEUM). This glass building chronicles Germanic art and culture from pre-history to the present. Highlights include Dürer's woodcuts, Rembrandt's etchings, and Cranach's paintings, including his portrait of Martin Luther. Outside the entrance, the **Straße der Menschenrechte** (Avenue of Human Rights) has 27 white pillars engraved in 50 languages with the United Nations Universal Declaration of Human Rights. *(Kartäusergasse 1. U2 to "Opernhaus." ☎ 0911 133 10. English tours every other Su 2pm. Open Tu-Su 10am-6pm, W 10am-9pm. Upper floors of the museum close at 5pm. Audio tours €1.50. €6, students and seniors €4. Free W from 6-9pm, Tu, Th, F-Su from 5-6pm.)*

JÜDISCHES MUSEUM FRANKEN (JEWISH MUSEUM OF FRANCONIA). Housed in nearby Fürth, once the largest urban Jewish community in southern Germany, this museum chronicles the history and culture of Jews in Franconia, displaying everything from medieval religious manuscripts to everyday artifacts. Most notable are the *mikva* (ritual bath) in the cellar, and the moveable roof that separates up to become a *sukkah*, an open-roof structure for Sukkot, the Jewish harvest holiday. *(Königstr. 89, Fürth. U1 (dir.: Fürth Klinikum) to "Rathaus." ☎ 0911 77 05 77. Open Tu 10am-8pm, W-Su 10am-5pm.€3, students and seniors €2.)*

STADTMUSEUM FEMBOHAUS (FEMBO HOUSE MUNICIPIAL MUSEUM). Through lively audio tours and engaging exhibits, Fembohaus introduces you to Nuremberg's past and to the building's inhabitants, once Europe's most important cartographers. The museum also offers an excellent multimedia presentation chronicling the history and development of the city. *(Burgstr. 15. Uphill from the Rathaus. ☎ 0911 231 25 95. Open Tu-F 10am-5pm, Sa-Su 10am-6pm. €4, students €2. Ticket also valid for the Dürerhaus. Multimedia presentation €4/2.)*

NICOLAUS-COPERNICUS-PLANETARIUM. Sit back and watch the nighttime sky projected on a concrete dome above you. *(Am Plärrer 41. U1 or U2 to "Plärrer." ☎ 0911 929 65 53; www.planetarium-nuernberg.de. Shows W and Th 4 and 7pm, 1st and 3rd weekend of the month Sa-Su 4pm. During school holidays also Tu 2 and 4pm. Children's shows Th 4pm, 1st and 3rd weekend of the month Sa-Su 4pm. €6, students €3.50, families €13.50.)*

ENTERTAINMENT AND NIGHTLIFE

Nuremberg's Altstadt is packed with bars and clubs, the best of which can be found just down the hill from the Kaiserburg. Every July, Nuremberg holds the **Bardenfest** and **Klassik Open** music festivals, which combine all genres for an event-filled few weekends. Pick up the monthly *Plärrer* (€2) for cultural events and the addresses of bars, discos, and cafes. Bars and discos also hand out the free guides *Doppelpunkt* (www.doppelpunkt.de) and *Curt* (www.curt.de). Visit www.rosawebworld.eu for up-to-date information on the city's gay scene.

The **Staatstheater Nürnberg** opera house and theater offers a 25% student discount (40% 1hr. before performances), and a 50% discount to Nürnberg Card holders. (Richard-Wagner-Pl. 2-10. ☎01805 23 16 00. Box office open M-F 9am-6pm, Sa 9am-1pm. MC/V.) **Cine Città,** Gewerbemuseumspl. 3, is near the river on the eastern side of the Altstadt and has 17 German-language cinemas and the biggest IMAX theater in Europe. (U2 to "Wöhrder Wiese." ☎0911 20 66 606; www.cinecitta.de. Tickets €8.40; discounts before 4pm and on M and Tu. Open M-Th and Su until 2am, F-Sa until 3am.) **Roxy,** Julius-Loßman-Str. 116, shows mostly recent American releases. (Tram #8 (dir: "Worzeldorfer Str.) to "Nürnberg-Südfriedhof." ☎0911 480 1064; www.roxy-nuernberg.de. M-Th €6.50, F-Su €7.50, students €7. More for long films.)

Hirsch, Vogelweiherstr. 66 (☎0911 42 94 14; www.der-hirsch.de). Nightbus N6 to "Vogelweiherstr." Energetic crowds dance late into the night at this huge club with disco F-Sa and concerts (110+ annually) M-Th. Multiple bars and Biergarten out front. Beer €3 (0.5L). Mixed drinks from €5.50. Cover €3-15. Open F-Sa 10pm-5am, M-Th for frequent concerts (check online for schedule). Cash only.

Club Stereo, Kornmarkt 7 (www.club-stereo.net). Plays rock and indie music in its entirely black interior with large dance floor and classy, alternative vibe. Busiest after 2am. More of a hangout spot than a dance club. Beer €2.90. Mixed drinks €6.50-7.50. Cover €5-8. Open Tu and F-Sa 11pm-5am. Cash only.

Matahari, Weißgerbergasse 31 (☎0911 194 95 00; www.mataharibar.de). This small, crowded bar is one of the few without a contract with any particular brewery; each month they serve 2 different beers. Beer €2.80 (05L). Mixed drinks €5.50-8. Happy hour W-Th 8-9pm, with €2 beer and €4.50 mixed drinks. Th ladies' night. Occasional concerts on W. Open W-Th 9pm-2am, F-Sa 8pm-3am. Cash only.

Downtown, Obere Schmiedgasse 5 (☎0911 22 23 81). A young, casual crowd gathers in this intimate underground lair of disco balls, tiger-print walls, and 80s music. Entrance in a dark alley. Beer €3 (0.5L). Open W-Th 9pm-3am, F-Sa 9pm-4am. Cash only.

Schleuder, Unschlittpl. 9 (www.schleuder.de). A very small, casual, and eclectic place with irregular events (check the website), a quirky crowd, and an offbeat owner who bartends with personality. Beer €2.80. Long drinks €5. Nightly DJ music. Open W-Sa 8:15pm-5am. Band night every Th. 21+ F-Sa. Cash only.

Saigon, Lammsgasse 8 (☎0911 24 48 56 57; www.saigon-bar.de). A classic late-night hangout, this intimate "bartender's bar" keeps to the bare basics—no special nights, no happy hours, just innovative DJs and a crowd that changes with the hour. Free internet. Beer €3 (0.4L). Mixed drinks €6.50-8.50. Open daily 9pm-5am. Cash only.

BAYREUTH ☎0921

Broad streets, resplendent 18th-century buildings, and a large English-style park give Bayreuth (buy-ROYT; pop. 74,000) an unexpectedly cosmopolitan flair. In the 18th century, the cultivated and ambitious Margravine Wilhelmine shaped Bayreuth according to her ideal of enlightened absolutism. In the 19th century, Richard Wagner, great *Meister* of opera, made it the center of his musical cult, and the city is an opera-lover's destination. Each year, it swells for the legendary Festspiele (annual operatic delirium from July 25 to August 28), and the wealth generated is evident in the array of international restaurants and carefully groomed neighborhoods. Allied bombs obliterated the dark traces of Bayreuth's Nazi interlude, yet spared most of its Italianate architecture.

TRANSPORTATION AND PRACTICAL INFORMATION

The central **Altstadt** of Bayreuth is south of the train station, while the **Festspielhaus,** epicenter of all things Wagnerian, is just to the north. To get to the Altstadt, go left out of the train station and follow Bahnhofstr. until it becomes Luitpoldpl. and then ends at Kanalstr. One block ahead, a pedestrian zone stretches from the Markt to Richard-Wagner-Str. The latter leads to the **Hofgarten,** a park and the city's museums. South of the Altstadt is the university.

Trains: Train station is just north of the Altstadt. To: **Bamberg** (1½hr., every hr., €16.10); **Nuremberg** (1hr., 1-2 per hr., €16.10); **Regensburg** (2hr., 2 per hr., €27-38).

Bike Rental: Radgarten, Friderichstr. 40 (☎0921 169 19 01; www.radgarten.de). €7 per day. Ask about special week rates. Open M-Sa 9am-1pm, M and F also 4pm-8pm.

Tourist Office: Luitpoldpl. 9 (☎0921 885 88; www.bayreuth.de), 4 blocks to the left of the station in the "Reisebüro Bayreuth" building just past the Rathaus. Books rooms for free (except during Festspiel when reservations cost €8), and offers maps, a monthly calendar of events, and 2hr. walking tours in German. **Tours** May-Oct. daily 10:30am; Nov.-Apr. Sa only (€5.50, students €3). Sells tickets to Bayreuth entertainment (except the Festspiele). Open M-F 9am-6pm, Sa 9am-2pm; May-Oct. also Su 10am-2pm. City maps and hotel lists are posted outside the door after hours.

Currency Exchange: Citibank, Maximilianstr. 46. Open M-Tu and Th 9am-1pm and 2-6pm, W and F 9am-1pm and 2-4pm.

Pharmacy: Hof Apotheke, Richard-Wagner-Str. 2 (☎0921 652 10). Open M-F 8am-6pm, Sa 8am-2pm.

Internet Access: Zoom, Wittelsbacherring 2-6 (www.casino-zoom.de). 18+. €2 per hr. Open daily 6am-5am. **Engin's Ponte Cafe,** Opernstr. 26 (☎0921 871 05 03). In a trendy cafe right in the city center. €2 per 30min. Open daily 8am-1am.

Post Office: Bürgerreutherstr. 1 (☎0921 78 03 30). To the right and across the street from the train station. Open M-F 8am-6:30pm, Sa 8:30am-1pm. **Postal Code:** 95444.

ACCOMMODATIONS

If you visit within a week of the **Festspiele,** be advised: everybody raises rates.

Jugendherberge (HI), Universitätsstr. 28 (☎0921 76 43 80). Bayreuth's hostel is a bit far outside the city center, past the Hofgarten near the university. On weekdays, take any bus from the station to "Marktpl.," then bus #6 (dir.: Campus) or #10 (dir: Kreuzsteinbad) to "Mensa" (€1.70). Or, walk down Ludwigstr. from the city center, take a left onto Friedrichstr., then veer left onto Jean-Paul-Str., which merges with Universitätsstr. (30min.) Located right next to the university grounds and a public swimming pool, this large, welcoming hostel has small, rustic rooms, billiards, bowling, and tennis and volleyball courts. Breakfast included. Reception 7am-noon and 5-10pm. Free lockers. Check-in (strictly observed) 11am-noon, 5-7pm, and 9:30-10pm. Curfew 10pm; ask at desk for door code. Open Feb. to mid-Dec. Dorms €17.90; singles €21.90. MC/V. ❶

Gasthof Zum Herzog, Herzog 2 (☎0921 413 34). Located about 15min. from the city center. From Sternplatz, head west on Maximilianstr. and follow it around the bend until it reaches Hohenzollernring. Cross over the busy road onto Kulmbacherstr. and follow the street up the hill bearing right with the road until you reach Herzog. Breakfast included. Reception 9am-9pm. Check out 11am. Singles €30, doubles €52. AmEx/MC/V. ❸

Gasthof Schindler, Bahnhofstr. 9 (☎0921 262 49). A block from the train station right next to Hotel Weihenstephan. Basic rooms with an eclectic mix of home decorations over a noisy Biergarten. Breakfast included. Reception M-Sa 8am-10pm, Su 9am-2pm. Singles €35; doubles €60; triples €75. Cash only. ❷

FOOD

Plus, Badstr. 10, sells groceries. (Open M-Sa 8am-8pm.) **Bäckerei Görl,** Sophienstr. 32, has sandwiches. (☎0921 608 0678. Open M-F 6am-6pm, Sa 6am-12:30pm.)

Kraftraum, Sophienstr. 16 (☎0921 800 25 15; www.cafe-kraftraum.de). This organic cafe serves yummy breakfast, noodles, salads, and sandwiches (€5-8) on its terrace. Weekend brunch €11. English menu available. Happy hour daily 5-7pm: mixed drinks €3.50-4. Open M-F 8am-1am, Sa-Su 9am-1am. Cash only. ❷

Gaststätte Porsch, Maximilianstr. 63 (☎0921 646 49). This little Biergarten serves heaps of Franconian fare on bistro seats in the middle of the pedestrian zone. Schnitzel €6-9. Beer €2.20 (0.5L). Open M-Sa 8:30am-10pm, Su 10am-8pm. Cash only. ❸

Hansl's Holzofen Pizzeria, Friedrichstr. 15 (☎0921 543 44), at Jean-Paul-Pl. Enjoy delicious wood oven pizzas in this little corner Mom and Pop joint. Pizzas €4-8.50. Salads €3-6. Limited seating. Open daily 10am-10:30pm. Cash only. ❷

SIGHTS

MARKGRÄFLICHES OPERNHAUS. Commissioned in 1744 by Margravine Wilhelmine, sister of Frederich the Great, this pristine Baroque opera house and its gargantuan stage were the reason for Wagner's initial interest in Bayreuth. Amazingly, the ceiling fresco is painted in the wrong direction. About 80 shows still take place annually, but on off-days, the opera house offers a bombastic 25min. **multimedia tour** featuring the disembodied voice of the Margravine—a very Bayreuth (read: theatrical) experience. *(Opernpl. 14. ☎0921 759 6922. Open Apr.-Sept. 9am-6pm; Oct.-Mar. 10am-4pm. Shows every 45min. in German, English handout available. €5, students €4. Combo with Schloß €8/7. For opera tickets (€5-80), call ☎0921 690 01.)*

RICHARD-WAGNER-MUSEUM. *Haus Wahnfried* (Delusional Peace) was once Wagner's custom-built home. It now exhaustively documents the composer's career and relationships with Ludwig II, father-in-law Franz Liszt, and Friedrich Nietzsche. Wagner music thunders throughout the remarkable exhibition, which winds up and down stairs. Exhibits in German; English guide booklets are available (€2.50). Behind the house are the graves of Wagner and his wife Cosima. *(Richard-Wagner-Str. 48. ☎0921 757 28 16. Open Apr.-Oct. M, W, F-Su 9am-5pm, Tu and Th 9am-8pm; Nov.-Mar. daily 10am-5pm. Music in the drawing room daily 10am, noon, 2pm; videos 11am and 3pm. July-Aug. €4.50, students €2, under 14 free; Sept.-June €4/2.)*

NEUES SCHLOSS. Margravine Wilhelmine, thought to be one of Europe's most cultured women, was forced to wed the Margrave of Bayreuth. To make the best of life in a small town, Wilhelmine built herself a gigantic palace. The walnut-paneled "palm room" and collection of Bayreuth porcelain are among the home's highlights. Also features an extensive collection of 18th- and 19th-century Dutch paintings. *(Ludwigstr. 21. Bus #2 to "Stadthalle." ☎0921 759 69 21. Open Apr.-Sept. daily 9am-6pm; Oct.-Mar. Tu-Su 10am-4pm. €5, students €4, under 18 free.)*

FESTSPIELHAUS (FESTIVAL HOUSE). Wagner's 1872 construction is famed for its acoustics and aesthetic. Wagnerophile Ludwig II could only offer modest funds, resulting in a spartan structure—Wagner fans must endure rigid seats and limited leg room. Nonetheless, the Festspielhaus revolutionized European theatrics, with the first covered orchestra pit and forward-facing seats to focus the audience on the performers. *(Festspielhügel 1-2. From the train station, take a right on Bürgerreuther Str. and follow it until it forks into Siegfried-Wagner-Allee. ☎0921 787 80. Tours Tu-Su Sept.-Oct. at 10, 10:45am, 2:15, 3pm; Dec.-Apr. 10:45am and 2:15pm. €2.50, students €2.)*

FESTIVALS

For Wagnerians, a visit to Bayreuth is a pilgrimage. Since 1876, every summer from July 25 to August 28, thousands have poured in for the **Wagner Festspiele,** held in the Festspielhaus that Wagner built for his "music of the future." All of his repertoire is performed annually, excepting his Ring Cycle operas, which show every four years (next in 2010). Tickets (€13-208, obstructed view €12, no view €6.50) go on sale mid-October and sell out immediately. Fanatics write to **Bayreuther Festspiele,** Postfach 100262, 95402 Bayreuth, well before September and hope for the best. Tickets are not available by phone or online.

BAMBERG ☎0951

Once known as the Rome of the north, windy Bamberg (pop. 71,000) straddles seven hills, covering the islands at the confluence of the Main-Donau canal and the two arms of the Regnitz river. Bamberg has been powerful and pious since 1007, when Heinrich II made it the center of the Holy Roman Empire in an attempt to push Christianity eastward. Crowned with a colossal cathedral and an imperial palace, Bamberg, which escaped WWII unscathed, is a thriving university town that once housed Hegel. Despite its location in wine-loving Franconia, this UNESCO World Heritage site has more breweries than Munich. One can't help but get caught up in the town's bustle, nightlife, and history.

TRANSPORTATION

Trains: The main station is on Ludwigstr. Trains run to: **Frankfurt** (3hr., every hr., €33-46); **Munich** (2-3½hr., 1-2 per hr., €34-54); **Nuremberg** (1hr., 3 per hr., €10.90); **Würzburg** (1hr., every hr., €16.90).

Public Transportation: An excellent transportation network centers on the ZOB (bus station) on Promenadestr. off Schönleinspl, where there is also an information center. To get there, walk down Luitpoldstr. from the train station and take the 2nd right after the bridge, or get on any bus with ZOB on the front. Single ride within the inner zone €1.20, 4-ride ticket €3.50. The 2-day **Touristenticket** (€6.60) offers unlimited travel within both zones. Family day cards €9.50.

Taxis: ☎0951 194 10, 150 15, or 430 43.

Bike Rental: Fahrradhaus Griesmann, Obere Königsstr. 36 (☎09851 229 67). €7.50 per day. Open M-F 9:30am-1pm and 2-6pm, Sa 10am-2pm.

ORIENTATION AND PRACTICAL INFORMATION

The heart of Bamberg lies on an island, **Sand,** between the **Main-Danube** canal and the **Regnitz River** (the Regen and Pegnitz Rivers combined). The Altstadt's winding streets weave through Sand and across the Regnitz away from the train station. To get to town from the station, walk down Luitpoldstr., cross the canal, and walk straight on Willy-Lessing-Str. until it empties into Schönleinspl. Turn right onto Lange Str. (to reach the island section of the pedestrian zone); hang a left up Obere Brückestr., through the archway of the Rathaus and across the Regnitz (to reach the far section of the Altstadt, 25-30min.). Or, take any bus in front of the station to "ZOB." The **Bamberg Card,** available at the tourist office or the Deutsche Bahn Service point, is valid for 48hr., and is good for free public transportation, a tour of Bamberg, and admission to 5 museums (€8.50; children under 6 free with parent).

Tourist Office: Geyerswörthstr. 3 (☎0951 297 6200; www.bamberg.info), on an island in the Regnitz. Follow the directions to Lange Str., above, then follow signs over the footbridge and around the building. The staff books rooms for free and gives out good maps and the free pamphlet *Bamberger* (in German), which lists performances and exhibits. Open M-F 9:30am-6pm, Sa-Su 9:30am-2:30pm; closed Su Jan.-Mar. After hours, a machine outside dispenses a map and hotel list (free).

Tours: 2hr. city tours in German meet in front of the tourist office Apr.-Oct. M-Sa 10:30am and 2pm, Nov.-Mar. M-Sa 2pm (€6, students €4, under 10 free). English audio/visual guides €8.50. Horse-drawn carriage tours of the Altstadt are offered Easter-Oct. Th-Su 1-6pm. Inquire at the tourist office (€8, ages 6-18 €5). Also ask about the 5hr. **canoe** tour (Tu-Su 6:30am, €25/15) or the brewery tour, with 5 beer vouchers and an inside look at the history and brewing process of **Bamberg's local breweries** (€24).

Budget Travel: Reisebüro Flugreise, Am Kranen 8 (☎0951 986 42 33; www.deinurlaub.de). STA services: books travel and prints ISICs. Open M-F 9am-6pm, Sa 9am-2pm.

Currency Exchange: Citibank, Hainstr. 2-4 (☎0951 98 24 60), on Schönleinspl. Open M-Tu and Th 9am-1pm and 2-6pm, W and F 9am-1pm and 2-4pm.

Laundromat: SB Waschsaloon, Obere Königsstr. 14 (☎0951 208 44 83; www.sb-waschsaloon.de). Wash €3.50. Dry €0.50 per 10min. Open M-Sa 7am-11pm.

Emergency: Police ☎110. **Fire** and **Ambulance** ☎112.

Pharmacy: Martin Apotheke, Grüner Markt 21 (☎0951 221 22). Open M-W and F 8:30am-6pm, Th 8:30am-7pm, Sa 9am-3pm.

Internet Access: ND's Internet Telecafe, Untere Königstr. 19 (☎0951 297 5717). €2 per hr. Happy hour noon-2pm and 8-9pm, €1.50 per hr. Open M-F 9am-10pm, Sa 10am-10pm, Su 12:30pm-10pm.

Post Office: Ludwigstr. 25, across from the train station. Open M-F 8am-6pm, Sa 8am-12:30pm. **Postal Code:** 96052.

ACCOMMODATIONS AND CAMPING

Budget lodgings surround **Luitpoldstraße,** in front of the train station.

Fässla, Obere Königstr. 19-21 (☎0951 265 16). From the Hauptbahnhof, walk straight on Luitpoldstr. and turn right a block before the bridge. Above a popular *Biergarten,* spacious rooms with luxurious new black marble baths, and a sophisticated feel. Breakfast included. Singles €40, doubles €60, triples €75. Call ahead in summer. Cash only. ❹

Jugendherberge Wolfsschlucht (HI), Oberer Leinritt 70 (☎0951 560 02). Bus #18 (dir.: Burg) from the ZOB to "Rodelbahn" (until 8pm M-F every 20min., Sa-Su every hr.; €1). Walk downhill and turn left onto Oberer Leinritt just before the river. Next to a former boathouse and far from the city center, with cozy rooms and old wooden windows. Breakfast included. Free internet. Reception 8am-8pm. Curfew 10pm, key available. Reservations strongly recommended in summer. Closed mid-Dec. to mid-Jan. 4- or 6-bed dorms €18.20, doubles €36.40. MC/V. ❷

Campingplatz Insel, Am Campingpl. 1 (☎0951 563 20). Bus #18 (dir.: Bug to "Campingpl." Far from town, the small campsite is right by the river. Wash €2.50. Dry €3. Reception 7:30am-12:30pm and 1-11pm. €4.50 per adult, €3 per child, €7 per campsite. Electricity €1.10 plus €0.50 per kW. Cash only. ❶

Bamberger Weissbierhaus, Obere Königstr. 38 (☎0951 255 03), 10min. from the station. Walk straight from the station on Luitpoldstr. and take a left 1 block before the river. Simple rooms with new wooden floors and shared balconies overlooking a secluded courtyard and Biergarten. Breakfast included. Dinner from €7. Reception 8am-2pm and 4:30-11pm. Singles €24-26, doubles €41-48, triples €61-65. Cash only. ❷

FOOD

When looking for food, **Austraße** is a good place to start, although the surrounding hills conceal wonderful beer gardens. Bamberg and its countryside has the highest concentration of breweries in the world, its most unusual specialty being *Rauchbier* (smoked beer). The daring can try its sharp taste at **Brauerei Schlenkerla,** Dominikanerstr. 6, Rauchbier's traditional home since 1678. (☎0951 560 60. €2 for 0.5L. Open M and W-Su 9:30am-11:30pm. Kitchen open until 10pm.) **Norma,** 12 Promenadenstr., by the ZOB, has cheap groceries. (Open M-F 7am-8pm, Sa 7am-6pm.) **Bäckerei Postler,** Lange Str. 35, uses organic grains for baked goods. (☎0951 219 36. Open M-F 6:30am-6pm, Sa 6:30am-1:30pm.) Pick up everything from fresh strawberries and cherries to asparagus and wurst at the farmer's **market** on Grüner Markt. (M-F 8am-4pm, Sa 8am-2pm.)

Spezial-Keller, Oberer Stephansberg 47 (☎0951 548 87). From Judenstr., head past the Stephanskirche up the Stephansberg. Turn left onto Sternwartstr. at the *Rauchbier* shield, bear right past the Gymnasium, and turn in right at the small iron gate. Walk all the way along the hedge, then turn left, and the Keller will soon be in view (20min.). This Biergarten is Bamberg's best-kept secret, offering a stunning hilltop view of the city, a playground, and house *Rauchbier.* Entrees €4-9. Beer €2.40 (0.5L). Open Tu-Sa 3-11pm, Su 10am-11pm. Cash only. ❷

Hofcafe, Austr. 14 (☎0951 254 47; www.hofcafe-bamberg.de). In a peaceful courtyard. Extensive menu with breakfast (€3-10) until 4pm. Weekly lunch specials are a steal. Vegetarian options (€7). On nice days, dine on their popular upstairs balcony. Open M-W 8am-1am, Th-F 8am-2am, Sa 9am-2am, Su 9am-1am. Cash only. ❷

Brauerei Greifenklau, Laurenzipl. 20 (☎0951 532 19), unbeknownst to tourists, has been serving its own brew at the top of the Kaulberg since 1719. Head up the Kaulberg road from the Schranne, following Laurenzistr. when it forks off to the right (15min.). Franconian pork roast with dumplings €7.40. Entrees €7-9. Beer €2.30 (0.5L). Open Tu-Sa 9am-11pm, Su 9:30am-2pm. Kitchen open 11:30am-9:30pm. Cash only. ❷

SIGHTS

DOM. Commissioned by Emperor Heinrich II, the cathedral was consecrated in 1012, burned down twice, and rebuilt to its present-day form in 1237. The most famous object inside, the equestrian statue of the **Bamberger Reiter** (Bamberg Rider), dates to the 13th century. Just beneath the rider is the tomb of **Heinrich II** and **Queen Kunigunde,** with their life-size figures on top. Kunigunde walked over coals to prove her loyalty to her suspicious husband—both were later canonized. On the left side of the Dom is the **Diözesanmuseum** (Diocesan Museum), with the **Domschatz** (Cathedral Treasury) and beautiful ritual garments, including Heinrich's star-spangled cloak. *(Across the river and up Karolinenstr. from the Rathaus. Dom ☎0951 50 23 30. Open daily Apr.-Oct. 8am-6pm, Nov.-Mar. 8am-5pm. Free. Museum ☎0951 50 23 16. Open Tu-Su 10am-5pm. €3, students and seniors €2.50, under 15 free. Tours of the cathedral M-Th 10:30am and 2pm; F 10:30am, 2, 3pm; Sa 10:30am, 1, 2, 3pm, Su 1 and 3pm. €3, students €2.50. Tu-Su meet at entrance to Dom museum; M meet at the Lady Portal. 30min. Organ concerts May-Oct. Sa noon.)*

NEUE RESIDENZ. The largest building in Bamberg was built between 1600 and 1703 to serve as the home of Bamberg's lavish rulers. One wing is now a museum displaying medieval religious art, Cranach the Elder's famous *Lucretia*, and a comically inaccurate Noah's Ark. Admission includes a tour of the **parade rooms** and entry to the serene **rose garden.** *(Dompl. 8. Opposite the Dom. ☎0951 51 93 90. Open daily Apr.-Sept. 9am-6pm, Oct.-Mar. 10am-4pm. Obligatory tours meet Apr.-Oct. daily every 15min., 1 floor above the cashier's desk. English and French translations available. €4, students and seniors €3, under 18 free.)*

FESTIVALS AND NIGHTLIFE

The third week of August is **Sandkerwa.** Originally a celebration of the Sand area churches, it is now a folk festival. The rest of the year, **Sandstraße** is a well-known pub mile, but **Austraße** and **Lange Straße** also buzz with students.

Live Club, Obere Sandstr. 7 (☎0951 50 04 58; www.live-club.de), features live acts and a regular club night on M and Sa. Even on Monday, this wildly popular scene features R&B, hip-hop, and rock. Cover €4+. Hours vary; check website for details. Open M and F-Sa. One floor up, **Haas Säle,** Obere Sandstr. 7 (☎0951 93 53 29), is a classy open-air terrace with golden stucco, tall palm trees, and swings. Beer €2.50 (0.5L). Open M-F 5pm-2am, Sa 2pm-2am, Su 10am-2am, later when busy. Cash only.

Morph Club, Siechenstr. 7 (☎0951 208 41 33; www.morphclub.org), at the intersection of Außere Löwenstr. and Untere Konigstr. Take bus #6 to "Löwenstr." Cool scene with nightly techno, dance hall, reggae, and pop. Occasional concerts. Mixed drinks €5-7.50, beer €2.70 (0.5L). Cover €2.50-8. Open W-Sa 10pm-4am. Cash only.

Calimeros, Lange Str. 8 (☎0951 20 11 79), undergoes a nightly transformation from Tex-Mex restaurant to raging club; you can tell it's a good night when everyone's dancing on the tables. M-W and Su happy hour 6-7:30pm and 11pm-12:30am with €3 caipirinha or margarita. Th Beer €1. Open M-Th 5pm-2am, F-Sa 5pm-3am. Cash only.

THÜRINGEN

Thüringen (Thuringia) has recovered spectacularly since reunification. Today, the home of *Bratwurst* is bursting at the seams with opportunities for history buffs to walk, hike, eat, and sleep in the footsteps of cultural luminaries like Luther, Goethe, Schiller, and Wagner. Outdoor enthusiasts will be delighted by the trails cutting through the rolling hills, misty highlands, and idyllic Thüringer Wald.

HIGHLIGHTS OF THÜRINGEN

CLIMB THE TOWER of **Eisenach's Wartburg,** which once sheltered Luther, and look over J.S. Bach's birthplace and the surrounding forest (p. 430).

LOSE YOURSELF among the ample trails of the gorgeous **Thüringer Wald** (p. 428), from the 6hr. *Goethewanderweg* to the 5-day Rennsteig.

CHANNEL THE SPIRITS of Goethe, Schiller, Hegel, and Novalis in the cultural center of **Weimar** (p. 414) and the university town of **Jena** (p. 420).

WEIMAR ☎03643

In its heyday, Weimar (pop. 64,400) attracted such cultural giants as Goethe, Schiller, and Johann Gottfried von Herder (grandfather of the Romantics), and the fame of these long-dead men still draws thousands to the city. Weimar residents are quick to point out that in 1999, their little city was declared the cultural capital of Europe. During the months leading up to the big celebration the city received a thorough facelift, making it one of the most renovated cities in the former DDR. Although Goethe's presence is inescapable, Weimar's importance does not begin or end with the author. As the capital and namesake of the Weimar Republic, Germany's attempt at a democratic state after WWI, Weimar has a unique political significance in Germany's recent history. Hitler, too, was attracted by Weimar's rich culture, and founded the Hitler Youth movement here in 1926. The Bauhaus architectural movement also took root here, and students at the internationally renowned conservatory and Bauhaus Universität bring cultural energy to the city.

TRANSPORTATION

Trains: To: **Dresden** (2hr., every hr., €39); **Eisenach** (1hr., every hr., €11.70); **Erfurt** (15min., every hr., €4.40); **Frankfurt** (3hr., every hr., €49); **Jena** (20min., 2-3 per hr., €4.40); **Leipzig** (1hr., every hr., €22).

Public Transportation: Most of Weimar is easily walkable, but has an extensive bus network. Most buses run until midnight. Single tickets (€1.70) can be bought on board. Book of 4 tickets €4.80; day pass €4.20; weekly pass €9.50, students and seniors €7.20. Buy tickets at tourist offices, the main ticket office on Goethepl., or at newsstands with green and yellow "H" signs. Tickets must be validated on the buses.

ORIENTATION AND PRACTICAL INFORMATION

A series of open squares strung together by sidestreets makes up Weimar's city center, which contains most of its sights. From the train station, Carl-August-Allee stretches downhill past the Neues Museum to Karl-Liebknecht-Str., which

leads into Goethepl. (15min.). From there, Theaterpl. is down Wielandstr. to the left, and the Marktpl. is a short walk from Theaterpl. down Schillerstr. The **Thuringen Card** (24hr. €14, 3-day €33, 6-day €53) provides free or reduced entry to Weimar's major sights, excluding Goethe's Wohnhaus, as well as to sights in other Thuringen cities. The **WeimarCard** (€10 for 72hr.) provides transportation, free or reduced entry to sights, and 50% off tours. Purchase at tourist offices.

Tourist Offices: The modern **Weimar Information,** Markt 10 (☎036 43 74 50; www.weimar.de), is on the Markt across from the Rathaus. The staff sells maps (€0.20), a brochure detailing major sights (€0.50), theater tickets, and books rooms for free. Walking tours (2hr., in German) leave the office daily at 10am and 2pm. €7, with WeimarCard €3.50, students €4, children under 14 free. Guide yourself with a handheld audio-visual **IGuide** (€7 for 2hr., €7.50 for 4hr.). A separate desk supplies information on Buchenwald, and yet another on the classical museums of the city. Open Apr.-Oct. M-F 9:30am-6pm, Sa-Su 9:30am-3pm; Nov.-Mar. M-F 10am-6pm, Sa-Su 10am-2pm.

Currency Exchange: 4 banks with **24hr. ATMs** are spread out on Schillerstr. and Frauentorstr. **Deutsche Bank,** Frauentorstr. 3, is at their intersection. Open M 9:30am-1pm, 2-4pm; Tu and Th 9:30am-1pm and 2-6pm, W and F 9:30am-1pm.

Bookstore: Eckermann Buchhhandlung, Marktstr. 2 (☎03643 415 90), sells English-language paperbacks. Open M-Sa 9:30am-8pm, Su 9:30-7pm.

Laundromat: SB-Waschsalon, Graben 47, a few blocks from Goethepl. Wash €3.50. Dry €0.50 per 15min. Open M-Sa 8am-10pm; last wash at 8:30pm.

Pharmacy: Stadt Apotheke, Frauentorstr. 3 (☎03643 20 20 93). Has a *Notdienst* (emergency service) buzzer. Open M-F 8am-7pm, Sa 9am-2pm.

Internet Access: Roxanne, Markt 21, is a bar, cafe, and amateur record store. €2 per hr. Open M-Sa from 10am Su from 1pm.

Post Office: Am Goethepl. 7-8. Open M-F 9am-6:30pm, Sa 9am-noon. **24hr. ATM. Postal Code:** 99421.

ACCOMMODATIONS

Hababusch Hostel, Geleitstr. 4 (☎03643 85 07 37; www.hababusch.de). Young bohemians tired of sterile HI hostels will find something a little more soulful here. Art and design students run the hostel–and supply it accordingly with ironic decor. Reserve singles and doubles ahead in summer. Reception 24hr. 7-bed dorms €10, 4-bed dorms €12, 2-bed dorms €15, singles €20. Cash only. ❶

Jugendherberge Germania (HI), Carl-August-Allee 13 (☎03643 85 04 90). From the train station, walk directly straight downhill for 2min.; it's on your right. Though convenient to the train station, it's deceptively far from town. A bed and a roof. Internet €2 per hr. Breakfast included. 24hr. reception. Dorms €20, over 27 €23. MC/V. ❷

Jugendherberge Am Poseckschen Garten (HI), Humboldtstr. 17 (☎03643 85 07 92). A big turn-of-the-century brownstone a few blocks from the city center with 8- to 10-bed rooms. The hostel hosts many school groups, so book early. Internet access €0.10 per min. Breakfast included. 24hr. reception. Dorms €24, over 27 €27; subsequent nights €22.50/25.50. AmEx/MC/V. ❷

FOOD

For groceries, try the produce market at the Marktpl. (open M-Sa 6am-4pm), or supermarkets **Rewe** in the small shopping complex on Theaterpl. and **Na Kauf** on the corner of Frauenplan and Steubenstr. (Open M-F 7am-11pm, Sa 7am-8pm.) If a restaurant in Weimar has any visible connection to Goethe—in its name, on its door, in its decor—it's probably overpriced. However, Weimar's restaurants don't have to drain your wallet; chances are there's a more reasonable, if less historic, option just down the road.

Creperie du Palais, Am Palais 1 (☎03643 40 15 81). French expats serve delicious crepes large enough to satisfy German appetites, in a plant-filled dining room or on a tree-shaded terrace. Try the *Schinken und Spargel* (ham and asparagus). Dinner and dessert crepe combo €5-9. Open daily 11am-midnight. Cash only. ❷

ACC, Burgpl. 1-2 (☎03643 85 11 61; www.acc-cafe.de). This cafe, cultural center, and gallery offers daily specials ranging from casseroles to curries (€5, with soup for €6.50). A variety of vegetarian options, salads, and classic *Abendbrote* (cheese and cold cuts) complete the menu. Mondays, professors from Bauhaus lecture about art in English. Free Wi-Fi, even after hours. Open daily 11am-1am. AmEx/MC/V. ❷

Cafe Bauhaus, Marienstr. 3 (☎01791 13 05 65), serves coffee and foot-long, toasted baguettes (€2) to trendy students near the *Uni.* Open M-F 9am-6pm. Cash only. ❶

Residenz-Cafe, Grüner Markt 4 (☎0364 35 94 08; www.residenz-cafe.de). Weimar's oldest restaurant offers a taste of Thuringian cuisine at its best. Try the *Thüringer Grillplatte* (€11.20) for a taste of 3 local meats with sinus-clearing mustard. Vegetarian entrees available. Open daily 8am-1am. MC/V with €20 minimum. ❸

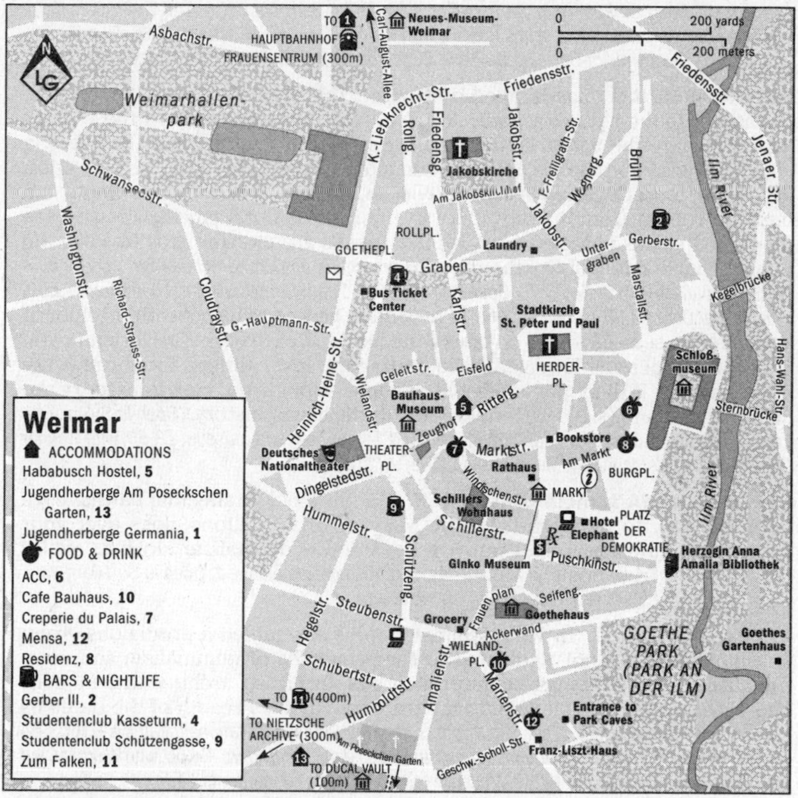

SIGHTS AND MUSEUMS

Weimar will always belong to its poets, whose plays, houses, and gravestones attract pilgrims from around the world. Beyond the relics of Germany's lyrical titans, the **Neues Museum** and **Bauhaus Museum** house surprisingly fresh collections of art, and the **Stadtmuseum** sheds light on Weimar's fascinating and oft-neglected history. At all museums, the last entry is 15min. before closing.

GOETHEHAUS. While countless German towns leap at any excuse to build memorial *Goethehäuser* (Goethe slept here, Goethe tripped on this rock, Goethe stole my wife), this one is the real thing. The **Goethewohnhaus** presents the immaculate chambers where the genius entertained, wrote, studied, and ultimately died after 50 years in Weimar. The rooms are crammed with busts, paintings, and sculptures from his art collection, including over 18,000 cabbage-like rocks—not only could the man write, but he knew his geology. The entry hall, decorated with classical statues, was inspired by his visit to Italy. Easy to miss, Goethe's badass yellow buggy is stashed in the barn under the house. To preserve the exhibit's authenticity, no explanatory signs are posted in the Goethehaus, so grab an English audio tour (€1). The rest of the Goethe-Nationalmuseum consists of an exhibit on Weimar's history. *(Frauenplan 1. Open*

Apr.-Sept. Tu-F and Su 9am-6pm, Sa 9am-7pm; Oct. Tu-Su 9am-6pm; Nov.-Mar. Tu-Su 9am-4pm. Expect to wait on summer weekends. €6.50, with Weimar Card €5.30, students €5. Tours in German Tu and F-Sa 1pm; Apr-Oct. also Sa 3pm; €2, students €1.50. Museum exhibit €2.50/2.)

PARK AN DER ILM. Landscaped by Goethe, this sprawling park flanking the Ilm attests to the writer's artistic skill. Note the fake ruins built by the Weimar shooting club, the **Sphinx Grotto** from the late 18th century, and the **Kubus,** a gigantic black cube used as a theater and movie screen. On the park's far slopes, across the footbridge, is **Goethe's Gartenhaus,** the poet's first Weimar home and later his retreat from the city. Take in the intense floral smellscape and see more of Goethe's possessions. A replica travels around Germany to slake the unquenchable national Goethe-thirst. *(Gartenhaus on Corona-Schöfer-Str., access from inside the park. ☎ 03643 54 33 75. Open daily Apr.-Oct. 10am-6pm, Nov.-Mar. 10am-4pm. €3.50, with Weimar Card €2.90, students €2.50.)* The watery **park caves** lie beneath the floor of a prehistoric sea—if you go on one of the hard-hat cave tours (in German), you can nearly touch the Ice Age fossils dotting the low ceilings. Tours run every hour, but only if there are at least six people—2pm is the best time to try. An adjacent museum (signs in German) details the caves' history. *(Open Tu-Su Apr.-Oct. 10am-noon and 1-6pm, Nov.-Mar. 10am-noon and 1-4pm. Tour and museum €3.50, with Weimar Card €2.90, students €2.50. Museum only €2.50/2.10/2.)*

HERZOGIN ANNA AMALIA BIBLIOTHEK. Goethe's old intellectual batting cage is on the way to the park from the Markt. Don ridiculous clogs over your shoes and shuffle around the newly renovated Rococo hall, an sky-blue ovular library that is frighteningly well-designed. *(Pl. der Demokratie 1. Open Tu-Su 10am-3pm. €6.50, students €5.50. Audio tour in English included.)*

BAUHAUS-MUSEUM. In 1919, Walter Gropius assembled a prodigious group at Weimar's art school, dedicated to the principles of minimalism and functionalism. Their weavings, sculptures, prints, furniture, architectural models, and even tea kettles—all displayed here—convey the breadth of the Bauhaus school's undertakings. *(Theaterpl., across from the Deutsches Nationaltheater. ☎ 03643 54 59 61; www.uni-weimar.de/bauhausspaziergang. Open daily 10am-6pm. €4.50, with Weimar Card €3.70, students and seniors €3.50. Museum tours Su 11am €2, students €1.50.)*

SCHILLERS WOHNHAUS. Sitting a neighborly distance from Goethe's residence, this yellow house was Schiller's home during the last three years of his life. As well as chronicling the poet's life, the museum exhibits the backgrounds to *The Maid of Orleans* and *William Tell*—both written here—and houses original drafts of his plays. One room displays over 600 medallions imprinted with Schiller's head. Keep an eye out for the funky wallpaper (replicas of the original patterns) adorning the walls upstairs. *(Schillerstr. 12. ☎ 03643 54 54 01. Open M and W-Su Apr.-Oct. 9am-6pm, Apr.-Sept. Sa until 7pm; Nov.-Mar. 9am-4pm. €4, students €3. Tours in German M 1pm €3/1. Audio tour in English €2.)*

HISTORISCHER FRIEDHOF (HISTORIC CEMETERY). South of the town center, Goethe and Schiller rest side-by-side in the basement of the **Fürstengruft** (Ducal Vault) with a dozen or so Prussian nobles. Schiller died in an epidemic and was originally buried in a mass grave, but Goethe later combed through the remains until he found Schiller and had him interred here. Skeptics long argued that Goethe had chosen the wrong body, but Russian scientists confirmed the poet's identification in the 1960s. Goethe himself arranged to be buried in an airtight steel case. Unless it's sweltering, stick to the cemetery grounds. Otherwise, the chilly underground vault is a good place to cool off. *(Open daily Mar.-Sept. 8am-9pm, Oct.-Feb. 8am-6pm. Free. Tomb open daily Apr.-Oct. 10am-6pm, Nov.-Mar. 10am-4pm. €2.50, with Weimar Card €2.10, students €2.)*

SCHLOSSMUSEUM (PALACE MUSEUM). The palace and tower from the former city walls now house three floors of art. The collection is organized roughly on a "newer is higher" scheme. The first floor is a major Lucas Cranach fest (the painter lived in the Marktpl.), featuring his portraits, as well as religious icons and carved Renaissance altars. The second moves into 17th- and 18th-century German works, with a real emphasis on Romantic natural landscapes and town life. Much of the artwork is dramatically integrated into museum walls, insulated by ornate ceilings and trim, a holdover from the palace's pre-retirement days. The third floor displays more modern work, some Impressionism, and refreshingly nude bodies. Monet and Rodin are sprinkled around this floor. *(Burgpl. 4. To the left of the Marktpl. Enter the archway and head through the courtyard. Open Tu-Su Apr.-Oct. 10am-6pm, Nov.-Mar. 10am-4pm. €5, with Weimar Card €4.10, students €4.)*

NIETZSCHE-ARCHIV. Nietzsche lived here for three years, suffering from mental and physical illness, before his death in 1900. His sister, who returned from a struggling colony in Paraguay to care for him, archived the philosopher's work after his death, but distorted it during the process. Her totalitarian control over Nietzsche's papers contributed to the Nazis' misappropriation of parts of his philosophy to horrifying ends. On display is a history of the archive, many portraits—and a death mask—of the man with his famous mustache, documents in his own hand, and an enviable flat designed by Henry van de Velde. *(Humboldtstr. 36. Open Apr.-Oct. Tu-Su 1-6pm. €2.50, with Weimar Card €2.10, students €2.)*

ENTERTAINMENT AND NIGHTLIFE

The best resource for theater and music in Weimar is the **Deutsches Nationaltheater,** Theaterpl. 2. The theater that inspired Goethe and Schiller still presents *Faust* regularly, along with Shakespeare and classic operas from Mozart, Verdi, Puccini, Rossini, Bizet, and Wagner. It's also the site where the **Weimar Constitution** was signed in 1919. (☎03643 75 53 34. Box office open M 2-6pm, Tu-Sa 10am-6pm, Su 10am-1pm, and 1hr. before performances. Nov.-Mar closed Sa 1-4pm.) Tickets are also available at **Tourist Information.** (Tickets €8-55.)

Weimar's nightlife consists of an eclectic collection of bars, student clubs and cafes. Pick up a copy of the German-language *Blitz,* or check the posters and bulletin boards at the Mensa for the latest goings-on.

Studentenclub Kasseturm, Goethepl. 10 (☎03643 85 16 70; www.kasseturm.de). The oldest student club in Germany serves cheap drinks (shots €1-1.20; beer €2) in a medieval tower, with dancing on the top 2 floors and a rowdy cellar below. Disco W and F or Sa. Cover €3-6, students €1-4, more for concerts. Open daily 2pm-late. Cash only.

Studentenclub Schützengasse, Schützengasse 2 (☎03643 90 43 23; www.schuetzengasse.de), has live rock upstairs Tu and F-Sa and a DJ downstairs, with a (slightly) quieter *Biergarten* out back. Disco Tu and Sa at 9pm. A variety of activities—from dance classes to jam sessions—other nights. Check the board outside for weekly schedule. 18+. Cover €1.50-2.50, students €1 off. Open M-Sa 8pm-3am. Cash only.

Gerber III, Gerberstr. 3. This former squatters' house now shelters an improvised bar. The topsy-turvy, graffiti-covered interior feels like something out of a grungy Soviet-style *Alice in Wonderland.* The building also hosts an occasional disco and a climbing wall. Look for the Bob Marley mural. Bar open M-Sa 8pm-late. Cash only.

DAYTRIP FROM WEIMAR

BUCHENWALD

Take bus #6 from Weimar's train station or Goethepl. (20min., every hr. M 8:45 to 5:45, T-F from 6:45. Sa-Su roughly every hr. 8:30am-5:45pm). Check schedule; some #6 buses go to "Ettersburg" rather than "Gedenkstätte Buchenwald," but routes are combined on weekends. Buses to Weimar stop at the KZ-Lager parking lot and the road by the Glockenturm.

A quarter-million Jews, Gypsies, homosexuals, communists, and political prisoners were incarcerated at the Buchenwald labor camp during WWII. Buchenwald was not explicitly an extermination camp, but over 50,000 prisoners died from malnutrition, mistreatment, or medical experimentation. The compound is now a vast gray expanse of gravel with the former location of the prison blocks marked by numbers and crumbling foundations. Some of the remaining buildings around the perimeter can still be visited, including the SS officers' quarters and the crematorium. The uncompromising starkness of the compound and the horror of its history stand in wrenching contrast to the Thuringian forests surrounding the site.

The **Nationale Mahnmal und Gedenkstätte Buchenwald** (National Buchenwald Memorial) has two principal sights: the **KZ-Lager** and the DDR-designed **Mahnmal** (memorial). The former refers to the camp itself, while the latter is a solemn monument overlooking the surrounding countryside. The main exhibit of the camp, in the large storehouse building, documents the history of Buchenwald (1937-1945) and the general history of Nazism and German anti-Semitism. An exhibit about the Soviet internment camp is in the basement. Many tributes are scattered around the camp; the stones of the Jewish memorial at block #22 read: "So that the generation to come might know, the children, yet to be born, that they too may rise and declare to their children." The camp archives are open by appointment. (Archives ☎03643 43 00, library 03643 01 60. Exhibits open Tu-Su Apr.-Oct. 10am-6pm, Nov.-Mar. 10am-4pm. Last entry 30min. before closing. Outdoor camp area open daily until sundown.) The Mahnmal and **Glockenturm** (bell tower) are 15min. from the camp on the other side of the hilltop, and are visually the most moving feature of the camp. From the main semicircular parking lot, take the gravel path near the cafe up past the old train station, and walk next to the road until the parking lot on your right; the memorial is just beyond it. Behind the bell tower, a commanding view of the region unfolds, overseen by the **Plastikgruppe,** a sculpture of ragged, stern-jawed socialist prisoners claiming their freedom.

An **information center** near the Buchenwald bus stop shows a 30min. video with English subtitles on the hour, and has helpful English-language brochures (€0.25), a self-guided walking tour booklet with several routes (€1.80), and audio (€3, students €2) and video (€5/4) guides. Brochures and electronic guides are available in nine languages, including English. (☎03643 43 02 00; www.buchenwald.de. Open Tu-F Apr.-Oct. 9am-5pm, Sa-Su 9am-6pm; Nov.-Mar. Tu-F 9am-4pm, Sa-Su 9am-4:30pm. 90min. guided tours leave from the visitor center Tu-Su 10:30am and 1:30pm. A branch next to Weimar's Tourist Information on the Marktpl. has more information.)

JENA ☎03641

Jena's life is its university. Once the country's finest, the institution proudly displays its illustrious past, especially professor Friedrich Schiller, who lectured here in 1789 on the ideals of the French Revolution. His students, Novalis and Hölderlin, joined other literary greats, such as Schlegel and Tieck, to plant the seeds of the German Romantic movement. The 19th century also saw Jena become a world leader in the field of optics with the founding of microscope company Carl Zeiss. In-depth museums celebrate Jena's tradition of intellectualism, and the students strolling through the city's streets at all hours keep this town a haven for bookish and fun-loving travelers alike.

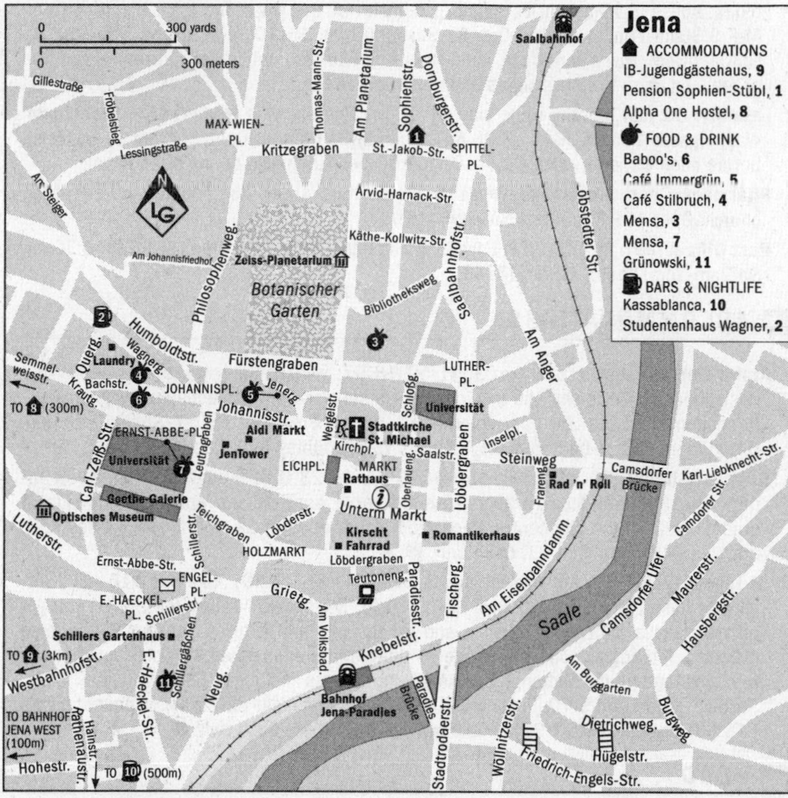

TRANSPORTATION

Trains: Jena is in the Saale River Valley, 25km east of Weimar by train (20min., 2 per hr., €4.50). Three major train stations serve the town. Trains between Dresden and Erfurt stop at **Bahnhof Jena-West,** a 10min. walk from town, while trains on the Berlin-Munich and Saalfeld-Naumburg lines stop at **Jena Saalbahnhof,** 15min. north of the center. Trains from the Saalbahnhof also stop at **Bahnhof Jena-Paradies,** 5min. from town.

Public Transportation: Most of the city is connected by a bus and tram system centered on the "Zentrum" stop (€1.70; pay on board).

Bikes: Kirscht Fahrrad, Löbdergraben 8, rents spanking new mountain bikes with full suspension. (☎03641 44 15 39. €15 for the 1st day, €10 per additional day. Open M-F 9am-7pm, Sa 9am-4pm.) A better deal might be to join the sturdy orange fleet of city bikes housed at **Rad 'n Roll,** Steinweg 24 (☎03641 62 87 97). Located off Löbdergraben, across the tracks. (€7.50 per day. Open M-F 9am-7pm, Sa 9am-1pm.)

Taxis: ☎03641 45 88 88.

PRACTICAL INFORMATION

Tourist office, Markt 16 (☎03641 49 80 50; www.jena.de). Hands out free maps, leads city tours in German (€4), and books private rooms (from €19) for free. It sits in the oldest house in Jena, but it's tough to tell with all the glass and laser displays. Open M-F 9:30am-7pm; also Apr.-Oct. Sa 9:30am-4pm, Su 10am-3pm and Nov.-Mar. Sa 9:30am-3pm. Buy a **JenaCard,** good for a free tour, free public transportation, and free or reduced entry to Jena's sights and museums (€9).

Laundry: Do your laundry while sipping a drink and enjoying **free Wi-Fi** at **Cleanicum,** Wagnergasse 11 (☎03641 63 88 84). Open M-Sa from 9:30am, Su from 11am. Wash before noon €2, after noon €2.50. Dry €0.50 per 10min. No drying after 10pm.

Pharmacy: Goethe-Apotheke, Weigelstr. 7 (☎03641 45 45 45). Located in front of the church. Open M-F 8am-8pm, Sa 8am-4pm.

Post Office: The post office is at Engelpl. 8 and has a **24hr. ATM.** Open M-F 9am-6:30pm, Sa 9am-1pm. **Postal Code:** 07743.

ACCOMMODATIONS

Alpha One, 8 Lassallestr. 8 (☎03641 59 78 97; www.hostel-jena.de). A new 40-bed hostel near the university, and a quick walk—or stagger—from the action on Wagnergasse. Reception is on the 3rd floor. Internet €1 per hr. Breakfast €3.50. Sheets included. 6-bed room €15, 4-bed dorm €17, singles €25, doubles €20. Cash only. ❶

Sophien-Stueb'l, St.-Jakob-Str. 15 (☎036 41 44 23 03). Though far from Westbahnhof and Bahnhof Jena-Paradies, this adorable pension sits above a little pub, a quiet walk from the city center. Reception at bar open M-Sa 5pm-1am. Singles €30, doubles €45. Breakfast €3. Cash only. ❸

IB-Jugendgästehaus, Am Herrenberge 3 (☎03641 68 72 30). Take bus #10 (dir.: Burgau) or buses #13 and #40 (dir: Göshwitz) to "Zeiss-Werk." Follow the bus as you get off and take a right on Mühlenstr. and up the hill until it turns into Am Herrenberge (15min.). The bright rooms have huge windows and are furnished with pine wood, green furniture, and fluffy bedding. Breakfast and sheets included. Reception M-F 24hr., Sa-Su 7-11am and 5-10pm. 3- and 4-bed rooms first night €20.10, subsequent nights €18.60; singles €28.50/27; double with bath €47/44. Cash only. ❷

FOOD

A **market** in front of the Rathaus sells fresh produce (Tu and Th-F 6am-5pm, Sa 6am-1pm), and there's an **Aldi** supermarket in the basement of the Neue Mitte shopping center. (Open M-Sa 8am-8pm.)

Baboo's Internationale Spezialitäten, Johannispl. 12 (☎03641 42 66 66). Offers everything from chicken curry (€7.50) to inches-high stuffed pizza (€3). Don't leave town without trying the *Lahmacun* for €3.20. Student lunch deals: salad, dessert and drink with pasta or pizza €2.50/3. Open daily 10am-2am. Cash only. ❷

Cafe Immergrün, Jenergasse 6 (☎03641 44 73 13). Comfortable couches and modern art against spring green walls. Daily vegetarian and meat specials (€3-5). Go for the *Fladenbrot* €3. Open M-Sa 11am-1am, Su 10am-2:30pm and 3-10pm. Cash only. ❶

Cafe Stilbruch, Wagnergasse 1-2 (☎03641 82 71 71), offers a large selection of salads, baguettes, and piping hot *Pfannengerichte* (pan-cooked meals €7-10) in a rich atmosphere. Later in the evening this cafe fills with cocktail patrons. Open M-Th 8:30am-2am, F 8:30am-3am, Sa 9am-3am, Su 9am-2am. Cash only. ❸

Grünowski, Schillergässchen 5 (☎03641 44 66 20; www.gruenowski.de), is a quiet restaurant and bar with a diversely landscaped outdoor seating. Soups and pastas €3-7. Open daily from 2pm. Cash only. ❶

Jena's Mensa, Ernst-Abbe-Pl., across Leutragraben from the tower. Full meals €4-4.50, with ISIC €1.40-1.60. Open M-F 8am-3pm. Sa 11am-2pm. Cash only. A **smaller Mensa**

is located downstairs in the university building on the corner of Fürstengraben and Am Planetarium, near the botanical garden. Open M-Th 9:30am-7pm, Sa 1-4pm. ❶

SIGHTS

ZEISS-PLANETARIUM. The world's oldest planetarium also features the latest, recently installed technology. Zeiss dazzles stargazers and classic rock fans alike with laser shows ranging from children's musicals to an English-language Queen extravaganza. *(Am Planetarium 5. ☎06341 88 54 88; www.planetarium-jena.de. Check the poster on the gate for event times, usually 11am-7:30pm. Ticket office open Tu-F 10am-2pm and 7-8pm, Sa 1pm-9:30pm, Su 1-7:30pm, and 30min. before all shows. Shows 30-75min. Admission €9 for musical, €8 for scientific; students €7.50/6.50. Combination Optical museum and science show ticket €11/9.)*

ROMANTIKERHAUS (ROMANTIC HOUSE). This house once bubbled with the raw creative energy of the Romantic period. Owned by philosopher and fiery democrat Johann Fichte from 1794-99, it hosted the poetic, philosophical, and musical get-togethers of the Romantics. Rather than reconstruct the house's furnishings, creative permanent and rotating exhibits teach visitors about the Romantic movement and its origins. On the top floor, a varying exhibit displays a worthwhile collection of Romantic-inspired art. *(Unterm Markt 12a. ☎06341 44 32 63. Signs in German. Open Tu-Su 10am-5pm. €4, seniors €3, students €2.50.)*

OPTISCHES MUSEUM (OPTICAL MUSEUM). Presents the history of optics with emphasis on the contributions of *Wunderkind* Carl Zeiss. See the history of eyeglasses, from classy monacles to fetching lunettes and hilarious specialty goggles. The collection also features a variety of cameras, including a replica of one meant to be strapped to a bird's chest. Downstairs is a painstakingly detailed replication of Zeiss' laboratory and a hologram gallery. *(Carl-Zeiß-Pl. 12. ☎06341 44 31 65; www.optischesmuseum.de. Open Tu-F 10am-4:30pm, Sa 11am-5pm. €5, students and seniors €4. Signs in German; English audio tour €1 with €5 deposit.)* Be sure to visit the surrounding **Botanischer Garten.** *(Open daily May 15-Sept. 14 9am-6pm, Sept. 15-May 14 9am-5pm. Last entry 30min. before closing. €3, students €1.50.)*

STADTKIRCHE ST. MICHAEL. This church has three treasures: a 13th-century wooden St. Michael, a pulpit from which Luther twice preached, and Luther's tombstone designed by Cranach the Elder, conspicuously not on Luther's grave in Wittenberg. Evidently, a battle interrupted the stone's shipment—a story that Wittenbergers find hard to swallow. *(Off Eichpl. Open M 12:30-5pm, Tu-Sa 10-11:45am and 12:30-5pm. Tour guides roam the building Th 3-5pm.)*

FESTIVALS AND NIGHTLIFE

This university town has plenty going on. Pick up the monthly *Blitz guide* at the tourist office, or start on **Wagnergasse,** an area popular with students and lined with bars and restaurants. At night, the street becomes a continuous boardwalk of outdoor seating. Towards the end of the strip, set behind a garden, you'll find the **Studentenhaus Wagner,** Wagnergasse 26, headquarters for a bohemian student culture with plays, live music, and film screenings. (☎06341 47 21 53; www.wagnerverein-jena.de. Open M-F 11am-1am, Sa-Su 7:30pm-1am.) **Kassablanca,** Felsenkellerstr. 13a, sponsors an array of discos, concerts, and political discussions in a renovated, graffitied train depot in the wooded outskirts of town. To get there from the center, turn left off Westbahnhofstr. to Rathenaustr., and take a left at the fork; this becomes Hainstr. Turn right on Felsenkellerstr. and climb the hill—the psychedelic trains will be hard to miss on your right. (☎03641 82 60; www.kassablanca.de. Cover €3-8. Usually open W-Sa from 8pm; check website for special events.)

During **Kulturarena Jena,** a festival from early July to mid-August, the area in front of Jena's theater at Engelpl. becomes a performance space. Two audiences gather for the concerts: the excited crowd in the arena itself, and the chill group lining the sidewalks and listening in for free. (☎03641 49 26 85; www.kulturarena.de. €9-17, students €7-14.)

ERFURT ☎0361

Street after street of ornate facades line this capital city, the *Thüringisches Rom* (Thuringian Rome). Erfurt (pop. 200,000) benefited from its strategic position on the trade route connecting medieval Europe with the Silk Road. The city's wealthy merchants funded the construction of 37 churches and several monasteries, one of which housed Martin Luther during his formative years as a monk. As a capital, Erfurt has a dynamic political history: Napoleon called a meeting of princes here and chatted with Goethe in what is now the Thüringer Staatskanzlei. More recently, West German Chancellor Willy Brandt met here in 1970 with East German leader Willi Stoph, commencing Ostpolitik, the arduous process of East-West reconciliation.

TRANSPORTATION

Flights: Flughafen Erfurt (☎0361 656 22 00). Take tram #4 toward "Bindersleben." Flights to major European airports via Munich.

Trains: To: **Berlin** (2hr., every 2hr., €50); **Dresden** (2hr., every hr., €42); **Frankfurt** (2hr., every hr., €46); **Leipzig** (1hr., every hr., €25); **Weimar** (15min., 4 per hr., €7).

Public Transportation: Buses and **trams** run through the pedestrian zones and beyond. Single ticket €1.70, 4 tickets €5.60. **Tageskarte** (day ticket) €54.20. Every 10min., after 7pm, every 15min., after 9pm, every 30min. Night trams (numbered with an "N" prefix) cover most daytime routes, running every 15-30min. until 1am on weekdays and throughout the night on weekends, except 4-5am. Timetable information: ☎036 11 94 49. The tourist office sells **Erfurt Cards** (€10, valid for 48hr. from time of purchase), good for unlimited transportation, city tours, and admission to the city's museums.

Taxis:☎ 036 15 55 55 (remember: 5 times 5) or 03 61 66 66 66 (6 times 6).

Bike Rental: Radhaus am Dom, Kettenstr. 13. (☎0361 602 0640). A stone's throw away from the Mariendom. City bikes €9, mountain bikes €11. Open M-F 10am-6pm, Sa 10am-2pm. www.radhaus-erfurt.de. The city is eminently bikeable, and nearly every shop has a rack for its patrons.

ORIENTATION AND PRACTICAL INFORMATION

Erfurt lies in the heart of Thuringia, only 15min. from Weimar. Its large train station and proximity to the **Thüringer Wald** make it a convenient gateway to the forest. The train station is south of the city center. Head straight down Bahnhofstr. to reach the **Anger**—the main drag—and then the **Altstadt,** which is split by the Gera River. Across the river lies the **Fischmarkt,** dominated by the **Rathaus.** From there, continue on Marktstr. to **Domplatz,** home of Erfurt's cathedral.

Tourist Office: Erfurt Tourismus Gesellschaft, Benediktspl. 1 (☎036 16 64 00; www.erfurt-tourismus.de), between the Rathaus and the Krämerbrücke. Pick up a copy of the free monthly *Erfurter Magazin* for event listings. Ask for a free walking tour of Erfurt and a brochure (€0.50). The staff also books rooms and reserves theater tickets. Open M-F 10am-7pm (Jan.-Mar. closes 6pm), Sa 10am-6pm, Su 10am-4pm.

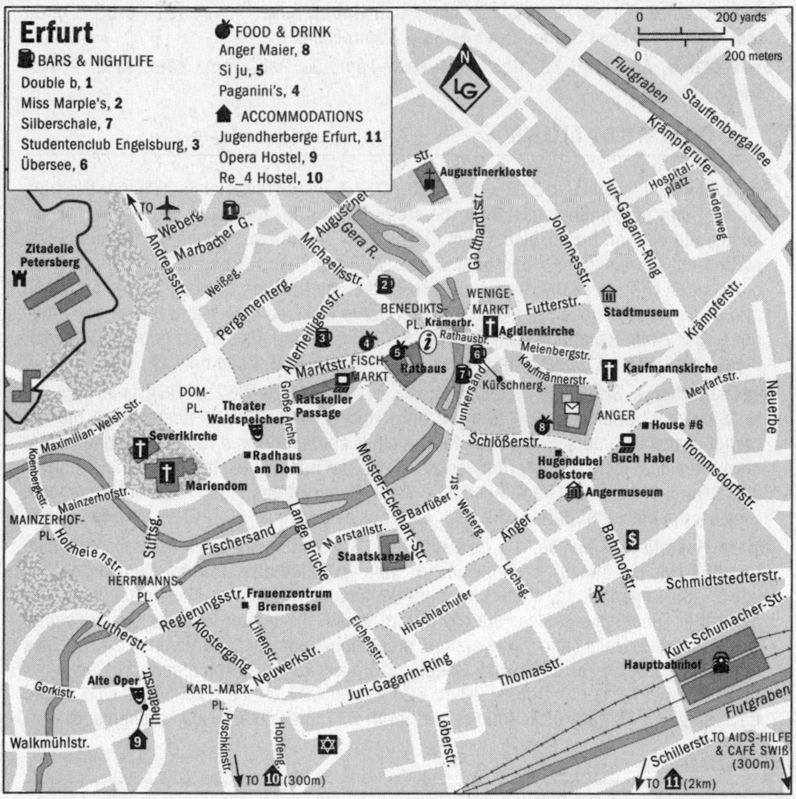

Currency Exchange: Deutsche Bank, Bahnhofstr. 7a, changes currency and has a **24hr. ATM.** Open M, W, F 9am-4pm, Tu and Th 9am-6pm.

Gay and Lesbian Resources: At the **AIDS-Hilfe,** Windthorststr. 43a (☎036 17 31 22 33). Tram #3 (dir.: Urbicher Kreuz) or #4 (dir.: Wiesenhügel) to "Robert-Koch-Str.," then continue another block. AIDS counseling available Tu 1-6pm, W 2-9pm. **Cafe Swiß** open Tu and W 7pm-midnight, Su 4-10pm. Women's **Frauencafe** on 1st and 3rd F of the month 7pm-midnight. Cafe contains library with information on AIDS and sexuality.

Women's Resources: Brennessel Frauenzentrum, Regierungsstr. 28 (☎036 15 65 65 10; www.frauenzentrum-brennessel.de). Specializing in support for abused women, the center offers information, counseling, and arranges emergency overnight stays. Cafe and cultural programs. Open M-Th 9am-6pm, F 9am-4pm.

Bookstore: Hugendubel, Am Anger 62 (☎03 61 48 44 84), has many English-language books, mostly novels. Open M-Sa 9:30am-8pm.

Emergency: Police ☎110. **Fire** and **Ambulance** ☎112.

Pharmacy: Apollo-Apotheke, Juri-Gagarin-Ring 94 (☎03 61 24 11 66). Open M-F 7:30am-7pm, Sa 8am-2pm.

Internet Access: Internet Cafe (☎036 12 62 38 34) in the Ratskeller Passage across from the Rathaus. €1.50 per 30min. €5 back for every 5hr. you buy. Open M-F

10am-8pm, Sa 11am-7pm, Su 3-8pm. **Buch Habel,** Anger 7 (☎0361 59 85 80), on the 3rd fl. €1.50 per 30min. Open M-Sa 9:30am-8pm.

Post Office, Anger 66-73. Open M-F 9am-7pm, Sa 9am-1pm. **24hr. ATM. Postal Code:** 99084.

ACCOMMODATIONS

Re_4 Hostel, Puschkinstr. 21 (☎0361 600 0110; www.re4hostel.com). From the train station, turn on Bahnhofstr. toward the steps in front of the Stadtpark, right on Schillerstr., and right on Puschkinstr. (15min). This may be the most glamorous former police station out there. Fall into bed behind bars in Room 13, a 3-bed room occupying the old weapon chamber. Table tennis and foosball in the basement, a cafe on the first floor, and a streetside terrace. Breakfast €4.50. Sheets €2. Free coffee and tea all day. Internet €3 for 24 hr. Reception daily 8am-9pm. Check-in 2pm. Check-out noon. 4-bed €13; 3-bed 16; singles €22.50, with shower €26; doubles €52. Cash only. ❶

Jugendherberge Erfurt (HI), Hochheimer Str. 12 (☎0361 562 6705). Take tram #6 to "Steigerstr." Backtrack and turn left onto Hochheimer Str.; the hostel is on the left corner at the 1st intersection. Look for the classical facade and metal sculpture on the lawn. Breakfast included. Internet access €0.05 per min. Wheelchair-accessible. Check-in 3-10pm. Check-out 10am. Reception 24hr. Reservations recommended in summer. Singles, doubles, and dorms with bath €24 per person, over €27. Cash only. ❷

Opera Hostel, Walkmuhlstr. 13 (☎0361 60 13 13 60; www.opera-hostel.com). Take bus #51 (dir. Hochheim) to "Alte Oper," or walk up Bahnhofstr. toward town, and take a left on Juri-Gagarin-Ring, which turns into Walkmuhlstr. (20min.). The hostel is on your right after Dalbergsweg. Near the old opera house, the hostel features swanky suede chairs, marble stairs, and hand-crafted steel bunkbeds for 3. Breakfast €4.50. Bike rental €1.50 per hr. or €10 a day. Sheets and towel €2.50. 24hr. reception. Check-out noon. Internet €2 per hr. Dorms: 2-bed €24, 3-bed €22, 5-bed €18, 6-bed €16, 7-bed €13. Singles with bath €37, doubles with bath €27. AmEx/MC/V €2 surcharge. ❷

FOOD

The region's specialty, *Thüringer Bratwurst,* is a plump, oversized sausage on an small roll sold at stands all over the city (€1.50-2). Check out the many outdoor *Eiscafes,* especially on the Fischmarkt, that sell colorful sundaes in eyeball-high flutes. For **groceries,** try **Tegut,** Anger 74-75, next to the Kaufmannskirche. (Open M-Sa 7:30am-8pm.) There is also a fresh fruit and vegetable **market** on Dompl. (M-Sa 6am-2pm.) Many of Erfurt's *Biergärten* like Engelsburg (see **Nightlife;** weekly specials €3-7) also serve inexpensive meals.

Anger Maier, Schlößerstr. 8 (☎036 15 66 10 58; www.angermaier.de), at the edge of Angerpl. heading toward the Fischmarkt. One of the oldest bars in Erfurt, with an herbaceous bricked beer garden where guests find shaded tables, a fountain, and an extensive menu, with historical details. Specials €4-8, entrees €6-9. English menu upon request. Open M-Sa 9am-1am, Su 10am-6pm. MC/V ❸

Paganini's, Fischmarkt 13-16 (☎036 16 43 06 92; www.paganini-erfurt.de), slices its own spaghetti and stuffs its own tortellinis daily. Locals dine on the Sicilian chef's pasta and gourmet pizza (€5-7) in the bustling interior or while serenaded by street musicians outside. In back, the charming garden will transport you to Naples. Open daily 11:30am-midnight. AmEx/MC/V. ❸

Si ju, Fischmarkt 1 (☎036 16 55 22 95; www.si-ju-erfurt.de.), adjoining the Rathaus. This intensely sleek, modern cafe and lounge serves reasonably-priced entrees (7-11) in a prime location. Open daily 9am-1am. MC/V. ❷

SIGHTS

MARIENDOM. Eight-hundred-year-old steps lead up to the heavenly cathedral towering over the Dompl. Today, it is a Gothic extravaganza, though its 1154 foundation is Romanesque. Fifteen 14th-century stained-glass windows portray Biblical stories and the lives of the saints. A life-size candelabra in the form of a saint is the oldest free-standing piece of bronze artwork in Germany, and a Romanesque sculpture of an enthroned Mary dates back to the 12th century. Opposite the ornate altar and choir stalls is a gigantic baptismal font, connected to the ceiling, symbolizing baptism's power to connect Earth to Heaven. Out of sight hangs the 12-ton **Gloriosa bell,** the biggest in medieval Europe, which only rings on important church holidays. Pause for a moment by the gigantic **mural** of St. Christophorus, the patron of travelers, who is said to protect them against untimely death. *(Dompl. ☎0361 646 1265. Open May-Oct. M-Sa 9am-5pm, Su 1-5pm; Nov.-Apr. M-Sa 10am-4pm, Su 1-4pm. English translations available. Free.)*

SEVERIKIRCHE. The muted sandstone interior and Gothic exterior of this church are similar to, and outshone by, the Mariendom, for which it served as a model with its unusual three towers. The smaller neighbor asserts itself with its enormous Baroque organ with flying golden angels, flames, and fake pastel marble. The sarcophagus near the entrance supposedly holds the bones of St. Severus, for whom the church is named. *(Enter up the stairs, opposite the Mariendom. ☎0361 57 69 60 Open May-Oct. M-Sa 10am-12:30pm and 1:30-4pm Nov.-Apr. M-Sa.10:30am-12:30pm and 1:30-3:30pm. Jan.-Feb. closed M. Free.)*

KRÄMERBRÜCKE. Funded in the 1400s by sales of awful-smelling Thuringian blue dye, the bridge—one of Erfurt's most interesting architectural attractions—still serves a commercial function, lined on both sides with shops that completely block the Gera from view. At the end of the bridge, the tower of the Ägidienkirche offers glimpses of Erfurt's red-roofed houses. Wander beneath the bridge, accessible from the flanking Rathausbrüke, to take the architectural marvel. There you can also relax on the grass, or wade in the Gera. *(☎0361 373 3301. Tower open Tu-Su 11am-5pm. €1.50, students €1.)*

ANGER. Erfurt's wide pedestrian promenade, the *Anger* (meadow), is one of the most attractive shopping areas in eastern Germany, and it buzzes with activity. Nineteenth-century Neoclassical and Jugendstil architecture lines the street, interlaced with modern constructions. Across from the post office is **House #6,** where Russian Tsar Alexander I stayed when he came to Erfurt to meet with Napoleon in 1808. The Kaufmannskirche, once the site of business transactions, sits at the end of the Anger behind the post office. The **Angermuseum,** Anger 18, housed in a yellow mansion, displays a small collection of medieval religious art from around Erfurt as well as rotating exhibitions of local contemporary art. *(☎0361 554 50. The museum is currently closed for renovations, but is expected to reopen in 2009. Ask at the tourist office for hours and prices.)*

RATHAUS. The stony neo-Gothic facade of Erfurt's Rathaus belies its more playful red, gold and blue interior, which dates from the Romantic period. Along its staircases and hallways, murals depict fictional and factual events related to Erfurt, including Dr. Faust conjuring up a vision of the cyclops Polyphemus before bewildered Erfurt University students. *(Fischmarkt 1. ☎0361 65 50. Signs in English. Open M-Tu and Th 8am-6pm, W 8am-4pm, F 8am-2pm, Sa-Su 10am-5pm. Free.)*

ENTERTAINMENT AND NIGHTLIFE

For nightlife, the German-language monthly *Blitz* lists upcoming shows, concerts, parties, and special events. The **Theater Erfurt** puts on shows, ranging from operas and ballet to youth theater, at the **Schauspielhaus,** Dalbersweg 2. (☎0361 223 30. **Box office,** Schlöesserstr. 4, open M-F 8am-7pm, Sa 9am-3pm. Tickets €10-22; student discounts available.) Tickets to these and most other performances in Erfurt can also be purchased at the tourist office. Just off Dompl., the **Theater Waidspeicher** runs a marionette and puppet theater, and holds cabaret shows on weekends. (Box office Dompl.18. ☎0361 598 2924; www.waidspeicher.de. Puppet shows €5 regular and €5 reduced price, cabaret €8.50-12. Open Tu-F 3-5:30pm, Sa 10am-1pm.) For a drinking scene, check out the area near Dompl. and the Krämerbrücke. The following spots are worthwhile.

Double b, Marbacher Gasse 10 (☎0361 211 5122), fuses Irish pub with German Biergarten. Trendy Erfurters show up for the cordial atmosphere, good food, and cheap beers. Entrees €4-8. Open M-F 8am-1am, Sa-Su 9am-1am. Kitchen open until 11pm.

Silberschale, Kürschnergasse 3 (☎0361 262 0885). Reasonably priced drinks and a back deck with seating right over the shallow Gera. Open Tu-Th 9am-1am or later, F-Sa 9am-2am, Su 9am-6pm. English menu available. Cash only.)

Überbersee, Kürschnergasse 8 (☎0361 644 7607; www.uebersee-erfurt.de). Eat all three meals in unconventional seating and a terrace overlooking the river. Daily drink specials. Th all beers €2. Free Wi-Fi. Open daily from 9am. MC/V.

Miss Marple's, Michaelisstr. 42 (☎0361 540 3399), features photos of Agatha Christie's humorous private eye on the walls and an entrance that is a dead ringer for a London phone booth. Kitchen serves great baguette sandwiches and *Thüringer* specialties (€3.50-10.50) until 2am. Open M-Th and Su 6pm-2am, F-Sa 6pm-3am. Cash only.

THÜRINGER WALD (THURINGIAN FOREST)

Extending from Eisenach in the northwest to the Saale river in the east, the vast Thüringen Wald is one of Germany's most magnificent landscapes. Because of the forest's proximity to Weimar and Jena, historical university cities that once sheltered many of Germany's foremost intellectuals, the region enjoys the reputation that only poets can bestow. Following Goethe and Schiller's lead, droves of Romantic thinkers found inspiration in the shadows of these trees.

Today, the Romantic sensibility of the forest is more accessible than ever. One of the most popular routes through the region is the 168km long Rennsteig. Starting in Hörschel, cutting across southern Thuringia, and running south to Bavaria, the Rennsteig links the gorgeous scenery and villages scattered along its path. While history books date the trail to 1330, locals claim that it was first trod upon by prehistoric hunter-gatherers. In the middle of the route, Ilmenau is a good starting point in either direction: take Ilmenau's bus #300 (dir.: Suhl) to "Rennsteigkreuzung" (€2). The tourist offices in Ilmenau, Erfurt (p. 424), or Eisenach (p. 429) sell guides and maps for an extended jaunt. If you're planning a multi-day hike, reserve trail-side huts far in advance. For more info, contact **Fremdenverkehrsband Thüringer Wald,** Postfach 124, 98501 Suhl (☎03681 394 50; www.thueringer-wald.com), or **Gästeinformation Brotterode,** Bad-Vilbeler-Pl. 4, 98599 Brotterode (☎036840 33 33).

EISENACH ☎03691

Birthplace of Johann Sebastian Bach, residence-in-exile of Martin Luther, and site of the famous Wartburg castle, Eisenach (pop. 44,000) has garnered national and international attention for almost a millennium. Tourists started visiting the castle as early as the 16th century, primarily to see the black stain that Luther supposedly made on the wall of his small room while "fighting the devil with ink." By the 19th century, Wartburg, one of Goethe's favorite spots, had became a national symbol. Eisenach is also the perfect place to start a journey into the Thuringian Forest to the south or the Hainich National Park to the north. Buses run from Eisenach to the heads of various trails (the distance is also bikeable), and unlike Wartburg, the national park is refreshingly undiscovered. Goethe came for the scenery, though he hated the castle itself—or the "old dirty box," as he so eloquently put it. Pilgrims coming to the Lutherstube have carved their names into the wood all around the door.

TRANSPORTATION AND PRACTICAL INFORMATION

Trains go to Eisenach from Bebra in the west (45min., every hr.), Meiningen in the south (1hr., every hr.), and Erfurt in the east (50min., every 30min.). **Buses** (20min., every hr.) go to Wartburg from the Hauptbanhof, stopping at Karlsplatz and Wandelhalle along the way; don't miss the last bus back to town at 5:25pm—it's a long, hilly walk. Buy tickets at the Busbahnhof (€1.50; open M 6:30am-noon and 1-4pm, Tu and Th-F 7:45am-noon and 1-4pm, W 7:45am-noon and 1-3pm), on board (€1.50) or at the tourist office (€1.10). For a **taxi,** call ☎03691 290 00. Rent **bikes** at **Fahrrad-Service Helm,** Katharinenstr. 139. (☎03 69 17 73 74. €10 per day. Open M-F 9am-6pm, Sa 9am-1pm.) Eisenach's **tourist office,** Markt 9, has information on Wartburg, hands out free maps, offers daily city tours (2hr. Apr.-Oct. M-F 10:30am and 2pm, Sa-Su 3-4 per day; Nov.-Mar. Sa-Su 10am and 2pm; €5; German only), and books rooms for free. From the train station, walk on Bahnhofstr. through the arched tunnel under the darkened tower and follow it left until you can turn right onto the pedestrian Karlstr. (☎03691 792 30; www.eisenach.info. Open M-F 10am-6pm, Sa 10am-4pm; Apr.-Oct. also Su 10am-4pm.) **Rats Apotheke,** Karlstr. 1, is a centrally located **pharmacy.** (☎03691 297 30. Open M-F 8am-7pm, Sa 8:30am-4pm.). **Die Eule,** Karlstr. 3, in the pedestrian zone near the Markt, is a **bookstore** that offers **internet**. (☎03691 89 05 05. €2 per 40min. Open M-F 9am-7pm, Sa 10am-6pm, Su 11am-5pm.) The internet cafe **Diakonie Verbund,** Goldschmiedenstr. 14, is open later. (☎03691 708 4812. €1.60 per hr. Open M-F 11am-10pm, Sa-Su 2pm-10pm.) The **post office** is at Markt 16. (Open M-F 8:30am-6pm, Sa 8:30am-2pm.) **Postal Code:** 99817.

ACCOMMODATIONS AND FOOD

Residenz Haus ❷, Auf der Esplanade, is around the corner from the tourist office. Miniature witches decorate the spiraling staircase up to spacious rooms off an 18th-century stone tower. Impeccably clean, white fluffy bedding and bathrobe. (☎03691 21 41 33; www.residenzhaus-eisenach.de. €20 per person in rooms of three or more, singles €25, doubles €50. Breakfast €6. Cash only.) **Jugendherberge Arthur Becker (HI) ❶,** Mariental 24, occupies a golden Mediterranean-style villa far from town, but close to the Wartburg. From the train station, take Bahnhofstr. to Wartburger Allee, veering left before the tunnel. This road runs into Mariental. Pass the pond; it's on your right. Or, take bus #3 (dir.: Mariental) to "Liliengrund Parkpl." and continue up Mariental for 5min. Recently renovated, the hostel has an elegant dining room and terraces.

(☎03691 74 32 59. Breakfast included. Reception M-F 7am-10pm, Sa-Su 7-10am and 3-10pm. Dorms €18.50, over 27 €21.50. Cash only.)

For groceries, head to the **Edeka,** Johannispl. 2-4. (Open M-F 7am-5pm. Sa 7am-4pm.) The centrally located **La Fontana ❷,** Georgenstr. 22, serves pizzas, pastas, and salads (€3-5) on a lovely delta with a fountain by the Markt. (☎03691 74 35 39. Open M-Th and Su 11:30am-10:30pm, F-Sa 11:30am-11pm. Cash only.) **Cafe-Restaurant Möritz ❸,** Bahnhofstr. 7, dishes out local specialties like *Rostbrätel* and *Jager Schnitzel*, named after the town's most notable guests (€3-9.50). Indulge in a fortress-sized sundae, perhaps inspired by the Wartburg. (☎036 91 74 65 75. Open M-F 8am-6:30pm, Sa-Su 10am-6:30pm. Cash only.) Bask in the classical climate of the Bachhaus at nearby

SIGHTS

WARTBURG FORTRESS

Buses run between the train station and the castle parking lot (every hr. 9am-5pm; €1.50, €1.10 at the tourist office). Wartburgallee leads to the foot of the hill, and footpaths snake up to the gates. If you weigh 64kg (about 140 lb.) or less, you can ride a donkey up the last stretch. (☎03691 21 04 04; www.wartburg.de. Donkeys Tu-Su 10am-4pm. €4 roundtrip.) Gates open daily Mar.-Oct. 8:30am-8pm, last tour 5pm; Nov.-Feb. 9am-5pm, last tour 3:30pm. To see the inside of the palace, you must take a tour. Tours in English daily at 1:30pm. Tours in German leave every 15min., but ask for a leaflet with English narration (free). Admission €7, students and children €4, seniors and the disabled €6. Museum and Luther study without tour €3.50, students €2. Photography permit €1.

The castle perches 200m above Eisenach's half-timbered streets and lords over the northwestern slope of the rolling Thüringer Wald. It was founded in 1067 by the Franconian **Count Ludwig the Jumper,** who didn't own the land, but covered it with soil from his estate in order to build the castle "on his own land" with a clear conscience. By the turn of the 13th century, Wartburg's court was a famed cultural center. Six talented *Minnesänger* (medieval troubadours who established German choral music) competed here in the *Sängerkrieg* (singers' battles), the loser narrowly escaping death. These events, which inspired Wagner's opera *Tannhäuser*, are depicted in the castle's **Sängersaal** (Singers' Hall).

Another important medieval resident was **St. Elizabeth,** the humble queen from Hungary whose legendary deeds are represented in a 20th-century mosaiced hall, covered in just under four million pieces of glass. After its medieval heyday, Wartburg lay low for a few hundred years before receiving its most important guest, the refugee **Martin Luther,** in 1521. Disguised as a wanderer under the pseudonym Squire Jörg, Luther spent 10 months here growing a mustache and translating the New Testament into High German. The castle then stagnated for a few hundred years, but due in part to Goethe's efforts, Wartburg found new life in the 19th century with the installation of an art gallery.

The castle's **Festsaal** (festival hall), which is replicated in Ludwig II's famous Neuschwanstein (p. 360), housed an 1817 meeting of 500 representatives of university fraternities, the group that formed Germany's first bourgeois opposition to the monarchy. A copy of the flag they toasted hangs in the room—its red, gold, and black colors inspired Germany's present flag. The renovated interior of the castle now matches the Romantic idea of the Middle Ages more closely than historical reality, but the structure itself has remained remarkably unchanged in the last 850 years. Each stage of the castle's renovations over the last 800 years can be tracked with a different type of brick. The view from the walls of the courtyard or from atop the south tower (entrance €0.50) is spectacular. If you look opposite Eisenach, you can see from the Thüringer Wald extend all the way to Hessen.

BACHHAUS. Next to an imposing Bach statue on Frauenplan are the recreated Bach family living quarters where Johann Sebastian is thought to have been born in 1685. The museum below showcases instruments Bach used in his compositions, including those he played at home—he kept 19 private instruments—and wackier ones from the era, like a violin with an internal trumpet and a Benjamin Franklin invention: a glass harmonica to be played with wet fingers. Roughly every hour, one of the museum's guides plays Bach selections on a gamut of keyboard instruments, including two "house organs," a clavichord, and a spinet, and provides historical context in German. Another exhibit reveals a forensic reconstruction of Bach, obtained from his cadaver. *(Frauenplan 21. Turn off Wartburgallee down Grimmelgasse to reach the house. ☎03691 793 40. Open daily 10am-6pm. English translations at all exhibits. €6, students €3.50.)*

OTHER SIGHTS. Town life centers on the pastel **Markt,** bounded by the tilting pink Rathaus and the **Georgenkirche,** an 800-year-old church where Bach's family members were organists for 132 years, where **J.S. Bach** was baptized, and where Martin Luther sang in the boys choir. The ornate diptych on the left side of the altar is where Martin Luther and Jan Hus, a Dutch minister and one of Luther's forerunners in the Reformation, once preached. *(Open daily 10am-noon and 2-5pm. Entrance free. English translations available. www.bachhaus.de.)* Just up the street from the Markt is the latticed **Lutherhaus,** where Luther spent his school days studying Latin at the top of his class. *(Lutherpl. 8. ☎03691 298 30; www.lutherhaus-eisenach.de. Open daily 10am-5pm. €3, students and children €1.50. English translations available.)*

SACHSEN-ANHALT (SAXONY-ANHALT)

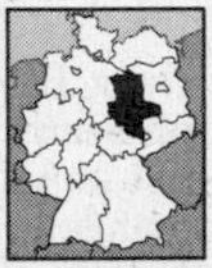

Saxony-Anhalt's tranquil grass plains encircle cities of international cultural significance. Despite drawing thousands of tourists each year, villages like Wittenberg and Dessau remain small enough to harbor traditional German character. The region suffers from the highest unemployment rate in Germany, but it is rapidly modernizing. Ancient cathedral spires now share the skyline with scaffolding and cranes. Nature enthusiasts will delight in the Harz Mountains, a skiing and hiking paradise virtually undiscovered by English-speaking travelers.

HIGHLIGHTS OF SAXONY-ANHALT

RELIVE THE REFORMATION in **Wittenberg** (see this page), the city where Martin Luther posted his 95 Theses. The city still celebrates its native superstar and was recently blessed with a Hundertwasser-designed high school.

SUBORDINATE FORM TO FUNCTION at the original Bauhaus, which imbues the city of **Dessau** (p. 435) with design-school hipness.

FOLLOW GOETHE to the half-timbered town of **Wernigerode** (p. 441) in the **Harz mountains** (p. 438).

WITTENBERG ☎03491

In an effort to keep the memory of Martin Luther alive, the city even renamed itself Lutherstadt Wittenberg in 1938. It was here that Luther nailed his 95 Theses to the Schloßkirche in 1517, igniting the Protestant Reformation that irrevocably changed Europe. His scandalous wedding—conducted despite his vows of celibacy as a final snub to Rome—was so perfectly dramatic that the town reenacts it every June in a three-day festival. Even in the officially atheistic DDR, many East Germans clung to the image of the maverick Luther as an emblem of courageous resistance. Since the fall of the wall, religious pilgrims have returned in full force to Luther's city.

TRANSPORTATION

Trains run to: **Berlin** (45min., every hr., €22); **Dessau** (40min., every hr., €6); **Leipzig** (1hr., every hr., €10); **Magdeburg** (2hr., every hr., €15).

Bike Rental: Fahrradladen, Coswiger Str. 21. (☎03491 40 28 49. €7 per day. Open M-F 9am-6pm, Sa 10am-noon.)

ORIENTATION AND PRACTICAL INFORMATION

To get to the pedestrian zone from the station, go toward the bus stop, turn left through the parking lot and down the street, and follow the curve right, where it becomes Lutherstr. Continue on Lutherstr., then take a left on Wilhelm-Weber-Str. The Lutherhaus is straight ahead; once there, the road off to the right is Collegienstr., the beginning of the pedestrian zone.

Tourist Office: Schloßpl. 2 (☎03491 49 86 10; www.wittenberg.de), at the western end of the pedestrian zone, provides maps in a dozen languages, including English and

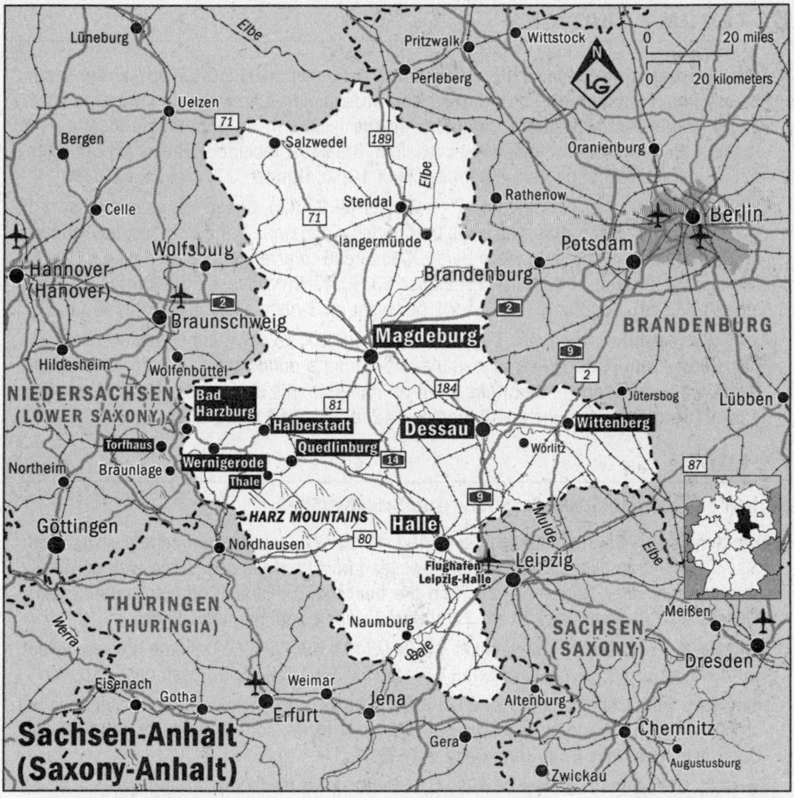

German (€0.50), books rooms for free, and gives tours in German. Private rooms start from €18. English tours are available at additional cost with advance arrangements. Open Apr.-Oct. M-F 9am-6:30pm, Sa-Su 10am-4pm; Nov.-Mar. M-F 10am-4pm, Sa 10am-2pm, Su 11am-3pm. Jan.-Feb. closed Sa-Su.

Tours: If you have a good mobile phone plan, pick up a free "Mobile Audio Guide" flyer from the tourist office. At each of seventeen city sights, you can call a phone number with a special extension and hear a 2min. blurb, brought to you by the History Channel.

Banks: One of many banks near the Rathaus, **Sparkasse,** Markt 20, immediately behind the Rathaus, has several 24hr. ATMs. Open M-F 8:30am-6pm, Sa 9am-11:30am.

Pharmacy: Apotheke am Collegienhof, Collegienstr. 74, sells pharmaceuticals in a central location. (☎03491 496 90. Open M-F 7:30am-7pm, Sa 8am-noon.)

Internet: Head to the **public library,** Schloßstr. 7 (☎03491 402 1600). €0.41 per 15min. Open Tu-F 11am-6pm. **New York Bagels,** Coswiger Str. 18 (☎03491 69 54 46), near the tourist office. Open daily 8:30am-10pm. €0.50 per 15min. Pop into the **Rathaus** for the free internet terminal in the lobby.

Post office: Wilhelm-Weber-Str. 1, on the corner with Fleischerstr. (Open M-F 9am-12:30pm and 2-6pm, Sa 9am-noon.) **Postal Code:** 06886.

ACCOMMODATIONS

Jugendherberge im Schloß (HI), Schlossstr. 14-15 (☎03491 50 52 05), in the castle across from tourist office. Enter through the wheat-colored archway, and then the glass cube. Medieval on the outside, modern on the inside, in an unbeatable location. All rooms with bath, some wheelchair-accessible. Breakfast included. Sheets €3.50. Internet €6 per hr. Reception 8am-10pm. Lockout 10pm. Dorms €17, over 27 €20. ❷

CVJM Gloecknerstift, Fleischerstr. 17 (☎03491 67 86 39). Cheap rooms in the heart of town. High-ceilinged rooms with beds that match. From behind the Rathaus, take Jüdenstr., which delivers you onto Fleischerstr. Call ahead to arrange reception times. Check-out flexible. Shared bathrooms. Breakfast €3.50. Kitchen use €1.50. Dorms €14.50, singles €18.50, doubles €31. Save €1 per night on 3-night stays. Cash only. ❷

Am Schwanenteich, Töpferstr. 1 (☎03491 40 28 07; www.wittenberg-schwanenteich.de). Rooms with TV and Wi-Fi across the street from a pond ringed by willows. From the Markt, walk up Jüdenstr., then take a left on Töpferstr.; it's at the next corner. Reception 11am-10pm. Breakfast included. Singles €42, doubles €71. MC/V. ❹

FOOD

Budget eateries line **Collegienstraße** and **Schloßstraße.**

Zum Schwarzen Bär, Schloßstr. 2 (☎03491 41 12 00), serves spud-centric dishes with a sense of humor. Sleds and wheelbarrows leap from shelves, deer skulls with comically small antlers hang from the walls, and the beer menu includes off-color commentary. Entrees €4-12. Open daily 11am-1am. Kitchen open until midnight. V. ❸

Eiscaffe & Restaurant, Collegienstr. 70 (☎03491 43 76 82). Delicate crepes. Sweet €3-4.50, savory €5-6.20, vegetarian €5. Open M-Sa 10am-6pm. Cash only. ❷

Irish Harp Pub, Collegienstr. 71 (☎03491 41 01 50). This lively pub has Guinness on tap (€3.50 a pint) and serves over 100 whiskeys, to the sound of live rock or blues on Saturday. Open daily 4pm-3am. Cash only. ❷

Barrick, Collegienstr. 81 (☎03491 40 32 60; www.barrik.de), draws people of all ages on the weekend to its secluded patio just off the main drive. Barrick features in-house cabaret (€13-20) on select dates; check the website for information. Open W-Sa 6pm-2am, Su 3-10pm. Cash only. ❺

SIGHTS

To the delight of some citizens and the chagrin of others, Wittenberg truly is an open-air museum, the living scene of Martin Luther. Plan your sightseeing around Collegienstr., the historic row.

LUTHERHAUS. Once the site of an old monastery, this museum now chronicles the history of the Reformation through letters, texts, art, and artifacts (signs in English). Hundreds of early printed pamphlets, for and against Luther's ideas, show how the Reformation was also a media revolution. Among these is a first-edition copy of Luther's ground breaking translation of the Bible, and a replica of the printing press used to proliferate his ideas. The top floor shows modern renderings of the preacher, with an emphasis on contemporary interpretations of the Reformation. *(Collegienstr. 54. ☎03491 420 30; www.martinluther.de. Open Apr.-Oct. daily 9am-6pm, Nov.-Mar. Tu-Su 10am-5pm. €5, students €3, under 6 free.)* Continue a block down Collegienstr. away from the town center to see the **Luther Oak,** the site at which the reformer allegedly burned a papal bull.

HAUPTKIRCHE ST. MARIEN. In the 725-year-old church, nicknamed "the Mother of the Reformation" and known for its dazzling paintings by hometown prodigy Lucas Cranach the Elder, you will find a life-size picture, on location, of the tiny pulplit from which Luther gave his famous *Invocavit* sermon. The actual pulpit, now in the Lutherhaus, befits the man's figure: though slightly plump, he stood barely 5 ft. tall. *(Jüdenstr. 35. ☎03491 40 44 15. Open May-Oct. M-Sa 10am-6pm Su 11:30-6pm; Nov.-Apr. M-Sa10am-4pm S. Free information in English.)* The **Cranachhoefe,** the two houses where Cranach lived and worked, are now museums about the artist; the courtyard hosts lively open-air performances. The **Galerie im Cranach-Haus** showcases modern art exhibitions. Facing the Rathaus, take the alley called Kirchpl. on your right. *(Markt 4. ☎03491 42 0 1911; www.cranach-stiftung.de. Museum and gallery open. May-Oct. M-Sa 10am-5pm, Su 1-5pm; Nov.-Apr. Tu-Sa 10am-5pm, Su 1-5pm. €4, students €3. Gallery only, €2.)*

ALTES RATHAUS. Wittenberg's elegant Altes Rathaus, Markt 26, dominates the Markt with its arctic facade. Inside, a sleek modern room displays a terrific collection of 20th-century Christian graphic art. A maze of walls shows series of prints of Biblical scenes by German expressionists like Otto Dix, Max Beckmann, and Karl Schmidt-Rotluff. Other artists include Chagall, Picasso, and even Günter Grass. The departure from classical oil paintings is stark, and not just in the composition: check out George Grosz's image of Jesus on the cross being heckled by WWI soldiers. *(☎03491 40 11 49 www.christlichekunst-wb.de. Open Tu-Su 10am-5pm. €3, students €2.)* Statues of Luther and fellow reformer Philip Melanchthon share the plaza in front of the Rathaus with one of Wittenberg's famous **Jungfernröhrwässer,** the 16th-century wells whose waters flow through original wooden pipes (the other is in the Cranachhof).

SCHLOSSKIRCHE. On October 31, 1517, Martin Luther nailed his **95 Theses** to the door of this church. These doors are now nail-proof as the originals have been replaced by bronze ones inscribed with the 95 Theses in their original Latin. Luther is buried in the church, as are Melanchthon and Saxon Electors Johann the Steadfast and Friedrich the Wise. The tower offers a panoramic view of the area. *(Located on Schloßpl., down Scloßstr. from the Markt. ☎03491 40 25 85. Church open Apr.-Oct. M-Sa 10am-6pm, Su 11:30am-6pm; Nov.-Mar. M-Sa 10am-4pm, Su 11:30am-4pm. Services Su 10am. Free. 30min. organ concerts May-Oct. Tu 2:30pm. Tower open May-Oct. M-F noon-4pm, Sa-Su 10am-5pm. Last entry to tower 30min. before closing. Tower €2, students €1. Call ahead for guided tours €3/1.50.)*

LUTHER-MELANCHTHON GYMNASIUM. In 1995, an art class at the local high school asked Austrian architect Friedensreich Hundertwasser to redesign their decrepit school building in his whimsically eccentric style. Using both the students' drawings and his own ideas about nature and architecture as inspiration, he created the funkiest high school in Germany. The product was the Luther-Melanchthon Gymnasium, which looks like Gaudi on acid. Follow Sternstr. out of the city center (walking in the direction that the Lutherhalle faces) and turn right at Schillerstr. *(Schillerstr. 22a. ☎03491 88 11 31. Open Apr.-Oct. M-F 1-5pm, Sa-Su 10am-5pm; Nov.-Mar. M-F 1pm-4pm, Sa-Su 10am-4pm. 45min. tours €2, students €1.)*

DESSAU ☎0340

Founded as a medieval fortress in 1341, Dessau flourished under Princess Henrietta Katharina von Oranien in the 18th century. Famous residents include Moses Mendelssohn, a great German-Jewish philosopher and a fervent proponent of religious tolerance in the 19th century, and composer/playwright Kurt Weill, whose works encouraged artistic resistance against Nazism. Today, Dessau draws international visitors to its two UNESCO world treasures: the Bauhaus experiment in Modernist architecture, and the stunning gardens of Schloß Georgium.

TRANSPORTATION AND PRACTICAL INFORMATION

Trains: To: **Berlin** (2hr., every hr., €18.30); **Leipzig** (45min., 2 per hr., €9); **Wittenberg** (40min., every hr., €6.20). Claim a **locker** in the train station for €2-3.

Rent Bikes: Mobilitätszentrale kiosk, left of the train station's main exit. (☎0340 21 33 66. €7 per day. Open M-F 6:30am-5pm, Sa-Su 9am-1pm. Drop-off until 9pm.)

Tourist office: Zerbster Str. 2c (☎0340 204 14 42; www.dessau.de), finds private rooms and books hotel and pension rooms for free. Take tram #1, 3, or 4 from the train station's main exit to "Hauptpost." The office is behind the huge Rathaus-Center shopping mall; walk toward the center and turn left into Ratsgasse. When you reach the Rathaus proper, turn right, and the office will be on your left. The staff also sells the **Dessau Card** (€8), a 3-day ticket that allows 1 adult and 1 child unlimited access to all buses and trams in Dessau, free entry into city museums, and discounts on Bauhaus sights, tours, and bike rental. Open Apr.-Oct. M-F 9am-6pm, Sa 9am-1pm; Nov.-Mar. M-F 9am-5pm, Sa 10am-1pm. Tours depart from the tourist office; English-language tours are available for groups if arranged in advance. (Sa 11am, Apr.-Oct. also Sa 10am, Jun.-Sept. also daily 11am. €5, students €4, children free.)

Internet: Hauptbibliotek, Zerbstr. 10 (☎0340 204 26 48). €1 library use fee plus €1 per 30min. Open M-Tu and Th-F 10am-6pm, Sa 10am-1pm. With a drink, you can use the PCs at **Coffeshop Company** (☎0340 53 23 420), on the 2nd fl. of the Rathaus-Center, for free. Open M-Sa 8am-8pm, Su 11am-6pm.

Bookstore: Thalia, in the Rathaus, sells English paperbacks. Open M-Sa 8am-8pm.

Post Office, Friedrichstr. 2, is at the corner with Kavalierstr. and harbors a **24hr. ATM.** (Open M-F 8am-6:30pm, Sa 9am-12:30pm.) **Postal Code:** 06844.

ACCOMMODATIONS AND FOOD

Street market on Zerbstr., north of the Rathaus. (Open Tu and Th 7am-5pm.)

Jugendherberge (HI), Ebertallee 151 (☎0340 619 803). Airy and open 2- to 6-bed rooms feign the Bauhaus aesthetic. Exit train station to the west of tracks, away from town center. Take Schwabestr., make a slight left onto Bauhausstr., and continue through the Bauhaus complex. After passing under a walkway, turn right onto Gropius-Allee. At the first major intersection, turn left onto Elbertallee; continue for 15min. Breakfast included. Sheets €3.50. Reception 8am-10pm. Check-out 10am. Curfew midnight, but keys available. €16.50, over 27 €20. 1-night stay add €2. ❷

Klub im Bauhaus (☎0340 650 84 44; www.klubimbauhaus.de). This tragically hip club in the Bauhaus school basement offers omelettes (€4.30) and spaghetti (€6.50) that won't disappoint. Open daily 9am-midnight. AmEx/MC/V, min. €10. ❸

Essbar, on Ferdinand-von-Schill-Str., off Antoinettenstr. (☎0340 576 8815). This trendy little bistro has high-back chairs against green walls and tall bookshelves. Breakfasts €3-6, baguettes €2.60-4. Open M-F 8am-3pm and 7-10pm, Sa 10am-2pm. ❷

Ratskeller, Zerbster Str. 4a (☎0340 221 5283; www.ratskeller-dessau.de), at the pedestrian end of Ratsgasse, serves hearty *Ratsherren* (beef steak with shallot crust) and *Ratsfrauen* (pork steak with mushrooms) for €12.40. For lighter fare, try local specialties, like the *Anhaltische Milchreis* with *Knackwurst* (€4.80) and unfiltered *Dessauer Zwickelbier.* Open daily 11am-midnight. MC/V. ❹

Kiez Cafe, Bertolt-Brecht-Str. 29a (☎0340 21 20 32; www.kiez-ev.de), two blocks off Kurt-Weill-Str. The offbeat art scene congregates at this cafe, featuring a theater

(€1-3), art-film cinema (€5, students €4; M and Th €4/3), and art studios. Open M-Th 7pm-midnight, F-Sa 7pm-2am. Cash only. ❷

SIGHTS

BAUHAUS. The Bauhaus school, an icon of 20th-century Modernism, sought to marry art and industry while simultaneously forming a synthesis of the arts. Walter Gropius brought together craftsmen from across the disciplines to his avant garde **Hochschule für Gestaltung** (school of design) in 1910. For political reasons, the school moved to the new northwestern suburb of Dessau in 1925. Reacting against the notion that, at school, "art strangles life," the Bauhaus artists created sheer, functional designs for everyday use, intended for serial production. This Bauhaus building, designed by Gropius himself to house workshops, lecture halls, and student spaces, is now home to the **Bauhaus Foundation,** an urban planning research center. A permanent exhibit displays paintings by Kandinsky and Klee, architectural sketches, and the chrome tubular furniture of Marcel Breuer inspired by his bike handlebars. *(Gropiusallee 38. ☎0340 650 8251; www.bauhaus-dessau.de. Building and exhibition open daily 10am-6pm. 1hr. tour every hr. 11am and 2pm; extra tours Sa-Su. Call ahead to arrange a tour of all Bauhaus sights in Dessau. Guided tours €4, students €3, with Meisterhäuser (includes admission, see below) €9/6; Museum exhibit €4/3. English audio tour €4/3. A Bauhaus dayticket is good for audio tour and guided tours and exhibits at most Bauhaus sights, including the Meisterhäuser, €12/8.)*

BAUHAUS MEISTERHÄUSER. The six masters of the Bauhaus school lived with their families side by side in in a tranquil pine grove on Elbertallee. As expected, the artists lived according to Bauhaus principles. Gropius designed three nearly identical houses bisected into two living spaces, mirrored twice about perpendicular planes. The houses are composed of orthogonal fir wood elements, patched with generous glass expanses. The interiors, furnished by Marcel Breuer, are a calm gray and white, save for vivid splashes on the staircases and the occasional closet door. The first (#63) now houses the **Kurt Weill Center.** The composer is celebrated extensively in an annual festival (Feb. 27-Mar. 8, 2009; Feb. 26-Mar. 7, 2010). In the other two, the **Kandinsky/Klee House** and the **Muche Schlemmer House,** one of each pair of living spaces is on display, while the other shows a shifting exhibit of students of the Bauhaus. After almost completely crumbling in WWII, thanks to a 1996 renovation, the trio once again radiates elegant simplicity. *(Ebertallee. Odd numbers 63-71. ☎0340 650 8251; www.meisterhaeuser.de. Kurt Weill Festival info ☎0340 61 95 95; www.kurt-weill-fest.de. Open Tu-Su Mar.-Oct. 10am-6pm, Nov.-Feb. 10am-5pm. €5, students €3. Combination ticket to the Bauhaus exhibition and the Meisterhäuser €8/5. 1hr. Public guided tours leave the Bauhaus building Tu-Su 12:30pm, May.-Oct. also 3:30pm.)*

OTHER BAUHAUS BUILDINGS. Check out the English-language brochures *Bauhaus Buildings in Dessau* (€1) and *Bauhaus* (€0.50) at the tourist office or the Bauhaus. Continue down Elbertallee past the Meisterhäuser and turn right onto Elballee. Follow it to the end to **Kornhaus,** Kornhausstr. 146. This restaurant and dance hall was the crisp vision of Carl Fieger: It is essentially a white box with teal window trim, but it sports a breezy waterfront patio and flying-saucer glass terrace. *(☎0340 640 4141; www.kornhaus.de. Open M-W and F-Su 11am-11pm. Entrees €10-15.)* The **Laubenganghäuser** (housing with balcony access, desinged by Hannes Meyer) on Mittlebreite and Peterholzstr. is hard to distinguish from the neighboring DDR complexes, but still displays Bauhaus efficiency. The city-owned **Moses-Mendelssohn-Zentrum,** Mittelring 38, includes exhibits about the philosopher's life and work as a Jew in Dessau.

(Tram #1 (dir.: Dessau-Süd) to "Damaschkestr." (15min.) ☎0340 850 11 99. Open Mar-Oct. daily 10am-5pm, Nov.-Feb. M-F 10am-5pm, Sa-Su 1-4pm. €2, students €1.)

NON-BAUHAUS ARCHITECTURE SIGHTS. Dessau also has its share of old-school architecture as ornate as Bauhaus is spare. In the 17th-century country estate **Schloß Georgium,** built in 1780 as a summer home for prince Johann Georg, the **Anhaltische Gemäldegalerie** (Anhalt Picture Gallery) displays lesser-known paintings from the 16th-19th centuries along with some modern German art. The UNESCO-protected gardens surrounding the castle melt into lush forests that extend all the way to the Elbe. *(Puschkinallee 100. Walk down Bauhausstr. from the Bauhaus and take a left onto Kleiststr., and cross Puschkinallee to enter the park. ☎0340 661 260 16; www.georgium.de. Schloß open Tu-Su 10am-5pm; €3, students €2. Gardens open 24hr.)* With its off-beat exhibits on Dessau's history and contemporary concerns, the **Museum für Stadtgeschichte** (Municipal History Museum) in the Johannbau will satisfy all cravings for Dessau esoterica. *(Schloßpl. 3a. Walk south down Zerbster Str. and after Marienkirche walk through the gate on the left. ☎0340 220 96 12; www.stadtgeschichte.dessau.de. Open Tu-Su 10am-5pm. Last entry 30min. before close. €3, students €2.)*

HARZ MOUNTAINS

Poet Heinrich Heine wrote that even Mephistopheles (the devil's liaison in Goethe's *Faust*) trembled when he approached the Harz, the devil's own mountains. It's easy to see why Heine—and a host of others, including Goethe and Bismarck—were fascinated by this mist-shrouded terrain. The region has practical appeal, too. The Harz were Germany's main mineral source until the 20th century, but since the region straddled the Iron Curtain, both East and West declared much of it off-limits for mining during Germany's 50-year division. The effects of a shaky economy can still be felt, although a recent surge in tourism brings hope to this region still largely unknown to international visitors.

HARZ NATIONAL PARK

Hikers and spa-seekers populate the Harz National Park, which stretches from the northwestern Oberharz to the valleys of the south and Wernigerode in the east. Across the Harz, historic villages and misty mountains make for rewarding biking and hiking in summer and excellent skiing and sledding in winter.

HARZ NATIONAL PARK AT A GLANCE

AREA: 247 sq. km.

CLIMATE: Mild summers, snowy winters. Often foggy at high altitudes.

FEATURES: Dense deciduous forests, mountainous terrain, bogs, and moors.

CAMPING: Permitted only in designated campgrounds.

HIGHLIGHTS: Hiking in Goethe's footsteps, skiing the Harz, enjoying the view from the Brockenbahn.

GATEWAYS: Goslar (p. 208), Wernigerode (p. 441), Quedlinburg (p. 443).

TRANSPORTATION

The **Harzer Schmalspurbahn** (narrow-gauge railway) consists of two railroads that serve the Harz. The **Brockenbahn** runs from **Nordhausen** to **Wernigerode,** passes through the unfortunately named towns of **Sorge** (Sorrow) and **Elend** (Misery), and chugs along to the **Brocken.** The **Selketalbahn** cuts through the southeast

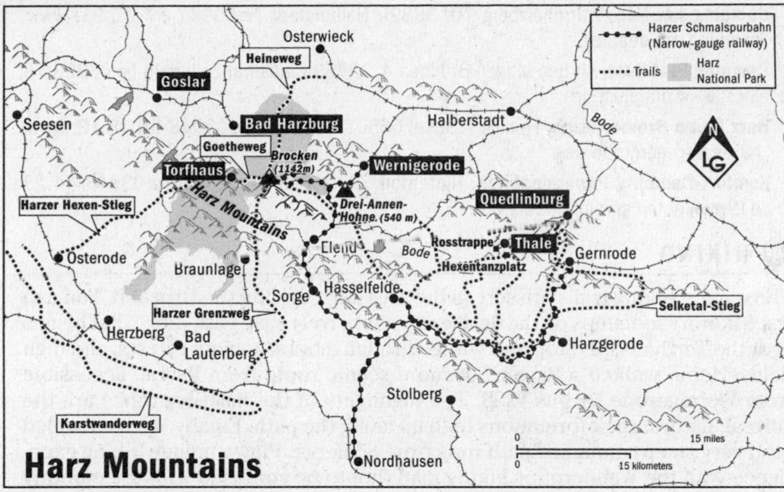

valleys. **Trains** run every hour in summer from 8:30am-8:30pm, although some routes only run until 4pm. Schedules are available at most tourist offices, online (www.hsb-wr.de), and in the free monthly pamphlet *Wandern Tips*. The Harz regional **bus station** is located in Wernigerode (p. 441). A bus and rail schedule for the eastern Harz (€2), and another for the Oberharz (€1), are invaluable and available at both the **tourist office** (in Goslar, p. 208) and bus station. Schedules vary greatly between seasons and some buses come only a few times per day. Although strenuous, **hiking** offers a more interesting way to experience this stunning landscape. Torfhaus, Braunlage, Gernrode, and most of the region's other towns are all within a day's hike of one another.

ORIENTATION AND PRACTICAL INFORMATION

The Harz National Park is located at the intersection of three *Länder:* Niedersachsen, Saxony-Anhalt, and Thuringia. The park itself resides within the wider Harz region, which supports a population of nearly 900,000 and extends 100km east to west and 40km north to south. **Brocken,** the highest mountain in northern Germany (1142m), sets near the center of the park's Saxony-Anhalt half, while glacial lakes and valleys lie to the south.

Emergency: Police ☎110. **Fire** ☎112.

Park Administration: Wernigerode (☎03943 55 020; www.nationalpark-harz.de).

Nationalparkhäuser (Visitors' Centers): Located throughout the park, in **Torfaus** (☎05320 263; open daily Apr.-Oct. 9am-5pm, Nov.-Mar. 10am-4pm), **Sankt Andreasberg** (☎05582 92 30; open daily Apr.-Oct. 9am-5pm, Nov.-Mar. 10am-5pm), and **Brocken** (☎03945 55 00 06; open daily 9:30am-5pm).

CAMPING

In addition to hostels and pensions listed below in the **Accommodations** sections of the Harz's gateway towns, visitors will find ample opportunity to camp near the park. The following campgrounds are good starting points; check with local tourist offices or visit www.harz-urlaub.com for a comprehensive listing.

Camping am See, Warmholzberg 70, 38820 Halberstadt (☎03941 57 07 91; www.camping-am-see.de).

Camping Prahljust, An den langen Brüchen 4, 38789 Clausthal-Zellerfeld (☎05323 78 393; www.prahljust.de).

Harz Camp Bremer Teich, Familie Krause, 06507 Gernrode (☎03948 56 08 10; www.harz-camp-gernrode.de).

Komfort-Camping Panoramablick, Hinterdorf 79, 06493 Dankerode (☎03948 44 23 41; www.hotelcamping-ludwig.de).

HIKING

Three main hiking trails crisscross the area surrounding the Brocken. You can trace literary footsteps on the **Goetheweg,** a relatively easy path (2hr.) that begins near the Torfhaus bus stop and winds through moors, ancient forests, and high fields. Heine walked a longer but more scenic route from Ilsetal, accessible from Wernigerode by bus #288. The highlights of the **Heineweg** (8hr.) are the surreal, natural rock formations high up along the path. Finally, a less-traveled (and very steep) unnamed path runs from Schierke. Plan a unique hiking experience with the Wanderntips hiking map (not to be confused with the monthly Wandern Tips), available at any regional tourist office.

The **Wurmberg Seilbahn** chairlift is an exhilarating way to approach the **hiking** paths around Braunlage, a small town on the park's southern fringe easily accessible by bus or train. Take the lift to the top (15min.) to reach the head of a 3hr. trail to Brocken. Or, get off at "Mittelstation" to reach the Schierke trail (2hr.). Wurmburg (971m) itself is the second-tallest peak in the Harz, topped by a high-tech ski jump used for national competitions. The lift departs from the mountain base in the parking lot behind a winter-time ice rink. From the tourist office, turn left, then right on Kurpromenade along the river. (☎05520 999 30; www.wurmberg-seilbahn.com. Open May-Oct. daily 9am-4:40pm. €5.50, round-trip €11. To "Mittelstation" €4.)

ACTIVITIES AND FESTIVALS

The Harz are famed for their skiing, sporting over 500km of cross-country and downhill trails. Skis can be rented in all of the Harz's gateway towns, many of which are trailheads for slopes and cross-country trails. Check www.harzwinter.de or www.skiharz.de to identify those most appropriate to your interests and abilities. Ice skating and tobogganing are also popular—the websites above list rinks and toboggan runs and detail winter festivals and special activities.

To see more of the Harz, consider renting a bike. The National Park features many trails suitable for **mountain biking.** For those less interested in strenuous activities, a day of rejuvenation may be a better bet. Relax just outside the park in Bad Harzburg's **Sole-Therme** (see below), or enjoy Braunlage's **Hallen- und Freizeitbad,** on Ramsenweg, which offers a pool and sauna. (☎05520 27 88. Open Tu-W and Sa 10am-7pm, Th 10am-9pm, F 10am-5pm, Su 10am-2pm. Sauna €8. Pool €3.50 for 1hr., €5 for 3hr. Last entrance 1hr. before closing.)

Spring in the Harz brings the immense regional celebration of **Walpurgisnacht** (April 30). The hedonistic festivities, immortalized by Goethe in his masterpiece *Faust*, center around legendary witches who sweep through the sky on broomsticks to alight on the peak of Brocken. Wandern Tips lists events and activities in Wernigerode, Goslar, and Quedlinburg. For more on cultural happenings, pick up a free copy of *Harz-Blick* at any Harz tourist office..

WERNIGERODE ☎03943

Wernigerode (pop. 35,500), crowned by one of Germany's most beautiful castles, was a hidden haunt of Goethe, but its central location between the western and eastern Harz makes this secret too good to keep.

TRANSPORTATION AND PRACTICAL INFORMATION. Wernigerode is part of the **Harz Elbe Express (HEX)** network. Trains to: Halberstadt (20min., every hr., €4.60), Halle (1hr., every hr., €19), and Hanover (2hr., every 2hr., €21.80). A **bus** travels to and from Bad Harzburg (40min., every 2hr., €3.40) and Braunlage (1hr., every 2hr.) Harz regional trains stop at **Bahnhof Wernigerode,** north of the city center. To get to the Markt, turn right onto Bahnhofstr., and stay right as it becomes a highway. At the traffic light, head left onto Albert-Bartels-Str.to Nicolaipl.; Breite Str. on the left leads to the Markt. The **Harzer Schmalspurbahn** (narrow gauge railway) has a terminus at Bahnhof Wernigerode, and another atop Brocken. Hop the train at the "Westerntor" station for a quicker ascent from to the city center. Take Westernstr. out of the Markt, then a right on Unter den Zindeln. (☎03943 55 80; www.hsb-wr.de. 100min., every hr.; €16, roundtrip €24.) For a cab, call **TAXI-Anger** ☎03943 90 30 90. Rent city **bikes** from **Wernigeröder Fahrradverleih,** Breitestr. 48 (☎03943 62 61 19. Open M-F 8am-6pm, Sa-Su 8am-2pm. €15 per day, €20 for 2 days.)
The **tourist office** adjoining the Rathaus, Marktpl. 10, books rooms for free, sells town guides (€1.50 in English). Ask for the free map produced by the Bimmelbahn company or buy a more extensive one for €0.50. (☎03943 553 78 35; www.wernigerode-tourismus.de. Open May-Oct. M-F 8:30am-7pm, Sa 10am-4pm, Su 10am-3pm; Nov.-Apr. M-F 8:30am-6pm, Sa 10am-4pm, Su 10am-3pm.) **Tours** also depart from the office. (Daily 10:30am, also Sa 2pm; €4.) The **Deutsche Bank,** at the corner of Kochstr. and Breite Str., **exchanges currency** (€5.50 commission) and provides a **24hr. ATM.** (Open M-Tu and Th 9am-1pm and 2-6pm, W and F 9am-2pm.) The **police** station is on Nikolaipl. ☎03943 65 30, **emergency** 110). **Raths-Apotheke,** a pharmacy, is on Nikolaipl. (☎03943 63 24 39. Open M-F 8am-6:30pm, Sa 9am-1pm.) The **post office,** Marktstr. 14, is located near the Bimmelbahn station. (Open M-F 9am-6pm, Sa 9am-noon.) **Postal Code:** 38855.

ACCOMMODATIONS AND FOOD. Wernigerode's **Jugendherberge (HI) ❷,** Am Eichberg 5, hosts nightly events including live music and themed dinners. Don't miss the pool and ping-pong tables near the sauna. Take Bus #1, 4, or 5 to "Lutherstr." and climb the stairs leading up to Am Eichberg; the gate is to the left. (☎03943 60 61 76. Breakfast included. Sheets €3.50. Reception 7am-11pm. €16.50, over 27 €19.50. Cash only.) **Pension Am Nicolaiplatz ❹,** Breite Str. 17, rests amid the cobble and timber of the charming city center. The restaurant downstairs serves traditional German fare. (☎03943 63 23 29. Singles €35, doubles €55-60. Breakfast included. Reception in restaurant daily 11am-10pm. MC/V.) With golden landscapes on the wall and gold-standard prices, **Alt Wernigeröder Hof ❺,** Pfarrstr. 50a, has all the fixings: free Wi-Fi, a zippy elevator, and that hotel smell. From Nicolaipl., take Alber-Bartels-Str. until it intersects with Pfarrstr.; it's on the far left corner. Book well in advance. (☎03943 948 90. Breakfast included. Reception 24hr. Singles €55, doubles €75. AmEx/MC/V.)

Butchers, bakers and fresh produce makers congregate on the **Marktpl.** every Tu and F 9am-5pm. **Eurogrill ❶,** Breite Str. 79, crafts refined kebaps (€3-4) along with salads and Turkish platters on Nicolaipl. (☎03943 55 77 21. Open daily 10am-1am. Cash only.) Next door, **Brauhaus Wernigerode ❸,** Breite Str. 24, resembles an indoor half-timbered village with ferns spilling into the skylit alley. At night, the upper tier morphs into a bar. (☎03943 69 57 27. Open daily

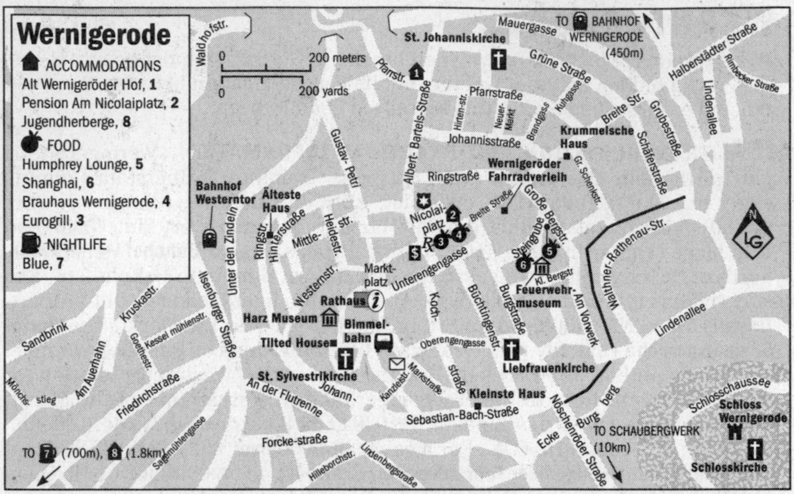

11am-midnight. Kitchen closes 10pm. €5-15. Cash only.) At **China-Restaurant Shanghai ❸,** Steingrube 6, the ornate dynastic decorations match the fish in the tank (not for consumption). Try the *Abendmenü* (from 5pm, €7-8.20) or curry dishes at lunchtime (11am-3pm €4.70-6). (☎03943 63 22 30. Open Tu-Su 11am-3pm and 5-11:30pm. Cash only.) Mr. Bogart welcomes you with tipped hat to **Humphrey Lounge ❷,** Grosse Bergstr. 2a. All-you-can-eat schnitzel (€6.66) or spaghetti (€5.55) until 8pm. 1.5L pitcher of *Hasseröder Pils* €6. Dancebar upstairs F-Sa from 10pm. (☎03943 172 34 64 194. Open Tu-Su from 6pm. Cash only.) Local students rely on **Blue,** Friedrichstr. 123, a 15min. walk from town, for cheap drinks (cocktails €2-4, beer €2), free Wi-Fi, and a dance floor. (☎0172 34 64 194; www.meinblue.de. Open M-Th and Su 8pm-1am, F-Sa 8am-5am.)

SIGHTS. Schloß Wernigerode, originally built around 1110, hovers in the hills above town. In the 1860s, Count Otto zu Stolberg-Wernigerode undertook renovations that lent the castle a Romantic flair. The perfectly preserved **Königszimmer** guest suite, where Otto hosted the Kaiser, flaunts gold-plated wallpaper and decadent adornments, while a flower-trimmed terrace looks out to the Brocken. (☎03943 55 30 30. Open May-Oct. daily 10am-6pm; Nov.-Apr. Tu-F 10am-4pm, Sa-Su 10am-6pm. Last entry 30min. before closing. Signs in English. €4.50, students €4.) To get there, walk up the white brick Burgberg path through the park to the castle (20min.). Take the **Bimmelbahn** from behind the Rathaus. (☎03943 60 40 00. May-Oct. daily every 20min. 9:30am-5:50pm; Nov.-Apr. every 45min. 10:30am-5:50pm. €3, under 10 €1, round-trip €4.50.) In the center of the Altstadt, the twin-horned **Rathaus** towers over the marketplace with strikingly sharp slopes and petite wooden figures of saints and miners decorating the facade. The **Krummelsche Haus,** Breite Str. 72, is a private home covered with ornate carvings visible from the street. Several of Wernigerode's other residences tell a tale of superlatives. The **Älteste Haus** (Oldest House), Hinterstr. 48, has undergone surprisingly little renovation since an overhaul in 1438. The **Kleinste Haus** (Smallest House), Kochstr. 43, once home to a family of nine, is 3m wide with a door only 1.7m high. (Open daily 10am-4pm. €1.) The **Normalste Haus** (Normal-est House), Witzestr. 13, has no distinguishing traits.

QUEDLINBURG ☎03946

Quedlinburg's narrow, winding streets are crowded with pastel half-timbered houses, towering churches, and a charming castle on a hill. Untouched by Allied bombers during WWII, the city (pop. 24,000) is a UNESCO world cultural treasure. Retaining the medieval charm that once made it the region's cultural and political center, Quedlinburg today draws visitors from across the world.

TRANSPORTATION AND PRACTICAL INFORMATION. **Trains** run every hour to Magdeburg (1hr., €11.70), Halberstadt (20min., €3.60) and Thale (10min., €1.80). **Buses** depart every hour from the train station to most towns in the Harz range. Rent a **bike** at **Zweirad Pavillon,** Bahnhofstr. 1b. (☎03946 70 95 07. €6 per day. Open M-F 9am-6pm, Sa 9am-12:30pm.) Quedlinburg's **tourist office,** Markt 2, books rooms (from €15) and dispenses maps for free. (☎03946 90 56 24; www.quedlinburg.de. Open May-Oct. M-Th 9am-6:30pm, F 9:30am-7pm, Sa 9:30am-4pm, Su 9:30am-2pm; Nov.-Apr. M-F 9:30am-5pm, Sa 9:30am-2pm.) City **tours** (€5) leave from the tourist office daily at 10am and 2pm; Fachwerk tours leave W 10am and Su 11am. Find a **24hr. ATM** in the **Commerzbank,** Am Markt 6. (Open M and W 8:30am-12:30pm and 2-4pm, Tu and Th 9am-1pm and 2-6pm, F 9am-1pm.) Use the **internet** at the **Hotel Theophano,** Markt 12-14; ask at reception behind the cafe. (☎03946 96300. Open daily 7am-10pm. €3 per hr.) The **post office** is at Bahnhofstr. 15, near the intersection with Turnstr. (Open M-F 9am-6pm, Sa 9am-noon.) **Postal Code:** 06484.

ACCOMMODATIONS AND FOOD. For a room, look for *"Zimmer frei"* signs on **Weberstraße** north of Steinweg. Also try **Pension Biehl ❷,** Blankenburger Str. 39, run by a pensioner with a green thumb. To get there, head up Marktstr. away from the Markt, turn left onto Marschlingerhof, which becomes Blankenburger Str. Affordable rooms with sofa, TV, stereo, and bath in a quiet neighborhood. (☎03946 70 35 38. Breakfast included. Singles €25; doubles €50. Cash only.) Quedlinburg's half-timbered **Jugendherberge ❶,** Neuendorf 28, offers inexpensive rooms in the heart of town.With bright hallways circling a private couryard, it feels more like a pension than a hostel. From the Markt, walk to the left of the Rathaus and take a left after the church, then a quick right onto Neuendorf. Enter through the green gate on Goldstr. (☎03946 81 17 03; www.djh-sachsen-anhalt.de. Breakfast included. Sheets €3. Dorms Apr-Oct. €15.50, over 27 €18.50; Nov.-Mar. €14.50/17.50. 1-night stays add €2. Cash only.)

Twice a week, local farmers sell their harvest on the **Marktplatz** (M and Sa 8am-4pm.) At **Brauhaus Lüdde ❷,** Blasiistr. 14, the ceilings soar over copper brewing kettles. The house brews a nutty *Schwarzbier,* milky *Weizen,* and sweet *Pubarschknal* (€2). Snacks run €2.50-8, and heartier pub fare goes for €8-18. (☎03946 70 52 06; www.hotel-brauhaus-luedde.de. Open M-Sa 11am-midnight, Su 11am-10pm. MC/V.) **Wispel-Pub ❶,** Steinweg 81, serves German staples (€3.60-5.80). 0.3L beer starts at €1.60 (☎03946 70 22 54. Open M-F 10am-11pm, Sa-Su 11am-11pm. Kitchen closes M-Sa 10:30pm, Su 10pm. Cash only.) **Pizzeria Zur Hölle ❷,** Stieg 20, makes wonderfully doughy pizzas, including a sauerkraut variety, in a quiet alley. (☎03946 42 41. Open M-Th noon-2:30pm and 5-11pm, Sa-Su 5-11pm. Small €3.20-4.40, large €5-7. Cash only.)

SIGHTS. Coated in ivy, the 17th-century stone **Rathaus** overlooks the Markt. A statue of Roland once again guards the stately building, after having spent nearly four centuries buried underground as a punishment to the people of Quedlinburg for an attempted insurrection in the mid-14th century. With the aid of smooth helical columns covered in gilded foliage, the **Marktkirche,**

tucked behind the Rathaus, shelters a spectacular altar from 1700. (Open daily 10am-4pm.) The winding roads of **Schloßberg** insulate the *Schloß* complex within a narrow ring of half-timbered cottages. The 16th-century Renaissance castle overlooks the labyrinthine town below and the Harz Mountains beyond. The **Schloßmuseum** (Castle Museum) depicts city history from the Paleolithic era to the present with dusty bones, crumbled pillars, and medieval iron relics. Visitors can also stroll through the castle, home to shiny fabrics and ornate wood. (☎03946 27 30. Signs in German. Open daily 10am-6pm. Last entry 30min. before closing. €3.50, students €2.) Also on the hill, **Stiftskirche St. Servatius** houses a treasure trove of gilded relics and a crypt. (☎03946 70 99 00. Open Tu-Sa 10am-4pm, Su noon-4pm. Dom and Domschatz €4, students €3; with Schloßmuseum €6/4.) Below the entrance to the *Schloß*, the vine-covered **Lyonel Feininger Galerie,** Finkenherd 5a, displays the watercolors, woodcuts, oil paintings, and comic strips of the influential Modernist painter. (☎03946 22 38. Open Tu-Su Apr.-Oct. 10am-6pm, Nov.-Mar. 10am-5pm. €6, students €3.

SACHSEN (SAXONY)

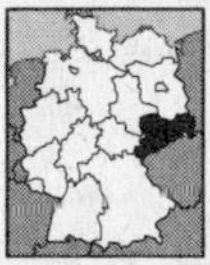

Freed from the stagnation of the DDR and bent on revitalization, Sachsen (Saxony) has embarked on some of Europe's most ambitious reconstruction projects. While older Saxons—most of whom were taught Russian in school—pass on the region's history, and dialect, a hopeful new generation keeps its cities lively and forward-looking. Though student-driven Leipzig, resurgent Dresden, and the legendary castles of August the Strong on the Elbe draw crowds from across the world, some of Saxony's greatest treasures have yet to be discovered by international tourists. Home to Germany's only native ethnic minority, the Sorbs, Saxony is marked by the verve and diversity of a region rebuilding itself in grand design.

HIGHLIGHTS OF SACHSEN

CHILL OUT in the **University of Leipzig** (p. 468), which harbors an active student population, a relaxed cafe scene, and an almost alarmingly incredible club culture.

CLIMB, HIKE, OR SKI the cliffs and mountains of the **Sächsische Schweiz** (p. 458).

ENLIGHTEN YOURSELF amid the world-class museums and grand Baroque architecture of **Dresden** (see this page), before losing your head in the throes of its feverish nightlife.

DRESDEN ☎0351

Over the course of two nights in February 1945, Allied firebombs incinerated over three quarters of Dresden, killing between 25,000 and 50,000 civilians. With most of the Altstadt in ruins, the surviving 19th-century Neustadt became Dresden's nerve center. Today, it is still an energetic nexus of nightlife and alternative culture. Since the war, the Altstadt has resurrected its regal grandeur, living up to its nickname the "Florence of the Elbe." Today, modern buildings like the futuristic **Volkswagen Gläserne Manufaktur** (Transparent Factory) are just blocks from restored Baroque masterpieces by Pöppelmann and Bährs. With the largest university in the *Land*, the capital of Saxony is a city of vibrance and intensity that backpackers on the road from Berlin to Prague won't want to ignore.

TRANSPORTATION

Flights: Dresden's airport (☎0351 881 33 60; www.dresden-airport.de) is 9km from the city center. S2 runs there from both main train stations, but is closer to Dresden-Neustadt. (25min. from Hauptbahnhof, 15min. from Neustadt Bahnhof. 2 per hr. 4am-11:30pm, €1.80.)

Trains: Dresden has 2 main train stations: the **Hauptbahnhof** south of the Altstadt and **Bahnhof Dresden Neustadt** across the Elbe on the western edge of the Neustadt. Most trains stop at both stations. A 3rd station, **Dresden Mitte,** lies between the two but is rarely used because of its location. Trains to: **Bautzen** (1hr., every hr., €9); **Berlin** (3hr., 1 per hr., €32); **Budapest, Hungary** (11hr., 2 per day, €81); **Frankfurt am Main** (4hr., every hr., €76); **Görlitz** (1hr., every hr., €16); **Leipzig** (1hr., 1-2 per hr., €18.30); **Munich** (7hr., 1-2 per hr., €108); **Prague, Czech Republic** (2hr., 7 per day, €25.80);

Warsaw, Poland (8hr., 2 per day, €71); **Zittau** (2hr., every 2hr., €16).

Ferries: Sächsische Dampfschifffahrt (☎0351 86 60 90 www.saechsische-dampfschiff-farhrt.de). Ships leave from the Elbe between Augustusbrücke and Carolabrücke in the Altstadt for Seußlitz in the north and to the Czech border town Decín in the south. Office and info desk open M-Th and Su 8am-6pm, F-Sa 8am-7:30pm.

Ferries: Meißen (2hr., €11.40, round-trip €16.80) and **Pillnitz** (1½hr., €9.60, round-trip €14.80). Day pass €20.50, children €10.25.

Ride Share: Mitfahrzentrale, Dr.-Friedrich-Wolf-Str. 2 (☎0351 194 40; www.mitfahren-online.de; www.shuttlenet.de). On Schlesischer Pl., across from Bahnhof Neustadt. Open M-F 9am-8pm, Sa-Su 10am-4pm.

Public Transportation: Most of Dresden is manageable on foot, but **buses** and **trams** help with quick jaunts between districts. Single ride €1.80, children €1.30. Day pass €4.50/3.50; weekly pass €17/13. Tickets are available from *Fahrkarten* dispensers at major stops, and on the trams. For information and maps, go to one of the Service Punkt stands in front of the Hauptbahnhof or at Postpl., Albertpl., and Pirnaischer Pl. Most major lines run every 30min. after midnight—look for the moon sign marked "Gute-Nacht-Linie." Dresden's **S-Bahn** network travels along the Elbe from Meißen to the Czech border. Buy tickets from the *Automaten* and validate them in the red machines at the bottom of the stairwells to each track. Validate your ticket aboard buses and trams.

Taxis: ☎0351 211 211 or 888 88 88.

Car Rental: Sixt-Budget, An der Frauenkirche 5 (☎0351 25 25 25), in the Hilton Hotel (open M-F 7am-7pm, Sa-Su 8am-noon), or the Hauptbahnhof (open M-F 7am-8pm). **Europcar,** Strehlener Str. 5 (☎0351 87 73 20), at the Bayerische Str. exit of the Hauptbahnhof (open 24hr.), or at Bahnhof Neustadt, out the Schlesischer Pl. exit and up the stairs, then left. (☎0351 82 82 40. Open M-F 7am-6pm, Sa 8am-noon, Su 9-11am).

Bike Rental: Rent city bikes in either train station. In the Hauptbahnhof, look for **Gepäck Center** (☎0351 461 3262; open M-F daily 6:15am-9:30pm) or the **Fahrradverleih** in the Neustadt Bahnhof. (☎0351 804 1370; open daily 6am-10pm. €7 per day.)

Hitchhiking: *Let's Go* does not recommend hitchhiking as a safe mode of transportation. Hitchers reportedly stand in front of the Autobahn signs at on-ramps.

ORIENTATION

With a population of 500,000, Dresden crowds the banks of the Elbe river 60km northwest of the Czech border and 200km south of Berlin. A 60-degree hook in the **Elbe** bisects Dresden, pointing toward the Altstadt in the south, separating it from the Neustadt above. The **Hauptbahnof** is to the south. **Prager Straße,** a pedestrian zone lined with modern shops and fountains, leads from the train station to the **Altmarkt.** The **Neustadt** north of the Elbe is, ironically, one of the oldest parts of the city. The central walking bridge, **Augustusbrucke,** links the Altstadt with the Neustadt's pedestrian **Haupstraße,** at the Golden Rider statue. **Antonstraße** connects the Dresden-Neustadt train station to **Albertplatz.** The neighborhoods off of Albertpl. pulse with the energy of Dresden's young alternative scene. Five romantic bridges—**Marienbrücke, Augustusbrücke, Carolabrücke, Albertbrücke,** and the "Blue Marvel" **Loschwitzbrücke**—connect the city's two halves.

PRACTICAL INFORMATION

Tourist Office: 2 locations: Prager Str. 2, near the Hauptbahnhof in the Prager Spitze shopping center (open M-Sa 10am-7pm), and Theaterpl. in the Schinkelwache (open M-F 10am-6pm, Sa-Su 10am-4pm). The staffs of both offices book rooms (from €25) for free, hand out city maps, and sell English-language city guides (€0.50). Audio walking tour in English (€7.50 for 4hr., €10 for 8hr.). The **Dresden City-Card,** valid for 48hr., gives unlimited city transport (€21); the **Dresden Regio-Card,** good for 72hr., covers the Oberelbe region, including Meißen and Sächsische Schweiz (€32). Both cards grant free entry to State Art Collections, including the Zwinger Palace museums, and give discounts at many others. Cards can also be purchased online or at DVB transportation centers. Visit www.dresden-tourist.de, or call special city hotlines for general information (☎0351 49 19 21 00), room reservations (☎0351 49 19 22 22), group tours (☎0351 49 19 21 40), and advance ticket purchases (☎0351 49 19 22 33).

Tours: The double-decker **Stadtrundfahrt tour bus** roams Dresden Apr.-Oct. 9:30am-10pm, Nov.-Mar. 9:30am-8pm, departing from Theaterpl. every 30min. Buy a day pass (€20, children free) on the bus and stay for the 90min. tour, or board as you please at any of the 22 stops. Ticket includes 30min. walking tours of the Zwinger Palace and Frauenkirche (☎0351 899 5650; www.stadtrundfahrt.de).

Currency Exchange: ReiseBank (☎0351 471 2177), in the Hauptbahnhof. €5 commission over €25; €3 for less.; 1.5% commission on all traveler's checks. Window, with Western Union money transfer service, open M-F 8am-8pm, Sa 9am-6pm, Su 10am-6pm. A Deutsche Bank and Sparkasse are diagonally across from one another at the corner of Königsbrücker Str. and Katharinenstr. in the Neustadt, but the Deutsche Bank, Königs-

brücker Str. 15, offers far superior commission rates (☎0351 48240. Exchange commission €4.50. Open M-F 9am-1pm, M-Tu also 2-6pm, Th 2-7pm, F 2-4pm.)

Luggage Storage: Lockers in all train stations; follow suitcase icon. €2-2.50 per 24hr.

Bookstore: Das Internationale Buch, Altmarkt 24 (☎0351 65 64 80; www.buch-kunst.de), in the arcade off the Altmarkt. English books on 2nd fl. Open M-Sa 10am-8pm.

Library: Haupt- und Musikbibliothek, Freiberger Str. 35 (☎0351 864 8233), in World Trade Center. Some English books. Free internet 30min. at a time. Music scores, CDs, and DVDs. Bring a passport to check out items. Open M-F 11am-7pm, Sa 10am-2pm.

Home Share: Mitwohnzentrale, Dr.-Friedrich-Wolf-Str. 2 (☎0351 194 30; www.dresdner-mitwohnzentrale.de). On Schlesischer Pl., same building as Mitfahrzentrale. Open M-F 10am-8pm, Sa-Su 10am-2pm. Flats available in outer districts from €150/month.

Gay and Lesbian Resources: Gerede, Prießnitzstr. 18, at the outlet of Louisenstr. (☎03051 802 22 51, counseling ☎0351 804 44 80; www.gerede-dresden.de). Open M-F 8am-5pm. Informal advice at **Cafe Kontakt** daily 3-9pm. Professional services by phone or in person for men Tu 3-5pm, women Th 3-5pm, and transgender Th 3-6pm.

Women's Resources: Frauenzentrum "sowieso," Angelikastr. 1 (☎0351 804 1470; www.frauenzentrumsowieso.de). Open M, W, F 9am-3pm, Th 9am-6pm. Specializes in addressing sexual harrassment and assault, eating disorders, and employment.Advice in person or by

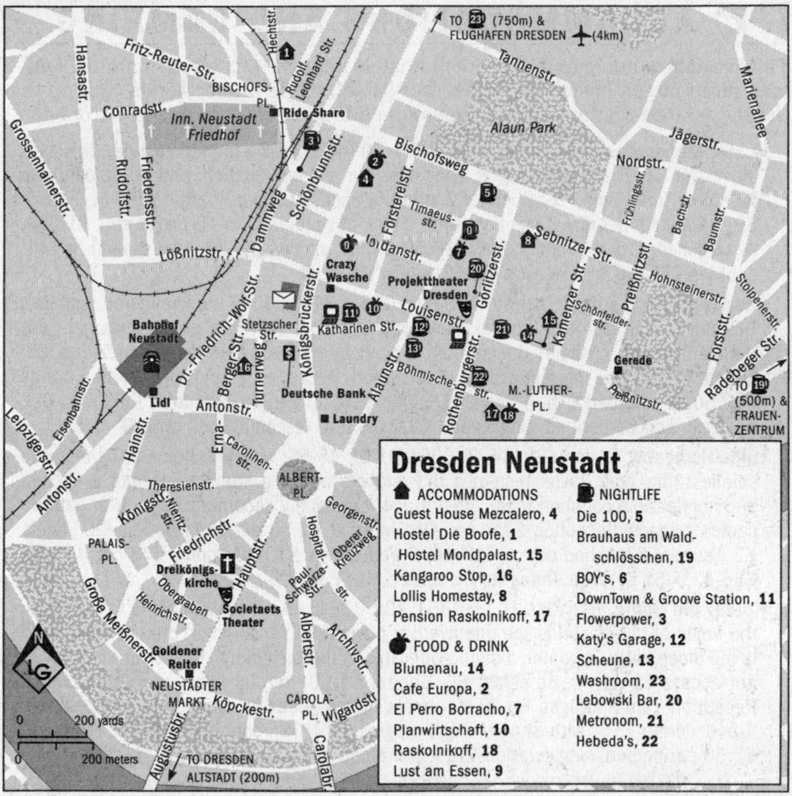

phone M, W, F 9-11am, Th 3-6pm. Psychologist by appointment M-F or walk-in Th 3-6pm. Tram #11 (dir: Bühlau) to Angelikastr., or walk 30min. up Bautzner Str. from Albertpl.

Laundromat: Eco-Express, 2 Königsbrücker Str., on Albertpl. Wash €1.90 before 11am, €2.40 after 11am. Dry €0.50 per 10min. Soap €0.30. Open M-Sa 6am-11pm. Also try **Crazy Waschsalon,** 6 Louisenstr. Wash €2.50 before 11am, €2.70 after 11am. Dry €0.50 per 10min. Soap €0.30. Open M-Sa 7am-11pm.

Emergency: Police ☎110. **Ambulance** and **Fire** ☎112.

Pharmacy: Saxonia Apotheke Internationale, Prager Str. 8a (☎0351 490 4949; www.saxoniaapotheke.de). Open M-F 9am-8pm, Sa 9:30am-5pm. Carries international medicines. The Notdienst sign outside lists rotating 24hr. pharmacies.

Internet Access: Mondial, Rothenburgerstr. 43 (☎0351 896 1470), in Neustadt. Enter on Louisenstr. €2 per hr. Wi-Fi available. Open M-F 10am-1am, Sa-Su 11am-1am.

Post Office: Königsbrücker Str. 21-29 (☎0351 819 1373), in the Neustadt. Open M-F 9am-7pm, Sa 10am-1pm. **Branches** in the Altstadt are on Wallstr. at the Altmarkt Galerie (open M-F 8am-6pm, Sa 9am-noon), and near the Postpl. at Annenstr. 10 (open M-F 9am-12:30pm and 1:30-6pm, Sa 9:30am-noon). **Postal Code:** 01099.

ACCOMMODATIONS AND CAMPING

The **Neustadt** is home to independent hostels near the city's best nightlife. Quieter, often larger, hostels lie below the **Altstadt,** while pricier hotels cozy up to the sights. Reservations strongly recommended between April and October.

Hostel Mondpalast, Louisenstr. 77 (☎0351 563 4050; www.mondpalast.de). This stellar hostel has it all: good prices, spacious rooms, large kitchen, and downstairs bar. Breakfast (until 2pm) €5. Sheets €2. Internet access €2 per hr.; free Wi-Fi at the bar. Bike rental €7 per day. Reception 24hr. Check-out noon. 8- to 10-bed dorms €13.50, 4- to 6-bed €15-17, with shower €18.50-19.50; singles 29/39, high season 34/44; doubles €37/50, high season 44/52. AmEx/MC/V. ❷

Kangaroo-Stop, Erna-Berger-Str. 8-10 (☎0351 314 3455; www.kangaroo-stop.de). This newly built Outback-themed backpackers' hostel sits on a quiet street near the Neustadt Bahnhof. Koalas dangle from a giant tree trunk in the lounge. Breakfast €5. Sheets €2.20. Free internet access at reception. Reception 8am-10pm. 10-bed dorms €12.50, 5- to 6-bed €14, 4-bed €15, 3-bed €16; singles €27; doubles €36. Mar.-Oct. and Dec. add €1 per bed, singles add €2. 10% ISIC discount. Cash only. ❸

Lollis Homestay, Görlitzer Str. 34. (☎0351 81 08 45 58; www.lollishome.de). Dresden's smallest, this cozy hostel recreates the relaxed feel of a student flat with a kitchen and comfortable common room. Most rooms exquisitely decorated, some with bathtub cactus gardens. Reception 24hr. Apr.-Oct. Internet €2.50 per hr. Breakfast €3. Sheets €2. Laundry €3. 8-bed dorms €13-14, 6-bed dorms €13-16, triples €48-57, doubles €36-42. F-Sa €1 extra. Rates vary in winter. MC/V. ❶

Hostel Die Boofe, Hechtstr. 10 (☎0351 801 3361; www.boofe.de). True to its name, the focus of this hostel is the beehive bar downstairs. In summer, the cozy courtyard is the place to be. In winter, a sauna operates in the basement (€6.50 for 1hr.). Internet access €1 per hr. Breakfast €6. Sheets €1.50, free for stays over three nights. Reception 7am-midnight. The hostel hosts many groups in summer, so book ahead. 4-bed dorms €15, with shower €18; singles €29/39; doubles €40/50. F-Sa add €1.50 per person, singles add €2.50. Handicap-accessible. ❸

Pension Raskolnikoff, Böhmische Str. 34 (☎0351 804 5706; www.raskolnikoff.de). This 6-room pension shares a building with the eponymous restaurant and gallery. The bohemian atmosphere and fold-out couches are an escape from the standard hostel scene. Singles €35-43, doubles €47-55. MC/V. ❸

Guest House Mezcalero, Königsbrücker Str. 64 (☎0351 81 07 70; www.mezcalero.de). Though named for a tequila, this Mexican-themed guest house goes down much smoother. Lofted beds in ranchy rooms in a quiet courtyard. Private bar open noon-5am every day. Reception 24hr. Free Wi-Fi. Breakfast €6. Sheets €2.50. Dorms from €17 per person. Singles with shared bath €35, doubles from €55. MC/V. ❸

Jugendherberge Dresden Rudi Arndt (HI), Hübnerstr. 11 (☎0351 471 0667). Tram #3 (dir.: Coschütz) or #8 (dir.: Südvorstadt) to "Nürnberger Pl." Take a left on Nürnbergerstr. behind you and then a right onto Hübnerstr.; the hostel is at the 2nd corner on the right. Located in a quiet residential neighborhood, this hostel is a little more mature than your typical HI. Fresh popcorn in the lobby. Downstairs bar. Breakfast included. Laundry €1.50. Sheets €1. Lockout 1-6am. Reservations recommended. Dorms €15.40, over 27 €18.40; doubles add €1.50 per person, singles add €2.50. Cash only. ❶

FOOD

In the Altstadt, almost all of the restaurants target tourists and price gouge accordingly, especially around **Münzgasse** and the **Frauenkirche.** The cheapest eats are at the *Imbiße* (snack bars) along **Prager Straße** and the World Trade Center mall on Freiberger Str. The Neustadt area between **Albertplatz** and **Alaunplatz** is home to most of Dresden's quirky, ethnic, vegetarian, and student-friendly restaurants. The free monthly *Spot*, available at the tourist office, details culinary options. The **Lidl** grocery store in the Neustadt Bahnhof is the backpacker refueling station. (Open M-Sa 8am-9pm, Su 8am-7pm.)

Cafe Aha, Kreuzstr. 7 (☎0351 496 0673, www.laden-Cafe.de). This maverick restaurant celebrates ecologically sound foods. Each dish (€4-11) promotes fair trade; the Cafe introduces food from a different developing country each month. Try the fried goat cheese with mango-chili sauce. Store downstairs sells international spices, crafts and chocolates. Store open M-F 10am-7pm, Sa 10am-6pm. Cafe open daily 10am-midnight; kitchen closes at 10:30pm. AmEx/MC/V. ❷

Planwirtschaft, Louisenstr. 20 (☎0351 801 3187; www.planwirtschaft.de). Offers traditional and contemporary cuisine made with ingredients direct from local farms. Inventive soups, fresh salads (€3.50-7), and entrees (€7-13). In a room filled with vacuums, sewing machines, and typewriters, enjoy the giant breakfast buffet (€9 daily 9am-3pm. Viewed from the garden, the lower portion of the house is plastered with LP covers, including David Hasselhoff's. Open M-Th and Su 9am-1am, F-Sa 9am-2am. MC/V. ❸

Cafe Europa, Königsbrücker Str. 68 (☎0351 804 4810; www.cafe-europa-dresden.de). Open 24hr., this self-consciously cosmopolitan cafe draws a student and 20-something crowd with 120 drinks and 14 international newspapers on offer. Breakfasts from around the world (€3.10-7.50) 6am-4pm. Pastas €6-10. Free Wi-Fi. AmEx/MC/V. ❷

Rauschenbach Deli, Weissegasse 2 ☎0351 821 2760; www.rauschenbach-deli.de). Chandelier crystals dangle from soft red lights as waiters serve tapas (€3-3.60) and sandwiches (€3.80) to young locals. Reservations recommended F-Sa nights. Open M-Th and Su 9am-1am, F-Sa 9am-3am. Kitchen open till midnight. AmEx/MC/V. ❷

Blumenau, Louisenstr. 67 (☎0351 802 6502; www.cafe-blumenau.de). One of the most popular restaurants in the Neustadt. Friendly environment makes for a perfect morning *Milchkaffee* or evening drink. Vast selection of aroma-infused coffees and teas. Wonderful pastas €6.80-8.20; fish and flesh €9.30-12.40. Breakfast until 4pm. Food until 11pm. Extensive mixed drink menu. Open M-Th 8:30am-midnight, F 8:30am-2am, Sa 9am-2pam, Su 9am-midnight. AmEx/MC/V for purchases over €10. ❸

TOO GOOD TO BE BREW

The receptionist at the hostel in Dresden showed me to the six-bed dorm. The two guys living there had left a crate of empty beer bottles in the room: glass jugs, made for giants, shaped like industrial flasks. At around 7pm, in walked the two hulking German boys, each clutching his own magnificent brown jug. Tony struck up a conversation with me, explaining that they were, in fact, apprentice brewers. How exciting, I thought! Germans with an interested in replenishing the malty reservoirs they so heartily deplete.

Tony spent two years studying biochemistry at University until he decided he wanted to be a brewer. Now an apprentice in Dresden, he splits his time between the factory and brewing classes. At work, he only drinks about a half-liter a day, sampling the various casks to check for progress and freshness. At school, he'll drink much more. He had just returned from his "sensorium" exam, where was made to sample eleven different brews, rating them for their carbonation, hops quality, the clarity of the taste, and other categories that elude translation.

For the rest of the night, Tony regailed me with brewing stories, repeatedly refilling my mug with his own varieties. "The experience of a beer," he explained, "should be a deep kiss, not just a peck."

-Scott McKinney

This was at Kangaroo Stop, Dresden, where I stayed June 25-26, 2008.

El Perro Borracho, Alaunstr. 70 (☎0351 803 6723; www.elperro.de), through the passageway and into the courtyard. Free-flowing Spanish wine and bright decor evoke a Mallorcan beach vacation. Tasty tapas (€3.30, 5 for €15), from calamari to potato tortillas. Lunch €5.80, dinner €8-14. Buffet breakfast 10am-3pm on weekends (€8). Open M 4pm-2am and Tu-F 11:30am-2am, tapas from 6pm; Sa-Su 10am-3am, tapas from 3:30pm. Cash only. ❸

SIGHTS

ALTSTADT (OLD TOWN)

Destroyed during WWII and partially rebuilt during Communist times, Dresden's Altstadt is one of Europe's undisputed cultural centers. A gigantic restoration effort, though largely completed, still chugs along. The Altmarkt is at present a cordoned pit, and it's hard to find a skyline without a crane. Still, the view from across the Elbe evokes unmistakable majesty. Most of Dresden's celebrated sights are near the Theaterplatz.

DRESDENER RESIDENZ SCHLOSS (ROYAL PALACE). Saxony's Wettin dynasty of electors, whose portraits adorn the northern wall of the **Fürstenzug** (a block-long mural that depicts over 900 years of Saxon kings), built their grand residential palace here. Like most of the Altstadt, it was ruined in the Allied firebombing, but restoration was successful. Today, the **Schloß** houses the **Grünes Gewölbe** (Green Vault), a remarkably intimate display of the Saxon electors' precious stones, many designed by jeweler Johann Melchior Dinglinger. Highlights of the collection include rare medieval chalices, cherry stones inscribed with over 100 pinhead-sized faces, and exquisitely diverse uses of mother-of-pearl-coated mollusks. *(☎0351 49 14 20 00. Open M and W-Su 10am-6pm. €6, students €3.50. Audio tours in English €3.)* The 100m tall **Hausmannsturm** has a collection of sobering photographs of the Altstadt after the February 1945 bombings that, combined with the 360° view of the city from the top, illustrate the immensity of the reconstruction project. *(Across from the Zwinger; enter on Sophienstr. Open M and W-Su 10am-6pm. Captions in German. €3, students and seniors €2.)* The beautiful exterior sculptures of the **Katholische Hofkirche** (Catholic Court Cathedral), best viewed from the **Brühlsche Terrasse,** hint at the building's striking white interior, with green and red marbled accents. The church was destroyed in WWII, but restoration quickly returned it to near-perfect condition. The organ in the balcony miraculously survived the bombing and is the last and largest work of the world-famous organ-builder Gottfried Silbermann. *(Schlosspl. ☎0351 4844812; www.kathedrale-dresden.de. Open M-Tu 9am-6pm, W-Th 9am-5pm, F 1-5pm, Sa 10am-5pm, Su noon-4pm. Free. Guided tours M-Th 2pm, F-Su 1pm, Sa also 2pm.)*

ZWINGER. The extravagant collection of **Friedrich August I,** a.k.a. August the Strong, Prince Elector of Saxony and King of Poland, is housed in this elaborate palace, designed by August's senior state architect, **Matthäus Daniel Pöppelmann.** Championed as one of the most successful examples of Baroque design, the palace narrowly escaped destruction in the 1945 bombings. Some of the statues lining the grounds are still charred, but workers continually sandblast the statues in attempts to recapture their perfection. **Gottfried Semper,** revolutionary activist and master architect, designed the northern wing addition. The palace interior now houses the Saxon State Art Collection. *(North of Postpl., next to the Semper-Oper. Courtyard free. Palace open to Museum visitors only.)*

SEMPER-OPER. Dresden's famed opera house displays the same opulence as the northern wing of the Zwinger. Its bulging facade is perforated with more than 20 arches. Painstaking restoration has returned the building to its original state, making it one of Dresden's most prominent attractions. *(Theaterpl. 2. ☎ 0351 44 84 38 48; www.semperoper-fuehrungen.de. Entrance only on guided tours; 45min., occasionally in English. The main entrance lists tour times, most often 1-3pm. €7, students €3.50.)*

FRAUENKIRCHE. Dresden's most famous silhouette was reduced to rubble by the 1945 bombings. The most complex and expensive project of its kind in Germany, reconstruction of the Frauenkirche began in 1994 and ended on Oct. 31, 2005. The cathedral's completion brought floods of German tourists into Dresden. On weekends, the quickly moving line curls around the Neumarkt. The speckled, bulbous exterior is just a prelude to the delicious, easter egg interior. Climb the magnificent cupola. *(Neumarkt. ☎ 0351 498 11 31; www.frauenkirche-dresden.de. Open M-F 10am-noon and 1-6pm. Sa-Su hours vary, check the information center on Neumarkt for details or pick up a free copy of the German-language Leben in der Frauenkirche schedule at the tourist office and look for "Offene Kirche." Entry free. Audio tours (€2.50) available in English. Open mass M-F at noon and 6pm, except for Th 6pm. Afterward, a short tour in German is given. Cupola open daily 10am-1pm; also 2-6pm Apr.-Oct., Nov.-Mar. 2-4pm. €8, students €5.)*

SACHSEN

NEUSTADT (NEW TOWN)

Across the Elbe, the some of Germany's best-preserved turn-of-the-century neighborhoods and a handful of Baroque holdouts are home to Dresden's busy cultural scene. A walk down the pedestrian Hauptstr. hits most of the sights and brings you to Albertplatz, with its magnificent twin fountains.

GOLDENER REITER (GILDED HORSEMAN). A gold-plated August the Strong statue faces the Augustusbrücke on Neustädter Markt. August's nickname has two sources: his physical strength, supposedly proved by an indented thumbprint on the Brühlsche Terrasse (more miraculous still since it was imprinted after his death), and his virility—legend has it he fathered 365 children, though the official tally is 15. Day and night, August shines with cocky gallantry.

DREIKÖNIGSKIRCHE (CHURCH OF THE MAGI). Designed in 1730, this church was destroyed in 1945. Now the original crumbling altar still stands tall like a tombstone amid the stark white halls of the newly rebuilt (1991) church. Inside, check out the *Dresden Danse Macabre*, a 12.5m Renaissance fresco, or climb the tower for a panoramic view. *(Hauptstr. 23. ☎ 0351 812 4100. Church free. Tower open Mar.-Oct. Tu 11:30am-4pm, W-Sa 11am-5pm, Su 11:30am-5pm. Nov.-Feb. W noon-4pm, Th-F 1am-4pm, Su 11:30am-4:30pm. €2.50, students €1.25.)*

ELSEWHERE IN DRESDEN

Virtually untouched by the bombings, Dresden's outskirts are appealing suburbs, well worth a venture. The paved paths on the banks of the Elbe make for a lovely stroll. Alaun Park, bordered below by the Neustadt's Bischofsweg, has a pleasant green and wooded bike trails.

DIE GLÄSERNE MANUFAKTUR. This nearly transparent €180 million Volkswagen factory was built to manufacture the company's new luxury car, the Phaeton. It features bold, curvaceous architecture with steel cones, glass walls, and a giant central orb. Take a tour culminating in a virtual test drive at Autobahn speeds. *(Lennestr. 1. ☎ 0180 589 6268; www.glaesernemanufaktur.de. Open daily 8am-8pm. €4, students €2. Tours in German, free with entry every hr. English tour M 9pm.)*

GROSSER GARTEN. This idyllic, sprawling garden, hedgy and florid, was once used by the House of Wettin for games, theater, and feasts. It was generously opened to the public in the 19th century. A Baroque palace, the first in Germany, sits as the centerpiece, with a gorgeous pond behind. The palace now contains an exhibit on Saxon Baroque sculpture. Smooth walkways beg for rollerskates.

There is a zoo on the southern edge, and a botanical garden opposite. *(Enter from Lennestr. Take trams #10 or 13 to Grosser Garten. Park open until dusk. Sculpture exhibit open Apr.-Oct. Sa 2-5pm and Su 11am-6pm, Nov.-Mar. Sa-Su 11am-6pm. €3, students €2.)*

MUSEUMS

After several years of renovations, Dresden's museums once again to stand with the best in Europe. If you are planning on visiting more than one museum in a day, consider investing in a **Tageskarte** (€12, students and seniors €7), which covers one-day admission to the Albertinum museums, the *Schloß*, most of the **Zwinger** museums, and a number of other sights. Both **Dresden Cards** (p. 447) also include free or reduced entrance to many of the major museums.

ZWINGER COMPLEX

A €5 pass entitles you to take photos (without flash) at any Zwinger museum. All Zwinger museums are free with either Dresden Card.

GEMÄLDEGALERIE ALTE MEISTER (GALLERY OF THE OLD MASTERS). This museum displays a world-class collection of paintings dating from 1400 to 1800, predominantly Italian and Dutch. Thanks to a particularly prudent museum director, these masterpieces were kept hidden during WWII. Raphael's **Sistine Madonna** tops the collection, which also includes such treasures as Cranach the Elder's luminous Adam and Eve paintings, and Rubens' *Leda and the Swan.* Designed explicitly to house the collections of August the Strong, these rooms have displayed some of the same paintings for over 200 years. *(Theaterpl. 1. From the Semper-Oper side, walk through the archway toward the courtyard, and the entrance is on the right. ☎0351 491 4678. Open Tu-Su 10am-6pm. 1hr. gallery tours in German F-Su 4pm. €2. Audio tours in English and German €3. €6, students and seniors €3.50.)*

PORZELLANSAMMLUNG (PORCELAIN COLLECTION). With over 20,000 pieces, this museum boasts the largest collection of porcelain in Europe, with a spectacular selection of Meißen china. Exhibits of Asian porcelain from the 15th-18th-centuries are also exceptional. August the Strong invested in intricate religious icons, centerpieces, and a whole menagerie of life-size animals,with oddly humanoid faces. Many of the pieces have been meticulously glued together from cracker-sized fragments. Upstairs is a collection of less-spectacular 18th-century German porcelain, apparently made before the craft had been perfected. *(Entry in the southern archway on Sophienstr. ☎0351 491 4622. Open Tu-Su 10am-6pm. €56, students and seniors €33.50. Signs in English. Tours in German Su 2pm.)*

RÜSTKAMMER (ARMORY). Rekindle dreams of chivalric valor with this collection of shiny but deadly toys from the court of the Wettin princes (16th-18th centuries). Cringe at spiky hatchets, surely too delicate and beautiful for battle, and real jousting lances, those human skewers. Other highlights include stately silver- and gold-plated armor for man and steed, and bejewelled firearms. The collection of diminutive armor belonged to Wettin toddlers. *(In the archway nearest Theaterpl., across from the Alte Meister. ☎0351 491 4682. Open Tu-Su 10am-6pm. €3, students and seniors €2, included in Gemäldegalerie Alte Meister admission fee. Signs in German only.)*

MATHEMATISCH-PHYSIKALISCHER SALON. Europe's oldest "science museum," these two large rooms host an impressive collection of 16th- to 19th-century scientific instruments, far more stylish than their modern equivalents. Also serving as a science laboratory, this salon once set the official time for all of Saxony. *(In the west corner of the Zwinger courtyard. ☎0351 94 01 46 66. The museum is closed for remodelling until 2010.)*

ELSEWHERE IN DRESDEN

DEUTSCHES HYGIENEMUSEUM (GERMAN HEALTH MUSEUM). Better described as a museum of mankind, this unique collection is famous for its "Glass Man," a transparent human model with illuminated organs. The world's first public health museum enlightens visitors with exhibits like "Life and Death," "Food and Drink," and "Sexuality" in a charmingly straightforward way that smacks of DDR days. The museum also hosts rotating exhibits. *(Lingnerpl. 1, enter via Blüherstr. Or take tram #10 or 13 to Grosser Garten. ☎0351 484 6400; www.dhmd.de. English translations. Open Tu-Su 10am-6pm, last entry 5:30pm. €6, students and seniors €3.)*

ALBERTINUM. Yet another construction project of August the Strong, this Baroque museum along the Elbe was designed by the inexhaustible Pöppelmann. Destroyed during WWII, it was quickly rebuilt, and now houses several renowned museums. The brilliant **Gemäldegalerie Neue Meister** (Gallery of the New Masters), displaying choice art from the 19th- and 20th-centuries will be under construction until 2010. The adjacent **Skupturensammlung** (Sculpture Collection) displays an immense collection of classical sculpture was rescued from a basement depot during the floods that struck Eastern Europe in 2002. Although several regular exhibition rooms upstairs are filled with the finest pieces, the majority of the collection is piled up for visitors to view in the Albertinum's vaulted cellar. Sculptured wall sections from a 2000-year-old Assyrian temple compose the museum's most prized collection. *(Open Tu-Su 1am-6pm. €2.50, students and seniors €1.50. Free admission with Dresden City Card or Zwinger day pass.*

ENTERTAINMENT

Dresden has been a leader in the realms of theater, opera, and music for centuries. The **Semper-Oper** is the city's crown jewel, but there are enough smaller theaters to suit any taste. The tourist office by the Semper-Oper is a great resource for performances, but individual box offices offer better deals. Although most theaters take a *Pause* (summer break) from mid-July to early September, open-air festivals fill the gap. The **Filmnächte am Elbufer** (Film Nights on the Elbe) festival in July and August sets up an enormous movie screen and stage against the illuminated Altstadt. Most shows start at 9:30pm and cost €6.50. (Office at Alaunstr. 62. ☎0351 89 93 20; complete schedule at www.filmnaechte-am-elbufer.de.) Like many palaces in the area the **Zwinger** hosts classical concerts on summer evenings (shows at 6:30pm, tickets at tourist office).

Sächsische Staatsoper (Semper-Oper), Theaterpl. 2 (☎0351 491 10; www.semperoper.de). See opera's finest in this stately opera house. The **Staatskapelle Dresden,** the city's first class orchestra, performs here as well. Smaller productions take place in the **Kleine Szene,** Bautzner Str. 107, across the river. Box office at Schinkelwache, across from the **Semper Oper,** open M-F 10am-6pm, Sa-Su 10am-4pm, and 1hr. before shows.

Kulturpalast, Schloßstr. 2, am Altmarkt (☎0351 486 6666; www.kulturpalast-dresden.de). This civic center is home to the **Dresdner Philharmonie** (☎0351 486 63 06; www.dresdnerphilharmonie.de), a close second to the Staatskapelle, and hosts a wide variety of performances. Box office, Schloßstr. 2, open M-F 10am-7pm, Sa 10am-2pm.

Staatsoperette Dresden, Pirnaer Landstr. 131 (☎0351 20 79 90; www.staatsoperette-dresden.de). Musical theater and operetta from Lerner and Loewe to Sondheim. €5-24, students €5-19. Premieres €2.50-4 extra. Discounted shows Tu-Th. Open M 11am-4pm, Tu-Th 10am-7pm, F 11am-7pm, Sa 4-7pm, Su 1hr. before shows.

Staatsschauspiel (☎0351 491 3500; www.staatsschauspiel-dresden.de) operates 4 venues at 2 different locations: the main **Schauspielhaus** (tickets €20-64) and the

Kleines Haus, (Glacisstr. 28, tickets €12-15), which also houses the **neubau** theater (tickets €9). Big discounts M, pay extra on Sa. Students half price. Shakespeare and Molière, alongside contemporary comedy. Box office (Theaterstr. 2, ☎0351 491 3555) open M-F 10am-6:30pm, Sa 10am-2pm, and 1hr. before performances.

Theater Junge Generation, Meißner Landstr. 4 (☎0351 429 1220; www.tjg-dresden.de). Performs opera and summer theater in the Dresdner *Schloß*. The city's puppet theater. Tickets €9, students €5, children €4.50. Phone booking service M-F 8am-4pm. Box office, Rundkino Prager Str., open Tu-F 2-6pm and 1hr. before shows.

projekttheater dresden, Louisenstr. 47 (☎0351 810 7610; www.projekttheater.de). Cutting-edge, international experimental theater in the heart of the Neustadt. Tickets €11, students €7-9. €1 off each ticket if you call to book in advance. Shows 8 or 9pm, matinees 10am or noon. Box office open M-F 10am-4pm and 1hr. before shows.

NIGHTLIFE

The entire Neustadt seems to spend the day anticipating 10pm. Ten years ago, the area north of Albertpl. was a maze of gray streets and crumbling buildings. Now a fast-paced, underground community has sprung up among the 50 bars and clubs crammed into the square kilometer roughly bounded by **Königsbrückerstraße, Bischofsweg, Kamenzerstraße,** and **Albertplatz** *Kneipen Surfer* (free at Neustadt hostels and restaurants) describes every bar. Peruse the back of *SAX* (€3 at the tourist office, or ask to see one at any bar) or websites like www.dresden-nightlife.de for upcoming concerts. The free German-language monthlies *Dresdner* and *Frizz*, available in many pubs, also list nighttime entertainment. For gay and lesbian nightlife, grab a free *gegenpol* at the tourist office.

Brauhaus am Waldschlößchen, am Brauhaus 8b (☎0351 652 3900; www.waldschloesschen.de). Tram #11 to "Waldschlößchen" or walk 25min. up Baunitzerstr. A castle wall supports a terrace, home to the most pleasent cafe in Dresden. Soups and wurst (€3-6.50). The restaurant inside is filled with the smell of hops from beer brewed according to a Bavarian recipe, brought to Dresden in 1836. German pub fare cooked in beer sauce (€5-13). House brews €2.90 for 0.5L. Open daily 11am-1am. AmEx/MC/V.

DownTown, Katharinenstr. 11-13 (☎0351 801 3923; www.downtown-dresden.de). Constantly packed, DownTown caters to those who want more than conversation. The music is loud, seating rare, and the crowd enthusiastic. Evenings begin upstairs at the bar, billiard hall, and tattoo parlor, **Groove Station** (☎0351 80 29 59; www.groovestation.de). Expect rock and electronic music. Cover €4, students €3. Drinks €3-9. €1 cover F-Sa, mixed drinks €4-5. Open daily 7pm-5am. Club open Th-Sa 10pm-5am. Cash only.

Wash Room, Hermann-Mende-Str. 1 (☎0351 441 5708). Take tram #7 or 8 to "Industriegelaende." Indoor waterfalls, films of crashing waves, and an indoor beach volleyball court fill this club, pulsating with electronica and frenetically colorful lights. Open F-Sa 9:22pm-5am. Cover F €5, Sa €4-8; 50% off 9:22-10:23pm. Cash only.

Flowerpower, Eschenstr. 11 (☎0351 804 9799; www.flower-power.de). From Albertpl., walk up Königsbrücker Str. and take a left on Eschenstr.; it's on the left. A low-key hippie hangout clad in cushions and tie-dye. Lively until 5am with a dedicated crowd of 20-somethings. Beer €2.30. M student nights feature discounted beer and wine, discos F-Sa. Open daily 8pm-5am. Cash only.

Die 100, Alaunstr. 100 (☎0351 801 3957; www.Cafe100.de). With over 300 German, French, and Israeli wines (from €3.50 per glass, bottles from €13) on the menu, this Weinkeller caters to the thrifty connoisseur. Unpolished, relaxed atmosphere in candlelit interior and intimate stone courtyard. In the cellar, there's often music, from flamenco to jazz, played in front of the face of Bakos, the Greek wine god. Salads and sandwiches €3-4.20. Open daily 5pm-3am. Cash only.

Katy's Garage, Alaunstr. 48 (☎0351 656 7701; www.katysgarage.de). Guarded by a gigantic stone armadillo, Katy's is one of the area's more energetic venues. A young, edgy crowd fills this small, smoky, crimson-colored club for dancing and drinking. M student night (no cover, beer and wine €1.50), Tu alternative, W over 30 night with 70s-90s music., Th reggae, F Britpop and indie. Sa disco. Cover up to €4. Open daily 8pm-5am. Free entry and reduced drinks until 10pm. Cash only.

Scheune, Alaunstr. 36-40 (☎0351 802 6619; www.scheune.org). The granddaddy of the Neustadt scene, this bar serves as a starting point for many nights out. Performance space upstairs and Indian cafe downstairs (€4-12). Hosts the fantastic Schaubudensommer festival in July and the Schaubudenwinter in December. A jazz band plays M nights. Cover €5-15. Cafe open M-F 5pm-2am, Sa-Su 10am-2am. Club opens at 8pm.

DAYTRIPS FROM DRESDEN

MORITZBURG

Take bus #326 (dir: Radeburg über Moritzburg) from Bahnhof-Neustadt to "Moritzburg, Schloß" (25min., M-F every 30min. 5:15am-11:25pm, Sa-Su every hr. 8am-11pm; €3.50 round-trip; buy a daypass, €5.10, before you go). Return trip from "Moritzburg Markt" on Marktstr., parallel to Schloßallee on the west. For a more nostalgic journey, take the S-Bahn from Dresen to "Radebeul-Ost" (15min.), and then board the 124-year-old narrow-gauge steam train Loessnitzgrudbahn—the "Loessnitz Dachsund"—as it trundles up to "Moritzburg" (30min. every 2hr. daily 8:26am-8:26pm, €5.80, roundtrip €11.60. ☎0352 078 93 90; www.loessnitzgrundbahn.de). From the station, follow Bahnhofstr. up the hill to Schloßallee and take a right. Moritzburg's tourist office is at Schloßallee 3b, just before the bus station. ☎0352 07 85 40. Open Tu-Sa 11am-5pm.

Never one to be bashful about leaving his mark on the Saxon landscape, August the Strong tore down a little palace in 1723 and replaced it with **Schloß Moritzburg,** a titanic Baroque hunting lodge. The immense saffron *Schloß*, towers at all four corners, stands at the foot of Moritzburg's main street, Schloßallee, occupying much of a tree-rimmed island in an artificial lake. The palace's rooms, each named for its contents, is on display in museum fashion. The **Federzimmer** (feather room), shows a featherbed constructed inside out: its ornate exterior was woven from the fluffy dyed feathers of European waterbirds. Upstairs, look for the 8000-year-old fossil antlers of the now extinct giant red deer in the **Stone Hall,** and the 66-point (counting generously) "Moritzburger" in the **Hall of Monstrosities,** a 1696 gift of Frederick III of Brandenburg. (☎0352 07 87 30; www.schloss-moritzburg.de. Open daily Apr.-Oct. 10am-5:30pm last entry 5pm, Nov.-Mar. guided tours in German; Feb.-Mar. and Nov.-Dec. Tu-Su 10am-4pm; Jan. Sa-Su 10am-4pm. Palace grounds free, interior and exhibition €6, students €3. Pick up an English-language audio tour, €2, or free translation booklet from the museum shop.) A 30min. walk from the main palace, the **Fasanenschlößchen** (little pheasant palace), was built by the great-grandson of August, Friedrich August III. Girded by tall hedges and crumbling statues, the pink hunting lodge is a monument to elegant restraint, a sensibility clearly absent in August. A small jetty creates a cove on the adjacent **Grossteich,** and supports the **Leuchtturm** (lighthouse), painted to match the lodge. This miniature sea was once the stage of the mock sea battles of bored, rich princes. A pleasant loop through the wild game reserve connects the *Fasanenschlößchen* and the *Schloß*. Walk around the *Schloß* and take the path bordering the lake to the right, and follow signs. (☎035207 87 36 10. Tours May-Sept. 10am-6pm, Apr. and Oct. 10am-5pm. €5.) If you're still in the hunting spirit after the palace, head to **Adam's Gasthof ❸,** Markt 9, near the bus stop, for some gamey fare, like *Wildgulasch.* (☎035207 85 70; www.adamsgasthof.com. Open daily from 11am.)

SÄCHSISCHE SCHWEIZ NATIONAL PARK (SAXON SWITZERLAND)

Sheer sandstone cliffs and mountains draped with lush forests distinguish the national park Germany has claimed as its own "Switzerland." Once an ancient lakebed, the Elbe etched out the now-inhabited valleys, leaving monolithic peaks standing up to 600m tall. Although archaeologists can trace settlements in the area back to the Bronze Age, the region truly flourished under the auspices of the Saxon electors of the Holy Roman Empire, for whom it served as the perfect destination for such activities as hunting expeditions and various court festivals. Over the past century, it has become one of the most popular national vacation destinations, but it's virtually unknown outside of Germany. Transportation within the park is very thorough and affordable, and hiking, biking, kayaking, and canoeing opportunities abound in this exceptional corner of Germany just kilometers down the river from Dresden.

SÄCHSISCHE SCHWEIZ NATIONAL PARK AT A GLANCE

AREA: 368 sq. km.

CLIMATE: Temperate. Summers 20-30°C (68-86°F).

FEATURES: Sandstone cliffs, tabled mountains, and river gorges.

CAMPING: Only in designated areas. Most campgrounds close Nov.-Mar.

GATEWAYS: Bad Schandau (p. 461).

HIGHLIGHTS: Dramatic cliffs and valleys seen from atop the numerous rock formations, particularly stunning from the Bastei lookout point or the Königstein Festung.

FEES: No entrance or trail fees.

TRANSPORTATION

The park is easily accessible by Dresden's S1, running from Meißen to the Dresden Hauptbahnhof along the southern bank of the Elbe River (every 30min.), stopping at Bad Schandau or Schöna. Some towns must be reached via ferry across the river from the station. A fleet of **Sächsische Dampfschifffahrt** paddle-steamers connect the towns along this section of the Elbe (☎0351 8 66 090; www.saechsische-dampfschifffahrt.de). If you plan to explore more than one town in a day, buy a *Tageskarte* (€4.50, children and seniors €3.50) from any *Fahrausweis* machine, located at most train stops, for the S-Bahn, buses, and many ferries until 4am. The **Kirnitzschtalbahn,** an antique trolley, travels from Bad Schandau east into the canyon, turning back at **Lichtenhainer Wasserfall** (30min.; Apr.-Oct. 2 per hr. 9:30am-7pm, less frequently in winter; €3, 14 and under €1.50). *Wanderwege* (footpaths) connect towns via winding park paths.

ORIENTATION AND PRACTICAL INFORMATION

The national park is divided into the *vorderer Teil* (front section) and the *hinterer Teil* (back section). The **Elbe River,** along which most of the region's towns lie, runs from the Czech Republic in the southeast toward Dresden in the northwest, cutting the park in half. The best source of park information is the **Nationalpark Zentrum,** Dresdner Str. 2b. In addition to the knowledgeable, English-speaking staff, the house has an exhibit on the park's history and wildlife. (☎0350 225 0240; www.lanu.de. Open Apr.-Oct. daily 9am-6pm, Nov.-Mar. Tu-Su 9am-5pm; closed Jan. 2009. Exhibit €4, students €3.) The park website, www.saechsische-schweiz.de, contains useful information for tourists, and www.nationalpark-saechsische-schweiz.de has information about the wildlife and

conservation efforts. Tourist offices in towns near the park supply fundamental brochures, and can offer specific recommendations for accessing the park. For information on group travel, contact the **Tourismusverband,** Bahnhofstr. 21, 01796 Pirna (☎3501 47 01 47). For **emergencies** dial ☎110 for police, ☎112 for fire, or ☎115 for medical emergencies. There are no telephones within the park, but there is often cell phone service. Dialing ☎112 will relay your call to **Bergrettungsstationen** (mountain rescue stations) located throughout the park.

CAMPING

The entire region can be seen on a daytrip from Dresden, but vacationers looking for an extended stay can choose from many types of accommodations. Private rooms can be booked through tourist offices. For the most rustic experience, guests are permitted to *Boofe* (sleep under the sky) outside the Kernzonen in specially marked locations, as an informal concession to visitors who had been visiting the region before the area was designated as a national park. These improvised overnights must leave no trace on the forest, and fires are prohibited; for those desiring even the slightest material comforts, seeking out a formal campgound is recommended. The following campgrounds vary widely in services offered and space available, so call ahead. Whatever the type of accommodation, reservations are a good idea between April and October.

Campingplatz Ostrauer Mühle, im Kirnitzschtal, Bad Schandau (☎035022 427 42; www.ostrauer-muehle.de). Open year-round.

Campingplatz Thorwaldblick, Schandauer Str. 37, Hinterhermsdorf (☎035974 506 48; www.thorwaldblick.de). Open year-round.

Camping Königstein, Schandauer Str. 25e, Königstein (☎035021 682 24; www.camping-koenigstein.de). Open Apr.-Oct.

Waldcamping Pirna-Copitz, Äußere Pillnitzer Str., Pirna (☎03501 52 37 73; www.waldcamping-pirna.de). Open Apr.-Oct. Handicapped facilities available.

Camping Stoplen, Am Stadtbad, Stolpen (☎0172 809 4923; wwww.stolpen.de). Open mid-Mar. to mid-Oct. Many amenities and recreational facilities.

Camping- & Freizeitpark LuxOase, Arnsdorfer Str. 1, Kleinrohrsdorf/Dresden (☎03595 25 66 66; www.luxoase.de).

HIKING

With nearly 100km of trails, hikes of all lengths and difficulty levels are available, and only a few are listed here. Trails are often well marked, but a green stripe can be difficult to distinguish from a blue one when painted on a tree trunk, so a map available at various degrees of magnification (€5.50-9.60), from the Nationalparkzentrum or any tourist office, is strongly recommended. Within *Kernzonen*, hikers must stay on posted paths. Be sure to wear proper hiking shoes or boots, and bring your passport if you want to cross over to the nearby Czech Republic through the officially sanctioned checkpoints.

Basteiaussicht (2hr.). Starting in Rathen, this easy hike with lots of stairs passes the startling outcrops and dramatic plunges of the **Bastei** cliffs in all their splendor. The lookout point offers a dizzying view of the forested Elbe valley. Rent boats at the Amselsee, a section of river in the middle of the hike (€2.60 per 30min.).

Schrammsteinaussicht (4hr.). This hike begins in Bad Schandau and includes the Kipphorn lookout point (480m), a stone ridge next to the Elbe valley. Among the highest spots in the park, this is the perfect vantage point from which to watch the sun rise or set. On a clear day, you can see all the way to Dresden. A relatively easy hike, excepting the 30min. ascent to the top of the ridge.

Kuhstall und Raubschloß (3hr.). Begins at the Lichtenhainer Wasserfall. Includes the cavernous Kuhstall rock formation and the site of the **Raubschloß** (Robbers' Castle) ruins. (Bus #241 from Bad Schandau or Königstein,.every 2hr. 8am-6:30pm. Or, Kirnitzschtalbahn from Bad Schandau. Every 30min. 9:30am-8:30pm.)

Großer Zschirnstein (4hr.). Begins in Schöna (S1, every 30min. 5:30am-10:30pm). Leads to the **Kohlbornstein** (Cabbage Spring Stone) lookout point (372m), with a view of sandstone rock formations and the **Böhmische Schweiz** (Bohemian Switzerland).

Pfaffenstein (2hr.). Begins in Königstein. A moderately difficult hike among the park's many "stone needles," with stairs to the **Pfaffenstein** (Priest Stone) rock formation.

BIKING

Cyclists will enjoy the formidable **Elberadweg,** a 860km bike path that traces the Elbe as it slices through Germany from the Czech Republic and empties into the North Sea. A 30km segment runs through the Sächsishe Schweiz region, marked with a cursive 'e' on trail maps (www.elberadweg.de); pick up a handbook at tourist offices. The park website (www.saechsische-schweiz.de) suggests bike tours with lengths ranging from 20-70km. The **Nationalparkhaus** in Bad Schandau (p. 461) can supply more information on paths. **Spaß Tours,** Mennickestr. 29, in Stadt Wehlen, will drive you and your bike up to the Bastei, and let you coast back to town. (☎035024 710 84. €8 with your own bike, €10 with theirs.) Rent bikes in Pirna at **Fahhrader Kurt Baessler,** Hauptstr. 4, 01796 Pirna. (☎03501 52 32 68. Open M-F 9am-6pm, Sa 9am-noon. €8 per day.)

Dresden to Schöna (3hr.). The paved Elberadweg follows the river from Dresden to Schöna. Pick up the path by the docks on the southern side of the Elbe. To avoid riding on streets with car traffic, cross the river with the ferry at **Königstein** and then again at Bad Schandau. Offers fantastic views of the Elbe and the park's rock formations.

Bad Schandau to Hinterhermsdorf (3hr.). The Elberadweg heads off to the right as soon as you get off the ferry in Bad Schandau. Follow the marked bike paths through the back part of the park to Hinterhermsdorf. Includes the **Lindigtblick** ("pleasing view") lookout point and the **Lichtenhainer Wasserfall.**

OTHER ACTIVITIES

CLIMBING. The rock formations and sheer cliff faces of the Sächsische Schweiz make it a natural attraction for rock climbers. Locals claim that "free climbing" was first practiced on these very bluffs. Although experienced climbers are permitted to brave the challenging cliffs on their own, *Let's Go* recommends that all visitors first stop by the Nationalparkhaus, which can inform climbers about park rules and direct the less experienced toward guides and climbing courses. **Bergsport Arnold,** in Bad Schandau (Marktstr. 4; ☎035022 423 72) and in Hohnstein (Obere Str. 2; ☎035975 812 46), is the best resource for climbers: they recommend agreeable cliffs, rent equipment, and offer climbing courses and guided excursions from beginner to advanced. (www.bergsport-arnold.de. 1-day course €50, 2-day guided climbs €150 beginner, €135 advanced. Equipment included. AmEx/MC/V.) Another good place to hunt for climbs is www.gipfelbuch.de. In the interest of preserving the rock, metal safety devices like clamps and stakes are forbidden, as are chemical climbing aids such as magnesia. Some of the most popular climbing regions include Bielatal (239m), Rathener Gebiet (145m), Schmilkaer Gebiet (124m), Affensteine (115m), Großer Zschand (87m), Schrammsteingebiet (80m), and Brandgebiet (80m).

WATER SPORTS. Canoeing on the broad and tranquil Elbe lets you float between the raised sandstone plateaus, swallowed between the pined hills, and peer up at the occasional castle. **Kanu-Aktiv-Tours,** Elbpromenade Schadauer Str. 17-19, Königstein, rents canoes and rubber dinghies for up to 12 people and offers guided water tours aboard boxy party boats. (☎035021 59960; www.kanu-aktiv-tours.de. Boats €30-90 per day. 5½hr. tours €30-36 per person.) **Spaß Tours,** Mennicke Str. 29, Stadt Wehlen, rents charter boats for trips anywhere between Schmilka and Meißen. They also rent muscle-propelled vessels for up to 10 people (2-person kayaks €25, 3-person canoe, €30, 4-person raft €30, 10-person raft €65.) The whole stretch of river offers about 12hr. of non-stop paddling. Ever beneficent, they will let you float down river from Stadt Wehlen and pick you up on a motorboat at Dresden, or deposit you up river at Bad Schandau and let you meander back (☎035024 710 84; www.elbe-erleben.de.3hr. in either direction; €22 per person).

BAD SCHANDAU ☎035022

The most bustling town in the Sächsische Schweiz, Bad Schandau (pop. 3000) offers plenty of outdoor opportunities. The river Kirnitzsch flows off the Elbe through town and down into the canyon, its mossy ferned banks insulated by narrow parkgrounds. Take the Kirnitzschtalbahn trolley car (from the Markt, take Marktstr. straight, turn right on Poststr., and then left on Kirnitzschtalstr.) along the river to the modest but pleasant **Lichtenhain waterfall,** a favorite starting point for 3-4hr. hikes on the **Schrammsteine.** (Trolley runs Apr.-Oct. 2 per hr. 9:30am-7pm, Nov-Mar. every 70min. 10:15am-4pm. €3, day pass €5.)

Bad Schandau's hotels fill up quickly when the weather is pleasant. The **Jugendherberge Bad Schandau (HI) ❷,** Dorfstr. 14, is perched above town, about 35min. from the Markt. Take Kirchstr. away from the Church, turn right on Poststr., and make a left on Kirnitzschtalstr. shortly after. Follow this for 20min. until Ostrauer Berg on the right, and trudge up the hill. The hostel will be to the left at the summit. Take bus #255 from "Bad Schandau Bahnhof" or "Bad Shandau Elbkai," to the left of the ferry dock on the north bank to "Ostauer

Zur Falkensteinklinik" and follow signs to the Jugendherberge. (20min. Buses run every hr., 8:30am-5:30pm, €1.80.) Though far from the center of town, the hostel, which has singles, doubles, and some dorms, is near several trailheads. (☎035022 424 08. Breakfast included. Reception 7:30-9am and 4:30-7pm. All rooms €18, over 27 €21. Singles €28/31, doubles €44/50. Cash only.) In a town that closes down before 11pm, **Sigl's ❸,** Kirnitzschtalstr. 17, a relaxed bar and bistro, offers food and a wide selection of beers from 5pm until midnight during the week, and until 2am F and Sa (entrees €9-12). The restaurant doubles as a hotel that's cheaper than those by the ferry dock. (☎035022 407 02. Apr.-Oct. singles €38; doubles €66-72. Nov.-Mar. €30/44-50. MC/V.)

Bad Schandau is connected to the rest of Saxony; the **S-Bahn** runs to **Dresden** (1hr., 2 per hr. 6:30am-7pm, €5.10). To get to town from the Bad Schandau train station, take the **ferry** (every 30min. M-F 5:30am-10pm, Sa-Su from 6:50am, €0.90, roundtrip €1.50.) and walk up from the dock to the Markt, to find the **tourist office,** Markt 12, in the **Haus des Gastes** on your left. The staff finds rooms (from €20) and suggests hikes. They also house two **internet** terminals in the waiting room and rent **bikes.** (☎035022 900 30; www.bad-schandau.de. Open May-Sept. daily 9am-9pm; Apr. and Oct. daily 9am-6pm; Nov.-Mar. M-F 9am-6pm and Sa-Su 9am-1pm. Internet €2 per hr. Bikes €8 per day.) For a **taxi,** call ☎035022 428 85. The **ticket office** in the **Bahnhof,** Am Bahnhof 6, also serves as a rudimentary tourist office. (☎035022 412 47. Open Apr. M-F 8am-5pm, May-Oct. M-F 8am-6pm, Nov-Mr M-Tu and Th-F 9am-5pm.) There is a **Sparkasse** across from the **Nationalparkzentrum** at Dresdnerstr. 1a that has a 24hr **ATM.** (Open M and F 9am-noon and 1-4pm, Tu and Th 9am-noon and 1-6pm, W 9am-noon.) The **post office,** Basteiplatz 5, is at the intersection of Kirnitzschtalstr. and Rudolf-Sendig-Str. (Open M-F 9am-noon and 2-6pm, Sa 9am-noon.) **Postal Code:** 01814.

OBERLAUSITZ (UPPER LUSTATIA)

Originally a Bohemian territory, Oberlausitz became part of Saxony when the Bohemian king could not repay the 72 tons of gold he borrowed from the Saxon king. Bordering two of Germany's former Warsaw Pact neighbors (Poland and the Czech Republic), Oberlausitz has worked hard to overcome the economic stagnation it experienced prior to reunification, and has had remarkable success. Many building projects in the area have been devoted to breathing new life into long-neglected architecture and removing overbearing Socialist structures. The area around Bautzen exemplifies the successful rejuvenation of this pleasantly rural region on the edge of eastern Germany.

BUDYŠIN (BAUTZEN) ☎03591

Millennium-old Bautzen (pop. 42,200) displays its history on every corner. Above the Spree river, the city's ancient towers guard architectural treasures, be they Gothic, Baroque, or from the Gründerzeit—a prosperous period of industrial expansion in the late 19th century. Ruins dating back hundreds of years attest to the ravages of war and time. Before German invasions and fortifications came to Oberlausitz in the 10th century, however, the region was settled by Slavic Sorbs (see **The Absorbing Sorbs,** p. 472), who continue to live in and around Bautzen, still speaking Sorbian and now on good terms with the former German invaders.

SACHSEN

TRANSPORTATION AND PRACTICAL INFORMATION

Trains: S-Bahn runs from Dresden (1hr., 2 per hr., €9).

Tourist Office: Hauptmarkt 1 (☎03591 420 16; www.bautzen.de). Take a left out of the train station and continue to the first intersection. Stay right and follow Aussere Lauenstr. into town. Two blocks after passing a bridge on your left, you'll come to the Hauptmarkt. The office has accommodations listings and finds rooms in hotels, pensions, and private homes (from €23) for free. To learn more about the Sorbs, visit the **Sorbische Kulturinformation office,** Postpl. 2. The staff has abundant pamphlets in English, and information on cultural events and **homestays** with local Sorbs. (☎03591 421 05; www.sorben.com/ski. Open M-F 10am-5pm.) Open Apr.-Oct. M-F 9am-6pm and Sa-Su 9am-3pm, Nov.-Mar. M-F 9am-5pm and Sa-Su 9am-2pm.

Internet: Get Connect, Steinstr. 13, off the Kornmarkt. Open M-Sa 10am-11pm and Su 2-11pm; €1.80 per 30min.

Post office: Postpl. Open M-F 8:30am-6:30pm, Sa 9am-noon. **Postal Code:** 02625.

ACCOMMODATIONS

Jugendherberge (HI), Am Zwinger 1 (☎03591 403 47), Built around an ancient tower, Bautzen's hostel has spacious rooms and 3 floors of recreation rooms. From the Hauptmarkt, follow Kornstr. as it turns into Schulerstr.; take a left after you go through the Schülertor. Breakfast included. Reception M-F 7am-8pm and Sa-Su 6-8pm. Reservations recommended. Dorms €15.80, over 27 €18.80. Single room add €10 per night, double add €4 per person per night. 1 night stay add €1.50. Cash only. ❷

Spree Pension, Fischergasse 6 (☎03591 489 60; www.spree-pension.de), is in a quiet spot by the Spree at the foot of the city's cliffs. From the train station, take a left onto Tzschirnerstr., and make a right at its end. After 50m, go left down the winding Dresdener Str. and stay right for Fischergasse; it's on the right before the bridge. Breakfast included. Singles €40, doubles €60, triples €77. AmEx/MC/V. ❸

FOOD

The **Fleischmarkt,** behind the Rathaus, and the Hauptmarkt alternately host markets close to one another (Tu 9am-1pm, Th 9am-5pm, Sa 8am-noon). Grocery stores line **Karl-Marx-Straße** (Most open M-F 8am-6pm Sa 8am-noon), and **Reichenstraße,** joining the Reichenturm and the Markt, has cafes and bakeries.

Wjelbik, Kornstr. 7 (☎03591 420 60). Immerse yourself in Sorbian tradition by trying the *Stulle* (pork sandwich; €8.50) or *Hochzeitsuppe* (wedding soup; €3.90) at this local favorite. Pick up a few words of Sorbish along the way. Open M-F 11am-3pm and 5-11pm, Sa-Su 11am-11pm. MC/V. ❸

Mönchshof, Burglehn 1 (☎03591 49 01 41; www.moenchshof.de). Over 400-year-old recipes (including roasted stag) and a monastic air make this medieval restaurant worth a visit. Entrees €6.70-13.50. Reservations recommended. Open M-Th 11:30am-midnight, F-Sa 11:30am-1am, and Su 11:30am-11pm. AmEx/MC/V. ❸

Zur Apotheke, Schloßstr. 21 (☎03591 48 00 35). In the site of the old town pharmacy. this restaurant serves meals rich in herbs (€7-11) and much tastier than the offerings of actual pharmacies. Open Tu-Su 11:30am-2pm and 5pm-midnight. Cash only. ❸

SIGHTS

SORBISCHES MUSEUM. The museum details the intriguing history and culture of the Sorbs. The displays include everything from handwritten Bible translations to model houses, Easter eggs, modern Sorbian art, *Dudelsacks* (bagpipes), and Sorbish violins. *(Ortenburg 3. On Schloßstr., through the Matthiasturm. ☎03591 424 03. Open Apr.-Oct. M-F 10am-5pm, Sa-Su 10am-6pm; Nov.-Mar. M-F 10am-4pm, Sa-Su 10am-5pm. €2.50, students and children €1.50.)*

HAUPTMARKT. This square contains the grand yellow 13th-century **Rathaus,** backed up by the **Fleischmarkt** and the Gothic **Dom St. Petri.** First consecrated in 1221, the elegant Dom became eastern Germany's only *Simultankirche* (simultaneous church) in 1524. Two sets of pews in the church look up at two altars, one Catholic and one Protestant. Each week the church switches not only religions, but also entrances: Catholic week uses a door on the southeast side, while during Protestant week, a door on the west side opens. Until 1952, this division was made more clear by a 4m high screen down the middle of the church. The 83m tower provides a beautiful view of the city and of the Spree. *(Left from the Reichenturm and down Reichenstr. Open Apr.-Oct. M-Sa 10am-5:30pm, Su 1-5:30pm; Nov.-Mar. M-Sa 10am-4pm, Su 1-4pm. Free.)* The **Domstift,** the flashy red-and-gold structure behind the cathedral, houses the **Domschatz** (Cathedral Treasury), a collection of jewel-studded gowns, bishop staffs (the bishop lived in Bautzen until he moved to Dresden, and an army of chalices. Ring the bell and ask to see the *Domschatzkammer. (Open M-F 10am-noon and 1-4pm. Free.)*

TOWERS. Bautzen has an unusual number of towers (17, to be precise), some offering excellent views of the city and countryside. The white **Reichenturm** (Realm Tower) is the leaning tower of Bautzen. Built in 1490, it is now a full 1.44m from the perpendicular. The reason for the incline is that, until 1953, the foundation for the 3200-ton tower was only 80cm deep. *(At the intersection of Kornmarkt and Reichenstr. Open daily Apr.-Oct. 10am-5pm. Last entrance 4:30pm. Tours €6. €1.60, students €1.40, under 14 €1.)* A block away you'll find the stone **Wendischer Turm** (Sorb Tower), a tower built in 1490-92 that once served as the city's debtors prison. Its roof was changed in 1566. Locals claim that the ghostly face above the gate of the **Nikolaiturm,** down An der Petrikirche from the Dom and to the right on **Nikolaipforte,** is a likeness of a former mayor who was bricked into the tower alive for opening the city to 16th-century Hussite attackers. Next door at the cemetery stand the eerie columns and empty window-arches of the ruined Nikolaikirche, destroyed in 1634 during the Thirty Years' War. To the left of the Sorbisches Museum, follow the scenic Osterweg and Reymannweg paths around the western city walls above the Spree, taking in the views of the 1480 **Mühlbastei** (Mill Tower), the spire of the 1429 **Michaelskirche,** and the 1558 **Alte Wasserkunst** (Old Water Works), now a technical museum. *(Museum open Feb.-Nov. daily 10am-4pm, Jan. Sa-Su only 10am-4pm. €1.50, students €1.)*

GEDENKSTÄTTE BAUTZEN (BAUTZEN MEMORIAL). Far grimmer than the stony towers above, Bautzen II held the enemies of two generations of oppressive polical regimes. Beginning in 1933, the Bautzen prisons (I and II) housed those who opposed Hitler—in 1945 it came under Soviet control. During the DDR years, Bautzen II became the only prison under direct command of the Ministry of State Security, and was kept hidden from the public. The Stasi (secret police) incarcerated opponents of the Stalinist regime and conducted brutal interrogations within these walls. Amble the hopeless hallways, see the living quarters, and listen to official recordings made inside the prison. **Bautzen I,** nicknamed "Yellow Misery," has become a modern penitentary closed to the public. *(Weingangstr. 8a. Take Steinstr. away from the Reichenturm, turn right on Wallstr., then left onto Weingang. ☎03591 40 474; www.gedenkstaette-bautzen.de. Open M-Th 10am-4pm, F 10am-8pm, Sa-Su 10am-6pm. Tours F 5pm, Sa-Su 2pm. Free.)*

ZITTAUER GEBIRGE (ZITTAU MOUNTAINS)

The rocky cliffs of the Zittau Mountains rise in a sliver of Germany wedged between the Czech Republic and Poland. Once a favorite spot of medieval monks, these beehive-shaped mountains are now the conquests of choice for skiers, hikers, and landscape lovers. In 1491, the region was the scene of the vicious *Bierkrieg* (Beer War), when incensed citizens of nearby Görlitz protested Zittau's beer-brewing success by destroying barrels of the brew. Despite unemployment rates of 20%, towns like Zittau keep the area vibrant.

CHEMNITZ ☎0371

For those interested in the history of the East German *Deutsche Demokratische Republik* (DDR), a visit to Chemnitz is a must. As the DDR's center of industry, Chemnitz was taken over by big new developments on the *Str. der Nationen* (Street of Nations), and was renamed Karl-Marx Stadt in 1952. As a result, the *Wende* (the "turn" of reunification) has been particularly challenging for Chemnitz, which struggles to rebuild its industry on capitalist terms.

TRANSPORTATION AND PRACTICAL INFORMATION

Trains: Run to: **Dresden** (1hr., every hr., €11.70); **Görlitz** (3hr., every hr., €25.80); **Leipzig** (1hr., every hr., €13.40); **Prague, Czech Republic** (4hr., 5 per day, €36).

Public Transportation: Sprawling Chemnitz is connected by a system of trams and buses, almost all of which stop at "Zentralhalestelle," comprised of Bahnhofstr. and Rathausstr. in the city center. The Omnibusbahnhof is a short walk down Georgstr. from the train station. Tickets are available at major stops and on board. A **Kurzstrecke ticket** (short distance ride; €1.10) covers rides up to 6 stops on the tram and 3 stops on the bus, an **Einzelfahrt** ticket (€1.60) covers all rides within 1hr., and a **Tageskarte** (day pass; €3.20) is valid until 3am the next morning. A **Wochenkarte** (week ticket; €13) covers all rides for 7 days. There's also an **Erweiterte Kurzstrecke** (extended short distance; €1.80) which has an even more complicated system.

Taxis: call ☎0371 330 0333.

Tourist Office: Markt 1 (☎0371 69 06 80), in the Rathaus. To get from the train station to the city center, head straight down Georgstr. or Carolastr. After a block, you'll come to Str. der Nationen, connecting the Markt. and Theaterpl. Turn left and continue toward the Markt to get to the office. The staff finds private rooms (from €13.50) for free, leads city tours (1hr. walking tour €5, 2hr. walking tour €8, 2hr. bus tour €13, students €11.50), and hands out free maps in English. Open M-F 9am-7pm, Sa 9am-4pm, Su 10am-4pm. **Tour** schedule varies; normally 1hr. walking tour Tu 2pm, bus tour Sa 10:30am.

Internet: Communication Center, Waisenstr. 13 (☎0371 666 3716), off Bahnhofstr., near Str. der Nationen. Open daily 10am-10pm. €2 per hr.

Pharmacy: Rathausstr. 1 (☎0371 666 4866.) Open M-F 7am-8pm, Sa 9am-5pm.

Post office: Str. der Nationen 2-4, just within the Innenstadt. Open M-F 9am-7pm, Sa 9am-2pm.) **Postal Code:** 09111.

ACCOMMODATIONS

Pension Art Nouveau, Hainstr. 130 (☎0371 402 50 72), is a 15min. walk from the station, away from town. Take an immediate right from Georgstr. onto Mauerstr. and go under the tunnel at the end on the right; turn left out of the tunnel and then right on Lessingstr., then left on Hainstr. You'll find clean, pleasant rooms with TV. Most have baths; some have kitchens. Breakfast included. Singles from €35, doubles €45. MC. ❸

Hotel Europark, Schulstr. 38 (☎0371 522 83 41; www.europark.de). A wide spectrum of rooms, from dorms to lavish hotel lodgings. It's far from the Innenstadt, but a straightforward commute. From the station take tram #6 (dir.: Altchemnitz) 20min. to "Altchemnitz Center." Facing the opposite direction of the train, turn left on Zöblitzerstr and stay left for Schulstr; don't be fooled by the hotel's rightward pointing logo. Reception 7am-3pm; info center 24hr. Breakfast €5. Hostel: singles from €17, doubles from €30. Hotel: singles from €33, doubles from €40. MC/V. ❷

Jugendherberge (HI), Augustusburger Str. 369 (☎0371 713 31; www.jugendherberge-chemnitz.de), is inexpensive but far-flung. Tram #5 (dir.: Gablenz) runs from "Brückenstr." to "Pappelhain." Follow signs for the Jugendherberge for 30min., cut through the field, and take a right on Augustusburger Str. During the week, bus #704 runs to "Walter-Kippel-Str.," 50m past the hostel. (45min., every 2hr. M-F 8am-5pm, €1.80.) The stocky white villa is surrounded by farmland, leaving ample space for pick-up soccer or crop circles. Reception daily 7am-9pm. Breakfast included. Check-in 1pm. Check-out 11am. €15.90, over 27 €18.90. 1-night stays add €1.50. Cash only. ❷

FOOD

For a quick bite, *Imbiße* and a fresh **market** (Th-Sa 9am-5pm) surround the Rathaus at the end of Str. der Nationen with everything from fresh fruit to fish dangling in a smoking box, right on the street. Larger appetites can be satisfied at the restaurants along Str. der Nationen near the Rathaus.

Turm Brauhaus, Neumarkt 2 (☎0371 909 5095; www.turmbrauhaus.de), serves heaping portions of German food, with an emphasis on steaks (entrees €4-10). Try the house beers, brewed according to the German purity regulations of 1516: the crisp *Helles* (bright), or the sweeter *Kupfer* (copper, made with herbs; both €1.50 for 0.5L). Or, treat yourself to a €14.50 brewery tour, including 0.5L. All-day specials (€7-9) include a *Turmbrau.* Open M-Th and Su 9am-1am, F-Sa 9am-3am. Kitchen closes at midnight. ❷

Pizzeria Dolomiti, Str. der Nationen 12 (☎ 0371 444 7796), between a McDonald's and a Marx statue. (Insert irony here.) Filling thin-crust *Studentenpizza* for €3.50; pastas €4-7. Open daily 11am-midnight. Cash only. ❷

Heck-Art, Mühlenstr. 2 (☎0371 694 6818; www.restaurant-heck-art.de). This hybrid gallery, chic bar, and bohemian cafe serves lunch specials like the *Mediterraneaner Fischauflauf* (€6) and an exhibition space upstairs. Open daily 11am-1am. Gallery open until 6pm; Kitchen closes at midnight. AmEx/MC/V. ❷

SIGHTS

GUNZENHAUSER MUSEUM. Recently opened, this museum in the renovated Sparkasse building now contains the private collection (2400 works) of Munich gallerist Alfred Gunzenhauser, including the world's largest collection of works by Otto Dix, and other 20th-century German notables. A wine-red staircaise slices through all three floors. The 1st fl. contains abstract, non-representational works and the 2nd houses Expressionist works, notably those of Max Beckmann. The top floor contains the fierce oeuvres of Otto Dix and Conrad

Felixmüller. If you thought watercolors couldn't be obscene, look for Dix's taboo-breaking depictions of society's marginals. His next period consisted of mostly landscapes. *(Stollberger Str. 2. ☎0371 488 7024. Open Tu-F noon-7pm, Sa-Su 11am-7pm. Free guided tours Tu-F 3pm, Sa-Su noon. €7, students €4.)*

STRASSE DER NATIONEN. The city's former identity as **Karl-Marx-Stadt** is embodied in the politically charged works of art along the Straße der Nationen. Statues of frolicking children or happily scrubbed workers are everywhere, inscribed with cautionary messages like "the Party has a thousand eyes." No statue outshines the clunky countenance of Karl Marx on Bruckenstr., his 7m tall head, cast in bronze, especially intimidating when lit at night.

KUNSTSAMMLUNGEN CHEMNITZ. To the left of Petrikirche, this art museum features a sampling of 19th- and 20th-century German art, and a huge collection of paintings and woodcuts by local Expressionist Karl Schmidt-Rotluff. *(From the corner of Bruckenstr. and the Str. der Nationen, walk past Karl Marx on your right until you reach Promenadenstr. ☎0371 488 4424; www.kunstammlungen-chemnitz.de. Open Tu-F noon-7pm, Sa-Su 11am-7pm. €7, students €4. English-language audio tour €1.)*

SCHLOSS. The reconstructed castle, destroyed in the Thirty Years' War, now contains an impressive collection of medieval art and a historical exhibit on the 800-year-old city, and a clover-shaped garden out front. *(Up the Promenadenstr. and follow footpaths up the Schloßberg, which surveys the lake. ☎0371 488 4501; www.chemnitz-schlossberg.de. Open Tu-F 1-87pm, Sa noon-9pm, Su 10am-6pm.)* Make sure to stop by the **Boat House,** Schlossteichstr. 20, soon on your left, which rents row- and paddle-boats, weather permitting. *(☎0371 331 1086. Open daily 10am-8pm. €4-7 per hr.)*

ENTERTAINMENT AND NIGHTLIFE

The **Theater Chemnitz** dominates Chemnitz's high culture scene with opera, ballet, symphony, theater, puppet shows, and its annual production of Wagner's *Ring*. Tickets are available at the opera house **Theater-Service,** Theaterpl. 2 (open Mo-Fr 9am-4:30pm and 1hr before performances) at in the Galerie Roter Turm, Neumarkt 2, on the second floor (open M-Th 10am-8pm, F-Sa 10am-9pm). Under 27 can sign up for a **JuniorCard** on the spot and receive 50% off all tickets (free). (☎037140 00 430; www.theater-chemnitz.de.Tickets €7-36.50 before reduction.) Though not known for nightlife, Chemnitz offers more dance venues than any neighboring towns. Pick up the magazines *Blitz* or *Streicher* from the tourist office for event listings.

Fuchsbau, Carolastr. 8 (☎0371 67 17 17; www.clubfx.de), hosts discos W, F, Sa at 10pm with various deals like 99-cent drinks or girls get in free. Cover €3-5.

Brauclub, Neumarkt 2 (☎0371 909 5095; www.brauclub.de). Right in Neumarkt, this club reaches for class with an underground leather and velvet lounge. Hip hop on W (€4), 80s and 90s on F (€5). Students ½-price. Open from 10pm.

DAYTRIP FROM CHEMNITZ

AUGUSTUSBURG

Augustusburg hamlet can be reached by bus #704 (dir.: Augustusburg) or #705 (dir.: Eppendorf) from the Chemnitz Busbahnhof. (20min., 6:20am-5:10pm, €2.80.) The bus stops at the foot of the path to the castle. Trains travel to Erdmannsdorf, located down the mountain from Augustusburg (20min., 6am-10pm, €2.40). The castle is a beautiful 3km walk uphill, but you can take a the Drahtseilbahn (cable car) up to the Schloß. (☎037291 202 65; www.drahtseilbahn-augustusburg.de. 8min., every 20min. daily 9am-6pm. Round-

trip €4.50, students €4.) On weekends and holidays, a bus also runs from Chemnitz right up to the entrance of the Schloß itself. (30min., every 2hr. 8:30am-4:30pm, €1.60.)

A day at the peach-trimmed **Schloß in Augustusburg** will help you recover from post-industrial, monochromatic Chemnitz. At 516m above the town, this Renaissance hunting lodge of the Saxon electors gives two mesmerizing views of the surrounding **Erzgebirge** mountains—the Czech Republic is visible on the horizon. The interior has been divided into six discrete buildings, two of which can only be entered on guided tours, which lead through the **Brunnenhaus** (well house) and the intimate **Schloßkapelle** (chapel), the only Renaissance chapel left in Saxony. The altar was painted by Cranach the Younger. (45min. tours daily Apr.-Oct. 10:30am, 12:30, 2, and 4:30pm; Nov.-Mar. 11:30am, 1:30 and 3:30pm. €3, students €2.20.) The adjacent **Jagdtier- und Vogelkundemuseum** (Hunting and Game Musuem) contains an exhaustive display of the local fauna and the machines the palace's guests used to kill them. In another corner of the main courtyard, descend into the dungeon to see gruesome intruments of punishment and humiliation. Also in the palace, the **Motorradmuseum** (Motorcycle Museum) documents the history of the motorcycle, from early proto-motos to shiny BMWs to racing video games at the end. With a more aristocratic flair, the **Kutschenmuseum** (Carriage Museum) houses a fleet of buggies, modest to magnificent—the 1790 carriage is a palace on wheels. (☎0372 913 8018; www.die-sehenswerten-drei.de. *Schloß* open daily Apr.-Oct. 9:30am-6pm; Nov.-Mar. 10am-5pm. Last entry 30min. before closing. Each museum €1.60-3.20, students €1.20-2.40. Day pass for all 4 €6.60/5.) The eagles and falcons that live under triangular shelters at the *Schloß* swoop and dive in **falconry exhibitions.** The hut is down the stairs to the right of the main gate. (45min. Mar.-Oct. Tu-Su 11am and 3pm. €6, students €5.) Get dinner and a drink in the **Augustuskeller ❸,** an original castle cellar kept aglow with candles and faux torch lighting.(☎037291 207 40. Entrees from €7.60. Open Tu-Su 11am-9pm, AmEx/MC/V.)

LEIPZIG ☎0341

Dubbed a "little Paris" by Goethe himself, Leipzig (pop. 500,000) is the perfect German university city: large enough to have a life beyond academia, yet not so big that the influence of its students is diluted. Surrounded by a ring road, Leipzig might appear small on the map, but it's bursting at the seams with activity: music lovers, art critics, club fanatics, and adventure seekers meet here to satisfy their passions. Once home to Bach, Mendelssohn, Schumann, Wagner, Nietzsche, Goethe, and Leibniz, the city enjoys an exceptionally rich cultural tradition and boasts world-class museums, churches, and restaurants.

TRANSPORTATION

Flights: Flughafen Leipzig-Halle (☎0341 241155), on Schkeuditzg., is 20km from Leipzig with international service throughout Europe. Outbound trains stop at the airport. (From the Hauptbahnhof, 15min., 2 per hr. 3:30am-12:10am, €3.40.)

Trains: To: **Berlin** (2½hr., 2 per hr., €40); **Dresden** (1½hr., every hr., €28); **Frankfurt** (4hr., every hr., €67); **Munich** (5hr., every 2hr., €84). The "Service Point" counter near track 14 is the quickest source of information and itineraries. For tickets, use *Automaten* (don't forget to validate at the small box on the entrance to the platform), or the *Reisezentrum* (travel center) on the ground floor near the main entrance; expect a line.

Public Transportation: Information ☎0341 194 49. Trams and buses cover the city; the hub is in front of the Hauptbahnhof. The Innenstadt is spared the congestion of public transportation except for lonely bus 89 which runs cuts through from the Hauptbahnhof via Thomaskirche. A *Kurzstrecke* ticket covers up to 4 stops (€1.40); a regular ticket

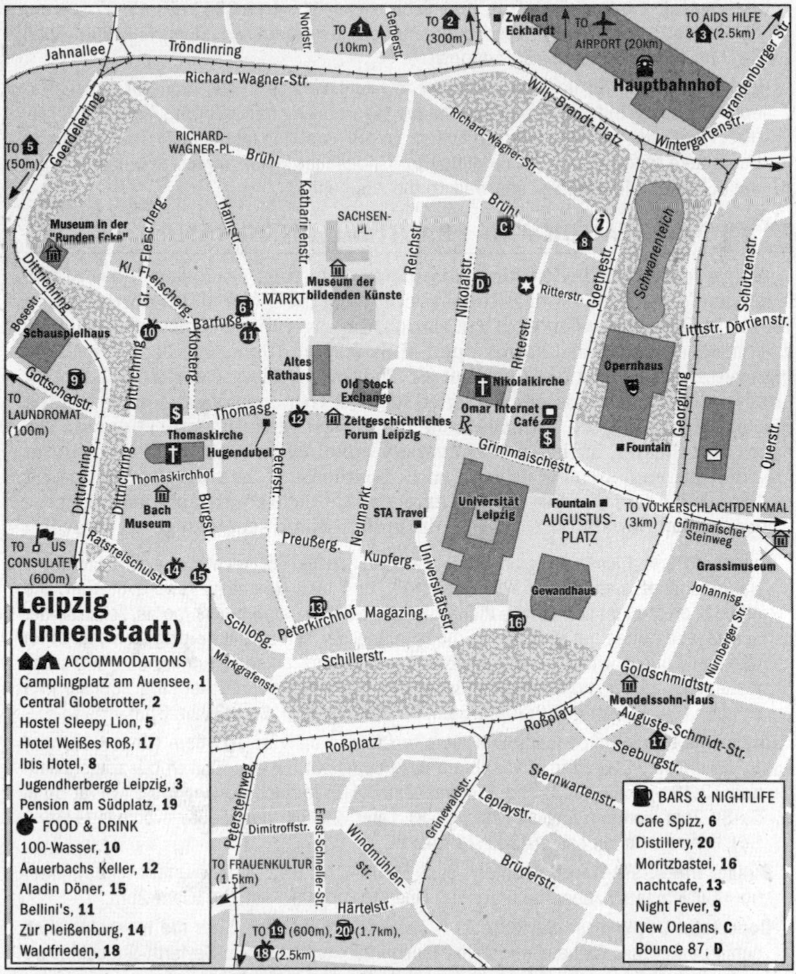

covers all rides within 1hr. (€2). A **Tageskarte** (day card) is valid until 4am the day after purchase (€5.20). Tickets available from the tourist office, the Mobi Zentrum on Willy-Brandt-Platz in front of the train station (open M-F 8am-8pm, Sa 8-10am, MC/V), some trams, and *Automaten*. Validate all tickets on board. Night buses (look for the "N" prefix and bat silhouette at the stop) leave from the Hauptbahnhof 1:11am, 2:22am and 3:33am, Sa-Su also 1:45am and 3am, covering most daytime tram routes.

Taxis: ☎0341 48 84. AmEx/MC/V. Toll-free ☎0800 800 42 33.

Car Rental: Sixt has an in the Hauptbahnhof at track 6. ☎0341 26 988 11; www.sixt.de. Open M-F 7am-10pm, Sa 8am-6:30pm, Su 10am-6pm. More offices at the airport.

Ride Share: Mitfahrzentrale, Goethestr. 7-10 (☎194 40), past the tourist office. To: **Berlin** (€12.50); **Dresden** (€9.50); **Frankfurt** (€22.50); **Munich** (€23.50); **Hamburg** (€23.50). Open daily 9am-7pm.

Bike Rental: Zweirad Eckhardt, Kurt-Schumacher-Str. 4 (☎0341 96 17 274; www.bikeandsport.de), close to the Hauptbahnhof's west entrance. Open M-F 6am-8pm, Sa 9am-8pm. €8 per day, €50 deposit.

Hitchhiking: *Let's Go* does not recommend hitchhiking as a safe mode of transportation. Hitchers going to Dresden and Prague report taking tram #3 (dir.: Taucha) to "Portitzer Allee" and continuing on Torgauerstr. to the Autobahn interchange. Those going to Berlin take tram #8 or 15 (dir.: Miltitz) to "Lindenauer Markt," switch to bus #131, get out at "Dölzig, Holl. Mühle," and walk to the Autobahn.

ORIENTATION AND PRACTICAL INFORMATION

Leipzig's **Innenstadt** lies within a kilometer-wide ring, enclosing most of the sights and nightlife, as well as the university. On the Innenstadt's north edge (a 10min. walk from the center of the Markt), the cavernous **Hauptbahnhof** doubles as a tri-level mall (most stores open M-Sa 9:30am-10pm, Su 10am-8pm) selling everything from shoes to schnitzel. The train station was Europe's largest until Berlin's Lehrter Bahnhof opened in 2006. Grimmaischestr. slices the the disc in half, joining the Thomaskirche in the west with Augustpl., home to the opera and theater, in the east. University buildings are scattered throughout city, but the main locus is situated in the southeast of the ring. But life doesn't extinguish beyond the ring; the city extends a tentacle south, culminating in the funky student-populated Karl-Liebknecht-Str., which seems to go on forever.

Tourist Office: Richard-Wagner-Str. 1 (☎0341 7104265; www.leipzig.de). From the Hauptbahnhof, walk across Willy-Brandt-Pl., and take Goethestr. toward the left; the office is on the first corner with Richard-Wagner-Str. The staff books rooms, sells theater tickets, and hands out several free maps in English. Pick up the **Leipzig Card,** good for trams and buses within the city, discounts on city tours, museum admissions, and some restaurants. (1-day, until 4am, €9; 3-day €18.50, 3-day group ticket for 2 adults and 3 children €34.) Open M-F 9:30am-6pm, Sa 9:30am-4pm, Su 9:30am-3pm.

Tours: The tourist office leads bus tours in German daily at 10:30am (2hr.; €13) and 1:30pm (2hr.; €16), and at variable times throughout the day. English bus tours 10am and 12:30pm (2hr., €13) and 1:30pm (2hr., €16). Themed walking tours M-F at 3pm, Sa-Su 2pm, some in English (2hr., €7-8). Later walking tours Friday evenings (1½hr. , €6). For information call ☎0341 710 42 80.

Budget Travel: STA Travel, Neumarkt 9-19 (☎0341 211 42 20; www.statravel.de). Enter from Universitätstr., near the university. Open M-F 10am-7pm, Sa 10am-2pm.

Consulate: US, Wilhelm-Seyferth-Str. 4 (☎0341 21 38 40). Cross the Innenstadt ring behind the Neues Rathaus and follow Tauchnitzstr. until Wilhelm-Seyferth-Str. comes up on the left. The entrance is through Grassistr., the next street to the left.

Currency Exchange: Commerzbank, Thomaskirchhof 22, across the street from the church on the western side of the Innenstadt. (☎0341 141 50. Open M and W 9am-4pm, Tu and Th 9am-6pm, F 9am-1pm.) **Citibank,** Goethestr. 1, just before the Opernhaus on the eastern side. Both exchange foreign currency and have **24hr ATMs.**

Women's Resources: Frauenkultur, Windscheidstr. 51 (☎0341 213 0030; www.frauenkultur.leipzig.w4w.net), is a center for art, meetings, and leisure. Take tram #9, 10, or 11 to "Connewitz, Kreuz," then make a right onto Selneckerstr. and turn right again onto Windscheidstr.; the building is located in 1st alley on the right. Office open M-F 9am-2pm, later for afternoon events. Runs evening women's cafe; call for schedule.

Gay and Lesbian Resources: AIDS-Hilfe, Ossietzkystr. 18 (☎0341 232 31 27). Take tram #1 (dir.: Schönefeld/Stannebeinpl.) to "Ossietzkystr./Gorkistr." The complex features a popular cafe (open Tu and Th 5-10pm), and distributes the magazine *gegen-*

pol, which has gay information for Saxony. Office open M and W 10am-6pm, Tu and Th 10am-10pm, F 10am-2pm.

Home Share: Mitwohnzentrale, Goethestr. 7-10 (☎0341 194 30; www.mwz-leipzig.de), in the same office as the Mitfahrzentrale. Arranges long-term accommodations (3 months and up, from €250 a month). Open daily 9am-7pm.

Laundromat: Maga Pon, Gottschedstr. 11 (☎0341 337 3782). A university town classic: sip espresso (€1.60) while you wash your clothes at this hip, domestic cafe. Breakfast until 3pm (€3.50-8). Wash €3.80. Dry €1.80. Detergent complimentary. Open M-F from 11am, Sa-Su from 10am until midnight or later

Emergency: Police ☎110. **Fire** and **Ambulance** ☎112.

Pharmacy: Löwen-Apotheke, Grimmaischestr. 19 (☎0341 246 0424). Open M-Th 8am-8pm, F 8am-9pm, Sa 9am-8pm.

Internet Access: IntertelCafe has two locations: one at Reichsstr. 16 (☎0341 225 5402), and another at Am Bruehl 64 (☎0341 225 5402), in the pedestrian passage connecting Bruehl and Nikolaistr. €2 per hr. Open daily 10am-10pm.

Post Office: Augustuspl. 2-4, across Georgiring from the Opernhaus. Open M-F 9am-8pm, Sa 9am-3pm. **Postal Code:** 04109.

SACHSEN

ACCOMMODATIONS AND CAMPING

Hostel Sleepy Lion, Käthe-Kollwitz-Str. 3 (☎0341 993 9480; www.hostel-leipzig.de). A 10min. walk from the station; cross the street and turn right onto Richard-Wagner-Str. After the skate park, turn left. Follow Gördelerring until Käthe-Kollwitz-Str. veers to the right. Or, take tram #1 (dir.: Lausen) or #14 (dir.: S-Bahnhof Plagwitz) to "Gottschedstr." Operated by young locals and close to nightlife, the Sleepy Lion draws an international crowd. In the lounge, pool balls crackle (€1 a game) and upbeat music blasts around the clock. Spacious rooms have personal lockers and showers. Sheets €2.50. Breakfast €3.50. Internet access €2 per hr. Bike rental €5 per day. Reception 24hr. 5-, 6-, and 8-bed dorms €13-16, singles €29.50, doubles €42; quads €68. AmEx/MC/V. ❶

Central Globetrotter, Kurt-Schumacher-Str. 41 (☎0341 149 89 60; www.globetrotter-leipzig.de). From the train station, take the west exit and turn right onto Kurt-Schumacher-Str. Wild spray-paint designs cover the walls of this backpacker's hostel, run by the same people as the Sleepy Lion. Kitchen access. Breakfast €3.50. Internet access €2 per hr. Sheets €2.50. Reception 24hr. 6- to 8-bed dorms €13-14, singles €24, doubles €36, triples €42, quads €60. AmEx/MC/V. ❶

Hotel Weißes Roß, Auguste-Schmidt-Str. 20 (☎0341 960 5951). From the station take tram #11 (dir.: Markkleeberg-Ost), #8 (dir.: Wilhelm-Leuschnerpl.) or #10 or 16 (dir.: Lößnig) to "Augustuspl.," and head to the left of the Gewandhaus. Or, walk left out of the train station, and right onto Georgiring. At Roßpl., take the pedestrian street to the left. Go through the archway opposite the skyscraper; the hotel is 100m ahead. Comfortable rooms in sepia tones. The attached restaurant serves dinner. Breakfast included. Reception M-F 5-10pm; call ahead at other times. Singles €31, with shower €35; doubles €49/55. Lower rates when less busy, longer stays negotiable. Cash only. ❸

Ibis Hotel, Brühl 69 (☎0341 218 60; www.ibishotel.com). From the Hauptbahnhof, cross the street and head a block down Goethestr., toward the left. Take a right onto the Brühl. If you run out of budget options, the classy Ibis (part of a large chain) is a 2min. walk from the train station. Impeccably clean with reliable service and no surprises. Reception 24hr. Breakfast €9.50. Ask for a floor with free Wi-Fi, or use the free PC downstairs. Rooms from €62. Book online 30 days in advance for discounts. AmEx/MC/V. ❺

JCamping & Motel Am Auensee, Gustav-Esche-Str. 5 (☎0341 465 16 00; www.camping-auensee.de), by a lake in the nearby suburb of Wahren 6km from the city center. From the station, take tram #10 (dir.: Wahren) or #11 (dir: Schkeuditz) to "Wahren."

THE ABSORBING SORBS

The Sorbs, Germany's only indigenous ethnic minority, are descended from Slavic tribes that settled the Spreewald and Lusatian mountains during the 6th and 7th centuries. The Sorbian language is similar to Czech and Polish and is divided into two basic dialects: *Niedersorbisch* (Low Sorbian), spoken around Cottbus, and *Obersorbisch* (High Sorbian), spoken near Bautzen. Since the formation of the Sorb nationalist movement in 1848, small Sorbisch-speaking communities have maintained regional identities.

The Sorbs are famous for intricately dyed Easter eggs and *Osterreiten,* horseback processions that take place every Easter Sunday. January 25 marks the *Vogelhochzeit* (birds' wedding), during which costumed children act as birds grateful for seeds left over from a marriage celebration. All winter, children feed the birds and are rewarded with sweets and cookies during this festival.

The Prussians all but destroyed the Sorbian culture in the 17th and 18th centuries, and the Nazis nearly wiped them out in 1937. Despite post-war laws protecting the Sorbian culture and language, both are in decline: only about 60,000 people still live in Sorbian communities. Younger generations are moving to big cities in large numbers, but many communities are working to ensure that children learn Sorbian in school and that their time-honored customs will continue for years to come.

Turn left before the Rathaus onto Linkelstr. and follow the twisting main road (10min.); it will be on your right. Reception daily 7:30am-1pm and 2-9:30pm. €4 per person, €3-5 per tent, €2-6 per car. 1-bed bungalows €29; 2-bed €39, with shower €59; 3-bed €55. Public showers €0.75. MC/V. ❶

FOOD

Leipzig's Innenstadt, especially **Grimmaischestraße,** is well supplied with *Imbiße* (snack bars), bistros, and bakeries, and has a **market** on Richard-Wagner-Pl., at the end of the Brühl (Tu and F 8am-4pm). Escape downtown crowds and Barfussg. prices with a jaunt to **Karl-Liebknecht-Straße,** packed with well-priced cafes and bars. To get there from the Markt, take Peterstr. to Petersteinweg (15min.), or hop on tram #11 (dir.: Markkleeberg-Ost) or #10 (dir.: Lößnig) to "Südpl." Most cafes offer Sunday brunch.

Bellini's, Barfussgässchen 3-7 (☎0341 961 7681), off the Markt. If you're itching to eat in the swarm of Barfussgasse, head here, the most reasonably priced eatery on the row. All dishes under €10. Crispy baguettes €4-5.50. Colorful salads and pastas €7.60-9.80. Open daily from noon. MC/V. ❸

100-Wasser Cafe, Barfussgasse 15 (☎0341 215 7927), on the corner with Grosse Fleischergasse. With a pelican mosaic and psychedelic puzzle pieces covering the ceiling, this two-tiered cafe and bar vividly evokes its namesake. Pastas €5.50-7.50. Other entrees €7-10. Lunch specials 11am-3pm, €4-4.50. Open daily from 8am. Kitchen closes midnight M-Th and Su, F-Sa at 1am. Bar open later. MC/V €15 minimum. ❹

Auerbachs Keller, Grimmaischestr. 2-4 (☎0341 21 61 00; www.auerbachs-keller-leipzig.de), across from the Altes Rathaus, inside the Mädlerpassage. First opening in 1525, this palatial cellar has endless dark wood and vaulted ceilings accented red and gold. It's truly a Leipzig institution. In Goethe's *Faust,* Mephistopheles tricks some drunkards here before carrying Faust away on an enchanted beer barrel. Check out Faust scenes on the walls, along with other intriguing paintings, over a long meal in this elegant but unpretentious restaurant. Entrees €12-25. Open daily 11:30am-midnight. Martin Luther sipped spirits in the historic wine room (entrees €26-32), open M-Sa 6pm-midnight. Kitchen closes 10pm. MC/V/AmEx. ❺

Aladin Döner, Burgstr. 12 (☎0170 97 66 67 07), just south of the Thomaskirche, on the corner with Ratsfreischulstr. Take their magic carpet ride to a whole new world of cylindrical meat—it's the best kebap in town.

Free cup of tea at the end of your meal. *Döner Kebap* €3, fries €1.50. Open M-W 10am-11pm, Th-Su 10am-1am. Cash only. ❶

Zur Pleißenburg, Ratsfreischulstr. 2 (☎0341 960 2653), located just down Burgstr. from the Thomaskirche. Classic street signs decorate the rafters, and the menu nostalgically retains its DM prices alongside the newfangled Euro. *Schnitzel, Rostbrätl, Goulasch,* and more €4.50-8.80. Lunch specials (M-F 11am-3pm) €4.80. English menu available. Open daily 9am-5am. Kitchen open until 4am. Cash only. ❸

SIGHTS

Leipzig's Innenstadt is surprisingly heterogeneous. Most streets are a mix of elegant old townhouses, institutional DDR relics, and gleaming new shopping malls—the product of Leipzig's post-1991 building spree. **Augustsplatz** reveals the breadth of Leipzig's architectural palette: the tidy Opera house, the glass-facaded Gewandhaus, the skyscraping Panorama tower, and Baroque residences. Most of Leipzig's museums and sights are near **Marktplatz,** currently under construction for a new bus station.

VÖLKERSCHLACHTDENKMAL (MONUMENT TO THE BATTLE OF NATIONS). Southeast of the city ring, this massive jagged temple, built in 1913 to look like a Mesopotamian ziggurat, memorializes the 120,000 soldiers who died in the 1813 Battle of Nations—a six-day struggle that turned the tide against Napoleon and determined many of Europe's national boundaries as they stand today. The cavernous interior bears witness to the extreme nationalism of the era in which it was built: gigantic stone soldiers lean sadly over their swords as war horses spiral up to the dome. Using the free elevator, the climb to the top is 364 steps. An additional mechanical boost (€1) cuts it down to 214. On the ground, the **Forum 1813 museum** describes the battle with paintings and soldiers' uniforms. *(Prager Str. Take tram #15 from the Hauptbahnhof (dir.: Meusdorf) to "Völkerschlachtdenkmal" (15min.), then take the street on the right and follow the hand-railed path up to the left. ☎0341 961 8538; www.voelkerschlachtdenkmal.de. Museum and memorial open daily Apr.-Oct. 10am-6pm, Nov.-Mar. 10am-4pm. Monument only €5, students €3. Museum only €3/2. Both €7/4.50. Free tour Sa 11am. English-language audio tour €1. Signs in English.)*

THOMASKIRCHE. Down Thomasgasse from the Altes Rathaus is the church where the famed composer Johann Sebastian Bach spent the last 27 years of his career, serving as as cantor until his death in 1750. Dressed in sparkling white and decorated in the neo-Gothic style, the church pays simple and fitting homage to the composer, buried beneath the floor of the choir room. Bach's beefy figure dwarfs the organ between two trees on Thomaskirchhof. The organ from Bach's day did not survive, but they do keep a Baroque instrument collection and baptismal certificates of the 12 Bach children born in Leipzig. The **Thomanerchor,** once directed by Bach, is one of Europe's most prestigious boys' choirs. *(☎0341 22 22 40; www.thomaskirche.org. Church open daily 9am-6pm. Free. Thomanerchor Motette F 6pm, and Sa 3pm; €2. Also during Sunday services 9:30am and 6pm.)*

MUSEUMS

Leipzig posesses two assets which conspire to produce a fabulous museum landscape: a rich past and intellectual demand. As the hometown of classical musicians and early 20th-century artists, and as the epicenter of DDR collapse, there's no shortage of history here. Research institutes, in partnership with the University of Leipzig, have meticulously tracked this heritage.

MUSEUM IN DER "RUNDEN ECKE" (MUSEUM IN THE "ROUND CORNER"). The East German *Staatssicherheit,* or simply *Stasi,* was the largest per capita secret police force in world history. Over 91,000 official employees produced miles of paper and mountains of cassettes and photographs in their attempts to keep tabs on suspected "enemies of the state." In 1950 the "Runden Ecke" building, comprised of a cylindrical domain and two wings projecting outward at a right angle, became Stasi district headquarters. When the Leipzig Citizens' Committee wrested the building from *Stasi* hands during the Peaceful Revolution, they preserved and put on display most of the tools used to play Big Brother, including machines to secretly open and reseal up to 2000 letters per day. The archive, including citizen profiles with everything from handwriting samples to scents, is the largest of its kind in Germany. The museum staff also gives tours of a bunker nearby (for *Stasi* refuge in the event of "tension") that contains an exhibit detailing the organization's unrealized plans. Every Saturday at 2pm a tour departs from the door of St. Nikolai's Church, stopping at major landmarks of the Peaceful Revolution. *(Dittrichring 24. ☎0341 961 2443; www.runde-ecke-leipzig.de. Open daily 10am-6pm. Free. Tours in German 3pm (€3, students €2), in English for groups by appointment. Ask for an English handout at the office. Bunker tours (€3) are at 1-4pm on the last Sa and Su of the month.)*

MUSEEN IM GRASSI. The newly renovated, coral-red Grassi complex houses three distinct museums, each more charming than the next. The **Museum für Musikinstrumente** (Musical Instrument Museum) shows anything that squawks, bellows, chimes, toots or buzzes from the 16th-century Rennaisance period through to the present. Make some noise of your own upstairs in the Klanglabor ("noise laboratory"), where a free-standing organ, transparent pianos, and a sea of percussion intruments invite your clumsy hands. *(☎0341 973 07 50; mfm.uni-leipzig.de. €4, students €2.)* Take a world tour in the **Museum für Völkerkunde** (Ethnographical Museum), which displays artifacts from all corners of the globe. Learn how the swastika appeared in its original Indian context, how to stay warm in Siberia, and how best to float on the Tigris. *(☎0341 97 31 100. €4, students €2. Special exhibitions €4/2. All receive student price entry every first Tu of the month.)* Western Europeans are spared gawking ethnographic scrutiny, but their wares and artifacts can be seen in the **Museum für Angewandte Kunst** (Applied Arts Museum). A labyrinth of thirty period-pegged rooms takes you through two millenia of human trinkets. In addition to regal Saxon metalwork and Meissen porcelain, there is also a focus on the private life: check out the personal drinking tankards, a fashion in the German baroque period, or the wall of 94 delicate cups and saucers. Pick up an English guide at the exhibition entrance. *(Johannisplatz 5-11. From Augustusplatz, take Grimmaischer Steinweg across Georgiring for 200m. ☎0341 22 29 100; www.grassimuseum.de. €5, students €3.50. Special exhibitions €6/4. Permanent and special €8/5.50. First W of the month free.) Museums open Tu-Su 9am-6pm. Völkerkunde and Angewandte Kunst combination ticket €8, students €6. All three €12/9. English audio tour €1.)*

MUSEUM DER BILDENDEN KÜNSTE LEIPZIG (LEIPZIG FINE ARTS MUSEUM). Leipzig's art collection breathes freely in this airy glass building. Highlights include classic modernist paintings by Leipziger Max Beckmann, and the magisterial 'Beethoven' statue by Max Klinger, another local, which broods deservingly in its own room. On the floors above hang paintings ranging from Old Masters like Cranach the Elder to giant splotchy 20th-century canvases by East German artists. The size of the museum lets you soak up paintings from a distance. *(Katharinenstr. 10. Take Katharinenstr. from the Markt and the museum appears conspicuously on your right after 150m. ☎0341 21 6990; www.mdbk.de. Open Tu and Th-Su 10am-6pm, W noon-8pm. €5, students €3.50. Special exhibits €6/4. Both €8/5.)*

JOHANN-SEBASTIAN-BACH-MUSEUM. The Bach Museum's informative exhibits emphasize his role as choir director, teacher, and city musician, focusing on the composer's life and work in Leipzig, where he wrote his Mass in B minor and both the St. John and St. Matthew Passions. In total, he composed over 300 *cantatas* here. The museum host to concerts during the fall. In addition, Leipzig holds an annual Bach festival every June. *(Thomaskirchhof 16, across from the Bach statue. ☎0341 913 7202; www.bach-leipzig.de. Open daily 11am-6pm. Admission free.)*

ZEITGESCHICHTLICHES FORUM LEIPZIG (FORUM FOR CONTEMPORARY HISTORY). Through the glass doors behind Wolfgang Mattheuer's long-legged *Jahrhundertschritt* statue, the forum provides a comprehensive and thoughtful look at the metamorphoses of east Germany and the SED since WWII. The museum transitions from Soviet Occupied Zone to Reunification. Old propaganda and cultural artifacts transport visitors to the various phases of DDR history, some tranquil, others turbulent. Special exhibits on the third floor cover contemporary issues in German society. *(Grimmaischestr. 6. ☎0341 222 00; www.hdg.de. Open Tu-F 9am-6pm, Sa-Su 10am-6pm. Free. 1½hr. tours in German Sa 3pm, Su 11am.)*

SACHSEN

MENDELSSOHN-HAUS. This gorgeous house was the residence of composer Felix Mendelssohn-Bartholdy for two of the years (1845-1847) that he lived in Leipzig. Mendelssohn, ever the nostalgic, led a revival of interest in Bach, conducting performances of his music at the Gewandhaus. Some rooms have been furnished to appear as Mendelssohn knew them, while others house exhibits on his life and work. The **Musiksalon** holds 1hr. concerts Su 11am, and also hosts the annual Leipzig Piano Summer series and Mendelssohn Festival. *(Goldschmidtstr. 12. Take Rosspl., a piece of the Innenstadt's outer ring, south away from the Opernhaus, then a left down Goldschmidtstr. ☎0341 127 0294; www.mendelsson-stiftung.de. Open daily 10am-6pm. €3.50, students €2.50 Concerts €12, students €8.)*

ENTERTAINMENT

The patrons who frequent the eclectic cafes scattered around Leipzig also support a world-class theater and music scene. Leipzig offers a variety of famous musical groups. The first is the **Gewandhaus-Orchester,** a major international orchestra that has been performing since 1843. Purchase tickets for all of their venues at the Gewandhaus box office, Augustuspl. 8. (☎0341 127 0280; www.gewandhaus.de. €9-26 and up. Most concerts 20% off for students. Open M-F 10am-6pm, Sa 10am-2pm, and 1hr. before performances.) Leipzig's boxy, gold-trimmed **Opera,** Augustuspl. 12, gives Dresden's Semperoper a run for its money in programming, if not architecturally. In the summer the opera hosts international music and ballet. Last-minute tickets cost €10, €6 for those under 27. (☎0341 126 12 61; www.oper-leipzig.de. Counter and phone lines open M-F 10am-8pm, Sa 10am-6pm, and 1hr. before performances. You can find a seat at every show for €12-33, students 30% off.) The opera house is also an entry point to Leipzig's diverse theater scene, hosting the experimental **Kellertheater** in its basement (tickets €15, students €11). The **Schauspielhaus,** Bosestr. 1 just off Dittrichring, produces the classics, and occasionally presents pieces of outdoor vertical theater, in which the theater's side becomes the stage, and actors block by climbing up the walls. The Schauspielhaus also runs the contemporary **Neue Szene,** nearby at Gottschedstr. 16. (☎0341 126 8168; www.schauspiel-leipzig.de. Tickets from €7-17. Check the schedule for the monthly Theatertag, when all tickets are €5.55. Box office open M-F 10am-7pm, Sa 10am-1pm, and 1½hr. before performance.) Leipzig has a prominent **cabaret** scene. The most popular with students is **academixer,** on Kupfergasse right by the university. They present both politial and social satire every night at 8pm, they are one of the few without summer closings. (☎0341 21 78 78 78; www.academixer.com. Box office open daily 10am-8pm. Tickets €10-17 and up.) The **Leipziger Pfeffermühle,** Gottschedstr. 1, the oldest cabaret in the city (founded 1954), puts on knee-slapper political satire nightly at 8pm for an older crowd (☎0341

960 3196; www.kabarett-leipziger-pfeffermuehle.de. Open M-F 10am-8pm, Sa 3-8pm, and Su 2hr. before shows. Tickets M-Th €15, students €10; F-Su €18.) **naTo,** Karl-Liebknecht-Str. 46 (☎0341 303 9133; www.nato-leipzig.de), shows foreign flicks in original languages with German subtitles in an old DDR mess hall on Suedplatz. (2 screenings daily, usually 8pm and 9:45m. tickets €5.50, students €4.50.) October brings Leipzig's renowned **International Festival for Documentary and Animated Film.** (☎0341 980 39 21; www.dok-leipzig.de.)

NIGHTLIFE

Free German-language magazines *Fritz* and *Blitz* will fill you in on nightlife, but *Kreuzer* is indispensible for the low-down on local bars, clubs, and events. **Barfußgäßchen,** a street just off the Markt, serves as the see-and-be-seen bar venue for everyone from students to *Schicki-Mickis* (yuppies). In the summer, there's only a narrow pedestrian channel between the packed parasol-covered cafe tables. **Zum Arabischen Coffe Baum,** the oldest coffee house in the city, **Zigarre,** and **Varadero** all fill by 10pm. Robert Schumann used to hang out at Coffe Baum. Though crowds dwindle by midnight, the most popular bars stay packed until 3am on a good night. Just across Dittrichring on **Gottschedstraße** and **Bosestraße,** a similar scene takes place in bars like **Neue Szene** and the **Milchbar,** but with a slightly younger and more boisterous crowd. Karl-Liebknecht-Str. hosts Leipzig's alternative scene. The bars are more spread out, but also more distinctive. Take tram #11 (dir.: Markkleeburg-Ost) or 10 (dir.: Lößnig) to "Südpl." The Irish pub Killiwilly at Karl-Liebknecht Str. 44 offers good cheer (and Murphy's Stout, Strongbow, and Guinness for €3.60 a pint), while farther south, Weißes Rössel is more chill. The cafe scene constantly hums in the background, but dance clubs welcome more active revelers Tu-W and F-Sa.

Moritzbastei, Universitätsstr. 9 (☎0341 70 25 90; www.moritzbastei.de), behind the university tower. University students spent 8 years excavating a series of medieval tunnels to create this subterranean dance club. The result: a huge complex housing cafes, hammock-filled Biergarten, movie theater, multilevel dance floor, and relaxed bars. The W and Sa **All You Can Dance** disco blasts pounding music in cavernous vaulted brick rooms, producing reverberations you won't find anywhere else in Leipzig. The 3 underground dance floors are connected by a perfectly lit, high-ceilinged tunnels, that imbue a nocturnal, medieval romanticism. The music ranges from metal to minimal techno so all ears are happy. Cover €4, students with ID €2.50; slightly more for concerts (some require advance ticket purchase; office on street level M-F 10am-6pm). Cash only.

Cafe Barbakan, in the Moritzbastei (☎0341 702 5930). Brunch, hammocks and free internet. On disco nights, Barbakan connects to the rest of the complex, providing respite from the underground madness. Opens M-F 10am-late, Sa noon-late, Su 9am-late. An **open-air movie theater** screens indie and foreign films July-Aug. daily at 10pm, weather permitting. €5, students €4. Cash only.

Night Fever, Gottschedstr. 4 (☎0341 149 9990; www.night-fever.net). This disco has more stamina than did John Travolta, who is painted inspirationally on the wall. Crowds relish in colorful lights, super-fly music from the 70s and 80s, and a free cover. Tu beer €1.30, wine €1.50, cocktails €2.10. Open Tu and F-Sa from 10pm.

nachtcafe limited, Petersstr. 39-41 (☎0341 221 0000; www.nachtcafe.com). The parties here feature hip hop and house on two floors as well as a celebrity air, red awning and all. Cover €5. Open W and F-Sa from 10pm-5am, last entry 3am.

Distillery, Kurt-Eisner-Str. 108a (☎0341 35 59 74 00; www.distillery.de), near the corner of Lößinger Str. Take tram #9 (dir.: Markkleeberg-West) to the "K.-Eisner/A.-Hoffman-Str.", stop, and turn left. A little out of the way, this edgy industrial-yard-turned-club plays house, techno, and rock. Cover €5 before midnight, €7 after; W no cover. Opens at 11pm, although things don't heat up until around 1am. Closed late July to early Sept.

Cafe Spizz, Markt 9 (☎0341 960 8043; www.spizz.org). The bar takes up two storefronts, and tables spill deep into Barfussgasse. Big jazz names show up occasionally for weekend concerts, while W "Piano Boogie Night" jam sessions attract an almost cult-like following. Weekend club nights in the disco below entertain a slightly older crowd. Club cover €3, W free, Sa ladies free until 1am; concerts €20-80. Club open W and F-Sa 10pm-5am, cafe daily from 10am. Cash only.

Schauhaus, Bosestr. 1 (☎0341 960 0596; www.schauhaus-leipzig.de) On the corner with Dittrichring, this club hosts the 18-21 crowd, lured in by weekday discos (Tu-Su) and cheap cover (€0.75). Free entry until 11pm. On F-Sa, a second floor opens.

GATEWAY CITY: PRAGUE

Home to the stately Prague Castle and Old Town Square's pastel facades, Prague (pop. 1,200,000) retains small-town charm despite its size. In the 14th century, Holy Roman Emperor Charles IV refurbished Prague with stone bridges and lavish palaces still visible today. Since the lifting of the Iron Curtain in 1989, outsiders have flooded the Czech capital. In summer, most locals leave for the countryside when the foreigner-to-resident ratio soars above nine-to-one. Despite rising prices and a hyper-touristed Staré Město (Old Town), Prague still commands the awe of its visitors.

PRAGUE

HIGHLIGHTS OF PRAGUE

GAZE hundreds of miles in every direction from **Prague Castle** (p. 489), one of the largest in the world and the seat of the Czech government for 1000 years.

RELIVE the legend at the **Franz Kafka Museum** (p. 490).

OGLE with the crowds at the Staré Město's impressive **astronomical clock** (p. 488).

INTERCITY TRANSPORTATION

Flights: Ruzyně Airport (PRG; ☎220 111 111), 20km northwest of the city. Take bus #119 to Metro A: Dejvická (12Kč, luggage 6Kč per bag); buy tickets from kiosks or machines. Airport **buses** run by Cedaz (☎220 114 296; 20-45 min., 2 per hr.) collect travelers from nám. Republiky (120Kč); try to settle on a price before departing.

Trains: (☎221 111 122, international 224 615 249; www.vlak.cz). Prague has 4 main terminals. **Hlavní nádraží** (☎224 615 786; Metro C: Hlavní nádraží) and **Nádraží Holešovice** (☎224 624 632; Metro C: Nádraží Holešovice) are the largest and cover most international service. Domestic trains leave **Masarykovo nádraží** (☎840 112 113; Metro B: nám. Republiky) and from **Smíchovské nádraží** (☎972 226 150; Metro B: Smíchovské nádraží). International trains run to: **Berlin, GER** (5hr., 6 per day, 1500Kč); **Bratislava, SLK** (5hr., 6 per day, 650Kč); **Budapest, HUN** (7-9hr., 5 per day, 1400Kč); **Kraków, POL** (7-8hr., 3 per day, 900Kč); **Moscow, RUS** (31hr., 1 per day, 3000Kč); **Munich, GER** (7hr., 3 per day, 1650Kč); **Vienna, AUT** (4-5hr., 7 per day, 1000Kč); **Warsaw, POL** (9hr., 2 per day, 1350Kč).

Buses (☎900 144 444; www.vlak-bus.cz). State-run **ČSAD** (☎257 319 016) has several terminals. The biggest is **Florenc,** Křižíkova 4 (☎900 149 044; Metro B or C: Florenc). Info office open daily 6am-9pm. To: **Berlin, GER** (7hr., 2 per day, 900Kč); **Budapest, HUN** (8hr., 3 per day, 1600Kč); **Paris, FRA** (15hr., 2 per day, 2200Kč); **Sofia, BUL** (24hr., 2 per day, 1600Kč); **Vienna, AUT** (5hr., 1 per day, 600Kč). 10% ISIC discount. **Tourbus** office (☎224 218 680; www.eurolines.cz), at the terminal, sells Eurolines and airport bus tickets. Open M-F 7am-7pm, Sa 8am-7pm, Su 9am-7pm.

ORIENTATION

Shouldering the river **Vltava,** greater Prague is a mess of suburbs and maze-like streets. All sightseeing destinations are in the compact downtown. The

Vltava runs south to north through central Prague, separating **Staré Město** (Old Town) and **Nové Město** (New Town) from **Malá Strana** (Lesser Side). On the right bank, **Staroměstské náměstí** (Old Town Square) is Prague's focal point. From the square, the elegant **Pařížská ulice** (Paris Street) leads north into Josefov, the old Jewish quarter. South of Staré Město, the Nové Město houses **Václavské náměstí** (Wenceslas Square), the city's commercial core. West of Staroměstské nám., **Karlův Most** (Charles Bridge) spans the Vltava, connecting Staré Město with **Malostranské náměstí** (Lesser Town Square). **Pražský Hrad** (Prague Castle) overlooks Malostranské nám. from Hradčany hill. The train station and bus station lie northeast of Václavské nám. To reach Staroměstské nám., take Metro A line to Staroměstská and follow Kaprova away from the river.

LOCAL TRANSPORTATION

Public Transportation: Buy **interchangeable tickets** for the bus, Metro, and tram at newsstands, *tabák* kiosks, machines in stations, or the DP (Dopravní podnik; transport authority) kiosks. Validate tickets in machines above escalators to avoid fines issued by plainclothes inspectors who roam transport lines. 3 **Metro** lines run daily 5am-midnight: A is green on maps, B yellow, C red. **Night trams** #51-58 and **buses** #502-514 and 601 run after the last Metro and cover the same areas as day trams and buses (2 per hr. 12:30am-4:30am); look for dark blue signs with white letters at bus stops. 18Kč tickets are good for a 20min. ride or 5 stops. 26Kč tickets are valid for 1hr., with transfers, for all travel in the same direction. Large bags and baby carriages 6Kč. DP offices (☎296 191 817; www.dpp.cz; open daily 7am-9pm), in the Muzeum stop on Metro A and C lines, sells **multi-day passes** (1-day 100Kč, 3-day 330Kč, 5-day 500Kč).

Taxis: City Taxi (☎257 257 257) and **AAA** (☎140 14). 40Kč base, 25Kč per km, 5Kč per min. waiting. Hail a cab anywhere, but call ahead to avoid getting ripped off.

> TIP **GOING THE DISTANCE.** To avoid being scammed by taxis, always ask in advance for a receipt *(Prosím, dejte mi paragon;* please, give me a receipt*)* with distance traveled and price paid.

PRACTICAL INFORMATION

Tourist Offices: Green "i"s mark tourist offices. **Pražská Informační Služba (PIS;** Prague Information Service; ☎12 444; www.pis.cz) is in the **Staroměstské Radnice** (Old Town Hall). Open Apr.-Oct. daily 9am-7pm; Nov.-Mar. daily 9am-6pm. Branches at Na příkopě 20 and Hlavní nádraží. Open in summer M-F 9am-7pm, Sa-Su 9am-5pm; winter M-F 9am-6pm, Sa 9am-3pm. Branch in the tower by the Malá Strana side of the Charles Bridge. Open Apr.-Oct. daily 10am-6pm.

Budget Travel: CKM, Mánesova 77 (☎222 721 595; www.ckm-praha.cz). Metro A: Jiřího z Poděbrad. Sells budget airline tickets to those under 26. Also books accommodations in Prague from 350Kč. Open M-Th 10am-6pm, F 10am-4pm. **GTS,** Ve smečkách 27 (☎222 119 700; www.gtsint.cz). Metro A or C: Muzeum. Offers student discounts on airline tickets (225-2500Kč in Europe). Open M-F 8am-10pm, Sa 10am-5pm.

Embassies and Consulates: Australia, Klimentská 10, 6th fl. (☎296 578 350; www.embassy.gov.au/cz.html; open M-Th 8:30am-5pm, F 8:30am-2pm) and **New Zealand,** Dykova 19 (☎222 514 672) have consulates, but citizens should contact the UK embassy in an emergency. **Canada,** Muchova 6 (☎272 101 800; www.canada.cz). Open M-F 8:30am-12:30pm and 1:30-4:30pm. Consular office open only in the morning.

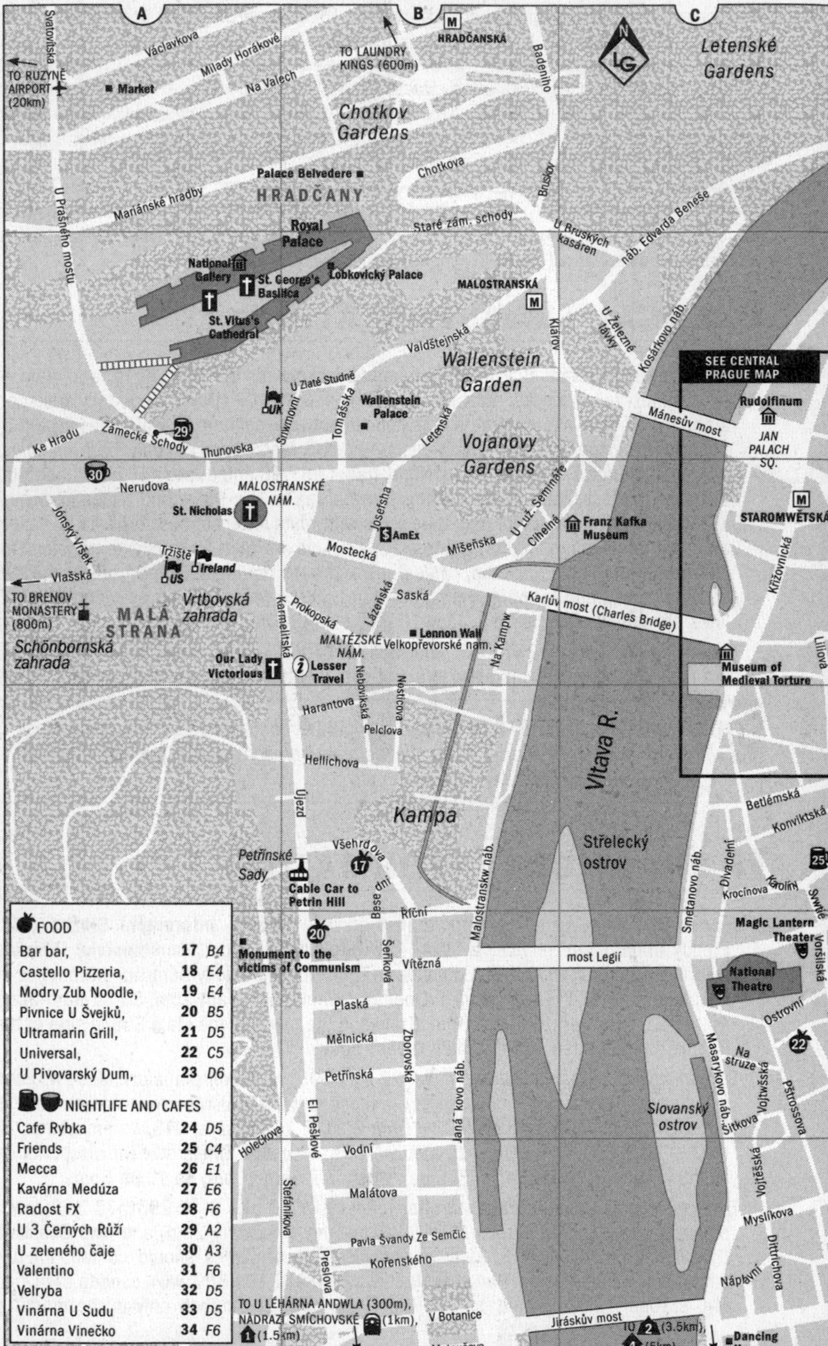
A
B
C
TO RUZYNĚ AIRPORT (20km)
Market
TO LAUNDRY KINGS (600m)
HRADČANSKÁ
Letenské Gardens
Chotkov Gardens
Palace Belvedere
HRADČANY
Royal Palace
National Gallery
St. George's Basilica
Lobkovický Palace
St. Vitus's Cathedral
MALOSTRANSKÁ
Wallenstein Garden
Wallenstein Palace
Vojanovy Gardens
SEE CENTRAL PRAGUE MAP
Rudolfinum
JAN PALACH SQ.
STAROMWĚTSKÁ
Mánesův most
MALOSTRANSKÉ NÁM.
St. Nicholas
AmEx
Franz Kafka Museum
Ireland
US
UK
TO BRENOV MONASTERY (800m)
MALÁ STRANA
Vrtbovská zahrada
Schönbornská zahrada
Karlův most (Charles Bridge)
Museum of Medieval Torture
Lennon Wall
MALTÉZSKÉ NÁM.
Velkopřevorské nám.
Our Lady Victorious
Lesser Travel
Vltava R.
Kampa
Střelecký ostrov
Petřínské Sady
Cable Car to Petrin Hill
Monument to the victims of Communism
Magic Lantern Theater
National Theatre
most Legií
Slovanský ostrov
Jiráskův most
Dancing House
Václavkova
Milady Horákové
Na Valech
Badeniho
Chotkova
Bruskov
Mariánské hradby
U Prašného mostu
Svatovítská
Staré zám. schody
U Bruských kasáren
náb. Edvarda Beneše
U Železné lávky
Kosárkovo náb.
Klárov
Valdštejnská
U Zlaté Studně
Tomášská
Letenská
Sněmovní
Ke Hradu
Zámecké Schody
Thunovska
Nerudova
Jánský Vršek
Vlašská
Tržiště
Josefsha
U Luž. Semináře
Cihelná
Mišeňska
Mostecká
Saská
Lázeňská
Prokopská
Karmelitská
Na Kampw
Křižovnická
Liliová
Harantova
Nebovidská
Nostícova
Pelclova
Hellichova
Újezd
Všehrdova
Besední
Říční
Šeříková
Vítězná
Plaská
Mělnická
Zborovská
Petřínská
Janá kovo náb.
Malostranskw náb.
Smetanovo náb.
Betlémská
Konviktská
Divadelní
Krocínova
Karolíny Světlé
Voršilská
Ostrovní
Na struze
Masarykovo náb.
Vojtěšská
Pštrossova
Šitkova
Myslíkova
Dittrichova
Náplavní
Holečkova
El. Peškové
Štefánikova
Vodní
Malátova
Pavla Švandy Ze Semčic
Kořenského
Preslova
V Botanice
Matoušova
TO U LÉHÁRNA ANDWLA (300m), NÁDRAŽÍ SMÍCHOVSKÉ (1km), 1 (1.5km)
TO 2 (3.5km), 4 (5km)
FOOD
Bar bar, 17 B4
Castello Pizzeria, 18 E4
Modry Zub Noodle, 19 E4
Pivnice U Švejků, 20 B5
Ultramarin Grill, 21 D5
Universal, 22 C5
U Pivovarský Dum, 23 D6
NIGHTLIFE AND CAFES
Cafe Rybka 24 D5
Friends 25 C4
Mecca 26 E1
Kavárna Medúza 27 E6
Radost FX 28 F6
U 3 Černých Růží 29 A2
U zeleného čaje 30 A3
Valentino 31 F6
Velryba 32 D5
Vinárna U Sudu 33 D5
Vinárna Vinečko 34 F6

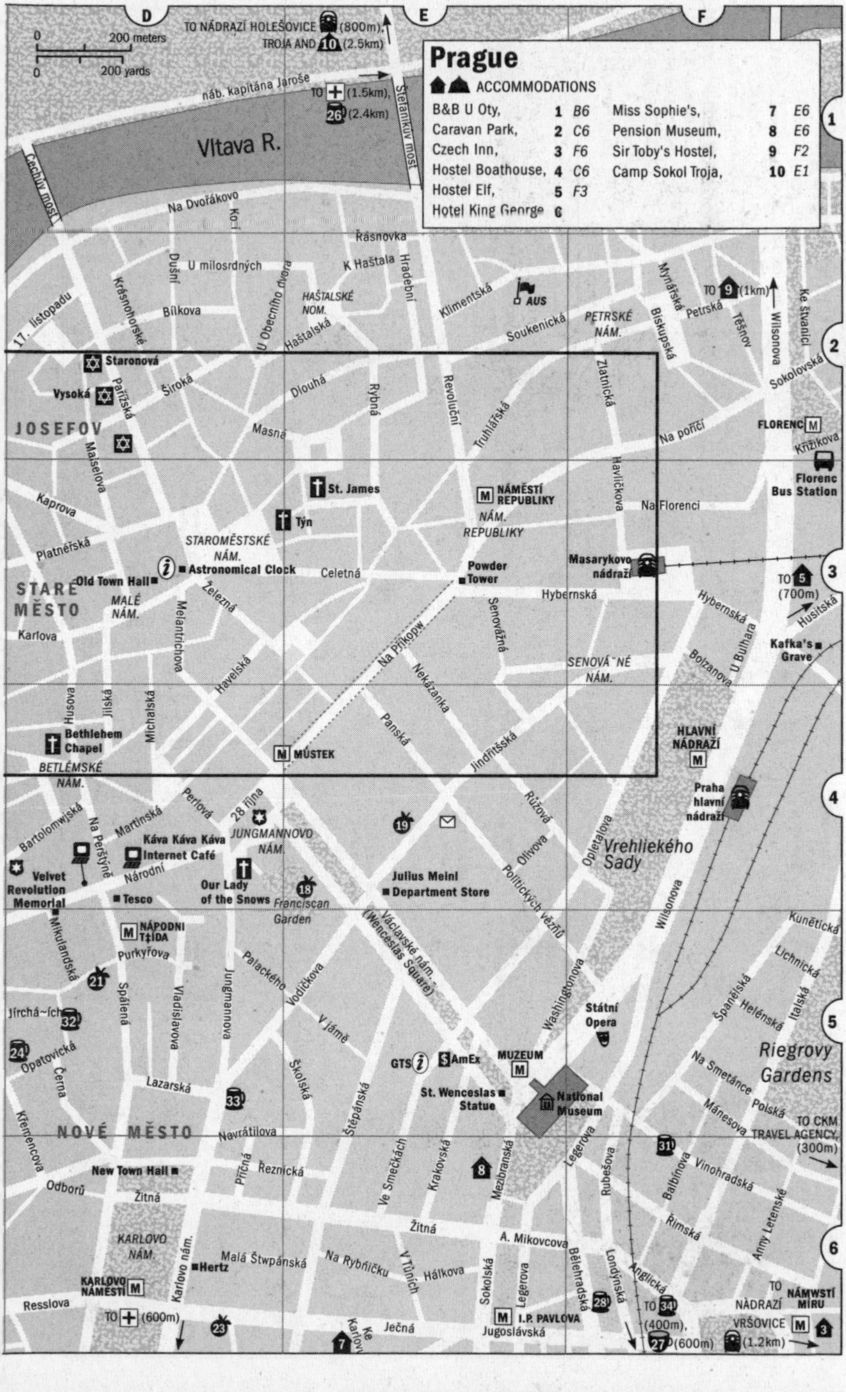
Prague
ACCOMMODATIONS
B&B U Oty, 1 B6
Caravan Park, 2 C6
Czech Inn, 3 F6
Hostel Boathouse, 4 C6
Hostel Elf, 5 F3
Hotel King George 6
Miss Sophie's, 7 E6
Pension Museum, 8 E6
Sir Toby's Hostel, 9 F2
Camp Sokol Troja, 10 E1
0 200 meters
0 200 yards
TO NÁDRAZÍ HOLEŠOVICE (800m),
TROJA AND 10 (2.5km)
TO (1.5km),
26 (2.4km)
Vltava R.
náb. kapitána Jaroše
Štefánikův most
Čechův most
Na Dvořákovo
Řásnovka
K Haštala
U milosrdných
Dušní
Bílkova
Kozí
Krásnohorské
17. listopadu
HAŠTALSKÉ NOM.
Haštalská
Klimentská
AUS
Soukenická
PETRSKÉ NÁM.
Petrská
Biskupská
Mynářská
TO 9 (1km)
Těšnov
Wilsonova
Ke Švanici
Sokolovská
Staronová
Vysoká
JOSEFOV
Pařížská
Široká
Dlouhá
Rybná
Revoluční
Truhlářská
Zlatnická
Masná
Maiselova
Na poříčí
FLORENC
Křižíkova
Florenc Bus Station
St. James
NÁMĚSTÍ REPUBLIKY
NÁM. REPUBLIKY
Havlíčkova
Na Florenci
Kaprova
Týn
STAROMĚSTSKÉ NÁM.
Platnéřská
Astronomical Clock
Celetná
Powder Tower
Masarykovo nádraží
TO 5 (700m)
Old Town Hall
STARÉ MĚSTO
MALÉ NÁM.
Železná
Hybernská
Husitská
Karlova
Melantrichova
Senovážná
Kafka's Grave
Na Příkopě
Havelská
Nekázanka
SENOVÁŽNÉ NÁM.
Bolzanova
U Bulhara
Husova
Jilská
Michalská
Panská
Bethlehem Chapel
BETLÉMSKÉ NÁM.
MŮSTEK
Jindřišská
HLAVNÍ NÁDRAŽÍ
Praha hlavní nádraží
Bartolomějská
Na Perštýně
Martinská
Perlová
28 října
JUNGMANNOVO NÁM.
Růžová
Opletalova
Vrehliekého Sady
Káva Káva Káva Internet Café
Velvet Revolution Memorial
Národní
Our Lady of the Snows
Olivova
Julius Meinl Department Store
Politických vězňů
Tesco
Franciscan Garden
Václavské nám. (Wenceslas Square)
Wilsonova
Mikulandská
NÁPODNI TŘIDA
Purkyňova
Palackého
Vodičkova
Kunětická
Lichnická
Spálená
Vladislavova
Jungmannova
Washingtonova
Státní Opera
Španělská
Helénská
Italská
Jirchá~ích
Opatovická
V jámě
Riegrovy Gardens
Černá
GTS
AmEx
MUZEUM
Na Smetánce
Školská
Lazarská
St. Wenceslas Statue
National Museum
Polská
Mánesova
Křemencova
NOVÉ MĚSTO
Navrátilova
Štěpánská
TO CKM TRAVEL AGENCY (300m)
Ve Smečkách
Krakovská
Mezibranská
Legerova
Rubešova
Balbínova
Vinohradská
New Town Hall
Příčná
Řeznická
Odborů
Žitná
Žitná
Římská
Anny Letenské
KARLOVO NÁM.
A. Mikovcova
Bělehradská
Londýnská
Anglická
Malá Štwpánská
Na Rybníčku
V Tůních
Hálkova
Sokolská
Karlovo nám.
Hertz
KARLOVO NÁMĚSTÍ
TO NÁMWSTÍ MÍRU
TO NÁDRAŽÍ VRŠOVICE (1.2km)
Resslova
TO (600m)
I.P. PAVLOVA
Jugoslávská
Ječná
Ke Karlovu
(400m),
(600m)
TO 34

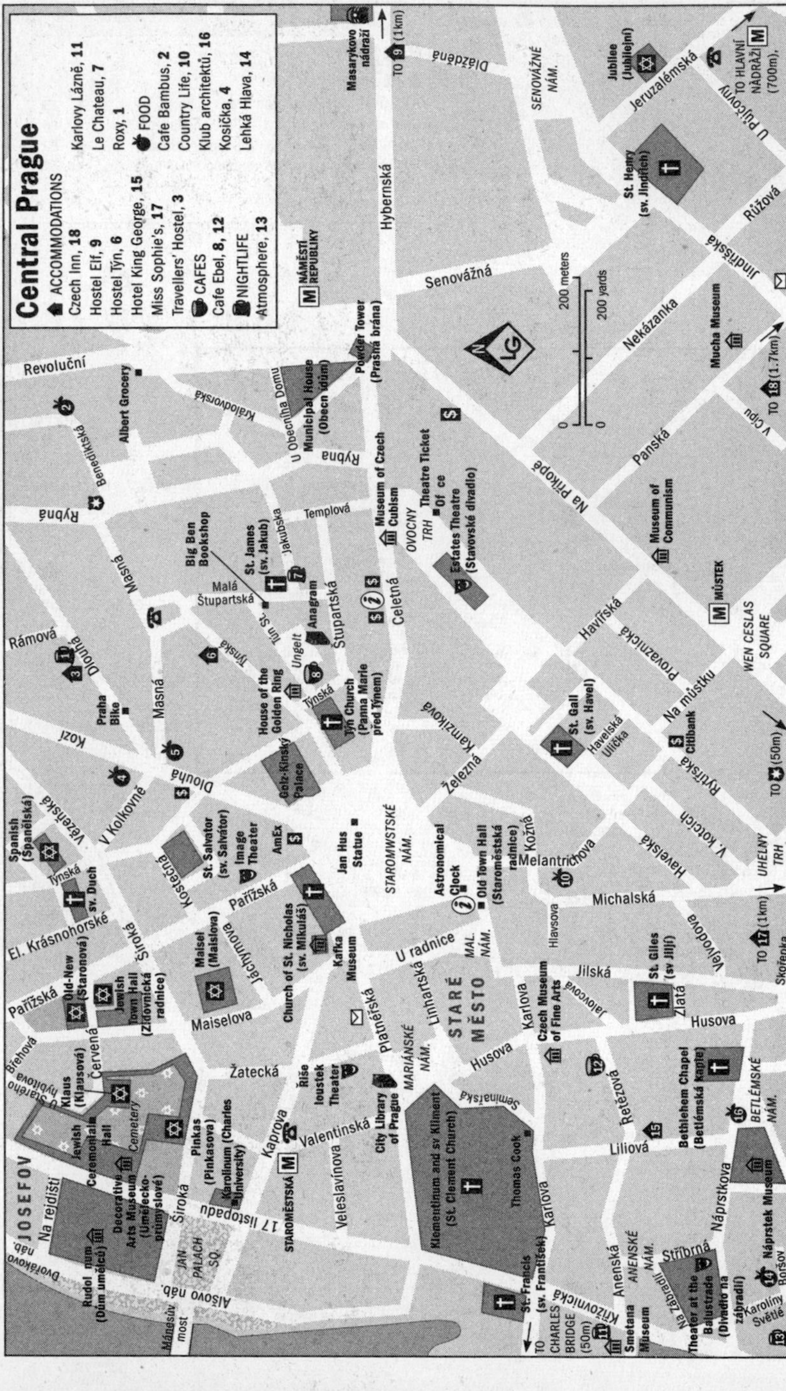
Central Prague
ACCOMMODATIONS
Czech Inn, 18
Hostel Elf, 9
Hostel Týn, 6
Hotel King George, 15
Miss Sophie's, 17
Travellers' Hostel, 3
Karlovy Lázně, 11
Le Chateau, 7
Roxy, 1
CAFES
Cafe Ebel, 8, 12
NIGHTLIFE
Atmosphere, 13
FOOD
Cafe Bambus, 2
Country Life, 10
Klub architektů, 16
Kosička, 4
Lehká Hlava, 14
200 meters
200 yards
JOSEFOV
STARÉ MĚSTO
STAROMĚSTSKÉ NÁM.
OVOCNY TRH
WEN CESLAS SQUARE
SENOVÁŽNÉ NÁM.
MARIÁNSKÉ NÁM.
MAL. NÁM.
BETLÉMSKÉ NÁM.
ANENSKÉ NÁM.
UHELNY TRH
JAN PALACH SQ.
NÁMĚSTÍ REPUBLIKY
MŮSTEK
STAROMĚSTSKÁ
Masarykovo nádraží
TO HLAVNÍ NÁDRAŽÍ (700m)
TO CHARLES BRIDGE (50m)
Municipal House (Obecní dům)
Powder Tower (Prašná brána)
Museum of Czech Cubism
Estates Theatre (Stavovské divadlo)
Theatre Ticket Office
St. James (sv. Jakub)
Big Ben Bookshop
Anagram
Ungelt
House of the Golden Ring
Týn Church (Panna Marie před Týnem)
Golz-Kinský Palace
Jan Hus Statue
AmEx
St. Salvator (sv. Salvátor)
Image Theater
Astronomical Clock
Old Town Hall (Staroměstská radnice)
Church of St. Nicholas (sv. Mikuláš)
Kafka Museum
Maisel (Maiselova)
Spanish (Španělská)
sv. Duch
Old-New (Staronová)
Jewish Town Hall (Židovnická radnice)
Klaus (Klausová)
Jewish Ceremonial Hall
Cemetery
Decorative Arts Museum (Umělecko-průmyslové)
Rudolfinum (Dům umělců)
Pinkas (Pinkasova)
Karolinum (Charles University)
Říše loutek Theater
City Library of Prague
Klementinum and sv Kliment (St. Clement Church)
Thomas Cook
St. Francis (sv. František)
Smetana Museum
Theater at the Balustrade (Divadlo na zábradlí)
Náprstek Museum
Bethlehem Chapel (Betlémská kaple)
Czech Museum of Fine Arts
St. Giles (sv Jiljí)
St. Gall (sv. Havel)
Havelská Ulička
Citibank
Museum of Communism
Mucha Museum
St. Henry (sv. Jindřich)
Jubilee (Jubilejní)
Albert Grocery
Praha Bike
Revoluční
Rybná
Benediktská
Králodvorská
U Obecního Domu
Templová
Jakubská
Malá Štupartská
Štupartská
Týnská
Týn St.
Celetná
Hybernská
Senovážná
Dlážděná
Jeruzalémská
Jindřišská
Růžová
U Půjčovny
Na Příkopě
Panská
Nekázanka
V Cípu
Havířská
Provaznická
Na můstku
Rytířská
Železná
Kamzíkova
Kožná
Melantrichova
Michalská
Havelská
V. kotcích
Vejvodova
Skořepka
Jilská
Jalovcova
Zlatá
Husova
Hlavsova
Karlova
Řetězová
Liliová
Náprstkova
Stříbrná
Na Zábradlí
Anenská
Křižovnická
Karolíny Světlé
Boršov
U radnice
Linhartská
Platnéřská
Mariánská
Seminářská
Valentinská
Veleslavínova
Kaprova
17 listopadu
Žatecká
Maiselova
Jáchymova
Pařížská
Kostečná
Široká
El. Krásnohorské
Červená
Břehová
U Starého hřbitova
Na rejdišti
Dvořákovo nábř.
Alšovo nábř.
Mánesův most
Vězeňská
V Kolkovně
Kozí
Dlouhá
Masná
Rámová
TO 9 (1km)
TO 18 (1.7km)
TO 17 (1km)
TO (50m)

Ireland, Tržiště 13 (☎257 530 061; irishembassy@iol.cz). Metro A: Malostranská. Open M-F 9:30am-12:30pm and 2:30-4:30pm. **UK,** Thunovská 14 (☎257 402 111; www.britishembassy.gov.uk/czechrepublic). Metro A: Malostranská. Open M-F 9am-noon. **US,** Tržiště 15 (☎257 022 000; www.prague.usembassy.gov). Metro A: Malostranská. Open M-F 8am-4:30pm. Consular section open M-F 8:30-11:30am.

Currency Exchange: Exchange counters are everywhere but rates vary wildly. Train stations have high rates. Never change money on the street. **Chequepoints** are plentiful and open late, but can charge large commissions. **Komerční banka,** Na příkopě 33 (☎222 432 111), buys notes and checks for 2% commission. Open M and W 8:30am-5pm, Tu, Th 8:30am-5pm, F 8:30am-5:30pm. A 24hr. **Citibank** is at Rytířska 24.

American Express/Interchange: Václavské nám. 56 (☎222 800 224). Metro A or C: Muzeum. AmEx **ATM** outside. Western Union services available. MC/V **cash advances** (3% commission). Western Union services available. Open daily 9am-7pm.

Luggage Storage: Lockers in train and bus stations take 2 5Kč coins. For storage over 24hr., use the luggage offices to the left in the basement of Hlavní nádraží. 25Kč per day, bags over 15kg 40Kč. Fine for forgotten lock code 30Kč. Open 24hr. with breaks 5:30-6am, 11-11:30am, and 5:30-6pm.

English-Language Bookstore: The Globe Bookstore, Pštrossova 6 (☎224 934 203; www.globebookstore.cz). Metro B: Národní třída. Exit Metro left on Spálená, take the 1st right on Ostrovní, then the 3rd left on Pštrossova. Wide variety of new and used books and periodicals. Cafe upstairs with an expansive menu of teas, coffees, and cocktails. Internet 1.50Kč per min. Open daily 9:30am-midnight.

Medical Services: Na Homolce (Hospital for Foreigners), Roentgenova 2 (☎257 271 111, after hours 257 272 146; www.homolka.cz). Bus #167. Open 24hr. **Canadian Medical Center,** Velesavínská 1 (☎235 360 133, after hours 724 300 301; www.cmc.praha.cz). Open M, W, F 8am-6pm, Tu and Th 8am-8pm.

24hr. Pharmacy: U Lékárna Anděla, Štefánikova 6 (☎257 320 918, after hours 257 324 686). Metro B: Anděl. For after-hours service, press the button marked "Pohotovost" to the left of the main door.

Telephones: Phone cards sold at kiosks, post offices, and some exchange establishments for 200Kč and 300Kč. Coins also accepted (local calls from 5Kč per min.).

Internet: Bohemia Bagel, Masná 2 (☎224 812 560; www.bohemiabagel.cz), Metro A: Staroměstská. 2Kč per min. Open M-F 7am-midnight, Sa, Su 8am-midnight.

Post Office: Jindřišská 14 (☎221 131 445). Metro A or B: Můstek. Internet 1Kč per min. Open daily 2am-midnight. Windows close 7:30pm. **Postal Code:** 11000.

ACCOMMODATIONS AND CAMPING

Nové Město is probably your best bet for a hostel: its accommodations are budget-friendly, conveniently located, and of good quality. **Staré Město** has hostels closest to the action, but you'll likely get something overpriced or unfurnished. Accomodations in **Žižkov** and **Holešovice** look more like resorts for hipsters than budget digs.

Campgrounds can be found on the Vltava Islands as well as on the outskirts of Prague. Bungalows must be reserved ahead, but tent sites are generally available without prior notice. Tourist offices sell a guide to sites near the city (20Kč). Just north of town in **Troja,** you can rent campsites from April through October at **Camp Sokol Troja** (☎233 542 908; www.camp-sokol-troja.cz; 120Kč per person; 100-170Kč per tent site; low-season reduced rates; cash only) or **Camp Herzog** (☎283 850 472; www.campherzog.cz; 80Kč per person, students 55Kč; 60-150Kč per tent site; cash only).

PRAGUE

2009
LET'S GO recommends
Prague Accommodation
10% off
comfort
low price
cool design
*Flash (this ad at) reception and receive 10% off your entire stay.
Featured in: New York Times. Elle. Glamour. Washington Post. The Guardian. Let's Go (too many years to count on one hand).
We invite you stay with us. We think we'll tickle your fancy too.
So escape the tourist masses and grab one of our dorm rooms, private rooms or apartments. Our properties are full of character, but it's best to get to know them before jumping in bed.
Check us out and Book online!
sirtobys.com / miss-sophies.com / czech-inn.com
SIR TOBY'S
Miss Sophie's
CZECHINN
MOSAIC HOUSE
Coming in 2010
mosaichouse.com

NOVÉ MĚSTO

Chili Hostel, Pštrossova 7 (☎603 119 113; www.chili.dj). ⓂB: Národní třída. From the metro station, walk south on Spálená, make a right on Myslíkova, and then another right on Pštrossova. Great location, spacious rooms, and an anime-poster-lined common room (open 24 hr). Linens and towels included. Free Wi-Fi. Reception 24hr. Check-in 2:30am. Check-out 11am. Dorms 322Kč; singles 1475Kč; doubles 966Kč. MC/V. ❶

Golden Sickle Hostel, Vodičkova 10 (☎222 230 773; www.goldensickle.com). ⓂB: Karlovo náměstí. From the metro station, cross the park and then turn left on Vodičkova; there will be small signs on the wall directing you to the hostel. Clean, comfortable dorms, each with its own bath and full kitchen. Hot breakfast can be arranged in advance for 100Kč. Towels and linens included. Free Wi-Fi and internet. Pickups from the airport 590Kč for groups of 1-4. Discounts at many nearby restaurants. Reception 9am-9pm, though arrangements can be made for late arrivals. Check-out 11am. Dorms 420Kč; 2-bed apartments 1680. Cash only. ❶

Miss Sophie's, Melounová 3 (☎296 303 530; www.missophies.com). ⓂC: IP Pavlova. Take 1st left from subway platform, then follow Katerinská to 1st right onto Melounová. Less centrally located, but it makes up for it with its sleek, ultra modern design. Kitchen available. Linens included. Free internet and Wi-Fi. Reception 24hr. Check-in 2pm. Check-out 11am. Dorms 590Kč; singles from 2100Kč. AmEx/MC/V. ❷

OTHER NEIGHBORHOODS

Sir Toby's, Dělnická 24 (☎246 032 610; www.sirtobys.com). ⓂC: Nádraží Holešovice. From the metro, take the tram to Dělnická, walk to the corner of Dělnická, and turn left. Welcoming and social, with 3 film nights per week and a social cellar pub (beer; 30Kč). Terrace garden or and well-equipped guest kitchen. Large rooms, some of which have paintings from former guests. Buffet breakfast 100Kč. Laundry service 150Kč, self-service 100Kč. Free Wi-Fi. Wheelchairs can be accommodated with advanced notice. Reception 24hr. Check-in 3pm. Check-out 11am. Dorms 380-530Kč; singles 1400Kč; doubles 1950Kč. AmEx/MC/V. ❷

Hostel Elf, Husitská 11 (☎222 540 963; www.hostelelf.com). Trams 5, 9, 26, Husinecká Tram stop. From the tram stop, follow Husinecká until you reach the square and then make a left at Orebitská, which will run into Husinecká right in front of the hostel. highly social common room. Communal kitchen. Clean dorms with shared hall baths. Bike storage available. Breakfast included. Free Wi-Fi. Reception 24hr. Check-in 2pm. Check-out 10am. Dorms from 340Kč; singles 980Kč, with private bath 1230Kč; doubles 580/730Kč. 5% discounts in dorms for students. Cash only. ❶

Travellers' Hostel, Dlouhá 33 (☎224 826 662; www.travellers.cz). ⓂB: Náměstí. Republiky. Branches at Husova 3, Střelecký Ostrov 36, and U Lanové Dráhy 3. Private kitchens for each dorm and set of single rooms. Convenient bar on the 3rd floor (beer; 25Kč). Breakfast and linens included. Laundry 150Kč. Internet and Wi-Fi. Reception 24hr. Check-in 1pm. Check-out 10am. Reserve ahead in summer. 16-bed dorms 350Kč, 6-bed 480Kč, 4-bed 500Kč; singles 1190Kč, with bath 1390Kč; doubles 1380Kč per person, with bath 1600Kč. 40Kč ISIC discount. AmEx/MC/V. ❶

Hostel Sokol, Nosticova 2 (☎257 007 397; www.sokol-cos.cz/index_en.htm). Hellichova tram stop, trams 12, 20, 22, 91. From the tram stop, walk south down Újezd and make a left on Hellichova; the hostel is in the Sokol Organization complex. The only hostel in Malá Strana proper. Basic, bunkless dorms and a rooftop terrace that provides the only real common space. Parking available 100Kč per night. Linens and lockers included. Free Wi-Fi. Reception 24hr. Check-in 11am. Check-out 10am. Dorms 350Kč; doubles 900Kč. Cash only. ❶

FOOD

As a general rule, the closer you are to a tourist center, the more you will pay. The most overpriced restaurants in the city can be found around Old Town Square and across the river in Malá Strana near the Charles Bridge. Some of the city's most reasonably-priced are in Nové Město (west of Spálená) and in Malá Strana around Újezd. Farther out, Holešovice also has its share of reasonably priced and delicious restaurants.

The major grocery store chains in the city are **Albert, Billa,** and **Tesco.** Albert and Billa have locations within a stone's throw of one another at Karlovo náměstí (Albert open Su 8am-9pm, M-Sa 7am-9pm; Billa open Su 8am-8pm, M-Sa 7am-9pm). There's also a Tesco at Národní třída 26 (Open M-F 7am-10pm, Sa 8am-9pm, Su 9am-8pm). Look for the daily **market** in Staré Město where you can grab better deals.

TIP **CASH, CZECH, OR CREDIT?** In the Czech Republic, everyone pays cash; very few establishments will accept credit cards. Your best bet is to take advantage of ATMs whenever you can. They will give you a much better rate than the ubiquitous currency exchanges, even if they're much less common.

T **Klub architektů,** Betlémské náměstí 169/5A (☎224 401 214). ⓂB: Národní třída. From the metro in Staré Město, take Spálená north and then make a left on Betlémské náměstí; the restaurant is through the courtyard on your right and in the basement. Rub elbows with the locals and stylish internationals in this intimate cavern. Wide selection of dishes. Chicken in cream sauce with peaches (160Kč). Salads 70-150Kč. Veggie dishes 70-150Kč. Meat entrees 160-320Kč. Open daily 11:30am-midnight. AmEx/MC/V. ❸

Bar bar, Všehrdova 17 (☎257 313 246; www.bar-bar.cz). ⓂA: Malostranská. From the metro in Malá Strana, take the tram to the Újezd stop, walk north on Újezd and then turn right on Všehrdova. Has a zeal for combining things you would never imagine together. Try the cheese- and spinach-stuffed pancake topped with fried egg and bacon (129Kč). Enjoy sculptures inside television sets. Savory pancakes 115-129Kč. Sweet pancakes 74-79Kč. Pasta 115-154Kč. Entrees 125-275Kč. Beer from 20Kč. Open M-Th and Su noon-midnight, F-Sa noon-2am. MC/V. ❷

La Crêperie, Janovského 4 (☎220 878 040; www.lacreperie.cz). ⓂC: Vltavská. From the metro in Holešovice, take Antoninská west and at the 5-way intersection turn left onto Janovského; the restaurant is on your left. A young and cool staff serves their young and cool customers delicious crepes and galettes. Galette with smoked ham, cheese, egg, and potatoes with garlic butter (125Kč). Galettes 105-145Kč. Crepes 35-85Kč. Open daily 9am-11pm. Cash only. ❷

Fraktal, Šmeralova 1 (☎777 794 094; www.fraktalbar.cz). ⓂC: Nádraží Holešovice. From the metro, take the tram to Letenské náměstí; the restaurant is at the corner of Šmeralova and Letenské náměstí. Delicious, hearty portions of American and Mexican food. High leather benches and a tree-stump table that appears to be reserved for hobbits. Goat cheese and pistachio burger with chili mayonnaise (185Kč). Appetizers 55-80Kč. Entrees 130-295Kč. Outdoor seating available. Open daily 11am-midnight. Cash only. ❷

Lehká Hlava, Boršov 2 (☎222 220 665; www.lehkahlava.cz). ⓂA: Staroměstská. From the metro, take Křižovnická south, then veer left on Karoliny Svétlé and turn left on Boršov. Tiny vegetarian and vegan restaurant in Staré Město filled with colorful tapestries. The "Small Clear Head" (eggplant, tabouli, and feta salad; 140Kč) will ease most hangovers. Su brunch (10:30am-3pm) comes in tiny (90Kč), standard (145Kč), and ideal (270Kč) portions. Entrees 95-210Kč. Open M-F 11:30am-11:30pm; Sa and Su noon-11:30pm. MC/V. ❷

Dynamo, Pštrossova 29 (☎224 932 020; www.restauracedynamo.com). ⓂB: Národní třída. From the metro stop, walk down Ostrovní toward the river and then turn left on Pštrossova; Dynamo is on the right. A great place to take a break while exploring the shops and bookstores in Nové Město. Full menu of duck, pork, and vegetarian options (135-180Kč); the real jewel is the tomato, mozzarella, and basil bruschetta (75Kč). Free Wi-Fi. Open daily 11:30am-midnight. AmEx/DC/MC/V. ❷

Restaurace Stará Doba, Gorazdoba 22 (☎224 922 511; www.staradoba.cz). ⓂB: Karlovo náměstí. From Karlovo náměstí in Nové Město, turn left on Resslova and then left on Gorazdoba. Unabashedly kitschy with delicious food. Ask for English menu to appreciate gems like the "Highlander's well-earned meal" (stuffed chicken breast with spinach and basil sauce; 150Kč). Open M-F 11am-11pm, Sa 5:30-11pm. Cash only. ❸

Restaurace Carmelita, Újezd 31 (☎257 312 564; www.restauracecarmelita.cz). ⓂA: Malostranská. From the metro in Malá Strana, take the tram to the Újezd stop. Classy, but not stuffy. Reasonably priced (if you avoid the entrees). The indecisive will appreciate the *quattro stagioni* pizza, which contains 4 specialty pizzas in 1 easily divided dish (145Kč). Appetizers 85-159Kč. Salads 98-169Kč. Pasta 109-169Kč. Entrees 175-349Kč. Wheelchair-accessible. Open M-Sa 11am-midnight. Cash only. ❸

PRAGUE

CAFES

Globe Bookstore and Cafe, Pštrossova 6 (☎224 934 203; www.globebookstore.cz). ⓂB: Karlovo náměstí. From the metro, take Resslova toward the river and then turn right on Na Zderaze, which becomes Pštrossova; the cafe is on your right. Largest collection of English-language books in Central Europe. Free classic movie screenings (Su 11pm). Live music most weekends. Printing available and Wi-Fi 1Kč per min. Coffee and tea 50Kč. Espresso drinks 60-95Kč. Open daily 9:30am-1am. Kitchen open 9:30am-midnight. AmEx/MC/V. ❶

Kavárna v Sedmém Nebi, Zborovská 68 (☎257 318 110). Trams 6, 9, 12, 20, 22, 91, Újezd tram stop. From the tram stop, take Vítězná toward the river, then turn right on Zborovská. Feels like a neighborhood establishment, though just off Malá Strana's main drag. Tea 25Kč. Espresso 29Kč. Beer 38Kč. Salads 75-95Kč. Sandwiches 75-90Kč. Free Wi-Fi. Open M-F 10am-1am, Sa noon-1am, Su noon-midnight. Cash only. ❸

Čajovna Pod Stromem Čajovým, Mánesova 55 (☎776 236 314). ⓂA: Jiřího z Poděbrad. From the metro station take Mánesova west (in Vinohrady); the teahouse is on your right. Vaguely Near Eastern-themed teahouse. Peruse a (non-English) menu of over 100 varieties of tea. Pita with edam cheese (50Kč). Couscous dishes (74-88Kč). Open daily 10am-11pm. Cash only. ❶

NoD Cafe and Art Gallery, Dlouhá 33 (☎736 152 015; www.roxy.cz). ⓂB: Náměstí Republiky. From the metro, walk north on Revoluční and then make a left on Dlouhá. Student favorite. Flexible performance area houses street art, nonverbal theater, and weekly techno DJs. Tea 30Kč. Coffee 35Kč. Mixed drinks 80-90Kč. Open daily 10am-2am. Cash only. ❶

SIGHTS

STARÉ MĚSTO

CHARLES BRIDGE. Thronged with tourists and the hawkers who feed on them, the Charles Bridge (Karlův Most) is Prague's most treasured landmark. Those seeking to avoid the crowds should visit late at night when the bridge is illuminated. The defensive towers on each side offer splendid views. *(ⓂA: Malostranská or Staroměstská. Tower open daily 10am-10pm. Last entry 30min. before closing. Entry to tower 70Kč, students 50Kč.)*

OLD TOWN SQUARE. Staroměstské náměstí (Old Town Square) is the heart of Staré Město, filled with tourists of all flavors snapping pictures, riding around in horse-drawn carriages, and gorging themselves on overpriced food. For the discerning visitor, the square still offers its share of (occasionally bizarre) historical value. The surrounding buildings—a mix of Gothic, Baroque, Art Nouveau, and even Cubist styles—would make your average architecture student giddy. *(Ⓜ A: Staroměstská; Ⓜ A or B: Můstek.)*

OLD TOWN HALL. A tour of the historical rooms inside the Staroměstské Radnice (Old Town Hall) will take you through various council chambers and conclude with a basement photography exhibit. The view from the top of the clocktower doesn't hold a candle to people-watching outside when the crowds form to watch the **astronomical clock** chime. On the hour, the windows open and a procession of apostles marches by 15th-century depictions of the four evils—a skeletal Death, a lute-playing Vanity, a corrupt Turk, and an avaricious Jew. After WWII, the Jew's horns and beard were removed and his name was changed to Greed. *(Exhibition hall open in summer M 10am-7pm, Tu-F 9am-7pm, Sa-Su 9am-6pm. Clock tower open M 11am-6pm, Tu-Su 9am-6pm; enter through 3rd fl. of Old Town Hall. Exhibition hall 100Kč, students 50Kč. Clock tower 100/50Kč.)*

TÝN CHURCH. At night, the glowing spires of **Chrám Matky Boží před Týnem** (Church of Our Lady Before Týn) are one of the most striking sights in the city. Even in an interior ornamented with gold, the altar stands out for its elaborate decor. *(Open daily Apr.-Sept. 10am-8pm, Oct.-Mar. 10am-6pm. Mass Tu-F 5pm, Sa 8am, Su 9:30am and 9pm. Free.)*

SAINT JAMES'S CHURCH. Barely a surface in Kostel sv. Jakuba (St. James's Church) remains un-figured or unpainted. Perhaps most striking is the mummified forearm that hangs to the left of the entrance. *(Ⓜ B: Staroměstská. On Malá Štupartská, behind Týn Church. Open M-Sa 10am-noon and 2-3:45pm. Mass Su 8, 9, and 10:30am. Free.)*

NOVÉ MĚSTO

NEW TOWN HALL. Built in the 14th century, Novoměstská radnice (New Town Hall) served as the administrative center of Nové Město for nearly 400 years. Constantly renovated and rebuilt, the hall is something of an architectural hodgepodge, with the distinctly Renaissance-style south wing set against the medieval **Outlook Tower.** *(Karlovo náměstí 23. Ⓜ B: Karlovo nám. From the metro station, turn left and look for the enormous tower. Open Tu-Su 10am-8pm.)*

WENCESLAS SQUARE. More a commercial boulevard than a square, Václavské náměstí (Wenceslas Square) owes its name to the statue of 10th-century Czech ruler and patron **Saint Wenceslas** (Václav) that stands in front of the National Museum. Today, the square is lined with overpriced restaurants, department stores, American fast food joints. The area is particularly dangerous in the evening. Traces of its rich history remain, however: a former publishing house turned luxury hotel, the **Melantrich Building** once served as a platform for speakers to address the crowds gathered in the square during the **Velvet Revolution.** *(Václavské náměstí 36. Ⓜ A or B: Můstek or Ⓜ A or C: Muzeum.)*

JOSEFOV

SYNAGOGUES

Ⓜ A: Staroměstská. Synagogues open M-F and Su Apr.-Oct. 9am-6pm; Nov.-Mar. 9am-4:30pm. Closed Jewish holidays. Admission to all synagogues except Staronová 300Kč,

students 200Kč. Staronová 200/140Kč. Combined tickets 480/320Kč. Men must cover their heads; yarmulke free. AmEx/MC/V.

Four of the five synagogues in Josefov are administered by the **Jewish Museum** of Prague (Židovské muzeum v Praze), which has ticket booths outside of each synagogue. Tickets are good for those four synagogues and also the **Old Jewish Cemetery** (Starý židovský hřbitov). The **Old-New Synagogue** (Staronová synagoga), the oldest operating synagogue in Europe, is administered separately from the Jewish Museum. The most dramatic of all the synagogues is the **Pinkas Synagogue** (Pinkasova synagoga), which has the names of Prague's Holocaust victims inscribed on its walls. Next to the richly decorated **Spanish Synagogue** (Španělská synagoga) stands the distinctive statue of **Franz Kafka.**

MALÁ STRANA

PETŘÍN HILL. This impossible-to-miss piece of the Prague skyline serves as a recreational area for locals and contains many of Malá Strana's landmarks. The **Petřínská rozhledna** (Petřín Lookout Tower) is the most notable, and looks suspiciously like Paris's famous Eiffel Tower. (Open Apr.-Oct. 7am-10pm daily. Open Nov.-Mar. Sa-Su 10am-5pm. Wheelchair-accessible. 100Kč, students 50Kč.) The **Štefánikova Hvězdárna** (Štefánik Observatory) has great views of sun spots on clear days, and of stars, galaxies, and nebulae on clear nights. (☎257 320 504; www.observatory.cz. Open Apr.-Aug. Tu-F 2-7pm and 9-11pm and Sa-Su 11am-7pm and 9-11pm. Check website for other hours. Wheelchair-accessible. 50Kč, students 35Kč. Audiovisual program 60/40Kč. Cash only.) At the top of the steep hill, hundreds of rose varieties bloom in the **Rose Gardens** in spring and summer.

SAINT NICHOLAS'S CATHEDRAL. This Baroque landmark's massive dome can be seen from all over Prague; it's second only to Prague Castle in the Malá Strana skyline. Inside, you'll find yourself surrounded by more marble statues than you know what to do with. *(Malostranské náměstí 26. ⓂA: Malostranská. From the metro, take Letenská to Malostranské náměstí. ☎257 534 215. Open Nov.-Feb. 9am-4pm daily, Mar.-Oct. 9am-5pm daily. Last entry 15min. before closing. Concerts from 6pm. Admission 70Kč, students 35Kč. Concerts 490/300Kč. Cash only.)*

HRADČANY

PRAGUE CASTLE (PRAŽSKÝ HRAD)

Take tram #22 or 23 from the center, get off at Pražský hrad, and go down U Prašného Mostu past the Royal Gardens and into the 2nd courtyard. Or, hike up Nerudova. ☎224 373 368; www.hrad.cz. Open daily Apr.-Oct. 9am-5pm; Nov.-Mar. 9am-4pm. Castle grounds open daily Apr.-Oct. 5am-midnight; Nov.-Mar. 9am-midnight. Ticket info and office located opposite St. Vitus's Cathedral, inside the castle walls. Tickets come in 5 different flavors. The Long Tour (350Kč, students 175Kč) gets you everything, while the Short Tour (250/125Kč) covers the most important things. Tickets valid for 2 successive days.

One of the largest castles in the world, Prague Castle (Pražský hrad) has been the seat of the Bohemian government since its construction more than a millenium ago. Arrive on the hour to catch the changing of the guard, complete with fanfare, daily from 5am-midnight. **Saint Vitus's Cathedral** (Katedrála sv. Víta), the centerpiece of the castle complex, is an architectural masterpiece visible from all over Prague. The cathedral boasts three magnificent towers and more flying buttresses than it knows what to do with. During tourist season, expect waits of 20 to 30 minutes just to step inside. The **Old Royal Palace** (Starý královský palác) holds the largest Gothic hall in the Czech Republic. The **Royal Summer Palace and Royal Gardens** make for a relaxing stroll at any time of day.

MUSEUMS

VELETRŽNÍ PALACE. The flagship (and largest) collection of Prague's dispersed National Gallery houses three full floors devoted to its impressive permanent collections of 20th- and 21st-century art, while the ground floor and mezzanine contain rotating galleries of contemporary art. *(Dukelských hrdinů 45. Ⓜ C: Vltavská. From the metro, take Antoninská west and turn right onto Dukelských hrdinů. ☎ 224 301 090; www.ngprague.cz. Open Tu-Su 10am-6pm. Last entry 30min. before closing. Free 1st W of every month 3-6pm. Wheelchair-accessible. 200Kč, students and seniors 100Kč. AmEx/D/MC/V.)*

FRANZ KAFKA MUSEUM. This fantastic museum eschews the stuffy display case approach to museums with a series of original and occasionally bizarre multimedia exhibits. *(Cihelná 2b. Ⓜ A: Malostranská. Go down Klárov toward the river, turn right on U. Luzické Semináré and left on Cilhená. ☎ 257 535 507; www.kafkamuseum.cz. Open daily 10am-6pm. 120Kč, students 60Kč. MC/V.)*

MUCHA MUSEUM. Devoted to the work of Alfons Mucha, the Czechs' most celebrated artist and an Art Nouveau pioneer. His graphic design work, particularly his many posters featuring "*la divine*" Sarah Bernhardt, remains the most impressive. *(Panská 7. Ⓜ A or B: Můstek. Walk up Václavské náměsti. toward the St. Wenceslas statue. Go left on Jindřišská and left again on Panská. ☎ 221 451 333; www.mucha.cz. Open daily 10am-6pm. 120Kč, students 60Kč. AmEx/MC/V.)*

MUSEUM OF CZECH CUBISM. Appropriately located inside the **House of the Black Madonna** (U Černé Matky Boží), itself a masterpiece of cubist architecture, the Museum of Czech Cubism demonstrates how Czech Cubism permeated all areas of the fine arts during its heyday (even areas where it maybe shouldn't have, such as home furniture). *(Ovocný trh 19. Ⓜ B: Náměstí Republiky. ☎ 224 301 803; www.ngprague.cz. Open daily 10am-6pm. Wheelchair-accessible. 100Kč, 50Kč for students, 50Kč after 4pm. Cash only.)*

MUSEUM OF MINIATURES. The collection features everything from miniature reproductions of works by Leonardo, Matisse, and Dalí to portraits of John Lennon and Václav Havel on poppy seeds. Some of the more exciting pieces include a menagerie on the wing of a mosquito and a caravan of camels passing through the eye of a needle. *(Strahovské nádvoří 11. ☎ 233 352 371. Tram 22, Pohořelec tram stop. From the tram stop, walk south, make a right on Dlabačov, and then make a sharp left onto Strahovské nádvoří. Wheelchair-accessible. Open daily 10am-5pm. 50Kč, students 30Kč. D/MC/V.)*

ENTERTAINMENT

For info on Prague's concerts and performances, consult *The Prague Post*, *Threshold*, *Do mesta-Downtown*, or *The Pill* (all free at many cafes and restaurants). Most performances start at 7 or 8pm and offer standby tickets 30min. before curtain. The majority of Prague's theaters close in July and August. For Czech opera, ballet, or drama, try the **National Theater**. (☎ 224 224 351; www.nationaltheatre.cz. Tickets 800-1200Kč. Box office open M-F 10am-5:30pm, Sa-Su 10am-12:30pm. AmEx/D/MC/V). For classical music, try the **Municipal House** (Náměstí Republiky 5. ☎ 222 002 101; www.obecni-dum.cz. Tickets 700-1300Kč. Box office open daily 10am-7pm. AmEx/MC/V). For tickets to the city's shows, try **Bohemia Ticket International**, Malé nám. 13, next to Čedok. (☎ 224 227 832; www.ticketsbti.cz. Open M-F 9am-5pm, Sa 9am-1pm). The **Prague Spring International Music Festival** (☎ 257 312 547; www.prague-spring.net), runs from mid-May to early June. June brings all things avant-garde with the **Prague Fringe Festival** (☎ 224 935 183; www.praguefringe.com) and the often-political **Prague**

Writers' Festival (☎224 241 312; www.pwf.cz). Now entering its sixth year, the **United Islands of Prague** (☎257 325 041; www.unitedislands.cz) attracts more than 100 bands from all musical genres.

NIGHTLIFE

Žižkov is the undisputed king of places to get triggity-trashed in Prague. Nearby Vinohrady has a less active pub scene, but several good wine bars and the majority of Prague's gay bars. If you want to stay closer to the center of town, Malá Strana has a good mix of bars and live music venues. Nové Město has several of the city's better music venues. In Staré Město expect expensive drinks and pub crawls.

Cross Club, Plynární 23 (☎736 535 053; www.crossclub.cz). Ⓜ C: Nádraží Holešovice. From the metro, take Verbenského east and then turn right onto Argentinská and right onto Plynární. Bar, cafe, club, and rock venue. Head down to the crowded techno-industrial-themed lower level, lit by all manner of glowing, flashing, and spinning contraptions. Beer 20Kč. Shots 50-100Kč. Mixed drinks 85-95Kč. Cover varies, usually 75-100Kč. Open daily 4pm-late. Cash only.

Hapu, Orlická 8 (☎775 109 331). Ⓜ A: Flora. From the metro, walk west on Vinohradská and then make a right on Orlická. Something of a bartender's bar, this inconspicuous little Žižkov haunt serves some of the most creative and best-mixed drinks in Prague. Try the "Alien Secretion" (120Kč). Beer 35Kč. Mixed drinks 80-140Kč. Open daily 6pm-2am. Cash only.

Blind Eye, Vlkova 26 (www.blindeye.cz). Trams 5, 9, 26, Husinecká tram stop (in Žižkov). From the tram stop, walk east on Seifertova, then make a right on Krásova; the bar is at the corner. Small, dark, rowdy, but much-loved. A wide assortment of drinks you couldn't describe to your mother, including the appropriately named "Adios, Motherfucker" (195Kč). Beer 22Kč. Most mixed drinks 60-100Kč. Karaoke M night. Wheelchair-accessible. Open 7pm-late. Cash only.

Klub Újezd, Újezd 18 (☎257 570 873; www.klubujezd.cz). Ⓜ A: Malostranská. From the metro, take the tram to the Újezd stop. Local gathering place for young Czech artists, poets, and punks. Weekend DJs spin a mix of punk, ska, and old school hip hop. Beer 35Kč. Shots 30-120Kč. Wheelchair-accessible. Open daily 2pm-4am. Cash only.

Harley's, Dlouhá 18 (☎227 195 195; www.harleys.cz). Ⓜ B: Náměstí Republiky. From the metro, walk north on Revoluční and then make a left on Dlouhá. The rough and tough exterior belies a surprisingly sophisticated bar, offering over 200 drinks. Rock and dance DJs nightly. Beer 55Kč. Mixed drinks 100-130Kč. Open daily 7pm-6am. Cash only.

The Saints, Polská 32 (☎222 250 326; www.praguesaints.cz). Ⓜ A: Jiřího z Poděbrad. From the metro, take Slavíkova north and then turn left onto Polská. Cozy basement bar in Vinohrady where Prague's GLBT tourists and English speakers of all ages meet and chat. Beer 26Kč. Wine (40Kč). Themed Quiz Night on the last Su of every month. Women and straight customers welcome but uncommon. Shots 60-120Kč. Open daily 7pm-4am. Cash only.

APPENDIX

CLIMATE

Germany enjoys a seasonal temperate climate. Throughout most of the country, summers are mild and winters are rarely snowy. Conditions in the mountainous south can be more extreme but usually just extreme enough to keep the slopes groomed for ski season. Summers, on the other hand, are frankly balmy. The plains in the north tend to be wet and windy throughout the year.

AVG. TEMP. (LOW/ HIGH), PRECIP.	JANUARY			APRIL			JULY			OCTOBER		
	°C	°F	mm	°C	°F	mm	°C	°F	mm	°C	°F	mm
Berlin	-3/2	26/35	43	4/13	39/55	43	13/23	55/73	53	6/13	42/55	36
Frankfurt	-3/1	26/34	38	4/13	39/55	41	13/23	56/74	53	6/13	43/56	38
Hamburg	-2/2	28/36	61	3/12	37/53	51	12/21	54/70	81	6/13	44/55	64
Munich	-5/1	23/34	46	3/13	37/55	56	12/23	53/73	99	4/13	40/56	48

To convert from degrees Fahrenheit to degrees Celsius, subtract 32 and multiply by 5/9. To convert from Celsius to Fahrenheit, multiply by 9/5 and add 32.

°CELSIUS	-5	0	5	10	15	20	25	30	35	40
°FAHRENHEIT	23	32	41	50	59	68	77	86	95	104

MEASUREMENTS

Like the rest of the rational world, Germany uses the metric system. The basic unit of length is the meter (m), which is divided into 100 centimeters (cm) or 1000 millimeters (mm). One thousand meters make up one kilometer (km). Fluids are measured in liters (L), each divided into 1000 milliliters (mL). A liter of pure water weighs one kilogram (kg), the unit of mass that is divided into 1000 grams (g). One metric ton is 1000kg. German recipe books use metric measurements (and usually measure ingredients by weight rather than volume). And, unfortunately, gasoline isn't as cheap as it looks: prices are *per liter*.

MEASUREMENT CONVERSIONS	
1 inch (in.) = 25.4mm	1 millimeter (mm) = 0.039 in.
1 foot (ft.) = 0.305m	1 meter (m) = 3.28 ft.
1 yard (yd.) = 0.914m	1 meter (m) = 1.094 yd.
1 mile (mi.) = 1.609km	1 kilometer (km) = 0.621 mi.
1 ounce (oz.) = 28.35g	1 gram (g) = 0.035 oz.
1 pound (lb.) = 0.454kg	1 kilogram (kg) = 2.205 lb.
1 fluid ounce (fl. oz.) = 29.57mL	1 milliliter (mL) = 0.034 fl. oz.
1 gallon (gal.) = 3.785L	1 liter (L) = 0.264 gal.

LANGUAGE

I can understand German as well as the maniac that invented it, but I talk it best through an interpreter.
—Mark Twain

Most Germans speak at least basic English, but you will encounter many that don't. When visiting smaller villages in the eastern parts of the country and Bavaria, carry a phrasebook and a bit of patience. Wherever you are, preface any questions with a polite *Sprechen Sie Englisch?* (Do you speak English?) When out at restaurants, bars, and attractions, a simple *Bitte* (Please) and *Danke* (Thank You) go a long way. Even if your command of German is shaky, most Germans will appreciate your effort to speak their native tongue.

PRONUNCIATION

With a little bit of effort, you can make yourself easily understood in German. German pronunciation, for the most part, is consistent with spelling. There are no silent letters, and all nouns are capitalized.

German vowels and diphthongs also differ from their English counterparts. An **umlaut** over a letter (e.g., ü) makes the pronunciation longer and more rounded. An umlaut is sometimes replaced by an E following the vowel, so that "schön" becomes "schoen." Germans are very forgiving toward foreigners who butcher their mother tongue. There is, however, one important exception: place names. If you learn nothing else in German, learn to pronounce the names of cities properly. Berlin is "bare-LEEN," Hamburg is "HAHM-boorg," Munich "MEUWN-shen," and Bayreuth is "BUY-royt."

Different pronounciations for certain letters and dipthongs are listen below.German also has one consonant that does not exist in English, the "ß," which is alternately referred to as the scharfes S (sharp S) or the Ess-tset. It is shorthand for a double-s , and is pronounced just like an "ss" in English. The letter appears only in lower case and shows up in two of the most important German words for travelers: Straße, "street," which is pronounced "SHTRAH-sseh" and abbreviated "Str."; and Schloß, "castle," pronounced "SHLOSS." The "ß" is being phased out by te German government in accordance with other German-speaking countries and replaced with "ss" in an effort to standardize spelling.

PHONETIC UNIT	PRONUNCIATION	PHONETIC UNIT	PRONUNCIATION
a	AH, as in "father"	**j**	Y, as in "young"
e	EH, as in "bet"	**k**	always K, as in "kelp"
i	IH, as in "wind"	**r**	gutteral RH, like French
o	OH, as in "oh"	**s**	Z, as in "zone"
u	OO, as in "fondue"	**v**	F, as in "fantasy"
au	OW, as in "cow"	**w**	V, as in "vacuum"
ie	EE, as in "thief"	**z**	TS, as in "cats"
ei	EY, as in "wine"	**ch**	CHH, as in "loch"
eu	OI, as in "boil"	**qu**	KV, as in "kvetch"
ä	similar to the E in "bet"	**sch**	SH, as in "shot"
ö	similar to the E in "perm"	**st/sp**	SHT/SHP, as in "spiel"
ü	close to the EU in "blue"	**th**	T, as in "time"

APPENDIX

PHRASEBOOK

The following phrasebook is meant to provide only the very rudimentary phrases you will need in your travels. Nothing can replace a full-fledged phrasebook or a pocket-sized English-German dictionary. German features both an informal and formal form of address; in the tables below, the polite form follows the familiar form in parentheses. In German, all nouns can take any one of three genders: masculine (taking the article **der;** pronounced DARE), feminine (**die;** pronounced DEE), and neuter (**das;** pronounced DAHSS). All plural nouns also take the *die* article, regardless of their gender in the singular.

ENGLISH	GERMAN	PRONUNCIATION
Hello!/Hi!	Hallo!/Tag!	Hahllo!/Tahk!
Goodbye!/Bye!	Auf Wiedersehen!/Tschüss!	Owf VEE-der-zain!/Chuess!
Yes.	Ja.	Yah.
No.	Nein.	Nine.
Sorry!	Es tut mir leid!	Ess toot meer lite!
	EMERGENCY	
Go away!	Geh weg!	Gay veck!
Help!	Hilfe!	HILL-fuh!
Call the police!	Ruf die Polizei!	Roof dee Pol-ee-TSEI!
Get a doctor!	Hol einen Arzt!	Hole EIN-en Ahrtst!

APPENDIX

GREETINGS

ENGLISH	GERMAN	ENGLISH	GERMAN
Good morning.	Guten Morgen.	**My name is...**	Ich heiße...
Good afternoon.	Guten Tag.	**What is your name?**	Wie heißt du (heißen Sie)?
Good evening.	Guten Abend.	**Where are you from?**	Woher kommst du (kommen Sie)?
Good night.	Guten Nacht.	**How are you?**	Wie geht's (geht es Ihnen)?
Excuse me/Sorry.	Enthschuldigung/Sorry.	**I'm well.**	Es geht mir good.
Could you please help me?	Kannst du (Können Sie) mir helfen, bitte?	**Do you speak English?**	Sprichst du (Sprechen Sie) Englisch?
How old are you?	Wie alt bist du (sind Sie)?	**I don't speak German.**	Ich spreche kein Deutsch.

USEFUL PHRASES

ENGLISH	GERMAN	ENGLISH	GERMAN
Thank you (very much).	Danke (schön).	**Please.**	Bitte.
What?	Was?	**No, thanks.**	Nein, danke.
When (what time)?	Wann?	**I don't care.**	Es ist mir egal.
Why?	Warum?	**No problem.**	Kein problem.
Where is...?	Wo ist...?	**I don't understand.**	Ich verstehe nicht.
I'm from...	Ich komme aus...	**Please speak slowly.**	Sprechen Sie bitte langsam.
America/USA	Amerika/den USA	**Please repeat.**	Bitte wiederholen Sie.
Australia	Australien	**Pardon? What was that?**	Wie, bitte?
Canada	Kanada	**How do you say that in German?**	Wie sagt man das auf Deutsch?
Great Britain	Großbritannien	**What does that mean?**	Was bedeutet das?